STUART HARRIS was born in Edinburgh in 1920. Educated at George Heriot's School and Edinburgh College of Art, he qualified as an architect and served on the staff of Edinburgh Corporation and the City of Edinburgh District Council from 1950 until he retired, as Senior Depute City Architect, in 1984. Amongst other projects, he led the design of the Napier College (now Napier University, Merchiston) and the Meadowbank Sports Centre, and personally directed the restoration of the fifteenth-century Tower of Merchiston.

From 1975 onwards one of his departmental responsibilities lay in the naming of streets, and it was this experience, combined with a lifelong interest in the city and its environs, as well as a lively curiosity about place names in general, that led to the present book, the first comprehensive study of the origins and history of the names of features, streets and places in the City of Edinburgh.

Stuart Harris died in 1997. He was married to Catherine and they had one daughter and three sons.

The Place Names of Edinburgh

THEIR ORIGINS AND HISTORY

STUART HARRIS

Steve Savage
LONDON AND EDINBURGH

Steve Savage Publishers Ltd
The Old Truman Brewery
91 Brick Lane
LONDON
E1 6QL

www.savagepublishers.com

Published in Great Britain by Steve Savage Publishers Ltd 2002

First published in hardback by Gordon Wright Publishing Ltd 1996
Copyright © Stuart Harris 1996

ISBN 1-904246-06-0

British Library Cataloguing in Publication Data
A catalogue entry for this book is available from the British Library

Typeset by Steve Savage Publishers Ltd
Printed and bound by The Cromwell Press Ltd

CONTENTS

Foreword

It is both a duty and a pleasure to acknowledge that this book owes almost everything to the work of others. In reviewing the older place names, it has leant heavily on the systematic studies by Norman Dixon in Midlothian and Angus Macdonald in West Lothian; on street names, the main sources have been the voluminous notes, published and unpublished, by Charles Boog Watson, together with the supplementary record published by the City Engineer for Edinburgh Corporation, and its continuation, up to 1994, by the City of Edinburgh District Council; and while many local historians and others have helped me with individual names, I must make particular mention of John Tweedie of Currie, Arnot Beveridge of Corstorphine and Donald Whyte of Kirkliston, for their collected notes on streets and places in western parts of the district.

The initial plan was to draw all this material together in a single book, written for general readers (including those still at school) and to amplify it so as to cover the names of places within the city district as defined in 1975 and to relate them to the ground and to local history. It meant that much had to be re-examined and many primary sources checked out—not least in our 400-year-old heritage of maps and plans, which show place names in their settings, and in many cases clarify or add to the written records; and since much of the earlier material was now over fifty years old, it obviously had to be reviewed in the light of more recent studies. In the particular matter of historic place names, I have tried to take account of the extensive work that has been done on Cornish, Welsh and English as well as Scottish place names since Macdonald and Dixon pioneered their studies in Lothian, and I have greatly valued kindly encouragement from Professor W. F. H. Nicolaisen.

Yet much remains to be investigated, and one aim in writing this book has been to encourage further local studies. Even in modern instances, there is often no specific record of the origin of a place name. Usually it has to be tracked down by a veritable detective process—searching for clues, direct or circumstantial and often very small, and piecing them together to arrive at a conclusion which may sometimes be firm, but often has to be provisional, open to change if new information comes to hand, and not seldom it has to be a frank 'don't know', with or without a hazarded guess at what it might possibly be.

The process must be rigorous. There are many pitfalls. Stories attached to names are simply not to be trusted, for almost always they will have been invented to explain them. The modern spelling or pronunciation of a name—and even its present use or location—can be quite misleading. Every effort needs to be made to trace its history in

7

these and other aspects, before starting to look at the name itself; and while the earliest mention of it will of course prove that it was by then in being, its origin will often remain a matter of possibility or probability, to be estimated from such clues as language, or the landscape, or the history of land use or local settlement or ownerships, or the relationship of the name to similar ones elsewhere. For such work in Edinburgh, powerful help is ready to hand: for besides the city archives and the large specialist collections in Edinburgh City Libraries, there are the immense resources of the National Library of Scotland and the Scottish Records Office, all with easy access made yet easier by skilled advice.

A book like this is a long job. The Scottish Arts Council assisted with the early costs of research and I am greatly indebted to Edinburgh City Libraries for their generous aid in the provision of illustrations. Besides this I am grateful for the encouragement and help I have had from so many at various times over the past eleven years. I hope the others will not think it invidious if I single out Gordon Wright, my publisher, whose faith has spurred me on ever since I first thought of the book, and Stewart Mossman, my friend and former colleague, whose constant and unsparing practical help has meant a great deal to me.

Stuart Harris, FSA Scot.
Edinburgh, Easter 1995

Introduction

The Perspective of Names

As they are used day by day, place names are simply labels standing for particular places but for the most part without meanings of their own. Yet each of them, when it was new, had such a meaning and therefore encapsulates, like a fly in amber, something about the place or of those who have lived in it; and so the thousands of names in the district of Edinburgh together make up a record of its past, a veritable stereo in time, in its depths going back for something in the order of 3,000 years. To take, as a random sample, the 58 names borrowed or invented in 1974 as labels for the wards of the new district council, half of them already existed in the time of Robert the Bruce, and one in six dates back at least twice as far as that. Yet although sheer age is of some interest, what is much more important is that the stereo shows a long sequence of change in landscape and settlement, and above all a long succession of different peoples, each bringing their own language and way of life into the area and evolving their own working set of place names.

Although some of these changes undoubtedly came by violence, the very place names themselves nevertheless bear witness that none of these incoming peoples drove out or wiped out their predecessors, but rather that they overran or infiltrated the existing population and eventually merged with them. There is some silent evidence of such intermingling of prehistoric peoples in the monuments and other traces they left behind them; but when we come to the Celts, the iron-working folk who began to arrive in Lothian perhaps as early as 800 BC and were still dominant in it more than a thousand years later, the fact that their language is known enables us to detect not only their surviving place names but at least one name, *Almond*, which is non-Celtic and which they probably borrowed from their Bronze Age predecessors. The same sort of thing happened when each later group of incomers arrived, for as may also be seen in the Scottish Highlands or the American West or indeed in many a modern housing estate, incomers are apt not only to coin or import place names of their own but also to adopt or adapt existing ones, whether phonetically or as translated for them by some obliging native. The effect is multiplied when, as in Lothian, a succession of incomers is coupled with an underlying continuity of population; and in much the same way as the genes of each group are still found in the local population, so are their place names represented in the current stock.

It is important, then, to view and understand the city's place names in this perspective of peoples in time. In the foreground there is the dense array of modern names, amounting to about three-quarters of all names in use, most of them street names generated since about 1760 by a tenfold growth in population and a hundredfold expansion of the built-up area. Then in the middle ground, ranging from the mid 18th century back to about 1100, we still have almost 1,300 of the names generated in the feudal settlement of countryside and burghs and in the subsequent development in and around this capital of Scotland—as the Duc de Rohan remarked in 1600, he could count over a hundred country seats of notables within six miles of it. And finally, behind all these and retreating into the depths of the picture towards the distant glimmer of the Bronze Age in the *Almond* name, there are about 220 names which (still going backwards into time) have been left us by Gaelic Scots, Norse vikings and Northumbrian Angles, and from perhaps a thousand years of a tribal kingdom of British Celts.

The Early Names

Since the first and fourth of these early peoples, although both Celtic, were quite distinct from each other and played quite different parts in the history of Lothian, it is first of all necessary to try to sort out which of the Celtic names are likely to have come from which of the two groups.

Language is the first clue, for although British and Gaelic had much in common, as cousin languages within the Celtic group, they also differed, in much the same way as their modern counterparts, Welsh and Scottish Gaelic, are both like and unlike each other. Where names contain terms special to one of them—e.g. British *maen*, stone, in *Dalmeny*, or Gaelic *baile*, farmstead, in *Balerno*—they can be readily classified; and on this basis about one third of the Celtic names in the district may be taken to be certainly British, while one tenth are as certainly Gaelic in the form they have come down to us. The remainder, amounting to just over half the Celtic names, might be classed as either British or Gaelic, inasmuch as they are made up of words, such as *crag* or *drum*, which are virtually the same in both tongues.

Yet the question can scarcely be left there, for how and when the two languages were in use in the district must have some bearing on their contributions to its place names. In point of fact, this is where they differed enormously. Briefly (it will be gone into more fully below) the British speakers were dominant in Lothian for hundreds of years before they were conquered by the Northumbrians in about 638, and for several centuries thereafter they continued to be the basic population, albeit as a subject people. By contrast, the direct impact of Gaelic speaking on Lothian was much later, more limited, and comparatively short-lived. Partly it came through a brief contact with the Irish-Gaelic Columban kirk in the 7th century, and partly it came three centuries later, when the Edinburgh area came finally under the control of the kingdom of the Gaelic Scots. There is no evidence that this political change was accompanied by any great immigration of Scots: it was an affair of overlords rather than a movement of people; the Gaelic influence seems to have been patchy, and by the 11th century it was already on the wane. No doubt, in both the 7th century and the later period, place names freshly generated by the activities of Gaelic speakers would be in Gaelic; but since these incomers were not unfamiliar with British they would feel no great urge to replace existing names—least of all, those that used terms common to both languages—although they might well give some of them a Gaelic colouring.

With all this in mind, it is reasonable to draw three broad conclusions about the Celtic names in the Edinburgh area. Firstly, any that are British are for the most part likely to date from before the 7th-century Northumbrian conquest, although some may belong to the centuries of subjection that followed. Secondly, but for any connected with the Columban kirk, Gaelic names are likely to be later than the mid 10th century, although the Scots may have coined a few of them earlier—for example, their translation of British *Din Eidyn* or Northumbrian *Edin Burh* as Gaelic *Dun Eidean*. Lastly, when the circumstances are given their proper weight, the realistic view of any Celtic name in the area is surely to presume it to be British, unless there is some particular and special reason for taking it to be Gaelic; and on this basis nearly nine out of ten of the Celtic names are either certainly or probably British in origin.

The British Names

When the Romans under Julius Agricola advanced into northern Britannia in AD 79, they found the coastal region between the Tees and the Forth in the possession of the *Votadini* tribe, part of a British-speaking culture that occupied the whole island from Kent and Cornwall to Forth and Clyde. The Romans pushed northwards to the Tay very rapidly; and indeed it would seem that during all three of their major incursions into Scotland, which between them occupied rather less than 50 years within the period AD 79 to 215 or thereby, they were able to treat the Votadins as 'friendlies'; and since their main operations were against tribes north of the Forth, the Edinburgh area was simply part of their support zone, traversed by their main roads from York and Carlisle, which apparently joined together just west of the Castle rock before heading for Stirling. Each road had its standard chain of marching forts, and by the 2nd century there was a special fort with a harbour at the mouth of the Almond. None of the names the Romans had for their installations within the district has been traced, although in Cramond we evidently have the native Votadinic name for that supply base.

11

Recent excavations, although restricted to small and marginal parts of the habitable platform of the rock of Edinburgh, have nevertheless confirmed that it was occupied at least as early as 900 BC, and that during the period of the Roman invasions it was a fortified hill town with a large and thriving community enjoying an abundant trade with the invaders. It seems that it was already an important native stronghold, which might well have borne the British name of *Alauna*, rock place, used by Ptolemy in about AD150 for 'the town of the Votadini'. Certainly it had this pre-eminence some four centuries later, when it figures as the tribal capital, *Din Eidyn* or Fortress Eidyn, in a set of poems believed to have been composed in Lothian shortly before the year 600. Their author was Aneurin, bard of the *Gododdin*—the Votadini name in its later Welsh form, nowadays pronounced approximately *Gau-'dauthin* (with *th* as in 'the') but earlier with the stress on the final -'*din*—and although his concern was to celebrate the heroic death of his comrades in battle with the Anglians in Northumbria, he gives in the by-going a remarkable portrait of the Gododdin in what was to prove the final flowering of their long history. In many ways they had changed since their first contact with the Romans: they were literate in Latin (witness their inscription on the Catstane, near Turnhouse) and had adopted some Roman names and military methods; and they were also Christian, probably evangelised by missions from Ninian's Whithorn in the 5th century. Yet in essence Aneurin's picture is of a vigorous Celtic society manifestly descended from those the Romans had encountered and described centuries earlier: a primitive yet courtly society of a Homeric sort, its warrior aristocrats finished products of a long tradition, delighting in finery, in banquets and in recitals of splendid and elaborate verse, recklessly brave in war, and yet with an ideal of kindness and gentleness in peace. Although destined soon to be overrun by the Anglians from the south, they were not destroyed but, as already noted, continued to inhabit the area, with at least some of their social structures remaining intact.

About 135 of their place names are recorded in the Edinburgh area, and most of them are still in use, although in the course of time many—like *Braid* or *Dalmeny*, not to mention the city's name itself—have come to have something much wider than their original meaning. As might be expected, almost nine out of ten of them belong to the landscape. Along with the pre-Celtic *Almond*, they include the names of every watercourse of any consequence, although in some instances—notably the pair of the *Peffer* and the *Lothian*—the original burn names have been partly supplanted by later names drawn from places along their banks. The simplicity of Leith, 'the water', suggests a period when life was so local that people felt no need to distinguish the river from any other, in much the same way as for Londoners 'the river' means the Thames; but other watercourse names seize on some distinguishing feature, such as the crooked courses of the *Gogar* and the *Anker*, or the sluggish pools of the *Pow*, or the bogginess of the *Cockle*, the clearness of the *Peffer* or the peat-stained waters of the *Lothian* or the *Tummel*.

As with the rivers, there was a primitive tendency to give hills names of a very local sort. Several were simply called *Crag*, and it was no doubt a later need for better distinction that led to such names being displaced by others, such as *Braid* or *Dalmahoy*, borrowed from lower ground. In the case of Corstorphine Hill, the original hill name seems to have descended to the lower ground at *Craigcrook*; and on a smaller scale the ridge name *Drumdryan* (intriguingly making a pair with the later Scots name *Thornybauk*) also became an estate name.

Distinctive forms of the land, like the original ravine of *Braid*, led to names such as *Currie* or *Inch* or *Cammo*, while other names give clues to its surface features or vegetation. Where *Gyle* occurs, there were sheets of water; and if many names, such as *Corslet* or *Megget* or *Cockle*, refer to bogs, it is scarcely to be wondered at, for the shallow valleys gouged out by the primeval ice sheet and the blanket of boulder clay it laid down when it melted created an ill-drained landscape that was about half of it water-logged until the 200 years of drainage works begun in the 17th century redeemed it as first class farm land. Yet names like *Lennie* and *Cockmalane* speak of well-watered meadows, and *Dalry* and *Minnifree* of heathery muirs; while *Dunsappie* mentions the tufted grass that still grows there, *Bonaly*, *Drumdryan* and *Drumselch* refer to broom, hawthorn and sauchs, and there were evidently woods or groves at *Calton* or *Leuchold* or *Inchkeith*.

Tormain, Caerketton, and perhaps *Carnodding*, as well as the first parts of *Lis*ton, *Cat*stane and *Cat*heaps, refer to monuments already ancient when the British first arrived. *Dalmahoy* and the *Annat* of Cramond may go back to the Ninianic kirk of the Gododdin. The term *lann*, for yard or farm, occurs in *Echline, Meggetland, Cumberland* or *Pentland*; while the term *tref*, for a farm, is found in *Niddrie, Dreghorn* and *Treverlen*—the last perhaps the name of the crannog or loch farm believed to have stood in Duddingston loch. At least seven names refer to fortified places, with British *caer*, fort or stockaded settlement, in *Cramond* and *Carlowrie* and perhaps *Keirhill*, while *din*, a fort, is heavily disguised in *Dalmeny*, wears Gaelic dress in *Dunsappie* or *Dundas* or *Dumbeg*, and appears as Edin*burgh* and *Dun* Eidean in the historic translations of British *Din Eidyn* into Anglian and Scots Gaelic.

This British 'Fortress Eidyn', as a hill-top fort with a difficult approach, would be of no military use to the Romans (except perhaps as a signal station) for theirs was an army of manoeuvre rather than static defence; but as a native stronghold it must have gained immensely from its position beside the junction of their great military roads, which even after centuries of neglect continued to give rapid access to the southeast and southwest, and to the west and north. The

13

resultant mobility in war is vividly illustrated in Aneurin's *Gododdin* poems: for they tell how Mynyddog 'the Magnificent', king of the Gododdin, was able to assemble in Din Eidyn a troop of mounted warriors, including champions from Wales and Dumbarton and Argyll as well as his own people, and to send them off—probably along the Roman route by Carlops, Carlisle and Stainmore—to deliver a lightning strike against the Anglian incomers based on Bamburgh and York, whose aggression was becoming more and more a threat to the British kingdoms north of the Humber.

It was a disaster. The British force was cut to pieces in a battle at Catterick; and although the Scots of Argyll made a similar thrust a few years later, bloodily repulsed by the Anglians at Degsastan in Liddesdale in 603, it seems that the Gododdin could no longer offer resistance to the Anglians in pitched battle, except perhaps in a last-ditch defence of Din Eidyn itself.

The Anglian Names

Nevertheless it seems to have been around 30 years after Catterick before the Anglians began to settle beyond the Tweed, for none of their pagan burials have been found north of it, and the inference is that their advance began some time after their king Edwin was baptised a Christian in 627. So far as Edinburgh is concerned, it is likely that the crux came in 638, when what is laconically chronicled as 'The siege of Eten' was probably a successful assault on Din Eidyn by Edwin's successor, Oswald of Northumbria. Once that fortress fell, the way was open to the west; and the chronicler's equally laconic note of 'The siege of Ritu' in 642 probably meant the capture of the rock of Stirling, commanding the ritu or ford of the Forth. Thus it may be that the Anglian advance from Tweed to Forth took rather less than fifteen years in all, and the second part of it, from Edinburgh westwards, perhaps only four.

This division of their advance into two distinct phases is supported by place-name evidence brought out by W. F. H. Nicolaisen in *Scottish Place-Names* in 1976: for along the coast from Berwick into East Lothian the pattern of Anglian place names is much the same as in the Merse and the Anglian homeland around Bamburgh, figuring such early elements as those in Whitt*ingham*, Mor*ham*, *Bol*ton or Hedder*wick*; but on the banks of the South Esk this ceases abruptly, and from here westwards such early elements are conspicuously absent, and Anglian settlement names are of a simple descriptive sort, such as *Granton* or *Morton* or *Pilton*. Yet although the difference surely indicates two phases, it can scarcely be put down to lapse of time, since the overall period was so short. Rather there must have been a difference in the character of the phases. The most likely guess is that whereas the first one had been an advance or infiltration by settlers, the second was basically a military operation, its objective not so much to promote settlement as to seize the whole Gododdin territory. Indeed it may have had nothing to do with the East Lothian colony, for Oswald may have come up by Roman Dere Street and Lauderdale to launch his attack on Din Eidyn directly from the south; and his campaign may have been the first stage of a plan, actively continued by his brother and successor Osiu, to establish a Northumbrian hegemony over eastern Scotland—a plan that was to meet with considerable success until 685, when the Northumbrians were decisively defeated by the Picts at Dunnichen in Angus, and forced to fall back on the Forth.

Most likely it was in Oswald's time that the Anglians had the name *Din Eidyn* translated for them as *Edinburgh*—a form which shows that even then Eidyn was untranslatable, either because it was a proper name or because the Gododdin had forgotten (or never known) what it meant. Similarly the name *Arthur's Seat*—if not invented five centuries later by the same romanticism that turned Edinburgh's castle into an Arthurian 'Castle of maidens'—may have been a translation of a Celtic hill name into Anglian, and some of the Anglian farm names may overlie Celtic originals; but names like *Hailes* or *Dean* or *Pilrig* are straightforward Anglian descriptions of land forms, while *Warklaw* and *Liston* and the several examples of *Mounthuly* and *Harlaw* referred to prehistoric monuments, and *Straiton* and *Chesterlaw* were perhaps named for vestiges of Roman works. Amongst farms, *Broughton* and *Clifton* were named for their position, *Liberton* for both its position and the barley it grew, and *Saughton* for its trees, on a broad ridge so full of springs that even in modern times it was remembered that 'ye could aye get a drink in ony o its fields'—and the same characteristic may account for the adjoining name of *Lerbar*, muddy ridge or pasture.

But for *Edinburgh*, none of these names is recorded before the 11th century; and since names of like sorts continued to be formed for several hundreds of years and into medieval times, it is often impossible to be sure which period a particular one belongs to: but even at the most liberal estimate, scarcely three dozen of them may go back to the time of the Northumbrian ascendency, and the fact that they are outnumbered 4 to 1 by the surviving British names would seem to confirm that the Anglian incomers were relatively few on the ground and probably a minority in the population. Nevertheless their language, although not the only one in use, remained dominant, and was destined to develop eventually into Early Scots; and while the subdivision of the land into small shires (the shire of Edinburgh was almost the same as the present Council area) seems to have come down from the British kingdom of the Gododdin, the Northumbrian administration is seen in the Anglian term *shire* and in the title of the *thane* or royal officer in charge of it, as well as in those of *hiredman* and (from Old Norse) *bondi* for yeoman and freeholder, enshrined in the farm names *Hermiston* and *Bonnington*.

Even in about 1100, after more than a century of rule by the Gaelic Scots, this former outpost of Northumbria was still to be described by Bishop Thurgot, Queen Margaret's confessor, as 'separated from Scotland by the Firth of Forth'. Yet it was an extremely mixed society, for from the 9th century onwards the original overlapping of Britons and Anglians was compounded by successive arrivals of Scandinavians and Gaelic Scots, as well as refugees from England in the 11th century, and the first of the NormanFrench adventurers who were to play such a great part in creating medieval Scotland. Intermarriage, certainly among leading families, produced an extraordinary ethnic mix—in a family in Coldingham in the 12th century, for example, there were five brothers, severally named British *Gospatric*, Anglian *Eggard*, Norse *Gamal*, British or Gaelic *Macbeth*, and NormanFrench *Reginald*. Yet the speed of this mixing should not be overestimated. To compare it with the absorption of immigrants into modern urbanised society could scarcely be more misleading: for typically the settlements of the day were self-sufficient farm touns with relatively little come and go between them; and when it is remembered that, despite vastly greater pressures towards integration, native Gaelic-speaking persisted in Perthshire and Aberdeenshire until the 20th century, the survival of British speech in Lothian for several hundred years after the Anglian conquest need not be wondered at, and something the same must have held for the other languages in Northumbrian society. Thus when a language or a personal name is found in a place name, like a coin in an archaelogical dig, it may fix its earliest possible date but cannot of itself shut out the possibility that it is later. For example, the *Merchiaun* whose British name is joined to Anglian *tún* in the name *Merchiston* evidently owned a farm there, and the earliest possibility is that he was a 7th-century survivor of the Gododdin aristocracy: but equally he might have been a descendant of many generations later, perhaps British-speaking but perhaps not, or else, like the Gospatric mentioned above, a scion of a 12th-century family of mixed stock, with a Briton somewhere in his family tree.

The Scandinavian Names

Names of Scandinavian origin account for at least one fifth of all the early Teutonic names in the area. The *Whale* brae and the *Coal* hill, like the *May* further down the coast, seem to have been named as sea marks. Among inland names there are *Figgate*, *Kellerstane*, *Keldelethe* (later 'Kinleith') and *Byerside*; while the Norse term *cleikimin*, for a stony outlet of a burn, occurs no fewer than three times in central Lothian and a fourth time just over the border in Lauderdale, although otherwise in Scotland there seem to be but single examples of it in Lanarkshire and Shetland. When it comes to place names incorporating personal names, the question of distribution arises even more forcibly,

16

for in a zone of 200 square miles in and around Edinburgh those in which the personal name is Scandinavian not only outnumber all the others in the zone, whether Celtic or Anglian, but also form a distinct and quite concentrated cluster among such Scandinavian names in south-eastern Scotland. In seven of them, such as *Humbie*, the Old Norse ending *byr*, a farm, shows that the name must have been given by Norse speakers. In other cases (including the interesting one of Smeaton, which is also recorded with the *-byr* ending) the ending is *tún*, another word for a farm in Old Norse; and although *tún* meant the same in Anglian, there is no compelling reason to suppose that the fifteen names of the *Ravelston* type were not wholly Norse and not given by Norse speakers. Thus the names themselves, as well as their place in the pattern of such names in Scotland, strongly suggest there was a concentration of settlements by Norse incomers, although not necessarily in a single generation.

It is unlikely that they came a-roving over the North Sea. Although their first reported attack on the coasts of Britain was at Lindisfarne in 793, when it came to settling down, the Vikings showed little interest in the seaboard between the Moray firth and the Northumbrian Tyne. No doubt this was partly because it lay in between their routes to richer pickings, from Denmark to the Humber and from Norway to the northern and western isles; but probably it was also that as sailormen they knew it would be hard to sustain beachheads of settlers along this 300-mile stretch of mainly rock-bound shore, scant of natural shelter and with estuaries beset by fast tides and fogs so frequent (four times as many as in the Hebrides) that the Viking name for the mouth of the Forth was 'mirky firth'. The evidence is rather that the movement into Lothian belonged to a later phase of Scandinavian activity. The distribution of the farm term *byr* in southern Scotland, as well as the fact that Moorfoot (originally *mor thveit*, outlying pasture in the muir) is the solitary example of the term *thveit* in the east of the country, suggest that these Lothian settlers came from the west and the region of the Irish Sea; and the most likely time would be after 870, when the Norse kings of Dublin attacked the Britons of Dumbarton and the Picts of central Scotland in order to secure the portage across the isthmus of Forth and Clyde (no doubt materially shortened by using the river Leven, Loch Lomond and the river Forth, or else the lower reaches of the Kelvin and the Carron) as part of their corridor for ship-borne forces between Norse Dublin and Danish York. With its score and more of farm touns, on average but three miles apart, their Lothian settlement must have become quite an important outpost of AngloScandinavian Northumbria; and perhaps it was this, rather than the weak Anglian hegemony which preceded it, that stamped on Lothian the strong Northumbrian character it has never quite lost.

The Gaelic Names

Although Lothian was not annexed to Gaelic Scotland until the 10th century, there had been earlier contact with Gaelic speakers. To begin with, in the 7th century there had been a brief connection with the Gaelic-speaking Columban kirk, for Oswald, future king of Northumbria, had been baptised in Iona when in exile, and shortly after coming to power in 634 he invited Aidan of Iona to set up a mission to Northumbria, and thus it came about that it was this Gaelic kirk that entered Lothian in the wake of Oswald's invasion in 638, no doubt peacefully absorbing the native British kirk of the Gododdin in the process; and although the mission was short-lived (for Northumbria broke with it soon after the synod of Whitby in 664, preferring the rule of Rome, and the Celtic bishop and all his people went back to Iona) certain place names in Lothian seem to reflect some of its work. Later on, and especially after the 9th-century merging of the Pictish and Scottish kingdoms had extended the use of Gaelic to eastern Scotland north of the Forth, it is quite likely (although scarcely to be proved) that there was some stray settlement in the Edinburgh area by Gaelic speakers moving down the Lothian coast or crossing over from Fife. In the 10th century, however, the political map was decisively changed by the three-sided power struggle that developed between the united kingdom of Picts and Scots, the English (now united under the kingdom of Wessex) and the Scandinavians of York and Dublin. Along with the rest of the English province of Bernicia (i.e. Northumbria north of the Tees) Lothian was in a frontier zone, controlled by sometimes one and sometimes another of the main contestants; until finally in 954 the Scandinavian power of York collapsed, and the English, now bent on consolidating their gains in southern Northumbria, evacuated Edinburgh and fell back on the Tweed, in effect ceding Lothian to the Scots.

This was to set the future course of Scottish history, but its immediate effects in Lothian appear to have been slight. Admittedly the records are scanty, but there is nothing to suggest that there was any great immigration of Gaelic Scots, the majority of the thanes or local administrators seems to have remained Northumbrian (even the name of Macbeth or Malbet of Liberton might have been as easily British as Gaelic) and the impression is that the Scots were in the position of being overlords of a continuing society, probably polyglot and including some Gaelic speakers but still dominated by the Anglian speech of Northumbria. More widely, the effect of the annexation of Lothian on Scotland as a whole was to draw the political centre southwards, and eventually to weaken the ascendancy of Gaelic. Both tendencies are to be seen in the reign of Malcolm Canmore, who seized the throne in 1058 with Northumbrian help, and made Dunfermline his main base. Himself half-Gaelic half-Northumbrian and brought up in the English court,

Malcolm's English and French were said to be as good as his Gaelic, and his marriage to the half-English half-Ukrainian princess Margaret underlined his view of Scotland as part of Britain and of Europe. From 1066 onwards his main concern was to consolidate, if not to extend, the southern part of his kingdom, and his policy for Lothian is illustrated by his grant of a huge tract of it to his cousin Cospatric, the refugee earl of Northumbria, made earl of Dunbar. Thus within 100 years of the annexation the Gaelic-speaking overlordship was on the wane—indeed, the impression given by Thurgot's contemporary *Life of Queen Margaret* is that in her day the Northumbrian character of Lothian was fully evident, and that if she and Malcolm often stayed in Edinburgh instead of Dunfermline, it was by choice and not merely for military reasons. The Gaelic Scots had made some impact on Lothian, for there certainly was some settlement (and, as already noted, some intermarriage) but it was limited, and the surviving Gaelic names probably reflect this in showing a tendency to occur in pockets. In Dalmeny the landscape names *Kingbowie* and *Glenpuntie*, apparently half-translations from the British, are only a few hundred yards apart; while *Colinton* and *Comiston*, together with field names like *Auchingane*, suggest that *Colgyn* and *Colman* were a pair of Gaelic farmer-lairds in an Anglian milieu. The characteristic Gaelic term *baile*, for a farm place, occurs in *Balerno* and its neighbour *Balleny*; and *Balgreen* is not far from the original site of *Corstorphine*, which although it could be British and referring to a Norseman, is perhaps as likely to be Gaelic and referring to an incomer from Gaelic Scotland, where the Norse name Thorfinn was already naturalised by the year 1000. The term *baile* is also found in *Blawearie* in Inverleith, and perhaps also in Ratho, where *Bellmansknowe* may imply that there was an early monastery beside the *Abthane* which must have originally belonged to the Celtic kirk. Lastly, there may be a shadow of *baile* in *Auld Walls*, a field in Wester Hailes next to the Celtic-named fort of *Dumbeg* and a half-mile from *Dumbryden*, a Gaelic description of a British settlement.

The Names of the Middle Period

By the time they died in 1093, Malcolm Canmore and Queen Margaret had brought Scotland to the threshhold of the Middle Ages, and the policies pursued by their descendents in the ensuing 150 years had profound effects, still visible, on the forms and names of its towns and countryside. The structure of society was adapted to the feudal principle, the kirk was reorganised, religious orders were introduced, and the new concept of the trading burgh was exploited by the crown and major landowners. All this required new leadership and new skills, mostly but not exclusively supplied by incomers from Flanders, northern France and Norman England, deliberately invited, as a matter of policy, to settle in Scotland. Yet there was apparently ample room for them, and the process of adaptation was so peaceful that a good deal of the old was carried on into the new. Nevertheless the changes went deep, and laid foundations for so much that followed in the ensuing six centuries that the towns and countryside of the early 18th century were recognisably descended from the medieval scheme; and it is therefore reasonable to take the 'middle ground' in the perspective of the history of Lothian's place names to be the period between 1100 and 1750—after which, as we shall see, that continuity was virtually shattered by revolutionary change.

The Estates

The basis of the feudalization of the countryside was the systematic granting of land. No doubt many of these grants took account of ancient boundaries, but not all estates were like *Hailes* or *Inverleith* in carrying forward a name which already attached to the whole of the ground. More often, local names were stretched to cover new and wider areas. For example, *Redhall* became the 'chymmes' or centre of a barony extending over two square miles, while AngloNorman lairds like Henry *of Braid* or Aleyn *of Liberton* or Thomas *of Lestalric* not only adopted these names for their broad estates but took them as surnames as well. In some cases, as at *Craiglockhart*, the incomer's name was simply tacked on to the ancient name of the place; but more often (especially perhaps where the place was not an old-established centre) such names as *Clermiston* or *Riccarton*, *Gilbertston* or *Duddingston* were made up by the simple and time-honoured method of adding Early Scots *-toun*, farm place, to the owner's name.

Under David I the kirk was reorganised in parishes which, although centred on existing kirks wherever this was possible, for the most part coincided with the new baronies. Each parish priest was provided with land for his subsistence, variously known as *glebe* or *vicar's acres* or *panny*, while larger kirks had *kirklands* or *kirktons* for their support. Still larger donations, such as the estates of *Kirkliston* or *Keldelethe* or *Kirk Cramond*, were made to bishoprics, and among David I's many gifts to his new abbey of Holyroodhouse was the great stretch of land from North Leith and the *St Leonard's lands* of South Leith southwards to *St Leonard's Crag*, which became the abbey's *barony of Broughton* and *burgh of the Canongate*. A *grange* was the technical term for a farm with barns for storing rents-in-kind for a distant landlord, whether clerical or lay: but in practice most granges were like Gilmerton Grange in being outposts of monasteries, for pious gifts of land were apt to be widely scattered throughout the countryside—in the case of the Grange of St Giles, as much as a hundred miles distant from its parent monastery of Holm Cultram in Cumbria. The same was true of the possessions of the Knights Templars and their heirs, the Knights of St John, whose Scottish headquarters were at Torphichen: for although the Knights held the whole barony of Auldliston, with *Templehouse* a centre on the hill ground attached to it, their many other holdings in both countryside and town were mostly small corners gifted as *templelands*. Unlike these militant orders and the monastics, however, the orders of friars chose not to be great landowners, but preferred to feu off donated land in order to generate cash income, holding on only to what they needed for subsistence—their friary gardens or *yards*, their orchards and their nearby glebes or crofts, such as the *Blackfriars croft* in the Pleasance or the *Friarscroft* of the Carmelites at Queensferry.

From the 14th century onwards the subdivision of estates and the growing practice of feuing off land to wealthy investors from the burghs led to a rapid increase in the number of recorded place names. Yet by no means all of them were new, for it is this period that many early names, kept alive over centuries by popular use, begin to surface in the written records—indeed it is astonishing how, despite the virtual reconstruction of the countryside by new-style farming in the 18th and 19th centuries, estate plans can still reveal ancient names like *Phantassie* or *Dumbeg* or *Carnodding*, surviving after a thousand years or more. Although many of these 'uncovered' names, such as *Bonaly* or *Pilton* or *Humbie*, emerged in forms that make their ancestry fairly clear, some, like *Fairafar* or *Fairmilehead*, have been garbled and then altered in an attempt to give a meaning (often faintly humorous) to the name; while in one or two cases, such as the hapless '*Croft-an-righ*', there has been a deliberate but misguided attempt to 'rectify' a perfectly proper name.

Where new names were needed, they were often systematically developed from existing ones. One very direct and ancient method (the Gododdin had used it) was simply to add the prefix *New-*, to produce such names as *Newliston*, *Newhaven*, or the several instances of *Newhouse* and *Newbiggin*—this last the earliest known name of the Grassmarket neighbourhood. Another old formula, already mentioned, was to add *-toun* to the owner's name—but now it was his newfangled surname, rather than his Christian name, that was used to produce such names as *Frogston* or *Scotstoun*; and if different endings were used for William Brune's *Brun(t)sfield* or Hugh le Ewer's *Ewerland*, it was perhaps because these royal officials were not normally resident on their small estates.

When an estate was divided, it was sometimes convenient to keep the original name for the original centre, but to modify it for any additional centre. One way was to combine it with a reference to some kenspeckle feature of the ground, such as (in a great many cases) a *haugh* or *haw*, clearly seen in *Deanhaugh* or *Haugh of Dalry* but half-concealed in *Craigiehall* or *Saughtonhall* or *Mortonhall*, bred from *Craigie*, *Saughton* and *Morton* respectively, in which (as in ninety-nine

21

out of a hundred such names in Britain) the *-hall* ending does not refer to any hall or mansion. Subdivisions might also be named for their position within the estate. Relatively few were labelled *north-* or *south-*, although there are examples in *Norton* and *Southhouse*. More often, parts of fields or estates would be classified according to their position relative to the sun: those perceived as lying more under the forenoon sun were said to be 'on the sunny side', while those under the afternoon sun were 'on the shadow side'. To those accustomed to think in terms of compass directions, this method might seem awkward: but on the ground it is remarkably easy to apply, and it generated the host of cases where sunny-side divisions bear the estate name with a prefix *Easter-* or *Over-* or *Upper-* or *Fore-*, while their shadow-side counterparts are *Wester-*, *Nether-*, *Under-* or *Back-*; and besides this, the method could cope with subsubdivision, as for example the *Overtoun of Nether Newliston*. A third way of distinguishing between subdivisions was by ownership, as in the cases of *King's Cramond* and *Kirk Cramond*, or *Bonaly* and *Bonaly Wallace*. The manorial system itself also generated special names. The term *mains* specifically meant a farm not feued off by the laird, but kept for his own use within his domain or 'demesne'; and in Saughton the unusual names of the *Lairdship* and the *Gentrice* muir suggest that *Saughton Mains* was not the only domain land on that estate. Although the name of *Burdiehouse* is obscure—except in the certainty that it had nothing to do with French *Bordeaux*—it may have referred to a manorial function of a similar sort.

A scattering of names were 'fancy', in the sense of being invented or else imported by an owner's caprice. In the 16th century the name *Champanyie*, for Blackford, was perhaps given nostalgically by a herald of France; and another early example is the enigmatic *Catelbok*, perhaps unique in Scotland (although not in Europe) and to all appearances descriptive, but hard to relate to any feature of its site. *Wheatfield*, *Canaan*, *Prestonfield* and *Newington* were deliberately selected as estate names, while *Powburn* was borrowed from an existing feature. *Morningside* and *Greenhill* were probably chosen in the same way; whereas *Lilliput*, given by one of Dean Swift's earliest readers, must be among the most delightful examples of a fancy name.

Besides all these names derived more or less deliberately from ownership, there was evidently a wealth of bynames in use among the folk of the countryside; and from the 15th century onwards these figure increasingly in charters, introduced by the phrase 'commonly called'. In the Plewlands of Braid, for example, *Over Plewlands* became *Greenbank*, while *Nether Plewlands* inherited the old general name of *Plewlands*; and in the adjoining estate of Braid, the name *Egypt*, tracing back to the early days of the 'Egyptians' or Romany in Scotland, ultimately displaced *Nether Braid*. The *Barrace* goes back to sport in the Middle Ages, the *Balm well* to their medicine, and the *Boothacre* to measures taken in time of plague. *Jocks Lodge* got its name from the Bluecoats or licensed beggars who lived there. In this category also belong the greatest single group of names—bynames derived from local features or connections, such as *Kaims* for ridges, *Merrylands* for marshy hollows, *Wantonwalls* for seasonal springs, *Redford* or *Winnelstraelee* for plants, *Laverockhall* and *Clapperknowe* for birds and animals, *Raivel* for enclosure, *Threestops* for fields, *Bowbridge* for an arched bridge, *Briggs* for a bridge tollhouse, and *Priestfield* or *Parson's Green* or *Niven's Green* for particular ownerships.

The Farming Names

The medieval farm system, itself largely inherited from earlier times, carried on for centuries with little or no fundamental change until it was swept away by the revolutionary 'improved' farming shown on *Roy* 1753 and *Laurie* 1763 as then just beginning here and there in Lothian; and although that revolution was to create a landscape so utterly new that it is hard to conceive the one it replaced, technical terms of the older system are still enshrined in many local names. The *plewland* (otherwise known, from an ancient valuation, as a '£2 or 40-shilling land of the old extent') was the chief measure of farm land. Embracing about 104 Scots acres (131 imperial acres) it got its name because in a notional way it was reckoned to contain, along with other unploughable land, as much arable as could be kept in normal production by means of a single plough drawn by eight oxen or their equivalent—a team vividly portrayed on the tombstone of William Straiton's wife at Liberton kirk. The eighth part of a plewland (13 Scots acres) was known as an *oxgang*, because its tenant had to supply the equivalent of one ox to the communal ploughing team; and the quarter of a plewland was the 26-acre *husbandland*, the minimum holding of a *husbandman* or *bondi*, whether as an independent farm or as a share in a larger one. Most farms were held by more than one tenant—sometimes there were as many as eight or ten; and since each tenant could have a *cottar* as subtenant, as well as several hinds or waged labourers, the number of families living in the farm *toun* could be considerable.

The farm was worked communally. Each tenant had rights in the pasturage or *soum*, and held named pieces of the *roum* or land in each of the various parts of the arable ground. This was worked in two *fields*, a term which did not imply enclosure, but simply a tract or zone of land. The first of these zones was the *croft* or *infield*, mostly arable 'mukkit land' that was nearhand enough to be conveniently dunged from the toun's midden and so enabled to bear a continuous rotation of pease and cereal crops. Beyond the infield was the *outfield*, also arable, but which for want of fertilizer had to lie half the time as *faich* or fallow grazing. Besides these fields, the farm included grazings on burnside *haughs* and on *bog* or *muir wastes*; and some of this might be *bruntland* or *brunthaugh*, occasionally

23

coaxed into bearing a crop by dint of ripping up the turf and burning it as fertilizer. Outwith the farm proper—indeed, sometimes quite distant from it, and reached by a green *loaning* that gave the beasts some grazing as they went—there was a *common muir* or (on lower ground) *links*, where summer grazing was shared by a number of farms, and the stock was looked after by women and children camping out in *shiels* or huts in the muir.

Conveniently near the farm toun were *byres* for cows, *bughts* for milking yowes and *stodfaulds* for horses or bulls, while in parts of the outfield animals were penned in temporary *faulds* on the faich next due for ploughing. Fencing or *haining*, often in the form of turf dykes, was also used to keep stock away from grass being grown for hay, or from the *broom parks* or *broomie knowes* where this plant, so useful in the rural economy, was deliberately cultivated and so highly valued that penalties for damaging it were extremely severe. Enclosed pasture was called a *park* or, using the Old Norse term, an *angr*, and a *croft angr* (as at Holyrood) was a 'grazing within the croft or infield', while an 'enclosure for grazing outwith the main infield' was an *angr croft*.

For cropping purposes, the ploughed land was divided (as it is today) into *breks* or *shots*, separated by unploughed strips or *bauks*; and the brek was ploughed (again, as it is today) in a series of *rigs*, so called because the plough, as it begins at the centre line and works clockwise up and down the length of the rig, naturally pitches each furrow towards the centre, creating a crown down the middle and finishing each side of the rig with a hollow or open furrow. Nowadays, because the farming unit is the whole brek and the land is drained by field drains at subsoil level, this ridging effect can be cancelled out by centring this year's rigs on last year's open furrows, leaving the field flat; but under the old system it was the rigs, not the breks, that were the legal units of tenant holdings and the open furrows the only means of drainage, and in consequence the sett of the ploughing had to stay the same, year after year. The result was that the topsoil became permanently humped up along the crown of the rig, developing that corrugated landscape of narrow cambered ridges characteristic of *Rothiemay* 1647 and early views by Hollar, Slezer and others, and still to be seen in many places (for example, in hollows in the Braid and Blackford hills) where cultivation long ago gave way to grass.

Where a field boundary was not parallel to the rigs, the irregular piece of ground in between was called a *gore* or *garbrage*, a 'gore breadth', and the furrows of unequal length within it were called *butts*; but wherever possible the length of a rig was a *furlong*, about as far as the ploughing team were able to drag the cumbersome plough without a breather. In the infield, the rigs were only about ten yards across, but the outfield arable was often worked in broader patches known as *dales*—i.e. deals or shares, not to be confused with the similar word for 'valleys'; and in order that each tenant should have his fair shares of good and poorer land, his holding was made up of rigs and dales (or parts of them) in each and every part of the farm.

The Mills

In every estate the corn mill provided an essential service to the farms, and they in turn were 'thirled' to it and bound to pay the *multures* or levies on their corn, even if they had some of it ground elsewhere. The income from multures was shared betweeen the estate owner and the miller, and the latter also had the *mil(l)ton* or farm that went with his tenancy of the mill. Similar arrangements were made for the waulking of cloth, and by the 16th century other mills were being set up for a wide variety of purposes, of which (in the Edinburgh area) paper making at the Braid and the Water of Leith were chief, and the crushing of ore at *Silvermills* perhaps the most exotic. Although there were windmills at the Timber Bush and the Back Dean, and a wind pump was erected in Bristo in 1599, water was the usual source of power, and the mention of mills at Liberton and the Dene in David I's foundation charter to Holyrood abbey shows that water mills were well established by the early 12th century. Virtually every watercourse was harnessed, and eventually there were upwards of a hundred mills at work in the area, the Water of Leith alone driving seventy-one. This involved very considerable engineering works, even in medieval times, for the water entering the mill lade or *dam* by the sluice or *damheid* was not usually released until it had powered a whole series of mills, sometimes extending miles downstream. For example, the mills of Gorgie and Dalry shared a single dam; and in the Dene, while an upper dam served a series of mills on the haugh north of the river, a lower dam (in an arrangement which lasted until the 1880s, but is clearly shown on the map of the *Siege of Leith* in 1560) not only drove another series on the south bank but was carried on through the gorge in a high-level timber aqueduct or *trows* so as to drive many more mills in Stockbridge, Silvermills and Canonmills before the water was at last returned to the river at Powderhall.

Mill names were many and various; and like the processes within the mills themselves, they were apt, some of them, to change with bewildering frequency. The corn mills and the waulk mills were usually named for estates; but the *Hole mill* was named for its site, the *Canonmills* for their original owners, the *Breistmill* and *Cocklemill* for their technical features. *Frenchmill* probably commemorates immigrant cloth workers, and *Jinkabout* perhaps shows a touch of molendinary humour; but *Mawr's*, *Mossie's*, *Lin's*, *Bell's* and *Dalyell's* represent a remarkable group that carry forward the names of tenants (some of them families in several generations) who had these mills in the 15th

25

or 16th centuries, or in the case of *Hunter's mill* in Niddrie, perhaps in the 14th century and for 500 years thereafter.

The Burghs

An important innovation under the feudal scheme, and one destined to last until 1975, was the creation of *burghs*, whether by the king or by major landowners. While this term had been used hundreds of years earlier—for example, in the Anglian naming of Edinburgh—it was now imported into Scotland with the very different meaning it had since acquired in Flanders and northern France: for in place of 'fortress' it now meant 'centre of commerce', and thus the name of the feudal *royal burgh of Edinburgh* combined new and old in meaning 'the king's commercial centre at Fortress Edin'. Indeed not only the name but the very concept of the thing was so novel that most of the early burgesses were incomers from abroad (which explains why so many burgh kirks, like *St Giles*, were dedicated to continental saints) and there is evidence that experienced administrators were deliberately imported to lead the new communities in their early years.

The significant point in the new meaning of *burgh* is that it was commerce, not defence, that shaped the town. In Edinburgh, for example, it was to be all of 200 years before part of the town was enclosed by the so-called 'king's wall', which seems to have been imposed (perhaps by an occupying army) for military rather than burghal purposes, and to have been soon ignored; and it was 1450 before the community petitioned the king for leave to fortify the burgh—and even then, action was so slow that the work was still unfinished 90 years later. When the king or a lord set up a burgh, his primary object was to make profits for himself, and to this end he equipped his burgesses with legal and mercantile privileges. Where the lord was a landowner, as in the case of Holyrood abbey's burgh of Canongate or Dunfermline abbey's Queensferry, these privileges were normally confined to the lord's estates (although the Canongate had exceptional rights in the Edinburgh market) but in the case of king's burghs like Edinburgh or the latterday Queensferry, they ran through whole zones of the kingdom and, as for example through Edinburgh's ownership of Leith harbour, could extend to seaborne trade. Since the privileges were tied to the burghal land (known, in the case of a royal burgh, as 'the royalty') it was a strict rule that burgesses had to reside within it; and thus the gates and dykes or (in the case of Edinburgh, after 1514) walls round its perimeter were there not so much to protect the burgesses in time of war as to define and police the bounds of their privileges in times of peace. It was this residential limit of trading advantage, rather than any constraint of defence, that bottled up expansion and forced growth in density and height of building rather than extension of area, especially in Edinburgh, where by the 17th century tenements of a dozen storeys were not uncommon and there was at least one of sixteen.

When the new trading burgh of Edinburgh was first set up, probably by Alexander I in about 1120, it was laid out on lines already established as standard for burghs of the kind, but with adjustments to take account of special features of the site: for irregularities in alignments suggest—not surprisingly, since Edinburgh had for long been the capital of a shire extending from the Esk to the Almond—that there was already an earlier settlement on Castlehill; and secondly the ridge was so steep-sided that the Upper Bow, probably the established way up to that ancient settlement and certainly the first practicable approach to the west end of the burgh, had to come in at right angles to the central street. Otherwise it was possible to follow the standard plan, dominated, not by the castle, but by the great central space for the market and twice-yearly fairs, the whole reason for the burgh's existence. This is still represented by the High Street and Lawnmarket, except that the space between the building frontages is now ten or twenty feet narrower than it used to be, besides being a little longer at its eastern end, where the gate was once in the vicinity of John Knox House, and may have been even further west (above Blackfriars Street) in the 12th century. Near the middle of it stood the burgh kirk, together with the *mercat cross* that gave religious and legal guarantee to all bargains struck, the *trone* or public weigh beam, and the *tolbooth* which was originally the burgh's custom house but soon became the meeting place of its court and council and the national parliament, as well as housing the burgh jail. Entrance to the burgh was controlled by gates at each end of the street. As already noted, the western one deviated from the standard burgh plan in that it was not at the head of the street but on a branch to the south of it; and this may explain the solitary reference, in 1214, to a 'south entrance' to the burgh. By the 14th century, both this *upper* entrance and the lower or *nether* one at the foot of the street were in the form of stone-arched gateways or *bows* (pronounced 'boughs'); but from the 15th century onwards the Netherbow and the six extra gates made necessary by development of the burgh (*Rothiemay* 1647 shows them all with stone arches) were generally called *ports*, a term that in its basic meaning of 'passage' underlined their essential civilian function as check points controlling movement in and out of the burgh.

In the 12th-century scheme, the *tofts* or plots held by the burgesses individually from the king were ranged along the sides of the market street, each giving the burgess a frontage of about 8 or 9 yards for his house and work place. Behind the house, his toft stretched about 130 yards down the slope in a long narrow strip, forming his private *close* (from Old French *clos*, an enclosed yard) in which he had a garden and kept his livestock, for in the absence of country trade, the early burgess was half a farmer. At the foot of his close, his *heid dyke*, along with those of his neighbours, kept the town 'firmly closit about', as a town council minute put it; and his private gate in the dyke gave access from his close to a public loaning which, as shown by the names *Welgate* and *Cowgate* for the one in the valley south of the town, contained the town's water supply and led to its common pastures. At intervals between the private tofts there were public ways connecting the market street with the outer loanings or routes out of town. Sometimes referred to as *vennels* (from Old French *venelle*, a lane) these cross streets were more often called wynds, a term which is from Old Norse *venda*, to wend or turn, and simply means 'a turning off a main street', without implying that it is curved—in point of fact, most wynds are straight.

From the beginning and until the *land market* or trade with the countryside developed, the burgh had to be self-sufficient. Hence the *new mill of Edinburgh*, mentioned in David I's charter for Holyrood abbey in 1128, a forerunner of a group of eleven mills which ground the town's corn in the Dean. Also a first essential to the early burgh's subsistence was its communal farm, worked by the burgesses and extending to over two square miles of arable, pasture, muir and myre; but with the growth of the land market the need for burgh farming declined, and the lands were progressively put to other uses. Some of the infield croft seems to have been turned into extra burgage land, for the southern slope above the Cowgate was probably once part of its arable, and the place names *Laplee* and *Stokwell* suggest that the Canongatehead and the vicinity of the Grassmarket were originally common pastures. Change came more slowly in the main grazings, which lay further south of the town, and were reached by the wide *Loaning* (i.e. a road with broad grassy borders, where the beasts could feed as they went along) that led from the Cowgatehead by Bristo to the *Burgh loch* and the wide commons of the *Burgh muir* and the *Common myre*. As time went on, surplus areas in the muir were leased out; and after 1508, when the town council got powers to feu it off, they began cautiously to part with it in small allotments of three acres apiece. Soon these were merged to form larger plots, and in less than a century virtually the whole of the muir except Bruntsfield Links had become a mosaic of properties surrounding that curious archipelago of independent estates (the Grange, Bruntsfield, and Hogistoun or Whitehouse) which had never been part of the Burgh muir, but had apparently been created at the same time as the burgh, if not before it.

By the 14th century, despite the ravages of war, expansion of the burgh had begun: for if Froissart, visiting Edinburgh in 1364, estimated that it had rather less than 400 houses, even this was about double the number of the original burgage houses in the High Street tofts. As has been mentioned, there was at first some room for expansion into redundant farm land—and the Grassmarket was already *the street called Newbygging* by 1363—but sooner or later it became a matter of increasing the density by subdividing tofts. By the 15th century this process was far advanced, and the Stent Roll of 1635 shows that by then (and probably for long before) there were on average about half a dozen different owners in each toft, and over a dozen in some.

Correspondingly, the plan of the town became more complex. When a burgess named (say) Telfer sold the lower part of his toft, he obviously had to preserve his own right of access down the toft to the common wells in the back loaning, but at the same time he had to allow the new proprietor access to the business world of the High street. Thus there had to be a throughgang for mutual uses down the whole length of the toft; and since the new property and the passage were both in the former yard or garden of Telfer's original toft—literally *in Telfer's close*—that became the new owner's address, and the throughgang came to be called *Telfer's Close*. Unlike the public wynds, these new-styled closes were on private ground. Many remain so to this day, even although they may be open to the public; but in most cases, as subdivision of property multiplied, the passageway became less and less private, and the close became as public as a wynd.

Despite this, the closes continued to be named mostly for owners, and the practice spread to many of the wynds, such as *Liberton's* or *Halkerston's*. In many cases, the close continued to be named in the old way, viz. for the owner of the *fore land* on the site of the original burgage house, and a considerable number of such names, like *Carruber's*, go far back into the early history of the burgh—indeed, although there can be no proof of it, some may go back to its very beginning; but as time went on, closes began to be named for kenspeckle owners in the back lands as well, and thus it came about that many closes—indeed, the majority—simultaneously bore the names of several owners, whether living or else recently or long since dead. For instance, *Melrose Close*, named for the abbots of Melrose who had a mansion in it from about 1400 until 1588, was also *Walter Mawer's* from the 1590s, and *Mackenzie's* or *Rosehaugh's* from the 1660s, and all four of these names continued in full use even after it also became *Strichen's* in about 1731. Again, *New Assembly Close*, named for the New Edinburgh Assembly who opened their ballroom here in 1736, was also known (for its position) as *Back o Bell's Wynd*, and (for ancient owners) as *Snadoun's* or *Murray's*, and yet as late as 1814 it also became *Commercial Bank Close* when that bank opened its head office in it. Besides those referring to persons, about a tenth of the names had various other origins. *Leith Wynd* and *Blackfriars Wynd* were named for where they led to. There were headquarters of trade corporations in closes such as *Baxters'* or *Shoemakers'* or *Skinners'*; and public institutions in *Parliament, Coinyiehouse* or *Fishmarket Closes*. Industry figures in names like *Sugarhouse* or *Candlemaker*, but often, as in *Campbell's Close*, it was represented by the owner of the business. While in one case *Society* referred to the Society for the Propagation of Christian Knowledge, in another it was the Society of Brewers, a large enterprise set up by the town in 1599. Entertainment gave names to the *Cachepele*, *Playhouse*, and *Assembly Closes*; *Bull's* and *Anchor Closes* and *Cap & Feather Close* were named for taverns; and there were also descriptive names like *Stinking* and *Stripping* (with meanings probably different from the obvious) as well as the mysterious *World's End*.

Altogether there are over 500 names for these passage ways in the Old Town (including the Canongate in the reckoning) and over a quarter of them go back to before 1600. If the system of addresses might seem bewildering, the fact is that in the conditions of high density and frequent change it worked where a modern system would probably have broken down. It was helped by an efficient team of caddies, operating as guides and messengers; and it is perhaps significant that it was not until 1790, when the Old Town was beginning to lose its vitality and the New Town was setting the fashion of street names and house numbers, that the authorities first tried to stabilise the names of closes by ordaining that they should be painted at the close mouths—and even then, as in the case of *Commercial Bank Close* already instanced, the townsfolk were still inventing new names a quarter of a century later.

The second of the medieval burghs now within the modern city was the *burgh of the Canongate*, set up by the canons of Holyroodhouse under powers granted them by David I when he founded the abbey in 1128. Inasmuch as the name is a street name, *canon gait* or canons' way, which must have taken a while to become established after the abbey was built, it must be presumed that the canons had been using the road for a considerable time before they formed their burgh round it, adapting it as the burgh's central market street, complete with mercat cross and tolbooth. If it was not as spacious as Edinburgh's market street, it was perhaps because David I had given the canons' burgesses special rights to trade in Edinburgh 'as freely as any of his Edinburgh burgesses'. Besides its *mercat cross* and *tolbooth*, there were two landmarks in the street: near its foot the *Girth Cross* showed the boundary of the *girth* or sanctuary of Holyrood, the refuge of those appealing to the Kirk for justice; while towards the upper end of the street the *Laplee Stane* (later also called *St John's Cross*) marked the north-east corner of the *Canongatehead*, the outshot part of Edinburgh on the south side of the ridge below the Netherbow. Otherwise, the burgh of the Canongate was laid out in the normal way on either side of the street, with the burgage tofts and half a dozen wynds stretching down to the loanings known as the *South* and *North Backs*. There were no defences other than the heid dykes of the tofts, shown on *Rothiemay* 1647, and the foot of each wynd was policed by a *yett* or gate, of which at least two were known as *water yetts* because they led to the common wells and Tummel burn in the North Back—one, at Leith Wynd, being shared with Edinburgh, while the other, at Canongatefoot, also served as customs entrance to the burgh of the Canongate from the east. Besides their outlet to the sea at *North Leith* (described below) the burgesses had their farm in the *St Leonard's lands* and their *common muir* near Shrubhill. The canons had conceived their burgh on a generous scale, for the total acreage of its tofts was virtually equal to that of the king's burgh of Edinburgh; but the burghal community was never more than a fraction of the size of Edinburgh's, and even although the development of Holyroodhouse as chief royal palace in the 15th century swelled the population with Court people and the households of the nobility (who indeed continued to build mansions and town houses here even after the Court departed to London in 1603) the density of building was far lower than in Edinburgh—a contrast shown dramatically on *Rothiemay* 1647. While there was some subdivision of tofts, accompanied by the familiar development of closes, for the most part the lands and mansions were concentrated along the frontages of the main street, and behind them about two thirds of the toft ground continued as gardens or open yards until the 19th century.

Queensferry, the third of the medieval burghs, was also owned by a monastic house: in this case, Dunfermline Abbey, which set up its little burgh at some date prior to 1300, on ground which was probably included in the lands granted by Malcolm IV (if not by his great grandfather, Malcolm Canmore) to support the abbey's half share in the responsibility of running the Queen's ferry and its associated hostels. The street of the burgh, with its *mercat cross* and *tolbooth*, was laid out along a curving flat between the shore and the 100-foot scarp of the raised beach behind it—a flat so narrow that there was no room for tofts on its seaward side, while those on the inland side (some of them still to this day undivided and showing themselves as 'closes' in the original sense of 'enclosed yards or gardens') occupied the lower slope of the bluff, where the 1 in 4 gradient gave rise to the distinctive terraces along the High Street frontage. A loan running along the heads of the tofts gave access to the burgh's arable land in the *Stonycroft* and also to loanings east and west which led further up the scarp to the common grazings in the *Back Braes* and the *Ferry muir*. A charter of 1364 describes the western boundary of the burgh as marked by a burn, probably that running in the *gote* or channel in *Gote Lane*, while the friary of Carmelites founded in about 1330 by Dundas of Dundas lay further west; and although the whereabouts of the ancient ferry hostel founded by Queen Margaret on the southern shore are quite unknown, the curious gap between the burgh and the friary suggests that the hostel might have been situated here, on the knowe at the *Bellstane*, immediately above the narrow guts in the *binks* or shelf-like rocks which served as boat landings. While these were adequate for boats, the development of shipping led to the construction of a harbour in the lee of the rocks. The burgh prospered, and in 1636 it was converted into a royal burgh. The boundary seems to have been adjusted to a line just east of the Bellstane; and in 1642 the market and fairs were moved to waste ground beside it. Upon the demise of Dunfermline abbey as a landowner, many of the richer burgesses acquired shares in the ferry and its lands, and the map of *Dundas* 1757 shows a great deal of these lands still in 'runrig' and shared out between several of them. It also shows many ancient names, such as *the Ravel, Muirball, Muirie Green, Ferry Acres,* the *Sword* and *Stoop parks,* the *Flasse shot* and *Thieves loch,* which have been lost in modern developments.

The tidal harbour at the mouth of the Water of Leith, by far the best of the few natural havens on the Lothian coast, was doubtless made use of from the earliest times; but the early name *Inverleith* seems to have embraced a large tract of country, and there is no evidence that there was any settlement around the harbour until after the burgh of Edinburgh and the abbey of Holyrood were separately granted rights to it in the early 12th century. Edinburgh's rights, although the earliest surviving record of them is Robert I's replacement of the burgh's earlier charters with a grant of feu in 1329, evidently dated back to the beginning of the burgh; but they extended to the harbour only, and the quays and township of *South Leith* generated by the burgh's seaborne trade grew up on land feued from Restalrig on the south bank of the river; whereas Holyrood's rights, conferred by David I in 1128, not only extended to the harbour but included grants of land on both sides of it, and led to the development of *North Leith* as part of the abbey's burgh of the Canongate.

On the south bank of the river, these Holyrood lands were the *St Leonard's lands of North Leith*, occupying the Coalhill, immediately above the river where it ran deep next to the steep *Shore*, and this gave the abbey a share in the shipborne commerce of the port. At its upstream end, the Coalhill was linked, at first by a ford and then by the *Brig o Leith* built by the abbey in 1493, with the more shelving north bank or *Roodside*, which was wholly owned by Holyrood and developed as a township chiefly of seafarers and shipbuilders, laid out in normal burghal fashion, with tofts and wynds flanking the central *street of North Leith*. At the north end was the *Sandport*, a little bay which remained sheltered even after the sea washed away the greater part of the considerable promontory of *North Leith Links* in the 16th century; and its sandy beach served as a slipway, and perhaps also as a source of ships' ballast. A quarter mile further west stood the chapel of *St Nicholas*, patron saint of seamen; and since its kirkyard was the township's burying ground, it may well have been the 'church of *Lye*' mentioned in 1335. In 1493 a chapel of *St Ninian* (destined to become the parish kirk of North Leith after the Reformation) was built in the wynd of the same name, leading from the new Brig o Leith to the main street. With remarkably few changes, other than the intrusion of the Cromwellian *Citadel* in 1656 and the resultant clearance of the St Nicholas kirk and the transfer of the burying ground to its present riverside site, the medieval plan of North Leith survived until 1789, when the superseding of the old Brig by the first *Drawbridge* (now most inappropriately named *Sandport Place*) signalled the beginning of modern Leith.

On the other side of the harbour, and initially in the space between the St Leonard's lands on the Coalhill and the royal residence and arsenal of the *King's Wark*, the township of *South Leith* gradually developed on the Restalrig ground behind the *Shore*. How quickly it grew up is not known; but since trade was brisk in the 13th century and by 1312 had made Leith Scotland's leading seaport, it is surely obvious that the earliest known charters permitting Edinburgh such essential facilities as wharfs, storage space and rights of passage through the lands of Restalrig, which are dated as late as 1398 and 1414, must have been to confirm or amplify arrangements made previously with some earlier lord of Restalrig. The strip of land 80 yards deep behind the Shore seems to have been subdivided as a regular set of yards opening off the quay; and while these *closes* may have been originally for storage of goods in the open, in course of time they were built up as warehouses and lodgings for merchants from Edinburgh and elsewhere; and the name of *Cortoun's Close* suggests that Canongate burgess families in North Leith could also rise to prominence in South Leith. Such names as the *Shore, Broad Wynd* and the *Links* survive from this medieval settlement, as also did the *Ratounraw, Dub Raw* and the *Paunchmarket*, before they fell victim to renaming in the late 18th century; but although the routes of the *Kirkgate* and *Tolbooth Wynd* must have been already ancient when they got these names after the St Mary's kirk and the Tolbooth were built in 1483 and 1565 respectively, their earlier names have been lost.

Much of Edinburgh's growing trade (it accounted for almost half the total returns of Scottish customs) was channelled through South Leith, and by the 1480s the population of the township was evidently large enough to justify the erection of St Mary's kirk as a chapel of Restalrig. The sense of community and identity in the port was no doubt further strengthened by the building of the Brig and then by the enclosure of both North and South Leith within the great bastioned fortification carried out by Peter Strozzi for Mary of Guise in 1548; and a few years later the people of South Leith raised funds to enable Mary to buy its freedom from Restalrig and make it a burgh of barony, at first under the crown, but soon afterwards transferred, in redemption of a mortgage, to the superiority of Edinburgh. Since Strozzi's work made Leith the most powerful fortress in Britain, it was a political as well as a military embarrassment, and the greater part of it was therefore hastily dismantled as soon as the French army departed in

1560. Yet it had lasting effects on Leith. For one thing, the ramparts had enclosed part of the lees or meadows that lay south of the town, and this had led swiftly to the development of the *Lees quarter* beyond the earlier boundary at Giles Street. Again, after the defences were slighted, the huge platform of the great bastion east of the harbour was made use of as a site for a timber exchange (a *burs* or *bush*) with *common closets* or communal yards for storage of timber, while elsewhere the great mounds and hollows left by the ramparts and ditches created a collar of open ground around the town, so uneven that it checked expansion for 200 years but at the same time preserved space for the great bypass roads which became essential to the development of modern Leith and its docks after 1800.

The Modern Names

It is no exaggeration to say that the changes which have taken place in the district since 1750 have affected (and in most cases transformed) the use of virtually every acre within it—even among the hills—with corresponding effects on its place names. Most obvious have been the huge increase in population and the even greater expansion of the built-up areas; and in the process a fair proportion of the older urban names have been retained, and several thousand new ones (mostly street names) added. But the other side of the medal is that the conversion of almost half of the original countryside of the 1750s to urban or suburban uses has entailed a heavy loss in rural names; and when this is taken together with further losses arising from radical changes in farms and farming, it appears that only something in the order of one third of the heritage of countryside names has survived.

Names in the Improved Countryside

Of all the changes since 1750, those in the countryside itself are the most difficult to visualise, simply because they have been so categoric, and so complete that scarcely a trace remains of what was there before. The detail on *Roy* 1753 suggests that at that time as much as nine tenths of the farm land was still being worked on the old open-field system, even although its decline in productivity through exhaustion of the soil had long been obvious. Many a drawing or print of the time faithfully depicts the resultant landscape—hedgeless, almost treeless, its bareness relieved only by the corrugated rigs of the ploughed land. The change, when it came, was nothing short of a revolution, even although at the time it was more coolly described as 'improvement'. Almost at a bound, Scottish agriculture, hitherto backward in the extreme, became one of the most advanced in the world; and although further changes were brought about by the scientific farming of the 19th century and by its mechanisation in the 20th, the rich pattern of the countryside as we now know it was basically created by the early 'Improvers'.

Their ideas had been already stirring in the 17th century. Laws had been passed to permit the necessary amalgamation of tenants' holdings; and at Prestonfield in the 1680s Sir James Dick pioneered enclosure of fields and the use of fertilizers—in this case, the 'polis dung' or street sweepings of Edinburgh. In 1698 the first book on Improvement was published; and by the 1720s the Earl of Stair was trying out the new turnip husbandry at Newliston, while in Edinburgh Thomas Hope of Rankeillour, who drained the Meadows, became the first chairman of the influential Society of Improvers. Yet although enthusiasm for improvement ran high, so did its costs. Bad times and other problems, not least the parlous state of the roads, held it back; but as soon as times grew better in the second half of the century, improvement came with a rush, and by 1790 it was well advanced throughout the district.

It was not only a matter of new fields and woodland shelter belts, of new systems of cultivation or new kinds of crop or breeds of animals or types of plough and other plenishings. It was nothing short of a total reorganisation of the countryside and its people. Holdings were slumped together to create farms of 100 acres or more. Many old farm touns were suppressed, and new ones were formed either by upgrading some old ones or by building afresh. New farmhouses were erected (superior to most manses, as the minister of Kirkliston ruefully noted in his *Statistical Account* of the parish in 1792) and the farm folk, much reduced in numbers when the new and more efficient methods were introduced, were transferred from their old blackhouses and farm touns to rows of cottages next the new farm steadings. Carts replaced pack horses; and the roads, until then unmetalled and unfit for wheeled transport, were thoroughly reconstructed, and in many cases rerouted to suit the new farms.

All this affected place names. Despite its bald appearance, the old unimproved landscape had been rich in names, not only because it contained more settlements but because the tenants needed to be able to identify the many small dispersed parts of their holdings. Under the old system, at a conservative estimate, upwards of sixteen names might have been needed within each hundred acres of land; but after improvement, with farms amalgamated and the multitude of rigs and dales merged into a very much simpler system of fields, the practical demand was reduced; and even though it must not be assumed that the maps of improved estates record every name in use among the farm folk, they show that for management purposes an average of about ten or a dozen names in a hundred acres of farm land usually sufficed. While some of these names were new and perhaps, like *Angle Park* or *Fore Shot* or *Fiorin Field*, described the shape or position or use of the field, a surprisingly large number—around half of them—seem to have come down from the land before its enclosure. Some, like *Scaudhinty* or *Stonyflatt*, described the ground; while others, such as *Garbrage* or

White Dales, continued technical terms of the old open-field system, or like *Skaithmuir*, harked back to the primitive days of the estate; and still others, like *Dumbeg*, preserved the names of long-forgotten settlements of over a thousand years before. Many of these ancient names still survive, despite the further weakening of the tradition in the 19th century, when fields were increasingly referred to by number rather than name, and the blows dealt it in the 20th century, not only where farms were split up by the advancing town, but more generally through the mechanisation of farming, which cut the working population to a small fraction of what it had been, and destroyed a great deal of folk memory in the by-going.

Most of the estates and farms in the improved countryside carried on old names, but others were re-named, either with importations, such as *Moredun* and (*New*) *Barnton* for the historic estates of Gutters and King's Cramond, or with names newly made up, such as Almondhill for the group of farms centred on Catelbok, or (much later) *Cockdurno* and *Cockburnhill* for Todholes and Shothead. The big difference was that whereas in the past most names had been given by the community, any new ones were now being chosen by the proprietors. A simple instance is in the change from *Nisbet's parks*, a name evidently given by the folk round about, to *Murrayfield*, the new owner's label for his family estate; and the practice became almost invariable when increased prosperity and ease of transport multiplied the number of small country estates round about the city. For example, when Corstorphinehill, the estate next to Murrayfield, was subdivided, one owner named his part *Beechwood* for his tree planting, while another part was called *Brucehill* by its Bruce owner and re-named *Bellmount* by the Campbell who succeeded him, and then later, when a third property was formed between the two, the name of *Beechmount* was compiled by borrowing half the name of each of them.

Names in the Expanded Towns

By the late 17th century the need to expand the capital city had become pressing and in 1688 James VII granted the town council the necessary powers, firstly to enlarge the 'royalty' or physical area within which the legal and commercial rights essential to the burgh applied, and secondly to build roads and bridges to overcome the difficulty that the potential sites for expansion were cut off from the central town by the deep and steep-sided valleys that flanked it. But James' charter was no sooner given than it was aborted by the abrupt ending of his reign; and political uncertainties and upheavals and the poor state of Scotland in the years that followed blocked effective action until 1752, when national proposals for the improvement of the city began a process which led to the North Bridge being started in 1765 and the New Town two years later. Gradually the process accelerated, assisted by the construction of the Mound and the six great flyover bridges north and south of the Old Town and at the gorges of Calton and the Dean; and by the 1830s the district's built-up areas (using that term broadly to include land taken into any sort of urban or suburban use, in the smaller centres as well as in Edinburgh and Leith) had become collectively more than four times as large as in the 1760s, when they had amounted to rather less than half a square mile. In the next 150 years, growth continued generally, but especially in two other great surges of expansion, the first in late Victorian times and the second in the period just before and just after the second world war; and the effect was to carry the total built-up area to about fourteen square miles by 1914 and to over forty-one by the 1980s.

Since conversion of countryside into town enormously increases the number of properties, each requiring an address, this huge expansion of the city meant that many more place names had to be created. On average they became rather more than twice as thick on the ground, and since (for reasons which will be touched on later) scarcely a quarter of the old countryside names were made use of, the vast majority of the town names were new. Not only so, but the unprecedented pace and manner of development meant that the very process of creating them had to change. Hitherto, as we have seen, the vast majority of place names had arisen, like nicknames, by use and wont among the populace, each deriving from the appearance or function or ownership or other association of the particular place. Given such distinctive characteristics and, more especially, a little time, names have continued to be created in this way, sometimes for streets like *New Street* or *Cuddy Lane*, but more often for routes like *the Glasgow Road* or *Leith Walk* or *the Lothian Road* or *the City Bypass*, or roads like *Society Road* or *Mansfield Road*, leading to or past well known places. Popular usage, often in connection with transport, has also made place names out of local resorts such as *Happy Valley* or *The Maybury*, or meeting points like *the West End* or (as a transferred name) *Tollcross*, or stopping places like *Western Corner* or *Holy Corner*; and names like *The Pillars* or the *Dummie Steps* probably represent a host of local names, mostly unrecorded, that have been coined in the first place by children. But obviously this way of creating names cannot cope with rapid development of whole neighbourhoods or with groups of streets in which one is very like another. It is no mere accident of fashion, but a matter of simple necessity, that in the period since 1750 the vast majority of names have been created or adapted by deliberate choice.

Although there are some earlier isolated examples of it, such as in the naming of *Milne's Square* in 1689 or *Argyle Square* in the 1730s, the new method came into its own in the choice of names for the streets of the New Town of 1767. In the original scheme of names (it was to be somewhat blurred by changes made in deference to George III) it is evident that they were not chosen singly but as a group designed to proclaim that, in the fashion then current in France, this New Town was being built to the greater glory of the reigning monarch. Thirty-five years later, the same national theme was taken up, on a bigger scale but in a less absolutist style, in the names of streets in the Northern New Town. Yet in the very nature of things the scope for celebration of the nation or of great events (as, for example, in *Waterloo Place*) is apt to be restricted, not only because the subjects themselves are limited, but because few developments are grand enough to carry such themes with any dignity. Already in 1802 other fashions were coming in—for example, naming to celebrate developers, as at *Heriot Row* and *Fettes Row*, or out of fancy, as at *Royal Crescent* or *Royal Circus*; and in the huge scheme for the Calton New Town in 1819—the last big development the town had a hand in before modern times, and aiming to be the grandest of them all, although less than half of it was built— the original plan shows street names not marshalled under one great theme, but grouped in various sets of compliments and historical commemorations.

But if the theme of national celebration had soon become more or less played out, celebration of the developer or the developer's connections, typified in the early examples of *Milne's Square* and *Argyle Square* already mentioned, had the merit of being freshly available for each new scheme. Thus in the development of the earl of Moray's estate of Drumsheugh in 1822, the street names were chosen to celebrate the earl himself, his family, his historic predecessors in the title, and his Scottish estates—albeit with omission of *Drumsheugh*, the very one of them he was developing. It was a model that could be easily extended to take in a great variety of private interests, from political heroes, as in *Peel Terrace*, to favourite holiday resorts, as in *Ventnor Terrace*. It was widely followed in the ensuing hundred years, especially in developments of personal or family estates, and was continued for a time by the local authority—for example, in naming *Harewood Drive* for the Princess Royal, or *Maybury Drive* for a civil servant, or (in surely the most overdone compliment of all) an entire block of ten new streets for the Lord Provost of the day, Thomas Hutchison. Another device was to make up fancy names. Some of these, such as *Royal Crescent*, sought fashionable prestige or, like *Buckingham Terrace* or *Belgrave Park*, openly imitated London addresses. Others simply sought prettiness or diversity, as in some developments by the Edinburgh Co-operative Building Company, in which the streets were named after flowers or shrubs or trees, or in Edinburgh Corporation's schemes at the Inch, where the three dozen individual street names were taken from Sir Walter Scott and his novels. Finally, there were names which might be termed 'site-related', derived in some way from the place itself. The great majority of them continued or recovered local place names; but sometimes the connection was a historical one, whether general to the district, as at *Canmore Street*, or to the neighbourhood, as at *Barony Street* or *Roull Road*, or else belonging to the site in particular, as at *Castle Avenue, Barrace Steps, Cromwell Street* or *King Edward's Way*; while in yet other cases, notably in Leith, names like *Bangor Road* or *Salamander Street* obliquely referred to businesses served by the streets concerned.

In this analysis, about two thirds of new names in the 19th century were developer-related, while the rest were related to their sites. In very few cases is there any direct record of who chose them and why, but the circumstances and the names themselves generally suggest that it was the developer who coined them. This is hardly surprising, for development was thought of as very much a private matter. Indeed, some of the earlier schemes, like Dr Young's *New Street* or George Bell's *Blacket Place*, were designed to be closed off to the public by gates; and in many cases the name was not attached to the public street itself, but was in the nature of an enhanced house name given to the buildings it served—an arrangement of 'side names' that persists in *Haddington Place* or *St Peter's Buildings*, for instance, while elsewhere, as in *Shandwick Place* or *Albert Terrace*, the original side name has eventually usurped the name of the street. Nevertheless, throughout the period, there was some public concern about names. It was probably the commissioners appointed by Parliament in 1771 for the improvement of Leith who promoted new and more high-sounding names for some of its medieval streets, such as *Queen Street* for the *Paunchmarket* or *St Andrew's Street* for the *Dub Raw*. In Edinburgh itself, the city's police commissioners (and after 1856, the town council) had to see to it that each street had its name properly displayed—a duty that must have entailed confirmation of names, if not some selection of them; and after 1879, when the town council was expressly empowered by statute to choose or to alter the names of streets, they began to regulate street naming, and to simplify addresses by adjusting or merging existing names and by suppressing many of the side names.

In the 1900s, the ratio between names related to developers and those related to the site began to change; and after 1919 the pace quickened so rapidly that in the two decades between the Wars the earlier ratio was almost exactly reversed, site-related names being now in the majority, and after 1946 more than eighty percent of new names derived in one way or another from the locality. Two factors combined to bring this about: change in the kind of developer, and change in the scale and pace of development. Typically the earlier developments had been in personal or family properties and were carried out more or less directly by their owners; and understandably the owners' sense of property, as well as personal or family pride, led them to be less concerned to continue local place names than to celebrate themselves and their interests. But increasingly after the turn of the century development came to be promoted by corporate agencies, whether local or national or multinational companies or else public authorities, who could scarcely have such private or personal interests. Furthermore, in the course of the vast expansion of the urban areas that set in after 1919 and went on yet more vigorously after 1946, schemes of development were apt to be individually much larger and to thrust out into the countryside more rapidly than ever before. The demand for names was not only much greater but more urgent; and names already connected with the place offered one ready source of supply.

But this pressing demand for groups of street names also had an effect on the method of coining them. Whereas it had been usual to give each street a distinctive specific name of its own, followed by the generic term for the type of street (so making names like *Great King Street* and *Heriot Row*) now there was a sudden extension of a fashion which reversed this normal style by giving one and the same specific name to every street in the group, and distinguished between them only by varying the terms for type of street. For example, in the development of Northfield in Duddingston in 1921, all ten of its original streets shared the specific name *Northfield*, while each had its own different street-type label, whether *Avenue, Broadway, Circus, Crescent, Eastway, Gardens, Highway, Road, Square* or *Terrace*. The fashion was not entirely new, for previously and in a limited way there had been some such sharing of names, mostly in pairs, but also in a handful of somewhat larger groups averaging four or five streets apiece. What was new after 1919 was not only that this method was used far more often, but that the number of streets involved in each case (often in double figures and, after 1946, even exceeding twenty or thirty) was generally so much greater as to change the scale and character of the group quite radically. Instead of being a compact and quite local cluster it became a whole neighbourhood, sometimes covering more than half a square kilometre. While the 'blanket' use of one single specific name for all streets within it bypassed the problem of finding or inventing a large number of individual names, at the same time it meant that many more street-type labels had to be supplied. Whereas only eleven different labels of this kind had been needed in a hundred and fifty years of street naming prior to 1919, by 1974 the number had shot up to thirty-two, and by 1990 it was thirty-nine. One result was almost to drain them of their distinctive meanings. *Place* had once implied something which was not so much a *street* as a space; *avenue*, an approach lined by trees or buildings; or *terrace*, a row of houses overlooking a road, as distinct from a *row* that simply lined it; but now it became commonplace for streets to differ in name but so little in form that a *crescent* might look virtually the same as a *drive*, and there was also the absurdity that if more than one street

40

happened to fit a particular description, only one of them could be given that distinctive label. Of its very nature, the method tended towards monotony and lack of distinction between streets, besides drabness and, in larger schemes where many of the names were apt to be somewhat forced, even a certain triviality. It may have begun as an administrative convenience; but when compared with the older method used (for example) at the Inch, where each street had its own individual name, it offered no social advantage, but only disadvantages: for in practice, nationally as well as in Edinburgh, it was found that a new neighbourhood soon acquired its own identity, no matter how the streets were named, and that the more distinct the street names were from one another the easier it became to memorise the layout of the whole place and to find particular addresses within it.

The common feature of any 'blanket' naming of streets, whether of the type just described or arising from the exclusive use of developer-related or fancy names, was that it resulted in suppression of local names. Among modern 'greenfield' developments, schemes like those in South Clermiston or Muirhall in Queensferry, which used only fancy or commemorative or complimentary street names, necessarily made a clean sweep of every name previously attached to the ground. Schemes that made blanket use of the farm or estate name were far more numerous; but even although they produced blocks of names that could be classed as site-related, their effect on local place names was scarcely less drastic. The Northfield scheme already mentioned was a typical case, for while it preserved the 200-year-old farm name, it suppressed half a dozen other highly distinctive (and probably much older) names belonging to the ground. Such a loss of about eighty or ninety percent of countryside names was fairly general, and it was only partly relieved by continuation of traditional names for adjoining main roads or burns or hills or other features.

Although expansion of the built-up area is seen from the urban point of view as 'development', it is more properly to be described as redevelopment of the countryside; and the question of the loss or survival of existing names in fact arises in redevelopment of every sort, whether within a town or beyond its bounds. Thus in the outskirts, land names were thinned out or else obliterated by redevelopment for housing or parks and golf courses, or for industrial installations, such as the colliery and railway yards that covered the Hunter's Haw in Niddrie or the huge area of farm land taken up by Edinburgh Airport; while redevelopment in the older parts of the city brought urban names similarly under threat, the more so because new works were usually radically different in form from those they replaced, and often vastly different in scale—the sort of thing seen most dramatically (although by no means uniquely) in central Leith, where the historic plan and texture of the town, already altered by sweeping improvements in the

19th century, was for the most part destroyed by later redevelopments on such a giant scale that not only the names but all vestiges of many places were lost. Yet in essence such processes were nothing different from what had happened in the farm land of the Lang Dykes when the New Town was built 200 years earlier, or in the densely built-up High Street in 1753, when over a dozen medieval properties and parts of three closes were slumped together to make a single quadrangular site for the Royal Exchange. In general, whenever there is a change of use, it is normal for the earlier users to be dispersed before redevelopment begins, taking their knowledge of local names with them, while the new users are essentially interested in what results from redevelopment, and often know little or even nothing about what was there before it took place; and because of this hiatus in interest as well as time, earlier names will not be carried forward unless they are among the few the incomers happen to know, or else are deliberately sought out and chosen for continued use. The larger or more drastic the redevelopment, the more acutely the question arises; and it is astonishing how quickly the full or accurate memory of the earlier pattern of names can be lost, or records mislaid.

In the 1970s, the need to grapple with such problems became obvious. Coupled with this was a growing awareness of the social importance of the heritage from the past and the practical value of place names in keeping it alive; and by 1984 it was settled policy that every new street should have its own distinctive name, that blanket use of common specific names was to be avoided, and that street names, wherever possible, should be used to strengthen the individuality of a neighbourhood by accurately continuing or recovering local place names, or making reference to historical associations of the ground. This was not to say that the invention of entirely new names could or should have no place in the living tradition, but it was recognised that it was merely perverse to allow new inventions unnecessarily to oust distinctive names that already belonged to the place or could in one way or another be associated with it. Furthermore it was clear that unless these local names were used accurately, their genuineness would be undermined and the whole purpose compromised—and to make matters worse, any corruption of their form or displacement from their proper location would threaten to damage the originals or even bar them from further use, as had happened all too often in the past. Indeed if they were to serve any practical purpose, place names had to be handled with care and respected as local monuments: some already familiar, some only to be discovered as it were by excavation in the records, but all of interest and value in lighting up the depths of the past and enriching the present and the future.

References Used in the Text

Generally, those listed here are mentioned in more than one entry in the list of place names. In other cases, details are given in the entry concerned.

* Indicates map, plan or print. Where possible, dates noted are dates of survey.

Abbreviations:

CA   City Archives.
ECL   Edinburgh City Libraries—Scottish Library and Edinburgh Room.
NLS   National Library of Scotland Map Room.
BOEC   Book of the Old Edinburgh Club.
PSAS   Proceedings of the Society of Antiquaries of Scotland.
RHP   Plans in Scottish Records Office, West Register House.

Accurate View: Peter Williamson: *An Accurate View*, broadsheet listing streets, wynds and closes 1783—EPL, also *BOEC Vol. XXII* p264.

Acts of Bailies of the Canongate: *Acts of Bailies of the Canongate*—CA.

* **Adair 1682:** MS maps of *Midlothian* and *West Lothian*—NLS.

* **Adair/Cooper 1735:** R Cooper's engravings of above MSS—NLS.

Agriculture in Midlothian: Robertson, *Agriculture in Midlothian* 1795—ECL Reference Library.

* **Ainslie 1780:** *City of Edinburgh* c1780—NLS; ECL.

* **Ainslie 1804:** *Old & New Town of Edinburgh & Leith*—NLS; ECL.

Anent Old Edinburgh: A H Dunlop, *Anent Old Edinburgh*. Edinburgh 1890.

* **Armstrongs 1773:** A & M Armstrong, *Map of the Three Lothians* with inset plan of city—NLS.

Arnot: Hugo Arnot, *History of Edinburgh*. Edinburgh 1779 & 1816.

Baird's Duddingston & Portobello: Wm. Baird, *Annals of Duddingston & Portobello*. Edinburgh 1900.

* **Barnbougle & Dalmeny:** Estate map by Ainslie c1800—RHP 3657.

Bain: *Calendar of Documents relating to Scotland* (Ed) J Bain. Edinburgh 1881-8.

* **Bartholomew 1876:** *Edinburgh & Leith* (for PO Directory) 1876—NLS.

Black's Surnames: G F Black, *Surnames of Scotland*. New York Public Library 1946.

* **Blaeu 1654:** 'Lothian & Linlitquo', in Blaeu's *Atlas Novus* 1654, based on survey by Timothy Pont c1596, edited by Gordon of Straloch—NLS.

Boog Watson: Charles Boog Watson (a) MS 'Notes', 6 vols. in ECL (including the volume on street names published by City Engineer—see below) and (b) 'Names of the Closes and Wynds', *BOEC Vol. XII*.

* **Braid 1772:** John Home, map of *The Barony of Braid*—NLS.

* **Braid & Niddrie Burns:** Kirkwood, *Draught of Braids Burn etc.*—RPH 582.

* **Brown & Watson 1793:** *City of Edinburgh*—NLS.

* **Brown 1809:** Thos. Brown, City of Edinburgh—NLS.

* **Brunstane 1761:** John Lesslie, Estate of Brunstane—RHP 14979/2.

Burgh Register: *Burgh Register*—CA.

* **Bypass Roads:** Anon. untitled and undated map (c1763) showing

proposed roads from North Bridge: see plate in *BOEC Vol. XXII* p4, and *BOEC Second Series Vol 2.* pp11-12. Notes 11 & 12.

* **Caldcoats 1815:** *Caldcoats, Bankfield & Wisp*—RHP 3716.

* **Calton 1819:** *Plan referred to ... at a meeting of the Joint Committee* 20 December 1819, with copy minute 27 September 1819—NLS.

Campbell: Alexander Campbell, *History of Leith*, 1827.

Canongate Charters: MS *Canongate Charters*—CA.

Canongate Burgh Court: *Court Book of Regality of Broughton and Burgh of Canongate 1569-73*, ed. Marguerite Wood. Edinburgh 1937.

* **Canongate, Regality of, 1813:** *Regality of the Canongate, comprising the liberties of Pleasance, North Leith, Coalhill and Citidal*—RHP 191.

* **Carlowrie c1800:** Ainslie, n.d. *Carlowrie—Wheatlands, Bourtreebush, Puncheonlaw, and West Carlowrie*—RHP 185.

Chambers 1825 & 1868: Robert Chambers, *Traditions of Edinburgh*. Edinburgh.

Charters relating to Edinburgh: *Charters & Documents relating to Edinburgh AD 1143-1540*, Scottish Burgh Records Society. Edinburgh 1871.

City Charters: MS *City Charters*—CA.

City Engineer: City Engineer's Department, *History & Derivation of Edinburgh Street Names* (incl. notes by C Boog Watson) Edinburgh 1975.

* **City Improvement 1866:** Royal Burgh, County of City and County of Edinburgh, *Edinburgh Improvements*. Index map and 6 sheets of details—ECL.

* **Coates Haugh 1761:** *Plan of Coateshaugh, now called Sunberry*—RHP 586.

Cockburn: Henry Cockburn, *Memorials of His Time*. Edinburgh 1858.

* **Colinton Mains & Oxgangs, 1813:** Plan of farms—RHP 31849 (copied in *Steuart's Colinton*).

* **Collins 1693:** *Mappe of Leith* in Capt. Greenvile Collins, *Coasting Pilot*—NLS, also copied on *Kirkwood's Ancient Plan*.

Common Good 1904: Thos. Hunter & Robt. Paton, *Report on the Common Good*. Edinburgh 1905—ECL.

* **Cooper 1759:** R Cooper, *Edinburgh with Adjacent Grounds*—small-scale summary engraving of MSS maps by *Scott* and *Fergus & Robinson* 1759—NLS.

* **Corstorphine 1754:** Robt. Johnstone, *Barony of Corstorphin*—RHP 1041.

* **Corstorphine 1777:** In Selway, *A Midlothian Village*, p5—ECL.

* **Corstorphine 1845:** Wm. Brooke, *Estate of Corstorphine*—SLP 149 NLS.

* **Corstorphinehill, 1885:** Plan of estates—Scottish Records Office GD 335/21.

* **County Roads 1902:** Chas. Robb, *Map of the Four Districts etc.*—NLS.

* **Craigentinny 1847:** Plan of (part of) estate—NLS.

* **Craiglockhart 1834:** G Craig, *Plan of Craiglockhart*—RHP 30763.

* **Craigour, Edmonston & Fernieside:** Plan 1815—RHP 3716.

* **Cramond 1815:** Bauchop, *Plan of Cramond*—1815—RHP 6866.

* **Cramond Roads:** J Leslie & Son, *Roads within and connected with Cramond District*, 1812—NLS.

* **Cultins 1776:** Thos. Johnston, *Roads—Ratho to Edinburgh*—RHP 3702/3.

Cumberland Hill: Cumberland Hill, *Historic Memorials of Stockbridge*, 2nd ed. Edinburgh 1887.

* **Currie Farm 1797:** *Corslet & Currie farm and Currie muir*—RHP 550/2.

* **Dall & Leslie 1831:** *Harbour & Docks of Leith and Coast adjacent*—NLS.
* **Dalmahoy 1749:** Thos. Winter, *Estate of Dalmahoy*—RHP 1021.
Dean of Guild Records: MS *Dean of Guild records*—CA.
Directories 1773 onwards: *Campbell, Denovan, New Edinburgh, Portobello, Post Office, Williamson*—ECL.
* **District Roads 1777:** Thos. Johnston, *Plans of all roads in the several districts of Midlothian ... with explanations*—NLS.
Diurnal of Occurrents: *Diurnal of Occurrents*, Bannatyne Club No. 43.
* **The Drum 1815:** Estate plan (lithograph 1842)—RHP 3716.
* **Duddingston c. 1800:** Estate plan, copied 1820—NLS.
* **Duddingston Parish Roads c1820:** Wm. Crawford Jnr., roads proposals, n.d.—RHP 486.
* **Duddingston Mills 1564:** Map drawn for Court of Session case—RHP 430.
* Dundas 1757: James Gordon, *Estate of Dundas*—RHP 3370.
Dunfermline Register: *Registrum de Dunfermelyn*, Bannatyne Club, Edinburgh 1842.
* **Edgar 1742 & 1765:** *City & Castle of Edinburgh*—NLS; EPL.
Edinburgh 1329-1929: Edinburgh Corporation, *Edinburgh 1329-1929*, (published on occasion of sexcentenary of Bruce charter) Edinburgh 1929.
Edinburgh in the Olden Time: T G Stevenson, *Edinburgh in the Olden Time*. Edinburgh 1880. Facsimiles of plates dating from 1717 to 1828.
* **Egypt 1834:** Jas. Knox, *Sketch of the farm*—RHP 12791.
Exchequer Rolls: *Exchequer Rolls of Scotland*, eds. Stuart and others. Edinburgh 1878-1908.
* **Fergus & Robinson:** MS map of *Lands belonging to Edinburgh and other Heritors north of the City* 1759—NLS.
* **Forrest, W:** *Linlithgowshire* 1818 (surveyed 1817)—NLS.
* **Fortification of Leith 1850:** Conjectural and erroneous map in Robertson's *Sculptured Stones of Leith*—see under *Siege of Leith*.
* **Fowler 1845:** *County of Edinburgh*—NLS.
* **Gellatly 1834:** *The Country 12 Miles round Edinburgh*—NLS.
* **Geological Survey:** *Geological Survey of Great Britain (Scotland) Drift Edition* 1 inch to 1 mile, Sheet 32, 1967.
* **George Square feus 1779:** Jas. Brown, *Plan of New Buildings in Ross Park* in *BOEC Vol. XXVI* p16.
Good's Liberton: George Good, *Liberton in Ancient & Modern Times*. Edinburgh 1892.
***Grange c1760:** Plan of part estate, overmarked with reference to defenders' sketch plan of 1766—RPH 5385.
* **Grange 1766:** Sketch plan of part estate—RHP 5386.
Grant: James Grant, *Old & New Edinburgh*, 3 vols. London 1882.
* **Hailes 1818:** Geo. Buchanan, *Part of Hailes*—RHP 3590.
* **Hailes Quarry 1837:** incl. Dumbryden & Kingsknowes—RHP 89 and 3529.
* **Hatton etc. 1797:** John Ainslie, *Lands of Hatton etc.*—RHP 724.
* **Hermiston 1793:** Thos. Johnston, *Plan of Hermiston*—RHP 547.
* **Hertford's Assault 1544:** *Attack on Edinburgh by English army under the Earl of Hertford in 1544*, Cottonian MS, British Library; facsimiles in *Bannatyne Club No. 19 Vol. 1*, and in EPL; reduced facsimile in *Grant*, Vol. I, p5.

45

Historie of James Sext: Anon. *Historie & Life of King James the Sext*, Bannatyne Club No. 13; extracts in *BOEC Vol. XVI*.

* **Hollar 1650:** Hollar W, *Edenburgh from the south*, c1650, etching published in 1670—ECL.

Holyrood Charters: *Book of Charters of Holyrood abbey*. Bannatyne Club No. 70.

* **Holyrood Park 1845:** Wm. Nixon, scheme of roads etc.—RHP 2821.

* **Humbie 1720:** Plan of *Humbie Farm* 1720—RHP 6728.

Hutchison's Leith: Wm. Hutchison, *Tales, Traditions & Antiquities of Leith*. 1865.

* **Johnston W & A K 1851:** see *Lancefield* 1851.

* **Johnston W & A K 1861:** *Edinburgh, Leith & Suburbs* (P O Directory)— NLS.

* **Johnston W & A K 1861:** *Four-sheet map of Edinburgh*—NLS.

* **Johnston W & A K 1888:** *Edinburgh, Leith, Portobello and Environs*—NLS.

* **Johnston W & A K 1898:** *Edinburgh, Leith, Portobello with Suburbs*—NLS.

* **Johnston W & A K 1905:** *Edinburgh, Leith, Portobello with Suburbs*—NLS.

* **Kay 1836:** *Plan of Edinburgh*—NLS.

Kelso Abbey Charters: *Register of Charters of Kelso abbey* 1160-70, Bannatyne Club No. 82.

* **Kerr H F:** *Edinburgh in Mid Eighteenth Century* 1918—*BOEC Vol. X*—ECL.

* **Kincaid 1784:** *Map of City and Suburbs of Edinburgh*—NLS.

Kincaid 1787: Alexr. Kincaid, *History of Edinburgh and Gazetteer of County*, Edinburgh 1787.

* **Kirk o Fields 1567:** Drawing *Our Lady Kirk of Field*, HM State Paper Office: and interpretation of it by Henry F Kerr, *PSAS Vol. 66*, 1932.

* **Kirkliston 1789:** John Lesslie, *Kirkliston*—RHP 6837.

* **Kirkliston 1812:** untitled, n.d.: Alternative schemes for turnpike—RHP 6840(2).

* **Kirkliston 1815:** J Lauder (?), *Plan of Kirkliston* RHP 35563.

* **Kirkwood's Ancient Plan:** Historical map compiled in 1817 from *Collins* 1693, *Edgar* 1742, *Scott* and *Fergus & Robinson* 1759, and *Wood's Leith* 1777—NLS.

* **Kirkwood 1817 & 1823:** *City of Edinburgh*—NLS; ECL.

* **Kirkwood's Environs 1817:** *Environs of Edinburgh*—NLS.

* **Knox 1812:** *Edinburgh and its Environs*—NLS; ECL.

* **Knox 1821:** *Edinburgh & its Environs* (City)—NLS.

Laing Charters: *Calendar of the Laing Charters* (ed.) J Anderson. Edinburgh 1899.

* **Lancefield 1851:** Johnson's *Edinburgh and Leith in 1851*—ECL; NLS.

* **Laurie 1763:** *The County of Midlothian or Shire of Edinburgh*—NLS.

* **Laurie 1766:** *Edinburgh & Places Adjacent*, 1766 (two editions—see *BOEC Series 2 Vol. 2*, p7) also 1786 and 1811—NLS.

* **Lauriston 1808:** *Laurieston* (Cramond)—RHP 3575.

Leith Burlaw Court Minutes 1725-50: David Robertson, 'Burlaw Court of Leith', *BOEC Vol. XV 1927*.

* **Leith River 1787:** J Ainslie, *Leith River from Harbour to Canonmills*—RHP 3282.

* Lothian 1829: *Edinburgh*—NLS.

* Lothian 1826: *Leith & its Vicinity*—NLS.

Maitland: Wm. Maitland, *History of Edinburgh*. Edinburgh 1753.

Mason's Queensferry: John Mason, *History of Queensferry* 1963, typescript in ECL.

* Mayfield 1862: David Cousins, *Feuing Plan of Mayfield* (superseded)— RHP 1385.

* Merchiston 1776: Walter Kerr & John Lesslie, *Merchiston* 1776, incl. survey by Lesslie 1772, and overmarked with realignment of Slateford road etc. by J Bell c.1800—RHP 20578.

Milne: *Gaelic Placenames of the Lothians* 1912—mentioned only as an unreliable and highly misleading book.

Morison's Queensferry: Alexander Morison, *Notes on the Ancient & Royal Burgh of Queensferry*. West Lothian Courier, 1927.

* Mortonhall 1770: Wm. Crawford, *Sketch Plan of Meadowhead, Buckstone, North Morton and Mortonhall* 1770—in estate office, Charterhall, Berwickshire.

* Mortonhall 1776: J Lesslie, *Mortonhall etc.* 1776—in Charterhall as the foregoing.

* Muirhouse: *Muirhouse (incl. Silverknowes)* c.1827—ECL.

* Naish 1709: John Naish, *Town of Leith*—MS survey in Public Record Office, London, copied as illustration in *PSAS Vol. 121.*

Newbattle Abbey charters: *Register of Charters of Newbattle abbey*, Bannatyne Club No. 89.

* Newhaven Roads: John Laurie, 'Plan of roads leading from the Netherbow port to Newhaven' 1765, MS in *Robertson v le Grand law Papers*—ECL.

* Newington 1795: Bell & Reid, *Feuing Plan of Newington* and other lands between Crosscausey and Mayfield Loan—plate in *BOEC Vol. XXIV.*

* Newington 1806: Benjamin Bell, *Feuing Plan*—RHP 85, see plate in *BOEC Vol. XXIV.*

* Newington 1826: *Newington & Belleville*—NLS.

* Newmains 1839: *Newmains Farm* (incl. Kirkliston village)—RHP 11583.

* New Town site plan: *Ground Plan* surveyed by Laurie 1766, printed in *BOEC Vol. XXIII* as overlay to engraved plan 1767 (see below)—modern copy in ECL.

* New Town 1767: MS *Plan* approved 29 July 1767—original in Huntly House Museum.

* New Town 1767: unfinished engraved *Plan* autumn 1767—plate in *BOEC Vol. XXIII.*

* New Town 1768: Feuing plan published 1 January 1768—NLS; ECL.

Nicoll's Diary: John Nicoll, *Diary*, Bannatyne Club No. 52, Edinburgh 1836; also extracts in *BOEC Vol. XVI.*

* Niddrie Coals: *Map of Niddrie Coals* 1760—RHP 33. Also see *Geological Survey* 6 inch = 1 mile, Sheet NT 37 SW, 1965.

* Norton 1813: Wm. Crawford & Son, *Estate of Norton*—RHP 9621.

Old Edinburgh Club (BOEC): *Book of the Old Edinburgh Club Vol. I-XXXV*, and New Series Vol. 1-2.

* **Ordnance Survey:** all in NLS—
   Six-inch (1:10560, now metric 1:10000) 1852 to date;
   Twenty-five inch (1:2500) Queensferry and Kirkliston 1856; and District generally 1893-4;
   Five-foot (1:1056) City area 1852.
Pathfinder Gazetteer: R A Hooker, *Pathfinder Gazetteer*, Hawick—gazetteer of all names shown on O.S. Pathfinder maps.
* **Pilton 1780s:** John Ainslie, *West & East Pilton, belonging to Sir Philip Ainslie* n.d.—RHP 6473.
* **Plewlandfield 1769:** J Leslie, *Plewlandfield* 1769, overmarked 1782—RHP 35555.
* **Plewlands 1887:** John Aitken, *Plewlands* (Queenferry)—RHP 11550.
* **Plewlands 1882:** *Proposed Development of Plewlands Estate* (South Morningside)—in Charles Smith's *Historic South Edinburgh* p274.
* **Pollock 1834:** *Plan of Edinburgh, Leith & Suburbs*—NLS.
* **Portobello 1832:** *Parliamentary boundaries*—NLS.
* **Portobello 1856:** Arch. Sutter, *Burgh of Portobello*—NLS.
* **Prestonfield 1824:** David Crawford, *Plan of Estate*—RHP 31863.
Protocols: Protocol books of *John Foular, Alexr. King, William Stewart, Adam Watt, James Young*—ECL.
* **Queensferry 1832:** *Parliamentary Boundaries*—NLS.
Ragman Rolls: *Ragman Rolls 1296*, Bannatyne Club No. 47.
* **Ravelrig 1764:** James Richmond, *Ravelrig ... in Currie*—NLS.
* **Ravelston 1820:** D Crawford, *Ravelston & Corstorphinehill*—RHP 2166.
RCAHMS Inventory: Royal Commission on Ancient & Historical Monuments of Scotland, *Midlothian and West Lothian* 1929, and *City of Edinburgh* 1951.
* **Riccarton 1772:** *Plan of Riccarton*—RHP 550/1.
* **Riccarton 1800:** *Plan* incl. farms from Currie to the Gyle—RHP 550/2.
RMS: *Register of the Great Seal of Scotland Vol. I-XI.* Reprinted by Scottish Record Society 1984.
* **Roads from Figget 1783:** John Ainslie, n.d.—RHP 98.
Robertson: D H Robertson, 'Map of Fortifications of Leith', *Sculptured Stones of Leith*, 1851: but see under Siege of Leith.
* **Rothiemay 1647:** James Gordon, untitled plan (bird's eye view) commissioned by Town Council 1647, engraved by Blaeu 1649, re-engraved by de Wit c1695, Andrew Johnston 1708-14 (with sketches)—NLS; ECL.
* **Roy 1753:** *Military Survey of Scotland* 1747-55: MS in British Library, best studied in colour slides—NLS.
RPC: *Register of the Privy Council of Scotland.* Edinburgh 1877.
RSS: *Register of the Privy Seal (Secreti Sigilli) of Scotland.* Edinburgh 1908.
* **Saughton 1795:** John Johnston, *Plan of Estate*—RHP 11151/2.
* **Saughtonhall 1795:** John Johnston, *Plan of Estate*—RHP 3705/1 & 2.
* **Scott 1759:** MS plan of *Lands South of the City*—NLS.
Selway: G Upton Selway, *A Midlothian Village*, Edinburgh 1890, facsimile ed. by City Libraries 1984.
* **Sheens 1761:** A Bell, plate, 'Ground of Sheens', *BOEC Vol. X.*
* **Siege of Edinburgh Castle 1573:** *Plan of the Siege*, plate in Holinshed's *Chronicles* 1577, facsimiles in *Bannatyne Miscellany Vol II*, and *Grant*

Vol. I p53; see also contemporary 'Journal of the Siege', Bannatyne Club No. 19 (a) and *BOEC Vol. XVI.*

* **Siege of Leith 1560:** Military engineer's MS plan of siege works, Petworth House Archives 4640, West Sussex Record Office; copies in CA and Huntly House Museum. (For interpretation, see Harris, 'Fortifications and Siege of Leith' *PSAS Vol. 121.*)

* **Silverknowes 1841:** G James: *Silverknowes*—RHP 31872. (Also see *Muirhouse.*)

Smith A H: *English Place-name Elements* (2 vols) 1970.

South Leith Records: David Robertson, *South Leith Records* Series I (1911) and II (1925) Edinburgh.

* **Spylaw 1769:** A Leslie, *Plan of the Farm*—RHP 47.

* **Spylaw 1798:** John Bell, *Plan of the Estate*—RHP 20580.

Statistical Account, Old: *Statistical Account of Scotland*, (ed) Sir John Sinclair, 1791-99, reissued 1975, Vol. II—*The Lothians.*

Statistical Account, New: *New Statistical Account of Scotland*, Vol. 1 *Edinburgh*, Edinburgh 1845.

Stent (or Valuation) Roll 1635: C B Boog Watson, 'Owners of Property' and select list of tenants, *BOEC Vol. XIII.*

Steuart's Colinton: James Steuart, *Notes for a History of Colinton Parish*, Edinburgh 1938.

* **Strangers Guide 1816:** map of Edinburgh & Leith—NLS.

* **Taylor & Skinner 1775 & 1805:** *Road Books of Scotland*—NLS.

* **Thomson 1822:** *Leith & its Environments*—NLS.

Town Council Minutes: *Extracts from the Records of Burgh of Edinburgh* 1403-1718, 12 vols. Edinburgh 1869-1967.

* **Turnpike Roads 1841:** Map showing turnpike gates—RHP 10231.

Tweedie & Jones: J Tweedie & C Jones, *Our District.* Currie 1975.

* **Union Canal 1816:** Francis Hall, (*Proposals*) *Dumbryden to Meggatland*—RHP 1862.

Valuation Roll 1635: see *Stent Roll* above.

Walker's Collington 1795: Revd John Walker, 'Collington', in his *Essays on Natural History & Rural Economy*, 1812; much abridged in *Statistical Account* 1795.

* **Wester Hailes 1818:** see *Hailes 1818* above.

* **Whitehouse & Adiefield c1788:** *Lands belonging to Mr Morison*—RHP 601.

White's Liberton 1786: Revd Thos. Whyte, 'Parish of Liberton', in Transactions of Society of Antiquaries of Scotland. Vol. I; much abridged in *Statistical Account* 1786.

Wilson: Daniel Wilson, *Memorials of Edinburgh in the Olden Time*, 2 vols. 2nd ed. Edinburgh 1891.

Wood's Cramond 1794: John P Wood, *Parish of Cramond*—ECL.

Wood's Corstorphine c1792: John P Wood, MS *draft history of Corstorphine*—typescript copy in ECL.

* **Wood's Leith or *Wood 1777*:** Alexr. Wood, *Town of Leith* 1777—NLS.

* **Wood 1823:** J Wood, *City of Edinburgh* (Brown's map of 1820 'altered to 1823')—NLS.

* **Wood's Portobello:** J Wood, *Town of Portobello* 1824—NLS.

A

ABBEY CLOSE (Holyrood) is shown on *Hertford's Assault* 1544 and named on *Edgar* 1742. The name, using close in its primary sense of 'enclosure', no doubt goes back to the medieval abbey.

ABBEYHILL is named on *Adair* 1682, and all maps concur in attaching the name to the road and the settlement beside it, rather than to any natural feature. It is possible, as suggested in *Edinburgh 1329-1929* pp263-5, that the road was a 12th-century diversion, to make room for the new abbey, of a road which had previously led straight on east from the foot of the Canongate; but what is certain is that it keeps to the low ground, circling north of the Tummel burn and the bogs that once lay in the vicinity of Milton Street; and it is likely that it is not the Calton slope that is referred to in the name *hill at the Abbey*, but the hillock of St Ann's Brae, which must have been prominent in the early landscape. ABBEYMOUNT, although medieval in date and shown on the map of the *Siege of Leith* 1560, appears from the alignments to have been a later branch off the Abbeyhill road; and its name—an obvious play on Abbeyhill—is perhaps no older than the 1840s. In *Town Council Minutes* 1500 this part of the easter road to Leith is referred to as 'Leyth hill besyde the Abbay', where as a precaution against the spread of the plague from Leith, goods being sent there were to be dumped by the Edinburgh carters and then uplifted by carters from Leith. ABBEYHILL CRESCENT, redeveloped in 1968 on the site of HOLYROOD TERRACE and other property, was named from the adjoining main road, missing an opportunity to restore the site's ancient name of IRNESIDE, *which see.*

ABBEY LANE (Abbeyhill) was a lane on the west side of Croftangry (the so-called 'Croft an Righ') shown on *Ordnance Survey* 1852 but suppressed by brewery development by 1899. The name was revived in 1966 as a new name for ROSE LANE at Comely Green, which itself seems to have been a late 19th-century name for the first section of the old road from Abbeyhill to Restalrig—*see* MARIONVILLE ROAD.

ABBEY STRAND (Holyrood) takes its name from the rivulet or (in Scots) *strand* that is shown on *Kincaid* 1784 as crossing the street on a line now marked by brass setts figured 'S'. Although the text and map in the *Historical Description of Holyroodhouse* 1819 records this as the boundary of the GIRTH OF HOLYROOD (*which see*) earlier records place the boundary further west, at the Girth Cross.

ABBEY STREET (Abbeymount) dates from 1876 and probably got its name from the adjoining *Abbey Church* of 1875, and ultimately from *Abbeyhill House* demolished in about 1870, both kirk and street being built in its grounds.

ABBOTSFORD PARK and **CRESCENT** (Church Hill) were laid out in the *Dow Croft* of Merchiston (*see under* DOW LOAN, Morningside) in 1859, when they were listed together as ABBOTSFORD PARK. ABBOTSFORD CRESCENT first appeared as a separate address in

PO Directory 1870. They are named for Sir Walter Scott's home near Melrose, probably out of the same enthusiasm which had led to the naming of BANNER PLACE in 1856 and was to prompt that of MARMION and WAVERLEY TERRACES nearby in 1861 and 1877.

ABERCORN AVENUE and **CRESCENT** (Willowbrae) were planned in the *North Park* of Meadowfield in 1909, but scarcely started before the early 1920s. The Crescent's extension, together with the development of ABERCORN GROVE and ABERCORN DRIVE, was planned in 1927. The name was in compliment to the duke of Abercorn, superior of Duddingston estate—*see also* PAISLEY CRESCENT etc *and* ULSTER DRIVE etc.

ABERCORN GARDENS (Jocks Lodge) lies within a field shown on *Duddingston* c1800 as *Dixon's Park*, in Northfield farm. *Kirkwood* 1817 shows part of the field feued off as *Beautyfield*; but by the 1840s it had become *Stuartfield*, presumably for a new owner. *Ordnance Survey* 1852 shows further changes: the original house is now named *Northfield Place*, and a new house called *Abercorn Place* has been erected, fronting the main road, while the rest of the ground is a nursery named *Abercorn Gardens*. The short street leading into these gardens was named STUART or STEWART STREET by 1842, but by 1894 the name had been displaced by ABERCORN GARDENS, derived from the gardens and ultimately from the Marquis of Abercorn, superior of Duddingston.

ABERCORN ROAD (Parson's Green) *see under* PARSON'S GREEN.

ABERCORN TERRACE (Joppa) is part of the coast road to Musselburgh and the south shown on *Adair* 1682. It is named as ABERCORN STREET on *Wood's Portobello* 1824 and *Portobello* 1832, but as part of the High Street on *Ordnance Survey* 1852 and *Sutter* 1856; and the name ABERCORN TERRACE first appears in *New Edinburgh Directory* 1868, along with ABERCORN VILLA, STREET and PLACE—all in Joppa but in locations not yet identified. The name evidently derived from the Marquis of Abercorn, the ground being part of his estate of Duddingston, see RABBIT HALL, Joppa.

ABERCROMBIE PLACE (New Town) *see under* NORTHERN NEW TOWN.

ABERNETHY'S CLOSE (High Street) see ALLAN'S CLOSE, High St.

ABINGER GARDENS (Murrayfield) is one of a group of streets planned by 1887, although not occupied until after 1900. They were all named for legal luminaries: appropriately enough, considering the place that the estate owners (the Campbells of Succoth, and the Murrays before them) had had in the history of the law. ABINGER GARDENS commemorated the English barrister and politician James Scarlett, Attorney General in 1827 and 1829 and created Baron Abinger in 1835, who as Sir Ilay Campbell's son-in-law was related by marriage to the owners of Murrayfield. KINGSBURGH ROAD was named for Sir John Hay Athole Macdonald, who sat in the Court of Session as Lord Kingsburgh, and became Lord Chief Justice in 1836;

and ORMIDALE TERRACE was named for another Scottish judge, Robert Macfarlane, sitting as Lord Ormidale from 1862. The tradition was continued in 1985, when STAIR PARK was named for Sir James Dalrymple, 1st Viscount Stair, renowned for his *Institutions of the Law of Scotland* 1681.

THE ABTHANE OF RATHO is recorded in 1547, but the name is much older, being the technical term, derived from Gaelic *abdhaine*, abbacy, for the land belonging to a monastic settlement in the Celtic kirk, and usually adjoining it. The one at Ratho included RATHOBYRES, (shown thus on *Blaeu* 1654, recorded as *Byres* in 1444 and *Rathobiris* in 1497 and evidently originating as the dairy of the kirk lands) together with the MERRYLANDS (which see) and RATHORIGG, thus on *Adair* 1682 but RATHOBANK on *Knox* 1812, and fancily renamed ASHLEY (ash-tree meadow) in about 1840.

ACADEMY STREET (South Leith) *see under* MORTON STREET, South Leith.

ADAM'S CLOSE or **COURT** (Cowgate) is listed on *Ainslie* 1780 but was later displaced by the buildings on the west side of the South Bridge. It was named for William Adam, architect, father of the Adam brothers, who bought it from John Strachey or Straitchy (*see under* STARCH CLOSE, Cowgate) prior to 1748. Probably the purchase also included the site of ADAM SQUARE (*which see*) immediately south of the close.

ADAMS LAW (Portobello) is shown on *Roads from Figget* 1783 as *Adams Laws*; but the earlier records are *Adams-law* 1627 and *Adames-law* 1653, and the plural may have arisen from the fact that the area was divided into two fields, shown on *Duddingston* c1800 as *East* and *West Adams Lawn*. The name appears to combine the personal name Adam or Adams with Scots *law*, a hillock. There were probably many hillocks in the Figgate Whins (see BLEAK LAW) and this one may have been in the east end of the property, where *Duddingston* c1800 shows a brickworks already started, no doubt with excavations already sweeping away surface features.

ADAM SQUARE (Old Town) is shown on *Edgar* 1765 as 'Mr Adam's New Building', the reference being either to William Adam (*see also* ADAM'S CLOSE, Cowgate) if the building was earlier than 1748, or else to his son John, eldest of the famous brothers and partner in charge of their Edinburgh practice, who was resident in the Square in 1773. The School of Arts and Watt Institute was housed here from the 1820s until 1872, when the construction of Chambers Street entailed the suppression of the Square and led to the transfer of the Institute to premises in the new street.

ADAMSON'S CLOSE (south side of High Street) is recorded in *City Charters 2448* in 1577 but its location remains to be found.

ADAMSON'S CLOSE (north side of High Street) *see* BROWN'S CLOSE, High Street, at St Giles Street.

ADAM STREET (Pleasance) appears as ELDIN STREET in *Campbell's Directory* 1804, although it is shown (probably through map error) as EDINBURGH STREET on *Ainslie* 1804; and it continues as Eldin Street until 1825, when *PO Directory* gives both this and ADAM STREET. It is clear from *Lothian* 1829 that Adam Street was the eastward and later extension of Eldin Street; and in *PO Directory* 1827 the latter is renamed as WEST ADAM STREET. Nevertheless, *Eldin Street* was still appearing on maps up to 1836; but the usage EAST & WEST ADAM STREET seems to have prevailed by 1850. The original naming was presumably for John Clerk of Eldin, noted for his books and splendid drawings and etchings, unless it was for his son, also John Clerk, advocate and later Lord Eldin: both of them were active around 1804, but their connection with the development is not known. Likewise the reason for the choice of the name Adam Street is not known: but that of a tribute to Robert Adam is possibly the least likely, considering that the name appears over thirty years after his death and at a time when his architectural style was well on the way out of fashion.

ADAM'S WELL (Redford) was named in 1994, its eastern branches being built within the *Adam's Well park* shown on a map of Redford in *Steuart's Colinton*. None of the maps show where the *well* or spring was. While it might have been named for a particular person, there are at least two other wells of the name in southern Scotland, and it is perhaps more likely that the reference is to the nickname *Adam's wine* or *ale*, for water.

ADDISTON (Ratho) is shown on *Blaeu* 1654. Recorded as *Ower and Nather Auldinstoun* in *RMS* 1556 and as *Adestoun* in 1589 and *Alderstoun* in 1610, it may be the *Aldeneston* and/or *Aldanston* referred to in 1292 and 1296 (*Black's Surnames* p15). It appears to be Anglian *Aldwines tún*, farm place of Aldwin, a personal name recorded more than once in Scotland in about 1100. ADDISTON MAINS is shown on *Roy* 1753, ADDISTON BANK (a short-lived name at JAW, *which see*) appears on *Knox* 1812, and ADDISTON BRIDGE, shown on *Adair/Cooper* 1735, is named on *Ordnance Survey* 1852.

ADDISTON CRESCENT (Balerno) *see under* DALMAHOY CRESCENT, Balerno.

ADELPHI PLACE (Portobello) is shown on Ainslie's *Roads from Figget* 1783 as a short branch off the highway beside William Jamieson's house of Rosefield. It was named by 1808, perhaps merely after the fashion set by the Adelphi terrace in London, created and named by the Adam brothers in 1772; but possibly the *brethren* involved in this case were the freemasons who set up their Portobello Lodge in 1808 and whose first office-bearers were installed in a room in Adelphi Place. The extension of the street in the 1860s led to the development of HENDERSON ROW, a scheme of working-class housing named for its promoter, the Revd Robert Henderson Ireland, minister of the Free Kirk in Portobello 1861-81; but in 1967, in order to obviate any confusion with Henderson Row in Stockbridge, the street was made part of Adelphi Place. A like fate overtook LIVINGSTON PLACE, built in about

1870 and named to commemorate Allan Livingston, provost of Portobello for but seven weeks before his death in 1867: for in 1966, to obviate confusion with Livingstone Place in Sciennes, this other local memorial was suppressed by being renamed ADELPHI GROVE.

ADMIRAL TERRACE (Merchiston) was formed along with WESTHALL GARDENS in 1881, in part of the grounds of Viewforth House (*see under* VIEWFORTH) which had long been occupied by Admiral Peat of Seggie prior to his death in 1879, aged eighty-six.

ADMIRALTY STREET (North Leith) was planned and named by 1816, as shown on *Kirkwood* 1817, but development did not start for some time and the street name first appears in *PO Directory* 1822. While it may have been given for the Royal Navy's presence in the new docks nearby, the name might alternatively have been in compliment to the Admiralty Court of Leith, a jurisdiction then conferred on the Lord Provost, Magistrates and Council of Edinburgh, and carried out through a court of Admirals-substitute presided over by an Admiral-depute. In the early 1960s redevelopment at Couper Street cut Admiralty Street in two, and the resultant awkwardness in addresses was not relieved until 1979, when the northern fragment was re-named CROMWELL STREET, *which see.*

THE ADVOCATE'S CLOSE (High Street) is shown on *Edgar* 1742 and was also known as STEWART'S or PROVOST STEWART'S or SIR JAMES STEWART'S CLOSE, all four names arising from Sir James Stewart of Coltness, provost of Edinburgh in 1648 and 1658, who bought a tenement in the close, and from his successors. His son, Sir James Stewart of Goodtrees (*see under* MOREDUN), Lord Advocate of Scotland 1692-1709 and 1711-13, rebuilt the house soon after 1688 and lived in it until his death in 1713; and thereafter it belonged to the family until 1769, when it was sold off by the Lord Advocate's grandson, also Sir James Stewart. Before the advent of the Stewarts, the close had been CANT'S—one of several closes confusingly so named for property belonging to the Cants of Liberton. At some time before 1749 it was also HOME'S, probably for John Hoome, vintner, owner and resident within it in 1635: the fact that Henry Home, Lord Kaims, had a house here in 1760 may indicate some family connection, but is obviously too late to account for the close name. Yet earlier, as recorded in 1635, it was CLEMENT COR'S CLOSE, named for Clement Cor or Cer, merchant, son of Andro Cor, burgess, and himself made a burgess in 1566. Active in the town council 1588-98 and three times bailie, Cor built or rebuilt his house near the head of the close in 1590, and its door heads, inscribed with his initials and *HB* for his wife Helen Bellenden, are still extant. His name seems to have been a variant of Ker.

AFFLECK COURT (East Craigs) *see under* CRAIGIEVAR WYND.

AFTON TERRACE (Wardie) appeared in 1886, and AFTON PLACE was derived from it in 1927. The name is obscure. It may refer to Burns' 'sweet Afton', the Ayrshire river; but there is also an Afton in the Isle of Wight.

AGNEW TERRACE (Bonnington) was named in about 1905, probably for Lt. Col. George Agnew of East Warriston.

AIKENHEAD'S CLOSE (High Street) *see* KENNEDY'S CLOSE.

AIKMAN'S CLOSE (71 High Street) *see* SANDILANDS'S CLOSE.

AIKMAN'S CLOSE (118 High Street) *see* DICKSON'S CLOSE.

AIKMAN'S CLOSE (276 High Street) *see* GOSFORD'S CLOSE.

AIKMAN'S CLOSE (374 High Street) is recorded in 1764 but the name evidently goes back at least as far as 1635, when Robert Aikman, merchant, was owner and occupier in the close. A later name KENNEDY'S seems to have been for John Kennedy, surgeon burgess, owner of Aikman's Land in the 1690s. The close is listed on *Ainslie* 1780 as LORD COLSTOUN'S, for George, son of Charles Brown of Coalston and a relative of James Brown, builder of George Square, who sat in the Court of Session as Lord Colston from 1756 onwards, and moved in 1757 to Castle hill, where he died in 1776. The area was cleared for the Tolbooth kirk before 1839.

AINSLIE PLACE (New Town) *see under* MORAY ESTATE, New Town.

AIRD'S CLOSE (next 87 Grassmarket) is not shown on *Ainslie* 1780 or 1804 but is given under its old number of 130 Grassmarket in *PO Directory* 1827 and shown on *Ordnance Survey* 1827. The origin of the name is not known, but George Aird, spirits merchant, was at 173 Grassmarket in 1817.

AITCHISON'S CLOSE (now 58 West Port) is listed as at 52 West Port in *PO Directory* 1827 and shown on *Ordnance Survey* 1852. It appears to be the passageway shown boldly on *Rothiemay* 1647 as leading south to the open ground that was later known as the Cordiners' Park. The Aitchison involved remains to be traced.

AITCHISON'S PLACE (Portobello) was named in 1981, carrying forward the name of an earlier street on this site, shown on *Wood's Portobello* 1824 and named on *Sutter* 1856. In a note attributed to *Baird* 1898, *Boog Watson* reports that the name derived from the owner, Aitchison, confectioner in Edinburgh. The further note that he was also known locally as 'Sweetie Mill' might suggest either that 'Mill' was a slip for the forename 'Will', or that this name belonged not to the man himself but to his sweetie factory.

AITKEN'S CLOSE (171 Canongate) *see* MILLER'S CLOSE, Canongate.

AITKEN'S CLOSE (253 Cowgate) is listed on *Ainslie* 1780 and was named for George Aitken, smith, recorded in 1758 as owning properties bought from the daughters of the late John Scott, wright, and also from the heirs of John Jack, slater. It is shown as SOUTH NIDDRY STREET on Kirkwood 1817.

ALAN BRECK GARDENS (Clermiston) *see under* CLERMISTON MAINS.

ALBANY STREET (Broughton) is named on *Ainslie* 1804 partly as *Albany Street* and partly as *Albion Row*. This division was there even before the street was built, for an *Albany Row* is mentioned in 1800, while a proposed *Albion Row* is shown, somewhat out of position, on the late edition (updated to 1 January 1801) of *Ainslie* 1780. Besides division, there was some confusion in the early years, for as many as four names—ALBANY or ALBION ROW and ALBANY or ALBION STREET—were in use, and it was about 1817 before the present name finally prevailed as the name of the whole street. While *Albion* and *Albany* are of course related, sharing the root *alb*, meaning white or else high ground, their history and meanings—and therefore the reasons for using them in street names—are distinctly different. *Albion* has come down to us from about 500 BC, when the Carthaginian explorer Himilico reported it as the name of the island of Great Britain, no doubt because he had heard something like it from the islanders or their Celtic cousins in France; and the reference might have been to the white cliffs of its south coast, or to its northern mountains. In Old Irish this island name became *Albe* or (later) *Alba*; and when Scots from Ireland colonised Argyll, they called their settlement *Albainn*, 'land or community in Alba', and those who lived there were *Albannaich*. In NormanFrench this became *Albanie*; and hence the royal title *duke of Albany*, first given by Robert III to his brother in 1398, means 'duke of Scots'. Thus ALBANY STREET, like YORK PLACE and DUKE STREET (*which see*) would seem to have been named for George III's second son, Frederick Augustus, Duke of York and Albany; whereas ALBION ROW, celebrating Great Britain, belonged with the 'United Kingdom' theme of street names in the NORTHERN NEW TOWN, which see. ALBANY STREET LANE was built as the meuse lane of the street; but ALBANY LANE, together with YORK LANE, developed from a track along the eastern fence of the Broughton Parks, shown in *Fergus & Robinson* 1759.

ALBERT PLACE and **STREET** (Leith Walk) were named in memory of Albert, Prince Consort, who had died in 1861. The first, a side terrace in Leith Walk, was occupied in 1870, and ALBERT STREET began a year later.

ALBERT ROAD (Leith Docks) was formed in course of constructing the Albert Dock (1869) and Edinburgh Dock (1881) but was apparently not named until the 1890s, taking its name from Albert Dock.

ALBERT TERRACE (Morningside) was a side name given by 1862 to a terrace of houses built in the historic DOW LOAN, *which see*. It obviously commemorated Albert, the Prince Consort, who had died in 1861. In the later 1890s it was allowed to displace the old street name—rather unfortunately, for although it suited the terrace, it is scarcely apt for the loan.

ALBION ROAD, PLACE and **TERRACE** (Lochend) were developed in about 1899 from a loan which gave access to the Hibernian Football Park; and the names clearly derive from this circumstance, drawing on the classical geography which went back to the explorations of Himilco of Carthage in about 500 BC, and regarded the *Britannic Isles* as a group consisting of Albion (Great Britain) and *Ierne* or *Hibernia* (Ireland)—*see also under* ALBANY STREET, Broughton.

ALBYN PLACE (New Town) is shown on *Wood* 1823 as part of Gillespie Graham's plan for the Moray estate, but like WEMYSS PLACE it is not named on that plan, evidently because these two streets were partly to be built on adjoining city land in the former Barjarg feu—the boundary is clearly indicated on *Kirkwood* 1823. The name is a variant of Gaelic *Albainn*, Scotland, and Highland Scotland in particular (*see also* ALBANY STREET), but since the word could also be used for *men of Scotland*, there is the more reason to suppose that its choice was connected with the Highland Society of Scotland, who were the first occupants of 6 Albyn Place by 1824.

ALCORN PARK (Wester Hailes) *see under* CLOVENSTONE DRIVE, Wester Hailes.

ALDERBANK GARDENS, PLACE and **TERRACE** (North Merchiston) *see under* SHAFTESBURY PARK, North Merchiston.

ALEXANDER DRIVE (Gorgie) was named in 1936, evidently for its developer, Alexander Glass.

ALFRED PLACE (Newington) was named thus in 1866, the year in which Victoria's second son, Alfred Ernest, was created Duke of Edinburgh and made a free burgess of Edinburgh. But this was the street's third name: it is shown on the plan of *Newington* 1826 as CANONBIE PLACE, from Canonbie in Eskdale, not far from Middlebie —*see under* MIDDLEBY STREET; and *PO Directory* 1865 lists it as ALFORD STREET.

ALISON'S CLOSE (34 Cowgate) is mentioned in 1708 and listed on *Ainslie* 1780, and was probably named for James Alison, merchant burgess, listed as owner and resident in 1635. Connected with the Lawnmarket through Riddle's Close, it was earlier named WARDLAW'S, for James Wardlaw (possibly the tailor burgess of that name in the 1590s) who owned property on the east side.

ALISON'S CLOSE (east end of Cowgate) *see* POT HOUSE CLOSE.

ALISON'S SQUARE (Bristo) was feued out in 1749 by Lady Nicholson to Colin Alison, wright, who built the large H-shaped tenement of housing shown on *Edgar* 1765. Its central range was destroyed in the building of MARSHALL STREET, *which see*.

ALLANFIELD (Bonnington) was a property formed by purchase in 1802 of part of Summerside in Northfield, Bonnington, by John Allan, who built the house and named it for himself. In the 1820s the family were concerned with development at MARY'S PLACE and ALLAN STREET, Stockbridge, *which see*. In 1871 another ALLAN STREET was developed on the site of Allanfield itself; and in 1966, to obviate confusion with the Stockbridge street, it was renamed DUDLEY AVENUE SOUTH—*see under* DUDLEY AVENUE, Bonnington.

ALLANFIELD (Hillside) was devised in 1984 as the name of this new development on ground which had been the Leith Walk Goods Station yard since 1866. For more than a century before that, it had been in use as market gardens or nurseries; maps such as *Kirkwood* 1817 show part of it as within *Dickson's nursery*, but the *PO Directories* for several years before 1866 show that another part was a nursery run by a Mrs Allan.

ALLAN PARK CRESCENT, DRIVE, GARDENS and **ROAD** (Slateford) were named in 1933, as being built in a field called *Allan's Park*; and ALLAN PARK LOAN was added in 1934. Shown on a map of Craiglockhart estate in *Steuart's Colinton*, the field was once part of Meggetland; and thus it may have been named for an owner or (more likely) a tenant in either of these estates.

ALLAN PARK (Kirkliston) was built in Newmains and named in 1974 for Robert Allan (1745-1818) a notable tenant of that farm.

ALLAN'S CLOSE (once 77 now about 49 Grassmarket) is listed on *Ainslie* 1780 and shown still open on *Ordnance Survey* 1852. The name may have derived immediately from James Allan, brewer in the south side of Grassmarket in 1773; but a John Allan owned land in the area in the early 1500s.

ALLAN'S CLOSE (High Street) is listed thus on *Edgar* 1742, but the origin of this particular name is obscure. Earlier it was LECHE'S or LEITCH'S CLOSE, from an owner David Leche, recorded in 1528, whose son Archibald, deacon of the furriers, was also connected with the close. The yet older name DOUGAL'S or DUELL'S, recorded as *Dowgallis* in *Dean of Guild records* 1554, traces back to a Symone Doweill mentioned in *RMS* 1507 as late owner of a tenement here, and it may also be remarked that, without saying exactly where it was, *RMS* 1425 mentions a burghal tenement in Edinburgh which had belonged to a deceased Symon Duwele. The close was also linked with John Dougal, probably one of a pair, father and son, who were prominent in the town council in the 16th century. It was also DUNLOP'S, deriving from owners of the name who included a John Dunlop as well as the Alexander Dunlop, advocate, listed as a resident in 1635. Yet another name, ABERNETHY'S, was recorded in 1750, but its origin is obscure. The close was largely suppressed in the redevelopment of Cockburn Street in 1859 and the extension of the City Chambers in 1930-34, but a remnant of it descends to the south side of Cockburn Street.

ALLAN STREET (Stockbridge) was named and feued out in about 1824 by Thomas Allan of ALLANFIELD, Bonnington (which *see*) along with the eastern part of MARY'S PLACE, Stockbridge.

ALLERMUIR (Pentland Hills) is *Allermore* on *Armstrongs* 1773 and *Allermuir* on *Knox* 1812, but in the *Statistical Account* 1794 Dr Walker seems to call it CAPELAW (*which see*) a name which would fit this hill better than its neighbour. The name appears to be Anglian or Old Norse *alra* or *elri mor* or Scots *aller muir*, muir where alders grow; and this suggests that it was once known as '(the hill above the) aller muir' although no such place has been identified.

ALLEY CLOSE (267 Canongate) *see* Dr SETON'S CLOSE, Canongate.

ALLISON PLACE (Kirkliston) is built in Almondhill and was named in 1975 for William Allison JP (1887-1960) who had farmed Newmains from 1911 and Almondhill from 1927 and was noted for his work not only in agriculture but in kirk and County Council as well.

ALLOWAY LOAN (Liberton) *see under* KIRK BRAE, Liberton.

THE ALMOND (West Clifton to Cramond) is recorded in 1420 as *Aumond*, and is evidently British *Ambona*, river, perhaps (as in the case of its Perthshire namesake) at one stage Gaelicised as *Aman*. Like the neighbouring Esk, Leith and Avon, it is an exceedingly primitive river name, given by people living on its banks, in the same way as Londoners refer to the Thames as 'the river'; and it may well be pre-Celtic, from a root *ombb*, water.

ALMONDBANK ROW (Cramond) is listed in *PO Directory* 1875, and was presumably an earlier name for ALMONDBANK COTTAGES. These are at the head of the bank of the Almond at this point.

ALMONDBANK TERRACE (North Merchiston) *see under* SHAFTESBURY PARK, North Merchiston.

ALMOND GROVE (Queensferry) was named in 1966, for the river ALMOND, *which see*.

ALMOND GREEN and **SQUARE** (Bughtlin) were named in 1973 after their developers, the Almond Housing Society.

ALMONDHILL (Kirkliston) was formed in about 1815 by merging the farms of CATELBUCK, MILTON, LOANHEAD and MEADOWS (*all of which see*) the main steading being at Catelbuck and still named thus on *Kirkwood's Environs* 1817 and *Gellatly* 1834. *Almondbill*, appearing on *Ordnance Survey* 1852, is fancy, describing the position of the farm on the higher ground north of the Almond. ALMONDHILL ROAD was built in the farm's *Toll field* in 1971.

ALMONDSIDE (Kirkliston) bears a name coined in about 1935, probably on the model of ALMONDHILL (also fancy) and referring to the street's position fairly near the river. It enters Station Road only a few yards north of where the *Cramond Brig road*, shown on *Kirkliston* 1759 and now called CARLOWRIE ROAD (*which see*) entered the village before the turnpike bypass was constructed in about 1810—*see under* MAIN STREET, Kirkliston.

ALNWICKHILL (Liberton) began as an imported name for a house at the STANEDYKEHEAD (*which see*) either when it was occupied by the Revd Dr James Begg after he left the parish kirk of Liberton for the Free Kirk in 1843, or when it became a home for 'fallen women', but certainly before 1852 when the name ousts *Stanedykehead* on the *Ordnance Survey*. The 'great south road' built in about 1812 (*see* LIBERTON BRAE and GARDENS) had bypassed the section of the ancient Penicuik road running past Stanedykehead, and this became the ALNWICKHILL ROAD, leading to Alnwickhill. In its northern section, apart from a terrace of houses built in about 1905, development started in 1926—*see under* LIBERTON. In 1972, development to the west of its southern section, named for it as well as the adjoining HOWDENHALL ROAD (*which see*) included ALNWICKHILL COURT, CRESCENT, DRIVE, GARDENS, LOAN, PARK and VIEW, together with HOWDENHALL COURT, CRESCENT, DRIVE, GARDENS, LOAN, PARK and WAY. All these streets were on the ground of the farm of

BACKSIDELEE. Shown on *Roy* 1753, its steading was in the vicinity of Alnwickhill Crescent. The name—partly continued in BACKLEE, named in 1983—is Scots *back side lee*, the *lee* or pasture on the *back* or west *side* or slope, and is thus a counterpart of Southfield and Northfield in Liberton. NETHERBANK and NETHERBANK VIEW were developed in the *nether* or western part of Backsidelee in 1993.

ALVANLEY TERRACE (Warrender Park) *see under* BRUNTSFIELD.

ALVA PLACE (Norton Park) *see under* MARYFIELD, Norton Park.

ALVA STREET (West End) is named and shown as proposed on *Kirkwood* 1817, but although *Kirkwood* 1823 shows building just started at its western end, little further progress was made until the 1830s. It was named for James Erskine (1726-96) who sat in the Court of Session first as Lord Barjarg and then as Lord Alva. His house in the Kirkbraehead, rather confusingly also described as 'in Drumsheugh', is shown on *Ainslie* 1804, and the street was built on its site and policies.

THE ANCHOR CLOSE (243 High Street) is recorded thus in 1714 and took this name from a tavern at its head, dating from before 1703. Later, as *Dannie Douglas's*, this was the meeting place of the Crochallan Fencibles, a club of some of the most distinguished men in the city, founded by William Smellie, printer in the close, who also founded the *Encyclopaedia Britannica* and printed the first Edinburgh edition of Burns in 1787. The close is recorded as FOWLER'S or FOULAR'S in 1521, for a William Fowler, merchant burgess. Considering the date, he is more likely to have been the William Fowler who was dean of guild in 1510 than the one who was bailie in 1565 and perhaps the father of a third William Fowler, parson of Hawick, sent to Denmark in 1589 as the city's representative in arranging the marriage of Anne of Denmark to James VI, *see under* NORTH FOULIS CLOSE. The close was also known as FORDYCE'S before 1711, for James Fordyce, described as a religious writer; and it is recorded in 1723 as having been BROWN'S, for Thomas Brown's property in it, and then DICKSON'S, for Thomas Dickson and the three sisters Agnes, Sibella and Elizabeth Dickson, who may have been his daughters.

ANCHORFIELD (Newhaven) *see* ANKERFIELD, Newhaven.

ANDERSON PLACE (Bonnington Road) first appears in *PO Directory* 1866 as ANDERSON'S PLACE, and was named after its builder Thomas Anderson, then based at Fox Lane.

ANDERSON'S CLOSE (14 Cowgate) is so listed in *PO Directory* 1827 and took this name from Alex Anderson, deacon of the Hammermen, who built *Deacon Anderson's Land* at the head of the close in the West Bow in 1678. It is recorded as STINKING CLOSE in 1635 and still given this apparently insalubrious name on *Kirkwood* 1817—*but see under* STINKAND STYLE for a discussion of its meaning. The 'Haunted Close' in *Wilson* is not a name for the close but the descriptive caption of his drawing of it, and refers to the tale of the apparition of a giantess looking for the warlock Major Weir in 1670.

ANDERSON'S COURT (Old Broughton) appears in *PO Directory* 1862-85, but information about it is lacking.

ANDERSON'S PLACE (Leith Walk) was named by 1831 for John Anderson of Gladswood, whose Leith Walk Foundry is shown here on *Ainslie* 1804.

ANDREW WOOD COURT (Newhaven) was named in 1970 for Sir Andrew Wood of Largo, merchant and shipowner in Leith, and kenspeckle naval commander under James III and James IV, famous for his action off Dunbar in 1489, when with his two ships, *Yellow Carvel* and *Flower*, he captured five of the English. He was knighted in about 1495 and made Admiral of the Seas in 1511, and became 'quartermaster' or commander of the *Great Michael*, launched at Newhaven in that year.

ANGLE PARK (Slateford) *see under* LONGSTONE, Slateford.

ANGLE PARK TERRACE (Dalry) was formed in about 1847, when the Lanark road was realigned to suit the Caledonian Railway. With the development of housing along its west side in about 1875, it was named for the *Angle park*—a normal name for a triangular field—which had existed here not only since the Tynecastle Brae had been developed in about 1801 (*see under* ARDMILLAN TERRACE) but even earlier, with a slightly different western boundary as shown on *Merchiston* 1776 and, somewhat faintly, on *Roy* 1753.

ANKERFIELD (Newhaven) is referred to in 1722 as *Ankerfield commonly called Holy Blood Acre*, and the name also attaches to the ANKERFIELD BURN. The name *Holy Blood Acre*, recorded from 1598 onwards, arose because the revenues of this arable land were attached to the altar of the Holy Blood in James IV's chapel of St Mary and St James in Newhaven before they passed to South Leith Kirk Session in 1614. The 'Anchorfield' spelling of the other name, appearing on *Ainslie* 1804, looks like a fanciful attempt to explain it as having to do with ships' anchors. In the absence of early forms, any explanation must be tentative: but there is nothing to suggest that any hermitage or nunnery (in Scots, an *anker*) was ever associated with the Haly Blude Acre, and it is perhaps most likely that the name, like *Ankerlaw* near Lasswade, contains British *anker*, a winding or hook-shaped watercourse—a description that fits the general course of the burn as well as the pronounced hook-shaped bend in it at Ankerfield, graphically shown on *Ainslie* 1804 and other maps.

ANNANDALE STREET (Broughton) was begun in 1825 in the course of development by the heirs of Dr John Hope, founder of the Botanic Garden, at the site vacated by the Garden when it was removed to Inverleith in 1822-24 (*see also* HOPE CRESCENT) and they evidently named the street for the Johnstone Hopes of Annandale, another branch of the family founded by Sir Thomas Hope of Craighall in the time of Charles I. ANNANDALE STREET LANE was begun in the early 1870s and completed in the 1880s. WEST ANNANDALE STREET, occupying ground which had been part of the Royal Zoological Park from 1840 to 1867, was formed in the 1880s but seems to have been named only in about 1910.

THE ANNAT (Cramond) is mentioned in *RMS* 1654 in terms which suggest that it was all or part of Kirk Cramond; but however that may be, and despite the late date of the record, this use of Gaelic *annaid*, a term for a sacred place, indicates that there was a Celtic kirk here, and might imply that the dedication to St Columba, recorded in *RMS* 1479, belonged to this earlier period.

ANNFIELD (Newhaven) is shown as a tenement on *Ainslie* 1804 and named on *Kirkwood* 1817. The name is recorded from 1763, when the land's owner John Steuart of Blairhaw, whose wife's name was Ann, began to style himself 'of Annfield'. The adjoining ANN STREET first appeared on *Ordnance Survey* 1893 and in *PO Directory* 1894. It was renamed ANNFIELD STREET in 1965, in order to obviate any confusion with Ann Street in Stockbridge.

ANN STREET (Stockbridge) *see under* DEAN HAUGH, Stockbridge.

ANN TERRACE (Abbeyhill) was formed at the end of Spring Gardens in the 1880s. The name looks as though derived from some relative of the builder, rather than from St Anne's Brae, a little to the west.

ANTIGUA STREET (Broughton) is shown on *Ainslie* 1804 and listed in *Campbell's Directory* of that year. No doubt it was named for the island, which like others in the West Indies was frequently in the news of the naval war with the French.

ANWOTH VILLAS (Corstorphine) *see* MEADOWHOUSE ROAD.

APPIN TERRACE (Gorgie) was named by 1891, evidently because its developer, Bailie Mackenzie of Mackenzie & Moncur, engineers, was a native of Appin.

ARBORETUM AVENUE (Inverleith) appears on *Ainslie* 1804 as an avenue to Inverleith House, and was named after the House policies were converted into the Botanic Gardens in 1877, part of them being planted as an *arboretum* or tree garden. A new west entrance to the Gardens was formed, and the access to it from Inverleith Place and Terrace was named ARBORETUM ROAD. In about 1896 this name was extended to a new section leading to Ferry Road; but in 1982, in order to provide independent addresses, the original southern section was renamed ARBORETUM PLACE.

THE ARCADE (North Bridge) is part of the *Scotsman* building of 1902, but as a passage it preserves the throughgang of the *Market Stairs* and the *Poultry & Veal Market* shown on *Ordnance Survey* 1852. The opening is shown on *Kincaid* 1784 as leading from North Bridge into the head of the Fleshmarket, hence probably the name of the stairs. While *arcade* is architecturally a series of arches in the same plane, it came to be used for a walk under a series of arches, and hence for a covered avenue.

ARCHIBALD PLACE (Lauriston) was named by and for its developer, George Archibald, seedsman in Nicholson Street. His father Joseph had established a nursery at Lauriston, shown on *Ainslie* 1804, and the scheme for the street followed the transfer of this side of the business to the Grange in about 1821. The street formed a new approach to the Merchant Maiden's Hospital (i.e. boarding school) built by William Burn in 1816, which was subsequently purchased to form George Watson's School in 1871 but was demolished in the course of the extension of the Royal Infirmary in 1934.

ARCHIBALD'S CLOSE (High Street & West Bow) *see* CLARK'S CLOSE.

ARDEN STREET (Marchmont) *see under* BRUNTSFIELD.

ARDMILLAN TERRACE (North Merchiston) is first shown as a proposed new road overmarked by J Bell on *Merchiston* 1776, probably in 1801. It was known as TYNECASTLE BRAE until 1876, when it was renamed for James Craufurd, who sat in the Court of Session 1855-76 as Lord Ardmillan, taking his title from Ardmillan, near Girvan. ARDMILLAN PLACE was formed in 1876, but was known as MacKENZIE PLACE until 1885.

ARDSHIEL AVENUE (Clermiston) *see under* CLERMISTON MAINS.

ARGYLE CRESCENT and **PLACE** (Portobello) were named by 1888. While there may have been an intention to commemorate the Campbells of Argyll as owners of Duddingston from 1701 to 1745, the naming may have had some connection with *Argyle Cottage*, existing in Hope Lane in 1824 and named in *Portobello Directory* 1836.

ARGYLE PARK TERRACE (Sciennes) *see under* ARGYLE PLACE, Sciennes.

ARGYLE PLACE (Sciennes) is on ground shown on *Scott* 1759 as 'Mr Campbell's' and listed in *PO Directory* 1826 as *Argyle Park*; and this clan connection evidently generated the names of streets built upon it. ARGYLE PLACE appears in *PO Directory* 1826 as the end house in Fingal Place (*see under* SYLVAN PLACE, Sciennes) and is shown as *Argyle Street* on *Pollock* 1837, and as *Argyle Place* on *Ordnance Survey* 1852. In about 1874 further developments in Argyle Park were named ARGYLE PARK TERRACE and ROSENEATH TERRACE, the latter named for the duke of Argyll's seat beside the Gareloch. In about 1890 a section of the ancient *common passage* from the Sciennes to the Links was named ROSENEATH PLACE; and in about 1897 Roseneath Terrace was extended westwards on the line of another existing lane, and gave its name to the tenement of ROSENEATH STREET.

ARGYLE SQUARE (Old Town) is shown on *Edgar* 1742. Suppressed in 1871, when the Royal Scottish Museum was built, its position is best seen on *City Improvements* 1866. To judge by a notice in the *Gentlemen's Magazine* of 1745, which describes it as 'lately begun', it was the first local essay in terraced houses in the London fashion, instead of the flatted tenements typical of Edinburgh. Since the same article reports it as named 'in honour of the late Duke' (John Campbell, 2nd Duke of Argyll, had died in 1743) it seems that it was also the first street in the town to be named for someone other than its builder or a kenspeckle resident. That a Campbell was involved in its development is confirmed on *Edgar* 1765, where its south side (not shown on *Edgar* 1742) is labelled *Campbell's New Buildings*; and the tradition given in *Chambers* 1825 Vol. 1, p43, that it was begun by a tailor named Campbell, using profits he had made from mournings for George I in 1727, may have some truth in it, however improbable it is in detail.

ARGYLE STREET (North Leith) although proposed in 1807 and shown on *Pollock* 1834 as though half-built, continued as little more than a lane until it was named in about 1871. The reason for the choice of name can only be guessed at. The detail on *Ordnance Survey* 1852 suggests that the street, together with ELLEN STREET, may have originated as a cart track or loaning leading to ground (now PRINCE REGENT STREET) which *Ainslie* 1804 shows as owned by a Campbell and which was not developed until about 1860.

ARGYLL TERRACE (Dalry) *see under* DALRY PLACE.

ARNISTON PLACE (Newington) *see* NEWINGTON ROAD.

ARNOTT GARDENS (Kingsknowe) was named in 1936 for its builders, Arnott and Lawend.

ARRAN PLACE (Portobello) was named in 1986 with reference to Anne, eldest daughter of the earl of Arran and third wife of John James Hamilton, 1st Marquess of Abercorn, for whom the adjoining JAMES STREET was named.

ARROL PLACE (Queensferry) was named in 1953 for William Arrol of Tancred, Arrol & Co, contractors for the Forth Bridge 1883-90.

ARTHUR'S SEAT is recorded in Walter Kennedy's *Flyting* of William Dunbar in 1508 as *Arthurissete*. At least eleven place names in south Argyll, Dumbarton, Lothian, Angus, Aberdeenshire and Glenlivet—i.e. in an arc skirting the Highlands—appear to celebrate the British hero Arthur. Four of them are 'Arthur's Seat', either in English or in Gaelic; and since British *suide Artur* would translate into Anglian just as readily as *Din Eidyn* became *Edinburgh*, it is possible that Edinburgh's 'Arthur's Seat' may represent such an earlier Celtic name. On the other hand, in a number of twelfth-century charters which refer to the division of this hill ground between the royal abbeys of Holyrood and Kelso there is no hint of an 'Arthur' name, and only the British names *Crag* or CRAGGENEMARF (which see) are used for the hill or the part of it involved in the boundary question. Furthermore, 'Mount Dolorous', a twelfth-century fanciful name for the hill, is almost a translation of *Craggenemarf*, dead men's crag. Thus the alternative possibility is that 'Arthur's Seat' was a romantic invention of the same period and of the same sort as the fanciful Arthurian name 'Castle of Maidens' for EDINBURGH CASTLE, *which see*.

ARTHUR STREET (Pilrig) is shown sketched on *Knox* 1812 as one of a set of eight streets planned to be built on part of James Balfour's Pilrig estate. All of them are named on *Kirkwood* 1817 but only ARTHUR STREET, together with MORAY STREET and St JAMES STREET (*see under* SPEY STREET) is shown as already started. The name's origin has not yet been traced, but it is likely to be connected with the Balfours or with the builder of the first houses on the north side of Pilrig Street.

ARTHUR STREET, EAST, MIDDLE & WEST ARTHUR PLACE, NEW ARTHUR PLACE (Pleasance) *see under* DALE STREET, Pleasance.

ASHBURNHAM ROAD (Queensferry) originated as part of the COMMON LOAN (*which see*) and formed part of a route between New Garden and the Kirkliston road long before it was developed as a housing street; but in 1948 it was named for nearby Ashburnham House, built in 1899 and itself named either for Ashburnham in Sussex (a place associated with Charles I) or else for the earls of Ashburnham. WHITEHEAD GROVE was named in 1952 for Admiral Whitehead, owner of the House; and ASHBURNHAM GARDENS was named in 1983 as being developed in its grounds, once the vicinity of the FLASH, *which see.*

ASHLEY GROVE (North Merchiston) was formed in about 1901-3, when the adjoining school and the first part of Cowan Road were built, and took its name from ASHLEY TERRACE—*see under* SHAFTESBURY PARK. The name was extended to ASHLEY DRIVE and GARDENS in 1932.

ASHLEY BUILDINGS (15 High Street) are shown on *Ordnance Survey* 1852. Consisting of three stairs of model flats for families, they were designed and built by the local firm W Beattie & Son, and named for Lord Ashley, the housing reformer, who had visited Scotland in 1850 to address meetings on improved housing and health.

ASHLEY PLACE (Pilrig) was formed and named in about 1895, when Bonnington Toll was redeveloped. The name probably commemorates Lord Ashley, 7th Earl of Shaftesbury, prominent in factory as well as housing reform—*see also* SHAFTESBURY PARK, North Merchiston.

ASHLEY TERRACE (North Merchiston) *see under* SHAFTESBURY PARK, North Merchiston.

ASHTON GROVE (Inch) *see under* THE INCH, Nether Liberton.

ASHVILLE TERRACE (South Leith) *see under* WOODBINE TERRACE, South Leith.

ASSEMBLY CLOSES (High Street) *see under* OLD *and* NEW ASSEMBLY CLOSE.

ASSEMBLY STREET (South Leith) was formed by 1804 and named by 1819 for the neighbouring *Assembly Rooms* at Constitution Hill, which were opened in 1785 and extended in 1810 as *Leith Exchange and Assembly Rooms.*

ATHELING GROVE (Queensferry) was named in 1971, evidently to commemorate Edgar Atheling, brother of Queen Margaret of Scotland, who claimed the English throne in 1066 but was forced to flee with his sister to Scotland in 1068. *See also* PORT EDGAR, Queensferry.

ATHOLL CRESCENT (West End) is shown on *Wood* 1823 as projected and already named, presumably by the developers, the Heriot Trust. ATHOLL PLACE and ATHOLL LANE, planned along with it, were named by 1828 and 1850 respectively. The name, spelt *Atholl*, *Athol*, and *Athole* in accordance with fashions prevailing at various periods, was probably given in compliment to John Duke of Atholl, who was prominent in national affairs at the time. He was one of the Commissioners for the National Monument scheme, and may have had some connection with the Trust.

ATHOLL STREET (Stockbridge) *see under* INDIA PLACE, Stockbridge.

ATHOLL TERRACE (Dalry) *see under* DALRY PLACE, Dalry.

AUBURN PLACE (North Leith) is shown on *Ordnance Survey* 1852 as a side name at 11-17 North Fort Street near Industry Lane, but is dropped in *PO Directory* 1888. The name was fancy, perhaps with a glance at Goldsmith's *Sweet Auburn, loveliest village of the plain...*

AUCHINGANE (Dreghorn and Swanston) is recorded from 1554 onwards and was joined to Dreghorn in 1606. Its exact bounds are not known, but charters show that it lay between Hunters Tryst and the Baads, with a part projecting south into Swanston; and since this part may be the *East Muir Park* shown on the map of Swanston in *Steuart's Colinton*, the street built within it in 1985 was given the ground's older name, which is Gaelic *achadh nan gaimhne*, field of the stirks or yearlings.

AUCHINLECK BRAE (Newhaven) appears in *Town Council Minutes* 1836 and *PO Directory* 1865 but the name probably had been in use for long before then, as that of the approach to the property shown as 'Auchinleck's' on Ainslie 1804. It was continued in AUCHINLECK COURT after the redevelopment of the village in 1970.

AULDGATE (Kirkliston) is partly on the site of Kirkliston Railway Station (1866-1966) but was named *auld gate*, old road, in 1982 because its southern section is a remnant of the ancient highroad which passed through here from Foxhall on the way to Linlithgow (*see also* HIGH STREET, PATH BRAE and GATESIDE, Kirkliston) as shown on *Adair* 1682 as well as *Taylor & Skinner* 1805 and in detail on *Kirkliston* 1759. In about 1810, it was bypassed (*see under* MAIN STREET, Kirkliston) and the section through Foxhall was suppressed; and in 1866 the section remaining east of the High Street became the access to the railway station.

AULDLISTON (Newbridge) is recorded from 1447 onwards, sometimes as the name of a barony, sometimes that of a property within it. The barony was one of a pair created, probably by David I, by dividing the original shire of LISTON (*which see*) in two. One part, described as 'Liston in the regality of St Andrews', was gifted to that bishopric and so became the barony of KIRKLISTON (*which see*) while the other part, described as 'Liston in the regality of Torphichen' and known as the barony of AULDLISTON, was given to the Knights Templars, whose headquarters in Scotland were at Torphichen. Extending on both sides of the river, this Templar barony included NEWLISTON (*which see*) as one of several estates within it, and whether the name of the barony had *auld-* added to it, as though to distinguish it from this 'new' part of it, must be at least doubtful. The record of the more limited use of AULDLISTON as a farm name begins in 1558, when a charter (quoted in *RMS* 1578) was given for a farm and estate of *Auldliston* 'within the barony of Auld Liston'. This was evidently not the modern *Old Liston*, south of Newbridge, for although this is on Auldliston ground, it was known as CORSENEUK (*which see*) until about 1850. The historic farm toun of Auldliston seems to have been north of Newbridge, at NT 125725, where it is shown as *Alistoun* on *Blaeu* 1654 (surveyed in 1596) and as *Haliston* on *Adair* 1682 and *Laurie* 1763, whereas on *Roy* 1753 and *Armstrongs* 1773 and later maps it is *Old Liston*, until 1852, when the *Ordnance Survey* notes it as *Hall Liston*. The place disappeared without trace before 1912. The name obviously calls for further investigation (along with others within the barony, such as HALYARDS and HALLBARNS and the *Listonhall* mentioned in *RMS* 1540) for although the evidence for the *auld-* form cannot be brushed aside, neither can the variants on the maps be ignored, and there is a strong suspicion that there may have been some remodelling, under influence of *New*liston, of an earlier *Halb-* or *Hawliston*, which as 'haugh of Liston' would have aptly described these Templar lands.

AULD PROVOST'S CLOSE (189 High Street) *see* OLD PROVOST'S CLOSE.

AULD WALLS (Wester Hailes) *see under* WESTER HAILES.

FIRST, SECOND and **THIRD AVENUES** (Newcraighall) originally made up the central part of the mining village, with a MAIN AVENUE across either end of the rows. The whole area was redeveloped in 1976 as NEWCRAIGHALL DRIVE and KLONDYKE STREET and WAY.

AVENUE VILLAS (Comely Bank) were named in 1914 as a development in part of BLACK'S ENTRY, so named on *Ordnance Survey* 1852 and 1913, which was itself developed on the site of Sir William Fettes's house of Comely Bank, shown on *Knox* 1812. It may have been the site of HOWMAINS, shown on *Roy* 1753.

AVONDALE PLACE (Stockbridge) *see under* THE COLONIES, Stockbridge.

AVON ROAD (Cramond) was named thus in 1934 at the suggestion of the developer's architect, John A W Grant, who gave no reasons for the choice; and the name was borrowed for the adjoining streets AVON GROVE and PLACE in 1972. *See also* ESSEX ROAD, Cramond.

AYR BANK CLOSE (249 Canongate) is listed on *Ainslie* 1780 and was named for the short-lived Ayr Bank, which had its Edinburgh branch here under the name of Douglas Heron & Co from 1769 until it failed in 1773. The close is also recorded in 1821 as having the name WILLIAM LOTHIAN'S, for William Lothian, wright, burgess of Canongate, in all probability from a much earlier period. It seems also to have been known as PASSIE'S in 1689.

AYRE'S CLOSE (115 Cowgate) *see* RATTERAY'S CLOSE, Cowgate.

B

BAADS (Dreghorn) is recorded in *RMS* 1540 as *Baddis*, along with the lost name PILMURE. It is shown on *Roy* 1753 as *Bauds*, and as *The Bards* on *Knox* 1812, across the road from FORDEL, *which see*. The spellings show the vowel as long; and the name, which occurs elsewhere in Lothian with or without the added *s*, is British *bod*, residence or place.

BABERTON (Currie) is recorded in *RMS* 1306-29 as *Kibabertone*, *Kilbabertoun* and *Kilbebirtoun*; but although the name still appears as *Kilbabertoun* in *RMS* 1642, it is shortened, apparently colloquially, to *Babertoun* in *RMS* 1599, while *Blaeu* 1654 (probably surveyed in 1596) shows the medieval tower as *Balberton*, on or near the site of the present Baberton House, built in 1622 and shown on *Adair* 1682 as *Babertoun*. Despite difference in spelling, this part of the original name shares its modern pronunciation '*ba-berton* with Balberton, near Kinghorn, which is *Babertane* in *RMS* 1540, but *Balbretane*, evidently Gaelic 'steading of Britons', in *RMS* 1329-71; and if the *Kil-* in the Currie name may be taken as Gaelic *coill*, a wood, or *cul*, back or upper-ground, the original place name may have been 'wood or ground above the steading of the Britons', fitting in with its position above DUMBEG and DUMBRYDEN (*which see*) where a British settlement seems to have been still recognisable by Gaelic speakers in the tenth century or thereby. BABERTON MAINS or home farm is so named on *Laurie* 1763 but is LITTLE BABERTON on *Roy* 1753. BABERTON MAINS BRAE, LEA, RISE and WAY (all 1976) are within that farm, but the earlier streets, BABERTON MAINS DRIVE, GARDENS, GROVE, PLACE, TERRACE and VIEW (all 1971) and BABERTON MAINS AVENUE, BANK, COURT, CRESCENT, DELL, GREEN, HILL, LOAN, PARK, ROW, WOOD and WYND (1973) are all on ground of FERNIEFLAT (*which see*) in Hailes, except for parts of Baberton Mains Hill and Wood. This has prejudiced the naming of BABERTON MAINS ROAD, leading from Slateford (*Roy* 1753) or Wester Hailes (*Knox* 1812) past the farm and on to the Corslet in Currie: part of it was renamed in 1970 as WESTBURN AVENUE, and in 1976 the rest was renamed partly as an extension of that and partly as BABERTON ROAD. BABERTON AVENUE, shown on *Knox* 1812 as developed from one of the avenues in the park of Woodhall (*see under* ENTERKIN'S YETT *and* JUNIPER GREEN) was so named by 1912, as the avenue leading to the south drive of Baberton; but it has led to the intrusion of a number of 'Baberton' names into what is properly Woodhall: BABERTON SQUARE (formed before 1893) and PARK (1962) and the absurdly misleading BABERTON LOAN given in 1967 as a new name for STATION LOAN, formed in 1874 to give access to the Juniper Green station on the new Balerno branch railway. BABERTON CRESCENT, named in 1937, is also in historic Woodhall, although the field seems to have been acquired by Baberton in the later 19th century.

BACK BRAES (Kirkliston) are shown on *Ordnance Survey* 1352. The name may use back in the sense of 'high bank' (see BACK BRAES, Queensferry) but if it is related to the *Back of the kirk* lands shown on *Kirkliston* 1759 as stretching back to the Branken, *back* may be used in the sense of 'west'.

BACK BRAES (Queensferry) are shown on *Ordnance Survey* 1354. The name is traditional, and probably means 'the steep slopes at the back', using that term in its sense of 'high bank' derived ultimately from Old Norse *bakki*, meaning the same.

BACK DEAN (Dean) is shown on *Kirkwood* 1817 and recorded as WESTER DEAN, the house built by Sir Henry Nisbet in about 1681, when he was fiar of Dean. In the Scots subdivision of land, the *Fore* part of an estate was the 'sunny' or *Easter* part, also termed *Upper* or *Over*, while the *Back* or *Nether* part was on its 'shadow' or *Wester* side. Until the 1890s, as shown on *Ordnance Survey* 1893, the name was used for the street now called, most inappropriately, Ravelston Terrace, *see under* RAVELSTON; but in 1981 it was restored to the approach to new flats built on the site of the Nisbet house.

BACKLEE and **BACKSIDELEE** (Liberton) *see under* ALNWICKHILL, Liberton.

BACK OF BETH'S or **BEST'S WYND** (High Street) is shown on *Edgar* 1742, and was named as a close backing on to the west side of BETH'S WYND. It seems to have been also known as FALCON'S CLOSE, from a family including a John and a William Falcon owning lands here before—perhaps very long before—1700. It ran along what is now the centre line of West Parliament Square, and was suppressed in the development of the Signet Library in 1811.

BACK OF BORTHWICK'S CLOSE (196 High Street) *see* OLD FISHMARKET CLOSE.

BACK O THE BUGHTS (8 Grassmarket) is shown on *Ainslie* 1780 and was evidently named as being behind the BUGHTS (*which see*) in the Grassmarket. It is given in *PO Directory* 1827 (under its earlier number, 16) as CRAWFORD'S CLOSE, named for John Crawford, stabler in Grassmarket in 1766, whose son and heir Gilbert, a musician, sold the property to James Brown, stabler, in 1811.

BACK O THE VOUTS (South Leith) *see under* THE VAULTS *or* VOUTS, South Leith.

THE BACKS OF THE CANONGATE were an integral part of the burgh of the Canongate from its inception, being the loanings that gave the burgesses access to the common wells, grazings and other lands of the burgh. The North Back is shown on *Hertford's Approach* 1544, and figures together with the South Back on *Siege of Edinburgh Castle* 1573. Between 1905 and 1912 the name of the NORTH BACK was displaced by that of CALTON ROAD, apparently by extension from *Calton Road* in the CALTON, *which see*. Prior to 1892 there had been attempts to call the SOUTH BACK *Holyrood Street*, but the historic name was displaced only in about 1913 by that of

HOLYROOD ROAD—'in the belief,' Charles Boog Watson tartly remarked, 'that change of label improves wine'.

BACK OF THE FISH MARKET (196 High Street) *see* OLD FISHMARKET CLOSE.

BACK O THE MILL (Kirkliston) is named as a path coming down at the back of Lamb's Mill(s), which is shown on *Kirkliston* 1759 as a considerable group of buildings. The path had developed by 1800, and the mills became a distillery in about 1817.

BACK OF THE WALL (Bristo and Pleasance) *see* THIEF *or* THIEVES ROW, Bristo and Pleasance.

BACK ROW (Pleasance) was the historic name of the loan (now ROXBURGH PLACE and RICHMOND STREET and LANE) which is shown on *Rothiemay* 1647 and *Regality of Canongate* 1813 as running between the Easter Croft of Bristo, and the North and South Crofts of the Pleasance. Mentioned in *Protocols of James Young* 1503 as the 'common way from the Blackfriars to the Borow mure' and described in *RSS* 1563 as issuing from the priory garden, it was certainly the medieval entrance to the Blackfriars from the south; but the alignment of streets, together with the fact that it was the march between Bristo and the abbey lands of the Canongate, strongly suggests that it may also represent the original line of the Dalkeith road, heading up Blackfriars wynd to an early NETHERBOW (*which see*) and indeed in yet earlier times it may have begun as a track from the south to the natural haven of Leith *via* the Calton gorge. The name, recorded in 1653, is expanded in 1716 as 'the Backraw of the Easter Croft of Bristo'; but this seems to be a late usage, for the name probably derived from the *back* or western *raw* or boundary bauk of the crofts of the DERENEUCH, *which see*.

BACK ROW (Slateford) is the traditional name for this road beside the *dam* or lade serving the mills on the haugh of Inglis Green and Graysmill. The term back could mean 'rear' or equally 'west' and either sense would fit in here.

BACKSIDELEE and **BACKLEE** (Liberton) *see under* ALNWICKHILL, Liberton.

THE BACK STAIRS (108 Cowgate) was the general name for the passage which led by three stages from the Cowgate up to the Parliament Close, beginning with the NEW or HENDERSON'S STAIRS, named for John Henderson, wright, who had a land west of them at some date before 1741, and continuing in a passage going eastwards across the slope to the foot of the MEAL MARKET STAIRS—*see* MEAL MARKET, Cowgate.

THE BAGLAP or **BALLOP** (Warrender Park) was part of the Burgh Muir feued off in 1586 and described in *Town Council Minutes* as 16 acres of arable land lying between Bruntsfield and Whitehouse. Since it also marched with Whitehouse Loan and with the Grange 500 yards to the east, it was evidently a cul-de-sac averaging only some 160 yards in width and centred more or less on the line of Thirlestane Road. Clearly this shape gave it its name, early Scots *bagge lappe*, bag-shaped

71

outshot of land, *see also* LAPLEE STANE and LOUPIELEES. Bought by John and Agnes Rig in 1641, it was also known as RIGSLAND, until after George Warrender added it to his estate of Bruntsfield in 1700.

BAILEYFIELD ROAD (Portobello) was built by 1833 as part of a new road from Leith to Dalkeith (*see also* DUDDINGSTON PARK) and it was known by that description until 1900, when the present name was adopted. No doubt this had been long in use informally, since the road led past BAILEYFIELD, a house built and named by William Bailey, provost of Portobello 1833-36, soon after he bought Astley's Chemical Works in Adams Laws in 1829 and set up his flint-glass factory here. The *Portobello Directory* 1836 also lists a BAILEYFIELD SQUARE— perhaps never built, since there is no sign of it on *Sutter* 1856.

BAILIE PLACE (Easter Duddingston) was named in 1936—with an evident misspelling of the name—for William Bailey, glass and bottle maker, the first Provost of Portobello 1833-36—*see also* BAILEYFIELD. BAILIE TERRACE followed in 1937, and BAILIE DRIVE, GROVE and PATH in 1956.

BAILLIE'S CLOSE (50 Cowgate) is listed thus in *PO Directory* 1827 and was named for William Baillie, whose advocate son James rebuilt their tenement *Bailie's Land* in the Cowgatehead. He left it to his sister Margaret, and she to her daughter Jean Mitchell, whose husband James Stoddart, merchant councillor in 1764 and Lord Provost in 1774-75, gave the close its name of STODDART'S. It got the further name of HAMILTON'S from the succeeding owner, Cornet John Hamilton, 17th Dragoons.

BAINFIELD (Fountainbridge) is recorded in 1729 in the styling of James Bain of Bainfield, which also shows how the name developed. The small estate is named on *Adair/Cooper* 1735 and prominently shown on *Roy* 1753. Its last owner was Thomas Gibson, iron fence maker, who began to develop it in about 1870 as GIBSON TERRACE, named for himself, and MURDOCH TERRACE—the derivation of which has not yet been traced but is no doubt connected with Gibson.

BAIRD AVENUE, DRIVE, GARDENS, GROVE and **TERRACE** (Saughtonhall) were planned in the early 1920s in the *Beggar's Acre* and the *House Park* of Balgreen farm, and were named for the superior, Baird of SAUGHTONHALL, *which see*.

BAIRD ROAD (Ratho) *see under* LIDGATE, Ratho.

BAIRD'S or **BAILIE BAIRD'S CLOSE** (404 High Street) *see* BLAIR'S CLOSE.

BAIRD'S CLOSE (West Port) is listed as 115 West Port in *PO Directory* 1827, and is shown on *Ainslie* 1780 and *Ordnance Survey* 1852, but is now part of the site of Argyle House. It was evidently named for an owner who remains to be traced.

BAKEHOUSE CLOSE (146 Canongate) is listed thus on *Kirkwood* 1817 along with its earlier name HAMMERMEN'S, which appears alone on *Ainslie* 1780 and 1804. This derived from the ownership by the Incorporation of Hammermen of Canongate of the tenement now called 'Huntly House', together with the land stretching south to the Strand at the south back of the Canongate, an ownership which lasted from 1647 until 1762. Meantime the Acheson property on the east side of the close, including the mansion built by Sir Archibald Acheson of Glencairney in 1633, was broken up; and the Incorporation of Bakers of Canongate bought the southern part of it in the later 18th century and built a bakehouse there—hence the other name of the close. There is no evidence for the assertions by J Bruce Home that it was anciently 'Huntly Close' and then 'Cordiners' Close'. The only connection of the place with the Huntly family was that Henrietta, widow of the 2nd duke of Gordon, followed by her son Lord Adam Gordon, rented a flat from the Hammermen for some years between 1728 and 1762.

(COMMON) BAKEHOUSE CLOSE (153 Canongate) is listed on *Ainslie* 1780, and must have been named for some bakehouse, as yet untraced, of the Incorporation of Bakers of the Canongate. Its other name, SMITH'S, is recorded in 1827, but its origin is obscure. A James Smith, stay maker, is listed in *Williamson's Directory* 1780 as resident 'below the Canongate kirk'.

BAKER'S PLACE (Stockbridge) is on the site of *Stockbridge Toll* and a building immediately south of it, as shown on *Ainslie* 1804 and *Wood* 1823. It is possible that the name, which goes back to before 1824, once attached to this building, which may be the same one as the *Baker's Place* shown on *Ordnance Survey* 1852, with *Stockbridge Flour Mill* immediately behind it. While the name may have arisen in this trade connection, the possibility that it was an owner's name cannot be ruled out.

BALBIRNIE PLACE (Wester Coates) was named in about 1876, perhaps for Balbirnie, near Meigle in Forfar, or perhaps more likely (considering the nearby coal yards) for some connection with the collieries at Balbirnie near Markinch, Fife.

BALCARRES STREET (South Morningside) is for the most part in the lands of PLEWLANDS—but *see under* BELHAVEN TERRACE for note about its eastern end. It is shown, named and planned to run westwards to Craighouse Road, on the feuing plan for Plewlands estate 1882. The name is first listed in *PO Directory* 1884 and appears on all maps, although until about 1900 it is accompanied on some maps (but not on the *Ordnance Survey* 1893) by the further name BALCARRES TERRACE for the second section of the street, beside the cemetery. The name may derive from Balcarres in the East Neuk of Fife or from the surname or the title derived from it, and such evidence as there is points to its having been chosen by the superiors, the Scottish Heritage Company. BALCARRES COURT was named in 1970.

BALDERSTONE GARDENS (Inch) *see under* THE INCH, Nether Liberton.

BALERNO is recorded from 1280 onwards, and the early spellings *Balhernoch*, *Balernache* and *Balernaugh* show the name to be Gaelic *bail(e) àirneach*, stressed in exactly the same way as the modern form and meaning 'farm at/with the sloe bushes'. By medieval times it was not only a farm, but a baronial estate within the barony of Balerno and (Kirk)newton, and the WAULK MILL of Balerno and BALERNO MILL (*see under* KINAULD, Currie) were within it. It is shown as *Bowlenny* on *Laurie* 1763, altered to *Balernoe* on *Laurie* 1766 and *Armstrongs* 1773; but on earlier maps the name is closer to BYRNIE (*which see*) which is either a corruption of 'Balerno' or a separate local name. The village grew up in the later 18th century, around quarrying in the vicinity and papermaking in the mills of Byrnie, Townhead and Balerno Bank, all three being merged under the latter name in the 1830s.

BALFOUR STREET (Pilrig) is shown proposed on *Bartholomew* 1876, laid out in Pilrig Park Nursery and named for the Balfour lairds of Pilrig. The development stopped at Cambridge Gardens until 1899, when it was extended to BALFOUR PLACE.

BALFRON LOAN (Clermiston) *see under* CLERMISTON MAINS.

BALGREEN (Saughtonhall) is *Bogreen* on *Roy* 1753, *Backgreen* on *Laurie* 1763 and in *Kincaid* 1787, and *Ballgreen* on *Saughtonhall* 1795. Earlier forms are lacking; but these ones suggest a name pronounced *baw-'green*, which would be consistent with the spelling *Balgreen* found here and in five other places, including examples near Ecclesmachan and Midcalder. The name appears to be associated with gravelly or sandy ground—nowhere more clearly than here, where the farm included a 10-acre patch of glacial gravel on the shore of a post-glacial loch, *see under* CORSTORPHINE—and it is probably Gaelic *baile griain*, gravelly farm, or else its similar British equivalent. BALGREEN ROAD, evidently named as the road *to or by Balgreen*, is shown (with a more curving line) on *Roy* but it follows its present line on *Saughtonhall* 1795. Housing began to be developed beside it in about 1902, and BALGREEN AVENUE branched off it into the *Meadowshot* of Carrick Knowes in 1905. BALGREEN PARK and GARDENS were named by 1926.

BALLANTYNE PLACE and **ROAD** (North Leith) were built in 1896, the latter being a rebuilding of a section of the ancient MILL LANE, *which see*. BALLANTYNE PLACE was suppressed by redevelopment in 1981, when BALLANTYNE LANE was constructed. The name derived from the builders, Messrs. Grieve Ballantyne, and there was no connection with Abbot Ballantyne or Bellenden of Holyrood who built the first bridge at Leith in the 15th century.

BALLANTYNE'S CLOSE (226 Canongate) *see* WATSON'S CLOSE, Canongate.

BALLANTYNE'S or **BELLENDEN'S CLOSE** (307 Canongate) *see* HIGH SCHOOL CLOSE, Canongate.

BALLANTYNE'S CLOSE (once 7 now behind 21/23 Grassmarket) is shown on *Ainslie* 1780, while two generations later the name appears in *PO Directory* 1827, with Robert Ballantyne listed as owning an inn and carriers quarters in the close.

THE BALLAST QUAY (North Leith) is mentioned in *Town Council Minutes* 1657, and is shown on both *Collins* 1693 and *Fergus &*

Robinson 1759 as having a pronounced westward curve. Reported in 1773 as being 'in danger of tumbling down', it was rebuilt by William Jameson in 1777, evidently in the straight and shorter form first shown on *Wood's Leith* 1777. As its name implies, it was used for loading or off-loading ships' ballast, some of it perhaps sand or gravel from the adjoining beach of the SANDPORT. The name still appears on *Ainslie* 1804 but was eventually displaced by that of CUSTOM HOUSE QUAY, probably soon after the CUSTOM HOUSE (*which see*) was built here in 1812, by which time also the first of Rennie's great docks was in use and ballasting may have been carried out elsewhere.

BALLENY (Balerno) is recorded in 1627 as *Baleny* and shown as *Balenie* on *Adair* 1682 and *Baleny* on *Roy* 1753. The name is probably Gaelic *baile lèanaidhe*, farm place at the swampy meadows—*see also* MALLENY, with which the place has often been confused. There is a later spelling *Balveny* which would not bear that interpretation, but it may have arisen from confusion with Balveny in Banff.

THE BALM WELL OF St KATHERINE (Liberton) is referred to in the name *Sanct Katrinis of the Oly Well* in the *Treasurer's Accounts* 1505 and is shown on *Blaeu* 1654 as *Oyly Well*. The name arose from the crude paraffin that persistently floats on the water of the spring and was found useful in healing skin diseases. It was called 'St Katherine's oil' in a legend (summarised by Hector Boece in 1526 and translated in *RCAHMS Midlothian* p135) which artlessly brings together the popular saints, the 11th-century Margaret of Scotland and the 14th-century Katherine of Siena. James VI built a well house in 1617. Slighted by Cromwell, it was repaired in the 1660s. The estate of St Katherine's is mentioned in *RMS* 1663 and its development began in 1956 with BALMWELL AVENUE, GROVE and TERRACE, and St KATHERINE'S BRAE and LOAN, and continued with BALMWELL PARK in 1958 and St KATHERINE'S CRESCENT in 1960.

BALTIC STREET (South Leith) is not shown, even as a path, on *Naish* 1709, but appears on *Roy* 1753 as a link giving direct access from the vicinity of the Shore to the coast road to Musselburgh, as well as to the first of the glass furnaces newly set up at South Leith Sands (*see under* SALAMANDER STREET) and the roperies a little further to the east. *Wood* 1777 shows the street still unbuilt-up; and its name first appears in *Williamson's Directory* 1790, which also lists the Danish consul as resident in it; but while the name may celebrate Leith's trading connections, it is more likely that it specifically refers to corn exchange, for *The Baltic* (like *Lloyds*, from a coffee-house) was then the usual name for the London corn exchange. It may not have been coincidence that when Leith's spacious new Corn Exchange was built in 1860, it was sited in Baltic Street.

BANGHOLM (Warriston) was a farm (later a 'nursery' or market garden) lying immediately south of the Ankerfield burn. Its steading, shown on *Roy* 1753 as *Bangam* and as *Bangholm Mains* on *Fergus & Robinson* 1759, stood east of the south end of Clark Road, where it is still shown on *Bartholomew* 1923. The spelling on *Roy* (also used on the same map at OXGANGS and again, a half mile west of Bonnyrigg) is probably phonetic, and if so would sound the same as the surname *Bangham* still found in Edinburgh; but the place name (despite the usual acrobatic effort in *Milne* to find it Gaelic) remains obscure. BANGHOLM TERRACE was developed by 1898; BANGHOLM AVENUE, PARK, PLACE and ROAD date from 1924; and BANGHOLM GROVE, LOAN and VIEW were formed in the extreme east of the farm in 1925. BANGHOLM BOWER, shown on *Ainslie* 1804 as a house in the estate of LILLIPUT (*which see*) evidently took its name from the adjoining farm; and BANGHOLM BOWER AVENUE was developed in the northern part of its garden in 1926.

BANGOR ROAD (South Leith) is shown as a track on *Ordnance Survey* 1852 but by 1860 it was developed into a road giving access to a slateworks developed by Field and Allan, slate merchants in Great Junction Street. The name appears in *PO Directory* 1865 and (like that of BURLINGTON STREET two years later) probably derived from that of a major centre of slate quarrying—in this case Bangor in North Wales. BANGOR LANE is shown on *Ordnance Survey* 1893 as an unnamed path or lane leading from Bangor Road to the west end of Bowling Green Street. Skirting a boundary fence which had been set up by the slate works in about 1867, it probably grew up shortly after this, when the bridge was built at the end of Bowling Green Street.

(OLD) BANK CLOSE (286 High Street) got the name of *Bank Close* after 1700, when *the bank* (i.e. the Bank of Scotland, none other being in existence) moved from its burnt-out premises in Parliament Close to a new office in Robert Gourlay's house (see below) in the close. It became *the old bank* in 1727, when its rival, *the new bank* or Royal Bank of Scotland appeared on the scene, and thus the address of the Bank of Scotland became 'the close of the Old Bank'. The Bank quitted the close for its new office in Bank Street in 1806; and the close itself was suppressed in the building of George IV Bridge in about 1830—its site is now the western pavement at the head of that street. In 1511 it had been known as MAUCHAN'S, evidently for Alexander Mauchan, merchant, who is recorded as building two lands, albeit in the Boothraw or Luckenbooths, in that same year. He is also recorded as former owner of the ground on which Robert Gourlay, collector of customs for the burghs, built a house in the close in 1569—hence the name GOURLAY'S, still used in 1635, when one of two properties then owned by David Gourlay was tenanted by Sir Thomas Hope of Craighall, King's Advocate. Craighall bought it in 1637, giving rise to the further names HOPE'S or CRAIGHALL'S CLOSE.

OLD BANK, (BACK) ENTRY TO (52 Cowgate) *see* BRODIE'S CLOSE, High Street

NEW BANK CLOSE (High Street at Parliament Square) *see* St MONAN'S WYND.

BANKFIELD (Edmondston) is shown as *Bank* on *Roy* 1753 and as *Bankfield* on *Knox* 1812, and is detailed as a 24-acre holding on *Caldcoats etc.* 1815. The name described its position at the foot of the slope of Niddrie Edge. Still shown on *W & A K Johnston* 1898, the steading seems to have disappeared thereafter, becoming the site of *Cloverfoot Cottages* before 1920, this fancy name being transferred from a house in The Wisp on the other side of the road, shown as *Cloverfoot* on *Ordnance Survey* 1852.

BANKHEAD (Balerno) is shown as a farm on *Ravelrigg* 1764. The name is Scots, and refers to its position on a spur of higher ground between the Water of Leith on the north and its tributary burn on the south.

BANKHEAD (Dalmeny) is recorded from 1565 onwards as *the Bankheid*, evidently named for its position at the head of the slope above the shore. BANKHEAD GROVE was named by 1970 for its position on the farm.

BANKHEAD (Saughton) is named on *Roy* 1753 as a steading on the north side of the Calder Road. Thomas Johnston's map *Cultins* 1776, shows a cot house in this location, and *Saughton* 1795 shows how this was just east of the junction of the then new Broomhouse Road. The holding is still shown and named on *Gellatly* 1834, but had disappeared by 1852. Its name derived from its position at the head of the slope north of the Calder road, named as *the Bank* in a charter of 1590 quoted in *RMS* 1662. This field extended westwards from the west boundary of Saughton's home parks (now represented by Broomhouse Crescent) perhaps as far as Sighthill; but however that may be, the streets named BANKHEAD AVENUE, CROSSWAY, DRIVE, LOAN, MEDWAY, STREET, PLACE, TERRACE and WAY in 1947 are all a clear half-mile away from the historic Bankhead.

BANK PLACE (North Leith) *see under* LARGO PLACE, North Leith.

BANK STREET (Old Town) is shown on *Kincaid* 1784 as a proposed access from the head of the *Earthen Mound* to the High Street. It was driven through the pattern of earlier closes in 1798, and was named for the Bank of Scotland, which moved here in 1806 from the BANK CLOSE (286 High Street), *which see*. NORTH BANK STREET was *Bank Street* prior to 1893.

BANK STREET (South Leith) was on the site of an older entry or close, but was named thus by 1817, evidently for the *West Leith Bank* whose elegant office was erected here in 1806. In 1965, to obviate any confusion with Bank Street in the Old Town, the street was renamed SEAPORT STREET, reportedly in vague and rather ponderous reference to the character of Leith, but it might have been for the *Sea Gate* in the ramparts, shown on *Siege of Leith* 1560 in a position which would be more or less directly opposite, on the north side of Bernard Street.

BANNATYNE or **BALLANTYNE'S CLOSE** (226 Canongate) *see* WATSON'S CLOSE.

BARCLAY PLACE (Wrightshouses) is a redevelopment built in 1885 and named for the adjoining Barclay Free Kirk, built in 1862-64 under a bequest by Miss Barclay. BARCLAY TERRACE followed in 1890.

BARCLAY'S CLOSE (327 High Street) *see under* DON'S CLOSE.

BARCLAY'S CLOSE (66 High Street) *see under* SKINNERS' CLOSE.

BARCLAY'S HOUSES (Bonnington Toll) is shown on Laurie's *Newhaven Roads* 1765 and was a group of houses built in the 1740s on five acres of Pilrig land by Robert Barclay, deacon of the tailors in Edinburgh. Some time after 1768 a toll bar was erected, and the name *Barclay's Houses* was displaced by that of BONNINGTON TOLL, *see under* BONNINGTON ROAD, Pilrig.

BARKER'S CLOSE (South Leith) may have been named for Thomas Barker, brewer in Yardheads in 1744, but its position has not been established.

BARM CLOSE (Coalhill, Leith) is shown on *Kirkwood* 1817 and *Ordnance Survey* 1852, and *PO Directory* 1827 lists the Barm (i.e. yeast) Company of Bakers here at Sheriffbrae.

BARNBOUGLE (Dalmeny) is recorded in charters of David II as *Barbogle* 1346 and *Barnebugele* 1362; but in *RMS* 1365 it is *Parnbogalle*, while the 16th-century index to the charters of Robert the Bruce 1306-29 gives it as *Pronbugele*. The name is British, possibly *pren bugel*, shepherd's tree, but more likely *brinn bugel*, shepherd's hill, or *bar an bugel*, shepherd's hill top; and it would fit the high ground which rises immediately behind the shore (*see under* DRUM SANDS, Dalmeny) and more particularly the steep spur immediately behind Barnbougle (or a tree on its summit) which indeed gives an excellent view of the grazings around the mouth of the Cockle. The tower house, recorded in 1539 but reduced to a shell after 1817, was restored in 1880. LITTLE BARNBOUGLE, recorded from 1473 onwards and still shown on *Knox* 1812, was suppressed before 1834, apparently in favour of *Dalmeny Home Farm*, although its name persists in that of BARNBOUGLE RIDE.

BARNES CLOSE (172 High Street) *see* OLD ASSEMBLY CLOSE.

BARNSHOT ROAD (Colinton) dates from about 1890 and is named for the field which lay between Woodhall Road and the north side of Grant Avenue, named on Leslie's *Spylaw* 1767 as the *Burn Shot*—i.e. the field beside the burn, a small one which, originating at the Bung Well at Torphin, flowed down the east side of Bonaly Road and, to judge by the 1767 map, along the north edge of the field (controversy anent its course is reported in *Steuart's Colinton* p385). The name appears, already corrupted to *Barnshot*, on Bell's *Spylaw* 1799.

BARNTALLOCH COURT (East Craigs) *see under* CRAIGIEVAR WYND, East Craigs.

BARNTON (Cramond) is recorded in *RMS* 1390-1406 in the forms *Bernetoun*, *Berntoun* and *Barntoun*, evidently derived from Anglian *beren tún*, farm with a storehouse for barley or other corn, but perhaps carrying the more specialised meaning of demesne farm, where the laird stored his crops and rents-in-kind. By about 1500 it had been divided into OVER (upper) BARNTON and NETHER (lower) BARNTON: *Blaeu* 1654 shows both, but *Adair* 1682 shows only *Barntoun*. In about 1790, William Ramsay merged the estate with that of KING'S CRAMOND (*which see*) and by 1811 the old house of King's Cramond *alias*

Cramond Regis was replaced by NEW BARNTON, the original Barnton becoming OLD BARNTON, as shown on *Knox* 1812, and later EASTER PARK. The new house stood immediately north of West Barnton Avenue, about 170 yards east of Barnton Brae; while the earlier house of Cramond Regis might have been on the same site, but was more probably on the little knoll a few yards further north at NT 18777559. The eastern part of EAST BARNTON AVENUE is a remnant of the old Queensferry road prior to 1824, and the eastern part of BARNTON AVENUE dates from the 1900s, but otherwise the modern BARNTON AVENUE, and EAST and WEST BARNTON AVENUES represent the winding drives formed in the new parkland in about 1810 and shown on *Cramond Roads* 1812 as entered from the old Queensferry road at BARNTONGATE, now represented by the crook in East Barnton Avenue. The East and West Barnton Avenues were distinguished from each other in 1924. BARNTON LOAN was named in 1924, and BARNTON BRAE in 1936. The opening of CRAMOND BRIG RAILWAY STATION in 1894 stimulated the construction of BARNTON GROVE at BONNYFIELD, in the south west corner of the parks. Similarly, the construction of BARNTONGATE STATION in the *Plover park* of Lauriston encouraged the development of BARNTON GARDENS and PARK, together with the eastern extension of BARNTON AVENUE, in the *Stony Butts* and *Lady's Knowes* of Lauriston, the streets being laid out by 1912. In 1958, following the closure of the railway, SOUTH BARNTON AVENUE was built on the site of Barntongate station; and EAST BARNTON GARDENS, on the site of Barntongate Nurseries in the Plover park, were named in 1978.

BARNTONGATE TERRACE (Drum Brae) was originally named SOUTHFIELD TERRACE, after the farm on which it stood; but for fear of this ancient name (shown on *Blaeu* 1654) being confused with *Southfield*-named streets in Duddingston, it was renamed in 1967, and SOUTHFIELD AVENUE and DRIVE became BARNTONGATE AVENUE and DRIVE in 1968. The new name was possibly influenced by the older *Barntongate* at Davidson's Mains (*see under* BARNTON) but was ostensibly suggested by the *gate to Barnton* opposite the foot of the Drum Brae, which is in fact a remnant of the old Queensferry road which continued north past Bonnyfield before turning sharply west for Cramond Brig, as shown on *Knox* and *Cramond Roads* 1812.

BARNTON PARK AVENUE, CRESCENT, DRIVE, PLACE, VIEW and **WOOD** (Barnton) were developed in 1959 in what had been the southern part of the park of New Barnton before it was cut off by the railway line in about 1893. BARNTON PARK DELL was added in 1973.

BARNTON TERRACE and **WEST BARNTON TERRACE** (Craigleith) *see under* CRAIGLEITH ROAD.

BARONSCOURT ROAD and **TERRACE** (Jocks Lodge) were developed in 1908 in fields shown on *Duddingston* c1800 as *Barnyard Park* and *South Park*. The streets were named for Baronscourt in Co. Tyrone, Ireland, seat of the Duke of Abercorn, superior of this Duddingston ground.

BARONY STREET (Broughton) is shown proposed on *Knox* 1821 and feuing began in 1829. As is shown very clearly on *Ainslie* 1804, its site was the centre of the ancient village of BROUGHTON (*which see*) and of the barony of regality of Broughton, which comprised great stretches of land around Edinburgh and Leith as well as elsewhere within the extensive lands granted to Holyrood by David I in 1128. The street name, fixed by 1831, commemorates the barony. BARONY PLACE, taking its name from Barony Street, went apparently unnamed until about 1890, but its beginnings are shown on *Kay* 1836, taking the place of a proposed mews entry sketched on *Knox* 1821.

BARONY TERRACE (Corstorphine) *see under* FORRESTER ROAD, Corstorphine.

THE BARRACE or **BARRES** (West Port) was a tilting ground west of the King's Stables, first laid out by the garrison (including several Scottish knights) who held the Castle for Edward III from 1335 to 1341 and reinstated it after it had lain waste since being put out of action by Robert the Bruce in 1313. A barrace was regarded as an important facility, and its construction is mentioned in *Bain* 1337. The name is from Old French *barres*, barriers defining the sides of the lists. Combats took place on the narrow flat beside the road to St Cuthbert's, there was a chapel for the dead or wounded (*see under* LADY WYND, West Port) and the steep bank on the west of the ground probably served as grandstand. The place was still available for combats in 1602. It is shown on *Rothiemay* 1647, and in 1752 *Maitland* describes it as a pleasant public green. In 1983 THE BARRACE STEPS, situated about halfway along the site, were named to commemorate it.

BARRIE'S CLOSE (196 High Street) *see* OLD FISHMARKET CLOSE.

BARRINGER'S CLOSE (91 High Street) is given thus on *Edgar* 1742, but no derivation has been found either for this name or for two others current in the previous century, which appear as 'MRS MURE'S, of old ALEXr DON'S in 1697, and in earlier forms such as *Mistress Mourisch's* in 1658, and *Mistress Murie's or Alex Doune's* in 1669, while the good lady (unless there was an unrecorded Mrs Menzies) was perhaps still remembered in 1764 as *Mrs Minish*.

BARRY'S CLOSE (107 High Street) *see* BAILIE FYFE'S CLOSE.

(JACOB or **JAMES) BARRON'S CLOSE** (251 High Street) *see* OLD POST OFFICE CLOSE.

JOHN BARTON'S CLOSE (28 High Street) *see* FOUNTAIN CLOSE.

BASSENDEN'S CLOSE (19 High Street) *see* PANMURE'S CLOSE.

(SOUTH) BASSENDEN'S CLOSE (28 High Street) *see* FOUNTAIN CLOSE.

BATHFIELD (North Leith) is noted in *South Leith Records* 1684 as a deserted farm called LODGE-ME-LOWNE (*which see*) but in 1784 it was redeveloped as BATHFIELD by one of the Bonnar family, painters and decorators in Edinburgh for over 200 years, who built a block of lodgings for families coming to North Leith Links for the sea bathing, noted in *Kincaid* 1784 as a leading industry in North Leith. Cut off from the sea by the advent of the Caledonian Railway and LINDSAY ROAD in the 1860s, it gave its name to BATHFIELD ROAD by 1901. Bonnar's original tenement, often called *Bathfield House*, served many purposes before it was demolished in 1984, when BATHFIELD ROAD and HAMILTON CRESCENT were amalgamated to form a new housing street named BATHFIELD, with a path or *gate* BATHFIELDGATE branching off it, together with a small park called NICHOLL GREEN on the site of NICHOLL PLACE, the name appearing in *PO Directory* 1898 and formally adopted by Leith Town Council in 1900 for a street feued out in the late 1890s by David and Albert Nicholl of Bathfield Dairy.

BATHGATE'S CLOSE (94 Cowgate) is listed on *Ainslie* 1780, but was cleared for the building of George IV Bridge in about 1829. The names of George and John Bathgate, both of them *messengers* or executors of summonses, are given as residents by *Williamson's Directories* for 1773 and 1780 respectively.

BATH ROAD (South Leith) is shown on Wood 1777 as an access to Leith Sands. The name *Bath Road* does not appear until 1885, and it would seem that until then the street and its extension to the south shared the name of BATH STREET, shown on *Ainslie* 1804. Clearly this derived from the sea bathing at the Sands, which as early as 1761 was being promoted by the hiring-out of a bathing machine from the Royal Oak public house near the 'Glass houses' or glassworks in what became Salamander Street. The separate name *Bath Road* was probably devised after the street became the access to the new Edinburgh Dock, opened in 1881. In 1967, to obviate any confusion with Bath Street in Portobello, Bath Street was renamed SALAMANDER PLACE, from the adjoining SALAMANDER STREET, *which see*.

BATH STREET (Portobello) was laid out by 1802, but little progress was made in feuing until after the *Portobello Hot and Cold Sea Water Baths*, planned in 1804, were opened in 1806. Recorded in 1805, the street name obviously derived from this, but perhaps not without a glance at the English watering place of the name, for Portobello was being strongly promoted as a fashionable resort at this time. BATH PLACE was named soon afterwards, as a branch off the original street.

THE BATTERY (North Leith) is shown on *Ainslie* 1804. In 1779, a threatened attack on Leith by a rebel American squadron of three ships commanded by Paul Jones had been repelled only by strong contrary winds; and this 9-gun battery was built soon afterwards to reinforce the defences by covering the entrance channel to the harbour. It was swept away in 1963 by the development of HAMILTON WYND and LINDSAY PLACE.

BAVELAW (Balerno) is recorded from about 1230 onwards. The earliest spellings are typically *Bavelay*, *Bavilley* and *Bauelay*, and the name is clearly Anglian, combining *beaw*, a cleg (or else the personal name *Beaw* or *Beawa* derived from the insect's) with *leah*, which although it came to mean 'meadow' primarily meant 'a clear space in woodland' and may therefore take the name back to a time when scrub forest covered most of the land. The present ending -*law* seems to have begun to challenge the earlier -*ley* around 1500 and to have prevailed over it by 1700. Sometimes given as -*laws*, it may be Scots *law*, a hillock, describing the main features in the treeless landscape of later times. The 17th-century BAVELAW HOUSE seems to be on or near the site of an earlier tower shown on *Blaeu* 1654 as *Brusley*— probably an engraver's error for *Bausley*. EASTER and WESTER BAVELAW are recorded in *RMS* 1529 and shown on *Roy* 1753 along with BAVELAW MILL. *Laurie* 1763 shows the mill's DAMHEAD on the BAVELAW BURN. The stretch of the burn where it is bridged by Harlaw Road is the BLACK LINN, Scots from Anglian *hlynn*, a cataract.

BAVELAW ROAD (Balerno) was built in 1973 to bypass Balerno and was named as the through route to Bavelaw. In 1979, BAVELAW GARDENS was named as a branch off it.

BAWS INCH (Duddingston) figures on *Duddingston* c1800 as an area of 11 Scots acres; it may be related to the *Baw Mure* noted in *Protocols of James Young* 1489 as owned by Margaret, sister of Simon Preston of Craigmillar. The second part of the name is Scots *inch* from Celtic *inis*, a waterside meadow. The first part may be early Scots *bawsen*, badger, or *bausand*, piebald or white-striped; but is possibly from British *bau*, muddy.

BAXTER'S BUILDINGS (Greenside) are shown on *Ainslie* 1804 and were built in about 1799 by John Baxter, architect in Princes Street, who had feued ground here since 1780. The adjoining BAXTER'S PLACE dates from about 1812.

BAXTERS CLOSE (South side of Canongate) *see under* BRODIE'S CLOSE, south side of foot of Canongate.

BAXTERS CLOSE (41 Canongate) *see* RAMSAY'S CLOSE, Canongate.

BAXTERS CLOSE (60 Cowgate) was one of several outlets from BRODIE'S CLOSE, 304 High St, *which see*, to the Cowgate. Listed on *Ainslie* 1780, it got this name from property purchased by the Incorporation of Baxters from the trustees of James Ferguson, still occupied by John Mason and other bakers in the 1770s. It was also HOPE'S or CRAIGHALL'S or (by confusion) CRAIGIEHALL'S.

BAXTERS CLOSE (High Street) was one of four closes named for the property of the Incorporation of Baxters (i.e. Bakers) which stood some 200 feet north of the High Street on a site now occupied by North Bank Street—*see also* WARDROP'S COURT, and MIDDLE and LOWER BAXTERS' CLOSES. It is listed as *Upper Baxter's Close* on *Edgar* 1742 and as *Old Baxter's Close* on *Ainslie* 1780, and is famous as being where Robert Burns lodged on his first visit to Edinburgh in 1786. It was also known as HOOPER'S CLOSE, from a family named Hooper (or Hopper or Happer) who held property in it before 1723. It also seems to have been one of the four closes in Edinburgh named BULL'S CLOSE for Robert Bull, deacon of the Wrights in 1680, who sold property 'on the north side of the High Street' to David Hopper, one of the family who owned a tenement in the close.

MIDDLE BAXTERS CLOSE (High Street) was one of three closes cleared to make way for Bank Street. Its name was transferred from WARDROP'S COURT (*which see*) by 1742, when it is shown here on *Edgar*.

LOWER or **LOW BAXTERS CLOSE** (High Street) is shown on *Edgar* 1742 and was cleared to make way for Bank Street in about 1798. Also called *Eastmost Baxters Close*, it was named for the Incorporation of Baxters in the same way as BAXTERS CLOSE, *which see*. Alternatively, it was called BAILIE REID'S CLOSE, and the form *William Reid's* recorded in 1641 shows that it was named for William Reid, bailie in 1624, he and his successors (three of them also bailies in their day) having several properties in the close. The further alternative name, RONALD'S CLOSE, recorded in 1648, is obscure.

JAMES BAYNE'S CLOSE (Old Town) was a little close on the east side of Blackfriars' Wynd, behind *Bain's land*, and named for its owner James Bayne, wright, at some date prior to 1747. He may have been the James Bane, wright, mentioned in *Town Council Minutes* 1665.

BAYTON TERRACE (Wardie) was a side name on the east side of Granton Road from 1879 until about 1900. It looks as though it were coined from Wardie *Bay*, with *-ton* added for Wardie farm.

BEACH LANE (Portobello) *see* RAMSAY LANE *under* RAMSAY PLACE, Portobello.

BEARFORD'S (BAREFOOT'S) PARKS (New Town) *see under* HALKERSTON'S CROFT, New Town.

BEATTIE'S CLOSE (at 84 Grassmarket) is shown on *Ordnance Survey* 1852 but is unnamed on earlier maps. It was evidently named for an owner, as yet untraced.

BEAUCHAMP ROAD and **GROVE** (Liberton) *see under* CADOGAN ROAD, Liberton.

BEAUFORT ROAD (Grange) was formed in the Grange estate as an extension of Grange Road to link up with Strathearn Road. Although it makes its appearance in *PO Directory* 1872, it was probably planned and named along with PALMERSTON ROAD and CHALMERS CRESCENT, *see under* THE GRANGE, Thus the *Beaufort* in question, whether a person or a place, is likely to have had some connection with the Dick Lauders or one of their enthusiasms, but this remains to be established.

BEAUMONT PLACE (St Leonards) *see* BOWMONT PLACE, St Leonards.

BEAVERBANK PLACE (Canonmills) was named in about 1882, evidently by association with Beaverhall, although the street was actually on the west side of the Clerk's Mill Bleachfield, 60 yards from the nearest part of Beaverhall.

BEAVERBANK TERRACE (Canonmills) appears to have been a side name in Beaverhall Road, perhaps dating from 1882, but dropped in 1903.

BEAVERHALL (Canonmills) is shown on *Fergus & Robinson* 1759 as well as *Ordnance Survey* 1852 as a large property, *Beaver Hall*. The name is believed to derive from the manufacture of *beaver* hats, on the ground that an advertisement in 1782 refers to 'a large building beside the house, formerly used as a hat factory'. In 1683 Capt. Thomas Hamilton, merchant in Edinburgh, petitioned the Privy Council for a monopoly in manufacture of beaver hats, which he intended to start up for the first time in the country, using skins which he imported from the Plantations in America, and bringing over two experts in the craft of beaver-hat making; and while there is no evidence connecting this enterprise with Beaverhall, it is at least a possibility. BEAVERHALL ROAD was developed in the eastern part of the property in the 1880s and was named by 1887.

BEDEMANS or **BEIDMANS CROFT** (St Leonard's) *see under* HERMITS AND TERMITS, St Leonard's.

BEDFORD CLOSE (South Leith) is shown off Giles Street on *Ordnance Survey* 1852, but the origin of the name remains to be traced.

BEDFORD STREET (Stockbridge) was developed in about 1825 in two properties in Dean Street (shown on *Ainslie* 1804 and *Kirkwood* 1817) one of which had already been partly developed as MARY'S PLACE and ALLAN STREET, Stockbridge, *which see*. How the name originated is not known, but it is more likely to have come from some local person or connection than from John 6th Duke of Bedford, by this time long retired from politics, although well known as an art collector and authority on agriculture and horticulture. BEDFORD CRESCENT was formed in 1903, and BEDFORD COURT was named in 1971.

BEDFORD TERRACE (Joppa) was envisaged as a meuse lane in the plan for development of RABBIT HAW (*which see*) in 1801, Shown on *W & A K Johnston* 1888, it was named *Bedford Place* by 1893, but this was altered to *Bedford Terrace* in 1912. James Hamilton, 1st Duke of Abercorn and superior of Duddingston (including Rabbit Haw) was married to a daughter of the Duke of Bedford. He died in 1885.

BEECHMOUNT (Corstorphine) was feued off from Beechwood Mains in 1903, and the new mansion was named by combining *Beech-* from the older name with *-mount* for the hill slope, possibly imitating the adjoining Belmont, often spelt *Belmount* on the earlier maps. The house was bequeathed to the Royal Infirmary of Edinburgh in 1926.

BEECHMOUNT CRESCENT (Saughtonhall) was formed in 1971. Branching off from Saughton Road (itself misnamed, since it is on Saughtonhall ground) the street is partly on what was once the *Langcotelee* of Balgreen farm but mainly on a haugh in Belmont north of the Stank. While it was agreed that existing confusion would be compounded if it were given a 'Saughton' name, a fresh confusion was risked by naming it for a mere view of Beechmount House across intervening land in Belmont.

BEECHWOOD (Corstorphine) was the central portion of the lands on the south side of Corstorphine Hill feued by John Dickie in 1720, and it is recorded in 1778 as *Corstorphinehill now called Beechwood*—a name probably derived from the tree plantings which figure prominently on the maps from *Roy* 1753 onwards. BEECHWOOD HOUSE was built by Francis Scott in 1780. Its home farm BEECHWOOD MAINS presumably dates from the same period, unless it was earlier a farm steading in the original Corstorphinehill estate, and it was adopted as a street name in 1984. SOUTH BEECHWOOD was so named in 1986 as a street built on the Beechwood ground along the north bank of the Stank burn.

BEECHWOOD TERRACE (South Leith) *see under* WOODBINE TERRACE, South Leith.

BEGBIE'S CLOSE (once 118 now 104 Grassmarket) is shown on *Ainslie* 1780 and 1804, and was evidently named for Charles Begbie, listed in *Williamson's Directory* 1773 as stabler in the north side of Grassmarket. In *PO Directory* 1827 it is given as DEWAR'S CLOSE: the name may be connected with the Dewar owners at DEWAR CLOSE, West Bow, *which see.*

DR BEGG'S BUILDING (Abbeyhill) was built in the 1850s as a block of sixty improved dwellings for the working class, named for the Revd Dr James Begg, then minister of the Free Kirk in Newington, one of the leading spirits in the reform of housing from the 1840s onwards (*see also under* THE COLONIES, Stockbridge) and author of the pamphlet *Happy Homes for Working Men.*

BELFORD ROAD (Drumsheugh and Dean) represents part of the old highroad to Queensferry which, as shown on *Roy* 1753 and *Armstrongs* 1773, branched westwards from Queensferry Street by Lynedoch Place Lane (*see under* DRUMSHEUGH LANE) and then followed its present line, crossing the river by the 3-arched *Bell's Mill Bridge* which, as shown on *Roy*, was on the same site as the present bridge. In the late 1770s or early 1780s, as shown on *Laurie* 1786, the eastern end of the road was altered, presumably to ease the gradient, by cutting it off from Drumsheugh Lane and forming the present connection with the road to the Dean at the head of Bell's Brae. After 1832, when the Dean Bridge was completed and the present Queensferry Road opened up, the earlier route was known as the OLD QUEENSFERRY ROAD until 1887, when the old bridge was replaced and the road and the new structure were named BELFORD ROAD and BELFORD BRIDGE. There is nothing to indicate that there was a ford here, and it seems likely that the name had been coined (originally as *Bellford*) as a name for BELFORD TERRACE in 1871. BELFORD PARK and PLACE followed in 1873 and 1874; and BELFORD MEWS in Sunbury took its name from Belford Road in 1890. BELFORD AVENUE and GARDENS, on ground once in Dean Park farm but latterly in Blinkbonny, took their name from Belford Road in 1932.

BELFRAGE LANE (High Riggs) is shown on *Kirkwood* 1817, but was named for Andrew Belfrage, farmer in Kingsknowes, Slateford, who got a large tenement in the lane in 1826, on land then known as *Crichan's Gardens.*

BELGRAVE CRESCENT etc. (Dean) see under BUCKINGHAM TERRACE, Dean.

BELGRAVE ROAD (Corstorphine) derived its name from a field, once the *East Bank* of Meadowhead, bought in 1870 by Robert Mason and renamed *Belgrave Park*, a fancy name doubtless borrowed from Westminster to provide a would-be fashionable address for feuing. This began along the main-road frontage; and in 1892 C F Gordon (*see also* GORDON STREET, Quarryholes) began a development in the whole of the Park and in Corstorphinehill ground north of it. *Ordnance Survey* 1893 shows the entries of BELGRAVE ROAD and KAIMES ROAD in process of formation. By 1912, the latter, named by 1902 for Kaimes in Gordon's estate of Halmyre, near Romanno Bridge, had reached Old Kirk Road; BELGRAVE PLACE, so named in 1902 but later made part of St John's Road, had been built up; BELGRAVE ROAD, so named by 1900, was more than half built, and the southern part of BELGRAVE GARDENS was at least envisaged; and at the north end of Gordon's ground an old quarry road, shown on *Ordnance Survey* 1852, was being developed as CAIRNMUIR ROAD, named in 1902 for Cairnmuir in Halmyre estate. GORDON LOAN was named in 1923, the northern stretch of KAIMES ROAD in 1924, and BELGRAVE GARDENS in 1926. For the rest of the development *see under* OLD KIRK ROAD and CORSTORPHINEHILL. BELGRAVE TERRACE was developed by 1903 in garden ground at the foot of Clermiston Road.

BELHAVEN TERRACE (Morningside) was built in 1880. The origin of the name, like that of BALCARRES STREET adjoining, is obscure. It may be from Belhaven, Dunbar.

BELL CLOSE (Castlehill) *see under* the BELL HOUSE, Castlehill.

BELLENDEN GARDENS (Inch) *see under* THE INCH, Nether Liberton.

BELLEVILLE (Newington) was a marketing name coined, with a play on their family name, by George, Robert, Joseph and William Bell, soon after they began to feu out NEWINGTON (*which see*) in 1806.

BELLEVUE, BELLEVUE CRESCENT etc. (Bellevue) *see under* NORTHERN NEW TOWN.

BELLFIELD (Joppa) was a property probably dating from about 1801, when the marquess of Abercorn began to feu out Rabbit Haw. Shown as *Bellsfield* on *Wood's Portobello* 1824, it was evidently named for someone called Bell. It remained virtually unaltered until after 1856, but its High Street frontage was built up by the 1880s and the rest was developed by 1893. BELLFIELD LANE, named on *Sutter's Portobello* 1856, is shown in 1824 as *Chapel Lane*, for the parish kirk which was then a chapel of ease of the parish kirk of Duddingston. For BELLFIELD STREET (formerly MELVILLE STREET) *see under* RABBIT HALL, Joppa.

THE BELL HOUSE (Castlehill) was a bell foundry built by John Meikle in 1684 on a site which although described as 'east' of Ramsay Lane appears to have been west of it, north of the reservoir and next to Allan Ramsay's garden—where a complex of buildings is in fact shown on *Edgar* 1742. The BELLHOUSE CLOSE mentioned in *Maitland* 1753 may have been the upper part of Ramsay Lane, but perhaps more likely was the entry off it into the foundry. It seems to be the same as the BELL CLOSE mentioned in 1762.

BELL HOUSE (High Street) *see* THE TOLBOOTH, High Street.

BELLMANSKNOWE (Ratho) is recorded on *Norton* 1813 in the field name *Bellman's Knowe Park*. The name is Scots *knowe*, small hill, attached to an earlier place name, perhaps Gaelic *baile manach*, monks' farm, which would fit in with the hill's location on the north of the historic glebe and ABTHANE OF RATHO *which see*.

BELL PLACE (Stockbridge) *see* THE COLONIES.

BELL'S BRAE (Water of Leith or Dean Village) is so named on *Ordnance Survey* 1852, which also shows BELL'S BRAES further upstream, opposite BELL'S MILLS, which see; but maps previous to 1852 name it *Water of Leith*, evidently as the main street of that village. It is possible that the Bell's Brae name has been transferred; but on the other hand, millers named Bell were associated not only with Bell's Mills but with the town's mills in the Water of Leith village: *Town Council Minutes* of 1525 record Adam Bell as a lease holder, and in 1598 Clement Bell was appointed 'ordinary miller' at the town's malt mills here.

BELL'S CLOSE (272 Canongate) is listed on *Ainslie* 1780, and evidently got this name from a family of stablers, represented by John Bell in 1773. *Bell's carriers' quarters* are advertised as in the Canongatehead in 1771; but the family business may go back to a considerably earlier date, since they got their property from Charles Hope, merchant—probably the one who was a councillor in 1704. The close was also known as COUDON'S, for a John Coudon, who also had stables in it at some time prior to 1744. It also seems to have been one of the many CANT'S CLOSES, but there is no record of ownership. Being in the south Canongatehead, the close was part of Edinburgh, not the burgh of Canongate.

BELL'S or **FRANCIS BELL'S CLOSE** (571 High Street) *see under* BLYTH'S CLOSE, 571 High Street.

BELL'S CLOSE or **COURT** (South Leith) is shown on *Kirkwood* 1817 as off New Kirk Lane (now Maritime Lane) and was occupied in 1800 by Wm. and Chas. Bell, wine merchants. In 1989 a new development on the site was named NEW BELL'S COURT.

BELL'S HILL (Currie) is named on *Knox* 1812. The name occurs elsewhere (e.g. *Bell's Law* in Newton) and may be early Scots *bellit hill*, hill with a bald or pale patch on it, but is more likely to be from Old Norse *bjalli*, bell-shaped or rounded hill, with the ending changed to *s*, and *hill* added.

BELL'S MILLS (Dean) are shown on *Blaeu* 1654 as *Den Mills*, and originated as the corn and waulk mills of the medieval barony of Dean, distinct from the royal mills and *new mill of Edinburgh* mentioned in David I's charter to Holyrood Abbey, and from the *Common mills* of Edinburgh, *see under* WATER OF LEITH VILLAGE. The name was evidently from the family who ran them. The Adam Bell mentioned in *RMS* 1559 as *in Deyn myllis* may have been, or have descended from, the Adam Bell mentioned in *Town Council Minutes* 1525 as tenant of the town's mills further downstream; and in *RMS* 1583 the styling of Walter Bell *of Bellismylne* suggests that by this time the family were owners of the mill. BELL'S MILL BRIDGE is shown on *Roy* 1753 and carried the Queensferry road over the river until 1887, when it was replaced by BELFORD BRIDGE, *which see*. The way to it across Coates was known as BELL'S LOAN or COATES BAUKS (see under COATES) and *Ordnance Survey* 1852 shows the slopes opposite the mills, now the vicinity of Douglas Crescent, as BELL'S BRAES.

THE BELLSTANE (Queensferry) is noted on *Ordnance Survey* 1854 as the name of an object just outwith the burgh boundary and in the southwest corner of the little square that now bears the name. While it has been surmised that it was a stone named for a handbell rung beside it on market days, in point of fact a burgh council minute of 1642 (quoted in *Morison's Queensferry* p131) records that a piece of ground hitherto waste and unused, within the burgh but *near the bellstane*, was to be set aside for markets and fairs *in time coming*; and the clear inference is that the name belonged to the stone before any markets were held near it. In absence of a reliable description of the stone or of early forms of its name, the origin of the name can only be guessed at. Similar names in Kirknewton and Whitburn are no better documented, but the early forms of *Belstane* in Lanarkshire (*Bellitstane, Bellistane, Belstane* and *Bellstane* prior to 1329, and *Beldstane* in 1452) suggest that its first part may be Anglian *ballede* or early Scots *bellit* (from a Celtic root *ball*, white) making the name 'the stone with a white or pale patch or stripe on it'—such as one with a band of quartz running through it. A conspicuous boulder or standing stone of this sort on this spur of higher ground above the shore would have been a useful meith or leading mark for boats making for the narrow landing place at the Binks.

BELL'S WYND (142 High Street and 178 Cowgate) is shown on *Rothiemay* 1647, but recorded much earlier in *RMS* 1500 as *Bellis Wynd* and in 1504 as *Ade Bell's vennel*. Since *RMS* 1505 records two brothers David and Adam (i.e. Ade) Bell and their late father Andrew as owners of properties adjoining each other on the south side of the High Street, and since *Protocols of John Foular* 1529 mention a deceased John Bell as an owner in the wynd, it is likely that it was named for this family. Andrew Bell was to the fore in 1450, but dead before 1488, while Adam witnessed a charter as early as 1484.

BELL'S WYND (Pleasance) gave entry to Bell's brewery, shown on *Edgar* 1765 as well as *Ordnance Survey* 1852 and later maps.

BELMONT (Corstorphine) was the most easterly part of a feu on the south side of Corstorphine Hill, taken by John Dickie in 1720, *see also* BEECHWOOD *and* CORSTORPHINEHILL. Purchased in the early 1730s by Charles Bruce, glazier in Edinburgh, it appears on *Adair/Cooper* 1735 as BRUCE NOCKE (i.e. Scots *knock* or hillock), and as BRUCEHILL on *Laurie* 1763. In about 1763 its next owner, David Campbell, lawyer in Edinburgh, named it BELMONT, perhaps for its *fine hill* situation, and perhaps with a glance at Portia's idyllic *Belmont* in *The Merchant of Venice*; but perhaps also, considering the frequent early spelling *Bellmount*, Campbell followed Bruce's example by enshrining part of his own surname in it. BELMONT CRESCENT and TERRACE were named in 1926, and BELMONT AVENUE, GARDENS, PARK and VIEW followed in 1930. EASTER BELMONT ROAD was given in 1935 as a name, apparently fancy, for that part of the *Kirk Road* which skirted round the north of Belmont. Shown on *Roy* 1753, it was an ancient right of way from Ravelston to the parish kirk at Corstorphine, *see also* OLD KIRK ROAD, Corstorphine.

BELMONT ROAD (Juniper Green) is shown developing but as yet unnamed on *Fowler* 1845 and *Ordnance Survey* 1852, probably taking its line from a path in the original park of Woodhall (*see under* ENTERKIN'S YETT *and* JUNIPER GREEN) at the same time and in the same way as another road developed off Lanark road further west. By 1893 these roads had joined and at some date before 1902 they were named BELMONT AVENUE, said to have been for a *Belmont Dairy* in the western section. By 1912, the northern section had been renamed BELMONT ROAD; and in 1967 the western section lost the original name, for fear of confusion with a street in Corstorphine, and was renamed JUNIPER AVENUE.

BELVEDERE PARK (Newhaven) was named in 1971 as a development in part of the grounds of Belvidere House, built about a hundred years earlier.

THE BERE HOLMS (Craiglockhart) appear on a map of Craiglockhart in *Steuart's Colinton* p240, as the name of a field or fields on the terrace immediately above the western bluff of Easter Craiglockhart Hill. *Holm* is early Scots from Old Norse *holmr*, an island or raised piece of ground; and the name implies that this was arable land, suitable for growing bere or barley, but occurring in patches separated in some way—e.g. by wet or broken ground.

BERESFORD GARDENS (Trinity) was built in Lixmount and named for one or other (or both) of two naval commanders of the family of the Marquis of Waterford: Admiral Sir John Beresford (1766-1844) who was made a free burgess of Edinburgh after serving as Commander in Leith from 1820 to 1823, and Admiral Baron Charles Beresford (1846-1919) who was promoted to command the Channel Fleet in 1907, the very year in which the street was named. BERESFORD AVENUE, built in the easter part of the grounds of Trinity House, followed in 1910; and BERESFORD PLACE and TERRACE, completing the redevelopment of Trinity House, were named in 1979.

BERNARD STREET (South Leith) runs along what was virtually the shore line before the ground to the north was reclaimed in the course of the fortification of Leith in 1548, *see under* TIMBER BUSH. The road is referred to in *RMS* 1577 as the *passage from the harbour to the sands*, and the detail on *Collins* 1693, *Naish* 1709 and *Wood* 1777 shows how the wide section of the street developed from the ruined ramparts. The street name is from Bernard Lindsay, who married Barbara Logan in Leith in 1589 and became a considerable local figure. In 1604, when he was a Groom of the Bedchamber to James VI, he was granted part of the KING'S WARK (*which see*) on the south side of the street. His improvement of the property included the building of a *cachepel* or royal tennis court west of Carpet Lane, and a merchant exchange (*see* THE BURSE, South Leith) and in 1623 his zeal was rewarded when the Wark was made a free bailiary under his own control and independent of the magistrates of Leith. Thus the whole corner or *neuk* became known as BARNIESNOWCK or BERNARD'S NEUK in the 17th century. It is listed thus in *Kincaid* 1787, but *Arnot* 1779 (written by a native of Leith) applies the name to the whole street, while *Ordnance Survey* 1852 restricts it to a building east of Carpet Lane. The city bought the King's Wark from Lindsay's heirs in 1647, and two years later converted the cachepel into a public trone or weighhouse, giving rise to the name WEIGHHOUSE WYND. *Williamson's Directory* 1773 lists the street as BERNARD STREET, whereas on *Wood* 1777, and in *Kincaid* 1787 it is *St Bernard's Street*. The map makers continued to show the 'St' until 1861, but on the evidence of the directories the public (and even then, only some of them) used it only between 1793 and 1850, by which time the plain *Bernard Street* prevailed. For this 'sanctification' of Leith streets, *see also* GILES STREET and JOHN STREET, South Leith.

BERNARD TERRACE (South Side) was formed in 1867, as a cul-de-sac in ground which was part of that owned by Lindsay or Preston heirs, as shown on *Kirkwood* 1823; and its extension through SPITALFIELD (*which see*) to Dalkeith Road did not take its present form until 1929. The name's derivation has not yet been traced; it is probably from the developer.

BETH'S or **BEST'S WYND** (High Street to Cowgate) is *Bethis wynd* in *RMS* 1532 and *Beth's wyne* on *Rothiemay* 1648, but *Bestis wynd* in *John Foular's Protocols* 1528 and *Best's* on *Edgar* 1742. Nevertheless it is clear from the details of both sets of sources that the two names referred to the same wynd, and it would also seem that it was a long time since anyone of either name had owned property in it. A prominent burgess Andrew Bet is mentioned in *RMS* 1375 in connection with a property on the south side of the High Street; and the John Best noted in *Town Council Minutes* 1457 as lessee of a booth on the south side of the Tolbooth might have been the 'late John Best' recorded in *RMS* 1513 and *Protocols of John Foular* 1528 as a former owner in the vicinity. The wynd was suppressed in 1809, in preparation for the building of the Signet Library in 1811.

BIGGAR ROAD (Fairmilehead) is one of several names (*Linton, Penicuik, Carlisle* etc.) traditionally attached to this *road to Biggar*.

BINGHAM GARDENS, TERRACE and **ROAD** (Duddingston) were named in 1936 for Lady Rosaline Bingham, wife of the Duke of Abercorn, owner of the estate; but in 1974 the first two were renamed

DUDDINGSTON RISE and VIEW respectively, and DUDDINGSTON ROW replaced Bingham Road in 1976—*see under* DUDDINGSTON. Meantime, in 1946, the name had been applied to another group of streets, mainly in the *Willow Pool* and *Bere* or *Barley Furlongs* fields of Southfield farm: BINGHAM AVENUE, BROADWAY, CIRCLE, CRESCENT, CROSSWAY, DRIVE, MEDWAY, PLACE and STREET; and BINGHAM WAY was added in 1966.

THE BINKS (Queensferry) are rocks named for their pronounced natural ledges, the word being early Scots *bynk*, a ledge or shelf. Until the early 19th century they were regularly made use of as quays for the ferry boats. Similar rocks at the north end of Cramond Island bear the same name.

BIRCH COURT (Barnton) was named in 1965, along with BLAEBERRY GARDENS, BLACKTHORN COURT and BRAMBLE DRIVE: all fancy names beginning with B, chosen to facilitate filing of tenant records by the developers, Link Housing Society.

BIRD'S CLOSE (South Leith) is shown on *Kirkwood* 1817, and was evidently named for a resident as yet untraced.

BIRKISIDE HEAD (Dreghorn) is recorded in 1709 as a landmark which is still in use at NT 217666 on the north side of Tarbrax Hill. The name is Scots *heid* with Old Norse *birkisíth* or Anglian or Scots *birkenside*, slope where birches grow. Possibly this is still represented by the Whitehill plantation.

BIRNIE'S CLOSE (265 High Street) *see* CRAIG'S CLOSE.

BISHOPS CLOSE (115 Cowgate) *see* RATTERAY'S CLOSE, Cowgate.

BISHOP'S CLOSE (131 High Street) is shown on *Ainslie* 1780. It takes its name from Thomas Sydserff, appointed minister in the burgh in 1610 and ordained a bishop (initially of Brechin) in 1634. He rebuilt a land in the close which he inherited from at least three generations of the family; but the connection possibly went much further back, for a William de Sydeserf was an officer of the *dusane* or council in 1403. The close was also EDWARD NISBET'S, for the owner of a back land in the close, who succeeded his late father William Nisbet as a burgess in 1596. It was also JAMES NISBET'S, perhaps for James, son of former provost Henry Nisbet, who was bailie in 1608; and it was PATRICK NISBET'S, for a member of the family as yet unidentified, unless he was Sir Patrick Nisbet of Southbank, who died some time before 1653. Thirdly the close was also called LINDSAY'S or ALEXANDER LINDSAY'S, relating to a tenement east of Bishop's land, at one time owned by a John Lindsay of Covingtoun and passing to a Robert Lindsay. These two may have been the father and son of the same names who are mentioned in *RMS* 1599 with reference to a grant of some earlier date (albeit unconnected with Edinburgh) and it is possible that the son was the Robert Lindesay recorded in *Town Council Minutes* 1555 as member of town council. Alexander Lindsay, a tailor, was a burgess in 1593. The same family may have been connected with LINDSAY'S CLOSE in Castlehill, *which see*.

BLACKBARONY ROAD (South Craigmillar Park) *see under* CRAIGMILLAR PARK.

BLACKCHAPEL ROAD (Niddrie) was named in 1979, borrowing the name (dating from before 1760) of the coal seam which outcrops alongside it—*see also* PEACOCKTAIL CLOSE *and* THE JEWEL.

BLACK BULL CLOSE (Pleasance) is shown on *Edgar* 1742. The name, noted on *Kincaid* 1784, was for the inn and stabling owned by John Sharp in 1760 and taken over after his death by James Robertson, formerly of the Black Bull in the head of Canongate, who reopened the Pleasance inn under the same name in 1775. In 1789 he transferred his business and the name for a second time, when he opened the commodious 50-room BLACK BULL which became a local place name in Leith Street.

BLACKET PLACE (Newington) was planned as the final phase of the development of NEWINGTON (*which see*) since the terms of feu of Newington House required building within its grounds to be delayed until after George Bell had developed the rest of his property. A plan by Gillespie Graham was advertised in 1825, and the street name first appeared in *PO Directory* in 1829. The central road, on the line of a drive to Newington House shown on Newington 1806, was originally part of BLACKET PLACE, but later became SOUTH BLACKET PLACE and then, in about 1900, BLACKET AVENUE. The name was imported from Blacket, the Bell family's ancestral home, near Middlebie in Annandale.

BLACKFORD is recorded in *Protocols of William Stewart* 1577 as *the Blakefurde* and also *Blakfurde alias Champanye*. The latter (*see under* CHAMPANYIE) was evidently an estate name, but Blackford, being Anglian *blaec* or Scots *blak* or *blake ford*, must have originated as the name of a dark or muddy crossing of the Pow burn at the head of the ancient loch (or its residual bogs) which stretched from here to Mayfield Road. The house is shown on *Blaeu* 1654 (somewhat out of position) as Blackford, and the variant Black Burn given on *Roy* 1753 is a map error, unless this was a local name for the Pow. The original estate lay south of the burn (i.e. outwith the Burgh Muir) but in 1723 a tract of the Muir westwards from Blackford Avenue and including the southern part of the grounds of Astley Ainslie Hospital was acquired from Wester Grange—*see under* THE GRANGE. BLACKFORD AVENUE began to be used as an address in about 1887, but it is shown on Roy 1753 as an avenue leading through this newly-acquired ground and across the burn to BLACKFORD HOUSE. Whether it existed before 1723 is an open question; but the tale that it was once the town's access to the Pow in time of plague, described in 1598 as 'by the old dike in the east end of Herbert Maxwell's feu', stems from a gross error by Dr Moir Bryce (in *Old Edinburgh Club X* p223) for Maxwell's ground extended to but 12½ Scots acres immediately east of Morningside Road, and had it continued as far as Blackford Avenue it would have been a mere strip of ground about 50 yards wide stretching for the best part of a mile along the burnside, something unlikely in itself but also at odds with the known feuing of the adjoining parts of the Muir. (The access referred to in 1598 seems to have been the early form of CANAAN LANE, *which see*.) Although BLACKFORD HILL is *Blackfoord Hill* on *Braid* 1772, it is *Bread* (i.e. Braid) *Crags* on *Adair* 1682 and is probably the *Easthill of Braid* mentioned along with Blackford in *RMS* 1665. The name BLACKFORD GLEN, misleadingly placed on the south side of the hill, seems to have been coined in the late 19th century, on the analogy of the somewhat earlier fancy name of *Braid Glen* within the policies of Hermitage of Braid. BLACKFORD PLACE was a side name at 156-62 Morningside Road from 1858 until 1892. BLACKFORD HILL RISE (1961) and BLACKFORD HILL GROVE and VIEW (1962) were named for their position on the lower slope of the Hill; and BLACKFORD BANK was named in 1978 as occupying the site of the former Blackford Nurseries on the steep bank above the Pow.

BLACKFORD ROAD (Whitehouse) *see under* WHITEHOUSE.

THE BLACKFRIARS (Old Town) was a priory of the Dominicans or Preaching Friars, founded by Alexander II in 1230 on the south side of the Cowgate. Their popular name *Blak freris*, black brothers (from the black cloaks they wore over their white gowns and scapulars) appears in *Town Council Minutes* 1553, but was doubtless currrent much earlier. As described in *Old Edinburgh Club III*, the priory and its gardens originally occupied virtually the whole block of land on the south side of the Cowgate and east of Robertson's Close, with east and south boundaries that were later followed by the Flodden Wall; and south of this was its arable croft land, known as the BLACKFRIARS CROFT or (later) the NORTH CROFT OF THE PLEASANCE, *see under* DERENEUCH, Pleasance. The priory's kirk is shown on *Hertford's Assault* 1544, but was wrecked by a mob in June 1559. The friars were dispersed in 1560, and the priory became the site of the town's High School in 1578, *see under* HIGH SCHOOL YARDS.

BLACKFRIARS WYND (Old Town) is recorded in *Town Council Minutes* 1477 as the *Frere Wynd* and also in *RMS* 1477 as the *venella* or wynd of the Preaching Friars, and the popular form *Blackfriars Wynd* appears in the 1550s. Although obviously named as the way from the high street down to the priory of the BLACKFRIARS (*which see*) it is clear from the early charters that it was already in existence when the priory was founded in 1230, and road alignments suggest that it was part of a very early approach to the town, *see under* BACK ROW, Pleasance, *and* THE NETHERBOW. As shown on *Ordnance Survey* 1852 the wynd was barely more than ten feet wide in places. As may be seen from *City Improvements* 1866, it is now represented by the western pavement of BLACKFRIARS STREET, while the construction of the rest of the modern street (the first work put in hand under the Improvement Act of 1867) involved drastic clearance of the east side of the wynd.

BLACKHALL is shown as a settlement on *Roy* 1753 and named on *Laurie* 1763. There is neither sign nor likelihood of any mansion in the small cluster of buildings shown; and as in the vast majority of names of this sort, the *-hall* ending is Anglian *halh* Scots *haw* or *haugh*, land beside or in the bend of a burn. This exactly fits the location upstream from the bridge on the Queensferry road, where the Cottage Park was known as *the Haugh* in 1770, and *Ravelston* 1820 shows the fields *Whitehall* Park and *Blackhall* Brae. Since *black-* could derive either from Anglian *blaec* Scots *blak*, meaning 'black or dark-coloured' or else from Old Norse *bleikr* Anglian *blac* meaning 'pale or whitish in colour', it may be that there were two haughs, one looking darker than the other, by reason of reeds or mossy ground, but the possibility that there was but a single one, rather pale in colour, cannot be excluded.

BLACK HILL (Balerno) is named on *Adair* 1682. The highest of the hills in the northern range of the Pentlands, it is also its most dominant feature. Made darker than its neighbours by its intrusive felsite rock and the thick cover of heather that goes with it, the difference is exaggerated by the hill's bulk and steep northern face, seen against the sun during most of the day.

BLACKIE ROAD (South Leith) was named in 1903 for Bailie John Blackie, who had a market garden here.

BLACK LAWS (Queensferry) is recorded as *Blaklaw* in 1576 and shown on *Plewlandfield* 1769 as the name of fields on the ridge north of the upper reach of the Ferry burn. While the name's second part is from Anglian *hlaw*, rounded hill or hillock, the first part may be either *blaec*, black, or *blac*, pale or whitish. Part of the ground is shown on *Plewlands* 1887 as *Hungry Hill*, indicating a thin soil which might have been heathery or 'black' before it was cultivated, or else bald and showing pale with thin grass.

BLACKLAWS BURN (Bonaly) is given on Bell's *Spylaw* 1799 as BLACK-MYRE SYKE or small burn, and this suits the topography so much better as to suggest that the *Blacklaws* name given on *Ordnance Survey* 1852 may stand for an earlier and unrecorded *Blacklache* or *Blacklatch*, from Anglian *laecc*, boggy stream, with *black-* referring to its course in the peat.

BLACK LINN (Balerno) *see under* BAVELAW BURN, Balerno.

BLACKLOCK'S CLOSE (High Street) *see* KINLOCH'S CLOSE, next Niddry Street.

BLACK MYRE SIKE (Bonaly) *see* BLACKLAWS BURN, Bonaly.

BLACK'S ENTRY (Comely Bank) *see under* AVENUE VILLAS, Comely Bank.

BLACKTHORN COURT (Barnton) *see under* BIRCH COURT, Barnton.

BLACKWOOD CRESCENT (Newington) was named in about 1868 for Thomas Blackwood, silk mercer and haberdasher, who was living in West Newington House (*see under* NEWINGTON ROAD) in 1812 and may well have built it some six or seven years earlier.

BLAEBERRY GARDENS (Barnton) *see under* BIRCH COURT, Barnton.

BLAIR'S CLOSE (404 High Street) is shown on *Ainslie* 1780 and was named for Archibald Blair, writer, who acquired properties here in about 1747. Earlier, the close was BAIRD'S, deriving from the family of the Bairds of Newbyth and of Saughtonhall, and in particular from Robert Baird, merchant burgess and bailie, who acquired Saughtonhall in 1660 and had a tenement, possibly his burgess house, here on Castle Hill. *Maitland* calls it BAILIE BAIRD'S, which could have derived from Sir Robert, as above, or else from David Baird, who owned the *Sclatehouse* in the close and was bailie in 1738. Yet earlier, the close was PATRICK EDGAR'S, for a previous owner of this Sclatehouse. At least two men of the name are mentioned in *Town Council Minutes* 1554-1613, and although there is no evidence of their direct connection with the close, the fact that Thomas Edgar, writer, was owner and resident in it in 1635 may be of some significance.

BLAIR STREET (High Street) and **HUNTER SQUARE** were planned in 1785 as part of the scheme for the SOUTH BRIDGE (*which see*) and are shown on *Brown & Watson* 1793. They were named for James Hunter Blair, Lord Provost 1784-86, who had played a leading part in the promotion of the bridge scheme. As James Hunter, he had married the heiress of John Blair of Dunskey, near Portpatrick in Galloway, and he took his wife's name when she inherited the estate. A partner in Coutts Bank and a friend of Robert Burns, he was made a baronet in 1786 but died in the following year. The streets and new frontages involved the suppression of KENNEDY'S CLOSE, PEEBLES WYND, and MARLIN'S WYND in the High Street, together with SAWERS CLOSE in the Cowgate; while the Tron kirk was severely truncated, losing half a bay at its west end to Blair Street, half a bay at its east end to the South Bridge, and the whole of its south or *Communion* aisle to Hunter Square, so that its east and west fronts became entirely new work, while the south front was refaced to match.

THE BLAKVOLTS (South Leith) *see under* THE VAULTS, South Leith.

BLANTYRE TERRACE (Merchiston) together with ROCHESTER TERRACE, MARDALE CRESCENT and the south side of MERCHISTON CRESCENT were developed in open ground, beginning with Blantyre Terrace (1878) and continuing at Rochester Terrace (1879) and Mardale Crescent (1881). The names may refer to Blantyre, David Livingstone's birthplace in Lanarkshire, Rochester in either Northumberland or Kent, and Mardale in Westmoreland; but apart from the first, which might well commemorate Livingstone's death in 1874, no reason for the choice of names is apparent.

BLAWEARIE (Inverleith) is recorded on *Knox* 1812, and was evidently an older or an alternative name for Inverleith Mains, shown in the same position on *Kirkwood* 1817. The name also occurs (on a very similar ridge above the sea) at Longniddry, and in Galloway, and may or may not be the same name as *Balwearie* in Fife. It appears to be Celtic: the first part either *blà*, a field, or *baile*, a farm, and the second part perhaps *fhuraidh*, making it 'cold field' or 'cold farm', or else *iarach*, making it 'west field' or 'west farm'.

BLEACHFIELD (Bonnington) *see under* BONNYHAUGH, Bonnington.

THE BLEAK LAW (Portobello) is shown on Ainslie's *Roads from Figget* 1783 and was evidently the most prominent feature north of the highway through Figgate Whins. Latterly it was crowned with trees and planted with shrubs, forming part of the garden of *Shrub Mount* certainly as late as the 1850s. The name is Scots *blaik*, pale-coloured, from Anglian *blac* or Old Norse *bleikr*, pale or shining, with *law*, a hillock and is an obvious description of a sandy knoll. The streets LAW PLACE and SHRUB MOUNT (*which see*) have been named for it.

BLENHEIM PLACE (Hillside) is shown (unnamed) on *Calton* 1819 as part of the CALTON NEW TOWN (*which see*) and was built to William Playfair's design in 1824 and named by the following year. The name appears to refer to Marlborough's victory over the French in 1704, and may have been suggested by the celebration of Wellington's one in the naming of WATERLOO PLACE (*which see*) not long before.

BLINKBONNY (Craigleith) was part of the estate of DEAN (*which see*) until 1739, when it was sold to Trinity Hospital. It is listed as a member farm in Leith burlaw court prior to 1750, and is shown on *Laurie* 1763. The name, fairly frequent in lowland Scotland, seems to be Scots *bonnie blink*, a fine view, although the reason for the inversion is not clear. Development of the farm for housing began in 1905 at BLINKBONNY CRESCENT, and was resumed at BLINKBONNY AVENUE and TERRACE (1926) ROAD, GARDENS and GROVE (1928) the last being extended westwards in 1936.

BLINKBONNY (Currie) is shown thus on *Armstrongs* 1773. It was the farm of the East Mill of Currie. For the probable derivation of the name, *see* BLINKBONNY, Craigleith.

BLOOMY HALL (Juniper Green) appears on *Knox* 1812, and it seems likely that it was a fancy name for a property in the early days of the development of Juniper Green.

BLYTH'S CLOSE (571 High Street) is listed on *Ainslie* 1780 and may have been named for a Sir Simon Blyth, who owned property near the Upper Bow before 1756. It was cleared for the building of the Free Kirk Assembly Hall 1858-59. As shown on *Ordnance Survey* 1852 and described in *Wilson*, there was a mansion in the close, evidently connected with Queen Mary of Guise and perhaps her residence within the period 1551-59. It seems also to have been BELL'S CLOSE (recorded in 1726) for Stephen Bell, owner of a tenement on its east side, and also known as FRANCIS BELL'S for his son, a skinner.

BOAT GREEN (Canonmills) is recorded as *Boothsgreen* in 1759, in a deed scheduled under the *Act for extension of the Royalty* 1767. The word *green*, together with the mention of an earlier tenancy by James MacDougall, clothier in Edinburgh, suggests that the property was a bleaching green and that it must have been set up considerably earlier; and the indication is that it had been owned, if not founded, by someone called Booth. The ground is shown as *Mr Somerville's feu* on *Fergus and Robinson* 1759 and labelled *Boat Green* on *Kirkwood* 1817—a spelling adopted when the new street was named in 1982, since it may echo a traditional pronunciation 'Boath'. Part of the land became a railway goods station in about 1847, but the name lingered on in the adjoining *Boothgreen Cottage* shown on *Ordnance Survey* 1852, only to be lost when the cottage was renamed *Warriston Green* some time before 1876.

BOGSMILL (Slateford) is recorded in 1598 as the *West Mill of Easter Hailes*, tenanted by Alexander Vernour. It is given as *Vernours miln alias Bogismiln* in 1631, and shown as *Boggismill* on *Roy* 1753. Although it is also referred to as the *Corn Mill of Redhall* it was changed into a white-paper mill in about 1720, and for decades after 1735 it supplied paper for the £1 notes of the Bank of Scotland. John Verner was a burgess in Edinburgh in 1428, and the surnames Vernour and Bog both occur in *Town Council Minutes* (although not in connection with milling) from 1462 and 1501 respectively. BOGSMILL ROAD, named traditionally as the road down to the mill, was the historic access to REDHALL TOWER (*which see*) crossing the river by a ford, until George Inglis of Redhall built the present bridge in the later 1750s.

BOLL O BERE (Balerno) is more staidly *Boll of Bear* on *Ordnance Survey* 1852 and *Armstrongs* 1773. This is clearly a reading of the form *Bow of Bear* shown on *Adair/Cooper* 1735, taking it to mean a *bow* or *boll*, a 6-bushel measure, of *bear*, the coarse type of barley grown generally in those days. But on the manuscript *Adair* 1682 (from which Cooper's plate was transcribed) the first word, although somewhat indistinct, is certainly not *bow* but almost certainly *berd*, making the name *Beard of Bear*, i.e. 'Beard of barley', which sounds very like that of an inn. If so, the later variant could have been a revised name for the hostelry, referring to bushels instead of awns; or it might embody a different word *bow* or *boo*, a house, which would be apt whether the building was still an inn or converted into a house or farm; or else it might be a deliberate pun on both words.

BONALY (Colinton) is recorded from 1280 onwards, and the typical early spellings *Bounaylin*, *Benhathelyn* and *Bonalyn* show the name to be British *banathel(an)*, (place of) the broom bushes— cf. Bonallack in Cornwall. The lands were originally part of the great estate of Redhall. Between 1462 and 1555 their eastern part was owned by the Wallaces of Craigie in Ayrshire, and so got the name BONALY WALLACE. In 1772 James Gillespie of Spylaw reunited it with the western part of Bonaly (then called FERNIELAW, *which see*) and added Bonaly to his estate of Spylaw, as shown on Spylaw 1799. In 1820 Lord Cockburn feued 20 acres in Bonaly Wallace and created what he called a paradise by doing up the farmhouse, building BONALY TOWER, and 'destroying' (as he himself put it) the village of Bonaly which stood at the confluence of the Dean and Lady burns. BONALY ROAD was the access to the farmhouse and village as well as to BONALY STEADING, partly retained in a new development in 1985. In 1959 BONALY AVENUE, CRESCENT, DRIVE and TERRACE were begun in the *Scaudhinty* field (a name for land on a ridge, apt to be parched in summer) and BONALY GARDENS (1961) GROVE (1969) BRAE, RISE and LOAN (1975) followed in the *East field*. The name BONALY WESTER, coined in the traditional style, was given to a new development in Fernielaw in 1987.

BONALY PLACE and **ROAD** (North Merchiston) were formed in the 1880s to give access to Merchiston Railway Station. Bonaly Road was named by 1893, for the farm of BONALY (*which see*) within the Spylaw estate owned by the Merchant Company, who were also the owners of North Merchiston. Bonaly Place was named by 1899; but in 1965 both streets were renamed, to obviate confusion with streets in Colinton: Bonaly Road became HARRISON GARDENS, and Bonaly Place, HARRISON PLACE, both names being from nearby HARRISON ROAD, *which see*.

BONAR PLACE (Bonnington) appears in *PO Directory* 1903. The ground had been in the hands of Andrew Bonar of East Warriston and his descendants since 1818.

BO'NESS ROAD (Queensferry) is shown on *Dundas* 1757 as *highway to Linlithgow*, and *Bo'ness Road* was probably a new usage resulting from the closing of the old SHORE ROAD (*which see*) some time after 1832.

BONKILL'S CLOSE (High Street) was one of the closes on the north side of the street, but remains to be identified. It is named in *Protocols of John Foular* 1534, along with a note that a tenement in it had been owned by the late John Bonkill. The Bonkill or Boncle family were prominent in Edinburgh from the early 15th century (in 1426, one was the town's treasurer and another the dean of guild) and the owner mentioned may have been the John of Bonkill who was treasurer in 1478.

BONNINGTON (North Leith) was part of the land granted to Holyrood Abbey by David I, and the name is recorded from 1465 onwards. While the modern neighbourhood name takes in ground south of the river as well as riverside haughs once held in common by Bonnington, Pilrig and Hillhousefield (*see under* BONNYHAUGH and BONNINGTON ROAD) the historic estate lay between the Water of Leith and the Ankerfield burn, marching with the Holyrood lands of Hillhousefield in the east and Warriston in the west. The medieval centre, shown (apparently roofless) on *Siege of Leith* 1560, stood on the left bank of the river, and was replaced in about 1630 by a new manor house (demolished in 1891) which is shown as BONNINGTON HOUSE on *Leith River* 1787 and as BONNINGTON OLD HOUSE on *Ordnance Survey* 1852. The early forms of the estate name (all three still current in local parlance) are *Bonyntoun* in *RMS* 1460, *Bonyngtoun* 1465 and *Bonytoun* 1587. Shared by over two dozen farms in lowland Scotland, the name seems to have originated as early Scots *Bondingtoun*, from Anglian *bondena tún*, 'farm run by bondis', a bondi or bonder (from Old Norse *bondi*) being a yeoman farmer, also termed a *colono* in Latin records, typically holding a 'husbandland' of about 26 Scots acres. It seems that *bondington* was the technical term for land let out, probably in the 12th or 13th centuries, to groups of such tenants; and since this

Holyrood ground was a plewgate of about 104 acres, it may have been worked by four of them. In 1787, BONNINGTON PARK was built in the northern corner of the estate; its policies became VICTORIA PARK in the 1890s. BONNINGTON FIELD (1817) or LODGE (1829) were earlier names for BLAIR PARK, now a primary school annexe. BONNINGTON PLACE, already partly built in 1817, was taken into NEWINGTON ROAD in about 1899. BONNINGTON TERRACE dates from about 1864. BONNINGTON GROVE was known as *Taaphall Lane* until about 1870: it originated in 1802 as a lane serving houses called *Bonnington Grove* and TAAPHALL, *which see*. Another property feued out in 1802 was called *Bonnington Brae*, and BONNINGTON AVENUE was developed in its grounds in 1930.

BONNINGTON (Ratho) is recorded as *Bondington* in about 1315, and as *Bonyntoun* and *Bendingtoun* 1329, *Bonyngtoun* 1371 and *Bonytoun* 1444. The name is the same as that of BONNINGTON, North Leith (*which see*) but since the Ratho estate is described in *RMS* 1528 as a '£10 land of the old extent' it must have comprised five plewgates (about 520 Scots acres) and may have been shared by as many as twenty bonders. Between these bonders and their associated cottars and other workers, there may have been upwards of forty families living in the farm toun. Only the estate name *Bonitoun* appears on *Blaeu* 1654; but *Adair* 1682 as well as *Roy* 1753 show the BONNINGTON HOUSE of 1622 as *Boni-* or *Bonnytonhead*, and the farm toun, in the vicinity of the present BONNINGTON MAINS and BONNINGTON, as *Boni-* or *Bonnyton*. On *Laurie* 1763 the farm toun area is labelled *Bonnyton Farms*, and this may indicate that improvement had started, with some subdivision of the old runrig. WEST BONNINGTON appears on *Gellatly* 1834, but is called BONNINGTON HEAD MAINS on *Fowler* 1845.

BONNINGTON ROAD (Pilrig) is a section of the 'new highway leading from Canonmills to Leith', mentioned in the original charter for Stewartfield in 1735. This was part of a new road system, vividly shown on *Roy* 1753, which was obviously intended to enable James Balfour, laird of Pilrig, to feu off the northern part of his estate in regular plots, such as Stewartfield and Barclay's Houses. The scheme also involved the suppression of the old 'common way to the mill of Bonnington' from South Leith, mentioned in *RMS* 1467, which inconveniently for Balfour's purpose wound its way up the riverside and past St Cuthbert's well at the foot of Bonnyhaugh; and Balfour replaced it with a branch off his new highway, so that the route from Leith took its present dog-legged form. With the growth of the Bonnington mills on the haugh and this feuing of Pilrig land, a new 'Bonnington' began to be created south of the river, as shown on *River Leith* 1787, and this led to the naming of BONNINGTON TOLL and the latter-day BONNINGTON HOUSE built by John Haig of Lochrin in 1805, east of the Toll and facing Pilrig House. As a result, the 19th-century maps showed the street north of the Toll as *Bonnington*, and the name *Bonnington Road* applied to the whole of the dog-legged route. Indeed, after the replacement of the ford at

Bonnyhaugh with a bridge, as shown on *Ainslie* 1804, there was a tendency to regard the road from there to Newhaven as a 'road to Bonnington', figured on *Thomson* 1822 as *Bonnington Street* and on *Ordnance Survey* 1853 as *Bonnington Road*; but already in 1804, when *Ainslie* notes the completion of the route (later called Pilrig Street) as a 'New Road from New Haven to Edinburgh', there was a leaning towards the older name NEWHAVEN ROAD (*which see*) and this is figured north of the bridge on *Bartholomew* 1876 and north of Bonnington Toll by all maps after 1890.

BONNYFIELD (Cramond) is shown on *Knox* 1812 as *Boneyfield*, in the angle of the old Queensferry road where it turned north at Parkneuk and then west for Cramond Brig, *see under* QUEENSFERRY ROAD. The house, still named on *Ordnance Survey* 1912 and still shown on *Ordnance Survey* 1938, was on the site of 'Barnton Court', and the road past it, converted into a drive after 1824 and shown on *Ordnance Survey* 1852 with a gate and lodge, is now the entry to BARNTON PARK VIEW. The name *Bonnyfield*, if modern, may have been fancy, 'pretty field'; but if it is ancient, the derivation of *bonny-* should be treated with caution, for it may relate to 'bonnage' service rendered by a tenant.

BONNYHAUGH (Bonnington) stands on a haugh which was part of the common grazings of Bonnington, Hillhousefield and Pilrig in medieval times, as well as the site of the corn mill of Bonnington mentioned in *RMS* 1467. Its more intensive use as a centre of industry began in 1621, when the town council of Edinburgh launched a training scheme for the improvement of cloth making, under the direction of experts brought from Holland. Cloth woven in the trade school in St PAUL'S WARK (*which see*) was brought for finishing to BONNYHAUGH HOUSE, built for the purpose 'apone the miln land of Bonieton', with plant for fulling and dyeing. The name *Bonnyhaugh* first appears in 1723, when the house and bleachfields were bought by Gilbert Stewart: he may have coined it, by adding -*haugh* to the first part of the estate name in its late form *Bonny-*; but perhaps it was already a traditional name for the haugh, possibly a shortened form of Bonny(ton)haugh, or else a separate but related name *bondis' haugh* with a derivation similar to that of BONNINGTON, *which see*. BONNINGTON HAUGH LANE, renamed BONNYHAUGH LANE in 1983, is a remnant of the road built by Balfour of Pilrig in about 1738 (*see* BONNINGTON ROAD) joining the old WHITING ROAD at a bridge over the mill lade as shown on *River Leith* 1787. The road was diverted to the east when a stone bridge at the river crossing, shown on *Ainslie* 1804, replaced the ford and wooden footbridge shown on the 1787 map. By 1983 the dense mass of industrial buildings on the haugh was cleared away, and the single access road to new housing on the site was given the place name BONNYHAUGH, while the pedestrian streets branching off it were named for historical features of the haugh: MILNACRE for the land attached to the medieval corn mill; WHITINGFORD for the river crossing by the Whiting road; BLEACHFIELD and PAULSFIELD for the greens used to bleach the cloth made in St Paul's Wark; and LADEHEAD for its position near the cauld of the dam or lade that had powered mills on the haugh for the best part of a thousand years.

BONNYTOUN (Corstorphine) appears on *Corstorphine* 1845 as the name of a field in Corstorphine Bank, lying between the Craigs and Glasgow roads and immediately west of Drum Brae. It may indicate that there was once a farm in this vicinity, extending to one or more husbandlands of 26 Scots acres and tenanted by one or more bondis or yeoman farmers, *see under* BONNINGTON, North Leith.

THE BOOTHACRE (South Leith) was one of several parts of the Links in which *booths* or *ludges* were set up in 1645 for isolation of the victims of the great plague, which killed three in every five of the inhabitants of South Leith in about six months. Apparently the only monument to this great disaster, the traditional name was continued for BOOTHACRE COTTAGES by 1868; and part of SEAFIELD AVENUE (*which see*) was renamed BOOTHACRE LANE in 1983.

BOOTHRAW (High Street) *see* BUTH RAW, High Street.

BORE STONE (Morningside) is a misnomer for the HARE STANE, Morningside, *which see*.

THE BOROUGHMUIR is a late 15th-century spelling of BURGH MUIR, *which see*.

THE BOROUGH or **BURGH LOCH** was an alternative name for the SOUTH LOCH, *which see*. BOROUGHLOCH is shown on *Roy* 1753 and *Scott* 1759 as a lane leading to the Boroughloch Brewery, rebuilt in 1897. BOROUGHLOCH SQUARE and BUILDINGS were named by 1907.

(LORD) BORTHWICK'S CLOSE (190 High Street and 150 Cowgate) is mentioned as *Lord Borthwick's* in *Town Council Minutes* 1514 and as *Borthwick's* in *RMS* 1537, and was named for the Lord Borthwick who built a house on the west side of the upper part of the close in about 1450. Along with the HORSE WYND and the POTTERROW (*which see*) it may have formed one of the earliest routes into Edinburgh from the south.

BORTHWICK PLACE (Wester Coates) *see under* DEVON PLACE, Wester Coates.

BOSWALL ROAD (Wardie) first appears in *PO Directory* 1853 and was apparently named after its existing eastward part was extended westwards to join the new Granton Road in the late 1840s. The name, for the Boswall family, owners of Wardie, was continued in 1921 to BOSWALL AVENUE, CRESCENT, DRIVE, GARDENS, GROVE, LOAN, PARKWAY, QUADRANT, TERRACE AND SQUARE; and to BOSWALL GREEN in 1925 and BOSWALL PLACE in 1931.

BOSWELL'S COURT (392 High Street) is given as *Boswell's Close* on *Ainslie* 1780 and derived this name from a medico, Dr Boswell, chief resident in the later 18th century. The earlier name of the close was LOWTHIAN'S, from Thomas Lowthiane, merchant burgess, recorded in *RMS* 1597 as having rebuilt two tenements here and being granted back lands previously owned by Robert Donaldson, executed for practising magic, sorcery, and devilish incantations, and resorting to spaewives. Lowthian's widow was still owner occupier in 1635. The south end of the close is still extant as steps east of St Columba's-by-the-Castle, on the south side of Johnston Terrace.

WILLIAM BOTHWELL'S CLOSE (577 High Street) *see* NAIRNE'S CLOSE.

BOTHWELL STREET (The Drum, South Leith) was formed in the Drum estate in about 1890. The naming is obscure: it may have been for the builder, or for the place in Lanarkshire or the river in the Lammermuirs. BOTHWELL HOUSE was given as a side name in 1988.

BOURSE (South Leith) *see* BURSE, South Leith.

BOURTREEBUSH (Kirkliston) is shown on *Carlowrie* c1800 as a holding of some 3 Scots acres in the vicinity of NT 13557515, while *Macdonald* notes a field *Bourtreebush park* in adjoining Almondhill. The name is from Scots *bourtree*, elder tree.

BOWBRIDGE (Swanston) is recorded in *Protocols of Gilbert Grote* 1573 as a land name *Bowbrig*; and since this derives from Scots *bow* (pron. 'bough'), an arch, it implies that a stone-arched bridge, probably of pack-horse type, had carried the Linton road over the Swanston burn for some considerable time before then. In 1957, evidence found in a cutting supported earlier reports by General Roy and in *White's Liberton* 1786, that the highway follows the line of a Roman road, *see under* ROMAN ROADS.

BOWERSHALL (Pilrig) is shown but not named on *Fergus & Robinson* 1759, appears as an address in *PO Directory* 1805, and is named on *Thomson* 1822. While the name may incorporate an owner's name in *Bowers' hall* or *haugh*, the first part is more likely to be Scots *bower*, a dairyman using rented grazing on this haugh.

THE BOWFOOT (Old Town) was named as the foot of the WEST BOW, *which see*. The *Bowfoot Well* was built by Robert Mylne in 1681, the water being supplied from Comiston by the town's scheme completed in 1677.

BOWHEID (Old Town) *see under* WEST BOW, Old Town.

BOWHILL TERRACE (Goldenacre) *see under* MONTAGU TERRACE, Goldenacre.

BOWIE'S CLOSE (South Leith) is shown on *Naish* 1709 and named as *Bowie's Lane* on *Wood* 1777, *Ainslie* 1804 and *Thomson* 1822, the variant *Close* appearing on *Kirkwood* 1817. It is clearly part of the 16th-century sett of the town and it is said to have been named for John Bowie, wright, treasurer of South Leith Kirk Session in 1646.

THE BOWLING GREEN, BOWLING LANE, THE QUILTS and **QUILTS WYND** (South Leith) were newly developed in 1981 on and around the site of the earlier BOWLING GREEN STREET, *which see*. As early as the 17th century this neighbourhood was a centre for the sports of *bowls*, *quilts* or *kyles* (i.e. skittles) and *cachepell*, real or royal tennis. The names of *keyls* and *caetspel*, and probably the games themselves, were imported from Holland in the 15th century, and a skittle-like game of *kyls* is played in Kirkcaldy on New Year's Day. All three names appear in *Town Council Minutes* 1823, but now as places. The original bowling green may have been that figured on Ainslie's *River Leith* 1787 in the gardens of a large property (also shown on *Fergus & Robinson* 1759) entered from Mill Lane; but the BOWLING GREEN of 1981 is somewhat northwest of this, being centred on the large circular green shown on *Ainslie* 1804, on a site shown on *River Leith* 1787 and *Naish* 1709 as a remnant of one of the bastions of the fortification of Leith of 1548. The QUILTS and QUILTS WYND (the *Qu* should be pronounced *K*) commemorate the skittle alley but may not stand on its site, which has still to be identified. Even by 1645 the name (in the odd form *The Toolls*) already stood for a locality rather than a particular building; and it is described in *Town Council Minutes* 1771 as 'the park at the head of King Street and Yardheads through which the great road runs from the West Docks to the Foot of Leith Walk'—a prophetic reference to JUNCTION STREET, *which see*. The detail shown on *Ainslie* 1804 and *Kirkwood* 1817 suggests that this park may have extended over most of the site of the 1981 development; but the northern parts of the Quilts and Quilts Wynd, together with the garden in the loop of the river, are on the site of the historic LEITH MILLS, *which see*.

BOWLING GREEN CLOSE or **ENTRY** (181 Canongate) *see* GLADSTONE COURT, Canongate.

BOWLING GREEN ROAD (Kirkliston) is named as the road passing the bowling green; but it is evident on *Kirkliston* 1759 and *Knox* 1812 that it was in existence long before the bowling green was formed in the *Little Park* of the Glebe in 1869, and that while its western section (still represented by skew boundaries at the head of Manse Road) was cut off when the turnpike bypass was formed in about 1810 (*see* MAIN STREET, Kirkliston) it had earlier led to NEWMAINS while its eastern section had probably originated as a lane to the *Back of the Kirk*, shown thus in 1759, but also known as the HOLMS. This term is early Scots *holm* or *howm* from Old Norse *holmr*, an island or a raised patch of land. It may be used of a waterside haugh (*see* PADDOCKHOLM) but also of ground at high level (*see* BERE HOLMS) and here it probably implies that the ground was in patches separated by boggy parts.

BOWLING GREEN STREET (South Leith) is shown planned on *Thomson* 1822 but is omitted on *Leith* 1826 and shown as only partly developed on *Pollock* 1834. It was named as being built over the site of the 18th-century bowling green shown on *Ainslie* 1804, *see under* THE BOWLING GREEN, South Leith, which replaced the street in 1981. WEST BOWLING GREEN STREET and its bridge over the river are shown on *Bartholomew* 1876, but the bridge is in fact dated 1886. They were part of the development of HILLHOUSEFIELD (*which see*) by the trustees of William Boyd, along with the sale of Hillhousefield mansion to David Bruce Peebles for his gas engineering works.

BOWMONT or **BEAUMONT PLACE** (St Leonards) was begun in 1812-13 by Alexander Thomson, who built the two tenements on the north side which are shown on *Stranger's Guide* 1816 and were to remain the only houses in the street until tenements were built opposite in the 1850s. The name, spelt *Bowmond* on *Kirkwood* 1817, evidently derived from some connection with Yetholm, Roxburghshire, or (more likely) celebrated the Kers of Roxburgh—possibly in a double sense, for while Robert Ker 1st Earl of Roxburgh had been the superior of the ground in the 1630s (and nearby HERIOT MOUNT was named for those who succeeded him) the book-loving John Ker 3rd Duke of Roxburgh, Marquess of Bowmont and last of his line, although he had died in 1804, was much in the news in 1812, when his great and famous library of early books was sold and the Roxburghe Club founded by a group of leading bibliophiles on the same day. The misspelling (and mispronunciation) BEAUMONT appears in the *PO Directory* 1815 and on *Knox* 1821; and the original was restored when the street was rebuilt in 1988.

BOYD'S CLOSE (opposite 65 Canongate) is shown on *Ainslie* 1780 and *Kincaid* 1784 as immediately west of Queensberry House; and this tallies with the name, since James Boyd, stabler (conceivably the owner of the White Horse in BOYD'S CLOSE, 276 Canongate, (*which see*) is recorded in *Canongate Charters* 1824 as having had property 'opposite Galloway's entry' (65 Canongate) in 1765.

BOYD'S CLOSE (276 Canongate) is listed on *Ainslie* 1780 and was named for James Boyd, owner of *Boyd's*, one of the chief coaching inns of the later 18th century, also known as the *White Horse*. It was patronised by the actors Samuel Foote and West Digges, but most famously as well as very briefly by Dr Johnson in 1773, for as soon as Boswell heard he was there he haled him up to his own house in James Court. Although Boyd was certainly an enthusiast for horse-racing, the tale that he named his inn for a particularly lucky winner is perhaps best taken, as it is in *Chambers* 1825, with a pinch of salt. Well enough established by 1757 to be elected High Constable for the Canongatehead, he is still listed as in Canongatehead in *Williamson's Directory* 1780, although it gives a James Dumbreck in the Whitehorse inn. The alternative name WHITEHORSE CLOSE, listed in *PO Directory* 1827, probably rose to prominence after the memory of Boyd had faded. The close was also ROSS'S, a name that continues to be obscure; but the earlier name YOUNG'S or JOHN YOUNG'S was evidently for John Young, maltman, listed as owner and resident in 1635, and also for an earlier owner, John Young, wright, who may have been his father-in-law. Being in the south Canongatehead, the close was in Edinburgh, not the burgh of Canongate.

BOYD'S CLOSE (81 High Street) *see* CHALMERS'S CLOSE.

BOYD'S ENTRY (Old Town) is shown on *Edgar* 1742. As a cross passage suitable for vehicles from St Mary's Wynd, it explains the presence of a coaching inn in BOYD'S CLOSE 276 Canongate (*which* *see*) but also suggests that this may have been much older than Boyd's establishment.

BOYS BRIGADE WALK (Meadows) *see* THE MEADOWS.

BRAEFOOT (Corstorphine) was a side name on the west side of Clermiston Road near its junction with St John's Road from the 1860s onwards, but it probably originated much earlier as the general name for the vicinity of the road-end *at the foot of Clermiston brae.*

BRAEFOOT TERRACE (Liberton Dams) is a side name applying to a terrace now representing the clachan of LIBERTON DAMS, *which see.* The date of the name is uncertain, but it obviously describes the position of the place at the foot of Liberton Brae, and it may have suggested or have been suggested by the nearby BRAESIDE COTTAGES (*which see*) named before 1893.

BRAEHEAD (Cramond) is the 17th-century name for the EWERLAND, a '40-shilling land of the old extent' (nominally 104 Scots acres) held in 1335 by Hugh le Ewer, evidently of the same family as the Thomas le Ewer who figures in the *Ragman Roll* of 1296. Their names imply that they were of AngloNorman descent, and were officers in the royal household with responsibility for the ceremony of serving water for those at table to wash their hands; and since there is also record of BUTLERLAND in King's Cramond in the 14th century, it appears that David II or his predecessors gave grants of land in this royal demesne to support such hereditary office bearers. It is fairly obvious that it was this, rather than any service in rescuing James V from a mugging at Cramond Brig, that was the origin of the estate name as well as the feu duty of a service of *Ewry* or *a basin of water* which is noted in *RMS* 1505 (i.e. in the time of James IV) and also mentioned in *RMS* 1668 as attaching to 'the house called *Lyliehouse*' and its garden, part of the Ewerland. The name BRAEHEAD is recorded in 1698 and the house appears to date from about then. It is shown on *Adair/Cooper* 1735, while the unnamed house shown on *Adair* 1682 may have been its predecessor. The name is Scots *brae heid,* referring to its position at the top of the steep road up from Cramond Brig, now rather unfortunately named BRAEPARK ROAD, *which see.* It is clear from *Cramond Roads* 1812 that the steading of the home farm was then still at Braehead House; but following the realignment of the QUEENSFERRY ROAD (*which see*) in 1824, a new BRAEHEAD MAINS was constructed at the SUTOR HOLE (*which see*) west of the approach to the new bridge over the Almond. Housing development began at BRAEHEAD AVENUE in 1927 and continued at BRAEHEAD ROAD in 1946. The eastern part of BRAEHEAD GROVE (1955) follows the line of the old Queensferry road by Cramond brig. Development continued at BRAEHEAD LOAN and VIEW (1960) and PARK (1967) and in 1976 the policies of Braehead House began to be built up as BRAEHEAD DRIVE (the former house drive) and BRAEHEAD CRESCENT and ROW.

BRAE PARK and **BRAE PARK ROAD** (Cramond) are old roads taking modern names from the *Brae park* field on the north side of Brae Park Road. The first of the two began as the access road to the

LONG ROW of cottages, prominent on the maps from *Knox* 1812 onwards but redeveloped as BRAE PARK by 1910. The other is the historic (probably medieval) road leading from Braehead and White House down to the old Cramond Brig, and was known as 'the old Cramond brig road' until it was named as BRAEPARK ROAD at some time after 1938. The unfortunate result has been that mapmakers have shown the field name BRAE PARK as a neighbourhood name extending over the historic farm of BRAEHEAD.

BRAESIDE COTTAGES (Liberton) is shown on *Ordnance Survey* 1893 as a name for houses in the lower part of Liberton Brae. The name is an obvious description, but it may be related to BRAEFOOT TERRACE, Liberton Dams.

BRAID was owned in the 12th century by Sir Henry de Brade, sheriff of Edinburgh and probably the son of an AngloNorman recruited to the service of David I. There is no reason to doubt that his surname derived from the name of his Scottish estate, which is Gaelic *bràghaid*, a throat or gorge (perhaps overlying a British equivalent) and refers to the deep cut of the Braid burn in its glacial ravine, which must have been even more prominent in the primitive landscape than it is today. The estate originally included OVER PLEWLANDS (*see* GREENBANK) and NETHER PLEWLANDS (see PLEWLANDS, South Morningside) and some small holdings at BRIGGS OF BRAID (*which see*) as well as the lands of OVER BRAID, NETHER or NORTH BRAID and EGYPT, which are shown on *Braid* 1772. The medieval tower house stood upon the northern lip of the gorge. The tower, or a mansion developed from it, figures on *Adair* 1682, but *Adair/Cooper* 1735 adds the fancifully-named HERMITAGE within the gorge; and this, rebuilt and greatly enlarged in the 1780s, eventually displaced the original centre, which continued under the name of Nether or North Braid, but disappeared by 1812. BRAID ROAD, named as the road *by Braid*, appears to follow a Roman line (*see under* ROMAN ROADS) except that BRAID ROAD STAIRS, originating as a footpath to Over Braid, marks the point where the later road looped west from the Roman line (still shown in the 1920s by the farm boundary) in order to ease the ascent for wheeled traffic. The road was bypassed in about 1830 by a new length of turnpike, later called COMISTON ROAD (*which see*) and housing development started at its north end in the1880s, *see also under* EGYPT *and* PLEWLANDS. The western part of BRAID CRESCENT, begun in Plewlands ground in 1887, was named for Braid Road; and building was also in progress at BRAIDBURN (*which see*) in the same year. BRAID HILLS APPROACH was formed when the town acquired the BRAID HILLS (*which see*) in 1889. The road to Upper or Over Braid farm steading was extended westwards to Pentland Terrace as BRAID HILLS ROAD in 1898, and the road eastwards from the farm was altered to form BRAID HILLS DRIVE in the mid 1920s. Development of Over Braid began in 1926 in its *Longlands* field with BRAID FARM ROAD and BRAID HILLS AVENUE and CRESCENT, although the last two go beyond Braid into Greenbank where they overlap the line of the Roman road. BRAID

MOUNT, its name ringing the changes on 'hill', was begun in 1934, and BRAID MOUNT CREST, RISE and VIEW were added in 1955. BRAMDEAN RISE was named in 1934 for Bramdean Lodge, Bramdean, near Winchester, family home of Mrs Elaeson Gordon, owner of Braid (the Hampshire name means *broom dene*) and BRAMDEAN GROVE, PLACE and VIEW followed in 1957.

BRAID AVENUE (South Morningside) *see under* EGYPT.

THE BRAID BURN is the historic name for the middle reaches of what was perhaps in British times the PEFFER BURN (*which see*) extending from the meeting of the HOWDEN and BONALY burns at Dreghorn downstream to Duddingston House, after which the lower reach is generally known as FIGGATE burn. Some documents use its name for the Pow burn, obviously because the latter was the north march of Braid.

BRAIDBURN (Braid) is noted on *Adair* 1682 and shown on *Braid* 1772 as a clachan on the west side of the Braid road, just north of the bridge over the burn, and it is still represented by *Braidburn Dairy* on *Ordnance Survey* 1893. In 1886 a *Braidburn Terrace*, fronting Braid Road, was named along with BRAIDBURN CRESCENT, which, although planned at this time, was apparently not occupied until about 1892. In 1905, the name BRAIDBURN TERRACE was transferred to the eastern section of GREENBANK ROAD, *which see*.

THE BRAID HILLS (Braid) derived their name from the gorge that generated the name of BRAID (*which see*) and they seem therefore to have included Blackford Hill, which is in fact the north side of the gorge, is shown on *Adair* 1682 as *Bread Crag*, and may be the *Eastirhill of Braid* which appears to be grouped with Blackford in *RMS* 1665. The town acquired Blackford Hill in 1884 and the Braid Hills in 1889, together with rights of way connecting these two great recreational areas, at the HOWE DENE and the LANG LINN PATH, *which see*.

BRAID PLACE (Causeyside) was begun in about 1878 by widening and extending JEWS CLOSE, *which see*. It was named by 1879, probably for Sir William Dick of Braid, purchaser of the Grange in 1631; but the ground was never part of the Grange, being part of the Burgh Muir feued out in 1512 for the chapel of St John-in-the-Muir, and passing in 1517 to the convent of the SCIENNES, *which see*. In 1968 the street was renamed SCIENNES HOUSE PLACE; but although this was done to remove the anomaly of a 'Braid' street so far from others of the name, it succeeded in creating another, by confusing the names of *Sciennes House* (*see under* SCIENNES) and SCIENNES HILL HOUSE, *which see*.

BRAID'S CLOSE (Foot of West Bow) is listed in 1800 as occupied by David Braid, stabler. Its exact location and other names remain to be established.

BRAMBLE DRIVE (Barnton) *see under* BIRCH COURT, Barnton.

BRAMDEAN RISE etc (Braid) *see under* BRAID.

BRAND DRIVE and **GARDENS** (Easter Duddingston) *see under* CHRISTIAN CRESCENT etc, Easter Duddingston.

BRANDFIELD STREET (Dalry) *see under* DALRY *and* THE GROVE, Dalry.

BRANDON STREET and **HUNTLY STREET** (Canonmills) were begun in 1822 and 1825 respectively, as a development within James Eyre's estate of Canonmills, but a gap between them remained until it was filled by BRANDON TERRACE in about 1878. The street names appear to be linked, inasmuch as Susan Beckford, wife of Alexander Douglas 10th Duke of Hamilton and 7th Duke of Brandon in Suffolk, was niece to George 9th Marquis of Huntly. Huntly may also have been connected with the naming of HOWARD PLACE (*which see*) in about 1816, for the 4th marquis had married Elizabeth Howard, daughter of the Duke of Norfolk, in 1676; but the connection of the family with either of these developments in Warriston and Canonmills remains obscure.

BRAND PLACE (Abbeyhill) is shown, unnamed, on *Brown & Watson* 1793, and is recorded as MISS BRAND'S PLACE in *PO Directory* 1808, relating obviously to further entries of *Miss Brand, Abbeyhill* in subsequent years but possibly also to that of *Mrs Brand, Abbeyhill* in *Denovan's Directory* 1804.

THE BRANKEN (Kirkliston) is the traditional name for the land flanking Manse Road, and appears to be early Scots from Middle English *brenke*, a brink, referring to the ground's position on the edge of the slopes, as steep as 1 in 6 in places, on the west side of the howe of the Glebe. It lent its name to MANSE ROAD (*which see*) and also to a loan constructed by the minister in about 1830, which branched off that road and passed through his glebe to his manse next the kirkyard, prompting a complaint in 1832 that he was permitting it to be used for evasion of turnpike dues at the Kirkliston toll bar.

BREADALBANE STREET (South Leith) was formed in 1864, apparently to give access to the Bonnington Sugar Refining Company's plant which was started after a fire had destroyed an earlier refinery, owned by a Mr Macfie, in Elbe Street. Possibly the street name reflects some connection of one of the company's directors with this district in Perthshire—Gaelic *Bra'id Albainn*, the high ridge of Alba, i.e. Pictland or Scotland.

BREADALBANE TERRACE (Dalry) *see under* DALRY PLACE.

BREAD STREET (Tollcross) is part of the ancient Linlithgow road. Long named ORCHARDFIELD (*which see*) it was partly renamed in about 1824, when its north side began to be built up as the start of the development of the Grindlay estate of Orchardfield. While the name ORCHARDFIELD STREET was retained east of Spittal Street (as shown on *Ordnance Survey* 1852), the rest was dubbed BREAD STREET. Only slender reasons have been found for this as yet: there was a baker in the street in 1825; a 'Bread Society' is said to have existed, without indication of when or where; and it seems at least possible that Scots *main*, fine white bread, lies behind the name of nearby MAIN POINT, *which see*.

BREISTMILL (Kirkliston) is recorded in *RMS* 1533 as the *Brest-mylne de Auld-Listoun*, indicating that it was the mill of the barony, and of a type in which the water falls on to the wheel at a higher level. It is shown on *Blaeu* 1654 as *The Mill*, and as *Breistmill* on *Adair* 1682, while *Roy* 1753 calls it *Bellsmil. Priestmill* (1834) is a corrupt form. Milling continued here until the 1930s, and in 1968 the building was converted into a dwellinghouse.

BREWERY CLOSE (Queensferry) is probably on a medieval line, but is named for a brewery shown on its east side on *Ordnance Survey* 1854 and still shown in 1914.

BREWERY LANE (South Leith) took shape around 1810, and is in a part of the Yardheads which was long a centre of brewing.

BREWLANDS (Currie) was land attached to a brewery here from before 1530, and the brewing was still on the go in 1725. The ground is now occupied partly by ROSEVALE COTTAGES and partly by the former site of Currie Railway Station.

BRIARBANK TERRACE (North Merchiston) *see under* SHAFTESBURY PARK, North Merchiston.

BRICKFIELD (Portobello) was the site of the original brickworks opened by William Jamieson in 1765, the beginning of modern Portobello. The name seems to have been attached to the place from the start, but fell out of use when brick-making was superseded, around 1800, by potteries and a remarkable range of other industry. In 1978 it was recovered and applied to the present street.

BRICKFIELD (South Leith) *see* PROSPECT BANK, South Leith.

BRICKWORK CLOSE (South Leith) is shown on *Naish* 1709, and is now represented by that part of the remodelled Giles Street which is nearest to Trinity House. Listed on *Kirkwood* 1817, but also as TILEWORK CLOSE in Williamson's *Accurate View* 1783, it was named for the brick and tile works set up on waste ground here by Gilbert and Alexander Mathison in 1725.

BRIDGEND (Craigmillar) is shown thus on *Blaeu* 1654 and is recorded as *Bridgend* in *RPC* 1584, as *the Brigend of Craigmyller* in *RMS* 1600, and also as *Lady-brig-end* in 1602 and *Ladiebridges* in *RMS* 1655. Evidently it was named as the Craigmillar end of the sequence of three bridges where the Dalkeith road crossed, within the space of 500 yards, the Pow and Braid burns and (probably from medieval times) a mill lade which ran for over 100 yards on the west side of the road before passing under it and flowing east to power the Peffer mill, an arrangement shown on *Roy* 1753 and *Laurie* 1763 as well as *Ordnance Survey* 1852. The *ladie* referred to was either this lade or else the burns, which are deep and slow-running (i.e. in Scots, *ladie*) at this point. According to *White's Liberton* 1792, James V had a hunting lodge here, and there was also a chapel in the vicinity.

THE BRIDGE or **BRIG OF LEITH** or **NORTH LEITH BRIDGE** is shown on *Siege of Leith* 1560. It was built in the later 1480s by Abbot Bellenden or Ballantyne of Holyrood in order to connect the St Leonard's lands of Coalhill with the Abbey's other lands of North Leith, *see also* St NINIAN'S LANE; but its stone arches prevented the development of shipbuilding further upstream, and in 1789 the old route was bypassed by the construction of the (UPPER) DRAWBRIDGE (*which see*) and the medieval structure was removed soon afterwards. *See also* OLD BRIDGE END, Coalhill.

BRIDGE OF STONES (Cramond) is shown on *Cramond Roads* 1812 as the bridge over a small watercourse at the south entrance gates to Cramond House. Two field names on Cramond 1815 indicate that there was once a *brighouse* here, implying that the bridge had been a toll bridge on the old (Roman) road to Cramond prior to its diversion in 1778, *see under* CRAMOND ROAD.

BRIDGE PLACE (Stockbridge) *see under* THE COLONIES, Stockbridge.

BRIDGE ROAD (Balerno) was named by 1912 for *Balerno Bridge* over the river. Its traditional name is the LONG BRAES, probably referring to the slopes rising on its west side.

BRIDGE ROAD (Colinton) *see under* COLINTON.

BRIDGE STREET (Newbridge) is obviously named as leading to the bridge; and since the inn, dating from 1683, stands beside it, the road probably takes substantially the line it took in the 16th century or even earlier—*see under* NEWBRIDGE.

BRIDGE STREET (North Leith) was formed in 1789 by enlarging the Broad Wynd of North Leith to give access to the new (UPPER) DRAWBRIDGE, *which see*. The name appears in *PO Directory* 1818; but in 1968, in order to obviate any confusion with Bridge Street in Portobello, it was renamed, quite absurdly as well as misleadingly, SANDPORT PLACE. The SAND PORT, (*which see*) is in an altogether different quarter of North Leith.

BRIDGE STREET (Portobello) is shown, along with BRIDGE STREET LANE, on *Wood's Portobello* 1824, and is listed in *Portobello Directory* 1836. It was evidently named as being a branch off the part of the main road east of the bridge over the Figgate, which was known as BRIDGEND in 1836. Bridge Street (or more precisely, a house in a back court entered from it) was the birthplace of Sir Harry Lauder in 1870. Bridge Street Lane is said to have been known earlier as TOBAGO STREET, but evidence is lacking.

BRIERY BAUKS (Pleasance) is shown on *Regality of Canongate* 1813 as the name of this part of the DISCHFLAT (*which see*) and obviously referred to the division of the ground by *bauks* (i.e. ridges or walks) with wild roses growing on them. Part of the site was developed in the 1820s as MIDDLE ARTHUR PLACE (*see under* DALE STREET, Pleasance) but the old name was given to the present street when the place was redeveloped in 1988.

BRIGGS (Kirkliston) is recorded from 1488 onwards and shown on *Blaeu* 1654. Although the spellings *Briggis* and *Brigs* are general from 1493 onwards, the earliest form *Brighous* shows that the name is not a plural but Scots *brig hous*, the house for the tollkeeper in charge of the bridge. By 1631 the lands attached to the brighouse were subdivided into EASTER and WESTER BRIGGS, Easter Briggs being the alternative name for the original Briggs. While *Adair* 1682 shows this as *Bridges*, *Adair/Cooper* 1735 shows a new name BOATHOUSE at the waterside; and it is clear from a report in 1761, anent the building of a new bridge, that the old bridge had collapsed, and that the crossing, shown as *Almondford* on *Laurie* 1763 and *Armstrongs* 1773, had been reduced to a ford for horses and vehicles, with a boat for foot passengers only. Thus the Boathouse was either a shed for the boat or (more likely) the house of the tollkeeper/ferryman.

BRIGGS OF BRAID (Morningside) was at the south end of the bridge carrying the Linton road over the Pow (later, Jordan) burn. The mentions of it in *RMS* 1528 and *Town Council Minutes* 1586 as 'land of Brighouse occupied by James Broune' and 'the Brighous callit Browms of the Brigs' (probably a misreading of 'Browns') show that *briggs* is not the plural 'bridges' but Scots *brig hous*, the house occupied by the man in charge of the brig and any toll levied for its upkeep. Some land went with the job; and its mention in *Protocols of James Young* 1497 as inherited by John Broune, son and heir of the late John Broune, burgess of Edinburgh, shows that the post had become hereditary. By 1652 the land was divided into smallholdings, as shown on *Braid* 1772, namely EISTERBRIGGS (the site of Hermitage Terrace) in Nether Braid or Egypt, and WESTERBRIGGS (the site of Maxwell Street etc.) which along with another job-related plot, the SMIDDIEGREEN, belonged to Plewlands.

BRIGHTON CRESCENTS, EAST and **WEST,** and **BRIGHTON PLACE** (Portobello) together with the adjoining Rosefield Place were designed in 1820 by John Baxter, architect; and *Wood's Portobello* shows progress made by 1824. The street names were probably chosen to emulate Brighton in Sussex, the most fashionable resort of the period. Since the streets were planned as a select residential area, Baxter as superior strenuously opposed a scheme to make Brighton Place a through way connecting Portobello with Duddingston, and did not give way until after the North British Railway was constructed in 1846, with a bridge designed to suit a proposed bypass road along the back of West Brighton Crescent.

BRIGHTON STREET (Bristo) is on a site shown on *Kirkwood* 1817 as still the garden of the Merchant Maiden Hospital, although that school moved to Lauriston in 1816. The street is shown on *Knox* 1821 as though built and named ANDERSON STREET, but *Kirkwood* 1823 shows it as BRIGHTON STREET, and for the most part still under construction. The origin of either name is obscure; but it is possible that the second one was for Brighton, Sussex, then the fashionable resort of George IV.

BRIGHT'S CRESCENT (Mayfield) *see under* McLAREN ROAD, Mayfield.

BRIGHT TERRACE (Dalry) *see under* DALRY PLACE.

BRISTO, recorded from 1502 onwards, included most or more likely all of the 23 Scots acres bounded on the east by the *Back Raw* (Roxburgh Place to Richmond Lane) and part of the Dalkeith road, on the west by the *Loaning* (Bristo Place to Chapel Street) that led to the Burgh Muir, on the north by a boundary later followed by the Flodden Wall, and on the south by the Crosscausey. The area was divided into two *crofts* by the Potterrow, which together with the Horse Wynd and Borthwick's Close seems to have formed an early route to the burgh's mercat cross. The early history of the ground is obscure; but by 1500 the five-acre *West Croft* and about a quarter of the *East Croft* had been acquired by the Touris family and added to the barony of Inverleith (eventually becoming part of the PORTSBURGH in 1649) while the rest of the East Croft had been annexed to the nearby lands of St Leonard's. The name appears as both *Birsto* and *Bristo* in 1502, but the internal evidence points to *Birsto* as the earlier form: in Anglian, the *byrh* or burgh's *stow*—a term that had several shades of meaning, but is perhaps best translated in this particular case as 'herding place', for the Loaning or Liberton road was the main route for moving stock to and from the grazings in the Burgh Muir (*see also under* CANDLEMAKER ROW *and* CAUSEYSIDE) and the Bristo ground would offer the first convenient space for herding the beasts outside the town, while the term *croft* could imply that it was fenced for the purpose. BRISTO(W) PORT, the latter-day name for the GREYFRIARS or SOCIETY PORT (*which see*) appears on *Edgar* 1742. It stood just west of the north corner of the entry which is now called BRISTO PORT but is in fact a remnant of the *Back Wall Vennel* or HORSE WYND OF BRISTO that ran immediately outside the Flodden Wall, as shown on *Rothiemay* 1647. As shown on *Edgar* 1742, the Loaning running south from the Port was known simply as BRISTO; but after 1756 its southern section began to be called CHAPEL STREET (*which see*) while the rest became BRISTO PORT or BRISTO STREET. BRISTO PLACE, shown on *Ordnance Survey* 1852 as a side name, became the name of the northern part of the street in 1858; and finally, in 1982, the remaining middle section of Bristo Street was suppressed in the development of BRISTO SQUARE.

BRITWELL CRESCENT (Craigentinny) *see under* CRAIGENTINNY.

BROAD WYND (South Leith) is shown on *Siege of Leith* 1560, and is mentioned in *RMS* 1564 as *Braid wynd* and in *Town Council Minutes* 1581 as the *Bred Wynd of Leith*. It may date from 1439, when John of Danielstoun, burgess of Edinburgh, granted a strip of land 12 feet wide 'next the king's tenement' (i.e. the King's Wark) as a common vennel or public way.

BROAD WYND (North Leith) is mentioned in *Protocols of James Young* 1491 as the *common vennel callit bradwynde*. It seems to have been on the site of BRIDGE STREET (*see under* SANDPORT PLACE) formed to serve the UPPER DRAWBRIDGE in 1789.

BRODIE'S CLOSE (south side of foot of Canongate) is listed on *Ainslie* 1780 and got this name from Francis Brodie, wright, who feued ground here in 1759 and built a tenement, which he promptly sold to his brother William Brodie, tailor, who apparently paid for it by granting Francis a wadset or mortgage on it. William's son, also William, was a barber and wigmaker in Holyrood Abbey. When Francis Brodie died in 1782, the wadset passed to his son and partner William, deacon of the wrights and secretly a skilful burglar, who sold the property when he went on the run after his fatal robbery of the Excise Office in March 1788. The close was also BAXTER'S, for two bakers in it, Robert Grieve and Thomas Greig, in about 1758; and it was also GREIG'S for the latter and his son Robert and grandson George, who lived in Lothian Vale— *see under* LOTHIAN HUT. It is also noted in 1800 as having been called KINLOCH'S CLOSE, for former owners Henry and John Kinloch—the first probably the Henry Kinloch, burgess of Canongate, who entertained the French ambassador Rambollat in 1565. Also recorded in 1800 is the name CHANCELLOR'S, giving access to CHANCELLOR'S COURT, described in Wilson as 'a curious and exceedingly picturesque court'; but the guess made in Chambers 1833 and since then embroidered by others, that the royal chancellor lived here, does not alter the fact that the name is quite obscure.

BRODIE'S CLOSE (Castle Hill) is listed in *Williamson's Directory* 1773 as the address of a Mrs Brodie, but nothing else is known about it.

BRODIE'S CLOSE (304 High Street and 52 Cowgate) is listed on *Ainslie* 1780 and was named (if not for Francis Brodie, merchant councillor in 1701 and bailie in 1709-10) for Francis Brodie, wright, listed in *Williamson's Directory* 1773 as already in business in the Lawnmarket with his son, the notorious William Brodie, deacon of the Wrights, who was hanged for burglary in 1788. Earlier, as recorded on *Edgar* 1742, it was LORD CULLEN'S CLOSE, for Sir Francis Grant of Cullen, resident in the close, who sat in the Court of Session as Lord Cullen from 1709 until his death in 1726. An older name was LITTLE'S, for William Little, burgess, who built a house here in 1570, still owned by a William Little in 1635 and still named for the family in 1799 but demolished in 1836. The close was also known as CANT'S, possibly in reference to property adjacent to that of Thomas Cant of the Grange on the site of Fisher's Land—*see under* FISHER'S CLOSE, 312 High Street. At its Cowgate end, where cross passages linked more than one close and gave rise to some confusion of names, it was sometimes called (BACK) ENTRY TO OLD BANK, the *old Bank* being the name for the Bank of Scotland in Bank Close after its rival the Royal or *new Bank* of Scotland was founded in 1727—*see under* OLD STAMP OFFICE CLOSE, 221 High Street.

BRODY'S CLOSE (131 Cowgate) is listed thus on *Ainslie* 1780 but the name remains obscure. It is mentioned in *Williamson's Directory* 1780 as HARDIE'S CLOSE, evidently for Nicolas Hardie, whose widow and son sold his property here before 1725. In 1827 it is listed as FISHER'S ENTRY, from Andrew Fisher, spirits dealer.

BROKEN BRIDGE (Gilmerton) is shown on *Adair* 1682 and named on *Adair/Cooper* 1735 and *Roy* 1753. The 18th-century spelling *Brokenbriggs* suggests that the second part is Scots *brig(hou)s*, house where bridge tolls were collected (*see also* BRIGGS, Kirkliston, and BRIGGS O BRAID) and the first part may be Scots *brooken*, streaked or grimy, or the closely-related word *brockit*, striped black and white.

BROOMFIELD CRESCENT (Corstorphine) along with BROOMHALL AVENUE and BROOMSIDE TERRACE in 1935, and BROOMBANK TERRACE, BROOMBURN GROVE and BROOMLEA CRESCENT in 1938, made up a set of names of streets in the historic BROOMHOUSE (*which see*) by fancy variation of the second part of the estate name. Later development at BROOMHALL CRESCENT (1948) BROOMHALL PLACE and ROAD (1952) BROOMHALL BANK, CRESCENT, GARDENS, LOAN and TERRACE (1955) and BROOMHALL DRIVE and PARK (1956) carried this particular variant into the CLAYCLOTE of Saughton, *which see*.

BROOMHILL(S) (Liberton) seems to have originated after 1509 as a mansion house which, together with STRAITONHALL farm and STRAITON MILL, became separate from STRAITON (*which see*) in 1546. Although shown as *Broomhil* on *Adair* 1682, the property is generally shown under the two names *Straitonhall* and *Straiton Mill* on maps up until 1852, when the *Ordnance Survey* shows BROOMHILL and BROOMHILL MILL (amalgamated as BROOMHILLS by 1893) in place of *Straitonmill*, with BROOMHILL COTTAGE in place of *Straitonhall*, and marks a 'site of Broomhill House' 240 yards further west. The name is Scots *brume hill*, a slope where broom grows—a plant of considerable importance in the days of thatched houses, *see under* BROOM PARK, Granton. It is sometimes given as *Brownhill*, but the pairing of *Broom/Broun* is so frequent in Scottish records generally that it must be put down to confusion between their not dissimilar sounds or else to misreading of their spellings. Thus one or other but not both of the variants will be the true name, and in this particular case the weight of the evidence is for *Broomhill*.

BROOMHOUSE is recorded from 1599 onwards as part of the lands of Saughton, and is shown on *Blaeu* 1654 and in detail on *Saughton* 1795. The mansion was west of Broomhouse Road, on a site now occupied by St Augustine's School. The name is Scots, *brume hous*, house where broom grows—a plant of considerable practical importance, *see under* BROOM PARK, Granton. BROOMHOUSE ROAD is the road *to Broomhouse*, originally from Corstorphine High Street (shown on *Roy* 1753, this section was renamed LADYWELL AVENUE in 1978) but shown on *Saughton* 1795 as also connected with the Calder road. Only the north-east quarter of the modern district of BROOMHOUSE is on Broomhouse land, the rest having been parts of Saughton Mains, Parkhead farm, and the policies of Saughton House. BROOMHOUSE AVENUE, CRESCENT, DRIVE, GARDENS, GROVE, LOAN, PARK, PATH, PLACE, SQUARE, STREET and WALK were named in 1947; BROOMHOUSE COURT, MEDWAY, ROW, TERRACE, WAY

114

and WYND followed in 1950, and BROOMHOUSE BANK, COTTAGES and MARKET were added in 1965, 1966 and 1976 respectively. In the northern part of the historic Broomhouse and the adjoining land of CLAYCLOTE (*which see*) a number of streets were named by variations on the element *Broom*—*see under* BROOMFIELD CRESCENT *and* WESTER BROOM PLACE, Corstorphine.

BROOMPARK (Granton) is shown on *Roy* 1753. In 1985 the eastern part of the house policies was redeveloped for industry and named NEW BROOMPARK. If *broom-* is frequent in place names it is not because the plant was plentiful but because it was much sought after for such purposes as making brooms or weaving wattles or tying down thatch. Not only was it conserved where it grew wild, but by 1450 there are records of farmers being required to cultivate it in special *broom parks* and to keep stock out of them by fencing, under pain of losing their leases.

BROOMPARK (Corstorphine) appears as a field name on *Corstorphine* 1777. BROOMPARK ROAD was begun in about 1938 on a site just north of the field. Broom was cultivated for practical uses—*see* BROOMPARK, Granton.

BROOMYKNOWE (Colinton) was named in 1981, continuing the historic name of the place (recorded in *Steuart's Colinton* p199) as the hillock or slope where broom grows. There is also a BROOMIEKNOWE in Swanston. The plant was deliberately cultivated for important practical purposes—*see* BROOM PARK, Granton.

BROUGHAM STREET (Tollcross) derives from a proposed new street shown and named on *Wood* 1823 as part of a scheme for developing J H Rigg's Drumdryan estate and the north side of the West Meadows. Thus it was named for Henry Brougham, advocate, jurist, Liberal MP, and one of the founders of *The Edinburgh Review*, in the period when he was at the height of his popularity after his brilliant defence of Queen Caroline in 1820. Although the entry at Tollcross is shown formed on *Lothian* 1829 and the name is listed in *PO Directory* from 1831 onwards, only some 15 yards of the street had been marked out before 1857, when the rest was finally laid out on a modified line. At first, the whole length running east to the Meadows was called *Brougham Street*, but the last section was renamed BROUGHAM PLACE in 1861.

BROUGHTON is first recorded in 1128, when it was listed among lands granted to Holyrood Abbey by David I, *see under* HOLYROODHOUSE. The name's early forms, such as *Broctuna* or *Bruchton*, show it to be Anglian *broc tún*, farm beside the brook; and the latter was evidently the BROUGHTON BURN, which flowed from the *Broughton parks* (in the vicinity of York Place) through the western part of the village in about Barony Street and down the east side of Broughton Street, thence winding its way by the hollow of Bellevue Road and Pilrig park to join the Greenside burn south of Pirrie Street and the Water of Leith just above the Bowling Green bridge. Lying mainly between Albany Street and London Street, the village was the ancient centre of the barony of regality of Broughton;

and its tolbooth, which served as courthouse and prison from about 1582 until such regalities were abolished in 1746, was pulled down only when Barony Street began to be feued out in 1829. This feuing fell short of its intention to redevelop the whole of OLD BROUGHTON, where BROUGHTON MARKET was built in the 1840s for sale of meat, fish and poultry, and the street of NEW BROUGHTON was formed in about 1860. BROUGHTON STREET was part of the historic *Broughton Loan*, which led to the village from Leith Wynd; and although its modern development began in about 1808, its present name first appears in 1821. BROUGHTON STREET LANE was part of the development of PICARDY, *which see*. BROUGHTON PLACE, part of the old village area, began to be feued out in 1807, and the alignment of BROUGHTON PLACE LANE follows the march with the grounds of Gayfield. EAST BROUGHTON PLACE is shown as proposed on *Ainslie* 1804, and is named on *Pollock* 1834. At BROUGHTON TOLL, as shown on *Ordnance Survey* 1852, the present level of Mansfield Place is 17 feet above that of the early road which led northeastward from this point, as shown on *Roy* 1753 and *Ordnance Survey* 1852, and was known as the *Broughton road* from Leith or the *Bonnington road* from Broughton. In 1870 the section west of Claremont Crescent was entirely suppressed and the name of EAST CLAREMONT STREET was extended as far as BROUGHTON POINT, while the name BROUGHTON ROAD was now confined to the section between the Point and Bonnington Toll. About the same time, the road between Broughton Point and Canonmills, which had been built shortly before 1735 as 'a new high road between Canonmills and Leith', was with dubious logic named LOWER BROUGHTON ROAD; and in 1912 this illogicality was compounded when it was renamed as part of BROUGHTON ROAD.

BROWN'S CLOSE (79 Canongate) is listed thus in *PO Directory* 1827 and was named for Joseph Brown, baxter, burgess of Edinburgh, recorded in 1800 as 'baker at the head of Rae's Close'—i.e. the adjoining CAMPBELL'S CLOSE. On *Ainslie* 1780 it is given as SOMMERVILLE'S, for John Sommerville, gunsmith, who owned the Golfer's Land in it and was probably the John Somervell, gunsmith in the Canongate, who advertised coach services to London in 1736 and 1754. His son Jack was still owner in 1798, and a Mrs Sommerville was resident in 1800. The close was also PATERSON'S, for a connection which began in 1609, when Nicol Paterson, maltman in Leith, bought property at the head of the close. His son John, inheriting in 1632, was captain of the Canongate's company mobilised at Stirling against Montrose in 1644, and he was a bailie of the Canongate in 1648. After his death in 1663, the property came to a younger John Paterson, probably the shoemaker who was treasurer of the Canongate in 1691-92 and trades councillor in Edinburgh in 1700. THE GOLFER'S LAND, demolished in the 1950s but recorded by *RCAHMS Inventory* and assigned to the 17th century, was also known as PATERSON'S LAND and is said in Joseph Brown's charter (*see above*) to have been built by John Paterson, merchant, burgess of Edinburgh. This is borne out, so far as the family is concerned, by the armorial once built into the frontage, bearing the Paterson arms; but it is made yet more explicit in a second panel from the house, inscribed firstly with a verse by Dr Pitcairne (1652-1713) saying that a Paterson built the house, and also with a motto 'I HATE NO PERSON', an anagram of JOHN PATERSONE. Considering Pitcairne's dates, the verse can scarcely be much earlier than 1680, and is likely to refer to his contemporary, the younger John Paterson—as indeed Lord Hailes (quoted in *Chambers* 1825) assumed in 1774. A family enthusiasm for the golf was also evinced in the armorial, in parts still legible in 1825 although defaced by 1847, for the crest was a hand grasping a golf club, and the motto was 'SURE AND FARRE' or (as Chambers gives it) 'FAR AND SURE'; and Pitcairne expressly links it with the house, for he says that Paterson, the tenth member of his family to win the golf championship, began to build it after his own victory. This must have been before 1691, when Paterson mortgaged the property; and thus the evidence for the building's date converges on the 1680s. This might be consistent with the story, retailed in *Chambers* 1825 based on an account 'lately printed by the Leith Club of Golfers', of a profitable day on the links with James Duke of Albany when he was the king's Commissioner in Scotland 1679-82; but otherwise the 'poor shoemaker' of the story is hard to seek, and Pitcairne's verse clearly refers to the winning of a championship rather than some *ad hoc* challenge match.

BROWN'S CLOSE (125 Canongate) is so named on *Ainslie* 1780 and *Kirkwood* 1817 but is given as BROWN'S COURT in *PO Directory* 1827. It was named for Andrew Brown of Greenbank and Blackford, who had a house in it at some date prior to 1757. The close was also WILKIE'S, for an earlier owner Andrew Wilkie, lorimer, prominent as deacon of the Hammermen of the Canongate in the mid 17th century. In 1691 it was also STRAITON'S, for John Straiton, merchant burgess and improver of the SOUTH LOCH (*which see*) who acquired Wilkie's property. According to the listing of former owners in *Canongate Charters* 1775, Straiton also acquired Brown's property, as mentioned above, but the dates are not easy to reconcile.

BROWN'S CLOSE (14 Grassmarket) *see* STEVENSON'S CLOSE, Grassmarket.

BROWN'S CLOSE (High Street, at St Giles Street) is listed on *Edgar* 1742. Also recorded in 1697 as BAILIE BROWN'S, it was named for Thomas Brown, bookseller, bailie in 1680 (*see also* DUNBAR'S CLOSE) who bought property at the head of the close ln 1691 and built a 'great stone tenement', later inherited by his son William and grandson James. An earlier name, HERIOT'S CLOSE, evidently derived from the fact that the property Brown bought had belonged in the 16th century to George Heriot the elder, father of the founder of Heriot's Hospital, and had passed through his heirs to the Heriot Trust, who eventually sold it in 1635. But the close had two other alternative names going back to the same period: firstly, ADAMSON'S, recorded in 1583, for John Adamson, bailie in 1573, who with his wife

Bessie Otterburne owned two houses here in the time of John Knox, who lodged in one of them in the last phase of his life 1568-69—*see* Robert Miller's *John Knox* 1895; and secondly it was TENNENT'S, for Kentigern (or Mungo) Tennent who owned property in the close, next to that of Adamson's son Alexander, and who was either Kentigern Tennent, bailie in 1537, or else an heir of the same name. The close was cleared in about 1870 for the construction of St GILES STREET and lies beneath its eastern pavement.

BROWN'S CLOSE (High Street) *see under* ALEXANDER KING'S CLOSE.

BROWN'S CLOSE (243 High Street) *see* THE ANCHOR CLOSE.

BROWN'S CLOSE (396 High Street) is listed on *Ainslie* 1780 and named from the Browns of Greenbank, who had purchased the adjoining property from the Bairds of Newbyth some time after 1757—*see under* BLAIR'S CLOSE, 404 High Street.

JAMES BROWN'S CLOSE (16 High Street) *see under* TWEEDDALE COURT.

HUGH BROWN'S or **BROWN'S CLOSE** (327 High Street) *see under* DON'S CLOSE.

BROWN'S PLACE (West Port) was evidently built by and named for James Brown, stabler, recorded as resident in the Vennel and building houses there in 1824. The street name appears in *PO Directory* 1825. From 1807 Brown had been a stabler and innkeeper in Brown's Close, 14 Grassmarket, *see under* STEVENSON'S CLOSE, Grassmarket.

BROWN'S SQUARE (Old Town) was developed in the SOCIETY (*which see*) by James Brown, later the developer of George Square. Begun in 1763, it was acclaimed as 'an extremely elegant improvement'. Three sides are shown completed on *Edgar* 1765, and the south side appears on *Armstrongs* 1773. The western part of the square gave way to George IV Bridge in 1827-36; and of the remnants (shown on *Ordnance Survey* 1852) the north and east sides were suppressed when Chambers Street was built in 1871, and the south side was cleared in the 1960s in preparation for an extension to the Royal Museum of Scotland. While the name may have been given by Brown himself, it is more likely that it arose in the community as a description of his scheme.

BROWN STREET (Pleasance) is named in *Town Council Minutes* 1815, when John Brown, builder, was granted water supply for it, and it is shown, albeit unnamed, on *Stranger's Guide* 1816. It was obviously named for its builder, who is not to be confused with the earlier builder James Brown, *see under* BROWN'S SQUARE.

BROX BURN (Newliston) is shown on *Knox* 1812 as *Brocks Burn*. From Anglian *brocc*, a brock or badger, it is 'badgers' burn'.

BRUCEHILL (Corstorphine) *see under* BELMONT, Corstorphine.

BRUCE'S CLOSE (now part of 31-35 Grassmarket) is shown on *Ainslie* 1780. It was cleared away for the building of the Corn

Exchange in 1849. No immediate source for the name has been traced; but *RMS* 1542 records Patrick Bruce as owning ground in the south side of the Grassmarket, and a Robert Bruce is recorded in 1582.

BRUCE'S CLOSE (118 High Street) *see* DICKSON'S CLOSE.

BRUCE'S CLOSE (323 High Street) *see under* WARRISTON'S CLOSE.

BRUCE STREET (South Morningside) was named by 1884 for James Bruce, owner and developer of the ground.

BRUNSTANE is shown on *Blaeu* 1654 as *Brunstoun*, but is recorded in 1337 as *Gilberdestone*, Gielberht's *tún* or farm place; and it continued as *Gilbertoun* for over 200 years. In 1547 its owner Alexander Crichton was arraigned for treasonably supporting Henry VIII's invasion of Lothian; and although he retained Gilbertoun, he forfeited his family's main estate of Brunstoun—a name which, as Anglian *burnes tún*, farm place at the burn, derived from its position on the banks of the North Esk, two miles south of Penicuik. Notwithstanding this loss of their ancestral home, his heirs continued to style themselves as 'of Brunstoun'; and although *Gilbertoun* is still mentioned in deeds as late as 1692, it is displaced by the transferred (and misspelt) name of *Brunstane* in *RMS* 1652, while in 1653 the lands are given as 'Gilberttoune, commonly called Bruntstoune'. BRUNSTANE HOUSE began as a rebuilding of the house of Gilbertoun in about 1565, was enlarged by John Maitland, Duke of Lauderdale, in 1672 (when he also had MAITLAND BRIDGE built) and was completed by William Adam for Lord Milton in 1735-44. BRUNSTANE MILL was evidently the medieval mill of Gilbertoun, while the 'new mills of Gilbertoun' mentioned in *RMS* 1653 were apparently on the right bank of the burn, in the Whitehill land of FARDINHAUCH, *which see*. BRUNSTANE MILL ROAD is shown on *Duddingston* c1800 as the access to the mills, with a branch to Brunstane House. BRUNSTANE ROAD, named as access to the estate, is figured on *Roy* 1753. Part of it was renamed BRUNSTANE ROAD SOUTH in the early 1920s; but BRUNSTANE ROAD NORTH, renamed thus in 1967, had nothing to do with the historic Brunstane road, having been HAMILTON STREET for over 150 years, *see under* RABBIT HALL. BRUNSTANE GARDENS (evidently named for the adjoining Brunstane Road, since it is well within Easter Duddingston) is shown on *W & A K Johnston* 1905 as a development in the *Irene Park* shown on *W & A K Johnston* 1898. BRUNSTANE GARDENS MEWS was named in 1974. BRUNSTANE BANK and CRESCENT, named in 1935, were developed within the property 'Brunstane Bank'; shown on *Ordnance Survey* 1893, this included the parks of HARDYFLATTS (*which see*) and possibly had taken its name from the *Bank* fields shown on *Duddingston* c1800 as lying west of these parks. BRUNSTANE DRIVE was developed in these Bank fields in 1935. BRUNSTANE LOAN is a right-of-way shown on *Ordnance Survey* 1852 as leading from Brunstane to Wanton Walls, but it was diverted to Newcraighall by means of a footbridge over the railway prior to 1893.

BRUNSWICK PLACE (Lothian Road) was named in about 1867 but the name was suppressed ten years later.

BRUNSWICK STREET (Hillside) is named on *Calton* 1819 as part of Playfair's original scheme for the CALTON NEW TOWN, *which see*. The name may commemorate Frederick, Duke of Brunswick, who served in the British army with his 'Black Brunswickers' in 1809 and fell at Quatre Bras in 1815; and if so, the naming would parallel that of nearby *Wellington Street*, named for the duke's commander in the Peninsular War. Alternatively, it may have been a compliment to Frederick's sister, Princess Caroline of Brunswick, estranged wife of the Prince Regent and mother-in-law of Leopold of Saxe Coburg, for whom the adjoining *Leopold Place* is named. The name was extended to BRUNSWICK PLACE in 1882, and to BRUNSWICK ROAD (in part a development of the existing LOVERS LOAN, Greenside, *which see*) and BRUNSWICK TERRACE in 1886. The latter was suppressed by redevelopment in 1978, but the name was continued by transferring it to a new terrace of houses in the scheme.

BRUNSWICK STREET (Trinity) was briefly the name of a street at the Chain Pier prior to 1828.

BRUNSWICK STREET (Stockbridge) *see* St STEPHEN STREET, Stockbridge.

BRUNTHEUCH or **BRYNTHAUCH** (Inverleith) *see under* TANFIELD, Canonmills.

BRUNTON PLACE (Hillside) is shown and named on *Calton* 1819 as part of William Playfair's scheme for the CALTON NEW TOWN (*which see*) and was partly occupied by 1827. The Revd Dr Brunton, minister of the Tron Kirk, and professor of oriental languages, was one of the Heriot Trust's representatives on the Joint Committee who adopted Playfair's plan in September 1819. BRUNTON TERRACE followed in about 1887 and BRUNTON GARDENS three years later.

BRUNTON'S CLOSE (South Leith) is named and shown on *Kirkwood* 1817 on a site now occupied by the north end of Henderson Street. It was evidently named for an owner, probably Robert Brunton (or a predecessor), wholesaler in Carron cast-iron goods in 1827.

BRUNTSFIELD traces back to the 'lands of Boroumore' recorded in *RMS* 1381-83 as having been held by 'the late Richard Broune', king's sergeant or agent. Still earlier, a William Brune *del Borumore* is recorded in about 1332; but even then the estate must have been in existence for two centuries or more, for along with THE GRANGE and WHITEHOUSE (*which see*) it was surrounded by the Burgh muir but was never part of it, and the inference is that it must have been created at or before the time when the muir was granted to the burgh in about 1120. The estate name *Brounisfeld*, although first recorded in 1452, obviously derived from this Broune family and must date from before 1381-83, when the estate passed to the Lauders of Hatton. The second part of it is early Scots *feld*, with the meaning of 'open country'. Despite the appearance of the intrusive *t* in *Bruntisfield* in the 17th century, leading to the confused reading *Burntfield* found on *Ainslie* 1804, the form *Brounsfield* is still used on *Knox* 1812, and even today the name is usually pronounced *Brunsfield*, as spelt on *Kirkwood* 1817 as well as *Adair* 1682. Although the name belonged to the lands lying east of Whitehouse Loan, centred on the 16th-century BRUNTSFIELD HOUSE, it spread to the neighbouring part of the Burgh muir, in the popular name BRUNTSFIELD LINKS (*which see*), and by 1810 this had led to the naming of a section of the main road (fronting a development shown on *Knox* 1812 as *Boroughmuirhead villas*) as BRUNTSFIELD PLACE. Thus a new neighbourhood of 'Bruntsfield' began to grow up, soon to be consolidated by the building of BRUNTSFIELD TERRACE (1858) CRESCENT (1871) and GARDENS (1884) in Greenhill, and BRUNTSFIELD AVENUE (1887) in Merchiston. Ironically enough, this extended use of 'Bruntsfield' was to deny the name to the estate of Bruntsfield proper when it came to be developed by Sir George Warrender in 1869. In his first scheme, for streets in the *North Park* of Bruntsfield, Warrender chose to compliment his wife Helen, daughter of Hugh Hume Campbell of Marchmont in Berwickshire in the names MARCHMONT TERRACE (later renamed ALVANLEY TERRACE, *see below*) and MARCHMONT STREET, and proposed to call a further street BRUNTSFIELD ROAD and to use his own surname for the rest; but in 1877 he reviewed and enlarged his plan: WARRENDER PARK CRESCENT was begun in VIEWPARK (*which see*) and while the names of WARRENDER PARK ROAD (begun in 1877) and WARRENDER PARK TERRACE (1878) were confirmed, the proposed 'Bruntsfield Road' gave way to MARCHMONT ROAD and CRESCENT (1877). Other new streets in the *South Park* of Bruntsfield were all named for connections of Warrender's: THIRLESTANE ROAD (1878) and LANE, and LAUDERDALE STREET (1882) for his mother's father James, Earl of Lauderdale and Baron of Thirlestane; SPOTTISWOODE ROAD (1877) and STREET (1881) for his wife's mother Margaret, daughter of Spottiswoode of Spottiswoode in Berwickshire; and ARDEN STREET (1905) for his step-mother's father Richard Arden, Baron Alvanley of Alvanley in Cheshire, whose title had been used to rename Marchmont Terrace ALVANLEY TERRACE in 1877.

BRUNTSFIELD LINKS (Bruntsfield) are now the only part of the 12th-century BURGH MUIR (*which see*) remaining unfeued. The ground was used for grazings, but quarrying was also so extensive that as early as 1554 the town's regulations required quarry holes to be filled in when worked out. It is possible that golf was played here in the 16th century; but certainly by 1695 *Town Council Minutes* mention it as an established practice, and in 1717 James Brownhill built his tavern of *Golfhall* on ground feued out of the Muir at Wrightshouses. The Links, or at least their northern half, were also known as the *Fore Burgh Muir* and as the *Society Muir* after being conveyed to the Society of Brewers in 1598, *see under* SOCIETY, Greyfriars; while the present name appears in 1649 in the phrase 'the Society Muire ... commonly callit *Bruntfield Lynks*' where the meaning was simply 'near Bruntsfield' (since the Links were never part of that estate) and the spelling shows influence of the farming term *brunt* (*see under* BRUNTHEUGH) which has nothing to do with the place name. Early Scots *lynkis* described this rising and undulating ground above the shore of the South Loch; but it is evident from *Town Council Minutes* 1539 that (by transference) the word could also be used for rabbit warrens.

BRYCE AVENUE and **GROVE** (Craigentinny) *see under* CRAIGENTINNY.

BRYCE CRESCENT, PLACE and **ROAD** (Currie) were built in 1959-60, and named for Marshall Bryce, a local worthy mentioned in *Tweedie & Jones*. BRYCE GARDENS was added ten years later.

BRYCE'S CLOSE (Leith Shore) *see* PRETIES CLOSE, South Leith.

BRYDEN'S CLOSE (Canongate) *see under* (BAILIE) REID'S CLOSE, 80 Canongate.

BRYSON ROAD (North Merchiston) was begun by 1880 and named for Robert Bryson, watchmaker, who in 1874-76 had been Master of the Merchant Company, the superiors of the ground. WEST BRYSON ROAD was driven through the Harrison Park (which previously stretched to the railwayside) by 1904; and *Merchiston* 1776 shows, in what is now the middle of the north side of the street, a house or farm called CRAIGINGLES—apparently Scots *craig* or rock 'of the English', or of someone surnamed Inglis.

ANDREW BRYSON'S CLOSE (55 High Street) *see* TRUNKS CLOSE.

BUBBLING WELL (Cramond) is shown on *Ordnance Survey* 1852, and referred to in the field name *Babling Well* on *Cramond* 1815 (*RHP 6866*). The name describes a bubbling spring—*see also* BUILYEON ROAD, Queensferry.

BUCCLEUCH PLACE (South Side) is mentioned in *Arnot* 1779 as a 'Buccleuch Street' which James Brown was planning, and it appears as *Buccleuch Place* on his feuing plan for George Square in 1779. Its naming, presumably in compliment to the Duke of Buccleuch, may be connected with Brown's naming of GEORGE SQUARE after his brother George Brown of Elliston: for although the duke seems to have had no connection with the site (it is described as owned by James Brown in both *Arnot* and the feu charter of 1783 for the *George's Square Assembly Rooms*) he and Elliston evidently had common interests, for both were members of the Poker Club in 1776 and subscribers of the Royal Academy riding school in 1804. *Kincaid* 1784 shows a proposal to extend a 'Buccleuch Street' to St Patrick's Street; but it was no doubt the return blocks at the end of Buccleuch Place, featured in the plan of 1779, that led to the name BUCCLEUCH STREET being given to the first part of Causeyside, as shown on *Ainslie* 1804; and this, coupled with the establishment of HOPE PARK END (*which see*) gradually eroded the use of the name CAUSEYSIDE in the northern section of that ancient street, eliminating it altogether in about 1830. BUCCLEUCH PEND or ENTRY was an arched opening in a five-storey tenement facing the opening of Buccleuch Place. Shown on *Ainslie* 1780 (but not on *Scott* 1759) and notable as where Robert Burns lodged in 1784, the building was needlessly demolished in 1947 leaving the present unhappy gap-site entry to St Patrick's Square. BUCCLEUCH TERRACE, taking its name from Buccleuch Street, was formed in 1881 on the site of the printing works of Thomas Nelson & Sons, built at *Springfield* in 1846 but destroyed by fire in 1878.

BUCHAN or **BUCHANAN'S CLOSE** (281 Cowgate) *see* BULL'S CLOSE, Cowgate.

BUCHANAN'S or **BUCHAN'S COURT** (300 High Street) is listed on *Ainslie* 1780 and 1804 as *Buchanan's Close* and as *Buchan's Close* on *Kincaid* 1784, and the form *Court* appears in *PO Directory* 1826. The name was no doubt connected with *Buchanan's land*, burned down in 1771, itself a replacement of the timber-built tenement of the abbot of Cambuskenneth burned down in 1725. *Edgar* 1742 lists the close as WALTER WILLES'S, and *Kirkwood* 1817 notes it as 'formerly WALTER WILLIS'S' (N.B. in *Old Edinburgh Club XII* both of these entries are wrongly quoted 'Willie's') but any link with a Wills or Willis remains to be traced. A third name was HUNTER'S CLOSE, likewise obscure, although it may be noted that *Williamson's Directory* 1780 lists a James Hunter, physician, as resident in nearby Old Bank Close.

BUCHANAN STREET (Quarryholes) began to be occupied in 1878 and may have been named for James Buchanan, then a member of the Town Council and of its Streets & Buildings Committee.

THE BUCHANS (Dalmeny) is a patch of drying rocks in the Drum Sands, named on *Armstrongs* 1773. The name may be British *buch an*, cow place, and perhaps related to the 'watching shepherd' implied in the British name of BARNBOUGLE (*which see*) which overlooks the Buchans from the shore. Innumerable rocks off the Scottish coast are named as 'cows'.

BUCKINGHAM TERRACE (Dean) was started in 1860 as the beginning of a development by the Heriot Trust and James Steel which also included BELGRAVE CRESCENT and PLACE, named by 1868, although the latter began to be occupied only in 1880. The choice of names is perhaps the height of snobbish aping of London. BELGRAVE CRESCENT MEUSE or LANE was built along with the street. BELGRAVE MEWS, serving Belgrave Place, is on the site of the historic Village of Dean.

THE BUCK STANE (Braid) has been moved twice, first to the head of Buckstane Park and then, in 1964, to Buckstane farm house; but until the early 1920s it stood about 250 yards further north, on the west side of the summit of the Braid road, where it is recorded in 1496 as the *Buk Stane*, standing at the meeting of the bounds of Braid (including Over Plewlands or Greenbank) with those of Mortonhall and Comiston. Certainly it was used as a boundary mark, but that is not to say that it originated as one. The story deriving its name—somewhat tortuously—from the unchaining of hounds for royal deer hunts is introduced in *Maitland* 1753 with the reservation 'as 'tis said ...', and it is fairly obvious that it was made up to fit the name. This may be Anglian *bucc stan*, stone of stag or he-goat; but otherwise it may well be Anglian *bug stan*, bogle stone, possibly deriving from the fact that, small though it is, the Stane must have been visible for miles from north or south, like a little mannikin etched sharply on the skyline. It was prominent enough to give its name to the BUCKSTANE SNAB, the steep western spur of the Braid hills, as well as to the 47-acre BUCKSTANE FARM in Mortonhall, shown on *Roy* 1753 and detailed on *Mortonhall* 1776. In each of the estates adjoining the Stane the corner field was named as the *Buckstane Park*, and the Comiston one gave its name to BUCKSTANE PARK when that street was developed in it in 1923. The farm name had been anglicised as 'Buckstone' as early as 1773 (and sometimes misspelt as 'Buckston', wrongly implying 'Buck's farm') and this form was used when BUCKSTONE TERRACE was begun in part of Morton in 1927, starting a drift of the name southwards and even westwards into Comiston. Development in Morton continued with BUCKSTONE AVENUE, GARDENS and ROAD in 1934; while a modest start was made in Buckstane itself with BUCKSTONE DRIVE in 1930 and BUCKSTONE VIEW in 1935. It was resumed with BUCKSTONE DELL (1963) BANK, CRESCENT, HILL, ROW, WAY and WOOD (1965) LOAN and PLACE (1971) GREEN, GROVE and WYND (1973) COURT and RISE (1974) LEA (1977) CLOSE (1978) and NEUK (1979). In 1981, when a large extension to the south beyond historic Buckstane was in prospect, an attempt was made to articulate the neighbourhood by introducing other local names belonging to the ground, but residents' associations insisted upon continued use of the *Buckstone* label, proposing BUCKSTONE CIRCLE as a new name for BUCKSTONE LOAN SOUTH and its somewhat curved extension. Also in 1981, another branch of Buckstone Loan was renamed BUCKSTONE GATE (using *gate* in its Scots sense of 'way') while BUCKSTONE HOWE was named for its site in a hollow and BUCKSTONE SHAW for its nearby shaw or wood; and in 1986 HIGH BUCKSTONE was named for its position at the summit of the area.

BUGHTLIN or **BOUCHTLIN** (Corstorphine) is the name of a burn which flows from Clermiston down to the Almond through the farm of SOUTHFIELD (shown on *Blaeu* 1654) which began to be developed for housing in 1978. It is Scots *boucht* (from the Flemish *bocht* or *bucht*, in about the 15th century) a sheepfold, especially one for milking ewes, with *lin(n)*, a waterfall or cataract (from Anglian *hlynn*) or else a pool (from Gaelic *linne*) either sense of the Scots word fitting the character of this 'linn by the sheepfold' at some point on its course. BUGHTLIN DRIVE, GARDENS, GREEN, PLACE and PARK were named in 1978, and BUGHTLIN LOAN and MARKET followed in 1979. Taking their name from the north branch of the burn, NORTH BUGHTLIN BANK, BRAE, GATE (i.e. way) NEUK (i.e. corner) and ROAD were added in 1978, and were followed by NORTH BUGHTLINFIELD, NORTH BUGHTLINRIG and then NORTH BUGHTLINSIDE in 1980. In 1981, the final large scheme at the north end of the farm was named FAULDBURN, with a play on the name of the 'sheep-fold burn'.

THE BUGHTS (Grassmarket) were sheep pens shown on *Edgar* 1742 and other maps up to 1793 as permanent features in the west end of the Grassmarket. The word is Scots *boucht*, a fold or pen, from

Flemish *bocht*. The evidence of the royal charter for markets, engrossed in *Town Council Minutes* 1477, is that the livestock market was concentrated here from that date, if not earlier.

BUILYEON ROAD (Queensferry) is part of the old road from Echline to Scotstoun, shown on *Roy* 1753, which was cut off and diverted when the Forth Road Bridge approaches were constructed in about 1963. The name, which also occurs in Linlithgow, Ecclesmachan, Borthwick and elsewhere, is Gaelic *builgean* or Scots *builyand*, the bubbling-up of a spring—in this case a source of the Ferry burn shown on *Dundas* 1757 as well as *Ordnance Survey* 1922 as having been on the north side of the old road, where this is now obliterated by the dual carriageway leading to the Bridge. The spelling *builyeon* was chosen out of many variants as the one which most nearly suggested the local pronunciation of the traditional name 'billion road'.

BUISELAW or **BOWSHILL** (Lothianburn) is from Scots *buss*, a bush, and *law*, a hill: it is the 'bushy hill'.

THE BULL CLOSE (181 High Street) is shown as *Bull's Close* on *Edgar* 1742 and got its name from the *Bull Tavern* or *Cellar* which was in the close from some date prior to 1705. Two taverns, the *Union* and the *Perthshire*, are shown in the close on *Ordnance Survey* 1852. The name also attached to the BULL TURNPIKE at 189 High Street, which may possibly have been the *Black Turnpike* mentioned in *Town Council Minutes* 1641 and once the mansion of Henderson of Fordell—*see under* OLD PROVOST'S CLOSE. The close was earlier ADAMSON'S, from John Adamson, burgess, who got a feu here from the Abbot of Newbattle in 1549, in return for the help he had given in rebuilding a tenement belonging to the Abbey but burned down by Hertford's army in 1544. It was also known in the 17th century as CAICHPELE CLOSE, for the *cachepele* or real tennis court which was approached by the Fleshmarket and Old Provost's Closes as well as this one. The close was swept away in the construction of Cockburn Street in 1859.

BULL'S CLOSE (106 Canongate) was named for Robert Bull, wright, burgess of Edinburgh, who got property here through his wife Jean or Joanna Wright. Since the naming would imply that they had had the property for some considerable time before they sold it in 1701, it seems likely that the Robert Bull referred to was the one who was deacon of the wrights in 1680, rather than the one known to have been connected with BULL'S CLOSES in the Cowgate, *which see*. The close is listed in *Williamson's Directory* 1779 as MAY DRUMMOND'S and on *Ainslie* 1780 as DRUMMOND'S. May or Marion or Mariana Drummond was the sister of George Drummond, Lord Provost, and was well known in England as well as Scotland as *the Preaching Quakeress*. In *Chambers* 1825 she is described as 'perhaps the most remarkable woman that Scotland ever produced, except the Duchess of Lauderdale'. She owned *Bull's Land*, which was bought after her death by Peter Lamont, lint manufacturer, and renamed *Lamont's Land* before 1779; while another small part of her property was purchased from her estate by an adjoining owner, John Carfrae, *see* CRICHTON'S ENTRY,

Canongate. In the later 19th century the close got the name of FORD'S ROW, from houses owned by William Ford of Holyrood Glassworks.

BULL'S CLOSES (281 and 307 Cowgate) are listed on *Ainslie* 1780 and got their names from John Bull, merchant, mentioned in a title in 1719, and probably also Robert Bull, merchant, mentioned in *Town Council Minutes* 1717 as having a house north of High Street Yards, and being troubled by schoolboys climbing upon its roof. The close at 281 Cowgate was also known as BUCHAN'S or BUCHANAN'S CLOSE, for George Buchan, wright, owner here in 1799.

BUNKERS HILL (East End) is shown at South St James Street on *Ainslie* 1780, and the name was still current in 1839. Tales in *Chambers* 1825 and *Old Edinburgh Club II* both aver that it was given in 1775, because the foundation of the first house to be built here was laid on the very day that news of the British 'victory' at Bunkers Hill arrived in Edinburgh: but since the stories differ in every other particular and yet come so pat as explanations of the naming, it is scarcely surprising that Chambers dropped his one from his later editions. In all probability the name was local to the steep slope above the Leith road; and if Scots *bunkers*, sandy hollows or else banks of stones had once been prominent on it, they would swiftly be forgotten after it was built up, as shown on *Brown & Watson* 1793.

BUNKERS HILL (Joppa) figures on *Duddingston* c1800 as the name of the settlement at Joppa Salt Pans. While it may have been named for the British 'victory' in America in 1775, the date of the map (not later than 1801) would rule out any connection with the fact that the earl of Moira, distinguished in that battle, rented the Duddingston estate in 1803. Yet there is nothing to relate the name positively to the battle; and the alternative suggestion, that it derived from some hillock marked by *bunkers* (Scots for banks or heaps of stones, or for sandpits) is equally plausible and perhaps more likely.

BURDIEHOUSE (Liberton) is given as *Burdehous* on *Adair* 1682, and is *Burdiehouse* on *Armstrongs* 1773 and *Bordie House* on *Knox* 1812; but it is *Bourdeaux* on *Laurie* 1763 as against *Burdihouse* on *Laurie* 1766; and the same two forms appear in *Kincaid* 1787, the first in the gazeteer, the other on the accompanying map. Five years later, *White's Liberton* adopted the 'Bordeaux' form, and suggested that the place was 'so called, perhaps, by some French attending on Queen Mary in 1561'. But alas for that *perhaps*! for later writers have not scrupled to embroider White's tentative suggestion as though it were fact. Much the same has happened in the case of another *Burdiehouse* near Beith, Cunningham (only with weavers instead of courtiers) but the truth is that there is no evidence whatsoever for a French connection, apart from the interpretation of the name—and in the Lothian example this is certainly wrong, In 1763, Laurie's *Bourdeaux* may have arisen simply from taking the name to be *Burdeous*, one of the customary ways of spelling the French town's name in Scots, and his change to *Burdihous* in 1766 looks very like a correction of an error; but the decisive evidence is on *Roy* 1753 (a map which generally records names as then spoken) where the settlement is shown as *Bardy Burn*. The *-burn* was probably a mere alternative to *-house*; but the significant thing is that the first part of the name is shown to be an independent element, as it is on *Knox* 1812, quoted above. Possibly akin to *Bordy*, recorded in Culross in 1543, or to *Beard* in Derbyshire, it may be from Anglian *brerd*, early Scots *borde*, a rim or bank or border, aptly describing this place above the burn, and even more so the position of BURDIEHOUSE MAINS, shown on *Knox* 1812; or else it may be a variant of early Scots *bordland*, the mains or home farm which supplied the laird's *bord* or table. BURDIEHOUSE BURN is the local reach of the LOTHIAN BURN. BURDIEHOUSE ROAD is a section of the PENICUIK ROAD (*which see*) renamed in 1927 as the *road to Burdiehouse*; and part of it, by-passed when the main road was rebuilt as a dual carriageway, was further renamed OLD BURDIEHOUSE ROAD in 1969. BURDIEHOUSE SQUARE dates from 1938. In the same year two new streets in SOUTHHOUSE were named BURDIEHOUSE AVENUE and TERRACE, only because they were near the Burdiehouse road; and they in turn passed the name on to further streets in Southhouse: BURDIEHOUSE CRESCENT, CROSSWAY, DRIVE, LOAN, MEDWAY and PLACE in 1947, and BURDIEHOUSE STREET in 1964.

BURGESS ROAD (Queensferry) was formed by 1914 but may not have been named for some years thereafter. The reason for the name is not known.

BURGESS STREET (South Leith) was created in about 1890 by widening BURGESS CLOSE. While this was in the oldest part of Leith, and while a door lintel inscribed 'NISI DNS FRUSTRA 1573' is noted in *Wilson* as being at the foot of the close, there is no evidence for the story, appearing in *Maitland* 1753, that it was named in the 14th century as the only access to the Shore permitted to the burgesses of Edinburgh by Logan of Restalrig; and the tale is improbable, if only because at that period a *close* was not a public passage (which was a *wynd*) but an enclosure, and usually private ground. Recorded as *Burges Close* in 1717 and *Burge's Close* in 1777, it is more likely to have been named in the customary way for some prominent resident; and the surname Burges or Burgess, although it does not appear in Edinburgh's burgess roll until after these dates, was already in use in Aberdeenshire as early as 1382, and in Lothian by the early 17th century.

BURGESS TERRACE (Mayfield) *see under* McLAREN ROAD, Mayfield.

THE BURGH, BURROW, BORROW or **BOROUGH MUIR** is first mentioned in about 1332 in the name of William Brune *del Borumore* (*see under* BRUNTSFIELD) and it is 'the muir of the burgh of Edinburgh' in *RMS* 1444, and *le burrowmure* in 1449; but by then it was already hundreds of years old, for its teinds were among the pertinents of St Cuthbert's given to Holyrood abbey by David I in 1128; and furthermore, since this common land and the COMMON MYRE (*which see*) were essential to the farming which the burgesses had to carry on in their own support in the early burgh, it must be assumed that this grant of land out of the royal forest of Drumselch was made when the king's trading burgh was first set up, *see under* EDINBURGH. As time went on and trade with the countryside developed, the need for burghal farming declined; and powers to raise income by feuing out parts of the Muir were sought in 1490 and granted by James IV in 1508. Out of an original area of about a square mile (the bounds are described in *Old Edinburgh Club X*) only Bruntsfield Links remains unfeued.

BURGHMUIRHEAD (Morningside) originated as the name of the summit of the Muir, immediately west of the Linton highroad, but also attached to the gushet or triangle of ground beside the road (between Colinton Road and Abbotsford Park) feued out of the Muir in 1586. Shown thus on *Laurie* 1763, it later extended as a neighbourhood name to cover the vicinity of Bruntsfield Place, as shown on *Knox* 1812; and subsequent to the transfer of the 'Burghmuirhead' branch Post Office (along with its name) from its old position south of Colinton Road to a new one at Merchiston Place, the neighbourhood name has tended to drift northwards as well, no doubt assisted by the suppression of the old name in the historic Burghmuirhead.

BURGHTOFT (Gilmerton) was coined in 1986 as a name for a new development on this site, shown on *Roy* 1753 as built up within the village. The term *burgh* was used very loosely, for Gilmerton was never a burgh; while *toft*, the Scots term for a homestead and its plot of ground, was suggested by the TOFTS (*which see*) nearby.

BURIANRIDGE (Wester Norton) is preserved in the field name *Burianridge Park* shown on *Norton* 1813, in the vicinity of NT 133725, now Hillwood Gardens. It appears to be Scots *burian rigg*, ridge with a tumulus or a fortified settlement on it, but nothing of the kind has as yet been identified in the neighbourhood.

BURLINGTON STREET (South Leith) was first developed in the 1860s in connection with Field and Allan's slate works; and the name, first listed in *PO Directory* 1867, probably derived from the notable slate quarry of *Burlington* in North Lancashire—cf. BANGOR ROAD.

BURNBRAE (Bughtlin) was named in 1973 for its position above the South Bughtlin burn.

BURNDALE (Gilmerton) is shown on *Ordnance Survey* 1852 as a cottage, and is mentioned in *Good's Liberton* as an alternative name for Gilmerton Grange. The name is probably Scots *dale* or *deal*, portion of ground, *near the burn*, and may be linked with that of *Back Dale* (i.e. west dale) further upstream at Wester Grange.

BURNECRUIK (Gogar) is described in *RMS* 1602 as lying to the north of the Kirklandcroft of Gogar. This would place it at or in the direction of Kellerstain, near the centre of the land within the great *cruik* of the Gogar between Over Gogar, Redheughs and Gogarburn; and it is at least possible that *Burncruik* was once the general name for this half square mile of land.

BURNET'S CLOSE (156 High Street & 170 Cowgate) is shown on *Edgar* 1742 and was named for Samuel Burnet, brewer, who had a tenement in the High Street at the head of the close and was one of the nineteen burgesses who set up THE SOCIETY (*which see*) in 1598. The close was also JOHNSTON'S, for James Johnston, deacon of the Hammermen in 1537 and named in 1564 as having property here. It was also MORIES or MORICE CLOSE, for Peter Mories or Morice, recorded in *Protocols of William Forbes* 1746 as a later owner of Johnston's property.

BURNETT STREET (South Leith) made a brief appearance in *PO Directory* from 1813 until 1822—*see under* BURNS STREET, South Leith.

BURNHEAD CRESCENT, GROVE and **LOAN** (Liberton) followed by BURNHEAD PATH, were named in 1956 and 1959 for the clachan or farm of *Burnhead* shown on *Laurie* 1763 and *Armstrong* 1773 as lying south of Stenhouse burn and west of the Lasswade road, on a site later named *Gracemount Farm*. It is indicated on *Roy* 1753, with the names *Damhead* and *Willy's Dry* close behind it. The place was probably named as the settlement nearest the head of the burn—certainly the only place name higher up belongs to what seems to have been a purely natural feature, *see* HOWDENHALL, Liberton. After the disappearance of the clachan, the name was taken by John Duncan of Duncan & Flockhart, chemists in Edinburgh, for the house he built for himself on the east side of the Lasswade road, as shown on *Ordnance Survey* 1852, on a site now occupied by Lockerby Crescent and Cottages.

BURNS BRAE (Balerno) is the traditional name of RAVELRIG ROAD (*which see*) but possibly belonged to the whole slope below Pilmuir, where there are burns running down both east and west of the road, and a number of springs in between. Indeed, the name is almost a Scots translation of PILMUIR, *which see*.

BURNSHOT (Dalmeny) appears on *Barnbougle & Dalmeny* c.1800 as a field name, and certainly originated as such, since it is Scots *shot* or arable field *beside the* (Cockle) *burn*; but since it is shown with a farm symbol on *Blaeu* 1654 and listed in *RMS* 1622 among lands of Dalmeny and Barnbougle, it is evident that by the late 16th century the field name was used for a farm. In 1800, two of the estate roads converged on the BURNSHOT GATE; but *Ordnance Survey* 1854 shows one of them running to a NEW BURNSHOT GATE. It also shows a BURNSHOT WOOD on land which had belonged to Craigiehall in 1800.

BURNSIDE (Bughtlin) was named in 1973 for its position beside the South Bughtlin burn.

THE BURN SIDE (Longstone to Stenhousemill) describes this path *beside the burn*—in this case, the Water of Leith. Shown on *Roy* 1753 as a path beside the mill dam serving Stenhouse mill, it may outdate the Long Stone (*see under* LONGSTONE) which formed a bridge for it over the Murray burn, for the mill (and presumably the cauld and dam serving it) existed before 1511, *see under* STENHOUSE, Saughton.

BURNSIDE PARK (Balerno) was named in 1981, as being built in the field of this traditional name, which describes its position beside the Water of Leith.

BURN'S STREET (South Leith) was an early development in the Hermitage House estate. It is shown unnamed on *Kirkwood* 1817, but is named on *Thomson* 1822 and in *PO Directory* 1824; and since the latter lists an Alexander Burn as resident in Hermitage House, the street was probably named *Burn's Street* after him. Nevertheless there is as yet nothing to connect Burn with Hermitage House prior to this, and it may be that the street was earlier known as BURNETT STREET, which figures in *PO Directory* from 1813 to 1822 and which, although not named on any map, is described as being in this vicinity. In 1822 the *Directory* gives an Alexander Burnet as resident in 'Hermitage Cottage, foot of Lochend Road'; and to judge by *Ordnance Survey* 1852 this was the name of a detached house at the east end of Burn's Street.

BURNWYND (Currie) is shown on *Roy* 1753 and *Riccarton* 1772, and is perhaps shown as BURNHOUSE on *Blaeu* 1654. It was on the north bank of the Murray burn, upstream from the Corslet, at about NT 177683, and the name evidently derived from the marked *wynd* or bend in the course of the burn at this point. The place had disappeared by 1800.

BURNWYND (Dalmahoy) is recorded as part of Dalmahoy in *RMS* 1614 and is shown on *Dalmahoy* 1749 and *Hatton etc* 1797. The maps suggest that the name belonged to the *wynd* or bend formed by the combined courses of the Green and Gogar burns at this point.

BURSE or **BURS** (South Leith) became fashionable in Leith in the later 16th century as a term (originating in Bruges) for an exchange building. Apparently there was more than one of them, for *Town Council Minutes* 1578 mention land, evidently north of the King's Wark, 'sumtyme callit the *common closetis* and of new callit the *burs*' (later to be the TIMBER BUSH, *which see*) while over 30 years later, in *RMS* 1612, there is a grant of wine taxes to Bernard Lindsay, owner of the King's Wark, to help to finance the building of an elegant arcaded *burs* adjoining the Wark and overlooking the harbour, for the benefit of foreign as well as local merchants. The suggestion in *Maitland* 1753 that there had been a burse at the foot of the Paunchmarket (*see under* QUEEN STREET, South Leith) is admitted to be merely 'in some measure' corroborated by the remains of three 'piazzas' still visible in Maitland's time, and it was certainly based upon a wholly wrong interpretation of the above-mentioned *common closets* as being the closes in this part of the Shore: but notwithstanding this, there may have been a burse here, if (as he avers) one of the closes in the vicinity was known as *the Burss* in 1753.

BURT'S CLOSE (Grassmarket) *see* WARDEN'S CLOSE, Grassmarket.

BUTELAND (Balerno) is recorded in 1280 as *Botland*, and is shown on *Blaeu* 1654 as *Butlonds*. In *RMS* 1618 the lands of *Buitland* and *Buitlandhill* are described as comprising the OVIRTOUN OF

BUITLAND (shown on *Gellatly* 1834) the NETHERTOUN (now called BUTELAND farm) BUITLANDHILL (also shown on *Blaeu*) LONEHEID (still shown on *Laurie* 1763 at the head of a loan running westward to the BUT FORD at Pathhead) and the TEMPILLS and the TEMPILHOUSE. The name is Scots *bute* or *butt lands*, a detached part of an estate, and possibly arises from the fact, referred to in a charter of 1596 quoted in *RMS* 1613, that these lands, although originally Templar lands, were for some time annexed to the lordship of Borthwick.

THE BUTH or **BUITH RAW** (High Street) originated before 1497, as the name of the row of booths or shops which together with the Auld Tolbooth occupied an island site in the street north of St Giles. The letting of 22 booths is recorded in *Town Council Minutes* 1457. By the 17th century they were also called THE LUCKENBOOTHS—i.e. booths that could be shuttered and *locken* or locked up, as distinct from *crames* or open stalls. Both names, *Buth Raw* and *Luckenbooths*, were extended to the tall lands built several storeys high above the shops, as shown on *Rothiemay* 1647 as well as in many sketches of the High Street prior to the demolition of the Luckenbooths in 1817; but *Buth Raw* was also used for the narrow roadway of the High Street where it passed north of the booths.

BUTLAR'S CLOSE (High Street) is mentioned in *RMS* 1500, and was evidently named for a burgess family prominent in the 15th century. Five of them are mentioned in *Town Council Minutes* and *RMS*: two named John, bailies in 1429; two Thomases, mentioned in 1456 and 1501; and in 1475, Agnes, who like the earlier Thomas had property on the south side of the High Street, next to Niddry's Wynd. The close seems to have been west of that wynd, in an area subsequently disturbed by the building of the Tron kirk and the South Bridge. No doubt it had other names, but none has been identified.

BUTLAW (Queensferry) is recorded from 1695 onwards. The name is Scots *butt*, a detached piece of land (*see also* BUTELAND, Balerno) with *law*, a hill, and refers to the fact that, as shown on *Dundas* 1769, the ground was a detached part of Duddingston, with a part of Banks intervening between it and the main estate.

THE BUTTER TRON (High Street) is named in *Town Council Minutes* 1457 and was authorised by royal charter in 1477 as a weighbeam set at the Bowheid to serve markets for butter, cheese, wool and 'siclike gudis that suld be weyit'. It was also known as the OVER (i.e. upper) TRON, distinguishing it from the main TRON or SALT TRON (*which see*) below the Cross. A WEIGH HOUSE, with thatched roof and a steeple, as shown on *Rothiemay* 1647, was built in 1612 for more extensive weighing and measuring, but was cleared away by the Cromwellians in 1650 because it would give cover to troops attacking the Castle. A replacement was built in 1655, but finally removed in 1822 on the ground that it was no longer needed and only obstructed the street.

BUTTER WELL (Dalmeny) is shown on *Ordnance Survey* 1852 in the corner of the field shown as *Butter Well Park* on *Barnbougle &*

Dalmeny c1800. In absence of early forms, the term *butter* is obscure. The suggestion that it might mean that the well was useful for cooling butter overlooks the obvious point that any spring, except a hot one, will do the same; and any idea of 'richness in butter production', while it might apply to a farm or (at a stretch) to pasture, would seem impossible to apply to water. The word might be Scots *butter*, a bittern, a frequenter of marshy places.

THE BYERSIDE (Swanston) is recorded thus in 1709 and is shown as *Byerside Hill* on *Ordnance Survey* 1852. The name may be from Old Norse *byjar sítha*, side or slope above the farm steading, in this case, Sveinn's farm or SWANSTON, *which see*.

BYER'S MOUNT (North Leith) *see under* MOUNT PELHAM etc.

BYRES CLOSE (373 High Street) is listed thus on *Edgar* 1742 and was named for John Byres, merchant burgess (1569-1629) who retained his burgess house here even after he purchased COATES (*which see*) in 1610. Adam Bothwell, Bishop of Orkney (d.1593) also had his house here, still noted for its half-octagon gable and curious 'bee holes' on its east front. *Protocols of John Foular* record two earlier names for the close: in 1525 it is noted as MALCOLM'S CLOSE, for a family of that name, owners of a land on its east side; and in 1534 it is given as WILLIAM LAUDER'S CLOSE, evidently named for William Lauder, bailie in 1528, or quite probably for his namesake, a bailie in 1453.

BYRNIE (Balerno) appears (on the same site as does *Balerno* on later maps) as *Byrney* on *Blaeu* 1654 and *Bearna* on *Adair* 1682. In *RMS* 1528-90, charters variously use the forms *Bawerno, Biarno, Buirnoch, Byirnoch, Byreno* and *Byrno*; but since in each case the charter is clearly dealing with BALERNO (*which see*) these forms must be taken to be variants of that name, with the initial *Bal-* part shortened. While the sequence continues in *RMS* 1607-63 as *Byerno, Byreno, Byrent, Byrenalie* and *Byrna*, these later charters apply the name only to a particular farm, the *Overtoun of Byerno*, and they list it, side by side with *Balerno*, among properties within the barony of Balerno. Thus it is likely that the shortened form became a name in its own right, now belonging to the Overtoun farm and its mill; and this could explain the naming of BYRNIE PAPER MILL in 1799, as well as the continued use of 'Byrnie' for 'Balerno' in local parlance.

C

CABLES WYND (South Leith) is an amalgam of three separate streets still distinguishable even although their discontinuity has been largely smoothed out by modern road alterations. The oldest section, north of the junction with the historic Giles Street, was part of the medieval township; and since *Wood* 1777 and others label it *Cables Wynd continued* and *Ordnance Survey* 1852 gives it as SHEEPHEID WYND (*which see*) it is evident that it is called *Cables Wynd* only by extension from the middle section of the street. This last seems to have been the veritable *Cables Wynd*: a *wynd* or public way in the system of *closes* or yards laid out south of Giles Street prior to 1560, *see under* YARDHEADS, South Leith. The third or westmost part of the modern street was also named by extension: it is clear from *Naish* 1709 that the wynd was not originally continuous with the Bonnington road, although *Wood* 1777 shows it made so; and the *Cables Wynd* name was not extended south of the Yardheads until Great Junction Street was built in the 1820s. Recorded from 1743 onwards as *Cable* or *Cable's* or *Capill's Wynd*, the name incorporates the Dutch or Flemish surname Kappel; but although this is found in Scotland as early as the 15th century, it is likely that this street in Leith was named for Henry Capell or Capill, maltman and brewer in Leith, who was made a free maltster in 1660. Since *Town Council Minutes* 1659 report that Capell was formerly a veteran in the Cromwellian army under George Monck, it is likely that he hailed from England, where at least one person of the name, Richard Capel, was a kenspeckle Puritan in the time of the Civil War.

CADELL'S ROW (Cramond) is a row of cottages built for workers in the ironworks in the Cockle Mill and further upstream. William Cadell was one of the founders of the Carron Company which acquired the works in 1759, and he and his family owned them from 1770 until 1860.

CADIZ STREET (South Leith) was developed in about 1891 and seems to have been named for Leith's trade connections, following the style set earlier by ELBE STREET.

CADOGAN ROAD (Liberton) was named in 1926 for the Hon. Victoria Laura Cadogan, daughter of Viscount Chelsea, who married Sir John Little Gilmour of Liberton and Craigmillar in 1922. Celebration of the Gilmours' connections by marriage continued in 1930 when BEAUCHAMP ROAD and GROVE were named for Lady Susan Lygon, daughter of the earl of Beauchamp, who married Robert Wolrige Gordon Gilmour in 1889 (*see also* LYGON ROAD) and HAWKHEAD CRESCENT and GROVE were named for a connection with Ross of Hawkhead in Renfrewshire, through Lady Grizel Ross, daughter of Lord Ross of Melville, who had married Sir Alexander Gilmour of Craigmillar and Nether Liberton in 1678. Likewise in 1935, ORCHARDHEAD LOAN and ROAD were named for Gabriel Rankin of Orchardhead in Stirlingshire, who inherited Over Liberton from his mother's uncle, William Little, in 1685 (*see also* RANKIN AVENUE, West Mains) and also in 1935 WOLRIGE ROAD was named for the marriage of Henry Wolrige and Anne Gordon Gilmour in 1856, the family subsequently calling themselves Wolrige Gordon Gilmour.

CADZOW PLACE (Abbeymount) was named in about 1894, but the reason for the choice of name has not yet been traced. It may derive directly from Cadzow near Hamilton, or else indirectly through the surname which developed from that place name in the 13th century. The place name is British, although its meaning is obscure; and it is one of those names threatened by mispronunciation of the printed *z*, which stands for the old Scots 'yogh' letter ȝ, the variant spelling *Cadyow* being nearest to the proper sound.

CAER DUFF KNOWES (Mortonhall) are described in *White's Liberton* 1792 as 'two small tumuli close to the march with Upper Liberton', while on *Mortonhall* 1776 the prominent knowe at NT 261692 is shown as *Carduff Knowe*. The name is British, either *caer duv*, black fort or stockade, of which no remains have been discovered, or else *carn duv*, black rocky summit or cairn, which fits the knowe very well.

CAERKETTON (Swanston) appears on *Adair* 1682 as *Kairnketten*, and on later maps as *Kirkyetten* 1763, *Kirketton* 1773, *Kirkyetton* 1817 and *Caerketton* 1852. The forms *Caerketan-craig* and *Caerketan commonly Kirkyetton* appearing in the *Statistical Accounts* 1794 and 1839 give the impression of a deliberate attempt to read the first part of the name as *caer*, a fort; but although there is a fort on the spur above Hillend, the name clearly belongs to the main hill. Here the two distinctive features are the crags on its north face and the large (once much larger) burial cairn on its summit; and the hill name appears to be British, coupling *carn*, rocky summit, with *caid*, burial cairn, and the suffix -*an*, meaning 'place of', and making it the 'rocky summit at the burial-cairn place', the latter referring to the summit cairn, or else to the whole group of four conspicuous cairns here and at the CATHEAPS and MOUNTHOOLY at Fairmilehead. It is unlikely that the name is from some Celtic chief *Catel* buried at the cairn (which may have been 1,000 years old by the time the Celts arrived in the area) even although there is evidence (e.g. at Cairnpapple in the Bathgate hills) that the Celts sometimes buried their dead beside such ancient monuments.

CAERLAVEROCK COURT (East Craigs) *see under* CRAIGIEVAR WYND, East Craigs.

CAIRNEBUKKIS (Wester Duddingston) is given in *RMS* 1595 and *Laing Charters* 1599 as the name of croft land of Wester Duddingston, within which 1½ Scots acres were part of the Kirklands of Duddingston. Also recorded as *Carnebukis* 1599, *Carnbuck* 1707 and *Carin Buck* 1752, the name is probably Scots *bucht*, sheepfold or pen for milking yowes, *at the cairn*. Where it was is not known, but the name and the term 'croft' both suggest that it would be close to the township.

CAIRNMUIR ROAD (Corstorphine) *see under* BELGRAVE ROAD, Corstorphine.

CAIRNS DRIVE etc. (Balerno) *see under* COCKBURN CRESCENT, Balerno.

CAIRNTOWS (Craigmillar) is recorded in *RMS* 1550 as *Carnetowis*. On the strength of the fact that *Laurie* 1763 shows a toll to the west of it (it is still shown on *Ordnance Survey* 1852, and functioned until 1870) it has been suggested that the name is Scots *tow* or toll *at the cairn*; but it is neither evident nor likely that there was a toll here two centuries earlier, and the variant *Cairnfield* appearing on *Adair/ Cooper* 1735 strengthens the impression that it is a land name. It might be Celtic *carn toll(aigh)*, rock or cairn at the hollow, for some kenspeckle feature on the rise overlooking the wide flat of the Peffer or Braid burn; but the early *Carne-* forms, as well as the *Karintowis* on *Roy* 1753 (probably noted phonetically) suggest that the first part might be British *carden*, making the name 'thicket or wood at the hollow'. The farm steading was northeast of the crossroads; and NORTH CAIRNTOWS, so named in 1983 and previously part of *Cairntows* railway yard, lies just within the northern boundary of its fields. CAIRNTOWS CLOSE, near the farm centre, was named in 1989.

CAITHNESS PLACE (Trinity) was named in 1988, for the Earl of Caithness, resident in this estate of DENHAM GREEN in the 1830s.

THE CAIY STANE (Comiston) is named thus in *Maitland* 1753 and shown as *Kay's Stone* on *Armstrongs* 1773, while the CAIYSIDE is shown on *Ordnance Survey* 1852 and a map in *Steuart's Colinton* as the ridge or slope south of Oxgangs Road. Taken together, these names suggest that *caiy* was the name of the place: probably British *cai*, a bank or defence, and referring to some lost earthwork on the ridge, if not to the ridge itself. Thus it is likely that *Caiyside* is Anglian *side* or slope 'at the cai', while the prehistoric standing stone is Anglian *stán* 'at the cai', possibly a translation of British *maen cai*, of the same meaning, which occurs at Menkee in Cornwall. Since Maitland's time, no fewer than four other names for the Stane have been reported, with fanciful explanations which take no account of the adjoining Caiyside name but are all fixed on the notion, by no means supported by archaeology, that all standing stones are war memorials. The *Statistical Account* 1794 offers two of them: *Kel Stane*, 'an old British word signifying Battle Stone'; and *Camus Stone*, 'for some Danish commander'—obviously a wild attempt to explain the name of COMISTON, *which see*. Later reports, naming it as *Cat* or *Ket Stone* and seeking a connection with Gaelic *cath*, a battle, seem merely to pursue a remark by Maitland, who after reporting the name *Caiy Stane* goes on to say '... whether this be a corruption of Catstean [*sic*] I know not'. There may also have been some confusion with the CAT HEAPS (*which see*) which stood some 200 yards east of the Stane. Housing development nearby in Comiston began in 1934 with CAIYSTANE AVENUE and CRESCENT, EAST CAIYSTANE PLACE, and EAST and WEST CAIYSTANE ROAD, while CAIYSTANE DRIVE, GARDENS, HILL and VIEW followed in 1956. The spurious form 'Camus' was used for CAMUS AVENUE, EAST and WEST CAMUS PLACE and EAST and WEST CAMUS ROAD in 1937, and for CAMUS PARK in 1968. The new street of CAIYSIDE (Easter Swanston) lying within the *Caiyside parks* shown in *Steuart's Colinton*, was named in 1985.

CALDER ROAD (Saughton) is shown on *Adair/Cooper* 1735 as the main route to Midcalder; but since *Adair* 1682 shows a different arrangement, with the road branching from the Newbridge road and passing to Addiston by Over Gogar, it seems likely that the early road through Saughton followed the line of the 'old road' shown on *Cultins* 1775, through Saughton, Lairdship and Cultins and across a bridge at Gogar Bank, there to join the road shown on *Adair* 1682. On *Cultins* 1775 and *Saughton* 1795 it is noted as the 'great road from Glasgow by Whitburn', but it was probably also called 'the Calder road' from the beginning, and is figured *Midcalder road* on *Bartholomew* 1876. In 1967 its name was borrowed for the new streets CALDER COURT, CRESCENT, DRIVE, GARDENS, GROVE, PARK, PLACE and VIEW built in parts of SIGHTHILL and LERBAR, *which see*. The group has been nicknamed The Calders—most unfortunately, since this is of course proper and traditional for the three Calders nine miles further along the road.

CALEDONIAN CRESCENT, PLACE, ROAD and **TERRACE** (Dalry) were formed in the policies of Dalry House in 1869-70, and their name was probably suggested by the presence of the Caledonian Distillery, then one of the largest in Scotland, which had been set up on the opposite side of Dalry Road in 1855. Caledonian Crescent included ORWELL TERRACE (*which see*) until 1875; and Caledonian Terrace, fronting the main road, was renamed as part of DALRY ROAD in 1885.

CALLENDER'S CLOSE (117 High Street) *see* MORRISON'S CLOSE.

CALLENDER'S ENTRY (67 Canongate) is listed thus in *PO Directory* 1827 but is CALLENDER'S CLOSE on *Ainslie* 1780 and *Kirkwood* 1817. It was named for John Callender of Craigforth, advocate (grandson of John Callender of Craigforth, once deacon of the Blacksmiths) who according to *Canongate Charters* 1769 and 1782 purchased the ground from Gilbert Duncan, wright, in 1768 and built CALLENDER HOUSE. The fact that *Edgar* 1765 shows a house on the site and labels it *Mr Calender's* suggests either that Callender contemplated building for long in advance, or that he built the house before fully acquiring the land. The omission of the House from *Ainslie* 1780 and 1804 and other maps prior to *Kirkwood* 1817 seems to have been by surveyor's error, for it certainly dates to before 1782 and its style suggests the 1760s.

CALM CRAIG (Dalmeny) appears on *Dundas* 1757 on the north side of the road from Standing Stone to Milton of Dundas, at about NT 137762. While the name, on the face of it, might be Scots *caum craig*, limestone crag, the outcrop is of igneous rock, and thus the name is probably Celtic *cam crag* or *creag*, crooked or curving crag.

THE CALTON is *Caldtoun* in *South Leith Records* 1591, and this spelling (or sometimes *Coldtoun*) is general until about 1700, although the second edition of *Laurie* 1766 shows it still in use. Until about 1700 also it is used only for the settlement or neighbourhood, the hill having other names (*see under* CRAIGINGALT) and in the grant of West Restalrig to the town in 1725 the lands of *Calton* and *Caltonhill* are separately listed. The name appears to be Celtic, probably British, akin to Gaelic *coilltean*, place of or at groves. The name LOW CALTON survives from the curious arrangement (still shown on *Ordnance Survey* 1893, but abolished a year or two later) whereby the western half of the highway, lying in Edinburgh and fronted by St NINIAN'S ROW (*which see*) was at a lower level than the eastern half, which lay within the latter-day *barony of the Calton* and was known as the HIGH CALTON, fronted by the village of that name, also called CRAIGEND. *Edgar* 1742 shows a road branching from the High Calton up to the *Caltoun* burying ground, *Armstrongs* 1773 shows houses built along its north side, and it is variously named CALTON STREET on *Kincaid* 1784, HIGH CALTON on *Ainslie* 1801 and CALTON HILL on *Bartholomew* 1876. The street may be the *Calton hill* listed in the *Accurate View* 1783, but this name enters *PO Directory* only in 1833, five years after *High Calton* had been removed from it, and the double use of *High Calton* or *Calton Hill* continued at least until 1905. CALTON STREET and PLACE are shown on *Ordnance Survey* 1852 as side names in Leith Street and Low Calton. In about 1895 (probably when the two-level highway was abolished) these and other parts of the street through the Calton were renamed CALTON ROAD; and between 1905 and 1912 this name was extended to displace the name of NORTH BACK OF THE CANONGATE, *which see.*

THE CALTON NEW TOWN was planned as an ambitious scheme covering some 250 acres, extending from Regent Road to Duke Street and from Leith Walk to Lochend Road. In 1811, at the suggestion of Lord Provost William Calder, the proprietors of 86 percent of the ground (the Heriot Trust, Trinity Hospital, Alexander Allan of Hillside and Mrs Hume of Whitfield) proposed that the town as owners of 33 acres at the Calton Hill, should join them in adopting a single scheme for development of the whole area. A competition for the plan, held in 1813, proved abortive, even although it attracted 32 entries; but it prompted a report by William Stark, broken off by his death, which outlined an approach to the design that was closely followed by his erstwhile pupil William Playfair when he developed the final scheme in 1818-19, as shown on *Calton* 1819. Building started quite promptly, but progress was hindered not only by competition of new building in the Moray estate and Easter Coates and other parts of the New Town, but by difficulties in rating arising where buildings were beyond the bounds of the barony of Calton; and as a result development was virtually confined to Calton Hill and Allan's property of Hillside until after the advent of the railway in 1868. This finally blocked the completion of the original plan; and of the later developments, only Montgomery Street, Brunswick Street, Hillside Street and Wellington Street followed the Playfair alignments. The map of 1819 proposed thirty street names, of which a dozen survive: four connected with royalty (*see* CARLTON TERRACE, REGENT ROAD, ROYAL TERRACE and WINDSOR STREET) three in compliment to national personages (BRUNSWICK STREET, LEOPOLD PLACE, WELLINGTON STREET) three borrowing names already connected with the site (ELM ROW, HILLSIDE CRESCENT, MONTGOMERY STREET) one a new main road (GREAT LONDON ROAD) and lastly BRUNTON PLACE, one of an original six streets proposed to be named for members of the Joint Committee for the Calton New Town.

CALTON STREET (East End) *see under* LEITH STREET (East End).

CAMBRIDGE AVENUE (Pilrig) is shown on *Bartholomew* 1876 as proposed in the BALFOUR STREET development (*which see*) and appears in *PO Directory* 1882, named probably for Field Marshal George, 2nd Duke of Cambridge, who was the Queen's cousin and

Commander-in-chief from 1856 to 1895. CAMBRIDGE GARDENS followed on, and appears on *W & A K Johnston* 1888.

CAMBRIDGE STREET (Tollcross) *see under* ORCHARDFIELD, Tollcross.

CAMBUSNETHAN STREET (Meadowbank) began to be occupied in 1897, and like DALZIEL PLACE (1896) and WISHAW TERRACE (1901) was developed by James Steele, builder, Lord Provost 1900-3 and later Sir James Steele, Bt., of Murieston, who was the son of a farmer in Cambusnethan, Wishaw, and lived there and in the adjoining parish of Dalziel before he came to Edinburgh in 1866.

THE CAMERON is shown as *Kameron* on *Blaeu* 1654, but is first recorded in Kelso Abbey charters relating to 'the marsh called *Cameri*' in 1150, or *peatmoss of Camerun, Camberun* or *Cambrun* in 1211-26. This stretched from the Cameron to Forkenford, and there is no reason to doubt that the feature that gave it its name was in the historic Cameron area, where the spur of the Cellarknowe thrusts southwards and the Pow burn originally wound round its base, in a great crook that defined the edge of the bog, as shown on *Kirkwood* 1817 and *Ordnance Survey* 1852. The early forms quoted above, as well as the later ones *Cambrun* or *Kambrun* 1264-90, *Cambroun* 1337 and *Cam(e)ro(u)n*, frequent after 1475, suggest that the *b* (where it occurs) belongs to the first part of the name, and since the stress is on the first syllable, it is likely that the *-e-* (where it occurs) was inserted simply to make the name easier to say. It is probably British *cam rynn*, either the *rynn* or point of land 'at the *cam* or crook', or else (since *cam* could also mean a crooked burn) 'at the crooked burn'. Alternatively, but perhaps less likely, the name could be Anglian *kambr ryn*, belonging to the *ryn* or burn 'at the kame or ridge'—and it might be noted that in 1759 and 1824 the field name *Camb* or *Camp head* is recorded some 800 yards north of Cameron Bridge. There are eight other places called Cameron in Scotland, two in Lothian and all south of the Highland line, and the natural features of a point of high land and a burn curving round its base are prominent in each of them. In 1678 Sir James Dick added the lands of Cameron to those of Priestfield and Clearburn, and in 1689 he named the combined estate *Prestonfield*. CAMERON HOUSE was built by the Dicks in 1770, but replaced an earlier estate centre shown on *Roy* 1753 as well as *Adair* 1682, *Blaeu* 1654, and a curious map of the area in *Court of Session Papers* 1564. CAMERON HOUSE AVENUE was developed from the House drive in 1931. Although *Good's Liberton* asserts that CAMERON BRIDGE was built in 1752 in place of a ford over the Pow, a bridge is shown very positively on *Adair* 1682, *see also* BRIDGEND, Craigmillar. The vicinity was known as *The Cameron* or *Cameron Bridge* until recently, when these names have tended to be displaced by that of CAMERON TOLL, a toll bar officially known as *Cameron Bank Toll* and operating at the foot of Lady Road from 1820 until 1878. *Cameron Bank* appears as a house name on *Knox* 1812. CAMERON CRESCENT and TERRACE were built on Cameron land by 1887; but prior to 1898 CAMERON PARK was called DOW'S AVENUE, presumably for its builder. CAMERON TOLL GARDENS was named in 1967—rather unfortunately, inasmuch as it is in Bridgend and all of 300 yards from the site of the Toll.

CAMERON MARCH (Nether Liberton) was named in 1991, as being on the march of Liberton next the Cameron.

CAMERON'S ENTRY (32 and 36 Grassmarket) is shown on *Ainslie* 1780, the name evidently that of a proprietor who remains to be traced. On *Kincaid* 1784 it is PAXTON'S YARD, probably for James Paxton, listed in *Williamson's Directory* 1773 as vintner in the New Inn, Grassmarket. Its later name DUNLOP'S COURT, given in *PO Directory* 1827, is evidently connected with that of William Dunlop & Co, wine and spirits merchants, listed next door in 1827.

CAMMO is recorded in 1296 both as *Cambo* and *Cambok*, and is shown on *Blaeu* 1654 as *Kammock*. The name is British *cambaco*, 'place in the bend' of the Almond, and CRUMBLANDS (*which see*) less than a mile away is its exact Anglian counterpart. It was renamed NEW SAUGHTON in 1741, *see under* SAUGHTON. CAMMO ROAD, traditionally the road *by Cammo* between the Queensferry and Stirling roads, was formally named in 1956, along with CAMMO WALK. Both these roads are shown on *Roy* 1753; and *Cramond Roads* 1812, besides listing them both as public roads, confirms that Cammo Road then took a more direct line westwards (its northward loop dates from 1840 or thereby) and was known as LENY PATH. Its westermost section was renamed LENNYMUIR in 1985, *see under* LENNIE. CAMMO CRESCENT began beside the Queensferry road in about 1900. CAMMO GARDENS began in 1931, and CAMMO BANK, GROVE, HILL, PARKWAY and PLACE followed in 1957.

CAMPBELL AVENUE and **ROAD** (Murrayfield) *see under* GARSCUBE TERRACE, Murrayfield.

CAMPBELL'S CLOSE (87 Canongate) is listed on *Ainslie* 1780 and was evidently named for George Campbell, meal merchant, bailie of Canongate, who had a tenement here before 1682. The close is called RAE'S in *Canongate Charters* 1586, but the origin of this older name is obscure. The family name was prominent in the early history of the Canongate, *see* RAE'S CLOSE, 281 Canongate.

(EAST) CAMPBELL'S CLOSE (145 Cowgate) is listed on *Ainslie* 1780 and was named for the family of Campbell, brewers (see WEST CAMPBELL CLOSE) but more particularly for Archibald Campbell, who acquired a house on the east side of the close from John Adamson, advocate, who is listed in 1635 as owning the whole of it.

(WEST) CAMPBELL'S CLOSE (109 Cowgate) is listed on *Ainslie* 1780 and was named as an access to the premises of Alexander Campbell, brewer here in 1773, whose enterprise subsequently developed into the famous brewery of Campbell, Hope & King. Earlier, the close was BAILIE ROBERTSON'S, for Thomas Robertson of Lochbank, bailie in 1681 and 1684, who had a tenement on the east side of the close, adjoining RATTERAY'S CLOSE, *which see*.

CAMPBELL PARK CRESCENT and **DRIVE** (Woodhall) were built in 1958 in the *Alder Park* or *Willowbed* field of Woodhall, but were named for the adjacent CAMPBELL PARK, gifted as a public park by Duncan Campbell of Woodhall.

CANAAN (Morningside) was made up of several parcels of ground feued out of the wester Burgh Muir from 1595 onwards, ultimately forming an estate lying between Grange Loan and the Pow burn, and between Morningside Road and Wester Grange, *see under* THE GRANGE. First recorded in 1661 as a name already in common use, *Canaan* was an obvious response to the earlier EGYPT (*which see*) on the opposite bank of the Pow burn: and indeed *Adair* 1682 almost pointedly shows the two over against each other, and *Roy* 1753 adds the *Jordan* name for the burn, *see under* POW BURN. On *Laurie* 1763 and 1766 the placing of Canaan south of the burn is a palpable error. The name could have been coined at any time after feuing began in 1595, for the biblical notion of Canaan 'flowing with milk and honey' and contrasting with Egypt was familiar to everyone, and indeed this notion of blessedness was continued in later names within the estate, such as GOSHEN, EDEN, HEBRON and even PARADISE—now a pub. The estate centre was at CANAAN HOUSE (11 Canaan Lane) and *Scott* 1759 shows CANAAN FARM about 100 yards further south, just south of the future line of the east/west part of Canaan Lane. The same map shows only the eastern (north/south) section of CANAAN LANE, which (contrary to a misinterpretation of evidence in *Old Edinburgh Club X, see under* BLACKFORD AVENUE) is the remnant of a way that led from Grange Loan straight down to the Pow burn at Little Egypt. Its southern section, now lost but still marked by a wall east of Woodburn House, is mentioned in *Town Council Minutes* 1598 as reserved 'for the use of the town in time of pest and all other times as has been of auld' and as forming the east boundary of the plots feued to Herbert Maxwell in 1595, which together made up the 12½ Scots acres that lie between here and Morningside Road and between the Pow and what is now the western leg of Canaan Lane. The Lane is shown in its modern form on *Knox* 1812, but is listed in *PO Directory* 1827 as Egypt Lane, a name which may have belonged to its earlier function. The modern name appears on *Pollock* 1834.

CANAL STREET (East End) is mentioned in 1771 and shown on *Armstrongs* 1773 along with the ornamental canal which from 1723 onwards was proposed to replace the Nor Loch, but was never constructed. The street was suppressed in the redevelopment of the Waverley Station in 1868.

CANDLEMAKER ROW (Old Town) is part of the ancient route from the south by Bristo to the Upper Bow, by which James IV came to the town with his bride Margaret Tudor on 7 August 1503. Recorded in *RMS* 1496 as *the king's road called The Lonyng*, the name indicates that it was a broad way with wide grassy margins, evidently leading to pastures further south. It was known as the SOCIETY WYND or VENNEL after the SOCIETY (*which see*) set up their brewery east of it in 1598. By this time at least half of the original width of loaning alongside the Greyfriars dyke had become redundant; and in 1654 the town council, alarmed by a recent fire in the town set off by candlemaking, allocated this well-isolated strip of waste ground to the candlemakers for their workshops, and forbade them to operate anywhere else. The name CANDLEMAKER ROW originally applied to these workshops; but by the time the candlemakers built their trade hall here in 1728, it had become the name of the street.

CANDLEMAKERS PARK and **CRESCENT** (Gilmerton) were named in 1989, continuing the name of the *Candlemakers park* field shown on *The Drum* 1842. The mining of coal and limestone (the latter dramatically described in *Good's Liberton*) were the principal industries in Gilmerton from the 15th century until recent times, and created a strong demand for candles. On account of the stench and fire risk of candlemaking, it was usually kept on the outskirts of villages or towns.

CANMORE STREET (Queensferry) is built in the SKAITH MUIR (*which see*) in Plewlands, and was named by 1970 for Malcolm III, known in Gaelic as *ceann mor* or 'high chief', who reigned as king of Scots from 1058 until 1093, and whose second wife Margaret endowed the Queen's ferry

CANNING PLACE (Causeyside) is shown on *Ordnance Survey* 1852, and was a side name in Causeyside from 1848 until 1884 for a terrace of houses opposite East Sciennes, which seems (from the map detail) to have replaced an earlier terrace shown on *Scott* 1759 and *Kirkwood* 1817 and perhaps *Pollock* 1834, if the last is not showing its projected replacement. The name may have derived from a *Canning House* at the north end of the terrace, probably named for George Canning MP, who became Prime Minister shortly before his death in 1827.

CANNING STREET (West End) is shown projected and already named on *Wood* 1823, but the scheme lay fallow until about 1874. CANNING STREET LANE was formed by 1887 and named possibly by then but certainly by 1892. The original naming was evidently for George Canning (1770-1827) who became Foreign Minister in 1822 after the suicide of his great rival Lord Castlereagh, with whom he had fought a duel at Putney in 1809.

CANNON STREET (North Leith) was planned in 1817 and partly built by 1821. Its name presumably derived from the *Battery* immediately west of it, *see under* LEITH FORT. In 1968 it was renamed HELEN PLACE, borrowing this from the adjoining HELEN STREET; but in 1979 the street itself was suppressed by the development of LINDSAY PLACE. CANNON WYND, on part of the site of the Fort, was named in 1963.

THE CANONGATE is mentioned in *RMS* 1363 and *Exchequer Rolls* 1366 as Latin *vicus canonicorum* and Scots *canoungait*, way of the canons. Clearly the name referred to the Augustinian regular canons of Holyrood and had arisen, probably soon after their house was founded in 1128, as a name for the 'king's street' between the abbey and the king's burgh of Edinburgh. Along with Edinburgh's HIGH STREET, this was probably part of an earlier road or track which led eastwards from the ancient settlement on the ridge, and which seems to have been diverted at the foot of the Canongate in a northwards loop through Abbeyhill, apparently to accommodate the developing abbey. *The Canongate* must have been already established as the street name before it came also to be used for the burgh flanking the street, set up by the canons (at some unknown date) under powers granted them by David I in 1128. In a court case in 1554 it was averred that this burgh had originally been known as 'Harbargary'; but in the course of the action (the record is quoted in full in *Bannatyne Club Vol. 19, Appendix I to Preface*) it was shown conclusively that this was a false assumption, resting solely upon a misreading of the Latin of David's charter, mistaking the verb *herbergare*, to establish, for a proper name. In *RMS* 1363, *vicus canonicorum* clearly refers to the street, for the charter is about a property in Edinburgh's CANONGATEHEAD, *which see*; but in a charter of 1423 (quoted in *RMS* 1426) it is mentioned in connection with property within the canons' burgh, and in *RMS* 1493 all is made plain, albeit clumsily, in the phrase 'the king's street in the burgh of the street-of-the-canons'. The burgh's TOLBOOTH, dated 1591, replaced an earlier one mentioned in *RMS* 1477. Its MERCAT CROSS, now on its third site and mounted on a base made for the Cross of Edinburgh in 1866, is mentioned in *Protocols of James Young* 1497 as the *canon-corse*, and *Rothiemay* 1647 probably shows it in its medieval position, mounted on a substantial cross house virtually in front of the entry to Bakehouse Close. As shown on *Regality of Canongate* 1813 the burgh included not only the Canongate itself, but the lands of MEADOWFLATT, DISCHFLAT and PLEASANCE, as well as NORTH LEITH and the COALHILL. It came under Edinburgh's control in 1636, and was merged with it in 1856.

CANONGATEHEAD is shown on *Ordnance Survey* 1852 as bounded on the north by the centreline of the roadway from the Netherbow down to the Laplee Stane or St John's Cross, on the east by the west backs of St John's Close, and on the south by the frontages (once the course of the Stank) on the north side of the South Back of the Canongate, now called Holyrood Road. Referred to in RMS as 'beneath the burgh of Edinburgh' (1363) 'beneath the Netherbow' (1472) 'Canongate of Edinburgh' (1499) or 'Canongate next Edinburgh' (1515) and in *Town Council Minutes* 1625 as 'the head of the Canongait', this ground seems to have been always part of Edinburgh, and to judge by the name of its boundary mark, the LAPLEE STANE (*which see*) it may have originated as a common grazing of the early royal burgh, known as the *lap lee* or outskirt pasture.

CANONMILLS derives its name from mills built here by the canons of Holyrood on their lands of Broughton, probably not long after the lands were granted to them by David I in the 12th century, and long before the earliest record of the mills in 1423, by which time they were an established part of the pension of the abbot of Holyrood.

They were powered by water running in a mill dam (part of it an elevated wooden aqueduct in the Dean gorge, *see* THE TROWS) which served the lower mills of the Dean as well as those of Stockbridge and Silvermills before entering CANONMILLS LOCH and going on to serve a number of mills in Canonmills and Beaverhall and (at one time) Powderhall. The loch, still represented in 1893 by a pond south of Eyre Place, is shown as a sizeable sheet of water on *Roy* 1753, and earlier still it extended over the whole of the CANONMILLS HAUGH shown on *Ainslie* 1804, bounded by East Silvermills Lane, Fettes Row and Royal Circus, Scotland Street and Summer Bank, and Eyre Place and the south backs of Henderson Row. The street CANONMILLS is shown on *Fergus and Robinson* 1759 as passing through the complex of mills and turning sharply along Warriston Road to the ford at PUDDOCKY, *which see*; and it was modified in the 1760s to form the approach to the then new CANONMILLS BRIDGE. CANONMILLS HOUSE, shown on *Blaeu* 1654 and *Adair* 1682, was cleared away for the Davidson Church, built within Eyre Crescent in 1881, but now replaced by housing.

CANON STREET (Canonmills) is shown on *Ainslie* 1804 but began to be developed in the later 1820s as part of Robert Brown's scheme for housing in James Eyre's estate of Canonmills House—*also see* BRANDON STREET etc, Canonmills. Shown on *Lothian* 1829, the name clearly derived from CANONMILLS, *which see*. CANON LANE, which was originally an access drive to Canonmills House, as shown on *Ainslie* 1804 and *Ordnance Survey* 1852, is shown on *Lothian* 1829 as planned to be converted into a meuse lane; but this had to await the building of BRANDON TERRACE in the late 1870s.

CANT'S CLOSE (272 Canongate) *see* BELL'S CLOSE, Canongate.

CANT'S CLOSE (High Street) *see* ADVOCATE'S CLOSE.

CANT'S CLOSE (108 High Street and 220 Cowgate) is listed on *Edgar* 1742. Recorded in *RMS* 1588, its name is from the Cant family, prominent in the town from the days of Adam Cant, bailie in 1403, and probably even earlier. Members of the family had property on both sides of the High Street; but one in the vicinity of this close, next to land owned by Melrose abbey (*see under* STRICHEN'S CLOSE) is mentioned in *RMS* 1492 as owned by Henry Cant junior, who figures along with his father Henry in a list of *gude nychtbouris* or burgesses in *Town Council Minutes* 1501.

CANT'S or **ALEXANDER CANT'S CLOSE** (265 High Street) *see* CRAIG'S CLOSE.

CANT'S CLOSE (341 High Street) *see* ROXBURGH'S CLOSE.

CANT'S LOAN (Mayfield) *see under* EAST and WEST MAYFIELD, Mayfield.

CAPELAW HILL (Pentland Hills) is shown as *Caplaw* on *Armstrongs* 1773, but the *Statistical Account* 1794 seems to apply the name (as *Capelaw*) to ALLERMUIR, *which see*. The name combines Celtic *ceap*, pointed hill (frequent in Lothian, as at the nearby *Kips*) with Anglian *law*, also meaning conical hill, and English *hill* has been added for good measure. CAPELAW ROAD (Colinton) was named for it in 1923.

CAP & FEATHER CLOSE (High Street) is shown on *Edgar* 1742 but was swept away for the building of the North Bridge in 1765. The name came from the Cap & Feather Tavern at the head of the close, mentioned in *Kincaid* 1787 in the account of the bridge works. The older names LOCKHART'S or CAMERON'S CLOSE are recorded in 1731, but their origins are unknown.

CAPTAIN'S ROAD (Liberton) is shown as a route on *Laurie* 1763, but the name first appears in *PO Directory* 1900. Stories such as that of a Napoleonic prisoner of war, supposedly fond of riding this way, bear every mark of having been invented to account for its origin, and it remains obscure. CAPTAIN'S DRIVE and LOAN took their name from the Road in 1956.

CARBERRY PLACE (Wester Coates) *see under* DEVON PLACE, Wester Coates.

CARFRAE ROAD etc. (Craigcrook) *see under* CRAIGCROOK.

CARFRAE'S ENTRY (112 Canongate) *see* CRICHTON'S ENTRY.

CARFRAE'S CLOSE (High Street) *see* TURK'S CLOSE.

CARGILFIELD (Trinity) is spoken of by *Grant* as though it had once been an alternative name for Wardie Mains, but is shown on *Ainslie* 1804 as one of a group of properties on the west side of South Trinity Road; and the name probably derives from some early owner called Cargil. CARGIL TERRACE was formed along the land's north boundary by 1892, and CARGIL COURT was named in 1963. DARNELL ROAD was named in 1904, a year or two after Cargilfield School, founded here by the Revd Daniel Darnell, removed to its new building at King's Cramond.

CARLOWRIE (Kirkliston) is recorded in *Bain* 1337 as both *Carlouryn* and *Carlouri*, and is shown on *Blaeu* 1654 as *Kaerloury*. The name is probably British *caer lowern*, fort or stockaded place of the fox. Although no traces of a fort have been found, Carlowrie stands on a spur of higher ground, well placed to command any river crossing near the prehistoric and British burial ground at the Catstane on the opposite bank. The 'fox' part of the name shows the same shift of the *r* as found in the Cornish forms *lowren* and *lewren*; and it may not be simply coincidence that the name *Todshauch* (*see* FOXHALL) occurs half a mile upstream. The present CARLOWRIE HOUSE dates from 1855, but seems to be on the same site as the house shown on *Blaeu*, while *Roy* 1753 shows the policies very much as they are today. *Blaeu* shows *Over Kaerloury* and *N(ether) Kaerloury* as well as *Kaerloury*, and this subdivision must have taken place before 1337, when NETHER CARLOWRIE is recorded as *Carlouri inferior*, although EASTER CARLOWRIE is not directly recorded until 1427. CARLOWRIE HAUGH(S) is recorded in 1573, and seems to have been beside the river and not far from Todshauch. On *Carlowrie* c1800, the terms *Easter* and *Wester* are used in place of their equivalents *Over* and

Nether. EASTER CARLOWRIE appears as a separate property, soon (in 1858) to be reorganised round a new steading 500 yards east of the older site near the present EASTER CARLOWRIE COTTAGES; while WESTER CARLOWRIE (its centre now OLD CARLOWRIE or CARLOWRIE COTTAGES) is grouped with WHEATLANDS, PUNCHINLAW and BOURTREEBUSH (*all of which see*) together with the house policies, to form a 300-acre estate of CARLOWRIE. CARLOWRIE ROAD, named as leading to the old steading sites and Easter Carlowrie, is shown on *Kirkliston* 1759 as branching off the Queensferry road (now Station Road) on an alignment that clearly suggests that it once led straight from Kirkliston Kirk, and the map styles it (*Cramond*) *Bridge road*.

CARLOWRIE AVENUE and **CRESCENT** (Dalmeny) were named in about 1954 as branching off the road leading out from Dalmeny towards Standingstone and Carlowrie.

CARLTON STREET (Stockbridge) was constructed in 1824 as part of the revised scheme for the development of Sir Henry Raeburn's estate at DEANHAUGH, *which see*. It involved the demolition of his house of St Bernard's, which stood on its east side. Its name, shown on *Wood* 1823, may commemorate George IV's visit to Edinburgh in 1822 by recalling the town house which had been his headquarters in London before his accession in 1820; but it is also a surname, and moreover there are over three dozen places named *Carlton* or *Carleton*, including several in the Stewartry and Ayrshire.

CARLTON TERRACE (Calton) was planned as part of the CALTON NEW TOWN (*which see*) and is named on *Calton* 1819 as *Carlton Place*, evidently for the Prince Regent's London home, Carlton House. It is shown on *Ordnance Survey* 1852 as *Carlton Terrace*. CARLTON TERRACE MEWS is part of a mews planned in 1819 to serve all three tarraces on the Hill. CARLTON TERRACE BRAE, originally intended to descend to London Road, was built on its present line in the 1840s, and its name seems to have arisen from local use and wont.

CARLUMBY (Newbridge) is shown west of Briggs on *Roy* 1753 and *Armstrongs* 1773 and was noted in 1933 as still surviving in the field name *Carlumbie haugh*. Almost exactly mirrored in the Cornish name *Carlumb*, it appears to be British, 'settlement at the bare place'.

CARLYLE PLACE (Norton Park) *see under* MARYFIELD, Norton Park.

CARMEL HILL (Kirkliston) is shown as a steading on *Forrest* 1818, but figures on *Humbie* 1720 in the name of the *Carmel Hill Park*, a field immediately west of the hill named *Carmel Hill* on *Ordnance Survey* 1852. There is no reason to suppose that it is fancy—and in any case, a fancy name would surely have taken the Biblical form, 'Mount Carmel'. It appears to be Scots *hill* tacked on to an earlier hill name, perhaps (even although no traces of a fort have been reported) British *caer mail*, fort on the bare hill. See also CARNODDING, another apparently British name, south of the hill. CARMEL AVENUE and ROAD in Kirkliston were named for the place in about 1950.

CARMELITE ROAD (Queensferry) is in Plewlands, partly at the BLACK LAWS (*which see*) and was named by 1970 for the Carmelite or Whitefriars friary of Queensferry, known to have existed in 1440 but believed to date back to about 1330.

CARMICHAEL'S CLOSE (196 High Street) *see* OLD FISHMARKET CLOSE.

CARMICHAEL'S CLOSE (once 66, now 54 Grassmarket) is shown thus on *Ainslie* 1780. Two men of the name are known to have resided in the north side of Grassmarket: Robert Carmichael, who died before 1754, and James Carmichael, nailer, listed in *Williamson's Directory* 1773. In 1635 it was called LAURENCE LOCKIE'S, for a resident of that name. In *PO Directory* 1827 it is THOMSON'S COURT, for a family of merchants and corn merchants of that name, then occupying several properties in the court.

CARMICHAEL'S or **HALIBURTON'S CLOSE** (off 251 and 265 High Street) was a cross passage, not shown on any map, connecting CRAIG'S and OLD POST OFFICE CLOSES, *which see*. Its names came from William Carmichael, merchant and bailie in 1673, who had a house on the west side of Old Post Office Close, and from a family which included a Robert Halyburton before 1635 and a John Haliburton of Garvock at some date prior to 1758.

CARNEGIE STREET (St Leonards) is shown on *Ainslie* 1804 as *St Leonard's Street*, already part-built on ground belonging to 'Mr Carnegie'—possibly the man referred to in the note 'Property of Mr D Carnegie's Heirs' on *Kirkwood* 1817, but perhaps an earlier Thomas Carnegie whose house was advertised for sale in 1775. The name CARNEGIE STREET appeared in *PO Directory* 1810. In 1965, the site was redeveloped, and named CARNEGIE COURT.

CARNETHY AVENUE and **WEST CARNETHY AVENUE** (Colinton) were formed in 1923, partly in the *Scaudhinty* field of Spylaw and partly in Fernielaw. The names are fancy, from *Carnethy*, second highest summit in the Pentland hills. The hill's name is British *carneddau*, (hill of) the cairns.

CARNODDING (Kirkliston) is shown on a plan of *Humbie* 1720 as a field name immediately south of what is now the site of Carmelhill. It seems possible that it refers to the rocky hill in the field and that it is an older British form of Welsh *carneddog*, rocky place or one with cairns, dating from the time before the *dd* became *th*, as in CARNETHY, Pentlands.

CAROLINE PARK (Granton) was a new name given in 1739 to the house of Royston or Easter Granton—*see under* GRANTON. CAROLINE PARK GROVE was named for it in 1971.

CAROLINE TERRACE (Corstorphine) was proposed in 1910 and the first set of feus, evidently named for Caroline Dunsmure, wife of the superior Heatley Dickson, was known as *Caroline Terrace* by 1913. The street name was confirmed in 1927, and was continued to CAROLINE GARDENS and PLACE in 1978 and 1982.

CARPET LANE (South Leith) is shown on *Collins* 1693. Its lack of alignment with the Ratoun Row (Water Street) is evident on *Naish* 1709 and arose because it was within the KING'S WARK (*which see*) and this also explains why *Ordnance Survey* 1852 shows *Bernard's Neuk* on the east side of the Lane. Although *Kirkwood* 1817 still labels the street as *Water Lane continued*, the name *Carpet Lane* appears in *Aitchison's Directory* 1801. It presumably derived from a carpet factory or warehouse hereabouts, as yet unidentified.

CARRICK KNOWES, recorded in 1594 as the *Carrick* field and shown on *Roy* 1753 as *Carrick Knows*, was part of Saughtonhall. The name is probably Anglian *cnolls* or Scots *knowes* (for the hillocks that cluster near its historic centre, now occupied by the golf clubhouse) tacked on to an earlier name, British *carecc* or Gaelic *carraig*, a rock; and since *carecc* had the more particular meaning of a rock jutting out into water, the name may well go back to the time when the knowes were on the shore of the loch that once stretched from Gogar to Dalry, *see under* CORSTORPHINE. CARRICK KNOWE AVENUE was begun in 1928 on the western edge of the farm, in the *West Parks of Carrick Knowes*, shown on *Saughtonhall* 1795; and in 1935 the name was borrowed for CARRICKKNOWE DRIVE, GARDENS, GROVE, HILL, LOAN, PARKWAY, PLACE, ROAD and TERRACE, even although these nine streets were being built on the other side of the boundary, in SAUGHTON MAINS, on ground quite unconnected with Carrick Knowes.

CARRINGTON ROAD (Comely Bank) was laid out along with Fettes College in 1870. Named for Lord Carrington, a governor of the College, it was first used as an address in 1900. CARRINGTON CRESCENT was formerly MOREDUN CRESCENT (Craigleith) *which see*.

CARRON PLACE (South Leith) was developed in 1983 and so named because its northern section is on the site of CARRON COURT, shown on *Ordnance Survey* 1852, within the neighbourhood which was known as LITTLE CARRON from some date prior to 1772. Although the location of any forge here remains to be established, there may be a connection with Carron, Falkirk, for the Smith & Wrightwork Co. of Leith began to make small forgings and farm equipment in 1747 (the year in which industry, in the shape of the glassworks, started up in the vicinity of the Sands) but were taken over in 1759 by the newly-formed Carron Company, whose great blast-furnace works began production at Falkirk in the following year.

CARRUBBERS CLOSE (135 High Street) is recorded in *Protocols of John Foular* before 1513. The personal name, recorded in 1296 as *de Caribre*, is from *Carriber*, near Linlithgow; and the name of the close is probably from William de Carriberis, a burgess in 1450 (when he also bought Clermiston estate) and a bailie in 1454, and almost certainly the shipowner and merchant who was prominent in relations with the English in the mid 15th century. While he is mentioned in *RMS* 1473 as deceased owner of property in Blackfriars Wynd, south of the High Street, there is no direct evidence that he owned any in the close on the north side of the street; but the fact, recorded in *RMS* 1491, that his widow Agnes Faulaw, after her second marriage to Robert Lauder of the Bass, granted the annual income from a 10-mark property 'on the north side of the High Street' and a 5-mark one in South Leith as a gift to the kirk of the Blessed Apostle Andrew in North Berwick in memory of her first husband, strongly suggests that she had inherited them from Carriber.

CARSON STREET (Broughton) is shown on *Lothian* 1829 as part of the plan for the Hope estate (*see under* HOPETOUN CRESCENT) but it remained unbuilt and unnamed until the 1880s; and by 1899 its name was suppressed and it was made part of McDONALD ROAD, *which see*. The origin of the Carson name has not yet been traced; but in view of the street's history, it might have been named for Aglionby Ross Carson, a teacher at the Royal High School for 39 years, and its rector from 1820 to 1845.

CART'S CLOSE (101 Cowgate) *see* HUME'S CLOSE, Cowgate.

CASCHILIS (Queensferry) is recorded in the *Wardlaw MS* (*SHS* I.47) 1666-69 as the ancient Gaelic name for the straits at Queensferry: *cas chaolas*, the narrows with the fast, twisting tide—a graphic description of the difficult boat crossing.

CASSELS PLACE (South Leith) appears in *Campbell's Directory* 1803, and is shown on *Ainslie* 1804 as a terrace fronting Leith Walk, built on land owned by Walker Cassels, merchant in Leith. CASSELS LANE, the meuse serving it, was named in its own right by 1893. Development of Cassels' small estate continued at HOPE STREET in 1807, named for some connection with the Cassels family, or else for Charles Hope of Granton, who was exceedingly prominent at this time, not only in politics and the law, but in organising local defence against Napoleon; but in 1966, to obviate any confusion with Hope Street in the New Town, the name was changed (with rather careless spelling, for the man's name was *Cassels*) to CASSELBANK STREET.

CASTLE AVENUE (Corstorphine) was named in about 1929 for 15th-century Corstorphine castle, sited near the middle of the north side of the modern street. Its remains were still visible to a considerable extent in 1777, as shown in a sketch published in *Selway*, and the site is marked on *Ordnance Survey* 1893.

CASTLE BANK or **HILL** (Balerno) *see* RAVELRIG HILL, Balerno.

CASTLE BANK (Old Town) is mentioned in *RMS* 1603 as the banks and brays north and south of the approach to the Castle; and if the use of the name for the southern one (still shown on *W & A K Johnston* 1888) has declined, it is probably because the names of Johnston Terrace and Castle Wynd are available to define the public places hereabouts.

CASTLEBARNS (Tollcross) is shown on *Roy* 1753 and named on *Laurie* 1763 and *Kincaid* 1784, and the name continued to be used for the 150-yard stretch of the Linlithgow road west of Semple Street until it was supplanted in about 1887 by the extension of the name of MORRISON STREET, *which see*. Unrecorded prior to the early 18th century (when it is mentioned in the minutes of the burlaw court of Leith) the name's age and origin must be uncertain; but it might well be medieval and (as has been widely assumed, but simply on the strength of the name) connected with storage of crops at the ORCHARDFIELD, *which see.*

CASTLE HILL (Old Town) was separated from the Castle by a considerable dip or saddle in the ridge, shown on *Rothiemay* 1647 and concealed only in modern times by the construction of the ESPLANADE, *which see*; and this no doubt explains why the name *Castle Hill*, recorded from 1484 onwards, has always meant *the hill on the way to the castle*, and not the hill on which the Castle actually stands, which has to be differentiated, rather awkwardly, as the CASTLE ROCK. Differences in the alignment of the street and the sett of the tofts or building plots, as compared with those of the High Street, suggest that the Castle Hill was not laid out at the same time as the royal burgh; and since there are indications that the ancient route from the south originally climbed straight up the slope from Cowgatehead to the head of the Upper Bow, it is possible that the settlement on Castle Hill was earlier—perhaps much earlier—than the royal burgh.

CASTLELAW ROAD (Colinton) was built in 1925 in the *Scaudhinty* field of Spylaw, and like other neighbouring streets was named by fancy for one of the hills in the Pentlands, in this case Castlelaw Hill above Easter Howgate. The name of the hill originated more particularly as the name of its southeasterly spur, the *castle law*, a distinct knowe or *law* crowned by the triple ramparts of a fort; and the appearance of the name on *Blaeu* 1654 shows that it had been already transferred also to the nearby farm.

CASTLE O CLOUTS (Parkside) was a four-storeyed tenement built in about 1724 by William Hunter, tailor burgess of Edinburgh. He named it *Huntershall*, but as early as 1738 this was being ousted by the nickname *Castle o Clouts*, castle of rags. It was demolished in 1970.

CASTLE PLACE (Old Town) was a side name taken into JOHNSTON TERRACE by 1861.

EAST and **WEST CASTLE ROAD** (Merchiston) *see under* MERCHISTON.

CASTLE STREET (New Town) *see under* NEW TOWN.

CASTLE TERRACE (Tollcross) *see under* ORCHARDFIELD, Tollcross.

THE CASTLE WALL (Old Town) is referred to from 1426 onwards in the phrase 'under the castle wall' used to describe properties in the West Bow and Grassmarket. It seems to have run westwards from the Upper Bow on the line of Victoria Terrace; but how it was connected with the castle's defences is uncertain, although the line of the town's boundary shown on *Ordnance Survey* 1852 may offer a clue. When it was built is not known; but it might have been connected with the KING'S WALL, *which see.*

CASTLE WYND (Old Town) is named on *Edgar* 1742 as an entry off the Grassmarket, and is still primarily a Grassmarket address in *PO*

Directory 1827; but although maps prior to *Kincaid* 1784 show its upper part either vaguely or as a winding path, it is clear from the early records, beginning in 1529, that the wynd led to ground belonging to the Castle, and since this stretched as far east as the summit of CASTLE HILL, the form 'public lane leading to the castle hill' used in *RMS* 1542 may represent the original and more precise name. Yet it is possible (if the early GRASSMARKET (*which see*) was only about half as long as it eventually became) that the Wynd originated as a route to the castle immediately outwith the burgh's jurisdiction.

CATELBOK (Kirkliston) is now ALMONDHILL, *which see*. Shown on *Blaeu* 1654 as *Catelboch*, the name is recorded from 1535 onwards, and its early forms *Cattelbok* and *Catelbo*, as well as its traditional pronunciation *cat-él-bi*, show that it is Anglian *catt elboga* or Scots *catt elbok*, cat's elbow, a name almost exactly parallelled by that of Katzenelnbogen, near Koblenz, Germany. Presumably the meaning was something similar to 'dog-leg' and referred to some angular feature—perhaps the strangely-shaped parcel of land shown northeast of the steading on *Kirkliston* 1759. In *RMS* 1593 the farm is identified as the *demesne* or mains of the barony of Kirkliston, until then belonging to the archbishopric of St Andrews.

CATHCART PLACE (Dalry) was formed and named by 1879, one of a group of streets (*see also* DOWNFIELD *and* SPRINGWELL PLACE *and* DUFF STREET) developed in land shown on *Kirkwood* 1823 as owned by the Home Rigg family. The reason for the choice of name has not yet been traced.

THE CAT HEAPS (Fairmilehead) are so named in *Maitland* 1753, while in *White's Liberton* they are called the CAT STONES. They were two great cairns, so prominent on the ridge that they were represented by special conical symbols on *Adair* 1682, and so massive that even although they were largely carted off as road metal in the 1780s, their bases still show in the 185-metre contour at NT 24406826 in the south backs of Oxgangs Road. *Cat Heap* occurs elsewhere in Scotland as a name for a cairn. Maitland interpreted it as 'battle cairn', on the faulty assumption, general in his day, that prehistoric cairns and standing stones were war memorials; but the first part of the name is Celtic *caid*, stony top, while the second (added) part is Anglian *heap*, for the piled stones, making the name literally 'cairn cairn'.

CATHEDRAL LANE (East End) is shown on the *Stranger's Guide* 1816 beside the Roman Catholic Chapel, built here by Gillespie Graham in 1813 and erected into a cathedral in 1878. The street was long known as CATHOLIC CHAPEL LANE, latterly shortened to CHAPEL LANE; but in 1968 the name was changed to CATHEDRAL LANE, to obviate any confusion with CHAPEL LANE in Leith.

CATHERINE BANK (Queensferry) lies immediately outwith the south-east corner of the royal burgh as shown on *Ordnance Survey* 1854. The name is obscure: it perhaps related to the row of cottages shown on *Ordnance Survey* 1893 as above the road, which may be the CATHERINE TERRACE referred to in *PO Directory* 1924.

CATHERINE STREET (East End) is shown on *Brown & Watson* 1793 and was named for Catherine Swinton, wife of Walter Ferguson, owner of the ground on the north side of the lower part of Leith Street and also developer of the adjoining St James Square—*see also* SWINTON ROW, East End. The name continued in use as a side name in Leith Street until 1892.

CATHKIN'S or **CATCHKAN'S CLOSE** (151 High Street) *see* KINLOCH'S CLOSE

THE CAT NICK or **NEUK** (Coalhill, Leith) was a timber-framed tenement, probably of the 16th century, at the foot of Tolbooth Wynd. It was demolished in about 1820. The origin of the name is obscure.

THE CAT NICK (Salisbury Crags) is named on *Kirkwood* 1817, and is probably *cat neuk*, nook or corner where there was once a wildcat den.

CAT SKIN CLOSE (South Leith) *see under* LAWSON'S WYND, South Leith.

THE CAT STANE (Inch) was earlier at Nether Liberton, and may have been originally sited there. Since it is mentioned in *Good's Liberton* as one of four 'cat- or battle-stones' (it being generally assumed at that time that *Cat* was from *cath*, a battle, and that standing stones were war memorials) the stone's name may be of no greater antiquity; but *see next* for probable derivation of ancient names of this sort.

THE CATSTANE (Kirkliston) is a standing stone associated with a Bronze Age burial cairn, but adapted as an early Christian grave stone. The first part of the name is Celtic *caid*, stony top, or (more likely in this case) derives from the related word *càd*, holy or sacred, *also see* CAT HEAPS, Fairmilehead.

CATTLE ROAD (West Gorgie) was formed by 1912 and so named because it was the way for bringing animals to the Slaughterhouse.

CAULDHAME in Currie and also Slateford are both lost farms. The first is shown midway between Torphin and Kinleith on *Laurie* 1763 and *Armstrongs* 1773, while the second, shown at Stoneypath on a map of Hailes in *Steuart's Colinton* opp. p24, is mentioned in 1682 in the marriage contract of James Brand, younger of Baberton. The name occurs fairly often in Scotland and may be Scots *cauld hame*, cold home, for a farm in an exposed situation, which would fit the Currie site well enough, and possibly, although less aptly, the Slateford one; but *cauld* was also a farming term for *stiff* land, and *-hame* may sometimes be a corruption of Anglian *holmr*, which could mean 'enclosed marginal land'.

CAULIE'S or **CAUTIE'S CLOSE** (Lawnmarket) *see under* JOHNSTON'S CLOSE, 332 High Street.

THE CAUSEWAY (Duddingston) is shown on *Roy* 1753 and named on *Kirkwood* 1817 as *Wester Duddingston*—in other words, as the main street of that village. The present name seems to be recent, and not only an anglicised form but a misunderstanding of Scots *causey*, a paved or metalled road, or its surfacing. There is nothing to suggest that the village street was elevated, as now implied by the English term *causeway*; and while the villagers probably referred to the village street as 'the causey' in the same general sense as it might be called 'the street', the use of *The Causey* as a proper name would be as rare as the similar use of *The Street*.

CAUSEYSIDE, misspelled **CAUSEWAYSIDE** (South Side and Newington) got its name as that part of the highway that traversed the Burgh Muir on the way to Liberton, recorded as being *causeyed* by the town soon after it feued out parts of the Easter Muir in 1586. Scots *causey* or *calsay* (the pronunciation is identical) is from Old French *caucie*, a beaten way, and it means (as a noun) a road properly built and surfaced with metalling or pavings, or (as a verb) the making of one. Since about the mid 18th century, would-be 'improvers' of uncouth Scots have confused the term with English *causeway*, which was once 'a causey(ed) way' but (unlike the Scots word) has come to mean 'a raised roadway'. Fortunately, popular parlance in Edinburgh still resists corruption and sticks to the proper form of the street name *Causeyside*. The ending *-side* shows that it originally meant the land flanking the causeyed highway, which in early times was a loaning in which cattle could graze as they went along, *see under* BRISTO. Thus there were the farm lands of CAUSEYSIDE, represented in the burlaw court of Leith 1724-50, and when the Causeyside was recognised as a suburb by Act of Parliament in 1771, it was defined as the district extending from Crosscausey to Grange Toll (*see under* MAYFIELD ROAD) and embracing the SCIENNES and KITTLENAKIT, *which see*. In about 1800 the name in the northern half of the street began to be displaced by those of BUCCLEUCH STREET, HOPE PARK END (later TERRACE) and SUMMERHALL; and its southern end became RATCLIFFE TERRACE in about 1915.

CELLARBANK and **ECHOBANK** (Prestonfield) combined with GRAYFIELD TOLL (*which see*) to form a considerable settlement, including a school, at the point where the main road to Niddrie once branched off the Dalkeith road, on a line now represented by Prestonfield Terrace and the western part of Prestonfield Avenue. Marked on *Roy* 1753, the township is shown in detail on *Kirkwood* 1817 and *Ordnance Survey* 1852; but in 1893 it is shown half supplanted by the new tenements of Dalkeith Road. Although *Cellarbank* figures more prominently on the earlier maps, and *Echobank* on those later than 1850, the names are also shown together, and both derive from fields recorded in 1759 and shown on *Prestonfield* 1824. Cellarbank, south of the road junction, was in the northwest corner of the *Cellar* park, which took its name from the CELLAR or SILLER KNOWE, the great bank rising above the Dalkeith Road and Cameron Bridge. Described in *Good's Liberton* as the oldest grazing in the parish, the name is Scots *siller knowe* (also found as SILVERKNOWES in Cramond) and probably referred to the silvery gleam of its grasses as they bloomed. Echobank was north of the junction, in the southwest corner of the *Echo Park* of Priestfield, evidently named as the place where the echo from the ECHOING ROCK on Arthur's Seat could be heard.

CEMETERY ROAD (Queensferry) originated as part of the *kirk road* shown on *Dundas* 1757 as leading from Echline to Dalmeny kirk. In about 1910, when part of the road was adopted as the approach to the new cemetery in the Stonyflatts, a bypass farm road was formed immediately south of it, as shown on *Ordnance Survey* 1914, and this eventually became FERRYMUIR LANE, *which see*.

CESSFORD'S CLOSE (230 Cowgate) is recorded in 1720 and listed on *Ainslie* 1780, and derived its name from Thomas Cessford senior, stabler, who built a great stone tenement here, possibly in the 1680s. It was later HALL'S CLOSE, for the stabler William Hall, resident here in 1773. It may also have been DOBIE'S, recorded as THOMAS DOBIE'S CLOSE in *RMS* 1631 and named for a burgess family who held property here over several generations in the 17th century and very likely even before that, since Thomas Dobie may have been the one of that name mentioned in *Town Council Minutes* 1553. The close was cleared away in 1922.

THE CHAIN PIER (Trinity) was made up of three spans suspended from iron chains, and ran 500ft out to sea, opposite Trinity Crescent. It was built in 1821 for the local steamer service in the Forth, but was made redundant by the improvement of Leith Docks and the opening of Granton Harbour in 1833. By 1852 it was in decay, and it was finally dismantled in about 1900.

CHALMERS BUILDINGS (Fountainbridge) was one of the earliest essays in improved houses for the working class, initiated by a Mr Matheson and built in 1854 along with the adjoining Fountainbridge Free Kirk, a congregation who later set up the Fountainbridge Church Building Society to carry out similar projects elsewhere. The tenement was probably named for Dr Thomas Chalmers, the great leader of the Free Kirk, who had died in 1847.

CHALMER'S CLOSE (Castlehill) is mentioned in *City Charters* 1543 as giving access to property of Henry Chalmer, son of the late Alexander Chalmer, baker, which is also mentioned in *RMS* 1516 and 1533. The close's location remains to be ascertained.

CHALMERS'S CLOSE (81 High Street) is listed on *Edgar* 1742 and derived its name from Patrick Chalmers, belt maker, Captain of the Trained Bands in 1682, who had a tenement in the close. It was also known by 1726 as BOYD'S, from Hugh Boyd, merchant, who had a property at the close head, known as *Boyd's Land* or the *Blue Land*. Its earlier name was DUNSYRE'S, mentioned in *Protocols of John Foular* 1529 and named for William de Dunsyre, member of the *great dosane* or council in 1480 who owned land here as well as near Kirk o Fields.

CHALMERS CRESCENT (Grange) *see under* THE GRANGE.

CHALMERS STREET (Lauriston) was named by 1858 to commemorate George Chalmers, plumber in Edinburgh, who had died in 1836, leaving £30,000 to found a hospital. Lauriston House, built in the West Park of Lauriston by the Earl of Wemyss in about 1802, was purchased in 1854 by the Chalmers trustees, who feued out most of the ground to form the street, but kept back two acres, including the mansion house site, for the *Chalmers Hospital* which was opened in 1864.

CHAMBERLAIN ROAD (Greenhill) *see under* GREENHILL.

CHAMBERS STREET (Old Town) is shown proposed on *Edinburgh Improvements* 1866 and was carried out in 1871 under the Improvement Act of 1867, suppressing NORTH COLLEGE STREET, ARGYLE SQUARE and most of BROWN SQUARE—*which see*. It was named for Sir William Chambers of Glenormiston, Lord Provost 1865-69, who had taken a leading part in promoting the City Improvement Scheme.

CHAMPANYIE (Blackford) is recorded in *Protocols of William Stewart* 1577 as *Champnye*, alternative name for Blackford; in *RMS* 1631 the estate is *Blackfuird alias Champunyie*, and the pair of names continue to be used in deeds until 1784, the *y* standing for the 'yogh' letter ӡ sometimes written as *z*. The 1577 spelling resembles the name of Champnay in Lennox which was owned by a George Champnay in 1480; while a George Champnay is mentioned in *RMS* 1478 as a deceased proprietor in Edinburgh, and three other Champnays or Champneys (two of them heralds) were connected with the Scottish court between 1509 and 1547. This surname might have come from the French *champenois*, native of Champagne (with the stress anglicised in the normal way) and would fit in with both the surname *Champenay* recorded in 1343, and the local tradition at Champany, West Lothian, which (unlike incomers or visitors, who follow the spelling) pronounces it *'Champ-ni*. On the other hand, the longer form *Champunyie* recorded at Blackford in 1631 and used, with obvious corruptions, from then on, suggests the surnames of *de Chaumpagne*, introduced into Scotland prior to 1219, and of *Tschampany*, herald of France in the Scottish court in 1517, as well as a pronunciation *Shawm-* or *Cham-'pa-nyi*. Although the traditional pronunciation of the West Lothian name may show how the shorter form could evolve from the longer one, the fact that at Blackford the longer form comes later is puzzling, unless we can assume that Stewart used a colloquial form in his protocol, and that the longer one was used in formal deeds now lost. Be that as it may, this early example of a fancy name might prove even more interesting were its history known. It was revived at EAST CHAMPANYIE in 1984.

CHANCELLOR'S CLOSE and **COURT** (Canongate) *see under* BRODIE'S CLOSE, Canongate.

CHANCELOT (Bonnington) is shown on *Ainslie* 1804 as a property of 18 acres in Bonnington, marching with Easter Warriston in the west and stretching up from the Water of Leith to the Ferry road. The name seems to have been given after it was bought by John Robertson, accountant in Edinburgh, in about 1790. It has been ingeniously explained, on the assumption that *chance* here carried its modern meaning of 'accidental'; but the probability is simply that the name is

Scots *chance lot* in the contemporary meanings of 'fortunate or lucky' feu or plot—the same usage that led to hostelries being called Chance Inn. In about 1890 the frontage to Ferry Road was built up as CHANCELOT TERRACE, and this was followed by CHANCELOT CRESCENT, named in 1901. CHANCELOT GROVE, actually in Easter Warriston, was named in about 1937.

CHAPEL LANE (East End) *see* CATHEDRAL LANE, East End.

CHAPEL LANE (South Leith) is given thus on *Kirkwood* 1817 but is CHAPEL STREET on *Wood* 1777 and in *Aitchison's Directory* 1801. The name derived from the Episcopal chapel which functioned here from about 1730 until 1788; and it must have displaced an older name, since the street is shown as already well-established on *Siege of Leith* 1560, and the building which later housed the chapel seems to have been a dwelling house of the same period, for according to *Robertson* its front door had a 'marriage lintel' (now removed to St James' Church Hall in John's Place) bearing the initials TF and AM, together with the lines 'THAY AR WELCOME HEIR THAT GOD DOIS LOVE AND FEIR' and the date 1590.

CHAPEL STREET (Bristo) is a short section of the ancient way into the town by Bristo which got this special name shortly after a *chapel of ease* of St Cuthbert's parish (later to become Buccleuch Parish Church) was opened here in 1756. Although *Ainslie* 1780 and other maps prior to *Ainslie* 1804 attach the name to the street later styled WEST NICHOLSON STREET, it is clear that this was a map error, for in the charter of 1768 which extended the chapel's ground to include the WINDMILL (*which see*) the street fronting the site is named as *Chapple Street*.

CHAPEL WYND (West Port) *see under* LADY WYND, West Port,

CHARLES STREET (Bristo) was laid out as part of James Brown's George Square development. It was named by 1771, evidently because the site was a bleaching field which Charles Jackson had set up some 60 or 70 years earlier and named *Charlesfield*, not only for himself but also for his godfather, Charles II. The name CHARLESFIELD was revived for a part of the street pedestrianised in 1982. CHARLES STREET LANE, shown thus on *Ordnance Survey* 1893, is shown as *George's Mews Street* on the feuing plan of George Square in 1779; *also see* GEORGE SQUARE.

CHARLOTTE LANE and **PLACE** (West End) *see under* RANDOLPH PLACE, West End.

CHARLOTTE SQUARE and **STREET** (New Town) *see under* NEW TOWN.

CHARLOTTE STREET and **LANE** (South Leith) *see* QUEEN CHARLOTTE STREET, South Leith.

CHARTERHALL ROAD (Blackford) was developed in 1897 and named for Charterhall, near Duns, which like Blackford was owned by the Trotters of Mortonhall. The name was carried on to CHARTERHALL GROVE in 1960.

CHARTERIS CLOSE (south side of foot of Canongate) is listed in *Williamson's Directory* 1779 and still shown on *Brown & Watson* 1793, but like its neighbour PENMAN'S CLOSE (*which see*) it is omitted on *Ainslie* 1804. The naming is obscure.

CHARTERIS' CLOSE (50 High Street) *see* HYNDFORD'S CLOSE.

CHARTERIS CLOSE (South Leith) is mentioned in *Williamson's Directory* 1780, but remains to be identified.

CHARTERS CLOSE (188 Canongate) *see* St JOHN'S CLOSE, Canongate.

CHATTERRIG (Oxgangs) was the name of a field in Oxgangs, shown on *Colinton Mains & Oxgangs* 1813 and *Ordnance Survey* 1852-1938, bounded on its south side by a right of way now represented by OXGANGS AVENUE. The name is Scots for a *rig* or ridge made up of numerous *chats* or pebbles: in this case a mound of glacial gravel that may have formed the dam of the post-glacial loch which once stretched from here up to Colinton Mains and Colinton, as shown on the *Geological Survey*. In 1983 the name was adopted for a path at the west end of the mound.

CHERRY TREE GARDENS and **PARK** (Currie) were begun in 1964, and development continued in CHERRY TREE GROVE (1966) AVENUE and CRESCENT (1968) and CHERRY TREE LOAN, PLACE and VIEW in 1970. As in the case of the adjoining ROWAN TREE AVENUE and GROVE (1969) the group names were fancy, although backed up by planting trees of these sorts. As a further variation of the theme, WILLOW TREE PLACE was added in 1994.

CHESNUT STREET (Granton) *see under* GRANTON HARBOUR.

CHESSEL'S COURT (240 Canongate) is listed on *Ainslie* 1780, but the court and the building on its south side, figured as *Chesel Building*, appear on *Edgar* 1765. It was built by Archibald Chessel, wright, on land acquired from David, son of Alexander Pirie, merchant (*see under* PIRIE'S CLOSE, 246 Canongate) and also from David Milne, mason, *see* MILNE'S CLOSE, 218 Canongate. Chessel had a seat in the Tron Kirk in 1745, and still owned the Court in 1767; but by 1779 he was dead, and his widow was managing the property. Being in the south CANONGATEHEAD, the court was part of Edinburgh, not the burgh of Canongate.

CHESSER AVENUE (West Gorgie) was formed in about 1909 to give access to the New Markets, built in western fields of Gorgie farm in 1909-12. Councillor John William Chesser was convener of the Markets Committee of the Town Council at the time, and the street is shown on *Ordnance Survey* 1912 as named for him. He became Lord Provost in 1919, and in 1921, just before his term of office expired, the name was extended to CHESSER CRESCENT, GARDENS, GROVE and LOAN.

CHESTERLAW (Newliston) is recorded in *RMS* 1649 and shown on *Blaeu* 1654 as well as on a plan of Newliston 1767 (*RHP 2155*) while the CHESTERHALL shown on *Adair/Cooper* 1735 may be an error or else a related place name on the nearby *haugh*. The name is Anglian *caester hlaw* or Scots *chester law*, small hill with traces of ancient fortifications. The terrain suggests that such a feature would have been in the upper part of the farm, which judging by the field pattern shown in 1767 (virtually repeated on *Ordnance Survey* 1852) must have been drastically remodelled, north of an arbitrary line, when Newliston policies were laid out by William Adam in 1730. While 'chester' could imply either a British or a Roman fort, the probability that Roman Dere Street ran through this locality on its way to Linlithgow (*see under* ROMAN ROADS) would also make it likely that there was a Roman fort hereabouts, covering the crossing of the Almond.

CHESTER STREET (Coates) *see under* COATES.

CHEYNE'S CLOSE (Canongatehead) is mentioned in *Protocols of George Home* 1715 and *Adam Watt* 1716; and this was evidently an alternative name for one of the closes (as yet unidentified) between St Mary Wynd and Old Playhouse Close.

CHEYNE'S CLOSE (7 West Bow and High Street) *see* DONALDSON'S CLOSE.

CHEYNE STREET (Stockbridge) was formed in about 1824 in a property in Dean Street which had already been partly developed as HERMITAGE PLACE, Stockbridge, *which see*. It enters the *PO Directory* in 1825, when a Captain Cheyne RE, shown in the previous year as resident (along with a Colonel Cheyne RE) in Great King Street, is listed as at 19 Cheyne Street; and it is a fair assumption that the captain had bought the ground and named the development for himself.

CHRISTIAN CRESCENT and **GROVE** (Easter Duddingston) together with BRAND DRIVE and GARDENS, were formed in 1957 in the *Clays park* and *Thorntree park* of the early 19th-century farm of *Duddingston Bank* or *Mains*, and also on the site of its steading, which was just south of the south entry to Brand Drive. Yet although this ground was outwith the former burgh of Portobello, the streets were named for two of its Provosts. Major Hugh Christian had served two terms as Provost with distinction, from 1882 to 1888, before his election for a third term had to be declared invalid because he had neither a residence nor business within the burgh. Alexander Brand, elected in 1894, was the last Provost of Portobello; and it was he who chaired the final meeting of its Council in 1896, two days before the burgh was amalgamated with Edinburgh.

CHRISTIAN PATH (Portobello) originated as a track alongside the *leche* or slow-running burn which was one of the medieval boundaries of FIGGATE—*which see*. The maps of the 1850s show it as a short cut from the railway station to Sandford Street—as Sandford Gardens was then called; but in about 1886 it was made up as a proper path, connected to the rebuilt railway station by an underpass and extended eastwards to Hope Lane; and it was named for Hugh Christian, then Provost of Portobello, because he had led the campaign for replacement of the ruinous sheds which had served as a railway station since 1844.

CHRISTIE MILLER AVENUE, GROVE and **PLACE** (Craigentinny) *see under* CRAIGENTINNY.

CHRISTIE'S CLOSE (72 Cowgate) is shown on *Ainslie* 1780 and *Kirkwood* 1817, but was cleared for the building of George IV Bridge in about 1829. The origin of the name has not been traced.

CHUCKIE PEND (Tollcross) *see under* St ANTHONY'S PLACE, Tollcross.

CHUCKLIE KNOWE (Dreghorn) is shown as a quarry on *Ordnance Survey* 1852. The name is Scots '*knowe* known for *chuckies* or pebbles'.

CHURCH HILL (Morningside) *see under* GREENHILL.

CHURCH LANE and **STREET** (Stockbridge) along with WEMYSS PLACE were directly developed from the *kirk loan* shown on *Roy* 1753, which led from Stockbridge to the parish kirk of St Cuthbert's, while CHURCH LANE SQUARE appears on *Wood* 1823 as part of the development of the MORAY ESTATE, *which see*. In 1966, a proposal to eliminate duplication of street names included a grand clear-out of *Church-* street names in Edinburgh and Leith—only *Church Lane* in Duddingston escaped, by having an unnecessary (and untrue) *Old* tacked on in front of it. Apparently the reasoning was that *there were now no churches in these streets*: it was not appreciated that few had ever had such a thing in them, and that the term *kirk road* or *lane* normally meant a route to the parish kirk from an outlying part of the parish. Thus this lane from Stockbridge was renamed by borrowing from the nearby Gloucester Place, and became GLOUCESTER LANE and STREET, with its offshoot (rather pretentiously, for a triangular meuse?) GLOUCESTER SQUARE.

CHURCH PLACE (Queensferry) is a side name in the LOAN, in the vicinity of the parish church of St Andrew, opened in 1894 as a United Presbyterian church.

CHURCH STREET (North Leith) *see under* St NINIAN'S LANE, North Leith.

CIRCUS LANE (Northern New Town) is the meuse lane serving the northern half of ROYAL CIRCUS (*which see*) and as such was an integral part of Playfair's design. It is shown on *Knox* 1821 as already in course of building, and is named on *Pollock* 1834.

CIRCUS PLACE (Northern New Town) was probably adopted from the beginning as the general name for the four terraces branching from Playfair's ROYAL CIRCUS, *which see*. Two of them are named on *Kirkwood* 1823: one, shown as *East Circus Place*, appears on *Pollock* 1834 as SOUTHEAST CIRCUS PLACE; the other, *West Circus Place*, appears on Pollock as *Southwest Circus Place*, but reverted to *West Circus Place*, as shown on *Ordnance Survey* 1893, and was finally renamed CIRCUS GARDENS in 1898, at a resident's request. The other two terraces are shown on *Pollock* as NORTHEAST and NORTHWEST CIRCUS PLACE.

THE CITADEL (North Leith) was a fortress built in 1656 by the Cromwellians under General Monk, on the site of the ST NICHOLAS KIRK of North Leith, *which see*. It was pentagonal on plan, some 250 yards in diameter, and COMMERCIAL STREET represents its centre line. It cost Edinburgh a levy of £5,000 at the time, and a further £6,000 only seven years later, when the astute and unscrupulous Earl of Lauderdale forced the town to buy it back from the government. It was hardly built before the sea began to erode it: *Collins* 1693 shows it with its north bastion washed away; on *Naish* 1709 the east and west bastions have also gone; and *Fergus & Robinson* 1759 and *Wood* 1777 show only half the fortress left. Apart from the lower storey of its eastern gatehouse, still standing west of Dock Street, only the ghost of the great fortification remains in the sett of Dock Street, Coburg Street, Couper Street and Prince Regent Street, which run parallel with its ramparts and ditches. CITADEL GREEN was originally the central parade ground within the fortresss, but became the site of North Leith Railway Station in about 1844 and was redeveloped as CITADEL PLACE in 1979. In 1979 also, CITADEL STREET, shown on *Regality of Canongate* 1813 as already developed as the first new access to the Docks, was reduced to a mere rump.

THE CITY CHAMBERS (High Street) originated as the ROYAL EXCHANGE, built in 1754-61 to a design by John Adam, amended by John Fergus. It was the town's third attempt to provide a covered place of exchange for the merchants, but like the others (built in the Parliament Close in 1685, and shortly after 1700) it failed to wean them from their practice of dealing in the open air, and much of the accommodation was sold off, only to be laboriously bought back again after 1810, when it was decided to remove the city administration to this building from the TOLBOOTH, *which see*. In 1898-1904 Robert Morham, City Architect, rebuilt the arcade fronting the High Street, replaced the great 8-storey tenement of the Writers (*see under* WRITERS' COURT) which had continued to form the northwest frontage of the quadrangle of the Exchange, and extended the building in a northwest wing; and in 1930-34 Ebenezer MacRae, City Architect, developed east and west wings on the High Street frontage.

CLACKMAE ROAD and **COURT** (Liberton) *see under* LEADERVALE ROAD, Liberton.

THE CLAPPERFIELD (Nether Liberton) is the traditional name for the flat ground stretching westwards from Double Hedges Road to the crest of the bank above the Braid burn. There is no evidence for the suggestion in *Good's Liberton* that it was somehow associated with the mill or 'clapper' of Nether Liberton; and the name is much more likely to be from Scots *clapper* (from Old French *clapier*), a rabbit warren. Before the introduction of the turnip and other means of wintering stock, rabbits were an important source of meat, and clappers were often specially built for them. EAST CLAPPERFIELD was named in 1978 as being immediately east of the Clapperfield and perhaps originally part of it.

CLAPPER KNOWE (Cramond) is named on *Roy* 1753, apparently as a farm; but the knowe is a spur in the slope some 500 yards north of Lauriston farm steading, shown on *Silverknowes* 1841 along with the Golden knowe about 150 yards further east. The name is Scots *clapper* from Old French *clapier*, a rabbit warren, *see above*.

CLAPPER LANE (Nether Liberton) was named in 1990. The name derived from CLAPPERFIELD (*which see*) imported here as a house name, in the belief that (as suggested in *Good's Liberton*) it referred to the ancient mill of Nether Liberton—'clapper', the Scots term for a kenspeckle and noisy part of a mill's machinery, being often used colloquially for the mill itself.

CLAPPERTON PLACE (Abbeymount) was developed by 1887 and was presumably named for its builder.

CLAREBANK CRESCENT (South Leith) *see under* CLAREMONT PARK.

CLAREMONT CRESCENT (Broughton) is shown planned and named on Knox 1821, and was begun by 1823. Like other streets of the time it was named for Claremont, the Surrey home of Prince Leopold of Saxe Coburg (*see under* CLAREMONT PARK, South Leith). (EAST) CLAREMONT STREET is sketched on *Knox* 1821 and was begun in 1824. The name originally belonged only to the section west of Claremont Crescent: it was extended eastwards to Broughton Point when the western part of BROUGHTON ROAD (*which see*) was suppressed in about 1870. CLAREMONT BANK and GROVE were developed and named in 1935.

(WEST) CLAREMONT STREET and **CLAREMONT PLACE** (Stockbridge) *see under* SAXE-COBURG PLACE, Stockbridge.

CLARENCE STREET (Stockbridge) was begun, under the name SILVERMILLS STREET, in 1825, but by 1828 it was renamed for William, Duke of Clarence, who became heir presumptive in 1827 and came to the throne as William IV upon the death of his eldest brother, George IV, in 1830.

CLARENDON CRESCENT (Dean) was begun in 1850, the first scheme to take advantage of the provision, almost 20 years earlier, of the DEAN BRIDGE, *which see*. Planned to be named for Queen Victoria, in the event it was named for George Villiers, 4th Earl of Clarendon, highly successful at this time as Viceroy of Ireland. It was followed by a pair of streets intended to be named for the two English universities, but although OXFORD TERRACE (1853) was so named, the proposed *Cambridge Terrace* became ETON TERRACE, after the English public school, in 1855. The reason for the naming of LENNOX STREET (1861) has yet to be discovered.

CLARINDA TERRACE (Liberton) *see under* KIRK BRAE, Liberton.

CLARK'S or **BAILIE CLARK'S CLOSE** (High Street) is shown on *Ainslie* 1780 and was 'at the back of the Weighhouse', a site now in the roadway in front of the Tolbooth kirk. It was named for George Clark, merchant, bailie in 1698 and 1700, who owned the house at the foot of 7 West Bow, later belonging to Provost Steward and Alexander Donaldson, *see* DONALDSON'S CLOSE. The close is also recorded in 1635 as COCHRANE'S, for James Cochrane, merchant, bailie in 1629, who had his house here. It seems also to have been called ARCHIBALD'S, listed in *PO Directory* as 3 West Bow. *Williamson's Directory* lists a Mrs Archibald in Castlehill in 1773 and 1780, and John Archibald was a merchant at the Bowheid in 1799.

CLARK PLACE (Queensferry) is shown on *Ordnance Survey* 1893, and was presumably named for its developer. After a period when it was put to commercial use, the site is now part of PLEWLANDCROFT, *see under* PLEWLANDS, Queensferry.

CLARK ROAD (Bangholm) was developed in 1899 on part of Bangholm farm, owned by the Heriot Trust, and was named for Sir Thomas Clark, then convener of the Trust's finance committee. The name was extended to CLARK AVENUE, on the east side of the farm place, in 1910, and to CLARK PLACE in 1980.

CLAVERHOUSE DRIVE (Liberton) *see under* NORTHFIELD, Liberton.

CLAYCLOTE (Corstorphine) is shown on *Saughton* 1795 as the most northerly part of Saughton estate, although the detail on several maps suggests that it was worked from Corstorphine, by means of a bridge over the Stank. The name, which seems to have been wrongly interpreted in modern times as 'clay cott(age)' is early Scots *clay clote* or *clout*, a patch of clayey land; and this ground, now the site of most of the *Broomhall* and *Wester Broom* streets, was in fact once part of the bed of the ancient Gyle Loch, *see under* CORSTORPHINE *and* THE GYLE.

CLAYHILLS (Balerno) is shown on *Fowler* 1845 as a farm which seems to have been worked along with DEAN PARK, Balerno (*which see*) from about 1850 onwards, and was renamed LOVEDALE for the farmer David Love of Dean Park or his family. The name was revived at CLAYHILLS PARK (1979) and GROVE (1989).

CLAYLANDS (Newbridge) appears on *Ordnance Survey* 1852. The name is descriptive and may have been a field name before the farm was formed.

CLAYPOTTS (Newhaven) *see under* HAWTHORNVALE, Newhaven.

CLEARBURN (Prestonfield) is mentioned in 1677 among lands added to PRIESTFIELD (*which see*) and in *White's Liberton* 1786 the name is attached to the lower reach of the Pow burn (now culverted) that flows in a loop from Cameron round the north boundary of the Common Myre and joins the Braid or Peffer burn at Forkenford. The name could be read as an exact translation of PEFFER BURN (*which see*) and while this is difficult to dismiss as mere coincidence it would imply that the meaning of British *pefr* was not forgotten before the NormanFrench word *clere* came into early Scots in about 1100. CLEARBURN HOUSE figures on *Roy* 1753 and is shown in detail on *Prestonfield* 1824. It was built before 1708, but was demolished in about 1890, and its policies and the adjoining field *Clearburn Park* are now occupied bv Priestfield Gardens and Avenue. CLEARBURN ROAD, CRESCENT and GARDENS were formed in 1927: the first in the *Common Myre park* (part of the town's common grazings in the Middle Ages) and the other two in the *Cellar* or *Siller park, see under* CELLARBANK, Prestonfield.

CLEEKIM DRIVE and **ROAD** (Niddrie) *see under* CLEIKIMIN.

CLEGHORN'S CLOSE (once 15 now about 27 or 29 Grassmarket) is listed on *Ainslie* 1780, and was probably named for Thomas Cleghorn, wine merchant in Grassmarket, and Old Bailie in 1773. In *PO Directory* 1827 it is KINNIBURGH'S, a personal name also occurring as Kinnieburgh and Kennieburgh (but not with Grassmarket addresses) in *Williamson's Directory* 1773. The close is said to have been also GEDDES' and HUTCHISON'S, but nothing is known of them. The properties on the site of the close are now entered from PORTEOUS LAND, *which see.*

CLEIKIMIN (Niddrie) is recorded in 1690 and 1741, mentioned as *Klikhimin* in *White's Liberton* 1786 and shown on *Laurie* 1763 as a farm 300 yards south of Niddrie Mill crossroads. The name is Old Norse, from *klaki*, stony ground, and *minni*, a mouth, and means the stony outlet of a watercourse. Another *Cleikimin* (later a quarry) is shown on *Roy* 1753 at Wester Melville, and the name also occurs at Howgate in Midlothian, and Addinston in Lauderdale (where the landscape above Cleikimin Bridge vividly illustrates the meaning of the name) as well as in Lanarkshire and Shetland. The form *Cleickhim in's*, used in Cramond Kirk Session minutes 1690, attempts to interpret the name as though it were a Scots phrase, and this was probably also the origin of a local form *Cleekim* used in 1976 for CLEEKIM DRIVE and ROAD in Niddrie Mill, outwith the Cleikimin farm. In 1980, however, new streets within it, on ground already called *Cleikiminfield*, were named CLEIKIMINFIELD and CLEIKIMINRIG.

CLERICS HILL (Kirkliston) was coined in 1968 as the name of this new development on GREIG'S HILL (*which see*), the reputed and indeed probable site of the camp of Edward I at 'Temple Liston' in June 1298, prior to the battle of Falkirk—*see also* KING EDWARD'S WAY. In particular the name commemorates the 18 English churchmen in the camp who were murdered by some of Edward's Welsh levies in the course of a drunken brawl.

CLERK STREET (South Side) is sketched on *Newington* 1795 and *Ainslie* 1804 as part of an 'intended road to London by Coldstream, Kelso, Jedburgh, Selkirk etc.'. While *Town Council Minutes* 1814 refer to the way south from St Patrick's Square as still a 'footpath' it is shown as a roadway on *Kirkwood* 1817 and labelled CLERK STREET throughout its length. This map also shows proposals for St Patrick's Square and Dr Hope's ground as far south as Montague Street, and *Kirkwood* 1823 shows these as largely carried out. Meantime the ground further south to Preston Street remained undeveloped, even although an ambitious plan for a 'new town' here had been shown on *Ainslie* 1804 as well as *Stranger's Guide* 1816. A simpler plan appears on *Lothian* 1829, but no progress is shown on *Pollock* 1834. *Ordnance Survey* 1852 shows the name SOUTH CLERK STREET, but only patchy and irregular developments; and the area was not substantially built up much before 1870. The name *Clerk Street* probably derived from William Clerk, Clerk to the Signet, recorded in *Town Council Minutes* 1816 as owning various grounds in and near St Patrick's Square.

CLERMISTON is recorded in *Dunfermline Register* c.1250, and the early spellings *Clerbaudiston or terram de Clerribaldi* show that it incorporates an AngloNorman name of Flemish or German origin in *Clerembald's toun* or farm place. It is shown on *Adair/Cooper* 1735; and *Roy* 1753 shows it connected to Corstorphine and to the Queensferry road by a road passing west of its policies, but this seems to have been suppressed quite soon afterwards, *see under* FERRIEGATE, Corstorphine. CLERMISTON ROAD, referred to in 1646 as *the walk that goes to Cramond*, is shown on *Corstorphine* 1754 and was evidently named as leading to the estate; while its alternative (or sectional) name CLERMISTON BRAE referred to its steepness, although the name CLERMISTONHILL, shown on *Cramond Roads* 1812 at NT 202744 near the summit of the road, might be related to it. The subdivision of the estate into NORTH CLERMISTON and (SOUTH) CLERMISTON is shown on *Corstorphine* 1754. *Laurie* 1763 shows the two farms; and *Knox* 1812 shows CLERMISTON HOUSE, built in 1792. *Cramond Roads* 1812 calls North Clermiston *Nether Clermiston*. South *Clermiston* steading is shown as such on *Ordnance Survey* 1852, but on *Fowler* 1845 it is *Mid Clermiston*, and on *Ordnance Survey* 1893 it is CLERMISTON MAINS, *which see*. CLERMISTON TERRACE was built by 1912, and was named as fronting Clermiston Road. Another twelve *Clermiston* streets are in North Clermiston, where CLERMISTON AVENUE, named in 1937, prompted the naming in 1953 of CLERMISTON CRESCENT, DRIVE, GARDENS, GREEN, GROVE, HILL, LOAN, MEDWAY, PARK, PLACE and VIEW, with the rather unfortunate outcome that later streets in the historic heart of Clermiston were denied the use of that proper name, and were called after the Victorian houses of CLERWOOD and FOX COVERT *which see*.

CLERMISTON MAINS or **SOUTH CLERMISTON** (Clermiston) together with land to the west shown on *Corstorphine* 1754 as still part of CRAMOND MUIR, was developed for housing in 1957; and the town council chose to follow the precedent set earlier at THE INCH by naming the streets after characters and places in Sir Walter Scott's novels—in this case, taking names from Robert Louis Stevenson's *Kidnapped*, which had a certain aptness in the locality, since in the story young David Balfour approaches his uncle's 'House of Shaws' (which Stevenson partly modelled on Craigcrook Tower) by going over 'Clermiston Hill'. Hence the names of ALAN BRECK GARDENS, ARDSHIEL AVENUE, BALFRON LOAN, DOCHART DRIVE, DUART CRESCENT, DURAR DRIVE (it should have been 'Duror') ESSENDEAN PLACE and TERRACE, GLENURE LOAN, HOSEASON GARDENS,

MORVERN STREET, RANNOCH TERRACE, RANSOME GARDENS and TORRANCE PARK. RANNOCH GROVE and ROAD were added in 1960 and RANNOCH PLACE in 1968, the novel being perhaps exhausted of other names.

CLERWOOD BANK, GARDENS etc (Clermiston) were planned in 1963 as a group of streets within the policies of the 18th-century CLERMISTON HOUSE (since displaced by Queen Margaret College) and accordingly it was proposed to call them *Clermiston House Bank, Gardens* etc; but the developers pressed for the less clumsy but graceless *Clerwood*, which had been coined from Cler(miston) and the wood(s) of Corstorphine Hill as a name for a mid Victorian mansion on the other side of Clermiston Road: hence CLERWOOD BANK, GARDENS, GROVE, LOAN, PARK, PLACE, ROW, TERRACE, VIEW and WAY.

CLEUCHMAID GATE (Currie) *see* CLOCHMEAD, Currie.

CLIFTON (Newbridge) is recorded in *RMS* 1430 as *Clyftoun*, while the two names *Clyftoun* and *Clyftounhall* appear together in *RMS* 1503. The first is Anglian *clife tún*, farm place at the cliff, referring to the 100-foot scarp above the Almond; but the first part is perhaps more likely to carry the meanings of Old Norse *kleif*, a steep slope or the steep way up it. CLIFTONHALL and CLIFTON appear on a par with each other on *Blaeu* 1654, probably surveyed in 1596; and even if on *Adair* 1682 *Cliftonhal* is shown boldly and with Adair's mansionhouse symbol, while *Clifton toun* figures more humbly, it is likely that Cliftonhall was a 15th-century subdivision of Clifton, and that the ending *-hall* does not mean that it was the 'hall of Clifton', but is Anglian *halh*, haugh or land in the neuk or bend of the river: a description that fits the northern part of the estate very well indeed. CLIFTONHALL ROAD is simply the modern descriptive name of the road leading to it. The historic CLIFTON, still named thus in 1921, became WEST CLIFTON before 1971. CLIFTON MAINS is shown on *Roy* 1753 as *Mains* beside the name *Clifton Hall*; and while some of the later maps show it as *Cliftonhall Mains*, on others it is *Clifton Mains*. CLIFTONHALL MILL, recorded in 1591, had become LIN'S MILL (*which see*) by 1645. 'Clifton Staithe' is a fancy name, importing English *staithe*, a landing place, given to the house in the 1930s.

CLIFTON TERRACE (Haymarket) *see under* MAITLAND STREET, West End.

CLIFTON TERRACE (Portobello) was begun by 1888 and was apparently named for or along with the adjoining *Clifton House*. It was renamed in 1967 as part of BAILEYFIELD ROAD, *which see*. CLIFTON SQUARE was formed by 1893.

CLINTON ROAD (Greenhill) *see under* GREENHILL.

CLOCHMEAD (Currie) figures thus on *Roy* 1753 as a name written along the ancient route through the hills from Currie to Glencorse, and the variants CLOCHMAID GATE recorded in 1900, and CLEUCHMAID GATE still in current use, tend to confirm that the name refers to the *gate* or road itself rather than the saddle it crosses. Since this last is scarcely a *cleuch* (typically a deep and steep-sided ravine) it is likely that *cleuch* has replaced *cloch* only recently and by false analogy with the nearby ravine names of Dens Cleuch and White Cleuch; and there is no room for doubt that the further variant MAIDEN'S CLEUCH, appearing in the 20th century, is merely a corrupt attempt to impose a Scots word order on 'cleuch maid', which has every appearance of being Celtic *cloch* or *clach*, a stone, followed by an adjective in the normal position. Indeed, the *Statistical Account* 1845 refers to 'the ravine at Cleuchmaidstone'; and there is a vast stone near the summit of the path, a disc-shaped boulder weighing upwards of 2 tons, forming a stile in the march dyke but being altogether too massive to have been brought to the site for the purpose. Its position suggests that the name may be early Gaelic *cloch meid*, stone at the neck or middle (of the pass).

CLOCK (SORROW) MILL (Abbeyhill) is recorded as *Clocksorrow mill* 1540, *Clokisholm mylne* 1569 and *Clokisholow mill* 1570, while the building (or a house replacing it) is shown on *Ainslie* 1804 as *Clock Mill*. Since the name also occurs as *Clocksorrow mill* at Linlithgow, it evidently related to mills: and indeed the first part is a variant of *clack*, the Scots term for the noisy clapper of a mill, and by extension for the mill itself, as also found at *Clockmill*, near Duns. Each of the three variants of the second part of the name is evidently a land name: -*sorrow* from Old Norse *saurrar*, plural of *saurr*, swampy ground; -*holm* from Old Norse *holmr*, an island or dry patch in a boggy area; and -*holow*, if not a misreading of the charter, would be early Scots *holwe*, a hollow. Each of them would fit the site at Abbeyhill, and equally that mentioned in West Lothian, where the mill stood on the *bog haugh* at the outfall to Linlithgow loch. At Abbeyhill, the mill gave its name to the CLOCKMILL BRIDGE over the Tummel burn, and this in turn gave it to CLOCKMILL LANE, the old road to Restalrig, passing St MARGARET'S WELL, *which see*. The Lane was altered in about 1818 to suit the new London Road, and again in about 1845 to suit the new railway; but its eastern half was altogether suppressed in the development of Meadowbank Sports Centre in 1968.

CLOVE(N) CRAIG (Dalmeny) is shown on *Adair* 1682. The name is Scots, evidently referring to the south spur of Craigie Hill, which is divided from the main part of the craigs by a dramatic cleft, for the most part natural, although it looks like a road cutting. A cist burial was found near the east end of this gully, and just east of this again *Knox* 1812 shows a clachan *Cloven Houses*, given as *Clove* on *Ordnance Survey* 1852.

THE CLOVENSTONE (Slateford) was a standing stone, shown on *Knox* 1812 and *Ordnance Survey* 1852, which stood at about NT 214700 in a field named *Clovenstone park* (now the southwestern part of Kingsknowe Public Park) until it was lost in the final extension of Old Redhall Quarry in the 1870s. The name suggests that it may have been more than a single stone *see under* KNOCKILLBRAE.

Among the lands in Redhall valued for teinds in 1631 (listed in *Steuart's Colinton* p327) *Clovingstoun* appears to be land named for the stone, despite the spelling, which is clearly wrong.

CLOVENSTONE DRIVE, GARDENS, PARK and **ROAD** (Wester Hailes) were named in 1970 under the mistaken impression that THE CLOVENSTONE (*which see*) was 'nearby', whereas in fact it was half a mile away, in Easter Hailes. The streets for the most part occupy the site of the historic centre of WESTER HAILES, (*which see*) and inby fields shown on *Wester Hailes* 1818. This plan of the farm shows the field stretching from the vicinity of Clovenstone Primary School eastwards to the Lanark Road as the *Alcorn Park*. This might be from the surname Alcorn or Auldcorn recorded in Edinburgh in the 1690s; but alternatively it is conceivable that the field name belongs to the group of Celtic names found at DUMBRYDEN and WESTER HAILES, *which see*: at a guess, it might be *allt cornadh*, curving burn.

CLUBBIEDEAN (Colinton) is shown on *Ordnance Survey* 1852 as the name of the burn feeding the *Clubbiedean reservoir*; but since the name is Scots *clabby*, miry, and *dene*, a long winding valley, it may have attached more generally to the course of the main LADY BURN (*which see*) before it was dammed to form the reservoirs in 1845.

CLUFFLAT (Queensferry) is described in 1440 as lying between the Echline burn and the *Milburn*, presumably the burn at Linn Mill; and this would imply that the Clufflat was more or less what *Dundas* 1757 shows as the *Netherfields* of Echline, together with smaller parks at Sentry Knowe. The name crops up on the same map at *Clayflat Knowe Park* (now built up as ECHLINE GROVE) immediately west of the Echline burn, and thus marking the east end of the Clufflat. The name is Anglian *cloh flat*, level ground (or, in a later meaning, a division of land) at or near the cleuch or dene—the latter probably the one at the Linn, although the *Ordnance Surveys* 1854 and 1893 also show a much smaller dene near the mouth of the Echline burn. The name was continued in 1989 in the street names CLUFFLAT and CLUFFLAT BRAE.

CLUNY AVENUE etc (South Morningside) *see under* EGYPT, South Morningside.

CLYDE STREET (New Town) is shown and named on *Ainslie* 1804; but parts of it, together with CLYDE STREET LANE, had been in existence for several years previously, and are shown on *Brown & Watson* 1793 as a meuse. It was presumably named for the river, probably in response to the naming of FORTH STREET in 1802.

THE COALHILL (Leith) is approximately the area now bounded by Tolbooth Wynd, Henderson Street, a line about 35 yards west of Parliament Street, and the river frontage. Along with the OLD BRIDGE END and North Leith, it was granted to Holyrood Abbey by David I in 1128 and became part of the St Leonard's lands within the regality of the Canongate. Thus it was often called St LEONARD'S; and the chief entry into it was St LEONARD'S WYND or LANE, a name still in use up until about 1830, when the area was considerably altered, *see under* PARLIAMENT CLOSE. While the name COALHILL is recorded in 1606, most early references are to THE HILL (the waterfront being THE SHORE, *which see*) and this clearly reflects the fact that it was the summit of the higher ground in the early settlement, a promontory somewhat detached from its hinterland by the hollow or saddle occupied by the DUB RAW, *which see*; and before the quays were built it rose steeply above the river, in a gradient of nearly 1 in 2. There is nothing to connect the name with coal: there are no outcrops, and no references to the trade in early times—indeed, a *Town Council Minute* of 1616 specifies coal storage at the Timber Howff or Bush, at the opposite end of the harbour. The name is a hill name, perhaps akin to *Calehill*, which incorporates Old English *calu*, bald or bare, frequently used in hill names; but more likely it is from Old Norse *kollr*, bald summit, a term which is still represented in Scots by *cole*, a heap, and has produced names like *Collhill* elsewhere.

COALIE PARK (North Leith) was laid out in the 1970s on the site of the coal depot in Coburg Street, familiarly known as *the Coalie*, which dated from the 1880s.

COATES is shown on *Blaeu* 1654 as *Cots* and is listed in *RMS* 1581 as *Coittis*, among properties of Holyrood abbey. The name is early Scots *cotes*, often meaning 'cottages' but in this case more likely to mean 'enclosures or shelters for animals'. The mansion of COATES, later EASTER COATES, was built in about 1615 by John Byres, merchant burgess of Edinburgh, *see also* BYRES CLOSE, High Street. COATES BAUKS, from Scots *bauk*, a ridge, often marking a boundary, was also called BELL'S LOAN (*see under* BELL'S MILLS) and was a loaning which divided Easter and Wester Coates from each other. WESTER COATES HOUSE, shown but not named on *Roy* 1753, was demolished in 1869, giving place to the gardens of Lansdowne Crescent immediately north of Grosvenor Street. SOUTH COATES, named on *Ordnance Survey* 1852 but confusingly given as *Whitehouse* on *Knox* 1812 (*see also* WHITEHOUSE, Haymarket) is shown on *Kirkwood* 1817, along with the farm of WESTER COATES some 120 yards further west along the Glasgow road. In 1813 William Walker of Easter Coates began to develop his estate at COATES CRESCENT, following a revised version of a plan he had drawn up in 1808, in which the principal street was named MELVILLE STREET, for Robert Dundas, 2nd Viscount Melville, MP for Midlothian in 1801 and first lord of the Admiralty 1822-27. The revised plan named MELVILLE CRESCENT (where Dundas's statue was eventually put up in 1857) and MELVILLE PLACE. By 1823 WILLIAM STREET and WALKER STREET (earlier called COATES STREET) had been named for the original developer, and MANOR PLACE had been named for its site in the policies of Easter Coates House, shown as *Manor Place* on an estate plan in 1799. Despite a wide gap between dates, it seems likely that the naming of CHESTER STREET in 1862 and ROTHESAY TERRACE in 1880 was prompted by the 21st birthday of Albert Edward, Prince of Wales, Earl of Chester and Duke of Rothesay, in 1862. ROTHESAY MEWS, in its present form, was named by 1890. COATES PLACE, taking its name from Coates Crescent, was begun in 1864, along with PALMERSTON PLACE, jointly developed by the Walker estate and the Heriot Trust (as superiors of Wester Coates) on the line of Coates Bauks, and evidently named for Lord Palmerston, the Prime Minister, who had been made a burgess of Edinburgh in 1863. The development of WESTER COATES began in 1865 with a scheme that included LANSDOWNE CRESCENT, named for the 3rd Marquis of Lansdowne, a graduate of Edinburgh University and a minister along with Palmerston in several governments; GROSVENOR STREET and CRESCENT (GROSVENOR GARDENS was added in 1891) presumably named for some connection, still obscure, with the dukes of Westminster; and ROSEBERY CRESCENT, a name no doubt recalling the Heriot Trust's purchase of Coates from Lord Rosebery in 1704. MAGDALA CRESCENT (briefly known as *Magdala Terrace*) was named in 1869 for Lord Napier's brilliant victory at Magdala in Abyssinia in 1868, a feat which also won him the freedom of the city. COATES GARDENS (1869) was probably named for the farm steading of West Coates, which it displaced. GLENCAIRN and EGLINTON CRESCENTS were designed as a pair and built in 1873 and 1875, along with MAGDALA PLACE (taken into Eglinton Crescent in 1915) and MAGDALA MEWS. The tale of the two crescents being named for families confronting each other with dislike is a typical joke after the event. In naming Glencairn Crescent, the Heriot Trust were no doubt recalling that they had feued Wester Coates House to Elizabeth, dowager Countess of Glencairn and mother of the 13th earl (friend and patron of Robert Burns) and that she had lived in it for ten years before she died in 1802. It seems likely that Eglinton Crescent and nearby DOUGLAS CRESCENT (1874) were named for other great ladies of Edinburgh: the first for Susanna, Countess of Eglinton (1689-1780) renowned not only for her own beauty and that of her seven daughters, but for her grace and patronage of authors; and the second for her close friend Lady Jane Douglas of Grantully (1698-1753) the tragic heroine of the 'Douglas Cause', who had lived in Easter Coates (in the house later dubbed DRUMSHEUGH HOUSE, *which see*) from 1740 until 1746. DOUGLAS GARDENS followed in 1889, originally as part of Palmerston Place; but was named in its own right, along with DOUGLAS GARDENS MEWS, about ten years later. WEST COATES, continuing the farm name, began to be developed north of the highway in about 1850. For developments south of the highway, *see under* OSBORNE TERRACE, Wester Coates. WESTER COATES AVENUE, TERRACE and ROAD were planned in the northwest of the farm in 1896, and WESTER COATES GARDENS was added by 1904.

COATESHAUGH (Coates) *see* SUNBURY, Coates.

COATFIELD (South Leith) was an estate within the barony of Restalrig. Recorded from 1470, the name is Anglian *cote feld* or Scots *cot field*, in which 'cote' was probably plural and meant 'shelters for stock', while 'field' meant an open tract of pasture, not an enclosed area in the modern sense. COATFIELD MAINS (also known as LAUGH-AT-LEITH, *which see*) was where Vanbrugh Place now stands at the foot of Lochend Road. There was ground belonging to the estate at COATFIELD LANE, which is shown on *Collins* 1693 as extending to Queen Charlotte Street, and was the 'road to the altarstone' entering St Mary's kirkyard by the *kirkstyle*—the general term for a footpath to a kirk. The houses bordering it were known as THE BACKSIDE—i.e. of the Kirkgate.

COBBLER'S CLOSE (Kirkliston) is shown but not named on *Kirkliston* 1759. When or why it got its name is not recorded, but in 1941 it was reported that it had always been known by this name in living memory; and the business of Robert Paterson, shoemaker, which continued until 1945 at 21 High Street, on the west side of the close, may have been the last phase of a long connection with that trade.

COBDEN CRESCENT and **ROAD** (Mayfield) *see under* McLAREN ROAD, Mayfield.

COBDEN TERRACE (Dalry) *see under* DALRY PLACE.

THE COBLE (Dalmeny) is mentioned in *RMS* 1556 as *cimba 'lie cobill'*, which was attached to East Craigie, along with the mill and fishing in the Almond. Here the Latin *cimba* or *cumba*, ferry skiff (as used by Charon over Styx!) seems simply to parallel the Scots term *cobill* or *cowbill* (from British *caubal*) for a flat-bottomed ferry boat, which then, as now, plied across the river here. Nevertheless, *Coble* appears as a place name on *Barnbougle & Dalmeny* c1800 and *Forrest* 1818—the latter showing the *Ferry* quite separately; and the fact that the house becomes *Ferry Coble* on *Gellatly* 1834 and *Coble Cottage* on *Ordnance Survey* 1852 would not rule out the possibility that the word coble is being used in the land name in its other sense in Scots: that of a flat-bottomed malting vat, sometimes standing in as a term for the brewhouse itself.

COBURG STREET (North Leith) was part of the ancient *Wester Road* into North Leith from Bonnington, shown on *Naish* 1709 and *Fergus & Robinson* 1759 as joining up with the 'road from the Citadel' (*see* DOCK STREET) before entering the main street of North Leith. Figuring on *Kirkwood* 1817 and in *PO Directory* 1818, the name was given in compliment to Prince Leopold of Saxe Coburg (later Victoria's beloved 'Uncle Leopold') who had married Princess Charlotte, daughter of the Prince Regent, in 1816, and visited Edinburgh in 1817, not long after her death in childbirth. His popularity continued to grow; he was made a free burgess of Edinburgh in 1819, and several streets were named after him or for his home at Esher, in Surrey—*see* LEOPOLD PLACE, SAXE COBURG PLACE, CLAREMONT PARK, and other *Claremont* streets. COBURG LANE, indicated on *Naish* 1709, is shown named (obviously as a branch off Coburg Street) on *Ordnance Survey* 1852.

JAMES COCHRANE'S CLOSE (High Street and West Bow) *see* CLARK'S CLOSE.

COCHRANE PLACE (South Leith) *see under* INDUSTRIAL ROAD, South Leith.

COCKBURN (Balerno) is recorded in 1627 as *Cokburn*; but the spellings *Coleburn* on *Blaeu* 1654 (probably recorded by Pont in 1596) and *Colburn* on *Adair* 1682, in which the *ol* would tend to be pronounced *ow*, correspond very well with the current local pronunciation *Cow burn* for the Cock burn which gave the estate its name. The first part could be from Anglian *col*, cool, or from Old Norse *kol*, used of dark-coloured streams, or from British *cau* or Anglian *cole*, a hollow: but considering the topography, there is nothing to suggest that the water would be colder than usual, and it is likely that the reference is either to water somewhat more darkly stained with peat than in other nearby burns, or to the fact that the course of the Cock burn is more deeply engraved in a ravine than any of its neighbours except the Leith itself. COCKBURN HOUSE, dating from 1627, is at the ancient estate centre. HOUSE OF COCKBURN is a modern name for the property shown on *Knox* 1812 as 'West Brook'.

COCKBURN CRESCENT (Balerno) was begun in 1968 as part of the final development of the farm of Dean Park (*see under* TOWNHEAD *and* DEAN PARK, Balerno) and the streets were complete some six years later. While records which might show why their names were chosen are missing, it is fairly evident that COCKBURN CRESCENT was named for the neighbouring estate of COCKBURN (*which see*) and that THREIPMUIR AVENUE, GARDENS and PLACE, and CROSSWOOD CRESCENT and AVENUE, and CAIRNS DRIVE and GARDENS may have been named respectively for the reservoir at THREIPMUIR (*which see*) and for the two places associated with reservoirs in the Lang Whang: Crosswood, and Cairns Castle at the head of Harperrig. The names of GREENFIELD CRESCENT and ROAD, WHITELEA ROAD and CRESCENT, and HIGHLEA CIRCLE and GROVE appear to have been fancy.

COCKBURN STREET (Old Town) was originally named *Lord Cockburn Street*, for Henry Cockburn (1779-1854) who sat in the Court of Session as Lord Cockburn from 1834 onwards and was noted, among other things, for his concern for the development of Edinburgh. Planned in the year of his death by the Edinburgh Railway Station Access Company, which had been set up by Act of Parliament in 1853, the construction of the street did not begin until 1859. The shortened form of the name seems to have prevailed by 1863.

COCKDURNO (Balerno) *see under* SHOTHEAD, Balerno.

COCK HILL (Dalmeny) is named on *Barnbougle & Dalmeny* c.1800, and the name is probably from Anglian *cocc hyll*, hillock hill.

THE COCKIT HAT (Oxgangs) is a plantation shown on *Knox* 1812 and specifically mentioned in 1802 as the triangular piece of ground at the junction of the then-new eastern section of REDFORD ROAD (*which see*) with the road from Oxgangs to Sourhole. Derived from the three-cornered hat or tricorne, the expression *cockit hat* was used in the 18th century to describe anything (e.g. a curling stone) of a triangular shape, and it is still current as a technical term in land surveying or navigation.

COCKLAW (Currie) is shown on *Roy* 1753. The name is Anglian *cocc hlaw* or Scots *cock law*, hillock of a smoothly rounded sort, and there is a summit like this northeast of the steading.

COCKLE BURN (Dalmeny) is recorded from 1567 onwards as *Cokilburne* or *Cokkil burn*, and appears on *Blaeu* 1654 as *Cocle B(urn)*. Although *Ordnance Survey* 1852 calls its upper reaches *Dolphington Burn*, from the farm it flows through, *Dalmeny & Barnbougle* c1800 gives its whole length as *Cockle burn*. Like the burn of the same name in Gogar (*see next*) it follows a marshy course —indeed, it drained the GYLE BOGS in the howe south of Kirk Dalmeny—and the name may be related to British *cagal* or Gaelic *cacail*, mire or bog.

COCKLE BURN (Gogar) is the lower reach of the Ratho burn (shown on *Hatton etc* 1797 but since then largely diverted into the Union Canal) and enters the Gogar at Gogarburn. Its character throughout its course would support the suggestion that the name might be from British *cagal* (Gaelic *cacail*) mire or bog.

COCKLE MILL (Cramond) is recorded as the *mill of Cramond* in 1178, and appears as *Cocle M(ill)* on *Adair* 1682. It is hard to see why its name should be linked with the COCKLE BURN, Dalmeny (*which see*) or with any of the plants—burdock, campion, tares or periwinkle —which go variously under the name *cockle*. The mention in *RMS* 1626 of a *Cokkilmilne* in East Lothian strengthens the probability that *cockle* is here the milling term, from Middle Dutch *cakele*, for a drying kiln, a normal adjunct to corn milling.

COCKLERAE (Currie) is marked on *Ordnance Survey* 1852, and named on its 1912 revision. Possibly a transferred name of no great antiquity, it may otherwise be a minor land name, related to *Cockleroy* in the Bathgate hills and *Cocklerow* near Woolmet. Here in Currie, it occurs where there is a slack behind a knowe on a gentle slope down to a burn, and a map of 1793 (*RHP 547*) shows a moss between the burn and the park dyke of Riccarton 300 yards further east. Thus the site supports the suggestion that, if ancient, the name is British *cagal ruth*, reddish-coloured mire; and the interpretation would fit both the other places mentioned, if (as seems likely) *Cockleroy hill* in West Lothian got its name from the ground at its foot.

COCKMALANE (Comiston) is given on *Ordnance Survey* 1852 as the name of the hollow south of the cistern collecting the Comiston springs. The same name occurs at Kirkton in Bathgate, at Ormiston near Kirknewton and in West Calder; and the striking similarity of the terrain in all four places points to the name being British or Gaelic *cuach na leanaidh*, cup or hollow in the bosom of the slope of meadow land with springs in it. It may well have applied originally to the whole basin of the Comiston springs, which as a well-defined patch of glacial gravels was probably always a distinct feature in the landscape; but *Ordnance Survey* 1893, misinterpreting the ending *-lane* as English *lane*, attaches the name to the farm road crossing the hollow, and hence the still more recent deviant *Cooksy Lane* for the right of way.

COCK RIG (Balerno) is named on *Ordnance Survey* 1852. The name is probably Anglian *cocc hrigg* or Scots *cok rig*, ridge noted for its wild birds.

COFFIN LANE (Dalry) is a footpath formed in the railway ground immediately next Dalry Cemetery in about 1890 and nicknamed in whimsical reference to what is over the wall.

COILLESDENE (Joppa) is Scots *coillis dene*, meaning (and properly pronounced as) 'coals dene', the shallow valley of the Duddingston burn's final reach towards the sea, where coal was mined for over 300 years before the pits closed down in the 1840s. Although the name is first recorded as that of a mansion house built on the site of the last of the mines (immediately east of Coillesdene Drive) it is quite likely that it was chosen for the house because it was traditional for the neighbourhood. COILLESDENE AVENUE (1931) was followed by COILLESDENE CRESCENT, DRIVE, GARDENS and TERRACE (1934) GROVE (1955) and LOAN (1967).

COINYIEHOUSE CLOSE (Old Town) was named in 1981, recovering the old name of the *close* or yard of the *Coinyie House* or Scottish Mint that operated here from 1574 until 1707, in a large group of buildings which were finally swept away in 1877. Scots *coinyie*, from Old French *cuigne*, means 'coinage' as well as the process of striking coins. The typical medieval spelling was *cunʒie*, including the 'yogh' letter ʒ and pronounced *'kune-yi*; but in fixing the modern street name one of the later variant spellings *coinye* was adopted, partly because it gives a clue to the meaning and partly because it encourages the proper pronunciation of the 'yogh' letter—unlike the *z* used by printers, which to the modern eye suggests, quite wrongly, that the word is pronounced *'kune-zee* or even *'kunn-zee*. CUNYIEHOUSE CLOSE was also a name for SOUTH GRAY'S CLOSE, *which see*.

COLINTON was an estate within the medieval barony of REDHALL (*which see*) until 1540, when it became the *chymmes* or headquarters of a new barony embracing Dreghorn, Swanston, Comiston, Oxgangs, Pilmure and the Baads, as well as Colinton itself. All this was only part of the ancient parish of HAILES (*which see*) but by 1700 the Colinton barony had become so prominent locally that Hailes kirk began to be called *Colinton kirk*, and the parish *Colinton*. The name is first recorded in the *Ragman Roll* of 1296 as *Colgyntoun* (only through misreading of charter evidence has it been taken to be *Colbanestoun*, now *Covington*, also listed in the Roll) and it is evidently Anglian or early Scots *Colgan(nis) tún*, the farm place of someone bearing the Celtic name *Colgan*. With an entirely normal smoothing of *-gyn* to *-ing*, it is given as *Colingtoun* in *Dunfermline Abbey records* 1557-85, and this form, given as *Collington* in *RMS* 1610, as *Colington* on *Adair* 1682 and still as *Collington* in the *Statistical Account* 1794 and on *Spylaw* 1798, prevails in local parlance to this day, despite the written form first recorded as *Colyntoun* in 1438 and misspelt *Cobinton* on *Blaeu* 1654, the engraver evidently substituting 'h' for 'll'. The original *Mains* or home farm of Colinton was on the site occupied since 1970 by OLD FARM ROAD, AVENUE and PLACE; for the *New* mains, *see under* COLINTON MAINS. The clachan at the river crossing was known as HAILES BRIG as early as 1574, and *Spylaw* 1757 shows it in detail, with the name *Collingtoun* written on the left bank, beside the kirk. *Adair* 1682 shows the western approach to it by the Kirk Brae (*see under* SPYLAW BANK ROAD) while *Roy* 1753 also shows the eastern approach, traditionally named COLINTON ROAD, as leading to the estate as well as to Woodhall. Its branch down to Hailes Brig, with an access to Spylaw mill or house, is shown on *Spylaw* 1767 and 1798; it was greatly altered in 1874, when BRIDGE ROAD was formed to suit the new bridge spanning the river and the new Balerno branch railway, but its old line and level is still represented by CUDDIES LANE, so named after 1874 for the horses who stood in it waiting their turn in the smiddy at its south end; and the lower part of it continued to be known simply as the *main road* until 1913, when it was named SPYLAW STREET, the whole village being within that estate. COLINTON GROVE (1932) and WEST COLINTON GROVE are in Meggatland and a mile outwith the historic estate of Colinton, and got their rather confusing name by association with Colinton Road.

COLINTON DELL is so named on *Ordnance Survey* 1893. Since 'dell' occurs in ancient place names only in southern England, the name has been imported, probably in the late 19th century. CRAIGLOCKHART DELL was copied from it in the mid 20th century. The native name for the ravine was probably a *den* or *dene*, but it has not been traced.

COLINTON MAINS (Colinton) is recorded in *RMS* 1654 as *Newmains of Colingtoune* (for the original Mains, *see under* COLINTON) and appears on *Adair* 1682 as *Colington Mains*. It is possible that it was created as the new home farm of Colinton when part of that estate was separated off as REDFORD (*which see*) at some date prior to 1674. It is detailed on *Colinton Mains and Oxgangs* 1813 as a farm of 112 acres, lying between Wester Craiglockhart and the Braid Burn, and marching with Greenbank in the east and Redford in the west. The steading was on the east side of Oxgangs Road, just north of the entry to Firhill Loan. In 1937 the southeast corner of the farm was developed along with a much greater area in neighbouring Oxgangs: COLINTON MAINS DRIVE was formed by extending an existing cul-de-sac to bisect the *Wester Haugh of Oxgangs*; and COLINTON MAINS CRESCENT, GROVE, PLACE, ROAD and TERRACE were all built in this field, while COLINTON MAINS GREEN and LOAN were built in another Oxgangs field, the *Short Bog Park* on the north side of the burn. COLINTON MAINS GARDENS (1954) was sited in the *West Scrimgers* field of Colinton Mains, the field name perhaps containing the personal name Scrimgeour.

COLLEGE STREET (Old Town) was developed from three existing streets around the new building designed by Robert Adam for the university or *town's college* (*see* OLD QUAD) which was built in two stages, in 1789-93 and 1819-27. It is shown on *Brown & Watson* 1793, and it is clear from *Ainslie* 1804 and *Kirkwood* 1817 that the intention was to have a single *College Street* running round three sides of the block, with *South*, *West* and *North* tacked on to the name of each section. SOUTH COLLEGE STREET was developed from part of the THIEVES RAW (*which see*) which ran immediately outside the Flodden Wall and was therefore known also as BACK OF THE WALL, as shown on *Ainslie* 1780. WEST COLLEGE STREET was developed from the HORSE WYND and the KIRK O FIELD or POTTERROW PORT, *which see*. NORTH COLLEGE STREET originated as part of the KIRK O FIELD WYND (*which see*) and was altered in 1871 to become part of CHAMBERS STREET.

COLLEGE WYND (205 Cowgate) was earlier KIRK O FIELD WYND, named as leading to that kirk, and got its alternative name COLLEGE WYND after the town's college (later the University of Edinburgh) was founded in the premises of the Kirk o Field in 1583, and it goes under this name on *Rothiemay* 1647. It was also SCHOOL HOUSE or SCHOOL CHIEF WYND, for the high school (i.e. grammar school) which seems to have been in the east side of the wynd for a time (perhaps from 1555, when there was certainly an intention to build here, but more likely from 1570, when the older premises at the foot of Blackfriars Wynd were finally given up) before the new school building in Blackfriars kirkyard was opened in 1579, *see* HIGH SCHOOL YARDS. As shown on *City Improvements* 1866, the Wynd was almost completely suppressed in the building of GUTHRIE STREET, *which see*.

COLLINGTOUN'S CLOSE (50 High Street) *see* HYNDFORD'S CLOSE.

COLLINS PLACE (Stockbridge) *see under* THE COLONIES, Stockbridge.

COLMESTONE GATE (Comiston) was named in 1991, with the intention of commemorating Katherine Cant, Lady Colmestoune, who feued the Toddie well in Comiston to the town for its water supply in 1674. By an unfortunate error, her spelling *Colmestoune* for COMISTON (*which see*) was inaccurately copied in the street name.

COLM'S CLOSE (South Leith) *see* COMB'S CLOSE, South Leith.

THE COLONIES (Stockbridge) is a nickname which has prevailed over the name *Glenogle Park* originally intended for this group of fifeen terraces by the Edinburgh Co-operative Building Company. This was set up in 1861 by a group of stonemasons, under the inspiration of three outstanding men of the Free Kirk, ardent for the improvement of working-class housing. The first of them, Hugh Miller, editor of *The Witness*, had died in 1856, but his ideas were carried on by his friend the Revd Dr James Begg (*see under* Dr BEGG'S BUILDING) and Hugh Gilzean Reid, editor of the *Edinburgh*

Weekly News and later to be author of a book on the Co-operative. The site was a riverside haugh known as *The Whins* or *Distillery Haugh*, bordered on the south by WATER LANE, shown on *Roy* 1753 as leading from Canonmills to a ford just below Stockbridge. The design of the terraced flats was developed from that of James Gowan's ROSEBANK COTTAGES (Fountainbridge) and since 'Terrace' or 'Place' still meant a building, rather than the street in front of it, the street names are side names, each applying to either side of the same block, serving the *low doors* on one side, and the forestairs to the *high doors* on the other. REID TERRACE was named for Hugh Reid in 1861, and HUGH MILLER PLACE followed in 1862. Three of the original seven stonemason subscribers were honoured in RINTOUL PLACE (1863) for David Rintoul, first chairman of the Co-operative, COLVILLE PLACE for its first manager, James Colville, and COLLINS PLACE, named in 1866 for James Collins, chairman in that year. BELL PLACE (1867) was named for David Bell, joiner, who followed Collins in the chair. In 1868 GLENOGLE PLACE was named and GLENOGLE PARK was chosen as neighbourhood name, possibly in compliment to James Haig of the family of distillers (who were the superiors), since he lived in Glenogle, Perthshire. In the same year KEMP PLACE was named for William Kemp, Governor of the Poors House and active in the Co-operative as its Vice President. GLENOGLE TERRACE followed Glenogle Place in 1869. AVONDALE PLACE (1869) and TEVIOTDALE, DUNROBIN and BALMORAL PLACES (all 1872) seem to be fancy names. BRIDGE PLACE (1813) was named for the wooden footbridge beside the ford in Water Lane, soon to be replaced by the iron FALSHAW BRIDGE, named for the Lord Provost who opened it in 1877. In 1875, the *Canonmills Cottages*, a century old, were converted to form GLENOGLE HOUSE, and the same ubiquitous label was used to rename Water Lane GLENOGLE ROAD.

LORD COLSTON'S CLOSE (374 High Street) *see* AIKMAN'S CLOSE.

COLSTON STREET (Leith Walk) *see* DALMENY STREET, Leith Walk.

COLTBRIDGE appears on *Blaeu* 1654 (probably surveyed in 1596) as *Kowbridge*, and the crossing is at least as old as the medieval road to Linlithgow from the West Port. The spellings *Cot Bridge*, *Coitbridge* and *Coltbridge* on *Adair* 1682, *Roy* 1753 and *Laurie* 1763 respectively seem to illustrate the name's history. The first part appears to be early Scots *cote*, a cottage or a shelter (as in *doocot*) or enclosure for animals. While the bridge is at the west end of the lands of COATES (*which see*) there is nothing to indicate that it was specifically the 'brig of or at Coates'; and since the field name *Langcote leys* occurs 500 yards away on the Balgreen land at the Stank, the reference might otherwise be to some long row of cottages or shelter of some kind west of the bridge. COLTBRIDGE TERRACE and AVENUE (formerly part of SKINNER'S LOAN, *which see*) were named by 1875, and COLTBRIDGE GARDENS by 1892. UPPER COLTBRIDGE TERRACE seems to have followed in about 1902; but COLTBRIDGE VALE, although formed by 1876, was not so named until 1963. For COLTBRIDGE ROAD, *see under* WESTFIELD ROAD, Gorgie.

COLUMBA ROAD etc (Craigcrook) *see under* CRAIGCROOK.

COLVILLE PLACE (Stockbridge) *see under* THE COLONIES, Stockbridge.

COMB'S CLOSE (South Leith) is shown on *Kirkwood* 1817 and was perhaps named for Matthew Combe, brewer in the Kirkgate in 1718.

COMELY BANK (Inverleith) is recorded in *RMS* 1662 as *Cumliebank*, a name evidently celebrating the homely beauty of this holding on a south-facing slope in Inverleith. COMELY BANK HOUSE, later replaced by AVENUE VILLAS (*which see*), is recorded in 1774, and is shown on Knox 1812 as the mansion of Sir William Fettes's estate of *Comely Bank*, which lay for the most part between East Fettes Avenue and Crewe Road. *Knox* also shows the name *Comely Bank* further to the east, across the future line of East Fettes Avenue about 100 yards from its south end, while *Ordnance Survey* 1852 shows a *Comely Bank Park* in the same vicinity, and it may be that these names recall the position of the early Cumliebank. The street name COMELY BANK derived by use and wont from that of the terrace of houses along its north side, designed for Sir William Fettes in 1817, shown part-built on *Kirkwood* 1823, and listed in *PO Directory* 1825 as *Comely Bank*. Likewise, the road 'to Comely Bank' was no doubt known as COMELY BANK ROAD long before this was formalised in about 1892. The other 'Comely Bank' streets were all in Dean estate, and the naming of COMELY BANK AVENUE and PLACE (1892) TERRACE (1897) ROW and STREET (1898) GROVE (1910) and COMELY BANK PLACE MEWS (1913) has almost transferred the place name from its proper ground in Inverleith.

COMELY GARDENS (Abbeyhill) are shown on *Ainslie* 1804. Together with a mansion known as the *Green House* they were run as a kind of Vauxhall or Tivoli Gardens in the mid 18th century, with regular open-air dances and light refreshments; and it was here that, in 1784, James Tytler took off on his historic half-mile flight in a hot-air balloon, the first manned ascent in Britain. The name of the Gardens was evidently chosen as a literal description, and it was probably imitated at COMELY GREEN, shown on *Kirkwood* 1817. COMELY GREEN CRESCENT and PLACE were developed within this later property by 1834.

COMISTON is recorded from 1337 onwards, and is shown on *Adair* 1682 as *Comeston*. The early spellings *Colemanstone* and *Colmanstoun* show the name to be Anglian *Colman's tún*, the farm belonging to someone bearing the Celtic name of Colman. The estate was part of the medieval barony of REDHALL, and its bounds are now approximately represented by Braid Road, Buckstone Terrace and Fairmile Avenue in the east, thence by Oxgangs Road to Oxgangs Path and by Oxgangs Park, Rise and Avenue to the Braid burn, and thence eastwards on the line of the south end of Braidburn Valley park to the

Braid road at Buckstane Snab, where the BUCK STANE (*which see*) once marked the junction of the four estates of Comiston, Greenbank, Braid and Mortonhall. The historic centre is still marked by a fragment of a 16th-century tower house southwest of its successor COMISTON HOUSE, which dates from 1815. In about 1830, in order to bypass the steep braes of the old Braid road, a new length of turnpike was built through Plewlands, Greenbank and a corner of Comiston. It was known simply as the *new Penicuik road* until 1885, when it was named COMISTON ROAD or road *by Comiston*, on the analogy of the earlier Braid road *by Braid*. The outcome was that five new streets in Plewlands, all of them half a mile from Comiston and separated from it by Greenbank, were named COMISTON PLACE and DRIVE (1891) GARDENS (1893) TERRACE (1897) and LANE, not for any connection with Comiston estate, but simply because they were branches off this new main road. Development within the Comiston estate began in 1923, when BUCKSTANE PARK and COMISTON RISE were laid out in its *Buckstane Park* field. It was resumed in 1934 at PENTLAND GARDENS, CRESCENT, GROVE and VIEW, named by association with an extension of PENTLAND TERRACE, Braid, *which see*. Pentland View for the most part followed the line of the old road to the steading of COMISTON or COMISTON MAINS, while COMISTON VIEW followed the fence between the *Buckstane Park* and the *Fore Shot* or 'east field' of the farm. Together with the *Back Side* or 'west slope' stretching from Cockmalane to Oxgangs Rise, this Fore Shot formed the basin of the COMISTON SPRINGS, source of Edinburgh's first piped water supply in 1681. Although the waters are now discharged into the Braid burn, they are still first collected in the cistern at Cockmalane, while the lead figures of animals which stood over the inlets to illustrate the names of the springs are now kept in Huntly House museum. COMISTON SPRINGS AVENUE (1934) was named for the springs; and the names of two of them were taken in 1959 for SWAN SPRING AVENUE and FOX SPRING CRESCENT and RISE in 1959. COMISTON GROVE was added in 1958 and PENTLAND DRIVE in 1965. For other streets in Comiston, *see under* FAIRMILEHEAD, CAIYSTANE *and* OXGANGS.

COMMERCIAL STREET (North Leith) was formed to serve the warehouses of Rennie's new docks, completed in 1806 and 1817. *Kirkwood* 1817 shows its eastern section as JOHNSTON STREET and the rest as DOCK STREET, but *Ainslie* 1804, *Thomson* 1822 and *Lothian* 1826 all apply the *Dock Street* name to the roadway north of the warehouses. Johnston Street became COMMERCIAL PLACE by 1825, and by 1834 the whole street had become COMMERCIAL STREET.

COMMERCIAL WHARF (North Leith) is shown on *Fergus & Robinson* 1759 as well as *Ordnance Survey* 1852 as a wharf at Kirkpatrick's shipyard between the graving dock on the south and a basin on the north. In about 1870 the latter was filled in, and the wharf was extended to Commercial Street and named for it.

THE COMMON CLOSES (287, 295 and 307 Canongate) were so named as three closes giving *common* or public access to the High

School of the Canongate. All three are listed on *Ainslie* 1780. The most easterly was EAST COMMON CLOSE (No. 287) which was also known as LOGAN'S, for property owned by more than one generation of a family prominent in the affairs of the Canongate, notably James Logan and his son James, clerks of the Canongate 1568-1615. The MIDCOMMON CLOSE (No. 295) also called the *Middle Common Close*, or simply *Common Close*, was otherwise (as recorded in *Maitland* 1753) known as VEITCH'S, for property owned by more than one Edinburgh burgess of that name, including John and William Veatche, mentioned in 1658 and 1671 respectively. The WEST COMMON CLOSE (No. 307) was also known as the HIGH SCHOOL CLOSE, *which see*.

THE COMMON CLOSETS (South Leith) *see under* TIMBER BUSH, South Leith.

THE COMMON LOAN or **EASTER LOANING** (Queensferry) is shown on *Dundas* 1757 and named on *Barnbougle & Dalmeny* c1800 as a loan running from the common at Niven's Green, past Muirie Wells and Muirhaw Common to the Kirk Road or LOVERS LOAN. Its northern section became ASHBURNHAM ROAD (*which see*) while its southern section continues as a loan east of Dundas Park.

THE COMMON MYRE (Prestonfield) was a 52-acre marsh lying east of Cameron and apparently between the Pow and Braid burns. Presumably granted to the burgh as a common grazing at the same time as the BURGH MUIR (*which see*) it is bracketed with the Muir in James IV's charter in *RMS* 1508, giving the town powers to feu out their common lands. Their feu of the Myre to George Steill of Edinburgh in 1536 is recorded in *RMS* 1541.

CONNAUGHT PLACE (Bonnington) was named in about 1903, probably in honour of the Duke of Connaught, younger brother of Edward VII.

CONN'S CLOSE (162 High Street and 162 Cowgate) is named in *RMS* 1620 and on *Rothiemay* 1647, evidently for John Con, flesher, who is mentioned in *Town Council Minutes* 1508 and noted in *Protocols of John Foular* 1529 as an owner on the south side of the High Street. An alternative name was STEELE'S, but nothing is known about it. The close seems to have lost its direct entry from the High Street in the mid 18th century, and most of it was swept away when TRON SQUARE was developed in 1899, but a fragment of its south entry remains in the Cowgate.

CONSIDINE GARDENS etc (Parson's Green) *see under* PARSON'S GREEN.

CONSTITUTION STREET (South Leith) began, as shown on *Siege of Leith* 1560, as a military zone immediately behind the ramparts of 1548. *Naish* 1709 shows lanes and paths in that part of it north of St Mary's kirkyard, and on *Fergus & Robinson* 1759 these have become regular roads, the section north of (Queen) Charlotte Street widened to some 60 feet overall. *Wood* 1777 shows substantially the same arrangement and names it CONSTITUTION ROAD, with CONSTITUTION HILL immediately east of it, on the future site of the Assembly Rooms. Since *Williamson's Directory* 1775 lists the Hill, but not the Road, it may well be that the name was attached first of all to the great mounds left from fortifications, and may have been inspired by London's *Constitution Hill*, dated at least 30 years earlier. In 1784 a *Memorial* was published, urging completion of the road as a bypass connecting the new commerce and industry at Bernard Street and Leith Sands directly to the Foot of Leith Walk; the necessary Act of Parliament was obtained in 1787 and the connection completed in the early 1790s; and this work no doubt accounts for the appearance of CONSTITUTION STREET in *Williamson's Directory* 1788. CONSTITUTION PLACE appeared in the 1820s as a side name at 26 Constitution Street; but in about 1881, when the Edinburgh Dock was constructed, the name was transferred to the northward extension of Constitution Street, and by the 1920s was continued westwards on the site of former timber yards.

CONVENING COURT (Dean) is shown but not named on *Ordnance Survey* 1852 and 1893, and the name appears in *PO Directory* 1902. Presumably it refers to a meeting place of trades in Water of Leith village, but information is as yet lacking.

COOKSY LANE (Comiston) is a corrupt form of COCKMALANE, *which see*.

COOPER'S CLOSE (130 Canongate) is figured on *Edgar* 1742 and listed on *Ainslie* 1780. Given as COOPER'S ENTRY in *PO Directory* 1827, it was named for Richard Cooper, engraver, who trained under John Pine in London but settled in Edinburgh. He was treasurer of the short-lived *Edinburgh School of Painting etc* founded by Allan Ramsay the elder and others in 1729; and after its demise in 1731 he opened his own *Winter Academy*, believed to have been held in *Cooper's Land* in the close. He died in 1764. His son Richard, also a painter and engraver, practised in England and was drawing master at Eton; but Margaret Cooper or Baines, granddaughter of Richard Cooper the elder, still owned property in the close in 1840.

COOPER'S CLOSE (80 Cowgate) is listed on *Ainslie* but was cleared for the building of George IV Bridge in about 1829. The origin of the name, which may be the trade's or else the surname, has not been traced.

CORBETT'S CLOSE (South Leith) is mentioned in *Williamson's Directory* 1780 but remains to be identified.

CORBIE HILL (Colinton) is shown as *Corbielaw* on *Laurie* 1763 but as *Corbiehill* on *Laurie* 1766; and it is named as the hill (or conical hill looking like a cairn or a barrow) known for ravens.

CORBIEHILL (Davidson's Mains) is shown on the east side of the turnpike on *Laurie* 1763, on both sides of it on *Cramond Roads* 1812, and west of it on *Ordnance Survey* 1852. The variant *-hall* appearing on *Laurie* 1766 (but not 1763) and *Ordnance Survey* 1852 seems to be an error, and the name probably belonged to the hill immediately southeast of the clachan, later the site of HOUSE O HILL. It was evidently known for ravens, for even as late as the 1790s the distinction between corbies and crows was still being drawn, and it is possible that it may be seen in the names of this hill and of CROWHILL, less than a half mile away. The southern part of CORBIEHILL ROAD was altered to link up with the new line taken by the Queensferry road in the 1820s (*see under* HILLHOUSE ROAD, Blackhall) but the northern section is part of the ancient Queensferry road, and of the Roman road to Cramond. CORBIEHILL AVENUE, GARDENS and GROVE were named in 1928, CORBIEHILL CRESCENT and PLACE in 1936, and CORBIEHILL PARK in 1970.

CORBIESHOT (Niddrie) *see under* THE JEWEL, Niddrie.

CORNHILL TERRACE (South Leith) named by 1892, and RYEHILL TERRACE and PLACE (1896) GARDENS (1899) and AVENUE (1901) were all named by their builders, the Edinburgh Co-operative Building Company (*see under* THE COLONIES, Stockbridge) in their usual fanciful style, in this case referring to crops of oats or rye.

CORNTOUN'S or **CORTON'S CLOSE** (Shore, South Leith) *see under* WATERS' CLOSE, South Leith.

CORNWALLIS PLACE (Bellevue) *see under* NORTHERN NEW TOWN.

CORNWALL STREET (Tollcross) *see under* ORCHARDFIELD, Tollcross.

CORONATION WALK (Meadows) *see* THE MEADOWS.

CORRENNIE DRIVE etc (South Morningside) *see under* EGYPT, South Morningside.

CLEMENT COR'S CLOSE (High Street) *see* ADVOCATE'S CLOSE.

CORSE NEUK (Newbridge) is shown on *Fowler* 1845 and maps back to *Laurie* 1763 and is described by its name as Scots *neuk*, corner, in the *corse* (from British *cors*, a bog) or riverside flat. The steading seems to have been cleared away when the railway was built, and the present steading of OLDLISTON (*which see*) was built near by.

CORSLET (Currie) is shown on *Riccarton* 1772, while *Currie Farm* 1797 shows a steading on the site of the present *Corslet Cottage*, as well as a field *Corslet Park* on the south side of the Murray burn. The traditional CORSLET ROAD (insensitively renamed RICCARTON MAINS ROAD in 1959) is shown on *Roy* 1753 as not only leading from Currie 'by the Corslet' to Hermiston, but forking westwards across the Murray burn at BURNWYND (*which see*) and continuing past the CORSLET CROSS (*see below*) to the old house of Riccarton. The place name also occurs in Wester Duddingston, where it is recorded in 1707, and in Temple, Midlothian and since the terrain at all three sites would suggest that it is a waterside name, probably British *cors laid*, miry bog, it is likely that here in Currie it originally referred to the narrow half-mile stretch of the flood plain of the Murray (i.e. 'miry') burn where it runs through the howe between Currie and Riccarton; but considering all the local names, and the fact that the Cross was named when it stood on its original site in the South Strip of Riccarton policies, it is evident that *Corslet* became the chief name in the howe. Thus, although built in 1959-61 in Nether Currie, the modern group of CORSLET ROAD, CRESCENT and PLACE, may be within the ambit of the ancient neighbourhood name.

THE CORSLET CROSS (Currie) is shown on *Ordnance Survey* 1912 in what was probably its original position on a knowe at NT 176688 in the South Strip woodland of Riccarton. Although the map terms it a 'market cross' there is neither record nor likelihood of any market being held at it: it appears to have been a medieval wayside cross, overlooking the road from Currie to Riccarton by the CORSLET (*which see*) and became the meeting place of the local *birlaw court*, a convention of farmers who met to regulate agricultural affairs in the district—in *Old Edinburgh Club XV* there is a description of the Leith birlaw court, which ruled as far west as Curriemuirend. The Cross was transferred to its present site in Currie village in about 1970.

CORSTORPHINE is recorded as *Crostorfin* in 1128, *Crorstorfin* in 1140, and is both *Corstorfyn* and *Corstorphyn* in the *Ragman Roll* 1296. A 'vulgar opinion' deriving the name from the supposed French 'croix d'or fine' was rightly passed over in the *Statistical Account* 1793 and roundly dismissed in *Wood's Corstorphine* 1794 as 'a silly fable'. The name is British or Gaelic *crois Torfin*, Torfin's crossing, and like many names in the locality, such as THE GYLE, THE FLASSCHES, CLAYCLOTE, STANK, CARRICK KNOWE and BALGREEN, it relates to the water barrier which until modern times was the dominant feature south of Corstorphine Hill. This originated as a shallow post-glacial lake stretching for four miles from Dalry to the Gyle, where it was fed by the Gogar until that burn was captured by the Almond. There was a narrows at Corstorphine, between shores in the vicinity of Dovecot Road and Broomhall Avenue, with an island where Saughton Road passes Roull Road. Although the waters began to recede in prehistoric times, *Blaeu* 1654 and *Adair* 1682 still show a pair of half-mile lochs east and west of Corstorphine, linked by the boggy course of the Stank; and in 1650 the barrier was still formidable enough to play a major part in Leslie's repulse of Cromwell. From the 1660s onwards it was progressively reduced by drainage to the single loch and array of ponds shown at the Gyle on *Roy* 1753 and then to the Flasschès or flushing meadows shown on *Laurie* 1763. While field names (*see* LADIEMEADOW *and* HONEYMUG) indicate that much of the peninsula at Corstorphine remained boggy, the kist burial found at Broompark proves that by Bronze Age times the future site of Corstorphine Castle (around NT 19957230) was already dry, and it was obviously an excellent position for a strongpoint commanding the crossing of the Stank. The personal name *Torfin*, a Gaelicised form of Old Norse *Thorfinnr*, was probably brought into Southern Scotland from the Irish Sea area in the late 9th century, and there was more than one Torfin in Scotland in 1000. The place name could date from the same period, but hardly much later, for it was already extended and firmly attached to the adjoining chapel and kirklands by the time David I gifted them to his new abbey of Holyrood in 1128. CORSTORPHINE ROAD, named as the *road to Corstorphine*, is part of the ancient Stirling road (*see also* St JOHN'S ROAD) which always passed north of the village, as shown on *Adair* 1682, and the connection to the castle, kirk and village was the CORSTORPHINE LOAN or TOUNGAITT, also known as KIRK LOAN or the VENNEL or EAST LOAN. The sett of the village, as shown on *Corstorphine* 1754, suggests that CORSTORPHINE HIGH STREET (named thus in 1968, but HIGH STREET in the 19th century, and before that known simply as THE STREET OF CORSTORPHINE) originated as a branch from the Loan, giving access to a set of manorial crofts lying next earlier kirk lands. A most unusual feature in it was THE CROSS, shown on *Corstorphine* 1754 and described in *Selway* 1890 as consisting of five great trees.

CORSTORPHINE BANK (Corstorphine) is shown thus on *Corstorphine* 1845, and may have been the CORSTORPHINE RIGG farm shown on *Laurie* 1763; but its earlier name, shown on *Corstorphine* 1754 and referred to in *RMS* 1654, was WHITEHOUSE. The steading was on the west side of the Drum brae (between Craigmount Approach and Craigmount View) but the farm extended on both sides of the road, and CORSTORPHINE BANK DRIVE, AVENUE and TERRACES were built in its *North Bank* and *West Bank* fields in 1924.

CORSTORPHINE HILL is shown thus on *Adair* 1682, and is probably the *Roche de Corstorfyn* mentioned in the *Ragman Roll* in 1296; but obviously these names cannot be older than the settlement name of CORSTORPHINE (*which see*) and must be presumed to have displaced an earlier hill name: in all probability, the British name *crag cruc*, later transferred to the estate of CRAIGCROOK, *which see*. In 1720 John Dickie acquired the land along the southern face of the hill, between Meadowhead and Murrayfield, under the general name of CORSTORPHINEHILL, and this continued to be the name of its most westerly part after BEECHWOOD and BRUCEHILL (later called BELMONT, *which see*) were separated off by subdivision of Dickie's feu. CORSTORPHINEHILL HOUSE, built by William Keith in 1793, eventually became the centre of the Edinburgh Zoo; but its steading was further west, on the north side of Old Kirk Road, some 150 yards east of Clermiston Road; and the farm's *West Parks*, together with part of the *High Bank* of Meadowhead (shown on *Corstorphine* 1845 and *Corstorphinehill* 1885) were developed for housing at CORSTORPHINEHILL CRESCENT, GARDENS and ROAD in 1931 and CORSTORPHINEHILL AVENUE in 1932.

CORSTORPHINE HOUSE dates from 1832. CORSTORPHINE PARK GARDENS was so named in 1926 because it was built in a park attached to the House; and CORSTORPHINE HOUSE AVENUE was also developed in its grounds in 1931. Prior to 1966 CORSTORPHINE HOUSE TERRACE was named WHITEHOUSE TERRACE, Corstorphine—*which see*.

CORTON'S CLOSE (South Leith) *see* WATER'S CLOSE, South Leith.

CORUNNA PLACE (South Leith) was developed in about 1827 by Peter McCraw, tax collector in Leith, who as a sergeant serving under

Sir John Moore in Spain in 1809 had lost an arm in the battle of Corunna.

COSSAR'S CLOSE (West Port) is numbered 145 *West Port* in 1827 and was probably named for David Cossar, saddler in West Port in 1780.

COTLAW(S) (Kirkliston) is recorded from 1534 onwards as an alternative name for GATESIDE, *which see*. The earliest spellings are *Cotlaw(is)* and *Coitlaw*, and the name is Anglian *cote hlaw(s)* or Scots *cot law(s)*, hill(s) with or beside a cottage or shelter for animals. It was revived in 1968 as an address for new housing on the site of Gateside farm steading.

COTMUIR (Dalmeny) is recorded in 1491 and shown on *Blaeu* 1654. It stood northwest of the junction of the Cloven Craig road with the Queensferry road, opposite New Burnshot Gate, but was swept away, along with nearby MUIRHOUSE, Dalmeny, when the dual carriageway was constructed in the early 1960s. The name was Anglian *cote mor* or Scots *cot muir*, muir with a cottage or some kind of shelter for animals on it.

COTTAGE GREEN (Cramond) was named in 1984 by adaptation of the name *Cottagefield* belonging to the house on the original property.

COTTAGE PARK (Ravelston) was so named in 1984, reviving the field name shown on *Ravelston* 1820 along with a 'cottage' (shown on *Ordnance Survey* 1852 as 'Ravelston Cottage') which had probably given the field its name. The 'Park Cottage' shown west of the field on *Ordnance Survey* 1893 probably took its name from the field.

COUDON'S CLOSE (272 Canongate) *see* BELL'S CLOSE, Canongate.

COUL'S CLOSE (317 Canongate) is given thus on *Ainslie* 1780 and as COULL'S in *Accurate View* 1783, but as COULT'S in *Town Council Minutes* 1814. It was evidently named for *Coull's Land*, a house formerly owned by William Coult or Colt of Garturk in Monkland, Lanarkshire, heir of Sir Robert Colt, advocate. Since this property fronted Leith Wynd, it probably existed before the fleshmarket was set up hereabouts (*see under* OLD FLESHMARKET CLOSE, Canongate) and it seems likely that Sir Robert Colt was one of a family who came from Perth, apparently in the 1570s, and included a succession of advocates, beginning with Maister Oliver Colt, sheriff depute of Edinburgh and an elder in St Giles in 1580.

COUNCIL CHAMBER CLOSE (High Street) is shown on *Edgar* 1742 and named on *Ainslie* 1804. It was probably the TOLBOOTH CLOSE mentioned in *Maitland* 1753, both names deriving from the fact that it ran between the west end of St Giles and the *New Tolbooth* erected in 1564, which housed the High Court on an upper flat, above the *laigh council house* used by the town council until they flitted to the Royal Exchange in 1811. The close was cleared away shortly afterwards.

COUPER STREET (North Leith) is shown on *Fergus & Robinson* 1759 as 'the road from Newhaven to Leith'. To judge by the sharp bend at

Portland Place, and by the detail on *Siege of Leith* 1560, this route had originally continued eastwards past the St Nicholas kirk; and it was when this was blocked by the building of the Cromwellian Citadel in 1656 that a diversion, now represented by Couper Street, was formed along the outer edge of the Citadel's ditch. Urbanised after 1807, and listed in *PO Directory* from 1813 onwards, the street is shown on *Regality of Canongate* 1813, which also shows that most of the ground being feued belonged to a lawyer named Couper. The street's central section was suppressed by redevelopment in 1961-65.

COUTTS CLOSE (Canongatehead) is described in *Protocols of Adam Watt* 1722 as the first close east of St Mary Wynd, in which there was a tenement owned originally by John Coutts, stabler, and thereafter by a succession of owners, of which the third was Alexander Meikle, writer. This accounts for the name of the close, and it also agrees with the *Valuation Roll* 1635, which records an Alexander Meikell as an owner occupier in the west side of the first close (left unnamed) east of the Wynd. The *Roll* also lists this as the only close between the Wynd and Boyd's Close. This would conflict with *Ainslie* 1804, which shows two, although it names only the more easterly one, as the *Stinking Close*; but since all the earlier maps show the more westerly passage (and vestiges of it appear on *Ordnance Survey* 1852) as not being entered from the Canongate, but only from Boyd's Entry at its south end, it is reasonable to conclude that *Coutts Close*, as the first entry in the Canongatehead, was one and the same as the STINKING CLOSE, 284 Canongate, *which see.*

COVENANT CLOSE (162 High Street) is shown on *Edgar* 1742 and *Ordnance Survey* 1852 as a short cul-de-sac, with a side entrance into Burnet's Close. It is said to have been rebuilt in about 1600 by John Hamilton, wright and burgess. In 1635 it was known as Mr JOHN DAULING'S, for the late John Dauling, advocate, whose widow was still living in the close, along with their advocate son Thomas. The name COVENANT CLOSE derived from the circumstance that the house at the foot of the close was one of the places where a copy of the *Covenant*—either the National Covenant of 1638 or, more likely, the Solemn League & Covenant of 1643—was made available for public signature.

COVENANTER LANE (Queensferry) for the most part supersedes and derives its name from COVENANTER CLOSE, running from Hopetoun Road to the sea front, which in turn got its name from an incident in 1680 when two Cameronian leaders, Donald Cargill and Henry Hall, were lodging at an inn in the close and were almost caught by soldiers from Blackness, Hall being fatally wounded as he fled. The inn was in a substantial 17th century-building known as *The Palace* as well as *Covenanters' House*, demolished in about 1939.

COWAN ROAD (North Merchiston) was named by 1903 for Sir John Cowan, a former Master of the Merchant Company, owners of the estate.

COWAN'S CLOSE (South side of Cowgate) is listed (but unnamed) in the *Valuation Roll* 1635, and is shown on *Ainslie* 1780 and *Ordnance Survey* 1852. It was named (if not for some predecessor, for a Robert Cowan was prominent in Edinburgh in 1521) for George Cowan, wright, listed in *Williamson's Directory* 1773 as resident in the close. A John Cowan, candlemaker, was resident before 1799, and a William Cowan, also a candlemaker, by 1818. The close was also HARLAW'S (or, following a normal pronunciation of the same, HARLIE'S) before 1716, but this remains obscure.

COWAN'S CLOSE (Crosscausey) is shown as an entry on *Ainslie* 1780 but as a more developed close on *Ainslie* 1804. The name, shown on *Kirkwood* 1817, probably derived from James Cowan, shoemaker in Crosscausey in 1800.

COWAN'S CLOSE (South Leith) was the name of two closes: the first, in Water Lane (now Street) is shown on *Kirkwood* 1817 but information is otherwise lacking; the second, listed in 1828 as at 28 Tolbooth Wynd, may have been named for some connection of Charles Cowan, grocer, listed in *Williamson's Directory* 1780 as at 13 Tolbooth Wynd.

COWFEEDER ROW (Tollcross) *see under* HIGH RIGGS, South Side and Tollcross.

THE COWGATE (Old Town) is probably the *new street* and *newgat(e)* recorded in 1335 and 1369 (*see RCAHMS Inventory p. xli*) and named as the first addition to the original High Street of the burgh. It may also be the *street called Newbygging under the castle* in *RMS* 1363, unless (as is likely) the phrase 'under the castle' even then referred specifically to the Grassmarket area, as it certainly did later. The description of the High Street as *the north street* in *RMS* 1367 implies that the Cowgate was already known as *the south street*, even although that term is first used directly in *RMS* 1425. Chepman and Myllar, Scotland's first printers, used *Southgaitt* as their address in 1508; but earlier popular names of *the south street* are recorded in *RMS* in the phrases *commonly or of old called Cowgate* (1450) and *commonly called Welgate or of old Kowgate* (1480). Early Scots *well gate* was apt for this *gate* or way along the floor of the ravine south of the burgh, where numerous springs or *wells* supplied the town (and later on, many of its breweries) with water, and also fed the *strand* or little burn that flowed down to Holyrood; while as early Scots *cu gata* or *coo gait* it was the way or loan along which the cows each burgess kept in a byre in his *close* or yard were driven out to pasture—or the name may even hark back to a more primitive arrangement, for *gata* could mean grazing in the ravine itself. Yet despite this humble origin, the Cowgate became the town's most fashionable quarter, described by Alexander Alesse in 1529 as the place 'where the nobility and chief men of the city reside and in which are the palaces of the officers of state, and where nothing is mean or tasteless but all is magnificent'—an encomium borne out by pictures of many of the street's ancient buildings pulled down in modern times. The COWGATE PORT, still shown on *Ainslie* 1804, was built before 1554 as a town gate opening from the Cowgate into St Mary Wynd, *see under* St MARY'S STREET. At the other end of the street, at the watershed in the valley floor between Cowgate and Grassmarket, is the COWGATEHEAD, defined in the *Valuation Roll* 1635 as the buildings on the corner between Grassmarket and Candlemaker Row, which were considerably altered when the roadway was widened, as shown on *City Improvements* 1866.

COWIE'S CLOSE (Grassmarket) is shown but unnamed on *Ainslie* 1780. It appears as *Cowie's* in *PO Directory* 1827 and on *Ordnance Survey* 1852, but the derivation of the name has not yet been traced. It seems also to have been known as EASTER GILMORE'S CLOSE (*see under* GILMORE'S CLOSE) and as shown on *Kincaid* 1784 it certainly reads as though part of the Gilmore roperie.

COWSLAP (Currie) is shown on *Knox* 1812 and *Gellatly* 1834 as a building of some sort about 300 yards along the road from Wester Kinleith to Harlaw. The name contains Scots *slap*, probably in its sense of 'a miry place', for a small burn crosses the road at this point. Since the pronunciation is lost, the whole name is open to several interpretations: if it was *coos' slap* it might indicate a place for cattle to drink; but *kow(s)* could imply bushes of a straggly sort or a scarecrow or hobgoblin.

COXFIELD (Gorgie) was named in 1984, as being in the western part of the site of Cox's glue works, the last mills on the historic site of Gorgie mills.

CRAGGENEMARF (Arthur's Seat) was also known as THE CRAG, and is referred to in the foundation charter of Holyrood in 1128 and in other charters of David I's time as territory divided between Holyrood and the adjoining lands of TREVERLEN (*which see*) belonging to Kelso abbey and later known as DUDDINGSTON. *Craggenemarf* is British for 'dead men's rock'. It may have prompted the fanciful name *Mount Dolorous* used once for Arthur's Seat in a 12th-century chronicle of Holyrood; but since the 12th-century annalist John of Hexham calls Holyrood 'the monastery of the Crag', and an indulgence granted to Kelso abbey in 1426 describes St Anthony's chapel as both 'on the Crag' and 'within the territory of Duddingston', it is reasonably clear that *Craggenemarf* and *the Crag* were names for Arthur's Seat, certainly for a large part of the hill, and probably for the whole of it.

CRAIGBRAE (Dalmeny) is shown on *Adair* 1682 and recorded from 1488 onwards. The early spellings *Cragbrey* 1488, *Cragbray* 1506 and *Cragbrie* 1552 suggest that the name may be wholly Celtic, British *crag bre*, crag or rocky summit of the hill; but otherwise (and rather less likely) the second part might be early Scots *brae*, making the name 'hill slope at the rocky summit called Crag'.

CRAIGCROOK is recorded from 1335 onwards as an estate name, but its early forms *Cragruk*, *Cragcroke* and *Craigcruke* show that it originated as a hill name, British *creg crug*, rocky hill with hillocks or cairns on it. It was probably the Celtic name for CORSTORPHINE HILL (*which see*) where the summit, nowadays obscured by trees, is described in *Wood's Corstorphine* 1794 as 'a craggy and rocky ridge, indented like a cock's comb'. CRAIGCROOK ROAD, indicated on *Roy* 1753, got its name as the approach to the 16th-century tower house of CRAIGCROOK (no doubt a replacement of the medieval estate centre) but the road's northern section was also known as *the loch road*, since (as shown on *Ordnance Survey* 1852) it skirted a small loch at what is now the west end of March Road. In 1719 the estate was left in trust for charitable purposes by John Strachan WS. Development began in the *South Croft* and *Southhead Park* in 1903, when CRAIGCROOK TERRACE, PLACE and GARDENS were erected beside existing roads and St Columba's Church was built, with a small section of COLUMBA ROAD beside it. GARDINER ROAD, begun in 1921, was named for the Revd Dr Gardiner, minister of Kirknewton and chairman of the trustees of Craigcrook Mortification; and GARDINER GROVE and TERRACE continued his name in 1931 and 1932. Columba Road was extended in 1926, but still in two parts, with Craigcrook farm steading in between; and although COLUMBA AVENUE, to be built on the farm road, was named in 1936, *Ordnance Survey* 1938 shows the steading as still in existence, and these streets still incomplete. CRAIGCROOK AVENUE, GROVE, PARK and SQUARE were named in 1926. JEFFREY AVENUE was named in 1924 for Francis Jeffrey, Senator of Justice and one of the founders of the *Edinburgh Review*, who had been the Trust's tenant in Craigcrook Tower for 34 years before his death in 1850 (*see also* JEFFREY STREET, Old Town). John Strachan, the benefactor, was commemorated in the naming of STRACHAN ROAD in 1926; and STRACHAN GARDENS followed in 1931. LOCH ROAD, although some 300 yards from the site of the loch mentioned above, probably got its name in 1926 because it was being developed in the *Loch park* field of the farm. Also in 1926, MARCH ROAD was named because it ran along the northern march of the estate; and MARCH GROVE and PLACE were named from it in 1934. CARFRAE ROAD, PARK and GROVE were named in 1926 for the senior partner of Carfrae & Morrison, civil engineers, who had laid out the estate roads for the Trust; and CARFRAE GARDENS was added in 1931.

CRAIGEND (Calton) is recorded in 1631 as an alternative to CALTON (*which see*) for the name of the clachan at the west end of the Craigingalt or Calton Craigs. The name obviously describes the site, and there is neither reason nor evidence to pair it with LOCHEND, Restalrig, *which see*.

CRAIGEND (Dalmeny) is recorded from 1599 onwards and shown on *Blaeu* 1654. The name is Scots, describing its position at the east end of the bold crags of Dundas Hill.

CRAIGEND (Liberton) is shown on *Ordnance Survey* 1852 and appears to have been earlier a part of Craigs—*see under* KINGSTON GRANGE, Liberton. The name possibly forms a pair with GREENEND, further south.

CRAIGENTERRIE (Currie) is recorded in 1720, and given on *Roy* 1753 as *Craigintary*. Evidently Celtic, the name may be British *crag an taru*, bull's rock, but *crag an tarren*, rock of the knowe, would be an apt description of the prominent rocky scaur above the burn about 300 yards south of the house.

CRAIGENTINNY was part of Restalrig until about 1604, when it was sold as a separate 652-acre estate to James Nisbet, eldest son of Nisbet of Dean, and builder of CRAIGENTINNY HOUSE. The name is Celtic: Gaelic *creag an t-sionnaich*, fox's rock, has been suggested; but it is perhaps more likely to be British, possibly *cragen tanan*, (little) rock 'at a narrow place' or 'of a narrow sort'. Evidently it referred to a local feature, but where or what this was is a matter of guesswork, for in a bare landscape even a tiny one can generate a place name; but if, as is conceivable, it were the early name for RESTALRIG (*which see*) or for a central part of it, it might have referred to the outcrop of volcanic rock at Lochend House, on the east shore of the loch. The farm eventually known as CRAIGENTINNY by about 1890 had previously been called the SOUTH MAINS OF RESTALRIG in the 18th century, TELFER'S MAINS by 1783, and SOUTHBANK by 1813. Its steading was near the Portobello Road, on the west side of Kekewich Avenue, and its fields marched with Duddingston on the earlier line of the FISHWIVES CAUSEY, *which see*. In 1764 the estate was bought from the Nisbets by William Miller, Quaker and seed merchant; and it was the Christie Miller branch of his family who succeeded to it in 1864 and began its development for housing in 1906. BRYCE AVENUE (1906) was named for the estate factor Andrew Bryce, while the names of GOFF AVENUE (1906) SYDNEY TERRACE (1907) and WAKEFIELD AVENUE (1910) incorporate forenames of members of the Christie Miller family. Development resumed in 1929, when KEKEWICH AVENUE was named for G C Kekewich, who had acted as the estate's solicitor since 1898. In 1931, CHRISTIE MILLER AVENUE, PLACE and GROVE were named for the family, and VANDELEUR AVENUE for Evelyn Vandeleur, who had married Sydney R Christie Miller in 1904; while BRITWELL CRESCENT and STAPELEY AVENUE (1931) and NANTWICH DRIVE (1932) were named for the family's properties in Buckinghamshire and Cheshire, along with CRAIGENTINNY AVENUE (1931) GROVE and CRESCENT (1932) and CRAIGENTINNY AVENUE NORTH (1933). VANDELEUR GROVE and PLACE were added in 1933, and CRAIGENTINNY PLACE in 1954. PARKER AVENUE, ROAD and TERRACE were named for a trustee of the estate in 1937; and two connections of William Christie Miller, his godparent Gaspard Farrer and his wife's grandfather Sir William Farrer, were commemorated in the naming of FARRER TERRACE in 1937, echoed in FARRER GROVE in 1966.

CRAIGHALL ROAD (Newhaven and Bonnington) first appears, labelled 'New Road to Edinburgh', on *Dall & Leslie* 1831. Evidently a revision of more ambitious proposals (shown on *Knox* 1812 and *Kirkwood* 1817) for a road from Newhaven to Canonmills, it also displaced a plan (shown on *Lothian* 1826) for building up the east side of Laverock Terrace. Extending southwards as the NEW CUT, shown on *Pollock* 1834 and *Ordnance Survey* 1852, it crossed over the Ankerfield burn into Bonnington before joining Ferry Road. The name *Craighall Road*, first listed in *PO Directory* 1884, obviously arose from this Bonnington section of the road, for Craighall, near Blairgowrie, was a seat of the Clerk-Rattray family, lairds of Bonnington; and this explains why the road is still popularly known in Newhaven by its older names of THE CUT and GRASSY BANK. CRAIGHALL GARDENS was also named by 1884; and CRAIGHALL CRESCENT (1898) TERRACE (1907) and AVENUE and BANK (1910) took their names from Craighall Road.

CRAIGHILL GARDENS (South Morningside) *see under* PLEWLANDS, South Morningside.

CRAIGHOUSE (Cramond) appears as *Craghous* in *RMS* 1465, as *Craighouse* on *Roy* 1753 and as *Craig House* in *Wood's Cramond* 1794; but is given as *Craigend* on *Laurie* 1766 and *Armstrongs* 1773. The house seems to have disappeared by about the turn of the century, but *Cramond Roads* 1812 shows the Craig*house* Whinstone *Quarry*, which is named *Barnton Quarry* on *Ordnance Survey* 1893. The name is early Scots *crag hous*, house at the (Corstorphine) crags.

CRAIGHOUSE (South Morningside) is referred to in a charter of Newbattle abbey in 1278 as *Easter Crag*, owned by the heirs of William de Lamberton; while *RMS* 1368 refers to lands out of *Crag, namely ... Meduespot and ... Stodfald*, donated from Braid to Newbattle, and a later index to the same grant names the place as *Cragy Meadowspot*. Echoed in the current name *Old Craig* for the 16th-century mansionhouse which became part of the Craighouse Asylum in 1878, the name *Crag* evidently relates to the medieval hill name *Eastercrag of Gorgie* and yet more directly to the British place name *Crag* found in CRAIGLOCKHART, *which see*. The form *Craighouse* appears in a Newbattle Abbey charter of 1528, and the place is shown on *Blaeu* 1654 as *Craighous*, with *Krag* to the south of it. The name is evidently 'house at *Crag*'. CRAIGHOUSE ROAD, shown on *Knox* 1812, was named as an access to Craighouse and originally included MYRESIDE ROAD; and later streets in PLEWLANDS (*which see*) took their names from it.

CRAIGIE (Dalmeny) is recorded as *Cragin* in 1178 and *Cragyn* and *Cragy* in 1296 and figures on *Blaeu* 1654 as *Kragy*. Celtic, probably British *creg an*, place of/at crags, it is likely that the name originated as the name of the hill ridge itself, with its array of crags, *see under* DALMENY, while the later name CRAIGIE HILLS, appearing on *Armstrongs* 1773, was probably a back formation from the estate name. By the 14th century the estate had been subdivided. WESTER CRAIGIE, recorded in 1323, may have been the ancient as well as the modern CRAIGIE; and since it appears on *Adair* 1682 as the *Toun of Craigiehall*, it may have been the MAYNIS OF CRAIGIEHALL recorded in 1551 and 1653, *see also under* CRAIGIEHALL. EASTER CRAIGIE, recorded in 1364, is shown as *E. Kragy* on *Blaeu* 1654 and as *E. Craigie* on *Barnbougle & Dalmeny* c.1800, in the vicinity of NT 187770; but on *Forrest* 1818 it seems to be covered by a note 'Craigie in ruin', and the modern steading appears on *Ordnance Survey* 1852, half a mile upstream. UPCRAGY, mentioned in *RMS* from 1539 to 1621, is described as part of the demesne land of Craigiehall; while the 2-acre PRIESTLANDS OF DISCRAIGIE, mentioned in *RMS* 1662, seem to have been part of East Craigie, distinguished by *dic(s)*, ditch(es) or dyke(s). The COBLE (*which see*) is also in East Craigie. CRAIGIE MILL is listed in *RMS* 1556 and 1622 as attached to East Craigie. Shown thus on *Adair* 1682 and *Armstrongs* 1773, it is *Craigmill* on *Barnbougle & Dalmeny* c1800, and seems to be displaced by CRAIGMILL QUARRY on *Ordnance Survey* 1852.

CRAIGIEHALL (Dalmeny) is shown on *Blaeu* 1654 as *Kraggy hal*, and is recorded in *RMS* 1474 as *Cragyhall* and in the name *de Cragyhale* in 1482. It is evident that the ending *-hall* does not refer to a house, and that the name combines Anglian *halh* (or its dative *hale*) land in the river bend, with the territorial name of CRAIGIE (*which see*) to describe this part of it as 'the Craigie haugh or haw' or, more likely, 'the part of Craigie at the haw'. Nevertheless, the description of the modern Craigie as the MAYNES OF CRAIGIEHALL in 1551 shows that by then this riverside subdivision had become the estate centre.

CRAIGIEVAR WYND (Corstorphine) was given this fancy name in 1974, apparently because it shared the term *craig* with the name of the farm of East Craigs. It derives from the towerhouse of Craigievar in Aberdeenshire, with *wynd* added, under the mistaken impression that it means a curving street like this one. The branch streets off it, all called COURTS, followed the same fancy in being named for Scottish castles: AFFLECK near Monikie, BARNTALLOCH near Langholm, CAERLAVEROCK near Dumfries, DUNOLLIE near Oban, FINLAGGAN in Islay, KILCHURN in Glen Orchy, KISIMUL in Barra, NEIDPATH near Peebles, ROWALLAN near Kilmarnock, and TOWARD in Cowal. CRAIGIEVAR SQUARE was added to the head of the Wynd in 1983.

CRAIGINGALT (Calton) was the earliest known name of the Calton Hill. Appearing thus in *RMS* 1456, it is recorded from 1589 onwards with variant endings *-gatt*, *-gait* or *-(g)ate*, and was still in legal use in 1743. The name occurs in several places on either side of the Forth; and it is of interest that a 13th-century record in *Bannatyne Club* 74 groups one of them, Craigencat in the Cleish hills, with a place called Caltin. The name is British *crag an gallt*, crag on the hill or wooded hillside—and this second meaning would link with the nearby name of CALTON, *which see*. After John McNeill, clerk of the Canongate, purchased the hill in 1588, it began to be called McNElLL'S CRAGS; but while *Rothiemay* 1647 names it as *North craigs or Neils craigs*, the re-engraving of this map about 60 years later shows *The Calton Craigs* as an additional name.

CRAIGINGLES (North Merchiston) *see under* WEST BRYSON ROAD, North Merchiston.

CRAIGLEA DRIVE and **PLACE** (South Morningside) *see under* PLEWLANDS, South Morningside.

CRAIGLEITH is given on *Blaeu* 1654 as *Kraig* and is recorded from 1171 onwards as lands of *Crag of* or *at Inverleith*. Thus the form *Craigleith*, recorded in 1591 and on *Adair* 1682, seems to have developed from the estate name *Crag*, derived from the British hill name *creg*, a rock. The Royal Victoria Hospital is sited in the historic centre. Another house, west of Craigleith Hill Crescent, is given on *Knox* 1812 as CRAIGLEITH PARK, but as CRAIGLEITH HILL on *Ordnance Survey* 1852. *Roy* 1753 shows these properties as approached from the north, but *Armstrongs* 1773 shows CRAIGLEITH ROAD running south of them, giving access also to CRAIGLEITH QUARRY and TOLL, as shown on *Cramond Roads* 1812. Houses along the north side of Craigleith Road were named BARNTON TERRACE in about 1885; and this misleading side name (Barnton being a good mile away) lingered on as the yet more misleading WEST BARNTON TERRACE until 1968. CRAIGLEITH CRESCENT and VIEW were built in Blinkbonny in 1926, followed by CRAIGLEITH GARDENS (1927) DRIVE and GROVE (1928) BANK (1931) and AVENUES NORTH & SOUTH and RISE (1937). CRAIGLEITH HILL AVENUE and GARDENS were named in 1930, CRAIGLEITH HILL CRESCENT in 1931, and CRAIGLEITH HILL GREEN, LOAN, PARK and ROW in 1932. CRAIGLEITH HILL, developed in a *Barnton Nursery* considerably to the south of the site of the house of Craigleith Hill, was named in 1964.

CRAIGLOCKHART is recorded in 1278 (in a charter of the neighbouring lands of *Easter Crag* or CRAIGHOUSE, *which see*) as *Crag that Sir Stephen Loccard had held*: in other words, it was 'Crag, once Loccard's place', and the *Craglokkart* recorded in 1505 is like such names as *Niddrie Seton* or *Bonaly Wallace* in simply tacking an owner's name on to the original British place name. This is borne out by 13th-century reference to the Craiglockhart hills as the *Craggis of Gorgin*, and by the name *Krag* on *Blaeu* 1654; and the phrase used in 1278 is almost exactly echoed in a 17th-century reference to *Loccart's Rock, commonly called Craiglokart*. The history of nearby CRAIGHOUSE (*which see*) also suggests that *Crag*, from British *creg*, a rock, was the general name for this hilly ground; and while it has been suggested that *Craiglockhart* is Gaelic *creag luchairte*, crag of the (Iron Age) fort on the Wester hill, the evidence is all against it. The surname *Loccard* (from Old Norse *Loker*) is Flemish, and the spellings *Lokert* and *Lokhart* occur elsewhere in the 15th century. A Stephen Loccard evidently arrived in Scotland in the mid 12th century, holding Stevenston in Cunninghame in 1160, and giving it his first name; and it would seem that the charter of 1278 quoted above refers either to him or to a later namesake as former owner of this part of Crag in Edinburgh. The names EASTER and WESTER CRAIGLOCKHART HILLS appear on *Ordnance Survey* 1852, having displaced, at some unknown period, the medieval names EASTER and WESTER CRAGS OF GORGIE which, as already noted, go back to the 13th century at least. The 15th-century CRAIGLOCKHART TOWER, shown on *Blaeu* 1654 as *Krag*, and on *Adair* 1682 as *c. lockhart*, is noted as 'ruined' on *Armstrongs* 1773; and CRAIGLOCKHART HOUSE was built in about 1819 on a different site and as a property within the estate. The northern boundary of the historic estate was on the line of Allan Park Crescent and the pond in Craiglockhart Sports Centre; but under the influence of the naming of CRAIGLOCKHART STATION on the suburban railway in 1887, the estate name was drawn northwards over Meggetland and even part of Myreside, where CRAIGLOCKHART TERRACE was formed in 1897. The ancient road CRAIGLOCKHART BRAE, shown on *Roy* 1753 and probably dating from the Middle Ages as the access to Craiglockhart from the Lanark road, was renamed CRAIGLOCKHART AVENUE after housing began to be developed beside it in about 1904; and its branch to Redhall, latterly styled KATESMILL ROAD (*which see*) was partly renamed CRAIGLOCKHART DRIVE in 1923. Meantime the building of Redford Barracks in 1909-15 had made it necessary to construct a sewer through the Craiglockhart fields, with a bridge over the Canal at Allan Park. As may be seen on *Ordnance Survey* 1912, the route of the pipes was designed to become a road; and in 1923 part of it, in the *Langlands* and *Threshiedale* fields south of Craiglockhart Avenue, began to be developed as CRAIGLOCKHART ROAD, while the northern section, in the *Broom Park*, followed in the 1930s. Also in 1923, CRAIGLOCKHART CRESCENT began to be built in the *Langlands*, and CRAIGLOCKHART GARDENS and LOAN were formed in the *Middle Shot* of the estate. Development continued thereafter at CRAIGLOCKHART CRESCENT (1927) QUADRANT (1930) GROVE (1931) PLACE and VIEW (1932) and BANK (1933). CRAIGLOCKHART DELL ROAD (1947) took its name from the recently-coined name for the lower part of COLINTON DELL, *which see.*

CRAIGMILL (Balerno) is shown on *Ravelrigg* 1764 and *Armstrongs* 1773 as a farm stretching down to the river on the south side of Ravelrig hill, with its steading on the south side of Lanark road, opposite modern Hannahfield. The *craig* referred to is probably Ravelrig hill; there is no trace of a mill within the farm, but the reference may be to the ROYAL MILN shown in 1764 a little further downstream, opposite the mouth of the John's burn. Since *Adair/Cooper* 1735 shows a RAVILRIGE MILL, it seems likely that there was but one mill in the vicinity, and that *royal* derived from *ravel*. The possibility that it was once a king's mill seems remote.

CRAIGMILLAR is recorded from about 1124 onwards and is shown on *Blaeu* 1654 as *Crayggmillor*. The early spellings *Cragmilor* (c1130) and *Craigmelor* (1374) suggest that the name is British *creg* or rock, at or on the *meol ard*, the brow of the hill, or the bare summit. The rock was fortified from early times, and the Preston family, acquiring it in 1374, developed a powerful castle on the crag over the next 200 years. The MAINS OF CRAIGMILLAR, although first recorded in 1630, was probably the medieval home farm. The Gilmour family, acquiring the estate in 1660, left the castle derelict in the 18th century, and in consequence the name has increasingly tended to apply to modern developments in the northern estate farm of CAIRNTOWS (*which see*) where a railway station was built in 1883 and manufacture of 'butterine' (a form of margarine) began, followed by brewing in 1892 and a large housing scheme in 1938. This had an effect on the naming of the ancient roads to the castle from Duddingston and Little France, shown on *Roy* 1753, which were combined under the name CRAIGMILLAR ROAD until 1958, when the section from Duddingston to Cairntows was renamed DUDDINGSTON ROAD WEST, and the name of the remainder was rather needlessly altered to CRAIGMILLAR CASTLE ROAD, presumably to harmonise with the names CRAIGMILLAR CASTLE AVENUE, GARDENS, GROVE, LOAN, PLACE and TERRACE given to the new streets in 1938.

CRAIGMILLAR PARK (Newington) was a part of Liberton which W J Little Gilmour of Liberton and Craigmillar began to feu out in 1872, under the names of *East* and *West Craigmillar Parks*. CRAIGMILLAR PARK was given as a street name to the existing Liberton highway where it passed between the two. The names CRAWFURD ROAD, SAVILE ROAD and GRANBY TERRACE were fixed on by 1875 (the last being changed to GRANBY ROAD in 1882) and SUFFOLK ROAD and WILTON ROAD followed in about 1886. Why these names were chosen is not known, but the last four are titles in the English peerage, and *Crawfurd*, if it is not for Crawford and Balcarres in the Scots peerage, might be for George Crawfurd, genealogist, author of a book on the Scots peerage in 1716. SAVILE TERRACE was envisaged in 1875 and formed by 1887, but was apparently not named until 1892. GILMOUR ROAD (about 1887) was named for the family, and LYGON ROAD (about 1896) for Lady Susan Lygon, wife of R W Gordon Gilmour, who had succeeded to the estate in 1887. Development continued in about 1889 at SOUTH CRAIGMILLAR PARK, renamed GORDON TERRACE by 1897; and ESSLEMONT ROAD (1889) and HALLHEAD ROAD (about 1897) were named for Gordon Gilmour properties in Aberdeenshire. The final pair of streets were named in 1910 and 1937 for early connections of the Little Gilmour family: ROSS ROAD for Grizel Ross, wife of Sir Alexander Gilmour of Craigmillar, whose grandson William Little of Over Liberton inherited Craigmillar in 1792 and so brought the two estates together; and BLACKBARONY ROAD for a double connection with the Murrays of Blackbarony in Peeblesshire, firstly through Margaret Murray, wife of William Little, Provost of Edinburgh 1586-91, the first of the name to own part of Liberton, and secondly through a later Margaret Murray, third wife of Sir John Gilmour, purchaser of Craigmillar in 1660.

CRAIGMOUNT AVENUE, GARDENS, GROVE and **PARK** (Drum Brae) were built in fields of Corstorphine Bank farm and named in 1933, the first of seventeen streets to be given this name, coined by combining *craig-*, taken from the adjoining Craigs Road, with *-mount*, referring to the same slope as the *bank* in the farm name or the *brae* in the Drum Brae. Thereafter the name was extended to CRAIGMOUNT TERRACE (1936) and CRESCENT, GROVE NORTH, and VIEW (1939); and relentlessly proliferated in CRAIGMOUNT DRIVE, LOAN and PLACE (1953) WAY (1959) AVENUE NORTH and

CRAIGMOUNT HILL (1964) CRAIGMOUNT APPROACH (1966) BANK and BANK WEST (1969) COURT (1971) and finally, it is to be hoped, to CRAIGMOUNT BRAE (1978).

CRAIG O FLEURES (Swanston) is recorded in 1709, apparently as the name of the eastern part of Caerketton or a feature thereabout. While the place may have been itself 'the crag of flowers', it is perhaps more likely that it was named as 'the crag near the *Fleures*', this field name being quite frequent in Lothian and meaning 'the flats'.

CRAIGOUR (Edmondston) is listed in about 1724 as *Craigoer*, a member farm of Leith burlaw court, and figures as *Craigover* on *Laurie* 1763. But for -*ower* in the estate plan *Craigower, Edmonston & Fernyside Parks* 1815, the spellings up until the 1930s are generally -*oer*, -*over* and *o'er*, and -*our* seems to be entirely modern. Although its stress is typically Celtic, there is no reason to suppose that the name has been imported from elsewhere. It may refer to rock outcrops on Edmonston Edge; and since both British *gover* or Gaelic *gobhar* (in one of its senses) are terms for watercourses, the name may well be 'crag or rock at the burn'. The plan of 1815 shows the farm steading at what is now CRAIGOUR COTTAGES, while *Gellatly* 1834 shows it in its later position 200 yards down the road, opposite PENTECOX (*which see*), and four-fifths of the 99-acre farm lay east of the Dalkeith road and north of the Edmonston policies. CRAIGOUR DRIVE and ROAD (1947) are partly in Craigour and partly in Moredun; but CRAIGOUR AVENUE (1947) CRESCENT, GARDENS, GROVE and TERRACE (1948) and CRAIGOUR GREEN and PLACE (1966) are all on Moredun ground. In 1983 the names UPPER and NETHER CRAIGOUR were coined in order to retain the farm name for streets in the *West Park* and *South Haugh of Craigower* and in its *North Haugh* on the other side of the burn.

CRAIGPARK (Ratho) was formed as a new property in Westhall in about 1850. The name may have been fancy, but very possibly it was the name of the field, which had broken ground at its north end. CRAIGPARK AVENUE and CRESCENT were named for it in 1951, even although built in the adjoining *North Crofts of Ratho*, shown on *Hatton* etc. 1797.

CRAIGROYSTON (Granton) was coined as a house name in about 1800, combining *craig*, for Granton Craigs nearby, with ROYSTON, *which see*.

CRAIGS (Corstorphine) simply describes the rocky summits at the head of the hollow of the Bughtlin burn, and although the name is now in a Scots form, it may be British or Gaelic in origin. The lands are recorded as EAST and WEST CRAIGS from 1506 onwards, and both places appear on *Blaeu* 1654. CRAIGS ROAD got this traditional name as the road *by the Craigs* to Linlithgow and Stirling. Anciently, as shown on *Adair* 1682 and *Roy* 1753, it was continuous with St John's Road; but in about 1750, as shown on *Corstorphine* 1754, the eastmost section between the Drum and a point now represented by the south entry of Templeland Road was suppressed. CRAIGS

AVENUE, CRESCENT and LOAN (1931) and BANK and GARDENS (1932) were built in the BONNYTOUN field (*which see*) of Corstorphine Bank farm, and took their names from Craigs Road, rather than from the Craigs themselves; but CRAIGS DRIVE and PARK (1976) are in East Craigs, and WEST CRAIGS AVENUE and CRESCENT (1937) in West Craigs.

CRAIGS (Liberton) *see under* KINGSTON GRANGE and THE INCH, Liberton.

CRAIG'S CLOSE (Canongate, off Abbey Strand) *see* FERRIE'S CLOSE, Canongate.

CRAIG'S CLOSE (101 Cowgate) *see* HOME'S CLOSE, Cowgate.

CRAIG'S CLOSE (265 High Street) is listed on *Edgar* 1742 and took this name from John Craig, wright and burgess, who acquired property here from the estate of David Callen, as recorded in *Protocols of William Forbes* 1758. It was also called DENNISTON'S, for Alexander Denniston or Danielston, merchant, bailie in 1634, and owner and resident in the close in 1635; it was also BURNE'S, for Patrick Burne, who had a house and tannery by the lochside at the close foot in 1635; and it was probably also BYRNIE'S, for Richard Byrnie, who had property at the close head at some date prior to 1744. Fifthly, it was one of several closes called CANT'S. From mentions of Litill and Leche as adjoining owners (*see under* OLD POST OFFICE CLOSE and ALLAN'S CLOSE) it is clear that this was the *Cantis clois* referred to in *RMS* 1565; and since property owned hereabouts by an Alexander Cant can be traced back to 1507 in *RMS*, it is virtually certain that the close is the ALEXANDER CANT'S CLOSE mentioned in *Town Council Minutes* 1514 as the dividing line between the northeast and northwest quarters of the town. In the same period, as witnessed by a reference in *Birrel's Diary* 1598, it was known as JOUSSIE'S or JOSIAH'S CLOSE. Six persons of the name are mentioned in *Town Council Minutes* in the 16th century, and all of them seem to be mentioned in later protocols regarding properties in the close; but since a burnt-out tenement rebuilt by a Robert Joussie or Joysie was later owned by Alexander Cant, it is likely that the close was named for Robert Jossy, town councillor in 1500, or a predecessor. The upper part of it was removed almost completely in the eastward extension of the City Chambers in 1930-34, but its most northerly section still descends from Cockburn Street to Market Street.

CRAIG'S CLOSE (323 High Street) *see under* WARRISTON'S CLOSE.

JAMES CRAIG WALK (East End) was named in 1972 for James Craig, architect, since it gives access to the St James' Centre built in 1965-70 on the site of St JAMES' SQUARE (*which see*) designed by Craig for Walter Ferguson in 1773. For Craig's more dubious role in the design of the first New Town in 1766-67, *see under* THE NEW TOWN.

CRAIGWELL (Calton) is recorded from 1647 onwards and was the general name for the southern district in the barony of Calton, marching with the North Back of the Canongate from the foot of Leith

Wynd to the boundary of Erneside, now represented by that of the New Calton Burial Ground. It evidently derived from the earliest of the three wells shown on *Rothiemay* 1647 along the foot of the Calton crags, one opposite Jack's Close (about 40 yards east of New Street) another opposite Tolbooth Wynd, and the third, the NETHER CRAIGWELL, opposite Campbell's Close; and the last gave its name to new housing around it in 1986.

CRAMOND is recorded in the 1170s, in the spellings *Karramunt* or *Caramonde*; and since the name was spoken with the normal Celtic stress *karr-'amund*, its first syllable shortened, and it became *Cramond* by 1250. It is British *caer Amond*, fortified place on the ALMOND (*which see*) and was evidently the native Votadinic name for the Roman fort and annexes of the 2nd and early 3rd centuries, and probably also for the native settlement within the ruins after the Romans withdrew. CRAMOND KIRK is built over the Roman fort's headquarters, and this together with the local name ANNAT (*which see*) suggests that a kirk was founded very early on, perhaps by a Ninianic mission, at a time when the Roman building could still be adapted for this purpose. The names of the subdivisions of Cramond are given as *Kirke Craumond* (in Scots) and *Craumond of the king's demesne* (in Latin) in *Bain* 1336. Lying round about the kirk and granted to the bishops of Dunkeld in the late 12th century, KIRK CRAMOND figures in *Protocols of James Young* 1489 as 'the lands and burgh of Kyrk Crawmond'. Its alternative name NETHER CRAMOND appears in *RMS* 1479, but 'Bishop's Cramond' seems to have been a historians' invention. Since its centre is represented by CRAMOND TOWER, succeeded in 1808 by CRAMOND HOUSE, the name KIRK CRAMOND was revived in 1984 for the entry, formed in 1778, that leads to both. CRAMOND ROAD SOUTH is partly on a Roman line (*see under* ROMAN ROADS) and originally continued straight to the east gate of the fort at Kirk Cramond, as shown on *Roy* 1753 and on a line still marked by trees in 1960; but in 1778 this northern section was cut off at the *Bridge of Stones*, and diverted by what is now known as CRAMOND ROAD NORTH, crossing the middle of the minister's glebe and going on to the foot of the old village street, as shown on *Cramond* 1815. Hence the names of GLEBE ROAD for part of it, and of GLEBE TERRACE, built in the western glebe in about 1900. In 1967, for fear of confusion with other *Glebe* street names in the city, these were renamed CRAMOND GLEBE ROAD and TERRACE; and in 1971 CRAMOND GLEBE GARDENS, built in a market garden in the eastern glebe, followed suit. Building-up of the *Fairafar* and *East Parks* of Fairafar farm in Kirk Cramond began at CRAMOND CRESCENT in 1931 and continued at CRAMOND AVENUE (1935) GARDENS and PARK (1936) PLACE (1953) and GROVE and TERRACE (1955). CRAMOND VALE was started in another part of the farm in 1972. The other large historic estate in Cramond stretched southwards from Gamekeepers Road to the foot of the CRAMOND MUIR or COMMON on the Drum. Its name CRAMOND REGIS or KING'S CRAMOND appears in both Latin and Scots in *RMS* 1391-1406 and like the earlier description in

Bain, already quoted, implies that these lands had continued in royal ownership for some time after the grant of Kirk Cramond to Dunkeld. It was also known as OVER or UPPER CRAMOND, since it was centred rather more easterly than Nether Cramond. Suppressed under the name of BARNTON (*which see*) in about 1811, these historic names have been commemorated in the naming of four small streets: CRAMOND REGIS (1968) REGIS COURT and UPPER CRAMOND COURT (1974) and KING'S CRAMOND (1989).

CRAMOND BRIG (Cramond) is shown on *Blaeu* 1654 and *Adair* 1682, and its existing structure (probably not the first) carried the road to Queensferry from about 1500 until 1824, when a new bridge was built further upstream for the new turnpike, *see also under* HILLHOUSE ROAD. To fit in with this arrangement, CRAMOND TOLL was transferred from the east side of the old Brig to the west bank of the river; and in 1986 its name was revived for the rump of the ancient road on the west bank, cut off from Braehead when the Brig was finally closed to vehicles.

CRAMOND ISLAND (Cramond) is described in the 12th century as 'the island in front of the harbour of Cramond', and by the 16th century it is named as the *Yle of Cramond* or *Cramondinch*.

CRANNES BRIG (Wester Duddingston) is mentioned in *Duddingston Kirk Session Minutes* 1693, and carried the road from Wester Duddingston to Niddrie over the Braid burn near NT 29407225. Shown on *Roy* 1753, the road was suppressed when the policies of DUDDINGSTON HOUSE (*which see*) were laid out in about 1768. The name is evidently for the waterbird, early Scots *cran*, a crane or heron, and appeared also in the adjoining field name *Cranies* recorded in 1707 and figured in the corrupt form *Cranvas Park* on *Duddingston* c1800.

CRANSTON'S CLOSE (517 High Street) *see* MILNE'S CLOSE.

CRANSTON STREET (Canongate) is shown proposed on *City Improvements* 1866, starting at the entry of COULL'S CLOSE and curving westwards to overlie the lower part of LEITH WYND. It was named by 1874 for Robert Cranston, founder of the Cranston Temperance Hotels, then councillor for Canongate, who may have owned ground west of the street—as his son, Lord Provost Robert Cranston, did in 1891. The northern half of the street was suppressed when the Waverley Station goods yard and EAST MARKET STREET were constructed in the mid 1890s.

CRARAE AVENUE (Murrayfield) *see under* GARSCUBE TERRACE, Murrayfield.

CRAUFURDLAND (Cramond) was developed in 1987, and the name was coined to commemorate the Howison-Craufurd family, owners of Braehead.

CRAWFORD BRIDGE (Norton Park) was named in 1986 for Gerald Crawford, musician, who was elected to the Town Council in 1926 and represented Calton Ward until his death in 1945. His proposal for this footbridge was approved in 1927 and it was opened in 1929.

CRAWFORD'S CLOSE (8 Grassmarket) *see* BACK O THE BUGHTS, Grassmarket.

CRAWFURD ROAD (Craigmillar Park) *see under* CRAIGMILLAR PARK.

CRAW HILL (Ratho) was evidently named for the presence of crows.

CRAW'S CLOSE (Queensferry) is named on *Ordnance Survey* 1854, and is now represented approximately by the west front of HILL COURT. The curved line of the close, together with that of GOTE LANE, suggests that it was set by a watercourse—*see* WESTER LOANING BURN, Queensferry. The close is evidently named for a proprietor, but who Craw was is not known.

THE CRESCENT (South Morningside) was adopted in 1970 as a side name in Morningside Drive, to obviate renumbering of that street in order to accommodate new housing on its north side. The name was coined by the builders, evidently under the impression that a *crescent* is anything curved. *See also* NORTH WALK, South Morningside.

THE CREW (Inverleith) was a farm steading immediately southeast of Crewe Toll. Shown on *Adair* 1682 as *Creue*, the name was variously spelt *Crue*, *Crew* or *the Crew* until after 1900, when the spelling *Crewe* began to be used, probably under the influence of the Cheshire railway junction. While it might be Scots *crue* or Gaelic *cro*, a fold or hut, the terrain points to British *cryw*, a ford or crossing by stepping stones: for not only does the Crew road cross the Wardie burn less than 200 yards from the farm site, but the array of ditches shown on *Kirkwood* 1817 and *Ordnance Survey* 1852 bears witness to the wetness of the whole area round the steading at the crossroads. Since *cryw* could also mean 'weir', there may be some connection with the nearby name of WERBER, *which see*. CREWE ROAD was known, certainly north of Crewe Toll, but perhaps further south as well, as the WHITING ROAD, *which see*; but it was probably known as the road *by the Crew* from Dean to Granton long before it was noted on *W & A K Johnston* 1905 as *Crewe Road*. CREWE TOLL is shown on *Gellatly* 1834 and listed as *crue* among toll bars in 1844, but is not shown as such on *Ordnance Survey* 1852. Crewe Road was divided into NORTH and SOUTH sections in 1926; and later streets adjoining it, all on Pilton ground, took their names from Crewe Road North rather than from the Crew itself: CREWE BANK CRESCENT, GROVE, LOAN, PLACE and TERRACE in 1934, CREWE PATH in 1935, and CREWE GARDENS and CREWE ROAD WEST in 1938.

CRICHTON'S CLOSE and **ENTRY** (116 and 112 Canongate) are listed in *Ainslie* 1780, and were named for Alexander Crichton, son of Patrick Crichton of Newington, who set up a coachworks here (shown on *Edgar* 1765) in about 1762, on ground that had previously belonged to Patrick Jackson, burgess of Edinburgh and treasurer of the Canongate in 1705, and to his son David, also an Edinburgh burgess. Crichton and his partner Field moved to Greenside in 1794, but the coach building at Crichton's Entry was carried on by John Carfrae and his successors, hence the later name CARFRAE'S ENTRY.

CRICHTON STREET (Bristo) was developed as part of James Brown's scheme for George Square and was named by 1771, evidently for James Crichton, mason, who took up residence in one of the houses in 1780 and was probably the builder of the street.

CRIGHTON PLACE (Leith Walk) appears in *PO Directory* 1876 and was named for James Crighton, convener of the Trinity Hospital Committee, owners of the ground.

CROCKET'S CLOSE (South Leith) is shown on *Kirkwood* 1817 as lying south of Tolbooth Wynd. It was evidently named for the same owner or family as was CROCKET'S LAND within it; and there might be some connection with the John Crokat mentioned in *RMS* 1591 as late owner of land in South Leith.

CROFTANGRY (Abbeyhill) is recorded in 1724 as *Croftangrie*, but the house which also bears the name is shown on *Rothiemay* 1647 and partly dates from the previous century. The street name appears on *Kincaid* 1784 and *Kirkwood* 1817 as *Croftangry* and *Croft Angry*, and it is given as *Croft Angery* on *Regality of Canongate* 1813. Pronounced *croft-'ang-ry*, it is a field name widely recorded in the Lowlands from 1497 onwards, deriving from Anglian *croft angr*, a fenced grazing in the croft or arable infield, as distinct from unfenced grazings on outby land. The pseudo-Gaelic spelling 'Croft an righ' appears only at Holyrood and only since the 1820s, when the progressive change in map spellings from *-angry* and *-anry* to *an' rhi* and *an righ* shows that it was deliberately altered to suit a notion that it was Gaelic for 'king's croft'. This was assumed without a shred of evidence for royal ownership, and despite the fact that by the time the king came to own his residence at Holyrood in the 15th century Gaelic had long since fallen out of use in Lothian. Even if this were not so, the Gaelic sounds and stress of *croft-an-'ree* could never fit the historic form *Croftangry*; and the modern and quite unGaelic rhyming of the name with English *nigh*, even although it also corrupts the original, probably arose out of resistance of tradition to the fake.

CROMBIE'S CLOSE (101 Cowgate) *see* HUME'S CLOSE, Cowgate.

CROMBIE'S LAND (West Port) seems to have been named for Alexander Crombie, formerly a builder of canal boats at St Anthony's Place. It was demolished in 1869 and its position remains to be identified.

(OLIVER) CROMWELL'S CAMP (Fairmilehead) was a large earthwork, described in *Maitland* 1753 and *White's Liberton* 1792 and figured on *Armstrongs* 1773 in the same place as *Laurie* 1766 shows a Roman Camp. Since this would place it athwart the Roman route from Carlops (*see under* ROMAN ROADS) a Roman connection is at least possible; but since the remains visible in the 18th century are reported by some as square and by others as oval, their origin remains in doubt. Although Cromwell certainly camped in this neighbourhood in August 1650, no record suggests that he made any use of an earthwork. In advancing from Musselburgh on 13 and 18 August, as well as in his subsequent retreat from Gogar on 29 August, his route was by Niddrie Marischal, the Kames, Fairmilehead, Colinton and Slateford, and the most detailed contemporary accounts report that he camped somewhere between the Pentlands and 'Braid Craigs', the name shown on *Adair* 1682 at Blackford Hill. Since it is likely that he used the Frogston road for his guns and wagons, he probably found a defensible position, with access to water, at or near Morton or the Galachlaw.

CROMWELL STREET (North Leith) was planned in 1807 but not occupied until 1821. By 1845 it had been cut into two by the railway and North Leith Station. EAST CROMWELL STREET was further truncated by industrial development, and WEST CROMWELL STREET was rebuilt as new housing in 1980. CROMWELL PLACE was a new name given in 1979 to a part of ADMIRALTY STREET, *which see*. The streets are named for Oliver Cromwell because they were aligned along two sides of the fortress which the Cromwellian army under Monck erected here in 1656—*see under* THE CITADEL.

CROOKED DYKES (South Side) is shown on *Ainslie* 1804 and *Ordnance Survey* 1852, and the name aptly described this narrow passage between walls and turning four sharp corners. It was almost wholly cleared to make way for HOWDEN STREET, *which see*.

CROOKS' CLOSE (62 Grassmarket) is shown on *Ainslie* 1780 & 1804 but is omitted in *PO Directory* 1827 and left unnamed on *Ordnance Survey* 1852. The name was evidently from Thomas Crooks, listed in *Williamson's Directory* 1773 as a baxter on the north side of the Grassmarket.

THE CROSS or **MERCAT CROSS** (Old Town) is mentioned in *RMS* 1365 as a landmark in the town, but an edict of 1175 'that merchandize sal be presentit at the mercat croce of burghis', undoubtedly applied to Edinburgh as one of the four royal burghs, and illustrates the fact that the cross was the centre of any burgh from the very start, giving a religious and legal guarantee to all bargains struck in the market. In the Middle Ages, the Cross stood on a 'cross house' in the middle of the High Street, about 12 yards north of the present structure. Moved in 1617 to a site near the head of Old Fishmarket Close, it was demolished in 1756, on plea of road improvement but perhaps not without intention to persuade the merchants to transfer their activity from the Cross to the new Exchange built for them in 1753; but as *Arnot* points out in 1779, the site had to be marked in the causey (as it still is) for legal purposes, and 'there also company resort, from one to three o'clock, for news, business or meeting their acquaintances, nobody frequenting the exchange.' Indeed, since the Middle Ages *The Cross* had meant not merely the Mercat Cross itself but the section of the High Street in which it stood, from the Luckenbooths nearly to the Tron: a usage still shown on *Ainslie* 1804, and still lingering about 180 years later in the name of *The Cross* Post Office, closed down in the 1980s. Meantime, the capital of the Cross, together with five fragments of the medieval shaft (representing only about two thirds of the great single stone which had been dropped and shattered in the course of demolition) had been rescued in 1756 and kept at the Drum, Gilmerton, until 1866, when they were re-erected at the north side of St Giles. A new unicorn finial was added in 1869; and then in 1885, through the generosity of W E Gladstone, MP for Midlothian, the Cross was transferred to a new cross house, a free variation of the design of 1617, built east of St Giles. The present shaft, dating from 1970, is a replica of the old fragments as re-erected in 1885 and is therefore about 7 or 8 feet shorter than the medieval one. These fragments showed that the shaft had been at least as old as the surviving capital, which dates from the early 15th century, a time when a marked upsurge in the city's fortunes may well have led to an enhancement of its Cross or even a replacement with something bigger and better.

CROSSALL (Dalmeny) is probably the *C Roshall* shown garbled and out of position on *Blaeu* 1654. Recorded as *Corshall* in 1598 and *Corsehall* in 1692, it figures as *Corsha* on *Adair* 1682, *Corse hall* on *Dundas* 1757, and *Crosshall* on *Armstrongs* 1773, but *Barnbougle & Dalmeny* c1800 shows only the field name *Crosshall Park* (given as *Chamberlain Shot* in 1757) and *Ordnance Survey* 1852 names the spur of higher ground east of it as *Crossall Hill*. Although all maps up to and including *Armstrongs* 1773 indicate buildings beside the main road, there is nothing to suggest that these were more than farm buildings of an unpretentious sort; and as is normally the case, the ending -*hall* is unlikely to be Anglian *heall*, a hall, but is rather the land name *halh*, Scots *haw* or *haugh*. The first part of the name shows the *r* changing position in a way normal in Scots: it may be from British *cors*, a marsh, or else from Anglian *cros*, a cross, or Gaelic *crois*, a crossing. Thus the name may be 'marshy haugh', which would fit the lie of the land south and west of the hill; or it may be 'crossing haugh' or floor of the valley which runs between the Shepherd's Bog in the east to the great flat of *Fluirs park* in the west; or it may be the 'haugh at the cross', referring to a wayside cross, probably medieval and still represented by its socket stone, which stood on the south slope of Crossall Hill.

CROSSBANK (Corstorphine) was a side name at 174 St JOHN'S ROAD. Although developed apparently by James Younger in 1899, it seems to have been named for Robert Cross, owner of the ground 1885-1896.

CROSSCAUSEY (South Side) is shown on *Adair* 1682 as the link between the ancient roads to Liberton and Dalkeith; and this accounts for its early name of *Croce Gaitt*, a general term for a 'cross way' between two roads. In May 1599 this way that 'leids fra the Societie towre (or WINDMILL, *which see*) to Plesance' was *calsayed* or *causeyed* (the second shows the pronunciation of both) at the joint expense of the town and the adjoining landowner Crighton of Lugton; and by 1661 the name *Crosscausey* was in use. Scots *causey* (from Old French *caucie*) is a metalled or paved road, or the metalling itself. The spelling *Cross Causway* used on *Scott* 1759 already shows confusion with English *causeway* (which was a 'causey(ed) way', but has come to mean a raised one) yet popular usage has resisted this corruption, and the proper Scots 'Crosscausey' is still current in local parlance.

CROSSFERRY WA'S (Ingliston) is shown on *Knox* 1812 and 1852 and is *West Ingliston Cottages* on later maps. It seems to combine an earlier place name, perhaps Gaelic *crois feurach*, grassy crossing, or *crois fuarain* crossing place with springs, with Scots *walls*, springs, either explaining or half-translating the original.

CROSSGATE TOLL (West End) was the toll at Kirkbraehead, mentioned in 1766 and taking its name from the CROSSGATE or LANGDYKES road (*which see*) that branched eastwards from the Queensferry road at this point, linking it with the road to Leith at Moutrie's Hill.

CROSSWOOD CRESCENT etc (Balerno) *see under* COCKBURN CRESCENT, Balerno.

CROW HILL (Arthur's Seat) is named as a hill frequented by crows. *Kirkwood* 1817 and *Ordnance Survey* prior to 1893 attach the name to the summit a quarter-mile north-east of the main summit of Arthur's Seat (at NT 278734) whereas later maps show it further south, above Duddingston (at NT 277729).

CROWN STREET (South Leith) is shown constructed on *Ainslie* 1804 and was named before 1825, possibly to celebrate the rediscovery of the Scottish regalia in the Castle in 1818, but perhaps in emulation of nearby Queen's Place, which was named by 1815. The street appears to have been developed within the grounds of Whitfield House, shown (unnamed) on *Fergus & Robinson* 1759 as well as *Wood* 1777, but lost through redevelopment in about 1880. *Kirkwood* 1817 shows a lane on the north side of the house, and the name WHITFIELD PLACE appears in *PO Directory* 1834. This became WHITFIELD LANE shortly afterwards: but by 1893 it began to be displaced by CROWN PLACE (obviously modelled on *Crown Street*) although the Lane name continued in the directories until 1899).

CRUICKLAW (Currie) was a farm on the south side of the river, upstream from Currie, recorded in 1716 and 1771, and shown (misspelt as *Cocklaw*) on *Laurie* 1763. The site was in the hollow east of Lennox Tower, and the name, Anglian *croc hlaw* or Scots *cruik law*, hill or mound at the crook, probably referred to the bend of the river below the spur and cairn at DUNCAN'S BELT (*which see*) and indeed the *hlaw* could have been the cairn itself.

CRUICK'S CLOSE (341 High Street) *see* ROXBURGH'S CLOSE.

CRUIKNESS BURN (Redford) is recorded in 1586 as a name for the Braid Burn in the vicinity of Redford. As Scots, from Anglian *croc nes*, nose or projecting piece of land at the crook or bend, it might refer to the confluence of the Bonaly and Howden burns, where there is a long narrow spit of land between these tributaries and also a sharp bend in the main burn.

CRUMBLANDS (Lennie) is shown on *Roy* 1753 as *Crumlins*. As Anglian *crumb lands*, land in the crook (of the Almond) the name is to all appearances a translation of the nearby British name CAMMO (*which see*) and, if so, may date from a period when the Celtic name's meaning was still understood.

CUDDIES LANE (Colinton) *see under* COLINTON.

CUDDY LANE (Greenside) was a branch off Greenside Court, along the backs of the buildings fronting Greenside Row. It is listed in *PO Directory* 1911 but is shown, unnamed, on all maps from *Kirkwood* 1817 onwards. The evidence of *Ainslie* 1804 and *Kirkwood* 1817 is that it may have been developed in connection with the coach works of Crichton & Fields (later Gall & Thompson) and since it is likely that they included stabling or even a smiddy, the lane was probably named as a passage for horses. The area was cleared in 1969.

CUDDY LANE (Morningside) is shown on *Kirkwood* 1817 as the entry to a field that lay behind Denholm's smiddy, now the site of the public library. The name is traditional, and one that is frequently if not invariably associated with a smiddy. Evidently horses were brought in this way for shoeing; and it shows the tenacity of tradition that the name was still current a hundred years after the lane had become entirely a residential cul-de-sac in the 1840s, as shown on *Ordnance Survey* 1852. An attempt made in about 1860 to name it *Rosewood Place* failed, and the lane was awkwardly named as in Springvalley Terrace but numbered as part of Morningside Road until 1984, when *Cuddy Lane* was formally adopted.

CUDDY PARK (Lauriston) appears, from the description given in *Anent Old Edinburgh*, to have been the field shown as *Mr Kier's* on *Ainslie* 1804 (*see* KEIR STREET) and was perhaps named, not for *cuddies* as donkeys or horses, but for George Cuddie, coach hirer on the south side of Grassmarket in 1799. The cattle market removed here from the Grassmarket in 1843.

LORD CULLEN'S CLOSE (304 High Street) *see* BRODIE'S CLOSE.

CULTINS (Sighthill) is shown as CULTON MAINS on *Cultins* 1776 and noted on *Riccarton* 1800 as a farm of 65 acres. It seems to have been broken up when the Edinburgh & Glasgow Railway line was built in the 1840s; and the site of its steading, immediately north of the railway, is now occupied by an electricity substation. CULTINS ROAD is shown on *Cultins* 1776 as a proposed new road connecting Culton Mains with the Calder road. MID NEW CULTINS was developed in the south of the farm in 1990. The place name, recorded as *Cultins, Culton(s)* or *Cultens*, is Celtic: perhaps *coilltean*, (place of) woods or groves, but more likely *cuiltean*, (place of) nooks or corners, referring to the abrupt turns in the course of the Gogar hereabouts. In either case, the Celtic plural seems to be preserved in the English *s*.

CUMBERLAND (Dalmahoy) is shown on *Dalmahoy* 1749 as a place beside the meeting point of the various sources of the Murray burn on the south of Long Dalmahoy. While the evidence is slender, it is possible that the name is British *comber lann* or Gaelic *comar lainn*, meeting of waters at the enclosure or kirk. This 'kirk' meaning of *lann* may be appropriate here, since DALMAHOY (*which see*) is a Celtic kirk name, and the *New Statistical Account* 1839 reports that 'within living memory' there was once a 'Gothic arch, perhaps chapel ruins' at Long Dalmahoy.

CUMBERLAND STREET (New Town) *see under* NORTHERN NEW TOWN.

CUMIN PLACE (Grange) *see under* THE GRANGE.

CUMLODDEN AVENUE (Murrayfield) *see under* GARSCUBE TERRACE, Murrayfield.

CUMMING'S CLOSE (52 Canongate) is listed on *Ainslie* 1780. George and John Cuming, both brewers, are mentioned, without dates, in *Canongate Charters* 1888, along with a John Cuming of Gayswood, Haslemere, Surrey, owner of property in the close in 1835. A George Cumming owned the Anchor tavern in Anchor Close prior to 1734: there might be a connection, although there is no evidence for it.

CUMNOR CRESCENT (Inch) *see under* THE INCH, Nether Liberton.

CUNNINGHAM PLACE (South Leith) was named by 1895 for its developer, Peter Cunningham of James Cunningham & Sons, builders in Leith.

CURRIE is recorded from 1210 onwards in such early spellings as *Curey* 1210, *Cory* 1230, *Curri* 1246, *Curry* 1392, *Corry* 1434 and *Currie* 1402. Although the name is spread over a considerable area north of the river (*see also* CURRIEHEADRIG, CURRIEHILL, CURRIEMUIREND and the modern CURRIEVALE) the impression remains that it originated on the banks of the Water of Leith, where *Blaeu* 1654 shows *Curry* and *Over Curry*, and *Adair* 1682 shows *Currie K(irk)* and *Currie toun* or farm place. The name also occurs at Borthwick, Midlothian, in a closely similar setting. Derivation from Gaelic *currach*, boggy plain, is possible, but unconvincing, insofar as any haughs here or at Borthwick are small and unremarkable. What both places have in common is a steep river bank with a way down it to a crossing place; and this, together with a striking similarity in early forms with the names *Cory*, *Corry* and *Curry* in Somerset, Devon and Cornwall, suggest that the name is British *curi*, a hollow, akin to Welsh *cwr* or Gaelic *curra*, a corner. While CURRIE KIRK, mentioned in *RMS* 1493, traces back at least to the 13th century, speculation about a Celtic church foundation seems to rest upon a misinterpretation of the nearby name KELDELEITH, *which see*. CURRIE BRIG is recorded in 1599; but the crossing here must have been the ancient access to the kirk and to Keldelethe as well as the route through the hills by the CLOCHMEADGATE. The MAINS OF CURRIE recorded in 1495 may have included OVER and NETHER CURRIE mentioned in *RMS* 1530 (*Over/Nether* or *Easter/Wester* being the normal classification of lands on the 'sunny' or 'shadow' sides of an estate) and *Riccarton* 1772 shows WESTER and MID CURRIE west of the Corslet road, and EASTER and NETHER CURRIE east of it, while *Currie Farm* 1797 shows the latter pair amalgamated with the CORSLET, *which see*. Easter Currie began to be developed for housing in about 1960 at EASTER CURRIE CRESCENT, PLACE and TERRACE; and EASTER CURRIE COURT was built on the site of the farm steading in 1970. Nether Currie, once an *oxgang* of 13 Scots acres, centred at what is now Corslet Place; and the streets named for it in about 1960—NETHER CURRIE CRESCENT, PLACE and ROAD—lie in CURRIE MUIR, *which see*.

CURRIE HEADRIG (Riccarton) is shown on *Roy* 1753 (which does not show any Riccarton Mains) while *Riccarton* 1772 shows *Currie Head Rigg* at about NT 186694, some 600 yards east of *Riccarton Mains*, and the latter farm seems to have absorbed it by 1800. The site is on a low rigg or ridge with a knowe on it, which may have been seen as the *head* of Currie muir in the approach from Hermiston.

CURRIEHILL (Currie) is recorded in *Bain* 1337 as *Hille* and in *RMS* 1527 as '*the Hill* in the barony of Balerno', but it is shown on *Blaeu* 1654 (probably surveyed in 1596) as *Curry hill*, and mentioned in *RMS* 1604 as *Hill, commonly called Curriehill*. By then—and probably long before—it boasted a towerhouse on the spur above the Murray burn, about 150 yards west of the later CURRIEHILL HOUSE of 1856, and CURRIEHILL CASTLE DRIVE was named for it in 1978. CURRIEHILL ROAD originated as a loaning shown on *Riccarton* 1772 as leading from Currie to Malcolmston. In about 1847 it was developed as the access to *Currie Station* on the main Glasgow line of the Caledonian Railway; but with the opening of a new *Currie Station* on the Balerno branch in 1874, the mainline station was renamed *Curriehill Station* (possibly through its association with the Curriehill Strip, *see below*) and the road in turn became CURRIEHILL STATION ROAD. In the 1950s the station was closed, and in about 1970 the street name was shortened to CURRIEHILL ROAD—ironically enough, for with the reopening of the mainline station in the 1980s the street once more became a 'station road'. The CURRIEHILL STRIP, originally the name of the woodland on the eastern fringe of Curriehill estate, was in use before 1893 as the name of the pathway shown on *Ordnance Survey* 1852 as leading through it to Currie(hill) station. CURRIEHILL TERRACE was the side name (now suppressed) of the terrace of council housing built in Lanark Road opposite the Red Row in 1923.

CURRIE MUIR (Juniper Green and Currie) is shown on *Adair* 1682 and recorded in the same year as the *Common Muir of Currie* in which the owners of the Kirklands of Hailes (i.e. Spylaw) shared grazing rights with others. It extended for over a mile from Curriemuirend nearly to the centre of Currie—*see also* JUNIPER GREEN *and* MUIR WOOD.

CURRIEMUIREND (Hailes) is recorded in 1682, shown on *Roy* 1753 and detailed on *Hailes* 1818 as a 32-acre farm with its steading on the north side of the Lanark road about 300 yards west of the Wester Hailes road junction. The name obviously derived from its position at the east end of the CURRIE MUIR, *which see. Ordnance Survey* 1852 shows a fancy name VIEWFIELD at the farm, but continues to attach the earlier name to the inn and cottages on the opposite side of the road.

MOOREND AVENUE, developed before 1912, derived its name from Curriemuirend; while the later fancy name was given to VIEWFIELD ROAD, built in 1938 in part of the southern half of the farm.

CURRIE'S or **CURROR'S CLOSE** (384 High Street and once 110 but now 94 Grassmarket) was the only close, other than Castle Wynd, to run between Castlehill and the Grasssmarket; but its upper part was swept away by the development of Johnston Terrace and the Tolbooth Kirk in about 1840. Its earlier name, given on *Rothiemay* 1647 as *Currer's*, derived from a John Corrour, probably the one mentioned in *Town Council Minutes* 1480 as tenant of a booth under the Tolbooth, whose property in Castlehill was eventually inherited by seven sisters, as recorded in *Protocols of John Foular* 1532. The later name *Currie's*, appearing on *Edgar* 1742, may then have been quite recent, given for Andrew Currie, deacon of the Weavers in 1736, and resident in the close.

CURRIEVALE (Currie) dates from about 1865, as a name coined for a new farm in the howe or (more fancily) *vale* of Curriehill. CURRIEVALE DRIVE, lying south of the farm, was named for it in June 1977 and CURRIEVALE PARK was added four months later. CURRIEVALE PARK GROVE was named in 1986.

CURRISLATTS (Queensferry) is recorded in *RMS* 1662 as a field name in MUIRHALL (*which see*) and seems to be a hybrid of Gaelic *curraich*, (place) at the wet plain, and Scots *slatt*, from Old Norse *slétta*, level field. Its exact location remains to be traced.

CUSTOM HOUSE QUAY or **WHARF** (North Leith) *see under* BALLAST QUAY, North Leith.

THE CUT or **NEW CUT** (Newhaven) was the name used from the early 1830s for CRAIGHALL ROAD—*which see*.

D

DAIRIES ROAD (Corstorphine) *see* GYLEMUIR ROAD, Corstorphine.

DAIRSIE PLACE (Abbeymount) was developed in about 1870, and was probably named for its builder.

DAISY TERRACE (North Merchiston) *see under* PRIMROSE TERRACE, North Merchiston.

DALE STREET (Pleasance) appears on *Kirkwood* 1817 as a new development, including three branches called SALISBURY, ORCHARD and CALEDONIA STREETS, in the part of the historic DISHFLAT known as the BRIERY BAUKS. Building began in 1817, but the names were changed: *Knox* 1821 shows the main street as ARTHUR STREET, while *Kirkwood* 1823 shows the side streets as EAST, MIDDLE and WEST ARTHUR PLACE. All the names were fancy: *Dale* for the valley to the east, *Salisbury* and *Arthur* for the crags and hill beyond it, *Orchard* probably for the character of the site (shown on *Regality of Canongate* 1813 as 'Mr Alexander's') and *Caledonia* as a patriotic flourish akin to SCOTLAND STREET in the NORTHERN NEW TOWN, *which see*. The entire area was cleared in the late 1930s, and later occupied by VIEWCRAIG GARDENS, NEW ARTHUR PLACE and BRIERY BAUKS, *which see*.

DALHOUSIE TERRACE (South Morningside) *see under* PLEWLANDS, South Morningside.

DALGETY STREET, ROAD and **AVENUE** (Abbeymount) were developed in about 1892, 1894 and 1897 within lands of Restalrig owned by the earls of Moray, and were named for another Moray property at Dalgety, near Donisbristle, Fife.

DALKEITH ROAD is shown on *Blaeu* 1654 and was evidently established as a main route to the south long before 1586, when the town council's feuing plan for the easter Burgh Muir included a reservation 24 ells (almost 25 yards) wide for this *hie commoun gate*, as compared with 18 ells for the Liberton road, *see* MAYFIELD ROAD. The variant name OLD DALKEITH ROAD seems to date from the 1890s, when the 'new' one was said to be that by Minto Street, Greenend and Gilmerton—the greater part of it, ironically enough, as old as the Romans, *see* DERE STREET. DALKEITH ROAD LANE was developed opposite Echobank in about 1890.

DALKEITH STREET (Joppa) was developed in the *Old Engine Park* of Easter Duddingston, the field name referring to the mining pump in its north-eastern corner (later Mount Pleasant at the foot of Morton Street at Joppa Road) which is shown on *Laurie* 1763 and was in fact installed by the Earl of Abercorn in that very year. Listed in *New Edinburgh Directory* 1868, the street is named for the daughter of the 1st Duke of Abercorn, who married the Earl of Dalkeith.

DALLAS'S CLOSE (200 Canongate) *see* (UPPER) PLAYHOUSE CLOSE.

DALMAHOY (Ratho) is shown on *Blaeu* 1654 and recorded from 1296 onwards. The early spellings *Dalmahoy(e)*, *Dalmihoi*, *Dalmehoy* and *Dalmohoy* show the name to be Celtic, British or Gaelic *da(i)l mo Thuae*, meadow of St Tua, one of four saints of that name in the Celtic kirk, dating from the 9th century or earlier; and since Celtic kirk dedication usually meant that the saint worked there, Tua probably had some direct connection with the place. *See also under* CUMBERLAND, Dalmahoy. The home farm DALMAHOY MAINS or *Maynes of Dalmahoy* is named in *RMS* 1636. LONG DALMAHOY is mentioned in *RMS* 1657, and *Dalmahoy* 1749 shows the 'long row' of tofts or cottage plots, with the associated CROFTS OF DALMAHOY. DALMAHOY CRAIGS, shown on *Blaeu* 1654, is one of two general names for the group of hills, including KAIMES and RAVELRIG HILLS as well as DALMAHOY HILL, and names them for their location, whereas their other general name THE KAIMES (*which see*) refers to their form. The 76-acre DALMAHOY MOSS to the south of Dalmahoy Hill, graphically depicted on *Roy* 1753, was drained in 1840. DALMAHOY ROAD is the traditional name of the road leading out of Ratho to Dalmahoy. It is shown on *Hatton etc* 1797 as on its present alignment; but *Roy* 1753 and *Armstrongs* 1773 show that it was once continuous with the LIDGATE (*which see*) and the alteration is still marked by the kink in the road some 70 yards south of the village.

DALMAHOY CRESCENT (Balerno) was developed in part of Pilmuir in 1963, and appears to have been named for Dalmahoy, which faces Pilmuir across the valley of the Murray burn. ADDISTON CRESCENT, PARK and GROVE (1964) seem also to bear an estate name, from Addiston, north of Dalmahoy. Of the other two groups of streets in this development, TURNER AVENUE and PARK (1963) were named for the Revd David Turner, minister in Balerno from 1901 to 1940, while HORSBURGH GROVE, GARDENS and BANK (1965-68) commemorate Thomas Horsburgh, blacksmith in Johnsburn smiddy and a kenspeckle figure in the local community.

DALMENY is recorded from 1214 onwards, not primarily as DALMENY KIRK (recorded in 1363) but first as an estate and then as a barony centred on Barnbougle and extending as far west as Echline; and accordingly the kirk village, although it figures on *Blaeu* 1654 as *Dummany*, may not have been the point of the name's origin. Of the spellings, *Dunmanyn* was typical in the 13th century but was still in use in 1471, while *Dummany* 1325 and *Dumany* 1378 remained current long after *Dalmeny* appeared in 1587, and the present local pronunciation is still close to the *Damenie* appearing on *Adair* 1682. Clearly the first part of the name is not *dal-* but British *din* or Gaelic *dun*, a fort. The suggestion that the second part might be *manach* or *menegh*, would make the name 'fort of the monk(s)', odd in itself and unsupported by evidence of an early monastic settlement; whereas the presence within Dalmeny of the powerful fort and settlement on Craigie hill, with its triple ramparts partly built in stone, would account for names such as *din meyni*, stone fort, or *din meyn an*, place of the stone fort. The village of DALMENY or DALMENY KIRK is shown in some detail on *Roy* 1753, *Dundas* 1757, and *Barnbougle & Dalmeny* c1800; and *Roy* also shows DALMENY MUIR to the west of it. WESTER DALMENY may have been the original centre of the farm or *villa de Dunmanyn* mentioned in *RMS* 1428, which was subdivided in about 1850, and supplied with a new steading for EASTER DALMENY. DALMENY HOUSE, built in 1817 as a replacement of Barnbougle Castle, is shown on *Forrest* 1818 as *Dalmeny Park*. Soon after this, the estate was reorganised, Little Barnbougle was suppressed, and DALMENY HOME FARM formed. The original DALMENY STATION was opened in 1866 on the Queensferry branch railway line, but was converted to DALMENY SOUTH JUNCTION when the Forth Bridge line and a new DALMENY STATION were completed in 1889.

DALMENY ROAD (Bonnington) was named in about 1886, at the same time as GOSFORD PLACE. The streets originally intersected, and it is likely that they were named as a pair: one to honour the Earl of Rosebery, whose seat was at *Dalmeny* on the west of the city; and the other to honour the Earl of Wemyss, whose seat was at *Gosford* on the east of the city.

DALMENY STREET (Leith Walk) was originally named in 1876 as COLSTON STREET, for James Colston, city treasurer and convener of Trinity Hospital, superiors of the ground; but in 1885, although Colston was still prominent in the town council, it was renamed (at the same time as IONA STREET, *which see*) as DALMENY STREET, apparently in compliment to Lord Rosebery, owner of Dalmeny and then prominent in the Liberal party.

DALRY is recorded in *RMS* in about 1328. Early spellings *Dalry*, *Dalrye* and *Dailry* show the name to be Celtic, British *dol rug* or Gaelic *dail fhraoigh*, heathery dale, reflecting the character of the drier ground above the waterside haughs. Neither history nor pronunciation supports derivation from *dail righ*, king's meadow. In modern terms, the lands stretched from Semple Street and Thornybauk to Westfield and Roseburn, and included the DALRY HAUGHS mentioned in *RMS* 1545, on which stood the estate's DALRY MILLS, detailed in *RMS* 1478 as three mills for waulking cloth as well as grinding corn, and shown on *Blaeu* 1654 as *Darry Mill*, and as *Dary mil* on *Adair* 1682, but as ROSEBURN (*which see*) on *Adair/Cooper* 1735. Paper making, the earliest recorded in Scotland, was on the go at Dalry before 1591, and part of Roseburn House was altered to assist the process. *Blaeu* 1654 shows no estate centre, but the mid 17th-century DALRY HOUSE figures on *Adair* 1682. EASTER DALRY HOUSE dates from about a century later, and WESTER DALRY HOUSE from the 1840s. In 1696 Sir Alexander Brand renamed the estate BRAND(S)FIELD, but Dalry House reverted to its old name when it was separated from the lands in 1714. DALRY ROAD, known as *Dalry Lane* until about 1870, was little more than a local access until after West Maitland Street linked it with the New Town in the 1800s. The latter-day DALRY LANE (off Orwell Terrace) appears on *Pollock* 1834 as an access to Dalry House policies from Dalry Road, while *Ordnance Survey* 1852 shows it cut off by the drive to the new Wester Dalry House. It was named by 1876. DALRY PLACE (a name once used for ORWELL PLACE, *which see*) was earlier called DALRY PARK and was built in 1867 as the entry to a housing scheme by the Edinburgh Co-operative Building Company (*see under* THE COLONIES, Stockbridge) in which at least four streets were named for politicians, all Anti-Corn Law Leaguers (*see also under* McLAREN ROAD, Mayfield) viz: McLAREN TERRACE for Duncan McLaren, MP for Edinburgh 1865-81; BRIGHT TERRACE for his brother-in-law John Bright MP; COBDEN TERRACE for their leader Richard Cobden MP, and WALKER TERRACE for their younger colleague Sir Samuel Walker QC. LEWIS TERRACE may have been named for Bailie David Lewis, editor of the weekly *Reformer*, mouthpiece of the Advanced Liberals led by McLaren; or else it was for the Isle of Lewis, since ARGYLL, ATHOLL, BREADALBANE and DOUGLAS TERRACES seem to have been named for districts in Scotland. For DALRY PARK PLACE (North Merchiston) *see under* DUNDEE PLACE, North Merchiston.

DALRYMPLE CRESCENT (Grange) *see under* THE GRANGE.

DALRYMPLE PLACE (St Leonards) appears (unnamed) on *Knox* 1821 but is listed in *PO Directory* 1825. The origin of the name has not been traced, but there may be some connection with the 'D Carnegie's heirs' noted on *Kirkwood* 1817 as owners of the ground.

DALYELL'S MILL (Saughtonhall) got its name from John Dalyell, recorded in *RMS* 1574 as 'of Saughtonhall', although later entries show that he held only a portion of it. Shown on *Adair* 1682 as *Dalyelsmil*, the mill and the farm attached to it continued under this name until about 1850, when the farm was renamed SAUGHTONHALL MAINS, *see under* SAUGHTONHALL.

DALZIEL PLACE (Meadowbank) *see under* CAMBUSNETHAN STREET, Meadowbank.

DAMHEAD (Westfield) is recorded as SMITHIS LAND in 1626 and as *now commonly called Damhead* in *RMS* 1654. It was here that the *dam* or lade, after serving the mills in Gorgie, entered Dalry ground on its way to power the mills at Roseburn, and so the place was the *heid of the dam* so far as Dalry was concerned. For DAMHEAD ROAD *see* WESTFIELD ROAD, Gorgie.

DAMHEID (Gogar) *see under* GOGAR.

DAMSIDE (Water-of-Leith or Dean Village) is indicated on *Roy* 1753, and got its traditional name as the way along the south side of the *dam* or lade that carried the water from the cauld at the west end of the village through the haugh to the West Mills at its east end. As shown on *Ordnance Survey* 1852 and vividly illustrated in contemporary photographs by Thomas Begbie (in Edinburgh City Libraries) a series of stone slabs bridged across the water to the buildings on the north side of the dam. DAMHEAD was at the head of the dam, where sluices controlled the flow of water from the river. UPPER DAMSIDE was named in 1984 as a branch off the Damside, forming a terrace in the slope above it.

DANUBE STREET (Stockbridge) was built in about 1825 as part of the revised scheme for Sir Henry Raeburn's estate at DEANHAUGH, *which see*. The name appears on *Wood* 1823, but the choice of it remains obscure.

DARLING'S LAND (South Leith) is recorded in 1828 and was presumably in DARLING'S BRAE, named on *Ordnance Survey* 1852 and shown on *Wood* 1777 as a house with an extensive garden.

DARNAWAY STREET (New Town) *see under* MORAY ESTATE, New Town.

DARNELL ROAD (Trinity) *see under* CARGILFIELD, Trinity.

THE DASSES (Arthur's Seat) are shown on *Kirkwood* 1817 on the west side of the Crow Hill, where a sequence of rocky knowes, rising one above the other, form a ridge overlooking Hunter's Bog. In the little howe behind the second-top one are the remains of a hut settlement, believed to be the oldest of those on Arthur's Seat. The name, which is Scots *dasses* or *daisses*, ledges or platforms, is also attached to the man-made cultivation terraces on the eastern slopes of Arthur's Seat and Dunsappie Hill, above Duddingston.

DA(U)LING'S CLOSE (162 High Street) *see* COVENANT CLOSE.

DAVIDSON'S CLOSE (31 Canongate) *see* WHITEHORSE CLOSE, Canongate.

DAVIDSON'S MAINS is the latterday name of MUTTONHOLE (*which see*) but originated as the name of the mains or home farm of the Muirhouse estate after it had been acquired by William Davidson in 1776. On *Cramond Roads* 1812 the farm steading is shown in the vicinity of the (modern) Green; and although the farm as such disappeared shortly afterwards in the course of a reorganisation of the estate, the plans of *Muirhouse* c1827 and *Silverknowes* 1841 show its name persisting in the field names *Mains Park* and *Little Mains Park*, as well as in the label *Davidson's Mains* for the new part of Muttonhole village. In 1852 the *Ordnance Survey* evidently found that this was the preferred name for the whole village—yet perhaps amongst incomers, one suspects, since the old name *Muttonhole* still lingers in local parlance. DAVIDSON GARDENS was named by extension from the village name, in 1925.

DAVIDSON PARK and **ROAD** (Drylaw) were named in 1935 for William C Davidson, factor for the Steele-Maitland estate, who were the developers.

DAVIE STREET (South Side) was formed by 1814 on land which had belonged to the late John Davie, owner of chemical works and resident in Nicholson's Street.

THE DEAN or **DENE** is mentioned, as already a centre of milling, in the foundation charter of Holyrood abbey in 1128. The name's early spellings are *Den, dene* and *denne*, and it is Anglian *denu*, narrow and winding valley, obviously referring to the great ravine of the Water of Leith from Coltbridge down to Stockbridge. The Nisbets' estate of DEAN (which was soon also to include BLINKBONNY, CRAIGLEITH, DEAN HAUGH, DEAN PARK and MURRAYFIELD or NISBET'S PARKS, *all of which see*) began in 1609, when William Nisbet, bailie and later provost of Edinburgh, and his wife Janet bought the mills of Dean (even then called BELL'S MILLS, *which see*) together with the lands and *farm toun* of Dean, including its share in the *hieland mure*, grazed in common with Ravelston, and probably lying on the ridge of Ravelston Dykes. Since the charters make no mention of a mansion, and since *Blaeu* 1654, surveyed by Pont in 1596, shows only *Den mills*, it is likely that there was no considerable house at the Dean until the Nisbets built their baronial DEAN HOUSE in 1614. Shown on *Adair* 1682 as *Dean*, and used by Scott as one of his models for the Baron of Bradwardine's 'Tully-veolan' in *Waverley* (1814) it was demolished in 1845, to make way for Dean Cemetery. The home farm and DEAN VILLAGE (not to be confused with the latter-day 'Dean Village' down in the Dean, *see* WATER OF LEITH VILLAGE) stood at the head of DEAN PATH, *which see*. Figured on

Siege of Leith 1560 as *The Denne*, still shown on *Ordnance Survey* 1852, and marked as *The Dean* on *W & A K Johnston* 1861, the steading and village were swept away by 1881, but for the parish kirk (replaced in 1902), and all that is left is an 'echo' of village buildings in the frontage of Belgrave Mews.

DEAN BANK (Dean) recorded in 1690 and shown on a plan of *Coatshaugh or Sunberry* c1761 (*RHP 586*) as well as *Ordnance Survey* 1852, is the traditional name for the steep west bank of the Water of Leith between Bell's Mills and the Dean Village.

DEANBANK (Stockbridge) is shown on *Ainslie* 1804 as the name of *Deanbank House*. Although the *bank* was there, sloping steeply down to the river on the west and north sides of the property, it was separate from the Dean estate, and the name was fancy, probably coined when the house was built in the late 18th century. Cist burials, found in 1823 in the course of digging the foundations of the Deanbank Institution, bore witness to early habitation of this riverside haugh. DEANBANK LANE is shown formed on *Ainslie* 1804 and was probably named long before it was recorded in 1893. DEANBANK TERRACE was developed in the grounds of Deanbank House in the early 1870s, although the name first appears in *PO Directory* 1883. It was renamed SAXE COBURG TERRACE in 1980, as a side name in Saxe Coburg Street, because new owner-occupiers of the flats, unlike their previous tenants, complained that the earlier name was obscure. DEAN BANK PLACE (1873) came to be included in HAMILTON PLACE (*which see*) by 1904.

THE DEAN BRIDGE is a masterly work by Thomas Telford, built in 1831-32 to carry the turnpike to Queensferry on a new line, but largely financed by Lord Provost John Learmonth, to open the way for development of the Dean estate which he had purchased in 1825— *see under* CLARENDON CRESCENT, BUCKINGHAM TERRACE and LEARMONTH TERRACE.

DEAN BURN (Bonaly) obviously takes its name from the deep dene in which it descends to Bonaly.

DEANERY CLOSE (Restalrig) was named in 1981 as a new precinct built on part of the site of the Deanery of Restalrig founded by James III in 1487. All that remains of the deanery are the enlarged parish kirk and the main gateway to the other parts of the establishment; but close study of the remarkable picture of it given on *Siege of Leith* 1560 together with consideration of local boundaries shown on *Kirkwood* 1817 suggests that the Sangschule and the Prebendaries' quarters stood in this area to the south of the entrance gateway.

DEAN HAUGH (Stockbridge) is recorded in 1532 as a village name; but this evidently derived from its more general use as the name for the lands that sloped down from the village of THE DEAN (*which see*) to a march with Inverleith, and included (indeed, perhaps constituted) the *Poultrylands* attached to the hereditary office of Poulterer to the King, long held by the Napiers of Merchiston, but sold by them to

Nisbet of the Dean in 1610. The name is Anglian *den(u) halh*, land in the river bend at the dene or 'at Dean'. The later Scots use of *haw* or *haugh* more specifically for flats beside the water is probably to be seen in the name HAUGH given for the village on *Roy* 1753, and in HAUGH STREET, named on *Kirkwood* 1817, but shown on *Ainslie* 1804 as already developed on the MILL HAUGH named on *Fergus & Robinson* 1759. Notwithstanding this, the village is labelled DEAN HAUGH on *Ainslie* 1804 and maps of 1812, and the main street is entered as DEANHAUGH STREET in *PO Directory* 1833. (OLD) DEANHAUGH HOUSE, sited south of Leslie Place and pulled down in 1880, seems to have been only a little older than a second mansion built nearby, apparently in the 1750s, by Walter Ross WS, who laid out gardens in his part of Deanhaugh and built a tower house, northwest of the future Ann Street, as a folly in which he incorporated many fragments of historic buildings demolished in Edinburgh—among them, THE MERCAT CROSS, *which see*. He may well have had a hand in naming St BERNARD'S WELL (*which see*) but certainly by 1774 he had adopted St BERNARD'S as the name of his house, probably to distinguish it from the adjoining Old Deanhaugh House. In 1780, Old Deanhaugh was acquired by the up-and-coming painter Henry Raeburn, through his marriage with Ann Edgar, widow of Count Leslie, former owner of the House; and after Walter Ross died in 1789, Raeburn bought St Bernard's House and moved into it, giving Old Deanhaugh House to members of his family, including his stepdaughter Ann Inglis or Leslie. In 1812, Raeburn began to develop the estate at RAEBURN PLACE and DEAN STREET (*which see*) and followed them with ANN STREET, named for his wife, in 1816. This scheme, shown on *Kirkwood* 1817, continued with MINERAL STREET (*see under* DEAN TERRACE) but two further streets in the same suburban style as Ann Street (their chosen names *Charlotte* and *Elizabeth* possibly also running in the family) were not built, being overtaken by a new plan, devised shortly before Raeburn's death and published on *Wood* 1823, for St BERNARD'S CRESCENT and other streets of a more urban sort, see CARLTON STREET, DANUBE STREET and LESLIE PLACE.

DEAN PARK (Balerno) developed rapidly as a place name in the 1840s, although it may well have originated as a much older field name—the *park* or grass field beside the *den* or hollow of a burn in the woodland strip west of the farm. *Fowler* 1845 shows a *Dean Park House* just east of the strip, in the same place as *Ordnance Survey* 1852 shows a now-vanished *Dean Park Tile Works* at NT 15997515, about 200 yards south of Cockburn Crescent. The latter map also shows UPPER DEAN PARK, apparently a new farm, while the name DEAN PARK displaces that of the historic TOWNHEAD farm of Balerno, *which see*. Housing development was begun by the county in 1930, and was continued after 1952 in DEANPARK AVENUE and BRAE, followed by DEANPARK GROVE and PLACE, and finally by DEANPARK GARDENS, COURT, CRESCENT, BANK and SQUARE. For streets in the southern half of the farm *see under* COCKBURN CRESCENT and MARCHBANK, Balerno.

DEAN PARK (Dean) was a farm in the western part of Dean estate until 1739, when it was sold to Trinity College Hospital. Its steading, shown on *Roy* 1753 and sited midway along the west side of Queensferry Terrace, was demolished in 1874 to make way for a cricket ground for Daniel Stewart's College.

DEAN PARK CRESCENT (Dean) is part of the early road shown on *Roy* 1753 as leading from the historic Dean village (*see under* THE DEAN) to Deanhaugh and Stockbridge. It was cut off from the Dean when the Dean Bridge and new Queensferry road were opened in 1832. The name does not seem to relate to the farm of DEAN PARK (*which see*) but may have belonged to one or other of the open fields that still adjoined the street when it was named in about 1872. DEAN PARK STREET and MEWS followed a year later, on ground which had been the Dean Nursery, immediately east of a public park which was developed for housing about 20 years later, *see under* COMELY BANK.

DEAN PATH (Dean) is part of the ancient route from Edinburgh to Granton by the Water of Leith and Dean villages and the Crew. The name is Scots *peth*, a steep track (*see also* STANYPATH, Slateford *and* PETH BRAE, Kirkliston) leading up out of the *dene*.

DEAN STREET (Stockbridge) together with DEAN PARK CRESCENT was part of the old road from the historic Dean village (*see under* THE DEAN) to the village of Deanhaugh, shown on *Roy* 1753, and although it is not listed in *PO Directory* until 1826, it is shown on *Kirkwood* 1817 as named and partly built up. UPPER DEAN TERRACE and the upper part of DEAN TERRACE originated in a MINERAL STREET, shown planned on *Kirkwood* 1817 and obviously named for the waters of St Bernard's Well across the valley. *Wood* 1823 shows it extended to its present form, following clearance of St Bernard's House, and it began to be occupied in 1825. The name DEAN TERRACE was in use by 1826, is shown in the most easterly part of the street on *Lothian* 1829, but did not finally oust the name of *Mineral Street* until 1833. UPPER DEAN TERRACE is named thus on *Ordnance Survey* 1852, although not listed in *PO Directory* until 1859.

DEAN VILLAGE (Dean) was historically the village at the head of Dean Path, at the gates of Dean House (*see under* THE DEAN) but since it was finally cleared in 1881, giving way to Belgrave Mews (*see under* BUCKINGHAM TERRACE) its name became available for transfer to the historic WATER OF LEITH VILLAGE (*which see*) at the foot of Dean Path. The transfer was perhaps begun by J R Findlay, developer of Well Court, who used the new name at the opening of the Court in 1885; but the old name continued in the *PO Directory* until 1923 and was still used by some for decades thereafter. There was a certain logic in the change, for the village was truly in the valley or dene, and the old name was not only unwieldy but was apt to be confused with Leith.

DEARENOUGH (Pleasance) *see* DERENEUCH, Pleasance.

DECHMONT ROAD (North Gyle) was proposed in 1934 to be named *Allison Road* for the then owner of North Gyle farm. This is said to have been against his wishes; and the name *Dechmont Road*, presumably reflecting some connection of Allison or the developer with Dechmont in West Lothian, was adopted in 1936.

THE DELF WELL (Duddingston) was so named because its waters were gathered in a *delf* or pit dug in this marshy patch of ground.

DELHAIG (Gorgie) was developed in about 1890 in a field of Gorgie farm, possibly in connection with Saughton Leather Works, built on the other side of the main road at the same time. The name was in use by 1893 but its origin is obscure. It seems to be fancy, and may have been the name of one or more of the cottages built at the foot of Robb's Loan by 1845.

DELL ROAD (Colinton) is shown on *Ordnance Survey* 1852 as the access to the mill north of Colinton kirk, which was burned down in about 1880 and was the last of a long sequence of mills on this site, generally known as the HOLE MILL, *which see*. The street was named for Colinton Dell by about 1913.

DEMPSTER'S CLOSE (264 Canongate) *see* GULLAN'S CLOSE.

THE DENE (Dean Village to Stockbridge) was given in 1989 as the name of this public path which had been formed in the lower gorge of the DEAN after the removal of THE TROWS (*which see*) almost a century earlier, the new arrangement being detailed on *Ordnance Survey* 1893. In his *Water of Leith* 1896, John Geddie mentions its construction as 'a pleasant promenade of red asphalte', and this was obviously the origin of the name RED WALK which Geddie uses first in *Old Edinburgh Club I* 1908. Since it is otherwise unrecorded, it is likely that he invented it: but be that as it may, it did not take, and enquiries in 1989 failed to discover any use or memory of a specific name for the path.

DENHAM GREEN (Trinity) is shown on *Ainslie* 1804 as a house and grounds then owned by the Revd Sir Henry Moncrieff, minister of the West Kirk of St Cuthbert 1775-1827. The name was fancy, possibly derived from some connection with Denholm or Denholm Dean in Roxburghshire, but perhaps more likely from the surname variously spelt *Denholm, Denham,* or *Dennam,* for there were several people of that name in Edinburgh about this time—e.g. James Denholm, hatter in North Bridge, who was political agent for Robert Dundas, Viscount Melville, elected MP for Midlothian in 1801. DENHAM GREEN AVENUE (1897) and DENHAM GREEN PLACE and TERRACE (1898) were sited on ground which was once part of the adjoining estate of LILLIPUT (*which see*) but had become a market garden by 1850 and part of Denham Green some 40 years later.

DENNISTON'S CLOSE (265 High Street) *see* CRAIG'S CLOSE.

DENS CLEUCH (Balerno) is recorded on *Knox* 1812. The name is Scots *cleuch* from Middle English *cloghe*, a ravine, with the *dens*, the conspicuous group of deep-cut gullies near the watershed in the pass.

DERBY STREET (Newhaven) *see under* STANLEY ROAD.

DERENEUCH or **DEIRENEUCH** (Pleasance) appears in *Protocols of James Young* 1514 as the name of part of the tongue or neuk of land which extends some 350 yards southwards from the eastern section of Drummond Street and is shown on *Regality of Canongate* 1813 by the later names of NORTH and SOUTH CROFTS OF THE PLEASANCE. Given also as *Deyreneuch* 1537, *Deiraneuch* 1563 and *Diraneuch* 1630, the name is early Scots *derne neuk*, overgrown corner of an angular shape, and suggests that the place was once a waste of whins or scrub. Whether it was originally (as it sometimes was later) the name of the whole wedge of land making up the two crofts is a matter of conjecture; but what is certain is that in 1514 it applied to a property of 2 Scots acres in the southern tip of the neuk, bounded on the north by 'the lands and gardens of *the Plesans*'. The latter property is defined in 1507, in another of Young's protocols, and when the two are put together it emerges that the PLEASANCE (*which see*) was then but a small property, apparently in the extreme north of the South Croft (perhaps about 160 yards south of Drummond Street) and that the rest of the South Croft, nowadays bounded by the street of the Pleasance in the east and Richmond Lane and Place in the west, was Dereneuch. By 1537 Dereneuch and Pleasance were in the same ownership; and thereafter the names were almost always used together—no doubt in order to distinguish between the property and the street, for part of St LEONARD'S WYND or GATE was already being called *the Pleasance* by 1553. By 1639 *Dereneuch or Pleasance* had become the alternative name for the whole wedge of land, including the North Croft; and in 1799 this North or *Blackfriars* croft is described as being 'in *Dearenough*'—a late spelling that obviously attempts to interpret what had become an obscure name.

DERNECRUKE (Hillhousefield) is so described in *Protocols of James Young* 1496 and 1508 as to place it in the sharp crook of the river at West Bowling-Green Street, extending some 270 yards westwards from the bridge to the boundary between Hillhousefield and Bonnington. The name is early Scots *derne cruik*, hidden land in the bend of the river, 'hidden' by being overgrown with bushes of some sort.

DEVON PLACE (Wester Coates) was the first of a group of streets developed for working-class housing by James McKelvie, coal merchant. Named by 1863, it was followed by EGLINTON STREET and SUTHERLAND STREET (1864) WEST CATHERINE PLACE and STANHOPE PLACE (1865) PEMBROKE PLACE and CARBERRY PLACE (1866) BORTHWICK PLACE (1868) ELGIN PLACE (1871) and SURREY PLACE and SQUARE (1874). There is no obvious pattern in these names; if one contains a personal name *Catherine*, the others may be in each case from a surname or a title or a place name—*also see* DORSET PLACE, North Merchiston. STANHOPE STREET was added in 1949. In 1982 the name SUTHERLAND STREET was transferred to a new street built on the sites of the original Sutherland Street, Elgin Place, Eglinton Street, and Surrey Place and Square.

DEWAR PLACE (Haymarket) was formed and named in about 1811, evidently for James Dewar, recorded as grocer and builder at Tobago Street in 1800. It is shown on *Ordnance Survey* 1852 as a side name on the east side of St CUTHBERT'S STREET (*which see*)—an arrangement which persisted until about 1868, when a small terrace shown on the same map as WALLACE PLACE was also taken into *Dewar Place*. DEWAR (PLACE) LANE developed informally in the 1840s, and is unnamed on *Ordnance Survey* 1852 but named on the 1893 edition.

DEWAR'S CLOSE and **COURT** (100 West Bow) is shown on *Edgar* 1742 and was named for James Dewar of Vogrie, bailie in 1713, and John Dewar, also a bailie, after him. The family may also have had property in DEWAR CLOSE, Grassmarket: *see* BEGBIE'S CLOSE, Grassmarket.

DICK PLACE (Grange) *see under* THE GRANGE.

DICK'S CLOSE (195 Cowgate) is listed on *Ainslie* 1780 and was named for a succession of brewers named Dick: William Dick before 1743, James Dick in 1773, and David Dick in 1780.

DICKSON'S CLOSE (263 Cowgate) *see* ROBERTSON'S CLOSE, Cowgate.

DICKSON'S CLOSE (118 High Street and 212 Cowgate) is named on *Rothiemay* 1647, but there are indications that by then the Dickson connection was in decline, for the only owner-occupier of the name listed in 1635 is the widow of John Dickson, and the sale of a house in the close by a Charles Dickson (mentioned in a title deed of 1724) may have been a winding-up of the widow's estate, if the Thomas Leishman mentioned as its purchaser was the merchant of that name who flourished in the 1640s. A title deed of 1749 mentions a Thomas Dickson, son of John Dickson, as an early owner: the father may have been John Dickson, burgess, mentioned in *Town Council Minutes* 1514 as quartermaster in this part of the town, and the son the Thomas Dickson who was a burgess in 1537. Other possible connections might have been with Thomas Dickson, furrier deacon 1578-99, or John Dickson, flesher deacon 1606-28. In deeds of 1717 and 1724 the close is noted as having also been called AIKMAN'S, which certainly goes back to James Aikman, resident in it in 1538, who was probably the James Aikman made burgess in 1530, and possibly descended from the James Aikman who was made burgess in 1487 in right of his late father of the same name. The same deeds also give the close as formerly BRUCE'S, but although there are over 50 Bruces on the burgess roll prior to 1700, no connection has yet been traced. The name HALYBURTON'S, listed in 1635, seems to have belonged to the subsidiary close on the east side of the main one (as shown on *Ordnance Survey* 1852) and evidently originated with Maister James Halyburton, advocate, who built himself a house here in about 1500-10, described in *Wilson* as on the east side of Dickson's Close and bearing the Halyburton arms.

DICKSON'S CLOSE (243 High Street) *see* THE ANCHOR CLOSE.

DICKSON'S CLOSE (276 High Street) *see* GOSFORD'S CLOSE.

JOHN DICKSON OF HARTREE'S CLOSE (493 High Street) *see under* JAMES COURT.

DICKSON STREET (Quarryholes) was begun (near Albert Street) in 1884, and it is likely that it was named for Dickson & Co., who worked extensive nurseries east of Leith Walk, as shown on *Kirkwood* 1817, and were probably connected with Dickson and Fair, nurserymen at Leith Walk, mentioned in *Town Council Minutes* 1790. The completion of the street involved the demolition of the farmhouse and steading of QUARRYHOLES—*which see*.

DIN EIDYN, pronounced *din 'aid-in*, is the original British form of the name EDINBURGH, *which see*.

DINGWALL'S CASTLE (Low Calton) is mentioned in *Town Council Minutes* 1578 as the *low valts or Dingwallis hous* in Trinity College. It was built by Sir (i.e. the Reverend) John Dingwall, provost of the College 1525-32, and is shown, apparently ruinous, on *Rothiemay* 1647. In 1642 the town council authorised use of its stones in repair of the nearby Trinity hospital, but at least part of it was patched up to serve as a house for the poor and the insane, as well as a *correction house* or prison for beggars and vagabonds. By 1677 other arrangements had been made, and the place was let as a base for coaches.

DINMONT DRIVE (Inch) *see under* THE INCH, Nether Liberton.

DISHFLAT (Dummiedykes) is recorded as *Dischflat* in *Protocols of James Young* 1485 and as *Dissiflat* in *RMS* 1587. Shown as *Dishingflat* on *Regality of Canongate* 1813, it lay between Holyrood Park and the Pleasance, and between St Leonard's Hill and the South Back of the Canongate (Holyrood Road) while on the northeast it adjoined the MEADOWFLAT (*which see*) about 75 yards east of the present entry to Dummiedykes Road. The name, which also occurs in Linlithgow, is Early Scots, probably using *flat* in its sense of 'division of the field'. *Dis(ch)* is an Anglo-Norman form of Anglian *dic* or Old Norse *diki*, and while this could mean a ditch as well as a bank or ridge, the later alternative name of BRIERY BAUKS (*which see*) for at least part of the ground would suggest that the *Dishflat*, in contrast to the *Meadowflat* or hayfield, was the arable division of the great field, divided into strips by *dikes* in the form of rigs or bauks; and doubtless it is this meaning that is enshrined in the second half of the much later name DUMMIEDYKES (*which see*) that now covers most of the ancient Dishflat.

DOBIE'S CLOSE (230 Cowgate) *see* CESSFORD'S CLOSE.

DOCHART DRIVE (Clermiston) *see under* CLERMISTON MAINS.

DOCK PLACE (North Leith) is to the west of the ancient Sand Port, and on the site of the approach to the old North Pier shown on *Collins* 1693, but took its present form as the approach to Rennie's (Old) East Dock, opened in 1806. It is given as *Dock Street* in *PO Directory* 1827, but as *Dock Place* in 1830.

DOCK STREET (North Leith) developed out of the approach lane from North Leith to the Citadel, shown on *Fergus & Robinson* 1759 as well as *Wood* 1777, which skirted the eastern ditch of the fortress and probably dated from its construction in 1656. The area obviously gained importance when Rennie's East Dock was opened in 1806, and by 1813 the lane was redeveloped and named HAGGART STREET, for the North Leith wine merchant who owned the ground. This is still shown on *Dall & Leslie* 1831, but it is omitted from *PO Directory* 1827 and by 1829 it was supplanted by the name *Dock Street*, previously and variously attached to the wharves of the East and West Docks, as well as to the whole or part of what was to become COMMERCIAL STREET and to DOCK PLACE, *which see.*

DOLPHINGTON (Dalmeny) is shown on *Blaeu* 1654 and recorded from 1489 onwards in spellings such as *Dolfingtoun* and *Doffyntoun*. The name, meaning 'Dolfinn's farm place', may be pure Norse, implying that Dolfinn was one of a group of first-generation settlers in the area, probably in about the late 9th century; but equally the name may be Anglian, implying that he was a remote descendant of such a settler, whether in Lothian or Northumbria. A connection with Dolfin, son of Gospatric, in Malcolm Canmore's day is unlikely, even although Gospatric was earl of Dunbar and lord of Dundas.

DOLPHIN ROAD (Currie) was begun in the 1930s and was named for Robert Cuming Gibson Laing of Riccarton, tragically drowned in Plymouth in 1930, while serving in a submarine mother-ship HMS *Dolphin*. In 1951 the road was extended, and DOLPHIN AVENUE and GARDENS EAST and WEST were added to the group.

DONALDSON'S CLOSE (7 West Bow) ran up from the Bow to the High Street in Castle hill, as shown on *Ainslie* 1780, and was named for Alexander Donaldson, printer, who bought a house here from Archibald Stewart, provost 1744-45, arrested in 1745 on a charge of failing to defend Edinburgh from the Jacobites. (Acquitted two years later, Stewart went on to make a fortune in London.) By successfully defending an action brought against him by London printers in 1748, Donaldson established the freedom of printing in Scotland. His son Alexander founded the *Edinburgh Advertiser* in 1764, and his grandson James, dying in 1830, left the money which built and endowed Donaldson's Hospital, originally for orphans, but later for deaf children. The close was also CHEYNE'S, apparently for John Cheyne, surgeon burgess in 1697, one of a family of surgeons at New Quay in the Shore of Leith who were still to the fore in 1800. The close was cleared to make way for Tolbooth kirk and Johnston Terrace before 1839.

DON'S CLOSE (327 High Street) is listed on *Edgar* 1742 and was named for William Don, vintner, who was resident at the foot of the close in 1704. His wife had been the widow of the previous occupant, John Mitchell, also a vintner, from whom (or his forbears) the close got its earlier name of MITCHELL'S. Its earliest known name was TELFER'S, for Laurence Telfer or Taillefer who moved here from

STEVENLAW'S CLOSE (*which see*) in the late 16th century, and two members of the family, Alexander and Patrick Tailfeir, were residents in 1635. It was also BROWN'S or HUGH BROWN'S, perhaps from the Hew Brown, mason, who was active in the town in the 1580s; and if so it was probably also the BARCLAY'S CLOSE mentioned in 1596, when Hugh Brown acquired a tenement in it: but although James Barclay, skinner and member of town council, as well as Mr Alexander Barclay, apothecary, were also active in the town during this period, their connection with the close remains to be ascertained. The close was also TAIT'S, for John Tait, tailor, later owner of Brown's tenement; and in 1718 it was styled PLAINSTANES CLOSE, indicating that it was paved with flagstones rather than setts. *Ordnance Survey* 1852 shows the lower part of the close still open.

ALEXANDER DON'S CLOSE (91 High Street) *see* BARRINGER'S CLOSE.

DOOCOT or **DUCATT YARD** (South Leith) was adjacent to COATFIELD MAINS or LAUGH-AT-LEITH (*which see*) in the vicinity of Vanburgh Place, and was evidently named for a doocot. It was appointed in 1715 as the meeting place of the burlaw court of Leith.

DORSET PLACE (North Merchiston) was developed in 1873 by James McKelvie, coal merchant in Clifton Terrace, who adopted fancy names of a similar kind at DEVON PLACE, Wester Coates, *which see.*

DOUBLE DYKES (Cramond) appears on *Ordnance Survey* 1852 at the *Double Dykes Plantation*, which seems to be a remnant of the woodland strip or hedge along the north march of King's Cramond, figured prominently on *Knox* 1812 as well as *Roy* 1753; and the reference may be to the two banks of a 'double hedge', *see under* DOUBLE HEDGES ROAD, Nether Liberton.

DOUBLE HEDGES ROAD (Nether Liberton) is shown on *Roy* 1753 and named among county roads in 1902 as *Double Hedges Cross Road*. In Robertson's *Agriculture in Midlothian* 1795 a 'double hedge' is defined as being planted on the banks thrown up on either side of a deep ditch, sometimes with a row of trees added in the narrow space between. Several such hedges are noted on *Muirhouse* c.1827 and are called 'double fences' on *Silverknowes* 1841, and the DOUBLE DYKES in Cramond was probably another form of the same thing. DOUBLE HEDGES PARK was coined in 1982, for a new branch of the original road.

DOUGLAS CRESCENT, GARDENS and its **MEWS** (Coates) *see under* COATES.

DOUGLAS'S CLOSE (20 Grassmarket) is shown on *Ainslie* 1780, and is given as GLADSTONE'S on *Ordnance Survey* 1852. The proprietors remain to be traced.

DOUGLAS TERRACE (Dalry) *see under* DALRY PLACE.

DOUNE TERRACE (New Town) *see under* MORAY ESTATE, New Town.

DOVECOT PARK (Queensferry) is shown on *Plewlandfield* 1769 and named on *Queensferry* 1832. The name is obviously from a doocot, but there is nothing to show where it was. The (DOVECOT PARK) WELL is shown in 1832 and named on *Ordnance Survey* 1856, and its wellhead still exists.

DOVECOT PARK (Slateford) was begun in 1928 in the *Doocot Park* of Hailes, named for the Hailes House doocot which stood at its southern end. The middle part of its later extension in a crescent rejoining Lanark Road some 400 yards further north was suppressed in 1953, leaving its northern part, renamed DOVECOT GROVE, and its later offshoot DOVECOT LOAN (1962) quite detached from the source of the street name. In the 1980s, the name *Dovecot Park* began to be used for KINGSKNOWE PUBLIC PARK, *which see.*

DOVECOT ROAD (Corstorphine) was formed by 1881 in fields shown on *Corstorphine* 1777 as the *Ladie Meadow* and *Dovecot Park*, the latter as well as the street being named for the 16th-century dovecot of Corstorphine Castle, near the east end of the street.

THE DOW CRAIGS (Calton Hill) is the oldest name for the crags on the south side of the hill. It is recorded in 1555, but was soon to be displaced by a new name McNEILL'S CRAIGS, *see under* CRAIGINGALT. While both parts of the name could be Celtic (British *du* or Gaelic *dubh*, black, and *creg* or *creag*, rocky place) the word order suggests that it is Scots *dow craig*, derived from the Celtic and with the same meaning.

DOWGALL'S or **DUELL'S CLOSE** (High Street) *see* ALLAN'S CLOSE.

DOWIE'S MILL (Cramond) seems to be marked, but not named, on *Adair* 1682. Considering its position, it might be the *miln of Cramond Regis* mentioned in the 16th century. Recorded as *Old Mill* in 1697 and as *Dowie's Mill* in 1782, it is evidently named for an owner or tenant, the surname being found in the Edinburgh area before 1616. In 1985 the name of the lane leading to it but earlier labelled part of Braepark Road was confirmed to be DOWIE'S MILL LANE.

DOW LOAN (Morningside) is now known by the former side name ALBERT TERRACE, *which see.* It is described in a feu charter of 1587 as 'a pathway of six ells' width in between Merchiston and the part of the West Muir being feued off (the future West Morningside). It is shown on *Roy* 1753 as leading on to Meggetland, but the western section was suppressed when Myreside farm was enclosed between 1772 and 1776. The name evidently derived from the Dow Croft of Merchiston, lying immediately north of the loan and recorded in 1586. *Merchiston* 1776 gives this as *Dovecroft*, and *Ordnance Survey* 1852 gives the street as *Dove Loan*, both interpreting the name as Scots *dow* or *doo*, a dove: but almost certainly (the more so because the estate doocot was not here, but north of Merchiston Tower) the word is Scots *dow*, black, frequent in place names and derived from Celtic *du* or *dubh*.

DOWNFIELD PLACE (Dalry) was formed and named by 1877 as one of a group of streets (*see also* SPRINGWELL and CATHCART PLACE, and DUFF STREET, Dalry) built in land of Wester Dalry shown on *Kirkwood* 1823 as owned by the Home Rigg family of Morton and Downfield. Downfield is five miles from St Andrews, Fife; and the name *Downfield Place* had figured earlier (as shown on *Lothian* 1829) on abortive plans for developing the other Home Rigg estate at Drumdryan.

DOWNIE PLACE (Tollcross) was the name given in about 1822, in honour of Robert Downie of Appin, first chairman of the Union Canal Company, to the section of the Lothian Road between Bread Street and Fountainbridge, which then overlooked the quays of the new PORT HOPETOUN (*which see*) the terminal basin of the Canal. The name was suppressed in 1886.

DOWNIE TERRACE (Corstorphine) was built in about 1879 on part of some ground feued by John Downie and Robert Laird in 1877 and thereafter operated by the Downie family as Meadow Park Nursery. DOWNIE GROVE was added in 1960.

DOW'S AVENUE (Prestonfield) *see under* THE CAMERON.

(OLD or UPPER) DRAWBRIDGE (Leith) was opened in 1789, enabling the medieval BRIG OF LEITH (*which see*) to be demolished, so that ships might ascend Leith river as far as the tide would permit. Since 1968 it has languished under the wildly inappropriate name of SANDPORT PLACE, *which see*. In 1800, the NEW or LOWER DRAWBRIDGE was added at Bernard Street, to facilitate traffic to the new docks.

DREGHORN is recorded as *Dregerne* 1240, *Dregarne* 1374 or *Dreggarne* 1438, and the spelling *Dragorn* on *Adair* 1682 (altered to *Dreghorn* on *Adair/Cooper* 1735) testifies to the persistence of an early pronunciation, despite the form *Dreghorne* appearing in 1529. A suggested derivation from Anglian *draeg hyrne*, spit of land where a boat could be dragged across, makes no sense in the locality, and it is clear that the name is British, from *dre*, the farm, and *gronn(a)*, a bog, making the name 'the farm at/of the bog', with subsequent changes in Scots very like those of the similar British name *Kyngorn*, now Kinghorn in Fife. DREGHORN LOAN, until 1916 known simply as *the Loan*, is shown on *Roy* 1753; and while it was indeed the *road to Dreghorn* figured on *Spylaw* 1767, it is recorded in 1709 as part of the common loan giving the estates of Colinton and Redhall access to the common grazings in the hills, *see also* THE LANG STEPS, Colinton. DREGHORN MAINS, the home farm, is figured on *Laurie* 1763; and DREGHORN MAINS ROAD was formally named in 1966. DREGHORN GARDENS (1951) and DRIVE, GROVE and PLACE (1966) are on ground at the Baads (perhaps anciently part of Auchingane) acquired from Oxgangs when Redford Road was extended in 1800, while DREGHORN PARK was built in Little Fordell or the Gallolee—all these street names being doubtless influenced by the Army's ownership of Dreghorn.

DREGHORN SNAB (Colinton) is recorded in 1709, as the spur of Capelaw between the Lyon Dean and the Kirk burn. The name is probably transferred from DREGHORN, since this is the most southerly corner of the common lands of the barony of Redhall (which included Dreghorn) and although this part of them was allocated to the 'Colinton Share' when the commonty was divided up in 1709, it may have been loosely associated with Dreghorn in some earlier period.

THE DRUM (Gilmerton) is mentioned in 1406 and shown on *Adair* 1682. The name is British *drum* or Gaelic *druim*, ridge or back, and may have attached originally to the whole spur or edge which thrusts northeastwards from Straiton to Edmonston and Niddrie, *see also* EDGEHEAD, WEST EDGE and NIDDRIE EDGE. DRUM HOUSE, incorporating part of a house of 1584, dates from 1726. DRUM STREET was formally adopted as a street name in 1925, along with DRUM COTTAGES; but its remarkably early appearance as *Drum Street* on *The Drum* 1842, coupled with the fact that it is now known to be part of DERE STREET (*see under* ROMAN ROADS) and that *street* was the normal Anglian term for traces of Roman roads, suggests the name may be older than the village or the Drum estate, and may combine British *drum* and Anglian *straet* in an early name for this section of Roman road over the ridge. DRUM AVENUE, CRESCENT and PLACE were named in 1967.

THE DRUM (Restalrig) is mentioned in *RMS* 1577. As British *drum* or Gaelic *druim*, a back or ridge, it seems to have been the general name for the ridge north of Restalrig (now Lochend) loch and its tail burn, the strype which ran westwards in the vicinity of Bothwell Street and joined the Greenside burn near Allanfield. The subdivisions SOUTH and WEST DRUM recorded in 1605 may be the same as the FORE and BACK DRUM mentioned as Trinity Hospital lands in 1718, and the latter is shown on *Ordnance Survey* 1852. DRUM HOUSE, also named on that map, is shown on *Roy* 1753; and DRUM TERRACE and the EASTERN CEMETERY were formed in its grounds in about 1883.

THE DRUM or **DRUM BRAE** (Corstorphine) is shown on *Roy* 1753 as a minor road leading north from Craigs road past Corstorphine Bank to Parkneuk on the old Queensferry road. In the early 1750s it was extended southwards to the Newbridge road and upgraded as a link between it and the Queensferry road—*see under* FERRYGATE, Corstorphine. As shown on *Ordnance Survey* 1893, the name belongs to the road itself, using Scots *brae* in its sense of 'a steep road' over the Drum, which is British *drum* or Gaelic *druim*, a ridge. It was also known as DRUM ROAD; and in 1930, in order to obviate any confusion with similar names in Lochend and Gilmerton, the rather clumsy bureaucratic forms DRUM BRAE NORTH and SOUTH were adopted. In 1953, DRUM BRAE DRIVE and TERRACE were named, using *brae* as though it meant 'hill', and this was followed by DRUM BRAE CRESCENT and GROVE (1956) GARDENS (1978) PLACE (1979) AVENUE and PARK (1960) WALK (1964) NEUK (1971) and the 'four-decker' DRUMBRAE PARK APPROACH (1973).

DRUMDRYAN (Tollcross) was an 11-acre estate on the east side of the Linton road, as shown on *Ainslie* 1804. Recorded in 1458 as *Drumdriain*, the name is British *drum (an) drein* or Gaelic *druim drioghionn*, ridge of sloe or blackthorn. Thus it is virtually identical with the later Scots THORNYBAUK (*which see*) occurring immediately northwest of it, and the implication seems to be that this feature, described in 1824 as 'a ridge covered with thorns, long unploughed and untouched', had been prominent in this boggy terrain at least as early as the 10th or 11th centuries, when Gaelic was being spoken in Lothian, and quite possibly as far back as British-speaking times—for speculation anent a Roman connection, *see under* ROMAN ROADS. In about 1730 Patrick McDowall built DRUMDRYAN HOUSE; and this became LEVEN LODGE in 1750, and then part of a brewery in 1760, and was finally pulled down in 1905 to make way for the King's Theatre. Meantime, a Dr Spens had built a second DRUMDRYAN HOUSE northeast of it, as shown on *Ainslie* 1804; and it was this house, which stood until 1958, that passed on the name to DRUMDRYAN STREET when the surrounding area was developed as housing in 1867-70.

(MAY) DRUMMOND'S CLOSE (106 Canongate) *see* BULL'S CLOSE, Canongate.

DRUMMOND PLACE (New Town) *see under* NORTHERN NEW TOWN.

DRUMMOND STREET (Pleasance) originated as part of the historic BACK OF THE WALL or THEIF RAW (*which see*) which is shown on *Kirk o Fields* 1567 and *Rothiemay* 1647 as running immediately outside the Flodden Wall. In 1788, the year in which the South Bridge was opened, Dr Alex Munro launched a scheme for development of his property at *Bristo Green*, on the south side of that part of the Theif Raw which lay between its intersections with the Back Raw (Roxburgh Place) and the new link between the South Bridge and Nicolson Street; and it is this section of Theif Raw which is named *Drummond Street* on *Brown & Watson* 1793, evidently to commemorate Lord Provost George Drummond, who had taken a leading part in developing the Royal Infirmary on the ground opposite Dr Munro's. *Lothian* 1829 extends the name to the junction with Roxburgh Street, and *Ordnance Survey* 1852 continues it to the Pleasance. Munro's scheme is discussed in *Old Edinburgh Club XXIV*.

DRUM SANDS (Dalmeny) are shown thus on *Adair/Cooper* 1735. The name evidently derives from a name, British *drum* or Gaelic *druim*, a ridge, which must have attached to the high ground which runs behind the shore for a mile southwards from the Hound.

DRUMSELCH (not to be confused with DRUMSHEUGH, *which see*) is recorded in the *Holyrood Ordinale* c1450 as 'the great forest called *Drumselth*' in the time of David I, and in *RMS* 1507 as 'the forest of *Drumselch*, of old the name of the common (or Burgh) muir of Edinburgh'. How far it extended is not known; but the name, British *drum selig*, sauchie or willow ridge, scarcely suggests (as has been frequently assumed) the great undulating stretch of country north of the Pentlands, but rather would fit the broad ridge running on the north side of the Pow from Merchiston to Prestonfield—as indeed the entry in *RMS* 1507 implies.

DRUMSHEUGH (not to be confused, as it has been by *Grant* and others, with the entirely different name DRUMSELCH, *which see*) is mentioned in *Protocols of John Foular* 1509 as *Drumysheuch*, but this is clearly short for the *Maldrummysheuch* or *Meldrummisheuch*—i.e. Meldrum's heuch—recorded in *Protocols of James Young* 1507 and in *RMS* 1587. Part of the barony of Broughton, the original estate extended to about 35 Scots acres, and had a mill of its own, described by Foular as 'near the town's common mills' in the Dene, *see under* GREENLAND MILL. It marched with Broughton (at Gloucester Street and Lane) and with Coates (at Lynedoch Place Lane, formerly DRUMSHEUGH LANE) and the Scots term *heuch*, land on a rocky height, aptly fitted the location, which is described by *Grant* as 'on the crest of high rocks that overhang the ravine where the Leith runs brawling to the sea'. Its Meldrum owner remains to be identified (Young's protocol makes it clear that it had been owned by Henry de Liberton for some time before 1507) but he might have been Hector Meldrum, royal macer from 1460 until his death in 1495, who was resident in Leith Wynd in the Canongate and perhaps was the Hector Meldrum (or else his father) who rented one of the few shops in the High Street in 1480 and 1482, as recorded in *Town Council Minutes*. Shown on *Laurie* 1763, the historic DRUMSHEUGH HOUSE, latterly the home of the earls of Moray, stood south of the present junction of Great Stuart Street and Randolph Crescent; but in 1822, along with the very name of the land, it was swept away in the development of the MORAY ESTATE, *which see*. Since Lord Alva's house at Kirkbraehead, which latterly had borrowed the name 'Drumsheugh House', was pulled down about the same time, the only Drumsheugh names remaining were those of the street DRUMSHEUGH and the DRUMSHEUGH TOLL (*see under* QUEENSFERRY ROAD) together with the 3-acre 'Drumsheugh gushet', a wedge of land cut off from Drumsheugh by the Queensferry road, now for the most part the site of Lynedoch Place. This was taken advantage of by the Walker family, who as owners of part of this gushet as well as the adjoining estate of Easter Coates began to style themselves as 'of Easter Coates and Drumsheugh' and called their house *Drumsheugh House* even although it stood in Easter Coates, on the west side of Lynedoch Place Lane. The process was taken further in 1845, when the Misses Walker bought a smaller house within the gushet and christened it *Old Drumsheugh House*; and it was these two Walker mansions, both pulled down on 1872, that transmitted the *Drumsheugh* name into Easter Coates and led to the naming of DRUMSHEUGH GARDENS in about 1874, and DRUMSHEUGH PLACE in 1890.

DRUMSHEUGH LANE (Drumsheugh) formed the western march of Drumsheugh. It is clearly shown on *Roy* 1753 as part of the historic road to Queensferry by Bell's Mills, but in about 1780 it was cut off when that road was altered to pass at a lower level through the north end of the Drumsheugh gushet, *see under* BELFORD ROAD. *Ainslie* 1804 shows the northern half of the lane stopped up, while the rest gives access to Capt. Weir's property in the gushet and to the house in Easter Coates which was to become a latter-day 'Drumsheugh House' after 1822, *see under* DRUMSHEUGH. *Ordnance Survey* 1852 shows the lane redeveloped as a meuse to Lynedoch Place, and it was renamed LYNEDOCH PLACE LANE in the 1920s.

DRUM TERRACE (South Leith) *see under* THE DRUM, Restalrig.

DRYBURN PARK (Wester Hailes) *see under* HAILESLAND, Wester Hailes.

THE DRY DAM (Arthur's Seat) is shown on *Kirkwood* 1817. It is a sloping valley of remarkably regular form; and the name—a *dam* or burn, and one that is most often dry—implies that a 'winter burn' runs only occasionally down the hollow.

DRYDEN PLACE (Newington) appears in *PO Directory* 1866 as *Drydon Place*. The name may derive from some personal interest of Duncan McLaren MP, then owner of Newington House.

DRYDEN STREET (Pilrig) was developed in 1866, apparently at the same time as Rosslyn Street (see ROSSLYN CRESCENT, Pilrig) was being planned, for it is said that an original intention of naming it *Reynold Street* was dropped when the superior, John Balfour of Pilrig, suggested that *Dryden* would go well with *Rosslyn*, since Dryden and Roslin are only a mile apart and are mentioned together in Scott's *Lay of the Last Minstrel*, Canto VI. DRYDEN TERRACE and GARDENS were named in 1934 and 1936.

DRYLAW is recorded in 1296 as *Drilawe*, which is Anglian *dryge blaw* or Scots *dry law*, dried-up hill, and probably referred to its position on the sunny eastern slope of the Corbie Hill. It was already divided into *Easter* and *Wester Drylaw* by 1491. *Blaeu* 1654 shows *E* and *W Dryley*, but *Knox* 1812 shows the house and farms as they were before housing development began. DRYLAW HOUSE dates from 1718 but is probably on the site of the original centre; and DRYLAW HOUSE GARDEN and PADDOCK were so named in 1981 because they occupied such parts of its grounds. DRYLAW MAINS was on the south side of Ferry Road, immediately east of the Groathill road junction. EASTER DRYLAW was on the west side of Easter Drylaw Bank, about 100 yards south of Easter Drylaw Place. DRYLAW AVENUE was begun in about 1923 and development continued in this corner of the estate at DRYLAW CRESCENT in 1925, GARDENS and GROVE in 1926, and DRYLAW GREEN in 1934. Development in Easter Drylaw began in 1936 at EASTER DRYLAW DRIVE, PLACE and VIEW, and resumed at EASTER DRYLAW AVENUE, BANK and LOAN in 1952, and at EASTER DRYLAW WAY (1971) GARDENS and GREEN (1972). WESTER DRYLAW AVENUE, DRIVE, PLACE and ROAD were named in 1952, and WESTER DRYLAW PARK (within the House park) in 1978.

DUART CRESCENT (Clermiston) *see under* CLERMISTON MAINS.

DUBLIN STREET and **DUBLIN STREET MEUSE** (Broughton) were part of Reid & Sibbald's scheme of 1802 for the NORTHERN NEW TOWN—*which see*. As HIBERNIA STREET it was to be one of a group using the Latin names for the parts of the United Kingdom, but it became DUBLIN STREET by 1817, perhaps because *London Street* had already displaced the unfamiliar *Anglia Street*. In 1967 the name was extended to take in DUKE STREET (Broughton) *which see*.

THE DUB RAW(S) (South Leith) originated as a branch off the Kirkgate, leading westwards up the middle of a shallow valley, and the ancient name probably derives from wet ground, being Anglian or early Scots *dubb raw(s)*, row(s) of houses beside pools or puddles. On *Wood* 1777 it is shown as St ANDREW'S STREET, evidently as part of a scheme of more elegant names for principal streets in Leith; but it is still referred to as *Dubrow* in *Town Council Minutes* 1775, and the *Directories* show that the grander name did not catch on at all until 1781, and that the auldfarrant *Dub Raw* was still in use as an address in 1813—indeed, it lingered on in popular parlance for several decades more. In about 1889 the *St Andrew's Street* name was extended to take in the SHEEPHEID WYND, *which see*; but in 1964 the wynd was suppressed and made into public open space (except that the causey setts of its north entry were left in place) while the rest of St Andrew's Street was taken into GILES STREET, *which see*.

DUDDINGSTON stretched from Arthur's Seat and the Cameron to Magdalen Bridge. There were Bronze Age settlements near Magdalen Bridge and on and around Arthur's Seat, as well as later Celtic settlements and fortifications on Arthur's Seat and at DUNSAPPIE, and there may have been a crannog in Duddingston Loch. The estate, including lands bearing the British name of TREVERLEN (*which see*) in the west of it, was gifted to Kelso abbey in about 1130, probably by David I. The abbey soon afterwards feued it to Dodin de Berwic, evidently (from his name) an AngloNorman of continental extraction; and since by the 1150s he was styling himself Dodin de Dodinestoun, it is evident that by then the name *Duddingston*—i.e. early Scots 'Dodin's *toun* or farm place'—was already displacing any British name for the estate, although *Treverlen* continued into the next century as the parish name. DUDDINGSTON KIRK dates from this period, and the fact that it figures as 'Traverlen' in a list of thirteen parish kirks confirmed as belonging to Kelso in about 1200 might suggest that there was a kirk here before Dodin's time. By 1210 the estate was divided into EASTER and WESTER DUDDINGSTON. In 1600 the two were brought together again, with Easter Duddingston (sited northeast of the junction of South Morton Street with Milton Road) as the *chymmis* or centre of the combined estate; but the centre was moved westwards after 1745, when the Earl of Abercorn bought the estate and proceeded to reorganise the land (hitherto, as shown on *Roy* 1753, worked on the medieval runrig system) in a number of farms on the new 'improved' model. In 1768 he built DUDDINGSTON HOUSE on a virgin site in Wester Duddingston. DUDDINGSTON HUT was on the site of WOODLANDS GROVE, Duddingston, *which see*. WEST DUDDINGSTON ROAD (the *West* added only in 1958) is shown on *Roy* 1753, and was named as leading to (Wester) Duddingston from both Cairntows and the Willowbrae road. Its extension (now DUDDINGSTON ROAD) to connect with the Leith road at Baileyfield dates from about 1833. DUDDINGSTON ROW (so named in 1975, but formerly called BINGHAM ROAD, *which see*) represents part of the old route from Leith by Restalrig and the Wisp to Dalkeith. Although this route is still shown on *Fowler* 1845, the map also shows a link road from Baileyfield to Niddrie Mill, which, as shown on *Ordnance Survey* 1852, became the new route from Leith to Dalkeith. The link was named NIDDRIE ROAD; but by 1930, in the section north of Milton Road, this was displaced by the name DUDDINGSTON PARK, originally a side name given in the 1860s to houses built on the east side of the road, in the *Whinny Park* of Duddingston; and in 1976 the rest of the road to Niddrie was renamed DUDDINGSTON PARK SOUTH. DUDDINGSTON CRESCENT was named in the 1880s, as fronting the road to Easter Duddingston. DUDDINGSTON MAINS (*see also under* HOPE LANE, Portobello) was a new farm built in about 1830, and gave its name to DUDDINGSTON MAINS COTTAGES. DUDDINGSTON MILL was the site of mills from the early Middle Ages until recent times. DUDDINGSTON AVENUE was built at the *Millbraehead* in 1933. DUDDINGSTON SQUARE and GARDENS NORTH (1933) GROVE (1937) and GARDENS SOUTH (1954) were built in fields shown on *Duddingston* c1800 still under the technical names they had had in the medieval runrig farm: viz. *Mid Langlands*, recorded in 1595 and referring to the division of arable into long narrow strips or rigs; and *Garbrage*, early Scots *gar brede*, 'gore-shaped breadth', the triangle of ground left after the parallel rigs had been marked out within a non-rectangular field—*see also* GUARD WELL, Moredun. DUDDINGSTON RISE and VIEW were renamed thus in 1974, having been previously BINGHAM GARDENS and TERRACE, *which see*. DUDDINGSTON YARDS, on the former site of Portobello Combination or Fever Hospital, were named in 1983 as a group of workshops for light industry just within the boundary of Duddingston at the Niddrie burn.

DUDGEON PLACE (Kirkliston) is built in what was the Toll field of Almondhill, and was named in about 1971 for the Dudgeon family, farmers in Humbie for nearly 200 years but also tenants in Almondhill until 1927.

DUDLEY AVENUE (Bonnington) was planned before 1888 in Northfield of Bonnington and began to be occupied in 1890. The origin of the name, probably English, has still to be traced. Further development, apparently also envisaged in the 1880s, followed at DUDLEY GARDENS (1893) CRESCENT (1898) TERRACE (1902) and GROVE (1904). DUDLEY BANK was a development of WARD'S LANE, which appears to have dated from the 1920s. Prior to 1966, DUDLEY AVENUE SOUTH was ALLAN STREET *see under* ALLANFIELD, Bonnington.

DUELL'S or **DOWGAL'S CLOSE** (High Street) *see* ALLAN'S CLOSE.

DUFF STREET (Dalry) was formed and named *Maxwell Street* by 1879, as part of a group of streets (see also DOWNFIELD, SPRINGWELL and CATHCART PLACES) developed in ground shown on *Kirkwood* 1823 as owned by the Home Rigg family, who also owned Drumdryan at Tollcross. The reason for choice of name is obscure, but for the faint possibility that it may be somehow connected with the fact that in the 1650s a Janet Moodie or Maxwell owned land in Dalry as well as at Tollcross, next to Drumdryan. The street was renamed in 1890, evidently because of confusion with Maxwell Street in Morningside, which had also been named in about 1879; but the reason for the choice of *Duff Street* has not yet been traced. DUFF STREET LANE was added in 1910.

DUKE STREET (Broughton) figured in Reid & Sibbald's scheme of 1802 for the NORTHERN NEW TOWN (*which see*) and seems to have been named as linking the streets named for the King's second son, as Duke of York and Duke of Albany—*see* YORK PLACE and ALBANY STREET. It was renamed in 1967 in order to obviate confusion with Duke Street in Leith, the street itself becoming part of DUBLIN STREET and its Lane DUBLIN STREET LANE.

DUKE STREET (South Leith) is indicated on *Adair* 1682 and *Naish* 1709 as a route which must have been influenced, if not generated, by the fortifications of 1548, the frontage on its north side showing the alignment of the ditch of the bastion *Bartholemeus Bulwark* shown on the *Siege of Leith* 1560. The name appears in *PO Directory* 1818 and is said to be for Charles, Earl of Dalkeith, so keen on the golf that he rented a house here, close to the Golf House of the Links, in about 1800. He succeeded as 4th Duke of Buccleuch and 6th Duke of Queensberry in 1812. Prior to 1968, DUKE PLACE was DUNCAN STREET, South Leith, *which see*.

THE DUKE'S WALK (Holyrood) is named on *Roy* 1753 and shown on *Kirkwood* 1817 as a footpath running from the palace yards eastwards to the entrance to the king's park near Muschat's Cairn, on a line just north of the modern road (dating from 1845) which partly continues its name. The tradition is that it was so called because it was a favourite walk of James, Duke of Albany, when he lived in Holyrood as the king's Commissioner 1679-82. In *Baird's Duddingston* p114 the name is said to attach 'to this day' to a path from the Palace to Priestfield, but evidence is lacking and no such path is shown on plans of the Park.

DUMBEG (Wester Hailes) is recorded in the field name *Dumbeg Park* shown on *Wester Hailes* 1818. The field, centred about NT 20086957, continued to exist until it was redeveloped as WESTER HAILES DRIVE. The name is evidently Celtic, British *din bicc*, Gaelic *dun beag*, little fort, and was possibly given in comparison with nearby DUMBRYDEN, *which see*. It is possible that other adjoining field names are of Celtic origin, *see under* WESTER HAILES.

DUMBRYDEN (Longstone and Wester Hailes) is shown on *Laurie* 1763 as *Dumbredin*, and as *Dumbraiden* on *Armstrongs* 1773. The name, like that of Dumbarton on the Clyde, is Gaelic *dun Breatann*, township or fort of the British, and would suggest that a settlement of the British Gododdin folk (or the remains of one) was recognisable here when Gaelic speakers began to dominate Lothian in about the 10th century. It may be related to the Celtic name DUMBEG (*which see*) recorded half a mile to the southwest. DUMBRYDEN ROAD is the remnant of the road leading to the farm, which stood in the vicinity of Dumbryden Grove. Latterly the farm was subdivided into smallholdings, and its house and cottages were occupied by the manager and staff of Hailes Quarry, until DUMBRYDEN DRIVE, GARDENS and GROVE were developed in 1967.

DUMMIEDYKES is the late 18th-century name for part of the DISCHFLAT, (*which see*) arising from the circumstance that in about 1764 Thomas Braidwood set up his pioneering *Academy for the Deaf and Dumb* in a house on the east side of the St Leonard's road which led through the Dischflat to St Leonard's chapel and hospice at St Leonard's Crag. As reported in *Arnot* 1779, Braidwood's work soon achieved international renown; but by a process which was to be repeated later at the DUMMIE STEPS, Stockbridge (*which see*) the house was soon nicknamed the DUMMIE HOOSE, from Scots *dummie*, a dumb person, and by combining this with the *dikes* of the Dischflat the area came to be known as THE DUMMIEDYKES. This continued even although the Academy closed down in 1783: the house is shown as *Dumby Dykes* on *Regality of Canongate* 1813, and *Kirkwood* 1817 shows both DUMBIE HOUSE and DUMBIEDYKES ROAD, the latter simply displacing the old *St Leonard's road* name. Unfortunately when Scott borrowed 'Dumbiedykes' as the title of his comical laird in *The Heart of Midlothian* in 1818 he had to wrench it out of context, and this together with the English spelling has led generations of readers who would never dream of pronouncing the *b* in 'dumb' to suppose that the place name is the nonsensical 'Dum-bi-dykes', with the bizarre outcome that the proper pronunciation *Dummi-dykes*, still current locally, is often with unconscious irony looked down on as 'uneducated'. The Dummie House, latterly called *Craigside*, was demolished in about 1939, but the historic road continues, although its southern section was turned into a footpath when the Dummiedykes was redeveloped in 1964.

THE DUMMIE ROAD and **STEPS** (Stockbridge) are part of GABRIEL'S ROAD (*which see*) but got their local name after 1823, when the Deaf & Dumb Institution was built beside the path. The nicknaming, from Scots *dummie*, a dumb person, exactly duplicated what had happened 60 years earlier at the DUMMIEDYKES, *which see*.

DUN-ARD GARDEN (Blackford) was named in 1985 as a development within the garden of the house called Dun Ard, dating from about 1870.

DUNBAR'S CLOSE (137 Canongate) is shown on *Ainslie* 1780 and evidently named for David Dunbar, writer, recorded in *Canongate Charters* 1773 as owner of tenements here.

DUNBAR'S CLOSE (High Street) is shown on *Edgar* 1742. As recorded in 1557, it was earlier called IRELAND'S, for a tenement at its foot owned by Bailie John Ireland and his son Bailie Patrick Ireland and their successors; and it was also known as BAILIE BROWN'S, from Thomas Brown, bailie in 1680, although his connection with this close is obscure—*see* BROWN'S CLOSE. A third early name, recorded in 1698, was PENSTON'S, for John Painstoun, merchant burgess, who seems to have owned at least two properties in the close, giving one to his daughter Christian and selling another to John Dunbar, glover, whose successors included Andrew Dunbar of Leuchold and his son George, bailie in 1737. It may also have been DAVID MURRAY'S CLOSE, for David Murray, merchant, who had property on its east side in 1635, and *Protocols of Adam Watt* 1707 and 1722 mention a land once owned by Sir David Murray of Halmyre, west of Patrick Ireland's but east of John Galloway's, which might seem to place it on the *west* side of Dunbar's Close: *but see also* SELLAR'S CLOSE, 399 High Street, which may have a stronger claim to the name. Dunbar's Close was cleared away for the new Sheriff Courthouse in 1934.

DUNBAR STREET (Tollcross) is shown on *Kirkwood* 1817 as a projected scheme, and *Kirkwood* 1823 shows it as though partly built; but *Knox* 1821 shows a different scheme, and *Lothian* 1829 shows it as proceeding. On its east side, the housing that was intended failed to develop, and most of the ground was taken into the site of the Central Hall in 1899. The street name makes its appearance in the *PO Directory* in 1827, but its origin is not yet traced.

DUNCAN PLACE (South Leith) is part of a route not shown on *Naish* 1709 but appearing on *Roy* 1753 and figured *Road through the Links* on Wood 1777. The earliest entries of the name in *PO Directory* from 1829 onwards spell it *Duncan's Place*, which would suggest that it had originated as a name for property beside the street and called after its owner; and there are indeed two entries of the name Duncan, pipemakers in Duke Street, in the *Directory* for 1829. There is nothing to link the street with Admiral Duncan, who had died in Edinburgh 25 years earlier. DUNCAN STREET, developed by 1834, had taken its name from Duncan Place by 1852; but in 1968 it was renamed DUKE PLACE, from nearby Duke Street, in order to obviate any confusion with Duncan Street in Newington.

DUNCAN'S BELT (Currie) is a woodland strip, figured on maps from *Knox* 1812 onwards and presumably named for someone who had to do with its planting. It is noted for a cemetery, dating from about the year 500, which was marked by a cairn, shown on *Ordnance Survey* 1852 but removed by 1893 and now represented by a memorial stone.

DUNCAN'S CLOSE (35 Canongate) is listed on *Ainslie* 1780 and was named for Gilbert Duncan, mason, who owned property here, probably about 1768, when he had land in CALLENDER'S CLOSE, *which see*. *Canongate Charters* 1818 record descendants of his still owning houses at the foot of the close, near the well.

DUNCANSGAIT (Kingsknowe) was named in 1984 for Duncan Colquhoun JP, who despite severe disablement had taken a notable part in local affairs and community service before his death in 1976 at the age of 29 years.

DUNCAN STREET (Newington) was not proposed in the *Plan of Newington* 1806 but was added to the feuing scheme before 1810 by the superiors, the heirs of Dr Benjamin Bell, and evidently named after his distinguished patient and friend Admiral Duncan, victor of Camperdown in 1797, whose widow lived on in their house at 5 George Square for 28 years after her husband's death in 1804.

DUNCAN STREET (New Town) now DUNDONALD STREET—*see under* NORTHERN NEW TOWN.

DUNDAS (Dalmeny) is recorded from 1180 onwards. The name appears to be Gaelic *dun deas*, south fort, but could have originated in the British form *din des*. The suggestion that it was named as the counterpart of some unrecorded 'north fort' on land at Inverkeithing owned by the family of Gospatric (the refugee Northumbrian earl of British extraction, who got Dundas from Malcolm Canmore) seems to be a shaky guess. The *dun* or *din* must have preceded the motte at MOAT KNOWE (*which see*) which in turn was displaced by the existing tower house in the early 15th century. DUNDAS MAINS, the demesne or home farm, is recorded from 1594 onwards; while DUNDAS HOME FARM is modern.

DUNDAS AVENUE (Queensferry) together with STEWART CLARK AVENUE are built in the vicinity shown as *Muiry Green* on *Dundas* 1757, and were named by 1972 for the Dundas estate and its owners.

DUNDAS PLACE (Kirkliston) was named in about 1971 as being built in the Toll field of Almondhill, then part of the estate of Dundas.

DUNDAS STREET (New Town) *see under* NORTHERN NEW TOWN.

DUNDEE TERRACE (North Merchiston) was named by 1879, evidently for the city of Dundee, the adjoining TAY STREET being named for the river estuary by 1882. In 1885 the western extension of Fountainbridge was renamed DUNDEE STREET, and Dalry Park Place DUNDEE PLACE.

DUNDONALD STREET (New Town) *see under* NORTHERN NEW TOWN.

DUNDRENNAN COTTAGES (Inch) *see under* THE INCH.

DUNEDIN or **DUN EIDEAN**, pronounced *doon 'aid-in*, is the Gaelic translation of British *din Eidyn*, the original form of the name EDINBURGH, *which see*. Although the Gaelic-speaking Scots came into possession of the place only in about 960, they must have known of it as a foreign capital for centuries before then and the translation may date back to British times.

DUNEDIN STREET (Canonmills) is shown half-built on *W & A K Johnston* 1888 but on *Ordnance Survey* 1893 its eastern half is also developed. The street was named by 1889, perhaps referring directly to the city's British name *Din Eidyn* (see under EDINBURGH) or else to some local interest making use of the name. DUNEDIN STREET LANE was also developed by 1893.

DUNG PORT (Old Town) *see* WATERYETT, Old Town.

DUNLOP'S COURT (36 Grassmarket) *see* CAMERON'S ENTRY, Grassmarket.

DUNLOP'S CLOSE (High Street) *see* ALLAN'S CLOSE.

DUNOLLIE COURT (East Craigs) *see under* CRAIGIEVAR WYND, East Craigs.

DUNROBIN PLACE (Stockbridge) *see under* THE COLONIES, Stockbridge.

DUNSAPPIE (Arthur's Seat) is an Iron-Age fort, and the remains of its stone ramparts ring an area of one acre on the summit of the crag. The name probably goes back to the British form of the Gaelic *dun sopaich*, fort of the tufted grass—a growth which is still a marked feature of the slopes around the loch. While the name is sometimes spelt *Dunsapie*, *Dunsappie* better represents the pronunciation. The fort gives its name to the hill on which it stands; and DUNSAPPIE LOCH is so named on *Kirkwood* 1817, although it is shown as a bog or reed bed; its level was raised in about 1845 by a cauld at its tail burn.

DUNSMUIR COURT (Corstorphine) was named as being on a site shown on *Corstorphine* 1754 and named as *Mr Dunsmuir's* on *Corstorphine Village* 1777, the property having come to John Dunsmuir through his marriage with Margaret Cleland, whose father had acquired it in 1713. Redevelopment for housing began in the grounds of the early 19th-century Dunsmure House in 1951, and the house itself was demolished in 1959.

DUNSYRE'S CLOSE (81 High Street) *see* CHALMER'S CLOSE.

DUNTER HILL (Dalmeny) is shown on *Barnbougle & Dalmeny* c1800, and the name seems to be Scots 'hill frequented by *dunter* (i.e. eider) ducks'.

THE DUNTIE KNOWES (Lothianburn) rise immediately west of the old smiddy. The name seems to be Scots, 'the small hills frequented by *dunters* or eider ducks'.

DURAR DRIVE (Clermiston) *see under* CLERMISTON MAINS.

DURHAM ROAD (Duddingston) was named in about 1880, evidently in memory of Beatrix, second daughter of the 1st Duke of Abercorn, owner of Duddingston, and of her husband the 2nd Earl of Durham. They were married in 1854; but she had died in 1871 and he in 1879. The later development of Southfield in Duddingston included DURHAM AVENUE, PLACE and TERRACE (1931) and DURHAM DRIVE, GARDENS, GROVE, SQUARE and DURHAM ROAD SOUTH, named in 1932.

DURIE'S CLOSE (172 High Street) *see* OLD ASSEMBLY CLOSE.

DURWARD GROVE (Nether Liberton) *see under* THE INCH, Nether Liberton.

DYER'S CLOSE (101 Cowgate) *see* HUME'S CLOSE, Cowgate.

DYSTER'S CLOSE (77 Cowgate) is listed on *Ainslie* 1780 but was suppressed in the building of George IV Bridge in about 1829. It was evidently named for dyer work going on in it. It is mentioned as a *little close* in 1635.

E

EARL CAIRNIE (Dalmeny) seems to have been derived in error from HARLAW, Dalmeny, *which see*.

EARL GREY STREET (Tollcross) was constructed in 1785 as part of the LOTHIAN ROAD (*which see*) and was known as such until about 1824, when it was given the independent name of WELLINGTON STREET, probably by Jean Ponton, widow of Major James Weir RM, continuing here and also at RIEGO STREET the practice that her husband had begun at LYNEDOCH PLACE, of naming streets on the family's lands after heroes with a Spanish connection. In 1832, however, it was renamed EARL GREY STREET, evidently to celebrate the passing of the Reform Bill under the leadership of Charles, Earl Grey, against (ironically enough) the opposition of the Duke of Wellington. Whatever the truth of the story of an overnight change of label on 15 September 1834, when Grey was made a free burgess and dined in a special pavilion in the grounds of the High School, it was not the beginning of the street name, which is used in *PO Directory* 1833.

EARL HAIG GARDENS (Trinity) was built in Trinity Mains by the Scottish Veterans Garden City Association and named for Field Marshal Earl Haig, who formally opened the settlement in 1921.

EARLSTON PLACE (Norton Park) *see under* MARYFIELD, Norton Park.

EAST and **WEST CROFTS** (Ratho) were developed in the early 1970s and apparently named for the *East* and *West Lidgate crofts* shown on *Hatton etc* 1797 as lying somewhat further west, on either side of the LIDGATE (*which see*) now called *Baird Road*.

THE EAST and **WEST ENDS** (New Town) are named as meeting points of streets at either end of Princes Street; and if the names are used in the sense of neighbourhoods it is with the meaning of 'at or round about these ends of Princes Street' and not (as in London) 'in the east or west ends of the town'. The names do not seem to have been in use much before 1900, and it is likely that they were promoted to mark fare stages in the tramway system.

EAST and **WEST OLD DOCKS** (Leith) were part of Rennie's scheme, designed in 1799, for a sequence of three wet docks and a new harbour at Newhaven, as shown on *Ainslie* 1804 and later maps up until about 1830. The harbour and the westermost dock were never built; but the EAST DOCK was constructed in 1800-06 and the WEST

DOCK in 1811-17. The description 'OLD' was added by the 1880s, no doubt to obviate confusion with the newer docks built east of the river mouth. Both docks are now filled in.

EAST and **WEST RIG** (Balerno) are on ground shown on *Laurie* 1766 as part of the *commonty* or common land of Balerno. *Knox* 1812 and *Kirkwood's Environs* 1817 show East Rig as *Back of the Rig*, but while the first shows West Rig, the second shows UNTHANK (*which see*) in a somewhat different position. The names include Scots *rig* for the fields on the slope, and *back* either in the sense of 'further part' or as 'part near the crest of the slope'.

EAST CHAMPANYIE (Blackford) *see under* CHAMPANYIE.

EAST COMMON CLOSE (287 Canongate) *see under the* COMMON CLOSES, Canongate.

EAST CRAIGS (Corstorphine) *see under* CRAIGS, Corstorphine.

EASTER CURRIE CRESCENT etc (Currie) *see under* CURRIE.

EASTER HAUGH (Oxgangs) was named for its position within the *Easter Haugh* field of Oxgangs, shown on *Colinton Mains & Oxgangs* 1813. The name is Scots *haugh*, for the flat land beside the burn. *See also* INCHERATHRYNE, Oxgangs.

EASTER PARK (Barnton) occupies the site of the original BARNTON, *which see*. Shown as *Old Barnton* or *Old Mansion* up until 1845, it is given as EASTER PARK by 1912, obviously from its position in the parks of New Barnton. EASTER PARK DRIVE was named in 1973, along with its offshoots NORTHLAWN and GARDEN TERRACES named for the parts of the house grounds they occupied.

EASTER ROAD (Abbeyhill to South Leith) is shown on *Siege of Leith* 1560. Its alignments suggest that it originated as a local road in Restalrig rather than as a medieval route to Leith, and it doubtless gained in importance from the branch which led off at Upper Quarryholes, linking Holyrood with its Rood chapel at Greenside; but by 1602 the town was responsible for maintaining it as a *hiegait betwixt Leyth and the Cannogaitt*, and in 1717 it is described as the *Easter highway from the Watergate in Canongate to Leith*, as distinct from the *Wester Road* which later became LEITH WALK, *which see*. *Kirkwood* 1817 shows a proposal to carry the new London road over it on a bridge; but in the event, as proposed on *Calton* 1819, the Easter road was carried up to the new road's level by a westward loop, the original line and street level still showing in West Norton Place.

EAST FARM OF GILMERTON was named in 1985 as a modern development within the historic farm of that name, shown on *Ordnance Survey* 1852, and indeed includes some of its buildings restored and remodelled as housing.

EASTFIELD (Ingliston) *see under* INGLISTON.

EASTFIELD (Joppa) is shown on *Duddingston* c1800 as a narrow field of 5 Scots acres behind the shore, extending westwards from the mouth of the Magdalen burn. On *Ordnance Survey* 1852, its eastern half is shown developed as *Magdalen Chemical Works* and as housing at MAGDALEN STREET and WELLINGTON PLACE; while the *Eastfield* name is attached to a little group of properties further west. At the turn of the century these became a complete terrace of houses; but it was about 1910 before the residential name EASTFIELD displaced the ancient but latterly industrial name of MAGDALEN (*which see*) as the name of the neighbourhood, and Magdalen Street and Wellington Place were renamed EASTFIELD PLACE. EASTFIELD GARDENS, named in 1931, was part of the development of the *Snab Neuk* field of Easter Duddingston, the angle of the ridge that thrusts towards Magdalen Bridge.

EASTFIELD (South Leith) is recorded at Leith Links in 1803. EASTFIELD PLACE and COURT, Seafield, are named on *Ordnance Survey* 1852, but were affected by the advent of Seafield branch railway in 1903 and dropped from the *PO Directory* in 1913. The name was descriptive of the position of the place relative to Leith.

EAST MILL(S) (Currie) has been a milling centre since before 1625 and is named as being in the extreme east of Currie.

EAST TERRACE (Queensferry) *see under* HIGH STREET, Queensferry.

ECHLINE (Queensferry) is recorded from 1214 onwards, and appears on *Blaeu* 1654 as *Echlyin*. The spellings prior to 1300 are *Ekelyn* and *Egbelin*, and the name is Celtic, and Gaelic in form: *each lann*, (place at) the horse park, or simply 'horse farm'. The ECHLINE BURN, still partly shown on *Ordnance Survey* 1895 but now entirely culverted, was the historic march with the Friars Croft and Plewlands. The footpath that curves round the east side of the Clufflat Knowe is almost the only remaining visible sign of its course. From here, the Echline farm stretched westwards to the Linn Mill burn, and from the sea southwards to the ECHLINE STRIP in Dundas. Its development for housing began in 1976 with ECHLINE AVENUE and DRIVE, followed by ECHLINE PARK, PLACE, TERRACE and VIEW (1977) and ECHLINE GREEN (1987). ECHLINE GROVE, on the Clufflat Knowe, was named in 1982, together with ECHLINE RIGG, which occupies part of the *Lang Rigg* field or (earlier) the *East Whinny Muir* of Echline. The farmhouse and hinds' cottages, together with the steading (reconstructed as housing in 1985) retain the ancient farm name.

ECHOBANK (Prestonfield) *see* CELLARBANK & ECHOBANK.

THE ECHO (Queen's Park) is quoted in *BOEC XVI* as an established place name in use in 1677 at the *Echo(ing) Rock* opposite the *Echo Park—see under* CELLARBANK and ECHOBANK.

EDEN LANE (Morningside) is shown on *Kirkwood* 1817 as giving access to Canaan Cottage and a north entrance to Canaan House. On *Pollock* 1834 and other maps including *W & A K Johnston* 1861 it is shown as *Union Lane*, a name possibly related to that of a property on its west side, shown on *Pollock* and named on *Ordnance Survey* 1852 as 'Harmony House'. The name EDEN LANE appears in *PO*

Directory 1863. This fancy name, continuing the Biblical and idyllic theme started in CANAAN two centuries earlier, is shown on *Ordnance Survey* 1852 as attached to no fewer than four properties west of the Lane; and one of them, *Eden Villa*, was rebuilt in about 1891 as EDEN PLACE, later called EDEN TERRACE.

EDGEHEAD (Gilmerton) is named thus on *Roy* 1753 and shown as a clachan on the west side of the Lasswade road, just north of the junction with the Lang Loan; but *Knox* 1812 and *Ordnance Survey* 1852 both add the name EDGE to the northerly part of the settlement (at the head of Gilmerton Dykes Road) while *Ordnance Survey* 1893 shows no settlement at the Lang Loan entry, but gives EDGEHEAD as the name of the rest. Clearly the name arose from the *head* or summit of the Lasswade road's crossing of the Gilmerton *edge* or ridge, but moved with the settlement as it grew in a northerly direction; and *Edge* was probably a local shortening of the name by the Gilmerton folk.

EDINA PLACE (Norton Park) was named in about 1881, evidently taking its name from the *Edina Works* set up here in 1878 by W and A K Johnston, map makers, the name being the city's name in the fancy form popularised by Robert Burns—*see under* EDINBURGH. It was extended to EDINA STREET (Hillside) in about 1900.

EDINBURGH perhaps emerges from prehistory in the first half of the 2nd century, inasmuch as it may have been the British *Alauna*, rockplace, which Ptolemy lists among the 'towns' of the *Votadini*, a British tribe who inhabited southeast Scotland and northeast England in Roman times; but it is clearly identified in the late 6th century, when the heroic poems of the *Gododdin* (the Votadini name in its later Welsh form, to be pronounced roughly as *gau-'dauth-een*, with *th* as in 'the') named the place both as *Eidyn* and as *Din Eidyn* or 'Fort Eidyn', and also described it as *Eidyn ysgor* or *Eidyn gaer*, the stronghold or fortified town of Eidyn. All these forms use 'Eidyn' (pronounced *'aid-in*) as a proper name, and the same is true of the later versions made for the invading groups of Anglians and Gaelic-speaking Scots, typified in the note '*Dunedene*, which is in English *Edineburg*' given in the 9th-century Life of St Monenna: for while British *din* could be translated (no doubt, as usually happens in such circumstances, by conquered Britons for the benefit of new overlords) as equivalent to Anglian *burh* or Gaelic *dun*, it is evident that *Eidyn* had to be left untranslated. Not to be confused with Anglian *eoten* or Scots *etin*, a giant, or with Gaelic *eadainn* or *aodainn*, a slope, it seems to have been the name of the place, rather than a district, but is otherwise obscure. The fanciful form 'Edwinesburgh' is a palpable fake that appears in the time of David I and was probably an attempt to manufacture a link with Edwin, first Christian king of Northumbria; but there is no evidence that Edwin ever campaigned in Scotland, and fair evidence that Eidyn did not fall to the Northumbrians until some five years after he died in 633, and in any case there are the decisive objections that the native Gododdin called their capital *Eidyn* long before any Anglian set foot in Lothian, and that even if (with a stretch) the forms *Eden* or *Edine* might be derived from

'Edwin's', it is simply impossible that that could be the origin of British *Eidyn* or Gaelic *Eidean*. It is not known exactly when the settlement east of the Rock was made a royal *burgh* (a title which used the word no longer as 'fortress' but in its new sense of 'trading centre') but it was certainly before 1128, when the foundation charter of Holyrood abbey frequently mentions it as already existing, and it may have been before Alexander I rebuilt St Giles kirk in about 1120. The term *burgh* appears in both its old and new senses in the medieval title *The royal burgh of Edinburgh*: 'the royal trading centre of fortress Edin'. EDINA and EMBRO are late 18th-century forms, the first devised to personify the town, chiefly for poetical purposes, and the second a colloquial reduction of the name, showing the same tendency to change *n* into *m* as occurs in names like *Dumbryden* and (in normal parlance) *Dunfermline*.

EDINBURGH CASTLE was a fortified hill town in the Iron Age and Roman times. As noted under EDINBURGH, it was *Din Eidyn*, the stronghold of the Gododdin folk in the 6th century; it was also the *Etin* that the Anglians besieged in 638, and the *oppidum Eden* that they abandoned to the Gaelic Scots in about 960; and although the chapel dedicated to Margaret of Scotland was built perhaps 30 years after she died, there is evidence that in her time (1070-93) the place was fortified, was frequently used as a royal residence, and contained a kirk of St Mary. Since the name *Edinburgh* no doubt extended beyond the fortress on the CASTLE ROCK, to cover any early settlement on the CASTLEHILL (*which see*) it is understandable that the beginning of the organised *burgh of Edinburgh* resulted in the emergence, in a charter of David I in 1142, of a specific name for the Castle: yet surprisingly it was not the workaday *castrum de Edynburgh* (which makes its appearance in 1265) but the flowery title of *castellum puellarum*, castle of maidens or nuns. There is nothing whatsoever to suggest that this was a translation of some earlier Celtic or Anglian 'Maiden Castle'; and when that name appears in English in about 1200, it is clearly as a translation from the Latin, given above, or from its Old French equivalent, *le castel des pucelles*. Beginning with the *Chronicle of Lanercost* in about 1300, this curious name has often been explained by the romantic fiction of a 'safe house' (so oddly far from home!) for Anglian or else Pictish princesses, while more recently it has been supposed to refer to the 6th-century St Monnena and her nuns, said to have founded a kirk of St Michael in Din Eidyn; but in the 16th century George Buchanan maintained that the name had come from early French romances, and in 1955, in a paper in *PSAS* XXXIX, R S Loomis pointed out that Geoffrey of Monmouth, writing his highly romanticised *History of the Kings of Britain* in about 1135, not only mentions a Castellum Puellarum 'facing Albany' (the land of the Picts and Scots north of the Forth) but also seems to have invented *Lot* or *Loth*, duke of Lothian, with a wife who is a sister of Arthur and figures in other Arthurian tales as 'a queen in a castle of ladies'. Moreover, Geoffrey lived in Oxford, and his chief patron was Robert of Gloucester, a nephew of David I; and since David and Robert were together in Oxford for several weeks in 1141, they could have discussed the *History* with each other, or even with the author himself. Taking one thing with another, it seems not unlikely that it was David who began to call his fortress of Edinburgh *Castrum Puellarum*, in the fond belief that this was its proper name in the great romantic story of Arthur.

EDINBURGH DOCK (Leith) was named for Alfred, Duke of Edinburgh, Queen Victoria's second son, and opened by him in 1881.

EDINBURGH PARK (Gogar) was named in 1993 as the entry to the business park of that name; and LOCHSIDE CRESCENT was named as skirting an artificial lochan in the Gogar burn.

EDINBURGH ROAD (Queensferry) is shown on *Blaeu* 1654, and is named as the historic road *to Edinburgh* from Queensferry. In all probability it originated in very early times as a track from the crossing of the strait at CASCHILIS, leading southeast by the gully of the Hawes.

EDMONDSTON is recorded as a place from 1248 onwards, but since a Henry de Edmundistun witnessed a charter by Henry de Brade in about 1200, the name dates back to the 12th century or earlier. The typical early spellings *Edmunistune* and *Edmonstoun* show it to be Anglian, *Edmund's tún* or farm place. The personal name Aedmund is recorded in Scotland in about 1150. The modern spelling is properly *Edmondston*, not 'Edmondstone'. EDMONDSTON MAINS or home farm is first recorded in 1499. EDMONSTON EDGE, the *edge* or ridge on which the estate is planted, is mentioned in 1547 as the campsite of the Scottish army before the disastrous battle of Pinkie. The village of EDMONDSTON was well established by 1812, but is now struggling for identity with the modern growth of Danderhall. EDMONDSTON ROAD, named as leading to it, was renamed in 1978 as THE WISP, *which see.*

EDMONSTON'S CLOSE (112 West Bow) is listed in *PO Directory* 1827 and appears to have been named for Thomas Edmonston, ironmonger here at the Bowfoot in 1799.

EGLINTON CRESCENT (Coates) *see under* COATES.

EGLINTON STREET (Wester Coates) *see under* DEVON PLACE, Wester Coates.

EGYPT (South Morningside) is recorded as a farm in Nether Braid from 1585 onwards, and is named on *Adair* 1682 and shown in detail on the map of *Braid* 1772. It stretched from Braid Road eastwards to the park dykes of Blackford Hill and Pond, and from the Pow or Jordan burn southwards to a road, somewhat north of Hermitage Drive, which divided it from the smaller farm of North Braid. Like the term *gypsy*, the name derived from the medieval supposition that the Romany folk originated in Egypt; and *Egypt* or *Little Egypt* for their encampments was established Scots usage by 1500 or thereby. The reference to *Littil Egypt besyde the common mure* in *Town Council Minutes* 1585 illustrates the point that since it lay south of the Pow,

Egypt was outwith the Burgh Muir and thus immediately outwith the jurisdiction of the town; and it is therefore reasonable to assume that gypsies were apt to take refuge here whenever they were expelled from Edinburgh, as happened in 1540. The steading was still extant in 1880, with its farmhouse sited in the southwest corner of the junction of Nile Grove with Braid Avenue; but apart from a tentative labelling of Cluny Drive as *Egypt Avenue*, the farm name was suppressed in subsequent development until a group of properties, originating in the 1880s as stables in the *Meadow Field* of Egypt and long called by that name but latterly and awkwardly addressed as part of Cluny Place, was renamed EGYPT MEWS in 1985. Nevertheless, the medieval farm name generated many other local names, including CANAAN and JORDAN (*which see*) and a flock of lesser Biblical names north of the burn, as well as NILE GROVE for the first street in the redevelopment of Egypt, started in 1881. Subsequent streets were named for Braid or other estates owned by the Gordon family. One of them, sketched in 1885 on the line of the old road leading from Egypt up to North Braid, was then temporarily labelled *Centre Avenue*, but named BRAID AVENUE in 1890, and HERMITAGE TERRACE (1884) GARDENS (1890) and DRIVE (1893) were named for the Hermitage of Braid; but otherwise, names were taken from the family's Aberdeenshire properties of *Cluny*, *Corrennie* and *Midmar*. CLUNY AVENUE (1884) and GARDENS (1885) were followed by CLUNY DRIVE in 1890, while CLUNY TERRACE and PLACE, proposed in 1885 as *Meadowfield Terrace* and *Place*, were named by 1888, although building did not start until 1894 and 1895. CORRENNIE GARDENS and DRIVE, planned in 1890, began in 1898 and 1903; and MIDMAR GARDENS, planned in 1893, and MIDMAR AVENUE and DRIVE came into the *PO Directory* in 1902, 1905 and 1910.

EILDON STREET and **TERRACE** (Warriston) *see under* WARRISTON.

ELBE STREET (South Leith) is shown on *Naish* 1709 and *Roy* 1753 as the earliest connection through the eastern ramparts to the shore road at Leith Sands. It is labelled *Road to Glasshouses* on *Wood* 1777, and named as WHISKY ROW on *Ainslie* 1804 and as ELBE STREET on *Thomson* 1822. Both these names appear in *PO Directories* 1804-27. The first was used as an address by traders in wines and spirits, who outnumbered other residents in the early years, and it continued as a side name for 16 Elbe Street until 1827. Meantime the less playful ELBE STREET represented the port's more general trade connection with the Continent.

ELCHO TERRACE (Joppa) was developed at some time after 1856, when *Sutter's Portobello* shows no sign of it, and before 1868, when it is listed in the *New Edinburgh Directory*. It deviated from the original plan for streets in RABBIT HALL, *which see*. While the name may be connected with Elcho, near Perth, it is more likely that it relates to the Earl of Wemyss, Lord Elcho, a prominent figure at the time. Some thirty years later a distant cousin of his, Rosaline Bingham, married the 3rd Duke of Abercorn, superior of Duddingston, and there may have been some earlier friendship between the families.

ELDER STREET (New Town) was begun in 1799 and named for Thomas Elder, wine merchant opposite the Tron, Postmaster General for Scotland and three times Lord Provost of Edinburgh in the decade 1788-98, who died at his estate of Forneth near Blairgowrie in 1799.

ELDIN STREET (Pleasance) *see under* ADAM STREET, Pleasance.

ELECTRA PLACE (Portobello) *see under* WESTBANK, Portobello.

ELF or **ELFIN LOCH** (Braid) is shown on *Braid* 1772 as *Elff Loch*, a pond (now overgrown and seasonal) in a howe near the summit of the south ridge of the Braid Hills, known in 1890 as *Elfin Loch*, and today as *Deidman's Pool*; but the name is also attached to another pond in the lower ground some 200 yards further south, marked as *Elff Loch* on *Mortonhall* 1770 and 1776, and as *Elf Loch* on *Ordnance Survey* 1852. In *White's Liberton* 1786 there is mention of a hollow 'on the south side of the hills of Braid, called *Eve's* or *Elf's Kirk*, with a pretty natural pond'; and it also describes the site of *Kilmorton* (now lost) as 'at some distance below Elf's Kirk, near Mortonhall'. As they stand, the names obviously have been taken to refer to fairies, but they may conceal an early name for the hill, for British *elfin* or Gaelic *ailbhinn*, rocky steep, would be apt indeed for this ridge with its abrupt 100-foot fall to the south.

ELGIN PLACE (Wester Coates) *see under* DEVON PLACE, Wester Coates.

SOUTH ELGIN STREET (Hillside) was named *Elgin Street* by 1869, in all probability for James Bruce, 8th Earl of Elgin and latterly Viceroy of India, who had died in 1863. After some years of confusion between *Elgin Street*, *Elgin Place* and *Elgin Streets* (*sic*), the name *South Elgin Street* prevailed, even although no counterpart *North Elgin Street* survived. ELGIN TERRACE, indicated on *Ordnance Survey* 1893, was named by 1895; and NORTH ELGIN STREET was created in 1968 by renaming EAST WILLIAM STREET, only to be suppressed by redevelopment at Brunswick Terrace in 1978.

ELIZAFIELD (Pilrig) appears in *PO Directory* 1845, when Patrick Dall, supervisor of Leith Docks, was resident there. The house, shown on *Ordnance Survey* 1852 and still extant as 48 Newhaven Road, is not shown on *Pollock* 1834. It was probably named for the wife or daughter of Dall or some other owner in about 1844. The name, still carved on the original house in the terrace, continued as a side name in Newhaven Road until 1901; and it was revived in 1986 for a new street in the property adjoining the original Elizafield on the east.

ELLANGOWAN TERRACE (Inch) *see under* THE INCH, Nether Liberton.

ELLEN'S GLEN (Liberton) is recorded from 1870 as a fancy name south of Stenhouse Mill, although there is no mention of it in *Good's Liberton* of 1892, and its origin is unknown. In 1966, because the name 'Stenhouse' and 'Stenhouse Mill' had been used for streets in STENHOUSE in Saughton (where the name is in fact a corruption of *Stenhope*) the traditionally named STENHOUSE ROAD was renamed

ELLEN'S GLEN ROAD, and in 1969 a section of HYVOT'S LOAN was renamed ELLEN'S GLEN LOAN. The unfortunate outcome was that ELLEN'S GLEN began to displace the name of Stenhouse itself.

ELLEN'S STREET (North Leith) *see under* HELEN'S WALK, North Leith.

ELLERSLY ROAD (Murrayfield) is shown on *Gellatly* 1834, but it was about 1908 before the Campbell owners of Murrayfield named it for Ellerslie, near Paisley, home of Sir William Wallace in the 13th century, which came to Sir Islay Campbell, Lord Succoth (*see under* GARSCUBE TERRACE, Murrayfield) through his mother, heiresss of John Wallace of Elderslie. The Renfrewshire name is recorded as *Eldersly* in 1398 but as *Ellirsly* in 1499, and may be Anglian *ellerns*, elder trees, or else Old Norse *elris*, alder trees, along with Anglian *leah*, most likely in its early sense of 'wood' or 'glade'.

ELLIOT ROAD (Colinton) was developed in the most northerly part of Colinton estate and named in 1926 by Miss Margaret Trotter of Colinton House for Lady Mary Elliot, daughter of the 2nd Earl of Minto, and Miss Trotter's grandmother on her mother's side: a connection detailed in *Steuart's Colinton* p125. ELLIOT PLACE and PARK followed in 1930 and 1931, and ELLIOT GARDENS was added in 1974.

ELLIOT'S CLOSE (380 High Street) is named on *Ainslie* 1780 and may have been named for Cornelius Elliot, Clerk to the Signet, who was resident in Castle hill in 1773. The close is given in *PO Directory* 1827 as ROSS'S, which may also have been a recent name, referring to Matthew Ross, advocate, and Alexander Ross, depute clerk of session, who moved into the close from Dunbar's Close in the 1770s; but the name might have been of much longer standing, inasmuch as a charter of 1704 refers to a tenement somewhere in this vicinity west of the Upper Bow, once owned by a James Ross, merchant, and his son Thomas, who were likely to have been the James Ross, merchant, who was active in the town council 1573-87, and his second son, Thomas, who was arraigned by the council in 1580 for paying tax as a skinner when he was in fact trading as a merchant.

ELLIOT STREET (Quarryholes) was built in 1876 by J & W Elliot, builders, and named for them.

ELM PLACE (South Leith) *see under* INDUSTRIAL ROAD, South Leith.

ELM ROW (Hillside) was built in the early 1820s as part of W H Playfair's *Proposed New Town between Edinburgh and Leith* 1819 (*see under* CALTON NEW TOWN) and was so named because Playfair set back its frontage some 30 feet from the old boundary of Leith Walk, in response to the suggestion made in 1813 by the City Architect, William Stark, that the fine double row of elms along the west side of the grounds of Hillside House should be preserved and made a prominent feature of the new plan; but the space was clearly much too narrow, and *Ordnance Survey* 1852 shows but one tree surviving.

ELMWOOD TERRACE (South Leith) *see under* WOODBINE TERRACE, South Leith.

ELTRINGHAM GARDENS and **GROVE** (West Gorgie) were named in 1927 for Councillor Mrs Adam Miller, whose maiden name was Eltringham, in recognition of the help she had been to their developers. ELTRINGHAM TERRACE was named by association in 1934.

ELWALDSIDE (West Port) is recorded in 1454 as the alternative name of POKITSCLEIFF, *which see*. Like the later spellings *Elwand-*, *Elwod-* and *Elvand-*, *Elwald-* was a normal variant of the surname Eliot, and the name is 'Eliot's bank'. A Nicholas Elwald owned property in the vicinity of Edinburgh at some time before 1427.

ENTERKIN'S YETT (Juniper Green) is shown on *Ordnance Survey* 1852 and is referred to in the field name *Entriken's Yett Park* shown north of the Lanark road on *Riccarton* 1800, and in property names noted in *Ordnance Survey* 1893 and still current, on the south side of the road. The name evidently belongs to the point where the Lanark road enters Juniper Green. Once part of Currie muir, the land which was to become Juniper Green was brought into Woodhall by John Cunynghame of Enterkine in Ayrshire, who became laird of Woodhall in 1671, and by 1686 acquired this part of the common muir so that he might create a park (shown on *Roy* 1753) stretching northwards from Woodhall, crossing the river and public road, and continuing to the march with Baberton. It would appear that in order to control traffic through his park, either he or his son (the only other Enterkin laird of Woodhall) threw a *yett* or gate across the highway where it entered his land from the west.

ENTRYHEAD (Dalmahoy) is shown on *Roy* 1753, and is named as the place at the head of the entry to the estate.

ERNESYDE or **ARNESYDE** (Abbeyhill) *see* IRNESIDE, Abbeyhill.

ERSKINE PLACE (West End) is shown on *Kirkwood* 1823, and was evidently named for Lord Erskine of Alva, although this site was apparently separate from Alva's main property in the Kirkbraehead— *see under* ALVA STREET, West End. It was renamed as part of Shandwick Place in 1979.

ESPLANADE TERRACE (Joppa) was in use by 1894 as a side name for a terrace of houses built in Joppa Park and fronting a length of promenade which had been completed some three years earlier.

ESPLIN PLACE (Morningside) is shown on *W & A K Johnston* 1861 and was one of the six side names in Morningside Road suppressed in 1885. A property belonging to a Mr Esplin is shown on *Kirkwood* 1817, and a Mrs Charles Esplin kept lodgings in Morningside from 1832 to 1855.

ESPLIN'S CLOSE (once 37, now part of 31-35 Grassmarket) is listed on *Ainslie* 1780 and in *PO Directory* 1827, but was cleared for the contruction of the Corn Exchange in 1849. It was probably named for Robert Esplin, brewer in Grassmarket in 1780, or very possibly for a predecessor, for a Henry Esplin was plying the same trade in the Canongate in 1678.

ESSENDEAN PLACE and **TERRACE** (Clermiston) *see under* CLERMISTON MAINS.

ESSEX ROAD (Cramond) was named thus in 1932 at the suggestion of the developer's architect, John A W Grant, who gave no reason for the choice; and the name was borrowed for the adjoining streets ESSEX BRAE and ESSEX PARK in 1955 and 1960. *See also* AVON ROAD, Cramond.

ESSLEMONT ROAD (South Craigmillar Park) *see under* CRAIGMILLAR PARK.

ETHEL TERRACE (South Morningside) *see under* PLEWLANDS, South Morningside.

ETON TERRACE (Dean) *see under* CLARENDON CRESCENT, Dean.

ETTRICKDALE PLACE (Stockbridge) was named in 1980, continuing the style of the existing fancy names of Avondale and Teviotdale Place—*see under* THE COLONIES, Stockbridge.

ETTRICK ROAD (Merchiston) was named by 1873 for Sir Francis Napier, Baron Napier, created Baron Ettrick of Ettrick in 1872 when he retired to Scotland from India. ETTRICK GROVE was named in 1933, to provide an address for developments in the southern section of Ettrick Road, but was superseded in 1985, when this section was renamed SOUTH ETTRICK ROAD, in order to provide addresses for further new properties on the street.

EVA PLACE (Blackford) was named in about 1899 for Eva, daughter of the 2nd Baron Gifford, who had married Henry Trotter of Mortonhall, owner of Blackford, in 1866. Possibly at the same time, but certainly by 1901, MAURICE PLACE was named for her brother, Maurice Raymond Elton.

EWE & LAMB CLOSE (once 23 now 31 Grassmarket) is listed on *Ainslie* 1780 and was probably named for a tavern in it. The later name LAMOND'S, appearing in *PO Directory* 1827, may have derived from some proprietor as yet untraced, but may have been simply a corruption of the older name, after demise of the tavern.

EWERLAND (Cramond) *see* BRAEHEAD, Cramond.

OLD EXCISE OFFICE CLOSE (South side of Cowgate) is listed on *Ainslie* 1780 and was named for the Excise Office, which leased Merchant's Hall here in 1730. The Merchant's Hall (*see* MERCHANT STREET, Old Town) had once been the town house of Thomas Hamilton, Lord Drumcairn, who was nicknamed *Tam o the Cougate* by James VI and was created Earl of Haddington in 1626.

EYRE PLACE (Canonmills) was part of an old loan that led from Stockbridge to Leith by Silvermills, Canonmills, Logie Mill and Broughton Point. In 1822 it was included in Robert Brown's scheme for housing in James Eyre's estate of Canonmills (*see also under* BRANDON STREET and CANON STREET, Canonmills) but apart from the corner block at the west end of the street (best shown on *Ordnance Survey* 1852) development was delayed until 1891, when EYRE CRESCENT was also put in hand. Nevertheless, *Lothian* 1829 shows both streets named, obviously for James Eyre, brewer in

Canonmills and owner of Canonmills House in the first decades of the century. He or his father may well have been the Ayre recorded as a brewer in the Cowgate in 1780—*see under* RATTERAY'S or AYRE'S CLOSE, Cowgate. EYRE TERRACE was developed in 1897 from an earlier lane shown on *Bartholomew* 1876.

F

FACTOR'S PARK (Saughtonhall) is shown on *Saughtonhall* 1795 as some 18 Scots acres lying east of the river, now bounded by the north-west back of Hutchison View and the north-east back of Stevenson Avenue and a line (still evident in property boundaries) running north between them. The name suggests that the estate factor worked these fields, as a perquisite of his job and for his own benefit.

FACTORY WYND (South Leith) is listed in directories in 1783, and 1800 but is not shown on *Ainslie* 1804. The source of the name is not known.

FAIRAFAR (Cramond) is recorded in 1676 and shown on *Adair* 1682 as *Fairafar m(ill)*. *Laurie* 1766 shows both mill and farm, labelling the latter *Fairfar*; and in *Sasines* 1781 the name is given as *Fairyfare*. The suggestion that it was a whimsical name for the farm would scarcely explain how the mill, which was not approached from the farm, should come to share it, if indeed it did not have it first. It is more likely that both mill and farm were named for some local feature, such as the east side of the river gorge, which comes dramatically to its steepest at this point. The stress of the name suggests that it is Celtic, and British or Gaelic *fair a' bharr(adh)*, ridge or skyline of the brow or height, would fit the place exactly. FAIRAFAR ROW is shown on *Ordnance Survey* 1893 and is built along the frontage of a field known as *Mr Cadell's Park* in 1815. The housing development named FAIRAFAR in 1971 occupies the site of the farm steading and (along with CRAMOND VALE) the *Northwest park* of the farm.

FAIRBRAE (Saughton) is mentioned in a deed of 1590 (quoted in *RMS* 1662) and appears from the description to have been the name of the higher ground west of Stenhousemill. Considering the lie of the land, the name may have been Celtic *faithir*, shelving slope, with Scots *brae* for its steep ascent by the Calder road.

FAIRHOLM'S CLOSE (15 West Bow) is recorded in 1800 and seems to have been named for Thomas Fairholm, merchant, whose son Thomas Fairholm of Pilton owned a tenement here in 1780. Free St John's (now St Columba's) Church was built on the site in 1845.

FAIRLIE'S CLOSE or **ENTRY** (182 Cowgate) is listed in *Maitland* 1753. Numerous persons of the name were prominent in the town from 1300 to 1600 in particular, and it may be that the close name is connected with land on the north side of the Cowgate, recorded in 1529 as having been owned by Clement Fairlie.

FAIRMILEHEAD is shown on *Ordnance Survey* 1852 about a hundred yards west of the present crossroads, as a group of buildings at the former crossroads in the original high road, which had followed the line (still represented by the east backs of Fairmile Avenue) of the Roman road from Carlops, *see under* ROMAN ROADS. The modern crossroads or FAIRMILEHEAD TOLL is shown on *Knox* 1812, having been created in the 1780s, when the highroad was altered, looping eastwards in order to ease the stiff climb up from Bowbridge. In 1682 and for a century thereafter the name was spelt *Farmil(l)head*, and the version *Farmilehead* appearing on *Armstrongs* 1773 might have been an attempt to explain the name, having regard to the fact that there was neither record nor likelihood of any mill being on this site. The clue to the name may lie in the two great cairns of the CATHEAPS (*which see*) that stood some 250 yards west of the Roman road: for before they were robbed for road metal in the 1780s, these cairns were so prominent on the ridge that *Adair* 1682 uses special conical symbols to mark them; and this suggests that the place name may be Anglian *heafod* or Scots *heid*, for the summit in the ancient Carlops road, combined with an earlier name for the place, possibly British or Gaelic *fair* or *faithir mill*, ridge or slope of the mounds or heaps. Thus the name FAIRMILE AVENUE, although coined in 1934 in the fanciful belief that *Fairmilehead* referred to a 'fair mile' from somewhere, may accidentally reflect the ancient Celtic name.

FAIRNINGTON PLACE (Stockbridge) enters the *PO Directory* in 1833 and is shown on *Ordnance Survey* 1852 as a side name in Deanhaugh Street, presumably named for the builder or an owner of the property.

FALA KNOWE (Pentlands) is *the Falaw* in *RMS* 1542, and the name is Anglian *fáh hlaw* or early Scots *faw law*, speckled hill of a conical or cairnlike shape, with Scots *knowe* added. Since it is mentioned as one of the subdivisions of PENTLANDMUIR, it is possible that the *Falaw* name originally attached to Castlelaw hill itself, the *knowe* being added for this outlier.

FALCONER'S CLOSE (96 Canongate) *see* STEWART'S CLOSE, Canongate.

FALCON HALL (Morningside) was a mansion, shown on *Knox* 1812 and sited at what is now the middle of the south backs of Falcon Avenue, built by Andrew Falconer, sometime Chief Secretary to the Governor of Madras, who had retired in 1811; and its name was an obvious play on his surname. When it was pulled down in 1909, its last owner, John George Bartholomew the cartographer, had its west front re-erected as the entrance to his firm's premises in Duncan Street; and the pillars at its gates, transferred to Corstorphinehill House, now flank the entrance to the Edinburgh Zoo. Housing developed on the east side of Morningside Road (later replaced by tenements) was named FALCON PLACE by 1869, but was taken into MORNINGSIDE ROAD in 1885. FALCON AVENUE was named and opened by 1893, including the north part of what became FALCON GARDENS by 1907. FALCON ROAD was named by 1912, but FALCON ROAD WEST was not developed until 1938. FALCON COURT followed in 1961.

FALCON'S CLOSE (High Street) *see* BACK OF BETH'S WYND.

FALKLAND GARDENS (Clermiston) was named in 1966, taking its name from that of a house which stood on the site, shown as 'Carsebrae', on maps of 1912 and 1921 but renamed, presumably for Falkland, Fife, by a later owner, Lambert, wine merchant.

FALSHAW BRIDGE (Stockbridge) was built in 1877 to the design of David C Proudfoot, and named for Sir James Falshaw Bt., then Lord Provost. FALSHAW STREET is now IONA STREET, *which see*.

FANTASY (Straiton) *see* PHANTASSIE, Straiton.

FARQUHARSON PLACE (Newington) is shown on *Ordnance Survey* 1852 as a side name in West Preston Street, and appears to have been named for Charles Farquharson, watchmaker there in 1853.

FARQUHAR TERRACE (Queensferry) is a side name given to council housing built in Hopetoun Road in the early 1920s, in compliment to Councillor Canon William Farquhar.

FARRER GROVE etc (Craigentinny) *see under* CRAIGENTINNY.

FAULDBURN (Corstorphine) *see under* BUGHTLIN, Corstorphine.

FEATHERHALL (Corstorphine) appears on *Corstorphine* 1845 as the name of two farms, *Featherhall No. I* to the north of the Glasgow road, and *Featherhall No. II* to the south if it, stretching down to the Stank on the west and south of the village. The latter included an inby field *Featherhall park*, west of the steading which apparently served both farms and was eventually cleared in 1928, making way for 210-221 St John's Road. The steading is shown but not named on *Roy* 1753 and *Corstorphine* 1754 and 1777, but the latter shows the field name. The ending -*hall* is Anglian *halh* or Scots *haw*, land in the bend of the burn; but *feather* appears to be Celtic, possibly British *fethir*, a shelving slope, or *fother*, woodland, akin to Gaelic *faithir* or *foithre*. Either would be apt enough as a general name for the northern part of Corstorphine, and *haw* would describe the part of it reaching down towards the Stank. FEATHERHALL AVENUE (on the line of a path known as THE SLEEPERS, *which see*) and FEATHERHALL CRESCENT and TERRACE were named in 1927, and were followed by FEATHERHALL PLACE (1929) CRESCENT SOUTH (1931) and GROVE (1936).

FERDINGHEUGH (New Hailes & Brunstane) is mentioned in *RMS* 1661, as the name of a part of Whitehill (later *New Hailes*) adjacent to Brunstane Mill and extending to some 53 Scots acres. The variant *Ferdinhaugh* appears in *RMS* 1653. *Ferding* or *Farding*, probably meaning 'a fourth part' rather than a 'farthing (rental) land', occurs elsewhere, often with a distinguishing suffix which may be a personal name, as in Ferding*james*, or else a description of the ground, as in Ferding*wells*, or as here, where -*heugh* refers to the projecting spur rising steeply above the back of the shore.

FERNIEFLAT (Wester Hailes) is shown on *Laurie* 1763. The name, Scots *fernie flat*, level ground where bracken grows, was virtually suppressed in 1971 by a development of streets inappropriately named as though the land were in BABERTON MAINS (*which see*), Baberton Mains Gardens being built on the site of Fernieflat steading.

FERNIEHILL (Gilmerton) is shown on *Craigour etc* 1815 as *Fernyside Hill*, and since the name also applies to the *Fernyside Hill Park* it clearly originated as a land name for *the hill above Fernieside*, already shortened to *Ferniehill* on *Ordnance Survey* 1852. FERNIEHILL ROAD is the road which led to it. FERNIEHILL DRIVE was begun on part of the Drum in 1947. FERNIEHILL AVENUE, GARDENS, GROVE, PLACE, SQUARE, STREET, TERRACE and WAY were named in 1966.

FERNIELAW (Bonaly) is shown on *Roy* 1753 and is named as *Fairnielaw* in 1772, when it was reunited with BONALY WALLACE (*which see*) in James Gillespie's extended estate of SPYLAW, as shown on *Spylaw* 1799. The name is Scots *fernie law*, the hill or hillock with bracken on it. The land was part of BONALY from before 1337, and its western march with Woodhall is represented by the east side of Torphin Road. FERNIELAW AVENUE had served as access to the farm for centuries before it was formally named in about 1910.

FERNIESIDE (Gilmerton) is shown as *N(orth) Summerside* on *Laurie* 1763 but as *Fairnyside* on *Knox* 1812. The name is Scots *fernie side*, slope where bracken grows. FERNIESIDE AVENUE, DRIVE, CRESCENT and GROVE were named in 1947, the Drive being formed out of the drive to *Fernieside Lodge* or *House*, which appears on *Ordnance Survey* 1852.

FERRIEGATE (Corstorphine) is shown on *Ordnance Survey* 1852 as a loaning on the site of Victor Park Terrace, branching from the main road at FERRYBANK COTTAGES. The second part of the name is from Old Norse *gata*, a road; but in absence of early forms the derivation of the first part must be tentative. Apart from vague and doubtful references in *Selway* there is nothing to connect the road with any ferry over the Stank; and although *Roy* 1753 shows it continuing past Clermiston and joining the Ferry (Queensferry) road at Parkneuk, the suggestion that the name was 'road to the Ferry' is not altogether convincing, if only because *Roy* shows it duplicated by the Drum Brae route. Considering that both *Roy* and *Adair/Cooper* 1735 show it as the access to Clermiston (soon to be replaced by the present Clermiston road, shown on *Corstorphine* 1754) the name may be from Anglian *fergen gata*, hill road or path, describing its character and destination.

FERRIER STREET (Quarryholes) *see under* GORDON STREET, Quarryholes.

FERRIE'S CLOSE (Canongate, off Abbey Strand) is shown on *Ainslie* 1780, but appears as CRAIG'S CLOSE on *Ainslie* 1804. Both names remain obscure. *See also* WAUCHOPE CLOSE, Canongate.

FERRY ACRES (Queensferry) appear on *Dundas* 1757 as an area subdivided in runrig in the neighbourhood which was named SOUTH SCOTSTOUN in 1983. The legend on the 1757 map groups it with MUIRHALL (*which see*) and the name *ferry* supports the view that it was part of the endowment of the Queen's ferry. Scots *aiker*, from Old Norse *akr*, was a general term for a plot of land, before it became a unit of land measurement.

FERRY BURN (Queensferry) is named on *Dundas* 1757, evidently as the burn *at the Ferry*, a form of the burgh's name which has been in use since the time of Robert the Bruce, if not earlier. FERRYBURN GREEN was named in 1982 for its position beside the burn.

FERRYFIELD (Wardie) was developed in 1982 on the ancient farm of WINNELSTRAELEE, *which see*. Although the farm name continued in use until 1939, it had begun to be supplanted in about 1920, when the Edinburgh Institution (Melville College) acquired the central part of the farm and coined a new name from its nearness to *Ferry* road and its new use as a playing *field*. Regrettably this trivial name was continued for the housing street, despite a plea for recovery of the proper name of the ground.

THE FERRY MUIR or **HILL** (Queensferry) is recorded as *the Ferriehill* in 1618 and was evidently named as the high ground above and attached to *the Ferry*, the regular alternative name for QUEENSFERRY, *which see*. On the evidence of field names on *Dundas* 1757, *Plewlandfield* 1769 and *Barnbougle & Dalmeny* c.1800, it stretched from the *Ferriemuir parks* (about 650 yards to the west of the Kirkliston Road, next to Windyedge) eastwards virtually to Dalmeny. It included the MUIRHALL, FERRY ACRES and SCOTSTOUN (*which see*) which were apparently all part of the kirk lands granted to endow the Queen's ferry; but by the 17th century the first two had become runrig and common owned by burgesses and the kirk session of Queensferry. FERRYMUIR LANE originated as a farm road bypassing the cemetery when this took over part of the old kirk road, *see under* CEMETERY ROAD. Houses developed alongside the lane were addressed as in Cemetery Road until 1982, when the lane was named in its own right: not for any connection with the Muir, but simply to commemorate it, for the lane itself is within the BLACKLAWS of Plewlands (*which see*) and about 100 yards north of the march with the Muir at the Ferry burn. FERRYMUIR GATE was named in 1992, as a *gait* or way leading in the direction of the Muir.

FERRY ROAD (Leith to Davidson's Mains) probably existed long before it was shown on *Roy* 1753 but seems to have functioned more as a connection with the various properties along its length than as the main through route it became in the later 1750s, after upgrading and a certain amount of straightening at Bonnington and Drylaw. From *Fergus & Robinson* 1759 to *Pollock* 1834 the maps figure it as the *road from Queensferry*; *Queensferry Road* appears on the *PO Directory Map* of 1807 and *Ferry Road* on *Pollock* 1834, but only for the sections east of the Crew; and finally FERRY ROAD appears in *PO Directory* 1854 after names such as Jamaica Street had failed to win acceptance for sections of the road within Leith itself.

FERRY ROAD AVENUE, DRIVE, GARDENS, GROVE, LANE and **PLACE** (West Pilton) were built in fields of Pirniehall and West Pilton in 1938 and named for a nearness to *Ferry Road* which is shared by many other streets along its 3-mile length.

FETTES AVENUE and **EAST FETTES AVENUE** (Comely Bank) were laid out along with Fettes College, which was completed in 1870, but the names—in both cases sometimes given as *Road* in place of *Avenue*—seem to have been fixed much later: EAST FETTES AVENUE in about 1893 and FETTES AVENUE in about 1900. The streets were named for Lord Provost Sir William Fettes (1750-1836) who was doubly associated with the place, for as well as leaving £166,000 to found the College, he had owned the land at Comely Bank on which the streets are sited. FETTES RISE was named in 1970, perpetuating an existing house name of a style scarcely in keeping with the district.

FETTES ROW (New Town) *see under* NORTHERN NEW TOWN.

FIGGATE or **FIGGATE WHINS** was the coastal strip of dunes, links and (in places) bogs shown on *Roy* 1753 and *Knox* 1812 as stretching from Fillyside to Joppa. Recorded from 1466 onwards, the name's early forms *fegot* and *fegat* show it to be from Old Norse *fé*, cattle or sheep, and *gata*, a way, probably used here in its sense of 'pasture'. While the coast road is shown on *Adair* 1682, the whin bushes (a coastal feature still evident at Port Seton) gave such cover to highwaymen that a route along the sands was apt to be preferred, *see under* KING'S ROAD, Portobello. The *lands of Fegot* in Duddingston, as defined in 1466 in a charter of Kelso Abbey, are exactly the same as the *Village of Figget* shown on *Roads from Figget* 1783: in modern terms bounded on the east by Hope Lane and the east backs of Marlborough Street, on the north by the shore, on the west by the Figgate burn, and on the south by a *lech* or slow-running burn, long since culverted, on the north side of Harry Lauder Way, *see also under* CHRISTIAN PATH, Portobello. FIGGATE BURN is the local name for the final reach of the PEFFER or BRAID BURN, *which see*. FIGGATE BANK and STREET were new names coined in 1965 for TOWER BANK and STREET, Portobello, *which see*; and FIGGATE LANE was named in 1981 as a new street on the site of part of Figgate Street.

FINGAL PLACE (Sciennes) *see* SYLVAN PLACE, Sciennes.

FILLYSIDE (Craigentinny) is recorded as *Grenebank alias Fillisydebank* in 1553 and as *Fillyside alias Greenbank* in 1596; and although shown as the *North* or *East Mains* of Restalrig on *Roy* 1753 and *Laurie* 1763, it is *Fillysidebank* on *Armstrongs* 1773, *Knox* 1812 and *Kirkwood* 1817, while the last also shows *Fillyside Meadow* north of the steading, now displaced by the golf clubhouse. The duplication of *-side* by *-bank* witnesses to the age of the name, which is Anglian *fealu* or early Scots *falu*, yellowish, with *side*, a slope: a description perhaps translated by the 16th-century Greenbank. FILLYSIDE ROAD, partly the old road to the farm, was formed and named in 1933, along with FILLYSIDE AVENUE and TERRACE. In the 1810s the name was borrowed as a fancy name, noted on *Kirkwood* 1817, for a house in Seafield, north of Fillyside.

FINDHORN PLACE (Grange) *see under* THE GRANGE.

FINDLAY AVENUE, COTTAGES, GARDENS, GROVE, MEDWAY (Restalrig) were built in 1926 as a Government-sponsored scheme of steel houses, erected by the Second Scottish National Housing Company (Housing Trust) Ltd, Sir John R Findlay Bt. being their chairman at the time—*also see* FRASER AVENUE etc, a scheme of the same sort.

FINGAL PLACE (Sciennes) *see* SYLVAN PLACE, Sciennes.

FINGIES or **FINZIES PLACE** (South Leith) *see under* INDUSTRIAL ROAD.

FINLAGGAN COURT (East Craigs) *see under* CRAIGIEVAR WYND, East Craigs.

FINLAYSON'S CLOSE (160 Canongate) is listed on *Ainslie* 1780 and was named for James Finlayson, mason, burgess of Canongate, who built *Finlayson's land*, now part of 168 Canongate, immediately east of Moray House.

FIRHILL (Colinton Mains) is recorded in 1719 as lands and park attached to the Mains of Colinton, now COLINTON MAINS, *which see*. The name evidently refers to the south-west outlier of Wester Craiglockhart Hill, and since there is no reason to suppose that it does not also refer to firs growing on the hill, the *Firr* spelling appearing on *Ordnance Survey* 1893 seems scarcely justified. FIRHILL CRESCENT, DRIVE and LOAN were named in 1954. FIRHILL PATH, shown on *Ordnance Survey* 1912, restored (on a more northerly line) a right-of-way shown on *Colinton Mains* 1813 as a 'farm road to Edinburgh' from Oxgangs road to Plewlands.

FISHER'S CLOSE (312 High Street) is shown on *Edgar* 1742 and was evidently named for a Thomas Fisher, who formed *Fisher's Land* at its head by rebuilding an earlier tenement, once owned by Thomas Cant of St Giles Grange. It is possible that the rebuilding was by the Thomas Fisher who was prominent in town affairs 1589 until 1609; but there is nothing to connect him with this side of the Lawnmarket. No Fisher is listed as an owner in this vicinity in 1635. The style of the present building would fit the dates of a later Thomas Fisher, merchant, member of council in 1694 and town chamberlain in 1700, when he was in a position to let a house in the Lawnmarket to the newly-elected Lord Provost, Sir Patrick Johnston. The close ran down to the Cowgate (*see under* MacCONNOCHIE'S, BAILLIE'S and BRODIE'S CLOSES, 44, 50 and 52 Cowgate) and got its other name of HAMILTON'S from James Hamilton, one of the ministers of the town kirks, who was made a burgess upon his arrival in Edinburgh in 1647, and purchased a house, originally belonging to the late Thomas Hope of Craighall, at the south end of the close.

FISHER'S CLOSE (about 481 High Street) *see* GLADSTANES CLOSE.

NEW FISHMARKET (Cowgate) was a small court at the foot of Marlin's Wynd, entered by a close from the Cowgate. Swept away when the South Bridge was built in 1785-88, it is shown on *Rothiemay* 1647, and is described in *Maitland* 1753 as having been used successively as a marketplace for corn and for coal before it became a fish market.

(OLD) FISHMARKET CLOSE (196 High Street and 144 Cowgate) is recorded in 1592 and was evidently named for the fish market set up within it, as noted in *Town Council Minutes* 1539; but interpretation of records is made difficult by the fact that the close as it is at present is a combination (first shown on *Ainslie* 1780) of a pair of closes shown, with the fish market between them, on *Rothiemay* 1647. The one on the east (196 High Street) is *Fishmarkett wyne* on *Rothiemay* but BACK OF BORTHWICK'S CLOSE on *Edgar* 1742, and becomes the upper part of *Old Fishmarket Close* on *Ainslie* 1780; and it would seem that it was also known by the names, as yet obscure, of CARMICHAEL'S (mentioned in 1722) GOURLAY'S (1756) and HOME (1707). The last of these might perhaps be the origin of the strange name HUMPH CLOSE shown on *Ordnance Survey* 1852 as attached to its southern remnant. The western close of the pair is unnamed on *Rothiemay*, but is given as *Fishmarket Close* on *Edgar* 1742, while *Ainslie* 1780 continues that name for its southern half, but adds *Old*, and shows the northern part suppressed by new buildings. On the assumption that the arrangement shown on *Edgar* 1742 and 1765 is the one referred to in charters dated between 1719 and 1765, it is likely that this close was once BARRIE'S *later* JOLLY'S, mentioned in 1724 but as yet obscure, and also SUITTIE'S (1741), perhaps from a connection with the family of wool merchants (in particular, George Suittie and his son George) who were prominent in the town from 1620 to the 1660s. The most ancient name of all is SWIFT'S WYND, recorded in 1539 but apparently going back to John Swift and his wife Alison, who acquired a tenement south of the High Street and *near the Cross* in 1427. Various references in *RMS* 1433-1527 show that John and his son Thomas had more than one property between St Giles kirkyard and Borthwick's Close. The name BACK OF THE FISHMARKET is mentioned as an alternative to *Barrie's*, but it is also listed in 1635 as though it were the next close west of Borthwick's— i.e. the foot of the Fishmarket Wynd marked on *Rothiemay* 1647.

FISHMARKET SQUARE (Newhaven) *see under* St ANDREW'S SQUARE, Newhaven.

FIVEHOUSES (Liberton) is so named on *Knox* 1812, but is marked on *Roy* 1753 and named on *Laurie* 1763 as *S(outh) Camps*—i.e. KAIMS (*which see*) the little ridge or *kaim* being obvious, immediately west of the hamlet. The later name probably refers to the five cottages shown here on *Ordnance Survey* 1852—still there in 1931, but named *Janefield*, presumably for the owner or a relative; and the street name JANEFIELD was formally adopted upon redevelopment of the site in 1983.

FISHWIVES CAUSEY (Portobello and Craigentinny) has undergone so many changes that not one yard of it is original. Both end sections are shown on *Roads from Figget* 1783 with notes confirming that they once followed different lines, and since then the central section has been drastically altered to suit the developments of the North British Railway in 1845 and TELFERTON (*which see*) in 1984. Nevertheless it is evident that the Causey was never part of the ancient road from Musselburgh (possibly representing a Roman road from Inveresk) which is shown on *Blaeu* 1654 and *Roy* 1753 as going more or less in a straight line from Magdalene Pans to Jock's Lodge, *see under* PORTOBELLO; but since that road passed through Duddingston land and was wholly suppressed when that estate was enclosed in about 1760 (there is not a trace of it on *Duddingston* c1800) and since the Causey followed the march between Duddingston and Craigentinny and was a short cut across the corner of the new road from Musselburgh by Portobello and the Portobello Road, it seems possible that it was provided and *causeyed* (i.e. paved) as a footpath six feet wide, to compensate for the closure of the old right of way, which must have been of particular concern to the fishwives of Fisherrow who were walking with their creels to Edinburgh by Jocks' Lodge at least as early as the 17th century.

THE FLASH (Queensferry) is recorded from 1573 onwards and shown on *Dundas* 1757 as the *Flass shot*, a field beside the Rosshill burn. The name, frequent in the north of England as well as lowland Scotland, describes the character of the ground, for it is early Scots *flasche* or *flasshe* from Scandinavian *flask*, low and perhaps marshy land liable to be flooded by the burn in times of spate.

THE FLASHES or **FLASSHES** (Corstorphine) is reported as the traditional name (the same as the foregoing) of the low ground south of the Stank at the Gyle. It certainly describes the terrain; and the ground, shown as a loch on *Blaeu* 1654 and still described on *Laurie* 1763 as *loch or meadow*, was the last part of the primeval Corstorphine loch (*see under* CORSTORPHINE) to be drained by deepening of the Stank. Even so, the *Statistical Account* 1793 reports that much inconvenience and damage was still being caused by flooding and stagnant water.

FLEMING'S CLOSE (171 Cowgate) *see* KITCHEN'S CLOSE, Cowgate.

FLEMING'S CLOSE (61 High Street) *see* MONTEITH'S CLOSE.

JOHN FLEMING'S CLOSE (587 High Street) *see* TOD'S CLOSE.

FLESHMARKET CLOSE (199 High Street) is listed on *Edgar* 1742 as the westmost of three leading to the Fleshmarket (*see also* OLD PROVOST'S CLOSE and THE BULL CLOSE) and obviously got its name after the market was moved from the south side of the Tron Kirk, as shown on *Rothiemay* 1647, to the lower part of the slope down to the Nor Loch, at some time prior to 1691. It must have had an earlier name; but the only suggestion, that it was *Provost's Close*, is of doubtful authority and not very plausible.

(NEW) FLESHMARKET CLOSE (South Leith) was named for the new flesh or meat market planned by the town in 1768 and shown on *Wood* 1777. It was adjacent to an earlier one.

OLD FLESHMARKET CLOSE (355 Canongate) is listed on *Ainslie* 1780. *Rothiemay* 1647 shows the earlier market, with the crames or stalls of the fleshers in the middle of the street of the Canongate, near its head, and shows garden ground where *Edgar* 1742 shows the Fleshmarket.

FLETCHER'S LODGING (90 Canongate) *see* MILTON HOUSE, Canongate.

THE FLODDEN WALL (Old Town) is shown on *Rothiemay* 1647, except for the parts made redundant by the building of the salient of TELFER'S WALL (*which see*) after 1618. The name is in the nature of a historian's term for defensive building which, although perhaps accelerated by the disaster of Flodden field, had been on the go long before 1513. It probably began some time after James II granted licence in 1450 to fortify the town against 'the evil and skath of oure enemies of England'; but if that purpose was military, it was not the only one, for even in the year after Flodden the town council's immediate anxiety was to enclose the town against anyone infected with the plague. The wall incorporated several ports built before 1513, as well as the extensive walls of the Blackfriars and the Kirk o Fields. The east end of the burgh was never completely walled: in the wynds flanking the Netherbow the owners were obliged to keep their doors and windows securely steikit or locked at all times, and to build them up as soon as war threatened; and in 1561 the council were still dealing with gaps by building walls along the frontages of waste ground in Leith Wynd, even although by this time the example of Piero di Strozzi's immense new-style fortifications of Leith in 1548 must have convinced most people that the military value of walls of this outmoded medieval type was now slight.

FLY or **FLAE WALK** (Greenbank) is shown on *Ordnance Survey* 1852 as a footpath from Greenbank, branching south by Cockmalane to Comiston and west by Chatterrig to Oxgangs and the Baads. The name is traditional, recorded in 1926, and probably referred to the path's route on a *flaw* or *flae*, a grassed strip along the brink of the slope down to the Braid burn, where the land was too steep for ploughing.

FOORD'S CLOSE (246 Canongate) *see* PIRRIE'S CLOSE.

FORBES ROAD (Greenhill) *see under* GREENHILL.

FORBES STREET (St Leonards) was begun at its northern end with the building of a tenement of family flats, sponsored by a Mr Forbes in 1853 and, like ASHLEY BUILDINGS in the Netherbow (*which see*) designed and built by the local firm of W Beattie & Son. The southern half of the street was completed by 1875.

FORDEL(L) (Dreghorn) included *Little Fordell* and the *muir of Fordale*, was recorded in 1563 and added to Dreghorn in 1603; and *Fordelbank* is mentioned in 1671. The lands are now difficult to identify, but Little Fordel seems to have extended over the rising ground east of Redford Bridge (possibly including the Gallolee) and is noted as lying both east and west of the Baads, while the muir stretched along its south side. The site (NT 22956855) of the house of *Fordel* shown on *Laurie* 1763 was cleared in the 1980s. The name occurs twice in Lothian and three times on the other side of the Forth, and also in Ayrshire, Melrose and Dunkeld. It is Celtic, probably British *gor-dol*, upper meadow (the prefix also changes to *vor-* in Cornwall) easily Gaelicised as *for dail*.

FORD'S ROAD (Saughtonhall), together with its bridge and its branch and path continuing up the west bank of the river, represents the old line of the Calder road before it was altered, at some time between 1773 and 1795, to carry on straight on from Gorgie and over a new bridge at Stenhousemill. The plan of *Saughtonhall* 1795 shows both arrangements, and the older one is shown on *Adair* 1682, with the bridge clearly figured. No doubt there would have been a ford beside this bridge, but the *foord of Sauchtounhall* mentioned in *Laing Charters* 1643 seems to be that shown in 1795 as further downstream, on the branch road to Balgreen, and in any case the traditional name FORD'S ROAD must date from some time after this old section of Calder road was bypassed. It probably derives from an owner or tenant in DALYELL'S MILLS (*which see*) at some time after 1795.

FORD'S ROW (106 Canongate) *see* BULL'S CLOSE, Canongate.

FORDYCE CLOSE (243 High Street) *see* THE ANCHOR CLOSE.

FORKENFORD (Craigmillar) is Scots *ford at the forkin* or confluence. A map of Peffermill in 1839 (*RHP 3022*) shows the Braid and Pow burns entering a Y-shaped culvert and meeting under the centre of the highway which is now Duddingston Road West, and it is evident that the culverting simply replaced an earlier ford.

FORRES STREET (New Town) *see under* MORAY ESTATE, New Town.

FORREST ROAD (Bristo) originated as an access to the Back or Inner Yard of Greyfriars, part of the High Riggs ground which the town purchased in 1618 and enclosed within the Telfer Wall by 1636, *see under* FLODDEN WALL. Used as a prison for Covenanters in 1679, the ground was later the site of the head office of the Darien Company, built in 1698, and of the paternal home of the Quaker beauty Miss Mally Bontine, who eventually ran off with the young minister of Currie; but with the establishment of a bedlam and the building of the Charity Workhouse in 1743 it became the main centre for the insane and the poor until they were better provided for at Morningside and Greenbank in 1813 and 1870 respectively. Access was by a new gateway slapped in the Flodden Wall immediately west of the existing Bristo Port, as shown on *Edgar* 1742—an arrangement which was the beginnings of the later forked junction of Forrest Road and Bristo Place—and a wicket in the Telfer Wall continued the path to the Middle Meadow Walk created by Hope of Rankeillor after 1722. Redevelopment of the area was sketched in the *Scots Magazine* in 1817 and envisaged in the scheme for George IV Bridge in 1827, but obviously had to await clearance of the site. The roadway of FORREST ROAD was opened in the 1840s and named for Sir James Forrest of Comiston, Lord Provost 1837-43; but otherwise development was delayed until 1870, when the opening of the new City Poorshouse at Greenbank enabled the old Workhouse to be closed down, although part of it still stands in FORREST HILL, named in 1873.

FORRESTER PARK (Corstorphine) was developed in 1965 in a field of Broomhouse in Saughton, quite outwith the lands of the Forresters of Corstorphine; but notwithstanding this the name was coined for FORRESTER PARK AVENUE, DRIVE, GARDENS, GREEN, GROVE and LOAN.

FORRESTER ROAD (Corstorphine) was begun at its eastern end in 1884, and was named for the Forrester family, whose connection with Corstorphine lasted over 300 years, beginning in 1377, when Adam Forrester, later laird of the barony, feued the Mains of Corstorphine from William More of Abercorn. BARONY TERRACE, developed along with the western part of Forrester Road in the mid 1920s in the *South* and *Mid Bank* fields of Featherhall, was named for their estate.

FORRESTER'S WYND (South side of High Street, and 98 Cowgate) is mentioned in *RMS* 1473 as *the public lane commonly called the Forestaris wynde*. Sir Alexander Forrester of Corstorphine, who died in about 1467, is mentioned in *RMS* 1478 as a former owner in the wynd; and although the connection may go back to the remarkable Adam Forrester, burgess in 1362 and alderman in 1373, he is not recorded as owning property on the south side of the High Street. The wynd is shown on *Rothiemay* 1647; and although its upper end was suppressed when the Signet Library began to be built in 1811, its south end is still shown on *Ordnance Survey* 1893.

FORSYTH'S CLOSE (57 Canongate) is listed on *Ainslie* 1780, and was named for Alexander Forsyth, coachmaker, burgesss of Edinburgh, who acquired property here in 1719.

FORSYTH'S CLOSE (221 High Street) *see* OLD STAMP OFFICE CLOSE.

THE FORTH is mentioned by Tacitus, in his record of the campaigns of his father-in-law Agricola in Scotland from AD 79 to 83. The name, which of course belongs to the river in Stirlingshire, seems to have been British *Voritia*, becoming Gaelic *Foirthe*, river with the strong undercurrent, an apt description of its tidal reaches. The Norsemen called the estuary MURKFJORTH, for its frequent sea fogs or haar; and the name FIRTH OF FORTH contains Old Norse *firth*, Scots *firth* or *frith*, an estuary. The alternative name SCOTTIS SEA, recorded in the 12th century but probably dating back to Anglian times, arose because *Scotland*, as the 'land of the Scots', lay beyond its northern shore. The FORTH BRIDGE was opened in 1890, and the FORTH ROAD BRIDGE in 1964.

FORTH PLACE (Queensferry) was built athwart a burn in the Netherfields of Echline, and was named in 1974, in a rather limited flight of fancy, for the estuary to the north of it.

FORTH STREET (Broughton) *see under* PICARDY, Broughton.

FORTH TERRACE (Dalmeny) was built in about 1883 to house workers on the Forth Bridge, and named for the estuary.

FORTHVIEW (Dalmeny) was named by 1970 for a house previously occupying the site.

FORTHVIEW TERRACE (Blackhall) was named by 1904, evidently for the glimpse of the firth later obscured when the land to the northeast was built up. Prior to 1967 FORTHVIEW ROAD was named HILLVIEW ROAD, *which see*.

FORTHVIEW CRESCENT, ROAD and **AVENUE** (Currie) were built in 1957-58, and evidently named for the view from the ridge.

FORT PLACE (North Leith) was developed in the 1880s as a branch off North Fort Street and getting its name from it; but it was suppressed by redevelopment in 1984—*see under* HILLHOUSEFIELD.

THE FORTS (Queensferry) got its name as a gun site in the first world war.

FORT STREET (North Leith) was originally but briefly the name of NORTH FORT STREET, shown on *Knox* and *Cramond Roads* 1812 and first appearing in *PO Directory* 1813. The name was taken from the adjoining LEITH FORT (*which see*) and in 1966 it was extended to cover GEORGE STREET, also built in about 1812. SOUTH FORT STREET grew out of the access to HILLHOUSEFIELD HOUSE (*which see*) dating to 1657 or thereby. The street name was also given in 1813, evidently because it was opposite the entry of Fort Street, but although *Kirkwood* 1817 shows development planned as far as Pitt Street, it was about 60 years before building got further south.

FORTUNE'S CLOSE (221 High Street) *see* OLD STAMP OFFICE CLOSE.

FOULBRIGGIS or **FOULBRIDGE** (Fountainbridge) *see under* FOUNTAINBRIDGE.

(NORTH) FOULIS CLOSE (229 High Street) is given on *Edgar* 1742 and *Kirkwood* 1817 as FOWLER'S, a name which evidently dates at latest to 1635, when a Mr John Fouller is listed as owner and occupier on its west side. He appears in *RMS* 1627 as son of the late William Fowlar, merchant burgess, and the form of address *M* or *Mr* would suggest that he was a lawyer. The alternative FOULIS' for the close appears on *Ainslie* 1780 and possibly derives from John Foulis, apothecary and owner of a tenement in the close at some date prior to 1746: but it does not seem impossible that *Fouller* and *Foulis* might be one and the same. The prefix *North* was added to distinguish the close from the other *Foulis Close*, a name which is quite differently derived.

(SOUTH) FOULIS'S CLOSE (42 High Street) is given as *Fowler's* on *Edgar* 1742 but as *Foulis's* on *Ainslie* 1780 (the two showing that the pronunciation was *Fowlz-iz*) and took its name from Sir James Foulis, 7th of Colinton, son of the sixth laird by his first wife Barbara Ainslie (*see under* HYNDFORD'S CLOSE, 50 High Street) who owned property here prior to his death in 1711. There is no connection between this close and NORTH FOULIS' CLOSE (*which see*) for *North* and *South* were added to the names in the 1820s, simply to distinguish between them. Earlier the close was known as PURVES'S (sometimes rendered *Power's* or *Powrie's*) from an owner recorded as John Purves, burgess, who may have been the John Purves who was city treasurer in 1528 and dean of guild in 1539, or perhaps the later one made burgess in 1592 (*see also under* WORLD'S END CLOSE, 10 High Street). A further early name, ALEXANDER UDDART'S or UDWART'S CLOSE, derived from an owner of lands and a yard near the foot of the close, evidently the Alexander Uddart who first appears in *Town Council Minutes* as one of the leaders of a deputation of *burgess bairns* or unmarried sons of burgesses in 1557, but went on to be one of the most kenspeckle men in the town in the period 1566-82. The earliest name for the close appears to be MOUBRAY'S, going back to an Andrew Moubray mentioned in *RMS* 1528 as late owner of land on the south side of the street near the Netherbow. Feu charters give both Andrew and Robert Moubray as former owners of land on the east side of the close.

FOULIS CRESCENT (Juniper Green) lies within the estate of Woodhall north of the river (*see under* ENTERKIN'S YETT) and was named in 1934 for the Foulis family, who acquired Woodhall in 1701 and finally sold it in 1932.

FOUNTAINBRIDGE, recorded in 1713 and shown on *Plan of Bypass Roads* 1763, originated as a name for a suburb created by Sir Alexander Brand soon after his purchase of Dalry (*see under* BRANDSFIELD) in 1696. The new feus were on the north side of the Lanark road, but the name (as reported in the *Edinburgh Evening Courant* 1774) derived from the Foullbridge Well of 'singularly sweet water', south of the road and east of the burn and bridge, which was itself some 20 yards east of the entry to the present Gilmore Park. Evidently 'Fountainbridge' was newly coined as a more attractive name for the suburb than the ancient one still in use in 1705 and recorded in *Protocols of James Young* 1512 as the 'lands of FOULBRIGGS' lying south of the road and east of a 9-acre property of *Brigflat*. Scots *foul*, pronounced 'fool' and simply meaning 'muddy', is frequent in names of burns and fords; while *briggs* not only witnesses to a bridge in the Lanark road at this early date, but probably also to a *brighouse* and toll, as in the case of BRIGGS, Kirkliston, and BRIGGS O BRAID, *which see*. WEST FOUNTAINBRIDGE (1869) was named as a development further along the road to the west, but was renamed 16 years later as DUNDEE STREET, *which see*.

FOUNTAIN CLOSE (28 High Street) is named on *Edgar* 1742 and formed a group not only with the great tenement at the close head, called *the Fountain* in 1727, but with the *Fountain well*, recorded thus in 1736, and part of the water supply system completed in 1681. While the close could have been named for the house or vice versa, it is difficult to see why either should have been named for the well, for there are several other closes and many other buildings closer to it in its present position, which is substantially the same as that shown on *Edgar* 1742 and *Ainslie* 1804—a change of its position, instructed in 1813 (if it was carried out) must have been quite small. It is more reasonable to suppose that the present well got its name from being in the general vicinity of the mansion, and that the mansion and the close must have been named for another well, now lost, in the close or at its head. It is suggested in *Wilson*, but scarcely proved, that it was the *Endmyleis well* (a name fleetingly resembling that of WORLD'S END CLOSE, *which see*) which is mentioned in the evidence of the trial of Darnley's murderers in 1567. The close was also JOHN BARTON'S, evidently for the owner of a *cachepell* or royal-tennis court at its foot, whose widow is listed as an owner occupier in 1635. It was also STEVENSON'S or DAVID STEVENSON'S for some owner(s), at some date as yet unascertained, of the Fountain tenement. This was earlier owned by the Bassenden family, including James Bassenden, who was active in the Netherbow area from 1537 onwards, and also the famous Scottish printer Thomas Bassenden, who died in 1577. As well as being BASSENDEN'S (later *South Bassenden's*, simply to distinguish it from the close on the north side of the street) the close was FULLARTON'S, for Adam Fullartoun, merchant, prominent in the town, from 1552 to 1582, as councillor, bailie and finally dean of guild, who built or rebuilt his house on the east side of the close in 1573 after it had been used as a gun platform in the defence of Edinburgh by the Queen's Men under Kirkcaldy of Grange. But the earliest name of the close is given in *RMS* 1478 as *le* SOLTRAIS WYNDE, still in use in 1635 as *Soltray's Close*, and evidently derived from a connection with the hospice of Soltre or Soutra, founded by Malcolm IV in or before 1164 for shelter of travellers. Land in the Cowgate feued from the Master of the hospice is mentioned in *RMS* 1481, together with an adjoining owner, Thomas de Sowtre, who may have been the Master himself.

FOUNTAINHALL CLOSE (501 High St) *see under* JAMES COURT.

FOUNTAINHALL ROAD (Grange) *see under* THE GRANGE.

FOUR MILE HILL (West Craigs) is shown on *Knox* 1812. There is no evidence of there having been a milestone here; and the change of the name to *Five Mile Hill* on *Forrest* 1818 looks like an attempt to match it with its distance from Edinburgh, which is shown on *Taylor & Skinner* 1776 as rather more than five Scots miles. The name may be Scots *-hill* added to a British or Gaelic name such as *fuarmaol*, cold hill, or perhaps *fothuir maol*, rounded hill with a terraced slope, a description which would fit the topography admirably.

FOWLER'S CLOSE (243 High Street) *see* THE ANCHOR CLOSE.

FOWLER TERRACE (North Merchiston) was named by 1878 and seems to have been the first street begun in the redevelopment of the policies of North Merchiston House, which stood on the north side of its junction with Bryson Road. The source of the name is obscure, but it is evidently a surname and probably connected with the developer or builder.

FOX COVERT AVENUE and **GROVE** (Clermiston) were built in a paddock of Clermiston Mains and named in 1959 for 'Fox Covert', a late Victorian house immediately west of the paddock and entered by a drive immediately north of it, as shown on *Ordnance Survey* 1893. The site of this drive is shown on *Ordnance Survey* 1852 as a woodland strip, which might perhaps have been a recognised haunt of foxes, but it is altogether more likely that the Victorian house name was borrowed from the 5-acre woodland on the east side of Drum Brae (some of its trees still standing, north of Drum Brae Avenue and Drumbrae School) which is shown on *Knox* 1812 and named *Fox Covert* on *Ordnance Survey* 1893 and 1938.

FOXHALL (Kirkliston) is recorded as *Toddishauch* from 1539 onwards and shown on *Adair* 1682 as well as *Roy* 1753 as *Todshaugh*. Being pronounced *haw,* the name was evidently thought to be an illiterate rendering of a vernacular *Tod's Hall,* and was emended to English *Fox Hall* in about 1736. In point of fact, the *-haugh* was Scots *haw* from Anglian *halh,* riverside meadow; while the first part of the original name may contain early Scots *tod,* fox (perhaps not unconnected with nearby CARLOWRIE, *which see*) or else it may be the surname Todd, for these are Templar lands and an entry in the Templar records of Torphichen in 1540 refers to 'the haucht callit Toddis & Dovnis'. The surname, believed to have begun as a 'foxy' nickname, had been in use in Scotland for over 300 years before this.

FOX LANE (South Leith) is recorded on *Wood* 1777 as a lane leading off the north side of the Dub Raw or St Andrew's Street, still represented by an opening east of the Independent Baptist Tabernacle in the modern Giles Street. In about 1825 the name began to be given as FOXES LANE, probably to obviate confusion with *Fox Lane* off Bath Street (*see* FOX STREET) but it may also have been that the *Fox* spelling had always been pronounced *Fox's.* It is possible that, although in the early built-up area of the burgh, this name and that of *Todholes Close* could refer to the animal and its haunts, but in both cases it is more likely that they derived from surnames current in Scotland at least as early as the 17th century.

FOX SPRING CRESCENT and **RISE** *see under* COMISTON.

FOX STREET (South Leith) is shown laid out on *Wood* 1777 and is named FOX LANE on *Ainslie* 1804 and all maps up until 1893, when it becomes FOX STREET. The derivation of the name is uncertain, and while no one called Fox or Fawkes is recorded as connected with the place, the possibility of a fox having frequented the area before 1804, when the ground was still fairly open, is not altogether remote.

FRANCIS PLACE (Causeyside) was an early name for SUMMERHALL PLACE, *which see.*

FRASER AVENUE, CRESCENT, GARDENS and **GROVE** (Wardie) were developed in 1926 under a Government-sponsored scheme for steel housing erected by the Second Scottish National Housing Company (Housing Trust) Ltd, and were named for Provost Fraser of Dunfermline, one of the directors of the company—*also see* FINDLAY AVENUE etc, a scheme of the same sort.

FREDERICK STREET (New Town) *see under* NEW TOWN.

FREELANDS (Ratho) appears on *Ordnance Survey* 1852. The name may be related, either fancily or through a field name, to the strip of common land shown along the north bank of Ratho burn on *Hatton etc* 1797. FREELANDS ROAD is named as leading to it.

FREER STREET (Fountainbridge) was developed in 1863 on ground shown as 'Dr Smith's' on *Kirkwood* 1823 and still as open ground, except for a rope walk, on *Ordnance Survey* 1852. It seems to have been named for Adam Freer, one of the promoters of the Union Canal, or a descendant. FREER TERRACE was added in about 1888.

FRENCHMILL (Craigmillar) *see under* LITTLE FRANCE, Craigmillar.

THE FRIARS CROFT (Queensferry) is recorded in 1560 as the *Freyris Croft*, and is shown on *Dundas* 1757 as lying in the angle between the Shore Road and Hopetoun Road and bounded in the west by the den of the Echline burn. It was evidently a *croft* or enclosed field of arable land belonging to the Carmelites or Whitefriars, whose house was on the other side of ROSE LANE—*which see*.

FRITHFIELD BATHS (South Leith) are shown on the south side of Salamander Street on *Dall & Leslie* 1831 and *Ordnance Survey* 1877, and began in 1794 when James Whyte, merchant, built 'two houses for the use of salt water'. The name, for the *Frith* or Firth of Forth, was fancy, probably a play on the name of nearby SEAFIELD.

FROGSTON (Mortonhall) is shown on *Mortonhall* 1776 and later maps including *Fowler* 1845 as a holding on the north side of the sharp bend at the foot of FROGSTON BRAE; but by 1852 it had disappeared, and in the 1920s a new section of roadway was built across its site in order to straighten out the bend. The name is Scots, Frog's *toun* or farm, and probably derives from Alexander Frog, burgess of Edinburgh, who with his wife Marion and his sons took a lease of the lands of Straiton and Straitonhale in 1447, as recorded in *RMS* 1451. FROGSTON ROAD, shown on *Roy* 1753, was named as leading past Frogston, and WEST and EAST were tacked on to the names of its sections in the 1930s. FROGSTON AVENUE, GARDENS and TERRACE (1934) and FROGSTON GROVE (1965) were built on Morton ground, west of Mounthooly, and got their names not from Frogston, which is over half a mile away, but from Frogston Road West.

FULLARTOUN'S CLOSE (28 High Street) *see* FOUNTAIN CLOSE.

BAILIE FYFE'S CLOSE (107 High Street) is shown on *Edgar* 1742 and was named for Gilbert Fyfe, merchant and three times bailie within the period 1677-86, who had a house on its west side. It was earlier BARRY'S, of untraced derivation, although a Dr Samuel Barrow was made free burgess and freeman in 1657, and a Martin Barra was witness to a judgement of the bailies in 1542. Also before 1706 it was known as TROTTER'S, from John Trotter, elder, who owned a tenement on the west side of the close, and was living in it in 1635, the year in which he became laird of Mortonhall. EAST BAILIE FYFE'S CLOSE was a name for PAISLEY CLOSE (*which see*) entering the same court.

FYFE PLACE (Pilrig) is shown on *Ainslie* 1804 and maps up until 1888 as a side name in Leith Walk, for a terrace presumably developed by Dr Fyfe, resident there in 1794.

G

GABRIEL'S ROAD (East End and Stockbridge) was a loan, recorded in 1717 and shown on *Fergus & Robinson* 1759, that led from Moutrie's Hill to Silvermills and thence by a ford to Inverleith. Sections of it still exist as the footpath of GABRIEL'S ROAD at West Register Street, the right of way through the grounds of the Royal Bank of Scotland in St Andrew Square, and as the footpath of GABRIEL'S ROAD and the DUMMIE STEPS at Glenogle Road. Both EAST and WEST SILVERMILLS LANE were part of it; and there are other vestiges of it in feu boundaries within the New Town. The name's origin remains obscure: in the absence of a date for the 'Gabriel's Tavern' mentioned by Mackay in *The Barony of Broughton*, the description suggests that it may have taken its name from the road.

GAIRNSHALL or **GARDENHALL** (South Side) was a property totalling 14¼ acres south of Crosscausey and between the Causeyside and Dalkeith road, feued to James and John Gairns in 1659. While the name, recorded in 1688 as *Gairneshall*, is obviously from the brothers, the indications are that it was in use before John Gairns built a 'great stone tenement' there, and it is possible that the *-hall* element was Scots *haw* or *haugh*, referring to this flat land traversed by the tail burn from the GUSE DUB, *which see*. This may still have been true of the subdivisions *Yardhall* at the Guse Dub and *Cabbagehall* next to it, formed by 1708; but evidently *-hall* was soon read as 'house' and jocular names such as *Turniphall* and *Orangehall* appeared in the vicinity, *see also* SUMMERHALL.

GALACHLAW (Mortonhall) is named thus in *Maitland* 1753 and *White's Liberton* 1792, but is GALLOWLAW in 1666 and on *Mortonhall* 1770 and 1776. The second part of the name is Anglian *hlaw* Scots *law*, which usually means 'rounded hill' but perhaps in this case carried its earlier sense of 'burial mound', referring to the cairn on its summit, *see also* MOUNTHOOLY, Mortonhall. The first part of the name has been taken to mean 'gallows', which were of course a frequent wayside feature in the days before local baronial justice was abolished in 1746; but while this might fit some hills of the name, there are many others in Scotland and northern England which it would not fit at all. It is altogether more likely that the name is British, akin to Gaelic *gealach*, Welsh *golau*, or Cornish *golou*, a pale or shining place, perhaps (like the *white* in 'Whitehill') referring to grassiness in contrast to the darker colour of crags or heather—or whin-clad hills. Certainly the area was treeless (as well as gallows-free!) in 1650, when Cromwell found himself without means to hang a sergeant caught looting; and it may not be mere coincidence that *Mortonhall* 1770 shows the field on the north side of the Galachlaw as WHITE DALES. The street GALACHLAW SHOT was named in 1989, continuing the field name shown on *Mortonhall* 1770, *shot* being the Scots term for an arable field, coming second only to *Park* (a grass field) among field names in Lothian. GALACHLAWSIDE was named, also in 1989, for its position on the slope of the hill.

GALALAW (Dalmeny) appears on *Roy* 1753 as *Gallow law*, and shares the same meaning as GALACHLAW, Mortonhall, *which see.*

GALLOLEE (Dreghorn) was so named in 1984, continuing the traditional name of the ground, as recorded on a map of Dreghorn in *Steuart's Colinton*. While this might imply that it was the site of the baronial gallows (*see* GALLOWLEE, Pilrig) there is no evidence for this; and considering that it occurs beside the Braid or PEFFER BURN (*which see*) and the Celtic names of FORDEL and BAADS, it is likely that the name is Celtic, akin to Gaelic *geal ath*, clear-water ford (found also eight miles away in Gala Ford, Harperrig) with addition of Anglian *leah*, a clearing, or Scots *lea*, a pasture.

GALLONDEAN (Queensferry) appears on *Ordnance Survey* 1895. The name seems to have been fancy, and may be connected with the James Gallon, dairy keeper, resident in the district in 1883.

THE GALLOWGREEN (St Leonards) was a wedge-shaped outshot of the Burgh Muir on the west side of the Dalkeith road, extending at its base some 150 yards along the north side of East Preston Street, and tapering to a point about 400 yards further north, where (according to *Maitland* 1753) UMFRAVILLE'S CROSS stood opposite St Leonard's Lane. Named for the town's gibbet, which was maintained in the Green at East Preston Street from 1586 until 1675, the ground was then allotted to the students of the University as a playing field for several decades before it began to be feued out; and it was James Spittal, tanner, taking the feu in 1727, who changed its name to SPITTALFIELD, commemorated in the naming of SPITTALFIELD CRESCENT in 1872.

THE GALLOWLEE (Pilrig) was named as the grass field where, as shown graphically on *Adair* 1682 and *Fergus & Robinson* 1759 (copied on *Kirkwood's Ancient Plan*) the town gallows were put up on a knowe beside the road to Leith. They were in existence in 1570 and still in use in 1752; but by 1799 the knowe had become the site of the house of SHRUB HILL, *which see.*

GALLOWAY'S CLOSE (425 High Street) is shown on *Edgar* 1742 and was on a site now occupied by the Sheriff Court. It was named from a property Galloway's Land, owned by John Galloway and three successors of the name by 1722.

GALLOWAY'S ENTRY (65 Canongate) is shown thus on *Kirkwood* 1817 but as GALLOWAY'S CLOSE on *Ainslie* 1780. The name seems to have derived from Alexander Galloway, stabler, tenant of the lands of William Ramsay; and if Ramsay was the banker son of George Ramsay in the adjoining RAMSAY'S CLOSE (*which see*) it would place Galloway's tenancy in the earlier 18th century. *Edgar* 1742 shows the whole site vacant as *Ruins of the Earl of Winton's house*, but *Edgar* 1765 shows the front lands still built up. In 1769 WHITEFOORD HOUSE, designed by Robert Mylne for Sir John Whitefoord of Blairgunan and Ballochmyle, took entry from the close.

GAMEKEEPER'S ROAD (Cramond) is shown on *Roy* 1753 and on *District Roads* 1777, and since it runs along the march between Kirk Cramond and King's Cramond (*see under* CRAMOND) it may date back to the Middle Ages. The name, recorded in 1902, is probably modern and may have referred to estate staff living at the north lodge of New Barnton House, shown on *Cramond Roads* 1812 and named LANE END on *Ordnance Survey* 1852. The name was extended to GAMEKEEPER'S LOAN (1936) and PARK (1977) built in the Fairafar Park and South Park of Fairafar farm.

GARBRAGE or **GARE BREADS** (Duddingston) was a field name in SOUTHFIELD, Duddingston, *which see.*

GARDEN TERRACE (Barnton) *see under* EASTER PARK, Barnton.

GARDINER ROAD etc (Craigcrook) *see under* CRAIGCROOK.

GARDNER'S CRESCENT (Fountainbridge) is on the site of the *Gardeners Hall*, recorded in 1792 and shown on *Ainslie* 1804; but the only connection between the two names seems to be that William Gardner WS bought Gardeners Hall in 1821, and developed GARDNER'S CRESCENT, evidently named for himself, in the following year.

GARDNER'S STREET (Abbeymount) was named by 1868, presumably for its builder.

GARSCUBE TERRACE (Murrayfield) was named by 1884 for the estate of Garscube in Dunbartonshire, seat of the Campbells of Succoth, who had also become owners of Murrayfield in 1866. SUCCOTH PLACE and GARDENS were named by 1901, either for the family's ancient seat at Succoth, near Arrochar, or (as might be hinted by their proximity to HENDERLAND ROAD, *which see*) perhaps more particularly for Sir Islay Campbell, Lord Succoth, whose career in law and politics closely followed that of Lord Henderland, whose sister he married in 1766. SUCCOTH AVENUE was proposed by 1904 and developed by 1920, and SUCCOTH PARK was added in 1965. The family name was celebrated in CAMPBELL AVENUE and ROAD, named by 1906, the first being developed from the tree-lined west drive to Murrayfield House, figured on *Roy* 1753; and LENNEL AVENUE and CUMLODDEN AVENUE (1927) and CRARAE AVENUE (1930) were named for the family's properties of Lennel, near Coldstream, and Cumlodden and Crarae on Loch Fyne.

GATESIDE (Kirkliston) is recorded as *Gaitsyd(e)* from 1565 onwards and appears on *Blaeu* 1654 as *Gaitsyit*. The name is Anglian *gata side*, the slope at or land alongside the road, this latter being the ancient highway, shown on *Blaeu*, which ran through Kirkliston by the High Street and thence by Gateside and Charles Bridge to Muiryhall. As a main road it was bypassed in about 1810 (*see under* MAIN STREET, Kirkliston) and in about 1900 the eastern entry of GATESIDE ROAD was altered to permit expansion of the distillery, although its old line leading straight westwards from Peth Brae is still discernible. Whether the route is related to Roman Dere Street is a matter of conjecture; but it was certainly the medieval road to Stirling, and considering the terrain, it is probable that it was at Gateside that Edward I set up his army's camp when he paused for some days at 'Temple Liston' before engaging William Wallace at Falkirk in June 1298, *see also* CLERICS HILL and KING EDWARD'S WAY, Kirkliston.

GATESIDE (Ratho) is shown on *Hatton etc* 1797 and *Knox* 1812 as in two parts east and west of the junction of Dalmahoy Road with the Calder road. The name is Anglian *gata side* or Scots *gate side*, slope or place beside the gate or road, which in this case may be the Calder road or else Dalmahoy Road, which was originally continuous with the LIDGATE (*which see*) in Ratho village.

GAYFIELD (Broughton) is shown on *Fergus & Robinson* 1759 as open ground, but with a roadway outlined on *Spankie's Feu* and presaging the driveway to GAYFIELD HOUSE, built four or five years later. This name for the new estate appears to have been fancy, meaning 'happy place'. A plan for feuing part of it in the form of a Square was advertised in 1783, and GAYFIELD PLACE was begun by 1790. *Ainslie* 1804 shows the central garden of GAYFIELD SQUARE, and names the road on the south side of the Square, following the line of the original house drive, as *Gayfield Street*; but this last, although also shown on *Kirkwood* 1817 and 1823, seems not to have found favour as an address, *PO Directories* showing only Gayfield Place and Square. The modern GAYFIELD STREET, although shown (unnamed) on *Ainslie* 1804 and later maps, was named by the 1880s.

GEDDES'S CLOSE (233 High Street) is shown on *Ainslie* 1780, and given as GEDDES'S ENTRY on *Ordnance Survey* 1852. It was named for Robert Geddes of Scotstoun, surgeon, who had a tenement at the head of it, next to Anchor Close, prior to 1740. As shown on *Edgar* 1742 and *Kirkwood* 1817, it was also HUTCHESON'S: nothing certain is known about this name, but there may have been a connection with William Hutcheson, dean of guild 1712-13, or with his son, also William. The close was also RICHARDSON'S, from Robert Richardson, writer, who built a tenement in 1687 upon land bought from John Lauder of Fountainhall, merchant.

GENERAL'S ENTRY (Bristo) is shown on *Ordnance Survey* 1852 with entrances from both Potterrow and Bristo Street. As demonstrated in *Old Edinburgh Club XXII*, it dated from the 17th century and was probably named for the lodging of Major-General Joseph Wightman, Commander-in-Chief in Scotland from 1712. Mrs Agnes McLehose ('Clarinda') was living here when Robert Burns visited Edinburgh in 1786. The site was cleared for future development in 1965.

GENERAL'S WATCH (Balerno) is shown on *Ravelrigg* 1764 as a feature on the east end of Ravelrig hill, and is described in the *Statistical Account* 1791 as having the appearance of a fortification, although already much defaced by robbing of stones for dyke-building. The site is now the north-eastern part of Hannahfield Quarry.

GENTARIES or **GENTRICE MUIR** (Saughton) is described in a deed of 1590 anent Saughton, quoted in *RMS* 1662, as lying west of Saughton parks (a boundary now represented by the north-south section of Broomhouse Crescent) and along the south side of a road, shown on *Cultins* 1776, which led from Saughton to Gogar on a line now roughly represented by Bankhead Crossway North and the eastern part of Broomhouse Crescent. The name is a form of Old French *genterise*, becoming *gentrice* in later Scots, and suggests that the muir was not a common, but like THE LAIRDSHIP (*which see*) on the other side of the road, was retained in the ownership of the laird of Saughton.

GENTLE'S CLOSE (120 Canongate) is listed on *Ainslie* 1780 and was named for James Gentle, brewer, bailie of Canongate, who bought property here from Richard Cooper (*see* COOPER'S CLOSE, Canongate) in 1753. It was through his good offices that Burns got permission to erect the tombstone over the grave of Robert Fergusson in Canongate kirkyard.

GEORGE IV BRIDGE (Old Town) originated in a demand in 1824 for a new south approach to the High Street, which took definite form in 1827, in an Act of Parliament for a bridge in line with Bank Street. Designed by Thomas Hamilton and named for the reigning monarch, its foundation stone in Merchant Street, together with that of the KING'S BRIDGE at King's Stables Road, was laid on 15 August 1827, the fifth anniversary of George IV's landing on the Shore of Leith. Building was substantially started two years later, and was completed by 1834.

GEORGE PLACE (Pilrig) is shown on *Kirkwood* 1817. Since it was advertised in 1810 as '*George's Buildings* at Middlefield', it is likely that the terrace was named for its developer.

GEORGE SQUARE (South Side) is sketched on *Laurie* 1766. Its site was in the park of Ross House, a small estate which had been formed in 1738 by combining part of the Heriot Croft east of Middle Meadow Walk with the Windmill Acres next the highway from Bristo Port, *see* THE WINDMILL, Bristo. James Brown, builder, acquired the park in 1761, and began its development in 1766 with 'a Great Square' immediately to the south of Ross House. Almost ten times the area of his earlier successful speculation at BROWN'S SQUARE (*which see*) his new scheme was also a success, being completed within 20 years. He named the Square for his brother George Brown of Elliston; and the original spelling *George's Square* continued in use until after 1816. On Brown's feuing plan of 1779 for the Square and streets adjoining (*see* TEVIOT ROW, CRICHTON STREET, CHARLES STREET, WINDMILL STREET and BUCCLEUCH STREET) the name *George's Mews Street* embraces both GEORGE SQUARE LANE and CHARLES STREET LANE; and these separate names appear on *Ordnance Survey* 1893.

GEORGE STREET (New Town) *see under* NEW TOWN.

GEORGE STREET (North Leith) was planned by 1812, when it is shown on *Knox*, but is still unnamed on *Kirkwood* 1817 even although some house-building is shown in progress. The name appears in *PO Directory* 1823 and was presumably given in compliment to George IV, perhaps at the time of his landing at Leith in 1822. In 1966, to obviate confusion with George Street in the New Town, the name was suppressed and the street renamed as part of NORTH FORT STREET.

GIANT'S BRAE (South Leith) and **LADY FIFE'S BRAE** (*which see*) are named on *Ordnance Survey* 1852, which also follows Robertson's *Fortifications of Leith* in noting them as remains of emplacements of English guns deployed in the Siege of Leith in 1560. That this 'tradition', put about by Alexander Campbell in 1827, is wholly spurious is proved conclusively by the contemporary accounts of the siege and by the plans of the siege works drawn to scale on *Siege of Leith* 1560, showing the emplacements in detail—*see under* MOUNT PELHAM etc—and although the same map shows a number of ponds in the west end of the Links, together with what looks like a drain or an old entrenchment, it shows no sign of Giant's Brae or Lady Fife's. By contrast, maps such as *Thomson* 1822 and *Lancefield* 1851 show numerous natural hillocks in the Links, and it would seem that it was only because of the false tradition attached to the two Braes that they were spared when the Links were levelled as a public park in the 1880s.

GIBBET LOAN (Newington) was an alternative and later name for MOUNTHOOLY LOAN (*see under* MOUNTHOOLY, Newington) and was derived from the town's gibbet which operated at the GALLOWGREEN (*which see*) from 1586 onwards and is still shown on *Bypass Roads* 1763. The name was displaced by that of PRESTON STREET (*which see*) in about 1812, but it reappears on *Ordnance Survey* 1852, perhaps by mistake, as the name of Holyrood Park Road. The GIBBET TOLL, shown on the 1852 map but also on *Laurie* 1763, was on the east side of the Dalkeith road, just north of the entry to Holyrood Park Road.

(ROBERT) GIBB'S CLOSE (250 Canongate) is listed on *Ainslie* 1780 and seems to have been named for Robert Gibb, coachmaker, an owner at some time prior to 1744. According to *Kincaid*, coachmaking did not start in Edinburgh until 1696. Being in the south Canongatehead, the close was part of Edinburgh, not the burgh of Canongate.

GIB'S ENTRY (South Side) was named as the pend leading to the house of Adam Gib (1714-88) the kenspeckle minister of the First Associate Antiburger congregation, who built themselves a kirk (now the South Side Community Centre) in Nicolson Street soon after they were evicted from Bristo in 1753. Houses in the south end of Nicolson Street (distinct from any owned by the congregation) were advertised for sale in 1769 and 1792—the second, up for sale four years after Gib's death, being described as *Gib's Entry*.

GIBRALTAR HOUSE (St Leonards) is figured on *Kincaid* 1784; and the name, shown on *Kirkwood* 1817, was given by James Penman, recorded in 1764 as 'late surgeon-major to the Hospital in Gibraltar, now at Gibbet Toll'.

GIBSON'S CLOSE (Grassmarket) was about eleven yards west of the present entry of 79 Grassmarket. Listed on *Ainslie* 1780, it was probably named for Mrs Gibson, stabler in the Grassmarket in 1773. It is given as WEST SMITH'S CLOSE at the old number 121 Grassmarket in *PO Directory* 1827, but the proprietor has not yet been traced.

GIBSON STREET (Pilrig) was developed in Stewartfield in about 1869 and named for William Walker Gibson of Bonnington Steam Flour Mills, who had bought the estate in 1866 and lived there until his death in 1877.

GIBSON TERRACE (Fountainbridge) *see under* BAINFIELD, Fountainbridge.

GIFFORD PARK (South Side) is shown on *Ainslie* 1780 as already built up and named *Giffords Park*. Earlier part of Gairnshall, the site and the open ground east of it, both shown on *Scott* 1759 as *Mr Gifford's*, had been bought in 1751 by Thomas Gifford, smith and farrier, and the open ground was known as *Gifford's Park* until after his son sold it to Dr John Hope in 1772.

GILBERTOUN (Brunstane) was the original name of BRUNSTANE, *which see*. It was recovered at GILBERTOUN PLACE in 1990.

GILCHRIST LANE and **COURT** (Calton) appear to be shown on *Kirkwood* 1817 on the site shown as MUD ISLE on *Ainslie* 1804, and are named on *Ordnance Survey* 1852. The name was presumably a developer's.

GILES STREET (South Leith) was drastically altered in the early 1960s by the massive redevelopments of Kirkgate and Cables Wynd, and the U-shaped street now bearing the name is a composite of the middle third of the original Giles Street and the middle third of the historic DUB RAW (*which see*) joined together by an entirely new length of street parallel to the Kirkgate. Shown on *Siege of Leith* 1560, the historic Giles Street was a winding lane, evidently following a burn that formed the medieval boundary of the town, as given in the grant of the town to Edinburgh by Henry and Mary in 1565 and mapped in *Report on Common Good* 1904. The alignments suggest that it was also continuous with MILL LANE. South of it stretched the pastures known as THE LEES, later partly enclosed by a regular pattern of yards, and by 1630 these were so densely developed that this LEES QUARTER housed nearly half the population of Leith and served as their address. The GREEN TREE (shown on *Naish* 1709 as growing on the south side of Giles Street, at a point now just north of the entry of Spiers Place) provided a more local address for properties in its vicinity, while *Kirkwood* 1817 shows the south side of Giles Street as GREEN STREET, and *Ordnance Survey* 1852 shows a side name GREEN TREE PLACE opposite the entry to Back o the Vaults. While LANG-GATE SIDE is not shown on any map, it appears in *Williamson's Directories* 1773-1802 and is listed in *An Accurate View* 1783 in such a way as to suggest that it was in the Lees quarter, and 'lang gate' or way would have been a fair description of the whole of this winding street. Meantime the name

St GILES STREET appeared on *Wood* 1777. Evidently one of the 'improved' names suggested about this time in emulation of street names in the New Town of Edinburgh (where *St Giles Street* had been the original choice for Princes Street) it was slow to catch on; it was 1782 before it began to appear in *Williamson's Directory* (where the spellings *St Gill's* and *St Gilles* witness to its old pronunciation 'jeels') and by 1801 it was challenged by the less fantouche form GILES STREET, which finally prevailed by the 1820s. Since none of the Giles family, well-established local brewers, had an address in the street until 1793, it is unlikely that they had a hand in its original naming; but the later extension of their brewery into the street may have helped to promote the plainer form of its name.

GILLESPIE CRESCENT and **PLACE** (Wrightshouses) were named in 1870 as being built in the grounds of the GILLESPIE HOSPITAL, built in 1801 by the Gillespie Trust, on the site of the medieval mansion of WRIGHTSHOUSES (*which see*). The Hospital, later used by the Royal Blind Asylum, was replaced by sheltered housing in 1976.

GILLESPIE ROAD (Colinton) *see under* SPYLAW.

GILLESPIE'S CLOSE (172 High Street) *see* OLD ASSEMBLY CLOSE.

GILLESPIE STREET (Lochrin) was developed by 1816; but as shown on *Kirkwood* 1817 and like HAILES STREET (*which see*) it was numbered as part of Gilmore Place until 1837 when both these side streets were given independent names, derived from the Gillespie Trust, owners of the ground.

GILLSLAND ROAD (Merchiston) was part of the Merchant Company's development of their estate of Merchiston and was named in 1874, taking the name of a house built there by John Clapperton, Master of the Merchant Company. It was extended to a planned SOUTH GILLSLAND ROAD in 1897, although that address was not used until 1905. A section of Gillsland Road was renamed MID GILLSLAND ROAD in 1985, to assist the addressing of new developments. Clapperton chose his house name for unrecorded personal reasons: it may have been the name of a farm with which he had some connection. The spelling would suggest that it was not derived from Gilsland, near Brampton in Cumbria. GILLSLAND PARK was adopted in 1982 as the name of a new side street on the site of a house of that name.

GILMERTON is recorded from the late 12th century onwards. The early spellings *Gillemuristona* and *Gylmuriston* show the name to be Anglian *Gilmour's tún* or farm place, incorporating the Gaelic personal name *gille Moire*, servant of (Virgin) Mary. The 16th-century house at the west end of the village, is remembered in the name GILMERTON PLACE, given in 1989 to new housing built on its site. The detail on *Roy* 1753 shows the village virtually as it continued to be until development started in about 1890 at NEW (now NEWTOFT) STREET, *which see*. GILMERTON MAINS, now known as SOUTH FARM, is recorded in 1603 as *Maynes de Gilmerton*, the home farm of the estate. GILMERTON ROAD is the 'road to Gilmerton' which, before it was cut off by the new 'great road to the south' at Good's Corner, as shown on *Knox* 1812, was a branch off the old Liberton road (now Mayfield Road) at Powburn, as shown on *Roy* 1753 and *Armstrongs* 1773. The investigation of the Roman fort discovered at Elginhaugh in 1979 disclosed that Gilmerton Road represents a stretch of Roman DERE STREET, *see under* ROMAN ROADS. GILMERTON STATION ROAD is old enough to figure on *Roy* 1753, but got its present name (formally adopted in 1967) as leading past the station on the North British Railway's Loanhead & Roslin Branch.

GILMERTON DYKES was apparently coined in 1952 as a name for this large housing scheme, perhaps on the analogy of nearby MOREDUN DYKES, and possibly because the park dyke of Gilmerton House fronts the old road running from Gilmerton to Edgehead, shown on *Roy* 1753 and now called GILMERTON DYKES ROAD. Another old road, now represented by GILMERTON DYKES DRIVE, is shown on *Armstrongs* 1773 and was called THE KILNGATE, because it served the remarkable chain of limestone mines and works which, over 1,000 yards long and described in *Good's Liberton* (p161) as 'an enormous piazza' or 'colonnaded cavern', was the major feature of historic Gilmerton. GILMERTON DYKES AVENUE, CRESCENT, GARDENS, GROVE, LOAN, PLACE, STREET, TERRACE and VIEW were also named in 1952, while the public park at Brokenbriggs was given the fushionless and clumsy label HYVOTS BANK VALLEY PARK.

GILMERTON GRANGE, renamed MELVILLE GRANGE after it was joined to the Melville Castle estate in the late 19th century, is mentioned in *RMS* 1587 among the lands of Newbattle abbey, and the term grange implied that it was a detached farm supplying the abbey.

GILMORE PLACE (Lochrin) is indicated on *Ainslie* 1804 and was named by 1805 for the proprietor, Samuel Gilmore, ropemaker, *see also under* GILMORE'S CLOSE, Grassmarket. *Knox* 1812 shows the neighbourhood as *Gilmore Place*, while the street is given as *Gilmore Street* on the *Stranger's Guide* 1816 but as *Gilmour Place* on *Kirkwood* 1817. Both the latter maps show a rope walk on the north side of the street; but by 1850 it was replaced by a longer one further north, near the Lochrin basin of the Canal, now part of the site of GILMORE PLACE LANE. UPPER and LOWER GILMORE PLACE, shown on *Kirkwood* 1817, were named by 1850; and UPPER GILMORE TERRACE had branched off Upper Gilmore Place by 1892.

GILMORE'S CLOSE (once 101 now 65 Grassmarket) is shown on *Ainslie* 1780, while *Kincaid* 1784 shows *Gilmour's Roperie* at its south end. It was named for Samuel Gilmore, listed as rope maker in Grassmarket 1773—*see also* GILMORE PLACE, Lochrin. It seems also to have been one of the pair of closes *Easter* and *Wester Gilmore's*, recorded in 1862, and the first may have been COWIE'S CLOSE, *which see*.

GILMORE STREET (Canongate) *see under* McDOWALL STREET, Canongate.

GILMOUR ROAD (Craigmillar Park) *see under* CRAIGMILLAR PARK.

GILMOUR STREET (Pleasance) is shown on *Brown & Watson* 1793 and named on *Ainslie* 1804. The name is probably the developer's, possibly William Gilmour, shoemaker in Fisherrow, who set up a family business in tanning and leatherwork in the Pleasance prior to 1827. GILMOUR'S ENTRY was named as a branch off it in 1985.

GIPSY BRAE (Granton) is shown on *Cramond Roads* 1812, but the traditional name belongs to its northern section, shown on *Roy* 1753. While the name may have arisen from some connection with gipsies, it is perhaps more likely that *gipsy* is used here as the term for a seasonal burn.

GIRDWOOD'S ENTRY (26 Grassmarket) *see* STENTER'S CLOSE. Grassmarket.

GIRNAL CRAIG (Queen's Park) is shown on *Kirkwood* 1817 as *Girnal Craig or Hangman's Hill*; and it is clearly included in the 'Duddingston craggis' mention in *Town Council Minutes* 1554. Despite the elaborate tale of a melancholic hangman, purporting to explain the second one, both names remain obscure.

THE GIRTH or **SANCTUARY OF HOLYROOD** was concomitant with the foundation of the Abbey in 1128, since the Church offered sanctuary for accused persons, appointing *maisters of girth* to hold what amounted to preliminary trials before handing anyone over to the state. The word is from Old Norse *gerthi*, a fenced enclosure, and by the 14th century it was a term for immunity and a place of sanctuary. In the Middle Ages, the privilege applied within 'the haill boundis of the Abbacy and that pairt of the burgh of Canongait frae the Girth Croce doun to the Cloickisholm mylne'; but after the Reformation, when the Girth became royal, the bounds were extended to the whole of the royal park, and were apparently adjusted at the foot of the Canongate to run no longer from the Girth Cross but from the *strand* or little burn which, now culverted and marked S in the causey setts, crosses the road about forty yards further east. The GIRTH CROSS is shown on *Siege of Edinburgh Castle* 1573 and on maps up to and including *Edgar* 1765, but it was removed in 1767. Its position is plotted on *Kerr* 1918. It served latterly as a place of proclamation and also of execution—for example, in 1600 Lady Warriston was beheaded here, as accessory to her husband's murder.

GLADSTANES CLOSE (about 481 High Street) is listed in *Valuation Roll* 1635 as an unnamed close immediately east of Gladstanes Land, which had been acquired by Thomas Gladstanes, merchant burgess, in 1617. The entry from the High Street was evidently closed off some time after 1636, and entry to the lower part of the close (there are still traces of it west of Lady Stair's House) was from Lady Stair's Close, as shown on *Edgar* 1742. Prior to 1617, and certainly in 1620, the close was called FISHER'S, for Thomas Fisher, the previous owner of the Gladstanes property, and a prominent member of town council 1589-1609.

GLADSTONE COURT (181 Canongate) appears in *PO Directory* 1867 and was evidently named for William Ewart Gladstone MP, who became leader of the Liberal Party in that year. It is listed as BOWLING GREEN ENTRY in *Williamson's Directory* 1779 and as BOWLING GREEN CLOSE on *Ainslie* 1780; and was evidently named as access to the *bowling green* shown on *Edgar* 1742. By 1800 this green had become the site of the Magdalene Asylum: hence the name MAGDALENE ENTRY or ENTRY TO MAGDALENE ASYLUM, until this removed to Springwell House, Dalry, in about 1861.

GLADSTONE PLACE (South Leith) was developed in Summerfield and named by 1879, the year in which W E Gladstone campaigned in Midlothian, becoming its MP in 1880 and Prime Minister for the second time. According to *Grant*, the name was given in honour of his family generally, his father, Sir John Gladstone of Fasque, born in the Coalhill in 1764, having made notable benefactions to Leith.

GLADSTONE TERRACE (Sciennes) started by 1864, was evidently named for William Ewart Gladstone MP, at that time Chancellor of the Exchequer in Lord Palmerston's government.

GLADSTONE'S CLOSE (20 Grassmarket) *see* DOUGLAS'S CLOSE, Grassmarket.

GLANVILLE PLACE (Stockbridge) appears to be shown on *Ainslie* 1804 and was named by 1824. The name seems to be fancy, perhaps for Glanville in Dorset, but its origin is not yet traced.

GLASGOW ROAD (Corstorphine to Newbridge) is shown on *Blaeu* 1654. There is evidence to support the view that it represents the line of Roman *Dere Street* at least as far as the vicinity of Newbridge (*see under* ROMAN ROADS) and study of its junction with the old Linlithgow road (*see under* St JOHN'S ROAD) suggests that it originally ran eastwards to Back Dean. The term *Glasgow road* for long meant the Calder road, and it is still so used in *Kincaid's Gazetteer* 1787; but the suppression of part of the Linlithgow Road in Corstorphine in the 1750s (*see under* CRAIGS ROAD) clearly signalled the growing importance of the Newbridge road: in *Taylor & Skinner* 1775 it is the road *to Glasgow by Bathgate*, in Robertson's *Agriculture of Midlothian* 1795 it is shown as the *New Glasgow Road* running parallel to the *Glasgow Road* through the Calders, and by 1805 the development of the New Town and the opening of MAITLAND STREET (*which see*) as the 'new road to Glasgow' completed the process. Although the street name applies only westwards from St John's Road, in popular usage 'the Glasgow Road' begins at Haymarket.

GLASSLAND (Colinton) is recorded in 1709 as lying immediately south of LINNHEADS at the head of Torduff reservoir, and to judge by the ground, it probably stretched westwards to the Clubbiedean burn. The name is probably British *glas lann*, green enclosure, rather than a hybrid with Anglian *land*. It is a gentle well-watered slope; and it may be significant that the large fort at Clubbiedean is immediately west of it.

THE GLEBE (Dalmeny) was so named in about 1948 as being developed in the historic minister's glebe of Dalmeny, shown on *Barnbougle & Dalmeny* c1800.

THE GLEBE (Kirkliston) was developed in 1962 in what was the main part of the parish minister's glebe, as shown on *Kirkliston* 1759. The land had probably attached to the rectory from very early times, and although *gleib* came into Scots only in about 1400, it stemmed directly from the earlier Latin *gleba*.

GLEBE ROAD and **TERRACE** (Corstorphine) were so named by 1911, being developed in the glebe of Corstorphine Kirk, probably part of the kirklands mentioned in the Holyrood charter of 1128. GLEBE GARDENS and GROVE followed in 1924 and 1926.

GLEBE ROAD and **TERRACE** (Cramond) *see under* CRAMOND.

GLENALLAN DRIVE and **LOAN** (Inch) *see under* THE INCH, Nether Liberton.

GLEN BROOK (Balerno) appears on *Ordnance Survey* 1852 as the name of a property previously called *Birch Hill*, shown on *Knox* 1812. The name was fancy, conflating two adjoining property names *Glen Park* (in 1852, shown as 'Glendarroch') and West *Brook*, now 'House of Cockburn'.

GLENCAIRN CRESCENT (Coates) *see under* COATES.

GLENDEVON PLACE (Saughtonhall) was begun in 1903 in the *Meadow Shot* of Carrick Knowes by the Edinburgh Co-operative Building Company Ltd and named after Glendevon, Perthshire, birthplace of the second Chairman of the Company. The name was subsequently extended to GLENDEVON AVENUE (1926) GARDENS, GROVE, PARK and TERRACE (1934) and ROAD (1938).

GLENDINNING CRESCENT (Inch) *see under* THE INCH, Nether Liberton.

GLENFINLAS STREET (New Town) *see under* MORAY ESTATE, New Town.

GLENGYLE TERRACE (Tollcross) was developed in 1867-70 along the south frontage of VALLEYFIELD (*which see*) in a scheme which also embraced LEVEN TERRACE and VALLEYFIELD STREET; and the builders, William and Duncan MacGregor, evidently named the street for Glen Gyle at the head of Loch Katrine, one of the homelands of Clan Macgregor.

GLENISLA GARDENS (Blackford) was formed in Blackford farm and named by 1896, presumably for some connection (as yet untraced) of the Trotter family. Glenisla House is 13 miles north of Alyth in Angus.

GLENLEA COTTAGES (Gorgie) are in an area that (like nearby DELHAIG, *which see*) was rapidly built up in about 1890 on previously open ground, housing staff for the expanding industry at Gorgie under H B Cox. The name is fancy, and may reflect one of his interests.

GLENLEE AVENUE and **GARDENS** (Parson's Green) *see under* PARSON'S GREEN.

GLENLOCKHART ROAD (Craiglockhart and Greenbank) originated as the entrance drives to the City Poorshouse, built in 1870 in the *Steil* fields of Craiglockhart. Originally provided with gates and lodges at Comiston Road and at the west entrance to the grounds, some 200 yards east of Craiglockhart Tower, the pair of drives was opened as a public road in 1908, which continued to be known as the POORSHOUSE DRIVE until 1932, when its eastern section running beside the Plewland Sike was abandoned, and the rest of the road, now connected with GREENBANK DRIVE (*which see*) was renamed GLENLOCKHART ROAD, for a 'Glen Lockhart' invented for the purpose. GLENLOCKHART BANK was formed in the Dove Croft of Craiglockhart in 1933; and GLENLOCKHART VALLEY was named in 1974—a singularly clumsy tautology 'valley-of-Lockhart-valley', probably influenced by the nearby place name of HAPPY VALLEY.

GLENOGLE HOUSE, PLACE, ROAD and **TERRACE** (Stockbridge) *see under* THE COLONIES, Stockbridge.

GLENORCHY PLACE (Greenside) was named by 1875 for Lady Glenorchy's Free Church, built in Greenside Place in 1844 for a Free Kirk congregation descended from that of Lady Glenorchy's kirk built next to Trinity College in 1772. The original kirk was cleared away in 1848 for the NBR marshalling yard.

GLENORCHY TERRACE (Mayfield) *see under* McLAREN ROAD, Mayfield.

GLEN PARK (Balerno) is shown on *Knox* 1812, but is given as *Glendarroch* on *Ordnance Survey* 1852 and reverts to *Glen Park* on the 1893 survey. Both names are fancy.

GLENPUNTIE (Dalmeny) figures on *Barnbougle & Dalmeny* c1800 as a field name around the head of the Linklin burn, while *Ordnance Survey* 1854 shows *Glenpuntie Wood* in the north of the same area and extending southwards to Hags Brae. Presumably the name is the same as the (undated) 'Glenpuittie near Dalmeny' noted in *Celtic Placenames of Scotland*, which in face of the other evidence is probably misspelt. It appears to be a hybrid, adding Gaelic *gleann*, a valley, as a doublet to British *pant*, of the same meaning.

GLEN STREET (Tollcross) was formed by 1867 in part of Creichen's Gardens, so named as part of Drumdryan when that estate was bought by Patrick McDowall of Creichen in 1709. A property here was owned by Capt Nisbet Glen RN in 1840 and by the Misses Glen in 1850; and after their death it was leased as workshops for some time before it was cleared for the building of the street.

GLENURE LOAN (Clermiston) *see under* CLERMISTON MAINS.

GLENVARLOCH CRESCENT (Inch) *see under* THE INCH, Nether Liberton.

GLOUCESTER LANE, STREET and **SQUARE** (Stockbridge) *see under* CHURCH LANE, Stockbridge.

GLOUCESTER PLACE (Northern New Town) was planned by William Playfair in 1820 as part of an amendment of the original scheme for the NORTHERN NEW TOWN, *which see.* Shown unnamed on *Knox* 1821, it is *King Place* on *Kirkwood* 1823 (presumably intended as a reflection of (Great) King Street on the other side of Royal Circus), but appears in *PO Directory* 1825 as *Gloucester Place.* William Frederick, second Duke of Gloucester, was a first cousin of George IV and had married his sister Mary in 1816.

GLOVER'S CLOSE (South Leith) is shown on *Kirkwood* 1817 as running between Giles Street and Yardheads. The family name was quite frequent in Leith, but the connection with the close remains to be traced.

GLOVER STREET (South Leith) appears thus in *PO Directory* 1826, and seems to have been named either for William Glover, owner of ground hereabouts prior to 1813, or for the William Glover who was convener of Trades in Leith in 1822; but *Kirkwood* 1817 shows it as ALISON STREET, which may be the ALLISON PLACE listed in *PO Directory* 1822 as the address of James Allison & Son, vinegar manufacturers; and both *Thomson* 1822 and *Lothian* 1826 show it included, as GLADSWOOD LANE, in an elaborate but abortive scheme for development of the neighbourhood. The street was cut in two when the railway was built in 1898.

GOFF AVENUE (Craigentinny) *see under* CRAIGENTINNY.

GOGAR is recorded from the time of William the Lion (1165-1214) onwards, not only as a land name within an area of about four square miles but also as the *fluvius de Goger* recorded in 1233 and shown on *Adair* 1682 as GOGAR BURN and on *Hatton* 1797 as GOGAR WATER. The burn is remarkable for its twists and turns (some generating the local names BURNCRUIK and BURNWYND, *which see*) and it is noteworthy that the other Scottish Gogar, south of Blairlogie in Stirlingshire, adjoins a similar group of sharp bends in the river Devon. Prior to 1337 the spellings are *Gogyr, Goger, Coger, Gogar,* and *Gogger*—the last suggesting that it was spoken with a short *o*. The name is British: Watson tentatively suggests that it is *go cor*, a slight rise or perhaps a small bight of land; but this would scarcely fit the landscape or the spread of the name in either of the two locations, and it would seem more likely that the name first belonged to the burn, and that like the several *Cocker* or *Coker* river names in England, it is British *cocr* or *coger*, from earlier *cocra*, crooked stream. OVER or UPPER or EASTER GOGAR is mentioned in *RMS* 1306-1329; and it must be presumed that NETHER GOGAR was formed at the same time, even although it is first recorded in 1453. GOGAR HOUSE (fancily styled *Castle Gogar* after 1970) was built in Nether Gogar in 1625, and its home farm GOGAR MAINS, shown on *Roy* 1753 as *Mains*, is one or other of the *Easter Maynes of Nether Gogar* or the *Wester Maynes of Gogar* referred to in *RMS* 1656. *Blaeu* 1654 shows *Gogar* (in the position of Over Gogar) and *Nether Gogar. Adair* 1682 adds GOGARSTONE, evidently named for the nearby standing stone; and also GOGAR MILL, recorded thus in 1452 and as *mill of Over Gogar* in 1523. This is shown on *Roy* 1753 as *Old Mill*, working off a dam or lade which ran from a cauld near Kirklandcroft and re-entered the Gogar above Gogarburn House, giving rise to the names of DAMHEID (i.e. sluice controlling the flow) shown on *Adair/Cooper* 1735, and the later MILLBURN HOUSE. The mill is still shown on *Riccarton* 1772 as *Gogar Mill*, but was known as GOGAR BANK by 1775. The KIRKLANDS or KIRKLANDCROFT belonged to the medieval kirk of Gogar, as recorded in *RMS* 1570, and the name persists in the field name of *Kirkland* in Over Gogar, near the Trefoil School. The TEMPLELANDS of Over Gogar must have been gifted to the Knights Templars before their order was dissolved in about 1314; recorded in *RMS* 1561, they are shown on *Roy* 1753 as north of Jaw and south of GOGAR MUIR. GOGARBURN and GOGAR GREEN, MOUNT and PARK all appear on *Knox* 1812 as names for new properties.

GOGARLOCH ROAD (Corstorphine) at the Flassches was named in 1982 for the *Gogar Loch*, shown on *Blaeu* 1654, named on *Adair/Cooper* 1735, drained in about the 1750s and now represented by the FLASSCHES—*which see, together with* THE GYLE, Corstorphine. GOGARLOCH SYKE (1991) was followed by GOGARLOCH HAUGH and MUIR in 1993, all three names being fancy.

GOGAR STATION ROAD (Gogar) is shown on *Roy* 1753, and *Johnston's Cultins* 1776 (*RHP 3702/3*) confirms that its first dogleg section south of the bridge at Gogar Bank was part of the early road which ran by Cultins and the Lairdship to Saughton and was abandoned when a new link to the Glasgow road was constructed after 1775. The railway station is shown on *Ordnance Survey* 1852 and the road no doubt began to be thought of as the road to the station about this time. The name *Gogar Station Road* was adopted by the County Highways department by 1902.

GOGARSTONE (Gogar) appears on *Adair* 1682, and as *Gogarstane* on *Post Roads* 1777. Presumably it is named for the standing stone which is 400 yards south of the junction on the Glasgow road but close beside the old post road to Ratho. The field names on *Norton* 1813 suggest that the greater part of Easter Norton was earlier the *Gogarstone park* of Norton.

GOLDENACRE, shown on *Ainslie* 1804 and named on *Cramond Roads* 1812, was an 'island part' of Easter Granton, mentioned in *RMS* 1661 as *Goldenrigges* or *Goldenaikers*. The terms *acre* and *rigg* both imply that it was arable land. The *rigg* is the unit of ploughing, 'ridged' because it is high at the crown where the initial furrows are thrown together and low at the flanks, where the last furrows remain open, and in the old 'runrig' system of farming it was also the unit of tenancy. The other part of the name is quite frequent in field names, e.g. *Gildy-* or *Goldenknowe* in Silverknowes, *Goldylands* in Echline, *Goldriggs* in Balerno. It evidently meant land where yellow wildflowers grew in profusion, and it has been suggested that wild mustard would indicate that the soil was good; but it is perhaps more likely that the name referred to the *guild* or corn marigold, a weed so rampant and destructive of corn crops on land deficient in lime that it created a national problem for hundreds of years, despite stern laws aimed at controlling it. While there was some building within the property by the 1850s, its main development started in about 1878 (*see under* MONTAGU TERRACE) and GOLDENACRE TERRACE dates from 1887.

THE GOLFER'S LAND (79 Canongate) *see* BROWN'S CLOSE, Canongate.

GOLFHALL (Gogar) is shown thus on *Roy* 1753 and as *Gowfhall* on *Armstrongs* 1773. Apart from the spelling there is no reason to suppose that it was a fancy name for a house; and considering its position beside the Gogar burn, together with the fact that *-hall* in place names is almost invariably Anglian *halh* Scots *haw* or *haugh*, it is much more likely that the name is a land name, Scots *gouff haw*, a haugh which had a *gouff* or unpleasant smell about it.

GOODSPEED OF SCIENNES (Sciennes) is advertised in the *Courant* in December 1761 in terms which, taken along with *Sheens* 1761, suggest that this ground was either the eastern part or else the whole of the immediate policies of the House of Sheens, *see under* SCIENNES. In absence of early forms, the name remains obscure; but Anglian *sped*, meaning (like Scots *speed*) wealth or prosperity, is used in place names with the meaning of 'highly productive (land)'.

GOODTREES (Balerno) is shown on *Roy* 1753 in obvious confusion with nearby TODHOLES; but it is given on *Laurie* 1763 as *Gutters*, and as *Goodtrees* on Knox 1812. The local pronunciation is *gitters*. The name is quite frequent in lowland Scotland, as for example at MOREDUN (*which see*) where the recorded forms are earlier, and suggest that the name is British, from *guid* or *goth*, a stream, and means 'place beside the stream or bog'—which would fit the topography here in Balerno.

THE GOOSE- or **GUSE DUB** (Crosscausey) was a spring and goose pond in the angle between West Crosscausey and Causeyside (now Buccleuch Street). Shown on *Scott* 1759, even although the pond was drained in 1715, it was an established landmark before 1686, and also gave its name to the 2-acre property of *Goosedub* or *Yardhall* on the east side of Buccleuch Street. Its tail burn or stank ran south and then east round the ground which later became St Patrick's Square, continuing east by the north backs of Rankeillor Street to St Leonard's Crag, where it turned north down the hollow of Dummiedykes and joined the Tummel burn in Abbeyhill.

GORDON'S CLOSE (Grassmarket) is shown (unnamed) on *Ainslie* 1780, is named on *Ordnance Survey* 1852, and a vestige of it remains as an opening immediately west of Heriot Bridge. It was evidently named for James Gordon and his wife, brewers in Grassmarket west of Heriot Bridge in the 1770s, or for their predecessors.

GORDON'S CLOSE (388 High Street) *see* ROCKVILLE'S CLOSE.

ALEX GORDON'S CLOSE (South Leith) is recorded in 1764 as being at the NEW QUAY, *which see*.

GORDON STREET (Quarryholes) was named by 1869 for its developer Charles Ferrier Gordon, while FERRIER STREET was named for his wife, who owned the ground—it was probably her family who had earlier projected a street of the name in the vicinity, shown as *Ferrier Street* on *Thomson* 1822 but as *Crown Street* on *Kirkwood* 1817. HALMYRE STREET was named by 1880 for Gordon's estate of that name near Romanno Bridge, Peeblesshire.

GORDONS WEEL (Slateford) is the traditional name for a large pool at the bend of the river just above Bogsmill. The second part is Scots *weel* from Anglian *wael*, a deep pool or eddy; while the first part is unlikely to be a personal name, but may well conceal Scots *gour den* from Anglian *gor denu*, muddy valley—a fair description of the haughs in this part of the dell.

GORDON TERRACE (South Craigmillar Park) *see under* CRAIGMILLAR PARK.

GORGIE is recorded in charters of Holyrood abbey from the later 12th century. The name's early forms *Gorgin* and *Gorgyn* show it to be British *gor gyn*, upper wedge, probably referring to the tapering shape of this land between the river and the Craiglockhart hills, themselves known in the 13th century as the *Craggis de Gorgin*. GORGIE MILL and GORGIE HOUSE, mentioned in *RMS* 1494 and 1531 respectively, appear on *Blaeu* 1654. The dam or mill lade flowed from a cauld in the river below Ford's Road, giving DAMSIDE and DAMHEAD (*which see*) their names; and as shown on *Roy* 1753 it served mills in both Gorgie and Dalry before re-entering the river at Roseburn. The *Wester Mains of Gorgie*, the site of its steading now Robb's Loan Grove, is shown on *Roy* 1753 and 19th-century maps as GORGIE, but is WEST GORGIE on *Laurie* 1763 and *Armstrongs* 1773; and WEST GORGIE PARKS and PLACE were named for it in 1983, being built in its fields. GORGIE MUIR, its centre now enclosed within Merchiston Grove and Shandon Place, is also shown on *Roy*, but was displaced in about 1815 by GORGIE MAINS, east of Primrose Terrace. The steading of GORGIE PARK, shown on *Knox* 1812, was in Slateford Road, just east of Moat Drive. GORGIE ROAD, named traditionally as 'the road to Gorgie', was being used as an address by 1883.

GOSFORD PLACE (Bonnington) *see under* DALMENY ROAD, Bonnington.

GOSFORD'S CLOSE (276 High Street) was swept away in the building of George IV Bridge in about 1830. Shown as *Gosford's* on *Edgar* 1742, it got this name from Alexander Acheson of Gosford, East Lothian, who had a tenement here in the 1580s, although as a *burgess dwelling to landward* he was excused certain of the taxes upon burgesses. From a slightly earlier period the close was DICKSON'S, for Allan Dickson, frequently a bailie between 1550 and 1565; and in 1635 Andro and Charles Dikesone are listed among owner occupiers on the west side of the close. Yet earlier it was AIKMAN'S, for James Aikman, merchant, tenant of a booth in the Boothraw in 1482 and mentioned in *RMS* 1491 as owning property on the south side of the High Street.

GOTE LANE (Queensferry) bears every mark of having been the chief access from the High Street to the sea from the earliest times of the burgh. The name is Scots, from Middle English *gote*, creek or watercourse, and refers either to the creek which became the harbour, or more likely to a watercourse running down the west side of the lane. From 1364 onwards there are references to a sike or small burn that flowed down beside the Loan or West Loaning, also called the *Gutters*, and passed immediately west of the Cross: a position exactly that of Gote Lane—*see also* WEST LOANING BURN *and* CRAW'S CLOSE, Queensferry.

GOURLAY'S CLOSE (196 High Street) *see* OLD FISHMARKET CLOSE.

GOURLAY'S CLOSE (286 High Street) *see* OLD BANK CLOSE.

GOWANHILL (Currie) is recorded from 1691 onwards and shown on *Roy* 1753. The name may be from Scots *gowan*, a daisy, or *yellow gowan*, buttercup or marigold; or else it contains the surname Gowan or Govan, which, although prominent earlier in Lanarkshire and Peeblesshire, was current in the Edinburgh area by the 17th century.

GRACEMOUNT (Liberton) is so named on *Knox* 1812 but referred to in *White's Liberton* 1792 only by its pre-Reformation name of *Priesthill*, recorded in 1600 as land formerly pertaining to the vicar of Liberton Kirk. *Priest-* obviously referred to the vicar, and the later *Grace-* may echo the religious connection (cf. Mount Grace in Yorkshire) or else be a woman's name. Both *-hill* and *-mount* refer to the rise in the ground above the burn. GRACEMOUNT ROAD, shown on *Knox* 1812 as the access to the GRACEMOUNT HOUSE, was named as a street in 1934. GRACEMOUNT AVENUE, DRIVE, PLACE and SQUARE were named in 1956.

GRAHAM'S COURT (Bristo) figures on *Ainslie* 1780. The name, recorded in 1823 and on *Ordnance Survey* 1852, was connected with Graham & Anderson, jewellers in 1826. GRAHAM'S BUILDINGS, entered from the Court, are shown on *Kirkwood* 1823.

GRAHAM STREET (Bonnington) is built on the line of the former avenue to Bonnington House, which is shown on *Ordnance Survey* 1852 with a small development BRIDGE PLACE already formed at its west end. The street was planned by 1868 and appears as GRAHAME STREET (*sic*) in *PO Directory* 1870. Which Grahame it was named for is not known.

GRAHAM STREET (Lauriston) *see under* KEIR STREET, Lauriston.

GRANBY ROAD, earlier TERRACE (Craigmillar Park) *see under* CRAIGMILLAR PARK.

GRANDFIELD and **GRANDVILLE** (Bonnington) were named in 1989 and 1990. In 1741 the estate of Bonnington was bought by Alexander le Grand of *Grandville*, Co. Antrim, then collector of customs in Leith. Thirty years later, his grand-nephew Richard, the last of the Le Grand lairds (1771-82) styled himself *of Grandfield*, coined as his name for the Bonnington estate.

THE GRANGE, originally part of the forest of Drumselch, was a farm of a plewgate in extent given to St Giles kirk by Alexander I in about 1120; but after 1151, when David I gave it, along with St Giles, to his son's newly-founded Cistercian abbey of Holm Cultram on the Solway, near Wigton in Cumbria, it became a *grange*, Old French for a farm so detached from its owner's main estate that its produce had to be stored locally. In modern terms it was bounded on the north by Sciennes Road and the west and south backs of Sciennes Gardens, on the south by Grange Loan, on the east by a line roughly represented by Findhorn Place but running down to the Penny Well, and on the west by the east backs of Kilgraston Road and Marchmont Road and Crescent. In 1631 this original estate (but for 18 acres gifted to the convent of the Sciennes in 1517 and not brought back into the main estate until 1640) was bought by William Dick, merchant of Edinburgh, along with 63 acres which had been feued out of the Burgh Muir a century earlier, lying between Grange Loan and the Pow burn, and stretching from the Liberton road (Mayfield Road) to abut Canaan at what is now the west boundary of Astley Ainslie Hospital. This new property was styled NETHER (i.e. Wester) GRANGE, while the original became OVER (i.e. Easter) GRANGE. In 1704 forty acres of Nether Grange were sold off as WESTER GRANGE, and in 1723 the greater part of this, west of Blackford Avenue, became part of Blackford. GRANGE HOUSE, built in 1592, was demolished in 1936, giving place to GRANGE CRESCENT; while WESTER GRANGE HOUSE once stood where WESTER GRANGE GARDENS was developed in 1975. GRANGE LOAN was evidently an established landmark before it was mentioned in *Town Council Minutes* 1533, and as a 'common passage' across the Muir between the Linton and Liberton highroads it was probably as old as the Grange itself, since it ran along its southern march and was its principal access. Hence its name. Whether it was ever known as *Cant's Loan*, for the Cants who owned the Grange from 1506 until 1631, is doubtful (there seems to be some confusion with MAYFIELD LOAN, *which see*) but its western section was called CHURCH LANE from about 1838, when Morningside Parish Church was built, until 1885, when the name NEWBATTLE TERRACE prevailed, *see under* GREENHILL. Although Grange estate was freed for development by Act of Parliament in 1825, it was 20 years before GRANGE ROAD was constructed to give access to the new cemetery at the Fernielaw, opened in 1847. MANSIONHOUSE ROAD, its south end within the *Mansionhouse field* shown on an estate map of 1825 as immediately north of Grange House, appears in *PO Directory* 1847. DICK PLACE and (THE) LAUDER ROAD, named for the Dick Lauder family, owners of the estate, began to be feued in about 1850 and are listed in *PO Directory* 1853 and 1859 respectively. SETON PLACE, CUMIN PLACE and DALRYMPLE CRESCENT were planned in 1851 and named by 1858 for three ladies of the family: Lady Ann Seton, wife of William Dick, who entertained Prince Charles Edward to 'some bottles wine' at Grange House on 17 September 1745; Charlotte Cumin of Relugas, who married Sir Thomas Dick Lauder in 1808; and Lady Ann Dalrymple, daughter of the earl of Stair, who married Sir John Dick Lauder in 1845. TANTALLON PLACE (1864) and HATTON PLACE (1873) were named for the Lauders' medieval estates of the Bass (with Keepership of Tantallon Castle) and Hatton, Ratho; and FINDHORN PLACE, listed as *Findhorn Terrace* in 1878, was named for a Dick Lauder estate in Morayshire. St CATHERINE'S PLACE, beginning to be occupied in 1861, was named for the adjoining site of the convent of the Sisters of St Catherine of Siena, *see under* SCIENNES. CHALMERS CRESCENT and PALMERSTON ROAD (together with BEAUFORT ROAD, *which see*) were built in about 1866, and commemorate Thomas Chalmers, leading spirit of the early Free Kirk, who was buried in Grange Cemetery in 1847, and Lord Palmerston, twice Prime Minister and made burgess of Edinburgh two years before he died in 1865. Three new streets in Nether Grange were named by 1877: FOUNTAINHALL ROAD, for Sir Andrew Lauder's estate, joined to the Grange when he married Isobel Dick in 1755; St THOMAS ROAD, probably making some reference to Sir Thomas Dick Lauder; and St ALBAN'S ROAD, a name that is still obscure. GRANGE TERRACE was first recorded in 1879 as a side name for houses at the west end of Fountainhall Road. RELUGAS ROAD, named for the estate brought into the family by Charlotte Cumin (as above) was begun by 1879, although the greater part of it, like the western part of St Alban's Road, was not built up until the 1920s. RELUGAS LANE was named in 1924, and RELUGAS GARDENS and PLACE in 1970 and 1971. In the western part of the Grange, estate maps from 1766 show an area of ground named *Transilvania*, no doubt because it lay beyond a strip of woodland; GRANGE LOAN TERRACE was formed in part of it in 1922, and in 1986 another part was redeveloped as WYVERN PARK, named for the heraldic beast in the arms of Dick Lauder.

GRANGE COURT (Causeyside) is listed in *PO Directory* 1825, and some development is shown on *Scott* 1759 and *Bypass Roads* 1763 as well as on *Kirkwood* 1817. Shown on *Grange* 1766 as 'Baxter's feu', the ground was part of KITTLENAKIT (*which see*) and was the most northerly of the plots feued out of the Burgh Muir in 1537, later referred to as the *auld* (i.e. former) *Grange feus* because, although never part of the Grange, they had been held by the lairds of Grange from 1609 until 1654; and it seems likely that the court's name arose from this legal nickname, although the fact that the lane along the north of Baxter's feu was an access belonging to Grange ground to the west may have had something to do with it.

GRANGE TOLL (Mayfield) *see under* MAYFIELD ROAD.

GRANT AVENUE (Colinton) was named in 1913 for William Grant, master of the Merchant Company, developers of the ground.

GRANTON is recorded from 1478 onwards, and its division into EASTER and WESTER GRANTON dates from before 1612. The name is Anglian *grand tūn*, farm place of or at the gravel or sand. Easter Granton was also known as ROYSTON (*which see*) but in 1739 its mansion house, begun by Andrew Logan in about 1585 and remodelled and extended by George Mackenzie, Viscount Tarbat, a century later, was bought by the Duke of Argyll and renamed CAROLINE PARK, for his daughter Caroline, Countess of Dalkeith. At the same time, Argyll transferred the *Royston* name to the 16th-century GRANTON CASTLE (now demolished) sited 150 yards northwest of Caroline Park and commanding GRANTON CRAIGS, frequently mentioned in the 16th century as a landing place as well as the site of freestone quarries. The construction of GRANTON HARBOUR (*which see*) stimulated roads development from 1835 onwards. If *Adair* 1682 shows a road along the shore from Newhaven to Cramond, *Cramond Roads* 1812 confirms that it was by then eroded and of no account; but *Gellatly* 1834 shows it rebuilt as far west as to connect with West Granton Road. For a while it was the main access to the developing GRANTON HARBOUR and GRANTON SQUARE, formed by 1838; but it no doubt became LOWER GRANTON ROAD after the new GRANTON ROAD was completed in about 1848. As already mentioned, WEST GRANTON ROAD was an older road, part of the route shown on *Adair* 1682, but clearly shown on *Laurie* 1763; and it is named as leading past Easter Granton (shown on *Laurie* as *Royston Mains*) to Wester Granton (shown as *Granton Mains*). GRANTON CRESCENT, PLACE, TERRACE and VIEW were named in 1932, GRANTON GARDENS and GROVE in 1935 and GRANTON MEDWAY in 1936. Wester Granton began to be built up in 1965 at WEST GRANTON CRESCENT, DRIVE, GARDENS, GREEN, GROVE, LOAN, PLACE, ROW, TERRACE and VIEW. Built on and around the site of the steading of Granton Mains, GRANTON MAINS AVENUE, BANK, BRAE, COURT, GAIT, VALE and WYND were named in 1993.

GRANTON HARBOUR was constructed between 1835 and 1844, the main quays being at the MIDDLE PIER, which was founded on the rocks of the Ox Craig. WEST HARBOUR ROAD, and its extension WEST SHORE ROAD to the Gipsy Brae, were formed before 1850. In 1985, new streets formed by infilling the West Harbour were named for the WEST PIER and various local rocks: the OX CRAIG, already mentioned; the CHESNUT off the West Pier, perhaps so named for its smoothness and shape; and five rocks off Inchkeith: the PALLAS, perhaps from Scots *pallo*, porpoise or dolphin; SEAL CARR, seal rock, ultimately from British *carr*, a rock; the HERWIT, obscure, but possibly (on the analogy of Cornish names such as *Hervan*) containing British *hyr*, long; the IRON ROCK, possibly from Scots *erne*, sea eagle; and ROST BANK, which may be from Old Norse *rost*, Scots *roost*, and may mean a bank with a strong tidal eddy over it.

GRANTON PARK AVENUE (Granton) *see under* BROOM PARK, Granton.

BARON GRANT'S CLOSE (High Street) is listed on *Ainslie* 1780 and was evidently named for John Grant, Baron of Exchequer, who owned a house here, although in *Williamson's Directory* 1773 he has an address in New Street as well. *Edgar* 1742 gives the close as Dr SINCLAIR'S, a name which remains obscure. The close was probably also the SALUTATION CLOSE, described in 1737 as 'the second close within the Netherbow' and doubtless named for a tavern. It is likely that it was also known as MOUBRAY'S, for Robert Moubray, wright above the Netherbow, who seems to have bought up and redeveloped a number of properties in this vicinity in about 1700—*see under* PANMURE'S CLOSE and LITTLE GRANT'S CLOSE, High Street.

LITTLE GRANT'S or **GRANT'S LITTLE CLOSE** (9 High Street) is recorded as CAPT. GRANT'S in 1715 and listed as GRANT'S on *Edgar* 1742, and was evidently named for the family still represented by James Grant, merchant, listed in *Williamson's Directory* 1779 as in *Grant's Close*. The connection certainly goes at least as far back as David Grant, merchant, who was elected a master or treasurer of Trinity Hospital in 1713 and was involved with Robert Moubray, wright, in land deals in or near the close, which on the analogy of Moubray's similar activity at 19 High Street (*see* PANMURE'S CLOSE) may have been on the go some ten years earlier. The name is varied on *Ainslie* 1780 to BAILIE GRANT'S CLOSE; no direct connection has been traced, but the reference might be to one or more of the three Grants who held that office in the period: James Grant in 1711 and 1717, and another James and an Alexander Grant, simultaneously bailies in 1749, 1750 and 1752.

GRANTULLY PLACE (Newington) was named in 1985 for Sir George Stewart of Grantully who bought Newington House and grounds from George Bell in 1807.

GRANVILLE TERRACE (Merchiston) extended Gilmore Place in about 1871, and was probably named for Granville George Leveson-Gower, 2nd Earl Granville, Foreign Minister in Gladstone's government 1870-74.

THE GRASSMARKET (Old Town) had more or less taken its present form by 1500 (*see under* WEST PORT) with the important exception of the roadway across its western end, which (being outwith the royalty and therefore divided from it by the Flodden Wall) formed part of King's Stables Road, as shown on *City Improvements* 1866, until it was merged with the Grassmarket in about 1870. Considering the general alignment of King's Stables Road, this sharp turn southwards looks as though it were a diversion to fit in with the west boundary and entrance to the town; and it would seem likely that this road and the highway through West Port had originally continued on their general headings, converging and joining about 100 yards east of the historic West Port, and that there was an entrance here in an earlier burgh boundary now represented by the east side of the lower CASTLE WYND (*which see*) and enclosing a market place of only about half the present length. On one interpretation of the name of the STOK WELL (*which see*) the place—or its western half—may have originated as a grazing attached to the town; but the earliest record of it, in *RMS* 1363, is as *the street called Newbygging under the castle*, the phrase *under the castle* (*wall*) being the normal term for the neighbourhood even as late as 1648. The first mention of market use is in an edict by James III (engrossed in *Town Council Minutes* 1477) where it is the *Westirmart*, housing part of the timber market and also the *Friday merket* for secondhand goods, held in front of the Greyfriars (*see under* WARDENS CLOSE, Grassmarket) while livestock was to be kept 'far west at oure (i.e. the King's) stable, where indeed pens or BUCHTS (*which see*) are still shown on *Brown & Watson* 1793. The grass market was transferred from the Cowgate only a short time before 1601, when it is mentioned as *the girs merket under the wall*; but by 1635 *Grassmarket* was the established address of neighbouring properties, even although the place is shown on *Rothiemay* 1647 as *Horse Market Street*. In 1716 the corn market was brought from the old Mealmarket to a new exchange in the east end of the Grassmarket, as shown on *Edgar* 1742. In 1814 and 1849 successively it was moved to larger premises at the west end and south side of the marketplace (both buildings being shown on *Ordnance Survey* 1852) and finally it was transferred to Gorgie Corn Market in 1912.

LADY GRAY'S CLOSE (477 High Street) *see under* LADY STAIR'S CLOSE.

(NORTH) GRAY'S CLOSE (131 High Street) is GRAY'S in the Hammermen's records 1521 and on *Edgar* 1742, for the use of *North* and *South* to distinguish between the two *Gray's Closes* began only in about 1779, and the names are otherwise quite unconnected. The name of the north close is probably from Alexander Gray, burgess and one of the *greit dusane* (i.e. council) *and deikins* who met in 1480. His property stretched, possibly from the High Street, down to the yard or garden of the College of the Holy Trinity, now part of Waverley Station, at the foot of the close. By 1521 he had been succeeded by his son and heir Robert.

(SOUTH) GRAY'S CLOSE (56 High Street and 244 Cowgate) is shown on *Rothiemay* 1647. The name occurs in a charter of 1512 which also mentions a deceased John Gray as a previous owner—probably the John Gray mentioned in *RMS* 1492 as owner of property in this vicinity, and possibly the man of the same name mentioned in *Town Council Minutes* 1500 as a master waulker and cloth shearer. There is no connection with (NORTH) GRAY'S CLOSE: the *North* and *South*, coming into use in about 1779 and appearing on *Kirkwood* 1817, were merely added to distinguish between the two addresses. The close was also the CUNYIEHOUSE CLOSE, from the cunyie house or mint built on its west side near the Cowgate in 1574, although the name was also used (and probably originated) as that of the *close* or courtyard within the cunyie house itself—*see* COINYIEHOUSE CLOSE, Old Town. *Edgar* 1742, giving the close as *Gray's or* MINT CLOSE, shows the distinctive Scots term displaced by its English equivalent.

GRAY'S COURT (South Side) was originally entered at 95 Nicolson Street, and was built by and named for James Gray, wright. The entry is shown on *Ainslie* 1780, and the court appears more or less complete on *Ainslie* 1804. The name, shown on that map, is previously recorded in the *Edinburgh Evening Courant* in 1796. In the early 1820s the SOUTHREN MARKET was built further west, as a

284

lane with shops on each side, entered from Gray's Court through an archway bearing the market's name, as well as from West Nicolson Street and Chapel Street. The site of the court was cleared in the 1960s; but the name was continued in 1993 when the present court, entered from West Nicolson Street, was built on the ground, while the Southren Market archway was moved and rebuilt as a feature in West Nicolson Street.

GRAY'S LOAN (Merchiston) is shown on *Merchiston* 1776 as well as *Ordnance Survey* 1852 as a loan leading from Gorgie Road to Colinton Road and passing GORGIE MUIR (*which see*), and since there are no signs of it on *Roy* 1753 or *Laurie* 1763 (Merchiston estate seems to have been reorganised about this time) it is likely that it was named for, and perhaps built by, Thomas Gray, farmer in Merchiston in 1764. Although the side names STEWART TERRACE, SHANDON PLACE and ASHLEY TERRACE (*which see*) eventually displaced the name in its northern sections, its whole length was still being called *Gray's Loan* in the 1890s.

GRAY'S MILL (Slateford) is recorded in 1631 as *Graysmylne*, and shown as *Grays mil* on *Adair* 1682. Obviously incorporating the name of an early tenant of the mill, the name was also used for the farm attached to it. This included the field of *Graysknowe* on the south side of Inglis Green Road, hence the name given in 1984 to GRAYSKNOWE, built in part of it. The choice of 'Gray's Mill' as the name for a school at Redhall, half a mile away and on the other side of the river, was a strange blunder on the part of an education department normally careful not to confuse historic geography; and it was all the more regrettable because it was in the veritable Gray's Mill on 16 September 1745 that Prince Charles Edward commandeered the house of the tenant, David Wight, and used it as his base during negotiations with the magistrates for the surrender of Edinburgh. A later 18th-century farm house, probably on the same site as Wight's and perhaps incorporating it, was carelessly demolished in 1988.

GRAY STREET (Newington) figures in Benjamin Bell's feuing plan *Newington* 1806, and is shown on *Kirkwood* 1817 as well developed. The division into UPPER GRAY STREET and SOUTH GRAY STREET dates from about 1832. The origin of the name is obscure: and since nothing is known of any resident of the name in the locality, the most likely possibility is that it came from some connection of the Bell family.

GREAT CANNON BANK (Portobello) *see under* WESTBANK, Portobello.

GREAT CARLETON PLACE AND SQUARE (Niddrie) were named in 1992 for the *Great* and *Carleton* coal seams which, as shown on the *Geological Survey*, outcrop to the east of the streets.

GREAT JUNCTION STREET (South Leith) and **NORTH JUNCTION STREET** (North Leith) were conceived in about 1800 as a new great road effecting a *junction* between the Edinburgh road at the Foot of

Leith Walk and the new docks planned for North Leith Sands. Like its counterpart Constitution Street, built in the previous decade, it bypassed the congested streets of historic Leith and followed the line of the ramparts and ditches of 1548, which had left a broad strip of ground so uneven that it remained open and available for this new purpose. By 1811, road-building had begun at PORTLAND PLACE, and it continued at a fair pace in this northern section, JUNCTION BRIDGE being completed in 1818; but progress south of the river was much slower: on *Thomson* 1822 the road is still shown as 'proposed', and for some years after 1827 the section between Bonnington Road and Junction Bridge remained unbuilt. This hiatus put a strain on street naming: and the section north of the Bridge, originally given the temporary name of GREAT JUNCTION STREET NORTH, in turn became GREAT NORTH JUNCTION STREET and then NORTH JUNCTION STREET. JUNCTION PLACE, although existing as a side street from the 1870s and informally known as *Firebrigade Street*, because of the fire station built here in 1878, was counted part of Great Junction Street until 1969, when it was named as a street in its own right.

GREAT KING STREET (New Town) *see under* NORTHERN NEW TOWN.

GREAT MICHAEL RISE (Newhaven) was developed in 1967 in the *Free Fishermen's Park* and named for the warship *Great Michael*, launched at Newhaven in 1511, the pride of James IV's navy, and the most powerful ship of its day. The name was borrowed again in 1968, when the western part of Newhaven's PARLIAMENT SQUARE, so-called since 1864, was renamed GREAT MICHAEL SQUARE, lest there be any confusion with Parliament Square in the Old Town; and the eastern part of the square was renamed GREAT MICHAEL CLOSE in 1975.

GREAT STUART STREET (New Town) *see under* MORAY ESTATE, New Town.

THE GREEN (Balerno) was named in 1984 for its site on a bleaching green at Malleny Mills.

THE GREEN (Davidson's Mains) was so named in 1927 because the plan by the City Architect for a new housing street left an open space within the crescent which might be likened, fancifully, to a 'village green'. There was of course nothing of the sort here or elsewhere in Davidson's Mains before this, and the ground within the crescent had once included, amongst other things, the farm steading that gave its name to DAVIDSON'S MAINS, *which see.*

GREENBANK (Braid) is recorded from 1601 as an alternative name for Over Plewlands of Braid, *see* PLEWLANDS, South Morningside. Shown on *Adair* 1682, the name is a literal description of the situation of the place. Its steading, was southwest of the junction of Greenbank Crescent and Loan, and on the northern slope of a summit (in Greenbank Crescent) which appears to be the GREEN LAW referred to in nearby field names. The historic Greenbank was bounded by

Braid Road, from Braidburn Terrace up to the Buckstane Snab. From there, the southern march was with Comiston, by the head of Braidburn Valley Park and then, further up the burn, with Oxgangs. The western march, with Colinton Mains and Craiglockhart, is marked by the back gardens of Greenbank Road; and the march with Plewlands was along the *Plewland sike* or small burn that runs along the north side of Greenbank Drive. The historic approach to Greenbank was from the Braid road, and its first section was indeed called GREENBANK ROAD until 1905, when it was renamed BRAIDBURN TERRACE. Other earlier *Greenbank* street names also witness to the fact that the farm extended east of Comiston Road: GREENBANK PLACE (1887) marks its boundary with Plewlands, and GREENBANK TERRACE was begun about 1891. GREENBANK CRESCENT (1907) was for long an isolated development beside part of the old farm road. The development of GREENBANK AVENUE was overtaken in 1928 by the conversion of the HOSPITAL DRIVE, the access to the City Hospital built in 1903, to form GREENBANK DRIVE. The final development of Greenbank farm began in 1931 at GREENBANK ROAD, LOAN and LANE, and continued rapidly at GREENBANK GARDENS, GROVE, PARK and ROW (1932) and RISE (1933) while Greenbank Crescent was completed, and the fields east of it turned into BRAIDBURN VALLEY public park.

GREEN BURN (Dalmahoy) would seem to have been named for its grassy banks, as a means of distinguishing it from the Gogar at their confluence at Burnwynd.

GREEN CLEUCH (Balerno) is named for the grassiness of this ravine (Scots *cleuch*, from Middle English *cloghe*) between the Black Hill and Hare Hill, perhaps in contrast to the adjoining valley of Loganlee, where *lagan liath*, grey hollow, is also a colour name.

GREENDYKES (Niddrie) is recorded in 1470, and was the scene of the *Raid of Greendikes*, a skirmish at Niddrie Edge in 1594. Obviously descriptive, the name probably uses the word *dykes* in its earlier sense of grassy ditches, rather than walls. GREENDYKES ROAD, its eastern part shown as a local road on *Knox* 1812, was extended and formally named in 1947, along with GREENDYKES AVENUE, DRIVE and TERRACE; and GREENDYKES GARDENS and LOAN were added in 1962.

GREENEND (Liberton) is so named on *Roy* 1753 and *Laurie* 1763 and also in *White's Liberton* 1792; and while the name *Greenhead* shown on *Laurie* 1766 and *Armstrongs* 1773 may have been an alternative, it seems more likely to have been a misreading of Laurie's earlier map. The village and the place name seem to have originated on the east side of the main road, along with GREENPARK. The name describes the grassy terrain of this southern corner of Craigs estate and evidently made a pair with the contrasting CRAIGEND in the north-west corner, half a mile away. GREENEND DRIVE, GARDENS and GROVE were named in 1966.

GREENFIELD CRESCENT etc (Balerno) *see under* COCKBURN CRESCENT, Balerno.

GREENHILL is shown on *Adair* 1682 and recorded in 1666, by which time it was an estate merging several of the lots feued off in the wester Burgh Muir in 1586; but the name was probably coined by John Livingston, who acquired the main lot (8 Scots acres beside the main Linton road) in 1636. Dying of the plague only nine years later, he is buried in the little graveyard in Chamberlain Road. The name is descriptive of the cultivated land contrasting with the adjoining heathland of the Links, and the *-hill* would have been the slight eminence (between Bruntsfield Gardens and Forbes Road) which became the site of the mansion house of Greenhill. In modern terms, the estate stretched east to Whitehouse Loan and lay between the Links and Church Hill, with the addition of part of BURGHMUIRHEAD (*which see*) until 1735, and a part of East Morningside, down to Newbattle Terrace, after 1806. Development for housing started in about 1832 immediately opposite Burghmuirhead, at GREENHILL BANK, a side name in Morningside Road suppressed in 1885. CHURCH HILL was opened after Dr Thomas Chalmers built his house of *Kirkhill* (now 1 Church Hill) in 1842; and by 1849 a new road, then simply called GREENHILL but differentiated as BRUNTSFIELD TERRACE and GREENHILL GARDENS by 1858, connected Bruntsfield Place with the east end of Church Hill. By 1852, the east end of CHAMBERLAIN ROAD was formed, although it was not named until about 1860. A certain antiquarianism came into it, for it was first proposed to be *Banner Place*, derived from Scott's entirely spurious story of standard-raising before Flodden—*see under* HARE STANE; and the final choice seems to commemorate Adam Fairholm, owner of Greenhill and burgh treasurer (not 'chamberlain') in 1752, who is also buried in the graveyard here. GREENHILL PARK, probably continuing the local field name, was developing by 1859. FORBES ROAD, named for the estate's owner, Sir John Stuart Forbes of Greenhill and Pitsligo, was opened through the policies of Greenhill House in 1864, and the House itself was pulled down in the course of forming BRUNTSFIELD GARDENS in 1884. For a short time around 1860, Sir John was also commemorated in the side name STUART GREEN east of the grass plot in Greenhill Gardens. In about 1850, NEWBATTLE TERRACE was given as a side name on the north side of Church Lane (formerly GRANGE LOAN, *which see*) in about 1850, celebrating Sir John's wife's family, the Kerrs of Lothian, whose seat was at Newbattle Abbey. It became the street name in 1885. In about 1860, PITSLIGO ROAD was named for Sir John's Aberdeenshire estate, and the naming of CLINTON ROAD celebrated the marriage, in 1858, of his daughter and heiress Harriet to Charles Hepburn-Stuart-Forbes-Trefusis, 20th Baron Clinton. The development of the eastern part of Greenhill began in 1871 with BRUNTSFIELD CRESCENT (*see under* BRUNTSFIELD) and GREENHILL TERRACE, followed by STRATHEARN PLACE (*which see*) and, by 1875, GREENHILL PLACE and St MARGARET'S ROAD, this last being named for St Margaret's Convent at WHITEHOUSE—*which see*.

GREENLAND MILL(S) (Water of Leith or Dean Village) is mentioned in *Town Council Minutes* 1702 as a mill apparently old enough to need repairs. In 1713 it is mentioned as 'mills', and a double arrangement is shown on *Ainslie* 1804 and *Pollock* 1834; but *Ordnance Survey* 1852 shows it as a single mill. It is pictured in *Edinburgh in the Olden Time*, in a view of the Dene in 1816. Still shown on *W & A K Johnston* 1888, the building was removed (perhaps along with the TROWS, *which see*) before 1893. The name may have been from a tenant's surname. Although there is no evidence for it, other than its location, it is possible that it was descended from the medieval estate mill of DRUMSHEUGH, *which see*.

GREENLAW HEDGE and **RIG** (Colinton Mains) were named in 1986 for the field in which they were to be built, which is shown on *Colinton Mains & Oxgangs* 1813 as the *Greenlaw Hedge. Greenlaw* was the chief land name in the adjoining farm of GREENBANK (*which see*) and the *hedge* fenced the boundary between it and the Colinton ground; while *rig* is used here as a term for an arable field.

GREENMANTLE LOAN (Inch) *see under* THE INCH, Nether Liberton.

GREENSIDE (Calton) is recorded from 1180 onwards. The name is Anglian *grene side*, obviously for the steep grassy bank, no doubt later used by spectators after 1456, when James II gave the ground to the town for tournaments and plays—and a curious square structure shown here on *Siege of Leith* 1560 might have been an open-air stage. The ROOD CHAPEL OF GREENSIDE was founded in about 1456, no doubt to provide for the dead or wounded combatants in tourneys, *see also under* CHAPEL WYND, West Port. Originally a chapel of Holyrood Abbey, it became a house of the White Friars in 1518; by 1560, as shown on *Siege of Leith*, this was roofless; but it was reconstituted as a leper hospital in 1591. The ROOD WELL associated with it is still shown on *Ordnance Survey* 1852, at GREENSIDE END. But for MUD ISLAND (*which see*) Greenside is shown as open ground on *Kincaid* 1784; but *Ainslie* 1804 names GREENSIDE PLACE, gives GREENSIDE ROW as *Greenside*, and shows but does not name GREENSIDE STREET. The *Strangers Guide* 1816 names GREENSIDE ROW and NOTTINGHAM PLACE (*which see*) but in reverse of their later order; while *Kirkwood* 1817 names GREENSIDE STREET and LANE. *Ordnance Survey* 1852 shows a LOWER GREENSIDE STREET (now MARSHALL'S COURT, *which see*) as well as GREENSIDE COURT. GREENSIDE HOUSE is a fancy name given not long before 1850 to a house which is labelled *Mr Marshall's* on *Ainslie* 1804, *see under* LOVERS LOAN, Hillside. Its site, near the north end of Wellington Street, was a quarter of a mile from the historic Greenside.

GREEN STREET (Broughton) was formed and named in 1925, but the name appears earlier on the Hope Trust's plan for the development, dated 1916. Since the ground was then a nursery, the name is unlikely to have been a local place name: more probably it may have been connected with the Trust.

THE GREEN TREE (South Leith) and also GREENTREE PLACE and GREEN STREET, *see under* GILES STREET, South Leith.

THE GREEN WAY (Wester Hailes) *see under* WESTER HAILES.

GREIG'S CLOSE (Canongate) *see* BRODIE'S CLOSE, Canongate.

GREIG'S HILL (Kirkliston) is recorded on *Ordnance Survey* 1852. Although on the face of it the name contains the surname Greig, it is likely that it conceals some other name altogether, possibly a hill name such as *craig(s)*, but in the absence of early forms this remains obscure. In 1968 a development on the hill was given the new and unrelated name of CLERICS HILL, *which see.*

GREYFRIARS (Old Town) was a house of the Franciscan or Minor Friars, founded in 1447 and sited on the south side of Cowgatehead, with a yard extending up the slope. The friary was dissolved in 1559, and three years later the Friars Yard became the town's burying ground in place of St Giles' kirkyard. In 1612 the town council built a kirk in the yard, as shown on *Rothiemay* 1647. Extended in 1721 to form the twin kirks of Old and New Greyfriars, it was altered yet again in 1937 to make it into a single kirk. GREYFRIARS PLACE appeared in 1851 as the side name for a redevelopment in the southern section of CANDLEMAKER ROW (*which see*) between the kirkyard gate and the Flodden Wall.

GREYFRIARS PORT (Old Town) is shown on *Rothiemay* 1647 under its later name of SOCIETY PORT and on *Edgar* 1742 under its still later one of BRISTO PORT. It appears in *RMS* 1498 as 'the common port called the *Frere Port*'; and the fact that it is here used to define a boundary given only two years earlier in *RMS* 1496 as 'the king's way called *the Lonyng*' (*see under* CANDLEMAKER ROW) perhaps suggests that the port was then not long built. In 1558 (quoted in *RMS* 1587) it is called 'the Grey Friars port' and in *RMS* 1612 it is the *Grayfreir port*. Obviously it was named for the yards of the GREYFRIARS (*which see*) adjoining it on the west, granted to the brothers in 1447. By 1618 it was being called the *Society Port*, for the brewery set up on the opposite side of the road in 1598 by the SOCIETY (*which see*) as shown on *Rothiemay* 1647, where the name is also extended to cover the suburbs south of the port. The third name of *Bristo Port* reverts to the ancient name of the area of these suburbs (*see* BRISTO) and probably reflects their growing importance as part of the PORTSBURGH (*which see*) set up in 1649. The port was on the line of the heel of the north pavement of the side street now called Bristo Port, its centre about ten feet out into the roadway west of the Lindsay Place (earlier, Society) corner. Still shown as a gateway on *Edgar* 1765 and *Kincaid* 1784, it appears on *Ainslie* 1780 and 1804 as a mere gap in the town wall.

THE GREYFRIARS YETT or **GATE** (Old Town) mentioned in *RMS* 1614, was the entrance to the friary, and is probably represented by the existing gate to the kirkyard at the foot of Candlemaker Row, shown on *Rothiemay* 1647 as the main approach to the kirk.

GRIERSON AVENUE, CRESCENT, GARDENS, ROAD and **SQUARE** (Wardie) followed by GRIERSON VILLAS, were named in 1925 and 1926, evidently for Sir Andrew Grierson, Town Clerk of Edinburgh 1918-34.

GRIGOR AVENUE, DRIVE, GARDENS and **TERRACE** (Drylaw) were named in 1935, for a Mr Grigor, factor of the Steele-Maitland estate, who were the developers—*see also* DAVIDSON PARK, Drylaw.

GRINDIES WELL ROAD (Gilmerton) is so named on a plan by Carfrae & Clouston, lodged in an action *Harper v. Harper or Dow and husband* in 1863. The name is probably GRUNDIE'S, from some owner named Grundy, a surname recorded in Scotland as early as 1296.

GRINDLAY'S CLOSE (West Port) is shown on *Ainslie* 1780 and named on *Ordnance Survey* 1852. Now within the site of Argyle House, it led to King's Stables Lane past tanneries owned by the Grindlay family, leatherworkers in the West Bow, tanners in West Port, and owners of ORCHARDFIELD.

GRINDLAY STREET (Tollcross) *see under* ORCHARDFIELD, Tollcross.

GROATHILL (Drylaw) is recorded from 1350 onwards and shown on *Adair* 1682 as *Grotil*. The estate was taken into Drylaw in 1683; but the house, sited about 100 yards east of the junction of Groathill Road North with Telford Road, and still roofed with thatch, remained until Telford Road was constructed in 1925. Of over a dozen variant spellings, *Grothil* 1350, *Groutell* 1369, *Groithale* 1505 and *Grothoill* 1512 are typical. The first part of the name is Anglian *grot* or Old Norse *grjot*, pebbly; and while the second part could be *-hyll*, hill, or *-halh*, haugh, or *-hohl*, howe, the position of the place on the south slope of the Dry Law above the howe of the Blackhall burn might suggest it was either the first or the last. GROATHILL ROAD NORTH and SOUTH were the old approaches to the house. The southern part of Groathill Road South was renamed SOUTH GROATHILL AVENUE in 1977, in order to assist management of traffic to industries in the former Craigleith Quarry. GROATHILL AVENUE and GARDENS were named in 1935.

GROSVENOR CRESCENT, GARDENS, STREET (Coates) *see under* COATES.

THE GROVE (Dalry) was a part of the estate of Dalry *alias* Brandfield, separated from the rest in 1714 and sold in 1775 to John, Lord Colville, who named it *The Grove*. The house and park are shown on *Ainslie* 1804. A scheme for housing streets and a square is shown on *Knox* 1821, and some progress was made with the northern part of GROVE STREET; but the plan seems to have been dropped before 1834, when *Pollock* shows the greater part of that street as a mere lane, which is in fact called GROVE LANE on *Ordnance Survey* 1852; and after some piecemeal developments briefly named GROVE ROAD and TERRACE, Grove Street was completed in the 1860s or early 1870s, along with UPPER GROVE PLACE and BRANDFIELD STREET, the latter being named for the estate, *see under* DALRY.

GUARDIANSWOOD (Murrayfield) was named in 1983, by combining references to the grove of trees on the site and to the connection of the adjoining ELLERSLY ROAD (*which see*) with Sir William Wallace, Guardian of Scotland in 1298.

GUARDWELL (Moredun) is shown on *Roy* 1753 as the name of the settlement at Moredun Mill—*see under* MOREDUN, a name brought into Gilmerton in 1769. The first part of it is Anglian *gara*, a triangle or gore of land, *see also* GARBRAGE, *under* DUDDINGSTON SQUARE. The name is akin to *Gorebridge*, Midlothian, and *Guardbridge*, Fife, which is locally pronounced 'Garbrig'. The position of the well or spring is not known

GULLAN'S CLOSE (264 Canongate) is referred to as *Goolen's* in 1779, but the name, whether as that of the close or of a stabler in it, is recorded in at least eight variants. It seems to be from the East Lothian place name, which itself is variously pronounced *Gull-* or *Gooll-* or *Gill-*. Four references to a James Gullane suggest that he (with or without successors of the same Christian name) was a stabler in the close at some time before 1731. The close was also HALIBURTON'S from some date prior to 1705, possibly referring to a Robert Haliburton, the builder of a tenement in the Canongatehead, and to Sir John Haliburton, its owner. It was also DEMPSTER'S, for a James Dempster, weaver, apparently a resident as well as owner of a tannery which he sold in 1740. While it is also referred to as CANT'S CLOSE, other references suggest that this name belonged to the next close to the west—*see* BELL'S CLOSE (272 Canongate). Being in the south Canongatehead, the close was part of Edinburgh, not the burgh of Canongate.

THE GULLIONS (Redheughs, Gyle) appears on a plan of Redheughs in 1852 (*RHP 11162*) as a field name. It is Scots *gullion*, boggy gully, for the long steep-sided hollows which are a feature of the ground.

GUNSTONE'S CLOSE (North side of Cowgate, west of Niddry's Wynd) is shown (unnamed) on *Edgar* 1742 and *Kincaid* 1784 but was swept away shortly afterwards to clear the site for the South Bridge. Recorded as *Gunstone* in 1725, the close name is given as *Gunstone's* in 1691 and as *Gunstone's* and *Gun's* in 1756; and its earliest form suggests that it arose from the name of some owner, rather than the manufacture of *gun stanes* or flints for firelocks.

THE GUSE DUB (Crosscausey) *see* GOOSEDUB.

(ALEXANDER) GUTHRIE'S CLOSE (South side of Cowgate) is mentioned in *Maitland* 1753 as being between High School Wynd and College Wynd. There is nothing to link it with the naming of Guthrie Street, although it was in the same general locality.

GUTHRIE STREET (Old Town) is shown as proposed on *Edinburgh Improvements* 1866 and was carried out under the City Improvement Act by 1872. Its northern section was formed by widening the east side of the Horse Wynd, and its middle section bisected the College Wynd, now built over by the Edinburgh University Staff Club. A note in *Grant* implies that it was thought of as a *New College Wynd*, but in the event it was named GUTHRIE STREET after the Rev Thomas Guthrie, a leading spirit in the Free Kirk and a noted advocate of social and educational reform, who died in 1873.

THE GUTTIT HADDIE (Arthur's Seat) is a large Y-shaped gully on the western side of the hill, obviously named for its shape, and believed to be the 'channel or chasm' which the *Old Statistical Account* (Duddingston) reports as having been 'torn up' or spectacularly deepened by a cloudburst on 13 September 1744. The name is shown on *Ordnance Survey* 1852; but *Kirkwood* 1817 shows—albeit south, not north of the Ravens Craig—another name, THE SPELDRIN, which as 'a split and dried/smoked haddock' is so close in meaning to *guttit haddie* as to make it almost certainly an alternative and probably earlier name for the same feature, wrongly located on the map.

THE GYLE (Corstorphine) lies at the upper end of the bed of a post-glacial lake still represented by the flasshes or flushing meadows beside the Stank, *see under* CORSTORPHINE *and* THE FLASSHES. Recorded as *Goyle* in 1656, the name is Celtic, probably British and represented by Gaelic *goil*, swirl of water; and since this generally refers to some characteristic eddying on a sheet of water, it may well have been the loch's name, akin to Loch Goil, Argyllshire. GYLE PARK recreation ground lies in the bed of the loch, and GYLE PARK GARDENS was named for it in 1977. GYLE AVENUE and SERVICE LANE were named in 1993. *See also* NORTH and SOUTH GYLE, farms lying north and south of the loch.

GYLE BOGS COMMON (Dalmeny) is shown on *Plan of Dundas* 1757 as some 600 yards south-west of Dalmeny kirk, in the vicinity of NG 140770. The ground has been so disturbed by mining and by rail and road works that its early state is hard to establish, but the name possibly has to do with the swirl of water in floods at or near the Dolphington burn—*see also* THE GYLE, Corstorphine.

GYLE MUIR (Corstorphine) also called GYLE COMMON, was a common belonging to Corstorphine, lying south of the old road from South Gyle to Redheughs and east of the branch to Cultins. It was named after the loch to the north—*see* THE GYLE—and Scots *muir* frequently meant 'common land'. It is so named on *RHP 735* and shown as a 'detached part of Corstorphine' on *Ordnance Survey* 1852, and until recent times the approach to it was by SOUTH GYLE ROAD —*which see*. Thus the existing GYLEMUIR ROAD is misnamed. It was not built until the later 19th century, and although it is shown by its present name on *Ordnance Survey* 1893 it was commonly known as DAIRIES ROAD (from the number of such premises on it) until recent times. The confusion with Gyle Muir seems to have arisen because the meadows to the west of this road, lying in the bed of the ancient Gyle loch, were also common land (CORSTORPHINE COMMON north of the Stank, and MYRES COMMON south of it) and Selway reports that they were once known as the GOYLE MYRE.

H

HADDINGTON'S ENTRY or **CLOSE** and **COURT** (Canongate) *see* REID'S CLOSE, 80 Canongate.

HADDINGTON PLACE (Leith Walk) was begun in 1825 as part of the development of Major John Hope's land at the Physic Garden, and the name appears in *PO Directory* 1826. The reason for its choice remains to be traced, The guess that it derived from the temporary name *Road to Haddington* shown on *Ainslie* 1804 on the line of London Road is scarcely tenable, since the latter was already called the (*Great*) *London Road* by 1819.

HADDON'S COURT (South Side) is shown as partly built on *Ainslie* 1780 and is named on *Kirkwood* 1817. It was evidently named for an owner, as yet untraced.

HADDO'S HOLE (High Street) *see* WEST KIRK.

HAGGART STREET (North Leith) is shown on *Fergus & Robinson* 1759 as *Road from the Citadel* to North Leith and the old bridge of Leith, and while it undoubtedly dates back to the building of the Citadel in 1656 it may well represent an earlier access to the St Nicholas Kirk which was knocked down to make room for the Citadel. Its line originally followed the edge of the ditch of the Citadel's north-eastern ramparts, shown on *Nash* 1709, but was slightly altered to suit the Upper Drawbridge which replaced Abbot Ballantyne's bridge 170 yards upstream in about 1788. The street obviously gained in importance when the first of Rennie's new docks opened in 1806, but it was 1813 before the *PO Directory* listed it as HAGGART STREET, named for the North Leith wine merchant of that name, who owned the ground. While this name was still shown on *Lothian* 1826. the *PO Directory* 1821 shows that it was already beginning to be supplanted by the more utilitarian DOCK STREET—perhaps under the influence of the *Dock Street* (now the western part of Commercial Street) shown on *Kirkwood* 1817.

HAGGIS KNOWE (Queen's Park) is *Haggies Know* on *Kirkwood* 1817. The name is Scots *knowe*, knoll, with *haggs* or broken ground, in this case referring to the well-marked cultivation terraces, dating from the Dark Ages or earlier, on its north-easterly slope.

THE HAGGS (Dalmahoy) is shown on *Dalmahoy* 1749. While the name might be Scots *hag*, for a hollow in broken ground or else for coppiced woodland, the topography might suggest that it is a term for grazings, originally from Old Norse *hagi*, enclosed pastures.

HAGS BRAE (Dalmeny) is shown on *Ordnance Survey* 1854. The name is Scots, the *brae* probably referring as much to the stiff climb of the road as to the knowe itself, while the *hags*, if they were not natural broken ground or trenches opened in the muir for the cutting of peats, may have been coppiced woodland.

HAILES is first recorded in about 1095, when Ethelred, son of Malcolm Canmore, gave the lands to Dunfermline Abbey. The name is Anglian *halas*, in the sense perhaps of 'lands in the river bend' between Longstone and Curriemuirend, but more likely meaning 'lands between the waters' of Leith and the Murray burn, the historic estate's north boundary. By the 15th century this was divided into three main parts: OVER or EASTER HAILES, most of which became part of REDHALL, *which see*; NETHER or WESTER HAILES, *see under the latter*; and the KIRKLANDS OF HAILES, *see under* SPYLAW. HAILES HOUSE probably represents the original estate centre, but certainly was the centre of Easter Hailes, as shown on *Blaeu* 1654. HAILES KIRK was the name of Colinton Kirk until comparatively modern times; and since the evidence for an early kirk at Hailes House is altogether dubious, the present building is almost certainly the latest in a series of kirks on this site since the Dark Ages. HAILES BRIG is mentioned in 1574 and by then was such an established name that it was used for the locality as a whole. HAILES BRAE is traditional for the steep rise of the Lanark road up to Spylaw Bank, going south. HAILES QUARRY was opened in about 1750 and worked out by 1900, and is now HAILES QUARRY PARK. Development in the policies of Hailes House began in 1910, with HAILES APPROACH and the east end of HAILES GARDENS; and it continued with HAILES PARK (1932) AVENUE, GROVE and TERRACE (1936) and BANK (1963).

HAILESLAND (Wester Hailes) was coined in 1967, to supply names for HAILESLAND GARDENS and GROVE, built in *Dumbryden*, north of the culverted Union Canal, and HAILESLAND PARK, built south of the Canal in the *Mid Park* field of Wester Hailes. HAILESLAND PLACE, added in 1971, and HAILESLAND SCHOOL, together with WESTER HAILES PARK, are in what was the *Dryburn Park* of Wester Hailes, a field named for the little burn which ran along its south boundary, heading for Kingsknowe, and was apparently a 'winterburn', apt to be dry in summer.

HAILES STREET (Lochrin) was formed in about 1816 on ground owned by the Gillespie Trust and seems to have been named in about 1840 for James Gillespie's original estate of SPYLAW (*which see*) on the west bank of the Water of Leith, which had been earlier known as *the Kirklands of Hailes. See also* GILLESPIE STREET (Lochrin).

HAIN or **HEN BURN** (Swanston) is shown as *Hen burn* on a map in *Steuart's Colinton* but as *Swanston Burn* on *Ordnance Survey* 1852. The name is evidently from Old Norse *hegn* or Scots *hain(ing)*, enclosed pasture. The pronunciation *hen* is authentic in Lothian. HAINBURN PARK in New Swanston was named in 1987 as being beside a culverted reach of the burn.

HAIR'S or **YAIR'S CLOSE** (172 High Street) *see* OLD ASSEMBLY CLOSE.

HALBARNS (Kirkliston) *see under* HALLYARDS, Kirkliston.

HALIBURTON'S CLOSE (264 Canongate) *see* GULLAN'S CLOSE.

HALKERSTON'S CROFT (New Town) is mentioned in *Protocols of James Young* 1505 as a property of 7 Scots acres known as *Halkerston's Croft or Quhitcroft*, then inherited by William Halkerston as son and heir to William Halkerston, burgess; and the latter may have been the William Halkerston figuring in *RMS* 1478 and 1486, as well as the deceased owner of that name in HALKERSTON'S WYND (*which see*) referred to in 1530. Lying at the east end of the north bank of the Nor Loch (it is shown on *Edgar* 1742 and as 'Graham's Possession' on *New Town Site Plan* 1766) the croft was easily reached from the Wynd. As noted in *Common Good* 1904, it was still known as *Whitecroft alias Halkertson's croft* when it was acquired by the town in 1758; but since the Broughton lands of Holyrood listed in *RMS* 1581 included *Lochbank alias Halkerstoniscroft* as well as the Quhitcroft, it appears that the Halkerston's holding must have extended the whole length of the lochside (in modern terms, from the North Bridge to the line of Hope Street) while the alternative name LOCHBANK aptly described this steep slope between the LANG DYKES road (roughly on the line of Rose Street) and the 'green walk' that formed the march between Edinburgh and Broughton along the north shore of the loch. Lochbank got the further alternative name of BEARFORD'S or (corruptly) BAREFOOTS PARKS after it was bought by Hepburn of Bearford in 1645; and in purchasing it in 1717 the town took its first step in preparing for the New Town which became a reality 51 years later.

HALKERSTON'S WYND (165 High Street) was the only passage on the north side of the High Street to be termed *wynd* or 'public way' (Leith Wynd, except for its west side, was outwith the royalty) and this would suggest that it may have served as such from the very beginning of the burgh, as the most westerly route down the slope and past the foot of the Nor Loch to the Calton gorge. By 1584, a NEW PORT had been built to close the foot of the wynd; and *Rothiemay* 1647 shows a loan leading from it across the dam of the Loch and up to Multree's Hill. A Johan de Haukerstone figures in the *Ragman Roll* 1296 as a property owner in Edinburghshire; *Town Council Minutes* and the *RMS* show several of the family as prominent in Edinburgh in the 15th century, and John Halkerston, architect of the Holy Trinity kirk in about 1462, was probably one of them; and the *Protocols of John Foular* 1528-30 name the Wynd and show several Halkerstons (including William, owner of HALKERSTON'S CROFT, *which see*) as owners or deceased owners of more than one property in it. When the railways came, the Wynd gave access to the North British Railway's station at Waverley, and was known as NORTH BRITISH CLOSE for some years before it was finally suppressed in the redevelopment of the buildings on the east side of North Bridge in 1898.

HALLCROFT PARK, RISE, GREEN and **NEUK** (Ratho) were built in part of the *North Crofts* of Ratho and were named in 1977 in the belief that the land was part of the neighbouring estate of *Westhall*; but the

32 Scots acres of the North Crofts are shown on *Hatton etc* 1797 as lands of Ratho 'possessed by different people in the town of Ratho'. HALLCROFT CLOSE and GARDENS were added in 1978 and 1979.

HALLHEAD ROAD (South Craigmillar Park) *see under* CRAIGMILLAR PARK.

HALL'S CLOSE (South Leith) is listed on *Kirkwood* 1817 and may have been named for Robert Hall, miller in Kirkgate and Lawrie Street in 1826, or for a predecessor.

HALL LISTON (Newbridge) *see under* AULDLISTON, Newbridge.

HALL TERRACE (Corstorphine) was named in 1892 for a terrace of cottages opposite the Public Hall, which was begun in 1891 although it was not finished until 1903.

HALLBARNS (Newbridge) some 500 yards north of the historic HALLYARDS (*which see*) is coupled with it in *RMS* 1582, and again in 1619, when this pair of estates in the Templar barony of Liston were made into an independent barony 'of Hallyards'. In the 1619 charter *Halbarnis* is described as having been the *domain lands* or *mains* of Liston; and this at once explains the name element *-barnis*, for the mains of a barony was equipped to store not only its own produce but the rents paid in kind by all the other farms in the barony, which in this case stretched over a huge area including Briggs in the east and Newliston in the west. The name is probably early Scots *halh barnis*, barns in the haugh that extends about two square miles within the bend of the Almond. It appears on *Roy* 1753 and *Gellatly* 1834, but *Armstrongs* 1773 shows it already being displaced by the baronial name Hallyards, and the process seems to have been complete by 1840.

HALLYARDS (Newbridge) is recorded in *RMS* 1497 as the place of signing a charter, and it is likely that (as it certainly was in the 16th century) it was the administrative centre of the barony of Liston, owned by the priory of the Knights of St John at Torphichen. In *RMS* 1502 the estate is grouped with that of HALLBARNS (*which see*) and in 1619 the two together were made a barony in their own right. It seems that both of them had towerhouses in 1582; and the mansion of HALLYARDS CASTLE, demolished in the 1920s, was probably built after John Skene became laird of the barony in 1630. As may be seen on *Armstrong* 1773, the name began to include and displace that of Hallbarns, and this seems to have been completed by the 1840s. Since the historic site is in the centre of a knowe rising in the great floodplain of the Almond, it is possible that it was occupied at an early date. The early spellings of the name are *Halyardis* or *Halyairdis* (*Roy* 1753 gives it as *Hawyards*) and it is probably from Anglian *halh geard* or Scots *haw yaird*, fenced place in or of the haugh.

HALMYRE STREET (Quarryholes) *see under* GORDON STREET, Quarryholes.

HALYBURTON'S CLOSE (118 High Street) *see* DICKSON'S CLOSE.

HAMBURGH PLACE (North Leith) dates from 1979, but is a rebuilding of a terrace which was laid out by 1817 and partly built by

1822. The name, a variant spelling of Hamburg, celebrated trade links with that city.

HAMILTON PLACE (Stockbridge) was part of an old road, shown on *Roy* 1753, connecting Stockbridge, Silvermills and Canonmills. A Mrs Hamilton, widow of Dr Hamilton, moved here from 28 London Street in 1813, and her property (believed to be Nos. 10 and 11, later occupied by the Hamilton Place Academy) came to be addressed as *Hamilton Place* by 1822. The street name, not given on *Lothian* 1829, appears on *Pollock* 1834.

HAMILTON'S CLOSE (50 Cowgate) *see* BAILLIE'S CLOSE, Cowgate.

UNDER & UPPER HAMILTON'S CLOSES (once 57 and 65 now about 41 and 45 Grassmarket) are so named on *Ainslie* 1780 and are given as HAMILTON'S and LITTLE HAMILTON'S in *PO Directory* 1827 and on *Ordnance Survey* 1852. No immediate derivation has been traced, but William Hamilton figures amongst owners in the south side of Grassmarket in *Protocols of John Foular* 1512.

HAMILTON'S CLOSE (312 High Street) *see* FISHER'S CLOSE.

HAMILTON'S CLOSE (Queensferry) is indicated on *Ordnance Survey* 1854 and may be on a medieval line, inasmuch as closes are usually at one side of a burgage toft. The name is probably that of some former proprietor.

HAMILTON'S ENTRY (Bristo) was an entry off Bristo Street, named for Thomas Hamilton, mason, in about 1690. It was here that Sir Walter Scott first went to school in 1777. The street was swept away when MARSHALL STREET was formed in 1872

HAMILTON'S ENTRY (171 Canongate) *see under* MILLER'S CLOSE, Canongate.

HAMILTON'S FOLLY (St Leonard's) is shown on *Scott* 1759 as the name of the tenement which, together with a brewery, had been built in 1708 by Alexander Hamilton, merchant in Edinburgh, upon his newly-acquired property (which he called *Newgrange*) on the west side of St Leonard's Street, immediately south of Crosscausey. The nickname *Folly* no doubt arose from the fact that the scheme rendered him bankrupt by 1718.

HAMILTON STREET (Joppa) *see under* RABBIT HALL and BRUNSTANE ROAD NORTH.

HAMILTON STREET (North Leith) was named by 1884 and HAMILTON CRESCENT and TERRACE followed in 1886, the group being named for their developer, a builder in Great Junction Street; but all three were to be suppressed a century later in the redevelopment of BATHFIELD, *which see*. Meantime the name was borrowed for HAMILTON WYND, built on the site of the BATTERY (*which see*) in 1963.

HAMILTON TERRACE (Duddingston) is on land once the *Broom Hills* in Wester Duddingston, and was named in about 1900 for the Duke of Abercorn, owner of the estate, the family name being

Hamilton. Later streets, extending into the *Langlands* of Wester Duddingston, were named HAMILTON DRIVE, GROVE and PARK in 1935, and HAMILTON GARDENS was added in 1956.

HAMMERMEN'S CLOSE (146 Canongate) *see* BAKEHOUSE CLOSE.

HAMMERMEN'S CLOSE (55 Cowgate) is listed on *Ainslie* 1780 and given as an address in *Williamson's Directory* 1773. It was named for the Incorporation of the Hammermen of Edinburgh, which dated back to 1483. The Hammermen had *Hammermen's Land* here and they were also guardians of the Magdalen Chapel and hospital, built and endowed in 1541-44 by Janet Rynd in memory of her husband Michael MacQueen.

HAMPTON PLACE and **TERRACE** (Wester Coates) *see under* OSBORNE TERRACE, Wester Coates.

HANDYSIDE PLACE (Gorgie) *see under* ROBERTSON AVENUE, Gorgie.

HANGMAN'S CLOSE (140 Cowgate) is listed on *Ainslie* 1780 and was named for the public lockman or executioner. In 1681, John Whyt, the 'gude toun's lockman', built himself a house in Fishmarket Close 'on the east side of the dwelling formerly possessed by him'.

HANGMAN'S HILL or **CRAIG** (Queen's Park) *see under* GIRNAL CRAIG.

HANNAHFIELD (Balerno) is shown on *Knox* 1812, but *Ravelrigg* 1764 shows it to have been formed between these dates by combining parts of the *East* and *Craig* parks of Craigmill in Ravelrigg with a looping diversion of the Lanark road. While the *Hannah-* might be a woman's name, it is more likely to be the surname of the first owner of the new property. The 1764 plan shows a knowe (since then quarried away) bearing the name *General's Watch*, some 70 yards north of the original road. The name EAST HANNAHFIELD was coined in 1984 for a new street in the eastern part of the property.

HANOVER STREET (New Town) *see under* NEW TOWN.

HAPPERLAW'S CLOSE (231 Cowgate) *see* RAPPERLAW'S WYND, Cowgate.

HAPPY VALLEY (Craiglockhart) has become a place name for a part of Colinton Road, beside the entrance to an area which has been used for recreation from about 1880, when a boating pond and curling rink were formed on the flat boggy floor of the deep glacial valley of the Megget burn. In the 1920s this was developed as the *Happy Valley* amusement park and dance hall; and although it was redeveloped as a sports centre after 1945, its commercial name stuck to the adjoining part of the main road, where it dips on the south side of the *Partridge Knowe* and crosses the historic boundary between Meggetland and Craiglockhart.

THE HARBOUR (Portobello) is shown on *Wood's Portobello* 1824 and (with considerable detail) on *Portobello* 1856. It was an artificial basin, promoted by William Jamieson in about 1787; but by the 1860s it was silted up, and by the 1880s it was filled in and built up as A W Buchan & Co's pottery. The HARBOUR GREEN was originally on its east side; but on *Ordnance Survey* 1893 the name is extended to take in the remnant of filled-in basin and the western sea wall. HARBOUR PLACE was named in 1978 as occupying the southern part of the site of the harbour as shown on *Portobello* 1856. HARBOUR ROAD was named as in the vicinity of the harbour, although, as shown in 1856 and implied on *Wood's Portobello*, it led to the beach, rather than the harbour.

THE HARBOUR (Queensferry) was rebuilt in the 18th and early 19th centuries, but the corbelling of a lookout platform at HEAD OF THE HARBOUR appears to date from the 16th century, and shipping was the major activity in the town even before it became a royal burgh in 1636. HARBOUR LANE is traditionally named as leading to the harbour, but it is evident that the principal approach was by GOTE LANE, *which see.*

HARBOUR HILL (Currie) is named on *Knox* 1812. The term harbour occurs in at least four hill names in southern Scotland. In none of these cases would a derivation from early Scots *herbere*, shelter, seem to fit in with the terrain; but in each of them the hill is well placed as a grazing where stock could be brought together from the adjoining hills before being shorn or driven to market, and this suggests that the name is *harbour*, from Anglian *heorde-beorg*, hill of or for flocks or herds, with Scots *hill* added later.

HARDEN PLACE (Temple Park) *see under* POLWORTH TERRACE.

HARDWELL CLOSE (Coalhill, Leith; *also* Head of Pleasance) are both shown on *Kirkwood* 1817, and were probably named for wells yielding water notably hard and therefore excellent for drinking but not good for washing.

HARE BURN (Swanston) is recorded in 1709 as *Hary burn*, which suggests the name is from Anglian *haer*, rocky, referring to broken ground at its source.

HARE HILL (Balerno) is shown on *Roy* 1753. While it is not markedly rocky or stony, its red and yellow sandstones weather to greys and it is generally much lighter in colour than the adjoining Black Hill. This suggests that the name is Anglian *har hyll*, grey hill.

HARELAW ROAD (Colinton) was named in 1923, apparently for HARLAW (Balerno) which is also spelt *Harelaw*, but perhaps with some confusion of it with HARE HILL (Balerno).

HAREWOOD ROAD (Niddrie) was named in December 1929, apparently in compliment to HRH the Princess Mary, Countess of Harewood, who was given the freedom of Edinburgh in 1930. HAREWOOD CRESCENT and DRIVE were named in 1930.

THE HARE STANE (Church Hill) is named thus on *Ordnance Survey* 1852, which shows it some 40 yards north of its present site. This position tallies with its description in *Maitland* 1753, and with that of the *Standand Stane* referred to in *Town Council Minutes* 1586 as a landmark in defining some of the first feus in the West Muir, including the future East Morningside 'dew eist fra the Standard Stane' and West Morningside 'bewest' it 'toward Typperlin'. It may have been set up centuries earlier, to mark the sharp corner in the march between Merchiston and the Muir or the king's land that became the Muir; but equally that corner could have been made precisely because the Stane was already there, erected in some earlier era beside this Roman route—indeed it shares its somewhat unimpressive size with the BUCKSTANE (*which see*) and both stones were originally on a skyline beside the road. The one purpose it certainly did *not* serve was that of 'bearing' the standard when James IV mustered his army before Flodden. As shown by Henry Paton in *BOEC XXIV*, this romantic but untrue story was unheard of until Scott made it up in *Marmion*, published in 1808. Even then, Scott called the stone the Hare Stane, and the popular but manufactured and misleading name *Bore Stone* first appeared in 1822 and was not recognised by the *Ordnance Survey* until 1876. The historic name is Scots *hare stane* from Anglian *har stan*, grey or hoary stone, frequently a description of boundary marks, and in this case it could have been given at any time from the 7th century onwards.

HARLAW (Balerno) is recorded from 1280 onwards. The name's early forms *harlau*, *harlaw* and *hairlaw* would equally fit Anglian *har hlaw*, grey or hoary hill, or *haer hlaw*, hill with a rock or heap of stones: but the first is not strongly suggested by the place, whereas the second immediately fits in with the report in the *New Statistical Account* that 'an immense cairn of stones' containing a cist burial had been removed from Harlaw in about the 1800s, together with a group of five standing stones a quarter-mile further south—a feature which would call to mind the related Anglian word *haerg*, a heathen temple. The farm appears as *Harelaw* on *Blaeu* 1654. HARLAW ROAD, named as the approach to Harlaw from Balerno, is shown on *Laurie* 1763 as joining the route through the Pentlands by CLOCHMEAD, *which see*. HARLAW MARCH was named in 1981 as being formed just within the north march of Harlaw at the Bog Wood.

HARLAW CAIRN (Dalmeny) is noted in *RCAHMS Inventory* 1926 as an alternative name for the tumulus which is shown as *Airly Cairn* on *Barnbougle & Dalmeny* c1800 and as *Early Cairn* on *Forrest* 1818, but is given the somewhat different name of EARL CAIRNIE in the *Statistical Account* 1791 and on *Ordnance Survey* 1854. The fact that *Dundas* 1757 shows an *Airley Cairn* less than three miles away at SENTRY KNOWE, Queensferry, is independent evidence that *airly* or *early* (perhaps also the *hurly* in the HURLY BUTTS, Queensferry, also figured on *Dundas* 1757) must be a term having to do with cairns; and the perfect fit of Anglian *haer hlaw*, hill with heap of (sacred) stones, together with the occurrence of forms *Harla* (1682) and *Harlie* (1763) at HARLAW, Balerno, strongly suggests that *Airly* and *Early* are colloquial variants of Harlaw, and that 'Earl Cairnie' must have been either a muddled form or, more likely, the outcome of a deliberate attempt to make sense of *Early Cairn* when read as meaning a cairn which had something to do with an earl.

301

HARRISON ROAD (North Merchiston) was formed in the 1880s on Merchant Company ground and named for Sir George Harrison, Lord Provost 1882-85 and MP in 1885 shortly before his death. He is also commemorated by the HARRISON ARCH—*see under* OBSERVATORY ROAD, Blackford. HARRISON LANE was named by 1905. Prior to 1965, HARRISON GARDENS and PLACE were known as BONALY ROAD and PLACE, North Merchiston—*which see*.

HARTINGTON GARDENS and **PLACE** (Merchiston) were named by 1875 and 1876 respectively for Spencer Cavendish, Lord Hartington, who became leader of the Liberal Opposition in 1875, and succeeded as 8th Duke of Devonshire in 1891.

HARTINGTON TERRACE (Pilrig) was named in 1875 for Lord Hartington (*see preceding*) but the name was dropped in 1894.

HART'S CLOSE (Grassmarket) *see* WARDEN'S CLOSE, Grassmarket.

HART'S CLOSE (High Street) is shown on *Edgar* 1742 but was cleared away for the building of the North Bridge in 1765. It was named for Andro Hart, the celebrated Scots printer, who had a tenement at the close foot, inherited by his son John in 1621, and listed in 1635 as still owned and occupied by Andro Hart's widow. (Hart's printing house was further up the High Street, at CRAIG'S CLOSE.) The close may have been HENRY NISBET'S, recorded in 1660, and was also called BALLANTYNE'S, for James Ballantyne, writer, resident at some date prior to 1705. The name CRANSTON'S CLOSE, known to have belonged to a close lost when the North Bridge was built, may have been an alternative name for Hart's, or for one of the closes west of it (*see* LEYS'S CLOSE and MILNE SQUARE) and might have derived from any of a number of Cranstons who served on the town council, such as William Cranstoun (1403) Thomas (provost in 1450) or Patrick (1574).

HARTS KNOWES *see under* HILLSIDE.

HART STREET (Broughton) was developed in 1808, utilising an opening left for a *North Fort Street* in the scheme for PICARDY, *which see*. The name was *Hart Street* by 1814. Its origin has not yet been traced, but may be connected with ownership of the land. James Hairt, goldsmith in Canongate, had 16 acres in Broughton in 1600; and *Harts Knowes* at HILLSIDE (*which see*) were not far away.

HARVEST DRIVE and **PLACE** (Newbridge) were named in 1977. The name is fancy.

HASTIE'S CLOSE (225 Cowgate) is mentioned in 1725 and shown on *Edgar* 1742. A William Hastie, writer, had two houses here in 1765, but another William Hastie, jeweller, was on the east side of the College Wynd in or before 1747.

HATTON (Ratho) is recorded from 1288 onwards; and the early spellings *Halton, Haltoun* and *Hawtoun* show the name to be Anglian *halh tún*, farm place on the haugh beside the Gogar water. The 15th-century tower house is shown with an enclosed park on *Blaeu* 1654. HATTON MAINS or home farm is recorded from 1586 onwards and is shown on *Roy* 1753 although the place is named ENTRYHEAD—i.e. the head of the entry to Hatton House. *Hatton etc* 1797 shows a steading on the south side of the Calder road, and *Knox* 1812 adds an EASTER HATTON MAINS north of the road.

HATTON PLACE (Grange) *see under* THE GRANGE.

THE HAUGH (Newliston) is recorded from 1553 onwards and is shown on *Blaeu* 1654 as *Hauch*, the name describing the ground in this great haugh or river meadow between the Brox burn and the Almond. COTTARHAUGH, shown as *Cotairehaugh* on a plan of *Haugh etc* in 1767 (*RHP 2155*) was a separate smallholding (now traversed by the Almond railway viaduct) worked by a cottar. *Knox* 1812 shows the HAUGH TOLL BAR at the farm.

HAUGHHEAD (Balerno) is shown thus on *Laurie* 1763 and named for its position overlooking the riverside haugh. *Roy* 1753 shows it as *Pathead* (*sic*) and although the name Pathead occurs about a mile upstream it may also have belonged to Haughhead as the farm at the head of the *peth* or steep brae up from the ford and haugh.

HAUGH PARK (Longstone) developed by 1902 in part of the Haugh Park or riverside meadow of Kingsknowe.

HAUGH STREET (Stockbridge) *see under* DEANHAUGH, Stockbridge.

THE HAUSE (Arthur's Seat) is shown on *Kirkwood* 1817. The name is Scots *hause*, throat or narrow defile, apt enough for this gully leading to the upper part of the hill.

THE HAWES (Queensferry) is recorded from the 17th century variously as *Hawes*, *Halls* and *Newhalls*. The second is simply a standard spelling for the sound of the first, in which a long *a* was represented by *al*; while NEWHALLS seems to have been a property name (probably arising from a new building) for it did not displace the simple place name, and both continue to this day, although Newhalls, now read as though the spelling were modern, is of course mispronounced. The name is not plural, being Anglian or Old Norse *hals* or Scots *hause*, a defile or narrow pass, referring perhaps to the narrow foreshore leading round the bay below the bluffs (the road is shown on *Blaeu* 1654 as on the very shore) or else to the gully climbed by the HAWES BRAE road, or possibly even to both; but it is evident from *Adair* 1682 that even by that date the land name had also become a name for buildings represented by Hawes inn. NEWHALLS ROAD is now a side name in EDINBURGH ROAD, but the two probably overlapped for centuries, for the road is *to Edinburgh by the Hawes or Newhalls*.

HAWKHEAD CRESCENT and **GROVE** (Liberton) *see under* CADOGAN ROAD, Liberton.

HAWKHILL (Restalrig) is recorded in 1560 as *Halkehil* and shown on *Adair* 1682 as *Halkhil*. It is listed among lands of Trinity Hospital in 1718, along with the subdivisions MEIKLE and LITTLE HAWKHILL. The name is literal, hill noted for hawks, and *Ordnance Survey* 1852 attaches it to the knowe immediately east of Lochend road, *but see* *also* KIKERLAW, Restalrig. HAWKHILL HOUSE, built in 1757 by John Adam for Lord Alemoor, but demolished in the 1960s, stood immediately east of this knowe. HAWKHILL AVENUE, which is in West Drum, not Hawkhill, was named in 1928.

HAWTHORN BANK (Dean Village) appears on *Ordnance Survey* 1852 as the name of a house (also shown on *Kirkwood* 1817) fronting Belford Road. HAWTHORNBANK LANE, shown fully developed on *Kirkwood* 1817, was probably so called before 1893, when *Ordnance Survey* names the whole neighbourhood as *Hawthorn Bank*; and the naming of HAWTHORN TERRACE at its west end by 1862 suggests that this wider use was already established or at least in process of being so. It has been associated with a 'Covenanters Thorn', but mistakenly, since that particular tradition belongs to the haugh on the other side of the river and above Bell's Mills.

HAWTHORN BANK (Queensferry) appears to have originated as a loan between the backs of the tofts or burgage plots of the High Street and the Stonycroft further up the slope. Thus although it is first shown on *Queensferry* 1832, it is probably very much older. Its name, recorded on *Ordnance Survey* 1895, may have derived from the small trees shown along its south side on *Ordnance Survey* 1854.

HAWTHORNBANK PLACE and **TERRACE** (North Leith) were developed in 1864 and 1866 in a property shown as *Eliza Field* on *Pollock* 1834. If there was a 'hawthorn bank' it must have been very small, and the name may well be fancy.

HAWTHORNDEN PLACE (Pilrig) was named in 1989 for Hawthornden on the Esk, near Dryden and Roslin, both previously celebrated in the names of nearby DRYDEN STREET and ROSSLYN CRESCENT (Pilrig) *which see*.

HAWTHORNE PLACE (Gilmerton) is on the line of a loan shown on *Ordnance Survey* 1852 as running from Main Street to the Moredun Dykes; and by 1893 it had been widened to form a double path, with a grass plot in between. The date of the name is uncertain. It probably began as a house name; and the spelling *Hawthorne* suggests that it was not named for the tree but for someone with that Galloway surname.

HAWTHORNVALE (Newhaven) is part of the old road from Ankerfield to Trinity Mains, shown on *Fergus & Robinson* 1759 and recorded as the then regular route for carts and coaches to and from Newhaven, since the section of the Whiting Road at the Whale Brae could not be negotiated by wheeled traffic. The street name, dating from 1867, derives from that of the combined farm *Claypots and Hawthornvale* recorded in 1741 as worked by James Reid, burlaw bailie of Leith. A house or cottage *Hawthornville* is recorded in 1819 and shown in a corner of Claypotts on *Pollock* 1834. Scots clay pots, clay pits or else natural hollows with clay at the bottom, is frequent in place names; *hawthorn vale* is probably a much later romantic description.

HAY AVENUE, DRIVE, PLACE, ROAD and **TERRACE** (Niddrie) were named in 1932 for Councillor John Hay, then convener of the Housing Subcommittee of the Public Health Committee of the Town Council.

HAYFIELD (Bughtlin) was so named at the suggestion of the developers in 1975. Like nearby MEARNSIDE, it is a fancy name of an agricultural sort.

HAYMARKET is so named on *Knox* 1812, but there is no indication of a market on the earlier *Whitehouse and Adiefield* (*RHP 601*, undated but likely to be about 1788). The junction was earlier known as WHITEHOUSE TOLL, from the house and property which lay to the south of it, later the site of a railway goods yard. The toll bar was originally about what was to become the foot of Morrison Street, but by 1812 it had been transferred to the west end of Haymarket Terrace. Haymarket was also referred to as HAYWEIGHTS until the 1880s. The market and weighing machine, originally on the west of the junction, was later moved to the south of it, apparently when the railway station was built in 1840. HAYMARKET TERRACE, always part of the ancient Linlithgow road, got its particular name when it was developed for housing in the 1880s.

HAY'S CLOSE (once 93 now about 59 Grassmarket) *see* PRINGLE'S CLOSE, Grassmarket.

(HENRY) HAY'S CLOSE (South Leith) is shown on *Naish* 1709 and listed on *Wood* 1777. It was named for Henry Hay, treasurer of South Leith kirk in 1672.

HAY'S COURT (West Port) figures on *Ainslie* 1780 and is named on *Ordnance Survey* 1852. It was named for John Hay, brewer, who feued the ground in 1753.

HAY STREET (Nicolson Square, South Side) is shown on *Kincaid* 1784. The ground was feued in 1782 by Luke Fraser of Glenmaid and his wife Elizabeth, and the street was built by her father Alexander Hay.

HAZELBANK TERRACE (North Merchiston) *see under* SHAFTESBURY PARK, North Merchiston.

HAZELDEAN TERRACE (Inch) *see under* THE INCH, Nether Liberton.

HAZELSIDE or **HEASLESIDE** (Riccarton) was a 32-acre farm, shown on *Riccarton* 1772, but noted on *Riccarton* 1800 as 'now part of Malcolmston'. The name is literal, hazel slope.

HAZELWOOD GROVE (Inch) *see under* THE INCH, Nether Liberton.

HEADRIGG ROW (Inch) *see under* THE INCH, Nether Liberton.

HEELY HILL (Newbridge) *see* HULY HILL, Newbridge.

HELEN'S WALK (North Leith) is a footpath formed in 1979 and named for HELEN STREET (first recorded as ELLEN STREET in *PO Directory* 1830, and presumably named for a relative of its builder) then suppressed by redevelopment, together with HELEN PLACE—for which *see under* CANNON STREET (North Leith).

HENDERLAND ROAD (Murrayfield) *see under* MURRAYFIELD.

HENDERSON ROW (Canonmills) was developed from an early road, shown on *Roy* 1753, which ran from Stockbridge by Silvermills to Canonmills, *see also* HAMILTON PLACE *and* EYRE PLACE. Development had begun at its western end by about 1824 under the name *Claremont Place* (*see under* SAXE-COBURG PLACE) but also started at its eastern end in 1825, under the name *Henderson's Row*, in compliment to Alexander Henderson of Press, Lord Provost 1823-25, later the first president of the National Bank of Scotland. The name HENDERSON ROW was extended to include Claremont Place by about 1890, and was borrowed for the branch street HENDERSON PLACE in 1901.

HENDERSON'S or **HENRYSON'S CLOSE** (341 High Street) *see* ROXBURGH'S CLOSE.

HENDERSON'S CLOSE (High Street) *see under* WARDROP'S COURT.

HENDERSON & PATERSON'S COURT (High Street) *see under* PATERSON'S COURT.

HENDERSON'S STAIRS (108 Cowgate) *see* THE BACK STAIRS, Cowgate.

HENDERSON STREET (South Leith) was the main element of the Improvement Scheme of 1880 initiated by Dr John Henderson, Provost of Leith from 1875 to 1884. Contruction began in 1881, and the name first appeared in *PO Directory* 1885. For the most part the street cut across the historic sett of closes and wynds between Great Junction Street and Tolbooth Wynd, but HENDERSON GARDENS was in effect a widening of LAURIE'S CLOSE.

HENDERSON TERRACE (Dalry) is shown on *Adair/Cooper* 1735 as part of the Calder road, which until about 1847 (when the roads in this vicinity were altered to suit the Caledonian Railway) branched off a section of the old Lanark road, now represented by Dundee Terrace. It is likely that the name *Henderson Terrace*, appearing in 1875, began as a side name for the terrace of houses then being built on the south side of the old highway, and that it derived from some connection of the builder's, or from the builder himself.

HENRY ROSS PLACE (Queensferry) was built in about 1970 upon part of the SKAITH MUIR of Plewlandfield once owned by the Distillers Company. The Company were then major employers in the burgh, and the street appears to have been named for their president, Sir Henry James Ross.

HENRY'S CLOSE (South side of Cowgatehead) is listed on *Ainslie* 1780 and mentioned, along with a reference to a late Thomas Hendry, in *Town Council Minutes* 1836, but otherwise the name remains obscure.

HENRY STREET (Parkside) was developed along with Parkside Street in about 1825. Although given as *Hendry Street* in the *PO Directories* until 1833, the spelling *Henry* is used on *Lothian's Edinburgh* 1829.

HENRY PLACE appears in the *PO Directory* 1833 and on *Pollock* 1834. The reason for the choice of name has yet to be traced.

HERCULES STREET (St Leonards) was a section of the medieval *St Leonard's road* (*see under* DUMMIEDYKES) named as an independent street by 1820, evidently for the Hercules Insurance Company, who applied in 1819 for main-water supply to houses they were building. The local pronunciation of the name appears in variant spellings such as *Ercles Street*. The street was one of nine renamed as part of *Dumbiedykes Road* in 1885.

HERIOT (WARK) BRIDGE (Grassmarket) is shown on *Rothiemay* 1647 as the main entrance to Heriot's Hospital, although this map does not show its considerable projection into the Grassmarket (shown on *Edgar* 1742) which being partly carried on arches with a throughgang under, gave it the name of *bridge*. Its site may be that noted in the *Valuation roll* 1635 as a close and yard running back to the Flodden Wall, with a smiddy occupied by John Ormston, smith and *extentor* (i.e. assessor); but it may have been part of the land and garden, once belonging to a William Adamson, which was granted to the Heriot Trust for the use of the Hospital in 1629, the year after its foundation stone was laid. *Wark* was a general term for a large building like the hospital. HERIOT CROSS was redeveloped in 1923 and named for its cruciform plan.

HERIOT HILL (Canonmills) is named on *Ainslie* 1804, the House having been built in 1788, but the property is shown as 'James Hunter's Few' on *Fergus & Robinson* 1759. The name evidently derived from the ownership of Broughton from 1636 onwards by the Heriot Trust, who exercised the rights and duties of the baron of Broughton in the manor of Canonmills until such jurisdictions were abolished in 1747. HERIOTHILL TERRACE was named (at first as *Heriot Terrace*) in about 1862.

HERIOT MOUNT (St Leonards) was formed in about 1824 in a property shown as *St Leonard's* on *Ainslie* 1804 and as *Mr Ritchie's* on *Kirkwood* 1817 and 1823. The name was probably in compliment to the Heriot Trust as superiors of St Leonards—cf. the naming of BOWMONT PLACE for an earlier superior, about the same time.

HERIOT PLACE (Lauriston) *see under* THE VENNEL, West Port.

HERIOT ROW (New Town) *see under* NORTHERN NEW TOWN.

HERIOT'S CLOSE (High Street) *see* STEWART'S CLOSE.

HERIOT'S CLOSE (High Street) *see* BROWN'S CLOSE.

HERMAND TERRACE (Gorgie) was begun by 1890 and HERMAND CRESCENT and STREET were laid out by 1896. The name is said to be from Hermand Quarry, West Calder, which supplied the stone for at least the initial building.

HERMISTON is recorded from about 1214 onwards; and the early forms of the name, *Hyrdmanestoun* and *Hirdmanstoun*, show that it was the *tún* or farm place of a *hiredman* (literally a 'household man') a yeoman or freeholder of some substance and one of those assisting in the administration of the shire. LONG HERMISTON, an estate name, but implying that a *lang row* or village had been established, is recorded as early as 1320. Hermiston is shown on *Blaeu* 1654, and Long Hermiston is shown in some detail on *Roy* 1753 and on *RHP 547*, a plan of Hermiston in 1793. The farm of EAST HERMISTON is given as *Hermiston* on *Knox* 1812, but *Ordnance Survey* 1852 shows it as *East Hermiston*, together with MID HERMISTON; and the 1893 edition adds WEST HERMISTON. The alteration of the Calder road to bypass the village was completed in 1987.

HERMITAGE DRIVE, GARDENS and **TERRACE** (South Morningside) *see under* EGYPT, South Morningside.

HERMITAGE OF BRAID *see under* BRAID.

HERMITAGE PARK (South Leith) was a property shown on *Ainslie* 1804 as owned by a Mr Geddes, named on *Kirkwood* 1817 as *Hermitage Cottage* and on *Ordnance Survey* 1852 as *Hermitage Park*. The name evidently derived from Hermitage House, *see under* HERMITAGE PLACE, South Leith. Development began in about 1909, and the street giving access to the school was named HERMITAGE PARK. HERMITAGE PARK GROVE was developed in 1982 on the adjoining property known as *Upper Hermitage*, but the street name was invented to suit the local community association.

HERMITAGE PLACE (South Leith) was the first development of terraced housing beside the ancient road skirting the Links on the way to Figgate and Musselburgh. Dating from 1813, it took its name from its site within the grounds of HERMITAGE HOUSE, itself dating from perhaps 60 or 70 years earlier (it is named on *Cooper* 1759 and was advertised to let in 1761) and given a fanciful name, fashionable at the time—as for example at HERMITAGE of BRAID. EAST HERMITAGE PLACE and HERMITAGE TERRACE (later renamed ROSEVALE TERRACE) were both part of the final scheme for development of the Hermitage grounds, *see under* INDUSTRIAL ROAD, South Leith.

HERMITAGE PLACE (Stockbridge) is named on *Kirkwood* 1817 and shown lying within Henry Raeburn's ground as figured on *Ainslie* 1804, but reached by a road across an adjoining property in Dean Street, displacing its house. The street, originally secluded by gates at either end, may have been named for this house; but in any case the name was fancy. In 1968 it was changed to RAEBURN STREET (after the adjoining RAEBURN PLACE, *which see*) to obviate confusion with Hermitage Place, South Leith.

HERMITAGE TERRACE (South Leith) *see* ROSEVALE TERRACE *under* INDUSTRIAL ROAD, South Leith.

HERMITS AND TERMITS (St Leonard's) is the rhymed-slang name, recorded in 1649, for the pair of crofts attached to the Hospital or almshouse at St LEONARD'S, South Side (*which see*) which as mentioned in *RMS* 1493 were already 'commonly called' *the Hermitis croft and the Terraris croft*. Together they made up an area, roughly pentagonal in shape and extending to 5½ Scots acres, which later became the feus of St Leonard's Bank and the site of St Leonard's Station, terminus of the INNOCENT RAILWAY, *which see*. The names probably went back in Latin and Scots to the foundation of the almshouse in the 12th century, since the Hermits croft was so named because it was for the support of the six *hermits* or *bedemen* of the Hospital, pensioners required to say *bedes* or prayers daily for the souls of its founders and patrons, while the Hospital's *terrar* or manager had the Terrar's croft for his own keep. By 1578 the two were sometimes lumped together as the *Beidmannis croft*, although still divided into 'northmost' and 'southmost yards' within it; but the medieval names also persisted in several disguises, and *Scott* 1759 shows the ground as *St Hermans*. HERMITS CROFT and TERRAR'S CROFT were named in 1995, as new streets within the two crofts.

HERON'S CLOSE or **COURT** (134 Cowgate) is shown but not named on *Edgar* 1742, and is listed in *PO Directory* 1827. It was named for Patrick Heron of Heron, former proprietor of the Black Bull inn in Glasgow, who formed the *British Inn* here in 1787 by buying and converting a house which had been built in about 1741 by Alexander Lockhart, Lord Covington, sold in 1766 to Charles Campbell of Banbreck and thereafter purchased in 1784 by David Steuart Erskine, Earl of Buchan, for use by the newly-formed Society of Antiquaries as their meeting place and museum—hence the name *Antiquarian Society Hall* given on *Kincaid* 1784.

HERWIT STREET (Granton) *see under* GRANTON HARBOUR.

HIGHLEA CIRCLE etc (Balerno) *see under* COCKBURN CRESCENT, Balerno.

HIGH RIGGS (Tollcross and South Side) is recorded as *the Herygges* in 1387 and as *Hieriggis* from 1558 onwards. The name is early Scots *he rigges*, high or (more likely in this case) long strips of arable, and evidently described the medieval estate that lay on the ridge between Grassmarket and the South loch and stretched from the Linton road at Tollcross to the Liberton road at Bristo. By the 16th century this was being split up; and its name, subordinated to LAURISTON (*which see*) certainly by 1771 but probably long before, became confined to a relatively small area in the extreme west of the original lands. The modern street of HIGH RIGGS was the first section of the ancient Linton road, and as normally happened with such main routes, it gathered numerous side names long before it acquired any special name of its own. For the succession of names at its northern end, *see* TWOPENNY CUSTOM and MAIN POINT. The name COWFEEDER (i.e. dairymen) ROW, referring to a number of dairies beside the road, appears on *Ainslie* 1804, is still shown towards the north end of the street on *Ordnance Survey* 1852, and was not suppressed until 1885. More generally, properties were addressed as in the estates of High Riggs or Tollcross, depending on whether they were east or west of the road, but by about 1830 HIGH RIGGS began to prevail as the street name, and it figures as such on *Pollock* 1834.

HIGH SCHOOL CLOSE (307 Canongate) got its name as an access to the High School of the Canongate. Built on the east side of the close, on a site now in the middle of Lower Market Street, the school is described in Wilson as a large mansion bearing the date *1704* on a sundial in its central pediment. It is shown on *Edgar* 1742 and on maps up until the 1830s. In the Middle Ages, Holyrood Abbey ran both the burgh school of Canongate and the grammar school of Edinburgh, and a charter of 1524 (quoted in *RMS* 1530) concerns the transfer of staff from one to the other. The close was also known as the WEST COMMON CLOSE, being the westermost of the three common (viz. public) closes leading to the school. It also seems to have been BALLANTYNE'S, mentioned in 1805 and evidently named for the Henry Bellenden (or earlier members of his family) noted in 1711 as having more than one property in it.

HIGH SCHOOL WYND and **YARDS** (Old Town) got their names from the town's High School which, although founded considerably earlier, seems to have occupied rented premises until 1578, when it moved into a building newly erected for the purpose in the former kirk yard of the BLACKFRIARS (*which see*) laid waste in 1559. HIGH SCHOOL WYND, so named on *Rothiemay* 1647, originated in 1230 as the *transe* or access way granted to the Blackfriars along with the land for their priory; and the priory gate is now represented by the entry to HIGH SCHOOL YARDS—a plural name which may reflect the fact that the priory grounds were divided into a number of enclosures. A new school building, replacing that of 1578, was built in 1777; vacated when the High School moved to Regent Road in 1829, it has since served successively as part of the Royal Infirmary, the City Hospital, and the University of Edinburgh.

THE HIGH STREET of Edinburgh probably originated as a track leading from the east through the future site of Holyrood abbey and up by the crest of the ridge to the British fortress of Din Eidyn. Adopted as the spine of the 12th-century merchant burgh, it was set out wide enough to accommodate the markets which were the reason for the burgh's existence (a width eventually reduced by ten or twenty feet by encroachments of the frontages, especially in the 16th and 17th centuries) and it was therefore referred to as *vicus foralis*, market street; but it was also a thoroughfare, *vicus regis*, king's street, a *hie street* or *gate*—names which it shared with other thoroughfares in the town, although the term *magnus vicus*, great street, used in 1504, seems to have belonged to the main street alone, and by 1600, *High Street* had become its exclusive name. Although always recognised as a single whole, it embraced several subdivisions, as shown on *Ainslie* 1780—*see under* LAWNMARKET, LUCKENBOOTHS, THE CROSS, THE TRON, THE NETHERBOW. In charters, the term 'king's street/way' was apt to be used of any public route in town or country, whether a -gate or -way (from Old Norse *gata* or Anglian *weg*, a way or track) or a wynd (a side turning, from Old Norse *venda*, to turn off) or a vennel (from Old French *venelle*, a lane) or a loan or loaning (from

Anglian *lone*, a way bordered by grazings)—but it was not used of a close (from Old French *clos*) because this originally meant a private yard, and got the second meaning of a throughgang common to several owners only after the yard became subdivided between two or more of them.

HIGH STREET (Kirkliston) is part of the ancient road from Edinburgh to Linlithgow, shown on *Blaeu* 1654; and it was the centre of the village until the diversion of the highroad created a new MAIN STREET, *which see*.

HIGH STREET (Queensferry) was certainly the street of the medieval burgh of regality of QUEENSFERRY (*which see*) complete with mercat cross and tolbooth; but in all probability it originated much earlier, as a track along the foreshore linking the landing places on this side of the strait (used variously, depending upon the state of tide and weather) with a way to the south and east by the HAWES, *which see*. The distinctive feature of the TERRACES bears witness to the abruptness of the slope behind the shore. These pavements are public; but in the case of the EAST TERRACE the ground and vaults beneath it were part of the burgage plots, and it may be that the earliest development of houses combined with workplaces was at the street frontage.

HIGH TERRACE (East End) was a high-level terrace above the north side of Leith Street, based upon a design by Robert Adam 1786, shown on *Brown & Watson* 1793, and swept away for St James' Centre in 1965.

HILLCOAT LOAN and **PLACE** (Portobello) *see under* WESTBANK, Portobello.

HILL COURT (Queensferry) was built in 1964, on a site which seems to have included the HILL SQUARE listed in *PO Directory* 1924. The name may have been for David Hill, provost of the burgh 1871-73; or else for Bailie John Hill, who bought waste land at the west end of the town and south of the High Street in 1713. The surname had a long connection with the burgh, for a Robert Hill was bailie in about 1660.

HILLEND (Lothianburn) is shown on *Blaeu* 1654 and recorded from 1526 onwards as the descriptive name of the farm on the most easterly slope of the north range of the Pentland hills. It is immediately outside the bounds of the city.

HILLEND PLACE (Parsons Green) was named by 1885, presumably for its position near the foot of the Whinny Hill.

HILLHOUSEFIELD (North Leith) was an estate recorded from 1484 onwards and lying between the Water of Leith and the sea, bounded on the west by Bonnington and the Ankerfield burn, and on the east by the templelands of North Leith. The name would imply that the original manor house stood on higher ground, and since there is some indication that the sale of part of the estate to provide the site for Leith Citadel in 1657 included the old house, it would seem that it stood on some knoll in that area rather than on the ridge at Leith Fort. The laird, Archibald Kincaid, used the proceeds of the sale to build a new HILLHOUSEFIELD HOUSE (shown on *Adair/Cooper* 1735 and *Ainslie* 1804) which over two centuries later was sold to David Bruce Peebles, who renamed it TAY HOUSE in 1876 and built his gas engineering works in its policies. In 1985 a street formed in the course of redeveloping the area of FORT PLACE and HAMILTON STREET at Bathfield in the north of the historic Hillhousefield was named NORTH HILLHOUSEFIELD.

HILLHOUSE ROAD (Blackhall and Davidson's Mains) is made up of two sections of widely different date and origin. The Blackhall section is part of the old Queensferry road which carried straight on by Corbiehill to Muttonhole, *see* CORBIEHILL ROAD, Davidson's Mains, *and also under* ROMAN ROADS; whereas Hillhouse Road west of the Telford Road junction is part of the new Queensferry turnpike, built in about 1824 on an entirely new line through Marchfield, Craighouse, and King's Cramond or New Barnton, to a new Cramond bridge. The street name dates from 1927 and was a play on the name of nearby House o Hill farm.

HILLPARK AVENUE, DRIVE and **ROAD** (Craigcrook) took their name in 1937 from the field in which they were built, and HILLPARK GARDENS and GROVE were added in 1938. HILLPARK TERRACE (1970) BRAE and VIEW (1975) and GREEN (1979) carried on development in the adjoining *Hill Parks* of Craigcrook, the field names being obviously derived from their position on the slopes below Corstorphine Hill; but HILLPARK CRESCENT (1965) WAY (1968) LOAN (1970) COURT and PLACE (1975) and WOOD (1979) extended the name as a neighbourhood name over ground in Marchfield.

HILL PLACE (South Side) was developed from 1808 onwards by Peter Hill, bookseller in the High Street. HILL SQUARE followed in about 1822.

HILLSIDE (Calton) developed out of HART(S)KNOWES, a farm of 6 Scots acres, noted in 1724 as part of the barony of Calton and listed as *Heartknowe* in the contemporary records of the burlaw court of Leith. The north spur of the Calton Hill, named on *Kirkwood* 1817 in the garbled form *Heriot's Know*, was within the farm; but although the latter might have been named for a *hart's knowe* or stag's hillock, it is much more likely that it was for an owner or owners called Hart, probably represented by the advocate Mr John Hart, recorded in *RMS* 1621 and 1624 as owning ground somewhere in the vicinity of Greenside or Upper Quarryholes. Referred to as *Grant's feu* in 1749, it was later purchased by Alexander Allan, partly in 1758 and wholly in 1785. Since tle name HILLSIDE is first recorded in 1780, Allan probably coined it, on the model of adjoining Greenside, for his house and grounds shown on *Ainslie* 1804; and it would seem likely that the naming of HILLSIDE CRESCENT (shown on *Calton* 1819 and beginning to be occupied in 1824) was not only a reference to the estate but an oblique compliment to Alexander Allan (or a son of the same name) as one of those involved in the development of the CALTON NEW TOWN, *which see*. The name also continued in use as a neighbourhood name; and the street originally proposed on *Calton* 1819 as 'Hopetoun Street' first enters *PO Directory* in 1869 as HILLSIDE STREET.

HILLSIDE ROAD, HILLSIDE TERRACE and **RIVERSIDE ROAD** (Craigiehall) were named by the Army for their position on higher or lower ground within the estate.

HILL STREET (New Town) *see under* NEW TOWN.

HILLVIEW (Blackhall) was named in the early 1900s, evidently for the view westwards to Corstorphine Hill. HILLVIEW TERRACE was named before 1905, and HILLVIEW ROAD in 1925, but both were renamed in 1967 to obviate confusion with streets of the same names in Corstorphine, becoming SEAFORTH DRIVE and FORTHVIEW DRIVE, by association with the existing and adjoining Seaforth Terrace and Forthview Terrace.

HILLVIEW COTTAGES (Ratho) began to be developed by the county in 1923-24, and were evidently named for the view to the south.

HILLVIEW TERRACE (Corstorphine) was begun at its eastern end in 1911 and was developed in the *East* and *North Bank* fields of Featherhall along with HILLVIEW DRIVE and ROAD (1924) and CRESCENT (1931). The name is for the prospect from this high ground, or for the view of the Pentland Hills.

HILLWOOD (Ratho) was a new descriptive name given in about 1840 to the estate of North Platt—*see under* PLATT, Ratho. Shortly afterwards, it was divided into two by the railway, but it was not until about 1910 that the steading of HILLWOOD MAINS was set up north of the railway, opposite Wester Norton. In 1955 HILLWOOD AVENUE, CRESCENT, GARDENS, RISE, ROAD and TERRACE were named for it, although built on Wester Norton ground, shown on *Norton* 1813 as the Bank and Burianridge parks—*see also* BURIANRIDGE, Norton.

HILLWOOD PLACE (Queensferry) was named in 1910 for the local *Hillwood Co-operative Society* (named for Hillwood, Ratho) who had premises here.

WILLIAM HILTRAY'S CLOSE (Canongate) is mentioned in *Buik of the Canongate* 1546. Its whereabouts have still to be discovered.

HODGE'S CLOSE (Old Town) was a little close and court near the foot of the east side of Blackfriars Wynd, shown (unnamed) on *Edgar* 1742. It was named for James Hodge, brewer, who owned *Hodge's land* here at some time prior to 1740.

HOGGIES or **HUGGIES HOLE** (Ratho) is shown on *Hatton etc* 1797 and *Ordnance Survey* 1852. It was a 30-acre farm in Hatton, but the name probably refers to the narrow howe west of the spur of Craw Hill and is perhaps more likely to be Scots *haggies howe*, boggy hollow, than to refer to hoggs, yearling sheep—*yet see also* MUTTONHOLE.

HOGISTOUN (Whitehouse) was the early name of WHITEHOUSE, *which see.*

313

THE HOLE MILL (Colinton) was the name attached to a long succession of mills which stood in what is now the northern part of Colinton kirkyard and were approached by what is now DELL ROAD, *which see*. As noted in *Steuart's Colinton*, there were mills here from before 1226 until the last of them was burned down in about 1880, and they successively served Hailes, Easter Hailes and Wester Hailes. They were named as being in the *howe* or hollow, or on the *holm* or meadow beside the river.

HOLLYBANK TERRACE (North Merchiston) *see under* SHAFTESBURY PARK, North Merchiston.

THE HOLMS (Kirkliston) *see under* BOWLING GREEN ROAD, Kirkliston.

HOLY CORNER (Boroughmuirhead, Morningside) got its name from the cluster of three churches (later to be increased to five) built round the crossroads by the mid 1870s. Morningside Road was already a route for the horse trams, and bearing in mind the nicknaming habits of tram and bus conductors in later generations, it is likely that the name was coined for a tram stop.

HOLYROODHOUSE is recorded in 1387 as *Halyrudehouse*, the Scots form of the name of the monastery of *Sancta Crucis*, founded by David I in 1128. The tale that David did this out of gratitude for a miraculous delivery from an aggressive stag first appears three centuries later, in the *Holyrood Ordinale* c1450, and is manifestly borrowed from the much older legends of 8th-century St Eustace and 2nd-century St Hubert. The place may have had some sanctity already as an ancient burying ground; and the foundation of this centre of missionary Augustinian canons was in line with David's policy of strengthening and regularizing the Kirk in Scotland. The more local of his gifts for the abbey's support in 1128 included lands stretching from North Leith and circling Edinburgh, as well as the existing kirks of the Castle and St Cuthbert's, together with the latter's outpost chapels and kirklands at Liberton and Corstorphine. The dedication of the abbey probably arose from a general enthusiasm for the veneration of the Holy Rood or Cross that swept across Europe about this time; but it may also have reflected David's devotion to the *Black Rood*, reputed to contain a fragment of the True Cross, which he had inherited through his brothers from his mother Queen Margaret, and which, although never linked with Holyrood, continued to belong to the kings of Scotland until it was captured by the English in 1346. The abbey guest house was no doubt used from the start as a royal residence: at first, occasionally, and then with increasing frequency, as the old practice of king and court moving from place to place round the realm gradually declined. James II, born in Holyroodhouse in 1430, added to it in 1449; but it was James IV who began to build a palace here in 1501, and by 1542 it had displaced Edinburgh Castle as principal royal residence. Shown in some detail on *Rothiemay* 1647, this building was partly incorporated in the present one in the 1670s. The abbey kirk continued as the parish kirk of the

Canongate until this function was transferred to the new Canongate Kirk in 1687.

HOLYROOD PARK *see under* THE QUEEN'S PARK.

HOLYROOD PARK ROAD (Parkside) is referred to in 1786 as 'a new road from the Gibbet toll bar to the King's Park', and *Knox* 1812 shows it leading to a powder magazine at the Hause at the south end of the Crags. It was linked up with the new scheme of roads within the Park approved in 1845. On *Ordnance Survey* 1852 it is mistakenly identified as *Gibbet Loan*, a name properly belonging to PRESTON STREET, *which see*; but it was named PARK ROAD in 1888, possibly because it led between what had been the two parks of Parkside, but more likely because it gave entry to the royal Park: and this interpretation was certainly followed when it was renamed HOLYROOD PARK ROAD in 1967, to obviate any confusion with Park Road in Newhaven.

HOLYROOD ROAD (Canongate) *see under* THE SOUTH BACK OF CANONGATE.

HOLYROOD TERRACE (Abbeyhill) *see under* IRNESIDE.

HOME'S or **HUME'S CLOSE** (284 Canongate) *see* STINKING CLOSE, Canongate.

HOME'S CLOSE (High Street) *see* THE ADVOCATE'S CLOSE.

HOME'S CLOSE (196 High Street) *see* OLD FISHMARKET CLOSE.

HOME STREET (Tollcross) appears on *Wood* 1823 as part of a projected development of the Drumdryan estate of the family of Home Rigg of Tarvit, and occupation had begun by 1826, although the roadway itself, as part of the highroad to Linton, was of course hundreds of years older. The junction between Home Street and Tollcross marks where the road crosses the Lochrin burn, by what was once known as the *Lochrin brig*.

HONEYMUG PARK (Corstorphine) figures on *Corstorphine* 1777 as the name of a field now occupied by TYLER'S ACRE AVENUE etc. Once part of the bed of the loch at CORSTORPHINE (*which see*) the field was finally drained in about 1750, and the name may contain British *mig*, bog or meadow (see also MEGGETLAND) while in field names *honey* seems generally to mean 'wet' or 'sticky'.

HOPE CRESCENT (Broughton) was formed by 1827 as part of the redevelopment which followed the removal of the Botanic Garden from here to Inverleith. It was named for the founder of the Garden, Dr John Hope (1725-86) professor of botany and materia medica at Edinburgh University. Unfortunately this reference was virtually lost in 1966, when the street was renamed HOPETOUN CRESCENT (in imitation of nearby HOPETOUN STREET, *which see*) in order to obviate any difficulty which might arise from its distance from other streets of the *Hope-* name elsewhere in the city. Only a remote connection remains, inasmuch as Dr Hope descended through Hope of Rankeillor from Sir John Hope 2nd bt. of Craighall, while the Hopes of Hopetoun descended from one of Sir John's younger brothers.

315

HOPEFIELD TERRACE (North Leith) *see under* HOPE STREET, North Leith.

HOPE LANE (Portobello and Easter Duddingston) is shown on *Wood's Portobello* 1824. Lying on Abercorn land but closely skirting the Figgate boundary at its northern end, it had been built not long before 1824, on the initiative of Guthrie Wright, Abercorn's factor, as a connection between Duddingston and the developing Portobello, a half mile shorter than the earlier way round by the Brunstane road. It also led past the new steading of Duddingston Mains, then farmed by a Mr Hope.

HOPE PARK (South Side) is recorded on *Cooper* 1761 and was the name given by the Town Council to the area of the SOUTH LOCH (*which see*) after they had leased it to Thomas Hope of Rankeillor in 1722, for the express purpose of having it drained and laid out as meadows with walks and avenues of lime trees. As chairman of the new Society of Improvers in the Knowledge of Agriculture in Scotland, Hope was concerned to demonstrate the means and outcome of reclamation. His scheme is shown on *Roy* 1753 and *Scott* 1759, and the perimeter walks and the great *Middle Meadow Walk* still survive. These maps also show Hope's house, which dates from about 1725 but incorporated an older one and was itself modified in 1851 to form the nucleus of HOPE PARK SQUARE. If by about the 1830s the name *Hope Park* had finally failed to displace the 17th-century name of *The Meadows*, it was probably because HOPE PARK was being more widely used as the neighbourhood name round the fringe of the Meadows, especially on the south side, where *Roy* 1753 shows a string of large properties already developed in the strip of the Burgh Muir on the north side of Sciennes Road; and the *Hope Park* walk named on *Bartholomew* 1876 shows that this usage still lingered a full decade after these properties had been redeveloped as housing streets. As shown on *Kirkwood* 1817, a section of Causeyside was known as HOPE PARK END. In about 1861 it was renamed HOPE PARK CRESCENT; and HOPE PARK TERRACE was opened and named by 1863.

HOPE'S CLOSE (286 High Street) *see* OLD BANK CLOSE.

EDWARD HOPE'S CLOSE (587 High Street) *see* TOD'S CLOSE.

HOPE'S COURT (47 High Street) is HOPE'S CLOSE on *Ainslie* 1780 and was named for the Hope family, whose property in the close was finally sold by Archibald Hope to John Maule, Baron of Exchequer (*see* PANMURE'S CLOSE, 19 High Street) in about 1766.

HOPE STREET (Corstorphine) *see under* MANSE STREET, Corstorphine.

HOPE STREET (New Town) was named in 1803 in response to a complaint by a resident, Mrs Maxwell of Carriden, that she found it inconvenient to live in a street lacking a name. The name was probably chosen in compliment to Charles Hope of Granton, then Lord Advocate and recently elected MP for Edinburgh. In 1966, in order to obviate any confusion with this street, no fewer than three other *Hope Streets* in the city were renamed—*see under* CASSELLBANK STREET (South Leith) MANSE STREET (Corstorphine) *and* ROSEFIELD STREET (Portobello).

HOPE STREET (Queensferry) is built in part of the BLACK LAWS (*which see*) in Plewlands and was named by 1970 for the Hopes of Hopetoun, owners of Plewlands.

HOPE TERRACE (Whitehouse) *see under* WHITEHOUSE.

HOPETOUN ROAD (Queensferry) derives both its name and its form from the fact that it became a bypass to the old route to Hopetoun by the SHORE ROAD (*which see*) when this was affected by the development of the railway at Port Edgar in the 1860s. Its western section is part of a new road built parallel to the railway line (*see also* LOCH ROAD *and* STEWART TERRACE) and providing Hopetoun with a direct access from the Kirkliston road as well as a connection to the High Street via the first section of the old Linlithgow road. It was this latter connection that generated the name, as the route *from the burgh to Hopetoun*; and it also accounts for the unusual arrangement of a street name turning the corner at a crossroads. The name *Hopetoun* was imported by the Hope family in the 17th century, from their earlier seat in Lanarkshire.

HOPETOUN STREET (Broughton) was formed in about 1925, but had been named in 1916 on the Hope Trust's plan for building up their ground in this vicinity; and in view of the fact that the existing streets HOPE CRESCENT and ANNANDALE STREET already commemorated a Hope of Rankeillor and the Hope Johnstones of Annandale respectively, it would seem that the new street was named for the Hopes of Hopetoun, as another branch of the family begun by Thomas Hope of Craighall in the time of Charles I. If so, the scheme was spoiled in 1966 when HOPE CRESCENT (*which see*) was renamed HOPETOUN CRESCENT.

HORNE TERRACE (Merchiston) was begun in 1868, and McNEIL STREET and THISTLE PLACE branched off it in 1869 and 1871, but no convincing explanation of the choice of the three names has been offered.

HORSBURGH BANK etc (Balerno) *see under* DALMAHOY CRESCENT, Balerno.

HORSE WYND (Bristo) is mentioned in charters of Wester Bristo 1598-1655, quoted in *Old Edinburgh Club XXII*; it is shown on *Rothiemay* 1647 as Horse Market Street; and its position immediately south of the Flodden Wall between the Bristo and Potterrow ports accounts for its later name of *Back Wall Vennel*; but its earliest appearance is on *Kirk o Field* 1567, where its east end is shown and labelled *ye caichpill gait*, way to the cachepell, implying that *real tennis* was being played here in 1567; and it was still on the go eighty years later, for the charter of the Portsburgh in *RMS* 1649 mentions tennis courts in the Horse Wynd of Bristo, outwith the Society or Bristo port. There is nothing to suggest a connection with the HORSE

WYND, Cowgate: the wynds run at right angles to one another, the Bristo one was then outwith Edinburgh and in the barony of Inverleith, and *Rothiemay* gives the two names quite separately. His evidence is that the Bristo wynd got its name from a horse market in Wester Bristo. Part of the street still exists, misleadingly called BRISTO PORT, *see under* BRISTO.

HORSE WYND (Canongate) is represented on the oldest maps of the town, such as the *Siege of Edinburgh Castle* 1573, although the earliest record of the name appears to be in 1705. The name itself seems to be the only evidence to support the suggestion that the palace stables were entered from it. A simpler and more direct suggestion, clearly supported by the fact that it was a *wynd* or public passage, and by the way it is shown on *Rothiemay* 1647 and *Edgar* 1742, is that it was the normal route for riding into the Canongate from the south, by St Leonard's vennel (the Pleasance) and the South Back (Holyrood Road); for it has to be remembered that St Mary Wynd was part of Edinburgh, often barred by St Mary Wynd Port, and certainly not always friendly ground for travellers to and from the Court at Holyrood, nor perhaps for the folk of the Canongate before that burgh was purchased by Edinburgh in 1636.

THE HORSE WYND (179 Cowgate) is named on *Rothiemay* 1647, and as shown on *City Improvements* 1866, is now represented by the lower part of Guthrie Street, the west side of the steps up to Chambers street, and West College Street. Along with the Potterrow and Borthwick's Close it formed one of the oldest approaches to the burgh, and its name reflects the fact that it was one of the few routes for horse traffic. The suggestion in *Wilson* that name was from an inn is ruled out by *Rothiemay*'s Latin translation *Vicus Equorum*. It led through the Kirk o Field or POTTERROW PORT (*which see*) in the Flodden Wall, but the break in the wynd's alignment further north, in the vicinity of Chambers Street, which was evident until West College Street was widened on its western side in the late 1860s, perhaps indicated that there had once been a burgh gateway here, on the march between the burgh tofts south of the Cowgate and the lands of the Kirk o Field.

HORSE WYND (South Leith) is shown on *Naish* 1709 and named on *Wood* 1777, but was reduced to open ground in the redevelopment at Cables Wynd in 1963. The name may have derived from stabling, or a horse market.

HOSEASON GARDENS (Clermiston) *see under* CLERMISTON MAINS.

HOSIE RIGG (Niddrie) *see under* THE JEWEL, Niddrie.

THE HOUND (Dalmeny) is mentioned as *lie Hund* in *RMS* 1539, in a charter anent fishing rights; it is named on *Blaeu* 1654, and *Barnbougle & Dalmeny* c1800 shows it as the large offshore rock which has obviously given its name to HOUND POINT. From Anglian *hund* or Old Norse *hundr*, a dog, it is one of those animal names that seamen give to rocks, not always for any fancied resemblance but as labels for navigational purposes. As the rock on the corner where tides race in and out of the strait, the Hound was a danger to small coasting vessels, and the legend of a black hound bringing a Mowbray of Barnbougle to an untimely end may have been a folk memory of some fatal wreck on it.

HOUSE O HILL (Davidson's Mains) is shown on *Knox* 1812 and evidently got its name because the steading (in what is now House o Hill Brae) was prominent on the CORBIEHILL, *which see*. HOUSE O HILL TERRACE dates from the mid 1890s. HOUSE O HILL AVENUE, CRESCENT, GARDENS, GROVE, ROAD and ROW were named in 1926 and followed by HOUSE O HILL GREEN (1932) PLACE (1933) and BRAE (1937)—the last representing the old road to the farm.

HOWARD PLACE (West Warriston) is named on *Kirkwood* 1817, but HOWARD STREET, although part of the same highway, seems to have been named much later, making its appearance on *Ordnance Survey* 1852. The name perhaps celebrates the connection of the marquis of Huntly with the old line of the Howards, dukes of Norfolk, *see under* BRANDON STREET, Canonmills.

HOWDEN BURN (Dreghorn) is 'the burn of the howe den', the latter name being Scots from Anglian *holh den(u)*, narrow valley in or at the hollow. The burn runs in a deep cut where it issues from the howe between Capelaw and Allermuir.

HOWDENHALL (Kaims, Liberton) is given as *Howden's-hall* on *Laurie* 1763 and in *Kincaid's Gazetteer* 1787, and on the face of it this would suggest it was the *hall* of someone called *Howden*; but apart from the absence of any record of such a hall, the spellings *Houden's hal* in *White's Liberton* 1786 and *Howden Saw* on *Knox* 1812 are less confident in meaning, and since the name occurs just where the Stenhouse burn runs through a narrow dell, it is more likely that the *hall* is Scots *haw* or *haugh*, and that the name is Scots from Anglian *holh den(u) halh*, the *haugh* or land in the nook or bend of the burn at the *den* or narrow valley in the *howe* which opens out immediately below it. Until it was named separately in 1927, HOWDENHALL ROAD was part of PENICUIK ROAD. For HOWDENHALL COURT etc *see under* ALNWICKHILL, Liberton.

HOWDEN STREET (South Side) was formed in about 1876 by clearance of a close called CROOKED DYKES, shown on *Ordnance Survey* 1852 as considerably elaborated from a close shown on *Ainslie* 1780. This clearance was as proposed on *Edinburgh Improvements* 1866 and the street was named for Bailie Peter Howden, councillor for St Stephen's Ward 1865-76 and active in the City Improvement scheme.

HOWE DENE (Braid) is shown on *Braid* 1772 as the *Den*, the valley of a burn running down to the *Water of Braid* from a pair of small lochs in the east end of the Braid hills, and serving as the march between Liberton and Over Braid. The name, also to be found at the HOWDEN BURN and HOWDENHALL (*which see*) is Scots from Anglian *holh den(u)*, the dene or narrow valley at or in the hollow; and indeed, although it is small, this deep-cut ravine is the most prominent feature on the south side of the great howe of the Braid burn. The public footpath and bridge over the Braid burn, like those further west, were designed to link the two public recreation areas of Blackford and Braid hills, and were formed on ground expressly included for this purpose in the purchase of the Braid hills from Braid estate in 1890.

HOWE PARK (New Swanston) *see under* SOURHOWE *and* SWANSTON.

HOWE STREET (New Town) *see under* NORTHERN NEW TOWN.

HUGH RUSSELL PLACE (Queensferry) is built on the SKAITH MUIR (*which see*) in Plewlands, and was named in 1964 for Hugh Russell, builder, who became Provost of Queensferry in 1842, and for his grandson of the same name, who left a bequest in 1962 for the improvement of the burgh.

HULY or **HEELY HILL** (Newbridge) is a large prehistoric cairn and stone circle, and the name clearly derives from this, being Anglian *hulu* or *helan*, covering, or more specifically Old Norse *haéli*, shelter or house of the dead, with Anglian *hyll*, hill. *See also* MOUNTHOOLY, Mortonhall and Newington.

HUMBIE (Kirkliston) is recorded from 1290, and the name also occurs in Kirknewton, East Lothian and Fife. The spelling *Hundeby* in 1290 shows it to be Old Norse *Hunda byr*, Hundi's farm. That it was given by Norse speakers is clear from the use of *byr*, and the distribution of this element in Scottish names suggests that the settlers must have come from the area of the Irish Sea, in the late 9th or early 10th century. HUMBIE ROAD is in Newmains, but was named in about 1974 for the view towards Humbie.

HUME'S CLOSE (284 Canongate) *see* STINKING CLOSE, Canongate.

HUME'S CLOSE (101 Cowgate) is listed thus on *Ainslie* 1780 and was named either for David Home, litster, who acquired a tenement and dyer's yard here at some date prior to 1736, or else it was for Peter Home, who with his wife Agnes Rae built a land called *Cairthall* in the close (*see below*) some time before 1709. The close was also known as DYER'S, from David Home or his successors in the trade; and its other name CROMBIE'S was from an Andrew Crombie, silk dyer. It is listed on *Edgar* 1742 as CRAIG'S, but nothing is known about its derivation. Finally, the close is referred to in 1761 as CART'S, which seems to refer to the Cairthall mentioned above. Since Peter Home and his wife built another Cairthall on the south side of the Grassmarket, it is possible that they were in trade as carriers and that the close name was a plural CAIRTS.

HUMPH CLOSE (196 High Street and 144 Cowgate) *see* OLD FISHMARKET CLOSE.

HUNDEGRENELAND (Cramond) is mentioned in *Bain* 1337 as a *carucate* or plewland of about 104 Scots acres in Cramond, perhaps near Lauriston, but the name seems to be lost.

HUNTERS BOG (Arthur's Seat) is named on *Kirkwood* 1817. While it has been generally supposed (from the 19th century onwards) that the name is connected with hunting, there is no record of it—even although, as reported in *Arnot* 1779, a Company of Hunters was founded in Edinburgh in 1758; and it is more likely that it contains the surname *Hunter*, found frequently in Edinburgh from the 15th century onwards. A Thomas Hunter had a house within the girth or sanctuary of Holyrood in 1569.

HUNTER'S CLOSE (once 131 now 79 Grassmarket) is listed on *Ainslie* 1780 and was named for an Alexander Hunter, physician in York, who owned land here. It is noted in *Chambers* 1825 as being also CAMPBELL'S, a name probably derived from John Campbell, stabler in the south side of Grassmarket in 1773. As shown on *Ordnance Survey* 1852, the original entrance to the close, where the unfortunate Captain Porteous was hanged on a dyer's pole in 1736, was at what would now be between 83 and 85 Grassmarket, the present entrance at No. 79 being originally the entry of the next close westwards, EAST SMITH'S CLOSE, unnamed on *Ainslie* 1780.

HUNTER'S CLOSE (300 High Street) *see* BUCHANAN'S COURT.

HUNTER'S CRAIG or **EAGLE ROCK** (Dalmeny) *see under* KINGBOWIE, Dalmeny.

HUNTER'S HAW (Niddrie) appears on *Duddingston* c1800 as *Hunter's Ha'* and *Collins Houses*, shown as a cluster of cottages or perhaps a steading in a position which works out as about NT 31087195. The drawing was evidently added to the map when the Edinburgh & Dalkeith Railway (*see* INNOCENT RAILWAY) was being proposed, in about 1826. The place is shown on *Kirkwood's Environs* 1817, *Gellatly* 1834 and *Fowler* 1845 as *Huntershall* or *Hunters Hall*, but it had vanished by the time of *Ordnance Survey* 1852. The name is Scots *haw* or haugh, and may well have applied to the whole or some part of the east neuk of Niddrie that marched with Duddingston, Brunstane, Whitehill and Cauldcoats. *Hunter* is probably a tenant's name, and it is possible that the ground was attached to HUNTER'S MILL at Niddrie Mill, which according to *Good's Liberton* was occupied by millers and bakers of that name for almost 500 years before the family died out in the mid 19th century. HUNTER'S HALL PARK, originally the east park of Niddrie House policies, seems to have been named in ignorance of the location of the haw half a mile away. *See also* THE JEWEL *and* KINNAIRD PARK.

HUNTER SQUARE (Old Town) *see under* BLAIR STREET, Old Town.

HUNTERS TRYST (Comiston) is shown on *Roy* 1753 as on the main Linton road just south of Fairmilehead, but *Knox* 1812 shows it in its present position, displacing the name SOURHOLE (*which see*) shown on *Roy* and on *Armstrongs* 1773. It is possible, but unlikely, that *Roy* shows it out of position through map error: considering that the main highway and the roads linking it to Colinton were extensively altered in the late 18th century (*see under* FAIRMILEHEAD *and* REDFORD) it is more likely that the hostelry at Sourhole, where the building dates from about 1800, revived a name which had once been used at the other site. Whether it meant a tryst for hunters, or one run by someone called Hunter is not known. In 1985 it was referred to in the name of TRYST PARK in New Swanston, *see under* SWANSTON.

HUNTLY STREET (Canonmills) *see under* BRANDON STREET, Canonmills.

HURLY BUTTS (Queensferry) appears on *Dundas* 1757 as the name of a field, immediately south of the Builyeon road and at about NT 121176. The *butts* would be the normal ploughing term for the shortening furrows in a field of angular shape, but *hurly* might conceivably be a variant of *haer law* (*see* SENTRY KNOWE (for Airley Cairn) EARL CAIRNY *and* HARLAW) and if so it would imply that there were once stone remains of some sort here at KETTLESLAW, *which see*.

HUTCHESON'S CLOSE (233 High Street) *see* GEDDES'S CLOSE.

HUTCHISON AVENUE, COTTAGES, CROSSWAY, GARDENS, GROVE, MEDWAY, PLACE, ROAD and **TERRACE** (West Gorgie) were planned in fields of Gorgie farm in 1921, the scheme taking in a fragment of ROBB'S LOAN (*which see*) as HUTCHISON LOAN; and the streets were named in 1922 for Sir Thomas Hutchison, then Lord Provost. HUTCHISON VIEW was added in 1937, and HUTCHISON PARK in 1983.

HYNDFORD'S CLOSE (50 High Street) is shown on *Edgar* 1742. While James 2nd Earl of Hyndford certainly had property in it in 1710, the name might otherwise be from his father John Carmichael, Baron Carmichael, who was created earl of Hyndford in 1701. The close got its earlier name of COLLINGTOUN'S or COLINTON'S from the circumstance that a house in it, later to be Hyndford's or a part of it, was owned and lived in in 1635 by Andrew Ainslie, merchant, and thereafter came into the possession of the Foulis of Colinton through Ainslie's daughter Barbara, who married Sir James Foulis, 6th of Colinton, in 1644, and became the mother of their son James, seventh laird. Both sat in the Court of Session, the father as Lord Colinton from 1661 and his son as Lord Redford from 1674; but while the latter, who succeeded as laird of Colinton in 1688, certainly gave his name to SOUTH FOULIS'S CLOSE (*which see*) it is likely that *Colinton's Close* was named for the elder Sir James, made burgess in 1646 in right of his wife. Earlier still, the close was CHARTERIS', from an early owner recorded as John Charteris, burgess. This may have been the John Chartres listed as an owner in 1635; but since he was not a resident it is more likely that the name was from an earlier John Charteris, probably of the same family, who is mentioned in *RMS* 1538 and was a councillor in 1551 and dean of guild in 1559.

HYVOT'S BANK (Gilmerton) appears on *Ordnance Survey* 1852 as a farm name, evidently derived from the adjoining HYVOT'S MILL, shown thus on *Armstrongs* 1773 but as *Havit Mill* on *Laurie* 1763 and called *Haivock Mill* in *White's Liberton* 1786. The suggestion in *Good's Liberton*, that 'hyvots' is 'heavy oats', is mere havers, fitting neither the spellings nor any known crop; it was probably the name of a tenant of the mill (perhaps Hawok, an early form of the surname Hawke) but in absence of evidence it must remain obscure. In 1938 a footpath leading to Moredun Dykes was developed and named HYVOT'S BANK AVENUE; and shortly afterwards a scheme of *Hyvot-* street names, including the renaming of the northern stretch of MOREDUN DYKES as HYVOT LOAN, was drawn up; but although it is shown on *Ordnance Survey* 1944, it was 1952 before that renaming was confirmed, and 1962 before the rest of the names were adjusted and adopted for HYVOT AVENUE, COURT, GARDENS, GREEN, GROVE, BANK, TERRACE and VIEW.

I

IMPERIAL DOCK (Leith) was planned in 1891, built in 1896-1904, and named in accordance with the theme of Queen Victoria's Diamond Jubilee and final years.

THE INCH (Nether Liberton) was granted to Holyrood Abbey by James II in 1450. It became the chief house of NETHER LIBERTON (*which see*) and is shown as such on *Blaeu* 1654, but as *Inch* on *Adair* 1682. The name is British or Gaelic *innis*, used here in its meaning of haugh or riverside meadow, rather than 'island'. Thus the alternative name KING'S INCH is the same as KING'S MEADOW, east of the Dalkeith Road, and it seems likely that the two places were parts of one stretch of royal land prior to 1450. *King's Hill* is at least old enough to have been mentioned in *White's Liberton* 1786; and its alternative name of FIR HILL goes back to before 1739, when, according to White, a notable stand of trees on it was blown down on a windy Saturday. The adjoining farm of SOUTH or (from 1850) EAST MAINS OF NETHER LIBERTON, along with the ground of UNDER CRAIGS, was developed in 1950 in streets named for Sir Walter Scott (WALTER SCOTT AVENUE) and for places and characters in his poems and novels, viz. ASHTON GROVE, BALDERSTON GARDENS, BELLENDEN GARDENS, DINMONT DRIVE, DUNDRENNAN COTTAGES, HAZELWOOD GROVE, HEADRIGG ROW, LAMMERMOOR TERRACE, RAVENSWOOD AVENUE, REDGAUNTLET TERRACE, SADDLETREE LOAN and SUMMERTREES COURT. In 1952, ELLANGOWAN TERRACE, GLENALLAN DRIVE and LOAN, HAZELDEAN TERRACE and MARMION CRESCENT were added to this group. Meantime the same theme had been carried across to the west side of Gilmerton Road at CUMNOR CRESCENT in 1950, followed in 1952 by DURWARD GROVE, GLENDINNING CRESCENT, GLENVARLOCH CRESCENT, GREENMANTLE LOAN, INGLEWOOD PLACE, IVANHOE CRESCENT, KENILWORTH DRIVE, MANNERING PLACE, MONKBARNS GARDENS, NIGEL LOAN, PEVERIL TERRACE, PLEYDELL DRIVE, RINGWOOD PLACE,

RUTHERFORD DRIVE, TALISMAN PLACE and WOODSTOCK ROAD. In 1967, NORTHFIELD ROAD, which had been begun in the 1880s (*see under* NORTHFIELD, Liberton) was renamed CLAVERHOUSE DRIVE.

INCHCOLM TERRACE (Queensferry) is built in the STONYFLATTS (*which see*) in Plewlands and was named in 1964 either for the abbey of Inchcolm or more probably (considering the adjoining street name *Viewforth*) for the view of the island six miles away.

INCHERATHRYNE (Oxgangs) is mentioned in *RMS* 1425 as in the barony of Redhall and apparently next or near Oxgangs. Evidently Celtic, the name appears to be *innis* or riverside meadow of the *rath* in the *rynn* or triangle of ground, and since *rath* could mean a land measure of about two *oxgangs*, it is conceivable that *rath rynn* was a Celtic name for the land later called *Oxgangs*, and that the *innis* was the great haugh of Oxgangs beside the Braid burn.

INCHGARVIE (Queensferry) is shown on *Blaeu* 1654 as *Inch Garve* and is recorded from 1491 onwards, *Inchgarde* and *Inchgarvy* being typical of the early spellings. Evidently referring to the bold formation of the island's igneous rocks, the name is British, akin to Gaelic *innis garbh*, rough island. INCHGARVIE HOUSE at Sentry Knowe, built in about 1874 on the site of the earlier SPRINGFIELD, was probably named for the view of the island, while the name INCHGARVIE PARK given to housing in Hopetoun Road in the 1920s, probably derived from the House.

INCHKEITH AVENUE (Queensferry) was named in 1966 for Inchkeith island. This name, recorded before 1200 as *Insula keth* and as *Ynchketh* in 1451, is British *innis ceit*, island with a wood on it.

INCH MICKERY (Cramond) is *Mickry* on *Blaeu* 1654, *Muckrie* on *Collins* 1693, and *I. Mickrie* on *Adair* 1682. The name is Celtic, probably British (like neighbouring INCHKEITH and INCHGARVIE) akin to Gaelic *innis mucraidh*, seal island, for its denizens, the seal being *muc mhara*, sea pig.

INCHVIEW TERRACE (Craigentinny) was named in 1906 for its view of Inchkeith, now obscured by later development.

INDIA PLACE (Stockbridge) is shown (as proposed) on *Knox* 1821; and its name, given on *Wood* 1823, was evidently borrowed from the earlier India Street. If it was ever known as *Athole Street*, as reported by Cumberland Hill, it was only for a short time.

INDIA STREET (Northern New Town) was planned and named as part of the NORTHERN NEW TOWN, *which see*. Shown on *Ainslie* 1804, it began to be built in about 1807. Along with Jamaica Street, it appears to have been named to represent the colonies in the general scheme of names for this part of the New Town.

INDUSTRIAL ROAD (South Leith) although not recorded in *PO Directory* until 1878, was evidently named for the Industrial Building Society who had initiated the final development of the grounds of Hermitage House a decade earlier. A first group of streets, appearing in *PO Directory* 1869, included COCHRANE PLACE, named for the then owner of the House; ELM PLACE, probably named for trees in its gardens; HERMITAGE TERRACE, renamed ROSEVALE TERRACE (from Rosevale Place, *see below*) in 1968, to obviate any confusion with Hermitage Terrace, Morningside; and LIVINGSTONE PLACE, now called SOMERSET PLACE—*see under* LIVINGSTONE PLACE, South Leith. The second group of streets included SUMMERFIELD PLACE, its name borrowed from an earlier terrace in Restalrig Road—*see under* SUMMERFIELD, South Leith; NOBLE PLACE, named for Grace Noble, wife of William Finzies, the builder of the scheme; and WAVERLEY PLACE, appearing in *PO Directory* 1872 and one of no fewer than five Edinburgh streets named for Scott's novel about this time, but renamed LINDEAN PLACE (a fancy name chosen by the residents) in 1969, to obviate any confusion with Waverley Place in Abbeymount. The final group of streets, occupying the site of Hermitage House itself, included PARKVALE PLACE (1875) and ROSEVALE PLACE (1878) possibly named for the gardens of the House, and FINZIES PLACE (also spelt FINGIES, which is nearer its pronunciation *Fing-is*) named for the builder in 1878.

INDUSTRY LANE (North Leith) is shown named and part built on *Kirkwood* 1817. The origin of the name is not recorded; but considering the curious way in which the early maps show building beginning at the far end of the street (as also at LAPICIDE PLACE nearby) it may be that some cottage industry was on the go here in the first few years.

INFIRMARY STREET (Old Town) is part of a lane shown on *Rothiemay* 1647 as leading from the HIGH SCHOOL WYND to the HORSE WYND. Evidently an early loan along the march between the burgher tofts on the south side of the Cowgate and the ecclesiastical lands of the Blackfriars and Kirk o Fields that lay further south, it may have carried on westwards to the Greyfriars at Candlemaker Row. Its medieval name is unrecorded, unless it was that of KIRK O FIELDS WYND which was used for it later, or the interesting one of MYLK RAW which is shown attached to at least its eastern part on *Kirk o Fields* 1567. It is labelled *Jamaica Street* on *Ainslie* 1780, but *Kincaid* 1784 shows it as INFIRMARY STREET throughout its length, while the modern usage, limiting this name to the section east of South Bridge, appears on *Ainslie* 1804. It got this name as the access to the Royal Infirmary built in 1738 in the West Yards of the Blackfriars. Designed by William Adam, this building was demolished in 1884; but fragments of it were re-erected by R A Macfie of Dreghorn in a stable block at Redford and in the Covenanter's monument in Redford Road.

INGLIS CLOSE (200 Canongate) *see* (DOWNMOST) PLAYHOUSE CLOSE.

INGLIS COURT (West Port) is listed in *PO Directory* 1827 and is perhaps indicated on *Rothiemay* 1647. The origin of the name is as yet obscure, but it may be connected with the James Inglis who owned nearby ELWALDSIDE (*which see*) in 1714.

325

INGLIS GREEN (Slateford) originated as the name of an enterprise promoted by George Inglis of Redhall on his ground at the haughs of Slateford, Graysmill and the Powderhaugh in 1773, when he leased it to Joseph Reid for setting up works and greens for the bleaching and printing of cloth. INGLIS GREEN ROAD was traditionally named as the road to Inglis Green from Slateford. Before it was widened in about 1960 it was lined on both sides by INGLIS GREEN COTTAGES, built to house the Inglis Green works staff, and the name has been retained for some modern houses.

INGLISTON is recorded in 1478 as *Ingaldstoun*, showing the name to be *Ingjaldr's tún* or farm; but since the term *tún* occurs in both Old Norse and Anglian, the bearer of this Old Norse personal name might have been a Norse-speaking settler of the 9th or early 10th centuries, or else a somewhat later Northumbrian of Norse descent. By 1539 the estate had divided into *Eastfield* and *Westfield* and the first became so dominant that its alternative name RATTOUNRAW (for its interpretation, *see under* RATOUNRAW, Leith) displaced Ingliston as the estate name until after 1631, when James Inglis of Eastfield of Rattounraw had the estate erected into a barony and restored the old name. The subdivision EASTFIELD has continued to be so called; but although *Westfield* is shown by *Blaeu* 1654, later maps show it variously as *Wester Mains of Ingliston* (1747) *Westertoun* (1763) *Ingliston Mains* (1812 and 1852) and WEST INGLISTON (1912). INGLISTON TOLL, now also called WEST INGLISTON COTTAGES, is shown on both *Knox* 1812 and *Ordnance Survey* 1852 as CROSSFERRY WA'S—*which see.*

INGLISTON STREET (Pleasance) is shown planned on *Ainslie* 1804 on part of the site which had been shown on *Kincaid* 1784 as 'intended for new Prison & Bridewell'. Only the east side is shown as built on *Kirkwood* 1817, but the street was named by 1826, apparently for Laurence Inglis, superior of the ground in 1788. The form of the name suggests that some of the earlier buildings to the east had perhaps been called *Inglis' toun* or place.

THE INNOCENT RAILWAY was authorised in 1826, as a horse-drawn railway from St Leonards to Dalkeith. It was opened to goods traffic by 1831 and to passengers in 1832, and is shown on *Pollock* and *Gellatly* 1834. Formally the *Edinburgh & Dalkeith Railway*, it got the nickname *Innocent Railway* (perhaps as part of sales publicity) in contrast to the supposedly dangerous steam trains which came in in the 1840s.

INVERALMOND DRIVE, GARDENS and **GROVE** (Cramond) were named in 1972, being developed within the grounds of the midVictorian Inveralmond House. The site was earlier part of the Northwest Park of Fairafar farm, and the *Inveralmond* name (from Gaelic *inbhir Almond*, Almond mouth) was fancy.

INVERLEITH is mentioned in 1128 in David I's charter founding Holyroodhouse, which describes the land that was to become North Leith as 'that (part of) *Inverlet* nearest the harbour'; but the estate charters in *RMS* 1315-21 and later are concerned with *Inverlethe* as lands further upstream, and to judge by the mansion and gardens shown as *Inuerlythe* on *Siege of Leith* 1560, it seems that the medieval estate's centre must have been on or near the site where the present INVERLEITH HOUSE was built in 1774, not far from where the river emerges from the Dene, some two miles above North Leith. This stretch of the name so far inland suggests that it uses the Celtic word *inver* in its sense of 'lower basin of' rather than 'mouth of'. The term could be either British or Gaelic; but since it is coupled with the British river-name LEITH (*which see*) the odds are that it too is British in this particular case. INVERLEITH MAINS, mentioned in *RMS* 1642, seems to have been re-organised in the course of 18th-century improvements to create the NORTH and SOUTH INVERLEITH MAINS. Which (if either) of these steadings was the original one is an open question: the South Mains, converted into a clubhouse after the city created INVERLEITH PARK in 1890, is missing from many maps but appears on *Knox* 1812 as *Inverleith*, and as *Inverleith Mains* on *Lancefield* 1851; while North Inverleith Mains, cleared away when Inverleith Rugby Ground was formed in 1902, is *Inverleith Mains* on *Pollock* 1834, but BLAWEARIE (*which see*) on *Knox* 1812, *Gellatly* 1834 and *Fowler* 1845. If INVERLEITH ROW is shown somewhat inaccurately on *Laurie* 1766, it is probably because it was still only a proposal, awaiting completion of the Canonmills bridge in 1766 or 1767; but it is clearly shown on *Armstrongs* 1773, and was known as *Inverleith Road* until 1833. INVERLEITH PLACE was begun in about 1824, and the detail on *Lothian* 1826 suggests that its development was linked with that of the Botanic Gardens. By 1849, terraced houses had been built on the south side of Ferry Road, under the name of INVERLEITHFIELD; and in about 1882 the terrace was completed as INVERLEITH GARDENS, possibly named for the market garden that lay south of it. INVERLEITH AVENUE was named by 1888, SOUTH INVERLEITH AVENUE by 1905, and INVERLEITH GROVE was named in 1936.

IONA STREET (Leith Walk) was occupied in 1876 and named FALSHAW STREET, for the then Lord Provost, Sir James Falshaw; but in 1885 it was renamed IONA STREET, apparently in oblique compliment to that island's owner, the Duke of Argyll, a prominent Liberal of the day—*see also* DALMENY STREET, Leith Walk, renamed at the same time.

IRELAND'S CLOSE (High Street) *see* DUNBAR'S CLOSE.

IRNESIDE (Abbeyhill) is recorded thus from 1489 onwards and also as *Irnesyd* 1568, *Ernesyde* 1587 and *Ironside* 1741. The ground was part of the lands of St Leonard, granted to Holyrood Abbey in 1128, and slopes up from the west side of Abbeyhill road, immediately opposite the site of the manse of St Leonard's on the east side of the road near the Watergate. The name is probably Anglian *aerne side*, house slope, referring to its position as 'home field', or else it may be Anglian *hyrn*, Scots *hirne side*, corner slope, referring to the angular shape of the piece of ground. IRONSIDE PLACE is listed in *PO*

Directory 1827 and shown, along with IRONSIDE CLOSE and COURT, on *Ordnance Survey* 1852; but by 1872 they had given way to HOLYROOD TERRACE, listed from 1868 onwards but itself suppressed in the new development of ABBEYHILL CRESCENT in 1968.

IRONROCK STREET (Granton) *see under* GRANTON HARBOUR.

IVANHOE CRESCENT (Inch) *see under* THE INCH, Nether Liberton.

IVY TERRACE (North Merchiston) *see under* PRIMROSE TERRACE, North Merchiston.

J

(BIG) JACK'S CLOSE and **LITTLE JACK'S CLOSE** or **COURT** (225 and 231 Canongate) are shown on *Edgar* 1742 and named on *Ainslie* 1780. They were *big* or *little* according to their width, and were named for two brothers Robert and John Jack, slaters, who between them built *Jack's Land* between the two closes, Robert beginning it in 1738 and John, a bailie of the Canongate, completing it after his brother's death. David Hume lived here 1753-62, before he moved to James Court. Big Jack's Close was also MAUSIE SMITH'S, for the wife of Patrick Heart, who evidently owned property here in her own right at some date before 1784.

JACKSON'S CLOSE (209 High Street) is listed on *Edgar* 1742. A sasine of 1755 mentions property once acquired from a George Dougal by John Jackson, and subsequently owned by his son and grandson, both called John. The absence of any Jackson name from the *Valuation Roll* 1635 suggests that this sequence of ownerships must have been before or after that date: it remains a matter for conjecture, but there is record of Dowgall burgesses (but no George) from 1539 to 1584, and of three John Jacksons, burgesses: one in 1578; the other two, father and son, active in the 1590s and up to 1615.

JACOB'S LADDER (Calton) is shown on *Fergus & Robinson* 1759 as a way up to the Calton burying ground by the east end of the Dow Craig. The name, derived from the story in *Genesis* 28 of Jacob's dream of a stairs going up to heaven, may have been prompted not only by the length of the stairs, but by its use for funeral processions. Used in *Grant* 1882 as a name already established, there is no knowing when it was first applied to this particular footpath, but it was current as a nickname for a long ladder before 1750.

JAMAICA STREET (Bonnington) *see under* SUMMERSIDE.

JAMAICA STREET (Northern New Town) is shown on *Ainslie* 1804 and was planned in 1802 as the only street of artisan housing in the NORTHERN NEW TOWN, *which see*. Along with *India Street*, its name represented the colonies in the original scheme of street names chosen in 1802. The houses were cleared away in 1960; and in 1981 the site was redeveloped as JAMAICA MEWS, encircled by the original meuse lanes named JAMAICA STREET LANE NORTH and SOUTH.

JAMAICA STREET (Old Town) was fleetingly a name for INFIRMARY STREET, *which see.*

JAMES COURT (493 High Street) was also called BROWNHILL'S, both names being for James Brownhill, wright, who redeveloped this site in the Lawnmarket in 1725-27. Its present three entries, shown on *Kirkwood* 1817, are the remnants of four shown on the earlier maps and listed in *An Accurate View* 1783; and these in turn were the remains of a group of five closes listed in the *Valuation Roll* of 1635. The WEST ENTRY of 1783 (at 511 High Street) is unnamed in the *Roll* of 1635 but is recorded in 1705 as FOUNTAINHALL'S CLOSE, from Sir John Lauder, Lord Fountainhall (1646-1722) judge and diarist, who lived in it. It was stopped up before 1817, but parts of it still exist and it forms the west side of James Court. The UPPERMOST MAIN ENTRY of 1783 (507 High Street) is now called WEST ENTRY; in 1635 it was JOHN SLOWAN'S CLOSE, for a merchant of that name then resident owner in it. The MIDDLE MAIN ENTRY of 1783 (now MID ENTRY) is listed but unnamed in 1635. The close next to it on the east must have been in about 497 High Street: also unnamed in the 1635 Roll, it was apparently suppressed in the rebuilding of 1725-27. The entry at 493 High Street is listed as EASTMOST ENTRY in 1783, and is evidently the upper part of the close which is given in 1635 as DAVID JONSTON'S, for a tenant in it, but also bore the names of the two owners resident in it that year, being JARDIN'S (sometimes miscalled 'Fairden's') for George Jardin, merchant, as well as JOHN DICKSON OF HARTREE'S for John Dickson, writer—and very likely for his family, for it was also WHITSLADE'S, for another of their titles.

JAMES PLACE and **LANE**, and **JAMES PLACE LANE** (South Leith) *see under* LINKS PLACE *and* GARDENS.

JAMESON PLACE (Leith Walk) was named by 1895 for Dr Leander Jameson, who was made administrator of Matabeleland in 1894 and led the famous Jameson Raid into the Transvaal in December 1895. He was born in Edinburgh in 1853.

JAMES STREET (Pilrig) was renamed SPEY TERRACE, *which see.*

JAMES STREET (Joppa) *see under* RABBIT HALL.

JAMIESON'S CLOSE (68 Grassmarket) *see* MOYSE'S CLOSE, Grassmarket.

WILLIAM JAMIESON PLACE (Portobello) was named in 1978 for William Jamieson, the 'Father of Portobello', who began to exploit the brick clays here in the 1760s and was the leading spirit in the development of Portobello for half a century before his death in 1813. He had earlier been commemorated (but only for some decades) in the naming of JAMESON STREET, *see under* WINDSOR PLACE, Portobello.

JANEFIELD (Corstorphine) was a property shown on all maps from *Corstorphine* 1754 onwards on a site now occupied by the southern end of Featherhall Avenue. On *Corstorphine Village* 1777 it is shown as *Mr Alexr Patterson's*; and by the 1850s it was known as *Janefield,* probably named for an owner's wife or daughter. It was cleared away in 1956.

JANEFIELD (Liberton) *see* FIVEHOUSES, Liberton.

JANE STREET (South Leith) was formed by 1869 and named for Jane, wife of James Galloway, nephew and successor to Peter McCraw, superior of the ground.

JANE TERRACE (Abbeymount) was named by 1871, probably for the developer's wife or daughter.

JARDINE'S CLOSE (493 High Street) *see under* JAMES COURT.

JAW (Ratho) is shown on *Roy* 1753 and *Ordnance Survey* 1852, at or near where *Knox* 1812 shows ADDISTON BANK, and it gave its name to JAW BRIDGE on the Union Canal in about 1822. The name is Scots *gaw* from Old Norse *gall*, a barren spot, or spongy wet ground, or a drainage furrow.

JAWBONE WALK (Meadows) follows the line of a path shown on *Bartholomew* 1876 but bearing every mark of having been formed before Melville Drive was built in 1859; and it is named for the arch formed out of whales' jawbones, a relic of the Shetland display in the Great Exhibition in the Meadows in 1886.

JEAN ARMOUR AVENUE (Liberton) *see under* KIRKBRAE, Liberton.

JEFFREY AVENUE (Craigcrook) *see under* CRAIGCROOK *and also* JEFFREY STREET, Old Town.

JEFFREY STREET (Old Town) is shown proposed on *City Improvements* 1866, starting at the entry of LEITH WYND but curving westwards to cut across the sett of the historic closes and connect with what was then the east end of Market Street at the Fishmarket. It was named by 1872—probably as consciously parallel with the earlier COCKBURN STREET—in memory of Francis, Lord Jeffrey 1773-1850, not only advocate and judge and MP for Edinburgh in 1832, but editor of the *Edinburgh Review* 1803-29 and friend of Scott, Wordsworth, Dickens and Lord Cockburn, who wrote his biography in 1852.

JERICHO (Water of Leith or Dean Village) was a great granary built by the town, possibly in the early 17th century but certainly before it is mentioned in *Town Council Minutes* 1691. It may have replaced or incorporated a granary which the council instructed to be built in 1500 on the same site west of MAWR'S MILL, *which see*. It was burnt down in 1957, but a new structure follows its plan and incorporates or reproduces some of its features. In the 17th century *Jericho* was already in use in the phrase 'Go to Jericho!' but also seemed to carry a meaning of 'a place of concealment', and the name may have arisen because the place was a storehouse. In 1959 the name was still being used by children for ground in the vicinity.

JESSFIELD (Newhaven) appears in *Aitchison's Directory* 1800, with a Revd W F Ireland as resident. Other spellings *Jesse-* and *Jessiefield* occur a few years later, but it is probable that the place was named for a woman rather than the Jewish patriarch. Shown as *Jessfield* on

Knox 1812, it is given as *Whale Bank* on *Ainslie* 1804; but *Kirkwood* 1817 and *Pollock* 1834 both show the latter name transferred to property on the west side of Whale Brae. On *Ordnance Survey* 1852, Jessfield is shown subdivided, with JESSFIELD COTTAGE next its northern boundary, and it was probably this that gave the name JESSFIELD TERRACE to the street formed here in 1885.

THE JEWEL (Niddrie) was the colloquial name for the miners' row of the JEWEL COTTAGES, shown on *Ordnance Survey* 1893, both names arising from the *Jewel* coal, a notable seam worked here since before 1760, when it is shown on a map of the Niddrie coals (*RHP 33*). As a well-established place name it was given in 1983 to the spine road of a new development eastwards from the site of the Cottages. While this ground had been for centuries part of HUNTER'S HAW (*which see*), by 1831 it had been traversed by the INNOCENT RAILWAY, and most of it had latterly become anonymous after years of use as a railway yard. The new branch streets were named for the rock and coals which, outcropping here in a steep anticline, in fact determined the sett of the new development. Three are named for the coal seams which outcrop beside them: NORTH GREENS for the *North Greens*, and (with *shot*, after *park* the second most frequent type of field in Midlothian) CORBIESHOT for the *Corby Craig* or *Corbie* seam, and PARROTSHOT for the *Rough Parrot* seam of brightly burning or *cannel* coal. The other two streets are named for the limestone on which they are built: HOSIE RIGG for the *Top Hosie* stratum which forms the ridge and scarp above the Niddrie burn, and VEXHIM PARK for the broader band of *Lower Vexhim* rock.

JEWS CLOSE (Causeyside) is shown on *Kirkwood* 1817 and listed in *PO Directory* 1827, and was named as the entry giving access to the Jewish burial ground opened in 1816. In about 1878 it was altered and extended to form BRAID PLACE, *which see*.

JINKABOUT MILL (Slateford) was recorded as *Lumsdain's Mill* in 1506 and as the *New Mill of Redhall or Jinkabout* in 1714. It was cleared away in the late 1750s, when George Inglis of Redhall formed his walled garden partly on its site, but faint traces of its dam remain in the shape of the river. The curious name is also used for at least two mills elsewhere, near Inveravon in West Lothian (1682) and near Linlithgow (1773) and evidently refers to the jerky motion of the mill's wheel or some other kenspeckle part of its machinery.

JOCKS LODGE is mentioned in *Nicoll's Diary* as *Jokis Ludge*, where Cromwell posted his infantry in his first advance on Edinburgh in July 1650. Although the first part of the name begins to be given as *Jock's* on *Laurie* 1766, it is *Joks* in 1684, *Jokes* on *Adair/Cooper* 1735 and *Jocks* on *Roy* 1753 as well as *Laurie* 1763, and the impression that it was originally in the plural is confirmed by a sasine for THRIESTOPPIS, Piershill (*which see*) in 1736 which refers to 'the Bleugowns Lodge commonly called Jocks Lodge'. This also gives the clue to the name itself, for as noted by Sir Walter Scott in his 'Advertisement' in the 1828 edition of *The Antiquary*, the Bluegowns

331

were the king's bedesmen, with a royal licence to beg, and are recorded in 1683 as 'called by others, and by themselves, *Jockies*'. Thus the house was the *Jockies' Lodge*. The 1736 sasine shows that it stood on the west side of the entry to the Restalrig road; but a photograph printed in *Old Edinburgh Club XXIII* seems to show it replaced by an 18th-century house of some pretensions, including a 'Palladian' window, probably built by Louis Cauvin after 1758.

JOHN KNOX WAY (Mound) *see* PLAYFAIR STEPS, the Mound.

JOHN MASON COURT (Queensferry) was named in 1965 for John Mason, who became headmaster of Queensferry High School in 1922, and was the author of the (unpublished) *History of Queensferry* 1963.

JOHNSBURN (Balerno) is mentioned as a place in the early 19th century, and *Ordnance Survey* 1852 shows *John's Burn* and *John's Burn Cottage*. JOHNSBURN ROAD, shown on *Armstrongs* 1773, was locally the way to Cockburn and Buteland *by Johnsburn*; and the name was extended to JOHNSBURN PARK in 1983. JOHNSBURN HAUGH and GREEN were named in 1987, in consideration of the character of the ground east of the burn. The origin of the name is obscure; it is also somewhat difficult, for not only is it unusual to have a personal name attached to a burn, but settlement beside it seems to have been fairly recent, for the *Statistical Account* of 1792 remarks that the place had been a bare heath until Professor Adam Fergusson improved it in the previous decade or two.

JOHN'S LANE (South Leith) got its curious alignment ultimately from the north-east face of the bastion built here in 1548, or more directly from a road shown on *Naish* 1709 which skirted the ditch of the rampart and evidently determined the sett of the feus even although it was itself suppressed before *Wood* 1777 was surveyed. The first part of the modern Lane appears on *Ainslie* 1804. Shown fully developed on *Kirkwood* 1817 as a meuse serving the terrace of houses in John's Place, the lane shared the varying naming of the houses (*see* JOHN'S PLACE) being given as St JOHN'S LANE in the *PO Directory* 1817 but as JOHN'S PLACE from 1824 onwards.

JOHN'S PLACE (St Leonards) is shown on *Ordnance Survey* 1852, but the name's origin has yet to be traced. It was adapted in 1981 for the NEW JOHN'S PLACE built here and on adjoining ground, with entry from East Crosscausey rather than St Leonard's Street.

JOHN'S PLACE (South Leith) appears on *Wood* 1777 as a *road through the Links*, evidently replacing, on a line much further east, the road shown on *Naish* 1709 skirting the ramparts of 1548—*see under* JOHN'S LANE and WELLINGTON PLACE. The name certainly existed by 1801, and its absence from *Ainslie* 1804 and *Kirkwood* 1817 is explained by the way it is shown on *Thomson* 1822 and *Pollock* 1834 as the name not of the roadway but (as was the custom of the day) of the terrace of houses which was certainly built here by 1804, although altered or perhaps rebuilt in the 1820s. Given as St JOHN'S PLACE in *Aitchison's Directory* 1801 and on *Thomson* 1822, it appears in *PO Directory* 1806 not only thus but as JOHN'S PLACE, and this plainer version prevailed in the directories by the early 1820s, even although the maps continued to show the earlier one. The name may have been fancy or else connected with the original developer of the terrace, but it cannot have derived from St John's Church, which, although built in Constitution Hill in 1773, was called the New Kirk until 1834.

JOHN STREET (Joppa) *see under* RABBIT HALL.

JOHNSTON'S CLOSE (156 High Street) *see* BURNET'S CLOSE.

JOHNSTON'S CLOSE (332 High Street) is listed on *Ainslie* 1780 and still exists. In 1635 it is recorded as DAVID MAKALL'S or MacCALL'S, for the merchant who then owned all the property in it. He was bailie in 1633, and in making his will in 1639 set up a trust for the building and stipend of the new kirk at the Tron, for two bursaries at the university and the supply of books to its library, and for the benefit of the poor and hospitals in both Edinburgh and Leith. Among tenants in the close was James Jonston, while Christien Jonston owned property immediately east of it, in the High Street and Riddle's Close; and it is fairly evident that when MacCall's estate was dispersed (his heirs were his three daughters) the Johnstons increased their holdings hereabout. *Johnston's land* was on the east side of the close, next Riddle's; but although it may have been lived in by the Bailie Patrick Johnston who died in 1693 and Patrick (later Sir Patrick) Johnston who was elected to the council in 1694 and became bailie in the following year, it is clear from *Town Council Minutes* 1701 that Sir Patrick, when he was elected in 1700 for the first of his three terms as Lord provost, was persuaded to live, not in the house which then belonged to him, but in a more convenient and accessible one in the Lawnmarket, rented from Thomas Fisher, then town chamberlain. The close may also be the CAULIE'S or CAUTIE'S CLOSE mentioned in *Protocols of George Home* 1712 and 1737.

JOHNSTON STREET (North Leith) figures on *Stranger's Guide* 1816 and is named on *Thomson* 1822. It is said to have been named for the Revd Dr David Johnston, minister of North Leith 1765-1824.

JOHNSTON TERRACE (Old Town) is sketched on *Wood* 1823 and was adopted in Thomas Hamilton's design for a new Western Approach to the town, which was authorised by Act of Parliament in 1827. Shown as opened on *Kay* 1836, it seems to have been known as the *New Western Approach* until it was named in about 1850 for William Johnston, founder of the firm of W & A K Johnston, map makers, and Lord Provost 1848-51.

JOLLIE'S CLOSE (595 High Street) is listed on *Ainslie* 1780 and was named for a family, including Patrick Jollie and (later) Alexander Jollie, writer, who owned a tenement at the head of the close.

JOLLY'S CLOSE (196 High Street) *see* OLD FISHMARKET CLOSE.

DAVID JONSTON'S CLOSE (493 High Street) *see under* JAMES COURT.

JOPPA, shown as *Engine* (i.e. mining pump) on *Laurie* 1763 and named on *Armstrongs* 1773, is mentioned in the *Statistical Account* 1794 as the mining village attached to the coal workings in Easter Duddingston; and since there is no trace of it on *Roy* 1753 it was probably created and named in the period of improvement which followed the purchase of Duddingston by the earl of Abercorn in 1745. The reasons for naming it for the Palestinian town (now Jaffa or Tel Aviv) are obscure, unless it was in imitation of the other exotic names *Porto Bello* and *Bilbao* in nearby Figgate, and because the place was on the coast. JOPPA (SALT) PANS are shown thus on *Ordnance Survey* 1852, but they are *Duddingston Salt Pans* on earlier maps, and the *Statistical Account* 1794 refers to them as Maitland Pans (a name connected with BRUNSTANE, *which see*) and quite distinct from Magdalen Pans. JOPPA QUARRY PARK is on the site of the Joppa Quarry for sandstone, opened in the early 19th century. LOWER JOPPA was formed by 1832 and named before 1850. JOPPA LANE was the original name of NORTH MORTON STREET, which see. JOPPA TERRACE and PARK date from the mid 1890s, the latter being on the site of an 18th-century quarry which had been filled and laid out as Joppa Park football ground by 1893. JOPPA GARDENS and GROVE were named by 1914.

JORDAN BURN (Morningside) is a fancy name, first shown on *Roy* 1753, for the upper reach of the POW BURN (*which see*) in obvious allusion to its position between EGYPT and CANAAN, *which see.* JORDAN BURN COTTAGES, shown on *Kirkwood* 1817, were cleared away in about 1960 for a shop, later replaced by a post office. JORDAN LANE is shown on *Kirkwood* 1817 as partly developed; and *Pollock* 1834 shows it complete, and named JORDAN BANK. This name appears in *PO Directory* from 1833 until 1868, when it is replaced by JORDAN LANE, although that name had already been in use for a decade. JORDAN PLACE, in Morningside Road immediately north of the entry to the Lane, is listed from 1846 until 1885, when there was a general suppression of the numerous side names in Morningside Road.

JOUSSIE'S or **JOSIAH'S CLOSE** (265 High Street) *see* CRAIG'S CLOSE.

JUNCTION PLACE and **STREET** (Leith) *see* GREAT JUNCTION STREET, Leith.

JUNIPER GREEN evolved from a park, shown on *Roy* 1753 and *Armstrongs* 1773, that had been laid out in part of Currie Muir by John Cunyngham of Woodhall in about 1686, *see under* ENTERKIN'S YETT. A century later it is recorded in *Walker's Collington* as 'the farm called *Juniper Green*'; but in reporting that its lands 'were formerly moorish ground covered with juniper', Dr Walker seems to have some doubts of this as an explanation of the name, for as Professor of Natural History he adds that although he had found some 'juniper bugs' in the vicinity, there was not one plant of juniper growing there. The tradition may have been true, but equally may have been made up to explain the name, for the one thing that is certain is that by Walker's time no living memory of juniper plants remained. *Knox* 1812 gives the name as *Juniper Ley*, but it is *Juniper Green* on *Kirkwood's Environs* 1817, and evidently derived from one or more of the grass fields that lay between formal avenues in the original sett of the park—a sett still reflected in the subdivision of BLOOMIEHALL (*which see*) and in the alignment of streets. JUNIPER GROVE was named in 1967; and at the same time three other streets were renamed for fear of confusion with streets elsewhere: *Belmont Avenue* (*see under* BELMONT ROAD, Juniper Green) became JUNIPER AVENUE; *Pentland Terrace*, originally houses named for the view, became JUNIPER TERRACE; and *Park Road*, named when the grounds of Bloomiehall were opened as a public park in the 1900s, was renamed JUNIPER PARK ROAD. JUNIPER GARDENS (1971) and LANE (1989) were named as new streets, but the name of JUNIPERLEE (1985) was borrowed from *Knox* 1812 for a lane shown on *Ordnance Survey* 1852 but hitherto unnamed.

K

KAIMES (Ratho) is named on *Adair* 1682 as an estate house *Combs*; but the name, which is from Anglian *camb* or Scots *kame*, a ridge or hill crest, is clearly a hill name, probably covering Dalmahoy and Ravelrig Hills as well as Kaimes Hill, just as *Dalmahoy Craigs* also did duty for the whole group.

KAIMES ROAD (Corstorphine) *see under* GORDON LOAN, Corstorphine.

THE KAIMHEAD (Queen's Park) is the southern spur of St Leonard's Crag, the name being Scots kame Anglian *camb*, a crest or ridge, with *head* for its summit.

KAMES (Liberton) is shown as *Kames* on *Roy* 1753, while *Laurie* 1763 uses the same word in showing *N Camps* at the crossroads and *S Camps* at FIVEHOUSES, *which see*. The name is Scots *kames*, from Anglian *camb*, a crest or ridge, and evidently refers to the knowes on the high ground southwest of the crossroads, described in *White's Liberton* 1792 as 'the two kaims where there have been various fortifications'. Frogston Road and Captain's Road were formerly known as the *Kames road* from Fairmilehead.

KATE'S MILL (Redhall) was one of a series of mills working off the dam or lade on this haugh from before 1540, for long owned by Colinton but acquired by Redhall in 1800. Burnt down in 1890, Kate's Mill had been built as a white-paper mill in 1787 by John Balfour & Sons, booksellers in Edinburgh, and is believed to have been named for John Balfour's wife, Catherine Cant of Thurston. Along with the adjoining COLINTON BARLEY MILL, it probably shared an access through Colinton ground which may be still partly represented by PATIE'S ROAD and the final western section of KATESMILL ROAD.

With the transfer of the mills to Redhall, the access seems to have changed to a road through Redhall policies and along the brink of the Dell, as shown on *Knox* 1812 and *Gellatly* 1834; but by 1834, as indicated on a plan of Craiglockhart, *RHP 30763*, this was already being superseded by the present loop round the east and south marches of Redhall. The whole road from the junction at Craiglockhart Avenue was known as KATESMILL ROAD until 1923, when its northern half was needlessly renamed CRAIGLOCKHART DRIVE, *see under* CRAIGLOCKHART.

KAY'S CLOSE (east of 145 Cowgate) is listed on *Ainslie* 1780, but the name's origin is obscure. It was also POWER'S or (DAME) POOR'S or POWRIE'S, evidently from John Power, merchant in the close in 1635, unless the Laurence and Gilbert Power or Powrie, listed as former owners in titles of 1707, were his predecessors.

KEDDIE GARDENS (North Leith) is shown as open ground in Hillhousefield on *Ainslie* 1804, but *Kirkwood* 1817 shows it as part of the grounds of Bank Place and planned for housing development. This was never carried out, and the ground is shown as a *Public Park* from 1876 onwards, although the *Ordnance Survey* labels it *Drying Green* and it was not opened as a civic park until 1927, when Councillor Keddie was a member of the Public Parks Committee of Edinburgh Corporation.

KEDSLIE ROAD and **PLACE** (Liberton) *see under* LEADERVALE ROAD, Liberton.

KEIRHILL (Riccarton) is mentioned in *RMS* 1534 as *Keirhill*, shown on *Blaeu* 1654 as *Keyrhill* and spelt *Kier-* and *Keirs-* in 1796 and 1812. The first part of the name is almost certainly British *cair*, a fort, suggesting that there was some kind of fortification in the vicinity. The 18th-century maps show the name attached to a place in the region of NT 160695, and the name may have originally belonged to one of the knowes immediately south of this. KEIRHILL TOLL, at the junction of the Currie road with the Calder road, is shown on *Riccarton* 1800, as well as on *Ordnance Survey* 1852.

KEIR STREET (Lauriston) was developed by 1821 and named for the Keir family, bakers in Edinburgh, who had owned the land for over 50 years. In 1966 the name was extended to displace that of GRAHAM STREET, which had in fact been the earlier part of the development, completed by 1816 and named for a Mr Graham who had acquired the house on the land from the Keirs in about 1782.

KEITH ROW (Blackhall) was developing in the 1880s and KEITH CRESCENT and TERRACE followed in the mid 1890s, all three being named for the Keith family, owners of Ravelston.

KEKEWICH AVENUE (Craigentinny) *see under* CRAIGENTINNY.

KELDELETHE or **KYLDELETHE** (Currie) is recorded from 1250 onwards, as an estate owned by the archbishopric of St Andrews and the seat of the archdeacon in charge of all its estates south of the Forth. It centred on the tower of KELDELETHE, still represented by the 15th-century ruin known as LENNOX TOWER after the estate was acquired by the duke of Lennox in 1593. The early forms *Kylde-*, *Kelde-* or *Kildeleth(e)* show the name to be Old Norse *keldu blith*, slope of the spring(s), which would describe the immediate vicinity of Lennox Tower or equally the whole great slope from the hills to the river which still goes under the name in its modern form KINLEITH. An earlier shortened form *Killeith*, recorded in 1550 and noted in *RMS* 1618 as 'alias *Kildelicht*' obviously arose when Old Norse *kelda* evolved into Scots *kell*, also meaning a spring. In a decreet of the Regality of St Andrews in 1580 *Killeith* appears as the farm name, while another variant *Kyndeleyth* is used for the estate; but in *RMS* 1647 the two appear together as *Killeith alias Kendeleith*. On both *Blaeu* 1654 and *Adair* 1682 *Killyth* or *Killeth* are shown as distinct from the castle (Lennox Tower) at Lymphoy. *Roy* 1753 shows two farms, EAST and WEST KINLEITH, while *Knox* 1812 shows the three farms EAST, MID and WEST KENLEITH. The *Ordnance Survey* spells the name *Kenleith* in 1852, but *Kinleith* in 1893. The KINLEITH BURN probably took its name from the farms. A mill was operating on the haugh below the burn mouth in 1618, and the KINLEITH PAPER MILLS were set up in 1792 and worked until 1966.

KELLERSTANE (Gogar) appears on *Roy* 1753 as *Caller Stone*, and is *Callerstane* on *Laurie* 1763 and *Kellerstane* on *Gellatly* 1834 and *Ordnance Survey* 1852. In absence of early forms, derivation is risky: but Scots *caller*, cool or fresh, is impossible as a description of a stone, and the name might be Old Norse *kjalar stein*, stone of the (keel-shaped) ridge, conceivably (if the name has not migrated three-quarters of a mile from the Gogar Stone) referring to some lost standing stone on the ridge of Roddinglaw.

KEMFLET (Ratho) is shown on *Hatton etc* 1797 as a house and 19-acre field some 400 yards northwest of Hatton House. The name is probably Scots *kaim flat*, the level field below the kaim or ridge of the Craw Hill.

KEMP PLACE (Stockbridge) *see under* THE COLONIES.

KEMP'S CLOSE (South Leith) is shown thus on *Kirkwood* 1817 but is *Kemp's Lane* on *Wood* 1777. It may have been named for Robert Kemp, distiller, or a predecessor. It was also called BAIKIE'S CLOSE in 1831.

KEMPSTON PLACE (Queensferry) was named by 1972; but the origin of the name has yet to be traced.

KENILWORTH DRIVE (Inch) *see under* THE INCH, Nether Liberton.

KENMURE AVENUE (Parson's Green) *see under* PARSON'S GREEN.

KENNEDY'S CLOSE (374 High Street) *see* AIKMAN'S CLOSE.

KENNEDY'S CLOSE (High Street) is shown on *Edgar* 1742 and *Ainslie* 1780, but was suppressed when the west side of BLAIR STREET began to be built up in 1785. The close is listed in 1635 as AIKENHEAD'S, evidently for James Aikenhead, advocate, then resident at its foot. It is possible that it became KENNEDY'S for John Kennedy, vintner, listed as owner and resident at the same date; but it seems more likely that this name was for Quintin Kennedy, mentioned in 1710 as a former owner of a *cross house* or house set athwart the close, who may have been the Quintin Kennedy who was clerk to John Nicoll WS in 1613 or the Quintin Kennedy who figures as a WS in RMS 1634-56. Feu charters of 1710-34 refer to the close as *Tailyfiar's* or *Telfer's*, now Kennedy's, perhaps by confusion with TELFER'S CLOSE next door on the west, but more likely because there was some Telfer property east of it, between it and Peebles' Wynd.

KERR STREET (Stockbridge) is part of the old road by Kirk Loan (now Gloucester Street) to the bridge, but was named in about 1824, presumably for the developer of the houses on its west side, swept away in 1966.

KERSSHALL (Gogar) is shown on *Roy* 1753 and *Armstrongs* 1773, and appears to have been replaced by *Clay Wa's* shown on *Knox* 1812 and *Gellatly* 1834, but cleared away by 1845. The names are Scots *kerse haw*, flat land beside the burn in the carse, and *clay walls* or *wells*, springs in clayey ground.

KETTLESLAW (Queensferry) appears on *Plewlandfield* 1769 as an alternative name for WINDY EDGE (*which see*) and is probably much the older of the two, being Anglian *hlaw* combined with an Old Norse element. What this element is requires consideration of the two spellings given on the map: if the name is *Kettlelaw*, it might be *kettil*, a kettle, referring to the rounded shape of the *hlaw* or knowe; but if the other spelling *Kettleslaw* is preferred (as it perhaps should be, on the ground that the *s* is more likely to have been dropped than inserted) it would make the name *Kettil's law*, incorporating a personal name of Old Norse extraction found elsewhere in Lothian— e.g. at Kettlestoun, (Linlithgow) and Kirkettle (Midlothian).

KEW TERRACE (Wester Coates) *see under* OSBORNE TERRACE, Wester Coates.

KILCHURN COURT (East Craigs) *see under* CRAIGIEVAR WYND, East Craigs.

KIKERLAW (Restalrig) is recorded in 1605 in terms which indicate that it was in the vicinity of West Drum. The name is Scots *keeker law*, spy law or hill, and evidently refers to its position overlooking the coastal plain. It is possible that, through the notion of sharpness of eye, the nearby name of HAWKHILL bears some relation to it.

KILGRASTON ROAD (Whitehouse) *see under* WHITEHOUSE.

KILKERRAN'S COURT (High Street) lay near the head of FORRESTER'S WYND and was named for Sir James Fergusson (1688-1759) who sat in the Court of Session as Lord Kilkerran from 1735 onwards, and had a house on the west side of the court.

KILMAURS TERRACE and **ROAD** (Prestonfield) are built in what was the *Echo Park* of Prestonfield (*see under* CELLARBANK) and were respectively named in about 1879 and 1882 for Kilmaurs in Cunninghame, where Sir William Dick-Cunyngham of Prestonfield had property.

KINAULD (Currie) is a fancy name imported in the later 19th century for a house west of *Balerno Mill*. This mill, built for paper making in 1788, became a glue works in about 1882 and is now a tannery. KINAULD FARM is on the site of the *Waulk Mill of Balhernoch*, where cloth processing was on the go before 1376, and a small distillery operated in the 19th century.

KINCAID'S CLOSE or **COURT** (161 Cowgate) is listed on *Ainslie* 1780 and was named for Alexander Kincaid, King's Printer in Scotland, and partner of William Creech. He was a town councillor from 1737 until his death in 1777, becoming Lord Provost in 1776. He acquired his house here through his marriage with Caroline Kerr, granddaughter of the 1st Marquis of Lothian. The close is listed in 1635 as MAISTERTON'S, evidently for George Maisterton, whose heirs were then still owners in the close.

KINELLAN ROAD (Murrayfield) is shown on *Gellatly* 1834 together with a property which was named *Kinellan* at some time before 1875 and gave the street its name in about 1908. The house appears to have been named by Dr Cumming, sometime tutor to the family of the duke of Argyll. There is a Kinellan in Strathpeffer, but the name is of a kind which could occur elsewhere. KINELLAN GARDENS was added in 1991.

KINGBOWIE (Dalmeny) appears on *Barnbougle & Dalmeny* c1800 and *Knox* 1812 as the headland about 600 yards west of the mouth of the Almond. It seems to be Gaelic *ceann bocach* or *boin*, buck or ox head. Since the nearby name GLENPUNTIE (*which see*) is probably a Gaelic/British hybrid, it is conceivable that the headland name is a Gaelic translation of British *pen bogh* or *bowyn*, buck or ox head. THE HUNTER'S CRAIG and EAGLE ROCK are more specifically names for the carved rock on the point. *Eagle Rock* seems to be modern, and possibly derives from the note in *Wood's Cramond* 1794, which rather tentatively describes the weathered sculpture as 'bearing some resemblance to the figure of an eagle'; and since it is more likely that the carving portrayed some Roman god, such as Mercury, the name *The Hunter's Craig*, used by Wood, may go further back to a time when such an athletic figure was still discernible.

KING EDWARD'S WAY (Kirkliston) was coined in 1968 for this part of a housing development in Gateside in order to commemorate the passage of Edward I and his army through Kirkliston by the High Street and Gateside in 1298, on their way to do battle with the Scots under William Wallace at Falkirk—*see also under* GATESIDE *and* CLERICS HILL, Kirkliston.

KINGHORN PLACE (Bonnington) was built after 1893 (when *Ordnance Survey* shows the ground still open) and was named by 1896, probably for Hugh Kinghorn of H & W Kinghorn, builders in Leith, who was resident in 'Bonnington Villa' in 1827, or for his family.

THE KING'S BRIDGE (West Port) was designed by Thomas Hamilton, built in 1829-33 under the 1827 Act for a new Western Approach to Edinburgh, and named for George IV. The name had been proposed as early as 1823, as shown on *Wood* 1823, and its style was no doubt suggested by the medieval name of the King's Stables nearby.

KINGSBURGH ROAD (Murrayfield) *see under* ABINGER GARDENS, Murrayfield.

ALEXANDER or **MARY KING'S CLOSE** (High Street) is recorded in 1530 as John TOWRIS CLOSE, for Touris of Inverleith, owner on its east side, and also as LIVINGSTOUN'S, probably for Henry Livingstoun, a burgess in 1500 (or perhaps his father, also a burgess) since by 1530 Henry's daughters Isabella and Katherine had inherited a house in the close. In 1615 and 1621 it is recorded as M(r) ALEX(ANDER) KING'S CLOSE, which firmly links it with M. Alexander King of Dreden, advocate in Edinburgh from about 1580 until 1617. When King died in 1618, his heir was his brother Adam King; and the *Valuation Roll* 1635 lists the third of the six properties on the west side of the close as 'waste lands' belonging to 'Mr Alexr King or his heirs'. In *Town Council Minutes* 1694 the close is MARY KING'S, but in 1720 it is given as 'KING'S CLOSE, now ALEXr KING'S CLOSE' while a protocol of 1735 refers to it as 'BROWN'S, later KING'S, now MARY KING'S CLOSE'. Nothing is known of the origin of *Brown's*, but it appears that in the 17th century the name *Alexr King's* evolved into *King's* and then into *Mary King's*. It is also evident (contrary to what is supposed in *Wilson*) that Alexander King had no daughter Mary, nor is there a record of any Mary King resident in the close; but it is perhaps significant that the *Valuation Roll* of 1635 lists a Mary King as tenant in William Fairlie's property, not in the close but in the High Street immediately west of the close mouth, and also records a William King as an owner-occupier on the west side of Stewart's, the next close to the east of King's. How *King's Close* became *Mary King's* remains a matter of speculation: it is possible that Mary moved into it at some time after 1635; or alternatively, she being such a near neighbour, it might have become convenient to add her name to *King's Close* in order to distinguish it from nearby Stewart's, which could conceivably have been sometimes referred to as (*William*) *King's*; but it must be understood that there is not a scrap of evidence for either of these hypotheses. The ruinous state of the buildings in the close in 1754 has been exaggerated by *Wilson* and others: they were only partly demolished when the Royal Exchange was built, and the lower parts of their walls have proved sound enough to support much of that building ever since, while the eight-storeyed 17th-century tenement of the Writers continued in use until 1897, *see under* CITY CHAMBERS *and* WRITERS COURT.

KING'S CRAMOND or **CRAMOND REGIS** *see under* CRAMOND.

THE KINGS HAUGHS (Craigmillar) are described in a charter of 1530 as the Figgat Burn lands lying next the KING'S MEADOWS (*which see*) and in 1979 the name KING'S HAUGH was given to the access streets in the industrial development on the haugh beside the burn and below Peffermill.

KINGSKNOWE(S) (Slateford) is recorded from 1667 onwards and shown on *Roy* 1753. It was the largest farm in Easter Hailes. Its name, always given in the plural until the later 19th century, refers to the numerous steep knowes in the hilly terrain, and like the adjoining Graysknowe (see under GRAYSMILL) it contains a farmer's name, probably that of William King, tenant in Easter Hailes in 1656. The farm house and steading were cleared away in 1965 for the building of Kingsknowe Court; 'Kingsknowe House', now replaced by a public house, was a later dwelling built in about 1890. KINGSKNOWE ROAD SOUTH is clearly shown on *Knox* 1812, but KINGSKNOWE ROAD NORTH, built in about 1900 along the north side of the Cairn parks, replaced an earlier access to the farm from the Longstone road, which ran on a parallel line about 250 yards further west and was abandoned (together with Hailes village) to permit expansion of HAILES QUARRY, *which see*. KINGSKNOWE GARDENS was named in 1927, and was followed by KINGSKNOWE DRIVE, CRESCENT, AVENUE, TERRACE and PARK (1934) and KINGSKNOWE GROVE (1936). In 1965 KINGSKNOWE COURT and PLACE replaced a prefab housing scheme built in the 1940s as an extension of LONGSTONE STREET. KINGSKNOWE PUBLIC PARK, notable as the site of the CLOVENSTONE (*which see*) was formed in about 1950 after the infilling of Old Redhall Quarry (*see under* REDHALL) had been completed. *See also* DOVECOT PARK, Slateford.

THE KING'S LANDING (South Leith) is the spot on the Shore, marked by a handsome cast-iron plate bearing the loyal comment *O FELICEM DIEM!* 'O happy day!', where George IV stepped ashore on 15 August 1822, the first presence of a reigning monarch in Scotland since Charles II was crowned at Scone in 1651. A second plaque, on the face of the quay, records details of the event.

KING'S MEADOW (Craigmillar) is recorded in 1380 as property personal to the king. It is shown on *Roy* 1753 as east of Bridgend, but while it included the ground later called ROYAL NURSERIES, it is described in *White's Liberton* as lying on both sides of the Braid burn, and the name KING'S INCH, of identical meaning (see under THE INCH, Nether Liberton) would suggest that the royal meadows originally extended west of the Dalkeith road, possibly to the line of Gilmerton road or Roman Dere Street. An alternative name *Shairniehall*, dirty haugh, appears in 1634, obviously referring to miry flats beside the burn.

KING'S MEADOW (Holyrood) is shown on *Rothiemay* 1647 and named on *Kirkwood* 1817. It was evidently named as the king's grazing on the other side of the park dike from the St Leonard's land of MEADOWFLAT.

THE KING'S PARK *see under* THE QUEEN'S PARK.

KING'S PLACE (Pilrig) is shown on *Ordnance Survey* 1852 as a side name in Leith Walk, like the adjoining FYFE PLACE. It was named by

1780, evidently for John King, wright, then resident in the terrace, and no doubt its builder.

KING'S ROAD (Portobello) is shown on *Adair* 1682 and was probably a very old route on the firm ground leading up from the mouth of the Figgate burn, the first practicable landing place east of Leith, *see under* WESTBANK, Portobello. It is also clear from the memoirs of Dr Alexander Carlyle in 1745, as well as from *Laurie* 1766, that together with the sands at low water it served as a useful shortcut on the way to Musselburgh, bypassing the wilds of Figgate, a notorious haunt of highwaymen. The road was no doubt used when Leslie and Cromwell parleyed on the beach in 1650, and when Prince Charles Edward reviewed his troops there in 1745; and a similar event gave it its name, for as shown on *Wood's Portobello* 1824 it was in *King's Road* that George IV got out of his carriage and mounted a horse for the great military review on the sands which marked his visit to Edinburgh in 1822. In about 1907 the name was extended to KING'S PLACE, on the site of a gun emplacement in the coastal defences of the 1880s, and to KING'S TERRACE on the main road.

THE KING'S STABLES (West Port) began as a 'great stable' recorded in *Bain* in 1335 as being built by the English garrison who were then holding the Castle for Edward III; and the name *stabulo regis*, 'King's stable', appears in *Exchequer Rolls* in 1366. Sited just east of Lady Wynd, the stables declined in importance after the Castle gave place to Holyrood as royal residence, and were finally sold off in 1527. By this time the name was in the plural; and in its Scots form, recorded in *RMS* 1578 as *the Kingis stabilis*, it has belonged to the ground ever since. KING'S STABLES ROAD, shown on *Rothiemay* 1647, figures in David I's charter to Holyrood abbey in 1128 as 'the way that leads to the kirk of St Cuthbert'. The alignments suggest that it led to an early west port in the middle of the present GRASSMARKET (*which see*) and as the first practicable route passing west of the Nor Loch bogs it may be as old as any settlement on the Castle rock. It was known as *the way to St Cuthbert's* or *the Queensferry road* until the development of the New Town and the Maitland Street route to Glasgow in 1805 made it a link rather than a main road, variously called the *Low Castle road* or *South Back of the Castle* or *road by King's Stables* until *King's Stables Road* became normal in the 1880s. KING'S STABLES LANE is a modern name (deriving not from the stables but from the neighbourhood) for part of a lane, evidently medieval, which is shown on *Rothiemay* 1647 as skirting the south wall of the BARRACE, *which see*. On *Kincaid* 1784 it is TANNER STREET, from the tanneries on its south side, and it may have been thought of as part of TANNERS CLOSE, *which see*.

KINGSTON GRANGE (Liberton) is the southern part of lands once named CRAIGS, referring to the broken ground on them, or perhaps to the crags in Craigmillar immediately north-east of them. Until its development for housing in 1950 (*see under* THE INCH, Liberton) the northern section retained the name in various forms, such as the UPPER and UNDER CRAIGS and CRAIGEND shown on *Ordnance*

Survey 1852; but the property shown on *Laurie* 1763 as SOUTH CRAIGS is named SUNNYSIDE on *Armstrongs* 1773, and the mansion house by Robert Adam was completed in 1788. In about 1850 a new owner, a Mr Hay of Duns, altered it and renamed it KINGSTON GRANGE, for one of his forebears, the royalist Alexander Seton, created Viscount Kingston in 1651. KINGSTON AVENUE was CRAIGS ROAD until 1938, when it was renamed in order to obviate any confusion with Craigs Road, Corstorphine.

(LITTLE) KING STREET (East End) *see under* St JAMES' SQUARE, East End.

(GREAT) KING STREET (New Town) *see under* NORTHERN NEW TOWN.

KING STREET (South Leith) is listed as *King Street* in *Williamson's Directory* 1773, and appears as *King Street* on *Wood* 1779; but the reference to it in *Town Council Minutes* 1792 as 'the street now called King's Street' suggests that the name had been given not long before 1773, perhaps in compliment to George III. The street itself is much older than this: it is shown on *Naish* 1709, with every appearance of having been laid out when the LEES (*which see*) were originally feued, but its older name has not yet been identified.

KING'S WALL (Old Town) is the name attached to a wall which, on the evidence of a few vestiges and a number of references in charters, ran along the south slope of the burgh ridge, parallel to the High Street and roughly midway between it and the Cowgate; but although the *Kingiswall* is used as a proper name in *RMS* 1478, all earlier charters use the same phrase as if it were simply the term for any public wall belonging to what was 'the king's burgh', in the same way as 'the king's street' meant a public way therein. There is no record of its construction: the suggestion in *Maitland* that it was related to the licence to fortify issued to the town by James II in 1450 is altogether a red herring, if only because a charter in the *Register of St Giles* 1427 refers to the wall as then already existing. (It may be added that a letter of James III in 1472 referring to the earlier licence not only complains about inaction, but shows clearly that what was in question was not a wall within the town but the strengthening of the *heid dykes* on the outskirts of the burgh's *rowmes* or crofts.) On the assumption that the wall represents an early burgh boundary, it has been supposed that there must have been a time when the burgage tofts were only half a rood in area, and half their later length; but besides being most unlikely in itself, it is almost inconceivable that later extension of the tofts would not have left irregularities or other traces in their boundaries, whereas in fact most of them carry straight on across the line of the wall, and the above-mentioned charter of 1427 actually includes the wall in the area to be feued, implying that although it was public it had been built on burgage land. The evidence would suggest that the wall was placed halfway up the slope for purely military reasons, regardless of violence done to the tofts or of the fact that it left half the town defenceless; and the most plausible theory is that it was not built by the burgesses but by forces occupying the Castle and concerned to attach a fortified town to it, as Edward I did at Conway and Caernarvon in the 1280s. The most likely guess is that it was part of the works carried out by the English during their occupation in 1335-41; and that as soon as possible thereafter the burgesses began to breach the wall or to slap doorways through it, in order to resume unimpeded use of their tofts.

THE KING'S WARK (South Leith) was a royal residence and arsenal founded by James I in 1434. Its buildings eventually covered the area between Broad Wynd and Bernard Street, and from the Shore to Carpet Lane or (considering the use of the later name *Bernards Neuk*) more probably still further east towards Quality (now Maritime) Street. In 1555 Mary of Guise gave a towerhouse within it as a tolbooth for her new burgh of South Leith, and it served until replaced by a purpose-built one erected in Tolbooth Wynd in 1565. In 1604 James VI gave part of the King's Wark to Bernard Lindsay (*see under* BERNARD STREET) and in 1623 erected it into a free bailiary, with Lindsay as hereditary bailie. It was purchased by Edinburgh in 1647.

KINLEITH (Currie) *see under* **KELDELETHE**, Currie.

KINLOCH'S CLOSE (257 Canongate) is shown on *Ainslie* 1780. Like SETON'S CLOSE next door (*which see*) its various names all came from owners of the tenement built by John Oliphant, Sheriff Clerk of Edinburgh: it was successively OLIPHANT'S, then SETON'S MIDDLE CLOSE, for Dr Alexander Seton, Oliphant's daughter's brother-in-law, and then KINLOCH'S, for Hugh Kinloch, merchant, who got the house in about 1760, after it had passed through the hands of Seton's sisters Jean and Isabel and of Dr Thomas Young, the developer of New Street.

KINLOCH'S CLOSE (south side of foot of Canongate) *see* BRODIE'S CLOSE, Canongate.

KINLOCH'S CLOSE (High Street) was sited on what became the east side of Niddrie Street. It is still shown on *Ainslie* 1804 but noted as shut up on *Kirkwood* 1817. Sir Francis Kinloch of Gilmerton, merchant councillor in 1655 and Lord Provost 1677-79, lived in the close; but the name certainly dates from before his time, being recorded in 1635, and to judge by the names (David and Francis) of early Kinloch owners mentioned in the various feu charters, the close name may go even further back than the James Kinloch, merchant, and Andro Kinloch, listed in 1635 as adjoining owner occupiers in the close. There was a Francis Kinloch, burgess in 1605-10 but it is perhaps more significant that David Kinloch (*see* KINLOCH'S CLOSE 151 High Street) and his son Francis are mentioned in records of the 1570s, even although direct evidence of connection with this particular close is lacking. The close is noted in 1725 as also called BLACKLOCK'S, and the Walter Blacklock mentioned in title deeds of 1529 is probably the Walter Blaklock recorded as a *gude nychtbour* or burgess of the town in 1486 and 1501.

KINLOCH'S CLOSE (151 High Street) is shown on *Edgar* 1742 and was recorded as *Killoch's* in 1660. It was named for David Kinloch, baxter, who, with his son Francis and grandson David after him owned a tenement in the close. He appears as a spokesman for the deacons of crafts in 1539 and as assessor for the council in 1553, and both he and his son are witnesses to a charter in *RMS* 1573. A David Kinloch, skinner, is listed in 1635 as an owner in the High Street at or near the close mouth. The close was also CATHKIN'S or CATCHKAN'S, for a William Cathkine, owner of lands which were bought after his death by David Kinloch. He may have been of the same family as the brothers Edward and James Cathkin, booksellers and burgesses in the 1590s.

KINNAIRD PARK (Newcraighall) was developed in 1989 on ground once part of Hunter's Haw. It is named for John Kinnaird, ward councillor 1947-52.

KINNAIRD'S CLOSE (246 Canongate) *see* PIRRIE'S CLOSE.

KINNEAR ROAD (Inverleith) was named by 1901 for Lord Kinnear, a member of the Fettes Trust.

KINNIBURGH'S CLOSE (once 15 now about 27-29 Grassmarket) *see* CLEGHORN'S CLOSE, Grassmarket.

KIRK BRAE and **KIRKBRAEHEAD** (Colinton) *see under* SPYLAW BANK ROAD.

KIRK BRAE (Liberton) is named on *Ordnance Survey* 1852 in such a way as to show that it is primarily the name of the whole face of the hill below Liberton Kirk and only secondarily that of the section of the ancient LASSWADE ROAD (*which see*) that ascends it. The road's alignment at Liberton Dams with the old Liberton road (now Mayfield Road) suggests that it is older than the road to Over Liberton (now Alnwickhill Road) and this is borne out by the way it is shown on *Blaeu* 1654. Thus it was probably this road to Lasswade that prompted the original settlement of Liberton (according to *Good's Liberton*, Malbet's tower was beside it, at the head of the brae) and KIRKGATE probably originated as the access to it from the later LIBERTON TOWER. Streets on the eastern side of the Brae were named in 1975 to commemorate Robert Burns in ROBERT BURNS DRIVE, his Ayrshire birthplace in ALLOWAY LOAN, his wife in JEAN ARMOUR AVENUE and his *inamorata* Nancy Maclehose in CLARINDA TERRACE, while MOSSGIEL WALK is for the farm he worked 1784-88, and SHANTER WAY for the most famous character in his narrative poems.

KIRKBRAEHEAD (West End) was the name, shown on *Roy* 1753, for the clachan at the crossroads where the Lang Gate or Lang Dykes intersected the road to Queensferry by Kings Stables and Drumsheugh, and the overlay of plans published in *Old Edinburgh Club XXIII* confirms that this was exactly at the modern West End junction. The place was named as being at the head of the steep Kirk brae where the Queensferry road, still partly represented by Kings Stables Road, passed the West Kirk of St Cuthbert.

KIRK BURN (Colinton) is named for the medieval kirk of St Catherine in the Hope which (now submerged in Glencorse reservoir) stood at the burn foot, and for the adjoining kirk farm of Kirkton. Thus the name probably relates to that of LYON DENE, *which see*. It is also called the FALA BURN, *see under* FALA KNOWE.

KIRK CRAMOND *see under* **CRAMOND**.

KIRKGATE (Currie) is the traditional name of this *road to the kirk* at Currie, and it is at least possible that it also implied that it led by the Loan and the CLOCHMEADGATE (*which see*) to St Catherine's in the Hope, which was linked with Currie and Hailes kirks in 1574. The use of Scots *gate* (from Old Norse *gata*, a way) instead of *road* would suggest that the name dates to the 17th century at latest.

KIRKGATE (South Leith) figures on *Siege of Leith* 1560 and is recorded in 1585 as the *Kirkgate* or kirk road *of Leyth*. Clearly it got this name after St Mary's kirk was built in the 1480s as a chapel of Restalrig; but as clearly it had been for many centuries part of the main route from Edinburgh to the sea, referred to in 1398, in a grant to Edinburgh by Logan of Restalrig, as 'the wide road leading from the east side of the *villa* of Leith to the sea', *see also under* LEITH WALK. It continued as the principal street of Leith until the 1960s when it was reduced by redevelopment to a residential cul-de-sac, barred from Tolbooth Wynd by housing, and from the Foot of the Walk by the commercial development of NEW KIRKGATE.

KIRKGATE (Liberton) may date back to the early days of the parish kirk which was probably on the same site as the present building of 1815 but is mentioned in the 1140s, in David I's charter to Holyrood Abbey, as an existing chapel of St Cuthbert's kirk, certainly endowed and very likely founded by the local thane Macbeth in the eleventh century. The name is Anglian from Old Norse *kirkja gata*, way to the kirk: evidently from Liberton Tower, which dates from the late 14th or early 15th centuries but may well represent an older estate centre.

THE KIRKHEUCH (WYND) (130 Cowgate) is mentioned in *RMS* 1614 and was the *way up the heuch or steep bank below the* (*St Giles*) *kirk*, leading from the Cowgate to the High Street just east of the kirk. Its upper part (*see* THE PRESIDENT'S STAIRS) was suppressed in rebuilding after a fire in 1700, but its lower part continued as the OLD POST HOUSE STAIRS and CLOSE shown on *Ainslie* 1780 and named for the General Post Office which came to Parliament Close in the 1760s but moved to North Bridge in the next decade, as also shown on *Ainslie* 1780. A remnant of the close still exists at the Cowgate, but the rest disappeared when the law courts were extended eastwards after the Great Fire of 1824.

KIRKHILL ROAD (Prestonfield) is built in the *Echo Park* of Prestonfield and was named by 1909. The name may have been fancy, or might refer to any of half-a-dozen *Kirkhills* in Scotland; but since the adjacent earlier street was named for Kilmaurs in Ayrshire, the name may come from Kirkhill, near Colmonell, also in

Ayrshire. KIRKHILL DRIVE and GARDENS followed in 1927, and in 1928 KIRKHILL TERRACE was built in the *Kaimhead*, head of the ridge, recorded in 1759.

KIRKLANDCROFT (Gogar) *see under* GOGAR.

KIRKLANDS (Corstorphine) occupies part of the historic estate of BROOMHOUSE (*which see*) and the street name was coined in 1983 as a reference to the fact that the estate was also known as the Sacristan's Lands (e.g. in *RMS* 1599 No. 966) because its revenues, prior to the Reformation, were applied to the upkeep of the sacristy in the collegiate kirk of Corstorphine.

KIRKLANDS (Gogar) *see under* GOGAR.

KIRKLANDS OF HAILES *see under* SPYLAW.

KIRKLISTON, recorded in 1358, developed from the late 12th-century *kirk of Liston* as the name not merely of the township but of the large tract in the ancient district or shire of LISTON (*which see*) granted to the bishops of St Andrews in the 12th century, probably by David I. Among the lands in this *barony in the regality of St Andrews* were its *mains* (*see* CATELBOK) and its hill grazings in LISTONSHIELS, as well as HUMBIE, the ABTHANE OF RATHO (RATHOBYRES) KELDELETHE (KINLEITH) and Ecclesmachan and Lasswade. The mill of the barony, mentioned as the *mill of Liston* in 1290 (quoted in *RMS* 1596) was known as KIRKLISTON MILL in 1552, and its alternative name LAMB'S MILL, recorded as *Lammis-* or *Lammysmyln* in 1540, probably derived from a tennant named Lamb or Lammie. The historic KIRKLISTON PARISH was much wider than the barony, and included AULDLISTON, the Templar barony in Liston, as well as other estates to the west.

KIRKLISTON ROAD (Newbridge) is shown on *Roy* 1753 and is traditionally the *road to Kirkliston* from the Bathgate road at Newbridge.

KIRKLISTON ROAD (Queensferry) is shown on *Dundas* 1757 as part of the LOAN (*which see*) but bears its alternative name of the route *to Kirkliston*.

KIRK LOAN (Corstorphine) *see under* CORSTORPHINE.

KIRK O FIELD(S) (Old Town) is recorded in the later 13th century as St Mary *in campis*, one of the kirks belonging to Holyrood Abbey. The term 'fields' would imply that the land in this area was originally part of the *terra campestre* or arable held in common by the burgh, which as the burgesses became less and less directly concerned with farming, was put to other uses or passed into private hands as arable crofts. The kirk figures on *Hertford's Assault* 1544, and details of the place are shown on *Kirk o Field* 1567 and discussed in *Kerr's Interpretation* of this drawing in 1932. The grounds included the whole area now occupied by the Old Quad of Edinburgh University, together with land stretching about 45 yards further east of South Bridge; and the site of the murder of Darnley in 1567 is at the east front of the Old Quad, some 10 or 20 yards north of the corner of South College Street. The kirk was among those burnt by Hereford in 1544; and in 1564 the town council complained that its stonework was being taken down and sold at the very time they were trying to buy the place for a 'town's college' (the future university)—a goal finally achieved in 1583. KIRK O FIELD PORT was an early name for the POTTERROW PORT (*which see*) but since the name is recorded in 1505, there was evidently a gateway hereabouts (or else further north, on the line of the south backs of the Cowgate, *see under* HORSE WYND) long before the FLODDEN WALL (*which see*) was begun. The KIRK O FIELD WYND or VENNEL, mentioned in *RMS* 1500 and shown (unnamed) on *Rothiemay* 1647, led from the Cowgate to the Blackfriars (a section later called HIGH SCHOOL WYND, *which see*) and thence turned westwards, running along the south backs of the Cowgate and terminating at the Horse Wynd: *see also* INFIRMARY STREET. The lane that led direct from the Cowgate to the Kirk o Field was also known as the KIRK O FIELD WYND, later COLLEGE WYND, *which see*

KIRK PARK (Liberton) was so named in 1961 because it was developed in the grounds of the manse of Liberton Kirk, utilising part of its drive.

KIRK STREET and **UNION STREET** (South Leith) were merged as *Kirk Street* in 1967. While their entries from Leith Walk and Hope Street (now Casselbank Street) are shown on *Thomson* 1822, they continued otherwise undeveloped until the 1860s. Union Street is mentioned in *Town Council Minutes* 1812 and named on Ordnance Survey 1852, but the name's origin is not known. Kirk Street, unnamed in 1852, appears in *PO Directory* 1865 and commemorated Robert Kirk, shipowner, resident in *Kirk's Land* on the Leith Walk frontage here in 1827.

(OLD) KIRK STYLE (High Street) *see* STINKAND STYLE.

THE KIRKSTYLE (Kirkliston) originated as the name for the approach to the kirk from the east, but was naturally extended to the new approach from the north, shown on *Ordnance Survey* 1852, which followed the development of the village around Main Street after 1810. The Scots term *kirkstyle* is widely used in Lothian for a path leading to the kirk. Although in later use it does not imply that there is a stile in it, there is no doubt that this was the original meaning, for kirkyards were kept trim by letting them for grazing, and some device was needed to prevent sheep from straying.

KIRKTON (Ratho) is shown on *Hatton etc* 1797. The name implies a kirk farm larger than the glebe (which was north of the manse) and it may be connected with the fact that the whole teinds of Ratho belonged to the collegiate kirk of Corstorphine. It may also have some connection with the ABTHANE OF RATHO, *which see*. The KIRK MYLNE mentioned in *RMS* 1581 may have been the *watermill of Ratheu* mentioned in *Bain* 1336.

KIRKTOUN of St Cuthbert's (West End) is recorded as *Kyrchetun* in the foundation charter of Holyrood 1128. The name suggests that it was a kirk farm larger than a glebe, but it is probably represented (perhaps in part) by the *Minister's Glebe* shown on *Ainslie* 1780, extending westwards towards Dalry.

KIRKWOOD PLACE (Abbeymount) was named before 1887, presumably for its builder.

KISIMUL COURT (East Craigs) *see* CRAIGIEVAR WYND, East Craigs.

KITCHEN MOSS (Balerno) is noted on *Ordnance Survey* 1852. The name evidently combines early Scots *mos*, peat bog and grazing, with Gaelic *coitcheann*, common land or muir.

KITCHEN'S CLOSE (171 Cowgate) is recorded in 1827, and was named for John Caitcheon, carver, who became a burgess in 1763 and had his house here by 1768. The close was also FLEMING'S, from Robert Fleming, who sold the house to Caitcheon. It is listed on *Ainslie* 1780 as SIMPSON'S, and it would seem reasonable to link this with the fact that Andrew Symson, printer, had his printing house *at the foot of the Horse Wynd* in 1705.

KITTLEMACAVIE (Brunstane) has been reported from the 1920s onwards as a traditional name attaching to the vicinity of the Niddrie burn above the Maitland Bridge. The name is obscure, but its form and the stress on the second-last syllable suggests that it may be Celtic.

KITTLENAKIT (Causeyside) is recorded in the 17th and 18th centuries as a name for the narrow strip of the Burgh Muir, also known as *the auld Grange feus*, on the west of Causeyside and between Sciennes and Grange Loan. The name also occurs near Carnbee in Fife, where the pronunciation is *kittl-'nakkit*, with a short *a*; and it is perhaps significant that both sites are near a MOUNTHOOLY, *which see*. The name is obscure; but the stress suggests that it is Celtic, and the first part may be related to Scots *cuthill*, a grove, which is believed to be Celtic in origin. KITTLE YARD is within the site of Kittlenakit, and was named for it in 1990.

KLONDYKE STREET (Newcraighall) was named in 1981 for the Klondyke coal mine sunk at Newcraighall in 1897 at the time of the Klondyke gold rush. In Scots, klondyke has acquired the figurative meaning 'gold mine'.

THE KNOCKILLBRAE (Slateford) in the vicinity of the CLOVENSTONE (*which see*) is recorded in 1662 as *Knockillgbray*. The name may combine Celtic *cnoc(h)*, hillock or tumulus, with Anglian *hill*, Scots *brae* being added to apply it specifically to the slope of the Lanark road; but considering that the maps do not suggest that any hill here was prominent as a hill among those of Kingsknowe, and secondly that 'cloven stone' would aptly describe the twin standing stones with a very narrow gap between them, which were the main feature of the curved portals of neolithic chamber tombs, the recorded spelling of the middle word, *killg*, suggests that it might conceivably represent British *kylgh*, a (stone) circle or a grave. Either interpretation would suggest that the hillock was notable for an ancient burial of some kind on its summit. In 1984 the path running from the top of the brae down to the former railway halt in Easter Hailes Gate was named KNOCKILLBRAEHEAD.

KNOX CLOSE (High Street) *see* PEARSON'S CLOSE.

KYLE PLACE (Abbeymount) was developed in 1984 on the greater part of the ground which had been the Regent Road nursery in 1852. The name was taken from a property immediately west of it, shown on *Ainslie* 1804 in a manner which suggests that the nursery ground was part of it. It is figured on *Kirkwood* 1817 as owned by *Mrs Kyle*, and given by *Ordnance Survey* 1852 as *Kyle Place*, and James Kyle & Son, bootmakers, were occupiers in 1855.

L

LABURNUM or **JOHNSTON'S ROW** (Corstorphine) were cottages named initially for their builder David Johnston in 1832, and then for the laburnum trees along the frontage. They were demolished in 1936 and the site became 145-61 St John's Road.

THE LADE (Balerno) was named in 1984, for its site beside a former mill lade in Malleny Mills, serving a flax mill in 1852.

LADEHEAD (Bonnyhaugh) *see under* BONNYHAUGH, Bonnington.

LADIEBRIDGE (Corstorphine) is shown on *Corstorphine* 1754 as a bridge over the Stank to the Saughton ground of CLAYCLOTE, *which see*. The name is traditional, probably from Scots *ladie*, a descriptive term for the slow-running Stank; and it was formally recognised in 1983.

LADIEMEADOW (Corstorphine) was named in 1984 as being in the south corner of the Ladie Meadow park, recorded in *RMS* 1654 and shown on *Corstorphine* 1754, as well as the local maps of 1777 and 1845. The name is Scots, meaning either the meadow beside the *ladie*, slow-running stream (viz. the Stank) or more likely the meadow *with ladies* in it, referring to the drainage channels which figure prominently on the 1754 map.

LADY BURN (Bonaly) now the tail burn of Clubbiedean and Torduff reservoirs, is shown in its earlier course on *Bell's Spylaw* 1799. The name is Scots *ladie* from Anglian *lád*, a burn or channel.

LADYCROFT (Balerno) is the traditional Scots name of this *enclosed land* beside the *ladie*—viz. the lower and quieter reaches of Black Linn or Bavelaw Burn. There is no evidence of any dedication to the Virgin Mary.

LADYFIELD PLACE (Castlebarns) is named on *Ainslie* 1804, and enters *PO Directory* in 1805. The street stands within the ORCHARDFIELD (*which see*) and the name may be fancy and coined on that model; but more likely it may have been a field name, incorporating Scots *ladie*, a burn—perhaps referring to a tributary of the march burn at St Cuthbert's Lane, if not to that burn itself.

LADY FIFE'S BRAE (South Leith) has been wrongly identified as an earthwork raised in 1560 (*see under* GIANT'S BRAE, South Leith) but is probably one of a large number of natural hillocks shown on the Links by *Thomson* 1822 and *Lancefield* 1851. Since *Campbell* does not name it, but mentions it as 'at Lady Fife's Well', it is likely that name, first recorded by *Robertson* in 1851, was transferred by children to the hillock from the well; and since the LADY FIFE'S WELL shown on *Thomson* 1822 is *Well* on *Kirkwood* 1817, it could be that the 'Lady Fife's' form had quite recently derived from Lady Fife, tenant in Hermitage House in 1811, and was simply an elaboration of *ladie well*, a slow-running spring or pool—very close to one possible interpretation of the nearby name LAUGH-AT-LEITH, *which see*.

LADY GRAY'S CLOSE (477 High Street) *see* LADY STAIR'S CLOSE.

LADY LAWSON'S STREET (West Port) is shown as proposed on *City Improvements* 1866 and was constructed in the early 1880s. Its northern section cut across the ancient sett of closes to connect West Port with Spittal Street; but its southern section was formed by widening the earlier LADY LAWSON'S WYND on its east side. Curiously enough the Wynd is not shown on *Rothiemay* 1647 (although another one is shown, opposite the Websters' land) but it appears on *Roy* 1753, and since it was the road linking Easter and Wester Portsburgh, it must have gained in importance when the PORTSBURGH (*which see*) was founded in 1649. The family of the Lawsons of Highriggs seems to have begun with Richard Lawson, town clerk of Edinburgh in 1482; but the name of the Wynd is probably much later in date, *Scott* 1759 showing it flanked on both sides by *Lady Lawson's property*.

LADY MENZIES PLACE (Norton Park) *see* MARYFIELD, Norton Park.

LADY NAIRNE CRESCENT, GROVE, LOAN and **PLACE** (Duddingston) built in the Sandilands and Mill Park of MEADOWFIELD, were named in 1956 for Carolina Oliphant, Baroness Nairne, the Scottish song writer, who married her second cousin Major Nairne in 1806 and settled in Caroline Cottage (now Lady Nairne Hotel) in Willowbrae Road immediately east of the Mill park until his death in 1830.

LADY ROAD (Nether Liberton) was built between 1817 and 1833 and is said, in *Good's Liberton* 1892, to be *the Lady's Road*, named for Mrs Gilmour, mother of the last Gilmour laird of the Inch.

LADY St NINIAN'S or **MINNINS** or **MENENS CLOSE** (High Street) *see* St MONAN'S WYND.

LADYSMITH ROAD (Blackford) was named by 1901, evidently commemorating the relief of Ladysmith in Natal at the end of February 1900 after a three-month siege, which marked the turn of the tide after the first disastrous stage of the Boer War.

LADY STAIR'S CLOSE (477 High Street) is listed on *Edgar* 1742. It was earlier called LADY GRAY'S CLOSE, from Egidia, Lady Gray, widow of Sir William Gray of Pittendrum, who lived on in the close for some years after her husband's death in 1648, in the house he had built in 1622. The later name came from her granddaughter Elizabeth Dundas, Countess Dowager of Stair and widow of John 1st Earl of Stair, who acquired the house in 1719 and lived here until her death in 1731.

LADYWELL ROAD (Corstorphine) is shown on *Corstorphine* 1754 as a loaning leading west from the High Street of the village. It was named by 1890 for a spring said to be north of it, in Janefield, now covered by Featherhall Avenue. It seems most unlikely that its name, in the form 'Our Lady's Well' given by *Selway*, would have survived over 300 years of Presbyterianism, and if it had done so, we might be sure that the *Ordnance Survey* 1852 would have recorded it: what is much more than likely is that Selway jumped to conclusions about a simple Scots descriptive name, the *ladie well* or spring running slowly in a channel, and indeed this is only supported by his story of folk sitting round it all night, ladling out the water *by means of saucers*. LADYWELL GARDENS was named in 1964, apparently under the misapprehension that the name referred to the PHYSIC WELL; and the section of the historic BROOMHOUSE ROAD leading from the High Street to Broomhouse was renamed LADYWELL AVENUE in 1978, when road alterations at Broomhouse proper (*see under* BROOMHOUSE) finally removed any visible continuity between this section and the greater part of Broomhouse Road leading south to the Calder road and the modern neighbourhood misleadingly known as *Broomhouse*.

LADY WYND and **CHAPEL WYND** (West Port) are shown on *Rothiemay* 1647 and listed in *PO Directory* 1827 and 1828. Both were named for the chapel of St Mary below the castle recorded in 1578 and shown on *Rothiemay* on the north side of the junction of King's Stables Lane with Lady Wynd. A sketch by George Sandy, showing its ruins in 1788, appears in *Old Edinburgh Club XXIV*. The chapel was attached to the nearby tilting ground or BARRACE (*which see*) where a chaplain was needed for the taking of oaths before combat as well as for the care of the dead or wounded after it. The connection is clear in several records of the chapel 'newly biggit' in 1508 by James IV 'at the barreris'; but since there must have been some provision of the kind when the Barrace was set up almost 200 years earlier, it is likely that 'newly biggit' implies that James had simply repaired or extended an earlier building. Perhaps, considering that the Barrace was very much an adjunct of the Castle, it was the chapel of St Mary *infra* the castle recorded (also as 'newly constructed') in *Exchequer Rolls* 1366, even supposing that *infra* here carries its medieval-Latin meaning 'within' rather than the classical 'below'. The chaplaincy lapsed in 1592.

LAICHFIELD (West Gorgie) was named in 1983, by variation on the name of the adjoining Laich Park.

THE LAICH PARK (West Gorgie) along with LAICHPARK ROAD, LOAN, PLACE and CLOSE were named in 1981, Scots *laich park*, low(er) grazing, being a translation of Bottom Field, the name which has been used for the ground since about 1910.

JOHN LAING'S CLOSE (16 High Street) *see* TWEEDDALE COURT.

LAING TERRACE (Joppa) was built by 1824 as a meuse lane serving the houses in John Street and James Street, the latter including *East Villa*, a picturesque house at the sea front (demolished in the mid 1890s) in which David Laing, the great Scottish antiquarian scholar and first secretary of the Bannatyne Club founded by Sir Walter Scott and others in 1823, lived with his sisters from 1845 until his death in 1878; and the lane was named for him thereafter, appearing in the *Portobello Directory* in 1900.

THE LAIRDSHIP (Sighthill) was a farm of 28 Scots acres, detailed on *Saughton* 1795, which Watson of Saughton acquired in 1678 from George Girdwood, whose family had owned it since 1557. The steading, named on *Roy* 1753 and *Cultins* 1776, was sited about NT 19387116, on the east side of Bankhead Avenue and near its north end; but with the coming of the Edinburgh & Glasgow Railway in the 1840s the farm lost so much ground that it was broken up, and most of it taken into Sighthill. The name virtually translates the charter term *terra dominica*, the laird's land or domaine retained under his direct management when other parts of the estate were subfeued. Something similar seems to have applied to the GENTARIES MUIR (*which see*) lying immediately south of the Lairdship.

LAMB'S CLOSE (Crosscausey) is shown, but not named, on *Ainslie* 1780. The name, listed in *PO Directory* 1827, is probably from Andrew Lamb, resident in 1800.

LAMB'S CLOSE (Shore, South Leith) *see under* WATERS CLOSE, South Leith.

LAMMERMOOR TERRACE (Inch) *see under* THE INCH, Nether Liberton.

LAMOND'S CLOSE (once 23 now 31 Grassmarket) *see* EWE & LAMB CLOSE, Grassmarket.

LAMPACRE ROAD (Corstorphine) was named in 1928 at a considerable historical stretch, for it commemorates the fact that the practice of keeping a lamp shining from the east end of Corstorphine kirk to guide travellers through the nearby bogs was endowed by the revenues of the *Lampaiker*, a field well over a mile away on the north bank of the river near Coltbridge; whereas Lampacre Road follows the boundary of the TAYLOR'S-ACRE and HONEYMUG PARKS shown on *Corstorphine* 1777 and *Corstorphine* 1845.

LANARK ROAD is shown on *Blaeu* 1654 and is evidently an ancient route along the Lang Whang to Lanark. If a Roman road ran from Castledykes (Carstairs) along the north front of the Pentlands, it might have been on a similar line; but the only Roman find in its vicinity has been a carved slab built into a wall at Hailes House, which may have come from miles away. The addition of -WEST to the street name west of the former boundary of Midlothian at Enterkin's Yett, Juniper Green, was simply for convenience in postal addresses.

LANG CLOSE (Pleasance) is shown on *Edgar* 1742 and the name is given on *Regality of Canongate* 1813. Although short by Old Town standards, it was the longest close in the vicinity.

LANG DYKES or **GATE** or **CROSSGATE** (New Town) is recorded in 1561 and figures on *Siege of Edinburgh Castle* 1573. The name, incorporating Scots *gate* from Old Norse *gata*, a road, is neatly explained on *Laurie's New Town Site Plan* 1766 as the 'Road from the West Kirk between the LONG DIKES to Multrees Hill and Caldton'; and the relation of the road to the modern street pattern is best shown by the overlay of this survey and the New Town plan given in *Old Edinburgh Club XXIII*.

LANG-GATE SIDE (South Leith) *see under* GILES STREET, South Leith.

LANG LOAN (Straiton to Edgehead) is named on *Roy* 1753, simply for what it was: Scots *lang loan*, a long and perhaps grassy road or track along the summit of Gilmerton Edge.

THE LANG STEPS or **LONG STAIRS** (Colinton) together with Dreghorn Loan are part of a right of way confirmed in 1709, giving access to the kirk and also between Hailes brig and the common grazing of the barony of Redhall, in the Pentland Hills. The steps, occupying only part of its 30-foot width, are shown on *Ordnance Survey* 1893, and were salvaged from the old Royal Infirmary when it was demolished in 1884, *see also under* REDFORD, Colinton.

LANGTON ROAD (West Mains) was named in 1938 without record of reasons for its choice, but it may be from *Langton House*, near Duns and only some 15 miles from a property of the Gordon Gilmour family, owners of West Mains.

LANSDOWNE CRESCENT (Coates) *see under* COATES.

LAPICIDE PLACE (North Leith) is shown on *Kirkwood* 1817 unnamed but with some building in progress or completed at the inner end of the cul-de-sac. The name is a little-used alternative to *lapidary*, but when it first appears in *PO Directory* 1826 there is no reference to gem cutting going on. The circumstances are oddly parallelled in the case of the adjoining INDUSTRY LANE—*which see*; and the further point that *Ordnance Survey* 1852 shows the street as LAPICIDE LANE and the corner block fronting North Fort Street as LAPICIDE PLACE may have a bearing on the question. It seems possible that lapicide work went on in the buildings shown in 1817 but that it either ceased before 1826 or else was too small to be noted in *PO Directory*. The spelling 'Lapside' which appeared on the *PO Map* 1869 was clearly an engraver's error which escaped correction for several years after that.

THE LAPLEE STANE (Canongatehead) is recorded from 1490 onwards, and stood in the street about 180 yards below the Netherbow, marking the northeast corner of the boundary between *Edinburgh beneath the Netherbow* or CANONGATEHEAD (*which see*) and the separate *Burgh of the Canongate*. The site (given as 'St John's

Cross') is shown on *Ordnance Survey* 1852 as about two yards from the south side of the street, but since the Stane marked the turn of the boundary, it may well have been originally in the middle of the street. While it is not known for certain whether it was one and the same as the later *St John's Cross* (*see under* St JOHN'S LAND) the two certainly shared the same site and function and apparently the same form (for the Stane is called the *Loply corse* or cross in 1501) and the two names were used in parallel for over 100 years. Besides *Lople*, as in *Protocols of James Young* 1490, the first part of the name takes the forms *Laple*, *Loply*, *Lopli(e)* or *Lopelie* in the early 1500s, and clearly a solitary *Uplie* is an error in transcript, and the late forms *Laploke's* 1635 and *Laplies* 1717 are attempts to read a surname into it. The spelling *Laplee* (1558) is the best for the modern ear, inasmuch as it clarifies the second syllable; for the name is evidently early Scots *lappe lea*, pasture at the *lap* or outskirts: a name that clearly relates to the Stane's function as a marker of the curious outshot of the town below the Netherbow, and suggests that the Canongatehead originated as a common grazing outwith the burgage plots but easily accessible from them *via* the High Street or the Cowgate. *See also* THE BAGLAP, Warrender Park, *and* LOUPIELEES, Newbridge.

LARBOUR (Sighthill) *see* LERBAR, Sighthill.

LARCHFIELD and **LARCHFIELD NEUK** (Balerno) were named in 1984 for their position adjoining larch plantings beside the Water of Leith. Scots *neuk*, which can mean either an internal or an external angle, is apt for either the precinct of sheltered housing or its position at the traditional *Corner* of Balerno.

LARGO PLACE (North Leith) was built in 1876 on the site of the house BANK PLACE built by Archibald Cleghorn in 1809; but the street itself had begun to take shape in about 1870 as a loan leading to the PENNYWELL PARK—now KEDDIE GARDENS. The name presumably derives from Largo in Fife: how or why is not known, but it may celebrate Sir Andrew Wood of Largo, chief among sea captains under James III and James IV, and Quartermaster of the *Great Michael* when she was launched at Newhaven in 1511, the biggest and most powerful ship in the world. He was a native of Leith (probably North Leith) and leased land in Largo in 1483.

LASSWADE ROAD (Liberton) along with the KIRK BRAE is the ancient route to Lasswade; and its alignment with Mayfield Road at Liberton Dams suggests that, as shown on *Blaeu* 1654, it was older than the branch (now Alnwickhill Road) by Kames and Straiton to the south. LASSWADE itself is an early name for a crossing of the North Esk, Anglian *laeswe* (*ge*)*waed*, ford at the pasture, recorded in the 12th century as *Laswaid* or *Lesswade*. LASSWADE BANK and GROVE were named in 1930, obviously for the road rather than the village.

LATCH PARK (Redford) was named in 1994, being built partly within the earlier boundary of the field shown on *Knox* 1812 and named thus on the map of Redford printed in *Steuart's Colinton*. As shown on that map, and on *Ordnance Survey* 1852 and 1893, the field was bounded on the east by a latch—in early Scots, *leche*—a bog or slow-running burn, which might be fairly described as the final vestige of the post-glacial loch (its alluvium shown on the *Geological Survey*) that once covered the northern part of Redford, draining into the Braid burn.

LAUDERDALE STREET (Warrender Park) *see under* BRUNTSFIELD.

LAUDER ROAD (Grange) *see under* THE GRANGE. LAUDER LOAN was named as a branch off it in 1983.

SIR HARRY LAUDER ROAD (Portobello) was named in 1987 for Harry Lauder, comic singer, the most famous native of Portobello, born in Bridge Street in 1870.

(WILLIAM) LAUDER'S CLOSE (373 High Street) *see* BYRES CLOSE.

LAUGH-AT-LEITH (South Leith) occurs in minutes of Leith Burlaw Court 1724-50 as an alternative name for Coatfield Mains, and is shown on *Ainslie* 1804 as LOOK-AT-LEITH. These variants suggest, not so much a jocular name, as jocular attempts to make sense of a name no longer understood. As it stands, it must be considered obscure; but it may be a burn name (*see* LADY FIFE'S WELL) and its position at the foot of the slope down to the sandy flats of the Links would go with the term *lovat*: in Gaelic *lobhad*, a stagnant watercourse, often in a sea plain; in Anglian, akin to *lavant*, a seasonal stream, or a small one disappearing into the ground.

LAUREL TERRACE (North Merchiston) *see under* PRIMROSE TERRACE, North Merchiston.

LAURIE STREET (South Leith) is mentioned in *Kincaid's History* 1787 as 'just now forming', but it was 1794 before it appeared in *Williamson's Directory*. It is likely that it was named for the owner of the ground; and it may be significant—not as evidence, but as a clue—that the neighbouring King James Hospital leased ground, albeit at the eastern end of the Links, to a John Lawry in 1741.

LAURISTON (Cramond) is shown on *Blaeu* 1654 as *Laurencetoun* and is recorded in 1290 as *Laurancystun*. The name incorporates an Anglo-Norman personal name in early Scots *Laurence's tún* or farm place. The medieval centre was just east of LAURISTON CASTLE, a tower house of the 1590s extended as a mansion in 1827. As shown on *Lauriston* 1808, LAURISTON MAINS extended from Muttonhole (now Davidson's Mains) to the seashore, including land on both sides of the Cramond road, and was worked from a steading beside the tower. In about 1840 this was replaced by the existing steading, shown on *Silverknowes* 1841 together with a 'new road' to Silverknowes which has become LAURISTON FARM ROAD.

LAURISTON (South Side) is recorded in 1681 in the name of the *Lauriestoun Yairds*, which stretched southwards from Lauriston Place to the Meadows and eastwards from Lauriston Gardens to Lauriston Terrace. *Edgar* 1742 shows *Lauriston* as a general name for properties in the same locality, and by 1771 it was the recognised name for the whole suburb between Bristo and Tollcross, displacing the ancient name of HIGH RIGGS, *which see.* Although Laurence, son of Edmund of Edinburgh, acquired land near the West Port from Kelso Abbey in 1160, there is no record of a medieval 'Laurence's toun' in High Riggs, and it is likely that the name is from the family of Lowrie or Laurie (perhaps descended from Laurence) who were prominent in West Port in the 16th and 17th centuries, and may well have had a 'toun' or farm at or near the Yairds. LAURISTON PLACE developed from an old road through the High Riggs, shown on *Edgar* 1742 and *Scott* 1759 as curving into the Wester Portsburgh by Lady Lawson's Wynd. Its extension to Tollcross appears on *Armstrongs* 1773, and its name emerges in 1788, apparently coined for 'an elegant oblong square' proposed for the ground later and differently developed as Archibald Place. *Kirkwood* 1817 confines the name to the middle section of the modern street, and gives the north side of its extension to Tollcross (shown as LAURISTON LANE on *Ainslie* 1804) as PORTLAND PLACE, a side name given by 1812 (no doubt for William, 3rd Duke of Portland, prime minister 1807-09) and not dropped until 1886. LAURISTON STREET appears on *Armstrongs* 1773 and in *Williamson's Directory* in the same year; and for some years after 1827 it was also the address for 'Lauriston Lane' as above. The present LAURISTON LANE was formed in about 1760 by Gideon Shaw of Lauriston, who feued it out for the half dozen of houses named as NEW LAURISTON on *Kincaid* 1784. The lane is given as *Back Lane* in 1804, but as *Lauriston Lane* in 1816; and the side name LAURISTON TERRACE was added to it in about 1833. In 1861, LAURISTON GARDENS was formed in the grounds of Lauriston Lodge, a house built by Borthwick of Crookston in 1770, while LAURISTON PARK was laid out in the grounds of a mansion built by James Balmain but sold in 1790 to Thomas Hog of Newliston, the site of the house itself being developed as a maternity hospital.

LAVEROCK BANK (Trinity) is named as a property on *Roy* 1753. The land was bought from the Crown in 1660 by Maurice Trent, merchant in Leith, and sold in 1748 to Robert Anderson, wine merchant in Leith. It is quite possible that the crest of the slope above the shore was once frequented by larks or laverocks, and that this suggested the estate name *Larkbank*, varied to the Scots form by Anderson, when he built the dwelling house of LAVEROCK BANK. LAVEROCKBANK ROAD was formed by 1812, and up until the 1920s it was known quite simply as *Laverock Bank*. LAVEROCKBANK TERRACE, developed in 1859, was the western one of a pair of terraces shown on *Lothian* 1826 as 'proposed': the eastern one was overtaken by the development of CRAIGHALL ROAD. LAVEROCKBANK AVENUE, begun near the sea front in about 1904, was extended further into the policies of Laverockbank House in the 1920s, side by side with LAVEROCKBANK CRESCENT and the first part of SOUTH LAVEROCKBANK AVENUE; and the latter was completed, along with LAVEROCKBANK GARDENS and EAST MAYVILLE GARDENS, after the House was pulled down in 1933. LAVEROCKBANK GROVE, named in 1942, stands within the West Park of Laverockbank as figured on *Ainslie* 1804, and in part of a property shown as 'Mr Balfour's' on *Kirkwood* 1817 and as The Grove on *Ordnance Survey* 1852.

LAVEROCKDALE (Colinton) is shown on *Spylaw* 1767 with a building beside the burn and a small feu of the Bleachfield, while *Spylaw* 1798 shows a somewhat different building in much the same position, with a garden and ground extending to over 2 Scots acres and labelled *Lavrock-dale*. The report in the *Statistical Account* 1839 of a skinnery's name, 'having given place to the more poetical description of Laverockdale', tallies reasonably well with the evidence of the maps, although it may be wrong in supposing the name to be a poetical fancy for this little hollow, for it is perhaps more likely to have been the working name for this ground as a *dale* or share in the outfield of Bonaly, conveniently labelled for its laverocks or larks. LAVEROCKDALE HOUSE was rebuilt by Robert Lorimer in 1914. LAVEROCKDALE CRESCENT and LOAN were named in 1967, and LAVEROCKDALE PARK followed in 1969.

LAVEROCK HALL (Gilmerton) is shown on *Laurie* 1763 and on maps generally up to and including *Ordnance Survey* 1938, and is listed in *Kincaid's Gazetteer* 1787, but is shown on *Ordnance Survey* 1976 as *West End Cottages*. Doubtless the older name derived from the *laverock* or lark, perhaps given as a fancy name to some house or *hall*, but much more likely derived from a field name *laverock haw* or *heugh* for the flattish upland at the heel of the Edge, precisely the type of terrain frequented by larks. The newer name is difficult to interpret except as a confused form of 'West Edge cottages'.

LAWHOUSE (Niddrie) is shown on *Environs of Edinburgh* 1817, and appears on *Laurie* 1763 as *Lawhouse Toll*. Evidently named for the house on or at the law, the summit of the high ground in the east of Niddrie, the site is shown on *Ordnance Survey* 1852 as vacant ground east of Niddrie sandstone quarry; and in about 1890 it was developed as QUARRY COTTAGES, built for staff of the Niddrie Collieries, but so named because they were beside the quarry (by then disused) and had to be distinguished from NIDDRIE COTTAGES (*which see*) built about the same time.

THE LAWNMARKET (Old Town) got its name from *the countrey mercatt callit the landmercatt*, in which the vendors, being from outwith the burgh, were therefore 'unfree' and liable for taxes on their sales. In *Town Council Minutes* 1526 markets are appointed for both 'burgh' and 'land', but by 1656 it appears that there was a separate 'land' market on three days a week, and by 1690 the name had become attached to the upper part of the High Street, between the Tolbooth (the vicinity of St Giles Street entry) and the Bowheid. Pronounced *laun(d)merket*, it is given as *Land Market* on *Edgar* 1765, but as *Lawn Market* on *Bypass Roads* 1763 and in *Williamson's Directory* 1773.

LAW PLACE (Portobello) was named in 1978 as being partly on the site of the BLEAK LAW, *which see*.

LAWRIE'S CLOSE (South Leith) is shown on *Naish* 1709 and *Kirkwood* 1817 as running between Giles Street and the Yardheads, on a line which is now the west side of Henderson Gardens and part of Henderson Street. The name, given as *Lowrie* on *Kirkwood* 1817, is evidently that of an early owner, as yet untraced.

LAWSON CRESCENT (Queensferry) was originally developed in 1948 in what was once part of THE RAVEL (*which see*) and was named for James A Lawson, provost of Queensferry 1940-49.

LAWSON'S WYND (South Leith) is shown at the Sheriff Brae on *Kirkwood* 1817, and was named for John Lawson, kirk deacon in the Hill quarter, 1691. It is shown on *Ordnance Survey* 1852 as CAT SKIN CLOSE, an alternative which might go back to an early date, for *cattis skins* (i.e. furs) figure in a list of custom duties of the time of David I. The site is now open ground north of Cables Wynd.

LEADERVALE ROAD (Liberton) was named in 1956, along with CLACKMAE ROAD and GROVE and KEDSLIE ROAD and PLACE, for *Leadervale House* and the nearby farms of *Clackmae* and *Kedslie* on an estate belonging to the Gilmours of Liberton and Craigmillar, on the river Leader, a mile above Earlston. LEADERVALE GROVE followed in 1957.

LEAMINGTON PLACE, ROAD and **TERRACE** (Merchiston) all developed (along with GILMORE PARK, *which see*) from a path or loan shown on *Kirkwood* 1817 and *Pollock* 1834. The easter end of the Terrace is shown on *Ordnance Survey* 1852 as an access obviously retained in the scheme of villas which then lined Bruntsfield Place, in order to serve future development of the land behind them. LEAMINGTON TERRACE (1863) and PLACE (1879) were initially side names, the carriageway being called VIEWFORTH PLACE until this name was suppressed in 1885. LEAMINGTON ROAD was named by 1882. The name may derive from Leamington Spa in Warwickshire, which was rapidly growing in reputation in the 1860s, rivalling continental watering places such as Montpellier, already celebrated in the nearby street MONTPELIER, *which see*.

LEARMONTH TERRACE (Dean) was begun in 1873 and proved to be the only part of Dean to be developed directly by the family of John Learmonth, who had bought the estate for development in 1825; but the name was continued to the north of it, on the part of the estate bought by Sir James Steel in 1894: firstly in LEARMONTH GARDENS (1897) and SOUTH LEARMONTH GARDENS (1900) LEARMONTH PLACE (1903) and GROVE (1904), and then in LEARMONTH AVENUE and PARK (named in 1933) CRESCENT (1937) COURT (1945) and VIEW (1974).

LEE CRESCENT (Portobello) is in what had been the parks of *Middlefield* farm. It was feued out in about 1880 by J B W Lee, and named after himself.

THE LEES or **LEYS** (South Leith) are recorded from 1490 onwards. The name is Scots *leas*, grasslands, and implies that the ground south of the medieval boundary at GILES STREET (*which see*) was pasture land, possibly once the outfield of a farm sited in Leith. To judge by later boundaries, it may have stretched down to the Broughton burn; but the ramparts built in 1548 evidently struck a military line, cutting across the meadows and enclosing part of them within the fortified perimeter. The maps show that this area was feued off in a regular series of yards, and the detail on *Siege of Leith* 1560 suggests that these closes were speedily built up, giving their name to the LEES QUARTER, by 1645 the most populous part of Leith.

LEITCH'S CLOSE (High Street) *see* ALLAN'S CLOSE.

LEITH is first recorded in 1128, in the compound name INVERLEITH (*which see*) which means 'mouth of the Leith' and implies that *Leith* was the name of the river. It is British, akin to Welsh *llaith*, and meaning 'the water'. Even to this day this simple name is often used for the river; but by the late 12th century it was also being used for the harbour and the settlements beside it, and the expanded river name *Water of Leith*, first recorded in 1439 as *aque de Lyeth*, may have been coined in order to distinguish between the river and the place—yet it in turn soon came to be confused when it was used for the mill town in the Dene, *see under* WATER OF LEITH. Two distinct settlements grew up around Leith harbour. One lay on the south bank only: originally part of the barony of Restalrig, it had no rights of its own in the harbour, but grew up in dependence upon the trade generated by Edinburgh's rights in the harbour, probably granted when the burgh was created in about 1120 but certainly feued to it in 1329. The other settlement was on 'that part of Inverleith nearest the harbour', granted in 1128 to Holyrood abbey, along with some rights in the harbour. Part of the abbey's burgh of the Canongate, it included the Coalhill on the south bank as well as the whole of the ground on the *Roodside* or north bank. Both settlements were called *Leith*, occasionally with the phrase 'on the north (or south) side of the water' added, to show which of them was being referred to; but by 1370 the Canongate township was also being termed NORTH LEITH, and two centuries later its counterpart SOUTH LEITH is recorded as the name of a parish that now embraced the whole of the ancient estate of Restalrig. In 1555 the township of South Leith (not the whole parish) was bought by the Crown and made a burgh of barony in its own right. Edinburgh purchased this burgh twelve years later, and with the further acquisition of North Leith in 1636, soon followed by that of the other baronies of the KING'S WARK and the CITADEL (*which see*) it controlled the whole town until 1833, when Leith became an independent parliamentary burgh. In 1920, Edinburgh and Leith were amalgamated.

LEITH FORT (North Leith) was a further development of THE BATTERY, *which see*. While *Ainslie* 1804 shows a fortified building with two bastions south of the Battery, it is possible that it was planned but never built, since there is no sign of it on *Kirkwood* 1817, which shows the Fort apparently as it is detailed on *Ordnance Survey* 1852, where the Battery remains but the rest appears to be a base and barracks for horse artillery, lightly defended by an enclosing wall, of which a fragment is preserved in North Fort Street.

LEITHHEAD (Kirknewton) is left unnamed but indicated as a mill on *Blaeu* 1654. Recorded as *Lethishede* in 1454, the name is clearly 'at the head of the (river) Leith' in the sense that the place is at the head of its main valley, the final ravine running back but half a mile to the branch of the Dean burn.

LEITH LINKS (South Leith) were part of a larger area of common land which stretched along the coast behind South Leith Sands, including part of SEAFIELD. They were probably the *cuniculario* or rabbit warren which, as an important source of fresh meat, Logan of Restalrig reserved to himself in 1398, when he otherwise granted Edinburgh free right of access to Leith over his lands. Later, as a common, they were primarily used for pasture, but also for the *gouf*, which seems to have been imported into Scotland from Holland in the 15th century and was no doubt played in Leith from the first, although the earliest record is dated 1619. The name is Scots from Anglian *hlincas*, sandy ground with hillocks and dunes, and the present artificial flatness dates from about 1880—*see under* GIANT'S BRAE, South Leith.

LEITH MILLS (South Leith) are shown on *Siege of Leith* 1560 and stood on the haugh in the bend of the river north of the Quilts. The evidence is that they were not the 'mills' included in Robert I's charter to Edinburgh (which were probably at the Dene) but that they were Restalrig estate mills from early times, serving that estate (including South Leith) in the Middle Ages, and apparently continuing to serve South Leith after it was separated from Restalrig in 1555, even although the mills were not included in the new burgh. They are listed in *RMS* 1580 as 'mills of Leith' among lands purchased from Logan of Restalrig; and in 1725 Edinburgh acquired the superiority, along with that of the Yardheads and other parts of Restalrig, by purchase from Lord Balmerino.

LEITH MOUNT (North Leith) is shown on *Wood* 1777 and named on *Ainslie* 1804. Its site (now that of Leith Town Hall) had been part of the most powerful bastion in the defences of Leith in 1548, shown on *Siege of Leith* 1560 as the *Cittedale*, with a *mount* or battery of six guns.

LEITH STREET (East End) is shown proposed and named on the earliest engraved plan of the *New Town* 1767, and is shown formed on *Taylor & Skinner* 1775. The name, derived from the fact that it linked the North Bridge with the Wester Road to Leith (*see* LEITH WALK) belonged to the carriageway only until the 1890s, when the side names HIGH TERRACE and CATHERINE STREET on the west, and CALTON STREET and GREENSIDE STREET on the east (all shown on *Ordnance Survey* 1852) were suppressed.

LEITH WALK was formed in about 1766 by amalgamation of two earlier features, a road and a walk, shown separately on *Roy* 1753 and *Fergus & Robinson* 1759 but named jointly on the latter as *The Walk or Wester Road from Edinburgh to Leith*. The road, shown on *Siege of Leith* 1560 and *Blaeu* 1654, was evidently older than the medieval village of Leith, since the Kirkgate was merely its northerly section; and it is likely that it originated as a track leading through the Calton gorge and down the ridge between the Greenside and Broughton burns to the primitive natural harbour at the Shore, Contrary to what is averred by Chambers and Wilson and others, the maps and numerous references show that it continued in use as a road right up until the time of its reconstruction in the 1770s, *see below*. For long it was referred to simply as the *road to Leith*, but by the 17th century (and in particular, after the purchase of the Canongate by Edinburgh in 1639) it became necessary to distinguish between this and the EASTER ROAD (*which see*) and they began to be called roads to Leith *by the Calton* and *by the Quarryholes*, both maintained by the town, and shown prominently as a pair on *Adair* 1682. The names *Easter* and *Wester* seem to have come in after 1700. Back in 1650, however, the Wester road had been pressed into service as a military way, to serve a great rampart fully a mile long and over 30 yards wide at its base, which was thrown up immediately east of the road by the Scots under David Leslie in order to bar the north flank of Edinburgh against the English Parliamentarians under Oliver Cromwell; and it was the parapet walk of this earthwork, stretching from the Calton down to St Anthony's gate, that became *The Walk* or *High Foot Walk* to Leith. Running up to 18 feet above the adjoining ground, and barred to all horse traffic on pain of the considerable fine of 10s sterling, it was not only useful to local people but was a veritable tourist attraction, commended in Richardson's 1748 edition of Defoe's *Tour through the Whole Island* as 'a very handsome gravel walk twenty feet wide, kept in good repair at the public charge'. But if this could be said of the Walk, the state of the medieval Wester Road went from bad to worse with the increase in wheeled traffic, and in 1776 the town let a contract for the reconstruction of Road and Walk as a single metalled highway. This accounts for the street's unusual spaciousness, as well as its varying width, for although there were later encroachments, its sides generally followed the eastern edge of the rampart and the western edge of the road; and the spreading out of the huge mass of earth in the rampart also resulted in a roadway which is several feet higher than the ground adjoining it. As LEITH WALK, the new boulevard took the name of the more distinctive of its two components. Linked to Princes Street by LEITH STREET (*which see*) it met with immediate success, referred to in 1784 as giving added urgency to the proposed completion of CONSTITUTION STREET, *which see*. Because it was by far the longest street in the city, and even more because many properties bordering it had been established before the reconstruction of 1776, addresses were grouped under more than two dozen side names, of which most are still in use.

LEITH WYND (Old Town) is mentioned in *Town Council Minutes* 1514, and got its name as the first part of the way to Leith by the Calton gorge. As such it probably represented a very ancient track, but there are indications in the road alignments and in the sett of the closes west of it that its line had been altered more than once to suit the earlier site(s) of the NETHERBOW, *which see*. The wynd was mostly in the Canongate, the march with Edinburgh running down its west side. In the 16th century the houses on this side of the upper wynd were semi-fortified, as part of Edinburgh's defences; but lower down, where the frontage was open ground, the town took steps from 1540 onwards to build 'ane honest and substantious wall' along the side of the road, as shown on *Rothiemay* 1647. The same map shows the foot of the wynd closed with the LEITH WYN(D) PORT. Referred to in 1550 by its earlier name of *Water yett* (not to be confused—as it often is—with the Canongate's WATERGATE or YETT, *which see*) this gate's indispensible function in that period seems to have been to give access for tipping 'the town's filth' into the Tummel burn. As shown on *City Improvements* 1866, the Wynd's entry at the Netherbow is still represented by the west side of Jeffrey Street; but its lower half, still represented on *Ordnance Survey* 1893 by a lower section of Cranston Street and a tunnel under the railway, was finally swept away when Waverley Station was extended a few years later. Until the 1950s, the right of way was maintained by a pedestrian bridge over the railway, albeit on a more westerly line.

LENNEL AVENUE (Murrayfield) *see under* GARSCUBE TERRACE, Murrayfield.

LENNIE is recorded from 1169 onwards, and the early forms *Lanin* and *Lanyne* show the name to be British *lein an* or Gaelic *leanain*, (place) at the haugh or swampy meadow. The division into two estates evidently took place before 1179, when NETHER LENNIE is recorded as *Lanyne minorem*, and the Scots terms *Nether* and *Over* (for LENNIE MAINS) are used on *Blaeu* 1654. LENNIE MUIR (restored as a street name in 1985) is shown on *Adair* 1682, and *Laurie* 1763 shows the subsidiary OVER THE MUIR. LENNIE HILL is the *hill at Lennie*. It would appear that the historic LENNIE PORT, shown on *Roy* 1753 and possibly named according to an old usage of *port* as an outlying field, began to be 'improved' into LENNIE PARK in about the 1860s. LENNIE BRAE appears to be FOUR MILE HILL, *which see*.

LENNOX ROW (Trinity) is shown on *Dall & Leslie* 1831 but little of it was built-up until about 1860. It was named in about 1864, almost certainly for the ship *Lennox*, starting a local fashion of naming streets after ships registered in the port of Leith—*see* LOMOND *and* STIRLING ROADS *and* ZETLAND PLACE.

LENNOX STREET (Dean) *see under* CLARENDON CRESCENT, Dean.

LENNOX TOWER (Currie) *see under* KELDELETHE, Currie.

LENNOX TOWER GARDENS (Balerno) was named in 1973, for the association who built it, who had in turn taken their name from Lennox Tower or KELDELETHE, Currie, *which see*.

LEOPOLD PLACE (Hillside) is included in the scheme of names for CALTON NEW TOWN (*which see*) shown on *Calton* 1819. Designed in detail in 1820 by William Playfair, the street was named for Leopold of Saxe Coburg, the Prince Regent's popular son-in-law, who visited Edinburgh more than once and was made a free burgess when he formally opened the Regent Bridge in 1819. *See also* COBURG STREET, SAXE COBURG PLACE, CLAREMONT CRESCENT etc.

LERBAR (Sighthill) is shown on *Saughton* 1795 and *Knox* 1812 as a farm on the south side of the Calder road, its steading on the east side of the entry to the Thieves road (now Wester Hailes Road) and its fields on the slope above the Murray burn between what are now Sighthill Avenue and the east end of Calder Crescent. It was taken into Sighthill and its steading was removed by 1893, but the cottage rows on the west side of Thieves road remained until the area was developed for housing in the 1960s. Although early forms are lacking, the name seems to be of considerable age and is probably from Anglian *leir baer* or *beorg*, muddy pasture or ridge, an apt description for fields on the Saughton ridge, well known for its many springs. LARBOURFIELD was named in 1983, using the form *Larbour* given on *Knox* 1812, as a place in the middle of the old farm.

LESLIE PLACE (Stockbridge) is shown projected on *Wood* 1823 as part of the revised scheme for the development of Sir Henry Raeburn's estate at DEANHAUGH, *which see*. It was named by 1829 for Count Leslie, former owner of Old Deanhaugh House, or else for his daughter (and Raeburn's stepdaughter) Ann Inglis or Leslie, who lived on at Deanhaugh with her family well into the mid-19th century; but the street was scarcely developed, and this only at its extreme ends, until after Old Deanhaugh House was cleared away in 1880.

LEUCHOLD (Dalmeny) figures on *Adair* 1682, and is recorded as *Luchqweld* in 1392, *Luchald(e)* in *RMS* 1430 and 1474, and *Leuchald* in 1640. The same name occurs at Dalgety Bay, on the immediately opposite shore of the Firth, and here the typical early spellings are *Louhild* c1220, *Lowchald* 1420, *Luchald* 1517 and *Luquhet* 1528. Although it is pronounced locally with the stress on the first syllable, it seems to be Celtic, and since both places stand back from the shore above tidal bays, it may be British *luch*, tidal pool, with either *kald*, little wood, or *alt*, sloping shore.

LEVEN STREET (Tollcross) is part of the ancient highroad to Linton, but acquired this independent name by 1809, evidently to serve new development on the land of Leven Lodge, inherited by Major David Williamson in 1808. Originally the house of DRUMDRYAN (*which see*) this property had been purchased in 1750 by the Earl of Leven, who renamed it *Leven Lodge*, and this name continued even although his heir sold the house in 1757. It was eventually incorporated in the Drumdryan Brewery, founded next door to it in 1760, and was cleared in 1904 to make way for the King's Theatre. LEVEN TERRACE, so named because it formed the east frontage of the property of Leven Lodge and Valleyfield, follows the line of the west walk in the

Meadows, shown on *Scott* 1759, but was developed in 1867-68 along with VALLEYFIELD STREET and GLENGYLE TERRACE, *which see*.

LEWIS TERRACE (Dalry) *see under* DALRY PLACE.

LEYS'S CLOSE (High Street) was west of Hart's Close, and like it, was suppressed when the North Bridge was built in 1765. The list of owners in Edinburgh in 1635, printed in *Old Edinburgh Club XIII*, shows property owned by Marion Leys, wife of Alexander Lawe, and it is reasonable to suppose that she may have been a relative of William Leyis, merchant, recorded in 1600 and 1607, and perhaps also of the Adam Leyis, goldsmith (possibly father and son of the same name and trade) recorded in 1530 and 1550.

LIBERTON is recorded in the 11th century as part of a surname, and as a place from 1128 onwards. The early spellings Libertune and Libbertoun show the name to be Anglian *hlida beretûn*, the *bere* or barley *tûn* or farm at the *hlid* or slope; a description which fits the topography exactly, here and at the other Scottish Liberton at Quothquhan, Lanarkshire. (The popular explanation of the name as 'leper town' is not only fanciful but impossible, since the place name is much older than any use of the word 'leper' or 'lipper' in Scots.) LIBERTON KIRK had evidently been a chapel of St Cuthbert's parish for quite some time before David I gave it to his new abbey of Holyrood in 1128; and the KIRKTON OF LIBERTON was the centre for working its lands. By the 14th century the estate was divided into the two separate baronies of NETHER LIBERTON, centred at THE INCH (*which see*) and UPPER or OVER LIBERTON, centred at LIBERTON TOWER from about 1400, and at LIBERTON HOUSE from 1675. In about 1812, the old highroad to Liberton and the south (now represented by Mayfield Road, the lower part of Liberton Brae, and Alnwickhill Road) was bypassed by a new 'great road'. For long known as the PENICUIK ROAD, it was renamed in various parts in 1926: its southern section took the name, already a side name here from before 1900, of LIBERTON GARDENS; its middle section was given the old name of LIBERTON BRAE, previously belonging to ALNWICKHILL ROAD, *which see*; while its northern section, between the Dams and Mayfield Toll, was named partly CRAIGMILLAR PARK and partly (and rather misleadingly) NETHER LIBERTON—an arrangement altered in 1985, when the construction of a roundabout at Mayfield Toll enabled the road from here to the Dams to be renamed LIBERTON ROAD, freeing the old name for use at the old village of *Nether Liberton*. LIBERTON DRIVE, formerly part of Liberton's KIRKGATE (*which see*) was renamed in about 1925. LIBERTON GARDENS was named in 1993. LIBERTON MAINS ROAD leads to the former farm steading of that name. MID LIBERTON was newly coined in 1980 for a new housing precinct which, although it lies on a haugh in Nether Liberton, might reasonably be said to be between the two ancient places of Over and Nether Liberton.

LIBERTON DAMS is shown on *Adair* 1682; and the later 18th-century maps, as well as *Ordnance Survey* 1852, show how it got its name from the two *dams* (the Scots term for mill lades) which met here: one from a *cauld* or weir in the Braid burn 600 yards further upstream, the other supplied by a small burn rising near Liberton House and coming down the Liberton brae (now Alnwickhill Road) to power a waulk mill and perhaps other mills at the Dams before it merged with the first and ran on as a single lade to serve the mill at Nether Liberton. The Dams was also notable for a steam pump which was set up in 1788 with a staff of twenty men, to pump water from the Braid burn into the city's water supply at a rate of fifty gallons per minute.

LIBERTON'S WYND (260 High Street and 74 Cowgate) is shown on *Rothiemay* 1647 and referred to as a landmark in a letter from James III, engrossed in *Town Council Minutes* 1477. As a 'wynd' it was evidently a public street from the beginning. As noted in *Protocols of John Foular* 1531, a land on its west side had once belonged to Henry Liberton, also referred to as deceased in *RMS* 1501; and it is likely that the wynd was named for him or for others in the family, which included David de Liberton, laird of Over Liberton, who was made serjeant of the upper ward of Edinburgh in the time of David Bruce 1329-71, as well as William de Liberton, provost in 1426. The wynd was on the line of the east pavement of George IV Bridge, and was suppressed when that street was constructed.

LIDDESDALE PLACE (Stockbridge) was named in 1980, continuing the style of the existing fancy names of Avondale and Teviotdale Place—*see under* THE COLONIES, Stockbridge.

LIDGATE (Ratho) appears on *Hatton etc* 1797 in the names of the *Easter* and *Wester Lidgate* fields flanking a section of the road shown on *Roy* 1753 and *Armstrongs* 1773 as continuing straight from Ratho kirk to the junction with the Calder road at Gateside. The *Statistical Account* 1845 reports that although this part of the road had come to be regarded as part of the MAIN STREET of Ratho, it was still remembered as 'the Ludgate'—a spelling possibly suggested by the well-known London street name. The name persists (or was revived) in that of the LUD PATH, and was borrowed for the 'Ludgate Lodge', a property shown on *Gellatly* 1834 (and probably also on *Knox* 1812) which was redeveloped in 1990 and named LIDGATE SHOT, or 'field beside Lidgate'. The name is Anglian, the first part *hlid*, a hinged door, and the second part either *geat*, an opening, or else *gata*, a road. Thus it meant 'opening with hinged gate' (as distinct from the usual flake or hurdle, which could not be swung open but had to be lifted aside) or more probably it was 'the road with hinged gate(s)'; but in either case it evidently arose because, as shown on *Hatton etc* 1797, this section of the public road went through the middle of the croft or arable land of Ratho, and had to be equipped at both ends with gates to keep stock from straying into the croft. The plan of the village on *Hatton etc* shows that the route to Dalmahoy had been altered to its modern form before 1797; and in 1962 its northern part (originally the Lidgate) together with the road continuing past Ratho Kirk, was renamed BAIRD ROAD, for Hugh Baird, the engineer who designed the Union Canal in 1818.

LILLIPUT (Trinity) is shown on *Roy* 1753 as *Lilliputt Hall*, and the name is mentioned in Leith birlaw court minutes in 1744, less than twenty years after Swift published *Gulliver's Travels* in 1726. It was evidently given by Pierre de la Motte, dancing master in Edinburgh and farmer of a *half plough* (about 65 acres) at Trinity Hut at least as early as 1742. *Ainslie* 1804 shows the house and its 8½ acre policies approached from the Ferry road, apparently over Bangholm ground, by a *Lillypot Avenue*—a spelling perhaps influenced by *Lily Pot Lane* in London. By 1852 most of the policies had become a market garden, and by 1893 this had been taken into the adjoining property of DENHAM GREEN, *which see*; but the house appears as *Lilliput* in the *PO Directory* until 1852, and on *W & A K Johnston* 1861. EAST LILLIPUT was named in 1988: in point of fact, it lies within the original Denham Green, but the encroachment was excused by the earlier incursion of that name into Lilliput proper.

LILYHILL TERRACE (Parson's Green) *see under* PARSON'S GREEN.

LILY LOCH (Dalmeny) is the name—presumably derived from the water plants growing in it—given for Dundas Loch on a plan of Humbie in 1720 (*RHP 6728*) as well as *Ordnance Survey* 1852.

LILY TERRACE (North Merchiston) *see under* PRIMROSE TERRACE, North Merchiston.

LINDEAN PLACE (South Leith) once WAVERLEY PLACE—*see under* INDUSTRIAL ROAD.

LINDSAY PLACE (Old Town) appears on *Ordnance Survey* 1852 as a side name for a terrace of houses and shops in part of Society, opposite Greyfriars Place. It was cleared for museum development in the 1970s. The name was presumably the developer's, and there may have been a connection with Thomas Lindsay, shoemaker, who was living at 4 Lindsay Place in 1855.

LINDSAY ROAD (North Leith) dates from 1864, when the extension of the Caledonian Railway to a goods station newly built on made ground at the west end of Commercial Street gave opportunity to form a new and satisfactory road to Newhaven along a coast which had constantly suffered from dangerous erosion. It was named for William Lindsay, Provost of Leith 1860-66, who had played a leading part in the scheme. Part of the roadway was realigned after the closure and removal of the railway. The name was borrowed in 1963 when LINDSAY STREET was formed in the course of redeveloping the site of the BATTERY—*which see*; and it was borrowed again in 1979 for LINDSAY PLACE, a side name created when the adjoining area of LONDON ROW and HELEN STREET and PLACE (formerly CANNON STREET) was redeveloped.

LINDSAY'S or **ALEXANDER LINDSAY'S CLOSE** (131 High Street) *see* BISHOP'S CLOSE.

LINDSAY'S CLOSE (at about 350 High Street) stood on a site now immediately in front of the entrance to the Tolbooth kirk, and was cleared to make way for it by 1839. The earliest known connection of a Lindsay with the close was that of George Lindsay, born 1708 and becoming depute town clerk in 1757, who lived with his wife Christian Taylor in *Lindsay' Land*—a house which, being already a landmark in 1736, must have been named for some earlier member of the family. *Maitland* 1753 calls the close ALEXr LINDSAY'S, which might conceivably have referred to Alexander Lindsay, deacon of the Hammermen, active in town council from 1648 onwards. There may also have been some connection with the family in the other *Lindsay's Close* at 131 High Street—*see under* BISHOP'S CLOSE. The close is also recorded in 1687 as SHEEL'S, which may have been for William Shiel, merchant, mentioned in *Town Council Minutes* 1698; but again the name seems likely to be earlier—perhaps much earlier, for James and Simon de Schele were members of the *dusane* or council in 1403 and a James and Alexander Schele were bailies in 1457.

LINDSAY'S MILL (Water of Leith or Dean Village) is shown thus on *Ordnance Survey* 1852, is named as *Dean Distillery* on the *Survey* of 1893, but was demolished in 1931. Entries in *Town Council Minutes* 1556 show that it was built for the town in that year, by James Lindsay.

LINKLIN BURN (Dalmeny) is Anglian *blynn*, fast-running burn, coming down to a *blinc*, undulating sandy ground, behind the shore, Scots *burn* having been added later, when the meaning of *-lin* had become forgotten.

LINKS LANE (South Leith) evidently developed as a new access to the Links in the 18th century. There is no sign of it on *Naish* 1709, but *Wood* 1777 shows it as a loan cutting across the remains of the rampart of 1548. *Thomson* 1822 shows the name as at present, and the alternative LOVERS LANE given on *Ordnance Survey* 1852 may have been coined not long before.

LINKS OF LEITH included LEITH LINKS (*which see*) belonging to South Leith, and the WEST LINKS or NORTH LEITH LINKS. These last appear to have been greatly eroded by the sea in the 16th century (*see under* NORTH LEITH SANDS) and *Town Council Minutes* 1562 and 1573, in describing 'their West Links' as between the St Nicholas Chapel (which was sited roughly halfway along Commercial Street) and Wardie Brow, seem to lump together the Links of Newhaven with other coastal land east of Ankerfield burn.

LINKS PLACE and **GARDENS** (South Leith) are part of the *road to Restalrig* through Leith Links, shown on *Naish* 1709. By the late 18th century properties here were being addressed as at LINKS, but by 1806 property on the north side of the road east of the foot of Bath Street (now Salamander Place) was called St JAMES PLACE and by 1808 the service lane behind it was named St JAMES LANE. In similar fashion LINKS PLACE was adopted by 1827 as a side name for properties between the junctions with Elbe Street and Bath Street. It seems likely that St James Place was named more for its owner than for any saint, for the *St* was being dropped by the early 1820s. JAMES PLACE LANE began to be developed in about 1890 and was for long addressed as part of James Place. In 1966 the group was renamed 'because of duplication' (with what is not clear), James Place becoming LINKS GARDENS, James Place Lane LINKS GARDENS LANE and James Lane (with a touch of fantasy) LINKS GROVE.

LINNHEADS (Colinton) is recorded in 1709 as in the vicinity of the waterfall at what became the head of Torduff reservoir, which submerged the burn in the ravine further downstream. Scots *linn* has a double ancestry: from British *linn* or Gaelic *linne* it is 'a pool', whereas from Anglian *hlynn* it is 'a torrent', especially a noisy one; but often (as here) these features are combined.

LINN MILL (Queensferry) is shown on *Roy* 1753 and obviously is named as the mill adjoining the burn and waterfall. As noted above, Scots *linn* can refer to either a torrent or a pool. The LINN MILL BURN, referred to in 1441 as *the Mylburn*, has obviously lost some earlier independent name; but the evidence suggests that *the linn* is not the general name of the burn, but of the cataract and pools in and above the deep cleugh in which the burn finally runs out to the sea.

LIN'S MILL (Newbridge) is recorded in 1591 as *Cliftounhallmyln* (*see under* CLIFTON, Newbridge) occupied by a William Lyn; and since the inscription on LIN'S GRAVE on the slope above the Mill records the death in 1645 of William Lin *heritor of Linsmiln*, it is clear that the mill was named for one of that family before that date. Kirkliston parish records show yet another William Lin as tenant in *Lin's Mill* in 1663.

LISMORE AVENUE and **CRESCENT** (Parson's Green) *see under* PARSON'S GREEN.

LISTON is recorded from about 1165 onwards, but is now known only in the names of some of its medieval subdivisions, *see* LISTONSHIELS, KIRKLISTON, AULD- or OLDLISTON, and NEWLISTON. The name's early forms *Listun* or *Lyston* show it to be a hybrid, combining Anglian *tún*, farm place, with British *liss*. While this last word generally meant 'house or court of a chieftain', there is evidence in Cornish place names that it was sometimes used to name ancient ruins of unknown origin; and this would seem to be highly significant in the present case, for the most kenspeckle features by far in the primitive landscape must have been the immense Bronze-age monument of the Huly hill at Newbridge, with its cairn, stone circle and outlying monoliths, and the Catstane with its burial mound at West Briggs. Either might have been known as the *Liss*, and in either case 'farm at the Liss' would fit the heart-land of Liston.

LISTON DRIVE and **PLACE** (Kirkliston) were named in about 1950 for Sir Robert Liston (1742-1836) distinguished linguist, diplomat and privy councillor, who was born at Overtoun of Newliston. LISTON ROAD, in the same development, was named for the original name of the estates—*see* LISTON.

LISTONSHIELS (Balerno) is recorded from 1280 onwards, and is shown on *Blaeu* 1654. The name is early Scots *scheles* (from old Norse *skáli*) huts in which the women and children lived when looking after stock on summer grazings, in this case a large area of hill land attached to LISTON, *which see*. Certainly part of it belonged to the Templar barony of Auldliston (*see also under* BUTELAND) but it is also listed in *RMS* 1618 as part of the St Andrew's barony of Kirkliston: quite possibly each had a share of these uplands, and the connection may go back to a time before Liston was divided into these baronies in the 12th century.

LITTLE CARRON (South Leith) *see under* CARRON PLACE, South Leith.

LITTLE FRANCE (Craigmillar) is recorded from 1655 onwards. The rather thin story that it got its name from the residence of French servants of Mary Queen of Scots is mentioned, with appropriate caution, in *White's Liberton* 1786; and although it has since been elaborated with circumstantial detail, it remains a sheer guess. Considering that the name belonged to the mill, given as *Frenchmill* on *Roy* 1753, and that although included in a list of parts of the barony of Craigmillar in *RMS* 1655 it does not figure in earlier lists of the same sort, it is perhaps more likely that some French cloth workers settled here in the early 17th century, when there seems to have been a market for such enterprise, *see under* BONNYHAUGH, Bonnington.

LITTLE KING STREET (East End) *see under* St JAMES SQUARE.

LITTLE LONDON (South Leith) figures on *Siege of Leith* 1560, as also in Hayward's *Annals* of the siege, as the name of the northeast bastion of the fortifications, or possibly the ground immediately north of it. *Town Council Minutes* 1575 refer to a 'house upon the linkis callit lytill Loundoun' in terms that imply that the links, rather than the house, bore the name. In *City Charters* 1578 it is attached to meadow land within the ramparts (apparently the area now bounded by Maritime Street and Lane, Constitution Street and Bernard Street) while the Golden Charter of 1636 uses it for part of that meadow 'together with the fort(h) and mount thereof', which is presumably the nearby north-eastern bastion of the ramparts. There is nothing to link the name with the English capital. It is certainly earlier than 1560 and probably predates the fortification of 1548. The evidence is that it is a land name; and considering that *Lundin* and *Little Lun* are recorded as place names on the Fife coast opposite Leith in 1200 and 1605, and that the spelling *Loun-* may indicate an early pronunciation, it is perhaps Celtic, akin to Gaelic *lunndan*, smooth green or marshy spot. Features of this kind, conspicuous in the arid links, occur quite frequently among Lothian's coastal dunes; and the contours suggest that quite possibly a rivulet draining the east side of the Coalhill once flowed through this area.

LITTLE ROAD (Liberton) was named in 1931 in general reference to the Little family, owners in Liberton from the time of William Little, provost of Edinburgh 1586-91, who acquired part of Over Liberton in 1587. His descendent William Charles Little (Gilmour) of Over Liberton inherited Nether Liberton and Craigmillar in 1792.

(CLEMENT) LITTLE'S CLOSE (172 High Street) *see* OLD ASSEMBLY CLOSE.

(EDWARD) LITTLE'S CLOSE (251 High Street) *see* OLD POST OFFICE CLOSE.

LITTLE'S CLOSE (304 High Street) *see* BRODIE'S CLOSE.

LIVINGSTONE PLACE (Sciennes) was named by 1868 for David Livingstone, missionary and explorer, who had been made a free burgess of Edinburgh in 1857, and was by this time engaged in his last African journey which had started in 1866 and was to end with his death in Zambia in 1873.

LIVINGSTONE PLACE (South Leith) was in the first group of streets developed at INDUSTRIAL ROAD (*which see*) and was named for David Livingstone by 1868, at about the same time as LIVINGSTONE PLACE in Sciennes (*see above*) was named for him; and it was in order to obviate any confusion between the two that the street in South Leith was renamed SOMERSET PLACE in 1968. The new name was given in the general but wholly mistaken belief that the nearby GIANT'S BRAE (*which see*) in Leith Links is the remains of *Mount Somerset*, raised by the English army in the course of besieging Leith in 1560 and named for one of their captains; whereas in point of fact, as shown on *Siege of Leith* 1560, this large temporary fort was sited in Pilrig, while the south end of Somerset Place is within the site of the similar fort of *Mount Pelham*, constructed two or three weeks earlier.

LIVINGSTOUN'S CLOSE (High Street) *see under* ALEXANDER KING'S CLOSE.

LIXMOUNT (Trinity) was built in extensive grounds in 1794 and so named because the proprietor's wife hailed from Lix, in Glen Dochart, Perthshire. This curious name comes from a group of three places, each named in Gaelic *lic,* the place at the stone slab or slope, but known collectively in English as *the Lics*—hence, phonetically, *Lix*. Housing development began at the east end of the estate in 1882 under the name LIXMOUNT TERRACE, restyled LIXMOUNT VILLAS in 1895; but in 1903 the separate name was dropped and the houses were addressed as part of East Trinity Road. Meantime the old house had been demolished and redevelopment of the main part of the grounds began with LIXMOUNT GARDENS in 1903 and continued in 1907 with LIXMOUNT AVENUE and BERESFORD GARDENS—*which see*.

THE LOAN (Currie) *see* THE LONE, Currie.

THE LOAN or **WEST LOANING** (Queensferry) is clearly shown on both *Dundas* 1757 and *Barnbougle & Dalmeny* c1800 in the typical form of a loaning (i.e. a roadway flanked on each side by a strip of grazing) leading up from the west end of the burgh to a bridge over the Ferry burn, at which point (now the entry of Scotstoun Avenue) it changes character and continues as a highway to Kirkliston. It got its alternative name because it was the wester of the two loans (*Barnbougle & Dalmeny* c1800 shows both) that led up to the RAVEL, MUIRHALL, the FERRY ACRES and the FERRY MUIR, *all of which see*. The modern change of street name, where the burgh's *The Loan* gives way to the county highways name *Kirkliston Road*, arose simply because the road crossed the burgh boundary at the railway bridge.

LOANHEAD (Kirkliston) is recorded in 1669 and appears as *Lonehead* on *Roy* 1753. Evidently named as the place *at the head of the loan*, it is at the first summit in the road leading out of Kirkliston to Queensferry.

LOANHEAD (Newbridge) is shown on *Laurie* 1763 on the north side of the crossroads in Newbridge—i.e. at the *head of the loan* which leads northwards and used to connect with Hallyards and Maitland Bridge.

LOANHEID (Balerno) *see under* BUTELAND, Balerno.

LOANING ROAD (Restalrig) is the western remnant of a loan shown on *Roy* 1753, leading from Restalrig and Craigentinnie to Fillyside, joining the coast road from Leith at or near the present FILLYSIDE ROAD. The root is Anglian *lone*, Scots *loan*, originally a road or street but also a grassy track or farm road, and *loaning* implied a right of way for driving cattle. LOANING CRESCENT was developed in 1932 on land once part of the golf course.

LOCHBANK (New Town) *see under* HALKERSTON'S CROFT, New Town.

LOCHEND (Newbridge) is shown on *Knox* 1812. The name is either fancy (which seems unlikely) or else obscure, inasmuch as no map shows any sheet of water in the vicinity; but the *Geological Survey* indicates that the burn about 300 yards south of the steading has a considerable flood plain, and it is possible that there was once some standing water here.

LOCHEND (Restalrig) was probably a minor local name for land *at the end of the (Restalrig) loch* until after the slighting of Restalrig tower in about 1586 (*see under* RESTALRIG) but *Adair* 1682 shows it as having supplanted the Restalrig name. The present LOCHEND HOUSE, dating from 1816, incorporates a fragment of an older building. LOCHEND ROAD is named as the road leading to it, but was earlier the *road to Restalrig Place*, as shown on the *Siege of Leith* 1560. In 1925 part of *Lochend farm* was developed as LOCHEND AVENUE, CRESCENT, DRIVE, GARDENS, GROVE, SQUARE and QUADRANT. In 1926, LOCHEND PARK was built on *Logan's lea*, but was named for the adjoining public park.

LOCHEND CASTLE BARNS (Lochend) was coined in 1989 as a name for a development within ground which, later shown on *Kirkwood* 1817 as a park attached to Lochend House, is shown on *Siege of Leith* 1560 as the large fortified outer yard or barmkin of Restalrig tower, the forerunner of Lochend House.

(EAST or **NETHER) LOCHEND'S CLOSE** and **(LITTLE) LOCHEND'S CLOSE** (107 & 115 Canongate) are shown on *Ainslie* 1780 and were named for James Fergusson of Lochend, who had property in the north side of Canongate before 1682: probably the house and yard at the foot of the closes, recorded in 1703 as owned by John Ferguson, tanner, burgess of Edinburgh, and before him by William Ferguson of Lochend in Restalrig. The term *Little* simply distinguished this close as the narrower of the pair.

LOCHFLATT (South Side) is mentioned in *Protocols of James Young* 1492. In modern terms it lay between Lauriston Terrace and Buccleuch Street and between Lauriston Place and the Meadows. The name evidently originated in the low ground north-east of the Burgh Loch. The property was among those acquired by the Heriot Trust in 1639, and was thereafter also known as HERIOTSCROFT.

LOCHRIN got its name from the *rin* or tail burn which ran out of the South Loch at what is now the east end of Lonsdale Terrace and (in modern terms) followed a line along the east backs of Lauriston Gardens before turning west along the north backs of Panmure Place and thence through Lochrin and Dalry to the river at Coltbridge, as illustrated at p260 in *Old Edinburgh Club X*. LOCHRIN HOUSE, replaced by LOCHRIN BUILDINGS in 1897, was built by Samuel Gilmore in 1792 (*see under* GILMORE PLACE, Lochrin) but occupied in about 1795 by James Haig, one of the proprietors of the Lochrin Distillery, shown on *Ainslie* 1804; and LOCHRIN PLACE (1897) TERRACE (1898) and LANE were created by redevelopment of the distillery site.

LOCH ROAD (Craigcrook) *see under* CRAIGCROOK.

LOCH ROAD (Queensferry) continues a traditional name as part of the *road to the loch* shown on *Plewlandfield* 1769. Branching off the LOAN in a double curve that suggests that it was following a watercourse, this road led up over the Skaith muir to the east end of a loch which lay in what is still open space immediately north of Inchcolm Terrace. As shown on *Plewlands* 1887, its junction with the Loan was modified in the 1860s to suit the railway cutting, and at the same time it was intersected by the new bypass road to Hopetoun, *see* HOPETOUN ROAD *and* STEWART TERRACE. Feuing at the east end of this bypass in 1887 led to that section of it sharing the name of Loch Road until it was renamed STEWART TERRACE in about 1954. Part of the original Loch Road survives as a path to Loch Place, and the rest of it was redeveloped as VIEWFORTH ROAD, *which see*. LOCH PLACE was built in the Skaithmuir and named in 1970, evidently for Loch Road rather than the loch itself, for as noted above, the *place of the loch* is some 200 yards further south.

LOCHSIDE CRESCENT (Gogar) *see under* EDINBURGH PARK, Gogar.

LOCKERBY COTTAGES (Liberton) were named in about 1894 for Thomas Lockerby, who had left the Lockerby Trust fund for building and administering houses for decayed gentlemen. They were built in the southern part of the grounds of Burnhead House (*see under* BURNHEAD CRESCENT etc, Liberton) and the remainder of its grounds were developed and named in 1977 as LOCKERBY CRESCENT and GROVE.

LOCKHARTON AVENUE etc (Meggetland) *see under* MEGGETLAND.

LAURENCE LOCKIE'S CLOSE (54 Grassmarket) *see* CARMICHAEL'S CLOSE, Grassmarket.

LODGE-ME-LOWNE (North Leith) is recorded in *South Leith Records* 1684 as a deserted farm and a haunt of rogues, on a site which was later to be developed as BATHFIELD, *which see*. While on the face of it the earlier name may contain Scots *lodge* and *lown* in a whimsical phrase 'let me lie snug' or 'in peace' (perhaps apt enough for this place on an exposed coast) on the other hand it may be a corruption of some Celtic name containing *lon* or *luan*, a marshy spot—*see also* LITTLE LONDON, South Leith.

LOGANLEA AVENUE (Restalrig) together wlth LOGANLEA DRIVE, LOAN, ROAD and TERRACE (1932) and LOGANLEA GARDENS and PLACE (1933) got the name as being on the medieval estate of the Logans of Restalrig, but it may also have been transferred from *Logan's lea*, a field at the north end of Lochend Loch, mentioned in *Town Council Minutes* 1602 as *loganes ley*, the place appointed for the *wappenschaw* or military review of the townsfolk. While this name may have been Scots *Logan's lea*, for a meadow close beside the Logans' tower house (now Lochend House) it was obviously but one such meadow in their wide estate, and it is just possible that the name as recorded in 1602 was a late form of an earlier name, British or Gaelic *lagan liath*, little grey hollow, describing the site of the loch.

LOGAN'S CLOSE (287 Canongate) *see* EAST COMMON CLOSE, Canongate.

LOGAN STREET (Canonmills) was named by 1907. The property in it was initially owned by Thomas Anderson of 172 Easter Road, and he may have named the street for the Logans of Restalrig or (more likely) for some connection of his own.

LOGIE GREEN (Canonmills) is shown on *Fergus & Robinson* 1759 as open ground within BOAT GREEN (*which see*) and as *Provost Stoddart's House, Logie Hall* on *Ainslie's Leith River* 1787. It is probable that the house was built by James Stoddart, who was a merchant and Lord Provost in 1774-76. While the name may have been fancy, it is not impossible that it was an existing land name, Scots *logie haw*, haugh in the hollow, *haw* being often spelt as *hall*; and this is perhaps supported by the variation to Logie *Green*, appearing on *Ainslie* 1804, for the maps make it fairly clear that there were no working bleachfields here, of the sort found in the adjoining Boat Green and Clerk's Mill. The mansion was pulled down when LOGIE GREEN ROAD was being formed in about 1902, and its site is now occupied by LOGIE GREEN GARDENS, named in 1936 at the same time as LOGIE GREEN LOAN. The LOGIE MILL given on *Ordnance Survey* 1852 is shown (unnamed) on *Fergus & Robinson* 1759, *Leith River* 1787 and *Ainslie* 1804, and is given (by implication) as *Clerk's Mill* on *Kirkwood* 1817 and *Pollock* 1834, and it would seem that *Logie Mill* was a late name, derived from Logie Green.

LOMOND ROAD (Trinity) was named and beginning to be occupied in 1881. Possibly, like other streets in the neighbourhood (e.g.

LENNOX ROW, STIRLING ROAD), it was named for a ship registered in the port of Leith—in this case, the Ben Line's *Ben Lomond*, or else an earlier ship of the name which plied as a ferry in the Forth.

LONDON ROAD (Hillside to Meadowbank) is sketched on *Ainslie* 1804 as one of a pair of proposed approach roads diverging from the existing London road at Meadowbank and connecting with the expanding city at Drummond Street and Leith Walk. Both proposals also appear on *Knox* 1812, but the northern one is modified to show not only an additional loop south of the Calton (*see* REGENT ROAD) but alternative alignments for the northern section between Easter Road and Leith Walk—alternatives which were still a matter of debate in the Joint Committee for the CALTON NEW TOWN (*which see*) even as late as 1819, for Playfair argues strongly for his chosen line and levels in his report on the scheme finally accepted in December of that year. The view from Royal Terrace was his main consideration, the spacious street and gardens and the terrace frontages beyond them on the north forming an impressive foreground. *Calton* 1819 shows the street as GREAT LONDON ROAD; and it was apparently this plan that proposed the name REGENT ROAD for the southern loop which had been temporarily known as *Great London Road*, as shown on *Kirkwood* 1817.

LONDON ROW (North Leith) *see under* CANNON STREET.

LONDON STREET (New Town) *see under* NORTHERN NEW TOWN. The name was extended to EAST LONDON STREET in about 1872.

LONDON WHARF (North Leith) is shown on *Ordnance Survey* 1852 on the south side of the access now known as RONALDSON'S WHARF. It was the point of departure of ships of the London Steamship Company.

THE LONE or **LOAN** (Currie) is shown on *Armstrongs* 1773 and later maps up until 1852, when the *Ordnance Survey* shows *Kenleith Smiddy*, now a house called 'Crossroads'. The early name is mapped as a place name, and is mentioned in Jamie Thomson's poem *Mary Shanks* c1800 in a way that clearly implies a place; but notwithstanding this it would seem to have been transferred from the loan which, as shown on *Roy* 1753, combined with the KIRKGATE and CLOCHMEAD GATE to form an ancient way through the hills, as well as giving access to summer grazings.

LONG BRAES (Balerno) *see under* BRIDGE ROAD, Balerno.

LONG CRAIG (Queensferry) is the descriptive name of a reef of shale running 300 yards out to sea. It was extended by the LONGCRAIG PIER in about 1811 and LONGCRAIG ROAD is named as leading to it.

LONGCROOK (Queensferry) was named in 1986 as being built in the *Long Crook* and the *Stonyflatt* fields of Plewlands, shown on *Plewlandfield* 1769. The name is Scots, a ploughman's term for a field with something affecting the sett of his ploughing riggs, probably referring in the present case to the kink in its eastern boundary. Until the 1890s it was divided into two by the *kirk road* from Echline to Dalmeny, *see under* LOVERS LOAN, Queensferry.

LONGFORMACUS ROAD (Liberton) was named in 1930 for Jean, daughter of Sir Robert Sinclair of Longformacus, who married Sir Charles Gilmour of Craigmillar in 1733. Since their son died without issue, the family line was carried on through Sir Charles's sister, who had married a Little of Liberton. Recorded as *Langeford Makhous* in 1340, the Berwickshire place name is Gaelic *longphort Maccus*, home or shieling of Maccus.

LONG GREEN (Dalmeny) appears as a field name on *Barnbougle & Dalmeny* c1800, and describes this stretch of ground by the sea.

LONG LINN (Braid) appears as a field name on *Braid* 1772 in a position that suggests that it was the name of the long reach of the Braid burn through the gorge of Braid. It is probably Scots *linn*, from Anglian *hlynn*, a torrent.

LONGSTONE (Slateford) appears on *Knox* 1812 as *Long Stone*. This division into two words responds exactly to the traditional local pronunciation of the name, and indicates its origin, which was in a long narrow slab of Hailes stone, holed for a railing along one edge only, that served as a bridge over the Murray burn on the *Burnside* right-of-way along the riverside to Stenhouse mill. Replaced by a steel bridge in about 1930, the original stone now serves as a coping on the west bank of the burn, immediately upstream from the bridge. The village grew up in the late 19th century, after the quarry village of HAILES (*which see*) was cleared away to make room for extension of Hailes Quarry. LONGSTONE ROAD, traditionally known as the *Coal Road*, was renamed in about 1920, as leading to Longstone from Saughton. LONGSTONE CRESCENT was named in 1923 and LONGSTONE AVENUE and STREET in 1935, the latter being extended to serve a prefab development in 1947 and then shortened again in 1964, when the prefabs were replaced by permanent housing. LONGSTONE GROVE and PLACE were also named in 1947. LONGSTONE GARDENS and TERRACE, built on Saughtonmill ground, were named in 1952, and LONGSTONE VIEW was added in 1965. LONGSTONE PARK was named in 1964 as a replacement of the 19th-century ANGLE PARK development, which in turn had taken its name before 1870 from that of the triangular field in which it was built.

LONSDALE TERRACE (Tollcross), developed in Drumdryan by 1867, was in all probability named for William Lowther, 3rd Earl of Lonsdale, who besides being politically active in the same period as Henry Brougham (*see under* BROUGHAM STREET) was like him in being connected with Westmorland. A more local but less likely source of the name might be Henry Lonsdale, prominent as a physician in Edinburgh, partner and biographer of Robert Knox, the Anatomist.

THE LONYNG (near the Greyfriars) *see* CANDLEMAKER ROW, Old Town.

LOPLYSTANE (Canongate) *see under* LAPLEE STANE, Canongate.

LORD RUSSELL PLACE (Sciennes) is shown on *Pollock* 1834 and is named on *Ordnance Survey* 1852. It was named for Lord John Russell

(1792-1878) 1st Earl Russell, who was a graduate of Edinburgh University, introduced the Reform Bill in 1832, became Home Secretary in 1835 and Prime Minister in 1846, and was made a free burgess of Edinburgh in 1845.

LORNE STREET (Quarryholes) was occupied in 1870 and named for the Marquess of Lorne, heir of the Duke of Argyll, who was then engaged to the Princess Louise, Queen Victoria's daughter, and married her in March 1871. The branch streets LORNE SQUARE and PLACE were named in 1897 and 1900 respectively.

LORNE TERRACE (Abbeyhill) is a terrace of six houses, so named by 1871 but renamed in 1901 as Nos. 21-31 SPRING GARDENS. The reason for the choice of the original name may have been the same as in the case of LORNE STREET.

LOTHIAN is recorded from 1091 onwards in such forms as Latin *Laudonia* or *Lodoneium*, Scots *Lowthian* or *Loven*, and NormanFrench *Loeneis*, which is probably the original of the *Lyonesse* in Malory's Arthur story. In the 12th century, persons were freely invented to account for the name: the *Life of Kentigern* has the saint's grandfather as 'Leudonis' ruling 'Leudonia' from Dunpelder (Traprain Law) while Geoffrey of Monmouth summons up a 'Duke Loth' to rule 'Lothian': but in *Old Edinburgh Club XXXV* G W S Barrow points out that *Lothian* can be shown to be a stream name of British origin (*see* LOTHIAN BURN) and interprets the regional name as originating as (*the lands round*) *the Lothian* (*burn*). Despite this modest beginning, by the 10th century the name had been expanded to cover the area of the modern region, more or less; and the subdivision into *East, Mid* and *West Lothian* was similarly early, although these names are not recorded until the 15th and 16th centuries. In parallel with this local use, 'Lothian' was sometimes used in a looser way to cover south-east Scotland; and some foreign writers went even further, wrongly supposing it to be a name for Northumbria itself.

THE LOTHIAN BURN (Hillend to Magdalen Bridge) is recorded in about 1254 as the burn at Niddrie, showing that this is the primary name of the burn now also called *Burdiehouse, Niddrie, Brunstane* or *Magdalene burn* where it flows through these neighbourhoods. Early forms such as *Lodone, Louenyn* and *Louthyan* suggest that the name is British *lutna*, dark or muddy stream—a name perhaps given by contrast with the *pefr* or clear burn that flows closely parallel to it at Niddrie, *see under* PEFFERMILL. The burn's name seems to have generated the regional name of LOTHIAN, *which see*. LOTHIANBURN (Hillend) is shown on *Adair* 1682 as *Loudonburn*, and is so named as the place where the highway crosses the Lothian burn and probably has done so since the late 1st century, *see under* ROMAN ROADS.

THE LOTHIAN ROAD (West End and Tollcross) was completed in 1785. The story that it was built in a single day in order to win a bet is mere fairy tale: the facts are that the Town Council planned it in 1783 as a 'transverse great road' to link the west end of the New Town to the Linton or Midlothian road at Tollcross, and put the construction out to contract in 1784. Shown as 'New Road' (not quite on its final alignment) on *Kincaid* 1784, it was named by 1785 for its function, for although mapped as 'Lothian Road' it has always been more generally known as *the Lothian road*.

WILLIAM LOTHIAN'S CLOSE (249 Canongate) *see* AYR BANK CLOSE, Canongate.

LOTHIAN STREET (Bristo) was driven through earlier properties by 1796 and named, according to *Anent Old Edinburgh*, for a farm or dairy which stood northwest of its junction with Bristo Place.

LOUPIELEE (Newbridge) may be the *Wester Muir* farm shown on *Roy* 1753 but appears as *Loupley* on *Laurie* 1763 and *Armstrongs* 1773. The modern form *Loup-O-Lees* perhaps derives from the *Loupolees* shown on *Fowler* 1845 but is at odds with all other versions, including *Loupielee(s)* on *Ordnance Survey* 1852 and 1913. It is evidently a land name, with *-lee* for Anglian *leah* or Scots *ley*, a pasture; but while the first part might be Scots *loup*, for the bend in the Almond, it is more likely to be from Anglian *lappa*, (land) on the edge of an estate or outshot from it, aptly describing its position, *see also* LAPLEE STANE, Canongatehead, *and* BAGLAP, Warrender Park.

LOVEDALE (Balerno) was the name derived from David Love, farmer in Dean Park, or his family, and given to the ground of CLAYHILLS, Balerno (*which see*) after it was joined to Dean Park. LOVEDALE ROAD began to be developed in the later 1940s, and seems to have been known simply as *Lovedale* until it was followed by LOVEDALE AVENUE, CRESCENT, GARDENS and GROVE in 1951-52.

LOVERS LANE (South Leith) appears on *Ordnance Survey* 1852 for LINKS LANE—*which see*.

LOVERS LOAN (Grange) is named thus on *Kirkwood* 1817, but *Grange* 1766 shows it as the KIRK ROAD, leading to the West Kirk (i.e. St Cuthbert's) while on *Grange* c1760 it is noted as 'a private footpath connived at ... for use of Mr Forrest of Wester Grange'. The *Kirk/Lovers Loan* pairing of names occurs frequently in Scotland: not surprisingly, since dawn-to-dusk working hours six days a week made the long Sunday walks to and from the kirk an important courting occasion.

LOVERS LOAN (Hillside) was mostly lost in redevelopment in the 1870s, but its most westerly section was renamed as the western part of BRUNSWICK ROAD in 1885. The Loan may well have been the road shown on *Siege of Leith* 1560 as branching from the Easter road at Upper Quarryholes (the vicinity of Carlton Terrace) and joining the Wester road or Leith Walk immediately north of the Rood Chapel of Greenside (*see under* GREENSIDE, Calton). The name *Lovers Loan* probably dates much further back than its first entry in *PO Directory* 1850; but it was also known as *Marshall's Entry*, as shown on *Kirkwood* 1817, after James Marshall, a solicitor with a curious reputation for being foul-mouthed, who until his death in 1807 had long resided in a property served by the Loan, shown as 'Greenside House' on *Ordnance Survey* 1852—*but see under* GREENSIDE.

LOVERS LOAN (Queensferry) is shown on the 18th-century maps as a road or loaning from Echline 'to Dalmenie Kirk'; and *Plewlands* 1887 figures it as 'Church or Drove Road'.

LOWER GRANTON ROAD (Granton) *see under* GRANTON.

LOWER JOPPA (Joppa) *see under* JOPPA.

LOWER LONDON ROAD (Abbeymount) was developed in about 1870 as a residential adjunct to London Road.

LOWSIE- or **LUSIELAW** (Crosscausey) is recorded in 1661 and 1665 as a land name on the north side of Crosscausey, but references also show that it was a landmark. The name contains Old Norse or Anglian *lús*, literally a louse but in place names used in the sense of 'small', together with Anglian *hlaw* or Scots *law*, a hillock or burial mound. If a natural hillock, it may have been removed by quarrying in Bellsfield, *see under* QUARRY CLOSE; but the alternative meaning is made all the more likely by the fact that *lús* is often used of burial mounds, such as *Loose Howe* in Yorkshire.

LOWSIE- or **LUSIELAW** (Newington) is recorded in 1586 as the name of a feu in the East Burgh Muir. The description would place it in the vicinity of South Oxford Street or south of it, but north of East Mayfield; and in 1571 it was the scene of a short but sharp engagement between the King's men and the Queen's men, which they 'debaittit valiantlie at a part of the borrow mure callit the Lowsie Law'. *Good's Liberton* is certainly wrong in placing this south of the Pow burn. The meanings of the name are as discussed in the foregoing entry; but the suggestion of 'burial mound' is even stronger in this case, because it is in the close vicinity of MOUNTHOOLY, Newington, *which see*.

LOWTHIAN'S CLOSE (392 High Street) *see* BOSWELL'S COURT.

THE LUCKENBOOTHS (High Street) *see under* BUTH RAW.

LUDGATE (Ratho) *see* LIDGATE, Ratho.

LUFRA BANK (Wardie) was named in 1990, borrowing the name from Lufra Cottage, shown here on *Lancefield* 1851.

LUMPHOY (Dalmahoy) appears on *Dalmahoy* 1749 as a field name in Newhouse. The name also occurs as LYMPHOY, Currie, *which see*.

LUSSIELAW ROAD (West Mains) was named in 1936 in the mistaken belief, arising from a palpable error in *Good's Liberton* p5, that this hill-slope in Liberton was the location of the LOWSIE LAW in Newington, *which see*.

LUTTON PLACE (South Side) was begun at its western end in ground inherited by Sir Robert Preston of Valleyfield and Lutton, and took its name from the latter estate in 1848. Its eastward extension to Dalkeith Road through part of SPITALFIELD (*which see*) took place in the late 1870s or early 1880s.

LYGON ROAD (Craigmillar Park) *see under* CRAIGMILLAR PARK.

LYMPHOY (Currie) appears on *Blaeu* 1654 as *Lumphoy*, evidently standing for the tower of KELDELETH (*which see*) and this is quite explicit on *Adair* 1682, which shows *Lymphoy C(astle)*. The name, recorded as *Lumphoy* 1512, *Limphoy* 1551 and *Lymphoy* 1552, also occurs as a field name in Newhouse, on *Dalmahoy* 1749. It is Celtic, probably from British *lom*, bare, and -*fa* (the softened form of *ma*) a place.

LYNEDOCH PLACE (Drumsheugh) was begun in the gushet of DRUMSHEUGH (*which see*) in 1819, and was named in that year for Thomas Graham, distinguished as a general in the Peninsular War, created Baron Lynedoch of Balgowan in Glen Almond in 1814, and made free burgess of Edinburgh in 1815. The name evidently reflects a personal enthusiasm of Major James Weir RM, owner and resident here from 1808 until his death in 1820. His elder son was also named for Thomas Graham; and the Major's widow (a daughter of the developer of PONTON STREET, *which see*) seems to have continued his interest in things Spanish in the naming of streets developed after his death in the family property at Tollcross—*see* WELLINGTON STREET *under* EARL GREY STREET, *and* RIEGO STREET. LYNEDOCH PLACE LANE, renamed thus in the 1920s, as though it were the meuse lane of Lynedoch Place, is in reality many centuries older, being part of the historic road to Queensferry, *see* DRUMSHEUGH LANE.

LYNE STREET (Abbeymount) was formed and named as ROSLIN STREET by 1877, and was renamed LYNE STREET in 1885. The site, once part of Baron Norton's property of *Abbeyhill House*, was owned by a Mr Macleod in 1817 and is shown as *Regent Road Nursery* on *Ordnance Survey* 1852. Both street names appear to have been fancy—indeed, the second might have been suggested by the -*lin* of the first.

LYON DEAN (Colinton) is recorded thus in 1709. Since the 13th-century kirk of St Catherine's in the Hope (now submerged in Glencorse reservoir) lies at the foot of it and may well have been the site of a much earlier religious centre, the name may be a hybrid of Celtic *lann*, enclosure (often a sacred one) and Anglian *denu* or early Scots *dene*, 'the long narrow valley at the sacred place'.

LYON'S CLOSE (215 High Street) is shown on *Edgar* 1742 and was also known as STALKER'S CLOSE before 1756; but the derivations of both names are obscure. In 1581, at the King's request, his master cook John Lyoun was admitted burgess and gild brother; and in 1695 a mariner, Patrick Lyon, was likewise admitted, this having been made one of the conditions of a gift of five thousand pounds to Heriot's Hospital by Robert Sandilands.

M

DAVID MacCALL'S CLOSE (332 High Street) *see* JOHNSTON'S CLOSE.

MacCONNOCHIE'S CLOSE (44 Cowgate) is listed on *Ainslie* 1780 and was named for William MacConnochie, wright, who had a shop and yard here at some date prior to 1763. It was also called ROBERTSON'S CLOSE, but nothing further is known about this name.

McDONALD ROAD (Broughton) was formed by 1897 as an extension of CARSON STREET (*which see*) and named for Sir Andrew McDonald, Lord Provost 1895-97. Carson Street was merged with it by 1900; and in 1930 it gave its name to McDONALD PLACE and STREET, hitherto unnamed, although formed before 1912.

MacDOWALL ROAD (West Mains) was named in about 1907 for James-Anne Macdowall of Canonmills, who was married to Walter Little Gilmour of Liberton and Craigmillar in 1805.

McDOWALL and **GILMORE STREETS** (Canongate) were formed by 1810, are shown on *Regality of Canongate* 1813, and were named for their developers Mrs James Ann McDowall or Little Gilmour of Canonmills. Both streets were suppressed in the course of extension of the Waverley Station—Gilmore Street by 1894, and McDowall Street by 1897.

McGREGOR'S CLOSE (near 106 Canongate) is listed in *Williamson's Directory* 1779 and appears to have been named for John McGregor, writer, who along with Henry Arnot was a trustee for the late Peter Lamont's property in BULL'S CLOSE, 106 Canongate—*which see*. The close is noted on *Kirkwood* 1817 as 'now shut up'.

McINTYRE'S CLOSE (Grassmarket) is listed on *Ainslie* 1780 & 1804 and appears on *Ordnance Survey* 1852, unnamed land partly closed off, 18 yards east of Gilmore's Close. It may have been named for McIntyre & Buchanan, or else Coulter & McIntyre, both firms carriers in Grassmarket in 1773.

MacIVER BRAE (Queensferry) is a path, shown on *Ordnance Survey* 1854, that leads from the mouth of the Ferry Burn up to Stonycroft Road at Catherine Bank. The name is traditional, but its origin remains to be traced. A John McKiver, fishcurer, died in the burgh in 1854. The 1854 map shows the sloping ground as NIVEN'S BANK, *see under* NIVEN'S GREEN, Queensferry.

McKELL'S CLOSE (129 Canongate) *see* PANMURE CLOSE, Canongate.

MacKENZlE PLACE (Stockbridge) is shown planned as part of India Place on *Knox* 1821, and was named *Mackenzie's Place* and partly occupied by 1826. Samuel Mackenzie (1785-1847) portrait painter, had been a pupil of Sir Henry Raeburn, and the street name suggests that he was involved in the building development.

MacKENZIE'S CLOSE (104 High Street) *see* STRICHEN'S CLOSE.

McLAREN ROAD (Mayfield) appears thus in *PO Directory* 1881, but originally as *McLaren Street* in 1879. It was named for (and by) its developer, Duncan McLaren of Newington, Lord Provost 1851-54 and MP for Edinburgh 1865-81. Acquiring Mayfield estate in 1863, he commissioned plans for housing development in 1870, and pressed them to completion between 1877 and the mid 1880s. The name of BURGESS TERRACE reflected his civic status; QUEEN'S CRESCENT his loyalty to Victoria; and his enthusiasm for Reform is shown in the naming of PEEL TERRACE for Sir Robert Peel, and COBDEN CRESCENT and ROAD, for Richard Cobden MP. BRIGHT'S CRESCENT was for McLaren's fellow reformist and brother-in-law John Bright MP, and MOSTON TERRACE was for Bright's property of that name in Cheshire. The garden name WAVERLEY PARK evidently reflected McLaren's enthusiasm in literature, while GLENORCHY TERRACE celebrated his ancestral home, and MENTONE TERRACE and GARDENS and VENTNOR TERRACE his favourite holiday resorts in France and the Isle of Wight. In 1979 an offshoot from Ventnor Terrace, on the site of the former Ventnor Nursery, was named VENTNOR PLACE.

McLAREN TERRACE (Dalry) *see under* DALRY PLACE.

McLEOD STREET (Tynecastle) began to be built at its south end, on Tynecastle ground, and was named for its builder by 1885.

(JOHN) MacMORRAN'S CLOSE (322 High Street) *see* RIDDLE'S CLOSE.

McNAB STREET (Causeyside) *see under* SUMMERHALL SQUARE, Causeyside.

McNEIL STREET (Merchiston) *see under* HORNE TERRACE, Merchiston.

MADEIRA STREET (North Leith) appeared in *PO Directory* 1813 and was evidently named for the wine, because the greater part of its length was within the lands of Leith Mount, feued from Hillhousefield in about 1784 by James Chalmers, wine merchant in North Leith, Boulogne and Bordeaux, whose family continued to live there until 1866. As indicated by the detail on *Pollock* 1834, house-building went on very slowly indeed, despite the opening of William Burn's North Leith Parish Church in the street in 1816, and the name *Madeira Street* was either dropped or else inaccurately listed from 1827, when the *PO Directories* give MADEIRA PLACE only, until 1830, in which year MADEIRA STREET reappears and MADEIRA PLACE is retained as the name of the adjoining street which, according to the maps from *Kirkwood* 1817 onwards, had once been destined to be called LIDDEL STREET.

MAGDALA CRESCENT, MEWS and **PLACE** (Coates) *see under* COATES.

MAGDALEN BRIDGE and **BURN** derived their name from a medieval chapel of St Magdalen which stood some 200 yards east of the mouth of the burn which is variously known as MAGDALEN or MAITLAND WATER or NIDDRIE or BRUNSTANE BURN (*see* LOTHIAN BURN). The early spellings *Maidland(s)* in 1488, *Medlen* (*Brig*) in 1661 or *Maitland* all reflect the medieval pronunciation *maudlin*, and the third of them may have been influenced by (or confused with) the name of the Maitlands of Thirlestane, who owned nearby Brunstane from 1597 to 1696. The *Magdalene brig* is noted in *Town Council Minutes* 1557 as decayed to the point of falling down. The ground west of it is notable as one of the oldest known inhabited sites in Edinburgh, a cemetery of the Food Vessel folk having been found here in 1881. Named as MAGDALEN on *Blaeu* 1654, it was the site of salt pans belonging to Kelso Abbey in the Middle Ages, and of a variety of manufactures in later centuries. For MAITLAND or BRUNSTANE BRIDGE further upstream, *see under* BRUNSTANE. MAGDALENE AVENUE, DRIVE, GARDENS, LOAN, MEDWAY and PLACE, built on East Duddingston ground a mile upstream from the old settlement, were named for the burn in 1956; and MAGDALENE COURT was added to the group in 1975.

MAGDALENE ENTRY (181 Canongate) *see* GLADSTONE COURT.

MAIDENCRAIG (Blackhall) was the name of the ground before it began to be developed for housing. But it was also the name of the freestone quarry shown (apparently already worked out) on *Ordnance Survey* 1852; and the Articles of feuing in the Moray Estate in 1822 group *Maiden Craig* along with Redhall and Craigleith as the only stones which were allowed to be used in the main frontages. Evidently the name originally belonged to the small hill shown on *Roy* 1753 but later removed by the quarrying. It might be Scots or (perhaps more likely) Celtic; but in absence of early forms it remains obscure. MAIDENCRAIG CRESCENT was named in 1926; and was followed by MAIDENCRAIG GROVE (1928) and COURT (1955).

'MAIDEN'S CLEUCH' (Currie) is a misnomer for CLOCHMEAD, Currie, *which see*.

MAIN POINT (West Port) appears on *Kirkwood* 1817 as well as *Ordnance Survey* 1852 as an apparent replacement of the name TWOPENNY CUSTOM shown on *Armstrongs* 1773 as well as *Ainslie* 1804, at the point where the west-going route from the Grassmarket climbed out of the ravine and branched three ways to West Linton, Lanark and Linlithgow; but in both *Chambers* 1825 and *Anent Old Edinburgh* 1890 it is mentioned simply as the name of the building (4 High Riggs) erected here as a custom house in about 1770, and it should not be too readily assumed that the name originally belonged to the junction rather than the building. Nor is such a meaning as 'chief roads junction' altogether obvious, for not only is 'main point' far from usual as a term for such a thing, but the roads themselves lost much of their importance when the routes from the south and west were diverted to the New Town by the construction of the Lothian Road in 1785 and Maitland Street in 1807. The name remains obscure; but recalling that *main* is Scots for fine white bread, it is tempting to speculate that there might be a connection between the naming of the house and the equally obscure name of BREAD STREET (*which see*) which is first recorded soon after it.

MAIN STREET (Balerno) is shown on *Armstrongs* 1773 as part of the road to Redford and Bavelaw, and it is shown on *Ordnance Survey* 1852 as already considerably built up. It was cut off and pedestrianised when the village was bypassed by BAVELAW ROAD, *which see*.

MAIN STREET (Dalmeny) is shown on *Dundas* 1757 as laid out basically in the same form as it is today, and as the terminus of the kirk road from Barnbougle it is probably as old as the kirk itself.

MAIN STREET (Kirkliston) appears on *Knox* 1812 and *Kirkliston* 1815 but not on *Taylor & Skinner* 1805, and it is shown on *Kirkliston* c1810 as part of one of two schemes for improvement of the Linlithgow turnpike, involving a stretch of road, new but for a short length south of Newmains, forming a bypass to the ancient route (*see under* AULDGATE, HIGH STREET, PETH BRAE *and* GATESIDE) from a point about half a mile west of Boathouse bridge as far as Muiriehall. It speedily became an important part of the village: by 1812 there was a toll bar and some buildings south of the road, and by 1852 its north side was partly built up. The names *Market Street* and *Main Street* began to be used, and the latter became the accepted name by about 1920.

MAIN STREET (Newhaven) is clearly part of the Port of Grace set up by James IV in 1505, since it runs along the south boundary of the port as granted to Edinburgh in 1510. It was renamed NEWHAVEN MAIN STREET in 1968.

MAIN STREET (Ratho) is shown very clearly on *Roy* 1753 and in detail on *Hatton etc* 1797, and since *Ratho Town* is shown on *Adair* 1682 the street is likely to have been the main street of the village for years and perhaps centuries before that. *See also* LIDGATE, Ratho.

MAISTERTON'S CLOSE (161 Cowgate) *see* KINCAID'S CLOSE, Cowgate.

MAITLAND or **BRUNSTANE BRIDGE** and **MAITLAND BRAES** (Brunstane) *see under* BRUNSTANE.

MAITLAND BRIDGE (Kirkliston) is so named on *Ordnance Survey* 1852 and shown as a wooden bridge, with an associated *waggon ford* some 260 yards further downstream, while *Roy* 1753 shows a crossing at Breistmill, somewhat upstream of the present bridge. This was named for Sir Alexander Ramsay-Gibson-Maitland of Cliftonhall (1820-76) who took a keen interest in local affairs and was a president of the Edinburgh-Linlithgow Turnpike Trust. MAITLAND ROAD in Newmains was also named for him in about 1974.

MAITLAND-HOG LANE (Kirkliston) was named in 1972 for James Maitland-Hog (1799-1858) laird of Newliston, an advocate, prominent in local affairs and in the Free Kirk from 1843 onwards.

MAITLAND STREET (West End) is shown on *Ainslie* 1804 as a proposed 'New Road to Glasgow', connecting the New Town with the existing Glasgow road which passed through Haymarket from the West Port. It was begun in 1805 by Sir Alexander Charles Maitland of Cliftonhall, and is referred to in *Town Council Minutes* 1807 as the 'new western road called *Maitland Street*'. WEST MAITLAND STREET appears in *PO Directory* 1825, but is shown on *Pollock* 1834 as a side name on the south side of the section of street west of Torphichen Street; and it did not finally displace the name *Maitland Street* in the section west of Palmerston Place until its north side began to be built up in the mid 1860s. In about 1899 the remainder of *Maitland Street* was displaced by the name of SHANDWICK PLACE, *which see*. CLIFTON TERRACE (Haymarket) was named for the Maitland estate by 1863.

JOHN MAKNATH'S CLOSE (577 High Street) *see* NAIRNE'S CLOSE.

MALCOLM'S CLOSE (373 High Street) *see* BYRES CLOSE.

MALCOLMSTON (Currie) is recorded in *RMS* 1390 as (Latinised) *Macolmystona* and shortly afterwards as *Malcolmstoun*, and is shown on *Roy* 1753. It includes the personal name *Malcolm*, 'devotee of Columba', of Gaelic extraction, and the place name is Anglian or Scots *Malcolm's tún* or farm *toun*.

MALLENY (Balerno) is recorded in 1280, and MALLENY HOUSE, shown on *Adair* 1682 as *W Limphoy*, is *Moleany* on *Roy* 1753. The early forms *Maleny, Malemmy, Mallunny* or *Mallany* show the name to be Celtic, probably British *ma leyna*, plain of meadows, which would be virtually identical in Gaelic as *magh leanaidhe*. It seems to have belonged to a wide sweep of country, including the MALLENY MUIR shown on *Armstrongs* 1773 and the modern MALLENY RIFLE RANGE; and BALLENY (*which see*) was but one *baile* or farm within it. MALLENY MILLS, shown on *Knox* 1812 as *Balerno Mill*, but as *Milleny* on *Gellatly* 1834, were started in 1805 to make cloth for the Edinburgh Roperie and Sailcloth Company. MALLENY MILL GATE, shown on *Ordnance Survey* 1852 as a service road beside a reservoir, was named in 1984 as the *gate* or road leading to the Mills. MALLENY AVENUE was named by 1969 with only general reference to the local place name.

MALLOCH'S CLOSE (73 Canongate) is listed on *Ainslie* 1780, and was named for three owners of the tenement here at some dates prior to 1750: James, William and latterly Alexander Malloch, wright.

MALTA HOUSE (Stockbridge) is a later 19th-century replacement of a house of the same name dating from before 1804, listed in *Stark's Directory* 1805 as MALTA, residence of Donald Cameron Esq. The name, presumably fancy and arising from some connection of an early owner with the island, was later attached to MALTA TERRACE, as shown on *Knox* 1821, and also used then or shortly afterwards to name *Malta Green*, evidently a bleaching green later associated with a dyeworks, as shown on *Ordnance Survey* 1852; and hence the name MALTA GREEN for a new street on the site in 1984.

MANDERSTON PLACE (Leith Walk) appears on *Calton* 1819 as a proposed side name in Leith Walk, evidently in compliment to John Manderston, later Lord Provost 1819-21 but then City Treasurer and a member of the Joint Committee on Calton Plans. The terrace was never built, the frontage being taken up by Leith Walk Goods Station in the later 1860s; and it was possibly the prospect of this that enabled the name to be taken for MANDERSTON STREET (in the then separate burgh of Leith) in 1864, either in memory of John Manderston's shipping interest in Leith, or more likely in compliment to Sir William Miller, MP for Leith 1857-68, who was of a Leith family and acquired the estate of Manderston in Berwickshire in 1864.

MANNERING PLACE (Inch) *see under* THE INCH, Nether Liberton.

MANOR PLACE (Coates) *see under* COATES.

MANSE BRAE (Dalmeny) is the traditional name of this road, taken from the manse it passes on its way up from Bankhead and Newgarden to Dalmeny village.

MANSE ROAD (Corstorphine) is shown on *Corstorphine* 1754. It is recorded in 1766 as BARNEY'S SLAP or VENNEL, believed to have been named for a blacksmith, Bernard Hunter, and although it was formally named MANSE ROAD by 1885, Selway still uses the old name THE SLAP a few years later. In all probability, both names were in use from an early period: for it was the *manse road* because it led to the manse, which was there in 1754 and probably for centuries before that; and as a narrow gap and lane between the kirk lands on the east and other properties on the west, it was both a *slap* and a *vennel*. The name of MANSE STREET was coined in 1966 by borrowing from Manse Road, to replace the former name HOPE STREET given in about 1887, probably for James Hope of Belmont, whose son J E Hope was an early owner in the street.

MANSE ROAD (Kirkliston) appears on *Kirkliston* c1810 as a road or loan branching from the Newmains road before the new turnpike or MAIN STREET (*which see*) was built. It probably developed from a path along the west boundary of the Glebe, as shown on *Kirkliston* 1759, in the vicinity of the BRANKEN (*which see*) and it seems to have gone under that name until after 1865, when a new parish kirk manse was built here in the Glebe, replacing the old one on the north of the kirkyard. It was in turn sold off by the Kirk in 1941.

MANSFIELD PLACE (Bellevue) *see under* NORTHERN NEW TOWN.

MANSFIELD ROAD (Balerno) is listed in *County Roads* 1902 as *Marchbank Road* (*see* MARCHBANK, Balerno); but *Mansfield* appears as a house name on *Ordnance Survey* 1912, and displaced the earlier road name in 1963.

THE MANSION (Dalmeny) is recorded in *Protocols of James Young* 1503 in the phrase 'lands called *Mansione* of the manys of Bernbowgale'. The name, also given as *Mension* 1587 and *lie Mensioun* 1622, clearly implies a manor house; but the references show that it was distinct from Barnbougle, and none of them suggest that the house itself was still in existence. *Barnbougle & Dalmeny* c1800 shows a clump of trees called *Mansion house clump* in the same position (about NT 15907775) as *Ordnance Survey* 1854 notes *Site of Dalmeny House*; and both maps show MANSION HILL south of it, while *Roy* 1750 calls it *Mains hill*.

MANSIONHOUSE ROAD (Grange) *see under* THE GRANGE.

MARCH GROVE and **ROAD** (Craigcrook) *see under* CRAIGCROOK.

MARCHBANK (Balerno) is shown on *Knox* 1812 as *Muirbank*, a name describing its position on the bank above Balerno muir or common; while *Marchbank*, first appearing on *Ordnance Survey* 1852, may well have been an alternative name for the place, since it was on the march between farmland and muir. The road from Balerno is listed in *County Roads* 1902 as MARCHBANK ROAD, but by 1963 the name had been displaced by that of MANSFIELD ROAD, *which see*. In 1968 *Marchbank* was borrowed for the naming of MARCHBANK DRIVE, GARDENS, GROVE, PLACE and WAY in Dean Park, almost a mile further north.

MARCHFIELD (Davidson's Mains) is shown thus on maps dating back to *Laurie* 1763, but the spelling *Marchyfield* on *Roy* 1753 suggests that perhaps the name may not be from its position on any march or boundary, but from the shallow and rather boggy loch which was part of its march with CRAIGCROOK, *which see*. MARCHFIELD GROVE was named in 1925, MARCHFIELD TERRACE in 1929, and MARCHFIELD PARK in 1963.

MARCHHALL ROAD and **CRESCENT** (Prestonfield) were named in about 1876, although the northern part of Marchhall Crescent had been formed by 1860, as an access to a pair of houses. The site is part of the *Marchhall park* recorded in 1759 and shown on *Prestonfield* 1824; and while the field might have been named for a small property *March Hall*, recorded in 1811 and shown on *Kirkwood* 1817 as 70 yards west of the present property of this name, it is much more likely that the field was named first, as lying along the northern march of Prestonfield, and that the element *-hall* (as so often happens) represents another word altogether, in this case Scots *haugh* or *hough*, a heel or projecting ridge of land. Absorbing PRESTONFIELD TERRACE in 1885, Marchhall Road developed into a complex shape, and in 1929 this was adjusted by renaming parts of it MARCHHALL PLACE and CRESCENT and PRIESTFIELD ROAD NORTH.

MARCHMONT has become the neighbourhood name for the east end of BRUNTSFIELD, *which see* for the streets of the name.

MARCH PINES (Craigcrook) is built on the bed of a loch, still shown on *Ordnance Survey* 1938, that lay athwart the march between Craigcrook and Muttonhole or Davidson's Mains. It was named in 1989 for the march boundary and for the stand of Scots pines between the lochside and Craigcrook Road.

MARDALE CRESCENT (Merchiston) *see under* BLANTYRE TERRACE.

MARINE DRIVE (Muirhouse & Silverknowes) was named in 1956 as a drive beside the sea.

MARINE ESPLANADE (Leith Docks) is shown on *Bartholomew* 1876 as a proposed *promenade* along the sea front and was built and known as such by 1888, but is shown on *Ordnance Survey* 1893 as *Marine Esplanade*.

MARIONVILLE (Restalrig) is recorded in 1787 as the house of Capt. James Macrae of Houston, where he and his wife Maria Cecilie le Maistre staged fashionable theatricals, and it is likely that their house was named for her. According to *Chambers* 1825 it had been built by sisters named Ramsay, milliners, out of the profits of their business in Old Lyon Close, and was nicknamed *Lappet Ha'* for the hat ribands they made; but the assertion that the *Marion* name was for their favourite niece is a much later addition to the story. Curiously enough, *lappet* and *Ramsay* are also linked to Macrae, for in 1780 he was criticised for demolishing the castle of Houston and using the stones to build a village for lappet weavers, and in 1790 he had to flee the country after killing his friend Sir George Ramsay in a duel. MARIONVILLE TOLL is listed among toll bars in 1844 and shown on *Ordnance Survey* 1852; and MARIONVILLE COTTAGES had grouped round it by the 1880s. MARIONVILLE ROAD, obviously named as leading past Marionville, was in use as an address by 1922. Housing development began in 1934 with MARIONVILLE AVENUE, CRESCENT (immediately south of Marionville House) DRIVE and GROVE, and MARIONVILLE PARK followed in 1936. MARIONVILLE MEDWAY was added as a side name in Marionville Drive in 1989.

MARISCHAL PLACE (Blackhall) was named by 1909 for the office of great marischal of Scotland, held by the Keith family from the time of Robert the Bruce, and for that of knight marischal, conferred on Keith of Ravelston by George IV on the occasion of his visit to Edinburgh in 1822.

MARITIME STREET and **LANE** (South Leith) *see* QUALITY STREET and LANE, South Leith.

MARKET STREET (Old Town) is named on *Kirkwood* 1817 as the service access to the meat and fish markets, with a continuation on the north side of the latter which is later shown as LOW MARKET STREET on *Ordnance Survey* 1852. The *Sketch of Improvements* added to *Arnot* in 1816 describes the westward extension of the street as 'a new road', no doubt because a great deal of upfill was required to secure both a reasonable road-width and a satisfactory gradient up to the new level at the head of the Mound, but the entire street in fact overlaid the older *Back of the town* loan shown on *Edgar* 1742 and so named on *Kincaid* 1784, which led along the steep bank of the Nor Loch from Ramsay Lane to the Physic Garden and Leith Wynd. The section of Market Street below the North Bridge was remodelled in about 1872, as proposed on *City Improvements* 1866, except that EAST MARKET STREET was extended as far as Cranston Street; and its final extension to New Street followed in the mid 1890s.

MARLBOROUGH STREET (Portobello) was laid out in about 1815 and appropriately named WELLINGTON STREET, for the victor of Waterloo; but in 1968, in order to obviate any confusion with Wellington Street in Hillside, it was given a new name, borrowed from a tenement at the foot of the street (demolished in 1971) which had been named *Marlborough Mansions*, apparently on the principle that one ducal war hero suggests another.

MARLIN'S WYND (High Street) *see* MERLYON'S WYND, High Street.

MARMION CRESCENT (Inch) *see under* THE INCH, Nether Liberton.

MARSHALL'S CLOSE (once 3 now about 17-19 Grassmarket) is shown but not named on *Ainslie* 1780. The name is given in *PO Directory* 1827. Its origin remains to be traced.

MARSHALL'S COURT (Greenside) is shown on *Ainslie* 1804 as a lane with gardens on its west side. *Kirkwood* 1817 and *Ordnance Survey* 1852 show these as progressively built up, and the latter labels the street LOWER GREENSIDE STREET; but there is no entry in *PO Directory* until 1862, when it appears as *Marshall's Court*. There is no evidence of connection with James Marshall, owner of latterday Greenside House until 1807 (*see under* LOVERS LOAN, Hillside) but it is possible that the name goes back to Andrew Marshall, coachwright and feuar in Greenside in 1807.

MARSHALL STREET (Bristo) is shown as a proposal on *City Improvements* 1866, and was driven through older streets and properties by 1872. Its western section, itself cleared and left as a mere roadway in 1965, included the site of HAMILTON'S ENTRY, Bristo, *which see*. Its eastern half was driven through the middle of the great tenement of ALISON'S SQUARE (*which see*) and the new street was named in 1872 for John Marshall, surgeon, who had married a Margaret Alison and had, together with his three daughters, received a charter for this tenement in 1857.

MARSHALL WELL (Kirkliston) is a well in the High Street, now closed up and lacking its wrought ironwork, which was presented to the village in 1867 by Robert Marshall, tailor in Edinburgh but born in the village and resident at Gateside, who also endowed a school bursary, a local library, and a scheme for supplying coal to the poor. MARSHALL ROAD was also named for him in the 1950s.

MARYFIELD (West End) is shown on *Roy* 1753, named thus on *Kirkwood* 1817, and seems to have been cleared away in 1837, since it is dropped by *PO Directory* in 1838. It was probably named for an owner's wife.

MARYFIELD (Norton Park) probably originated as the name of a property, *Maryfield* (*House*) named for a female relative of its owner; but *Kirkwood* 1817 shows it as the name of the group of properties earlier shown as the QUARRYHOLES (*which see*), while *Ordnance Survey* 1852 and *Grant III* p158 use it as a general name for the neighbourhood. In 1866, the Edinburgh Co-operative Building Company, following the start of their first enterprise at the COLONIES in Stockbridge, began a development of artisan housing of a similar style at MARYFIELD, MARYFIELD PLACE, and ALVA PLACE—the latter apparently named for Johnston of Alva who owned some ground in the vicinity. Next came LADY MENZIES PLACE, named for Grace, daughter of Baron Norton, who had married Sir Neil Menzies of Castle Menzies in 1816 and was still living in Abbeyhill House when the street was named in 1869. REGENT PLACE, occupied in 1870, was presumably named in reference to Regent Road, and WAVERLEY PLACE (1871) for Scott's novel of that name. CARLYLE PLACE (1872) may have been named after Thomas Carlyle; but if the map spelling CARLISLE PLACE was what was intended, it may have been named after a town, as were PITLOCHRY PLACE in 1873 and EARLSTON PLACE in 1876. SALMOND PLACE (1887) may have been named for some director of the Company, but evidence is lacking. ROSSIE PLACE, somewhat earlier, may have been named for Rossie, near Montrose, or for someone of that surname.

MARYFIELD (Portobello) was developed in about 1804 in Wilson's Park and is thought to have been named after Mr Wilson's wife.

MARY KING'S CLOSE (High Street) *see under* (ALEXANDER or MARY) KING'S CLOSE, High Street.

MARYLANDS (Ratho) *see* MERRYLANDS, Ratho.

MARY'S PLACE (Stockbridge) is shown on *Cramond Roads* 1812 and named on *Kirkwood* 1817. Developed at the north end of a property in Deanhaugh, shown on *Ainslie* 1804, it was probably named for a member of the family of the original developer, who may or may not have been Thomas Allan of Allanfield in Bonnington, who was feuing out the east 'stance' of Mary's Place in 1824, along with ground in ALLAN STREET, Stockbridge—*which see*.

MAUCHAN'S CLOSE (286 High Street) *see* OLD BANK CLOSE.

BARON MAULE'S CLOSE (19 High Street) *see* PANMURE'S CLOSE.

MAURICE PLACE (Blackford) *see under* EVA PLACE, Blackford.

MAWR'S or **MAR'S MILL** (Water of Leith or Dean Village) is named in *Town Council Minutes* 1580 and on *Adair* 1682, and is shown on *Siege of Leith* 1560 with its outfall lade carrying on to Silvermills. The building is shown on *Ordnance Survey* 1852 as straddling the present Miller Row roadway 15 feet east of the granary of JERICHO, *which see*. One of the group of the town's common mills in the WATER OF LEITH VILLAGE (*which see*), it was probably the one referred to in *Town Council Minutes* 1463 as operated by 'John Mawar, wricht and servand to the mylne'.

MAXWELL STREET (Morningside) was developed in 1880 on land of the BRIGGS O BRAID—*which see*. Who the Maxwell was is as yet unknown. There is no evidence that the street was named for the Herbert Maxwell who had feued land in 1595, not here in Braid but in Canaan north of the Pow burn, and any such connection is unlikely.

MAYBANK VILLAS (Corstorphine) were developed in 1902 on ground feued by James Younger, opposite VICTOR PARK TERRACE, *which see*. The name is fancy, either for a woman relative or for the hawthorn.

MAYBURY ROAD (Corstorphine to Barnton) was built as part of a new route from Leith to the Glasgow road (*see also* TELFORD ROAD) and named for Sir Henry Maybury, Director General of Roads in the Ministry of Transport, who opened it on 21 April 1927. MAYBURY DRIVE was named as a branch off it in 1973. In the late 1930s the prominence of the *Maybury Roadhouse* at an otherwise undistinguished junction generated THE MAYBURY as a place name; and in 1984 SOUTH MAYBURY was given as a side name nearby.

MAYFIELD, also called NEWLANDS (*which see*) was an estate of 16 Scots acres created in 1704 by Walter Porterfield, surgeon and burgess of Edinburgh, who merged four of the 4-acre plots originally feued out of the Burgh Muir in 1530, including three which had been joined together by John Cant of the Grange in 1609. The name *Newlands* obviously referred to this merger, and Porterfield probably coined the alternative *Mayfield* in compliment to his wife, perhaps just before he conveyed the estate of 'Newlands or Mayfield' to her in 1735. The house of *Mayfield*, shown on *Scott* 1759, stood immediately southeast of the junction of East

Mayfield and Mayfield Gardens. With the addition of the lands of Powburn and Rosebank in 1805, the estate embraced virtually all the ground between Mayfield Loan (now East and West Mayfield) and the Pow burn; and in 1863 it was bought by Duncan McLaren of Newington for housing development, *see under* McLAREN ROAD. CANT'S LOAN, so named for John Cant as owner of the abovementioned 12-acre property from 1609 until 1637, figures in *Town Council Minutes* 1586 as a passage between the highroads to Dalkeith and Liberton 'besyde the heid of the awld (fewit) pairts of the mure', and it has the appearance of having been formed in 1530 as an access to these feus, along their north boundary. It became MAYFIELD LOAN in the 18th century, and EAST and WEST MAYFIELD (a subdivision of the street, never of the estate) in about 1892. ROSS STREET, part of the 1825 plan for Newington, was renamed MAYFIELD TERRACE in 1859, evidently because the houses on its south side overlooked Mayfield Loan. MAYFIELD GARDENS, called MAYFIELD STREET in the 1870s, was renamed in 1881; but MAYFIELD GARDENS LANE, although built at the same time, had to wait until 1981 for its statutory name. MOLLENDO TERRACE and St ANDREW'S PLACE began to be built beside the Liberton road in 1873 and 1875, but in about 1886 these side names were taken into the name MAYFIELD ROAD, for that part of the Liberton road passing the Mayfield estate and continuing south of the Pow burn. GRANGE TOLL was originally at its north end, at the entry of West Mayfield, but was moved in the 1850s to the vicinity of West Savile Terrace. MAYFIELD TOLL was on the new highway of 1812, at the junction of Craigmillar Park, Lady Road and Liberton Road; and although this was half a mile south of the historic Mayfield it was still known as *Mayfield* in 1914.

MAYFIELDGATE (North Leith) was named in 1984 as a *gate* or pathway on the site of the small property *Mayfield*, shown on *Ainslie* 1804 as then owned by the Revd Mr Walker next to Bathfield.

MAYFIELD PLACE (Corstorphine) was built in about 1910 by Thomas Moonie, and the name is fancy, either for the hawthorn or for some female relative of the developer's.

MAYVILLE GARDENS (Trinity) was built in 1880 in the southern part of a property shown as *Mr Balfour's* on *Kirkwood* 1817 and *Mayville* on *Ordnance Survey* 1852. EAST MAYVILLE GARDENS was developed in 1933 on the site of LAVEROCKBANK HOUSE, *which see.*

MEADOWBANK takes its name from the property shown as 'Mr Henderson's' on both *Ainslie* 1804 and *Kirkwood* 1817, where a house and small steading in what is now Royal Park Terrace is named *Meadow Bank*, while *Kirkwood* and *Ordnance Survey* 1852 also show *Meadowbank Tower* as a separate property further east. The street is MEADOWBANK in *PO Directory* 1825, but was of course part of the ancient highroad to Haddington and the south. The name evidently described the slope above Clockmill Lane, overlooking the flats of *Restalrig Meadow*, now the site of MEADOWBANK SPORTS CENTRE. MEADOWBANK AVENUE, CRESCENT, PLACE and TERRACE were developed in PARSON'S GREEN, *which see.*

MEADOW CAGE (Meadows) seems to be indicated on *Roy* 1753 as the terminal feature of Middle Meadow Walk. It is named on *Scott* 1759 as *Bird cage*, but in 1769, when the town council resolved to repair it, it was described as 'the summer house commonly called the Meadow Cage'. It was removed by the town council in 1824.

MEADOWFIELD (Duddingston) is not shown on *Armstrongs* 1773 but appears on *Figgate Roads* 1783; and its character and the name *Meadowlees* which belonged to the fields round about its steading suggest that it may have been developed from the outfield or even the common grazing of the original farm of Wester Duddingston. MEADOWFIELD AVENUE and TERRACE were built in 1936 and 1938; MEADOWFIELD DRIVE and GARDENS followed in 1956; and the steading was redeveloped as MEADOWFIELD COURT in 1982.

MEADOWFIELD (South Morningside) *see under* EGYPT.

MEADOWFIELD (West Craigs, Corstorphine) is recorded from 1424 onwards; and the name is early Scots *medow feld*, indicating grassland, perhaps of a marshy sort. The farm is named on *Laurie* 1763; but the *March hall* given on *Roy* 1753, if it is not a mistake, may have been an alternative name of the original farm (later much curtailed) as the *march haw*, haugh on the east side of Gogar Water, which formed the march with Gogar.

MEADOWFLAT (Holyrood) is mentioned from 1578 onwards as part of the lands of St Leonard granted to Holyrood Abbey in 1128. As shown on *Ordnance Survey* 1852 it extended for 300 yards west of the southern section (suppressed in 1845) of the Horse Wynd. The name is Early Scots, probably using *flat* in its sense of 'division of the field' in order to distinguish this *meadow*, or permanent grass that could be mown for hay, from the adjoining DISHFLAT, *which see*.

MEADOWHEAD (Mortonhall) is named on *Roy* 1753. The field name *Mortonhall Meadows* is shown in the south of the farm on the plan of *Mortonhall* 1770.

MEADOW HOUSE (Corstorphine) is shown thus on *Knox* 1812 (the farm steading being immediately west of Downie Grove) but *Armstrongs* 1773 shows it to be the EISTER MEADOW (with LADIE MEADOW and PARK) recorded in 1654, which together with the WEST MEADOW may have formed the MEADOWFIELD of Corstorphine, recorded from 1424 onwards—these *meadow* names all referring to the land beside or reclaimed from the lochs and bogs which were drained by the Stank. MEADOWHOUSE ROAD began at its western end as a terrace of houses built in the north end of Taylor's acre on land feued by Beach & Borthwick, plumbers, who named it ANWOTH VILLAS, for Anwoth, near Gatehouse of Fleet, with which Mr Beach had a family connection and which was also the parish of the redoubtable Covenanter Samuel Rutherford (1600-61). The street got its present name when it was extended eastwards in the late 1920s.

MEADOW LANE (South Side) is shown on *Roy* 1753 and (in detail) on *Scott* 1759 as a loaning passing Thomas Hope's house (now Hope Park Square) and entering the North Walk of the Meadows. Thus the name, shown on *Ordnance Survey* 1852, may go back to the 17th century, when at least part of the SOUTH LOCH (*which see*) was already known as the *South Meadows*. The form of the loaning near its western end, evident on Scott, shows that it was diverted perhaps in about 1725, when the grounds of Hope's house were formed, or it may have been to suit the earlier house on the site—*see under* HOPE PARK. The western section of the Lane was developed as a meuse to George Square, as shown on *Ainslie* 1780, later extended to serve Buccleuch Place and to link up with the older loaning, as shown on *Kirkwood* 1817.

MEADOW PLACE (Corstorphine) was, according to *Selway*, the earlier name of Dunsmure House. MEADOW PLACE ROAD is a development of the *West Loan* or *Loan* figured on *Corstorphine* 1754 and 1777 respectively. On *Ordnance Survey* 1893 it is shown as straightened out and named as the *road to Meadow Place*; and in 1958 it was extended to link with Broomhouse Road.

MEADOW PLACE (Marchmont) originated as an acre in the Burgh Muir, feued off from the Links in 1719 and shown as open ground on *Scott* 1759 and *Ainslie* 1804. Subdivided for a terrace of housing in about 1805, it was probably named more for the field than for the nearby Meadows; and since the name was equally apt as a neighbourhood name, it also attached itself to MEADOW PLACE LANE, shown on *Ainslie* 1804 and (now with its extra western loop) on *Kirkwood* 1817.

THE MEADOWS (South Side) occupy the site of the SOUTH or BURGH LOCH and the later HOPE PARK *which see*. The existing NORTH, SOUTH and MIDDLE MEADOW WALKS are part of the scheme for Hope Park shown on *Roy* 1753, and were apparently executed by 1759, when *Scott* shows drained meadows in between them, and the MEADOW CAGE (*which see*) at the terminus of the Middle Walk. Designated as a public park by Act of Parliament 1827, its fuller development for this purpose was hindered by sewerage problems at its eastern end, not finally overcome until 1862. The MELVILLE DRIVE (*which see*) dates from 1859. The pillars at its west end were built as the entrance to the great International Exhibition of Industry, Art & Science, held here in 1886, while a sundial in the West Meadows commemorates its opening by Prince Albert Victor, Duke of Clarence. The JAWBONE ARCH was originally part of the Zetland & Fair Isle stand. The pair of pillars at the east end of the Melville Drive date from 1896, and were once part of the printing works of Thomas Nelson & Sons at Hope Park End. While some of the diagonal paths in the Meadows had been formed by 1876, the present scheme was completed in the 1880s, either in connection with the Exhibition or just after it. The JAWBONE WALK was named for the Arch, but the other names were given much later: the CORONATION WALK in 1937, for the crowning of George VI; the BOYS BRIGADE

WALK in 1954, to mark the centenary of the birth of Sir William Smith, founder of the Brigade; and the TOWNSWOMEN'S GUILD WALK was named in 1973, in response to the Guild's gift of the trees that line it.

MEADOWSPOT (South Morningside) was revived in 1991 as the name of a new street in this meadow in the lands of Craighouse, mentioned in *RMS* 1368 as *Medeuspot*, early Scots for 'a small meadow'. A spring mentioned in the charter is probably the one which is the source of the Pow or Jordan Burn.

THE MEAL MARKET (110 & 122 Cowgate) is shown on *Rothiemay* 1647 with two arched entries from the Cowgate. The meal market was anciently held in the High Street, but latterly this became difficult to control; an effort was made in 1538 to resite it at the *foot of James Aikman's Close*, but the *Town Council Minutes* show that *some honest and gangand* (i.e. suitable) alternative to the High Street was still being sought two years later, and indeed this site in the Nether Kirkyard of St Giles was not fixed on until 1587, and even then the new market was not built until 1600. It gave its name to the MEAL MARKET STAIRS leading up the Parliament Close; and by 1852 an opening which represented its eastern entrance was being called OLD MEALMARKET CLOSE.

MEARENSIDE (Bughtlin) was named thus in 1973 at the suggestion of Craigs Building Society, with the express intention of using a Lowland farming term; and possibly it referred to the fact that the street was at the edge of development as then planned, Scots *mearing* being a *bauk* or strip of uncultivated ground marking a boundary. The ending -*side* seems to have been added in the sense of 'beside' rather than its stricter meaning of 'slope'.

MEETING HOUSE GREEN (South Leith) shown on *Naish* 1709 and so named on *Ordnance Survey* 1852 but given as GREEN STREET on *Thomson* 1822, is now represented by open ground on the south side of Leith Hospital Nurses Home. It was named for the *Meeting House* which served as a place of worship for dissenting Presbyterians from 1688 until 1693, when the congregation were able to return to South Leith Parish Kirk.

MEGGETLAND is recorded in *RMS* 1654 and shown on *Adair* 1682. The name is British, *lann*, yard or farm enclosure, with *miget*, (at the) boggy burn; and obviously relates to the burn (now mostly culverted, but clearly shown on *Ordnance Survey* 1852) that comes down the valley below the western crags of the Craiglockhart hills and turns to flow northwestwards across a wide flat haugh towards the Moat and the Water of Leith. The historic centre was on the spur above the crook of the burn, where the mansion house shown on *Knox* 1812 (and possibly also on *Laurie* 1763 or *Adair* 1682) was cleared away for MEGGATLAND TERRACE in 1932. Housebuilding began at the PERDRIXKNOWE (*which see*) in 1884, evidently stimulated by the coming of the suburban railway; and it was probably out of a desire to link it with the railway station, (named for Craiglockhart, although half a mile away from that estate) that the name *Lockharton*, from

Craig*lockhart* plus *-ton*, was coined for James Gowan's developments in the intervening estate of Meggetland, shown on *W & A K Johnston* 1888 and named on their edition of 1898 as LOCKHARTON TERRACE (a side name in Colinton Road, dropped by 1902) and LOCKHARTON GARDENS. LOCKHARTON CRESCENT (1902) and AVENUE (1931) followed suit. In 1986 a new development in the northern part of Meggetland, formerly Edinburgh University's *Canal Field* sports ground, was marked out as NORTH MEGGETLAND; and the name MEGGETLAND GATE (i.e. way) was given to the existing access from Slateford to the *Meggetland* sports field.

MEIKLE(JOHN)'S CLOSE (South Leith) is shown on *Naish* 1709 and named on *Kirkwood* 1817. The name was from James Meikle, brewer here in 1687; and the variant *Meiklejohn's* appearing on *Ordnance Survey* 1852 seems to be an error.

MEIN'S CLOSE (High Street) is recorded in *Burgh Register* 1742 as being on the north side of the High Street and evidently taking its name from a family of Bartholomew, Patrick and John Mein or Meyne, coopers, who were made burgesses in 1567, 1574 and 1603 respectively and had property in the close; but its exact whereabouts has still to be established.

MELBOURNE PLACE (Old Town) was named by 1836 for William Lamb, 2nd Viscount Melbourne, then Prime Minister. It was replaced by Midlothian County Council offices (later Lothian Regional Council's) in 1968.

MELDRUMSHEUGH (Drumsheugh) *see* DRUMSHEUGH.

MELGUND TERRACE (Broughton) is shown on *Bartholomew* 1876 as a continuation of Bellevue Place, but was named in its own right by 1878. The name must be connnected with either Melgund near Brechin, or the title Viscount Melgund, belonging to the heir of the Earl of Minto, but the link is as yet obscure.

MELROSE CLOSE (263 Cowgate) *see* ROBERTSON'S CLOSE, Cowgate.

(ABBOT OF) MELROSE CLOSE (104 High Street) *see* STRICHEN'S CLOSE.

MELVILLE CRESCENT, PLACE and **STREET** (Coates) *see under* COATES.

THE MELVILLE DRIVE (South Side) was a new road opened in 1859 and named for Sir John Melville, Lord Provost 1854-59, who had played a part in the opening up of Brougham Street, which made this new route across the town possible. The name was continued in MELVILLE TERRACE in about 1864.

MELVILLE GRANGE (Gilmerton) *see* GILMERTON GRANGE.

MELVILLE STREET (Joppa) renamed Bellfield Street, *see under* RABBIT HALL, Joppa.

MENTONE AVENUE (Portobello) was formed after 1870 in the grounds of Ramsay Lodge (*see under* RAMSAY PLACE, Portobello). The name is fancy, from the French watering place *Menton*.

MENTONE GARDENS and **TERRACE** (Mayfield) *see under* McLAREN ROAD, Mayfield.

MERCAT CROSS (Edinburgh) *see* THE CROSS, Edinburgh.

THE MERCAT CROSS (Queensferry) is recorded in 1364, as standing east of the rivulet which marked the western boundary of the burgh (*see* WEST LOANING BURN, Queensferry) but in 1764, on the grounds that 'it did greatly straiten the street' and that its shaft was in any case cracked and dangerous, it was removed in the course of a general improvement of the high street, and was replaced, for legal purposes, by a nominal 'Cross' in the form of a small platform three or four steps high, on the north side of the Tolbooth tower.

MERCHANT STREET (Old Town) was laid out in 1774 by James Craig, partly in what had been the garden of the Merchants' Hall, leased to the Excise Office in 1730. *See also* OLD EXCISE OFFICE CLOSE, Cowgate.

MERCHISTON, shown on *Blaeu* 1654, is recorded from 1266 onwards, and the early forms *Merchinstoun* 1266, *Merchammeston* 1278 and *Merchenstoun* 1371 show the name to be Anglian, incorporating a British personal name in *Merchiaun's tún* or farm place. The mention of *Overmerchampstone* in *Bain* 1337 shows that by then it had been subdivided; and in about 1433 Alexander Napier, merchant and Provost of Edinburgh, acquired *Nether Merchiston*, while his son later added *Over Merchiston* and built MERCHISTON TOWER at the centre of an estate stretching from the Gorgie road to the Pow or Jordan burn, and marching with Meggetland in the west and Wrightshouses and the Burgh Muir in the east. By 1776 the greater part of it, including the farms of *Myreside* and *Gorgie Muir* or *Mains* and *East Parks*, had been sold to George Watson's Hospital, and NORTH MERCHISTON (*which see*) had also been divided off. MERCHISTON PLACE was begun by 1861, and MERCHISTON TERRACE (a side name in Colinton Road) in 1863. MERCHISTON AVENUE (1867) replaced an early loan connecting the Burghmuirhead with Fountainbridge and flanking the East Parks, which were developed from 1876 onwards as MERCHISTON PARK. In 1867-68, MERCHISTON CRESCENT was planned along with EAST and WEST CASTLE ROADS (named for the Tower), to link up with James Gowan's earlier scheme at the south end of NAPIER ROAD, *which see*. For the westward development that followed, *see* SPYLAW, ETTRICK and GILLSLAND ROADS *and* POLWARTH TERRACE. MERCHISTON MEWS (1875) seems to have been intended as a general stabling for the neighbourhood. MERCHISTON GROVE (1896) was built in the grounds of a house of that name, earlier called 'Gorgie Cottage' and occupying the site of the steading of Gorgie Muir, shown on *Merchiston* 1776. MERCHISTON GARDENS (1897) occupied a playing field immediately west of Myreside farm steading.

MERCHISTON BANK AVENUE (Merchiston) was developed by 1892 on the site of a house shown as *Merchiston Bank* on *Knox* 1812 and *Ordnance Survey* 1852, and the house name seems to have been used for the street until 1902. MERCHISTON BANK GARDENS was formed in nursery ground in 1898 and appears in *PO Directory* 1899. MERCHISTON BANK TERRACE is noted as a side name in Colinton Road in *PO Directory* 1902.

MERLYON'S or **MARLIN'S WYND** (High Street) is named on *Rothiemay* 1647 and shown with its upper part diverted round the east end of the Tron Kirk, then newly built across the original head of the wynd. Still shown on *Kincaid* 1784, it disappeared in 1785 under the new developments of South Bridge, Hunter Square and Blair Street; but in the 1970s its original upper part was recovered by excavation beneath the floor level of the Tron Kirk. The fact that it is always referred to as a wynd or vennel suggests that it was never a (private) close but a public way, probably dating from the early days of the burgh. Presumably it had some earlier name; but it is scarcely to be doubted that that given as *Merlyeonis wynde* in *Town Council Minutes* 1558 and as *the vennel of the late Walter Merletone* in a charter of 1706 came from Walter Merlyoun, mason and burgess in Edinburgh, who witnessed a charter in Holyrood in 1490 and was still working on the new hall of the palace in 1502, but is referred to in a protocol of 1530 as 'the late Walter Merlyon' formerly owning property in the Cowgate, apparently at or near the foot of the wynd. He seems to have been one of a family of masons, possibly originating in Cupar, Fife, but also working in the royal service in Dysart and Dunkeld as well as at Holyrood palace; and the John Marlȝone mentioned in *Protocols of John Foular* 1531-32 as an owner in the south side of the High Street, although of the different trade of *causeymakar*, may have been his grandson. The story retailed in *Maitland* 1753, that Walter Merlyoun was a Frenchman hired in 1532 to pave the High Street for the very first time, is palpably untrue, not only because Merlyoun was not French, was not a causeymakar, and was dead before 1532, but because the contract for the paving work detailed in *Town Council Minutes* 1532, was not with any Merlyoun but with two Frenchmen called Mayser and Foliot, causeymakars; while the claim that it was for the first paving of the High street, rather than repair or extension of causeywork, is in contempt of the fact that cleansing contracts of 1505 and 1509 referred to forty roods (ten Scots acres) of causey, an area that must have included all the streets of the burgh. Indeed, considering that the technique of *caucé* had been introduced to Scotland from France before 1400, it would have been astonishing if Edinburgh had not made use of it before the 16th century.

MERRILEES' CLOSE (South Leith) is listed on *Kirkwood* 1817; and the name, evidently connected with John Merrilees, listed in *Williamson's Directory* 1773 as a brewer here in the Yardheads, may also have been connected with a John Merrilees, maltster, who acquired property in the Kirkgate in 1747.

MERRYLANDS (Ratho) is shown thus on *Roy* 1753 and as *Mirlands* on *Gellatly* 1834. It is fairly clear that the form *Mary lands* appearing on *Knox* 1812 gives a misleading impression of possible connection with the Church; for the other spellings, coupled with the evidence of the *Geological Survey* that the tail burn of the loch at RATHOMYRE (*which see*) once ran through a long narrow bog here in the howe south of Roddinglaw, point to the name being Scots *miry lands*. *Blaeu* 1654 shows the Ratho loch, and the name LOCHEND in the vicinity of Merrylands.

MERTOUN PLACE (Temple Park) *see under* POLWARTH TERRACE.

MEUSE LANE (New Town) *see under* NEW TOWN.

MICKLE'S or **MUCKLE'S CLOSE** (South Leith) is listed on *Kirkwood* 1817, and the name is probably connected with George Miekle, burgess and brewer in Leith in 1761, and listed in *Williamson's Directory* 1773 as George Muckle, brewer in Yardheads.

MIDCOMMON CLOSE (295 Canongate) *see under the* COMMON CLOSES, Canongate.

MIDDLEBY STREET (Newington) is shown as projected on *Kirkwood* 1817 and was named by the superior, George Bell, for Middlebie in Annandale, where his family's ancestral home was at Blacket. The *-by* spelling of the street name appears from the beginning.

MIDDLEFIELD (Pilrig) was advertised in 1793 as 'a house newly built', and the name may have been coined for it, or else taken from a field name. By 1804 *Ainslie* shows it as though it had become a side name for more than one property in Leith Walk, and *Kirkwood* 1817 shows this as MIDDLEFIELD PLACE. *Ordnance Survey* 1852 shows Middlefield House for the larger of the properties shown in 1804, and Middlefield Place for a short terrace which was taken into SHRUB PLACE by 1876. *Ordnance Survey* 1893 shows MIDDLEFIELD as the lane passing west of Middlefield House.

MIDDLEKNOWE, -PARK and **-SHOT** (Wester Hailes) *see under* WESTBURN, Wester Hailes.

MIDMAR AVENUE etc (South Morningside) *see under* EGYPT, South Morningside.

MID TERRACE (Queensferry) *see under* HIGH STREET, Queensferry.

MILLAR CRESCENT (Morningside) was begun by James Millar in 1896, as part of his redevelopment of the site of the East House of the Royal Edinburgh Asylum, vacated in 1894. In 1901 he added MILLAR PLACE and modified his plan to include MORNINGSIDE TERRACE.

MILL BRAE (Currie) is a name attaching to two distinct routes. The *big Mill Brae* as shown on *Ordnance Survey* 1852 and was formed in about 1831 as an access to the East Mills of Currie by the EAST MILLS or MUTTERS BRIDGE, the latter alternative apparently containing Scots *mutters* or *multures*, dues payable on grain brought to the mill. The *wee Mill Brae* is a path, also shown in 1852 as leading down to the river bank; but *Ordnance Survey* 1893 shows it joining the MILL STEPS and crossing the river to Kinleith Paper Mills by a footbridge. These mills closed in 1966.

MILL BRAE (Slateford) is the traditional name for the rise in the Inglis Green road (once much steeper than it is today) where this leaves the riverside near Longstone and continues eastward past the

Powderhaugh to Grays Mill. MILLBRAE WYND, a new road branching off at the foot of the Brae, was named for it in 1984.

MILLBURN (Gogar) *see under* GOGAR.

MILLERFIELD (Sciennes) was one of a succession of large villas, each within its own spacious grounds, which formed the suburb of Hope Park along the south side of the East Meadows. The grounds are shown on *Scott* 1759 as 'part of Mr Gardner's', but as 'Mr Miller's' on *Ainslie* 1804, and MILLARFIELD HOUSE, ultimately cleared away for the building of Sciennes Primary School in 1889, is shown on *Kirkwood* 1817. The name came from the owners, a branch of the Quaker family of Millers (*see under* CRAIGENTINNY) and it was William Miller (1796-1882) the notable engraver, who began to develop his land at MILLERFIELD PLACE in 1863.

MILLER ROW (Water of Leith or Dean Village) is named in *Town Council Minutes* 1713, and was probably the ten houses ordained in the *Minutes* 1695 to be built for the town's millers, apparently in a flatted tenement 'fyve howses laigh and fyve high'. The street name came into *PO Directory* in 1870, along with other addresses in the village.

MILLER'S CLOSE (171 Canongate) is listed on *Kirkwood* 1817 and was named for Daniel Miller, merchant, bailie of Canongate, who had a tenement here before 1799. Earlier the close was AITKEN'S, for Archibald Aitken, deacon of the Wrights of Canongate, who was the builder and previous owner of Miller's land, and seems to have become bankrupt in 1788. It may also have been known as HAMILTON'S ENTRY, recorded in 1799 and presumably named for William Hamilton, wright, recorded in *Williamson's Directory* 1773 as in Tolbooth Wynd, and also his successors Hamilton & Sons, upholsterers, active there in 1780; but the name may belong to TOLBOOTH WYND itself, *which see.*

MILL LANE (South Leith) is shown on all maps from *Collins* 1693 onwards and named *Road from Leith Mills* on *Wood* 1771 and *Mill Lane* on *Thomson* 1822. In view of the antiquity of milling on the river haugh above Junction Bridge, the road must be medieval; and it would seem to have been continuous with the original GILES STREET. The part west of Great Junction Street was rebuilt as BALLANTYNE ROAD in 1896.

MILLRIG (Kirkliston) is shown on *Armstrongs* 1773. The name is Scots *rigg*, in its later sense of field, *belonging to the mill*—presumably the Breistmill.

MILL STEPS (Currie) *see under* MILL BRAE, Currie.

MILNACRE (Bonnyhaugh) *see under* BONNYHAUGH, Bonnington.

MILNE'S CLOSE (218 Canongate) is given as *Miln's Court* on *Ainslie* 1780, and seems to have been named for more than one branch of the Milne family. Robert Milne, master mason, owning and probably building property here before 1709, is probably the same as the member of that illustrious family who developed MILNE'S COURT,

Lawnmarket, *which see*; and a Thomas Milne, mason, is recorded as selling property to Archibald Chessel (*see* CHESSEL'S COURT) who also got the main property in Milne's Close from David Miln, merchant, son of David Miln, tailor. A John Milne sold ground to George Weir, brewer in WEIR'S CLOSE, *which see*. As part of the south Canongatehead, the close was in Edinburgh, not the burgh of Canongate.

MILNE'S ENTRY (517 High Street) **MILNE'S COURT** and **CLOSE** are shown on *Edgar* 1742 and named for (and in the case of the Court, perhaps by) Robert Milne or Mylne, seventh of that family of royal Master Masons, who had built MILNE'S SQUARE (*which see*) in 1684-88 and followed it up with this development in the Lawnmarket in 1690. The Close was earlier CRANSTON'S, for James Cranston, owner of a tenement at the mouth of the close in 1682. The Court may have been called LINDSAY'S originally, but there is no clue as to why.

MILNE SQUARE (173 High Street) was built between 1684 and 1688 by Robert Milne or Mylne of Balfarg, royal Master Mason; and his own statement, that it was 'now and in all time coming to be called Mylne Square', suggests that he named it himself. It figures on *Edgar* 1742, and *Edgar* 1765 shows how part of it was cleared to form the *Greenmarket*. Since the buildings on the east side of the Square narrowed the approach to the North Bridge, in a way clearly shown on *Kincaid* 1784, the town bought them in 1787 and rebuilt them to suit the street, as shown in detail on *Ordnance Survey* 1852. In 1899 the Square was cleared to become part of the site of the *Scotsman Building*, completed in 1902. In forming his Square, Milne suppressed or truncated some older closes: among them SKLAITTER'S or SCLATER'S CLOSE, recorded in *Protocols of Alexander King* 1552 and perhaps named for Andrew Sclater, merchant, prominent in the town council from 1559 to 1588; and west of it, DUNCAN CAMPBELL'S CLOSE, which (at a guess) may have been connected with Duncan Campbell, merchant in Edinburgh in 1718.

MILTON (OF DUNDAS) (Dalmeny) is shown on *Blaeu* 1654 as *Mill of Dundas* and recorded thus from 1557 onwards, and in the derived names *Mylntounhill* 1583 and *Myltoun Myll* 1572. The name is Anglian *myln tún*, the village or farm place at the mill—in this case, the mill belonging to Dundas, to which all tenants in the estate were *thirled* or required to send their corn for grinding.

MILTON HOUSE (90 Canongate) is shown on *Edgar* 1765 on the former site of the Duke of Roxburgh's house, shown as vacant on *Edgar* 1742. The mansion was built by John Adam in 1755-58 for Andrew Fletcher, Lord Milton (1692-1766) Lord of Session from 1724 and Lord Justice Clerk 1735-48. It was also known as FLETCHER'S or LORD MILTON'S LODGING. All that remains of it is a quartet of mural paintings which Robert Wilson incorporated in the school building that replaced it in 1886.

MILTON ROAD (Duddingston) is shown on *Roy* 1753 as a branch of the Leith to Dalkeith road via Willowbrae and Niddrie, leading to

Easter Duddingston and joining the Musselburgh road at Magdalen. The 18th-century maps describe it as the parish road between Easter and Wester Duddingston. The section within Easter Duddingston was named in the 1880s for Andrew Fletcher, Lord Milton, who had acquired Brunstane and Figgate in 1747 and died in Brunstane House in 1766. As a Fletcher of Saltoun, he probably took his judicial title from the Milton—i.e. place of the estate corn mill—of West Saltoun, East Lothian. MILTON TERRACE (1931) and DRIVE (1934) were developed in the *Hardy Flatt* of Easter Duddingston, and MILTON GROVE was added in 1967. MILTON CRESCENT and GARDENS were formed in Wester Duddingston ground in 1932, and got their names from *Milton Road West*. MILTON LINK was named in 1987.

MILTON STREET (Abbeyhill) began to be developed in part of the ground in COMELY GREEN (*which see*) acquired in 1885 by James Milne & Son, gasfitters and engineers, formerly based in MILTON HOUSE, Canongate, *which see*. They continued their works' name in *Milton House Works* and named the street as the access to them.

MINERAL STREET (Stockbridge) since named DEAN TERRACE etc *see under* DEAN STREET & TERRACE, Stockbridge.

MRS MINISH'S CLOSE (91 High Street) *see* BARRINGER'S CLOSE.

LADY MINNES or **MENYIES CLOSE** (High Street) *see* St MONAN'S WYND.

MINNIFREE (Dalmeny) is shown thus on *Adair* 1682 and *Armstrongs* 1773 but has since disappeared. The name, recorded in 1652 as *Monifrie*, is British and/or Gaelic, describing the early landscape of the ridge where the place stood (in the vicinity of NT 131756) as 'heathery moor or hill'.

MINT CLOSE (56 High Street) *see* SOUTH GRAY'S CLOSE.

MINTO STREET (Newington) figures in Benjamin Bell's feuing scheme on *Newington* 1806, albeit not on the same grand scale in which it appeared on *Newington* 1795, and it eventually began to be built in about 1807. Shown simply as 'New Road' on *Stranger's Guide* 1816, it is named on *Kirkwood* 1817. There is nothing to connect the name directly with Minto, near Hawick, unless it be that Minto crags are mentioned in Scott's *Lay of the Last Minstrel*, published in 1805; and likewise there is no evidence of particular connection with Sir Gilbert Elliot, 1st Earl of Minto, except that he was prominent as Governor General of India 1807-13 and died in 1814, the period when the street was being developed.

MITCHELL'S CLOSE (327 High Street) *see under* DON'S CLOSE.

MITCHELL STREET (Craigmillar) *see* PEFFER STREET.

MITCHELL STREET (South Leith) is shown, unnamed, on *Ainslie* 1804 but appears in *PO Directory* 1808. It was named for the Mitchell family, merchants, who had owned this ground at Constitution Hill since before 1778.

MOAT (Gorgie) is named on *Roy* 1753 and shown in the same position as the name *Mount* on *Ordnance Survey* 1852, viz. on the west bank of the Meggetland burn immediately south of Slateford Road. It is possible that it was a transferred name, since Easter and Wester Gorgie were among the forfeited lands granted to James Duncan 'in the Mott of Errol' by the Cromwellian government in 1656; but on the other hand, there is no record of any residence or headquarters he might have had here, and the later form *mount* might suggest that the name, as Scots *mote*, a mound or embankment, simply described some feature of the sort in this boggy terrain. MOAT PLACE, opposite the Moat, was named by 1890. It was followed by MOAT STREET (1901) and TERRACE (1907); while MOAT DRIVE, occupying the site of the steading of Gorgie Park (*see under* GORGIE) was named in about 1925.

MOAT KNOWE (Dalmeny) is probably (as suggested on *Ordnance Survey* 1852) the site of a motte-and-bailey castle, predecessor of the nearby towerhouse of Dundas built in about 1424.

MOFFAT'S CLOSE (29 High Street) is shown on *Ainslie* 1780, and the name appears to have derived from William Moffat, merchant, who acquired property here through his wife Catherine from her father William Chalmers, writer, at some time prior to 1740. It was also PITCAIRLIE'S, from John Bayne of Pitcairlie, Fife, whose father Donald Baine, bowmaker, is listed in the *Valuation Roll* 1635 as owner occupier of two properties in the close (including a yard and a pair of butts) as well as another in the High Street but entered from the close. The family were still owners a century later.

MOIRA TERRACE (Craigentinny) was named by 1907, as part of the earliest housing development in CRAIGENTINNY, *which see*. If (as has been suggested) it was named for Francis Hastings, 2nd Earl of Moira in Co. Down, who had lived in Duddingston House when he was C-in-C Scotland in 1803, the connection with Craigentinny remains obscure, unless it be somehow related to the fact that Wakefield Christie, who succeeded his uncle in Craigentinny in 1889, was of Kircassock, also in Co. Down. The street name was extended to MOIRA PARK in 1986.

MONKBARNS GARDENS (Inch) *see under* THE INCH, Nether Liberton.

MONMOUTH TERRACE (Goldenacre) *see under* MONTAGU TERRACE, Goldenacre.

MONS HILL (Dalmeny) appears on *Blaeu* 1654 as *Munchhill*, in *RMS* 1622 as *Munghill*, and on *Roy* 1747 as *Munshill*. The first part is British *monid* or Gaelic *monadh*, a hill, while the second is Scots *hill*, added after the meaning of the original name was forgotten.

MONTAGUE STREET (South Side) is sketched on *Kirkwood* 1817 and shown planned on *Knox* 1821 and named on *Kirkwood* 1823. The development was on the property of the heirs of Dr John Hope (*see under* HOPE CRESCENT) and no connection with a Montagu, whether through the Buccleuch family or otherwise, has as yet been traced.

MONTAGU TERRACE (Goldenacre) was built in 1878 and like BOWHILL TERRACE (1880) and MONMOUTH TERRACE (1889) it derived its name from the ownership of GOLDENACRE (*which see*) by the owner of East Granton, the Duke of Buccleuch. The first of these street names was for his Montagu title, which had come into the family when the Lady Elizabeth, heiress of the Duke of Montagu, had married the 3rd Duke of Buccleuch in 1767. The second was for the Buccleuch's ancient seat of Bowhill, beside Gala Water. The third was for James, Duke of Monmouth, illegitimate son of Charles II, who married Anna Scott, daughter of the 2nd Earl of Buccleuch, took her surname, and was created 1st Duke of Buccleuch.

MONTEBELLO (Joppa) was the name of the south side of ARGYLE CRESCENT, shown on *W & A K Johnston* 1888 but noted as dropped in *PO Directory* 1914. A fancy name, perhaps suggested by the place in Italy or the battle there in 1800, or else made up as *monte bello*, bonny mount, or as a play on the names of Porto*bello* and nearby *Mount* Pleasant.

MONTEITH'S CLOSE (61 High Street) is listed on *Edgar* 1742 and mentioned in 1722, but beyond the fact that there was a *Monteith's Booth* or tenement in it, there is no information about this name. Earlier it was FLEMING'S, derived from a Patrick Fleming who is mentioned in 1733 as having had land 'near the Netherbow' and is probably the same as the Patrick Flemyng whose land is described in the same phrase in *RMS* 1573 and who may have been the son of Patrick Fleming, member of town council 1514-36. He is also said to have had a tennis court—i.e. a *cachepele* or royal-tennis court—in the close.

MONTGOMERY STREET (Hillside) is shown on *Calton* 1819 as part of the plan for the CALTON NEW TOWN (*which see*) and as already named, evidently for the owner(s) of the ground at its west end, noted in 1825 as 'heirs of William Montgomerie'. Some houses were completed at this end of the street by 1825, but progress was stopped at the city boundary, as shown on *Ordnance Survey* 1852, by reason of difficulties with local taxation on buildings beyond it. MONTGOMERY STREET LANE, unaffected by such problems, was substantially developed by 1850; but further east, the advent of the Leith & Granton branch of the NBR in 1866 finally put paid to the grandiose Calton scheme's extension: WEST and EAST MONTGOMERY PLACE were developed as local infill in about 1870, and Montgomery Street and East Montgomery Street were slowly completed in the 1880s.

MONTPELIER (Merchiston) is shown as a street *Montpellier* on *Kirkwood* 1817, but is also recorded in 1820 as the then current name of a mansion and 4-acre property here, originally known as *Wrighthouses Park*. It was evidently derived from Montpellier in Languedoc, esteemed as the very model of a genteel health resort—

in 1778, Inveresk was described 'as a kind of *Montpellier* to Edinburgh', and in 1820 the *Strangers Guide* acclaimed Morningside as 'the *Montpellier* of Midlothian' but the presence, less than a mile away, of the chapel of Montpellier's St ROQUE (*which see*) patron saint of those sick with the plague, and/or the fact that the house was inherited in 1810 by a physician, James Buchan, may have had something to do with it. The spelling followed the French style until about 1890, when MONTPELIER PARK was begun. MONTPELIER TERRACE followed by 1897.

MONTROSE TERRACE (Abbeymount) was named in about 1876; and since the nearby PITLOCHRY PLACE and EARLSTON PLACE were named in about 1873 and 1876 respectively, it may be that the reference is to yet another Scottish town, Montrose.

THE MORAY ESTATE (New Town) was the historic estate of DRUMSHEUGH (*which see*) acquired by the Earl of Moray in 1782 and feued out by the 10th Earl forty years later, in accordance with a design by Gillespie Graham. Except for two streets, dealt with separately because they partly involved land outwith Moray's (*see* ALBYN PLACE and WEMYSS PLACE) all the streets were named in the *Conditions of Sale* issued in 1822, and figure on *Wood* 1823. MORAY PLACE was named for the earldom, and DOUNE TERRACE for its heir, who is known as *Lord Doune*, from Doune in Perthshire. AINSLIE PLACE was named for the 10th Earl's second wife, Margaret, daughter of Sir Philip Ainslie of Pilton, while GREAT STUART STREET bears the Earl's own family name: the two streets together making something like a 'marriage lintol' in the middle of the scheme. St COLME STREET indirectly recalls the most illustrious of the Stewart earls of Moray, James Stuart, son of James V by Margaret Erskine, created Earl of Moray by his half-sister Mary Queen of Scots in 1562 and made Regent of Scotland in 1567, when she was incarcerated in Lochleven: amongst other things he was the lay abbot of Inchcolm, and this lordship continued with the family after 1620. RANDOLPH CRESCENT commemorates the first of the earlier line of Randolph earls of Moray, Sir Thomas Randolph, nephew and lieutenant of Robert the Bruce, created Earl of Moray in 1314 and Regent of Scotland after the Bruce died in 1329. The name was twice extended: first to RANDOLPH CLIFF in about 1837, the *cliff* being the rock face above the gorge of the Dean; and later to RANDOLPH PLACE, *which see*. The remaining streets in the group were named for Moray lands elsewhere: GLENFINLAS STREET for Glenfinlas, southwest of Callander; and FORRES and DARNAWAY STREETS for Darnaway, near Forres.

MORAY HOUSE (174 Canongate) was built in about 1625 by Mary, Dowager Duchess of Home, but got its present name from her daughter Margaret, Countess of Moray, who inherited it in 1643.

MORAY STREET (Pilrig) was renamed SPEY STREET, *which see*.

MOREDUN (Gilmerton) is a hill name from Moncrieff in Perthshire, imported into Gilmerton in 1769 by Baron David Stewart Moncrieff as a fancy name for his newly acquired estate of GUTTERS or GOODTREES. Shown on *Blaeu* 1654 as *Guters*, and found elsewhere in Scotland (*see* GOODTREES, Balerno), this earlier name is recorded here in the forms *Gutters* 1406, *Guttaris* 1501, *Gutteris* 1516, *Guters* 1596, *Gutheris* 1602, *Guttries* 1630 and *Goodtrees alias Guthers* 1663. The 'Guttries' form is clearly 'Gutters' with a normal shift of the *r*, and 'Goodtrees' probably arose as an attempt to fit a meaning to it. The name seems to be too early to be Scots *gutters* in its sense of 'place of dubs and mires', nor would this be notably apt for the topography; rather, it may be British, akin to the Cornish name *Gothers*, place at the watercourse, a fair description of its site within a pronounced bend of the Lothian or Burdiehouse burn, *but see also under* MOREDUN DYKES. The site of GUTTERS or MOREDUN HOUSE is now that of the Murray Home. The settlement and mill dam at MOREDUN MILL is clearly shown on *Roy* 1753 under its earlier name of GUARDWELL, *which see*. The site of the home farm steading of MOREDUN MAINS, shown on *Knox* 1812, is now open ground north of Moredunvale Place; and part of its approach road, skirting the north side of the *House parks*, began to be developed in 1933 as part of MOREDUN PARK ROAD, along with MOREDUN PARK GARDENS. Development continued at MOREDUN PARK DRIVE (1947) STREET and VIEW (1948) GREEN and GROVE (1963) WALK (1964) LOAN (1966) COURT and WAY (1967). Other streets in Moredun Mains were incongruously named for CRAIGOUR (*which see*) and in 1967 the name *Moredunvale* was invented for MOREDUNVALE BANK, GREEN, GROVE, LOAN, PARK, PLACE, ROAD, VIEW and WAY.

MOREDUN CRESCENT (Craigleith) was named in 1870 for David Anderson of Moredun, a trustee and governor of Fettes College. It was re-named CARRINGTON CRESCENT in 1968, to avoid confusion with the estate of Moredun—*see under* CARRINGTON ROAD, Comely Bank—but has since been cleared away for extension of Western General Hospital.

MOREDUN DYKES ROAD (Gilmerton) is shown on *Laurie* 1763 as a loan skirting the south and west boundaries of the park of Gutters; and while the first part of the name cannot be older than the renaming of that estate in 1769 (*see under* MOREDUN) the *dykes* may refer to the park wall or, more likely, to ditches running alongside the boundaries; and these might conceivably be related to the medieval name of the place, Gutters or Guthers. The southern section of the old road was developed and extended westwards in the mid 1930s; and this led to the northern section being renamed HYVOT LOAN, *see under* HYVOT'S BANK.

MORIES or **MORICE CLOSE** (156 High Street) *see* BURNET'S CLOSE.

MORISON GARDENS (Queensferry) was developed in about 1920 and named for Alexander Morison, Provost of Queensferry 1917-26 and author of *Historical Notes on the Ancient & Royal Burgh of Queensferry* 1927.

MORNINGSIDE is recorded in 1734 as the name already current for an estate which had been formed in 1657 by merging two properties, one on each side of the Linton highroad (Morningside Road) and both originally feued out of the Burgh Muir in 1586. Were the name to go back to the period before the Muir was granted to Edinburgh in the 12th century, it might well conceal some name other than 'morning slope'; but there is no evidence that it is of any great age, and it seems likely that it is a fancy name, coined for the estate at some time after 1657 and meaning just that. The estate centre, shown on *Roy* 1753 as *Morningside*, became EASTER MORNINGSIDE HOUSE after the estate was divided up again in 1764; while the working centre of the western part, shown on *Scott* 1759 as *Morningside farm*, on a site just north of the entry to present-day Morningside Park, became (WESTER) MORNINGSIDE HOUSE. The highway is believed to follow a Roman line (*see under* ROMAN ROADS) and until 1883, when it was formally named MORNINGSIDE ROAD, it was known simply as *Morningside*; and until 1885 the various groups of properties along its length were addressed under side names: on the east, GREENHILL BANK (1833) BANNER PLACE (1856) FALCON PLACE (1870) and JORDAN PLACE (1864); on the west, WAVERLEY TERRACE (1877) MARMION TERRACE (1861) MORNINGSIDE TERRACE (1852) MORNINGSIDE BANK (1890) ESPLIN PLACE (1870) BLACKFORD PLACE (1859) ALEXANDRA TERRACE (1882) and WATT TERRACE (1879). For some years after it was laid out in 1823, MORNINGSIDE PLACE was called DEUCHAR PLACE, for its developer William Deuchar of Wester Morningside. MORNINGSIDE PARK was formed and named (probably from a field name) in 1875, although until 1894 the first houses built in it, on its west side near the junction with Morningside Place, were called PENTLAND TERRACE, presumably for the view from rooms at the back. A second MORNINGSIDE TERRACE, in a locality entirely different from the first one mentioned above, was built by James Millar, as part of his redevelopment of the Royal Asylum's East House, *see under* MILLAR CRESCENT, Morningside. From about 1882, starting with the erection of the Morningside Hydropathic (replaced by MORNINGSIDE GROVE by 1905), a new neighbourhood of SOUTH MORNINGSIDE was created in Plewlands of Braid by the development of the Scottish Heritage Company's (SOUTH) MORNINGSIDE DRIVE and GARDENS, begun by 1883 and 1886 respectively. MORNINGSIDE STATION was opened in 1881 and speedily took over the function of landmark in the Braid road previously carried out by the medieval BRIGGS O BRAID (*which see*) and the MORNINGSIDE TOLL that had operated at the Briggs from about 1853 until 1883.

MOROCCO or **MOROCCO'S CLOSE** (High Street) was cleared in about 1798, to make way for Bank Street. It is recorded in 1645 as MOSCROP'S, evidently named for early owners within it, noted in 1764 as Patrick Moscrop of Castlewood, Jedburgh, followed by his son John—clearly members of a Border family who practised as lawyers in Edinburgh over at least four generations, and included Adam and John, made burgesses in 1494 and 1560, and Patrick and John, figuring in RMS 1575 and 1589. The close was also known to the end of its days as JAMESON'S, from Matthew (perhaps Matho Jameson, made burgess in 1566) and Robert and John Jameson, who successively owned a tenement in it at some time before 1635. There is nothing in the history to show the origin of its other names of MURROWS CLOSE, given in *Town Council Minutes* 1716, and MOROCCO or MORROCO'S given on *Edgar* 1742 and *Ainslie* 1780; but the fact that they are closely matched in the history of Morocco's Land in the Canongate may support some guesswork, *see under* MOROCCO'S CLOSE, Canongate.

MOROCCO'S CLOSE (273 Canongate) is listed on *Ainslie* 1780 and presumably took its name from *Morocco's* or *Morrows Land*, recorded in 1703. Rebuilt in 1957, this tenement had been much altered around the 1700s but was judged from its style to date from the 17th century; and the earliest record of it, in the *Acts of Bailies of the Canongate*, is that Thomas Gray, merchant burgess of Edinburgh, bought it from James Whyte, burgess of Canongate, in 1653. The name *Morrows* here and that of *Murrows* at MORROCO'S CLOSE in the High Street (*see above*) are surely the same; and although they might contain a surname, it is a reasonable guess that they are nicknames from Late Latin *morus* or Spanish *moro*, a Moor or Berber or negro, and that in both cases they simply parallel *Morocco's* in referring to some owner who was a Moor, or otherwise connected with Morocco—a thing in itself not in the least improbable, considering that one expatriate Scot, John McMath, 'lord major of Tangier', was made a burgess of Edinburgh in 1679. While in the High Street case this remains pure speculation, in the Canongate case the effigy of a Moor, mid 17th-century in style and displayed on the street front, might point to such a connection: but since it stood in a niche described in *RCAHMS Inventory* as 'roughly-formed', it seems to have been added to the original building, and there is no knowing when this was and how it was related to the name. There are also two widely different stories, both emerging in the 19th century, which purport to show how the building got its name. In the one retailed by *Chambers* (and he seems not to have known the other) a local merchant makes a fortune out of trade with Morocco through the good offices of his sister, who having been captured by pirates on the Barbary coast has become an influential favourite in the harem of the emperor of Morocco. The other story, given by *Wilson* as one of several known to him, is a more circumstantial tale, in which it is a young man, Andrew Gray, who is captured and enslaved in Morocco, after breaking jail in Edinburgh and fleeing the country; but rising to power under the emperor, he returns to Scotland in 1645 as a wealthy man, marries the daughter of Sir John Smith of Groathill, Lord Provost of the day, and settles in the Canongate. Yet so erratic is its play with historical circumstances and personages that the story only loses credibility; and although the Moorish statue bears the arms of Smith of Groathill, if anything this belies the story of a marriage, since it displays the family arms of the 'wife' without marshalling them with those of the 'husband' Gray. It is clear that both 'traditions' are merely fanciful attempts to explain the name, making use of stock romantic plots; and if any historical fact lies behind them, it is so heavily disguised as to be quite obscured.

MORRISON'S CLOSE (117 High Street) is listed on *Edgar* 1742 and recorded in 1750 as having a great house on its east side, owned of old by John Morison, merchant, and after him by John Morison of Dairsey. These may possibly have been the John Moresoun who was a bailie in 1582 and served on the town council in various capacities (including that of old or depute provost in 1590) until about 1603, and another John Morrison, merchant and member of town council in the 1630s, who was certainly connected with the close, being listed in 1635 as owner of property in it—albeit on the west side, not east. The close was also CALLENDER'S, for John Callender, deacon of the Hammermen in 1689—*see also* CALLENDER'S ENTRY, 67 Canongate.

MORRISON STREET (Haymarket) is part of the ancient route from Main Point to Linlithgow, named in about 1828, probably by the trustees of Thomas Morrison, builder in Edinburgh, who had died at Duke Street in 1820. Born in Muthill, he left money to found Morrison's Academy in Crieff; but his trustees also bought and developed the ground of *Morrison's Park*, stretching from Dewar Place westwards to Haymarket, which was named for William Morrison, lawyer, who had purchased it in 1788-90, and who also owned the properties of Whitehouse and Adiefield on the south side of the main road, as shown on *Whitehouse & Adiefield*, c1788. Thus the street name derived from William or Thomas Morrison or (most likely) from both. It originally applied only to the road west of Dewar Place; but by 1887 it had displaced the earlier names of CASTLE BARNS and TOBAGO STREET and the part of ORCHARDFIELD west of the junction with the Lothian Road.

MORTON (Fairmilehead) is recorded from 1182 onwards and shown as *Mortoun* on *Blaeu* 1654. The spellings *Mertona, Mertun*, and *Merton*, all prior to 1300, show the name to be Anglian *mere tún*, farm on the bank of the mere; and the *Geological Survey* shows the bed of an ancient lake at the confluence of the Lothian and Pentland burns, still partly visible as a patch of reedy ground less than half a mile east of the home farm of MORTON MAINS. The historic centre was probably in the vicinity of MORTON HOUSE, although the present building seems to have been remodelled from 1709 onwards, to serve as the dower house of Mortonhall. Its *belvidere* is noted on *Laurie* 1763. MORTON MAINS ROAD is named as the way to the home farm.

MORTONHALL, recorded from 1404 onwards as *Martonehall* or *Mortonhal*, clearly derived its name from MORTON, *which see*. There is no evidence that it was ever the 'hall of Morton', and it is much more likely that it was the *halh* or *haw* of Morton, referring to the great flat which stretches beside the Stenhouse burn immediately east of the mansion. It is shown on *Blaeu* 1654 as *Mortoun hall*, and *Roy* 1753 shows the estate centre more or less on the same site as the present house, which dates from 1769. In 1970 the name 'Mortonhall Park' was coined when development of the *Kaims Easter Park* and *Kaimes Partridge Park* began at MORTONHALL PARK AVENUE, GARDENS, GROVE and WAY, followed by MORTONHALL PARK GREEN, LOAN and VIEW in 1972, and MORTONHALL PARK BANK, CRESCENT, DRIVE, PLACE and TERRACE in 1973. In 1984, in order to provide addresses for new properties served by it, the former south drive of Mortonhall House was named MORTONHALL GATE, way to Mortonhall.

MORTONHALL ROAD (Blackford) is on ground added to Blackford by Trotter of Mortonhall in 1760. Partly planned by 1888, it was named for the main estate by 1889.

LORD MORTON'S CLOSE (119 Canongate) *see* MUNRO'S CLOSE, Canongate.

MORTON STREET (Joppa) together with SOUTH MORTON STREET in Easter Duddingston is shown on *Knox* 1812 as a road from Easter Duddingston to the sea, and the right of way was preserved by a footbridge when the railway was formed in about 1845. Housing development seems to have begun in the 1870s. By 1893 the names MORTON STREET and JOPPA LANE respectively attached to the sections from the footbridge to Joppa Road and from thence to the sea front. By 1898 this Joppa Lane was being styled NORTH MORTON STREET, and Morton Street SOUTH MORTON STREET; but by 1905 the present usage of MORTON STREET for the whole street north of the footbridge and SOUTH MORTON STREET south of it had become established. There is nothing to link the street name with Thomas Morton who succeeded William Jameson in his works at Brickfield or with a *Morton Cottage* in Windsor Place; and since Joppa was developed as part of Duddingston, it is probable that the street was named for the Dowager Countess of Morton, who rented Duddingston House in the mid 19th century.

MORTON STREET (South Leith) is shown (unnamed) on *Naish* 1709 and *Wood* 1777, as a loan outside the ditch of the ramparts of 1548. The name, shown on *Kirkwood* 1817, appears in *Aitchison's Directory* 1799 as *Morton's Street*, evidently named for a Hugh Morton, resident there. In 1968 the street was renamed ACADEMY STREET (with reference to Leith Academy nearby) to obviate any confusion with Morton Street, Portobello.

MORVERN STREET (Clermiston) *see under* CLERMISTON MAINS.

MOSSGIEL WALK (Liberton) *see under* KIRK BRAE, Liberton.

MOSSIE MILL (Woodhall) is mentioned in *RMS* 1621 as a waulk mill in Woodhall, and shown thus on *Roy* 1753. It is named for William Mosie, waulker and tenant of the mill in 1664, or possibly for one of his forebears, for as many as five waulkers of that name (a form of *Moses, Moyses* or *Moyes*) were burgesses in Edinburgh within the period 1583 to 1647.

MOSTON TERRACE (Mayfield) *see under* McLAREN ROAD, Mayfield.

MOUBRAY'S CLOSE (42 High Street) *see* SOUTH FOULIS'S CLOSE.

MOUBRAY'S CLOSE (High Street) *see* BARON GRANT'S CLOSE.

MOUBRAY GROVE (Queensferry) was named by 1972, evidently to commemorate the Moubray family, owners of Barnbougle and Dalmeny for over 400 years before 1620.

THE MOUND (New Town) began in about 1780 as an unofficial short cut from the Lawnmarket to the developing New Town, crossing the boggy ground left after the draining of the Nor Loch. Known as *Geordie Boyd's mud brig*, for a clothier in the Lawnmarket who took a lead in making a rough and ready causeway, it was also dubbed *Bailie Grieve's brig* for Bailie John Grieve, who had a house at 30 Princes Street and began the practice of using earth excavated from New Town site works to build a more substantial embankment. In 1781 the town council adopted this as policy (contrary to their earlier plan for an ornamental canal and gardens along the length of the valley) and a modest scheme for this *Lawnmarket Bridge* is shown on *Kincaid* 1784; but so much fill became available that the proposal developed into the wide high-level *Earthen Bridge* shown on *Brown & Watson* 1793, by which time over one and a half million tons had been deposited. It is shown on *Pollock* 1834 as still undeveloped, but for the Royal Institution building (now the RSA) begun in 1822. Various schemes were proposed (including a centrally heated shopping mall, first shown on *Kirkwood* 1823) but the final line of the roadway seems to have been settled only in 1848, with Playfair's first scheme for the National Gallery. While MOUND PLACE was named by 1810 and the MOUND is listed in *PO Directory* 1827, the *Earthen Mound* name on *Ainslie* 1804 is found on maps up to 1850, and was still in use in 1882. The traditional name for the space east of the RSA building is THE FOOT OF THE MOUND. THE MOUND STEPS are now the PLAYFAIR STEPS, *which see.*

THE LITTLE MOUND or **MOUND BRIDGE** (Old Town) is so named on *Ainslie* 1804 and *Kirkwood* 1817 respectively, and it is shown as a path on *Kincaid* 1784. The term 'bridge' (also used of THE MOUND, *which see*) does not imply that it was anything more than an earthen embankment. Part of it was replaced in 1844 by a three-arched bridge to suit the joint station of the Edinburgh & Glasgow and the North British railways; and its name WAVERLEY BRIDGE, for Scott's most celebrated novel, was no doubt suggested by its nearness to the Scott Monument, then nearing completion. The bridge was rebuilt in 1868 and again in 1895. In 1868 it gave its name to the WAVERLEY STATION, developed in 1868-74 out of the joint station of 1844 and the Edinburgh, Perth & Dundee station of 1847.

MOUNTCASTLE CRESCENT, DRIVE and **TERRACE** (Duddingston) were named in 1932 as the beginning of development in the *Crooked Furcheons* field of NORTHFIELD in Duddingston, *which see*. MOUNTCASTLE DRIVE SOUTH extended over the Figgate burn into Southfield; and MOUNTCASTLE GARDENS and GROVE were added in 1934. MOUNTCASTLE LOAN (1949) and BANK (1969) were built in the *Blacklands* of the farm, and MOUNTCASTLE GREEN and PLACE (1981) in the *Angle Park*. The name derived from the Irish title Lord Mountcastle dating from 1606 and belonging to the Duke of Abercorn, owner of the Duddingston estate.

MOUNT FALCON (North Leith) *see under* MOUNT PELHAM etc.

MOUNT GRANGE (Whitehouse) was named in 1985, continuing the name which had been attached to the site for over a century even although it was inaccurate in the first place, the place being some 150 yards outside the Grange. The developers' house name (which is of course not statutory) is a model of irrelevance, combining their policy of naming all their schemes *Home-* with the choice of *Ross* simply as 'a Scottish name'.

MOUNTHOOLY (Fairmilehead) is shown on *Knox* 1812 and *Ordnance Survey* 1852 as a farm on the south slope of the Galachlaw, also shown on *Mortonhall* 1770 as *North Morton*, still recognisable as the site of Princess Margaret Rose Hospital and Fairmile Marie Curie Centre. The name also occurs at Newington (*see below*) and at Ecclesmachan and in Fife near Kirkcaldy and Lochty: it is in fact fairly frequent in Solway and in the east of the country from Northumberland to Shetland. A check of a score of cases decisively rules out the suggestion in *Macdonald* that the name may be Scots 'mount huilie', climb slowly, for few are sited on a slope. Rather does the common factor seem to be a connection (as at the Galachlaw) with a cairn or ancient burial place. While the name may be akin to Anglian *mund hulu* or *helan*, mounded covering, its distribution suggests that it is from Old Norse *moenda háeli*, ridged shelter or house of the dead. *See also* HULY or HEELY HILL, Newbridge.

MOUNTHOOLY (Newington) is recorded in 1651 as *Munthully* in the vicinity of Preston Street, which is itself named as *the loan by Mountheulie* in 1659 and *Mounthooly loan* in 1699; and while *Maitland* 1753 rather vaguely places it 'opposite' Sciennes and 'on the eastern side of Newington', *Town Council Minutes* 1701 use *Mounthoully* as a reference point in Causeyside on the Liberton road. Thus it was certainly in the vicinity of West Preston Street, but how far it extended eastwards remains an open question. As noted above, the name is probably from Old Norse, meaning 'ridged house of the dead', and implying that there was once a burial mound is the vicinity; and the nearby place name LOWSIELAW (*which see*) and Maitland's mention of ancient graves found hereabouts may be significant.

MOUNT LODGE (Portobello) was a mansion, shown on *Wood's Portobello* 1824, built on the site of the second of William Jamieson's brickfields, shown on *Ainslie's Roads from Figget* 1783. Demolished to make way for MOUNT LODGE PLACE, named in 1932, the old house stood precisely at the angle of the new street.

MOUNT PARNASSUS (Currie) appears on *Ordnance Survey* 1893 as the name of the cottage that was until 1832 the home of Currie's weaver poet Jamie Thomson—*see under* THOMSON CRESCENT, Currie. Since it is also referred to as *Kenleith Cottage* in the 1890s, it seems likely that the fancier name (from Parnassos, in Greek mythology the home of the Muses) was given in memory of Thomson, rather than by the man himself; and this is borne out by the fact that while the *Ordnance Survey* 1852 simply shows the Kinleith burn running in the woodland strip below the cottage, the 1893 edition shows it as a *Poet's Burn* running in a *Poet's Glen* in which there are the *Poet's Seat* and *Poet's Well* and a new system of paths—all within the grounds of the new house *Braeburn* (now Glenburn) built by the Bruce family, owners of Kinleith Paper Mills.

MOUNT PELHAM and **MOUNT SOMERSET** (South Leith) and **MOUNT FALCON, BYER'S MOUNT** and **NEW MOUNT** (North Leith) are all shown on the map of the *Siege of Leith* 1560 as emplacements for English guns. The first four were named for captains in the English army, while the 'new mount' (shown without any guns) was perhaps formed at the very end of the siege and never used. The popular notion of where these sites were derives from wildly erroneous guesses made in 1827 and unfortunately endorsed by D H Robertson in 1850. Their true positions are in fact, shown to scale on *Siege of Leith* 1560: MOUNT PELHAM, a temporary fort of over three acres in area, was formed in the week before Easter 1560 on the rising ground of Restalrig Terrace, south of Somerset Place; MOUNT SOMERSET, a similar entrenchment belonging to the second phase of the siege, was a little to the northeast of the future Pilrig House; MOUNT FALCON (named on the map as 'the battery at the Pale') was just east of the southern part of South Fort Street; BYER'S MOUNT, a one-gun battery, stood more or less on the line of Ferry Road at Dudley Avenue South; and the NEW MOUNT was in the vicinity of the east end of Trafalgar Lane. The 1560 map also shows an unnamed battery of two heavy guns in the vicinity of Ferrier Street.

MOUNT PLEASANT (Joppa) is named on *Sutter's Portobello* 1856, but shown on *Wood's Portobello* 1824 as already begun. While the name obviously reflects the site of this terrace on rising ground overlooking the sea, it might also have been related to that of Mount Pleasant, Pennsylvania, settled in 1782 and incorporated as a town in 1828.

MOUNT SOMERSET (South Leith) *see under* MOUNT PELHAM etc.

MOUNT VERNON (Liberton) was a ten-acre property shown on *Adair/Cooper* 1735 and later maps as NELLFIELD (the KNELLHOUSE on *Roy* 1753 is probably an aberration) and was evidently named for an owner's wife or daughter; but by 1834 it had been renamed

MOUNT VERNON, perhaps for George Washington's family home, or in imitation of it as a tribute to Admiral Edward Vernon (1684-1757) captor of Puerto Bello in 1730, whose nickname *Old Grog* (from his *grogram* or silk-and-mohair coat) was passed on to the rum-and-water which he was the first to issue to crews in the Royal Navy. For some years around 1898 the house was styled LIBERTON LODGE. MOUNT VERNON ROAD, figured on *Roy* 1753 and evidently an old route to Liberton from Northfield and the Craigs, was so named in 1925. In 1983 the 18th-century name of NELLFIELD was revived for a development in the northern part of the original property.

MOUTRIE'S or **MULTRIE'S HILL** (East End) evidently took its name from owners, possibly going back to Robert Multrere, burgess of Edinburgh, recorded in *RMS* 1363-5 as acquiring land in the barony of Restalrig (which included the Calton); but the 16th-century references are to the place rather than the estate, and it is just possible that the *hill* in *Mowtrayis of the hill* 1571 refers to the Calton Hill rather than the high ground west of the gorge, on which the place stood. The house may have been the 'lowghe house' shown on *Siege of Leith* 1560; but a view drawn in about 1750 shows a substantial three-storeyed building. The position of the place relative to modern streets is best shown on the overlay of maps in *Old Edinburgh Club XXIII*.

MOYSE'S CLOSE (once 84 now 68 Grassmarket) is shown on *Ainslie* 1780 and was probably named for Andrew Moyse, listed in *Williamson's Directory* 1773 as a merchant in the north side of Grassmarket. In *PO Directory* 1827 it is JAMIESON'S, possibly for a connection with the George Jamieson listed as a tobacconist in the Grassmarket in 1773.

MUCK PORT (Old Town) *see* WATERYETT (Old Town).

MUD ISLAND (Greenside) is shown thus on *Kincaid* 1784 and as *Mud Isle* on *Ainslie* 1804 and *Brown* 1809. The name might have been whimsical, for what appears to have been a promontory of made ground jutting into the hollow of Greenside, which may have been marshy; but the possibility that it came by mapmaker's error from some unrecorded *Mudie's land* should not be excluded, for *Williamson's Directory* 1773 lists a Robert Muddie, merchant, at (Leith?) *walk side*.

MUILIEPUTCHIE (Swanston) is named thus on *Ordnance Survey* 1852. The name seems to be Celtic, and an interpretation of its first part as British *moel* or Gaelic *maoile*, hill brow, would fit the ground. In absence of early forms, the rest is guesswork: but one distinguishing feature of the hill is that it rises above the rather deep-sunk sources of the Swanston burn, which might relate to British *puth* or Gaelic *poiteag*, a pit or well.

MUIRBANK (Balerno) *see* MARCHBANK, Balerno.

MUIRBURGH (Sciennes) is described in *RMS* 1512 as a newly-built farm adjoining the lands destined for the chapel of St John in the Muir (*see under* SCIENNES) and it occupied the triangle of ground north of Sciennes Place.

MUIRDALE TERRACE (Blackhall) was named in about 1907 for A Muir, builder of the terrace.

MUIREND AVENUE (Hailes) *see under* CURRIEMUIREND, Hailes.

MUIRHALL or **MUIRIEHALL** (Queensferry) is referred to in *RMS* 1563 in terms which show that its revenue had heretofore belonged to Dunfermline Abbey, and it may well have been part of the endowment of the Queen's ferry by Malcolm IV. Lying in the neuk between the burn at the Flash (later Rosshill) in the north and the Ferry burn and Kirkliston road in the west, the land is recorded from 1630 as runrig divided into 32 parts, with a common attached. The charters and maps suggest that it was once very much larger than the 17 acres noted in the *Statistical Account* 1791, stretching south of the Kirk road (*see* LOVERS LOAN) and a considerable distance eastwards towards Dalmeny. The *Muirhill* appearing in 1663 is simply a misspelling, but the *common of Muirhalfield* mentioned in the same charter is probably represented by the *Muirhaw Common* shown beside the *Common Loan* on *Barnbougle & Dalmeny* c1800. There is no record of any 'hall' attached to the place, and everything points to Muirhall being a land name, Anglian *mor halh*, haugh (or land in a neuk) of the moor; and the names *Muirie Green*, recorded in 1575 and shown on *Dundas* 1757, and *Muirie Walls* or 'springs' and *Wellhead* also shown on *Dundas*, indicate that there was a well-watered flat or hollow in the vicinity of Dundas Avenue and Ashburnam Road, extending south-eastwards to the THIEVES LOCH, *which see*.

MUIRHOUSE (Cramond) is recorded from 1336 onwards and shown on *Siege of Leith* 1560 and *Blaeu* 1654. The early spellings *Morhus* 1336 and *Murehous* 1434 confirm that the name is Anglian *mor hus*, house on the muir; but the spellings *Moresse* on the 1560 map and *Murrayes* in *RMS* 1661 show the traditional pronunciation of this name both here and elsewhere—indeed, the present pronunciation 'muir house' dates only from the development of the land for housing. The present mansion of MUIRHOUSE dates from 1830 and stands some distance north of the site of its predecessor, which was immediately west of MUIRHOUSE MAINS. MUIRHOUSE AVENUE and PLACE were named in 1947 and were followed in 1956 by MUIRHOUSE TERRACE, DRIVE, GARDENS, GROVE, LOAN and PARKWAY, the last being developed from the great tree-lined avenue which traversed the estate from east to west, as shown on *Roy* 1753 as well as *Ordnance Survey* 1938. MUIRHOUSE MEDWAY followed in 1958, MUIRHOUSE BANK, GREEN and PARK in 1959, MUIRHOUSE VIEW and WAY in 1961 and 1964. For other streets built on Muirhouse ground *see under* PENNYWELL, Granton.

MUIRHOUSE (Gilmerton) is recorded from 1306 onwards, and is shown on *Adair* 1682. Early spellings *Morhuse* and *Murehous* show the name to be Anglian *mor hus*, house on the muir; while such spelling as *Murrois* 1634 or *Murrays* 1773 echo the traditional Scots pronunciation, which *Good's Liberton* also notes as current in 1892. This was taken advantage of in naming THE MURRAYS in 1990 and THE MURRAYS BRAE in 1991, both streets being in the heart of the ancient farm.

MUIRHOUSE (Dalmeny) is shown on *Blaeu* 1654 as *Mureshou*, a spelling that suggests that the name perhaps originated as 'howe in the muir'; but although this would fit the terrain very well, the other evidence is for *muir house*. Along with nearby COTMUIR, Dalmeny, the place was swept away when the dual carriageway was constructed in the early 1960s.

MUIRSIDE (New Swanston) *see under* SWANSTON.

MUIR WOOD (Currie) is shown on *Currie Farm* 1797 as several patches of rough grazing or scrub on CURRIE MUIR (*which see*) but appears on *Ordnance Survey* 1852 as a smaller area in the angle of the Muir Wood road. This road had been in existence since before 1797, but in 1960 it was developed as the housing street MUIR WOOD ROAD, followed in 1961 by MUIR WOOD CRESCENT, DRIVE, GROVE and PLACE.

MULBERRY PLACE (Bonnington) was built in about 1868. The name, appearing in *PO Directory* 1869, may have been fancy, for a local mulberry tree, but any connection with French weavers' silkworms is wholly fanciful.

MULTRIE'S HILL (New Town) *see* MOUTRIE'S HILL, New Town.

MUNRO DRIVE (Colinton) was named in 1935 for R H Munro, then master of the Merchant Company, developers of the ground.

MUNRO'S CLOSE (119 Canongate) was named for John Munro, musician, who bought property on its west side from Arthur Straiton, wig maker, at some date prior to 1751. The close was also LORD MORTON'S, from the 13th or 14th earls of Morton, who lived in Campbell's land, 87 Canongate, but had stables in Munro's Close prior to 1760. The 13th earl died in 1738; his successor, in 1768.

MUNRO PLACE (Canonmills) appears in *PO Directory* 1892, and seems to have been named for Daniel Munro, dairyman in Canonmills.

MURANO PLACE (Pilrig) was named in 1870 for Murano, the famous centre producing Venetian glass, probably at the suggestion of David Small, glass stainer and housepainter, listed in *PO Directory* 1871 as the first resident in the street.

MURDOCH'S CLOSE (70 High Street) is named thus on *Edgar* 1742 and *Ainslie* 1780 but is given as *Munloch's* on *Ainslie* 1804, probably in error. The name was probably from Robert Murdoch, writer, who owned a tenement in the close at some time before 1737; but an earlier name *Spotsewode's* (i.e. SPOTTISWOOD'S) is listed in 1635 and probably goes back to a James Spottiswod, mentioned in *RMS* 1504 along with Archibald Todrik (see TODRIG'S WYND, High Street) among owners adjoining a property on the south side of the High Street. A number of Spottiswoods continued to be prominent in town affairs in the 16th century.

MURDOCH TERRACE (Fountainbridge) *see under* BAINFIELD, Fountainbridge.

MRS MURE'S CLOSE (91 High Street) *see* BARRINGER'S CLOSE.

MURIESTON CRESCENT, PLACE, ROAD and **TERRACE** (West Dalry) were developed in 1887-89 by James Steel, builder, later Lord Provost Sir James Steel of Murieston, Bart, and were named for his estate in Midcalder, where *Murieston* is recorded from 1529 and appears to be Anglian *mor hus*, muir house, generally becoming *murrays* in Scots, with Scots *toun* or farm added, making the name *Muirhouse farm*. MURIESTON CRESCENT LANE was formed at the same time as the Crescent, and MURIESTON LANE was formed before 1893.

THE MURRAY BURN is *the muiry burn*, from Anglian *mor* Scots *muir*, which may refer to the muirland character of its catchment area in early times, witnessed also by such local names as *Fernieflat*, *Currie Muir* and *Pilmuir*, or else (and more probably) the word is being used in its early sense of low-lying swampy ground, which was equally characteristic of the more immediate surroundings of the burn throughout its course. MURRAYBURN ROAD was built on the line of the burn in 1967, along with MURRAYBURN PARK, GARDENS, GROVE and GREEN on the Dumbryden ground to the south of it. MURRAYBURN APPROACH and DRIVE were built in 1969, and MURRAYBURN PLACE followed in 1970.

MURRAYFIELD, shown on *Adair* 1682 under its earlier name of NISBET'S PARKS, was bought from Nisbet of Dean in 1733 by Archibald Murray, later Lord Henderland in the Court of Session, who renamed the estate after his family and built MURRAYFIELD HOUSE in about 1735. MURRAYFIELD ROAD, evidently an old connection between Ravelston and the Corstorphine road, is shown on *Roy* 1753 and is figured as *Road from Ravelston* on a feuing plan of 1823; although given its present name by 1888, when development east of it was planned, it first appears in *PO Directory* in 1903. MURRAYFIELD GARDENS and DRIVE are both part of a 'Murrayfield Avenue' planned in 1888: it was named and partly built as MURRAYFIELD GARDENS by 1893, and part of this was renamed MURRAYFIELD DRIVE in 1904. Meantime, a 'Henderland Road' was also planned in 1888 but was renamed MURRAYFIELD GRAND AVENUE in 1890, the *grand* being dropped in 1895; and in 1899 the HENDERLAND ROAD name (for Archibald Murray, mentioned above) was revived for its second half. MURRAYFIELD PLACE was named by 1895.

THE MURRAYS and **THE MURRAYS BRAE** (Gilmerton) *see under* MUIRHOUSE, Gilmerton.

MURRAY'S CLOSE (18 Cowgate) is so listed on *Kirkwood* 1817 and named for David Murray, listed in *Williamson's Directory* 1773 as a stabler here. In *PO Directory* 1827 it is called WINDING CLOSE, probably from its course.

(DAVID) MURRAY'S CLOSE (High Street) *see under* SELLAR'S CLOSE and DUNBAR'S CLOSE.

MURRAY STREET (Sciennes) *see* SCIENNES GARDENS.

THE MUSE WELL (Grassmarket) is recorded as a public well from 1502 onwards. It was on the south side of the street, about ten yards east of Gilmore's Close, and is shown on *Ordnance Survey* 1852 as well as *Rothiemay* 1647. The name's early spellings are *muse, mus(s), meus* and *mus(e)* and it seems to be an early example of Scots *meuse*, a stable. The King's Stables, dating from the 1340s, were of course over 200 yards further west; but the convent of the Greyfriars, founded in 1471 in the Cowgatehead only about fifty yards east of the Muse Well, certainly gave lodging to travellers of the more distinguished sort, and although no early record of stables here has come to light, it may be no accident that the only stables recorded in the *Valuation Roll* of 1635 as being on the south side of Grassmarket were in McIntyre's Close, which had its entry ten yards east of the Well.

MUSCHAT'S CAIRN (Holyrood) was set up in 1823 several yards west of the site of the original cairn which marked the spot where Nicol Mushat of Boghall murdered his wife in 1720.

MUTTONHOLE (Cramond) is shown on *Adair* 1682 as *Muttonhol* and subsequently as *Muttonhole* on maps up until *Fowler* 1845; and although this name is displaced by DAVIDSON'S MAINS (*which see*) on *Ordnance Survey* 1852, it still lingers in local parlance. There are more than half a dozen places named *Muttonhole* in lowland Scotland, three of them in Lothian and one in Fife, besides two instances of *Muttonhall* in Fife and Yarrow and no fewer than five of *Muttonbrae* in Aberdeenshire. The suggestion that *mutton-* derives from Anglian (*ge*)*mythe*, junction of roads or streams, quite fails to stand up when the various sites are examined. Rather the name is Early Scots *motoun holh* or *halh*, howe or haugh where *motouns* or wedder lambs were pastured. This term was from Old French *moton*; but since the latter was ultimately Celtic in origin, and closely parallelled in both British and Gaelic, it is possible that *motoun* in the place name stands for a native Celtic word which had continued to be used in Anglian times; and this might explain why such *Mutton-* names, quite frequent in south and north-east Scotland, should be so exceedingly rare in England.

MYRESIDE (Merchiston) is recorded in 1583 as *the myreside of Over Merchiston*, the name combining Old Norse *myrr* or early Scots *mire* with Anglian *side* and meaning the slope in Over Merchiston above the bog in the former bed of the loch which once extended from Myreside Road down to Maxwell Street and became the course of the Jordan burn. MYRESIDE, shown thus on *Laurie* 1763, becomes OLD MIRESIDE on *Pollock* 1834 and MYRESIDE COTTAGE on *Ordnance*

Survey 1852. The site of NEW MYRESIDE, shown on *Knox* 1812, is now on the north side of South Gillsland Road. MYRESIDE ROAD, a part of a road from Gorgie to Craighouse (*see under* GRAY'S LOAN) and named as *Craighouse Road* on *Ordnance Survey* 1893, was renamed in 1936, no doubt mainly for the school playing fields rather than the original farm, although it leads past Old Myreside; and MYRESIDE COURT was named in 1981 as an offshoot of it.

MYRKFJORD was the Norsemen's name for the FIRTH OF FORTH, *which see.*

MYRTLE TERRACE (North Merchiston) *see under* PRIMROSE TERRACE, North Merchiston.

N

NAIRNE'S CLOSE (577 High Street) is mentioned (as BAILIE NAIRNE'S) by *Maitland* 1752 and shown on *Ainslie* 1780. It was suppressed by the building of New College 1845-50, when the Free Kirk bought part of the site from the heirs of the James Nairne, bailie 1697-1706, for whom the close was named. It was also known as WILLIAM BOTHWELL'S CLOSE, from the owner of property later acquired by Bailie Nairne; and in 1635 it was called JOHN MAKNATH'S, from a merchant owner and resident of that name.

NANTWICH DRIVE (Craigentinny) *see under* CRAIGENTINNY.

NAPIER ROAD (Merchiston) was begun by 1860 and named either for the Napiers of Merchiston, who had owned the ground almost continuously until 1772, or more particularly for that family's most famous member, John Napier the mathematician. The upper and earlier part of the street is still distinguished for the work of Sir James Gowans, even although his masterwork *Rockville* was regrettably demolished, but for its boundary wall, in 1965.

NEIDPATH COURT (East Craigs) *see under* CRAIGIEVAR WYND, East Craigs.

NELLFIELD (Liberton) *see under* MOUNT VERNON, Liberton.

NELSON PLACE and **STREET** (New Town) *see under* NORTHERN NEW TOWN

NETHERBANK and **NETHERBANK VIEW** (Alnwickhill) *see under* ALNWICKHILL, Liberton.

THE NETHERBOW (Old Town) is recorded in 1369 as the *arcus inferior*: in Scots, *nether bow*. A *bow* (pronounced 'bough') is an arched gateway, which from its uses as a burgh entrance acquired special meanings as a checkpoint, a means of curfew, and a place for collection of customs; and in the present case it was *nether* or *lower* as counterpart to the *Over* or *Upper Bow* at the other and higher end of the town—*see* WEST BOW. In view of their functions, it is likely that both Bows were set up when the royal burgh was founded, as part of the mercantile boundary rather than military defence—and certainly until the end of its days in 1764 the Netherbow was flanked not by a wall but by partly fortified houses whose doors were hastily built up when danger threatened. While the final position of the Netherbow was that now marked out in brass setts in the causey, on the line of St Mary and Leith Wynds, it is certain from a rent roll of 1369 that at that period it stood further up the street, and in 1477 the space allocated to the market in iron goods seems to have been between the gate and St Mary Wynd. It is very likely that the gate was once where the High Street now narrows abruptly at 'John Knox House' (and the street from there downwards is labelled *Netherbow* on *Rothiemay* 1647) but it is also possible that at a yet earlier period it stood still further west at Blackfriars Wynd, which (as F C Mears, writing in *Edinburgh 1329-1929*, deduces from the sett of the early roads leading to the town) may have been the burgh's eastern boundary prior to the founding of the Blackfriars in 1230. The gateway, flanked by round towers, is shown in its final position on *Hertford* 1544 and *Siege of Edinburgh Castle* 1573; but in its final form, as shown on *Rothiemay* 1647 and in 18th-century drawings, it was a much more elaborate affair, with a two-storey gatehouse behind the round towers and a two-stage tower and steeple above that again. Although repairs and alterations of some sort were carried out in the 16th century, it is inconceivable that such an ambitious scheme could belong to this troubled period of bitter civil war, nor would it fit in with a *Town Council minute* of 1584, which noted the Port's visible decay and resolved that it should be 'upbiggett with expeditioun the narrest (i.e. cheapest) way'. Indeed, it appears that no action followed, until 1606, when a three-year contract was let to Johnne Taillefer, master mason, and Peter Grundestone, master of work; and there is every reason to believe that they were responsible for the 'handsome gateway' which *Arnot*, taking a little licence, says was built 'a few years' after 1571, and which, according to Claudero's *Sermon on the Condemnation of the Netherbow*, still bore a panel inscribed 1606 when, 'being thought to embarrass the street,' as Arnot dryly reports, 'the port was pulled down by the magistrates, AD 1764'.

NETHERBY ROAD (Trinity) began to be occupied in 1897. The choice of name is obscure, but it is more likely to have some connection with *Netherby* in Cumbria than to have been intended to describe the street as a 'nether' or 'lower town' in Trinity.

NETHER CRAIGWELL (Calton) *see under* CRAIGWELL, Calton.

NETHER CURRIE CRESCENT etc (Currie) *see under* CURRIE.

NETHER HILL (Arthur's Seat) is shown on *Kirkwood* 1817, the name meaning either the lower or the more westerly of the two summits of the main hill. The alternative LION'S HAUNCH also appears on *Ordnance Survey* 1852, perhaps indicating when the 19th-century imagination began to see the hill as a crouching lion.

NETHER LIBERTON is recorded in *RMS* 1369 as the subdivision of LIBERTON (*which see*) called 'nether' not so much because it is at a lower level but because it was on what was deemed the 'shadow side' of the original lands, *Over Liberton* being deemed the 'sunward side'. It stretched from the Pow burn south to the Kirk brae and Liberton Dams, and from West Mains to the Inch. It is shown on *Blaeu* 1654, while *Adair* 1682 shows the house as *Inch* and the farm steading (shown on the Gilmerton road on *Adair/Cooper* 1735) as *Nedder Libberton*. *Roy* 1753 shows the village in considerable detail, and labels it *N(ethe)r Liberton*. *Laurie* 1763 names the two farms of Nether Liberton as *South Mains* (by 1852 known as *Liberton East Mains*) and *Liberton Mains* (by 1852, *Liberton West Mains*). In 1927 part of the PENICUIK ROAD running through the estate, between Good's Corner and Liberton Dams, was renamed NETHER LIBERTON; with the unfortunate result that it became confused with the ancient village. This problem was removed in 1985, by renaming the main road as LIBERTON ROAD, but not before there had been a limp attempt to remedy it in 1961, by sacrificing the historic name of the village and coining the jejune name OLD MILL LANE for its street.

NEW ARTHUR PLACE (Pleasance) was named in 1988 as being partly on the sites of earlier streets called Arthur Street and West Arthur Place, *see under* DALE STREET, Pleasance.

NEW ASSEMBLY CLOSE (142 High Street) is listed on *Edgar* 1742 and was named for the Edinburgh Assembly which moved here from Old Assembly Close in 1736, and continued (on a new footing after 1746) until 1784. The close was also known, from its position, as BACK OF BELL'S WYND; and it is given as COMMERCIAL BANK CLOSE on *Kirkwood* 1817, from the Commercial Bank which built its head office in 1814, on the former site of the Assembly Room, and occupied it until 1847. Earlier, the close was MURRAY'S, for John Murray of Blackbarony, who in 1580 had the house at the head of the close formerly owned by the bishop of Dunkeld; and it was also SNADOUN'S or SNAWDOUN'S as early as 1525, probably named for a Snadoun Herald, since Thomas Tod, Snadoun herald, had a land in adjoining Bell's Wynd in 1579. (For another SNADOUN'S CLOSE *see under* PETER'S CLOSE, 179 Cowgate.)

NEWBANK CLOSE (221 High Street) *see* OLD STAMP OFFICE CLOSE.

NEWBATTLE TERRACE (Morningside) *see under* GREENHILL.

NEW BELFIELD (Willowbrae) was named in 1983 as a new development in part of the property shown as *Belfield* on *Kirkwood* 1817.

NEW BELL'S COURT (South Leith) *see under* BELL'S CLOSE or COURT, South Leith.

NEWBIGGING (Dalmeny) is recorded as *Newbigging* (of Dundas) from 1634 onwards and is shown on *Adair* 1682. The name, Scots for 'new building', evidently refers to a farm newly formed, at some date as yet unknown. *Also see under* NEWBYGGING, Old Town.

NEWBIGGING (Ratho) appears on the 18th-century maps as in the vicinity of Rathorigg or Rathobank (now Ashley) but west of the road. The name implies that it was a new house or farmstead: possibly replacing Rathorigg, but being itself replaced by Rathobank by 1812. On the other hand, the name is such that it could be much earlier, *see under* NEWBYGGING, Old Town.

NEWBRIDGE is evidently a literal name, probably implying replacement of an older bridge, rather than an addition to existing bridge(s). Since it appears on *Blaeu* 1654 it was probably recorded by survey in about 1596, and the bridge must have been new in the 16th century or earlier. The round barrow of HULY HILL (*which see*) witnesses to the importance of the place in the second millennium BC; and a Roman milestone was found about a kilometre further east, in the 17th century, *see under* ROMAN ROADS.

NEW BROOMPARK (Granton) *see under* BROOM PARK, Granton.

NEWBYGGING (Old Town) was a name in use in the neighbourhood of the future GRASSMARKET (*which see*) in 1363. Anglian 'new building or house', the name is noted in Northumbria from 1187 onwards.

NEWCRAIGHALL appears on *Ordnance Survey* 1853 as the name of a new village developing along the north side of Whitehill Street. The name was evidently a play on that of Craighall (now Old Craighall) an older village a mile to the south east. The original name is Scots *craig haw*, the haw or haugh beside the Esk, marked by some rocky outcrop. The new village gave its name to NEWCRAIGHALL ROAD, a much older road from Niddrie Mill to Wanton Walls and Fisherrow, shown on *Roy* 1753. NEWCRAIGHALL DRIVE was formed when the central part of the village was rebuilt in 1976.

NEW EDINBURGH (New Town) appears on the earlier of the two versions of *Laurie* 1766 as the name of a curiously inept scheme which (there is reason to believe) may represent James Craig's entry in the competition for the New Town plan. The amended version of the map published shortly afterwards shows a plan very like the final design and labels it NEW TOWN *which see*; but notwithstanding this the early title lingered on for a while, for Williamson's *Accurate View* of 1783 lists 'All the Squares and Streets in New Edinburgh'.

NEW GARDEN (Dalmeny) appears so named and noted as *Mr Liston's property* on *Barnbougle & Dalmeny* c.1800.

NEWGRANGE (St Leonard's) *see* HAMILTON'S FOLLY, St Leonard's.

NEWHAILES (Newcraighall) *see under* WHITEHILL, Newcraighall.

NEWHALLS (Queensferry) *see under* THE HAWES, Queensferry.

NEWHAVEN was founded by James IV in about 1505, when he purchased land from Holyrood Abbey and built his royal dockyard here, in place of inadequate facilities in Leith; but six years later he sold it to the town of Edinburgh, together with the lands along the shore between North Leith and the lands of Wardie. In *RMS* 1511 it is described as 'the new port called the Newhavin', while in *RMS* 1513 it is also named as the *Port of Grace*; and the ruins of the chapel of St Mary and St James, built by James in 1506-08, are still extant in Westmost Close. NEWHAVEN ROAD is shown on *Roy* 1753, and labelled 'Road to Newhaven' on *Fergus & Robinson* 1759, while *Newhaven Roads* 1765 shows its old name WHITING ROAD—a name that went back to before 1700 and probably had nothing to do with fish, *see under* WHITING ROAD, Granton. This map was produced in 1765, in the course of an action in the Court of Session about the status of the road, which witnesses described as little better than a track, and it is still shown as such on *River Leith* 1787 where it is named as *Newhavan Path*; but by 1792 it had been converted into a carriageway, and *Ainslie* 1804 shows a bridge in place of the old ford at Bonnington Mills, as well as a proposal to link the route with Leith Walk (*see* PILRIG STREET) and so to create a 'New Road from New Haven to Edinburgh'. Nevertheless the road north of the bridge was for long thought of as a 'road to Bonnington', being called *Bonnington Street* on *Thomson* 1822 and *Bonnington Road* on *Ordnance Survey* 1852; but by 1875 it had become *Newhaven Road*, and by 1892 this name was extended to Bonnington Toll, displacing the original name BONNINGTON or BONNINGTON ROAD, *which see*. NEWHAVEN PLACE was reclaimed from the shore by 1912.

NEWHOUSE (Dalmahoy) is recorded from 1614 onwards and shown on *Dalmahoy* 1749 as part of Dalmahoy, and was evidently named when it was newly a subdivision within the estate.

NEWINGTON began in 1586, when this part of the easter Burgh Muir, uncultivated and unnamed but for the LOWSIE LAW (*which see*) was feued out by the town in six lots of 8½ Scots acres each, lying between the old roads to Dalkeith (Dalkeith Road) and Liberton (Causeyside) and between the Gibbet or Mounthooly loan (Preston Street) in the north, and Cant's loan (East and West Mayfield) in the south. The name is a variant of Scots *Newton*, new farm, and was probably invented by Alexander Slowman and his wife Mariota after they had acquired half of the six lots in 1602, or else by their granddaughter Margaret, who added two more in 1628. Yet although Alexander Ellis, acquiring these five lots in 1649, began to style himself 'Ellis of Newington', there is no evidence of any estate mansion until 1766, when *Laurie* shows a house called *Newington* at the south end of the ground. This may have been a precursor of NEWINGTON HOUSE, built by Dr Benjamin Bell in 1805, but demolished in 1966. A so-called OLD NEWINGTON HOUSE, shown on *Kirkwood* 1817 and *Ordnance Survey* 1852 just north of the site of Longmore Hospital, was demolished in the 1860s, to make way for extension of West Newington Place. WEST NEWINGTON HOUSE was built in about 1806 and is still extant on the west side of the main road. As in the South Side and at Mayfield, housing development in Newington was stimulated by the prospect and progress of the new great road to the south prepared for by an Act of Parliament in 1794. NEWINGTON ROAD was formed as a part of it, after 1806, and building started on its east side at ARNISTON PLACE, shown on *Kirkwood* 1817 and no doubt named by the superior George Bell, son of Dr Benjamin Bell, for Dundas of Arniston, neighbour in George Square to Admiral and Lady Duncan, also friends of Dr Bell's—*see under* DUNCAN STREET, Newington. In about 1825 NEWINGTON PLACE and EAST NEWINGTON PLACE followed on adjoining ground, and a terrace named WEST NEWINGTON was begun opposite. WEST NEWINGTON PLACE was named by 1833 (although it was to be styled NEWINGTON TERRACE from 1858 to 1885) and on *Ordnance Survey* 1852 there is a NORTH NEWINGTON PLACE in West Preston Street. This plethora of *Newington* names was simplified in 1885, insofar as *Newington Place*, *West Newington* and *Arniston Place* were renamed as parts of NEWINGTON ROAD.

NEW JOHN'S PLACE (St Leonard's) *see under* JOHN'S PLACE, St Leonard's.

NEWKIRKGATE (South Leith) was completed in 1966 and named after the ancient KIRKGATE of Leith, which it partly displaced.

NEW LAIRDSHIP PLACE and **YARDS** (Broomhouse) were named in 1993 as being within the farm of THE LAIRDSHIP (*which see*) and about 600 yards east of its steading.

NEWLANDS (Mayfield) was an alternative name, probably dating from 1704, for MAYFIELD, *which see*. It continued in use as a name for the estate until some time after 1816, and was revived in the naming of NEWLANDS PARK in 1983.

NEW LANE (Newhaven) is shown on *Ainslie* 1804 as a development at Peter's Field, altered to St Peter's Field on *Kirkwood* 1817 and later maps, but named *New Lane* on *Ordnance Survey* 1852; and this was retained when the street was redeveloped in 1965.

NEWLISTON originated as a subdivision of LISTON (*which see*) at some date prior to 1461. While the name implies a new centre within Liston, it was not necessarily a counterpart to AULDLISTON (*which see*) for in a charter of 1533 (quoted in *RMS* 1543) the further subdivision of NETHER NEWLISTON is described as within the barony of Auldliston. This subdivision of Newliston into OVER and NETHER NEWLISTON dates from before 1516 and is shown on *Blaeu* 1654. *Over Newliston* appears to be now OVERTON (*which see*) while *Nether Newliston* seems to have become *Newliston*, as shown on *Adair* 1682. The name of the *Overtoun of Nether Newliston* recorded in 1576 reads as though it were a further subdivision of Nether Newliston, as yet unidentified and probably lost in the grand scheme for the policies of Newliston carried out by William Adam in about 1730 for John Dalrymple, second Earl of Stair. NEWLISTON HOUSE was built by Robert Adam in 1789 for Thomas Hog; and NEWLISTON ROAD, shown on *Roy* 1753 as part of the road from Broxburn to Kirkliston, is named as an access to the estate.

NEWMAINS (Kirkliston) is not shown on *Roy* 1753 but is marked *Mains* on *Armstrongs* 1773. Apparently part (along with CATELBOK, *which see*) of the *mains* or demesne farm of Kirkliston mentioned in *RMS* 1593, it seems to have been separated off after 1750, taking the term *mains* with it. Although joined with other farms in about 1815 to make up ALMONDHILL (*which see*) it retains its identity. NEWMAINS FARM ROAD is named as leading to it, and NEWMAINS ROAD was so named in 1974 because it stands on its ground.

NEW MARKET ROAD and **NEW MART ROAD** (West Gorgie) were formed and named as service roads in the New Markets for meat and corn built in western fields of Gorgie farm in 1909-12.

NEWMILLS (Currie) is recorded in *RMS* 1546 as *Newmylne* in the barony of Balerno; and while it appears as *Newmills* on *Laurie* 1763 and *Ordnance Survey* 1852 it is still shown as *New Mill* on maps between these dates. NEWMILLS AVENUE, CRESCENT, GROVE and ROAD were named in 1975 but the last, as the historic access to CURRIEHILL (*which see*) has existed since medieval times.

NEW MOUNT (North Leith) *see under* MOUNT PELHAM etc.

NEW ORCHARDFIELD (Pilrig) *see under* ORCHARDFIELD, Pilrig.

THE NEW PORT (Old Town) was at the foot of HALKERSTON'S WYND, *which see*.

NEWPORT STREET (Tollcross) was named in 1825 for the nearby and new PORT HOPETOUN basin of the Union Canal.

THE NEW QUAY (South Leith) is shown at the foot of Tolbooth Wynd on *Collins* 1693 and was built before 1645. In 1789 it was adapted as the south abutment of the new draw bridge which bypassed the medieval Bridge of Leith (*see under* OLD BRIDGE END, Coalhill) and has been itself in turn replaced by the present structure, inappropriately styled SANDPORT PLACE, *which see*.

NEW SKINNERS' CLOSE (Old Town) *see under* SKINNERS' CLOSE, 66 High Street.

THE NEW STAIRS (108 Cowgate) *see* THE BACK STAIRS, Cowgate.

THE 'NEWS' STEPS (Old Town) were for the most part formed along with St GILES STREET in 1869, connecting it with Advocate's Close by three long flights, the middle one following the ancient line of Byer's Close; but when the *Evening News* printing works was extended in 1928, the lowest flight, crossing to Advocate's Close, was suppressed and replaced by a new one descending to Market Street.

NEW STREET (Canongate) was developed by a Dr Thomas Young at some time between 1765, when his house was shown here on *Edgar* 1765, and 1773, when *New Street* is given as his address in *Williamson's Directory*. It is shown on *Ainslie* 1780. *Kincaid* 1787 says it was *formerly called Young's Street*; but since it was closed to the public until 1786, it is possible that it was previously referred to as *Dr Young's new street*—a phrase still used in 1826. The street displaced at least one earlier close, but its name is unrecorded.

NEW STREET (Gilmerton) *see* NEWTOFT STREET, Gilmerton.

NEW SWANSTON (Swanston) *see under* SWANSTON.

NEWTOFT STREET (Gilmerton) was built some time after 1852 and is shown as NEW STREET on *Ordnance Survey* 1893. In 1967, in order to obviate any confusion with New Street in the Canongate, the present name was concocted by combining the existing *New-* with the name of the Tofts (*which see*) shown on *Ordnance Survey* 1893 as a terrace at the west end of the street.

NEWTON'S CLOSE (341 High Street) *see* ROXBURGH'S CLOSE.

NEWTON STREET and **TERRACE** (Gorgie) were built in part of Gorgie Muir in about 1878. The name's origin has not yet been traced; it was probably connected with the developer.

NEW TOWER PLACE (Portobello) *see under* THE TOWER, Portobello.

THE NEW TOWN, now the collective name for the whole group of Georgian developments north of the medieval city, was earlier a term used individually of three of the six large schemes which together with a fringe of smaller ones make up the 'New Town' of today: the first NEW TOWN of 1767, the NORTHERN NEW TOWN (1802) DEANHAUGH (1812) COATES (1813) the CALTON NEW TOWN (1819) and the MORAY ESTATE (1822). The FIRST NEW TOWN (for the other schemes *see under the names listed*) was also briefly known as NEW EDINBURGH *which see*. It traces back to a scheme for the city's expansion envisaged as early as 1681 by James VII, then Duke of Albany and Commissioner to the Scottish Parliament for his brother Charles II; but although James followed this up in 1688 by granting a charter for improved access by roads and bridges and for the necessary extension of the royalty or area enjoying the royal burgh's privileges, it was almost at once aborted by his flight and removal from the throne. In 1728 the exiled John Erskine Earl of Mar suggested that extension might take the form of one long straight street along the Lang Dykes ridge with the gardens of its houses sloping down to north and south; and this was perhaps the germ of the plan finally adopted 39 years later in which Mar's single street was transformed into an array of three grand avenues and two squares. It has been widely assumed that this was the prize-winning plan produced by James Craig in competition in 1766; but the relevant minutes of the Town Council's Bridge Committee make it clear beyond doubt that while they judged Craig's entry to be the best of those submitted and therefore awarded him the prize, they nevertheless did not consider it good enough to be carried out; and the upshot was that the work went ahead on the basis of a 'rectified plan' produced for them by William Mylne two months later, although the youthful Craig was employed thereafter in working up its details and in making the finished drawing for the final approval of the Council in July 1767. This drawing was engraved in the late summer or autumn of 1767, and a print from the half-finished plate shows the names originally chosen for the principal streets of this

New Town at Edinburgh. In a fashion new to Britain they were to be named in a symmetrical group, the two squares as St ANDREW'S and St GEORGE'S for Scotland and England united by GEORGE STREET for George III, while the central cross street was to be QUEEN STREET for his consort and its neighbour to the east HANOVER STREET for their other dominion on the Continent. Clearly these were meant not so much as individual compliments but jointly as a celebration of George III in his realm; and although it was no doubt politic so soon after 1745 to make gestures of loyalty to the Union and the house of Hanover, it would seem that the inspiration for this novel scheme was the contemporary French notion widely publicised only two years earlier by Pierre Patte's *Monuments érigés à la gloire de Louis XV*, that new towns should be built to the glory of the reigning monarch. The three other names that appeared on this early print of the plan—CASTLE STREET for a cross street, and FORTH STREET and St GILES STREET for the northern and southern avenues—no doubt had their place in this celebratory scheme, standing for the King's northern capital, but they also set a fashion new to Edinburgh in referring not to the place but to the views from it. It was evidently a similar print or drawing that was shown to George III and Queen Charlotte by their physician Sir John Pringle later in 1767. Although the immediate object was to secure approval of the dedication of the scheme to his majesty, there was some discussion of the chosen street names; and in a letter to the Lord Provost (engrossed in *Town Council Minutes* 23 December 1767) Pringle recounts how the King, although gratified by the loyal set of names, jibbed at the name *St Giles Street*, for since he had never been in Edinburgh it suggested to him only an unsavoury quarter in London. Courtier as well as physician, Sir John at once suggested that it might be changed to PRINCE'S STREET for the Prince of Wales; and diplomatically he went on to balance this by proposing CHARLOTTE STREET for the northern avenue, in place of *Forth Street*; but upon reflection her majesty thought that QUEEN'S STREET would sound better. This of course robbed the central cross street of its intended name; but Pringle nimbly proposed that it might be FREDERICK STREET, for their majesties' second living son Frederick Augustus, then the four-year-old bishop of Osnaburg in Saxony. These adjustments were made in the final feuing plan issued on 1 January 1768 and others were added later. St DAVID'S STREET was named for Wales by 1772. While St ANDREW'S STREET and LANE took their name from the Square, MEUSE LANE simply retained its earlier and baldly functional title as a lane of stables and coach-houses. THISTLE COURT was called *Rose Court* at first but was renamed for the Scottish emblem by 1773. While THISTLE STREET and ROSE STREET are named on Craig's proposed amendment of the New Town plan in 1774, only the eastmost section of *Thistle Street* is named on *Ainslie* 1780 and *Rose Street* appears as *St David's Lane* or *Mews* until 1785 when the present names were formally added to the patriotic scheme—which did not however prevent HILL STREET and YOUNG

STREET from getting these names in the 1790s, after their developers James Hill, mason, and John Young, wright. Also in 1785, to avoid confusion with GEORGE SQUARE (*which see*) the proposed *St George's Square* (still seven years away from its start on the ground) was renamed CHARLOTTE SQUARE for the Queen, and CHARLOTTE STREET was apparently named at the same time. HOPE STREET (*which see*) and GLENFINLAS STREET (*see under* MORAY ESTATE) were named much later. The spelling of such names as *St Andrew's Square* or *Street* varied from the start; but by the mid 1820s the *'s* was dropped, with the notable exception of *Prince's Street*, which was indifferently *Prince's, Princes'* or *Princes* until the last became the settled form in the late 1830s—and it is instructive to note how explanations of the street name have been founded on this apparently plural spelling, each as confident as it is wrong.

NICOLLS PLACE (North Leith) was suppressed in the redevelopment of BATHFIELD, *which see.*

NICOLSON STREET (South Side) traces its name back to Sir James Nicholson, who bought land in the West Croft of Bristo not long before 1727 and built himself a house there, shown on *Edgar* 1742. In 1763 his widow Elizabeth Trotter or Nicolson leased out ground, in what was by then known as *Lady Nicolson's Park*, for the erection of the riding school of the Royal Academy for Teaching Exercises, opened in 1764 on what is now the site of Surgeons' Hall. At the same time she began a new street (affording access to the Academy at a roads charge of £118 : 18s) planned as an avenue on the axis of her house, as shown on *Edgar* 1765, and forking on either side of the house and a 25-foot high Corinthian column which she put up as a memorial to her husband; but soon after the completion of the South Bridge in 1788 both house and monument were cleared away and the street made continuous with the bridge, as shown on *Brown & Watson* 1793. Lady Nicolson named the street NICOLSON'S for her husband (or else folk named it for her: *Arnot* 1779 gives both stories, probably both true) and the name was in use by 1770. NICOLSON SQUARE is named on *Armstrongs* 1773 and shown as largely built-up. The same map shows WEST NICOLSON STREET as well developed, although without a name: for prior to *Ainslie* 1804, which shows the modern name, the maps as well as the *Accurate View* 1783 group the street with CHAPEL STREET, *which see.*

NIDDRIE is recorded from the 12th century onwards, and the early spellings *Nodrif* or *Nudreff* show the name to be British *newyth tref*, new farm. It is shown on *Blaeu* 1654 as NYDDRY MARSHAL, a medieval variant used to distinguish this estate from *Niddrie Seton* in East Lothian or *Niddry Forrester* in West Lothian. It has been said to derive from the fact that the Wauchopes of Niddrie were deputes in Midlothian for the Keiths, Earls Marischal of Scotland; but since *Niddrie Marischal* is recorded as early as 1363, it appears that the lairds of Niddrie exercised the local office of marshal for at least a century before the first of the Keiths was created Earl Marischal in

1455. NIDDRIE HOUSE, built in about 1636 on the site of the medieval towerhouse, was demolished in about 1968. It stood some twelve yards east of the chapel, dating from 1502, which is now represented by an 18th-century vaulted tomb house. NIDDRIE HOUSE AVENUE, DRIVE, GARDENS, GROVE, PARK and SQUARE were built in the house policies in 1969. NIDDRIE MARISCHAL CRESCENT, GROVE, PARK and ROAD were named in 1951, and NIDDRIE MARISCHAL DRIVE, GARDENS, GREEN, LOAN and STREET followed in 1954. NIDDRIE BURN is traditional as the local name of the LOTHIAN BURN, *which see*; but NIDDRIE GLEN is a modern invention, *see under* KITTLEMACAVIE, Brunstane. NIDDRIE MILL, shown on *Roy* 1753 and probably medieval, stood on the east bank of the burn just north of Niddrie Mains Road, all its arrangements being shown on *Ordnance Survey* 1852. NIDDRIE MILL AVENUE, CRESCENT, DRIVE, PLACE and TERRACE were named in 1956, and NIDDRIE MILL GROVE followed in 1965. NIDDRY ROAD was named as the *road to Niddrie* from Edmondston in the south and Baileyfield in the north, but the name has been supplanted by DUDDINGSTON PARK, DUDDINGSTON PARK SOUTH and THE WISP—*which see*. NIDDRIE MAINS, shown on *Laurie* 1763, was sited at NIDDRIE FARM GROVE, named for it in 1961. NIDDRIE MAINS DRIVE and TERRACE were named in 1931; NIDDRIE MAINS ROAD, part of the old road to Niddrie and Musselburgh, shown on *Roy* 1753, was formally named in 1932; and NIDDRIE MAINS COURT followed in 1963.

NIDDRIE COTTAGES (Niddrie) were built in about 1890, as housing for workers in the nearby Niddrie Pit. *See also* QUARRY COTTAGES, *under* LAWHOUSE, Niddrie.

NIDDRIE EDGE is the *edge* or ridge in the south of Niddrie, near Edmondston, and was the site of the Raid of Greendikes in 1594.

NIDDRY'S WYND (High Street) is mentioned in *Town Council Minutes* 1477 as *Nudreis wynde*, where the salt market was to be held, and the description in *RMS* 1477 of land on the south side of the High Street once belonging to the late Robert Nudry fits in with the suggestion in *Grant* that the wynd was named for Robert Niddry, said to have been a magistrate in 1437, and possibly the same Robert de Nudre who appears as a witness in *RMS* 1426. Presumably he was a member of the family who had been in Niddrie Marischal some sixty years earlier. The variation of the name ending between -*y* and -*ie* has no significance. After the inauguration of the scheme for the South Bridge in 1785, the wynd's name was perpetuated in that of NIDDRY STREET, given as *Niddry's Street* on *Brown & Watson* 1793 and as *Niddery Street* on *Ainslie* 1804; but although the map evidence suggests that little progress was made until the 1810s, the wynd itself became the site of the buildings on the east side of the new bridge, and Niddry Street was formed further east, bordering on KINLOCH'S CLOSE, *which see*. For SOUTH NIDDRY STREET, *see* AITKEN'S CLOSE, 253 Cowgate.

NIGEL LOAN (Inch) *see under* THE INCH, Nether Liberton.

NILE GROVE (South Morningside) *see under* EGYPT, South Morningside.

NIMMO'S CLOSE (South Leith) is listed on *Kirkwood* 1817 and was probably connected with James Nimmo, merchant in the Lees quarter, listed in *Williamson's Directory* 1773.

EDWARD or **JAMES** or **PATRICK NISBET'S CLOSE** (131 High Street) *see* BISHOP'S CLOSE.

NISBET'S PARKS (Murrayfield) *see under* MURRAYFIELD.

NIVEN'S GREEN (Queensferry) is recorded from 1692 onwards. In the normal usage of that period, the name implies a bleaching green; and this may well have been connected with or even set up by the John Niven, weaver, who was resident in Queensferry in 1647. The *Ordnance Survey* 1854 shows the name at the west side of the hollow (partly filled up by the railway embankment in the 1860s) beside the Ferry burn at Jock's Hole, with NIVEN'S BANK north of it, overlooking the Edinburgh road; but while *Dundas* 1757 shows the name centred in the same way, *Barnbougle & Dalmeny* c1800 shows it also extending between the burn and the Loan, as far south as Lover's Loan—a wider use which was probably a field name given by Dalmeny estate.

NOBLE PLACE (South Leith) *see under* INDUSTRIAL ROAD.

THE NOR LOCH (Old Town) is shown by the geological evidence to have stretched from the east side of the glebe of the West Kirk of St Cuthbert to the west side of the Trinity College garden, where *New Town Survey* 1766 shows the North Bridge crossing it some fifteen yards short of its eastern shore. The name (arising from the loch's position north of the town, and the fact that the town owned it) is used from as early as 1437 in defining feus north of the High Street. This suggests (although not conclusively) that the shore line had not greatly changed since the early days of the burgh, and this in turn would make it difficult to suppose that (as is so often assumed) the loch was artificial: it would seem much more likely that there was a natural sill, rather than a dam, at the College garden, and that when the loch was drained it was by deepening its outfall at the Tummel burn. The water is shown at its full extent on *Rothiemay* 1647 and *Roy* 1753, but *Edgar* 1742 shows its upper half as a marsh, while *Ainslie* 1804 shows it fully drained, divided by the MOUND and LITTLE MOUND (*which see*) and traversed by some functional paths. *Pollock* 1834 shows the area east of the Mound as *Cleghorn's Gardens*, probably connected with Home, Cleghorn & Wilson, who were coachmakers at 3 Princes Street in 1799. West of the Mound, the loch bed was still a noisome swamp when powers to improve it were obtained in 1816; a proposed scheme for gardens is shown on *Knox* 1821 and *Wood* 1823, but *Kirkwood* 1823 shows the one that was carried out.

NORTH BACK OF THE CANONGATE *see under* BACKS OF THE CANONGATE.

THE NORTH BRIDGE must be reckoned among the 'bridges and arches' seen as early as the 1680s to be essential to the city's growth (*see under* THE NEW TOWN) and in 1728 John Earl of Mar put forward a scheme for a high-level bridge more or less upon the present line; but it was 1753 before the necessary Act of Parliament was obtained, and another ten years before a design was put out to tender on 2 July 1763. Its author is unknown; but two engravings published in July and August 1763 (both from a drawing prepared by James Craig as draughtsman, not designer) show that it was to be a bridge of six arches. Building started in the following October, but the scheme was abandoned after only half of one pier had been completed. In 1765 a competition for a fresh design was won by David Henderson, but the scheme chosen for building was by the runner-up, William Mylne. After a setback in 1769, when part of the south abutment collapsed, the bridge was at last opened in 1772. Maps from 1773 onwards show it as *Bridge Street*, but with the advent of the South Bridge in 1785, the two streets were called *North Bridge Street* and *South Bridge Street*, as shown on *Brown & Watson* 1793; and this usage persists on maps until 1850, although *PO Directory* from 1825 onwards uses the shorter forms *North* and *South Bridge*. Mylne's bridge was widened by seven feet in 1873; but in 1894-97 it was replaced by a steel bridge designed to suit the reconstruction of the Waverley Station.

NORTH BRITISH CLOSE (High Street) *see* HALKERSTON'S WYND.

NORTH COLLEGE STREET (Old Town) *see* COLLEGE STREET.

NORTHCOTE STREET (Dalry) was formed and named by 1889, evidently in memory of Sir Stafford Northcote, a leading Conservative, who had been Rector of Edinburgh University in 1883, was created Earl of Iddesleigh in 1885 and made Foreign Secretary six months before he died in 1887.

THE NORTHERN NEW TOWN was developed by the Heriot Trust and the Town Council, on a plan by Robert Reid and William Sibbald. Begun in 1802, it was substantially carried out by 1830, with little modification except at ROYAL CIRCUS, where in 1820 an amendment by William Playfair brilliantly solved problems in designing a circus on such a steep slope and at the same time providing good access to Stockbridge and to the proposed development of the MORAY ESTATE, *which see*. Every street was named in 1802, and in the few cases where a change has been made, the new name has been derived from the original one. The scheme of names (also shown on *Ainslie* 1804) was clearly intended to be not a series of compliments to individuals but a general celebration of the nation, gathered round its sovereign George III, who was represented by the central avenue, originally named KING STREET but altered to GREAT KING STREET shortly after 1812, to obviate confusion with King Street (altered to Little King Street) in St JAMES

SQUARE, *which see*. Flanking it, NORTHUMBERLAND STREET and CUMBERLAND STREET were clearly named as a pair: the one probably for Hugh Percy, Duke of Northumberland, a distinguished general and an influential friend of the Prince of Wales; the other probably for Ernest Augustus, a younger brother of the Prince, also a general, and created Duke of Cumberland in 1795. Around this central group, other national heroes of the day are celebrated: among politicians, DUNDAS STREET for Henry Dundas, Viscount Melville (*see also under* MELVILLE STREET, Western New Town) and PITT STREET (merged with Dundas Street in 1967) for William Pitt, Prime Minister 1784-1801; among soldiers, ABERCROMBIE PLACE celebrated General Sir Ralph Abercromby, mortally wounded in the moment of victory at Alexandria in 1801; while among sailors, HOWE STREET was for Richard, Earl Howe, admiral of the Fleet in 1796; ST VINCENT STREET for Sir John Jervis, Earl St Vincent, First Lord of the Admiralty in 1801; NELSON PLACE and STREET for Sir Horatio Nelson, created viscount after the victory at Copenhagen in 1801; and CORNWALLIS PLACE (named in 1802, although not built until 1881) for Sir William Cornwallis, commander of the Channel Fleet in 1801; while DUNCAN STREET (renamed in 1885 as DUNDONALD STREET, for Rear Admiral Cochrane Earl of Dundonald, in order to obviate confusion with DUNCAN STREET in Newington) was originally named for the admiral Viscount Duncan of Camperdown. In the west of the scheme INDIA STREET and JAMAICA STREET represented the colonies; while in the east the incorporation of Ireland into the United Kingdom in 1801 was celebrated in the naming of CALEDONIA, ANGLIA and HIBERNIA STREETS, and the connection not entirely obscured when by 1806 they were renamed SCOTLAND STREET, LONDON STREET and DUBLIN STREET. ROYAL CIRCUS, originally named *The Circus*, and ROYAL CRESCENT were the first streets in Edinburgh to be conceived in these fashionable shapes (Abercrombie Place, irregularly curved to suit the site boundary, was not thought of as a crescent) and their names were fancy and fashionable, obviously emulating the Circus and Royal Crescent in Bath, Somerset. The other names in the scheme had more local origins. HERIOT ROW was named for the Heriot Trust, and FETTES ROW might be said to celebrate both developers, for Lord Provost William Fettes chaired both the Town Council and the Heriot Trust. DRUMMOND PLACE is on the site of *Drummond Lodge* shown on *Fergus & Robinson* 1759 which was from 1757 to 1766 the home of George Drummond, six times Lord Provost and above all others the man responsible for promoting the improvement of the city, *see also under* DRUMMOND STREET, South Side. BELLEVUE CRESCENT incorporates the new name given to Drummond's estate by General Scott of Balcomie when he bought it after Drummond's death and rebuilt the Lodge as the house of *Bellevue*. The name was later extended to BELLEVUE TERRACE (1835) PLACE (1875) STREET (1887) GARDENS (1933) and GROVE (1934) while the main road had the name BELLEVUE by

1893. MANSFIELD PLACE appears in the original scheme of 1802, named for the judge William Murray Earl of Mansfield, who was related to General Scott and was made a free burgess of Edinburgh after his defence of the town's conduct in the Porteous Riot case.

NORTHFIELD (Liberton) was in the barony of Stenhouse, and might have been the counterpart of SOUTHFIELD, *which see*; but since *Blaeu* 1654 and *Roy* 1753 show *Northhouse* in this vicinity (possibly the counterpart of SOUTHHOUSE, *which see*) and since *Northfield* reappears only in the 1880s as the name of development in what is shown on *Ordnance Survey* 1852 as open ground, more evidence is needed to show whether it derived from the ancient centre, or whether it was simply a local field name.

NORTHFIELD (Duddingston) was, like MEADOWFIELD, SOUTHFIELD, *Midfield* and *Eastfield*, one of the farms created by the earl of Abercorn by enclosure of the runrig farm of Wester Duddingston in the decades following his purchase of the estate in 1745; and it probably got its name as being formed out of the most northerly 'great field' of the original farm. The steading (in the vicinity of Northfield Park and Park Grove) was built in 1761 and appears as *North Mains* on *Laurie* 1763 and as *Northfield* on *Armstrongs* 1773. In 1919 the city held a competition for housing in its three western fields, shown on *Duddingston* c.1800 as the *Waterpans*, *Willow Head* and *Willow Cleeve* (*see under* WILLOWBRAE); and NORTHFIELD AVENUE, BROADWAY, CIRCUS, CRESCENT, EASTWAY, GARDENS, HIGHWAY, ROAD, SQUARE and TERRACE were named in 1921. NORTHFIELD FARM ROAD was developed in 1921 out of the western road to the farm, and NORTHFIELD FARM AVENUE, the old approach from Piershill, was named in 1929. In 1932, development continued (*see under* MOUNTCASTLE CRESCENT) in three eastern fields: the *Crookit Furcheons*, bent hindlegs, referring to the dog-legged shape of the field; the *Causeygates*, indicating that *causey gate*, paved way, was an early name for the so-called FISHWIVES CAUSEY, *which see*; and the *Blacklands*, no doubt named for rich soil. In the south of the farm, NORTHFIELD DRIVE and GROVE were formed in the *Mill Park* in 1947, and NORTHFIELD PARK and PARK GROVE were added in 1963 and 1973.

NORTH GRAY'S CLOSE (131 High Street) *see under* GRAY'S CLOSE.

NORTH GREENS (Niddrie) *see under* THE JEWEL, Niddrie.

NORTH GYLE (Corstorphine) is shown on *Roy* 1753 and was evidently named as the farm *on the northern shore* of the loch called THE GYLE—*which see*. Housing was developed from 1934 in NORTH GYLE AVENUE, DRIVE, LOAN, ROAD and TERRACE, and continued in 1936 with DECHMONT ROAD, *which see*. NORTH GYLE GROVE was named in 1953, and was followed by NORTH GYLE PARK (1960) and NORTH GYLE FARM ROAD and COURT (1970).

NORTHLAWN TERRACE (Barnton) *see under* EASTER PARK, Barnton.

NORTH LEITH, together with the Coalhill, was granted to Holyrood abbey by David I in 1128. For an outline of its subsequent history and eventual merging with South Leith and other elements in a single burgh in 1833 *see under* LEITH. It was laid out on the normal burgh plan with burgage tofts flanking a central street. As shown on *Wood* 1777 and *Thomson* 1822 this street was long known simply as NORTH LEITH; but in about 1817 it began to be called SANDPORT STREET, *see under* THE SANDPORT, North Leith.

NORTH LEITH SANDS (North Leith) was named in 1983 to commemorate the *North Leith Sands*, which until the East and West Old Docks were built in 1800-17 and the Caledonian Railway arrived in 1864, had stretched from the West Pier along to Anchorfield, the part between the West Pier and the Citadel being called the *Short Sands*. The Sands were the remnant of the LINKS OF NORTH LEITH which (to judge by the drying shoals shown on *Dall & Leslie* 1831) had extended a quarter mile seawards before they were lost to the sea by erosion, especially rapid in the 16th century.

NORTH MERCHISTON was part of the lands of MERCHISTON (*which see*) separated off by 1725, when it was bought by William Adam. The site of the House was at the northwest corner of the junction of Tay Street and Bryson Road. The estate stretched from the south backs of Polwarth Gardens to Dundee Terrace, and until 1878 it was for the most part a landscaped park, as shown on *Kirkwood* 1817, *see under* TEMPLE PARK, North Merchiston.

NORTH PARK TERRACE (Comely Bank) was named in about 1889, as being formed in the *North Park* field of Comely Bank.

NORTH RAW (Ratho) *see under* RATHO.

THE NORTH SIDE is in popular usage a general term for the part of the city that stretches north of the New Town ridge. No doubt it is because the centre of the town has always been on a ridge running from west to east that so much of the adjoining area has been perceived and named as *north* or *south* (*see also* SOUTH SIDE) whereas in the other directions the phrases *east of* and *west of* Edinburgh are used.

NORTH STREET (Ratho) was developed by the county in 1958 in the *North Crofts*, and was named, as the Crofts had been, for its position on the north of the main street of Ratho.

NORTHUMBERLAND STREET (New Town) *see under* NORTHERN NEW TOWN. NORTHUMBERLAND PLACE seems to have arisen after 1809 when the upper part of Nelson Street was realigned to suit a symmetrical design for Abercromby Place.

THE NORTH WALK (South Morningside) was introduced in 1981 as a side name in Morningside Drive to avoid the need to renumber that street to accommodate new housing on its north side—*see also* THE CRESCENT, South Morningside.

NORTON (Ratho) is recorded from 1290 onwards, the name being Anglian *north tún*, north farm town of Ratho. It is shown on *Adair* 1682, and *Laurie* 1763 adds NORTON EAST and WEST MAINS, while *Knox* 1812 adds MIDDLE NORTON. By 1893 a WESTER NORTON steading had been built east of Ratho Station Road, at the Newbridge road.

NORTON PARK (Abbeymount) was the general name for the northern part of the lands of Abbeyhill House, owned by the Hon. Fletcher Norton, Baron of the Scottish Exchequer for 44 years before his death in 1820. The street of the name dates from 1901; but NORTON PLACE is shown on *Knox* 1821 as the name of the southern frontage of the triangle of ground left between the Easter Road and the new London and Regent Roads; and WEST NORTON PLACE developed in the 1830s, EAST NORTON PLACE following about ten years later.

NOTTINGHAM PLACE (Greenside) arose as the name of a terrace of houses, also known as NOTTINGHAM TERRACE (occasionally at first, but regularly after 1861) and built in about 1812 by Samuel Wordsworth, stabler, who was certainly an Englishman and probably had some connection with Nottingham. His large stables at the south end of the terrace, are shown as a *Horse Bazaar* on *Ordnance Survey* 1852, and as *Horse Repository* in 1893. The street is much older than the terrace, and is shown on *Fergus & Robinson* 1759; and the indications are that *Nottingham Place* became the street name by about 1850.

O

OAKFIELD PLACE (Pleasance) was developed in 1988 on ground once part of the DISHFLAT (*which see*) where Alexander Forrest, bootmaker in Leith Street, began in about 1804 to tan and cure his hides. Although *Kirkwood* 1817 notes only the *tan yard*, it shows the development which was named *Oakfield House* and *Court* at some time before 1824. The name probably derived from the oak chips used in the tanning process.

OAK LANE (Clermiston) was given this unofficial name, derived from an oak tree at its entry, in about 1975.

OAKVILLE TERRACE (South Leith) *see under* WOODBINE TERRACE, South Leith.

OBSERVATORY ROAD (Blackford) was constructed in about 1884 to give vehicular access to Blackford Hill after it was purchased and opened as a public park, largely through the efforts of Lord Provost George Harrison, commemorated in the *Harrison Arch* at the entry to the street. The street was named after the transfer of the Royal Observatory from the Calton to Blackford in 1894; and in 1977 OBSERVATORY GREEN was named as a branch off it.

OCHIL COURT (Queensferry) was named by 1972, evidently for the Ochil Hills—a name which is British for *the height*.

OGILVIE TERRACE (North Merchiston) was built on Merchant Company ground in 1899 and named for Dr George Ogilvie, headmaster of George Watson's College.

OLD ASSEMBLY CLOSE (172 High Street and 158 Cowgate) is still shown on *Edgar* 1742 as ASSEMBLY CLOSE, named for the once 'new Edinburgh Assembly' which, as advertised, began to meet here 'in the great hall in Patrick Steil's Close' in 1723. This *Assembly House* was part of a tenement then newly built on the former site of Lord Durie's mansion (*see below*) which in 1839 became the site of the Heriot School building still extant on the west side of the close. The Assembly's dances, held weekly from November to April, continued here until 1736, when they were transferred to new premises in 142 High Street (*see* NEW ASSEMBLY CLOSE) and the close began to be called the *Old* or former *Assembly Close*. Much earlier it was YARIS CLOSE, recorded in 1537 and deriving from Thomas Yhare, burgess in 1473 and bailie in 1488. His surname originated from Yair, near Selkirk, prior to 1400, and the variant spellings of the close name, YAIR'S, ZAIR'S or HAIR'S, arise from its initial letter, the medieval ʒ or 'yogh', which is often printed confusingly as *z* (as it is in *Cockenzie*, for example) but is better represented by modern *y*. The close was also known as GILLESPIE'S, first recorded in 1570 and derived from David Gillespie, baxter, mentioned in *Town Council Minutes* 1523-31, and owner of *Gillespie's land* near the south end of the close in 1523. In 1580 it was also LITTLE'S or CLEMENT LITTLE'S CLOSE, presumably—for the name is the only direct evidence—for Maister Clement Little, advocate, whose bequest of books in 1580 became the nucleus of the University library. The close was also DURIE'S or, as recorded in 1635, LORD DURIE'S, and this last makes it clear that although a John Durie, fish curer, had property in the close at some time prior to 1720, the close was named not for him but for Sir Alexander Gibson, the eminent jurist, whose *Praticks* (published by his grandson in 1690) pioneered the collection of decisions in Scots law. He lived in a mansion on the west side of the close, as mentioned above, and is listed as its owner in 1635, under his judicial title Lord Durie, which he had assumed in 1621. A charter of 1759 notes the close as also known as BARNES'S; there is nothing to indicate when or why this was, but it would be interesting if it were found to be connected with James Barnes, member of town council in 1642 and treasurer of the town's College or University, for like Clement Little sixty years earlier, he became one of the College's benefactors. The close was also STEIL'S or PATRICK STEIL'S, from Patrick Steill, vintner, who kept the Crosskeys tavern in it in the last decades of the 17th century and whose enthusiasm for music, according to *Arnot*, led to the formation of a weekly music club in the Crosskeys and eventually to the founding of the Musical Society of Edinburgh in 1728. The variant name PATRICK SHIELS' CLOSE is probably a confused version, but may nevertheless refer to an Archibald Shiels, son of a merchant of the same name, who had property on the east side of the close at some date prior to 1767.

OLD BURDIEHOUSE ROAD (Burdiehouse) *see under* BURDIEHOUSE.

OLD CHURCH LANE (Duddingston) was originally formed in about 1760, probably in the course of the earl of Abercorn's remodelling of Duddingston village, as shown on a map of 1770 copied in *Baird's Duddingston* p88; but its eastern section of some 200 yards was realigned to suit the building of the new manse in 1805, its entry being moved about 100 yards north of its former position, still shown by a kink in Duddingston Road West. Its continuation westwards from the kirk gate dates only from 1856, when the road through the Park was constructed. It is named as *Church Lane* on *Ordnance Survey* 1852, but was renamed *Old Church Lane* in 1966, on the same day as the only other *Church Lane* in the city was renamed GLOUCESTER LANE 'to avoid duplication'.

OLD FARM AVENUE, PLACE and **ROAD** (Colinton) *see under* COLINTON.

OLD FISHMARKET CLOSE (Shore, South Leith) is shown on *Wood* 1777 and named (as the former place of the fish market) on *Kirkwood* 1817.

OLD HAY WEIGHTS (West Port) is so named on *Ordnance Survey* 1852 and evidently derived from the 'Steel Yard and Hay Weight' shown at a stables here on a plan of part of the east side of Lauriston Street in 1791. It is not clear whether the weighbeam was public or private.

OLD KIRK ROAD (Corstorphine) was named in 1923 when it was developed for housing (also see BELGRAVE ROAD, Corstorphine) on the site of part of a right-of-way from Ravelston Dykes to the parish kirk of Corstorphine, shown on *Roy* 1753 and *Knox* 1812, and named *Kirk Road* on *Corstorphinehill* 1885. Other parts of the same loaning form EASTER BELMONT ROAD and REST-AND-BE-THANKFUL (*which see*) as well as one of the main footpaths in the Zoo.

OLDLISTON (Newbridge) *see* AULDLISTON, Newbridge.

OLD MILL LANE (Nether Liberton) *see under* NETHER LIBERTON.

OLD POST HOUSE or **OFFICE STAIRS** and **CLOSE** (130 Cowgate and Parliament Square) *see* THE KIRKHEUCH.

OLD POST OFFICE CLOSE (251 High Street) is listed as *Old Posthouse Close* on *Edgar* 1742, and was named for the post office which was here in the 1720s before it was transferred to Parliament Close. Earlier, it was (EDWARD) LITTLE'S CLOSE, so named before 1563 for Edward Little of Badinsgill, who was a bailie in 1516; but it was also known as JACOB or JAMES BARRON'S CLOSE for another owner of property in it, probably Little's fellow councillor Jacob or

James Barron, who was treasurer in 1514, or else the James Barron (presumably a successor) who was Dean of Guild in 1556. The Close was suppressed in the eastward extension of the City Chambers in 1930.

OLD POST OFFICE LANE (Queensferry) is shown, with a Post Office in it, on *Ordnance Survey* 1856. The first post office in the burgh was established in 1747.

OLD or **AULD PROVOST'S CLOSE** (189 High Street) is now represented by the west side of the head of Cockburn Street. It is shown on *Ordnance Survey* 1852 as OLD GREENMARKET CLOSE, evidently from the *Green Market* first shown on *Edgar* 1765. The names MIDDLE FLESHMARKET CLOSE on *Edgar* 1742 and EAST FISHMARKET CLOSE on *Ainslie* 1780 cannot be older than the transfer of the meat market to this vicinity not long before 1691. The OLD PROVOST'S CLOSE name refers to the office of 'Old Provost' held by each Lord Provost after his retiral. First recorded in a 'neighbourhood book' of 1570, it may have been connected with Sir Simon Preston of Craigmillar who (as related in *Town Council Minutes* 1569, and discussed in *Old Edinburgh Club XXXV*) lived in a rented house here while he was Provost, from 1565 to 1569; or else the name may go further back to Patrick Hepburne, Lord Hailes, who was resident in the close in 1484 and chief magistrate (the first to be styled 'Lord Provost') in 1487; but it is not known whether either of them stayed in the close after becoming Old Provost.

OLD STAGE ENTRY (South Leith) is shown on *Kirkwood* 1817 as the first entry at the west end of Bernard Street. The name implies that it was once the starting point of a stage-coach service.

OLD STAMP OFFICE CLOSE (221 High Street) is named for the Stamp Office which was here from before 1779 until it was transferred to Waterloo Place in 1821, and the *Old* dates from after this. *Kirkwood* 1817 shows the close as *Stamp Office Close, formerly Newbank Close*. This NEWBANK name, shown on *Edgar* 1742 and still used on *Brown* 1809, referred to the original office of the Royal Bank (*new* in comparison with the *old* Bank of Scotland in (OLD) BANK CLOSE, *which see*) which was opened in 1727. The close, as shown on *Ainslie* 1780 and 1804, was also known as the SHIP CLOSE or the OLD SHIP or SHIP TAVERN CLOSE, for a tavern mentioned in *Dean of Guild Records* 1704 and built some time previously by a Thomas Wilson, perhaps the vintner of that name figuring in *Town Council Minutes* 1647. Fourthly, the close is referred to in *Williamson's Directory* 1773 as FORTUNE'S, for the tavern John Fortune opened here in the 1750s, which became famous not only as a meeting place for clubs, but for the levees held in it by the king's Commissioners to the General Assembly. Fifthly, the close seems also to have been FORSYTH'S, recorded in 1645 and probably named for the Robert Forsyth whose heirs are listed in 1635 as owners in the close.

THE OLD TOWN is a name which came into use only after the NEW TOWN (*which see*) was developed, from 1768 onwards. *Kincaid* 1787 uses the term strictly for the older part of the burgh of Edinburgh, expressly excluding the other burghs of Canongate, Portsburgh and Calton, which although owned by Edinburgh did not become part of it until 1856; but since that amalgamation the term has gradually been used more loosely as a description, covering not only the ancient royalty, which includes the Canongatehead as well as the area enclosed by the Flodden Wall, but also the Canongate.

OLIPHANT'S CLOSES (257 and 267 Canongate) *see* KINLOCH'S CLOSE *and* (Dr) SETON'S CLOSE, 257 and 267 Canongate.

OLIVER'S CAMP (Comiston) was a large earthwork lying athwart the high road between Fairmilehead and Buckstane Snab, its centre, as estimated from the 18th-century maps, being roughly in the vicinity of NT 245668. William Roy's expert witness (in his *Military Antiquities*) is that what was visible in about 1770 was oval in shape and judged not to be Roman, but that the remains seemed to have been originally more extensive. This perhaps explains why the oval shape figures on *Armstrongs* 1773 and in *White's Liberton* 1786, while *Laurie* 1766 shows a *Roman Camp* 500 yards square, and *Mortonhall* 1770 (covering only the eastern edge of the area) shows a small circular *Camp* straddling the boundary between Morton and Buckstane at about NT 24736885, near the northeast corner of the square on *Laurie*. *Maitland* 1753, while not sure whether the earthwork was originally Roman or Pictish or Danish, confidently asserts that Cromwell made use of it as a camp site during his attempt to outflank Leslie's position in Edinburgh in 1650, and *Armstrongs* 1773 and *White's Liberton* follow him in naming it *Oliver Cromwell's* or *Oliver's* camp; but the contemporary accounts are less specific, speaking of 'between Braid Crags (which could be BLACKFORD HILL, *which see*) and the Pentlands', and it is generally believed that his camp was in the slack between the Braid Hills and the Galachlaw, or even on the south side of the latter, the more so because his next move was through Colinton.

ORCHARD BRAE (Dean Park) is part of the ancient route by the Dean and the Crew to Granton, as shown on *Roy* 1753, although it was straightened and partly raised on an embankment in the later 1850s or the 1860s. It is named on *Ordnance Survey* 1852, which also shows it flanked on the east by the *Patriotic Society's Allotment Gardens* (perhaps connected with PATRIOT HALL, Stockbridge, *which see*) but in absence of any evidence for an orchard in its vicinity, the name remains obscure. ORCHARD BRAE WEST was named in 1931, ORCHARD BRAE AVENUE and GARDENS in 1958, and the western extension of the GARDENS in 1964. An earlier development to the north of this adopted the *Orchard* name for ORCHARD BANK, CRESCENT, DRIVE, PLACE, ROAD and TERRACE in 1927 and ORCHARD GROVE in 1929; and in 1981 this led to the naming of ORCHARD TOLL, which is a made-up name recalling the nearby *Dean Park Toll*, which was at the east side of the junction of Queensferry Road and Terrace.

ORCHARDFIELD (Corstorphine) appears in 1872 as the address of a gardener in Corstorphine High Street, and since his address had previously been simply *High Street* it is more likely that *Orchardfield* was coined as a description of his garden ground than as a reference to the *Pomarium* or orchard of Corstorphine Castle mentioned in a deed of 1473 (quoted in *Wood's Corstorphine* 1792) which apparently lay somewhat further south, possibly in the vicinity of the Dovecot Park. ORCHARDFIELD PLACE was named by 1904. ORCHARDFIELD AVENUE is shown on *Ordnance Survey* 1912 as already formed, and was named by 1914.

ORCHARDFIELD (Pilrig) appears in *PO Directory* 1827 and is shown on *Pollock* 1834 as attached to properties on the frontage which closely resemble those shown on *Kirkwood* 1817. The name was probably coined from the character of ground shown as *Mr Paton's* on both *Ainslie* 1804 and *Kirkwood* 1817. It was kept going, after the suppression of the side name, in the name of ORCHARDFIELD LANE (even although this is just over the boundary and in Springfield) and was re-established in 1988 in the form NEW ORCHARDFIELD, as the name of a redevelopment for housing within and west of Paton's garden ground.

ORCHARDFIELD (Tollcross) is referred to in David I's charter to St Cuthbert's in the mid 1120s as 'the king's garden' adjoining the kirk's glebe to the south, and in *Bain* 1336 it is called 'the castle orchard' and 'gardens below the castle', while in *RMS* 1431 it is referred to as *la Orchardfelde*, now no longer in royal use but feued out, evidently not for the first time, as a private property. The term *-felde* implies that there was open ground as well as an orchard, and it may have amounted to some 35 acres lying between St Cuthbert's glebe and the Linlithgow road (now Morrison Street) and stretching from the vicinity of Castle Terrace perhaps as far as Haymarket. In the late 18th century the name centred on the street (*see below*) and on a large part of the ground (shown on *Kirkwood* 1817 as acquired half by George and John Grindlay, tanners in King's Stables, and half by the Merchant Maidens' and Watson's hospitals) which was held by the Merchant Company, acting as the Grindlay Trust for the benefit of these schools together with James Gillespie's and the Royal Infirmary. The first of several abortive schemes for its development, boasting a large *Orchardfield Square*, is shown on *Ainslie* 1804; but progress was delayed by uncertainty about the form to be taken by the new 'Western Approach' (*see under* KING'S BRIDGE, SPITTAL STREET and JOHNSTON TERRACE) and difficulties continued even after the Trust's final plan appeared on *Lothian* 1829. It was 1836 before CASTLE TERRACE entered the *PO Directory*; grandiose plans for the area west of the Lothian Road were still on paper in 1848 when they were dropped in favour of the Caledonian Railway's goods and passenger stations; and *Ordnance Survey* 1852 shows the future Grindlay Street, Cornwall Street and half of Cambridge Street still as mere reservations of ground given over to temporary industrial use, with GRINDLAY STREET LANE (as yet unnamed) giving access to some parts of them. The name GRINDLAY STREET was originally proposed for a street in the abortive plan shown on *Kirkwood* 1823, and although this figured prematurely in *PO Directory* 1825, the present street was not opened until the mid 1860s. There was an intention to name a pair of streets for George *Watson* and Mary *Erskine*, as founders of Watson's and the Merchant Maidens' hospitals; but by 1859 the first of the pair was named CAMBRIDGE STREET, for Victoria's uncle Adolphus Frederick, Duke of Cambridge, who had died in 1850, and by 1865 the other was named CORNWALL STREET, for Albert Edward, Prince of Wales and Duke of Cornwall, perhaps on the occasion of his marriage in 1863. Meantime the ancient thoroughfare of ORCHARDFIELD, shown thus on *Ainslie* 1804 and partly thus on *Ordnance Survey* 1852, was progressively renamed BREAD STREET and MORRISON STREET (*which see*) and the side names of ORCHARDFIELD COURT and PLACE, shown in 1852 just west of Newport Street, have since been forgotten.

ORCHARDHEAD LOAN and **ROAD** (Liberton) *see under* CADOGAN ROAD, Liberton.

(LAURENCE) ORD'S CLOSE (31 Canongate) *see* WHITEHORSE CLOSE, Canongate.

ORMELIE TERRACE (Joppa) was developed in about 1906 in the grounds of a mansion in James Street shown as *Ormelie* on *Ordnance Survey* 1893 but as *Ko-lan-sao* on *W & A K Johnstone* 1888.

ORMIDALE TERRACE (Murrayfield) *see under* ABINGER GARDENS, Murrayfield.

ORMISTON TERRACE (Corstorphine) was built in 1885 by Charles and Thomas Blaikie, grocers, and named for their mother Matilda Ormiston.

ORROCK PARK (Nether Liberton) was named in 1988 as being on the site of the *Bawbee houses*, cleared away by 1850 and said in *Good's Liberton* to have been named from an advertisement for straw selling at 'five bawbees a wunnel' or bunch. The Scots bawbee or ha'penny got its nickname from Alexander Orrock of Sillebawbie in Fife, master of the cunyie or mint when the coin was first issued in the early 16th century.

ORWELL PLACE and **TERRACE** (Dalry) were formed in 1870, after the Walker family had given up residence in Dalry House. The first was initially named DALRY PLACE (i.e. for the House) and the second was evidently regarded as part of CALEDONIAN CRESCENT (*which see*) until 1875, when both streets got their *Orwell* names, which first appear in *PO Directory* 1876. No connection with the conversion of Dalry House into a Scottish Episcopal Church training centre in 1877 has been traced, and the reasons for both change and choice of street names remain obscure. Besides being a personal name, and a place name at Milnathort, *Orwell* is the name of a river and of several places in Suffolk and Cambridgeshire.

OSBORNE, KEW and **HAMPTON TERRACES** (Wester Coates) were built in successive years from 1862 and appear to have been named together for *Osborne*, the Queen's residence in the Isle of Wight; *Kew*, in Surrey, formerly a royal palace, developed as a great garden by George III and presented to the nation by Queen Victoria in 1840; and the royal palace *Hampton Court* in Middlesex. The last also gave the name to HAMPTON PLACE in West Catherine Street.

OSWALD and **SOUTH OSWALD ROADS** (Blackford) are on ground acquired by Trotter of Mortonhall in 1760, and Oswald Road was named in about 1870 for Mary Oswald, who had married Richard Trotter, 10th laird of Mortonhall, in 1836. SOUTH OSWALD ROAD was named by 1888 and OSWALD COURT in 1971.

OSWALD TERRACE (Corstorphine) was built in about 1903 by William Samuel, and named for his mother, Catherine Oswald.

OTTERBURN PARK (Redhall) is built in the East Park of Redhall and was named in 1980 for Sir Adam Otterburn of Redhall, a noted diplomat and seven times Lord Provost of Edinburgh in the period 1522 to 1548, who bought Redhall in 1527 and added Gorgie to it in 1535. He probably rebuilt or improved Redhall Tower, and the panel bearing his arms, built into the Redhall doocot in 1756, was evidently transferred from its ruins.

OVERTON (Newliston) is *Owir Newlistoun* in 1516 and shown as *Over Newlistoun* on *Blaeu* 1654, whereas on *Roy* 1753 and *Armstrongs* 1773 it is *Evertoun* and *Overtown*, and *Ordnance Survey* 1852 records it as *Over Newliston* or *Overtoun*. The explanation for the two names may be that whereas the medieval subdivision may have created *Over Newliston* and *Nether Newliston* (both shown on *Blaeu*, probably surveyed in 1596) as more or less equal properties, the latter became dominant and reverted to the name *Newlistoun*, as shown on *Adair* 1682 so that it became more appropriate to think of Over Newliston as the 'over toun or farm of Newliston'. The *Ovirtoun of Nether Newlistoun* recorded in 1576 may be a transitional form in this process. The terms *over* and *nether* belong to the ancient practice of labelling parts of a field or estate depending on how they were perceived in relation to the sun: if under the forenoon sun, they were 'sunny-side' and were labelled *over-*, *upper-*, *east-* or *fore-*; while those on the 'shadow side' under the sun after noon were *nether-*, *under-*, *west-* or *back-*.

THE OVER TRON (Old Town) was an alternative name for the BUTTER TRON, *which see*.

OXCRAIG STREET (Granton) *see under* GRANTON HARBOUR.

OXFORD STREET (St Leonard's) was built in the 1860s and took its name from the ground which, a part of the GALLOWGREEN or

SPITTALFIELD (*which see*) had latterly been called *Oxford Park*, for some unknown reason. SOUTH OXFORD STREET was formed on Newington ground in about 1880, and was evidently named as being opposite the entry to Oxford Street.

OXFORD TERRACE (Dean) *see under* CLARENDON CRESCENT, Dean.

OXGANGS (Colinton) is recorded in 1425 as *le Oxgangis* (*see also* INCHERATHRYNE) and is shown on *Adair* 1682 as *Oxengang*, while the entry *Bangam* on *Roy* 1753 may be a mistake, or else a tenant's name. *Colinton Mains & Oxgangs* 1813 shows the farm extending to 134 Scots acres, which in the traditional land measure was 10 *oxgangs*. The *plewgate* of about 104 Scots acres was notionally that area of arable which could be worked by one plough with a yoke of eight oxen, and the *oxgang*, being an eighth of a plewgate, was as it were the area that justified the keep of one ox in the team. The farm lay between the Braid burn and Redford Road, marching with Comiston in the east and the Baads in the west. Its steading is now represented by the police station in OXGANGS ROAD. This road, partly renamed OXGANGS ROAD NORTH in 1958, got its traditional name as leading *to* or *by the Oxgangs*; but whereas *Laurie* 1763 shows it (as now) leading to Fairmilehead by Sourhole or Hunter's Tryst, *Roy* 1753 shows it leading from Oxgangs past the north side of Comiston tower, heading straight for MOUNTHOOLY (*which see*) east of Fairmilehead. OXGANGS TERRACE was named in 1937 as part of the development called 'Colinton Mains', and marks the south border of the *West Haugh* of Oxgangs, on which the greater part of that housing scheme was built. In 1947 streets were developed in eastern fields of Oxgangs: OXGANGS CRESCENT in the *Chatterrigg* or stony ridge, OXGANGS DRIVE and PLACE in the *Bught Knowe* (Scots *bught* being a fold for milch yowes), OXGANGS AVENUE on the line of a right-of-way that ran along the south bounds of these fields (*see also* FLY WALK, Greenbank) and OXGANGS STREET in the *Lang Side* or 'long-slope field'. In 1954, development in the Lang Side continued with OXGANGS BRAE, PARK, PATH, RISE, ROW and VIEW, together with OXGANGS BANK, GREEN and LOAN on adjoining Comiston ground; followed in 1957 by OXGANGS BROADWAY, MEDWAY and PATH EAST, and in 1964 by OXGANGS HILL in Comiston and OXGANGS GARDENS and GROVE in the Bught Knowe. The streets west of Oxgangs Road were named in 1953, the extra element *-farm* being introduced simply to enable *avenue, drive, etc* to be used again. OXGANGS FARM GROVE (and part of COLINTON MAINS ROAD) were built in the *Mickle Park*, big park, and OXGANGS FARM AVENUE, DRIVE, GARDENS, LOAN and TERRACE in the *Gowk Law* or cuckoo-hill field. EASTER HAUGH was named in 1984, as being in the *Easter Haugh* of Oxgangs, which has also provided Colinton Mains Park.

P

PADDOCKHALL (Stockbridge) *see* PUDDOCKIE, Stockbridge.

THE PADDOCKHOLM (Corstorphine) is on the site of the terminus of the NBR Corstorphine branch, built in 1902 and superseding the earlier *Corstorphine Station* on the main line at Saughton, but finally closed in 1967. Before the railway came, the ground was part of the *Paddockholm*, and this name, shown on *Corstorphine Village* 1777, was revived for the new housing street in 1983. Anglian *holm*, from Old Norse *holmr*, here meant a meadow beside a water (the Stank) or marsh; and *paddock*, while it might be the fairly modern word for an inby grazing, is more likely to be early Scots *paddok*, implying that this waterside meadow was well known for its frogs and toads.

PAGE'S CLOSE (20 Shore Place, South Leith) is named on *Kirkwood* 1817, for an owner as yet untraced.

PAISLEY CRESCENT (Willowbrae) was developed in the *North Park* of MEADOWFIELD, Duddingston, and named in 1927 for the owner of the estate, the Duke of Abercorn and Baron Paisley—a title held by the Hamiltons since 1587. It was followed by PAISLEY AVENUE (1929) GARDENS and TERRACE (1934) and PAISLEY GROVE (1960).

PAISLEYS CLOSE (101 High Street) was named thus by 1679 for Henry Paisley, who owned property in it. *Edgar* 1742 lists its alternative name SMITH'S, recorded in 1660 as *George Smith's*, evidently from a predecessor of James Smith, mason, who was appointed overseer of Holyrood and other palaces in 1683, styled himself 'of Whitehill' after buying that estate near Brunstane in 1689, and built the Canongate kirk for the town in 1691, as well as his burgess house of *Smith's Land* within the close. On *Ainslie* 1780 and 1804 the close is shown as EAST BAILIE FYFE'S, linking it with BAILIE FYFE'S CLOSE, 107 High Street, *which see.*

PAISLEY STREET (planned in Joppa) *see under* RABBIT HALL.

PALLAS STREET (Granton) *see under* GRANTON HARBOUR.

PALMER PLACE and **ROAD** (Currie) were named by 1962 for Robert Palmer, born in Kirkcudbright in 1797, who was dominie of Currie school from 1828 to 1868, Session Clerk of Currie, a leading spirit in the development of curling as an organised sport, and maker of the sundial which stands in front of Currie kirk.

PALMERSTON PLACE (Coates) *see under* COATES.

PALMERSTON ROAD (Grange) *see under* THE GRANGE.

PANMURE CLOSE (129 Canongate) is listed on *Ainslie* 1780 and was named for James Maule, 4th Earl of Panmure and his successors in Panmure House. This mansion seems to have been built by Lieut-Col. George Murray, who bought the ground in 1691, added to it in 1693, and built the *lodging* which he sold to Panmure in 1696. After

443

Panmure's death in 1723, the house passed successively to James and William Maule, sons of the 4th earl's brother Harry (*see under* PANMURE'S CLOSE, 19 High Street) and William, created Earl Panmure of Forth in 1743, lived in it until his death, when it passed to his nephew, the Earl of Dalhousie. Adam Smith, author of *The Wealth of Nations*, was a tenant from 1778 until his death here in 1790. The close was also McKELL'S, for Jean and Catherine McKell, mentioned in *Canongate Charters* 1838 as former owners disponing some property in the close to William, 'Earl of Panmure'—presumably Earl Panmure of Forth.

PANMURE PLACE (Tollcross) was planned in about 1867, upon the site in Drumdryan of a *Rigg Street* proposed some half a century earlier, as shown on *Wood* 1823. In all probability it was named for Fox Maule, 11th Earl of Dalhousie, who as Baron Panmure had been Secretary of State for War 1855-58, the time of the Indian Mutiny.

PANMURE'S CLOSE (19 High Street) is listed on *Edgar* 1742, and was named for Henry Maule, who purchased a house at the foot of the close in 1711 and became titular Earl of Panmure after his brother James, 4th Earl, was forfeited in 1716. His grandson John Maule of Inverkeilor was appointed Baron of the Exchequer in 1748 and was still resident here in 1773: hence the name BARON MAULE'S CLOSE given on *Ainslie* 1780. Maule's house was taken over by the Society for Propagating Christian Knowledge as their offices and hall, and by 1799 the close was being called SOCIETY CLOSE. In the 17th century and perhaps earlier the close was known as BASSENDEN'S, for the same family (or a branch of it) who were settled at FOUNTAIN CLOSE, *which see*. In 1539, as recorded in *Town Council Minutes*, James Bassenden and his wife lent money on mortgage of the north vault of the Netherbow; and in 1624 Alison, daughter of Thomas Bassenden the printer and wife of John Ker, sold a property in the close, presumably part of her patrimony.

THE PANNY (Colinton Mains) is shown on *Colinton Mains & Oxgangs* 1813 as a field in Colinton Mains, now the west end of the City Hospital grounds. The name might have described a tendency of the subsoil to *pan* or pack hard in the bottom of the furrow, but although any particular connection with the parish kirk remains to be discovered, the more likely explanation is that the name is *pannie*, a Scots term for glebe land.

PAPE'S COTTAGES (Coltbridge) were endowed in 1854 as three cottages for widows of Coltbridge, by bequest of George Pape, whose wife Jessie Paterson had owned Coltbridge House since 1847.

PARK AVENUE (Easter Duddingston) was formed in about 1890. Originally called DUKE STREET (no doubt for the Duke of Abercorn, owner of Duddingston) it was renamed in about 1899, about the same time as the adjoining Portobello Park was laid out.

PARK CRESCENT, GARDENS and **GROVE** (Liberton) were so named in 1925 because this 5-acre site was said to have been known as 'Park Gardens' since the beginning of the century—a name which probably arose because it was part of the 17th-century property of Liberton Park.

PARKER DRIVE, PLACE and **TERRACE** (Craigentinny) *see under* CRAIGENTINNY.

PARKGROVE (North Clermiston) was coined in 1934 as a name for PARKGROVE AVENUE and DRIVE, by combining parts of two local names. *Park-* was taken from the farm of PARKNEUK, also known as *Muirpark*, shown on *Ordnance Survey* 1938 as well as *Roy* 1753. Sited at what became the entry to Parkgrove Drive from Drum Brae, it was named for its position at the foot of Cramond Muir and near the *neuk* or sharp corner, shown on *Roy* and still visible in field boundaries in 1938, where the old Queensferry road (now represented by part of Barntongate Avenue) doubled round the park of King's Cramond. some 240 yards west of the Drum Brae, and headed north on the line of Whitehouse Road. The other element - *grove* was borrowed from a well-wooded 18-acre property east of the Drum Brae and about 200 yards south of Parkneuk, recorded on *Knox* 1812 as MARY'S GROVE, but as MARGARET'S GROVE on *Cramond Roads* 1812 and *Fowler* 1845, and as THE GROVE on *Ordnance Survey* 1852 and 1938. Development continued at PARKGROVE ROAD (1937) CRESCENT (1938) and LOAN, GARDENS and TERRACE (1939) PLACE (1952) STREET (1953) PATH (1959) BANK, GREEN, ROW and VIEW (1961) and NEUK (1962). The western section of Parkgrove Crescent was taken into PARKGROVE LOAN in 1978.

PARKHEAD (Saughton) is named on *Roy* 1753, and shown on *Saughton* 1795 as an L-shaped farm marching with Broomhouse at what is now Broomhouse Place North and stretching south to the Murray burn and eastwards, on the south side of Calder Road, to Longstone Road. Its steading was in the angle of the L, at the head of Parkhead Gardens. The name is also recorded as *Park* in 1654 and shown as *Park Nook* on a map by Thomas Johnston in 1776 (*RHP 3702/3*) and all three variants obviously refer to its position just outside the park of Saughton House where this reached its highest point on the Calder road and also thrust out its southwest corner in an acute angle or neuk. PARKHEAD AVENUE, CRESCENT, DRIVE, GARDENS, GROVE, LOAN, PLACE, STREET, TERRACE and VIEW were named in 1936. Streets in Parkhead north of Calder Road were named as though they were in BROOMHOUSE, *which see.*

PARKNEUK (Inch) is named on *Laurie* 1763, which also shows how it lay on a road which led from Dalkeith Road to Nether Liberton, later superseded by LADY ROAD. According to *Good's Liberton* it was once quite considerable as a village, also known as LITTLE PAISLEY because of its weavers. The older name refers to its position on the *neuk* or corner of the park of the Inch.

PARK PLACE and **STREET** (Bristo) shown and named on *Ainslie* 1804 and probably dated from the late 1790s, were so named because they were built in the grounds of *Ross Park*, owned by the Lords Ross prior to the extinction of the line in 1754. Park Street was developed from the original driveway to the House and became TEVIOT ROW (*see under* TEVIOT PLACE) after the McEwan Hall was built in 1897; but both Teviot Row and Park Place were taken into BRISTO SQUARE in 1982.

PARK ROAD (Juniper Green) *see* JUNIPER PARK ROAD, Juniper Green.

PARK ROAD (Newhaven) was developed in about 1870 in the grounds of the property shown on *Ordnance Survey* 1852 as *Newhaven Park* and as *Mr Auchinleck's* on *Ainslie* 1804. PARK PLACE followed in 1883. SOUTH PARK was developed in 1983 in the southern park of the estate.

PARK ROAD (Parkside) *see* HOLYROOD PARK ROAD.

PARKSIDE (Newbridge) was developed by the county in 1946 and named for the adjoining public park.

PARKSIDE (St Leonards) was the southermost part of the lands of St Leonard's, an area of 26½ Scots acres stretching along the east side of the Dalkeith road to the boundary of Prestonfield at Marchhall. The name is Middle English or Scots *park side*, enclosed slope, and thus has to do with the ground itself and not (as it would if it were modern English) with any nearness to the Park of Holyroodhouse. After 1700, the name became especially associated with development in the northwest corner, as shown on *Ainslie* 1804: in about 1710 James Brown, surgeon and apothecary, built two houses here, one of them later called *Parkside House*; and in 1724 William Hunter, tailor burgess in Edinburgh, and his wife Jean Thomson not only bought these houses but built a third large tenement, speedily nicknamed *Castle o Clouts* for his trade, although he and his wife styled it *Hunter's Hall*, and it was also referred to later as *Parkside*. In about 1780 some ground was feued off at SALISBURY GREEN (*which see*) but otherwise the ground remained open until 1828, when a large strip along the east boundary was bought for the development of the INNOCENT RAILWAY (*which see*). PARKSIDE STREET was formed in about 1825. PARKSIDE PLACE (fronting St Leonard's Street) and TERRACE were conceived as a single scheme in about 1875. The first began to be occupied in 1877, but the separate side name was dropped in 1882 and the address became St Leonard's Street. PARKSIDE TERRACE began to be occupied in 1881. EAST PARKSIDE was coined in 1984 to establish a neighbourhood name for the considerable new housing precinct that was developing in the former railway ground in the east of Parkside.

PARK TERRACE and **VIEW** (Newcraighall) were named before 1938 for the nearby public park.

PARKVALE PLACE (South Leith) *see under* INDUSTRIAL ROAD.

PARLIAMENT CLOSE (Old Town) *see* PARLIAMENT SQUARE.

PARLIAMENT CLOSE (South Leith) is shown on *Naish* 1709 as a branch passage from the north side of the DUB RAW (*which see*) to St Leonard's Wynd in the COALHILL (*which see*) but the name first appears on *Kirkwood* 1817, and may have been then quite recent, arising from enthusiasm for a large mansion fronting the Shore in the Coalhill, referred to in *Maitland* 1753 as a handsome and spacious edifice erected by Mary of Guise in about 1555 for meetings of her Privy Council. Probably in the 1830s but certainly by 1850 the name extended to PARLIAMENT SQUARE, formed by alterations in the Peat Neuk area of Coalhill, as shown on *Ordnance Survey* 1852; and by 1892 the development of PARLIAMENT STREET on the line of Parliament Close had led to the suppression of the Close and the Square, as well as the last vestiges of St Leonard's Wynd.

PARLIAMENT SQUARE (Newhaven) was named by 1864 but renamed in 1968 and 1975 as GREAT MICHAEL SQUARE and CLOSE —*which see.*

PARLIAMENT SQUARE (Old Town) was formed in 1639 as the forecourt of the new PARLIAMENT HOUSE, and like it, occupied part of the former kirkyard of St Giles, which had gradually fallen out of use after Greyfriars' kirkyard was granted to the town as a burying ground in 1566. The open space was preserved more or less intact when the Parliament House and law courts were altered 1804-20, but it was lengthened by about ten yards to the eastward when the courts were extended after the Great Fire of 1824 destroyed the whole quarter between here and the Tron. Shown on *Rothiemay* 1647, it is referred to in *Town Council Minutes* in 1640 as the PARLIAMENT YARD and in 1643 as the PARLIAMENT CLOSE, the two names properly meaning exactly the same thing, and it is shown as the latter on *Edgar* 1742, *Kincaid* 1784 and *Ainslie* 1804. Notwithstanding this, *Ainslie* 1780, *Brown & Watson* 1793 and *Kirkwood* 1817 show the later variant PARLIAMENT SQUARE, a usage which *Cockburn* rightly in contempt and regret dismisses as 'foppery'; and by 1852 this had become absurdity through extension of the name to cover the square at the County Hall as well, although Edinburgh folk have had the sense to call it unofficially *West Parliament Square* or (before 1975) *County Square.*

PARROTSHOT (Niddrie) *see under* THE JEWEL, Niddrie.

PARSON'S GREEN is recorded thus from 1786 but was otherwise known as PARSON'S KNOWES, recorded as Personis Knowis in 1593. The name is Scots *parson*, parish priest, with *knowes*, hillocky ground, or *green*, grassland, and it arose because this was anciently church land belonging to the parson of Restalrig until after the Reformation, when it was acquired by the Logan family. It became a small estate with a house, shown on *Armstrongs* 1773, sited in the vicinity of the present Considine Terrace. Development started in the eastern fields in about 1881, when PARSON'S GREEN TERRACE was built, fronting the main road. LILYHILL TERRACE, running along the east side of the gardens of Parson's Green, was named in 1883, after the builder's daughter, it is said. WOLSELEY TERRACE appears in *PO Directory* 1884, probably named for Major-General Sir Garnett Wolseley, Commander-in-Chief in Egypt and Sudan 1882-84, and this was followed by WOLSELEY CRESCENT and PLACE in 1885 and WOLSELEY GARDENS in 1894. WILFRID TERRACE was named in 1883, possibly for Sir Wilfrid Lawson MP, prominent at the time in Parliament and the temperance movement, although positive evidence for the connection is lacking. ABERCORN ROAD and WILLOWBRAE AVENUE were planned in the 1880s and started, at their extreme eastern ends, by 1891. The first is named for the Abercorn family, who had owned the adjoining estate of Duddingston since 1745; and WILLOWBRAE AVENUE was so called as a branch off the road of that name—*see under* WILLOWBRAE. The naming of SCONE GARDENS in about 1891, after Scone Palace near Perth, seems to have started a theme of naming for Scottish country seats that was pursued in LISMORE CRESCENT (1899) and AVENUE (1906) for Lismore in Appin; KENMURE AVENUE (1906) for Kenmure in Kirkcudbright; and GLENLEE GARDENS and AVENUE (1907) for Glenlee, near St John's Town of Dalry, also in Kirkcudbrightshire. Meantime, development had started in the western part of the estate by 1893, when MEADOWBANK AVENUE was already formed, although its name (from MEADOWBANK, *which see*) first appears in *PO Directory* 1897, along with MEADOWBANK TERRACE. QUEEN'S PARK AVENUE, so named because it ran along the march with the Park, was named by 1898; and MEADOWBANK CRESCENT and PLACE followed in 1899. In 1934, the site of Parson's Green House was redeveloped as CONSIDINE GARDENS and TERRACE, named (at their own suggestion) for W & H Considine, lawyers concerned with the scheme.

PATERSON'S COURT (High Street) is on part of the site of the Old Meal Market. It is shown on *Edgar* 1742 and vestiges of its fore and back courts are still discernible on the east side of Wardrop's Court. It was built before 1724 by Andrew Paterson of Inch and Kirktoun, together with John Henderson of Leistoun, wright, and was also known as *Paterson and Henderson's* or *Henderson and Paterson's Court.*

PATERSON'S CLOSE and **GOLFER'S LAND** (79 Canongate) *see* BROWN'S CLOSE, Canongate.

PATERSON'S CLOSE (188 Canongate) *see* St JOHN'S CLOSE, Canongate.

PATH BRAE (Kirkliston) *see* PETH *or* PATH BRAE, Kirkliston.

PATIE'S ROAD (Colinton) probably originated in or before the 16th century as part of the access to the mills in Colinton Dell, and its historical development is bound up with that of Katesmill Road, *see under* KATE'S MILL, Colinton Dell. It began to be built up in 1926. The origin of the name is obscure, but it presumably referred to some indweller, and this probably before 1840, since the name still attaches to a section of road which was reduced to a path about that time. Given by *Ordnance Survey* 1893 as *Pattie's Road*, it evidently includes Scots *Pattie*, *Patie* or *Paty*, which is diminutive of *Peter* as well as of *Patrick*—a couple of names which have long tended to be interchangeable in Scotland, many a Peter being given *Patrick* as his 'Sunday name'. This being so, it may be significant that in the 1770s the Barley Mill in the Dell (later named Redhall Mill) was tenanted by a Peter Johnston.

PATRIOT HALL (Stockbridge) is recorded in 1775 as the name— apparently fancy—of a house and grounds for sale or to let; and *Ainslie* 1804 shows the latter extending to the west backs of Clarence Street. PATRIOTHALL BUILDINGS were built in the grounds in 1861. *Also see under* ORCHARD BRAE, Dean Park, for the *Patriotic Society's Allotment Gardens.*

PATTISON STREET (South Leith) first appears in *PO Directory* 1819, but is shown on *Kirkwood* 1817 as already partly formed on ground owned by John Pattison immediately north of his family's house at Links Place, which is shown (perhaps schematically) on *Wood* 1777 and was probably built by John Pattison, merchant in Leith, burgess of Edinburgh and Town Clerk of Leith, listed in *Williamson's Directory* 1780 as resident *at the Links.*

PAULSFIELD (Bonnyhaugh) *see under* BONNYHAUGH, Bonnington.

PAUNCH MARKET (South Leith) *see under* QUEEN STREET, South Leith.

PAXTON'S YARD (36 Grassmarket) *see* CAMERON'S ENTRY, Grassmarket.

PEACOCK COURT (Newhaven) was named by 1910, probably for the family of Thomas Peacock, who acquired land in Newhaven in 1767. The Peacock Inn is mentioned in 1779, and a Thomas Peacock was a vintner in Newhaven in 1793.

PEACOCKTAIL CLOSE (Cleikimin, Niddrie) was named in 1979 for the *Peacocktail* coal seam, recorded from 1760 onwards on maps of the Niddrie coals, which outcrops nearby and defines one side of the housing precinct or *close*. The name suggests the irridescence of the gleaming coal.

PEARCE AVENUE and **ROAD** (Drum Brae) were named in 1930 for Edward Pearce, who developed them in his nursery ground, earlier a field in Corstorphine Bank farm. The name was continued at PEARCE GROVE in 1966, nineteen years after his death.

PEARSON'S CLOSE (High Street) is shown on *Edgar* 1742, but was suppressed in 1753 in the building of the Royal Exchange, although some traces remain in the cellars. A sasine of 1615 shows that it was named for Alexander Pearson, merchant, who had previously obtained a tenement on its west side through his wife, Elizabeth Easton; and furthermore it records that before her father had this tenement it had belonged to Gilbert Knox, which accounts for the other name KNOX CLOSE, still referred to as late as 1720.

PEATDRAUGHT BAY (Dalmeny) is named on *Ordnance Survey* 1852. In absence of earlier forms, the name remains obscure; but if it is ancient, it might possibly contain the Pictish *pit-*, farm or piece of land, of which there are a few outlying examples south of the Forth.

PEAT NEUK (Coalhill, Leith) is recorded thus in 1684 and as *peit neuk* in 1691. Listed in *Williamson* 1783, it is shown on *Kirkwood* 1817 as entered from the quayside, whereas *PO Directory* 1827 gives it as 70 St Andrew Street. It was probably named for storage of peats, for in 1690 Sir Magnus Prince, ex-provost, had the *Old Guardhouse* (not far away, at the old Bridge of Leith) converted into a communal store for the fuel.

PEATVILLE TERRACE (Kingsknowe) was named in 1935 for its builder, Robert Peat of Currie, and the name was extended to PEATVILLE GARDENS in 1956.

PEEBLES WYND (High Street and Cowgate) figures on maps from *Rothiemay* 1647 to *Kincaid* 1784, but was swept away in 1785, its site becoming the west pavement of BLAIR STREET, *which see*. Its description in *RMS* 1504 as *the vennel of the late Ninian Peblis* probably refers to Ninian Peebles, town councillor in 1483; but since a letter from James III engrossed in *Town Council Minutes* 1477 refers to *Peblis Wynd* as an established landmark, the name seems to have gone still further back. A city charter of 1477 (as well as one in *RMS* 1489) mentions a deceased John de Peblis as former owner of property south of the High Street; and he might have been the Joannis Peiblis who made a gift to the chapel of St John in St Giles kirk in 1395, or the John de Pebly mentioned in *RMS* 1373 as son-in-law of Roger Hog, burgess of Edinburgh. The family evidently originated in Peebles.

PEEL TERRACE (Mayfield) *see under* McLAREN ROAD, Mayfield.

PEFFER, although recorded only in the name of PEFFERMILL (*see below*), appears to have been the Celtic name for the BRAID BURN, *which see*. Incorporating British *pefr* clear or bright, the name is frequent in Scotland as a stream name, and seems to have been translated in CLEARBURN, a name for the Pow burn immediately above its confluence with the Braid burn at Forkenford. Since the 'clear' Peffer burn and the Celtic-named 'dark or muddy' LOTHIAN BURN (*which see*) flow very close together near Niddrie Mill, it is possible that they were named in contrast to each other. PEFFERMILL is recorded in *RMS* 1630 in the phrase 'miller's lands of *Peppermylne*' and is shown as *Pepper mil* on *Adair* 1682 and other maps prior to *Kirkwood's Environs* 1817; but the *pepper-* is fairly obviously an attempt to give a meaning to *peffer-* after the ancient burn name had been displaced by *Braid-*, and notwithstanding these spellings the name is Scots *Peffer miln*, mill on the Peffer. PEFFERMILL ROAD got its name as the road *by Peffermill* to Craigmillar and Niddrie, which originally branched off the Dalkeith Road at Salisbury Green and passed to Peffermill by Clearburn, as shown on *Roy* 1753, but was subsequently altered, as shown on *Laurie* 1763, so as to branch off the Dalkeith road at Cellarbank (on the line of Prestonfield Avenue and Terrace) and altered again, in about 1820, by construction of its present western section from Cameron Bridge. PEFFER BANK was formed in 1893 on the bank above the flood plain of the burn, and was named by 1898. The nearby STATION ROAD, formed in 1884 as the access to the new *Duddingston & Craigmillar* railway station, was renamed PEFFER STREET in 1966; and MITCHELL STREET, constructed in about 1890 and named by 1905, was renamed PEFFER PLACE in 1967. NORTH PEFFER PLACE was added in 1984.

PEGGY'S MILL (Cramond) is recorded as *Pigies m(ill)* on *Adair* 1682, as *Peggiesmiln* in a sasine of 1782 and as *Pegies mill* on *Cramond Roads* 1812. The name evidently incorporates the surname of some early owner or tenant, Peggie or the Aberdeenshire Piggie. PEGGY'S MILL ROAD (the traditional name formally adopted in 1930) is the old approach to the mill, but altered at its east end.

PEMBROKE PLACE (Wester Coates) *see under* DEVON PLACE, Wester Coates.

THE PEND (Corstorphine) is traditionally named thus, from the pend or arched entry to the lane.

PENMAN'S CLOSE (south side of foot of Canongate) is listed in *Williamson's Directory* 1779 and still shown on *Brown & Watson* 1793, but like its neighbour CHARTERIS CLOSE (*which see*) it is omitted on *Ainslie* 1804. Nothing is known about the naming.

PENNY WELL (Grange) is referred to as a boundary mark in 1716. Since the name occurs elsewhere (*see* PENNY WELL, Granton) it must arise from some common circumstance. It probably derives from Scots *penny*, to feed, implying that the *well* or spring was a place where animals were brought to be fed and watered—a communal use obviously furthered if the well were on a boundary, and still more so if it were beside a public way, as in the two Edinburgh examples.

PENNY WELL (Granton) is shown on *Cramond Roads* 1812, and it may have been the *St Columba's well* mentioned in *RMS* 1601 as lying *between the lands of the common of Cramond and the seashore*. Its position near the west end of the north side of West Granton Road would fit in with use to *penny* animals (*see under* PENNY WELL, Grange) and it is in fact remembered as a watering place for horses, even although the memory has been embroidered with a fiction about a penny fee, brought in to explain the name after the original meaning of *penny* had been forgotten. PENNYWELL ROAD was developed in 1945 out of the access road to Pilton, Muirhouse and Granton Castle, shown on *Roy* 1753. The rest of the 'Pennywell' streets are built on Muirhouse ground: PENNYWELL GARDENS, GROVE, MEDWAY and PATH (1945) PLACE (1963) and COURT (1969).

PENSTON'S CLOSE (High Street) *see* DUNBAR'S CLOSE.

PENTECOX (Edmonston) figures, unnamed, on *Roy* 1753, but is named *Pentecocks* on *Knox* 1812, and while the cottages are not named on *Craigower etc* 1815, the field behind them is given as *Pentecox park*. Although earlier records are lacking, the name appears to contain British *pant*, valley, and *coxa*, foot, and to mean something like 'foot valley': apt enough, since the place is just where the Lothian or Burdiehouse burn emerges into a broad valley between Craigmillar and Niddrie Edge.

PENTLAND AVENUE and **ROAD** (Colinton) *see under* SPYLAW.

PENTLAND AVENUE, PLACE and **VIEW** (Currie) were named in 1958 for the view of the hills, and PENTLAND VIEW COURT followed three years later.

THE PENTLAND HILLS are named on *Blaeu* 1654 both as *Pentland Hill* and as *Penthlandt Hill*, while *Pentlandhilles* figures in *RMS* 1642 in connection with Dreghorn's share of grazings on their northern slopes. It seems fairly certain that the hill name derived from an earlier name *Muir of Pentland* or *Pentlandmuir*, mentioned in 1230 in a grant of tithes to Holyrood by Henry of Brade; and that this name in turn arose because a large area in the eastern part of the hill range was attached to PENTLAND (now Old Pentland), near Straiton. This place, recorded as *Pentlant* in about 1150 and shown as *Penthland* on *Blaeu* 1654, stands prominently on the higher ground overlooking the basin of the Lothian burn and the former mere at MORTON, *which see*; and both the site and the first-syllable stressing of the name suggest that it may be British *pen-llan*, head- or height-enclosure, while the map spelling *Penthland*, probably noted by Pont in 1596, may indicate that the *thl-* pronunciation of *ll-* was then still in use.

PENTLAND TERRACE (Comiston) was begun in about 1898 in the southeast of Greenbank and was named as a block of houses high above the Comiston road and looking over to the hills, a view which (unlike many streets named for a view) it continues to enjoy. In the later 1920s it was extended into the Buckstane park of Comiston; and the use of the name was continued, but neither so aptly nor so successfully, at PENTLAND CRESCENT, GARDENS, GROVE and VIEW 1934, and at PENTLAND DRIVE in 1965, all these streets being in Comiston.

PENTLAND TERRACE (Juniper Green) *see* JUNIPER TERRACE, Juniper Green.

PENTLAND VIEW ROAD (Kirkliston) was named in the 1950s, in all probability—as in so many cases of the kind—for the view from the site before the area was built up.

PERDRIXKNOWE (Meggetland) was named in 1990 as being on the west slope of the *Perdrix knowe*, partridge hill, shown as *Patrickes Know* on a map in *Steuart's Colinton* p240. The name of the bird came into Scots in the French form 'perdrix', generating many variants, including 'patrick'.

PERTH STREET (Canonmills) was named by 1829, it being sketched on *Lothian* 1829 as a proposed street connecting Fettes Row and Henderson Row with another formal street approximately on the line of Glenogle Road. Even although the name enters the *PO Directory* in 1830, the *Ordnance Survey* 1852 shows it as still a mere opening off Henderson Row, apparently nameless; and there seems to have been little development of consequence until after 1888. The connection with *Perth*—town, shire, peerage or surname—has not yet been traced.

PETER'S CLOSE (179 Cowgate) is listed on *Ainslie* 1780 and was named for Alexander Peter or Peters, wright, who built a great stone tenement for himself and his wife Isobel Dunbar before 1744. Oddly canonised as *St Peter* in *Wilson* and *Grant*, he was a Captain in the Trained Bands in 1738, had a seat in the Tron Kirk in 1745, and had stables on the east side of *Snadoun's Close on the south side of the Cowgate*. It is likely that this earlier name SNADOUN'S was for John Sawres, Snadoun herald, who had a tenement in College Wynd, later owned (in 1677) by Sir James Stanfield. (For another SNADOUN'S CLOSE *see* NEW ASSEMBLY CLOSE, High Street.)

PETH or **PATH BRAE** (Kirkliston) is recorded as *West Peth* in 1663, and is part of the ancient highroad to Linlithgow *see also* HIGH STREET *and* GATESIDE, Kirkliston. The name is Anglian *paeth* or Scots *peth*, a steep road out of a ravine (*see also* DEAN PATH *and* STANEYPETH) and the *brae* simply duplicates this and is probably a modern addition.

PEVERIL TERRACE (Inch) *see under* THE INCH, Nether Liberton.

PEW'S CLOSE (South Leith) is named on *Kirkwood* 1817 and still shown on *Ordnance Survey* 1913, occupying ground between Burgess Street and Bowie's Close. While it may have been named for Alexander Pew, wheelwright in Leith, listed in *Williamson's Directory* 1780, it is perhaps more likely that it was for one or more of a family of Pew, brewers and burgesses in Leith, noted in the period 1718-82, with the forenames Jeremiah, John and Jonathan.

PHANTASSIE or **FANTASY** (Straiton) is shown on all maps from *Roy* 1753 to *Fowler* 1845 in the position NT 280669 or thereby, but the holding evidently disappeared by 1852. The name, which also occurs near Haddington and East Linton and in Fife, is stressed on the second syllable, and is Celtic, probably British, akin to Gaelic *fàn taise*, soft or marshy slope.

THE PHYSIC WELL (Corstorphine) was a medicinal spring, shown on *Corstorphine* 1754 and 1777 and described in the *Old Statistical Account* in 1793 as having once been fashionable but 'now in total disrepute and disuse for a number of years'. The well head has been preserved, although transferred about forty yards from its original position, which was on the south side of the Stank and now within the back garden of a house in Broomhall Road.

PICARDY (Broughton) was a village of thirteen houses, shown on *Roy* 1753 and in some detail on *Fergus & Robinson* 1759, built in 1730 by the Board of Manufactures to accommodate a group of cambric weavers brought over from St Quentin, Picardy, in 1729, under a scheme by the Board's Linen Committee to establish this industry in Scotland. A documented account of this given in *BOEC XXV* shows that the other story, first published in *Wilson*, of an earlier abortive silk manufactory by Huguenot refugees is probably fanciful and quite certainly has nothing to do with the founding of the village. A redevelopment plan drawn up for the Board by William Burn in 1800 included PICARDY PLACE, named for the erstwhile village, FORTH STREET, named for the estuary, and UNION PLACE and STREET, named for the Union which brought Ireland into the United Kingdom on 1 January 1801. A projected *North Forth Street* was later developed as HART STREET, *which see*. The south side of Picardy Place (including the birthplace of Sir Arthur Conan Doyle) together with part of Union Place was swept away in misconceived roads development in 1969.

PIER PLACE (Newhaven) appears to have been formed, as a harbour work, not long before it was shown on *Lothian* 1826. The name, shown on *Ordnance Survey* 1852, describes it as an approach to Newhaven Pier.

PIERSFIELD PLACE and **TERRACE** (Piershill) were developed in 1907, followed by PIERSFIELD GROVE in 1910. The *Terrace* name was extended to take in part of the south side of Portobello Road in 1983. The name *Piersfield*, appearing at a property shown as *Piersfield Cottage* on the *Ordnance Survey* of 1852 but as *Piersfield Dairy* on that of 1893, is presumed to have been a fancy name coined from PIERSHILL, *which see*.

PIERSHILL is recorded in 1580 as *Peirieshill* and in a manner that indicates that it had been distinct as a property within Restalrig since before 1500. *The Peersback*, recorded in 1696, may be a variant form, using Anglian *baec* or Scots *back* in the sense of 'ridge'. While the name may contain the personal names *Piers* or *Perry* or *Pirrie*, all AngloNorman forms of French *Pierre*, there is no evidence for a house here much before 1700, and it is much more likely that the first part of the name is Anglian *persc* or Scots *persche*, osier, making the name akin to other 'willow' names in the vicinity of Arthur's Seat, *see under* WILLOWHEAD. EAST and WEST PIERSHILL SQUARES were formed in 1938 on the site of cavalry barracks built in 1794, which had themselves displaced the house built by John Crauford WS at Piershill in 1761. PIERSHILL PLACE (1899) and TERRACE (1908) were built in the field shown on *Duddingston* c.1800 as the *Barnyard Park*. RAMSAY LANE, shown on *Kirkwood* 1817 and presumably named for some owner or resident, was renamed PIERSHILL LANE in 1967, to obviate any confusion with Ramsay Lane in Castlehill.

PIKE-A-PLEA (Portobello) is shown on *Figgate Roads* 1783 as a piece of ground in the acute angle between the south side of the future High Street and the *common loan* (still represented by part of Hope Lane) which was the east march of Figgate. The name is rhyming slang—a *pike-a-plea body* is a person for ever pressing law cases—for a field name *pikit ley*, a grass field peak-shaped or running out to a point. There is a similar field name PIKE HOLE on Humbie farm, Kirkliston.

PILLANS PLACE (South Leith) is shown on *Pollock* 1832 and was named for James Pillans, shown on *Kirkwood* 1817 and *Thomson* 1822 as owner of the ground.

PILMUIR (Balerno) is recorded from 1437 onwards, in forms such as Pilmor and *Pilmure*, and is shown as *Pilmoore* on *Blaeu* 1654. The name is Anglian *pyll*, pool or small burn, with *mor*, muir: thus it is the 'pool or small burn in the muir'. It also occurs in Colinton—*see under* THE BAADS.

PILRIG is shown on *Blaeu* 1654 and recorded in 1448 as *Peilrig*. The name is Anglian *pyll hrycg*, ridge by the stream, and PILRIG HOUSE, built by Gilbert Kirkwood in 1638 but probably on or near the site of the earlier estate centre, stands on a ridge between the Broughton burn on the east and the Water of Leith on the north. PILRIG STREET is shown on *Ainslie* 1804 as part of a 'New Road from Newhaven to Edinburgh', and certainly this eastern stretch from Bonnington Toll was quite new. Development began at its east end in about 1810. The side name PILRIG PLACE first appears in *PO Directory* 1833. For PILRIG MODEL BUILDINGS *see under* SHAW'S PLACE, Pilrig. PILRIG AVENUE and GARDENS were named in 1933 and 1934. PILRIG HOUSE CLOSE was named in 1984 as a new close or precinct beside the restored Pilrig House.

PILRIG (Dalmeny) seems to have disappeared by 1750, but is shown on *Blaeu* 1654 as *Pilridge* and on *Adair* 1682 as *Pylridg*, very roughly in the location NT 152758. The name is Anglian *pyll hricg* or *hryggr*, ridge at the pool or stream, evidently referring to the small burn on the west side of Craigie hill.

PILTON is recorded from 1337 onwards. The name is Anglian *pyll tún*, farm toun or place beside the small stream, evidently the Wardie burn, which formed the south march of the estate. A plan of Pilton in about 1780 (*RHP 6473*) shows the main centre—probably the medieval centre—at WEST PILTON, in the vicinity of what is now West Pilton View, while the site of the steading of EAST PILTON is now in the playing field west of Pilton Drive. PILTON AVENUE, CRESCENT, DRIVE, GARDENS, LOAN, PARK and PLACE are in East Pilton and were named in 1933. WEST PILTON AVENUE, BANK, CIRCUS, CROSSWAY, GARDENS, GROVE, PARK, PLACE, RISE, ROAD,

STREET, TERRACE and VIEW were named in 1945. In 1987 West Pilton Circus was remodelled to form WEST PILTON DRIVE, GREEN, LEA and LOAN.

PINKHILL (Corstorphine) was a house and nursery ground from the early 19th century until 1971, when it was supplanted by the Post House Hotel. The name appears on *Corstorphinehill* 1885 and seems to have been a combination of *pink* for the flower and *-hill* from nearby Corstorphinehill estate. In 1902, as the nearest landmark name, it was borrowed for the station 400 yards away on the new Corstorphine Branch railway; and in 1990 it was borrowed from the station site (unfortunately in a form which usurps the original place name) as a name for the road which had originally been built to give access to the station, and was subsequently named EAST TRAQUAIR PARK, *which see.*

THE PIPES (South Leith) appears as an address in *Williamson's Directory* 1774, and is shown on *Wood* 1777 as the name for the vicinity of the water reservoir at the corner of Tolbooth Wynd and Water Lane (now Water Street) which was part of the improved water supply system brought into Leith under Act of Parliament in 1771.

PIPES CLOSE (619 High Street) is shown on *Ainslie* 1780 and was named for the pipes coming from the Water House of 1681.

PIPE STREET (Portobello) is shown on *Ainslie's Roads from Figget* 1783, and was so named because William Jamieson piped water from the Figgate burn above Rosefield to a large trough here, in order to supply his workers' houses at Brickfield. The redeveloped northern part of the street was named PIPE LANE in 1978, an earlier PIPE STREET LANE being suppressed by the same rebuilding of the neighbourhood.

PIRNIEFIELD (South Leith) appears in *PO Directory* 1805 and is shown on *Knox* 1812 as *Pirniefield* and *Pirniefield Cottage*, both owned by Rhind Esq., who is shown on *Kirkwood* 1817 as the developer of PIRNIEFIELD PLACE. It is possible that the name was coined by an owner in the same fashion as nearby SEAFIELD and SUMMERFIELD; but unless a connection with someone called Pirnie is found, it is more likely that it was a traditional name for the ground, as discussed under PIRNIEHAA *below.* PIRNIEFIELD TERRACE was named in 1932, and PIRNIEFIELD GARDENS and GROVE, together with the southward extension of PIRNIEFIELD PLACE, followed in 1937. PIRNIEFIELD BANK was added in 1954.

PIRNIEHAA (Balerno) is given on *Knox* 1812 and later maps as *Pirniehill.* Judging by the terrain and also the local pronunciation recorded on *Ordnance Survey* 1962, *-hill* was a map error for *-hall*, standing (as it does in PIRNIEHALL, Pilton) for Scots *haw* or *haugh.* While Scots *pirnie* might describe land 'marked by narrow stripes', perhaps by reedy growth in drainage channels, the terms *pirn* or *pirnie* occur in more than a dozen names in the east of Scotland,

and since in some of them the early form is *prin*, they may link up with further names like *Prinlaws*, and perhaps even with *Purin* in Fife. While early records of Edinburgh's *pirnie*-names are lacking, the evidence of other names in the group suggests that pirnie may derive from British *pren*, a tree, or else *peuran*, a pasture, and accordingly these names may be the *field* or burnside *haugh* at places earlier known as 'the place at the tree(s)' or as 'the pasture'.

PIRNIEHALL (Pilton) is shown on *Laurie* 1763 and later maps as lying between the Ferry road and the upper reach of the Wardie burn, just below the burn's source at the springs or wells of *Clay Walls* east of the Pilton road, now Pennywell Road. The name is probably the same as that of PIRNIEHAA, Balerno, *which see*.

PIRRIE'S CLOSE (246 Canongate) is given on *Ainslie* 1780 as *Perry's*, one of the many variants of the name Pirie or Pirrie, which may have originated as French *Pierre*. Feu charters suggest that a William or an Alexander Pirrie were among the earlier members of a family owning property in the close from some date prior to 1714. Mentions in the charters of pin making and of some links with Leith bring to mind the fact that, in the 1660s, pin makers from Leith were being encouraged to start up workshops in Edinburgh. In 1629 the close was also called FOORD'S or FUIRD'S, apparently for an Alexander Foord who had lands, barn and kiln here at some time prior to 1705. It may be the KINNAIRD'S CLOSE mentioned in *Maitland*, since a Malcolm Kinnaird had a tenement hereabouts, later owned by the Foords. Being in the south Canongatehead, the close was part of Edinburgh, not the burgh of Canongate.

PIRRIE STREET (South Leith) appears in *PO Directory* 1881 and was probably named for Pirrie, a builder and house agent in Duke Street at the time, who may have had some connection with David Pirie, wright in the Yardheads half a century earlier.

PITCAIRLIE'S CLOSE (29 High Street) *see* MOFFAT'S CLOSE.

PITLOCHRY PLACE (Norton Park) *see under* MARYFIELD, Norton Park.

PITSLIGO ROAD (Morningside) *see under* GREENHILL.

PITT STREET (Bonnington) was planned and named in about 1808 along with TRAFALGAR LANE, with obvious reference to the battle of 1805 and to William Pitt the younger, the Prime Minister who had led the country in the French war and had died in 1806. Development was exceedingly slow: for although TRAFALGAR LANE enters *PO Directory* in 1813 and PITT STREET in 1814, the *Ordnance Survey* 1852 shows little more than *Kirkwood* 1817, and TRAFALGAR STREET, described as 'projected' in 1828, made little or no progress until after 1870.

PITT STREET (New Town) *see under* NORTHERN NEW TOWN.

PITTVILLE STREET (earlier **PITT STREET**) and **LANE** (Joppa) *see under* RABBIT HALL, Joppa.

PLAINSTANE CLOSE (41 Canongate) *see* RAMSAY'S CLOSE, Canongate.

PLAINSTANES CLOSE (232 Canongate) is listed on *Ainslie* 1780, one of several closes so named because they were paved with flat flagstones instead of cobbles or setts. It is also recorded as THOMSON'S in 1716, for William Thomson WS, owner of a tenement on its east side. Its earlier name was YAIR'S (given as *Year's* in 1725) evidently for John Yaire, who owned property in it in 1635, or else his predecessors. Being in the south Canongatehead, the close was in Edinburgh, not the burgh of Canongate.

PLAINSTANE CLOSE (once 94 now at 78 Grassmarket) is shown on *Ainslie* 1780 but was suppressed at some time after 1852. The name indicates that it was paved with flat stones.

PLAINSTANES CLOSE (327 High Street) *see under* DON'S CLOSE.

PLATT (Ratho) is recorded as *Plat* 1379, *Platt* 1444 and *le Plat* 1452, the name being early Scots from Old French *plat*, something flat, or a spot or place, probably here referring to the flatter land west of the Ratho hills. *Roy* 1753 shows two steadings, NORTH and SOUTH PLATT, and *Armstrongs* 1773 extends the name to the PLATT HILLS of Tormain, Craw Hill and Ratho. South Platt disappears after 1812, perhaps with the advent of the Union Canal in about 1820; and North Platt was given the new descriptive name of HILLWOOD in about 1840.

PLAYFAIR STEPS (The Mound) were built soon after completion of the National Gallery in 1853. They were known as *the Mound Steps* until 1972, when in order to celebrate the quatercentenary of the death of John Knox they were named JOHN KNOX WAY—most inappropriately, considering that no way of any kind existed here in his time or for 200 years after it; and in 1978 they were renamed PLAYFAIR STEPS, to commemorate William Playfair, architect of not only the National Gallery but the Royal Scottish Academy and the New College, which make such an impressive trio of buildings in the centre of the city.

THE PLAYHOUSE CLOSES (200 Canongate) were a pair of closes in the Canongatehead, just within the boundary of Edinburgh, and were so named because they gave access to the Playhouse, the town's first purpose-built public theatre, opened in 1747 but deserted after the Theatre Royal was opened in Shakespeare Square in 1769. UPPER PLAYHOUSE CLOSE, so listed on *Ainslie* 1780, was also known as DALLAS'S, possibly for Charles Dallas, vintner in Edinburgh in 1700, although his connection with the close remains to be proved. The DOWNMOST or UNDERMOST or UNDER or OLD PLAYHOUSE CLOSE, as it is variously given on *Ainslie* 1780, *Kincaid* 1784, *Ainslie* 1804 or *Ordnance Survey* 1852, was also called INGLIS CLOSE, for Alexander Inglis, litster (i.e. dyer) in the close in 1635, as well as for a James Inglis and a (later) William Inglis WS, also owners in it.

THE PLEASANCE, as a street, is recorded from 1485 onwards as *St Leonard's vico* or *gait* or *wynd* (*see under* St LEONARD'S, Pleasance and South Side) and figures on *Siege of Edinburgh Castle* 1573. Together with St Mary Wynd (St Mary's Street) and Leith Wynd, it may have been a diversion of the approaches to suit a very early eastward extension of the burgh, *see under* NETHERBOW and BACK ROW, Pleasance. The story, started in *Maitland* 1753, that it got its 'Pleasance' name from a convent of 'St Mary of Placentia' is not merely fiction but nonsense, for no such saint, let alone a convent, ever existed. The name is simply Scots *plesance*, a park or garden, recorded in *Protocols of James Young* 1507 as the name of a house and garden, extending to half a Scots acre or thereby, on a site estimated to be round about NT 26257325, midway between Adam Street and West Richmond Street, *see under* DERENEUCH, Pleasance. But its use steadily expanded: by 1553 it had become a side name in St Leonard's Gait, *Rothiemay* 1647 shows it as the name of that suburb, and *Edgar* 1742 shows it as the street name. On *Kincaid* 1784, the section of the street beside the apex of the triangle of Dereneuch (where a tallow works or CRACKLING HOUSE stood at the head of Richmond Lane) is labelled HEAD OF THE PLEASANCE; and on *Knox* 1812 the Pleasance street name is continued yet further south, to the junction with the Crosscausey.

PLEWLAND(S) (Queensferry) figures in a charter of Robert the Bruce in *RMS* 1306-29 as *carucate land* in Queensferry and is recorded as *Plewland* from 1466 onwards or alternatively as *Plewlandfield* from 1478, while the plural forms *Plewlands* and *Plewlandsfield* appear about a century later. The area of 95 Scots acres given on the plan of *Plewlandfield* 1769 corresponds closely with the land measure of a *carucate* or *plewland*, notionally the acreage of arable that could be worked by one plough and a team of eight oxen. PLEWLANDS HOUSE, for all that it stands at the northeast corner of the little estate, was not the estate house, but was built on 'waste ground' by Samuel Wilson, merchant burgess in Queensferry, in 1641. PLEWLANDS PLACE, named in 1964, stands within the estate and in one of the fields of the SKAITH MUIR (*which see*) while PLEWLANDCROFT, named in 1988, is within the *Croft* fields shown on the estate map of 1769.

PLEWLANDS (South Morningside) was originally the name, recorded in 1497, of the whole division of BRAID west of the Linton or Braid road, which by 1599 (as recorded in *RMS* 1601) was further subdivided into *Over Plewlands* or GREENBANK (*which see*) and *Nether Plewlands*, later called PLEWLANDS. Both farms are shown on *Adair* 1682, and the march between them was at the PLEWLAND SIKE, the small tributary of the Jordan burn that runs along the south backs of Comiston Drive. The name is from Scots *plewland*, a measure of arable (also called a *pleughgate* or *carucate*) usually, but not invariably, 104 Scots acres or 8 oxgangs, notionally the area which could be worked by one plough and a team of eight oxen—

about twice the area reckoned in modern times to be workable with a pair of horses—and the original estate, extending from the Pow burn south to the Buck Stane on Buckstane Snab, evidently contained two of them. Development in (Nether) Plewlands began in the late 1870s. MORNINGSIDE DRIVE (at first named SOUTH MORNINGSIDE DRIVE, but listed by its present name when it entered *PO Directory* in 1883) replaced the old access to Plewlands and Craighouse which was blocked by the creation of Morningside Cemetery. By 1882 the Scottish Heritage Company had named and partly built the streets branching off its south side, as far west as St Fillan's Terrace: ETHEL TERRACE (1880) was named for Ethel Clarke, daughter of its builder; but the names of DALHOUSIE TERRACE, St RONAN'S TERRACE and St FILLAN'S TERRACE appear to have been fancy, as were those of St NINIAN'S TERRACE and St CLAIR TERRACE, following by 1887. CRAIGLEA DRIVE (1884) was named in 1882, by adding *-lea*, a field, to *Craig-* from adjoining Craighouse. COMISTON DRIVE (1892) was so named, not for any connection with that estate a mile away, but simply because it was a branch off the road to Comiston. By 1899 the demolition of Plewlands House (earlier Morningside Hydropathic and Morningside College) enabled the central section of MORNINGSIDE GROVE to be built on its site, approached by an extension of Craiglea Drive, as shown on *W & A K Johnston* 1905, and CRAIGLEA PLACE followed in 1909. CRAIGHILL GARDENS was named in 1923, making a further play on the Craighouse name. MORNINGSIDE GARDENS and PLEWLANDS TERRACE were begun by 1885, the latter leading to the west entrance of Plewlands farm steading. CRAIGHOUSE ROAD, shown on *Knox* 1812 as one approach to CRAIGHOUSE (*which see*) was occupied by 1899, along with CRAIGHOUSE AVENUE and TERRACE, and CRAIGHOUSE GARDENS and PARK had followed by 1905. The southern part of PLEWLANDS GARDENS was developed from the south entrance to the farm by 1912, and the street was extended over the site of the steading in about 1930. PLEWLANDS AVENUE (1923) represents the last remnant of the old road, shown on *Knox* 1812, from Briggs o Braid to Plewlands and Craighouse.

PLEYDELL PLACE (Inch) *see under* THE INCH, Nether Liberton.

POET'S BURN and **GLEN** (Currie) *see under* MOUNT PARNASSUS, Currie.

POKITSCLEIFF (West Port) is mentioned in *Protocols of James Young* 1491, with a reference to an earlier deed of 1454; and in 1492 another entry about '*Elwaldsid* now called *Pokitscleiff*' shows the latter as if it were the younger of two names for ELWALDSIDE (*which see*) a property described in a further entry as 'a pece of land callit the *polkit scleiff* abune the barras and next the kingis stabill'. In modern terms, it lay between King's Stables Lane and the highway of West Port and extended westwards from Lady Wynd, probably as far as the east backs of Spittal Street. Young's forms of the name are echoed in *Pocketsleive* 1640 and *Polkatslieve* 1649 and in all other variants except *Polcatsleis* in *RMS* 1578, where the final *s* may have been a copyist's error; but it is his two-word version *polkit scleiff* that shows the name to be Scots *scliff* or *slive*, from Anglian *scylfe*, a segment or shelf of land, which was *polkit*—i.e. noted for *polks* or *powks*, pools or puddles—a feature only to be expected in this low ground immediately under the steep banks to the south and west of it. Although Young's entry of 1492 can be read as though this landscape name was then emerging as a new name, it is more likely that it was a case of reverting to an ancient name which had been temporarily eclipsed by *Elwaldside*.

POLIS PARK (Kingsknowe) was the local name for the public park formed by infill of NEW REDHALL QUARRY (*see under* REDHALL) for long after it was officially named Redhall Public Park in about 1922. The name evidently refers to the infilling of the quarry with *polis* (i.e. civic) *rubbish*.

POLLOCK'S CLOSE (28 Cowgate) is listed on *Ainslie* 1780 and was named for John Pollock, who kept an inn and stables here in the early 1770s that served as headquarters for carriers to and from Jedburgh, Hawick, Broughton, Moffat, Stirling and Dunblane. Before that, the close was SKINNERS, possibly in connection with William Graham, skinner, who married a Catherine Alison of the family connected with the adjoining ALISON'S CLOSE; but since Grahams were skinners in Edinburgh from 1474 onwards, there could be some other family connection with the close.

POLWARTH TERRACE (Merchiston) was begun by 1870, as part of the Merchant Company's development of Merchiston, Myreside and Gorgie Muir, and was named for Walter Hugh Hepburne-Scott, 8th Baron Polwarth, who had succeeded his father in 1867, or else for his estate of Polwarth, near Duns. POLWARTH GROVE was named by 1891, although the section of main road so named seems to have been in existence ten or eleven years previously. POLWARTH CRESCENT (1879) and GARDENS (1880) were developed in the adjoining ground of North Merchiston (*see* TEMPLE PARK) and the name was continued in POLWARTH PLACE (1899) and PARK (1934). MERTOUN PLACE (1896) and HARDEN PLACE (1899) were named in the same connection, for the Polwarth family seats at Mertoun, near St Boswells, and Harden, near Hawick.

PONTON STREET (Tollcross) is shown on *Kincaid* 1784 as partly developed, and its name is recorded in 1790. Alexander Ponton, solicitor, was in practice about that time, and Ponton & Gray, solicitors, were advertising plots in the street in 1805; but the name probably goes back to Alexander Ponton, wright, who owned land in the vicinity and built a tenement on the west side of the street in 1766.

POPLAR LANE (South Leith) is shown on *Wood* 1777 and named in *PO Directory* 1807. The trees shown along its east side on *Ordnance Survey* 1852 may be some of those shown conventionally on *Ainslie* 1804 and may account for the name.

PORT EDGAR (Queensferry) appears on *Dundas* 1757, with an *Allum Works* beside the shore road (at that time still the high road to Bo'ness) and a limekiln on the western point of the bay, but without any indication of a pier or harbour. It is presumed to have been named for Edgar, the *atheling* or heir apparent to the throne of Edward the Confessor, who with his sister Margaret (later married to Malcolm III) took refuge in the Scottish court in Dunfermline in 1068; but if so, it commemorates him only in a general way, since there is nothing to connect him with the Queensferry shore in particular.

PORTERFIELD ROAD (Craigleith) was so named by 1922, but had long been the access to a small property *Porterfield*, shown on *Ordnance Survey* 1852 and probably named for A Porterfield, gardener in Stockbridge, listed in *PO Directory* 1812.

PORTGOWER PLACE (Stockbridge) is on the site of a *Rocheid Street,* sketched on *Wood* and *Kirkwood* 1823 and *Lothian* 1829 and evidently named for the Rocheid lairds of Inverleith; but it is shown on *Ordnance Survey* 1852 as still merely a secondary access to South Inverleith Mains, and it eventually took its name from *Portgower Place*, a short terrace of houses named in about 1880. The name was imported, probably by the builder and perhaps from the village of Portgower near Helmsdale, although there are other such 'goat harbours' of a lesser sort elsewhere.

PORTLAND PLACE (South Side) *see under* LAURISTON PLACE, South Side.

PORTLAND PLACE and **TERRACE** (North Leith) were conceived as parts of the GREAT JUNCTION STREET sketched on *Ainslie* 1804. PORTLAND PLACE was in fact the first part of it to be developed and is listed in *PO Directory* 1811. PORTLAND TERRACE followed in 1822. The name derived from the Duke of Portland, Prime Minister in 1807. Prior to 1966, PORTLAND STREET was ALBANY STREET (North Leith) *which see.*

PORTOBELLO got its name from a solitary house in the FIGGATE WHINS (*which see*) said by a witness in the Court of Session in 1787 to have been built by his father Peter Scott, tenant of the grazings there, as a house for his shepherd and for selling ale. In 1753 it is named as *Porto-Bello* in an advertisement of a horse race to be run from *George Hamilton's*, and in 1755 a similar notice refers to him as *George Hamilton, shoemaker, in Portobello House.* The *Statistical Account* 1794 calls it *Portobello Hut* and derives its name from the capture of Puerto Bello in Panama by Admiral Vernon in 1739, but shows no real knowledge of why the name was given, or any awareness of Scott or Hamilton or of the (later?) yarn about a sailor who had served under Vernon. The house figures on *Laurie* 1763 and apparently also on *Sutter* 1856, but was displaced in 1862 by the new town hall of Portobello, subsequently adapted as a Baptist church. Development in Figgate began with the opening of William Jamieson's brickworks in about 1765. In 1779 *Arnot* calls it *Brickfield or Portobello*; in the *Statistical Account* 1794 it is *the villages of*

Brickfield and Portobello, and by 1800 the latter name prevailed. The place grew so rapidly that it became a parliamentary burgh in 1832. PORTOBELLO ROAD (or one closely similar in alignment) is shown on *Adair* 1682 and probably originated along with KING'S ROAD (*which see*) as a way to the recognised landing place west of the mouth of the Figgate burn, although it also afforded some access to Musselburgh by a coast road along the foreshore, as shown on *Adair/Cooper* 1735, or (probably after erosion) along the PORTOBELLO SANDS themselves, as shown on *Laurie* 1763 and mentioned by Dr Alexander Carlyle in the story of his escape from Edinburgh in 1745. The existence of this route would explain why the Sands were used for a parley with Cromwell in 1650, and a review of the Jacobite army in 1745. Yet the road to Musselburgh shown on *Blaeu* 1654 ran more or less straight from Jocks Lodge to Magdalen Pans. It is still shown on *Roy* 1753, together with the new route (pointedly labelled *Road to Berwick*) that replaced it in about 1752, formed by upgrading the Portobello Road and linking it to the Pans by a new road through Figgate. Perhaps still notionally shown on *Roy*, this was to become the HIGH STREET of Portobello, so figured on *Wood's Portobello* 1824 but since then renamed PORTOBELLO HIGH STREET (to obviate any confusion with Edinburgh's High Street) not in 1896, when the burgh was amalgamated with the city, but 72 years later. PORTOBELLO PUBLIC PARK was once the *Langlands* of Easter Duddingston.

PORTSBURGH (West Port, Tollcross and Bristo) was a free burgh of barony created in 1649, when Edinburgh acquired the suburbs of HIGH RIGGS, DRUMDRYAN, TOLLCROSS, ELWALDSIDE or POKITSCLEIFF, and the East and West Crofts of BRISTO or POTTERRAW, *all of which see*. Named for the position of its two parts, the *Wester Portsburgh* outside the West Port and the *Easter Portsburgh* outside the Potterraw Port, it was administered by magistrates appointed by Edinburgh Town Council until it was finally made part of the city in 1856. PORTSBURGH SQUARE was built in 1900 on the site of a former tannery in the Wester Portsburgh.

POT HOUSE CLOSE (Cowgate) is recorded in 1761 and appears to be the entry and court immediately west of the Cowgate Port, which is shown on *Edgar* 1742 and listed on *Brown & Watson* 1793 as ALISON'S CLOSE. The first name suggests that there was a tavern in it.

THE POTTERROW (Bristo) is shown and named on *Kirk o Fields* 1567. It is frequently referred to in protocols from 1500 onwards as the 'common way' between the East and West Crofts of Bristo, but there is reason to believe that but for its new western section, so obtrusively engineered in 1965, it is part, along with the HORSE WYND (149 Cowgate) and BORTHWICK'S CLOSE (*which see*) of an ancient route which led straight to the mercat cross of the burgh. The name occurs in *Town Council Minutes* 1554, and the note in *Protocols of James Young* 1507 of a potter, John Robertson, among established owners on the west side of the street suggests that, even before then, pottery workshops had been concentrated here, clear of the town, probably in order to reduce fire risks. Shown on *Rothiemay* 1647 as *Potter ralb suburbs* (the spelling probably the Dutch engraver's) the settlement became part of the new barony of PORTSBURGH (*which see*) in 1649, and was known both as *the Potterrow* and *Easter Portsburgh*. By 1600, the name POTTERROW PORT was supplanting the original name of the Kirk o Field Port in the Flodden Wall (*see under* KIRK O FIELD) and it continued as a name for the immediate vicinity after the port was removed.

THE POTTERY (Portobello) was so named in 1978 as being a development on the site of the earliest of the Portobello potteries, shown on *Roads from Figget* 1783, founded by William Jamieson, and leased in 1810 by Thomas Yoole and his son-in-law and partner, Thomas Rathbone, the most famous of the Portobello potters, *see under* YOOLE PLACE *and* RATHBONE PLACE. As *Midlothian Pottery*, it was purchased by the town in 1942.

THE POW BURN (Craighouse to Prestonfield) ran in post-glacial times through a pair of lochs, each about half a mile long, one in the hollow along the north backs of Balcarres Street and the other east of Blackford, before entering Duddingston loch, which then stretched over one-and-a-half miles from Cameron to Niddrie Mains; and it was the residual pools and bogs, if not the lochs themselves, that gave the burn its name, recorded in 1500 as Scots *pow*, from British or Gaelic *poll*, a sluggish stream with pools and mires. It constituted the south boundary of the Burgh Muir from the 12th century onwards. By the early 18th century, as shown on *Roy* 1753, its upper reach acquired the fancy name of JORDAN BURN (*which see*) in obvious allusion to its course between the lands of Egypt in Braid and Canaan in the Muir; but below Egypt Mews, where it enters Blackford, it continues as the Pow to Cameron Bridge, where its lowest reach, variously diverted since 1880 and now running alongside the railway and entering the Braid Burn near Bridgend, was earlier also known as the CAMERON or CLEAR BURN and looped north by Clearburn in Prestonfield before picking up the tail burn from Duddingston loch at Bawsinch and joining the Braid or Peffer burn at Forkenford.

POWBURN (Mayfield) is shown on *Adair* 1682 as the place where the old Liberton road (now Mayfield Road) crossed the Pow burn; and since the Gilmerton road, representing the Roman *Dere Street*, came in in the vicinity of Savile Terrace, it appears that the Roman road crossed the Pow at or near the same point, *see under* ROMAN ROADS. Powburn is mentioned in the *Historie of James the Saxt* in connection with a skirmish in 1571 at nearby LOWSIELAW (*which see*) and it was also the name of a property of eight Scots acres feued out of the Burgh Muir in 1586, lying immediately east of the highway. POWBURN HOUSE was still extant here in 1898. WEST POWBURN was coined as a name for a new development in 1990.

POWDERHALL (Pilrig) is shown on *Adair/Cooper* 1735 as *Pouder Hall* and as *Powdiehall* on *Roy* 1753. While it is said that the name derives from a gunpowder factory set up by James Balfour and others after they were granted a monopoly in 1695, evidence that such a factory was here, or that it was called a *hall*, is lacking. It is possible that the story has been read back into the name, and that, as at POWDERHAUGH, Slateford (*which see*) this is Scots *poldre haw*, marshy haugh.

POWDERHAUGH (Slateford) is recorded in 1719, and there is mention in 1773 of 'a new mill called *Powderhaugh*'. The name is evidently early Scots *poldre haw*, marshy haugh, with the normal pronunciation *pow* for *pol* and equally normal change of *-dre* into *-der*. While it is true that, as noted in *Steuart's Colinton* (pp418-19), a county guide published in about 1647 mentions a *Powder mill* in the vicinity, it is likely that the author simply took the haugh name to be the mill name.

POWDERHOUSE CORNER (Arthur's Seat) is shown on *Ordnance Survey* 1852, as a turning in the Queen's Drive near the site of a powder magazine shown on *Kirkwood* 1817.

POWERS' or **POWRIE'S** or **POOR'S CLOSE** (Cowgate) *see* KAY'S CLOSE, Cowgate.

THE PRESIDENT'S STAIRS (Parliament Close, Old Town) were in the upper part of the ancient KIRKHEUCH (*which see*) and were named for Sir Hew Dalrymple, Lord North Berwick, lord president of session 1698-1737. They were also called the POST OFFICE STAIRS after the post office opened in the Kirkheuch in the 1760s.

PRESTON'S CLOSE (High Street) *see* STEWART'S CLOSE.

PRESTONFIELD *see under* PRIESTFIELD.

PRESTON STREET (Newington) originated as a loaning along the south march of the lands of St LEONARD'S (*which see*) with the BURGH MUIR. Thus it might be medieval or even earlier; but if the town's feuing plan of 1586 for the easter Burgh Muir did not create it, it certainly defined and established it as one of the two cross links between the Liberton and Dalkeith highgates, *see also* MAYFIELD LOAN. In the 17th century it was known as MOUNTHOOLY LOAN (*see under* MOUNTHOOLY, Newington) and it is shown on *Bypass Roads* 1763 as GIBBET LOAN (*which see*); but in 1801 Sir Robert Preston of Valleyfield and Lutton inherited the St Leonard's ground immediately to the north, and in about 1812 the loan was named PRESTON STREET, for Sir Robert or else his widow. Since the extension of the new great road to the south from Clerk Street was already envisaged, the resulting division into EAST and WEST PRESTON STREET seems to have been accepted from the beginning. PRESTON TERRACE was the side name of a property in East Preston Street from 1860 until 1880. PRESTON STREET LANE is shown on *Ordnance Survey* 1852 as a private meuse serving NEWINGTON PLACE (*which see*) and may well date back to when these houses were built in about 1825.

PRETIES CLOSE (South Leith) is named thus on *Wood* 1777 and Ainslie 1804 but is listed as *Precious Close* in the *Accurate View* 1783. *Kirkwood* 1817 lists it as BRYCE'S CLOSE, and the entry is still shown, but without a name, on *Ordnance Survey* 1852. The names were evidently from owners or tenants. The earlier one may contain a surname derived from Prathouse, near Crossgates in Fife, or from Pratis, near Largo.

PRIESTFIELD is recorded as *Prestisfeld* in a charter of 1376, which describes it as having been granted to the Cistercian monastery of Holm Cultram in Cumbria by David I, probably not long before his death in 1153, since his son Earl Henry, who had founded the monastery in 1150, himself died in 1152. The estate was secularised in 1376, but was still called *Priests Field* in 1678, when Sir James Dick combined it in a single estate (detailed on *Prestonfield* 1824) with the adjoining lands of CAMERON and CLEARBURN, *which see*; and it was perhaps in order to play down his Catholic connection, which had led to the house being burnt down in a riot in 1681, that Dick changed the name of the new barony in 1689 to PRESTONFIELD, which although its original meaning was *priest-farm field*, sounded as though it were 'Preston's field', referring to the former Preston owners of the Cameron. Nevertheless, it was the older name that was revived in about 1876, when PRIESTFIELD ROAD began to be developed out of the drive to the House; and this was continued in PRIESTFIELD AVENUE (1924) CRESCENT and GROVE (1964) and in PRIESTFIELD GARDENS, on the site of Clearburn, in 1964. The name PRESTONFIELD TERRACE appeared in *PO Directories* from 1884 until 1894, even although it was formally made part of MARCHHALL ROAD in 1885; and it became PRIESTFIELD ROAD NORTH in 1929. The present PRESTONFIELD TERRACE, which until the 1820s ran from CELLARBANK (*which see*) by Clearburn and Peffermill to Niddrie, was named in 1927, along with PRESTONFIELD ROAD and CRESCENT and two other streets which had been begun earlier under other names: PRESTONFIELD GARDENS, previously called ALSTON ROAD; and PRESTONFIELD AVENUE, once the main street of ECHOBANK (*which see*), by 1893 partly redeveloped as EASTER ROAD, and known as HAMMER or HANMER AVENUE from 1900 onwards. In 1985, PRESTONFIELD BANK was named as being on the site of Echobank.

PRIESTHILL (Liberton) *see under* GRACEMOUNT, Liberton.

PRIMROSE BANK ROAD (Trinity) was projected in the late 1870s and formed by about 1880. It took its name from the house *Primrose Bank* shown on *Pollock* 1834, but it seems that this naming was informal for some time, since the full title PRIMROSE BANK ROAD first occurs in the 1890s.

PRIMROSE GARDENS (Queensferry) was named in 1966, evidently for the family name of the earls of Rosebery, owners of Dalmeny since 1662.

PRIMROSE STREET (South Leith) is shown on *Kirkwood* 1817 as laid out, named, and just started building as one of the early developments on the Hermitage House estate, which the same map shows as *Miss Primrose's Property*.

PRIMROSE TERRACE (North Merchiston) was the first street in a housing scheme begun by the Edinburgh Co-operative Building Company (*see under* THE COLONIES, Stockbridge) in ground immediately east and west of the steading of GORGIE MAINS (*see under* GORGIE) in 1877. In naming the streets, the Company continued its earlier practice (*see under* WOODBINE TERRACE, South Leith) of basing fancy names on plants or trees, at PRIMROSE TERRACE (1877) MYRTLE and IVY TERRACES (1878) LAUREL and VIOLET TERRACES (1880) DAISY TERRACE (1882) and LILY TERRACE (1883).

PRINCE ALBERT BUILDINGS (Dummiedykes) were built in 1863, as a continuation of the VIEWCRAIGS scheme (*which see*) and were named in memory of the Prince Consort (d.1861) and perhaps more particularly because of his concern for improvement of working-class housing. They were renamed as part of Dumbiedykes Road in 1885.

PRINCE OF WALES TERRACE (Portobello) was the name given to the first completed section of the promenade, between Bath Street and Melville (now Bellfield) Street, which was opened in 1860 and named for Edward Albert, Prince of Wales, in particular because of his enthusiasm for sea bathing at Portobello, which he indulged in almost daily when residing at Holyrood. This is still commemorated by the PRINCE OF WALES FOUNTAIN erected on the promenade in that same year.

PRINCE REGENT STREET (North Leith) is sketched as a principal avenue on the *Map of Regality of Canongate* 1813, but was adjusted to provide a site for North Leith Parish Church. It was laid out by the time the church was completed in 1816, and *Kirkwood* 1817 shows it named for the Prince Regent, who became George IV four years later; but the street did not appear in *PO Directory* until 1824.

PRINCES STREET (New Town) *see under* NEW TOWN. The modern spelling has been settled since about 1840.

PRINGLE'S CLOSE (once 93 now near 59 Grassmarket) is listed on *Ainslie* 1780 and 1804, and may have been named for Stephen Pringill, owner of ground north of Greyfriars Kirkyard in 1513. The close is given in *PO Directory* 1827 as HAY'S, probably for Miss Hay & Co., grocers in 1780; but on *Ordnance Survey* 1852 the site is shown as a path on open ground.

PRIORY GROVE (Queensferry) is built in the STONYFLATTS (*which see*) in Plewlands, and was named in 1964 for the house of the Whitefriars in Queensferry—*see under* CARMELITE ROAD, Queensferry.

THE PROMENADE (Portobello and Joppa) dates from 1860, when the PRINCE OF WALES TERRACE (*which see*) was opened. By about 1890 it stretched from Pipe Street to Joppa, where ESPLANADE TERRACE was built up in the mid 1890s. Westwards, it was extended to the Harbour Green by 1900, to King's Road (as PROMENADE TERRACE) by 1905, and along the Craigentinny shore to the Black Rocks at Fillyside in the 1920s.

PROSPECT BANK (South Leith) evidently originated as a brick works, named as *Brickfield* on *Laurie* 1763, and appears to have been given its less utilitarian name (obviously for the view from this commanding site on the fifteen-metre contour above the sea) in about 1826. PROSPECT BANK ROAD was the access to the place from the beginning, but became an address for other properties after development started in about 1889. PROSPECT BANK CRESCENT was named in 1929, followed by PROSPECT BANK PLACE and TERRACE in 1932 and GARDENS and GROVE in 1935.

PROSPECT STREET (Dummiedykes) was developed in Dishflat in 1869, and PROSPECT PLACE and TERRACE followed in 1870. The name no doubt referred to the view of the Park and Crags, although—oddly enough—the streets were not built to face it.

PROVOST MILNE GROVE (Queensferry) was named in 1972 for James Milne, provost of Queensferry 1970-75, who was to be the last provost of the royal burgh and first representative of Queensferry in the City of Edinburgh District Council in 1974.

PUDDOCKIE (Canonmills) is recorded as *Paddockhall* in 1724, and in 1745 James Rannie, farmer of over 50 Scots acres at Trinity Mains and Paddockhall, was bailie of the Burlaw Court of Leith. The name is still in use for the vicinity of the ancient ford (some 150 yards upstream of the bridge at St Marks Place) which was the only crossing hereabouts until Canonmills bridge was built in 1768; and the detail on *Fergus & Robinson* 1759 suggests that Paddockhall was a holding on the north side of the river, probably losing its identity when the Warriston estate was reorganised in about 1774, and perhaps being affected by a change in the course of the river, in about the same period. The name is early Scots *paddok haw*, haugh noted for frogs or toads, *hall* being the typical spelling for *haw* in the 18th century, *see also* PADDOCKHOLM, Corstorphine.

PUNCHINLAW (Kirkliston) is thus on *Roy* 1753, *Punchen Head* on *Knox* 1812 but *Puncheonlaw* on *Carlowrie* c1800 (where it is shown and listed as a farm of 59 Scots acres in the northwest part of the estate) and on *Ordnance Survey* 1852. The *law* could refer to the slight rise at the site of the steading at NT 13737534, or (perhaps more likely) to the high ground covered by most of the farm, projecting south-eastwards parallel to Craig Brae. There is nothing with any resemblance to a *puncheon* or cask; but a derivation from Scots *punkin* or *punckin*, hoof marks in wet ground, is possible, for there is a sluggish burn in the slack that separates the ridge from Craig Brae, figured boldly on *Forrest* 1818. On the other hand, if early forms were to hand, it might be found that *punchin* stands for a place name in its own right, since there is a slight resemblance to some historic forms of the name Pinkie in Midlothian, which is from British *pant cyn*, valley-wedge, topographically possible here: but in absence of early forms this is pure speculation.

ANDRO PURVES'S CLOSE (10 High Street) *see* WORLD'S END CLOSE.

PURVES'S CLOSE (42 High Street) *see* SOUTH FOULIS'S CLOSE.

PURVIS'S CLOSE (55 High Street) *see* TRUNKS CLOSE.

Q

QUALITY STREET (Davidson's Mains) appears in *PO Directory* 1902 as the address of a single occupier, but does not reappear until some years later. Although the presumption must be that the resident invented his address sometime before the directory was edited in 1901, it is possible that it was connected with J M Barrie's *Quality Street*, despite the fact that that play was first staged in September 1902; and even if the address was borrowed from QUALITY STREET in Leith (*which see*) or North Berwick, there would still be a connection with the play, for Barrie picked up his title from these streets in 1899.

QUALITY STREET and **LANE** (South Leith) are perhaps indicated on *Siege of Leith* 1560 but are certainly shown on *Collins* 1695 and *Naish* 1709. QUALITY STREET is listed in *Williamson's Directory* 1773 and named on *Wood* 1779; but the *Quality Wynd* mentioned in *Maitland* 1753 is clearly the lane named QUALITY LANE on *Wood*. An eastern extension of this lane, leading to Constitution Street, is named as NEW KIRK LANE on *Wood* 1779 and as NEW KIRK STREET on *Ainslie* 1804, obviously because it led to the *New Kirk* (later St John's) built as a chapel-of-ease in Constitution Street in 1773; but a new name MEUSE LANE appeared in *PO Directory* 1812 and on *Thomson* 1822 and continued to be used as an address until 1865, even although the *Ordnance Survey* in 1852 noted the lane as an eastward part of QUALITY LANE. The same map shows the adjoining QUALITY COURT, which appeared in *PO Directories* from 1832 to 1893. The 'Quality Wynd' name may have been related to the house at its west end which Maitland believed to have been built by Mary of Guise; but considering that Leith was more or less deserted by the nobility soon after Mary's time, a hundred years before the phrase 'the quality', in the sense of persons of high birth, was first recorded in 1693, it seems likely that the street name was not traditional, but was invented for historical reasons, perhaps not long before 1753, and perhaps influenced by the name 'Quality Court' which had begun to be attached to a new and fashionable development in Chancery Lane, London, in 1720. Even so, it is surely regrettable that, to obviate any confusion with street names given in Davidson's Mains at least 150 years later, these streets were renamed MARITIME STREET and LANE in 1967, in a merely general reference to Leith's shipping interests. It would add an ironic twist if, as seems likely, there was some connection between J M Barrie's *Quality Street* and the appearance of that name in Davidson's Mains, for Barrie evidently evolved his play's title from a note he made in 1899 of 'Quality Streets, in Leith and North Berwick'.

QUARRY CLOSE (Crosscausey) is shown on *Kirkwood* 1817 (earlier maps show detail which suggests that it may have been entered by a pend) and its name, shown on *Ordnance Survey* 1852, arose because it gave access to a quarry recorded in 1734 as being open here in the property of Bellsfield.

QUARRY COTTAGES (Niddrie) *see under* LAWHOUSE, Niddrie.

QUARRYHOLES (South Leith and Calton) was the name of a pair of farms, separated by the *strype* or tailburn of Lochend loch which crossed Easter Road in the vicinity of Bothwell Street. They are shown on *Adair* 1682 as N(ETHER) QUARRYHOLE and O(VER) or UPPER QUARRYHOLE, but the reference to *Ovir Querrelholis* in *RMS* 1588 uses the plural form. The name is Scots for 'stone-quarry hollows', and the scanty map evidence suggests that any quarries were quite small and probably medieval. Nether Quarryholes stretched from the Greenside burn eastwards to the Lochend road, and its house and steading, cleared away in the 1930s, stood on the line of Dickson Street and about 50 yards north of Dalmeny Street. The steading and stackyard of Upper Quarryholes, shown on *Kirkwood* 1817, stretched back about 100 yards from the west side of West Norton Place; but it was suppressed in the 1820s when the south end of Easter Road was altered to make connection with the Regent Road.

QUARRY HOWE (Balerno) was named in 1985 by continuing the traditional name for this place in the hollow left by the quarrying that once was an important local industry.

QUARRYVIEW and **QUARRYBANK** (Wester Hailes) *see under* WESTBURN, Wester Hailes.

QUAYSIDE STREET (North Leith) *see under* St NINIAN'S WYND.

QUEEN ANNE DRIVE (Newbridge) was named by 1974 for the brand of whisky being bottled there.

QUEEN CHARLOTTE STREET (South Leith) figures on both *Collins* 1693 and *Naish* 1709. Its relationship to the 'Musselburgh gate' shown on *Map of the Siege of Leith* 1560 is uncertain, but *Naish* shows it as still the access to the shore road to Musselburgh as well as to Leith Links. Indeed, the street was known as the LINKS (road) until about 1776, when a number of Leith streets were renamed and this one was called CHARLOTTE STREET, for Charlotte Sophia of Mecklenburg, who had married George III in 1761. Nine years later the name was duplicated by the naming of CHARLOTTE STREET in the New Town; and in 1968, to obviate any confusion, the Leith street was renamed

QUEEN CHARLOTTE STREET. At the same time CHARLOTTE LANE, shown on *Naish* 1709 and named on *Knox* 1822, was restyled QUEEN CHARLOTTE LANE.

QUEEN MARGARET DRIVE (Queensferry) is built in MUIRHALL, probably in the vicinity of the RAVEL (*which see*) recorded in 1577. The street was named by 1948 for Margaret, second wife of Malcolm Canmore King of Scots, to commemorate her connection with the burgh of QUEENSFERRY, *which see*. Whether the connection of Muirhall with the endowment of the ferry was also in mind is not recorded.

QUEEN'S AVENUE and **QUEEN'S AVENUE LANE** (Blackhall) date from the later 1900s, and are therefore most likely to have been named for Queen Alexandra. QUEEN'S CRESCENT, begun in 1910, was inelegantly renamed QUEEN'S AVENUE SOUTH in 1968, in order to obviate any confusion with Queen's Crescent in Mayfield. QUEEN'S GARDENS and ROAD were named in 1923.

QUEEN'S BAY CRESCENT (Easter Duddingston) was developed in part of the grounds of Easter Duddingston Lodge by 1899. The name is fancy.

QUEENSBERRY HOUSE (64 Canongate) was built by James Smith, mason, in 1681-86 as a mansion for Charles Maitland, 3rd Earl of Lauderdale, who forthwith sold it to William Douglas, 1st Duke of Queensberry. After serving as the family's town house, it was converted into flats, and finally sold to form a barracks in 1803.

QUEEN'S CRESCENT (Mayfield) *see under* McLAREN ROAD, Mayfield.

THE QUEEN'S DRIVE (Queen's Park) was named as a new scenic drive round the royal park, opened by Queen Victoria in 1846.

QUEENSFERRY was a burgh of Dunfermline Abbey from before 1300. It became a royal burgh in 1636, and was included in the new City of Edinburgh District in 1975. Despite strong tidal currents that evidently generated its Gaelic name of CASCHILIS or *cas chaolas*, fast-running strait, the narrows in the firth must have been a crossing from earliest times. There is nowhere any suggestion that Margaret of Hungary, Queen of Scots 1069-93, founded the ferry; but the evidence of her chaplain Turgot, supported by the terms of later charters, is that she improved and consolidated it by endowing it with boats, hostels on either shore, and a right of free passage for poor folk and pilgrims. By 1150 it was being called 'the queen's ferry', and it is one of the three dozen features in Scotland named on the maps of Matthew Paris of St Albans in about 1250. Dunfermline Abbey had a half share in its operation, together with a grant from Malcolm IV (or possibly from his great grandfather Malcolm Canmore) of land on the south shore which included MUIRHALL (which see) and probably also the site of the burgh. In charters of Robert the Bruce 1306-29 the place is referred to as *Queensferry* and also (as it is today) as *The Ferry*; and the further alternative of *South Queensferry* first appears in 1558.

THE QUEENSFERRY ROAD (Grassmarket to Queensferry) is basically an ancient route, shown on *Blaeu* 1654 and in more detail on *Roy* 1753, which ran from the Grassmarket to Queensferry *via* Drumsheugh, Bell's Mills, Blackhall, Muttonhole (now Davidson's Mains) and the old Cramond Brig. At least part of it (from Blinkbonny to Muttonhole) followed the line of a Roman road, *see under* ROMAN ROADS. Its first section is now KING'S STABLES ROAD, *see under* KING'S STABLES. Its second section ran through KIRKBRAEHEAD and is now represented by QUEENSFERRY STREET, BELFORD ROAD and QUEENSFERRY TERRACE (*all of which see*) except that until about 1780 the route ran along the march between Drumsheugh and Coates, *see under* DRUMSHEUGH LANE *and* BELFORD ROAD. In 1832, most of this second section, from Drumsheugh to Deanpark Toll at the north end of Queensferry Terrace, was bypassed as main road by the opening of the DEAN BRIDGE and a new length of QUEENSFERRY ROAD looping through the Dean estate and rejoining the original road at Deanpark Toll. Passing through Blackhall, the third section of the original route struck straight for Muttonhole, on a line probably Roman and still represented by parts of HILLHOUSE ROAD and CORBIEHILL ROAD (*which see*) and thence turned westward along MAIN STREET and part of EAST BARNTON AVENUE, continuing on a line now lost (but still traceable in the plantings shown on *Ordnance Survey* 1852) to the corner of the Cramond Regis policies at PARKNEUK, where it turned sharply north past BONNYFIELD and then west by a connection largely lost, but for a portion of BRAEHEAD GROVE, leading to the old CRAMOND BRIG. In 1824 the greater part of this third section was bypassed by a new highway branching off north of Craigcrook and heading for a new bridge over the Almond just upstream of the old one, *see under* HILLHOUSE ROAD. Since the river, prior to 1975, was the county boundary, the fourth section of the route, now B924 and part of A90, is named EDINBURGH ROAD, as leading from Queensferry.

QUEENSFERRY ROAD (Kirkliston) is the historic *road to Queensferry*, originally starting at the east end of the High Street, as shown on *Kirkliston* 1759. With the coming of the railway in 1866, the lower part of it was named STATION ROAD—i.e. leading from Main Street to the station. For over 100 years the section between Main Street and Loanhead was known as the SCHOOL BRAE, for the school which was in Loanhead until it was transferred to a new building in the western part of the village in 1974.

QUEENSFERRY STREET (West End) was known by the general name of KIRKBRAEHEAD (*which see*) until about 1815, when the section south of Melville Place began to be called QUEENSFERRY STREET, as part of the Queensferry road. Similarly, its northern section, extending to Drumsheugh Toll at the head of Belford Road, was known simply as DRUMSHEUGH until after the Dean Bridge was opened in 1832. QUEENSFERRY STREET LANE, shown on

Kirkwood 1817, originated as a meuse lane to Shandwick Place. Its present name appears on *Ordnance Survey* 1852. QUEENSFERRY TERRACE appeared in the 1880s as a side name in Belford Road, and remained so until the west side of the street was developed for housing.

THE QUEEN'S PARK or **HOLYROOD ROYAL PARK** originated for the most part as the GIRTH or sanctuary of Holyrood abbey, taken over by the king at some unknown date before 1541, when *Town Council Minutes* record that James V had called upon the town to build the 'park dike', described in 1554 as 'circulit about Arthurs Sett, Salisborie and Duddingston craggis'. St Ann's Yard and other areas next the palace were added in the later 19th century, and the Park was completed in 1923 by the gift of Duddingston Loch. It has various names, of two distinct kinds. In the first place, from the city's point of view it has always been *the King's park*, changing to *the Queen's park* in 1837 and 1952, when Victoria and Elizabeth came to the throne; and *the Abbey park* or *park of Holyroodhouse* (1677) are names of a similar traditional sort, recalling its origin. But since 1841, when the earls of Haddington ceased to be its hereditary keepers, the park has been administered along with the other royal park in Linlithgow, and has been distinguished from it as *Holyrood Royal Park* or *Holyrood Park*. Only in recent years, assisted by their use in promotion of the Park for recreation, have these administrative names threatened to oust and suppress the traditional ones.

QUEEN'S PARK AVENUE (Parson's Green) *see under* PARSON'S GREEN.

QUEEN'S PLACE (Greenside) was named by 1806, perhaps for the reigning Queen Charlotte, but perhaps for Mary of Guise, Queen Regent, who had attended the nine-hour long performance of Lyndsay's *Ane Pleasand Satyre of the Thrie Estaits* here in Greenside in 1554. Named on *Ordnance Survey* 1852, the street was cleared away in the 1960s.

QUEEN'S PLACE (South Leith) is shown on *Kirkwood* 1817, when the terrace must have been quite new, since it appears in *PO Directory* only in 1819. It was probably named for Queen Charlotte, who died in 1818.

QUEEN STREET (New Town) *see under* NEW TOWN. The modern spelling appears on *Ainslie* 1804 and had prevailed by the 1820s.

QUEEN STREET (South Leith) seems to belong to the sett of the medieval streets of Leith, even although it is not shown on the *Siege of Leith* 1560. It is recorded in 1669 as the *Paunch* or *Pench* (i.e. pudding) *market*. According to *Maitland* 1753, a building at the north corner of the street with the Shore might have been a BOURSE, *which see*. The street is QUEEN STREET in *Williamson's Directory* 1773 and on *Wood* 1777: the naming may have been a counterpart to that of KING'S STREET, South Leith (*which see*) and if so, fairly recent. In

1966 it was changed to SHORE PLACE, for fear of confusion with Queen Street in the New Town.

QUHITCROFT or **WHITCROFT** (New Town) *see under* LOCHBANK, New Town.

THE QUILTS and **QUILTS WYND** (South Leith) *see under* THE BOWLING GREEN.

R

RABBIT HALL or **HAW** (Joppa) is shown on *Duddingston & Brunstane* c1800 as a farm stretching along the north side of the highroad, between the boundary of Figgate (now the east backs of Marlborough Street) and the village of Joppa, now represented by Lower Joppa. The steading was where the parish kirk now stands in Bellfield Street. The ground was also called the *Links of Duddingston*, and *North Links or Rabbit Ha'*, and it is clear that (as is true of nine out of ten *-hall* place names) the second part of the name is not Anglian *heall*, a house, but Anglian *halh* or Scots *haw* or *haugh*, nook of land; and *Baird's Duddingston & Portobello* testifies to the rabbits. It is possible that, as at LEITH LINKS and at St Andrews, these links were regularly used for farming rabbits as a supply of fresh meat. In 1801 the Marquis of Abercorn had a plan drawn up for development of the farm in six main streets, evidently named at the time. *Wood's Portobello* 1824 shows them all, although feuing was still sporadic and confined to the first four at that date. MELVILLE STREET was named for Henry Dundas, Viscount Melville, MP for Midlothian, and a leading member in the governments of William Pitt the Younger, whose name was given to PITT STREET; but both these streets have been renamed, to obviate any confusion with Melville Street in Coates or Pitt Street in Leith: in 1966 Pitt Street and its meuse became PITTVILLE STREET and LANE, *Pittville* having been a house name in the street since the mid 19th century and a recognised side name since 1929; and in 1968 Melville Street became BELLFIELD STREET, taking the nearby and assonant name of BELLFIELD, *which see*. JOHN STREET and JAMES STREET were given the Marquis's forenames, and HAMILTON STREET his surname; but in 1967 the latter was inelegantly renamed BRUNSTANE ROAD NORTH, to obviate any confusion with a minor street in Bathfield, North Leith—ironically enough, one that has since been suppressed by redevelopment. JAMES STREET LANE was named by 1898, and JOHN STREET LANE by 1912. The sixth and last of the main streets, named PAISLEY STREET for one of Abercorn's subsidiary titles, was planned but never built.

THE RADICAL ROAD (Salisbury Crags) figures on *Kincaid* 1784 as a *New Walk by the foot of the (Salisbury) Rock*. Scott, in *Heart of Midlothian* 1818, so praised 'that wild path' that in 1820 a committee running a scheme for relief of the unemployed in the West of Scotland brought over a squad of weavers to repair and upgrade it, and the name is said to come from their political persuasion.

RAEBURN PLACE (Stockbridge) is shown on *Ainslie* 1804 as *Road from Queensferry* but seems to have been little more than a local access road until after the stone bridge was built at Stockbridge in 1786. It began to be developed for housing in about 1814, and is shown on *Kirkwood* 1817 named for its position in the St Bernard's estate of Sir Henry Raeburn RA at DEAN HAUGH, *which see*. Until 1968, RAEBURN STREET was known as HERMITAGE PLACE, Stockbridge, *which see*. RAEBURN MEWS, coined in 1980 as the name for a precinct of housing on former industrial ground, is fancy, for the style of the place.

RAE'S CLOSE (87 Canongate) *see* CAMPBELL'S CLOSE, Canongate.

RAE'S CLOSE (281 Canongate) is mentioned as an established name in 1568, indicating that the Canongate's connection with someone of the name can scarcely be much later than Edinburgh's, which goes back to Thomas Ra, smith in 1492. The family's connection with the close continued for over 200 years. James Rae, the King's barber in the Canongate, was made burgess of Edinburgh and treasurer of the Canongate in 1678, and built or rebuilt the tenement in the close which his great grandson David inherited in 1765. In 1891 the close is referred to as NEW LOGAN'S *formerly Rae's*, but nothing more is known of this.

RAMSAY GARDEN (Old Town) is an exuberant development of 1892-95 incorporating the house, nicknamed the *Goose pie*, which Allan Ramsay the poet built for himself in about 1740, together with a terrace of houses added in 1768 by his son, Allan Ramsay the painter. The Goose pie is named on *Kincaid* 1784 in the engaging 18th-century style of *Ramsay Hut*, with (*Ramsay*) *Street* for the later terrace; but *Brown & Watson* 1793 and *Campell's Directory* 1804 name both *Ramsay Garden*, while *Ainslie* 1804 gives *Ramsay Gardens*. The name clearly derives from the two Ramsays; and the same is probably true of RAMSAY LANE, which appears unnamed on the 18th-century maps, but is listed in *PO Directory* 1827. Reports of connections of other and earlier Ramsays with this part of Castle Hill seem to be inconclusive in themselves, and offer no evidence of a street name.

RAMSAY LANE (Jocks Lodge) *see under* PIERSHILL.

RAMSAY PLACE (Portobello) was built after 1870 as an offshoot of RAMSAY LANE, the original entrance drive to RAMSAY LODGE, built in about 1780 by General Ramsay L'Amy, who retired here after service in the West Indies. By 1824, as shown on *Wood's Portobello*, the Lane had developed a link with Tower Lane (*see under* THE TOWER, Portobello) and by 1836 it had supplanted its name. The combined street continued as Ramsay Lane until 1967, when in order to obviate any confusion with Ramsay Lane in Castlehill it was renamed BEACH LANE (rather fatuously, considering that a score of streets in Portobello do the same) because it leads to the beach.

RAMSAY'S CLOSE (41 Canongate) is recorded in 1762 and shown on *Ainslie* 1780, and was named for Peter Ramsay, stabler, and a number of his successors, who had property here, acquired from John Hunter of Abbeyhill in 1694. The close was also called BAXTERS'S, for a house owned by the Incorporation of Bakers of the Canongate but acquired by James Ramsay in 1762. It is recorded in 1887 as having been PLAINSTANES CLOSE, indicating that it was paved with flagstones. A James Ramsay, burgess of Queensferry, is mentioned in *Canongate Charters* 1902 as having had ground in this vicinity, but the connection has not been traced.

RAMSAY ROW and **SQUARE** (Newhaven) appear on *Ordnance Survey* 1852, and were presumably named for their developer.

RAMSAY'S MOUNT (South Leith) *see under* TIMBER BUSH, South Leith.

RAMSLACK (Balerno) is shown on *Knox* 1812, and *Ordnance Survey* 1852 marks it as a ruin on the summit just east of NT 170643. Being Scots *slack* from Old Norse *slakki*, a hollow or small valley, the name presumably originated in the howe of the Bavelaw burn curving round south and east of the farmstead; and its first part is probably *ramsh*, from Anglian *hrammse*, wild garlic, and meaning 'with rank growth'. Another RAM SLACK is shown on *Spylaw* 1798 as immediately south of the modern Bonaly Reservoir.

RANDALSTON (Cramond) is recorded in *RMS* 1329-71 as *Randalistoun*, part of it is referred to in *RMS* 1654 as 'the lands commonly called the Outfield of Randerstone in the lordship of Lawriestone', and *Wood's Cramond* 1794 notes 'Randelston' as 'now included under Lauriston'. Part, or all of it appears to have become SILVERKNOWES (*which see*) but in charters it is always coupled with Lauriston, and it is possible that it was an earlier name for that estate. Evidently *Randulf's tún* or farm, it incorporates an Old Norse personal name; but since the word *tún* was common to both Anglian and Old Norse, this Randulf may have been a Norse-speaking settler of the 9th or 10th centuries or else some later Northumbrian of Norse descent.

RANDOLPH CLIFF and **CRESCENT** (Drumsheugh) were developed in the MORAY ESTATE, *which see*. RANDOLPH PLACE is an earlier development, shown on *Stranger's Guide* 1816 as CHARLOTTE PLACE; and this, evidently borrowed from CHARLOTTE SQUARE (*which see*) was the accepted name of the street until 1901. Nevertheless, *Ordnance Survey* 1852 shows it more precisely as a side name for the buildings on its south side and those round the corner in Queensferry Street, and the same map shows RANDOLPH PLACE (evidently derived from RANDOLPH CRESCENT) as a side name on the north side of the street. Both *Charlotte Place* and *Randolph Place* appear in *PO Directory* from 1859 until 1903, when the latter prevailed as the street name. CHARLOTTE LANE is shown in 1816 and named on *Ordnance Survey* 1852. RANDOLPH LANE is shown as open ground on *Knox* 1821, but as a plan for a mews on *Kirkwood* 1823.

RANKEILLOR STREET (South Side) is shown on *Kirkwood* 1817 as already named and just beginning to be built up in the middle of its north side. Developed by the heirs of Dr John Hope MD, Professor of Botany and founder of the Botanic Garden (*see under* HOPE CRESCENT, Leith Walk) on land which he had acquired in 1772, the street was named for Rankeillor in Fife, estate of his grandfather Archibald Hope, who sat in the Court of Session as Lord Rankeillor, and whose son, Thomas Hope of Rankeillor, drained the South Loch, *see under* HOPE PARK.

RANKIN ROAD (West Mains) was named in 1932 for William Rankine, nephew of William Little of Liberton, who inherited that estate from his uncle in 1686 and assumed the Little name. RANKIN AVENUE and DRIVE took their name from RANKIN ROAD in 1952.

RANKIN'S CLOSE (West Crosscausey) is shown on *Kirkwood* 1817 and named on *Ordnance Survey* 1852. It was named for William Rankin, tailor here in 1780.

RANNOCH GROVE, PLACE, ROAD and **TERRACE** (Clermiston) *see under* CLERMISTON MAINS.

RANSFIELD (Ratho) is shown on *Roy* 1753 and the name is probably Scots *rauns field*, a field marked by rowans or mountain ash. In the countryside (even more so in the bleaker landscape before the agricultural improvements of the 18th century) even a small feature can be distinctive enough to generate a place name.

RANSOME GARDENS (Clermiston) *see under* CLERMISTON MAINS.

RAPERLAW'S WYND (231 Cowgate) is also rendered corruptly as RAPLOCH'S or HAPPERLAW'S CLOSE, and is given as THRAPLE'S CLOSE on *Ainslie* 1780 and 1804. It is mentioned in *Protocols of John Foular* 1530 and 1532 as *Reparlawis* or *Raperlawis Wynd*; and the name possibly came from David Raperlawe, burgess in Edinburgh in 1438, or else from William Raperlawe, mentioned in 1471 and also in 1487 (quoted in *RMS* 1498) as a deceased former owner of land here on the south side of the Cowgate.

RATCLIFFE TERRACE (Causeyside) appeared in 1850 as the name of a terrace of houses in the rear of RATCLIFFE PLACE, itself recorded five years earlier, and shown on *Ordnance Survey* 1852 as on the west side of Causeyside, south of Grange Loan. Probably named for their builder, both groups were cleared in about 1880, to make room for tenements; but the name RATCLIFFE TERRACE reappeared some 35 years later, now as the name of part of Causeyside.

RATHBONE PLACE (Portobello) was named in 1981 as being partly on the site of a property shown on *Wood's Portobello* 1824 as *Rathbone Place*, residence of Thomas Rathbone, the most distinguished of the Portobello potters, who with the help of his father-in-law, Thomas Yoole (*see under* YOOLE PLACE) set up the firm of Thos. Rathbone & Co, stoneware makers, at the foot of Pipe Street in 1810; a business carried on into the 1850s by his son Samuel.

RATHO is recorded in 1258, and parts of its kirk date from the previous century. The early forms *Ratheu* 1258, *Ratho* 1292 and *Rethow* or *Rathow* 1315 suggest that the name is Celtic *ratha*, place of the *rath* or *raths*, a term which might have any of three meanings here. Firstly, as 'fort(s)', it might refer to the British forts still visible on nearby Dalmahoy and Kaimes Hills, which are within the parish, or more particularly to a stone 'encampment' of some sort on South Platt Hill, immediately west of the kirk, reported by an eyewitness in the *Statistical Account* 1792 as 'recently in great measure destroyed'. Secondly, the term might mean a monastic enclosure of the Columban kirk; and the antiquity of Ratho kirk, and the fact that it adjoined the extensive kirk lands of the ABTHANE OF RATHO, a Gaelic term for lands supporting a monastery, would suggest that there may have been foundation of the kind in the vicinity of the kirk, and the nearby name BELLMANSKNOWE (*which see*) might point in the same direction. Thirdly, *rath* was a term for a 26-acre holding, and this land name may figure as *raw* in the NORTH RAW and WEST RAW of Ratho, recorded in 1408 and 1659 respectively. *Blaeu* 1654 shows *Rathou*, but *Adair* 1682 shows *Ratho k(irk)* and *Ratho toun* or farm, and *Hatton etc* 1797 shows the same division, with the burn between the two. For *Rathobyres* and *Rathorigg* (later *Ratho Bank* and *Ashley*) *see under* ABTHANE OF RATHO. RATHO MYRE, recorded in *RMS* 1540 and shown on *Blaeu*, was once a loch three-quarters of a mile long, lying in the hollow between Ransfield and the village, and *Blaeu* shows a place LOCHEND in the same vicinity as MERRYLANDS, *which see*. RATHO HOUSE is shown on *Roy* 1753 and was renamed RATHO PARK between 1902 and 1912, and RATHO PARK ROAD is named as access to it. RATHO HALL dates from about 1800, but *Armstrongs* 1773 shows earlier buildings on the site. RATHO MAINS appears on *Gellatly* 1834 but its steading is shown considerably further south on *Knox* 1812. RATHO STATION was built in the later 1840s.

RATOUN or **ROTTEN ROW** (South Leith) may have been the *porta* or 'avenue' of John of Petendrech referred to in Robert Logan of Restalrig's grant of land in Leith to Edinburgh in 1314. It is recorded as *Ratoun raw* 1453, *Rantoneraw* 1489, *Rattounraw* 1505, and as *Rotten Row* in the 18th century. Frequent in both Scotland and England, this name has been taken to be from Old French *raton*, a rat, and implying a rat-ridden row of houses; but checks of several of the sites now suggest that it is a land name, with the root early Scots *roten* from Old Norse *rotinn*, soft, friable or yielding (ground); and here in early Leith it might have been a sandy way, contrasting with the bogginess of the DUB RAW, *which see*. A new name WATER LANE appears on *Wood* 1777. Probably part of the 'improvement' of Leith street names proposed in the 1770s, it obviously referred to the new water supply at THE PIPES, *which see*; but it was slow to catch on, for it was 1813 before it was used in the *PO Directory*, and forty years later *Hutchison* was still remarking that Leithers were more familiar with the street as the *Rotten Row*. It was raised to the further dignity of WATER STREET in 1872.

RATTERAY'S CLOSE (115 Cowgate) is listed on *Ainslie* 1780 as AYRE'S, being so named for Joseph Eayr or Ayer, brewer here some time before 1762, by which year the brewery was bought by James Rattray (hence the alternative name RATTERAY'S) but seems to have been shared by the heirs of Joseph Ayer, including James Ayer, still occupier here in 1780. By 1799, James, or some other member of the family of the same name, moved to Canonmills, *see under* EYRE PLACE, Canonmills. The close was also ROBERTSON'S, for Thomas Robertson of Lochbank, owning property here in the later 17th century, apparently on the east side of the close, adjoining West Campbell's Close at 109 Cowgate. Still later it was BISHOP'S, evidently for James Bishop, cowfeeder (i.e. dairyman) and spirits merchant, owner and resident in the close in 1824.

RATTOUN RAW (Ingliston) was an alternative name of Eastfield in INGLISTON, *which see. See also* RATOUN RAW, South Leith.

THE RAVEL (Queensferry) is recorded in 1577 and referred to in *RMS* 1629 as a part of the runrig farm of MUIRHALL, *which see*. The name is Scots (from the Scandinavian) *raivel*, a railing, and suggests that there was some sort of railed structure or enclosure in this corner of the Muirhaw—cf. RAVELRIG, Balerno, a name which might also suggest something special in part of a farm. The entries of RAVEL BANK on *Dundas* 1757 and *Barnbougle & Dalmeny* c1800 show between them that this subsidiary name belonged to the whole of the east bank of the Ferry burn (not merely as now, to the wooded bank south of Jock's hole), and it might be that the *raivel* was a fence along the brink of these steep slopes.

RAVELRIG (Balerno) is recorded from 1454 onwards. Possibly shown on *Blaeu* 1654 but misspelt as *Quailridge*, it appears on *Adair* 1682, and *Adair/Cooper* 1735 adds *Ravilrige Mill*, which is either the Royal Mill or the *Craigmiln* (farm) shown on *Ravelrig* 1764. The early forms *Ravilrig* and *Revelrig* show that the name includes Scots *ravel* or *raivel*, a railing or balustrade; and while it probably refers to a fenced *rig* or field (as distinct from unfenced outby land) it is perhaps possible that the name referred to the traces of a fortification with two defensive ditches on the ridge of RAVELRIG HILL, noted in the *Statistical Account* 1792 and sufficiently prominent for the hill to be known as *Castle Hill* in 1764 or *Castle Bank* in 1773 and 1792—*see also* GENERAL'S WATCH, Balerno. The name of RAVELRIG ROAD derived from that of *Ravelrig Entry* used by the county highways engineer and obviously local to its Dalmahoy end—more properly it might be said to be the *road to Pilmuir*. RAVELRIG PARK (1980) and RAVELRIG HILL (1987) were both named as being within the *Hill Park* field of Ravelrig, recorded thus in 1764.

RAVELSTON is recorded from 1363 onwards in the early forms *Raylistoun, Railstoun, Ralstoun* and *Ravelstoun*. The name is *Hrafnkell's tún* or farm; but since *tún* could be either Old Norse or Anglian, the bearer of this Old Norse personal name *Hrafnkell* might have been a Norse-speaking settler of the 9th or 10th century or else a somewhat later Northumbrian of Norse descent. There was no doubt a medieval tower house at the estate centre, shown on *Blaeu* 1654 and replaced in turn by George Foulis' mansion in 1624 and Alexander Keith's RAVELSTON HOUSE in 1790. RAVELSTON DYKES, shown on *Roy* 1753, was the approach to Ravelston through lands of Dean, Murrayfield and Blinkbonny, first reaching Ravelston ground in the vicinity of the future Craigleith Rise; and indeed it is listed on *Cramond Roads* 1812 as the road 'from Dean by the back [i.e. northern part] of Murrayfield'. The name appears on *Ordnance Survey* 1852, and derived either from stone dykes or ditched hedges, *see under* DOUBLE HEDGES ROAD. RAVELSTON DYKES ROAD was a road within Ravelston estate, and before the 1870s it took a more northerly line before turning south to make a T-junction with Ravelston Dykes. RAVELSTON DYKES LANE, so named only in 1963, is shown on *Knox* 1812, giving access to the quarries at Fountainhead. In 1875-76, by a curious aberration, terraces of houses built in Back Dean, a clear half mile from the nearest part of Ravelston, were nevertheless named RAVELSTON PLACE and TERRACE. The mischief was compounded in 1882 by the naming of RAVELSTON PARK, also in the Dean estate; and by the 1890s the side name *Ravelston Terrace* was already supplanting the ancient street name of BACK DEAN, *which see*. In 1961, four new streets formed in the *Longrigg* and *Avenue* parks of Ravelston were named RAVELSTON HOUSE GROVE, LOAN, PARK and ROAD. In 1974, RAVELSTON RISE was formed on Craigleith ground, and was named by association with the nearby names of Craigleith Rise, and the flats known as Ravelston Garden.

RAVENSCROFT STREET (Gilmerton) was formerly MAIN STREET, renamed in 1967 to obviate any confusion with Main Street in Davidson's Mains. The new name was taken from RAVENSCROFT PLACE which in turn had been named for *Ravenscroft Convalescent Home* in Newtoft Street. The name was extended to RAVENSCROFT GARDENS in 1968.

RAVENSWOOD AVENUE (Inch) *see under* THE INCH, Nether Liberton.

REDBRAES (Pilrig) is recorded in 1717 and was the descriptive name of this part of Pilrig, where the soil in banks above the river and bog shows a reddish colour. In 1729 a part of it extending to 6½ Scots acres was feued to Hew Crauford, Clerk to the Signet, who built Redbraes House. Swept away for road widening exactly 200 years later, this mansion stood some thirty yards north of the entry to REDBRAES PLACE, built in its grounds in 1931 and followed in 1961 by REDBRAES GROVE.

REDFORD (Balerno) is named on *Armstrongs* 1773 and shown as a ruin on *Ordnance Survey* 1852, which also shows the Bavelaw burn and *Redford Bridge* as they were before the new Threipmuir reservoir attained its present level. The original ford may have been named for reddish earth or stones in the bed of the burn, or because the crossing was through reeds, which still grow thick at the head of the reservoir—and the 1852 map shows a reedy patch south of the burn and just west of the bridge; but while it is most likely that the place was named as 'the reedy ford', a third possibility should be mentioned, for it may be that some of the *red-* names connected with burns in Lothian contain British *red*, a burn, or *rid*, a ford, with Anglian or Scots *burn* or *ford* tacked on.

REDFORD (Colinton) is recorded in 1674 as an estate name, but is probably much earlier, since it clearly originated as a name for a ford over the Braid burn, and since the crossing lies on a route between such early settlements as COLINTON, FORDEL, THE BAADS and COMISTON. While the name may have arisen in one or other of the ways mentioned under REDFORD, Balerno, the distinct flood plain along this stretch of the burn would have favoured the growth of reeds. Prior to 1960 the road looped some forty yards south of its present line, crossing the burn at REDFORD BRIDGE and heading up REDFORD BRAE to Fordel and the Baads. The line taken by the road eastwards from Fordel has been changed twice since the mid 18th century: the present road to the junction at the Cockit Hat plantation is shown on *Knox* 1812 and described in a deed of 1802 (quoted in *Steuart's Colinton* p194) as 'lately opened'; while *Laurie* 1766 shows the road on a different line, swinging south and leading to Fairmilehead by Sourhole, now Hunter's Tryst; whereas on *Roy* 1753 (which for the most part shows the countryside as it was when farmed in the ancient 'runrig' system, often with different local roads) the road is shown as heading east from Fordel and joining a loan (now lost, but recorded in field names as the *Lang Loan*) which then led more or less directly from Oxgangs to Fairmilehead, passing northwest of (Old) Comiston. REDFORD HOUSE dates from the later 1670s. The 'Drummond Scrolls' built into its stables, as well as the cluster of engaged columns that forms the 'Covenanters' Monument south of the road, are fragments rescued by R A Macfie of Dreghorn from William Adam's Royal Infirmary building of 1738 when it was demolished in 1884. REDFORD DRIVE (1929) and REDFORD AVENUE, CRESCENT and LOAN (1931) were built in the *Hungry* (i.e. infertile) *Hill* field; while REDFORD BANK, GARDENS and WALK (1950) REDFORD TERRACE (1952) and REDFORD GROVE, NEUK and PLACE (1953) stand in the *House Wood park* and *Sheep park* of Redford.

REDGAUNTLET TERRACE (Inch) *see under* THE INCH, Nether Liberton.

REDHALL (Pilrig) is shown, unnamed, on *Fergus & Robinson* 1759; but it was noted as 'Gardener's House' on *Ainslie's River Leith* in 1787, when the ground was owned by John Reid, gardener, and clearly it was named *Reid hall* for him, perhaps in imitation of REDBRAES, half a mile upstream. It was bought by the town in 1789, but was suppressed in the 1860s by the development of BANGOR ROAD and BREADALBANE STREET.

REDHALL is recorded in the reign of Alexander III (1249-86) as *Rubea Aula*, red hall, and this Latin form shows that the Scots forms *Redehalle* 1298 and *Redhalle* 1337 referred (or at least were understood to refer) to a red-coloured hall house, probably built in the red sandstone that outcrops in the ravine of the Water of Leith. Its builder may have been its first recorded owner, William le Grant, an AngloNorman immigrant from Lincoln in the 1250s, and it probably became the core of the medieval REDHALL TOWER. This stood at NT 21827025, on a spur above the river about 100 yards northwest of the later Redhall House (*see below*) and was the centre of the BARONY OF REDHALL, which besides REDHALL MAINS included COLINTON, OXGANGS, COMISTON, SWANSTON, DREGHORN, BONALY and WOODHALL. Soon after 1500 these subdivisions were sold off as separate estates, and in 1527 the remainder was acquired by Adam Otterburn, town clerk and provost of Edinburgh, king's advocate and diplomat; and it was he who by purchasing part of EASTER HAILES began the process which created the ESTATE OF REDHALL, still centred east of the river, but with most of its land west of it, *see* SLATEFORD, GRAYS MILL, KINGSKNOWES, CAULDHAME and BOGSMILL. Enlarged or replaced by Otterburn, the Tower was strong enough to offer a stout resistance to Cromwell's artillery in 1650, *see under* DOVECOT GROVE; but by 1755 it was demolished by George Inglis of Redhall, who built himself the present mansion of REDHALL House, as well as the handsome octagonal REDHALL DOOCOT, in which he incorporated an armorial of the Otterburns, apparently salvaged from the old Tower. Inglis also enclosed the estate, built a walled garden at Jinkabout Mill on the west bank of the river, and promoted industry at INGLIS GREEN (*which see*) as well as quarrying of white freestone south of Stanypath. This OLD REDHALL QUARRY, now represented by the greater part of Kingsknowe Public Park, was worked from 1763 until 1874 and latterly encroached so far into the Clovenstone park (*see under* CLOVENSTONE) that progress was hindered by the old Lanark road (*see under* REDHALL BANK ROAD) to such a degree that in 1863 the quarrymaster James Gowans constructed a bypass, at his own expense, to carry the Lanark road round the west side of the quarry. In 1873 Gowans opened NEW REDHALL QUARRY in the *Cow den* field of Kingsknowes: but it was closed soon after 1888, and was known as the POLIS PARK (*which see*) for long after it was officially named REDHALL PUBLIC PARK in about 1922.

REDHALL AVENUE, CRESCENT, DRIVE, GARDENS and **ROAD** (Slateford) were laid out in Graysknowe and the Cairn Parks of Kingsknowes and named in 1947 as being within the latterday estate of REDHALL, which see. REDHALL GROVE and PLACE were added in 1951. REDHALL VIEW, in another part of the estate, was named in 1952, either for the estate or for the prospect of its original centre on the other side of the river.

REDHALL BANK ROAD (Slateford) is a remnant of the section of the ancient Lanark road which was bypassed in 1863 in order to free ground for southward extension of OLD REDHALL QUARRY, *see under* REDHALL. It is distinguished by the cottages built by Sir James Gowans, in his characteristic style, for his quarry staff. He named them *Redhall Bank*, no doubt on the model of nearby *Millbank* (*see under* BOG'S MILL, Slateford) and the name was adopted for the street in the 1950s.

REDHEUGHS (Gyle) is recorded from about 1400 onwards, and the name's early forms, such as *Reidhewis* or *Redheuchis* show that it is Anglian *read hohes* (becoming *heuchs* in later Scots) evidently for the rising land at the steading and the reddish tint of the ground. REDHEUGHS ROAD was the road leading to it. A survey of the farm in 1852 (*RHP 11162*) records its field names, including the GULLIONS (*which see*) and the *Muir Park*, named for the GYLE MUIR. The latter is reflected in the naming of REDHEUGHS MUIR, along with REDHEUGHS AVENUE and RIGG, in 1988.

RED ROW (Currie) is a row of cottages built before 1845 and named, before 1893 and probably from the beginning, for the finish of their walls in red colour wash—rather unfortunately changed to white in recent times.

RED WALK (Dean Village to Stockbridge) *see under* THE DENE.

REGENT BRIDGE (Calton) is part of a scheme for 'a new London road over the Calton' mooted in 1787 but progressed as the 'Calton Bridge scheme' only after the necessary Acts of Parliament had been obtained in 1813 and 1814. The engineering structure, over 100 yards long, was designed by Robert Stevenson, and in November 1815 Archibald Elliot won the competition for the architectural design, including the buildings flanking the bridge as well as the graceful arch over the Low Calton. Passable by 1817, it was formally opened in 1819 by Prince Leopold of Saxe Coburg. The whole length of the carriageway is named as REGENT(S) BRIDGE on the competition drawings, and shown thus on *Strangers Guide* 1816 and *Kirkwood* 1817, the name being in compliment of the Prince Regent; and while Lord Cockburn refers to it as 'Waterloo Bridge', *Knox* 1821 shows the *Regent Bridge* as before, but with WATERLOO PLACE (celebrating Wellington's victory in June 1815) as the name of the flanking buildings; whereas *Kirkwood* and *Wood*, both 1823, show the street as *Waterloo Place* and confine *Regent Bridge* to the arch over Low Calton, and *PO Directory* 1824 rather contrariwise lists 'Waterloo Place, Regent's Bridge, east end of Princes Street'—but also 'Regent's Bridge, Waterloo Pl'. REGENT ARCH is listed in *PO Directory* 1844 and shown on *Ordnance Survey* 1852 as the name of the part of the Low Calton road immediately under the bridge.

REGENT PLACE (Norton Park) *see under* MARYFIELD, Norton Park.

REGENT ROAD (Calton) was mooted in 1787 and is shown on *Knox* 1812 as a southern branch of a proposed road running on the north side of the Calton Hill, *see under* LONDON ROAD. With the building of the REGENT BRIDGE (*which see*) under way, firmer proposals for this 'new London Road over the Calton or 'Greater London Road' appear on *Strangers Guide* 1816 and *Kirkwood* 1817 respectively. Since the latter shows it bridging the Easter Road at Abbeymount, it is evident that construction had not yet reached that point. *Knox* 1821 shows the final design of this junction, with Easter Road re-levelled and diverted to suit the gradient of Regent Road; but comparison of the detail on *Lothian* 1829 and *Pollock* 1834 suggests that the section of the road where it runs below REGENT TERRACE (*which see*) took its final form between these two dates. The name REGENT ROAD appears on *Calton* 1819 as one of the full set of street names proposed for the CALTON NEW TOWN (*which see*) and it was evidently chosen to compliment the Prince Regent, in the year before his accession to the throne as George IV.

REGENT STREET (Portobello) was laid out in about 1815 and evidently named before 1820, when the *Prince Regent* became George IV. REGENT STREET LANE is shown as a *meuse lane* on *Wood's Portobello* 1824.

REGENT TERRACE (Calton) appears on *Calton* 1819 as a terrace of houses proposed in the CALTON NEW TOWN, *which see*. The houses were designed in 1825, building began in 1826, and the name appears as REGENT'S TERRACE in *PO Directory* 1827 and as REGENT TERRACE on *Lothian* 1829. Although the name is missing on *Calton* 1819, there is no doubt that the terraced housing was intended from the beginning, and the omission may have something to do with the curiously uncertain design for the carriageway as shown in 1819, which appears in an amended form on *Lothian* 1829 and finally in its present shape on *Pollock* 1834.

REGIS COURT (Cramond) *see under* CRAMOND.

EAST and **WEST REGISTER STREETS** (East End) are shown proposed on James Craig's plan for *St James' Square* 1773, to be evolved from the entries of two old roads—GABRIEL'S ROAD in the west and a loan through Cleland's Yards to Broughton in the east—which flanked the site for the projected Register Office, started in 1774. The plan names the eastern street REGISTER STREET, but its counterpart seems to have continued to be known as GABRIEL'S ROAD, as shown on *Kincaid* 1784, until about 1800, when the streets began to be distinguished as EAST and WEST REGISTER STREET. REGISTER PLACE was named by 1815.

REIDFORD CLOSE (South Leith) is listed on *Kirkwood* 1817 and was probably connected with John Reidford, messenger in Giles Street in 1799.

(BAILIE) REID'S CLOSE (80 Canongate) is listed in *Williamson's Directory* 1779 and on *Ainslie* 1730, and was named for Andrew Reid, brewer, bailie of Canongate, who had property here in 1770, together with adjoining property he had purchased from creditors of Robert Reid (probably a relative) who is listed in *Williamson's Directory* 1773 as a brewer near Milton House. The close seems also to be that listed as BRYDEN'S in *Williamson* 1780, from a Major Bryden, feuar in 1740. HADDINGTON'S ENTRY or CLOSE, branching east of Reid's, was named for the Earl of Haddington, whose town house HADDINGTON COURT was built in about 1700 near the south back of the Canongate.

BAILIE REID'S CLOSE (High Street) *see under* LOWER BAXTERS CLOSE.

REID'S COURT (95 Canongate) is named thus on *Kirkwood* 1817, but the form REID'S COACH YARD in *Williamson's Directory* 1773 shows that the REID'S YARD on *Ainslie* 1780 is a reference to the work place of James Reid, coachmaker, listed in *Williamson* in 1773 as 'opposite Milton's Lodging'. The family connection went back at least as far as John Reid, smith, owner of property here at some date before 1682.

REID TERRACE (Stockbridge) *see under* THE COLONIES, Stockbridge.

REIKIE'S COURT (South Side) together with *Reikie's Land* is listed in *Directories* from 1800 onwards. The Court is shown on *Ainslie* 1804 but not on *Brown & Watson* 1793, and is named on *Ordnance Survey* 1852. Two glaziers of the name are listed in *Williamson's Directory* 1773, one in Fishmarket Close, the other in the High Street opposite Niddry's Wynd.

RELUGAS ROAD etc (Grange) *see under* THE GRANGE.

RESTALRIG is a 15th-century variant of the original LESTALRIC, recorded from the late 12th century, still current in 1752, and still occasionally heard in the locality. The medieval estate extended in a triangle from the Calton down to Leith Shore and eastwards to the Figgate burn, and its centre was the tower on the east shore of Lochend Loch, shown as RESTARYCKE PLACE on *Siege of Leith* 1560 and as RESTALRIGH on *Blaeu* 1654. The early spellings *Lastalric, -rik, -rich* or *-rig,* or *Lestalryk, -rich,* or *-ric* suggest that the name is Anglian *lastal* or *lestal,* mire, with *ric,* a narrow strip or else a ditch or drainage channel; and it may have referred to the boggy course of the Tummel burn from Meadowbank down to Fillyside, or more likely, to the upland valley in which Lochend loch is drained by the *strype* or little burn running westwards in the vicinity of Bothwell Street, through what must have been large marshy flats. The parish kirk was established by the 12th century, almost half a mile east of the estate centre. Erected into a Deanery in 1487 (*see under* DEANERY CLOSE) it became the nucleus of the village of RESTALRIG, while the original towerhouse was partly demolished in about 1586 and was eventually rebuilt as LOCHEND (*which see*).

This arrangement, shown on *Adair* 1682, led to the naming of the two main routes as LOCHEND ROAD, leading to the old estate centre, and RESTALRIG ROAD, leading to the secularized Deanery village. RESTALRIG TERRACE, formed by 1870, seems to have been named for the estate; and EAST RESTALRIG TERRACE was named by extension from it in 1897. In 1926, RESTALRIG CRESCENT, CIRCUS and SQUARE were named as offshoots from Restalrig Road; and in the same year RESTALRIG AVENUE was named as a new approach to the village from the southeast. RESTALRIG DRIVE and GARDENS were developed in about 1932 in the grounds of an 18th-century *Restalrig House*. RESTALRIG PARK was named in 1969 as a branch off Restalrig Road.

REST AND BE THANKFUL (Corstorphine Hill) is at the summit of the right of way of the *Kirk Road* from Ravelston to the parish kirk in Corstorphine. The name is given in *Selway* 1890 and noted by the *Ordnance Survey* in 1893, but not in 1852. There is no sign of it on *Corstorphinehill* 1885 or *Ravelston* 1826, but the field name *Kirk Steps Park* on the latter may preserve an earlier name for a stile in the march dyke.

RICCARTON (Currie) is recorded as *Richardeston* in 1296 and *Richardtoun* in *RMS* 1306-29, and is shown on *Blaeu* 1654 as *Ricartoune*. The name's early forms confirm that it was the *tún* or farm place belonging to an AngloNorman named *Richard*. RICCARTON HOUSE, a notable towerhouse of the 16th and 17th centuries, was swept away in the development of the Heriot Watt University in 1956. RICCARTON MAINS or home farm is recorded as the *Manys of Richardtoun* in 1508, and is shown on maps from *Laurie* 1763 onwards. RICCARTON MAINS ROAD, a name in use by the highways engineer in 1902, ousted the traditional name of THE CORSLET (*which see*) by about 1957.

RICCARTON AVENUE (Currie) was built in Wester Currie in 1957, and followed by RICCARTON DRIVE (1958) and CRESCENT and GROVE (1959). It is likely that the name came not directly from the estate, but from the adjoining RICCARTON MAINS ROAD, *which see*.

RICHARDSON'S CLOSE (233 High Street) *see* GEDDES'S CLOSE.

RICHMOND STREET (Pleasance) was formed before 1773, when it appears in *Williamson's Directory*, and was evidently named for James Richmond, land surveyor, who laid it out and probably also developed it. *Ainslie* 1804 shows NORTH and SOUTH RICHMOND STREETS forming a crossroads with the original Richmond Street, and it was renamed as EAST and WEST RICHMOND STREETS shortly afterwards. In the later 1920s this scheme was simplified, the original street becoming WEST RICHMOND STREET, while the *North* and *South* streets became RICHMOND STREET, only to be suppressed by clearance and redevelopment in about 1935. Parts of the ancient BACK ROW (*which see*) were developed as RICHMOND PLACE by 1795 and RICHMOND LANE by 1813.

RICHMOND TERRACE (Dalry) is named on *Bartholomew* 1876 and appears to have been built along with or soon after the Edinburgh Co-operative Building Company's scheme at DALRY PARK (*which see*) in 1869. The origin of the name is obscure.

RIDDEL'S CLOSE (South Leith) is shown on *Naish* 1709 and *Kirkwood* 1817 as running between the DUB RAW (*which see*) and Tolbooth Wynd. Recorded by about 1690, it was probably named for James Riddel of Kinglass, who owned *a loft in the Dubraw above the soap house* and let it out in 1655 as temporary premises for the grammar school of South Leith.

RIDDLE'S CLOSE (322 High Street) is listed on *Edgar* 1742, and was so named for George Riddell, wright and burgess, who rebuilt the foreland in 1726. It was in a flat in this *Riddal's land* that the 40-year-old philosopher David Hume first set himself up as a householder, with (as he reported to his friend Adam Smith) 'a maid and a cat as subsidiaries, and a sister for company'. In 1730 the close was referred to as SIR JAMES SMITH'S, *now* ROYSTON'S: the first referring to Sir James Smith of Groathill, Provost 1643-46, who lived in the cross house between the two courtyards; while the later name was for Sir James Mackenzie, who lived in the lower part of the MacMorran mansion (*see below*) and sat as Lord Royston in the Court of Session from 1710 until 1744. Yet another name for the close was SHAW'S, evidently for Bernard Shawe, one of the resident owners in 1635. While the northern courtyard is modern, created by clearances in 1893, the buildings round the north, west and south sides of the south courtyard (RIDDLE'S COURT is a modern misnomer) were built in about 1587 by John MacMorran. Both he and his younger brother Ninian were merchant burgesses by right of their father William MacMorran, and both served as bailies; but John's term of office was abruptly cut short in 1595 when he was shot dead by one of the rebellious pupils of the town's High School, who (not for the first time) had taken up arms against the authorities and had barricaded themselves into the school house. Ninian was a bailie in 1598, when the town council borrowed the MacMorran house for a banquet they gave, in the presence of James VI and Anne of Denmark, for the Queen's brother, the Duke of Holstein; and since MacMorran was one of those appointed to audit the £1,103 bill, it is probable that he or his nephew Ninian (John's son) was still connected with the house. The close was known as JOHN MacMORRAN'S for his brother; but the alternative name MacMORRAN'S may have been for other members of the family as well. In addition to their property in the close, John MacMorran owned a house immediately west of it; and other properties to the eastward, in Fisher's Close, were owned by George MacMorran in 1635.

RIDDLE'S ENTRY (Canongate) was at 35 New Street and is listed in *PO Directory* 1827. It was probably named for James Riddell, listed in *Williamson's Directory* 1780 as a smith in New Street.

RIDING PARK (Cramond) was so named in 1983 because it is sited in a small park or paddock which was immediately south of the ring-shaped Riding School built in the mid-19th century by W R Ramsay of Cramond Regis or New Barnton, a famous sportsman of the day. The School is illustrated in *The History of the Linlithgowshire Hunt.*

RIDING SCHOOL LANE (West End) *see* St CUTHBERT'S LANE, West End.

RIEGO STREET (Tollcross) is shown on *Kirkwood* 1817 as a scheme projected on ground owned by Major James Weir (*see also under* LYNEDOCH PLACE) and was developed and named by 1824, evidently in honour of Don Rafael Riego, major in the Astorian regiment, who had proclaimed a liberal constitution for Spain in 1820 and led a rebellion against the despotism of Ferdinand VII, but was defeated and barbarously executed at Madrid in 1823.

EAST and **WEST RIGS** (Balerno) appear on *Knox* 1812 but the first is named BACK O THE RIG, probably using *back* in the sense of the crest of the ridge which runs west from this point. The *rigs* are probably the fields on its south-facing slope

RILLBANK TERRACE and **CRESCENT** (Sciennes) were named by 1862 and 1863, clearly because they were built on part of a property which, shown as *Wilson's* on maps from 1759 to 1817, had been known as *Rill Bank* from 1846 (if not earlier) until 1858. It had been acquired by the Trades Maidens Hospital in 1854. The name appears to have been fancy: if there was a rill, it was too small to figure on any map, not even on *Ordnance Survey* 1852 which shows the property in close detail, the site of the streets being then plain open ground behind the house, which faced Sciennes Road.

RINGWOOD PLACE (Inch) *see under* THE INCH, Nether Liberton.

RINTOUL PLACE (Stockbridge) *see under* THE COLONIES, Stockbridge.

RISELAW ROAD (Braid) was named in 1905, and the name, evidently combining *rise* for the steep slope with *law* for the foothill of the Braid Hills, was extended to RISELAW CRESCENT, PLACE and TERRACE in 1910.

RITCHIE PLACE (Dummiedykes) was named *Ritchie's Place* in 1824, evidently for the developer, since *Kirkwood* 1817 shows the ground as belonging to 'Mrs Ritchie's Heirs'. The earlier houses (shown on *Pollock* 1834) were replaced in 1852 by a tenement of family flats, designed on the model of ASHLEY BUILDINGS in Netherbow (*which see*) and built by W Beattie and Son at the expense of Patrick Ritchie. The side name was one of nine suppressed in favour of DUMBIEDYKES ROAD in 1885.

RITCHIE PLACE (North Merchiston) was developed in the mid 1890s and named by 1897. The name's origin has yet to be traced.

RIVERSDALE ROAD (Saughtonhall) lies in the *Langcote Leys* of Balgreen and Carrickknowes, and the name was coined in 1926 from its position beside the river—but rather feebly, insofar as *dale* is not normally used for great flats such as those left by the post-glacial lake which stretched westwards from Dalry—*see under* CORSTORPHINE. RIVERSDALE CRESCENT and GROVE followed in 1931 and 1933.

RIVERSIDE (Cramond) is the descriptive name of this walk beside the river, shown unnamed on *Ordnance Survey* 1893.

RIVERSIDE (Newbridge) was developed by the Scottish Special Housing Association in 1947 and named for the nearby river Almond.

RIVERSIDE ROAD (Craigiehall) *see under* HILLSIDE ROAD, Craigiehall.

ROADING HILL (Dreghorn) is recorded thus in 1709, but its interpretation may not be straightforward, *see under* RODDLINGLAW, Gogar.

ROBB'S COURT (Castlebarns) is shown on *Kincaid* 1784 and named on *Ordnance Survey* 1852. A sasine of 1810 records it as a one-acre property then inherited by Barbara and Agnes Robb from James Robb.

ROBB'S LOAN (Gorgie) is shown on *Knox* 1812 but is much older, since it gave access from both the Saughton and the Slateford roads to the Wester Mains of Gorgie, shown as *Gorgie* on *Adair* 1682. The name is traditional, formally adopted in 1927, and evidently derived from some occupant of the farm; possibly someone surnamed Robb, but perhaps the Robert Fynnie who was tenant in 1620. The loan was cut in two by the railway in about 1910, its southern half later becoming HUTCHISON LOAN, *see under* HUTCHISON AVENUE, Wester Gorgie. Wester Gorgie farmhouse and steading were redeveloped in 1964 as ROBB'S LOAN GROVE.

ROBERT BURNS DRIVE (Liberton) *see under* KIRK BRAE, Liberton.

ROBERTSON AVENUE (Gorgie) is shown planned on *W & A K Johnston* 1888 and as opened, although still not named, on *Ordnance Survey* 1893. The name HANDYSIDE PLACE, probably for the developer of housing near its north end, became attached to it by 1896, and *W & A K Johnston* 1898 shows this together with the name ROBERTSON AVENUE—evidently given for W W Robertson, Master 1895-96 of the Merchant Company, owners of the ground. The *Handyside* name was dropped in about 1900.

ROBERTSON'S CLOSE (9 Canongate) is listed in *PO Directory* 1827 and was named for William Robertson, dairyman at Croftangry in Abbeyhill, who acquired bakehouses and dwellings here in 1797, shown on *Ordnance Survey* 1852 as *Robertson's Land*. It was formerly the CLOSE OF St ANDREW & St CATHERINE, recorded in 1678 as leading to the hospital of St Thomas, founded in 1541 by George Creichton, bishop of Dunkeld, and administered by the chaplains of

St Andrew and St Catherine in Holyrood Abbey. The site was redeveloped in 1971, but the name was retained as ROBERTSON'S CLOSE, opening off Calton Road.

ROBERTSON'S CLOSE (44 Cowgate) *see* MacCONNOCHIE'S CLOSE, Cowgate.

(BAILIE) ROBERTSON'S CLOSES (109 and 115 Cowgate) *see* WEST CAMPBELL'S CLOSE and RATTRAY'S CLOSE, Cowgate.

ROBERTSON'S CLOSE (263 Cowgate) is named on *Rothiemay* 1647. While it can be connected with several owners of the name after that date, including Thomas Robertson of Lochbank, treasurer of the town in 1671, it may be that the close was named for David Robesoun, mentioned in *RMS* 1598 as deceased owner of ground near the vennel of the Kirk o Field—*see under* KIRK O FIELD. It is also named in 1714 as DICKSON'S, with a reference to lands of the late Thomas Dickson, described as bounded on the south by the same vennel or transe; and there may be a further hint of family connection in the mention in *RMS* 1575 of an orchard occupied by Adam Diksoun, beside the *common close* of Kirk o Field. The close, or rather a western branch of it, is noted in 1709 as being called MELROSE CLOSE, for land belonging to Melrose Abbey, later the site of Lady Yester's kirk.

ROBERTSON'S COURT (Canongate) *see under* ROBERTSON'S CLOSE, 9 Canongate.

ROCHEAD'S COURT (370 High Street) is listed on *Kirkwood* 1817 and was probably named for Andrew Rochead & Son, musical instrument makers in the Castlehill in 1810. It was cleared away in about 1839 for the building of the Tolbooth Kirk.

ROCHEID PARK (Inverleith) was named in 1984 for the Rocheids of Inverleith. James Rocheid or Rucheid, merchant burgess and member of town council in 1635, acquired Craigleith in 1646, and the family were lairds of Inverleith from 1678 until the 19th century. ROCHEID PATH, formed prior to 1913 on the Inverleith bank of the river, was named by 1973.

ROCHESTER TERRACE (Merchiston) *see under* BLANTYRE TERRACE in the ilk.

ROCKVILLE'S CLOSE (388 High Street) is mentioned thus in 1830 but is given as GORDON'S CLOSE on *Ainslie* 1780 and 1804 and on *Kirkwood* 1817. Both names are from Alexander Gordon (1739-92) third son of the Earl of Aberdeen, listed in *Williamson's Directory* 1773 as an advocate in Castlehill, who was raised to the bench in 1784 and took his judicial title Lord Rockville from his East Lothian estate.

RODDINGLAW (Gogar) appears on *Laurie* 1763 as *Roadinlaw*, and is probably to be grouped with ROADING HILL, Dreghorn, as well as Roddinglaw near North Berwick, Rodanbraes near Burntisland, and perhaps Rodie Cleuch in Yarrow. The second part of the name presents no difficulty, being Anglian *hlaw* or Scots *law*, smoothly rounded hill; but while the first part might seem on the face of it to be Scots *rodding*, a narrow track, the earlier forms of Roddinghill in Cunningham (*Rodding-* and *Rodin-* in 1647, *Ridding-* in 1630, *Reddin-* and *Reddene-* in the 1570s, *Redding* and *Riding-* in the 1530s and *Reddin-* in 1525) show that it would be unwise to rely on the 18th-century spellings. There may be a connection with early Scots *redding*, in its sense of 'muir reclaimed as farm land'; but in the case of some of the hill names the terrain prompts the guess (otherwise quite unsupported) that British *reden*, bracken, may have lingered on in descriptive land names.

RODNEY STREET (Canonmills) is part of the ancient route through Broughton to Canonmills; but was named in about 1890 for Admiral George Rodney, Baron Rodney, another of the group of naval heroes earlier celebrated in the NORTHERN NEW TOWN. He had been made a free burgess of Edinburgh in 1783.

THE ROMAN ROADS in the area, although they became a legacy of trunk routes which enhanced the strategic importance of Edinburgh from British times onwards, played no direct part in shaping the burgh itself, since they swept past rather than through its site. For the same reason there was a certain lack of fit between them and the immediate approaches to the burgh, and this led to the disuse and eventual obliteration of Roman routes within a mile or so of the Castle rock, and so to a dearth of evidence for them in an area which, as it happens, is crucial to a full understanding of the Roman system. Thus even although there is hard evidence of the Roman scheme in the district as a whole (and every reason to hope that more will be found) guesses and speculation are still needed to bridge this and other notable gaps in information, and it is possible—indeed, very likely—that fresh discoveries may alter the picture outlined here.

Nevertheless it is clear that in the wake of Agricola's campaigns of AD 77-83, two trunk roads from the south and southwest were routed through Lothian, in support of operations and garrisons in the frontier zone between and north of Forth and Clyde. The first one was the main supply road from York, later known as *Dere Street*, which came in by Pathhead and Dalkeith to a fort at Elginhaugh, and thence passed through Gilmerton on the line of the A7, shown on the older maps as continuing to a point on the old Liberton road which is now at the junction of Savile Terrace with Mayfield Road. Beyond this no trace of the road has been found, except perhaps in the Celtic place name DRUMDRYAN (*which see*); but clearly it was heading for the gap at Tollcross between the water barriers of the South Loch and the four-mile stretch of the ancient loch between Dalry and the Gyle (*see under* CORSTORPHINE), and probably crossed the Water of Leith somewhere near Bells Mills. The second trunk road came up from Carlisle by Biggar and Carlops, and patently hugged the foot of the hills until it reached Lothianburn and could swing almost due north to the Buckstane Snab and the Boroughmuirhead—heading, like Dere Street, for the Tollcross gap, on a line which (but for two short looped diversions at Fairmilehead and at the Braid Hills Hotel, where in both cases the ancient estate boundaries show the original course of the road) is almost certainly represented by the Biggar, Braid and Morningside roads. It is therefore a fair assumption that these two trunk roads, Dere Street and the Carlops road, merged before crossing the river, and thereafter turned westwards, now as a single road heading for the frontier. Where exactly that turning was must still be guessed at: but the location of a pair of Roman camps near Millburn, Gogar, and a milestone near Newbridge may be some indication of the road's westward course; and when the barriers of Corstorphine Hill and the loch at the Gyle are taken into account, as well as some details of roads shown on *Roy* 1753 and other early maps, it seems reasonable to suggest that the Roman road struck directly westwards from the high ground above the river at Back Dean and carried straight on aslant the Murrayfield ridge and the southern shoulder of Corstorphine Hill, taking a line now represented by the western part of St John's Road and the Glasgow road as far as the crossing of the Gogar; and the geology of the area would suggest that it probably carried on from there more or less on the line of the A8 to the Almond at or near Newbridge.

It was normal practice to set up chains of forts along such roads, spaced about six or seven Roman miles apart. In the case of Dere Street, the last known fort on the way up from the south was that discovered at Elginhaugh in 1979; but if the normal system were followed, the chain may have been continued by forts, as yet undiscovered, commanding the crossing of the Leith (perhaps at Back Dean, where the terrain is very like that at Elginhaugh) and the crossing of the Almond, perhaps in Newliston, where the place names CHESTERHAW and CHESTERLAW seem to refer to a fortification of some kind, whether native or Roman. In the case of the road from Carlisle, there was a fort at Carlops, some 16 miles from Back Dean—a distance that would have somewhat strained the standard spacing if there were but one intermediate fort between these points, but which would have been relieved had OLIVER'S CAMP (*which see*) been a extra intermediate station, lying athwart the road near Fairmilehead and about 3½ miles from Back Dean.

In the mid 2nd century, new forts were built at Cramond and Inveresk and new roads were needed to connect them with the trunk system. In the case of Cramond, the road leading south-east from the fort has been identified by excavation, and the alignments of sections of Cramond Road South, Corbiehill Road and Hillhouse Road suggest that it ran almost straight to Back Dean, where it would have connected with both of the south-going trunk roads, and probably also (as suggested below) with Inveresk. By contrast, nothing is known of a west-going route from Cramond, and it is a pure guess, perhaps lent some support by the alignments of later roads, that there may have been a 6-mile link running by Clove Craig and the higher ground above the west bank of the Almond, to join

Dere Street at Newliston. In the case of Inveresk, where the 2nd-century fort seems to have taken over the function of the earlier one on Dere Street at Elginhaugh, it is a reasonable guess that its connections east and west amounted to a looping diversion of Dere Street between Pathhead and Back Dean; and it might be that the western half of the loop took a line later mapped by Pont in 1596 and shown on *Blaeu* 1654 and *Roy* 1753 as a road straight from Magdalen Bridge to Piershill, before rounding the north side of Arthur's Seat and heading for the river crossing below Back Dean. This would have given excellent communication with both Cramond and the west-going trunk road, as well as a connection with the Carlops road. A further and more direct link between the latter and Inveresk would clearly have been desirable; but although the place name STRAITON (normally meaning 'the farm at the Roman street') and its position on a line between Easter Howgate and the mouth of the Esk may be a pointer, such a link and its route are still matters for speculation.

ROMERO PLACE (Newington) was named in 1991, as a tribute to Archbishop Oscar Romero of San Salvador, whose denunciation of injustice and oppression had led to his assassination in 1980.

ROMILLY PLACE (Tollcross) appears in *PO Directory* 1826, although *Romilly Street* is shown on *Wood* 1823. Suppressed in 1885, the name was probably connected with Sir Samuel Romilly, lawyer, 1757-1818.

RONALDSON'S WHARF (North Leith) appears in *PO Directory* 1821 and the street is shown (unnamed) on *Ordnance Survey* 1852 as giving access to both *London Wharf* and *Ronaldson's Wharf*. The name would appear to be that of some owner of the wharf.

ROOD CHAPEL and **WELL** (Greenside) *see under* GREENSIDE.

ROODSIDE is recorded in 1569 as the popular name of NORTH LEITH (*which see*) evidently referring to the fact that it belonged to Holyrood abbey.

ROSEBANK (Currie), shown on *Knox* 1812, is more prosaically named WELLHEAD on *Armstrongs* 1773, presumably referring to the water supply.

ROSEBANK (Portobello) was part of the Figgate Whins in Craigentinny before it was developed as a brick and tile works by Edward and Alexander Colston in 1781. The name, shown on *Wood's Portobello* 1824, was fancy, probably influenced by the neighbouring *Westbank*. The site was cleared for Portobello Swimming Pool in 1937; and this swept away all vestiges of McEWAN SQUARE, named for Dugald McEwan, owner of the Rosebank works in the early 19th century, and ROSEBANK SQUARE, figured on *Wood* and listed in *Portobello Directory* 1836. ROSEBANK LANE, named as access to the brickworks, became the access to the new development of housing at WESTBANK (*which see*) in 1983, and was renamed WESTBANK STREET to suit this new function and to reduce the number of 'Rosebank' streets in the city.

ROSEBANK COTTAGES (Fountainbridge) were designed by Alexander McGregor for James Gowans in 1853. The name was a play on that of ROSEMOUNT, *which see.*

ROSEBANK ROAD (Wardie) was formed by 1887 by development of the entry to the steading of the *Wardie Gardens* nursery which had been formed in Wardie Mains in the late 1840s, after the suppression of the old road to WARDIE—*which see.* The name was fancy, although probably suggested by that of nearby ROSE PARK (*which see*) in Trinity Road. ROSEBANK GROVE was named in 1936; and ROSEBANK GARDENS, built on the site of the nursery steading, followed in 1955.

ROSEBERY AVENUE (Queensferry) in part represents a farm road shown on *Dundas* 1757 as branching off the Common or Easter Loan (now Ashburnham Road) and running as far west as the kink in the present road near its western junction with Lawson Crescent, to give access to some of the runrig fields of Muirhall. By 1832 it was extended westwards to the Kirkliston road, and by 1948 it was partly developed for housing, and named for Lord Rosebery as estate owner. ROSEBERY COURT, also developed by 1948, probably took its name from the Avenue.

ROSEBERY CRESCENT (Wester Coates) *see under* COATES.

ROSEBURN HOUSE, built by Mungo Russell, merchant burgess and city treasurer, in 1582, appears to have been the house of DALRY MILLS, recorded from 1592. *Adair* 1682 shows *Dalry mil* with his usual symbol for a house, but *Adair/Cooper* 1735 substitutes *Roseburn*, which is thus almost certainly a fancy name dating from the early 18th century. The 'burn' appears to have been the mill dam, which *Roy* 1753 shows running west of the house, although *Laurie* 1763 apparently shows the same arrangement as on *Ordnance Survey* 1852, in which it runs east of the house, but with a western branch controlled by a sluice and forming an ornamental burn in the policies. ROSEBURN PLACE was named by 1864, and ROSEBURN STREET and TERRACE by 1887. ROSEBURN GARDENS, on the site of a former nursery, was named by 1902, and there followed ROSEBURN AVENUE (1904) CLIFF (1906) CRESCENT and DRIVE (1913).

ROSEFIELD (Portobello) was the house that William Jamieson (*see under* WILLIAM JAMIESON PLACE) built for himself in 1767 and in which he died in 1813. Shown on *Roads from Figget* 1783 as *Mr Jamieson's House & Garden*, it appears unnamed on *Wood's Portobello* 1824; but on *Sutter's Portobello* 1856 it is shown as *Council Chambers*, being rented for this purpose from 1851 until 1863. The original name was fancy, and Jamieson also applied it to the subsidiary *Rosefield Cottage*, shown as *Rosefield* on the 1783 map, and now within ROSEFIELD PARK. ROSEFIELD AVENUE is outlined on *Taylor & Skinner* 1775, and originated as a lane to Rosefield Cottage, known as ROSEFIELD LANE until the mid 19th century. ROSEFIELD STREET was listed as HOPE STREET in 1836 but only partly developed by the 1880s: it was renamed in 1966 to obviate any confusion with Hope Street, West End. ROSEFIELD PLACE is shown on *Portobello* 1824 with its eastern part and the meuse ROSEFIELD LANE already established. The site of ROSEFIELD PLACE LANE is shown on *Portobello* 1856 as in the grounds of Burn House.

ROSEHALL (Newington) was a triangular piece of ground of some seven acres (clearly shown on *Ordnance Survey* 1852) recorded in *Town Council Minutes* 1586 as 'the gushat at Preistisfeyld', a part of the Burgh Muir lying east of the Dalkeith road, and bounded on the east by the old road to Prestonfield that forked off the Dalkeith road at NT 26917224. A house is shown on it on *Roy* 1753 and the property is given on *Laurie* 1763 as 'Rosehall', probably a fancy name, perhaps influenced by the adjoining field name MARCH HALL *which see*.

ROSEHAUGH'S CLOSE (104 High Street) *see* STRICHEN'S CLOSE.

ROSE LANE (Queensferry) is shown on *Dundas* 1757 and *Plewlandfield* 1769 as the entry to the SHORE ROAD (*which see*) and as such it probably formed the original east boundary of the FRIARS CROFT, *which see*. The first 150 yards of road along the shore was obviously vulnerable to erosion, and Forrest 1818 shows it bypassed by a 70-yard link to the Linlithgow road, creating the present fork between Shore Road and Hopetoun Road. Rose Lane continued, now reduced to a local access; and its name is probably fancy, from the flower.

ROSEMOUNT (Fountainbridge) is mentioned in 1792 as a house owned by William Morrison, one of the several properties shown on *RPH 601* as owned by him; and *Ainslie* 1804 shows a section of the Linlithgow road (now Morrison Street) as *Rose Mount*. The house name was dropped from *PO Directory* in 1854, at the same time as ROSEBANK COTTAGES (*which see*) came into it; and ROSEMOUNT BUILDINGS were named by 1859.

ROSENEATH PLACE etc (Marchmont) *see under* ARGYLE PLACE, Sciennes.

ROSE PARK (Trinity) was so named in 1983 because it is partly on the site of a property shown on *Ainslie* 1804 and *Strangers Guide* 1816 as *Trinity Park*, but as *Rose Park* on maps from *Kirkwood* 1817 onwards.

ROSEVALE PLACE and **TERRACE** (South Leith) *see under* INDUSTRIAL ROAD.

ROSEVILLE GARDENS (Trinity) was developed in 1938 on part of a property shown as *Mr Balfour's* on *Kirkwood* 1817, itself within the lands of Laverockbank as shown on *Ainslie* 1804. The large house, its site now the entry to the street, is given on *Ordnance Survey* 1852 as *The Grove*, and since this is perpetuated in the later street name of LAVEROCKBANK GROVE (*which see*) it would seem that *Roseville* was of quite recent coinage in 1938, possibly borrowing from the names of two nearby houses, *Rose* Villa and Wood*ville*.

ROSSHILL (Queensferry) is shown on *Knox* 1812 as a property of *Ross Esq.* on a site shown as open ground on *Barnbougle & Dalmeny* c1800 and all earlier maps except for *Blaeu* 1654, which shows *C. Roshall* and a 'farm place' symbol northwest of Dalmeny; but it is virtually certain that this last is an error for CROSSALL (*which see*) and that *Rosshill* is fancy, dating from the first decade of the 19th century and combining its owner's name with a reference to its position high above the shore. ROSSHILL TERRACE was named by 1895, and *Ordnance Survey* 1912-14 shows the name spreading further east at ROSSHILL SHALE MINE.

ROSSIE PLACE (Norton Park) *see under* MARYFIELD, Norton Park.

ROSSLYN CRESCENT (Pilrig) was originally named ROSSLYN STREET, out of a personal enthusiasm of its builder, James Cowie, for Roslin, Midlothian. The name entered the *PO Directory* in 1870 but may have been selected earlier, since its choice seems to have been bound up with the naming of nearby DRYDEN STREET, *which see*. The western half, developed as a closed loop, was named ROSSLYN CRESCENT in about 1880, and this name was extended to absorb *Rosslyn Street* in 1909. Meantime ROSSLYN TERRACE, already developing by 1876, was named by 1894. *Rosslyn* and *Roslin* are both variant spellings of a name which seems to be originally *Roskelyn*.

ROSS ROAD (South Craigmillar Park) and ROSS GARDENS and PLACE (West Mains) were named in 1910, 1924 and 1952 for Grizel Ross, daughter of Lord Ross of Melville and wife of Sir Alexander Gilmour of Craigmillar, who inherited the estate in 1671. Their daughter married William Little of Liberton, and her son inherited both estates and took the name Little Gilmour of Liberton and Craigmillar in 1792.

ROSS'S CLOSE (276 Canongate) *see* BOYD'S CLOSE.

ROSS'S CLOSE (380 High Street) *see* ELLIOT'S CLOSE.

ROSS STREET (Newington) *see under* MAYFIELD TERRACE, Mayfield.

ROSTBANK STREET (Granton) *see under* GRANTON HARBOUR.

ROTHESAY MEWS, PLACE and **TERRACE** (Coates) *see under* COATES.

ROTTEN ROW (South Leith) *see under* RATOUN RAW, South Leith.

ROULL ROAD (Corstorphine) was begun at its eastern end and named by 1890. The name's origin has not yet been traced. It may celebrate an early provost of the collegiate kirk in Corstorphine, a poet immortalized in Dunbar's *Lament for the Makaris* 1509 as 'gentill Rowll of Corstorphyne'; but at a guess it may derive from some connection or enthusiasm of Robert Rintoul, engineer and agent, the first and for some years the only resident in the street. The name was continued at ROULL GROVE in 1947 and ROULL PLACE in 1967.

ROWALLAN COURT (East Craigs) *see under* CRAIGIEVAR WYND, East Craigs.

ROWANTREE AVENUE and **GROVE** (Currie) *see under* CHERRYTREE AVENUE, Currie.

ROXBURGH PLACE and **STREET** (Pleasance) are shown and named on *Ainslie* 1804, but merely as proposals, for by 1810 only ROXBURGH PLACE had begun to be occupied, as a terrace in the BACK ROW (*which see*) together with a ROXBURGH SQUARE, which appears to have become ROXBURGH STREET in about 1814. ROXBURGH TERRACE, fronting Drummond Street, followed in about 1820. The site was part of the medieval *Blackfriars Croft*, which became the *North Croft of the Pleasance* when it was acquired by the town in 1639 and then *Roxburgh's Croft* or *Parks* after it was sold to the Earl of Roxburgh in 1657; and the street names arose either from the land name or in direct compliment to the duke of Roxburgh.

ROXBURGH'S CLOSE (341 High Street) is listed on *Edgar* 1742. It was named, not for any earl of Roxburgh (a story originating as a mere guess in *Wilson*) but for a professional cook, John Roxburgh, listed as owner and resident here in 1635, and presumably the cook of the same name who had been made a burgess in 1605—or else he was a son following the same trade. Earlier, like many another close in the town, including ADVOCATE'S CLOSE (*which see*) the close was CANT'S. Also, as early as 1578, it was CRUICK'S, for a William Crockie; and about the same time it was HENDERSON'S or HENRYSON'S, for Walter Henderson or Henryson of Granton, who had a house and property at the head of the close, part of it later becoming Roxburgh's. The close was also NEWTON'S, about which nothing is known.

ROYAL BANK CLOSE (High Street) *see* St MONAN'S WYND.

ROYAL CIRCUS and **CRESCENT** (New Town) *see under* NORTHERN NEW TOWN.

ROYAL EXCHANGE (High Street) *see under* CITY CHAMBERS.

THE 'ROYAL MILE' (High Street and Canongate) appears in W M Gilbert's *Edinburgh in the Nineteenth Century 1901* as a nickname in inverted commas, and it was further popularised as the title of a guidebook by Robert T Skinner published in 1920. While it may be convenient, especially in connection with tourism, to use this label for the combined length of the separate historic market streets of the king's burgh of Edinburgh and Holyrood abbey's burgh of the Canongate, it is at the cost of blurring the distinction between the two and distorting the very nature of the place. It is not only meaningless historically, but unhappily gives an impression that this was a route created to link castle and palace, whereas the truth is that it came into being hundreds of years before the kings of Scots had anything to do with the fortress or (still later) the palace; and even although the HIGH STREET of Edinburgh and the street of THE CANONGATE (*which see*) were each described in medieval charters as *via regia*, 'king's street', this was not a proper name but simply the term for any public highway, and each of the streets owed its development wholly to its particular burgh. Yet more unhappily, the nickname is now tending to supplant their historic names, with a regrettable loss of civic dignity.

ROYAL MILL (Balerno) *see under* CRAIGMILL and RAVELRIG, Balerno.

ROYAL PARK TERRACE (Meadowbank) is a section of the old hiegate to Haddington from Canongate. It was known generally as MEADOWBANK, from the property of that name which extended along its north side, until after 1873, when housing development starting in that property was called ROYAL PARK TERRACE because it overlooked the Queen's Park. The name was continued in ROYAL PARK PLACE in about 1893.

ROYAL TERRACE (Calton) was planned as the grandest street in the CALTON NEW TOWN (*which see*) and is named on *Calton* 1819, in general compliment to George III and the Prince Regent. ROYAL TERRACE MEWS and GARDENS, like those of REGENT TERRACE and CARLTON TERRACE were part of the original plan.

ROYSTON (Granton) was an alternative name, first recorded in 1611, for *Easter Granton* (*see under* GRANTON). The name is evidently *Roy's* (*ferm*)*toun*, derived from someone called Roy but as yet untraced. ROYSTON HOUSE, dating from about 1585 and shown as *Ranstoun* on *Adair* 1682, was rebuilt in a grand manner by George Mackenzie, Viscount Tarbat, between 1683 and 1696; but in 1739 it was renamed CAROLINE PARK (*see under* GRANTON) by its new owner the Duke of Argyll, who at the same time renamed the 16th-century Granton Castle as ROYSTON CASTLE. ROYSTON TERRACE was formed in about 1879 in Goldenacre, which was a detached part of Royston or Easter Granton. ROYSTON MAINS, shown as *Roystoun* on *Roy* 1753, was the home farm of the estate, and stood immediately east of the junction of Royston Mains Road with West Granton Road. Its development for housing began in 1936, when ROYSTON MAINS AVENUE, CRESCENT, GARDENS, GREEN, PLACE, ROAD and STREET were named. ROYSTON MAINS CLOSE was added in 1993.

ROYSTON'S CLOSE (322 High Street) *see* RIDDLE'S CLOSE.

RUSSELL PLACE (Trinity) was developed in the later 1850s on the site of a market garden owned by James Russell in 1842.

RUSSELL ROAD (Roseburn) was developed in the earlier 1890s (only its most northerly section is shown on *Ordnance Survey* 1893) from a lane, shown on *Ordnance Survey* 1852, which had evidently established the right of way under the North British railway lines. It was named by 1897, possibly for Sir James Russell, Lord Provost 1891-94, but perhaps, considering its site, for the Russells of Roseburn, who traced themselves back to Mungo Russell, city treasurer, builder of the original tower of Roseburn in 1582.

RUSTIC COTTAGES (Colinton) were so named as being designed in a 'rustic' style by Sir Robert Lorimer in 1902-4.

RUTHERFORD DRIVE (Inch) *see under* THE INCH, Nether Liberton.

RUTLAND STREET and **SQUARE** (West End) occupy a property shown as *Mrs Stewart's* on *Ainslie* 1804 and *Kirkwood* 1817, and were planned by Archibald Elliot for James Stuart in 1819. John Learmonth bought the ground in 1825, but the scheme lay fallow and apparently unnamed until RUTLAND STREET was begun in 1830, RUTLAND PLACE in 1832 and RUTLAND SQUARE in 1834. RUTLAND COURT, shown as a timber yard on *Ordnance Survey* 1852, was named by 1893. Presumably the *Rutland* name was chosen by Learmonth, but the reason for it remains obscure.

RYEHILL AVENUE etc (South Leith) *see under* CORNHILL TERRACE, South Leith.

S

SADDLETREE LOAN (Inch) *see under* THE INCH, Nether Liberton.

St ALBAN'S ROAD (Grange) *see under* THE GRANGE.

St ANDREW'S PLACE (South Leith) is shown on *Thomson* 1822 as the access to the High School, built in 1806; but in 1826, being still 'without any particular designation', the street was named by the congregation of St Andrew's Secession Kirk at the same time as they acquired the ground fronting it for a new kirk building. They in turn had taken their name from St Andrew's Street, South Leith, where they had built their original kirk in 1788.

St ANDREW SQUARE and **STREET** etc (New Town) *see under* NEW TOWN. The modern spellings appeared on *Kirkwood* 1823 and soon prevailed.

St ANDREW'S STREET (South Leith) *see under* DUB RAW.

St ANDREW'S SQUARE (Newhaven) is shown on *Ainslie* 1804 as an unnamed open space. Although given on *Ordnance Survey* 1852, the name is first listed in *PO Directory* 1864. In 1968, for fear of confusion with St Andrew Square in the New Town, it was changed to FISHMARKET SQUARE, referring to the market north of it, which had been opened in 1896.

St ANN(E) STREET (East End) was formed in about 1770 by a developer John Home. Descending steeply from Princes Street immediately west of the North Bridge, it is shown on *Armstrongs* 1773 and its name, evidently fancy, appears on *Ainslie* 1780. It was purchased and suppressed in 1816 by the town council, who built a new terrace of houses set back twelve feet from the Bridge and intended to improve the view of the Register House from it, the twelve-foot gap being arched over to form a wide pavement. The terrace was cleared away in 1896, for the building of the North British Hotel.

St ANN'S YARD (Holyrood) figures on *Rothiemay* 1647, and is shown on *W & A K Johnston* 1861 as added to the Queen's Park. It is reported in *Maitland* 1753 that it was named for a chapel of St Anne 'be-east the bowling green west of the palace' (now part of the palace gardens) but there is no record of such a chapel, and it is more likely that the ground was attached to the altar of St Anne within Holyrood Abbey, served by the Tailors of the Canongate and described in their letters of incorporation in 1554 as 'ane altar biggit within the abbey, quhair Sanct An, their patrone, now stands'.

St ANTHONY'S CHAPEL (Arthur's Seat) is recorded in 1426 as *St Anthonis on the Crag*, and is shown on *Hertford's Assault* 1544 and named and shown in some detail on *Siege of Leith* 1560. It may be presumed, although there is no evidence of it, that it was connected with the preceptory of St ANTHONY, South Leith (*which see*) founded in 1418. St ANTHONY'S WELL, shown on *Kirkwood* 1817 and mentioned in the old song 'O waly, waly' which may date back to the 1670s, is said by *Grant* to have altered its position about that period. St ANTHONY'S CAVE appears on *Ordnance Survey* 1852, and is probably a fancy extension of the name; and much the same may be true of St ANTHONY'S HERMITAGE, more prosaically thought to have been a storehouse.

St ANTHONY'S (South Leith) was a preceptory of the friars of St Anthony, founded in 1418 and situated on the west side of Kirkgate, south of Trinity House—i.e. on the present sites of NEWKIRKGATE and St ANTHONY'S LANE. St ANTHONY'S STREET (anciently, WYND) marks the site of *St Anthony's Yards*, and St ANTHONY'S PLACE is the modern name for the final section of the YARDHEADS which was cut off from the rest of that street when Henderson Street was driven across it in 1888. St ANTHONY'S PORT was part of the fortifications of 1548, giving entrance to Kirkgate from the Edinburgh road, as shown on *Siege of Leith* 1560; but it functioned for barely 20 years, for in 1560, as soon as the siege was over, the Government ordered the Town Council of Edinburgh to 'cast down and demolish the south part of the said town (i.e. Leith) begynand at Sanct Anthone's Port and passing westward, making the Blockhouse (i.e. the bastion at St Anthony's) and the curtain (wall) equal with the ground'. The Preceptory was dissolved in 1592 and its revenues passed in trust to South Leith Kirk Session, who applied them to the foundation of the *King James Hospital* in 1614.

St ANTHONY'S PLACE (Tollcross) is shown on *Kirkwood* 1823 as a terrace already built but part of a larger scheme proposed for the Lothian Road; and St ANTHONY'S LANE is shown also begun and planned as a mews lane to serve houses fronting that main road. The name is fancy, and the reasons for its choice remain to be traced. The side name was dropped in 1893, when the name MORRISON STREET was extended to include the terrace. The name CHUCKIE PEND for the arched entrance to the Lane would imply that the roadway was surfaced in gravel, rather than causey setts.

St BERNARD'S CRESCENT (Stockbridge) *see under* DEANHAUGH, Stockbridge.

St BERNARD'S WELL (Stockbridge) was given this fancy name in 1760, when a stone casing was built round the medicinal spring that three Heriot's boys, it is said, had discovered some time before. The present Roman Doric *tempietto* and pump room was built for Francis Gordon, Lord Gardenston, in 1789, to a design by Alexander Nasmyth, and was restored, with a new statue of Hygeia, in 1887. Meantime the name *St Bernard's* had been borrowed for part of the estate of DEANHAUGH (*which see*) and for St BERNARD'S ROW in Deanhaugh village, originating before 1817 as the name of a terrace of new houses along the west side of the old road leading by a ford and Water Lane (now Glenogle Road) to Canonmills; and also for St BERNARD'S BRIDGE, built in about 1822, and St BERNARD'S PLACE, *see under* SAUNDERS STREET, Stockbridge.

St CATHERINE'S GARDENS (Corstorphine) was built in 1898 and given the name of *St Catherine's*, one of three earlier houses on the site.

St CATHERINE PLACE (Grange) *see under* THE GRANGE.

St CLAIR STREET (Quarryholes, South Leith) was named in about 1902 for the *St Clair Works* of Dobson Molle, printers, who had moved here from an earlier works of the same name at 11 Elliot Street; and the choice of name evidently arose from the fact that in 1878 this ground at Elliot Street was owned by a Thomas Watson of St Clair Street, Aberdeen. Although planned along with St Clair Street, St CLAIR PLACE was not occupied until about 1910, and St CLAIR ROAD and AVENUE followed still later, the last being named in 1925.

St CLAIR TERRACE (Plewlands) *see under* PLEWLANDS, South Morningside.

St COLME STREET (New Town) *see under* MORAY ESTATE, New Town.

St CUTHBERT'S ENTRY (West Port) is listed as 145 West Port in *PO Directory* 1827 and is shown on *Ordnance Survey* 1852 as *St Cuthbert's Close*, leading past the south side of St Cuthbert's Free Kirk into Spittal Street; but obviously the reference in 1827 was to the West Kirk of St Cuthbert's, and this is borne out on *Ainslie* 1780, where the close leads to a path skirting Livingston's Yards and entering the main road to the West Kirk. The same arrangement appears to be shown in an earlier form on *Rothiemay* 1647, where the close is shown well developed as the way to Livingston's Yards.

St CUTHBERT'S LANE (West End) is shown on *Laurie* 1763 and (unchanged) on *Ordnance Survey* 1852, which also shows the riding academy that latterly gave it its other name RIDING SCHOOL LANE. It was diverted at its northern end when the first Prince Street Railway Station was built on the riding-school site in 1870, and was almost entirely suppressed when the station was rebuilt in 1893. A vestige survives at TOBAGO PLACE, *which see*. The lane was named as a 'kirk road' leading to St Cuthbert's Kirk, and more particularly because it formed a boundary of the kirk glebe.

St CUTHBERT'S STREET (Haymarket) *see under* TORPHICHEN STREET, Haymarket.

St DAVID'S PLACE and **TERRACE** (Haymarket) were built in Morrison Street in the early 1870s, on ground adjoining St David's Church, now replaced by an office block.

St DAVID STREET (New Town) *see under* NEW TOWN.

St FILLANS TERRACE (South Morningside) *see under* PLEWLANDS, South Morningside.

St GEORGE'S WELL (Dean Gorge) was built over a medicinal spring in 1810, and named in compliment to George III, who attained his jubilee in that year.

St GILES STREET (Old Town) was formed at BROWN'S CLOSE (*which see*) in about 1869, and was named for the High Kirk of St Giles, and possibly also for John Knox's connection with the close in 1568-69.

St JAMES' SQUARE (East End) was planned in 1773 by James Craig for Walter Ferguson, writer, who along with other lawyers named Gray and Steuart owned most of the site in Cleland's Yards. Building started in 1775 in Gray's ground at BUNKER HILL (*which see*) and progressed in succeeding decades to form the SQUARE, as well as SOUTH, NORTH and EAST St JAMES' STREET, St JAMES' PLACE, and (LITTLE) KING STREET, all shown on *Ainslie* 1804, although the name of St James' Place first appears on *Strangers Guide* 1816. Since all three of the developers were fervent Jacobites, meeting annually in Steuart's house to celebrate Prince Charles Edward's birthday (Robert Burns was among those present on the last occasion of the sort, a month before Charles's death in January 1788) it is likely that the *St James'* name was a covert reference, only 27 years after Culloden, to the Old Pretender, who had died in 1766; and that *King Street* (which acquired the *Little-* in about the 1840s) was named for the Young Pretender, Charles Edward himself. But for Nos. 27-31 St James' Square, the whole area was cleared for redevelopment in 1965.

St JAMES STREET (Pilrig) *see under* SPEY TERRACE, Pilrig.

St JOHN'S CLOSE (188 Canongate) is listed on *Ainslie* 1780, but does not figure in the *Valuation Roll* 1635 because it lay in the Canongate, immediately east of the march with the royalty of Edinburgh at the Laplee Stane. It took its name from St JOHN'S LAND, *which see*. It is shown on *Kincaid* 1784 as CHARTERS (CLOSE) but nothing is known about this name. In a deed of 1821 it is referred to as PATERSON'S, for a one-time owner of property west of St John's Street: George Paterson, architect, associated with Robert Mylne in the building of St Cecilia's Hall in 1761.

St JOHN'S CROSS (Canongate) *see under* St JOHN'S LAND *and also* LAPLEE STANE, Canongate.

St JOHN'S HILL (Pleasance) first appears on *Kincaid* 1784 as the name of a development shown on *Armstrong* 1773 as just beginning. It has been suggested that the land was once connected with St JOHN'S LAND in the Canongate, and with the Knights of St John; but there is not a shred of evidence for it, and it is wholly improbable that any property in the Canongate would as it were leapfrog the South Back (now Holyrood Road) where the *strand* was the general boundary of the burgage land. Everything points to *St John's Hill* being a fancy name for this new residential area facing the older one of St JOHN'S STREET across the valley. St JOHN'S SQUARE was created in 1893, when a space hitherto entered from the Pleasance was altered to take entry from the LANG CLOSE (*which see*) which was itself remodelled at this time and made part of St John's Hill.

St JOHN'S ROAD (Corstorphine) is made up of parts of two ancient roads which met where the street still kinks abruptly just west of the entry to Templeland Road. The eastern section was part of the old Linlithgow or Stirling road which, as shown on *Roy* 1753, originally carried straight on westwards to CRAIGS ROAD, *which see*. The western section of the street appears on *Adair* 1682 as if it were a branch off the Linlithgow road, leading to Bathgate; but the alignments suggest that the junction was perhaps originally a crossroads, and that this section may have continued eastwards to Back Dean, as a part of Roman Dere Street, *see under* ROMAN ROADS *and* GLASGOW ROAD. Thus the road, although not the main street of Corstorphine village, was always the main highway; and it was known simply as such until 1887, when the new development of the 'upper village' of Corstorphine required a more specific address, and this section of highway was named for the patron saint of the medieval chapel of St John the Baptist in the old village. By 1911 the name was borrowed for St JOHN'S TERRACE, built in the Paddockholm of Meadowhouse; and St JOHN'S AVENUE and GARDENS (1935) and CRESCENT (1966) followed suit.

St JOHN'S LAND (Canongate) is noted in *Protocols of John Foular* 1508 as the name of the 'land at the Loplie Stane under the Netherbow' feued out by the Black Friars, for a duty of 40s, and this was no doubt the same property 'of Lappie Stane' which shows a revenue of £2 in the rental book of the Friars in about 1560 (*Old Edinburgh Club III*, p82). There is nothing to support the guess by *Maitland* and others, that it was once owned by the Knights of St John; and the name remains obscure. The reference in *Foular* perhaps implies that in 1508 the LAPLEE STANE (*which see*) had not yet acquired its alternative name of St JOHN'S CROSS, first recorded 61 years later, and it seems likely it got it from *St John's Land*. The same is probably true of St JOHN'S CLOSE, *which see*; and since the Close lies on the Canongate side of the march with Edinburgh's CANONGATEHEAD (*which see*) it is likely that the Land was also in the Canongate, and gave its name directly to St JOHN'S STREET, a terrace of stylish houses begun in 1768 on ground shown on *Edgar* 1765 as for the most part open.

St KATHERINE'S BRAE etc (Liberton) *see under* the BALM WELL OF St KATHERINE, Liberton.

St LEONARDS (South Side) together with NORTH LEITH, the COALHILL, and IRNESIDE (*which see*) formed the lands of St Leonard's, included in David I's foundation grants to Holyrood abbey in 1128. This southerly part of the lands stretched from Holyrood southwards to a march with Prestonfield, and from Holyrood Park westwards to an irregular boundary running next the Pleasance, the Bristo crofts, and the ancient Causeyside (Buccleuch Street) and Mounthouly Loan (Preston Street) before doubling round the neuk of the Gallowgreen or Spittalfield and turning down the Dalkeith Road to Marchhall. The name is recorded in the late 12th century in the dedication of a hospital or almshouse, and the presence of a chapel beside it is confirmed in a charter of 1391. The *manse of St Leonard's* was on the north side of Abbey Strand; but the almshouse and chapel, reorganised in 1493 as a separate foundation (*see under* HERMITS and TERMITS) were at St LEONARD'S HILL or CRAGS. *Vico St Leonards* (1485) and St LEONARD'S GAIT (1507) or WYND (1632) were early names for THE PLEASANCE (*which see*) and St LEONARD'S ROAD (later DUMMIEDYKES ROAD) is shown on *Roy* 1753 and named on *Regality of Canongate* 1813. St LEONARD'S LANE, also shown on *Roy*, is named as *St Leonard's Hill* on most maps prior to the 1850s; and while the present street name St LEONARD'S HILL makes its appearance on *Ordnance Survey* 1852, it is shown as continuing southwards to include St LEONARD'S BANK, separately named in 1887. St LEONARD'S CRAG was utilised as a street name in 1986.

St LEONARD'S LANDS (Leith) were part of David I's grant to Holyrood abbey in about 1128, and as shown on *Regality of Canongate* 1813 they included NORTH LEITH and the COALHILL, *which see*. St LEONARD'S WYND in South Leith is named in 1439 (*XXVI of Charters relating to Edinburgh*) as forming, 'as it extended of old time', the southern boundary of the St Leonard's lands of the Coalhill, and this is still clearly shown on *Ordnance Survey* 1852. It is referred to as St Leonard's Gait in 1508, and listed as *St Leonard's Lane* on *Wood* 1777. It was suppressed in the later 19th century.

St MARGARET'S LOCH (Holyrood Park) is an artificial loch formed in about 1856. It is shown on *W & A K Johnston* 1861 as *St Anthony's Loch*, named for St ANTHONY'S CHAPEL, *which see*; but by 1876 it had been given the equally fancy name of *St Margaret's Loch*, probably influenced by the rebuilding of St MARGARET'S WELL, Meadowbank (*which see*) in the Holyrood Park.

St MARGARET'S WELL (Meadowbank, but now in Holyrood Park) was a medieval pilgrims' well beside the road to Restalrig, *see* CLOCKMILL LANE. In 1859, after the vaulted wellhouse had become virtually buried in the St Margaret's Works and Locomotive Depot (as shown on *Ordnance Survey* 1852), the 15th-century interior was pinned up in brickwork, so that its dressed stonework could be removed and used to build an exact replica at St David's Well in Holyrood Park, then renamed *St Margaret's Well*; and in 1969 the original vault, shorn of all dressings but still existing below ground in Meadowbank Sports Centre, was recorded and then filled with concrete.

St MARGARET'S WELL (Princes St Gardens) is the name now attached to the spring at the foot of the Castle rock, which was guarded by the WELLHOUSE TOWER and served as an auxiliary water supply for the Castle. This is assumed in *Maitland* 1753 and other later accounts to be the *Sanct Margarettis well* referred to in accounts of the siege of the Castle in 1573 and in *RMS* 1578 (quoting a charter of 1566) and *RMS* 1648; but the charter evidence is not only that that well was the spring mentioned in David I's charters to St Cuthbert's kirk and Holyrood abbey in 1127 and 1128 as rising 'near the corner of my garden', but that it lay at the west end of the 'tail' of the ground of the BARRACE (*which see*) and was clearly on the west side of the 'way to St Cuthbert's', now King's Stables Road. As a landmark it seems to have disappeared by Maitland's time, enabling the name to be transferred to the spring at the Wellhouse Tower, almost 300 yards further east.

St MARK'S LANE and **PLACE** (Portobello) were named for St Mark's Episcopal Chapel, erected 1824; but *Wood's Portobello* 1824 shows the LANE already built and serving as a meuse to houses on the High Street west of the chapel site. St MARK'S PLACE was developed by 1880.

St MARK'S PLACE (Warriston) appears as *Mark's Place* on *Kirkwood* 1817 and maps up until the 1870s, but for *Ordnance Survey* 1852, which introduces the *St*. It seems likely that it was named for a local resident, for the name was not unknown in the neighbourhood—a James Marks was a farmer in Broughton in the 1720s, and a member of the birlaw court of Leith.

St MARY'S PLACE (Portobello) was formed, together with its LANES, in the 1880s. The name was evidently suggested by that of nearby St MARK'S PLACE (*which see*) since a Mary was the mother of Mark.

St MARY(S) WYND (Old Town) was the medieval approach to the Netherbow from the south, mentioned by John of Fordoun in about 1380 and shown on *Hertford* 1544; but it may have originated as a diversion of an earlier route represented by the BACK ROW of the Pleasance, *which see*. It took its name from the chapel and hospice of St Mary (not to be confused with Maitland's fictitious convent 'St Mary of Placentia'—*see under* THE PLEASANCE) which stood on its west side, about forty yards south of the Netherbow, on land later entered from World's End Close. Said to have been originally Cistercian, it was in the control of the Town Council by 1499 and they were still operating it as a refuge for the destitute in 1589. Along with the south Canongatehead as far east as the Laplee Stane (*which see*) the wynd was part of Edinburgh even although it was outwith the town's main defences; it is mentioned in *Town Council Minutes* 1477 as the place of the ironwork market, and it was closed at its foot, on the line of the buildings and heid dykes along the north side of the South Back of Canongate (now Holyrood Road) by the St MARY WYND PORT, which (as very clearly shown on *Rothiemay* 1647) was south of the COWGATE PORT—an arrangement which is still reflected in the differing alignments of the Cowgate and Holyrood Road where they each intersect St Mary's Street. The houses on the west side of the wynd served as part of the town's defences between the Cowgate Port and the Netherbow: even in times of peace their doors and windows had to be maintained lockfast, and when warfare threatened they were hastily built up. As shown on *City Improvements* 1866, the wynd was more than doubled in width in 1867, by dint of sweeping away all the buildings on its east side, and it was renamed St MARY'S STREET.

St MONAN'S WYND (High Street) ran on a line now represented at its northern end by the eastern arcade of Parliament Square and at its southern end by HANGMAN'S CLOSE at 140 Cowgate, *which see*. Given on *Rothiemay* 1647 as *St Monans wyne* and said to be derived from a chapel in the close, the name took an astonishing number of corrupt forms, such as *St Ninian's Close, Lady St Ninian's, Ladie St Mennens* or *St Minnins, Lady Minnis* or *Lady Menyies*. The name STEIL'S CLOSE, given on *Edgar* 1742, remains obscure. The names NEW BANK CLOSE on *Ainslie* 1780 and ROYAL BANK CLOSE on *Kirkwood* 1817 both derive from the Royal Bank, 'new' as compared with the 'old' Bank of Scotland, which moved here from its first office in Old Stamp Office Close (also called New Bank Close) in about 1750.

St NICHOLAS CHAPEL (North Leith) stood on the western outskirts of North Leith, as shown on *Siege of Leith* 1560. Its dedication to the patron saint of seafarers fits in with the strong connection of North Leith with shipping. It must have dated back before 1488, when St NICHOLAS WYND, leading to it, is mentioned in *Protocols of James Young*; and since its kirkyard was the burying ground for North Leith, it is likely that it was 'the church of Lye', recorded in 1335. In 1569, along with the chapel of St NINIAN (*see under* St NINIAN'S WYND, North Leith) it was feued from the burgh of the Canongate to the inhabitants of North Leith. In 1656, when the site was cleared for the building of THE CITADEL (*which see*) the parish was given a new burying ground (at Coburg Street) in lieu of the kirkyard. Within thirty years thereafter, the part of the Citadel that had displaced the chapel was lost to the sea by coastal erosion; but the site was reclaimed when the West Dock was built in 1811-17.

St NICHOLAS PORT or **WEST GATE** (North Leith) is shown on *Siege of Leith* 1560 as a gateway in the ramparts of 1548, immediately south of the bastion which contained the St NICHOLAS CHAPEL.

St NINIAN'S CLOSE (High Street) *see* St MONAN'S WYND.

St NINIAN'S ROAD (Corstorphine) was developed in the *South Bank* field of Featherhall, and was named by 1903, evidently for the altar of St Ninian in the medieval kirk of Corstorphine. The street name was taken by the United Free Church in 1929, and by St NINIAN'S DRIVE ten years later.

St NINIAN'S ROW (Calton) is shown on *Rothiemay* 1647 as *St Ninian's* or *St Ringan's suburb* or the *Beggars Raw*, and the name has continued on the west side of the Low Calton (i.e. outwith the barony of Calton) despite huge parts of the ground being taken over for the development of REGENT BRIDGE and WATERLOO PLACE, and the North British Railway's goods yard. Holyrood Abbey records of 1554 mention the chapel dedicated to Ninian or Ringan, and *Arnot* 1778 describes it as converted into a house, on a site now occupied by the west abutment of the Regent Arch. In 1778 Walter Ross removed a font from it and built it into his folly at Deanhaugh; and in 1816, when the folly was cleared away for the building of Ann Street, the font found its way to Sir Walter Scott's garden at Abbotsford along with other historic fragments that Ross had collected.

St NINIAN'S TERRACE (South Morningside) *see under* PLEWLANDS, South Morningside.

St NINIAN'S WYND (North Leith) led from the medieval Brig of Leith to the CHAPEL OF St NINIAN and the single street of NORTH LEITH, *which see*. Both the bridge and the chapel were built by Robert Bellenden or Ballantyne, abbot of Holyrood, and his charter of 1493 endowed the chapel with the bridge tolls, as well as income from property in the Coalhill, which along with North Leith belonged to the abbey's regality of the Canongate. In 1569, along with the St NICHOLAS CHAPEL (*which see*) the chapel was feued from the Canongate to the inhabitants of North Leith, who altered it to make it their parish kirk; and it served as such until 1816, when it was replaced by a new kirk in Madeira Street. The old building was turned into a granary in 1825, and fragments of it are still to be seen in the east end of Quayside Mills. Mentioned as St NINIAN'S WYND in the 15th century, the street became a cul-de-sac when Bellenden's bridge was taken down in about 1789. By 1834 it was called St NINIAN'S LANE; but it became CHURCH STREET in 1890, and in 1966 the name was changed yet again (ostensibly to remedy duplication with Church Street in Stockbridge, *see under* CHURCH LANE, Stockbridge) the present name QUAYSIDE STREET referring not to any particular quay, but to the Quayside Mills.

St PATRICK'S STREET (South Side) is shown as in course of building on *Ainslie* 1780 and is named on *Kincaid* 1784 although not listed in the *Accurate View* 1783. The name may have been connected with Patrick Tod, an owner in the vicinity in 1767; or else reflects some Irish connection or enthusiasm of the developer, William Archibald, slater in the Goosedub immediately next to the site on the west. The site was in the *Cabbagehall*, feued from Gairnshall in 1708 by William Stevenson, gardener, and whimsically named for one of his products. St PATRICK'S SQUARE, also within Cabbagehall, is sketched and named on *Brown & Watson* 1793; its east and north sides, including SIBBALD PLACE, are shown built up on *Ainslie* 1804, but the west and south sides seem to have followed in the 1820s.

St PAUL'S WARK (Canongate) was set up in 1479 by Thomas Spence, bishop of Aberdeen, as a hospital and almshouse, *wark* being simply the Scots term for 'building'. A full account of it is given in *Old Edinburgh Club XVII*. In 1619 it became a trade school (*see also* BONNYHAUGH) and in 1632 part of it was altered or extended to provide a *House of Correction*, both being shown on *Rothiemay* 1647. Like Trinity College kirk, it was cleared away when the North British Railway's station was built in 1848, as shown on *Ordnance Survey* 1852.

St PETER'S PLACE and **BUILDINGS** (Merchiston) were named for St Peter's Free Kirk (Viewforth St David's & St Oswald's) built in 1871.

St RONAN'S TERRACE (South Morningside) *see under* PLEWLANDS, South Morningside.

St ROQUE'S (Morningside) was a chapel in the burgh muir south of Grange Loan, built in about 1502, probably by the town council, and dedicated to St Roque of Montpellier, patron saint of those stricken by the plague, and endowed with a strip of land running from the loan down to the Pow burn. Its site is marked on *Kirkwood* 1817 and *Ordnance Survey* 1852.

St STEPHEN'S STREET (Stockbridge) originated as two separate streets on either side of the Clarence Street junction. The western section is shown planned on *Wood* 1823 and was begun and named BRUNSWICK STREET in 1824—for possible derivations of the name, *see* BRUNSWICK STREET, Hillside. The other section began as one of a pair of quadrants planned to flank St Stephen's Church, as shown on *Lothian* 1829, and had taken its name from the church by 1832. In 1882 the Town Council extended the *St Stephen's* name to cover the whole street. MARKET PLACE, renamed St STEPHEN'S PLACE in 1882, was added to the plan for Brunswick Street in 1824, as a grand approach to the new STOCKBRIDGE MARKET, *which see*.

St TERESA PLACE (Merchiston) was named in 1985 as a new development on the site occupied between 1925 and 1982 by a Carmelite convent of St Teresa of Avila.

St THOMAS ROAD (Grange) *see under* THE GRANGE.

St VINCENT STREET (New Town) *see under* NORTHERN NEW TOWN.

SALAMANDER STREET (South Leith) is shown on *Wood* 1777 as developing from a section of the coast road to Musselburgh shown on *Roy* 1753. *Roy* also shows the first of the glass furnaces set up here in 1747, when the glass-making which had been started in North Leith in the previous century was transferred to South Leith Sands. The street is named on *Ainslie* 1804, which shows the number of furnaces increased to six; and it is fairly obvious that the street name alluded to this thriving industry and derived from the medieval legend of the fire-proof lizard. In 1967 the adjoining BATH STREET, South Leith (*which see*) was renamed SALAMANDER PLACE, in order to obviate any confusion with Bath Street, Portobello.

SALISBURY CRAGS (Holyrood) are referred to as *Cragge* in the 1170s and *Crag* in 1496, as 'crag called *salisbere*' in the *Holyrood Ordinale* c1450, and *Salisborie crag* or *craggis* in *Town Council Minutes* 1554; while the *Salisbrae* recorded in Holyrood in 1540 probably belongs here, even although crags are not mentioned. The suggestion in *Arnot* 1778 that the name derived from the earl of Salisbury, commander of the English army of occupation in 1335, is a wildly improbable guess. Rather it appears to be British *salis bre* or else Anglian *sales berig*, in either case meaning 'willows hill', and might have belonged to the whole western spur of Arthur's Seat, making the Crags more specifically 'the crag(s) at the willows hill'. For other 'willow' names in the vicinity of Arthur's Seat *see* DRUMSELCH, WILLOWBRAE and PIERSHILL.

SALISBURY PLACE and **ROAD** (Newington) are shown as proposed on Bell's *Plan of Newington* 1806 and as though largely built up on *Knox* 1812. They are named SALISBURY ROAD on *Kirkwood* 1817, and SALISBURY PLACE had its own separate name by 1826. The name was perhaps suggested by that of nearby *Salisbury Green*, built in about 1784; but in any case it derived from the view of the Crags and not from any local place name.

SALISBURY STREET (Pleasance) is sketched on *Strangers Guide* 1816 and shown named on *Knox* 1821, while SALISBURY SQUARE was named by 1824. SALISBURY TERRACE is listed from 1867 until 1885, when it was renamed as part of Dumbiedykes Road. The *Salisbury Street* name was in the air in 1816, since *Kirkwood* 1817 shows it at what was later to become East Arthur Place, and it evidently referred to the view of the Crags across the valley of Holyrood Park.

SALMOND PLACE (Norton Park) *see under* MARYFIELD, Norton Park.

SALUTATION CLOSE (High Street) *see* BARON GRANT'S CLOSE.

SALVESEN CRESCENT, GARDENS and **TERRACE** (Muirhouse) followed by SALVESEN GROVE were named in 1948 and 1950 for Lord Salvesen, then chairman of the Scottish Veterans Garden City Association, developers of the streets.

SAMSON'S GRAVE and **RIBS** (Arthur's Seat) are both shown on *Kirkwood* 1817 and named for their giant size: the Grave a natural howe west of the Whinny Hill; the Ribs an immense cliff of columnar basalt, with a prehistoric fort on its summit, above the road to Duddingston.

SANDFORD GARDENS (Portobello) was called *Sandford Street* until 1899, and dates from about 1825, when St John's Episcopal Chapel, Brighton Place, was consecrated by Bishop Sandford.

SANDILAND'S CLOSE (71 High Street) is listed on *Edgar* 1742. Also recorded in 1713 as BAILIE SANDILAND'S, it takes its name from Robert Sandilands, three times bailie between 1647 and 1661, dean of guild 1661-64, listed as a tenant in the close in 1635, but later having property on its east side. Earlier, the close was AIKMAN'S, from a family owning property on its west side. A family of Aikmans was prominent in the town from before 1482, and the names John, Francis and William Aikman mentioned in the feu charters might fit those of John and William Aikman, entered in the burgess roll in 1517 and 1535 respectively, and Francis Aikman, recorded as a burgess in *RMS* 1545, but their connection with the close is not proven.

THE SANDPORT (North Leith) is shown on *Fergus & Robinson* 1759 as the *Sandy Port*. Robertson's wholly unreliable *Fortifications of Leith* 1850 interprets 'port' as 'gateway', but this is altogether at variance with *Siege of Leith* 1560, which shows the place in great detail as a harbour defended to seaward by a great palisade of timber and with a beach open to the town. *Naish* 1709 appears to show a graving dock; while *Wood* 1777 notes the beach as 'Carpenter's Yard' and shows a large slip which may have been used when the battleship HMS *Fury* was built here in 1780. Since the beach adjoined the BALLAST QUAY, it may have been a source of sand or gravel for ships' ballast. In 1812 the CUSTOM HOUSE was built on top of it; but the name THE SANDPORT remained that of the basin until this was infilled in about 1890, and it was renewed in 1985 as the name of new housing built on its site. SANDPORT STREET is the name given in about 1817 to a remnant of the old street of NORTH LEITH (*which see*) which of course led to the Sandport; but SANDPORT PLACE is all of 200 yards from the Sandport and had nothing to do with it: originally the medieval BROAD WYND of North Leith (*which see*), it was widened in 1789 to serve as the approach to the new UPPER DRAWBRIDGE, and by 1812 it was known as BRIDGE STREET; but in 1968 in order to obviate any confusion with Bridge Street in Portobello, it was renamed, obviously by association with Sandport Street, but without thought to the misleading impression it gives of the historic site of the Sandport.

SAUCHIEBANK (West Dalry) was named in 1983 for the *sauchs* or willows planted on the bank beside it, as part of the landscaping of the new industrial estate.

SAUGHTON, recorded since 1128 in such early forms as *Salectun* and *Salchtone*, is Anglian *salig tún*, sauchie or willowy farm. Originally including SAUGHTONHALL (*which see*), the lands belonged to Holyrood Abbey from 1128 until they were secularized in 1587. *Saughton* 1795 shows the estate as then including SAUGHTON MAINS, evidently the home or *domaine* farm of

Saughton, as well as PARKHEAD, LERBAR, SIGHTHILL, THE LAIRDSHIP, BANKHEAD, BROOMHOUSE and CLAYCLOTE, together with STENHOPE MILL, *see under* STENHOUSE, Saughton. SAUGHTON HOUSE, dating from 1623, was ruined by fire in 1918 and finally cleared away in 1956, when Broomhouse Primary School was built on its site. It had tended to be called *Old Saughton* after 1741, when James Watson of Saughton, marrying a daughter of the earl of Hopetoun, flitted to the more pretentious house of CAMMO in Cramond and dubbed it *New Saughton*. SAUGHTON ROAD, shown on *Roy* 1753 and in detail on *Saughton* 1795, appears to be the *kirk road* or way to the parish kirk, which is mentioned in a deed of 1590 (quoted in *RMS* 1662 No. 308) but evidently got its present name as the road to Saughton from Corstorphine and from the Calder road. SAUGHTON LOAN (renamed SAUGHTON MAINS STREET in 1931) branched off it to Saughton Mains farm and thence to the clachan of LOANEND beside the Calder road. SAUGHTON MAINS steading was near the east end of Saughton Mains Drive; and development of the farm began in 1948 with SAUGHTON MAINS AVENUE, DRIVE, GARDENS, GROVE, LOAN, PLACE and TERRACE, and continued with SAUGHTON MAINS BANK (1955) COTTAGES (1958) and PARK (1964). SAUGHTON AVENUE and SAUGHTON CRESCENT, GARDENS, GROVE, LOAN and PARK, as well as SAUGHTON PUBLIC PARK are all confusingly misnamed, being in SAUGHTONHALL— *which see*—and the effect of this, coupled with the misnaming of the historic centre of Saughton as BROOMHOUSE and the interposing of an entirely modern STENHOUSE between Saughton and Saughtonhall, has been to make the location of *Saughton* as a modern neighbourhood variable, if not uncertain.

SAUGHTON AVENUE (Factor's Parks) developed from a lane shown on *Ordnance Survey* 1912, and was named in about 1922 on the assumption that it would continue straight on to the bridge leading to Balgreen, as shown on *Bartholomew* 1923, but this was frustrated by the development of Stevenson Road three years later. The *Saughton-* name is a misnomer, arising from misreading of the name SAUGHTONHALL, *which see*. The street was in fact built within the Factor's Parks of Saughtonhall.

SAUGHTONHALL is recorded from 1478 onwards, *Souchtonhall* being typical of the early spellings. The ground was originally that part of the Holyrood lands of SAUGHTON (*which see*) which lay 'on the haugh' or wedge of low ground in the neuk between the Water of Leith and the Stank, east of Saughton Mains Road and the west side of Carrick Knowe golf course; and the name *Saughtonhall* is not 'hall of Saughton' but 'haugh (Anglian *halh* Scots *haw*) of Saughton'. *Saughtonhall* 1795 lists the fields and shows the estate of 349 Scots acres made up of the farms of DALYELL'S MILL (later called SAUGHTONHALL MAINS), CARRICK KNOWES and BALGREEN, together with the 17-acre FACTOR'S PARKS (east of the river, and later sold to Gorgie) and the policies of SAUGHTONHALL HOUSE. Since *Blaeu* 1654 (surveyed in about 1596) shows two mansion houses, both named *Sauchton*, it is likely that there was a house at Saughtonhall by the 16th century; but it was superseded by the Saughtonhall House built by Robert Baird, merchant in Edinburgh, who bought the lands in 1660 and had them erected into a barony in 1667. The House was demolished in 1952, its site now a rose garden. Housing development began in the fields of Carrick Knowes and Balgreen called *Beggars Aiker* and *Langcote ley*, where SAUGHTONHALL DRIVE was named in 1908. SAUGHTONHALL AVENUE, CIRCUS, CRESCENT, GARDENS, GROVE, PLACE and TERRRACE followed in 1924, and the AVENUE was extended westwards in 1926. Meantime a lamentable confusion had arisen between the names *Saughton* and *Saughtonhall*, through misinterpreting the latter as 'hall of Saughton'; and this led to the inappropriate naming of SAUGHTON PUBLIC PARK, formed in the parks of Saughtonhall House in the 1890s, as well as SAUGHTON AVENUE (about 1906) in the Factor's Park, SAUGHTON CRESCENT (about 1910) in the Langcote Ley, and SAUGHTON GARDENS, GROVE, LOAN and PARK in 1926.

SAUNDERS STREET (Stockbridge) is shown on *Ainslie* 1804 as an access to properties along the river side; but a new development at its eastern end is named SAUNDERS PLACE on *Lothian* 1829 and the whole street is shown as SAUNDERS STREET on *Pollock* 1834. There may have been some link with a John Saunders, known to have had some business dealings with Sir Henry Raeburn, the superior.

SAVILE PLACE and **WEST SAVILE TERRACE** (West Mains of Liberton) got their names from the earlier SAVILE ROAD and TERRACE, *see under* CRAIGMILLAR PARK. West Savile Terrace was named and already developing from its eastern end in 1887. Although *-vile* remained the more frequent spelling, *-ville* (possibly influenced by 'Seville') appeared as early as 1888. SAVILE PLACE was named by 1902.

SAWER'S CLOSE (north side of Cowgate, east of Stevenlaw's Close) was a short blind close, shown on *Edgar* 1742 and named on *Ainslie* 1780. The origin of the name is still obscure.

SAXE-COBURG PLACE (Stockbridge) and the adjoining CLAREMONT PLACE were plannned together, as shown on *Wood* 1823. Both were named in honour of Prince Leopold of Saxe Coburg, widowed husband of Princess Charlotte, daughter of George IV. Leopold's popularity continued after his wife's untimely death in 1817, and he was given the freedom of Edinburgh in 1819. *Saxe Coburg* was his family name, and *Claremont* his home in Esher, Surrey. (*See also* LEOPOLD PLACE, Calton New Town; COBURG STREET, North Leith; CLAREMONT PARK, South Leith, and CLAREMONT STREET and CRESCENT, Broughton.) In 1828 the plan of the north end of Saxe-Coburg Place was changed, to make it a semicircular crescent (*Lothian* 1829 shows a proposal to connect it with a development on the haugh of the Whins, which was never built) but house-building ceased when the developer went bankrupt in 1834. By 1826, most of the east side of the original *Claremont Place* was built up; but its name had been changed to CLAREMONT STREET, while the name CLAREMONT PLACE reappeared round the corner by 1824, and continued until about 1890, when it was taken into HENDERSON ROW, *which see*. Also in about 1890, Claremont Street began to be called WEST CLAREMONT STREET, in order to distinguish it from (EAST) CLAREMONT STREET, in Broughton; and in 1968, for the same reason, the name was changed to SAXE-COBURG STREET. Its west side, built in 1870-76 as DEANBANK TERRACE (*see under* DEANBANK, Stockbridge) was renamed SAXE COBURG TERRACE in 1980.

SCHOOL BRAE (Cramond) is shown on *Cramond* 1815; and as access to the riverside it is clearly at least as old as the milling at FAIRAFAR (*which see*) and might conceivably go back to Roman times. The present name dates from after the building of the Board school in 1875.

SCHOOL BRAE (Queensferry) is the part of Hopetoun Road running westwards from the Shore Road corner for about 150 yards, and took its name from the school building (once the infants school) on that corner.

SCHOOL LANE (Queensferry) is shown on *Ordnance Survey* 1914. Its local name, obviously arising from the adjacent school, was formally adopted in 1984.

SCHOOL WYND (Ratho) was coined in 1983 as a name for an existing but unnamed opening which had been altered to give access to the new school built in the North Crofts of Ratho.

SCIENNES got its name from the convent set up here in 1517 by the Sisters of St Catherine of Siena—the Italian town name being *Seynis* or *Schiennes* in Scots, always pronounced and often spelt as *Sheens*. The 2-acre site of the convent lay in the angle between the east side of St Catherine's Place and Sciennes Road; and a kink in the latter's frontage still shows the position of the northeast corner of the nunnery's massive enclosing walls, 13 feet high, which were known as *Sheens Walls* until they were taken down in 1735, their stones being reused to enclose an enlarged area, including SCIENNES GARDENS, *see below*. In 1512, the land later called EAST SCIENNES (between the MUIRBURGH (*which see*) at Sciennes Place and the north back of Grange Court) was feued out of the Burgh Muir to John Crauford, canon of St Giles, who thereupon founded a chapel and hermitage of *St John in the Muir* (probably on the site of SCIENNES HILL HOUSE) and then donated it to the Sisters in 1517. The street of SCIENNES began as a path to the nunnery; but in 1606 the town had it *causeyed* or metalled as a road nine feet wide. As a neighbourhood name, *Sciennes* or *North Sciennes* spread westwards from this street over the strip of 16 Scots acres of the Burgh Muir between the South Loch and the Grange, its western boundary now marked by Roseneath Place. Feued out in 1538, it apparently included the GOODSPEED OF SCIENNES (*which see*) and the HOUSE

OF SHEENS mentioned as within it in 1593 probably stood near the corner of Sciennes and Sciennes Road. As shown on *Ordnance Survey* 1852, the name SCIENNES HOUSE eventually drifted 150 yards further north to a house shown on *Ainslie* 1804 as 'Mr Biggar's', no doubt connected with the firm of Walter Biggar & Co, weavers in the Sciennes in 1773. SCIENNES ROAD, mentioned in *RMS* 1538 (No.1827) as a loaning, probably originated as a track along the march between the Muir and the Grange. In 1758 it was widened to form a 27-foot roadway serving the various properties which had been developing in North Sciennes (*see under* HOPE PARK) and on *Grange* 1766 it is shown as a public road 'from back of the meadow (i.e. Bruntsfield Links) to Sheens'. Until about 1890 it was known as SCIENNES LOAN, except that from 1858 its most easterly section had been called SCIENNES HILL, *see under* SCIENNES HILL HOUSE. SCIENNES PLACE, so named in about 1832 but previously called SCIENNES ENTRY, gave access to the Sciennes between East Sciennes and the Muirburgh. SCIENNES GARDENS was formed in the late 1850s, within part of the hermitage of 1512 which became the convent's orchard and garden. Originally named MURRAY STREET, for the family of John Murray, accountant, who had acquired the ground in 1798, it was renamed in 1882. For SCIENNES HOUSE PLACE *see under* BRAID PLACE.

THE SCIENNES CROFT or **ACRES** (Old Town) was a croft of arable land lying east of the Greyfriars loan (now Candlemaker Row and Lindsay Place) and north of the Flodden Wall. It either was or else included the croft mentioned in *Town Council Minutes* 1510 as owned by Bartholomew Wawane and named in RMS 1528 and 1604 as WAWANISCROFT or WAWINSCROFT, but got the name *Sciennes* in 1517 when it was gifted to the new convent of the SCIENNES (*which see*) by the father of one of the founding Sisters, Beatrix Blakater or Blackadder. In 1541 it was feued from the Sisters by the town council, who transferred it in 1598 to the newly-founded Fellowship and Society of Brewers, and by 1619 the croft (or part of it) had come to be known simply as THE SOCIETY, *which see*. On *Rothiemay* 1647 as well as *Common Good* 1904 this name is restricted to a strip of about 2.7 Scots acres stretching alongside the highway from the Flodden Wall down to the south backs of the Canongate in the vicinity of Merchant Street; but it is certain that this was not the entire extent of the original croft, firstly because feu charters of properties in the Cowgate east of Scott's Close show that they backed on to Wawaniscroft, expressly noted in *RMS* 1604 as belonging to the Society, and secondly because the income of eight bolls of wheat and six of barley received by the Sisters from their land would have taken the whole crop from 2.7 acres, allowing neither expenses nor a living to the tenants who worked it. While research into sasines might give more information, the details of boundaries and gardens shown on *Rothiemay* suggest that the croft may have stretched most if not all the way eastwards to the Horse Wynd, now represented by West College Street.

SCIENNES HILL HOUSE (Sciennes) is shown on *Ainslie* 1804 as owned by 'Mr Gow', and it is built on ground which, shown as open on *Sheens* 1761 and *Bypass Roads* 1763, may have been the site of the chapel of St John in the Muir, erected by John Crauford in 1513, *see under Sciennes*. It is possible that SCIENNES HILL, although unrecorded, was the traditional name for the summit in the Causeyside or the ground in Sciennes adjoining it; but it was attached to the house by 1852, and from 1858 until about 1890 it was in use as the name of the most easterly section of Sciennes Loan or Road (*see under* SCIENNES), and SCIENNES HILL PLACE was named by 1860. In 1968, the renaming of BRAID PLACE (*which see*) as SCIENNES HOUSE PLACE evidently confused Sciennes Hill House with one or other of the earlier buildings known as 'Sciennes House', *see under* SCIENNES.

SCHOOL HOUSE or **SCHOOL CHIEF WYND** (205 Cowgate) *see* COLLEGE WYND.

THE SCLYVERS (Arthur's Seat) is shown on *Kirkwood* 1817, the name being Scots (from Anglian *scylfe*, shelf) for broken rocks of a thin-bedded sort.

SCONE GARDENS (Parson's Green) *see under* PARSON'S GREEN.

SCOTLAND STREET (New Town) *see under* NORTHERN NEW TOWN.

SCOTSTOUN (Queensferry) is recorded as *Scottistoun* from 1483 onwards, and its subdivision into *Over* and *Nether Scottistoun* is first mentioned in 1582; but the site of the house shown as SCOTSTOWN on *Forrest* 1818 and SCOTSTON PARK on *Ordnance Survey* 1854 (now replaced by a modern building, SCOTSTOUN HOUSE) is shown as open ground labelled *Baillie Dick's Park* on *Dundas* 1757 and *Mr Liston's* on *Barnbougle & Dalmeny* c1800. The name is Anglian or Scots *Scot's tún*, farm belonging either to someone of that name, or else to a *Scot*, which still meant specifically 'a Gaelic speaker' in the 14th century, as shown by several charters by Robert the Bruce, which address his subjects variously as *Frankish, Inglis, Scottis*, and *Gallovidians*. SCOTSTOUN AVENUE, GROVE and PARK (the last in part of the house policies) were named by 1970, and SCOTSTOUN GREEN and SOUTH SCOTSTOUN (the latter on the FERRY ACRES, *which see*) were named in 1982 and 1983.

SCOTTIS SEA *see under* FORTH.

SCOTT'S CLOSE (Canongate) was an entry off the east side of Leith Wynd, mentioned in *Canongate Burgh Court* in 1586, and shown but not named on *Edgar* 1742. Sasines mention as many as six Scotts as owners in the 17th century or earlier.

SCOT(T)'S CLOSE (123 Cowgate) is recorded in 1707 and shown on Edgar 1742. It was evidently named for Thomas Scott, listed in 1635 as an occupier owning a dyeworks and well, who may have been the Thomas Scott, burgess and brewer, mentioned in titles of 1707 as a former owner, along with Charles Scott of Bavelaw, of the *Moffat Well* brewery in the close.

SCOTT'S CLOSE (Water Street, South Leith) is shown on *Kirkwood* 1817 and *Ordnance Survey* 1852; and was evidently named for an owner as yet untraced.

SEACOT (South Leith) is shown on *Knox* 1812 and is listed in *PO Directory* 1807. The name is fancy, influenced by the adjoining *Seafield,* and was adopted for the street when the grounds of the house were developed in 1981.

SEAFIELD (South Leith) was a property formed in about 1774 and evidently named for its seaside location. Since it had suppressed part of the road from the Links, the latter's junction with the coast road had to be restored by constructing SEAFIELD PLACE and LANE, as shown on *Kirkwood* 1817, although these street names were not used until 1859. SEAFIELD BATHS were opened in 1813, and SEAFIELD ROAD stretched 500 yards from here to *Seafield Toll,* where SEAFIELD STREET was formed, at the extremity of the estate, in 1903. The coast road east of the Toll was known to Leithers as *Portobello road,* but in 1908 it was formally named as part of Seafield Road, modified as SEAFIELD ROAD EAST in 1968, and this has tended to draw the *Seafield* name along the Figgate Whins over a mile east of the historic Seafield—as illustrated by the naming of SEAFIELD WAY in Fillyside in 1976. An unidentified SEAFIELD ROW appears in *PO Directories* 1859-91, and SEAFIELD VILLAS were named by 1903. SEAFIELD AVENUE—actually in Pirniefield—was named by 1904, but its earlier section has since been renamed BOOTHACRE LANE, *which see.*

SEAFORTH TERRACE (Blackhall) dates from the mid 1890s and the name probably has some connection, unrecorded, with Mackenzie of Seaforth—the suggestion that it was constructed from *sea + Forth* is improbable. Prior to 1967, SEAFORTH DRIVE was known as HILLVIEW TERRACE—*which see.*

SEALCARR STREET (Granton) *see under* GRANTON HARBOUR.

SEAPORT STREET (South Leith) *see* BANK STREET, South Leith.

SEAVIEW TERRACE (Joppa) was developed in 1899 on the site of some old salt pans near BUNKERS HILL (*which see*) and was named for the view. SEAVIEW CRESCENT was named in 1934.

SELCHCRAIGS (Queensferry) are shown as *The Craigs* on *Ordnance Survey* 1852. The name is Scots *selch* from Anglian *sealh,* a seal, with *craigs,* for rocks frequented by seals. The map of *Queensferry* 1832 does not name the Craigs, but shows the bay between them and the harbour as the *Seal Hole.*

SELLAR'S CLOSE (399 High Street) is listed on *Edgar* 1742, and was cleared away for St Giles Street in about 1870. It was probably named for Patrick Sellars, known to have kept a tavern on the north side of the High Street. It may also have been DAVID MURRAY'S, for David Murray of Halmyre, merchant burgess, resident on the west side of the close in 1635, *but see also* DUNBAR'S CLOSE, High Street.

SEMPLE CLOSE or **COURT** (Castlebarns) was part of a brewery built before 1750 and bought in 1758 by John Semple. SEMPLE STREET, already a very old thoroughfare continuous with THORNYBAUK (*which see*) was named in 1766, when Robert Semple bought and began to develop a 2-acre site beside his brewery, as shown on *Kincaid* 1784 and *Ainslie* 1804. The street was also called the SLUNK, Scots for a wet hollow or rut or ditch. *See also* SLUNK, West Port.

SEMPLE'S or **SEMPILL'S CLOSE** (599 High Street) is listed on *Ainslie* 1780, and was named for the mansion at the foot of the close built by a David Brown in 1638, and occupied by Grissel, Lady Semple, widow of Francis, 8th Lord Semple, prior to 1734, when it was acquired by Hugh, 11th Lord Semple. It seems also to have been called WILLIAMSON'S CLOSE from a house in it owned by Joseph Williamson, advocate, of a family with a penchant for naming their properties humorously—e.g. *Fox-hall* at the head of the Mound and *Fox-ton* alias *Tax-ton* alias *Golf-hall* at Wrightshouses.

SENTRY KNOWE (Queensferry) is noted on *Ordnance Survey* 1854 and 1895 immediately northwest of Springfield or Inchgarvie House, whereas the revisions from 1914 onwards show it 400 yards away, southwest of the House. *Dundas* 1757 does not show a *Sentry Knowe*, but at the south end of a pair of *Sentry Knoll* parks, which stretch northwards to include the Inchgarvie land, it shows an *Earley Cairn* which on the analogy of HARLAW CAIRN, Dalmeny (*which see*) may mean 'cairn at the hill with the stones'. When plotted on the modern map, its site is in the middle of a field, some 170 yards south of Inchgarvie House and 250 yards ENE of the tumulus now shown as Sentry Knowe. The likeliest explanation of this varied record is that there was more than one tumulus in the area, and that the *Sentry Knowe* name may have belonged to the whole spur of the land here, rather than to any one cairn. *The Statistical Account* 1790 does not name the place, but reports that here 'there were, about forty or fifty years since, considerable ruins of probably an old Roman *speculatorium*'; and even if this notion of a *watchtower* sprang from a literal interpretation of the *Sentry-* part of the name, there were evidently ancient stone-built remains of some sort to be seen; and it is likely that the name is British *sen tre* or Gaelic *seann treabh*, old farmstead, with much later addition of Anglian or Scots *knowe*, hillock of a rounded shape.

(Dr) SETON'S CLOSE (267 Canongate) is recorded in 1765 and shown on *Ainslie* 1780. Along with the close adjoining it on the east (*see* KINLOCH'S CLOSE, 257 Canongate) it was named for Alexander Seton, son of Sir Alexander Seton, Lord Pitmedden, and at one time surgeon to General Wade's Regiment of Horse, who bought the house at the head of it from his sister-in-law Christian Oliphant. This had been built by her father, John Oliphant, Sheriff Clerk of Edinburgh:

hence the close's other name OLIPHANT'S, also shared by Kinloch's Close. There seems also to have been a third name for it, ALLEY CLOSE, its origin obscure.

SETON'S MIDDLE CLOSE (257 Canongate) *see* KINLOCH'S CLOSE, 257 Canongate.

SETON PLACE (Grange) *see under* THE GRANGE.

SHAFTESBURY PARK (North Merchiston) is the central street of a scheme begun by the Edinburgh Co-operative Building Company in 1885 at ASHLEY TERRACE, on the west side of an existing road then known as GRAY'S LOAN, Merchiston (*which see*) and both the street and the terrace were named for Antony Ashley Cooper, Lord Shaftesbury, the great reformer, who died in 1885 and whose visit to Edinburgh in 1850 had greatly stimulated the movement for housing reform which had led, amongst other things, to the formation of the Co-operative in 1860—*see under* THE COLONIES, Stockbridge. In naming the other streets in the scheme, the Company followed its practice (*see* PRIMROSE TERRACE, North Merchiston, or WOODBINE TERRACE, South Leith) of basing fancy names on plants and trees at HAZELBANK TERRACE (1885) HOLLYBANK TERRACE (1891) ALMONDBANK TERRACE (1892) BRIARBANK TERRACE (1896) and ALDERBANK PLACE and TERRACE (1902) and GARDENS (1904).

SHAKESPEARE SQUARE (East End) is shown on *Armstrongs* 1773 and named on *Ainslie* 1780; and *Ordnance Survey* 1852 shows it as it was shortly before it was cleared in 1860 for the building of the General Post Office. Its name simply celebrated the fact that it was a street round three sides of the Theatre Royal which had been built in 1768-69. The curtain was finally rung down on 25 May 1859.

SHANDON PLACE (North Merchiston) was originally part of the old road past Gorgie Muir farm (*see* MERCHISTON GROVE *and also* GRAY'S LOAN, Merchiston) but in 1881 it began to be developed for housing along its west side, along with SHANDON CRESCENT, followed by SHANDON STREET in 1883 and SHANDON ROAD and TERRACE within the next four years. The name is presumably related to Shandon on the Gareloch near Helensburgh, but the connection has not been traced.

SHANDWICK PLACE (West End) was initiated in 1806 by John Cockburn Ross of Shandwick in Nigg, Easter Ross. On *Ainslie* 1804 he is shown as owner of land in the Kirkbraehead, lying on the north side of the old road to Coates; and *Kirkwood* 1817 shows how he developed it as a terrace and meuse lane (later called QUEENSFERRY STREET LANE, *which see*) along the north frontage of the new MAITLAND STREET on the site of the old road. The name SHANDWICK PLACE attached to the terrace only, until it was adopted as the street name in the late 1890s, displacing *Maitland Street*. ERSKINE PLACE, on the south side of the street, was taken into it in 1979.

SHANTER WAY (Liberton) *see under* KIRKBRAE, Liberton.

SHARPDALE LOAN (Cameron Toll) was named in 1984 for a group of buildings, including a toll house, which had stood on the west side of the road at Cameron Bridge, until they were swept away in the course of constructing the present roundabout. Recorded from 1838 onwards, the name evidently derived from some owner named Sharp, with -*dale* added for the situation beside the burn, unless it referred, in the sense of *deal*, to his portion of ground.

SHAW'S CLOSE (322 High Street) *see* RIDDLE'S CLOSE.

SHAW'S PLACE, STREET and **TERRACE** (Pilrig) were built as a pioneering scheme of artisan housing by Patrick Wilson for the Pilrig Model Dwellings Company and were completed in 1850-51. They were known as *Pilrig Model Buildings* until 1896, when they were renamed for James Shaw, house agent.

SHAW'S SQUARE (Gayfield, Broughton) appears in *PO Directory* 1891 and on *Ordnance Survey* 1893. It was presumably named for its developer, who may have been the same agent whose name was attached to SHAW'S PLACE etc not long afterwards.

SHEARIE KNOWE (Swanston) is also recorded as *Shearing knowe*; but early forms are lacking, and derivation can only be tentative. The *Shearie* part appears to be Celtic, containing *siar*, west, or perhaps *sear*, dark or black, and making up either a hill name or a burn name. Thus it might be *West* or *Black hill*, with Scots *knowe* added for good measure later; or it might be *West* or *Black burn*, with *knowe* added when the name was transferred to the hill above it. Any of the four alternatives would fit the place well enough.

SHEELING or **SHILLING HILL** (Colinton) is the rising ground southwest of the foot of Bridge Road, where the wind was made use of in the sheeling or winnowing of corn. It is named on Leslie's *Spylaw* 1799.

SHEEL'S CLOSE (at 350 High Street) see **LINDSAY'S CLOSE**.

SHEEPHEAD WYND (South Leith) is shown on *Thomson* 1822, and the vestiges of its causeyed entry are still preserved in the garden ground on the south side of the Sheriffbrae. Referred to in 1439 as 'the common gate that passes to the ford' over the river, and forming as it did the west boundary of the St Leonard's lands on the COALHILL (*which see*), it may well have existed before David I granted these lands to the Abbey in 1128. *Wood* 1777 shows it as part of St ANDREW STREET (*which see*) and this change seems to have caught on by the 1820s, for the *PO Directory* 1827 lists it this way; but at the same time it uses the SHEEPHEAD WYND name for the street joining it from the west, labelled *Cables Wynd continued* on *Wood*, but given as *Sheephead Wynd* on *Ordnance Survey* 1852. The name probably originated as that of a tavern, and if this hostelry were on the corner between the two streets its curious double use could be explained.

SHERIFF BRAE (South Leith) took its name from Sir James Logan of Craighouse who built a house here in 1504 and became Sheriff of

Edinburgh. It is recorded as *Shireff Braye* in 1572 in a style which suggests that it was the name of the property or the place and not merely the street. Rebuilt by John Logan in 1636, the house was pulled down in 1840 to make way for St Thomas' Church, now converted into a mosque. SHERIFF PARK was named in 1988 as being on the haugh beside the brae and (to judge by the detail of the earlier maps) probably part of the lands or garden of the house of Sheriffbrae. SHERIFF BANK followed in 1991.

PATRICK SHIELS CLOSE (172 High Street) *see* OLD ASSEMBLY CLOSE.

THE SHIP or **OLD SHIP** or **SHIP TAVERN CLOSE** (221 High Street) *see* OLD STAMP OFFICE CLOSE.

SHOEMAKERS' CLOSE and **DARK** or **LITTLE** or **EAST SHOE-MAKERS' CLOSE** (215 and 195 Canongate) are shown on *Ainslie* 1780 and were named for the Incorporation of the Cordiners or Shoemakers of the Canongate, established in 1554, who acquired the site for the three *Shoemakers' Lands* in 1647. The eastmost one, known as *Bible Land* from the Bible carved below the craft insignia, dated from 1677 and contained their Hall. *Little* and *dark* simply distinguished the east close as being narrower and therefore somewhat darker than the other.

THE SHOOT (Colinton) developed in about 1900 as a short cut to the railway station, and got its name because it is like a channel down the steep slope.

THE SHORE (South Leith) is mentioned in a charter by Logan of Restalrig in 1398 as 'the bank or shore' of the Water of Leith, and it need not be doubted that the name *schoir of Leith* was in use long before it appeared in *Town Council Minutes* 1517. While the modern street name does not run further upstream than Tolbooth Wynd, 15th-century charters apply it to the quay below the Coalhill as well. Although as confirmed by Robert the Bruce in 1329 the harbour of Leith was part of the royal burgh of Edinburgh, Logan of Restalrig, by the charter already mentioned, was astute enough to require the town to purchase rights (or continuation of existing ones) to construct quays on his ground, and use or build roads to Edinburgh through his lands. Together with the land immediately behind it (which may have been the 'whole space' of land granted to the town by Logan of Restalrig in 1414, and was certainly occupied by various Edinburgh merchants later in the century), the Shore was the mercantile centre of Leith until the 19th century, as well as the setting of notable occasions such as the arrival of Mary Queen of Scots from France in 1560, of her son James VI with his Danish bride Anne 30 years later, and of their descendant George IV in 1822, the last of these events being commemorated by two cast-iron tablets built into the quay.

SHORE PLACE (South Leith) *see under* QUEEN STREET, South Leith.

SHORE ROAD (Queensferry) is an altered remnant of the highway that once ran *along the shore* from Queensferry to Bo'ness. Its original east end is represented by ROSE LANE (*which see*) but its present fork from Hopetoun Road was formed by 1818. Still shown as the *Bo'ness road* on *Gellatly* 1834, it was cut off at Society before 1854; and with the arrival of the railway at Port Edgar in the 1860s its eastern section as far as the Linnmill bridge was bypassed by the new and more convenient HOPETOUN ROAD (*which see*) and Shore Road eventually was reduced to an access to Port Edgar.

SHOTHEAD (Balerno) is shown on *Roy* 1753 but by an obvious map error its name is attached to TODHOLES—*which see*. The name was Scots, indicating that, as is graphically shown on *Laurie* 1766, the steading stood at the head of a shot or inby field of arable land in Cockburn, the land beyond it to the south being outby pasture and (as indicated by field names *Laigh* and *High Strother*) scrub land. In 1951 its owner, Sir Alick Buchanan Smith, renamed it COCKDURNO by combining *Cock-*, from the name of his estate of COCKBURN (*which see*), with *-durno*, from that of his wife's farm at Drumdurno, Aberdeenshire. Thus while it is reasonable as a name, Cockdurno is otherwise meaningless, as a pairing of the first part of Anglian *cole burna*, 'peat-water' burn, with the second part of Gaelic *druim dornach*, ridge 'of pebbles'.

SHRUB HILL (Pilrig) was once part of the GALLOWLEE (*which see*) and its present name, appearing as the address of a William Wilson in 1799, seems to have been coined when it was redeveloped for less grim purposes. Lady Maxwell was resident here in 1800, and her house, shown on *Ainslie* 1804, named as *Shrub Hill* on *Kirkwood* 1817 and as *Shrub House* on *Ordnance Survey* 1852, became part of the city's tramway depot in 1893. SHRUB PLACE appears in *PO Directory* 1815, and SHRUB PLACE LANE in 1908.

SHRUB MOUNT (Portobello) was so named in 1981 because it is on the site of the landscaped garden of *Shrub Mount*, one of the earliest houses in Portobello, probably built in about 1787, shown on *Wood's Portobello* 1824, and later noted as the home of Hugh Miller, the great geologist and reformer, for four years before his unhappy death in 1856. The name derived from the hillock of the BLEAK LAW (*which see*) which rose immediately behind the house and was partly in its garden.

SIBBALD PLACE (South Side) is shown on *Wood* 1823 as the name of the short branch street at the northwest corner of St Patrick Square, and it appears in *PO Directories* from 1826 until after it was merged with St PATRICK SQUARE in 1885. It was presumably named for its developer.

SIENNA GARDENS (Sciennes) stands on the site of the 16th-century *house of Sheens* (*see under* SCIENNES) and was named in 1987, rather labouring the point that Scots *Sciennes* referred to the Italian town, its name now normally spelt *Siena*.

SIGHTHILL (Saughton) is shown on *Roy* 1753, and recorded in *RMS* 1625 and 1631 as *Sythill* and *Sighthill*. For lack of early forms, the name is obscure. While it might be 'look-out hill', akin to SPYLAW in Hailes, it is perhaps more likely that the first part is from Anglian *sīd*, long or spacious, an apt description of this great sloping spur between the Gyle muir and the Murray burn. *Saughton* 1795 shows the farm with but one field south of the Calder road, west of LERBAR (*which see*) and in the area now occupied by Calder Crescent and the westerly parts of Calder Gardens and Grove; while on the north side of the high road the Sighthill fields are shown lying between the Broomhouse and the Cultins roads, marching on the north with the LAIRDSHIP (*which see*) on the line of the north side of Bankhead Crossway. The steading was just north of the Calder road, and was approached by the lane which is still extant about 120 yards east of Bankhead Avenue. In the 1840s the farm of Lerbar and the greater part of the Lairdship were taken into Sighthill. Housing development began in 1936 on former Lerbar ground at SIGHTHILL AVENUE, DRIVE, GARDENS, GROVE, LOAN, PARK and VIEW, followed by SIGHTHILL CRESCENT, PLACE, ROAD, STREET and TERRACE (1937) and NEUK and RISE (1944). A group of roads laid out along with SIGHTHILL COURT in 1953 were remodelled in 1966 and named SIGHTHILL BANK, GREEN and WYND.

THE SIGNAL TOWER (South Leith) was built by Robert Mylne in 1686 as a windmill for pressing rape-seed oil, but was converted into a signal tower in about 1805.

SILVERFIELD (Pilrig) appears thus in *PO Directory* 1811 and on *Kirkwood* 1817; but on *Ainslie* 1804, as well as *Knox* 1812, it is shown as Silver Mills Work, making its industrial origin evident. The *-field* form was no doubt suggested by earlier fancy names in the vicinity, such as *Swanfield* or *Stewartfield*. On *Fergus & Robinson* 1759 the site is shown as though part of the ground of BOWERSHALL, *which see*.

SILVERKNOWES (Cramond) appears to be the land known in the 14th century as RANDALISTOUN (*which see*) and still called *Randerstoune* in 1681. It is not shown on *Adair* 1682 but is added on *Adair/Cooper* 1735 as *Silver Knows*. *Laurie* 1763 and later maps also show CROWHILL to the southwest of it, but *Silverknowes* 1841 shows this ground as well as the later DAVIDSON'S MAINS (*which see*) apparently absorbed into Silverknowes, yet remembered in the field names *Crowhill Park* and *Mains Little Park*. The site of the house and steading of Silverknowes is now occupied by the golf club house. The name, which is frequent in Scotland (*see also under* CELLARBANK, Cameron) evidently derived from the silvery look of grasses in bloom on the knowes or spurs which are a prominent feature of the great slope down to the shore. *Silverknowes* 1841 shows the *Goldenknowe*, 500 yards north of the steading, where yellow flowers probably made a contrast with the silvery grass elsewhere. The southern half of SILVERKNOWES ROAD was developed from an old road, shown on *Roy* 1753 as well as *Silverknowes* 1841, leading from Ferry Road past *Burnside* (opposite

Silverknowes Court) to Silverknowes farm place and the west gate of Muirhouse. In 1934 housing development began beside it and in the *Curat Law* and *Crowhill* fields west of it, creating SILVERKNOWES AVENUE, CRESCENT, DRIVE, HILL, LOAN and TERRACE. In 1952, SILVERKNOWES COURT and PLACE were built in the *Burn Shot* and *Roberts Park*, and SILVERKNOWES EASTWAY, GARDENS and GROVE, and SILVERKNOWES BANK extended into the *Gardeners Park* and the *Whiteside Bank* in 1953-55. In 1954 the grand tree-lined west avenue to Muirhouse mansion was developed as SILVERKNOWES PARKWAY. SILVERKNOWES BRAE and ROAD EAST lie partly in the *Lang ley* of Silverknowes farm, but for the most part these streets, together with SILVERKNOWES GREEN, MIDWAY, SOUTHWAY and VIEW, were built in 1960 on Drylaw ground. SILVERKNOWES NEUK (1966) is also outwith the farm; but SILVERKNOWES DELL is in what was the south end of the *Lang ley* until it was cut off from the rest by the railway in 1894.

SILVERMILLS is shown on *Siege of Leith* 1560 and named on *Blaeu* 1654, a map probably surveyed in 1596. There is no reason to suppose that the name is not literal, or that silver ore was not milled in Scotland much earlier than the find at Torphichen in 1607, mentioned in *Chambers* 1868. EAST AND WEST SILVERMILLS LANES, both shown on *Fergus & Robinson* 1759, formed part of the village of Silvermills, and Silvermills House (c1760) still stands in the West Lane.

SILVER WELLS CLOSE (Cowgate) is shown on *Ainslie* 1780, on the south side of the street, next the Cowgate Port. The name may have been from *St Michael's Well*, recorded from 1459 onwards, which was on this side of the street and about 27 yards from the Port.

SIMMER FAUCH (Dalmeny) appearing in field names on *Dundas* 1757 is Scots for *summer fallow*.

SIMON SQUARE (South Side) is listed in *Campbell's Directory* and shown on *Ainslie* 1804 as *Simon's Square*, named for the builder Simon or Symon who developed it in about 1800.

SIMPSON'S CLOSE (171 Cowgate) *see* KITCHEN'S CLOSE, Cowgate.

SIMPSON'S COURT (Greenside) is shown as begun on *Ainslie* 1804 and was completed by Robert Simpson in 1809, shortly before he went bankrupt.

SIMPSON'S COURT (Potterrow, Bristo) is shown on *Ainslie* 1804 and detailed on *Ordnance Survey* 1852. It was named for John Simpson of Simpson & Bain, wrights in Potterrow, who was resident in 1799.

SKAITHMUIR (Queensferry) is recorded as *Skethmure* 1577 and *Skaythmure* 1596, while *Plewlandfield* 1769 shows the name variously spelt *Sketh-, Skeeth-* and *Sketch Moor* and attached to a belt of fields across the middle of that estate. The name is from Old Norse *skeith*; and while this has been interpreted in its meaning of 'race course' (since the ground is near Echline, the 'horse farm') the existence of *Skethmure* and *Overskaythmuir* in neighbouring Dundas (recorded in 1577 and 1599) suggests that the name once covered a wider stretch of muirland on the march between Plewlands and Dundas, and makes it more likely to derive from *skeith* in its other meanings of 'boundary' or 'boundary track'. There are other places of the name, near Stenhousemuir and Coldstream, and *Riccarton* c.1800 shows *Skaith* in the outfield of Currie.

SKINNERS' CLOSE (28 Cowgate) *see* POLLOCK'S CLOSE, Cowgate.

SKINNERS' CLOSE (66 High Street) is shown on *Edgar* 1742 and named in the *Stent roll* in 1635, which also lists among the proprietors the *Skinners Bretheren* or Incorporation of Skinners, whose hall still exists in the close, although adapted as part of the United Industrial School in 1847 and converted into housing in 1981. In 1710 the close is described as *formerly* BARCLAY'S and a John and a Gilbert Barclay are mentioned among previous owners; but while nothing is known about Gilbert and it can only be suggested that the other might have been the John Barclay who was a town councillor in 1530, the name Barclay was certainly associated with the Skinners, inasmuch as James Barclay was their deacon in 1588-89 and again in 1593-94; and since the Skinners, before they had a hall, met in their deacon's house, it is tempting to suppose some connection between these recorded meetings in Barclay's house and the premises they owned in the close less than forty years later. The original close was built over in the later 19th century; and in 1981 the name was revived by naming a new access from Blackfriars Street NEW SKINNERS' CLOSE, the Skinners' Hall now being No. 4 in the new close.

SKINNERS CLOSE (613 High Street) is shown on *Ainslie* 1780 and named in the *Stent roll* 1635, which lists not only Patrik Grahme, skinner, and his partner Thos Somervell amongst the resident owners, but also the *Skinners Brethrein* or Incorporation of Skinners as owners of a *laich house* or basement, endowed as a school, and also a *convening house* in an upper flat. See also SKINNERS' CLOSE at 66 High Street.

SKINNER'S LOAN (Murrayfield) connecting Coltbridge with Ravelston Dykes is shown possibly on *Laurie* 1763 but certainly on *Knox* 1812 and *Ordnance Survey* 1852, and presumably took its name from some owner or tenant of property in it. It was suppressed by 1888 by the development of Coltbridge Avenue and Garscube Terrace.

SLAESIDE (Balerno) is built in one of the quarries which had much to do with the establishment of the village. The name, coined in 1985, is Scots *side*, slope, with *slae* as a play on the name Balerno, which is Gaelic *baile àirneach*, farm toun with the slae or blackthorn.

SLATEFORD, recorded in 1654 as *Sklaitfoord*, is shown as *Sclatfoord* on *Adair* 1682 and *Slatefoord* on *Roy* 1753, the name obviously coming from the slaty rock which outcrops at the site of the ford in the Lanark road. SLATEFORD ROAD, a section of the ancient LANARK ROAD, was probably known thus, as the *road to Slateford*, long before the name entered *PO Directory* in 1879.

SLATER'S CLOSE (140 Canongate) is recorded in 1705 as *Sclaitter's*, and since an Andrew Slater, slater, was in it in 1856, it seems that property here was owned by many generations of a family whose surname had evolved from their trade.

SLATER'S CLOSE (High Street and Canongatehead) appears to have been the name of two or three closes in Edinburgh, as distinct from the one at 140 Canongate, *which see*. One of them, on the north side of the High Street opposite the Tron, was suppressed in the development of MYLNE'S SQUARE, *which see*. Another is mentioned in *George Home's Protocols* 1705 as being on the south side of Canongate 'below the Netherbow'—a phrase which would imply that it was in the CANONGATEHEAD, *which see*. A *Sclataris Close* is mentioned in *Protocols of John Foular* 1531 in connection with a land formerly owned by the late Andrew Robison *alias* Sclater or the late Robert Sclater *alias* Robison, somewhere on the south side of the High Street; and since Foular elsewhere calls land below the Netherbow as 'on the south side of the High Street', it is just possible that the close is the same as the one recorded in 1705.

THE SLEEPERS (Corstorphine) was a path, so named for the old railway sleepers used to fence it. Shown on *Ordnance Survey* 1893 and redeveloped as FEATHERHALL AVENUE in 1927, it was itself a replacement for a path or *vennel* about forty yards further east, shown on *Corstorphine* 1754 and *Ordnance Survey* 1852, but curiously not on *Corstorphine Village* 1777.

SLEIGH DRIVE and **GARDENS** (Lochend) were named in 1925 for Sir William Sleigh, Lord Provost of Edinburgh at the time.

SLOAN STREET (Quarryholes) was developed in 1898 and named for its builder Thomas Sloan, bailie of Edinburgh 1894-1900. Its extension SOUTH SLOAN STREET dates from 1935.

SLOCKENDRAUCHT (Jocks Lodge) is mentioned in 1774 as acres beside WATERPANS, *which see*. Evidently from Scots *slockindraucht*, a draught fit to quench your thirst, the name might conceivably have arisen from a copious spring in a field; but it is perhaps more likely that the field was named as beside or belonging to a tavern beside the main road, *see also* SLOCKINDRAUCHT, Gorgie.

SLOCKINDRAUGHT (Gorgie) is shown on *Laurie* 1763 and *Knox* 1812 on the south side of Gorgie road (about the foot of Wardlaw Street) and is listed in *Kincaid's Gazetteer* 1787. It is Scots *slockin draucht*, a drink fit to slake your thirst; and although *Ordnance Survey* 1852 shows a horsetrough here, there was no doubt a hostelry for the driver as well. The name also occurs at SLOCKENDRAUCHT, Jocks Lodge.

JOHN SLOWAN'S CLOSE (507 High Street) *see under* JAMES COURT.

SLUNK (West Port) was a name for a tannery yard (not yet identified) in West Port in the 1780s, and was also used of SEMPLE STREET. It is Scots for a muddy hollow or ditch.

SMEATON'S or **SMITON'S CLOSE** (South Leith) is shown on *Wood* 1777 and may have been connected with Patrick Smeaton, who bought property hereabouts in the East Lees quarter in 1776.

SMITHFIELD STREET (Dalry) was built on land of Wheatfield, latterly attached to the North British Distillery, and was named by 1897, probably for the developer, and on the model of the earlier name of WHEATFIELD, *which see*; but it may have been connected with SMITHLANDS, the early name of DAMHEAD (Westfield) *which see*.

SMITH'S CLOSE (153 Canongate) *see* BAKEHOUSE CLOSE, 153 Canongate.

MAUSIE SMITH'S CLOSE (225 Canongate) *see* BIG JACK'S CLOSE.

(WEST) SMITH'S CLOSE (Grassmarket) *see* GIBSON'S CLOSE, Grassmarket.

SMITH'S CLOSE (101 High Street) *see* PAISLEY'S CLOSE.

SIR JAMES SMITH'S CLOSE (322 High Street) *see* RIDDLE'S CLOSE.

SMITH'S LAND (Queensferry) appears to be an old name, referring to a person or else the trade. In 1713 there is record of a forge owned by Michael Gogar, smith, in the west end of the town.

SMITH'S PLACE (Leith Walk) is shown on *Kirkwood* 1817 on ground bought by James Smith of Leith in 1800 and shown as *Mr Smith's* on *Ainslie* 1804. Smith began to sell off land in 1814, but built himself a villa (still extant) at the east end of the street.

SMITHY CLEUCH (Dreghorn) is recorded as *Smylecleugh* in 1709 (quoted in *Steuart's Colinton* p263) and the name is probably from Anglian *smael*, Scots *smailly*, used in its early sense of 'narrow', which fits this cleuch exactly.

SNAB POINT (Dalmeny) appears as Snebe on *Barnbougle & Dalmeny* c1800 and the name is Scots from Middle English *snabbe*, a rugged point or projecting part of a hill (*see also* BUCKSTANE SNAB, Braid).

SNADOUN'S CLOSES (Old Town) *see under* (NEW) ASSEMBLY CLOSE, High Street, *and* PETER'S CLOSE, Cowgate.

SOCIETY (Balerno) was the name attached to a building or buildings (cleared away for the construction of BAVELAW ROAD, *which see*) which *Ordnance Survey* 1852 shows at the south end of Main Street. The local tradition is that it derived from the presence of the Co-operative Society here; but the usual nickname for that institution was *the Co-op*, and it seems possible that the usage was superimposed on an earlier reference to a co-operative brewing centre, which is the general Scots meaning of Society.

THE SOCIETY (Greyfriars) is shown on *Rothiemay* 1647 and on *Common Good* 1904, and got its name as land granted in 1598 from the town's Common Good to the Fellowship and Society of Ale and Beer Brewers of the Burgh of Edinburgh, which was then being set up by royal charter for monopoly supply of 'good and sufficient ale' to the burgh, at controlled prices. Supplied with water pumped from the Burgh Loch (*see* THE WINDMILL, Bristo) the place was the site of the Society's brewery; and although the Society was wound up in 1619, the name *the societie* (*of the burgh*) continued to be used for the land and buildings bought back by the town. Nevertheless it is clear, for reasons given under SCIENNES CROFT (*which see*) that this strip of land between the Flodden Wall and the south backs of the Cowgate in the vicinity of Merchant Street, averaging about 100 yards depth from the frontage at Candlemaker Row, was merely the western half of the original grant. It continued to be owned by the town for about 80 years. Four of the disused 'copper kettles' were melted down in 1639 to make field guns for the town's defence, and the Society's 'great copper' was sold in 1665. Finally feued off in 1697, most of the ground was built up as BROWN SQUARE in 1763 (all but its southern range being suppressed when CHAMBERS STREET was built a century later) and as MERCHANT STREET in 1774; but the neighbourhood and the southwest corner of the original croft in particular continued to be known as SOCIETY, even although the frontage facing Greyfriars was built up as LINDSAY PLACE in 1867, and the name has been forgotten only since the ground was cleared and temporarily landscaped in the 1960s, as the site of a new museum of Scotland.

SOCIETY (Queensferry) is recorded in 1693 and shown on *Adair/Cooper* 1737, but not on *Adair* 1682. As remarked in Sibbald's *History of Linlithgowshire* 1710, the name implies that at some earlier date (apparently unknown to Sibbald, but probably in the 17th century) a company or co-operative *society* had carried on brewing in this clachan on the shire road between Queensferry and Bo'ness. SOCIETY ROAD was named by 1974, as part of the road leading to Society as well as Hopetoun.

SOCIETY CLOSE (19 High Street) *see* PANMURE'S CLOSE.

SOCIETY PORT (Greyfriars) *see* GREYFRIARS PORT, Old Town.

SOCIETY WYND or **VENNEL** (Old Town) *see* CANDLEMAKER ROW, Old Town.

SOLTRAIS or **SOLTRAY'S WYND** or **CLOSE** (28 High Street) *see* FOUNTAIN CLOSE.

SOMERSET PLACE (South Leith) *see under* LIVINGSTONE PLACE, South Leith.

SOMMERVILLE'S CLOSE (79 Canongate) *see* BROWN'S CLOSE, Canongate.

SOMMERVILLE GARDENS (Queensferry) is built in the vicinity of the THIEVES LOCH (*which see*) and was named in 1972 for Bailie Peter Sommerville, headmaster of Queensferry Primary School 1949-72.

SOURHOWE or **SOURHOLE** (Swanston) originated as the name of the steep-sided hollow, originally scoured out by glacial melt-water, which interrupts the otherwise even slope of the land in NEW SWANSTON. The name is Scots from Old Norse *saurr hol*, muddy hollow, and evidently referred to the marshy bottom that drains south into the now-culverted Hain burn. The howe gave its name to the surrounding *Sourhowe park*, and also to the clachan shown on *Roy* 1753 as *Showerhole* (the *sh-* pronunciation is probably authentic) and given on *Armstrongs* 1773 as *Sour hole*, which was later to acquire the pub name HUNTER'S TRYST (*which see*) in about 1800; and the clachan in turn gave the name *Sourhole park* to the field on the other side of the road, in the southwest corner of Comiston. In 1985 the historic name was continued in SOURHOLE, a path leading into the howe, and in HOWE PARK, a street built in the Sourhowe park of Swanston.

SOUTERHOLE (Cramond) *see* SUTORHOLE, Cramond.

SOUTH BACK OF THE CANONGATE *see under* BACKS OF THE CANONGATE.

THE SOUTH BRIDGE (Old Town) was one of the improved accesses conceived in principle in the 1680s (*see under the* NEW TOWN) and the idea of it was quite considerably developed ln 1728 by the exiled earl of Mar, who rated it as almost equal to his proposed North Bridge in usefulness, not only as a better access to the main city (i.e. the Old Town) but as a means of opening up fine residential suburbs in Pleasance and Bristo. He suggested that the most economical scheme would be a bridge of three arches on the line of St Mary Wynd and the Pleasance; but it was no doubt the line of the North Bridge (1765) which fixed that of the present bridge, which is 1075 ft. long and is carried on 19 arches. A plan put forward in 1775 ran into difficulties; and according to *Kincaid* 1787 it was James Hunter Blair who got the scheme finally moving, after he became Lord Provost in 1784. The necessary Act of Parliament was obtained and the foundations were laid by August 1785; and the work, designed by Robert Kay and built by Alexander Laing, was carried on so rapidly that pedestrians were able to use the bridge by 19 November 1786, and it was completed by 1788. While the street name appears in *PO Directory* 1825 as *South Bridge*, the maps until 1850 show it as *South Bridge Street*.

SOUTH COLLEGE STREET (Old Town) *see* COLLEGE STREET.

SOUTHFIELD TERRACE, AVENUE and **DRIVE** (Drum Brae) renamed BARNTONGATE TERRACE etc—*which see*.

SOUTHFIELD (Duddingston) was one of the five farms (the others being NORTHFIELD and MEADOWFIELD (*which see*) and *Eastfield* and *Midfield*, near Magdalen Gardens and Southfield Square respectively) which were formed when the Earl of Abercorn enclosed the runrig farm of Wester Duddingston after buying it in 1745. Several of the field names noted on *Duddingston* c1800 show traces of the earlier runrig: *Langlands* (north of Southfield Road) for the long rigs of arable; *Garbrage* or *Gare Breads* as it is recorded in 1752 (between the Langlands and Milton Road) from early Scots *gar brede*, the gore-shaped or triangular strips needed to fit the rigs to the irregular boundary of the field; and *Bere Furlongs* (in the vicinity of Bingham Avenue) which were arable rigs devoted to bere or barley. The original steading of Southfield was built before 1770 on a site just north of Lismore Primary School (which is built in its *Fore Shot* or east field) but in about 1827 the farm was reorganised, and a new steading (now the site of DUDDINGSTON LOAN) was built at the *Millbraehead*, where the farm house still stands in SOUTHFIELD FARM GROVE, named for it in 1954. Development of the farm for housing began in about 1800 with SOUTHFIELD PLACE and VILLAS at SOUTHFIELD TOLL; and later developments included SOUTHFIELD GARDENS (1933) ROAD and TERRACE (1935) SQUARE (1938) LOAN (1958) and BANK (1960) together with many other streets named for titles or connections of the Abercorn family, *see under* BINGHAM, DURHAM, HAMILTON *and* MOUNTCASTLE. SOUTHFIELD PUBLIC PARK is sited in the *Clays* field shown on *Duddingston* c1800 and mentioned along with the *Langlands* (*see above*) in *RMS* 1595.

SOUTHFIELD (Liberton) has been a separate property since the mid 18th century, but its description in *White's Liberton* 1786 as 'a mere piece of outfield belonging to Stenhouse' indicates that it got its name as the *south field* of Stenhouse.

SOUTHGAIT (Old Town) *see under* COWGATE, Old Town.

SOUTH GRAY'S CLOSE (56 High Street) *see under* GRAY'S CLOSE.

SOUTH GRAY STREET (Newington) *see under* GRAY STREET, Newington.

SOUTH GYLE (Corstorphine) is shown on *Roy* 1753 and was evidently named as the southern one of the pair of farms on the shores of THE GYLE, *which see*. SOUTH GYLE ROAD, named as leading to the farm from Corstorphine High Street, was partly realigned in 1958, but originally led directly off the west end of Ladywell Road, on a line now represented by Wester Broom Place. SOUTH GYLE GARDENS is on the farm ground and was named in 1971. In 1977, new roads serving an industrial estate in the southwest corner of the farm and in the adjoining GYLE COMMON or MUIR were named SOUTH GYLE ACCESS, BROADWAY, CRESCENT, CROSSWAY and WYND. SOUTH GYLE LOAN and PARK were named in 1982. SOUTH GYLE CRESCENT followed in 1991. SOUTH GYLE MAINS 1984 occupies the site of the steading.

SOUTHHOUSE (Liberton) is recorded from 1509 onwards and shown as *Sudhous* on both *Adair* 1682 and *Roy* 1753—a spelling which may well echo the pronunciation at that time. The name is Scots *south hous*, evidently derived from the position of the estate in the south of Liberton. The mansion was in ruins by the end of the 18th century, but the steading still partly remains. SOUTHHOUSE AVENUE, BROADWAY, ROAD and TERRACE were named in 1930; SOUTHHOUSE CRESCENT and GROVE followed in 1947, and SOUTHHOUSE MEDWAY, PATH and SQUARE in 1962.

THE SOUTH LOCH, recorded in 1499, was named for its position south of the town and as one of a pair with the NOR LOCH, and its alternative name BURGH LOCH (also spelt *Burrow-* or *Borough-*), recorded in 1537, arose from the fact that the town owned it, presumably granted by the king in the early 12th century, along with the Burgh Muir which forms its southern shore. The extent of this post-glacial lake is fairly represented by the Meadows and the low ground south of the Melville Drive. Generally shallow, it was deepest near its eastern end but was drained westwards by the *loch rin* or tail burn which ran northwards in the vicinity of the east end of Lonsdale Terrace before turning westwards along what are now the north backs of Panmure Place and continuing through Lochrin and Dalry to join the Water of Leith just above Coltbridge. From the 1550s onwards there is mention of a dam at the rin to improve the supply of water. This was then still being carted or carried into the town, and there was talk of piping it; but the only scheme of that sort to come to fruition was the pumped supply operated by the Society of Brewers from about 1600 until 1617, *see under* THE WINDMILL, Bristo. By this time the loch had become so silted up or overgrown that it was described as *the burrow loch of Edinburgh now called the South Meadows*, and in 1657 it was resolved that it should be drained, but for a *watter pond* for horses at its east end. Accordingly, in 1658 it was leased for 19 years to John Straiton, merchant burgess, who made such considerable progress (at the cost of bankruptcy, as it turned out) that the loch became known as STRAITON'S PARK. It is probably Straiton's scheme of drainage and planting that is shown on *Adair* 1682; but its completion had to await the initiative of Hope of Rankeillour in 1722, *see under* HOPE PARK.

SOUTH MELLIS PARK (Northfield, Willowbrae) is on Northfield ground, but was named in 1984 for the *Mellis's Park* shown on *Ainslie's Roads from Figget* 1783 as immediately adjacent to the north of the street.

SOUTH MORTON STREET (Easter Duddingston) *see under* MORTON STREET, Joppa.

SOUTH PARK (Newhaven) *see under* PARK ROAD, Newhaven.

THE SOUTH SIDE may be said to be, in modern parlance, the general term for the whole area of the city between the Old Town and the Pentlands, and is thus the counterpart to THE NORTH SIDE, *which see*; but it is also still used in the more limited sense dating from sporadic developments in the county south of the ancient royalty of Edinburgh which began to be brought under the town's control in 1771 and 1786, when they were defined by Parliament as the eight *Southern Districts*. Taken together, these covered the area from Bristo and Lauriston to the Mayfield and Grange Loans, and from the Dalkeith road (from West Richmond Street southwards) to Wrightshouses and the district of Tollcross; and the modern notion of this special *South Side* embraces the same area together with the land sloping further south to the Pow or Jordan burn—virtually the extent of the Portsburgh and ancient burgh muir.

SPA PLACE (Portobello) was named in 1981 as a new development in the vicinity of one of the two mineral-water springs (the other at Joppa, shown on *Sutter* 1856 as just east of Morton Street) which helped to make Portobello a fashionable spa in the earlier 19th century, as noted in *Baird* p314.

SPARK'S CLOSE (South side of Cowgatehead) is listed on *Ainslie* 1780 but nothing is known about it.

THE SPELDRIN (Arthur's Seat) *see under* GUTTIT HADDIE, Arthur's Seat.

SPENCER PLACE (Trinity) was formed and named in the later 1850s or 1860, and since it is sited within what was Trinity Mains, it may have been named for John George, 2nd Earl Spencer, who as William Pitt's distinguished First Lord of the Admiralty from 1794 to 1801 was made an elder brother of Trinity House.

SPENCE'S PLACE (Castle Barns) is shown on *Kirkwood* 1817 and named in *PO Directory* 1825, evidently for John Spence, plumber there. Shown on *Ordnance Survey* 1852, as a side name, it was one of those suppressed in favour of MORRISON STREET in 1885.

SPENCE'S PLACE (South Leith) was the most northerly section of the present BONNINGTON ROAD, bearing this separate name from 1812 until about 1890. It derived from the owner of the ground on its east side, shown as *Spence's* on *Fergus & Robinson* 1759 and *Ainslie* 1804.

SPENCE STREET (Newington) was built in about 1872 in part of *Newington Gardens* which by that time may have become quite detached from Newington House. The name, appearing in *PO Directory* 1873, may have been that of the developer.

SPEY STREET and **TERRACE** (Pilrig) figure on *Knox* 1812 in a grand scheme of streets planned for James Balfour's Pilrig estate, and are named on *Kirkwood* 1817 as MORAY STREET and St JAMES STREET respectively. The names remain obscure, and were possibly connected with Balfour or the builder, who had already made progress by 1816. In 1885, presumably to obviate any confusion with Moray Place, Moray Street was renamed SPEY STREET, from the obvious association of the river with Moray. By 1864 St James Street had become simple JAMES STREET; and in 1965, to obviate any confusion with James Street in Portobello, it was renamed SPEY TERRACE, taking *Spey* from Spey Street, and *terrace* from its own main feature, the tenement erected in 1867 by the Edinburgh Artisan Building Company, in emulation of the pioneering Pilrig Model Buildings on the other side of the street, *see under* SHAW'S PLACE, Pilrig.

SPIERS PLACE (South Leith) was formed in about 1888 on cleared ground, along with HENDERSON STREET, and remained undeveloped and apparently unnamed until 1901, when a tenement was built on its north side. The origin of the name is unknown, but is more likely to be connected with the owner or builder of this tenement than with any unrecorded close or court cleared away a quarter of a century earlier.

SPITTALFIELD (St Leonards) *see under* GALLOWGREEN, St Leonards.

SPITTAL STREET (West Port) is sketched as part of a new West Approach road on *Wood* 1823, and is shown in its final form on *Lothian* 1829. Built by 1835, it was named for James Spittal, then Lord Provost.

SPOTTISWOODE ROAD and **STREET** (Warrender Park) *see under* BRUNTSFIELD.

SPOTTISWOOD'S CLOSE (70 High Street) *see* MURDOCH'S CLOSE.

SPRINGFIELD CRESCENT, PLACE, ROAD and **VIEW** (Queensferry) are built in Echline fields named on *Dundas* 1757 as the *South Park*, *Wester Whinny Muir*, and *Easter Netherfield*. The streets were named by 1972, and SPRINGFIELD GARDENS, LEA and TERRACE were added in 1977. While the intention may have been to revive the older name of Inchgarvie House (*see* SPRINGFIELD, Queensferry) there is no obvious connection between the two places, and it may be that the name described the housing site, which is bisected by a burn in a culvert entering the sea at Port Edgar.

SPRINGFIELD (Pilrig) is recorded in *Williamson's Directory* 1780 as the address of Arthur Miller, merchant. It is shown on *Ainslie* 1804 as a terrace of houses fronting Leith Walk, with a detached house and grounds behind. According to *Grant*, McCulloch of Ardwell occupied the central and largest house in the terrace in about 1780. SPRINGFIELD STREET was opened in about 1870, and the original houses began to give way to commercial development in about 1900. While the name may have been fancy, it is also possible that it was earlier a local field name, in which *spring* might have meant a spring of water, or else a grove or copse.

SPRINGFIELD (Queensferry) appears on *Forrest* 1818 as a property overlooking the Mill Braes at Linn Mill, at the north end of the *Sentry Knoll Parks* shown on *Dundas* 1757; and it may have been the farmhouse mentioned in the *Statistical Account* 1790. Although the name may have been fancy, it is perhaps more likely that it was a field name, using *spring* with the meaning of a copse or grove, or else a spring of water. By 1895 the grounds had been more than doubled in area, the house rebuilt, and the property renamed for INCHGARVIE, *which see*.

SPRING GARDENS (Abbeyhill) is a section of the ancient road by Watergate and Jocks Lodge. The name appears to have originated in the 1840s, at first as that of the most easterly of a number of properties formed about this time by breaking up COMELY GARDENS, *which*

532

see. Ordnance Survey 1852 names the street and gives this property as *Spring Gardens Villa*, and later it is *Spring Villa*. The name is probably fancy, but there is some evidence of water rising in the house grounds.

SPRING GARDENS (Stockbridge) appears on *Ainslie* 1804 as *Spring Garden*, one of a pair of streets originally proposed for the west side of *The Circus* but overtaken in 1820 by Playfair's new design of *Royal Circus*, in which *Spring Gardens*, listed in *PO Directory* 1825, became a side name in Northwest Circus Place, as it is still shown on *Ordnance Survey* 1852. While its origin is obscure, the name may well have belonged hereabouts before the Northern New Town was planned in 1802, and the *spring* may have been a grove or copse, or else a spring of water.

SPRINGVALLEY (Morningside) was the fancy name coined for a villa built in about 1830 at the west end of Cuddy Lane, shown in detail on *Ordnance Survey* 1852; but the name was possibly descriptive, insofar as there was a slight dip in the slope and a water supply within the garden of the house: *Kirkwood* 1817 shows a pond in one corner, and the 1852 map shows a draw well in the other. The *Ordnance Survey* 1893 shows it rather more as a neighbourhood name, and by 1897 SPRINGVALLEY GARDENS was begun in the next field further south, followed in 1901 by SPRINGVALLEY TERRACE, which eventually absorbed the site of Springvalley House in 1909.

SPRINGWELL PLACE (Dalry) was formed and named by 1877, one of a group of streets (*see also* CATHCART PLACE, DOWNFIELD PLACE and DUFF STREET) developed on ground shown on *Kirkwood* 1817 as owned by the Home Rigg family. The name is obscure; but it may have been suggested by a tributary of the Dalry burn, culverted by 1876, but shown on *Ordnance Survey* 1852 as crossing the middle of the site of the street.

SPRINGWELL TERRACE (Queensferry) is a side name, evidently fancy, given to the terrace of two properties dated 1888 and shown on *Ordnance Survey* 1895, at the entry to CLARK PLACE.

SPRINGWOOD PARK (Liberton) was so named in 1964 as a development for the most part on the site of a house of this name, dating back to 1874 or earlier. The name may not have been entirely fanciful, since there was a well not far away, within what is now the sharp angle on the south side of Kenilworth Drive. This is shown on *Ordnance Survey* 1852 as *Our Lady's Well*, with a public passage leading to it from Kirk Brae, all as described in *Good's Liberton* 1892; but since it is not mentioned in *White's Liberton* 1786 it is likely that the 'Our Lady' was a 19th-century interpretation of Scots *ladie well*, a spring with a channel flowing from it.

SPYLAW (Colinton) originated as the name of the *Spy Law* or lookout hill in Hailes, the ridge now crowned by Spylaw Bank Road, which commands immense views to the north, west and south. In the 17th century it became an alternative name for the KIRKLANDS OF HAILES (see under HAILES) lying between the river and Lanark road and stretching from the Law southwards to Curriemuirend. In 1759 James and John Gillespie feued the snuff mill of Spylaw, and began to extend the estate progressively, as shown on *Spylaw* 1767 and 1799, taking in land in Colinton, Bonaly and Fernielaw. Hence the name SPYLAW STREET given to the main street in Colinton village in about 1913. SPYLAW HOUSE, built as the mill house in about 1650 and rebuilt as a mansion in 1773, was formally listed as a 'street' in 1984, when it was converted into flats. SPYLAW BANK ROAD, shown on *Roy* 1753 and probably dating as far back as the foundation of Hailes kirk (see under HAILES) was for long known as the KIRK BRAE and KIRKBRAEHEAD, but by 1910 it had acquired its present name from the property shown as *Spylaw* on *Knox* 1812 and as *Spylaw Bank* on *Ordnance Survey* 1852. GILLESPIE ROAD, named for James Gillespie (although the elder brother, he survived John by five years and left the fortune by which their name is remembered), was constructed in the *Spylaw parks* in about 1874, as the approach to the railway station and goods yard and the new bridge spanning both rail and river; and in the later 1890s SPYLAW AVENUE and PARK were formed in the same fields and named for the ground, while PENTLAND AVENUE and ROAD were named for the view from it.

SPYLAW ROAD (Merchiston) started within Merchiston by 1861 and subsequently extended along the march between Myreside and Gorgie Muir (all lands owned by George Watson's Hospital under the Gillespie Trust), was named by 1871 for the Gillespies' estate of SPYLAW, Colinton, *which see.*

STABLE LANE (Morningside) was so named in 1980 in consideration of its original purpose, when built in about 1840, of providing a mews for future housing development in Morningside Place and Dow Loan.

STAFFORD STREET (West End) was planned in 1809 on ground shown on *Ainslie* 1804 and *Kirkwood* 1817 as divided between three ownerships: at its north end, Easter Coates; at its south end, the property of Cockburn Ross of Shandwick, and in between, the estate of Lord Alva. The name, appearing on *Kirkwood* 1817, remains obscure.

STAIR'S CLOSE (477 High Street) is short for LADY STAIR'S CLOSE, *which see.*

STAIR PARK (Murrayfield) *see under* ABINGER GARDENS, Murrayfield.

STALKER'S CLOSE (226 Canongate) *see* WATSON'S CLOSE.

STALKER'S CLOSE (215 High Street) *see* LYON'S CLOSE.

STANDINGSTANE (Dalmeny) is recorded as *Standandstane* (1576) *The Standand Stane* (1582) and *Standingstane* (1653) and is shown on *Dundas* 1757 and *Knox* 1812 virtually in the same position as

STANDALONE on *Adair* 1682 and *Armstrongs* 1773. They were either two places close together, or else (as seems more likely) *Standalone* is a map errror, perhaps attempting to make sense of the garbled form *Serand Alone* that occurs on *Blaeu* 1654, and echoing the name of Standalane, near Ballincrieff, East Lothian. STANDINGSTANE ROAD is the traditional name of the road to the crossroads from Dalmeny.

STANEDYKEHEAD (Liberton) is shown on maps from *Laurie* 1763 onwards and listed in *Kincaid's Gazetteer* 1787 as a clachan on the summit of the old post road to Penicuik, where the *Kirk Road* shown on *Mortonhall* 1770 came in from Fairmilehead and Mortonhall. The junction must have originally been marked by the *heid* or corner of a *stane dyke*. Although almost displaced by the later imported name of ALNWICKHILL (*which see*) the original *Stanedykehead* has stuck to the junction and the first section of the old kirk road.

SIR JAMES STANFIELD'S CLOSE (10 High Street) *see* WORLD'S END CLOSE.

STANHOPE PLACE and **STREET** (Wester Coates) *see under* DEVON PLACE, Wester Coates.

THE STANK (Corstorphine and Saughtonhall) is shown on all maps from *Blaeu* 1654 onwards, but since it is shown as *Corstorphine burn* on *Corstorphine* 1777 and is mentioned in *Wood's Corstorphine* 1790 as *the drain from Corstorphine Loch or Myre*, it is likely that the name stank was simply descriptive until the later 19th century, when *Selway* and *Ordnance Survey* 1893 use it as a proper name. It is the traditional term, early Scots from Old French *estanc*, originally for a pool or series of pools but latterly for a slow-running burn developed as a drain, and either or both these meanings would fit this particular example in the various stages of its development.

STANLEY PLACE (Abbeyhill) was named by 1872, probably for H M Stanley, after his successful search for David Livingstone in 1870.

STANLEY ROAD (Newhaven) is part of the old road from Ankerfield to Trinity Mains, shown on *Fergus & Robinson* 1759. Its present separate name first appears in *PO Directory* 1864, and the appearance of the adjoining DERBY STREET five years later suggests that both streets were named for Edward Stanley, 14th Earl of Derby, who was three times Prime Minister between 1858 and 1868, when he had to retire through ill health, dying in 1869. Eminent not only as a politician but as a scholar, he published his greatest work, a translation of *the Iliad*, in 1864. *Stanley Lodge, Newhaven*, occupied by J Peacock, gardener, and listed thus in *PO Directories* 1806-21, had nothing to do with this street name, *see under* STANWELL STREET, Pilrig.

STANLEY STREET (Bonnington) was named by 1873 (perhaps as a result of the furore caused by the meeting of H M Stanley with David Livingstone in 1870) but the name was dropped by 1893.

STANLEY STREET (Portobello) was named in the 1870s, possibly also for H M Stanley.

STANWELL STREET (Pilrig) was developed by 1880 in what had been the grounds of *Stanwell Lodge*, so named on *Kirkwood* 1817 and shown on this map and on *Ainslie* 1804 as 'Mr Peacock's'. In the *PO Directory*, J Peacock is listed as at *Stanwell Lodge, Bonnington*, from 1822 onwards, whereas from 1806 until 1821 a J Peacock, gardener, is listed as at *Stanley Lodge, Newhaven*, a house of which there is no trace on *Ainslie* 1804 or *Kirkwood* 1817, and the evidence suggests that the two places were the same. The surname *Peacock* has been long attached to Newhaven. The origin of the house name, whether it was *Stanley* or *Stanwell*, is obscure.

STANYPATH (Slateford) erroneously STONYPORT, is recorded from 1345 onwards. The early spellings *Stanipeth*, *Stenypath* and *Stonypethe* show it to be from Anglian *stanig*, stony or metalled or paved, and *paeth*, steep way or road; and it evidently referred to the way up from the ford at Slateford. The corruption *Stoneyport* appears on *Ordnance Survey* 1893 and probably derived from the presence of a wharf on the Union Canal (opened in 1822) which may have been used for loading stone from Old Redhall Quarry.

STAPELEY AVENUE (Craigentinny) *see under* CRAIGENTINNY.

STARBANK (Trinity) is shown on *Kirkwood* 1817 along with other properties evidently feued out from LAVEROCK BANK in the preceding decade. The name seems to have been fancy, following the fashion of the earlier *Laverock Bank* and *Christian Bank* in referring to the steep slope down to the sea. STARBANK COTTAGES and PLACE were developed in its grounds at the sea front, but were cleared in about 1890 to form STARBANK PUBLIC PARK. The landscaped 'star' on its bank is shown on *Ordnance Survey* 1893. STARBANK ROAD is part of the coast road shown on *Roy* 1753, but the name was not given until 1904.

STARCH CLOSE (219 Cowgate) is listed on *Ainslie* 1780. The name is obscure: starch-making cannot be ruled out, since it is known to have been carried out at other places nearby in the Cowgate; but the close may be that listed as STARK'S in *Maitland* 1753; or it may have been *Strachey's*, for John Strachey or Straitchy of St Margaret's, Westminister, mentioned in 1723 as owner of property near Rapperlaw's Close (231 Cowgate) and in 1766 as having sold ground to the Adam family—*see* ADAM COURT, Cowgate.

STARK'S COTTAGES (Oxgangs) date from the late 1920s and were presumably named for their builder or owner.

STATION BRAE (Portobello) was the traditional name of this way up to the railway, statutorily adopted in 1981.

STATION LOAN (Balerno) got its name as the access to the terminus of the Balerno Branch railway, opened in 1874.

STATION ROAD (Corstorphine) was formed in 1902 as access to the second Corstorphine railway station—the first was in Saughton Road, and *Ordnance Survey* 1912 shows them both. The Corstorphine branch line was closed in 1967—*see also under* PADDOCKHOLM, Corstorphine.

STATION ROAD (Craigmillar) *see* PEFFER PLACE.

STATION ROAD (Dalmeny) is named as leading to the second DALMENY STATION (*see under* DALMENY) but its eastern part from the Common Loan (*see* ASHBURNHAM ROAD) to New Garden was there before the railways came, being shown on *Barnbougle & Dalmeny* c1800 as a loan even then long established. Its extension westwards across Ravel Bank and Niven's Green to the Loan was evidently connected with its new role as access from the burgh to the station, and the name followed suit.

STATION ROAD (Kirkliston) originated as the QUEENSFERRY ROAD (*which see*) but got its new name as the road leading from Main Street to the railway station. Opened in 1866, this was closed to passenger traffic in 1930 and finally abandoned in 1966. STATION TERRACE, a block of buildings at the station entrance, was taken into AULDGATE (*which see*) in 1982.

STATION ROAD (Ratho) is shown on *Knox* 1812 as a route to Ratho and Dalmahoy. It got its present name after Ratho station was built on the Edinburgh & Glasgow Railway's line in the later 1840s.

STEDFASTGATE (Bonnington) was named in 1983 in honour of the Boys Brigade, whose motto is *Sure and Stedfast* and whose Leith Companies assisted in the landscaping of this *gate* or path in order to mark the Brigade's Centenary.

STEAD'S PLACE (South Leith) is shown on *Ainslie* 1804 as *Mr Stead's* ground and *Card Manufactory*. 'Near Mr Stead's card manufactory' was being used as an address in Leith Walk as early as 1792; and *Stead's Place* appears in *PO Directory* 1805.

STEELE'S CLOSE (162 High Street) *see* CONN'S CLOSE.

STEEL'S PLACE (Morningside) was named as a public street by 1832 but is shown incipiently on *Kirkwood* 1817 as the access to the magnesia works started in 1797 (on the site now occupied by Falcon Court) by Dr Thomas Steel of Burghmuirhead, who was also a co-founder of the Tipperlinn Chemical Works set up by Steel, Gladstanes and Company in 1770.

THE STEIL(S) (Craiglockhart) was the traditional name of the ground on which the City Poorshouse was built in 1865, and was recovered when the site was re-developed as housing in 1990. It is Scots *steil* or *steel*, a steep bank, referring to the northern slope of the 'tail' of Wester Craiglockhart Hill. The plural probably arose because there were three fields along the bank, forming the *Easter, Mid* and *Wester 'Steels'*. The same term occurs in the *Steelhead* in Duddingston, on the slope about 300 yards above the village. The street names THE STEILS and MID STEIL were adopted in 1990, and EASTER STEIL and SOUTH STEIL followed in 1992 and 1993.

STEIL'S CLOSE (High Street) *see* St MONAN'S CLOSE.

(PATRICK) STEIL'S CLOSE (172 High Street) *see* OLD ASSEMBLY CLOSE.

STENHOUSE (Liberton) is recorded as *Stanehouse* in 1478 and shown on *Blaeu* 1654. The name, from Anglian *stán hús*, evidently dates from a time when a stone building was a rarity in the locality. STANEHOUSE MILL is shown separately on *Armstrongs* 1773, and *Good's Liberton* says that there were mills here in the 12th century. The STENHOUSE BURN figures on *Adair* 1682, and *Roy* 1753 shows the curious name *Willy's Dry* where it is crossed by the Lasswade road. The discussion of local roads in *Good* is full of mistakes: *Roy* shows STENHOUSE ROAD (renamed in 1966, *see under* ELLEN'S GLEN) linking the place with Greenend on the ancient Dere Street and Burnhead on the Lasswade road; and also a minor road from Gilmerton by Hyvot's Mill, with a continuation (still existing, *see* VIA REGIS) which was probably a kirk road to the parish centre. The renaming of streets in 1966, when the ancient *Stenhouse* (Liberton) name was sacrificed for the sake of the latterday (and corrupt) name of STENHOUSE in Saughton (*which see*) unfortunately allowed the name of the place itself to be supplanted by the fancy name ELLEN'S GLEN. In 1991 the long-established colloquial form of the proper place name was used in naming STENNIS GARDENS.

STENHOUSE (Saughton) is unique among examples of this place name since it is derived, not from 'stone house' (cf. STENHOUSE in Liberton) but from *Stenhope*, the name of the family who were Holyrood Abbey's tacksmen in a mill or mills on the Water of Leith at Saughton in 1511 and for more than a century thereafter. Recorded in the 16th century as *Stennop* or *Stanehopps Milne(s)*, the name was still used along with an alternative *Saughton Mills* after Watson of Saughton purchased the mills in 1657, and the corruption into *Stenhouse* seems to have occurred in the 18th century. STENHOUSE MILL LANE and CRESCENT, so named only in 1950, are on the lands of the name. The other 'Stenhouse' streets (but for the western sections of STENHOUSE DRIVE and STREET, which are in Saughton Mains) are on Saughtonhall land, most of them in fields which were attached to SAUGHTONHALL MAINS, which is given on *Ordnance Survey* 1852 simply as SAUGHTON but was DALZIELL'S MILLS for long before that, certainly as far back as 1682, when it was recorded by *Adair*. STENHOUSE AVENUE, COTTAGES, CRESCENT, CROSS, DRIVE, GARDENS, GROVE, PLACE, ROAD, STREET and TERRACE were named in 1927, but the extension STENHOUSE AVENUE WEST dates from 1931. STEVENSON DRIVE, named for Lord Provost Sir Alexander Stevenson, dates from 1927; and the remaining streets in what amounted to a 'New Stenhouse', comprising WHITSON CRESCENT, GROVE, PLACE, ROAD, TERRACE, WALK and WAY, were laid out in 1931 and named for Lord Provost Sir Thomas Whitson.

STENNIS GARDENS (Liberton) *see under* STENHOUSE, Liberton.

STENTER'S CLOSE (26 Grassmarket) is given thus on *Ainslie* 1780 & 1804 but as *Stentor's* on *Kincaid* 1784. It does not incorporate a surname but the Scots term *stenter*, an assessor, probably one connected with the markets, for the *Valuation Roll* 1635 includes a John Ormston, smith and *extentor*, living on the south side of the street. The close is given on *Ordnance Survey* 1852 as GIRDWOOD'S ENTRY, but this proprietor has yet to be traced.

STEVENLAW'S CLOSE (132 High Street & 192 Cowgate) is named *Steven Laws Closs* on *Rothiemay* 1647, but the mention of *Stenelawis clois* in *RMS* 1593 shows the tendency to run the names together which resulted in the forms *Stanelaw's* and *Stonelaw's* given on *Edgar* 1742 and *Ainslie* 1780. In all probability the name goes back to Stephen Law, flesher, made burgess in 1501, who had property described in 1512 as being west of a property in Peebles Wynd, and is mentioned in *RMS* 1537 as late owner of a tavern or vault in the town. The close was also TELFER'S, recorded in many variant spellings of that name, which originated as NormanFrench *taillefer*, cutter of iron, and is first noted in Scotland in 1210. A deed of 1710 refers to a Laurence Telfer as an early owner in the close, probably to be identified as Laurence Taillyefer, burgess and town treasurer in 1485, who was evidently a man of wide business interests, since in the year he took leases of the town's mills as well as the flesh house. The close was apt also to be confused with the adjoining KENNEDY'S CLOSE, *which see*.

STEVENSON ROAD (Saughtonhall and Gorgie) was built for the most part in the FACTOR'S PARK (*which see*) in Saughtonhall, with its east end in Gorgie. It was named in 1926 for the then Lord Provost, Sir Alexander Stevenson. The name was extended in 1927 to STEVENSON DRIVE, in the part of Saughtonhall now wrongly called STENHOUSE (*which see*) and also to three streets in Factor's Park: STEVENSON AVENUE (1927) TERRACE (1934) and GROVE (1937).

STEVENSON'S CLOSE (once 22 now 14 Grassmarket) is recorded in the *Valuation Roll* 1635 as GAWEN STEINSON'S CLOSE, and the same roll lists Steinson as in partnership with John Walls, waulker, although a feu charter refers to him (or another owner of the same name) as a baxter. In *PO Directory* 1827 the close is given as BROWN'S, possibly for James Brown, brazier, and Patrick Brown, owners before Steinson, but more likely for James Brown, stabler, who purchased property here in 1811 from Gilbert Crawford (*see under* BACK O THE BUGHTS, Grassmarket) and was later developer of BROWN'S PLACE in the Vennel.

(DAVID) STEVENSON'S CLOSE (28 High Street) *see* FOUNTAIN CLOSE.

STEVENSON'S CLOSE (West Port) is listed in *PO Directory* 1827 as at 133 West Port, but is shown on *Ordnance Survey* 1852 on a site now occupied by 141 West Port. It was evidently named for an owner, as yet untraced.

STEWART AVENUE, GARDENS, PLACE and **ROAD** (Currie) were built in 1954, and STEWART CRESCENT followed in 1958. The streets were named for the Revd Dr David Stewart, minister of Currie 1898-1950.

STEWART CLARK AVENUE (Queensferry) *see under* DUNDAS AVENUE, Queensferry.

STEWARTFIELD (Pilrig) was so named in 1746 when this small estate was bought by James Stewart, magistrate, merchant and banker in Edinburgh. The house, built by Thomas and Robert Mylne of Powderhall in about 1743, was demolished by the Caledonian Railway Company in 1895; but the name was attached to a new street on its site in 1985.

STEWART PLACE (Kirkliston) stands partly on and partly north of the site of LOANHEAD (*which see*) and was named in 1975 for Dr Peter Stewart (1882-1975) who lived in Loanhead House and served the whole district as local doctor for many years.

STEWART'S CLOSE (96 Canongate) is named on *Ordnance Survey* 1852, but is FALCONER'S in *Williamson's Directory* 1779, and FALKNER'S on *Ainslie* 1780 & 1804 and *Kirkwood* 1817. *Williamson's Directory* 1780 and *Edinburgh Directory* 1799 mention a *Falconer's land* in the close. In 1773 *Williamson* has an entry 'John Falconer (bishop), near the foot of the Canongate': but no such bishop has been identified, and since (bishop) is actually printed as 'ditto.' below 'bishop' in the preceding entry, it may be an error. Nothing is known about the name *Stewart's*, and it may be later than 1817.

STEWART'S CLOSE (within 10 High Street) *see under* WORLD'S END CLOSE.

STEWART'S CLOSE (High Street) is shown on *Edgar* 1742; but its upper part was suppressed in the building of the Royal Exchange in 1753 (although some traces remain in its cellars) and the remainder was swept away in the development of Cockburn Street in the 1860s. In 1635 John Stewart is mentioned among owners and residents in the close, and a disposition of 1710 includes a reference back to William Stewart, merchant burgess, who with his son James, a druggist, and daughter Anna, owned a tenement on the east side of the close head. The close was also HERIOT'S, the name going back at least to Alexander Herriot, also an owner in 1635, who may have been the Alexander Heriot who was bailie in 1628. In 1615 it is recorded as PRESTON'S, for the Prestons of Craigmillar, who (as demonstrated by Peter Millar in a report of 1893, quoted in *Old Edinburgh Club XXXV*) held the land on the west side of the close and a mansion at its head in the 16th century—the mansion which in June 1567 had the unhappy distinction of being used to imprison Mary Queen of Scots during her last twenty-four hours in Edinburgh.

STEWART'S or **PROVOST STEWART'S** or **SIR JAMES STEWART'S CLOSE** (High Street) *see* ADVOCATE'S CLOSE.

STEWART TERRACE (Gorgie) originated as part of GRAY'S LOAN (*which see*) shown on *Merchiston* 1776. It was altered at its south end after it was cut by the railway in 1861, in order to restore its connection with Lanark Road. The name *Stewart Terrace* was given to tenements built at its north end in about 1879, on land owned by Charles Stewart of the North British Leather & Shoe Works in Gorgie Road. The road was still being called by its earlier name in 1892, but *Ordnance Survey* 1893 shows it as *Stewart Terrace*.

STEWART TERRACE (Queensferry) is part of a bypass built in the 1860s. While the road was for long known as the HOPETOUN ROAD (*which see*) *Stewart Terrace* originated as a side name for the row of houses built at its western end in 1922 and named for Councillor John Stewart, then convener of the burgh's Housing Committee. The name was adopted for the entire street in 1954.

THE STINKAND or **STINKING STYLE** (High Street) was a short pend giving access through the LUCKENBOOTHS to the north porch of St Giles kirk. Its alternative name of KIRK STYLE, recorded in 1463, was sometimes varied to OLD KIRK STYLE after St Giles was altered in the 1560s to house five separate congregations, since the Style then led directly to the *Old Kirk* in the middle of the group. In Scots, *style* means a pedestrian access, not necessarily with the steps implied by English *stile*. As regards the label *stinkand*, it is not altogether obvious why this entry or the two STINKING CLOSES (*which see*) should have been notably smelly, and the objection raised in William Dunbar's 'Address to the Merchants of Edinburgh' (written around or soon after 1500) was simply that the Style formed a dismally dark approach to the kirk. It seems likely that the word is from Scots *stank*, to make a ditch, and that it referred to a drainage channel in or beside the passageway.

STINKING CLOSE (284 Canongate) is shown on *Edgar* 1742 and named thus on *Ainslie* 1780 and 1804. The name was probably medieval, with a meaning discussed *under* STINKAND STYLE, High Street. A second name, COUTTS CLOSE (*which see*) probably dated from around 1600. A third name was HUME'S, given on *Kirkwood* 1817 but deriving from John Home, coachbuilder, who (as related in *Kincaid* 1787) trained in London and brought his craft to a new pitch of perfection when he returned and set up his workshop in the close in 1738. By 1773 the family business had transferred to the south side of Princes Street, and it is listed in 1799 as Home, Cleghorn & Wilson, coachmakers at 3 Princes Street. As may be seen from *City Improvements* 1866, the close became the site of new buildings on the east side of the widened St MARY'S STREET.

STINKING CLOSE (14 Cowgate) *see* ANDERSON'S CLOSE, Cowgate.

STIRLING ROAD (Trinity) was projected by 1887, and was named and beginning to be occupied by 1893. It has been suggested that like other nearby streets, such as LENNOX ROW and LOMOND ROAD, it was named for some ship registered in the port of Leith, in this case the *Stirling Castle*, built in 1884 and so registered until 1899.

STIRLING'S CLOSE (55 High Street) *see* TRUNKS CLOSE.

STOCKBRIDGE is shown on *Roy* 1753, and the spelling *Stoke Bridge* on *Fergus & Robinson* 1759 shows its traditional pronunciation. The name is Scots *stock brig* from Anglian *stocc brycg*, meaning a timber bridge and a footbridge in particular—indeed, the very word *stock*, used on its own, could mean a footbridge. Thus the 18th-century arrangement, whereby there was a ford near the site of the present bridge and a wooden footbridge some seventy yards upstream, was probably very much older, and possibly medieval, although the road was simply a local one until it was extended to the Queensferry road as CRAIGLEITH ROAD (*which see*) about the same time as Stockbridge got its first stone-built vehicular bridge in 1786. A similar name *Stokkis Briggs* near Niddrie is mentioned in *RMS* 1550.

STOCKBRIDGE MARKET (Stockbridge) opened in 1825 and finally closed down in 1906. Although it was also entered from Hamilton Place, the main entrance was planned as *Market Place*, now St STEPHEN'S PLACE (*which see*) where the entrance archway and side gates still survive.

STODDART'S CLOSE (50 Cowgate) *see* BAILLIE'S CLOSE, Cowgate.

THE STOK WELL (Grassmarket) is referred to as the *Stakwelle* in *RMS* 1363 and as the *Stok Well* from 1556 onwards, and is shown on *Rothiemay* 1647 as immediately east of the West Port. While the name may be from Anglian *staca*, a stake or boundary mark (and there is some evidence that the burgh boundary was moved westwards to this vicinity at some early date, *see under* GRASSMARKET) it might otherwise be from Anglian *stoc*, in its sense of an outlying steading, and this would explain how the Grassmarket came to be part of the burgh—i.e. as an extension of the Cowgate grazings, like the other early pasture at Canongatehead, *see under* LAPLEE STANE.

STONEYPORT (Slateford) *see under* STANIPATH, Slateford.

STONYCROFT (Queensferry) is referred to in 1648 in terms which confirm that it lay immediately within the southwest corner of the burgh, bounded by the Loan and by the south side of Stonycroft Road as shown on *Ordnance Survey* 1856—i.e. before the road was realigned to suit the railway in the 1860s. It was evidently a *croft* or enclosed piece of arable of a *stony* sort. As shown on *Barnbougle & Dalmeny* c1800 as well as *Ordnance Survey* 1856, STONYCROFT ROAD probably developed as a loan giving access eastwards to the COMMON LOAN (*which see*) and westwards to LOCH ROAD.

STONY FLATTS (Queensferry) is recorded as *Stainflatt* in 1577 and shown on *Plewlandfield* 1769 as a group of four fields in Plewlands extending westwards from the present Viewforth Road in the vicinity of Inchcolm Terrace, now including the streets STONYFLATTS and STONYFLATTS CRESCENT, named in 1987. The name is Scots, describing the more level ground south of the Skaithmuir, and the character of its soil.

THE STOOPS (Dalmeny) is a group of fields *Easter, Wester and Mid Stoop* shown in Wester Dalmeny on *Barnbougle & Dalmeny* c1800, with *Little Stoop Shot* added on *Dundas* 1757. Fairly frequent in field names, the name is from Anglian *stoppa*, a stoup or bucket, with the meaning of a hollow when it is used in place names. *Shot*, meaning a piece of arable ground, is the second most common term (after *park*, grass field) for a field in Lothian.

STORIE'S ALLEY (off Giles Street, South Leith) is shown on *Wood* 1777 and may have been named for James Storie, brewer, one of the victims of the plague in 1645, and/or for Gilbert Storie, resident in Leith in 1674.

STODFAULD CRAIGS (Swanston) is Scots for 'crags above the stodfauld'. Such folds are so frequent in place names (there was also a *Stodfald* at CRAIGHOUSE, *which see*, in 1368) that it would seem that they were not only a standard feature in farms, as might be expected, but that unlike other types of fold they remained in one place. While in later Scots *stot* meant a bullock, in early usage it meant horse or bull, and this is likely here in the place names.

STRACHAN GARDENS and **ROAD** (Craigcrook) *see under* CRAIGCROOK.

STRACHAN'S or **(LORD) STREIGHAN'S CLOSE** (104 High Street) *see* STRICHEN'S CLOSE.

STRACHIE'S or **STRATHIE'S CLOSE** (86 Canongate) is given as *Strachie's* in the *Accurate View* 1783 and on maps generally until after *Kirkwood* 1817; but a *Strathie's land* is mentioned here in a stent roll of 1775 and the close is *Strathie's* in *PO Directory* 1827. A John Strathy, haberdasher, was a burgess in 1819, but no connection with the close has been established.

STRAITON, shown on *Blaeu* 1654, is recorded from the 12th century, and the early forms *Stratun* or *Stratone* leave no room for doubt that the name is Anglian *straet tún*, farm place at the 'street'; and since this term in place names almost always means a Roman road, it would seem to point in this case to a link road, as yet untraced, branching to the forts at Elginhaugh or Inveresk from the known Roman trunk road that headed north from Carlops by Braid, *see under* ROMAN ROADS. The medieval estate included three working units: firstly, STRATOUN or MAINS OF STRATOUN, which seems to have centred at Straiton itself; secondly, STRAITON MILL, the mill of the whole barony, sited where Broomhills steading now stands; and thirdly, about 450 yards west of this, the farm of STRAITONHALL, where the ending *-hall* is shown by the early forms *Stratonhale* 1447 and *le hoill de Stratoun* 1509, to be Anglian *hale*, 'at the nook or haugh', or else *hole*, 'at the hollow', referring in either case to the shore of the mere or lake that lay to the west and gave MORTON (*which see*) its name on the other bank. In 1546, Straitonhall and the Mill were linked with BROOMHILL, *which see*. STRAITON ROAD is the road *by* *Straiton*, the part within the village being the old road bypassed by the dual carriageway in 1968. EAST, MID and WEST STRAITON COTTAGES were built in the later 19th century, and named for their position relative to the village.

STRAITON PLACE (Portobello) was laid out in about 1815 on the estate of the late John Rae. The name is given as *Straton* on *Wood's Portobello* 1824 and as *Stratton* in *Portobello Directory* 1836; but its origin has not yet been traced.

STRAITON'S CLOSE (125 Canongate) *see* BROWN'S CLOSE, Canongate.

THE STRAND (Canongate) was a burn that ran along the north side of the South Back of the Canongate (now Holyrood Road) and marked the boundary of all properties in the south side of the Canongate and the Canongatehead. The name is for a small burn or drainage channel, and occurs only in Scots.

STRATHALMOND COURT, GREEN, PARK and **ROAD** (Cammo) date from 1964. The name was coined in imitation of the Perthshire Glen Almond—like INVERALMOND (*which see*) but with less justification, since Gaelic *srath*, supposing it were applied to this Lowland valley, would have covered square miles of country and not just this single inby field of BRAEHEAD MAINS, a place earlier known as SOUTERHOLE, *which see*.

STRATHEARN PLACE (Greenhill) was named in about 1873, as a counterpart in Greenhill of STRATHEARN ROAD in the adjoining WHITEHOUSE, *which see*. The connection through to Greenhill Gardens and Church Hill was not made until 1897.

STRATHEARN ROAD (Whitehouse) *see under* WHITEHOUSE.

STRATHFILLAN ROAD (Whitehouse) *see under* WHITEHOUSE.

STRATHIE'S CLOSE (86 Canongate) *see* STRACHIE'S CLOSE, Canongate.

STRICHEN'S CLOSE (104 High Street) is given as *Lord Streighan's* on *Edgar* 1742. Also *Lord Strichen's* or *Strachan's*, the name was from Alexander Fraser of Strichen, who sat in the Court of Session as Lord Strichen, and probably acquired his house in the close through his marriage in 1731 with Anne Campbell, widow of the 2nd earl of Bute, grandson of its former owner Sir George Mackenzie of Rosehaugh (1630-91) king's advocate under Charles II, notorious as *Bluidy Mackenzie* in putting down Covenanters, but also the founder of the Advocate's Library. Hence the alternative close names MacKENZIE'S or ROSEHAUGH'S, still in use a century after his time. In 1635 it is listed as WALTER MAWER'S CLOSE, deriving from Walter Mawer, a writer in Edinburgh in 1593, and his son M(aister) Walter Mawer, advocate, who succeeded him in 1614. The father evidently acquired his house in the close through his marriage with Margaret Vaus, for Thomas Vaus, merchant in Edinburgh, had bought the *Abbot of Melrose ludgeing* in the west side of the close in 1588. This mansion, the residence of all the subsequent chief owners in the close, is described in *Wilson* as a large and substantial medieval building, greatly altered in about 1600—no doubt by Walter and Margaret Mawer. It was the house of Andrew Durie, abbot from 1528 until his death (from shock at a Protestant riot, says Knox) in 1558; but the name MELROSE or ABBOT OF MELROSE CLOSE (still in use in the mid 18th century) probably goes back to the early 15th century, for the abbey's land here, mentioned in *RMS* 1444 and 1473, seems to be that referred to in a grant noted in *RMS* 1390-1406.

STRIPPING CLOSE (356 High Street) appears on *Ainslie* 1780. Its site is now about the centre of the roadway at the head of Johnston Terrace. The explanation of the name, first given in *Chambers* 1825, that it was the place where criminals were stripped before being whipped all the way down the High Street, not only lacks supporting evidence but might be thought unlikely, considering that public humiliation was the object of the exercise. It is possible that the term was originally *strypand*, describing the close as having a *strype* or runnel or small drain from a spring on the slope.

STUART GREEN (Greenhill) *see under* GREENHILL (GARDENS).

STUART SQUARE (Drum Brae) was developed by the Royal British Legion Housing Association, and was named in 1978 for Alec S Stuart, a founder member of the Legion in Scotland. The name was continued in STUART GREEN, PARK and WYND in 1979, and in STUART CRESCENT in 1980.

SUCCOTH AVENUE etc (Murrayfield) *see under* GARSCUBE TERRACE, Murrayfield.

SUFFOLK and **EAST SUFFOLK ROADS** (Craigmillar Park) *see under* CRAIGMILLAR PARK.

SUGARHOUSE CLOSE (154 Canongate) is listed on *Ainslie* 1780 and was named for the refinery or *Sugar Work House* shown on *Edgar* 1765. Built on the site of the former house of the earl of Dunkeld, this was started up by the Edinburgh Sugar House company, formed in 1752, and David Jardine & Co, sugar refiners, were still operating here in the Edinburgh Sugar House in the 1820.

(OLD) SUGARHOUSE CLOSE (South Leith) is listed in *Williamson's Accurate View* 1783 and shown leading off Tolbooth Wynd on *Kirkwood* 1817. According to *Arnot*, the sugar refining industry in Leith started here in 1757. The later SUGAR HOUSE in Kirkgate is listed thus in 1783 and shown as SUGARWORK CLOSE on *Kirkwood* 1817.

SUGARWORK CLOSE (North Leith) is shown as a sugar refining works on *Regality of Canongate* 1813.

SUITTIE'S CLOSE (196 High Street) *see* OLD FISHMARKET CLOSE.

SUMMER BANK (Bellevue, Northern New Town) appears in *PO Directory* 1859 as the name (a somewhat brave fancy, considering its proximity to the mouth of the Scotland Street railway tunnel) for a row of houses later swept away when Cornwallis Place was formed in about 1881.

SUMMERFIELD (South Leith) was a property on the east side of the Restalrig road, listed in *PO Directory* 1805 and shown on *Knox* 1812. The name is fancy and idyllic, of a fashion typical of rural suburbia in the late 18th century. SUMMERFIELD GARDENS runs along the east boundary of the original property. It began as a lane beside the bowling green, in about 1900, and was first listed in *PO Directory* 1918. The name SUMMERFIELD PLACE was first used as a name for a terrace of houses on the east side of Restalrig Road, beside the original house, as shown on *Kirkwood* 1817; but in about 1872 the name was transferred to the present SUMMERFIELD PLACE, in the Industrial Road development in the grounds of Hermitage House, across Restalrig Road and on the side opposite Summerfield.

SUMMERHALL (Causeyside) originated as a property of 1¾ Scots acres, shown on *Scott* 1759 as fronting Causeyside for about 140 yards northwards from the corner of West Preston Street. Having feued it in 1704, Robert McClellan, gardener in Boroughloch, coined this name for it in 1705, building himself a house which may have been the 'Summerhall Cottage' shown on *Ordnance Survey* 1852 as just south of the main development of the ground, a brewery shown on *Scott* and named as *Summer Hall* on *Kirkwood* 1817. On *Pollock* 1834 this name is extended to include the frontage of a large house and grounds immediately north of the original feu, noted as 'Mrs Hislop's' on *Scott* but as a latter-day *Summerhall House* on *Ordnance Survey* 1852; and Hope Park Terrace was driven through its grounds, just north of the House, in 1873. Meanwhile in the southern part of the original feu, given as 'Mr McNab's' on *Ainslie* 1804, FRANCIS PLACE was developed in 1830 and was still listed as such until 1863, even although it is SUMMERHALL PLACE on *Ordnance Survey* 1852 and in *PO Directory* 1859. Adjoining it, McNAB STREET appears in 1852 and enters *PO Directory* in 1862, but becomes SUMMERHALL SQUARE by 1874.

SUMMER PLACE (Inverleith) appears thus in *PO Directory* 1843. The name may have been fancy, in the 'Summerfield' vein; but the variant *Summer's Place* attached to it on *Ordnance Survey* 1852 suggests that this free-standing tenement was named for its builder.

SUMMERSIDE (Bonnington) originated in the late 18th century as a fancy name for lands south of Northfield. It certainly applied to an easterly strip of ground (now the site of DUDLEY AVENUE) which was bought in 1802 by John Allan and renamed ALLANFIELD; but apparently its connection with the rest was strong enough to give the names SUMMERSIDE PLACE and STREET to new streets in 1869, despite the fact that an entirely different scheme of names had been planned five decades earlier, as shown on *Kirkwood* 1817. Only parts of this earlier scheme were implemented: JAMAICA STREET appeared in *PO Directory* 1814 and was not renamed as part of FERRY ROAD until 1882; and GREAT WELLINGTON STREET, listed in *PO Directory*

1821, did not progress very much before it was renamed as the southern section of SUMMERSIDE PLACE in 1910.

SUMMERTREES COURT (Inch) *see under* THE INCH, Nether Liberton.

SUNBURY (Coates) is a 4-acre haugh at Coates, recorded in 1690 as COATESHAUGH, and as *Coateshaugh now called* SUNBERRY on a plan (*RHP 586*) dating from shortly after 1761. This last shows the place as the house and grounds of William Loch (perhaps the William Loch, listed in *Williamson's Directory* 1773 as a writer in Patterson's Close) and the name, evidently fancy, may have come from Sunbury (anciently spelt *Suneberie*) in Middlesex. Loch's house was enlarged or rebuilt as *Sunbury House*, shown on *Ordnance Survey* 1852, and Haig's *Sunbury Distillery* appears on *Kirkwood* 1817. SUNBURY PLACE, STREET and MEWS were named in about 1890.

SUNNYBANK (Abbeymount) originated as the fancy name of *Sunnybank Cottage* shown on *Ordnance Survey* 1852. SUNNYBANK PLACE and TERRACE were developed in 1870.

SUNNYSIDE (Easter Road) is shown as a tollhouse on *Kirkwood's Environs* 1817, and was confirmed in 1988 as the name of the lane shown here on *W & A K Johnston* 1888.

SURGEON SQUARE (Old Town) appears on *Kincaid* 1784, developed from the garden (shown on *Edgar* 1742) of the old Surgeons' Hall. Still extant, if somewhat altered, this was built in 1697 on the site of the house of Skene of Curriehill, which is shown on *Rothiemay* 1647. After the Royal College of Surgeons removed to their new building at SURGEONS HALL, Southside, in 1832, the old Hall became successively part of the adjoining Royal Infirmary, the City Hospital, and the University of Edinburgh.

SURREY PLACE and **SQUARE** (Wester Coates) *see under* DEVON PLACE, Wester Coates.

SUTHERLAND STREET (Wester Coates) see under DEVON PLACE, Wester Coates.

SUTORHOLE (Cramond) is named thus on *Laurie* 1763 and *Armstrongs* 1773, and as *Souterhole* on *Knox* and *Cramond Roads* 1812 as well as *Kirkwood's Environs* 1817; it is shown but not named on *Gellatly* 1834, and appears on *Fowler* 1845 as BRAEHEAD MAINS, which see. It is probably akin to the seven names beginning with *Soiter-, Soyter-, Souter-, Sowter-* or *Suter-* found in *RMS* from 1476 onwards, including the *Souterland* of five rigs recorded in Straiton in 1628 and 1663. The second part is Anglian *holh* or early Scots *holl*, a howe or hollow. The first part seems to be early Scots from Anglian *sutere* or Old Norse *sútari*, a shoemaker; but it is perhaps worth noting that the latter could mean 'a tanner'.

SWANFIELD (South Leith) was a new street formed in 1982 on a property which was purchased from Haddoway, brewer in Leith, in 1804 by David Swan, merchant in the Yardheads, who built a house here and named the place after himself; and the name was continued in its later industrial development as *Swanfield Mills*.

SWAN'S CLOSE (High Street) is shown (as the next close east of Anchor Close) on *Edgar* 1742, but is noted on *Kirkwood* 1817 as 'now shut up'. Nothing is known about its name.

SWAN SPRING AVENUE (Comiston) *see under* COMISTON.

SWANSTON is recorded from 1214 onwards, *Swaynstoun* being typical of the early spellings. Combining the Old Norse personal name *Sveinn* with either Old Norse *tún* or Anglian *tún* (both meaning 'farm') the name is either Old Norse or else Anglian dating from about 900 or any of the succeeding three centuries. Part of the medieval barony of Redhall, the estate stretched from Oxgangs road to the hills and from Bowbridge to the Long Plantation of Dreghorn. The *Templelands* of Swanston, mentioned in *RMS* 1512 and in the huge list of templar lands granted to Thomas Hamilton, Lord Binning in 1614, must have been granted to the Knights Templar in the 12th or 13th centuries. In the 15th century the rest of the estate was subfeued into EASTER and WESTER SWANSTON, the march between them being the SWANSTON BURN. SWANSTON ROAD is the road to Swanston. Housing development began beside the Biggar road in about 1930. SWANSTON AVENUE, DRIVE and TERRACE were named in 1935, SWANSTON GARDENS, GROVE, PLACE and VIEW in 1956, and SWANSTON CRESCENT, GREEN, LOAN, PARK and WAY followed in 1971. Regrettably, no effort was made to distinguish these streets as being in a corner of Easter Swanston, and the group acquired the feeble nickname 'the Swanstons', which further development of the large estate has rendered only the more inept and confusing. In 1985, in order to mitigate this, new streets in the CAIYSIDE (*which see*) were named for the fields in which they were built, viz. CAIYSIDE and TRENCH KNOWE—a name which seems to have referred to the cutting in the face of the hill which developed into a small quarry at what is now the north end of Swanston Gardens; and in the same year the large development in the north of Wester Swanston was given the name of NEW SWANSTON (also the name of its spine road) and its street names were drawn from names of the ground on which it stands: SWANSTON MUIR and the MUIRSIDE path are in the *Muir Park*, AUCHINGANE and SOURHOLE path are both ancient names (*which see*) and HOWE PARK derived from the second of them, while TRYST PARK was named for nearby HUNTER'S TRYST, *which see*. HAINBURN PARK was named in 1987, as being beside the culverted HAIN BURN, *which see*.

SWEIT'S CLOSE (10 High Street) *see* WORLD'S END CLOSE.

SWIFT'S CLOSE (10 High Street) *see* WORLD'S END CLOSE.

SWIFT'S WYND (196 High Street) *see* OLD FISHMARKET CLOSE.

SWINEBURN (Kirkliston) is shown on *Forrest* 1818, and evidently took its name from the SWINE BURN. While it is likely that this is 'pig burn', the shape of its lower reach, as shown on *Kirkliston* 1759, might be described by Anglian *swin*, a channel or creek, or by Scots *swyn*, a slanting course.

SWINTON HOWE (Brunstane) was a field name still in use in the 1980s, but listed as *Swinton Holl* on *Brunstane* 1764, and probably derived from the ownership of Brunstane by John Swinton of Swinton in Berwickshire, recorded in *RMS* 1652.

SWINTON ROW (East End) is shown formed on *Kirkwood* 1817 but the name, for Catherine Swinton, wife of Walter Ferguson, who began the development of St James' Square in 1773, first appears in *PO Directory* 1829. It was closed in 1970. *See also* CATHERINE STREET, East End.

SYCAMORE TERRACE (Corstorphine) was developed by 1912 and named for the famous Corstorphine Sycamore, believed to be 500 years old, which grows opposite it. SYCAMORE GARDENS was developed in nursery ground and named in 1973.

SYDNEY PARK, PLACE and **TERRACE** (Craigentinny) *see under* CRAIGENTINNY.

SYLVAN PLACE and **FINGAL PLACE** (Sciennes) were both begun in 1825 in the Hope Park suburb in the north of Sciennes, in a property shown as *Mr Smollett's* on *Scott* 1759 and *Mr Warrender's* on *Ainslie* 1804 and *Kirkwood* 1817. SYLVAN PLACE is fancy, for the leafy suburb, if it was not borrowed from the earlier but still extant house shown on these maps. FINGAL PLACE might incorporate the Gaelic surname *Fingall* or *Fionnghal*; but more likely it is James Macpherson's *Fingal* for the Gaelic hero Fionn mac Cumhaill, chosen for the street out of the same enthusiasm that was to lead to Mendelssohn's 'Fingal's Cave' in 1829.

T

TAAPHALL (Bonnington) was the name given by Thomas Taap, shipmaster in Leith, to the villa he built here in 1802, shown as *Capt. Tap's* on *Ainslie* 1804. The later tenement on the site is listed as *Taap Hall Buildings* in *PO Directory* 1821, and *Ordnance Survey* 1852 shows TAAPHALL LANE, later to be BONNINGTON GROVE, *which see.*

TAILORS' CLOSE (137 Cowgate) is named for the Tailors' Hall, noted on *Edgar* 1742, built here by the Incorporation of Tailors in 1621.

TAIT'S CLOSE (327 High Street) *see under* DON'S CLOSE.

TAIT STREET (Hillside) appears in *PO Directory* 1872, apparently as a side name in Easter Road. It is dropped from the directory in 1889, but is given, together with TAIT PLACE, on *W & A K Johnston* 1888. The name was presumably from the developer.

TALISMAN PLACE (Inch) *see under* THE INCH, Nether Liberton.

TANFIELD (Inverleith) is recorded in 1827 as having once been known as *Bruntheugh* and was evidently part of 'the 50-shilling land of the *Brynthalch* in Inverleith', recorded in *Protocols of James Young* 1504. The nominal rental would suggest that it extended to more than 100 acres, and the name, Anglian *brynt halh* or Scots *brunt haugh*, would imply that it was once a 'brunt land', mossy ground occasionally able to bear crops when fertilised by stripping and burning the turf. The name TANFIELD appears on *Ainslie* 1804, attached to a house and 5-acre park owned by a Mr Galloway. An earlier tanyard here would seem unlikely, for there was neither ford nor bridge over the river at this point until 1768 or thereby. The name may have been fancy; but it might have been a field name on this riverside haugh, for Anglian *tanfeld* was 'a place where osiers grow'. The house continued in use until about 1870, but its southern policies were developed for industry in about 1825, with access by TANFIELD LANE. *Lothian* 1829 shows a 'portable gas works' as well as the 'oil gas works' which, converted into a hall, housed the historic first meeting of the Free Kirk in 1843.

TANNERS CLOSE (West Port) is listed at 47 West Port in 1827 and is shown on *Ainslie* 1780, but was cleared away for the building of Argyle House in 1966. Clearly it was named for a person or persons connected with the adjoining tanneries. Tanners and cordiners made leather work the staple trade of Portsburgh from early times. Archibald Lorymer, son of a beltmaker burgess in Edinburgh, was a tanner burgess of Portsburgh in 1638.

TANTALLON PLACE (Grange) *see under* THE GRANGE.

TAPACH (Dalmeny) occurs in two field names in West Muir (now Westfield) on *Dundas* 1757. It may be Gaelic *tapach*, bushy (place).

TARBRAX HILL (Dreghorn) lacks early record, but is British *tor brych* or Gaelic *tòrr breac*, speckled or brindled hill, with Scots *hill* added later.

TARVIT STREET (Tollcross) is a redevelopment of DRUMDRYAN LANE, shown on *Ainslie* 1804 and named on *Ordnance Survey* 1852 as access to the second Drumdryan House of 1774. It was remodelled by 1854 and named, like the earlier HOME STREET, for Home Rigg of Tarvit, who acquired the lands of Drumdryan in 1788, Tarvit being the family's seat near Cupar, Fife.

TAUCHIEFLATTS or **TURTLEFLATTS** (Queensferry) is recorded as a field in Muirhall in 1666, and the name is Scots *flatts*, level fields, frequented by *tauchies* or *teuchats*, peeweets.

TAVERNER'S CLOSE (High Street) lay between Niddrie's Wynd and Marlin's Wynd, and seems to have become the latter's outlet to the High Street after the Tron Kirk was begun in 1636. The line of the close was east of the kirk's gable, but since half a bay was lopped off each end of the kirk in 1785, the site of the close is now under the roadway of South Bridge. It is mentioned as *Tavernour's Wynd* in

Town Council Minutes 1488, and was probably named for John Tavernare, made burgess in 1486 and recorded in 1490 as owning a tenement at the head of the close.

TAY STREET (North Merchiston) *see under* DUNDEE TERRACE, North Merchiston.

TAYLOR GARDENS (South Leith) entered the *P O Directory* in 1914. Built on the former site of Leith Poorshouse, it was named for William Taylor, chairman of the Parish Council and partner in James Miller & Son, Leith, who had owned the ground.

TAYLOR PLACE (Abbeymount) was named by 1870, probably for its builder.

TAYLOR PLACE (Easter Road) appears briefly in *PO Directories* 1870-87, but nothing else is known about it.

TELEGRAPH KNOWE (Calton Hill) is marked on *Kirkwood* 1817. As shown on *Ainslie* 1804, the mast and yardarm used for signalling to ships in the Forth originally stood on the very summit of the Calton Hill; but in 1807 they were moved northwards, in order to free that site for the Nelson Monument.

TELFER'S CLOSE (132 High Street) *see* STEVENLAW'S CLOSE.

TELFER'S CLOSE (341 High Street) *see under* DON'S CLOSE.

TELFER SUBWAY (Fountainbridge–Dalry) dates from the mid 1890s, when Andrew Cowan Telfer was town councillor for St Cuthbert's Ward, which included Fountainbridge. Standing under the aegis of the Labour Electoral Association, he was elected in 1889 and became a bailie in 1899.

TELFERTON (Craigentinny) was coined in 1983 as a name for the main road into a new industrial estate, and WEST TELFERTON was named at the same time, as a branch off it. The name reflects the fact that, before it was used as a stockyard for fuel for Portobello Power Station, the ground was a field of the farm which, also known as *South Mains* (1750) *West Mains* (1763) *East Mains* (1773) *South Side Bank* (1812) and *Craigentinny* (1893), is shown as *Telfer's Mains* on *Figgate Roads* 1783. The new place name was formed by substituting Scots *-ton*, a farm, for *-mains*, in order to leave the older name intact as a name of the site of the steading, which is on the north side of the Portobello Road, just west of Kekewich Avenue.

TELFER'S WALL (Old Town) was instructed by the town council in November 1618, to be built to enclose an area of some ten Scots acres in High Riggs, outwith the Flodden Wall, which they had acquired from Inverleith as an addition to the royalty of the burgh, as confirmed by charter in *RMS* 1618. The boundaries of the salient are still marked by the west side of Bristo Place, the north sides of Teviot Place and Lauriston Place, and the east side of the Vennel, where the largest extant section of the Wall remains almost intact. It was named for John Tailepher, mason deacon in 1616, who evidently carried out at least part of the work. The greater part of the new enclosure was sold to the Heriot Trust in 1627, as a site for their Hospital.

TELFORD ROAD (Drylaw) was constructed as an improved route from Leith to Queensferry and (via Maybury Road) to Glasgow, and was named in 1929 for Thomas Telford (1757-1834) the great civil engineer. The name was extended to TELFORD DRIVE, GARDENS and PLACE in 1953.

TEMPLE and **TEMPLE HOUSE** (Balerno) *see under* BUTELAND (Balerno).

TEMPLELAND ROAD (Corstorphine) was named by 1904 for the *Templelands of Corstorphine*, mentioned in *RMS* 1429 and at some earlier date owned by the Knights Templars. The position of this property is uncertain, but it may have been hereabouts. The name was extended to TEMPLELAND GROVE in 1960.

TEMPLELANDS (Gogar) *see under* GOGAR.

TEMPLELANDS (Swanston) *see under* SWANSTON.

TEMPLE PARK (North Merchiston) is shown on *Kirkwood* 1817 as a large landscaped park attached to North Merchiston House and adorned with a folly in the form of a temple close to its south boundary, near the present entry to Mertoun Place; and although the park was bisected by the Union Canal in 1822, it continued with its halves linked by a bridge (now represented by Yeaman Place bridge) until North Merchiston estate began to be developed from 1878 onwards. TEMPLE PARK CRESCENT was named by 1897.

TEMPLE'S CLOSE (Cowgatehead) is listed as 149 Grassmarket in *PO Directory* 1827, shown unnamed on *Ainslie* 1780 and named on *Ordnance Survey* 1852; but it was swept away in the course of the road widening at Cowgatehead shown on *City Improvements* 1866. *Wilson II* p167 quotes a title referring to a building on the Cowgatehead frontage as a 'Templar tenement of land', and this indicates that it was one of the innumerable gifts of land to the Knights Templar or their successors the Knights of St John.

TENNANT STREET (South Leith) was developed in Bowershall and named by 1864 for James Tennant, engineer, of Bowershall Works, who was drowned in the ship *London* when bound for Australia on business.

TENNENT'S CLOSE (High Street) *see* BROWN'S CLOSE.

TERRAR'S CROFT (St Leonard's) *see under* HERMITS AND TERMITS.

TEVIOTDALE PLACE (Stockbridge) *see under* the COLONIES, Stockbridge.

TEVIOT PLACE (Bristo) together with Lauriston Place (*see under* LAURISTON, South Side) is shown on *Rothiemay* 1647 as a route along the High Riggs outside the Telfer Wall, and there is an indication of something of the kind in the siege works shown on *Siege of Edinburgh Castle* 1573. It was evidently a row of houses, shown on *Edgar* 1742 as developing in Ross Park, on the south side of the road, that generated the street's original name of TEVIOT ROW, listed in 1774 and figured on *Ainslie* 1780 and *Ordnance Survey* 1852: for the 13th Lord Ross was exceedingly fond of *Mount Teviot*, one of the seats of his uncle, the Marquis of Lothian—and indeed, as it happened, Ross died there in 1757, last of his line. In about 1871 the street name was altered to TEVIOT PLACE, probably because the original Row was about to be demolished in order to clear the site for the new Medical School; but by 1897 the name TEVIOT ROW reappeared, now attached to the eastern frontage of the McEwan Hall and ousting the earlier one of PARK STREET (*which see*) only to be itself displaced in 1982, when it became part of BRISTO SQUARE.

THIEVES LOCH (Queensferry) is shown on *Dundas* 1757 and represented by the field name *Thieves Loch Park* on *Barnbougle & Dalmeny* c1800, in the vicinity of Sommerville Gardens (NT 137774 or thereby). The name is probably early Scots *theves loch*, loch noted for thorny bushes or brambles along its shores.

THIEF or **THIEVES RAW** (Bristo and Pleasance) is shown on *Kirk o Fields* 1567 and *Rothiemay* 1647 as running immediately outside the Flodden Wall, hence its later alternative name BACK OF THE WALL, which was still shown on *Brown & Watson* 1793 although it was soon to be replaced by the current names SOUTH COLLEGE STREET and DRUMMOND STREET, *which see*. More than likely, the street existed, at least in part, before the Wall was built, for *Kirk o Fields* 1567 shows an ornamented gateway opening on to it, to all appearance an early or original main entrance to the Kirk o Fields from the south. A charter of 1563 (*RSS* V: 1218) indicates that its extension eastwards from the BACK RAW to the PLEASANCE was made at some later date, probably after the town wall was extended across the Blackfriars ground in 1567. Recorded from 1563 as *Theif Raw* and probably associated with the *Theifaker* recorded in 1579 as at the back of the Potterrow, the name is one of many such occurring in southern Scotland (*see under* THIEVES ROAD, Wester Hailes) and may refer to Scots *theif*, bramble or other thorny bush.

THIEVES ROAD (Wester Hailes) was the traditional name of WESTER HAILES ROAD, *which see*. The suggestion that it derived from use by highwaymen is pure guesswork and takes no account of the fact that this name *thieves road* is very frequent in southern Scotland. In 1832 it was noted as attaching to almost every king's highway in Selkirkshire. The reference is more likely to be to early Scots *theve*, later *theif*, hawthorn or bramble or other thorny bush growing along the roadside outwith areas of settlement, *see also* THIEF RAW.

THIMBLEHALL (Slateford) is the traditional name for this flat below the slope. Occurring elsewhere as a field name, it is Scots *thimmle haw*, the haugh noted for *thimmles*, foxgloves or (less likely in this particular ground) harebells.

THIRD AVENUE (Newcraighall) *see under* AVENUES, Newcraighall.

THIRLESTANE ROAD and **LANE** (Marchmont) *see under* BRUNTSFIELD.

THISTLE COURT and **STREET** (New Town) *see under* NEW TOWN.

THISTLE PLACE (Merchiston) *see under* HORNE TERRACE, Merchiston.

THOMAS STREET (Haymarket) *see under* TORPHICHEN STREET, Haymarket.

EAST THOMAS STREET (Hillside) was named by 1871, but the reason for the choice of name is not known.

THOMSON CRESCENT, DRIVE and **ROAD** (Currie) were built in Easter Currie in 1960, and THOMSON GROVE followed a year later. They were named to commemorate Jamie Thomson, Currie's weaver poet, who was born in Edinburgh but brought up in Currie, and settled there after his marriage in 1787, dying at Kinleith in 1832, *see* MOUNT PARNASSUS, Currie. His *Poems in the Scottish Dialect* were first published in 1801.

THOMSON'S CLOSE (40 Canongate) is given as *Thompson's* on *Ainslie* 1780 and 1804, but as *Thomson's* on *Kincaid* 1784 and in other references. Perhaps the *Bailey Thomson's Close* listed in *Maitland* 1753, it was probably named for the bailie Adam Thomson mentioned in *Town Council Minutes* 1803 as having been a brewer on the south side of the foot of the Canongate.

THOMSON'S CLOSE (232 Canongate) *see* PLAINSTANES CLOSE, Canongate.

THOMSON'S COURT (Abbey Strand, Holyrood) is figured on *Rothiemay* 1647 and named on *Ordnance Survey* 1852. The buildings no doubt provided lodgings for some of the 'abbey lairds' or refugees in the girth or sanctuary of Holyrood, which operated from early medieval times until 1913; but the date and origin of the name remain to be discovered.

THOMSON'S COURT (54 Grassmarket) *see* CARMICHAEL'S COURT, Grassmarket.

THOMSON'S PLACE (South Leith) appears as a side name in Duke Street in *PO Directory* 1816 and on *Thomson* 1822, at properties which are also shown on *Kirkwood* 1817 as belonging to *J Thomson*, who was probably James Thomson, builder, listed as in Constitution Street in 1799. The side name was dropped by 1874.

THORBURN ROAD (Dreghorn) evidently began in 1907 as access for cottages built by the Aged Christian Friend Society. The name is listed in *PO Directory* 1910 and was probably given for Alison Thorburn, mother of R A MacFie of Dreghorn (1811-93). Derivation of the street name from an alleged *Thor(n) burn* is folk etymology, for there is no sign of such a burn on *Ordnance Survey* 1893 and the supposed 'corruption' of *Thor(n)* is wholly improbable. The surname is from

Old English *Thurbrand*. The name was extended to THORBURN GROVE in 1930.

THORNTREE STREET (Quarryholes) was occupied in 1881 and named so as to continue the local place name of *the Thorn tree*, derived from a kenspeckle tree at Nether Quarryholes which was evidently well-established as a landmark in Easter Road when mentioned in *Town Council Minutes* in 1673. THORNTREESIDE, on a slope or *side* facing the site of the thorn tree across Easter Road, was named in 1981.

THORNYBAUK (Tollcross) is shown on *Roy* 1753, and is mentioned in *Town Council Minutes* 1718 as a landmark and in terms which show that the name included the present Semple Street as well as Thornybauk. Known also as the Brierybauk (not to be confused with the BRIERY BAUKS, Pleasance) it is described in the *Minutes* 1824 as 'a ridge covered with thorns, long unploughed and untouched'. Scots *bauk*, from Old Norse *balkr*, means a ridge, often of a man-made sort; and if the usage of *the Thornybauk* as a proper name suggests that this particular one was of considerable size and antiquity, this impression is deepened by the fact that, as a description, the name is exactly parallelled by the nearby Celtic place name of DRUMDRYAN, Tollcross, *which see*. While it is an open question whether *Thornybauk* is old enough to be a translation of the earlier name, it seems to be describing the same thing, which, on the evidence of the Celtic name, may have been old enough to be related to Roman roadworks, *see under* ROMAN ROADS.

THRAPLE'S CLOSE (231 Cowgate) *see* RAPPERLAW'S WYND, Cowgate.

THRASHIEDEAN (Balerno) is the Scots *dene* or deep valley where *thrashes* or rashes or rushes grow profusely. A cottage beside it is marked *Rushiedean* on *Armstrongs* 1773. The Dean burn is the southwesterly march of the city of Edinburgh.

THREE STONES (Dalmeny) is shown on *Barnbougle & Dalmeny* c1800 as a feature on Mons Hill, about 200 yards southwest of its main summit.

THREIPMUIR (Balerno) is given on *Knox* 1812 as *Threap Muir*. The name appears to be early Scots *threpe* or 'debatable' *muir*, and seems to imply that, lying as it does on the march between Malleny and Bavelaw and Kirkton, its ownership was sometimes in contention. THREIPMUIR RESERVOIR is shown on *Ordnance Survey* 1852 and was named for the farm lying east of it, rather than for the land now under water.

THREIPMUIR AVENUE, GARDENS and **PLACE** (Balerno) *see under* COCKBURN CRESCENT, Balerno.

THRIESTOPPIS or **THREESTEPS** (Piershill) was a 3-acre parcel of ground. Referred to in 1520 and named in a sasine of 1644, it was invariably grouped with Piershill prior to 1700. Lying immediately west of the Loneheid or Smoky Brae at Jocks Lodge, it is shown on *Kirkwood* 1817 as *Mr Cauvin's*. The second part of the name is Anglian *stoppa* or Scots *stoop*, a hollow, frequent in field names; and while the first part may be *three*, referring to the three Scots acres, it is more likely to be from Anglian *thyrre*, dry, making the name 'dry hollows', perhaps in contrast to the boggy howe of the Restalrig Meadow (now Meadowbank Sport Centre) at the foot of the slope.

THE TIMBER BUSH (South Leith) is recorded thus in 1698, but from 1609 onwards it is called the TIMBER HOWFF, using Scots *howff* in its primary meaning of 'yard', while in *RMS* 1603 it is the BURS (*bus* in 1636) or mercantile exchange. Both yard and exchange are mentioned in *Town Council Minutes* 1578, where it is resolved to buy from John of Dalmahoy 'the lands known heretofore as the common closets' or communal yards, but 'new callit the burs', *see also* THE BURSE, South Leith. From descriptions, as well as from maps such as *Collins* 1693 and *Naish* 1709, it is evident that the exchange and its yards occupied the whole area of the great stone bastion known as *Ramsay's fort*, built in 1548 and shown on *Siege of Leith* 1560 as mounting four guns to defend the entrance to the harbour, as well as the Sea Gate which adjoined the fort to the east. After the siege, the walls were slighted, and it was evidently their ashlar stones, belonging to the town but scattered and liable to be stolen, that the Council ordered *to be redd up* and properly stored in 1581. Nevertheless, the base platform of the fort remained: and it is clearly shown in a drawing by Slezer in 1690, still marked by the Shore on the west, the north side of Bernard Street, the boundary which strikes off northeast from the east side of 28 Bernard Street, and by Tower Street.

TINTO PLACE (Pilrig) was formed when Bonnington Toll was redeveloped in about 1895, and was named by 1896 either fancifully for the Lanarkshire hill or else for someone of the surname.

TIPPERLINN (Morningside) is recorded on *Blaeu* 1654 as a place, but in *Town Council Minutes* 1586 the context and the usage *the Tipperlyn* show that it was primarily the name of the burn. Clearly this in turn derived from the name of its source, the spring in the grounds of Viewfield House; and since this is recorded in 1813 as the *Tipperwell*, it seems likely that it was originally and simply Gaelic *an tobar*, the well, perhaps implying that it was singled out from other springs in the neighbourhood (*see* SPRINGVALLEY) as a holy one. Rather than Gaelic *linne*, which would make *Tipperlinn* a well name, 'well at the pool', the second part of the name is probably Scots *linn*, making it 'fast-running burn of/at the Tobar'. The burn was the western march of the Burgh muir, and the main part of TIPPERLINN ROAD (southwards from the end of the Dow Loan or Albert Terrace) originated in 1586, when the town council first feued out West Morningside and ordained that a strip of ground six yards wide should be reserved to form a passage down the east side of the burn to its junction with the Pow, and thence eastward to Briggs of Braid—a right of way that is still extant, although part of it looks as though it were within the grounds of the Royal Edinburgh Hospital. The northern section of the road, clearly not shown on *Roy* 1753, appears on *Merchiston* 1772, and was no doubt formed when that estate was reorganised shortly before that date.

THE TIRLESS (Duddingston) is the *style* or path leading west from the old main street or CAUSEWAY to the path by the Windy Gowl to St Leonard's Hill, as shown on *Kirkwood* 1817 and mentioned in the *Historical Description of Holyrood* 1819. The name is Scots *tirless* or *tirlies* (akin to *trellis*) a wicket or small barred gate, and by extension a right-of-way so gated to prevent stock straying.

THE TIRLIES (Hailes) is a right-of-way shown on *Armstrongs* 1773, the name being the same as the TIRLESS, Duddingston.

TOBAGO STREET (Castlebarns) was a section of the ancient Linlithgow road, named by 1792, evidently because of property here owned by Nathaniel Davidson 'of the Island of Tobago' in the West Indies. It was suppressed in favour of extension of the name MORRISON STREET in 1885. TOBAGO PLACE, derived from the name of a house built in St Cuthbert's Lane in about 1810, was given as the name of the southern section of St CUTHBERT'S LANE when this was bisected by the development of the Caledonian Railway Station in 1890.

TODD'S CLOSE or **WYND** (High Street) *see* TURK'S CLOSE.

TODDSHILL ROAD (Kirkliston) was named in 1960 for James Todd (1888-1973) County Councillor and energetic member of the community.

TODHOLE KNOWE (Dreghorn) is shown on *Ordnance Survey* 1852. The name is probably 'knowe with/near the fox's hole or den', but might be 'knowe beside the howe frequented by foxes'.

TODHOLES (Balerno) is shown on *Roy* 1753, although (probably by map error, since GOODTREES is shown as *Toddshall*) it is named as *Shothead*. It is shown on *Laurie* 1763 and 1766 as *Mains* and *Cockburn Mains*, but as *Todholes* on *Knox* 1812. An estate plan of about 1854 (*RHP 20590*) shows a *Todholes Knowe* nearby in SHOTHEAD (*which see*) and also a *Todshole park*, down by the burn; and while the name may be *tod holes*, dens of foxes, the earlier form *Toddishall* suggests that it was a *haw* or nook of land down by the burn, either tenanted by someone called Todd or else frequented by foxes. By 1893 the farm had been named COCKBURNHILL, the -*hill* no doubt being the Todholes Knowe.

TODMALANE (Stockbridge) is mentioned in *Anent Old Edinburgh* (p40) as a tree-lined path, apparently that shown on *Knox* 1812 as branching from Comely Bank on the present line of East Fettes Avenue. If ancient, the name may be Celtic; but in absence of evidence it remains obscure.

TODRICK'S WYND, (High Street) was once an important thoroughfare in the Old Town. Shown in *Rothiemay* 1647, it is marked on *City Improvements* 1866 to be closed at both ends, and but for a few vestiges it was suppressed in the development of Blackfriars Street immediately to the west of it. Mentioned as *Todrikkis Wynd* in *Town Council Minutes* 1456, its name probably went back to William Tothrik, recorded in *RMS* 1428 as an owner on the south side of the High Street, and Archibald Todrig, merchant burgess, certainly had land in the wynd, as recorded in a sasine of 1476 and in *City Charters* 1487.

TOD'S CLOSE (587 High Street) is listed on *Ainslie* 1780, but was suppressed by the building of New College 1845-50. It was named for a family of tanners and leatherworkers, one of whom, Thomas Tod, built *Tod's House* in the close towards the end of the 18th century. William Tod, leather merchant in Castle Hill, is listed in *Williamson's Directory* 1773 and the family's tan yard further down the slope is shown on *Kincaid* 1784. Earlier, the close was known as EDWARD HOPE'S CLOSE, for Edward Hope, ancestor of the Earls of Hopetoun, who had a mansion on the east side of the close in about 1560, occupied thereafter by several of his descendents. In 1635 the close is recorded as *now John Fleiming's*, from a merchant owner then resident.

TODS-HOLE CLOSE (South Leith) is recorded thus in 1683 and listed as *Tod's-hole Close* in *Williamson* 1783. On the face of it the name would be 'fox's den', but it is likely that it was a play on the surname *Tod*.

THE TOFTS (Gilmerton) appears on *Ordnance Survey* 1893 as a row of houses built in New Street (now NEWTOFT STREET) on ground shown on *Ordnance Survey* 1852 as completely open. Thus the name, using the Scots term *toft* for a homestead on its plot of ground, cannot be older than the street.

THE TOLBOOTH OF THE CANONGATE dates from 1591, but presumably replaced an earlier centre for the necessary functions of the burgh in tax collection, burgh council meetings, burgh court and jail. The building, considerably altered externally by Robert Morham in 1875, is shown on *Rothiemay* 1647, along with the TOLBOOTH WYND (165 Canongate) named for it. The Wynd may also have been HAMILTON'S ENTRY—*see under* MILLER'S CLOSE, Canongate.

THE TOLBOOTH (High Street) served not only as the headquarters, tax house, courts and prison of the burgh but, until the 17th century, as the meeting place of the high courts and the national Parliament. Before the town was sacked and burned by the English in 1385, this *pretorium* or headquarters was south-east of St Giles kirk; but its replacement was on a new site granted by Robert II in 1386, at the northwest corner of the kirk. Here the BELLHOUSE and AULD TOLBOOTH (this Scots term, referring to its function as a customs house, is increasingly used after 1436) stood until 1817; but long before this, despite alterations and extensions, it had become inadequate for its numerous purposes, and in 1560 steps were taken to supplement it, The three westermost bays of St Giles kirk were screened off and pressed into service for municipal and national purposes, and also partly as the TOLBOOTH KIRK and the WEST or HADDO(S) HOLE KIRK, *which see*. Meantime the NEW TOLBOOTH was built in 1564 at the south-west corner of St Giles (*see under* COUNCIL CHAMBER CLOSE) and the PARLIAMENT HOUSE was added in 1640. In 1811, the transfer of the town council to the Royal Exchange (now the CITY CHAMBERS) allowed the New Tolbooth to be demolished, freed the Parliament House for use of the Courts and enabled St Giles kirk to be restored; and a little later, in 1817, the opening of the new Bridewell prison on Calton Hill enabled the Auld Tolbooth to be demolished, its ancient stones being carted away to construct the common sewers in Fettes Row.

TOLBOOTH WYND (South Leith) was evidently named for the Tolbooth erected on its south side in 1565, replacing the temporary one provided in the King's Wark by Mary of Guise twenty years before; but the street must have had an earlier name, now lost, for it is shown on *Siege of Leith* 1560; and since of the two wynds or 'public ways' leading to the Shore, the BROAD WYND of South Leith (*which see*) seems to have been formed only in 1439, it is likely that the Tolbooth Wynd dates back to the very beginnings of the harbour over 200 years earlier. The yarn in *Maitland* about Burgess Close must be ignored (*see under* BURGESS STREET, South Leith) and it is probable that the Tolbooth Wynd was among the established 'common ways' made over to Edinburgh by Logan of Lestalryk in 1398, and that it was the town's 'common streitt to thair havin' mentioned in *Town Council Minutes* 1498 as being encroached upon by John Cant, indweller in Leith. The Tolbooth of 1565 was replaced in 1817 by a new one, castigated in *Wilson* as 'a nondescript building totally unfit for its purpose, afterwards converted to shops and offices'; while five years earlier the Custom House that stood next to it had been superseded by the new Custom House in Commercial Street.

TOLLCROSS is recorded from 1439 onwards, *Tolcors* being typical of the name's earliest forms; and although *Towcroce* and *Tolcroce* come in in 1529 and 1536, the ending *-cors(e)* continues to occur, even as late as 1787. Such interpretations as 'cross at a toll' or 'toll at crossroads' are quite unsupported by facts: there was no crossroads until modern times, and there is no record of any cross in the vicinity, nor of any toll except one further south at Wrightshouses; and the earliest records refer to a place or area, rather than a feature. Everything suggests that *cros* is a later form, derived from *cors* by the normal shift of *r*, and the place name appears to be British *toll cors*, boggy hollow, aptly describing this flat land beside the winding Lochrin burn in the dip between the slope of the burgh muir and the rising ground of the Hieriggs or Lauriston. The lands of Tollcross, described in *RMS* 1536 as extending to 10 Scots (i.e. 12½ imperial) acres in the lairdship of Dalry within the barony of Inverleith, were evidently bounded by the three ancient features of the Linton road (High Riggs etc) the Linlithgow road (Bread Street etc) and the Thornybauk (now partly Semple Street) except that, as shown on *Ordnance Survey* 1852, the tip of the triangle at Main Point was within the Portsburgh. The street of TOLLCROSS is of course part of the ancient Linton road; although it appears to be named on *Kirkwood* 1817, *Ordnance Survey* 1852 shows that this was still but a side name for the properties west of the road and between the foot of High Riggs and the entry of Thornybauk, while *Ordnance Survey* 1893 indicates its later use as a name for the modern crossroads. WEST TOLLCROSS originated as a subdivision of the *Tollcross* side name, specifically for the properties south or west of the entry to DUNBAR STREET (*which see*) and by 1904 it had become the street name for that entry, after its extension to Ponton Street in about 1898.

TORDUFF (Colinton) seems to be this hill's traditional name, but it is given as TORBRACK on *Armstrongs* 1773. Both names are British and/or Gaelic, the first part *torr*, steep-sided hill, and the second describing it as *dubh*, black or dark, or else *breac*, speckled, probably in contrast to the smooth and paler grassiness of its neighbour TORPHIN, *which see, and also* TARBRAX HILL, Dreghorn. TORDUFF ROAD was developed in about 1848 as access to the new reservoirs in the glen of the Ladie burn between the two hills. Originally extending from Fernielaw, it was cut off by the city bypass in about 1980 and given a new connection to Bonaly Road.

TORGEITH KNOWE (Swanston) is named on Ordnance Survey 1852. The name is British *torr goth* or Gaelic *tòrr gaoithe*, conical hill at the marsh, with Scots *knowe* added later. The knowe stands above the basin of the Hain burn, no doubt a marshy area in early times. The alternative reading of *gaoithe* as 'of the wind' would not be particularly apt to the situation.

TORMAIN HILL (Ratho) is remarkable for the cup-and-ring markings carved on its summit rocks. It was also the original site of the cross slab now at St Mary's Episcopal Church in Dalmahoy, and Kirkwood's *Environs of Edinburgh* 1817 notes a *Witches Stone* here. The name is British *torr maen*, hill of the stone(s).

TORPHICHEN STREET (Haymarket) was part of the scheme planned by Capt. Hugh Morrison (*see under* MORRISON STREET) shown as projected on *Kirkwood* 1817. It is named on *Knox* 1821 as St CUTHBERT'S STREET, obviously because of its connection with St CUTHBERT'S LANE, *which see*; and this name continued until 1870. Notwithstanding this, *Torphichen Street* appears on *Lothian* 1829 as the name of its western end, while *Ordnance Survey* 1852 shows *St Cuthbert's Street* attached to the south or Morrison side of the street, and *Torphichen Street* on the north or Heriot Trust side; and thus it is clear that the source of the *Torphichen* name, as yet untraced, is likely to be connected with the Heriot Trust or their builders. It was applied to the whole street in 1870. Meantime, a branch street in the Morrison estate, also shown on *Kirkwood* 1817, was named THOMAS STREET in 1828, evidently for Thomas Morrison, builder, *see under* MORRISON STREET. It was renamed TORPHICHEN PLACE by 1883.

TORPHIN (Colinton) is British and/or Gaelic *torr fionn*, white steep-sided hill, clearly named for its contrast with its dark rocky neighbour TORDUFF (*see also* WHITE HILL, Colinton) perhaps for its pale grassiness or, as suggested in *Walker's Collington* 1795, for 'the remarkable face of grey whinstone rocks above the farm, seen from a great distance.' *Armstrongs* 1773 shows the name transferred to the farm, giving the hill itself as LADY HILL, apparently by association with the LADY BURN (*which see*) to the south of it. TORPHIN ROAD is shown on *Knox* 1812, but must be as old as the farm, which is named on *Roy* 1753.

TORRANCE PARK (Clermiston) *see under* CLERMISTON MAINS.

TOTTLEYWELLS (Queensferry) is shown on *Forrest* 1818 as *Tottling Well*, which is Scots 'bubbling or rippling spring'.

TOWARD COURT (East Craigs) *see under* CRAIGIEVAR WYND, East Craigs.

THE TOWER (Portobello) was built in folly style in 1785, and was one of those 'gay and commodious new houses' in the fashionable Portobello, mentioned in the *Statistical Account* of Duddingston in 1794. TOWER STREET, laid out in 1802, was named as leading to it. TOWER BANK, a property built soon afterwards in *Wilson's Park*, east of the Tower, appears as *Flower Bank* on *Wood's Portobello* 1824, probably through a mapmaker's error. In 1965, in order to obviate any confusion with Tower Street in South Leith, Tower Street was renamed FIGGATE STREET, *which see*; and at the same time (but without the same reason) Tower Bank was made to follow suit as FIGGATE BANK, although the more pertinent local name has fortunately been continued in that of *Towerbank School*. TOWER LANE, shown thus on *Wood's Portobello* 1824, became RAMSAY LANE by 1836 (*see under* RAMSAY PLACE) but in 1967, in order to obviate any confusion with Ramsay Lane in Castlehill, it was renamed BEACH LANE—a rather fatuous choice, considering that a score of other streets in Portobello also lead to the beach. When the Figgate Street area was redeveloped in 1981, the opportunity was taken to restore the old place name at NEW TOWER PLACE.

TOWER STREET (South Leith) appears in *PO Directory* 1846, and seems to have been built when the North British Railway was extended to Leith Sands. It is named for the Tower at the north end of the Timber Bush, built by Robert Mylne in 1682 as a windmill for pressing oil from rape seed, and converted into a signal tower in about 1805. TOWER PLACE followed, when the Albert Dock was built in 1869; and TOWER STREET LANE was formed in the 1920s, taking in part of CONSTITUTION PLACE, *which see*.

TOWNHEAD (Balerno) is shown as a farm on *Laurie* 1763 and all maps up to *Fowler* 1845, but by 1852 it had been renamed DEAN PARK, *which see*. Recorded in *RMS* 1613 as the *Tounheid of Balerno*, the name uses toun in its early sense of 'arable farmland', and implies that it was at the southern or upper end of the medieval runrig farm of Balerno. The name was carried on in the naming of the TOWNHEAD PAPER MILL (amalgamated with Balerno Bank Mill in the 1830s) and still lingers in local parlance as a name for the area south of the junction of Mansefield and Harlaw Roads.

TOWNSWOMEN'S GUILD WALK (Meadows) *see* THE MEADOWS.

(JOHN) TOWRIS CLOSE (High Street) *see* ALEXANDER KING'S CLOSE.

TRAFALGAR LANE and **STREET** (Bonnington) *see under* PITT STREET, Bonnington.

TRANSILVANIA (Grange) *see under* THE GRANGE.

TRAQUAIR PARK (Corstorphine) was begun in 1903 in the *Paddockholm* of Meadowhouse as a cul-de-sac off Station Road, and was named for the Traquair Dickson family, owners of the ground. Elizabeth Traquair, daughter of an Edinburgh builder, had married John Dickson, farmer in Saughton, in the 1840s. The east end of the street was built separately in 1902, as access to Pinkhill railway station and to fields divided off by the new railway; and in 1925 the two parts were named as EAST and WEST TRAQUAIR PARK. In 1990 part of East Traquair Park was renamed PINKHILL, *which see*.

TRENCH KNOWE (Swanston) *see under* SWANSTON.

TREVERLEN (Duddingston) is recorded thus in a grant to Kelso abbey in 1136-47. As an estate name it was displaced by DUDDINGSTON (*which see*) in the 1150s, but as the parish name it continued into the next century. Noted as *Traverlen* in about 1170 and as *Treuerlene* in about 1250, the name is British, conceivably *tre war lyn*, farm at or on the loch—and it is tempting to think that it might have originated as the name of the crannog or lake dwelling believed to have existed in the south corner of the loch.

TRINITY COLLEGE (Old Town) was founded in about 1460. The kirk, with its aisled choir and transepts (the nave was never built) is shown on *Rothiemay* 1647 and was photographed in 1848 before it was taken down for the development of the NBR station, as shown on *Ordnance Survey* 1852. In 1872 it was re-erected, minus aisles and transepts, in Chalmers' Close.

TRINITY HOUSE (South Leith) dates from 1816-18, but is on the site of the earlier House or Hospital of 1555. It is named for its owners, the Corporation of Shipmasters of the Trinity House of Leith.

TRINITY (Newhaven) was part of the lands granted by David I to his new abbey of Holyrood in about 1128. In 1505, James IV purchased 143 acres from Holyrood, in order to set up his naval base or New Haven; and it was the western part of this crown land that was acquired in 1713 by Trinity Hospital (*see under* TRINITY HOUSE; South Leith) and developed as their farm of TRINITY MAINS, shown on *Roy* 1753. Along with LAVEROCK BANK and LILLIPUT (*which see*) the farm was served by a road from Ankerfield, as shown on *Fergus & Robinson* 1759. *Laurie* 1766 shows the road branching south, to join the Ferry road near Goldenacre, while *Ainslie* 1804 shows it branching north, to serve the villas which began to proliferate here in the 1780s. The awkwardness of this three-legged TRINITY ROAD was eventually relieved in 1928, by renaming parts of it SOUTH and EAST TRINITY ROAD. TRINITY CRESCENT, begun in 1824, was planned to exploit the presence of the CHAIN PIER (*which see*) but neither the Pier nor the later TRINITY RAILWAY STATION were able to survive competition with the development of Granton Harbour. TRINITY GROVE was built in the late 1920s in the grounds of William Creech's villa of that name, dating from 1789. TRINITY COURT, located outwith Trinity and a cul-de-sac rather than a court, was so named in 1964, apparently to satisfy a demand for a fashionable address.

THE TRON or **TRONE** (Old Town) was the burgh's main weighbeam, shown on *Rothiemay* 1647 as standing in the High Street at what is now the head of Blair Street. The name is Scots *tron* from Old French *trone*, a weighbeam. Recorded in *Exchequer Rolls* 1384 as having been repaired after its destruction by the English under Richard II, the tron was an essential facility which must have dated back to the beginning of the trading burgh. As time went on it was supplemented by the BUTTER TRON (*which see*) but the original one, like the Mercat Cross, gathered a variety of other functions (including that of pillory) and as a landmark gave its name to the locality. Hence the name of the TRON KIRK or 'Christ's kirk at the Tron', which was built in 1636-47 and has kept the place name going even after the demise of the Tron itself in the 18th century; and nearby TRON SQUARE, built by the town in 1899, was named on this basis.

TROTTER'S CLOSE (107 High Street) *see* BAILIE FYFE'S CLOSE.

TROTTER'S CLOSE (High Street & 9 West Bow) is given as *Potter's* in *Williamson's Directory* 1779 and on *Ainslie* 1780 and 1804, possibly in error. Property was owned here before 1750 by a Thomas Trotter, probably the merchant of that name mentioned in *Town Council Minutes* 1701. The site of its upper part is now roadway at the head of Johnston Terrace.

THE TROWS (Dean Gorge) were part of the dam or mill lade, shown on the *Siege of Leith* 1560, which ran from the cauld just above the Dean Bridge and powered Lindsay's, Mawr's and Greenland mills before it passed through the gorge to serve the mills in Stockbridge, Silvermills and Canonmills before rejoining the river at Powderhall. *The Trows*, Scots for a timber-built channel, was the name for the section of the waterway (still shown on *W & A K Johnston* 1888) where it was carried along the steep eastern bank of the river on a wooden aqueduct, shown on a drawing of 1816 printed in *Edinburgh in the Olden Time* 1853. It is evident from the sites and dates of the mills (Mawr's mill was operating in 1463 and Silvermills was already an established place name in 1596) that this structure or an earlier version of it must have existed in medieval times.

TRUNKS CLOSE (55 High Street) is listed on *Edgar* 1742. The name seems to be a corruption of TURING'S, from John Turing, burgess, mentioned in *RMS* 1478 as having property here, which was inherited by his son James before 1488. A John Turing, probably the same man, was bailie in 1467. A later name, ANDREW BRYSON'S CLOSE, derived from Andrew Bryson, merchant burgess, mentioned in *RMS* 1647 along with his son Alexander, and known to have rebuilt a tenement in the close. He was prominent in the town council in the 1650s, but must have been resident in the close for some time before this, since the close name occurs in *Town Council Minutes* 1650. The close also had names from two of the four previous owners of Bryson's tenement: PURVIS'S for the first of them, John Purvis, perhaps the merchant of that name elected burgess in 1592, or else the John Purves, wright, who was treasurer of the town in 1528 and dean of guild in 1539; and STIRLING'S for the third owner, William Stirling, of whom nothing more is known.

TRYST PARK (New Swanston) *see under* SWANSTON *and* HUNTERS TRYST.

THE TUMMEL or **TUMBLE** (this last obviously a would-be 'correct' spelling for a name pronounced *'tum-l*) is now wholly culverted as part of the city's sewerage system. With its tributaries it drained the valleys north and south of the Old Town ridge, and those east and west of St Leonard's Crag, as well as Hunter's Bog, and then flowed from Clockmill to Fillyside, where it entered the sea; and until almost 1800 this burn and its branches constituted the whole common sewer of Edinburgh. The curious usage of dignifying it as a *river* occurs not only on *Knox* 1812 but in numerous title deeds, which apply the term even to the *strands* or small burns which, as shown on *Regality of Canongate* 1813, defined the north and south backs of the Canongate. The name is probably British, perhaps from *timuil*, dark, referring to the peaty water of these burns in the flat bottoms of glacial valleys.

TURK'S CLOSE (south side of High Street) is noted in *Maitland* 1753 and shown on *Ainslie* 1780, but the name is obscure, and may not have been of long standing. Earlier the close was CARFRAE'S (given as *Carthrae's* on *Edgar* 1742) from William Carfrae, merchant, who had his house at the head of the close at some date prior to 1725. It also seems to have been known as TODD'S CLOSE or WYND. A *City Charter* of 1578 links this name with lands once belonging to Sir Thomas Tod, then deceased: he was a member of town council in 1492, and was perhaps the plain Thomas Tod listed as a councillor in 1480. The close was suppressed when the County Hall was built in 1817 on the site which is now occupied by Lothian Regional Chambers.

TURNDREICH (Dalmeny) is shown on *Barnbougle & Dalmeny* c.1800 as the name of the high ground behind the Snab, which has a knoll or point on its flattish top but also presents a steep and indeed remarkably abrupt northerly face to the Long Green. The name is Gaelic, very possibly standing for a British name of similar meaning and form, and might be *torr an dreich*, knoll of the hill face, or else— and perhaps more likely, for the settlement at the Long Green shown on *Blaeu* 1654 was probably not the first to be there—*treabhar an dreich*, farm at the hill face, the first *r* later dropping out, as it does elsewhere.

TURNER AVENUE etc (Balerno) *see under* DALMAHOY CRESCENT, Balerno.

TURNHOUSE (Lennie) is shown on *Armstrongs* 1773, but *Roy* 1753 shows *Dying house*, and *Laurie* 1763, *Pirnhouse*, apparently in the same place. These are presumably trade names, to do with weaving, but without fuller information and earlier forms the place name remains obscure. TURNHOUSE ROAD south of Lennie Port appears on *Gellatly* 1834. It was for long known as the *Stirling Road*, but also as *Turnhouse Road*, leading to Turnhouse farm and (later) aerodrome; and in 1968 the main road leading to the airport was renamed TURNHOUSE ROAD, while the section leading from Crumblands to Turnhouse farm was renamed TURNHOUSE FARM ROAD.

THE TWIRLIES (Colinton) is a right of way up the Sheeling Hill. Shown on *Spylaw* 1799 as a straight path, it may well have been known as a *tirless* or gated path, see THE TIRLIES, Hailes. Its present name, which also occurs in a similar situation in Hawick, possibly developed from this old term either by misundertanding or in play, after the path was altered in 1874 to wind up the hill from the new Bridge Road.

TWEEDDALE COURT (16 High Street) is given thus in *PO Directory* 1815 but is MARQUESS OF TWEEDDALE'S CLOSE on *Edgar* 1742 and *Kirkwood* 1817 and TWEEDALE'S CLOSE on *Ainslie* 1780 and 1804. It is named for John Hay, 2nd Earl of Tweeddale, created Marquis in 1694, who inherited the mansion at the foot of the close from his grandmother Margaret Ker, Lady Yester, in 1647. The last of the family to live in it was the 4th marquis, who died in 1762. Lady Yester 'built and repaired the great ludging', but it appears to have been earlier the house of Neil Laing WS, mentioned in the city treasurer's accounts 1554-55 as the meeting place of a conference on the repair of the Mercat Cross, and the close was known as JOHN LAING'S, for his successor, also a WS. The reference in 1750 to the close as ALEXANDER YOUNG'S *later* JAMES BROWN'S apparently goes back to 1564 and 1613, when (as noted in *Protocols of A Guthrie*) Young and Brown respectively got property in the close.

THE T-WOOD (Swanston) is shown on *Ordnance Survey* 1852 but is missing from earlier maps, although it is said to have been planted by Henry Trotter of Mortonhall in 1766. On plan its shape is an irregular Maltese cross (so irregular, indeed, that it looks as though its north and south arms have been added to an older plantation) but because it lies on the summit of the White Hill only three of its arms are visible in a T-shape in any one view of it, except from the air; and hence its popular name. There is no evidence that this was intended; and the internal evidence (as noted above) is rather against it.

TWOPENNY CUSTOM (West Port) is shown on *Scott* 1759 and was a collection point, strategically placed at the western entrance to the town via its subordinate burgh of Portsburgh, for the duty of 2d Scots on the pint of ale which began to be levied in 1690, as a means of financing public works and augmenting the stipends of the town's ministers and university professors. The toll house, still existing, was rebuilt in about 1770 and seems to have acquired the name MAIN POINT (*which see*) between 1809 and 1817.

TYLER'S ACRE ROAD (Corstorphine) was named in 1930 as being within the historic *Taylor's Acre Park* shown on *Corstorphine* 1777 and later maps. In 1714 a lease included an acre 'sometime possessed by William Stevenson Taylor', and seeing that prior to this there is record of a tenancy by William Stevenson, it is fairly clear that *Taylor* was not his name but that he was a tailor to trade. Since *tyler* is an authentic Scots variant of the word, its use suggests that the field name was still alive in local parlance when the street was named. Less appositely, it was extended in 1955 to TYLER'S ACRE AVENUE and GARDENS, the first partly and the second wholly within the adjoining field named the HONEYMUG PARK, *which see*.

TYNECASTLE, shown as an unnamed toll point on *Laurie* 1763, is named and shown on *Merchiston* 1776 as a 1½-acre property on the north side of the highroad, a site now immediately east of McLeod Street. In absence of earlier record, derivation must be guesswork; but the name would appear to be Celtic: perhaps (in Gaelic, or in British equivalents) *tigh*, house, described as either *na caiseil* or *'n caisteil*—two very similar terms, that would imply that this house was at a mound or a rock, or in or near a fenced settlement of some kind. While the name may have been transferred from elsewhere, one or other of such features might well have occurred around here, where the old Calder road branches off the yet more ancient Lanark road, and where the nearby name of CRAIGINGLIS (*see under* WEST BRYSON ROAD, North Merchiston) is not yet fully accounted for. TYNECASTLE BRAE, now ARDMILLAN TERRACE, was formed in about 1801. TYNECASTLE PLACE was developed within Tynecastle in about 1870, and TYNECASTLE TERRACE (1872) and LANE (1892) were named as being near it.

U

ALEXANDER UDDART'S or **UDWART'S CLOSE** (42 High Street) *see* SOUTH FOULIS'S CLOSE.

UPPER or OVER BOW (Old Town) *see* WEST BOW, Old Town.

UPPER CRAMOND COURT (Cramond) *see under* CRAMOND.

UPPER DAMSIDE (Dean Village) was named in 1984 as a new street branching off at a higher level from the DAMSIDE, *which see.*

ULSTER DRIVE, GARDENS, GROVE and **TERRACE** (Willowbrae) were developed in 1929 in the North Park and Black Ridge fields of Meadowfield, in the Duddingston estate of the Duke of Abercorn. Named at first for the Duke's barony of *Kilpatrick*, the streets were shortly afterwards renamed for *Ulster*, no doubt in view of his service as Governor of that province, which had begun in 1922 and was to continue until 1945. ULSTER CRESCENT was added in 1934.

UNION PLACE and **STREET** (Broughton) *see under* PICARDY, Broughton.

UNION STREET (South Leith) *see under* KIRK STREET, South Leith.

UNTHANK (Balerno) appears on *Kirkwood's Environs* 1817 near the position of West Rig, Balerno. Frequent as a farm or field name in England as well as in Scotland, the name derives from Anglian *unthanc*, thanklessness, and was the technical term for land which, being occupied by a squatter, did not produce a rent.

UPPER BOW (Old Town) *see under* WEST BOW.

UPPER DEAN TERRACE (Stockbridge) *see under* DEAN STREET, Stockbridge.

UPPER GRAY STREET (Newington) *see under* GRAY STREET, Newington.

V

VALLANCE'S CLOSE (74 Canongate) is listed as *Vallene's* on *Ainslie* 1780 and appears as *Valentine's* in *PO Directory* 1827. The surname was originally AngloFrench, brought into Scotland in the time of Malcolm IV, and assumes many forms, such as Vallange, Wallanche and Wallence. Property belonging to Adam Vallange is recorded here in 1775; but the close name might go back before his time, for a John Vallange was a 'maister hammerman of Canongate' in 1610.

VALLEYFIELD (Tollcross) was part of the Burgh Muir until 1687, when it was feued to John Marshall, merchant burgess, who built a house in its southwest corner (now the corner of Glengyle Terrace) shown and named on Scott 1759. It was later acquired by the Williamson family and merged with their adjoining property of Leven

Lodge, as shown on *Ainslie* 1804. Probably given by Marshall, the name describes the position of the place at the foot of the slope of the Muir. VALLEYFIELD STREET was formed in 1867, in the course of a development which also included GLENGYLE and LEVEN TERRACES, *which see*.

VANBRUGH PLACE (South Leith) was begun on the site of COATFIELD MAINS (*which see*) in 1825. Designed and built by William Lamb as a unified terrace, it seems to have been named by him, in compliment to Sir John Vanbrugh (1666-1726) the leading exponent of the English Baroque style.

VANDELEUR AVENUE, GROVE and **PLACE** (Craigentinny) *see under* CRAIGENTINNY.

THE VAULTS or **VOUTS** (South Leith) was a warehouse for the importing of wine, one of the chief trades in Leith from early medieval times onwards. The present building mostly dates from 1682, but the vaulted cellars may be much older, although they are not to be confused with other wine cellars immediately adjoining the east end of the Coalhill and recorded as the *gret volut of Villiam Logane* in *Charters relating to Edinburgh* 1439 and as the *Blakvolts* in *RMS* 1587. The local pronunciation *vouts* or *vowts* is not (as sometimes alleged) peculiar to Leith, but is from the Old French and has been normal in Scots since the early Middle Ages. BACK O THE VOUTS was a cross street on the southeast side of the building, still shown on *Ordnance Survey* 1931.

VEITCH'S CLOSE (295 Canongate) *see* MID COMMON CLOSE, Canongate.

VEITCH'S SQUARE (Stockbridge) is shown on *Ainslie* 1804 as already taking the shape shown more fully developed on *Kirkwood* 1817 and there labelled VEITCH'S COURT—a name that persisted until 1832, when the *Court* became VEITCH'S SQUARE and its approach from Deanhaugh Street became VEITCH'S PLACE. In all probability the name came from Thomas Veitch, listed as *feuar in Stockbridge* in 1806 and *baker in Stockbridge* from 1808 onwards; but (as noted) the place was established before his time, and *Cumberland Hill* reports that it was first of all known as VIRGIN SQUARE—a traditional street name that occurs in places as far apart as St Monans in Fife and St Ives in Cornwall.

THE VENNEL (Longstone) was developed soon after 1900, and since the name arose in local parlance, it shows how the term *vennel*, a narrow lane or public passage, has continued alive in Scots usage.

THE VENNEL (Queensferry) dates from before 1633 and was probably an early part of the medieval burgh. Its name, Scots from Old French *venelle*, a small street, indicates that (unlike a *close*, which would begin as private property) it was from the first a public way, leading up to the open ground above the tofts or burgage plots south of the High Street. Since the name was in the nature of a technical term, the records sometimes use it for other minor ways in the burgh, such as Hawthornbank or Stonycroft Road.

THE VENNEL (West Port) is strictly the *West Port Vennel*, as listed in *Williamson's Directory* 1773, or the *Lauriston Vennel* as shown on *Kirkwood* 1817, for the term (from Old French *venelle* or medieval Latin *venella*) means 'a small street or public passage', and there were many *vennels* in Edinburgh from medieval times onwards. Shown on *Rothiemay* 1647 and *Edgar* 1742, it runs immediately outside the FLODDEN and TELFER WALLS (*which see*) but since these followed earlier boundaries, the Vennel may be considerably older than them. The name properly applies to its whole length, from West Port to Lauriston Place; for HERIOT PLACE is properly the name of the tenements on its west side, named in 1826 for the Hospital they face.

VENTNOR PLACE and **TERRACE** (Mayfield) *see under* McLAREN ROAD, Mayfield.

VEXHIM PARK (Niddrie) *see under* THE JEWEL, Niddrie.

VIA REGIS (Liberton) was named thus in 1994. The path is what remains of part of a public road through Stenhouse, shown on *Roy* 1753 and reported in *Good's Liberton* as being referred to in a deed of 1760 as *regis via*; but Good wrongly took this to be a proper name, for *regis via* or *via regis* was simply the normal term in charters, in England as well as Scotland, for any public highway.

VICTORIA DOCK (North Leith) was opened in 1852 and named for the Queen.

VICTORIA PARK (Bonnington) was a new name, given in about 1900, for part of the grounds of BONNINGTON PARK, an estate which had been separated off from Bonnington in 1771, Bonnington Park House (later becoming Victoria Park House) being built in 1789.

VICTORIA PLACE (Newhaven) was built behind the south frontage of Main Street in the 1860s and presumably named for the Queen.

VICTORIA STREET (Old Town) was planned in 1827 as a *Grass Market Access* connected to the lower part of the West Bow and incorporating its middle section in a wider street continuing eastwards to the proposed George IV Bridge. It is shown as open on *Pollock* 1834 and the name, since it appears in *PO Directory* 1837, must have been given before Princess Victoria's accession to the throne in June of that year. VICTORIA TERRACE is named on *Ordnance Survey* 1852; and its western half approximately indicates the line of the CASTLE WALL, *which see*.

VICTOR PARK (Corstorphine) was named in about 1870 for Charles Victor Parker, owner of the property; and VICTOR PARK TERRACE began to be developed on it in 1898-99, on the site of the ancient FERRYGATE, *which see*.

VIEWCRAIGS ROW and **UPPER VIEWCRAIGS ROW** (Dummie-dykes) were built in 1862, the first developments in the DISHFLAT (*which see*) and facing the Crags which gave them their name. This was reduced to Viewcraig by 1876, and was carried forward into the redeveloped neighbourhood in 1971, in the names of VIEWCRAIG GARDENS and STREET.

VIEWFIELD ROAD (Hailes) *see under* CURRIEMUIREND, Hailes.

VIEWFORTH (Merchiston) began as a villa, mentioned in 1780 and shown perhaps on *Armstrongs* 1773 and certainly on *Kirkwood* 1817. Pulled down in 1911, when the ground was cleared for the building of Boroughmuir School, it was sited immediately west of the entry to Westhall Gardens, and was evidently named for the then unimpeded view of the estuary. As shown on *Pollock* 1834 the street is called *Viewforth Place*, probably in order to distinguish it from the house; but by the 1880s VIEWFORTH had prevailed as the name of the street, while the house became *Viewforth House*. VIEWFORTH PLACE was later reused as the name for the carriageway in front of LEAMINGTON TERRACE (*which see*) but was finally suppressed in 1885. VIEWFORTH TERRACE and PARK were named in 1862, but in 1885 the latter was renamed DUNDEE TERRACE, *which see*. VIEWFORTH GARDENS followed in 1889, and VIEWFORTH SQUARE in 1891.

VIEWFORTH ROAD and **PLACE** (Queensferry) were named by 1969 for the view over the estuary. The first was originally part of LOCH ROAD (*which see*) and crosses the SKAITHMUIR into the STONYFLATTS (*which see*) of Plewlands; while VIEWFORTH PLACE runs along the head of the Skaithmuir.

VILLA ROAD (Queensferry) is shown on *Ordnance Survey* 1895; and its name, recorded in 1933 as simply THE VILLAS, evidently derived from the flatted houses shown on its south side, the first of that sort to be built in the burgh.

VINEGAR CLOSE (South Leith) is listed on *Kirkwood* 1817, and appears as *Vinegar Street* in *Williamson's Directory* 1799. Named for the vinegar works of Hendry or Harry Smith (and perhaps his predecessors) who flourished about 1710, the close was swept away in the development of HENDERSON STREET (*which see*) but *Wilson* records Smith's house as ornamented with a panel bearing his arms impaled with those of Agnes Gray, his wife.

VIOLET BANK (Abbeyhill) was built in 1863. The name, partly echoing that of St Ann's Bank, may have been that of a relative of the developer, or else was fancy, for the flower.

VIOLET TERRACE (North Merchiston) *see under* PRIMROSE TERRACE, North Merchiston.

VIVIAN TERRACE (Davidson's Mains) was named in 1924 for Vivian, eldest daughter of the developer, Matthew Mather of Muirhouse.

W

WADDELL PLACE (South Leith) was named by 1881 for the contractors Andrew Waddell & Son, who maintained stables for their draught horses here.

WAKEFIELD AVENUE (Craigentinny) *see under* CRAIGENTINNY.

WALKER DRIVE (Queensferry) was begun in 1936 and named for Peter Walker, provost of the burgh 1936-39; and its western section, developed in 1947 for temporary housing, was completed in 1968 on a somewhat different plan.

WALKER'S CLOSE (Grassmarket) *see* WARDEN'S CLOSE, Grassmarket.

WALKERS RIGG, COURT and **WYND** (Wester Hailes) are fancy names given in 1992 and supported by a fictional tale of a pedestrian way in these parts. In point of fact the name *Walkers Rigg* was wrested from *Spylaw* 1767, where it is shown as belonging to a narrow 1-acre holm beside the Water of Leith, almost a mile from these streets and quite unconnected with them; and it is clear that this *rigg* or strip of arable was named, at some time before 1767, for some tenant called Walker.

WALKER STREET (Coates) *see under* COATES.

WALKER TERRACE (Dalry) *see under* DALRY PLACE.

WALTER SCOTT AVENUE (Inch) *see under* THE INCH, Nether Liberton.

WANTON WALLS (Newcraighall) is shown on *Laurie* 1763, and recorded as *Wantounwallis* from 1596 onwards, linked with Newhalls mains, Gaitsyde and Mairfield in the estate of New Hailes. It is one of five places of the name in eastern Scotland, the common feature in the various sites being the presence of a small burn with springs. These last are in Scots *walls* or *wells*; and the first part of the name is Scots *wantand* in its sense of being apt to wane or give out (cf. Anglian *waneting*) and thus the name is '(place of) intermittent or seasonal springs'.

WARDEN'S CLOSE (Grassmarket) is given thus on *Ordnance Survey* 1852, but as WALKER'S on *Ainslie* 1780 and 1804. Both names seem to derive from stablers in Grassmarket, Mrs Walker and George Warden, separately listed in *Williamson's Directory* 1773. *Kincaid* 1784 names an eastward branch to Candlemaker Row as HART'S CLOSE: it may be the same as the *alias* BURT CLOSE which appears with its old number 143 Grassmarket in *PO Directory* 1827, but no derivation has been found for either.

WARDIE is recorded from 1336 onwards, in spellings such as *Warda* and *Weirdie*; and the name is Anglian *wearda*, probably influenced by the Old Norse *varthi*, both meaning beacon or cairn, and evidently referring to the vantage point of WARDIE BROW, the steep bluff above WARDIE BAY. The mansion and surrounding buildings are shown as *Waredye* on *Siege of Leith* 1560, and *Ainslie* 1804 shows a group of buildings still represented by Wardie House and cottages in Boswall Road and WARDIEHOUSE LANE, named in 1956. The farm steading of WARDIE MAINS was on the north side of the Ferry road, midway between the present Wardie and Granton Roads, and the early road which led from here to Wardie House was suppressed when Granton Road was built to the west of it in about 1838. WARDIE CRESCENT began to be developed in 1853, partly as a curving access to Wardie Brick & Tile Works; and the fancy names WARDIE GROVE (1932) and DELL (1975) and WARDIEFIELD (1985) were given to spurs off it. WARDIE ROAD and AVENUE were opened by 1867, WARDIE SQUARE and STEPS were so named by 1903 and 1906, while WARDIE PARK dates from 1924.

WARDIEBURN DRIVE, PLACE, STREET and **TERRACE** (Royston Mains, Granton) were named in 1932, and WARDIEBURN PLACE WEST and ROAD followed in 1933. Ultimately derived from the Wardie burn, which runs some way to the south and east of the neighbourhood, the name seems to have been more directly suggested by the name of *Wardieburn House*, a villa erected in about 1853 on the site of an earlier *Wardie Burn Cottage* on ground between the burn and the Ferry road at West Winnelstrae.

WARDLAW PLACE, STREET and **TERRACE** (Gorgie) were built on part of Gorgie Muir and named by 1887 for General Wardlaw, a member of the Sir George Campbell Trust, owners of the ground.

WARDLAW'S CLOSE (28 Cowgate, and connecting with Riddle's Close, High Street) *see* ALISON'S CLOSE, Cowgate.

WARDROP'S COURT (High Street) originated as the name of a tenement in the close (then known as *Middle Baxters Close* from its connection with property belonging to that Incorporation—*see under* BAXTERS CLOSE) built by John Wardrop and John Henderson, wrights and burgesses, probably about 1712, when Wardrop acquired an existing house in the close. As shown on *Edgar* 1742, the old name was transferred to another close (*see* MIDDLE BAXTER CLOSE) and the tenement name became general to the close, while its entry became known as WARDROP'S or HENDERSON'S CLOSE.

WARKLAW HILL (Currie) is Anglian *werc hlaw*, law or hill at the 'work' or fortification (probably referring to the large fort with double earthen ramparts on the west bank of the Clubbiedean burn), with Scots *hill* added.

WARRENDER PARK (Bruntsfield) was coined in 1869 as the name for the housing development in Bruntsfield estate, and is still in use as the neighbourhood name for its western part—*see under* BRUNTSFIELD for streets of the name.

WARRISTON (Currie) is recorded from 1392 onwards, and appears on *Blaeu* 1654 as *Warestoun*. The early forms *Warynstone* and *Warnistoun* show that the name is Old Norse or Anglian *tún* or Scots *toun*, farm place, of someone bearing the Norse name *Warin*, or else its later AngloNorman version *Warin* or *Guerin*.

WARRISTON (North Edinburgh) is recorded from 1467 onwards, and is shown on *Blaeu* 1654 as *Warysto*. Also given as *Waranstone*, *Waristoun* or *Varestoun*, the name is the same as that of WARRISTON in Currie, *see above*. The lands stretched from the Water of Leith to the Ankerfield burn, marching with Bonnington on the east and Inverleith on the west. The detail on *Roy* 1753 and *Fergus & Robinson* 1759 suggests that the original centre was at Easter Warriston, and show that WARRISTON ROAD was the ancient *road to Warriston* by the ford at Puddockie. The part of it leading north from Easter Warriston appears to date from the realignment of the FERRY ROAD soon after 1750. In the late 18th century the estate was divided: William Ramsay built WEST WARRISTON HOUSE in about 1784, and Andrew Bonar acquired EAST WARRISTON in 1795. Planned in 1807, WARRISTON CRESCENT and HOWARD PLACE (*which see*) are named on *Kirkwood* 1817, while WARRISTON PLACE is shown, although the name first appears on *Pollock* 1834. In 1817 West Warriston was bought from the Ramsays by Alexander Henderson, and it was this family who continued its development in the 1870s, when a road called WARRISTON TERRACE was laid out, only to be suppressed later, when the Edinburgh Institution's cricket ground was developed in about 1900; and EILDON STREET, begun in 1879, was named for the Hendersons' property of Eildonhall, near Melrose. WARRISTON CEMETERY was laid out in 1842. In 1926 its access, CEMETERY ROAD, was renamed WARRISTON GARDENS; and development in West Warriston continued with WARRISTON GROVE (1930), EILDON TERRACE (begun in 1933 but not completed until after West Warriston House was cleared away in 1966) and WARRISTON AVENUE and DRIVE and a new WARRISTON TERRACE, named in 1955. EASTER WARRISTON, lost as a place name when the House was redeveloped as a crematorium in 1928, was recovered in 1984 as the name of new housing on ground partly within that division of the estate. Within this group, NORTH ENTRY was given as the name of a path entering from Ferry Road, CROSSGATES is a pair of paths linking roads in the middle of the group, and the parking and play areas were given some identity by naming them NORTH, MID, WOOD, EAST, WEST and SOUTH PARKS.

WARRISTON'S CLOSE (323 High Street) is shown on *Edgar* 1742 and was named for Sir Archibald Johnstoun of Warriston, Currie, the leading spirit in the framing of the National Covenant in 1638, who had his town house on the west side of the close. Earlier, the house (known as *Craig's Land* in 1582) had belonged to his uncle, Sir Thomas Craig of Riccarton—hence the name CRAIG'S CLOSE; but earlier still, in about 1566, it had been built or extended by Robert Bruce of Binnie, and the close had been known as BRUCE'S. A lintel of the house remains, inscribed GRATIA DEI ROBERTUS BRUISS, and John Knox's manse was immediately opposite. WARRISTON BRAE, shown on *Ordnance Survey* 1852 as a transe or passage at right angles to the closes, is now reduced to a short section with steps down into Cockburn Street at the foot of the Advocate's Close.

WASHINGTON PLACE and **STREET** (Dalry) are shown on *Ordnance Survey* 1878 and were named by 1870; but the reason for the choice of name has not yet been traced. WASHINGTON LANE and COTTAGES were named by 1892.

WATERGATES (Canongate & Leith Wynd) *see under* WATERYETTS.

THE WATERING STONE (Meadowbank) is mentioned in George Sandy's *Diary* of 1788 (in *Old Edinburgh Club XXIV*), named on *Knox* 1812 and shown in detail on *Ordnance Survey* 1852. Evidently a watering trough on the west side of the entrance to Holyrood Park, it was also used as a boundary mark—e.g. in the police regulations of 1822.

WATER LANE (South Leith) *see under* RATOUN RAW, South Leith.

WATERLOO PLACE (East End) *see under* REGENT BRIDGE, Calton.

WATER OF LEITH has been used since the 15th century as a form of the name of the river LEITH, *which see*; but in *Town Council Minutes* 1585 it is used as the name for the village on the town's ground in the Dene, referred to in 1535 as the *millers' village* and shown as *Common Mylles* on *Siege of Leith* 1560. With or without the suffix *Village*, it continued to be the regular name of the place until the 1920s, when it began to be ousted by the transferred name DEAN VILLAGE, *which see*. Since the site was part of the ancient royalty of Edinburgh, it was probably the site of the 'new mill of Edinburgh' mentioned in David I's charter to Holyrood abbey in 1128, as well as those mills confirmed to Edinburgh by Robert the Bruce in 1329. Early named buildings in the village include MAWR'S and LINDSAY'S MILLS and the granary of JERICHO (*all of which see*) and by the end of the 16th century there were eleven mills in the group.

WATERPANS (Jocks Lodge) appears on *Duddingston* c1800 as the name of a field, but in 1774 it is referred to as a place near SLOCKENDROCHT, *which see*. Since none of the maps indicate any ponds or cisterns which might have given rise to the name, it may be that there was a field where poor drainage, either natural or induced by *panning* of the subsoil in the course of ploughing, led to an abundance of puddles after rain.

(WILLIE) WATER'S CLOSE (South Leith) is recorded in *Laing's Charters* 1759 and *Williamson's Accurate View* 1783 as *Willie Water's*, but is listed on *Kirkwood* 1817 as *Water's*. The name is a form of Walter(s) and is said to have been that of an 18th-century owner in the close. Its older name was CORNTOUN'S, mentioned thus in *RMS* 1603 and listed on *Wood* 1777 and *Ainslie* 1804 as *Corton's*, and probably deriving from a family of merchants which may have included George Cornetoun of North Leith, dealer in hides, mentioned in *Town Council Minutes* 1516, as well as Florence Cornetoun, fish merchant in 1541, who may have been the Florence Carntoun who was among the first bailies of South Leith when it became a burgh in 1555. The close is said to have been also LAMB'S, for the owner of Lamb's House.

WATER STREET (South Leith) *see under* RATOUN RAW, South Leith.

WATERTOUN ROAD (West Mains) was named in 1931, the estate suggesting the name but giving no reason for its choice. Although *Ordnance Survey* 1893 shows a well in the field, the name is unlike a field name in form, and possibly derives from a personal name or else from one or other of the places of the name near Cumnock, Dyce or Elgin, or in Lincolnshire.

THE WATERYETT or **WATERGATE** (Canongate) is not to be confused with the WATERYETT or GATE in Leith Wynd (*see next*) to which the references in *Town Council Minutes* prior to 1639 generally apply. It is shown on *Hertford's Assault* 1544 as the way into the Canongate, and an arched entry is clearly shown on *Siege of Edinburgh Castle* 1573 and on *Rothiemay* 1647. It was not primarily a defensive port, but a lockable gate for normal security and police purposes. It was also a point for collection of the burgh's customs: when the ancient stone arch (shown in a print by Storer in 1820) was blown down in 1822, a timber one was put up in order to continue the administrative landmark; and although this disappeared within thirty years, the *Ordnance Survey* 1852 still marked the Watergate as 'Customs Station'. The name is Scots *yett* from Anglian *geat*, a gate in the modern sense (unlike the word in *Canongate*, which is from Norse *gata*, a road) while the *water-* part probably referred not only to the Tummel burn (the burgh boundary) which crossed the road at this point, but also the fact that the gate gave access to the common wells along the burnside.

THE WATERYETT or **GATE** (Old Town) is shown on *Rothiemay* 1647 as *Lieth Wyn Port* at the foot of Leith Wynd—a point still marked by a right of way over Waverley Station from Low Calton. Frequently mentioned in *Town Council Minutes* from 1550 onwards, it is not to be confused with the WATERYETT at the foot of the Canongate (*see above*) for the latter was outwith the jurisdiction of Edinburgh until after the purchase of the Canongate in 1639. The name is Scots *yett* from Anglian *geat*, and the gate was called *water yett* because it gave access to the Tummel burn which flowed along the foot of the Calton craigs and also to the common wells along the burn side. The yett was not intended for defence (indeed, when war threatened, the town council were apt to have it not merely locked but built up solid) but it assisted the policing of both Edinburgh and Canongate, for the march between the two burghs ran down the west side of Leith Wynd. While this wynd was part of the medieval way to Leith, it was inconveniently steep, and the opening of the *New Port* in HALKERSTON'S WYND (*which see*) reduced the importance of the Wateryett as a town entrance; so much so that by the 16th century its chief purpose seems to have been to enable the townsfolk 'to lead forth their muk' and (presumably) dump it in the Tummel; and in the 1730s the gateway was known as the MUCK or DUNG PORT.

WATSON CRESCENT (North Merchiston) was planned in about 1880 with Bryson Road, and was started and named (for Bailie James Watson) by 1887.

WATSON'S CLOSE (south side of High Street) is mentioned in *RMS* 1616, in a grant to Andrew Creich, merchant burgess, of land adjoining properties of John Adamson, merchant, Alexander Paterson, apothecary, and Watson's Close. The location is not established; but it might be noted that in *Stent Roll* 1635, while no one called Creich is mentioned, John Adamson, advocate, and Alexander Paterson are named among owners in Lady St Ninian's Close (*see* St MONAN'S CLOSE) and a George Watson, writer, is listed as an owner in the High Street just west of the close mouth.

WATSON'S CLOSE (226 Canongate) is shown on *Ainslie* 1780. Being in the south Canongatehead, it was part of Edinburgh, not of the burgh of Canongate. The name was from Thomas Watson, litster, who owned a tenement in it in 1716. The close was also BANNATYNE'S (or *Ballantyne's*) or STALKER'S (or by a slip, *Walker's*) for Henry Bannatyne and John Stalker of Drylaw, who are recorded in 1635 as owning property in the close both jointly and separately. Stalker was also a resident.

WAUCHOPE AVENUE, CRESCENT, PLACE and **TERRACE** (Niddrie) were named in 1931 for the Wauchope family, lairds of Niddrie Marischal for over 600 years from the late 14th century; and WAUCHOPE ROAD and SQUARE were added in 1932 and 1933.

WAUCHOPE CLOSE (Canongate) is mentioned in *Town Council Minutes* 1835 and appears from *Canongate Charters* 1888 to have been named for John Wauchope of Hill, father of Francis Wauchope of Caikmuir, advocate, who acquired property from Agnes and Jannet, daughters of James Kerr, maltman in the Horse Wynd. The close may have been on the east side of the wynd; or it may have been FERRIE'S CLOSE, *which see*.

WAULKMILL LOAN (Currie) was adopted in 1979 as the name for the road, shown on *Ordnance Survey* 1852 but evidently much older, which gave access to mills on the haugh here. These are shown on *Roy* 1753, and included the Waulk (i.e. cloth-processing) Mill of Balerno, mentioned in *RMS* 1376 and again in 1654.

WAVERLEY BRIDGE and **STATION** (Old Town) *see under* (LITTLE) MOUND.

WAVERLEY MARKET (Old Town) was built by the town in 1874-76 in order to rehouse the Vegetable Market, shown on *Ordnance Survey* 1852 but destined to be displaced by the expansion of the railway station planned in 1866. It took its name from WAVERLEY BRIDGE, *see under* (LITTLE) MOUND, The cast-iron structure was demolished as unsafe in 1974, but the name was continued by the new shopping centre developed on the site ten years later.

WAVERLEY PARK (Abbeyhill) appears in 1865 as a new name for the house of COMELY GARDENS, *which see*. The *Waverley* is but one more instance of the popularity of Scott's novel, and *Park* was still a fair description of the place. It was cleared for the street of the name in the mid 1890s; and WAVERLEY PARK TERRACE was added in about 1902.

WAVERLEY PARK (Mayfield) *see under* McLAREN ROAD, Mayfield.

WAVERLEY PLACE (Norton Park) *see under* MARYFIELD, Norton Park.

WAVERLEY PLACE (South Leith) now LINDEAN PLACE—*see under* INDUSTRIAL ROAD.

WAVERLEY STEPS (East End) was a new access created in 1868-76 in the course of the remodelling of the railway station (*see under* LITTLE MOUND) and the erection of WAVERLEY MARKET. It was evidently named for the station, and probably by those using it.

WAWANE'S or **WAWIN'S** or **WAIRIN'S CROFT** (Old Town) was the earlier name of the SCIENNES CROFT, *which see*.

WEAVERS CLOSE (West Port) *see* WEBSTER'S LAND, West Port.

WEAVER'S KNOWE (Currie) appears on *Ordnance Survey* 1912 as the name of a plantation beside the railway, on the north bank of the Murray burn opposite the Corslet. How or when the name arose is not known. It has been said that there was once a bleachfield at the Corslet, but this may have been supposed in order to explain the name. A house or hamlet of BURNWYND (*which see*) is shown hereabouts on *Roy* 1753, but there is no trace of it on *Riccarton* 1772. There is a little *knowe* just north of the railway; and the first part of the name might possibly refer not to a craftsman, but to a *weaver*, the Scots term for a spider. WEAVER'S KNOWE CRESCENT was built all of 200 yards further south in 1957.

WEBSTER'S CLOSE (High Street, at Castlehill) is shown on *Ainslie* 1780 and was named for Alexander Webster, appointed minister of the Tolbooth kirk in 1737, who built himself a house at the foot of this close (shown on *Kerr*) in 1739. He died in 1784.

WEBSTERS LAND (West Port) was newly built in 1983 on the site of a 19th-century tenement which had itself replaced a yet earlier *Weavers Close* and *Websters Land*. This last was the headquarters of the Incorporation of Websters (i.e. weavers) of the Portsburgh, one of the eight trade incorporations of the burgh given charters by John Touris of Inverleith in about 1600; and it seems to be shown on *Rothiemay* 1647 as a prominent building on the north side of the street. An armorial panel on the modern building is a copy (from a photograph) of a carving which was saved from the demolition of the early building, built in to the one that replaced it, but unfortunately lost when that was in turn pulled down. Above the date 1735 and the text from Job 7:6, MY DAYS ARE SWIFTER THAN A WEAVER'S SHUTTLE, it displays the Incorporation's arms: three red roses on a gold chevron, between three silver heads of leopards each with a shuttle in his mouth, all on a blue shield.

WEIGHHOUSE (Old Town) *see under* BUTTER TRON, Old Town.

WEIGHHOUSE WYND (South Leith) *see under* BERNARD STREET, South Leith.

WEIR'S CLOSE (208 Canongate) is shown on *Ainslie* 1780. Being in the south Canongatehead, it was within Edinburgh, not the burgh of Canongate. It was named for George Weir, brewer in Edinburgh prior to 1709, who built a great stone tenement *Weir's Land* here on the east side of the close.

WEIR'S CLOSE (South Leith) is listed in *PO Directory* 1827 as at 38 Kirkgate, and may have been named for James Weir, baker in Kirkgate in 1799.

WEIR'S or **MAJOR WEIR'S CLOSE** (24 West or Upper Bow) mentioned but not named in 1635, is shown, again unnamed, on *Edgar* 1742, and is listed in *PO Directory* 1827. It was named for *Weir's Land*, lodging of Major Thomas Weir of Kirkton and his sister Grizel, executed for necromancy in 1670.

WELL COURT (Dean/Water of Leith Village) was built in 1883-86 on a plan decidedly similar to the older buildings which it displaced, as shown on *Ordnance Survey* 1852. Designed by Sidney Mitchell as a scheme of model housing, including a community hall and a factor's house, it was evidently named for its ornamental well.

WELL CLOSE (South Leith) is listed in *PO Directory* 1827 at 115 Kirkgate, and is shown as CRAWLEY'S COURT on *Ordnance Survey* 1852; and the same map shows another WELL CLOSE on the south side of Giles Street, the name arising from the presence of a well in both cases. The origin of *Crawley's* remains to be traced.

WELL CLOSE (West Port) is mentioned in *Town Council Minutes* 1769 and listed in *PO Directory* 1826 as at the then 72 West Port. According to *Anent Old Edinburgh* there was but one public well in the Wester Portsburgh, and the cistern is shown on *Ordnance Survey* 1852.

WELLFLATT (Kirkliston) is recorded on a plan of Newmains in 1839 (*RHP 11583*) in the name *Wellflatt park* for a 19-acre field lying between the old turnpike at Wellflatts Road and the new one at Main Street; but it is likely that this name is 'the park beside the Wellflatt', since as Scots for 'flat land with or beside a spring' the latter name belongs to the riverside haugh immediately southeast of the village. Like AULDGATE (*which see*) the eastern leg of WELLFLATTS ROAD is part of the old turnpike, cut off at Foxhall in about 1810; its northern section is shown on *Kirkliston* 1759 as an entry to the part of the haugh that was once part of the minister's glebe; and the intermediate part of the street has been shaped and reshaped by the railway since 1866.

WELLGATE (Old Town) *see under* COWGATE, Old Town.

WELLINGTON PLACE (South Leith) originated from a road skirting the outer ditch of the ramparts of 1548. Comparison of *Naish* 1709 and *Wood* 1777 shows that the northern section of this road was altered between these dates, so as to swing further east; but the frontages of Wellington Place preserve the earlier line. Since the name appears in *PO Directory* 1813 it is evident that it was given in compliment to the victor in the Peninsular War before he became the hero of Waterloo.

(GREAT) WELLINGTON STREET (Bonnington) *see under* SUMMERSIDE.

WELLINGTON STREET (Hillside) was part of the plan for the CALTON NEW TOWN 1819 (*which see*) although its actual development came seventy years later. It is named on *Calton* 1819, evidently for the Duke of Wellington, hero of the Napoleonic wars.

WELLINGTON STREET (Portobello) *see* MARLBOROUGH STREET, Portobello.

WELLINGTON STREET (Tollcross) *see* EARL GREY STREET, Tollcross.

(THE) WELLS O WEARIE (Queen's Park) are shown on *Kirkwood* 1817. At a guess, the second part of the name might be Celtic; and if it were Gaelic *na fuarain*, (place) of the springs, the first part, *wells*, would be simply a Scots translation of it.

WEMYSS PLACE (New Town) was once part of the *kirk loan* from Stockbridge to the West Kirk of St Cuthbert, shown on *Roy* 1753 and as 'new road to Stockbridge' on Laurie's *New Town Site Plan* 1766; and the arrangement before its development is shown on *Kirkwood* 1817. *Wood* 1823 shows the new street planned as part of Gillespie Graham's scheme for the Moray estate, but along with ALBYN PLACE it was not yet named, evidently because these streets were partly on the Barjarg feu belonging to the city, outwith Moray's ground: and indeed it appears that Wemyss Place got its name (in about 1825) because the necessary widening of the Kirk Loan was at the expense of part of the garden attached to 64 Queen Street, residence of the Earl of Wemyss.

WEMYSS TERRACE (Grassmarket) is shown on *Kirkwood* 1817 and named for Andrew Wemyss, trunkmaker in the Vennel.

WERBER (Inverleith) is shown on *Knox* 1812 and *Ordnance Survey* 1852 as a farm steading on a site taken over in about 1864 for the west lodge of Fettes College. While early forms are lacking, the name has every appearance of being ancient: possibly Anglian *baer*, pasture, at the *wer*, weir or dam, perhaps connected with the nearby Celtic name of CREW, *which see*. NORTH WERBER PARK, PLACE and ROAD, together with EAST and WEST WERBERSIDE, were named in 1989.

WESTBANK (Portobello) was part of the Figgate Whins leased from Miller of Craigentinny in about 1770 by a Newcastle bricklayer Anthony Hillcoat, in order to exploit the brick clays discovered by William Jameson at nearby BRICKFIELD (*which see*) a few years earlier. The name Westbank seems to have been coined by Hillcoat, in order to distinguish his enterprise from Jameson's one on the opposite east bank of the Figgate burn. A street WESTBANK PLACE was formed in about 1907, only to be soon absorbed by the expansion of *Westbank Power Station*, founded in 1923 in the southern part of Westbank and later enlarged and renamed *Portobello Power Station*; but in 1983, when the power-station site was redeveloped for housing, the *Westbank* name was recovered in the naming of WESTBANK LOAN and a new WESTBANK PLACE, while Rosebank Lane (duplicated elsewhere in the city) was renamed WESTBANK STREET. In the same new development, the original founder of the brickworks was commemorated in HILLCOAT PLACE and LANE, and the later electrical industry in ELECTRA PLACE; while the naming of GREAT-CANNON BANK looked back to April 1560, when as noted in the contemporary *Diurnal of Occurrents* (p275) the English fleet under Vice Admiral Winter landed 'twelve great doubill and singill cannonis and fyfetene small pecis ... togedder with powder and munitions' at the mouth of the Figgate burn, for deployment in the siege of Leith: considering the terrain, it is reasonable to assume that the landing was here on the west bank of the burn, and that the guns were hauled up by KING'S ROAD, *which see*.

THE WEST or **OVER** or **UPPER BOW** (Old Town) is shown on *Rothiemay* 1647 and was the historic west gate of the burgh until the WEST PORT (*which see*) was built at some time before 1509. Recorded in *Kelso Abbey Charters* 1160-70 as the western *ianua* or gate of Edinburgh, and as *the Westbow* in *RMS* 1329-71, the name is Scots *bow* (pronounced *bough*) an arched port or gateway, and by extension the burgh's checkpoint and toll for local customs. Named in *RMS* 1425 as *arcus superior*, OVER or UPPER BOW, it formed a pair with the *arcus inferior* or NETHERBOW (*which see*) recorded in 1369; and in view of its functions as well as the 12th-century record quoted above, it probably dated from the foundation of the burgh. *Chambers* 1825 notes part of its east jamb as then still visible; but since its site was a yard or two south of the foot of the steps which now lead down from Upper Bow into Victoria Street (but of course at a level not far below that of Victoria Terrace) it was swept away when that street was formed in the 1830s. By 1538 its name had come to be used for the neighbourhood as well as the gateway itself, and by 1589 the street name of 'the common passage through the Ovirbow' had been shortened to the OVIRBOW, later subdivided into the BOWHEID and BOWFOOT (both still extant) linked by the narrow STRAIT BOW now represented (albeit at greater width and a much lower level) by the western section of Victoria Street. Until the 1920s, both the Bowfoot and Bowheid continued to be called WEST BOW, but more recently the latter has borne the alternative name UPPER BOW. This Upper Bow probably represents the line of an early approach to the Castlehill which (judging by the sett of later streets and closes) once descended from Bristo to the watershed in the valley floor at Cowgatehead and climbed directly up the south face of the Old Town ridge to the Bowhead; and it was evidently this that fixed the position of the Bow itself, while the Strait

Bow was a later route, probably demanded by the advent of wheeled traffic, which struck an easier gradient up the brae face below the port.

WEST BRIGGS (Kirkliston) *see under* BRIGGS, Kirkliston.

WESTBURN AVENUE (Wester Hailes) originated as a section of the historic BABERTON MAINS ROAD, *which see*; but in 1970, apparently because the name *Baberton Mains* was already destined to be misappropriated by another scheme in Fernieflat (*see* BABERTON MAINS DRIVE etc) this name was displaced by a new one, given at the same time to the adjoining WESTBURN GARDENS, GROVE and PARK, and derived—either directly or perhaps through a field name such as *West Burn park*—from the small burn which formed the west march of the farm of FERNIEFLAT (*which see*) in which the streets were built. WESTBURN MIDDLEFIELD, developed in Baberton Mains immediately west of this march burn, is sited in fields that were still known in the 1980s by the names *Middle* and *North Fields* recorded on a plan of Baberton (*RHP 595*) as long ago as 1755; and it was named in 1984 by combining *Westburn*, as above, with one of these historic field names. In 1993, three short branches off the Middlefield were named MIDDLEKNOWE, MIDDLEPARK and MIDDLESHOT, *park* and *shot* being terms for grass and arable fields respectively; and at the same time the larger branch roads QUARRYVIEW and QUARRYBANK, along with the adjoining QUARRYBANK COURT, CLOSE and END, were named for the nearby Baberton Sandstone Quarry, shown on *Ordnance Survey* 1852 but disused before 1893.

WEST CATHERINE PLACE (Wester Coates) *see under* DEVON PLACE, Wester Coates.

WEST or **WESTER COATES** *see under* **COATES**.

WEST COLLEGE STREET (Old Town) *see* COLLEGE STREET.

WEST COMMON CLOSE (307 Canongate) *see under* HIGH SCHOOL CLOSE *and also the* COMMON CLOSES, Canongate.

WEST CRAIGS (Corstorphine) *see under* CRAIGS, Corstorphine.

WEST CROFT (Ratho) *see* EAST & WEST CROFTS, Ratho.

THE WEST END (New Town) *see under* EAST and WEST ENDS, New Town.

WEST END PLACE (Dalry) was developed in about 1871, and was evidently named as being near the west end of the estate—there may have been an earlier field name such as *West End Park*.

WESTER BROOM PLACE (Corstorphine) was a new name given to a section of the South Gyle road when it was remodelled in 1959 and cut off from Meadow Place Road; and the name was immediately applied to further new streets in 1959—WESTER BROOM AVENUE, DRIVE, GARDENS, GROVE and TERRACE. The streets are in the CLAYCLOTE of Saughton (*which see*), but the name is coined from the adjoining *Broom*house—*see under* BROOMFIELD CRESCENT, Corstorphine.

WESTER CLOSE (Newhaven) is named on *Ordnance Survey* 1852. The naming of the WESTMOST CLOSE (*which see*) suggests that the Wester Close was the earlier of the two.

WESTER CLOSE (West Port) is indicated on *Kincaid* 1784, listed in *PO Directory* 1832 and named on *Ordnance Survey* 1852, the name obviously reflecting its position in the western part of the Wester Portsburgh.

WESTER COATES AVENUE, GARDENS, PLACE, ROAD and **TERRACE** (Wester Coates) *see under* COATES.

WESTER GRANGE (Grange & Blackford) *see under* THE GRANGE.

WESTER or **NETHER HAILES**, shown on *Blaeu* 1654, was part of HAILES, *which see*. The subdivision took place in the 15th century or earlier, and so far as is known the centre of Wester Hailes was always where the house and steading stood before they were cleared to make way for the present Green Way immediately east of Clovenstone Road. But for a part of it south of the railway, WESTER HAILES ROAD follows the line of the THIEVES ROAD (*which see*) or road by Wester Hailes between the Lanark and Calder roads, and continues the name formally adopted in 1931. WESTER HAILES PARK and DRIVE, named in 1970, occupy a group of fields with highly interesting names, as shown on a map of Wester Hailes in 1818 (*RHP 3590*). The northern section of Wester Hailes Park is in the *Dryburn Park* (*see also under* HAILESLAND); and south of this was the *Auld Walls* field, a name perhaps combining Celtic *allt*, a burn, with either Celtic *bhaile*, making the name 'burn of the farm place', or else Scots *walls*, making it 'springs of the Allt burn'. Immediately west of this, the middle part of Wester Hailes Drive occupied the *Dumbeg* field, which is plainly Gaelic, *dun beag*, little fort. It seems to be significant that this group of names (and *Alcorn Park* may just conceivably be another, *see under* CLOVENSTONE DRIVE, Wester Hailes) should be so close to the Gaelic name DUMBRYDEN, *which see*. The GREEN WAY is the descriptive, if somewhat stilted name given in 1970 to the great landscaped path which links the various parts of the Wester Hailes neighbourhood.

WESTER LOAN (Queensferry) *see* THE LOAN, Queensferry.

WESTERN TERRACE (Murrayfield) is shown on *W & A K Johnston* 1888, apparently as a name for a terrace of houses on the south side of the main road, referring to their westerly position beyond the city boundary, then at the foot of Ormidale Terrace. The name was extended to WESTERN CORNER, GARDENS and PLACE in 1933.

WESTER ROAD TO LEITH *see under* LEITH WALK.

WESTFIELD (Dalmeny) appears on *Forrest* 1818 but earlier maps back to *Adair* 1682 show the farm as *West Moor* and it is recorded as *Westmure* (*of Dundas*) as early as 1560. The name is literal, the muir in the western part of Dundas.

WESTFIELD ROAD (Gorgie) is shown on *Roy* 1753 substantially as it is today, but for some modification of its western end in about 1900.

Connecting Gorgie mill with Damhead, Dalry mill, Roseburn and Coltbridge, it was originally named, in the traditional way, according to where it led to: until the mid 1930s, its northern section was DAMHEAD ROAD, while the rest had been COLTBRIDGE ROAD until 1899, when it became WESTFIELD ROAD by association with WESTFIELD PLACE and STREET, then newly developing in the *west field* of Wheatfield in Wester Dalry; and WESTFIELD AVENUE followed suit in 1903.

WESTGARTH AVENUE (Colinton) was begun about 1888, but the name enters *PO Directory* only in 1914. By then the term *garth*, enclosure, was used only in some old farm names in Scotland, and it was evidently fancy in this location, perhaps brought in by the rectory of St Cuthbert's Episcopal Church.

WESTHALL (Ratho) is recorded in *Bain* in 1336. The early spellings are *-halle* or *-hall*; but no mansion house is mentioned in charters or shown on maps and the name is evidently Anglian or early Scots *west halh* or *haw*, for flat land beside the Cockle burn west of Ratho.

WESTHALL GARDENS (Merchiston) was formed in 1881 in part of the gardens of Viewforth House (*see under* VIEWFORTH, Merchiston) which included a sunken bowling green, possibly the remains of an old quarry. While this might account for the *Gardens* element, the choice of Westhall remains obscure. Possibly it had had some connection with Admiral Peat, long resident in the House, who had died in 1879 (*see* ADMIRAL TERRACE) or with his wife, a Miss Pratt of Seggie.

WEST HARBOUR ROAD (Granton) *see under* SHORE ROAD, Granton.

WEST or **HADDO'S HOLE KIRK** (High Street) was one of the four kirks created by subdivision of St Giles. The chief object was to secure better conditions for preaching; but at the west end of the nave the West and Tolbooth Kirks also served secular purposes as extensions of the facilities of the Auld and New Tolbooths (*see* THE TOLBOOTH) and *Haddo's Hole* within the West Kirk was a prison formed in 1563 and so named after it was used to incarcerate Sir John Gordon of Haddo before his execution in 1644.

WEST LOANING BURN (Queensferry) ran down beside the Loan or West Loaning, and appears to have been the 'rivulet' mentioned in a Dundas charter of 1364 (*Mac xxiv I*, in NLS) as the then western boundary of the burgh. Although *Morison's Queensferry* avers that this is culverted along the line of the burgh boundary as shown on *Ordnance Survey* 1854 (i.e. going on down the centre of the Loan and heading for the rocks west of the harbour) both the lie of the land and the name of GOTE LANE (*which see*) suggest that the burn, and therefore the medieval boundary, curved eastwards on the line of Craws Close (still approximately represented by the skew face of Hill's Court) and entered the sea at the foot of Gote Lane.

WEST MAINS (Nether Liberton) is named as *Liberton Mains*, together with *South Mains* for the other Nether-Liberton farm at the Inch, on *Laurie* 1763 and subsequent maps until 1852, when the *Ordnance Survey* gives the two as *Liberton West Mains* and *Liberton East Mains*. WEST MAINS ROAD, together with the loaning which continued it to Blackford, is shown on *Roy* 1753, and was named by use and wont as the road to the farm, which stood about forty yards east of the present opening of Langton Road, with the farmhouse north of the road and the steading opposite it, on the south side.

WEST MILLS (Colinton) was a group of mills on Woodhall ground south of the river, shown as *West Mill* on *Roy* 1753, which shows a single mill and also on *Spylaw* 1767, which shows two mills and other buildings. They included the EASTER WAULK MILL OF WOODHALL (counterpart of the Wester Waulk Mill or MOSSIE MILL, *which see*) recorded in 1688, as well as the WEST MILL OF COLLINTOUN recorded in 1725, and in 1796 the whole group is referred to as COLINTON WEST MILLS OF WOODHALL. WEST MILLS ROAD, shown on *Knox* 1812, is evidently as old as Mossie Mill or any of the West Mills, and probably medieval.

WEST or **WESTER MILLS** (Water of Leith or Dean Village) are mentioned in *Town Council Minutes* 1584, along with 'twa uther awld mylnis' apparently served by the same *dam* or lade on the north side of the river. While the *Minutes* ordain that two new mills are to be built in place of the wester mills, a further entry in April 1585 refers to 'the bigging of the foure new mylnis', and this suggests that it had been decided to replace the whole group of old mills. The present West Mill building, built in about 1805 and shown on *Kirkwood* 1817, occupies the same site, and operated as a double mill until 1891. WEST MILL LANE, named for it (or its predecessors) entered *PO Directory* in 1870.

WESTMOST CLOSE (Newhaven) is shown on *Ordnance Survey* 1852, and was evidently named as the most westerly of the closes in the village. Since it lies west of WESTER CLOSE (*which see*) it is likely that it was a later development, in the precinct of the 15th-century chapel of St Mary and St James which flanks it on the east.

WEST OLD DOCK (South Leith) *see under* EAST and WEST OLD DOCKS.

WEST PARK PLACE (Dalry) appears in 1870 under its original name WEST PARK TERRACE, displaced by *Place* in about 1885-88. The field in which it was built may well have been called the *West Park* of Easter Dalry.

WEST PIER (Granton) *see under* GRANTON HARBOUR.

WEST PILTON *see under* PILTON.

THE WEST PORT (Old Town) is mentioned in *Town Council Minutes* 1515 in a way which shows that by then it had effectively supplanted the UPPER BOW (*which see*) as the check point at the western entrance to the town; but even although *Protocols of John Foular* 1507 mention it as an established landmark, the striking absence of any reference to it in the description of market sites given in *Town Council Minutes* 1477 suggests that the port was formed at some time between these two dates.The gateway was demolished in 1786, but the gap it left continued to be called *The West Port*, as shown on *Kirkwood* 1817, because until the Portsburgh was merged with Edinburgh in 1856 it marked the boundary between the two. Nevertheless it had given its name to the ancient road that issued from it, and to the settlement that grew beside the road, within the barony of Inverleith. Although shown somewhat sketchily on *Siege of Edinburgh Castle* 1573, this township was big enough to begin to acquire its own trade incorporations in 1582; *Rothiemay* 1647 shows it in considerable detail, labelling it *West Port Suburbs*, and it kept this name WEST PORT even after 1649, when it became part of PORTSBURGH, *which see*. The lower part of the road was widened in the early 1880s, more or less in accordance with *City Improvements* 1866. It is labelled *Portsburgh* or *West Port* on the maps up until the 1830s, but from 1773 onwards the directories use the addresses WEST PORT and HEAD OF WEST PORT, later to be called MAIN POINT, *which see*.

WEST-PORT WELL CLOSE (West Port) is listed as 72 West Port in *PO Directory* 1827 and is shown, with the cistern beside it, on *Ordnance Survey* 1852. Alison Dunlop, in *Anent Old Edinburgh*, describes the well and the burgh court house which was up the close behind it as the two places round which Portsburgh life most congregated. The site was about 25 yards east of the eastern corner of Lady Lawson Street as altered by the *City Improvement* scheme of 1866.

WEST RIG (Balerno) *see under* EAST and WEST RIG, Balerno.

WEST SHORE ROAD (Granton) *see under* SHORE ROAD, Granton.

WEST TERRACE (Queensferry) *see under* HIGH STREET, Queensferry.

WEST TOLLCROSS (Tollcross) *see under* TOLLCROSS.

THE WHALE (Newhaven) is recorded thus in 1760 and later as WHALE BRAE, the first section of the WHITING ROAD (*which see*) to Edinburgh. The name is Old Norse *hvall*, rounded hill or knowe, and probably referred to the view of it from the sea and from the east, in which the inlet of the Ankerfield burn makes the ground north of it appear as a rounded snab with a distinct summit. The added Scots *brae* probably refers to the steep road in particular.

WHARTON LANE (South Side) is named thus on *Kirkwood* 1823, but on *Ainslie* 1804 it is HOSPITAL LANE, for George Watson's Hospital, built east of it in 1738. Still represented by the Royal Infirmary's West Gate, it formed the east boundary of Lauriston and Wester Portsburgh, and *Scott* 1759 shows it as the only public way between the future Lauriston Place and the Meadows. WHARTON PLACE is named on *Kirkwood* 1817, and like the lane it took its name from the house of Thomas Wharton, named on *Ainslie* 1804 but shown on *Ainslie* 1780 and probably feued in 1768. Wharton was a solicitor, Commissioner of Customs, and a colleague of Adam Smith. Both streets were taken into the site of the Royal Infirmary in 1872-79.

WHEATFIELD (Wester Dalry) first appears in *RMS* 1656 in a grant to Sir Daniel Carmichael of Hyndfoord of lands 'called the Haughe of Dalry'; and since the charter adds that it is 'to be called in all time hereafter *Wheatfeild*' it may be either that this was an existing field name promoted as an estate name for this part of the Haugh, or that it was a name newly coined, perhaps by Carmichael, and referring to the rich soil of this great plain, once part of the bed of a wide loch above Coltbridge. The feu duty of 'the just two parts and a half of six parts and a half of a pair of gilt spurs on Whitsunday if asked' might suggest that the Haugh was about 38 percent of a larger holding— perhaps the whole of Dalry. WHEATFIELD PLACE, ROAD and STREET are shown on *W & A K Johnston* 1888 as proposed developments. Only Wheatfield Street was open by 1893, serving as an (unnamed) access to the North British Distillery; but all three streets were named by 1897, and WHEATFIELD TERRACE had followed by 1902.

WHEATLANDS (Kirkliston) appears on *Roy* 1753 and is shown on *Ainslie's* Carlowrie as the largest single farm in that estate in the late 18th century. The name is literal, deriving ultimately from the richness of its alluvial soil.

WHELPSIDE (Balerno) is recorded as *Quhelpside* in 1582 and is shown on *Blaeu* 1654 as *Whelpsyid*. The name, which also occurred near Kirkliston, is Anglian *hwelp side* or Scots *whelp side*, slope of the cub(s).

WHINNY HILL (Arthur's Seat) is named for the whins growing on its side. *Kirkwood* 1817 and *Ordnance Survey* prior to 1893 show the name on the eastern slopes but call the summit CROW HILL, *which see*.

WHINS PLACE (Portobello) was named in 1981 for the *Figgate Whins*, the earliest name for the Portobello area, *see* FIGGATE.

WHISKY ROW (South Leith) *see under* ELBE STREET, South Leith.

WHITE DALES (Mortonhall) was named in 1989, recovering the name of the field as given on *Mortonhall* 1770. Anglian *hwit*, white, probably here describes the paleness of grassland in contrast to dark heath, and may be related to the adjoining name of the GALACHLAW, *which see*. While the second part may be Anglian from Old Norse *dalr*, valley or hollow, the plural would hardly fit unless (as might well be the case) the name once applied to more than one of the hollows between Braid Crags and the Galachlaw; but alternatively (and more likely) the word is Scots *dale*, a share, implying that the ground was once arable let out to tenants 'run-dale' i.e. in pieces much broader than the narrow strips of 'run-rig'.

WHITEHEAD GROVE (Queensferry) *see under* ASHBURNHAM ROAD, Queensferry.

WHITE HILL (Colinton) is recorded in 1709. The name is from Anglian *hwit hyll*, and probably referred to its pale grassiness in contrast to the dark rock and heather of its neighbour TORDUFF, *which see. See also* TORPHIN, Colinton.

WHITEHILL (Newcraighall) is shown thus on *Blaeu* 1654 and was the original name of NEW HAILES, renamed in 1708 when it was acquired by the owner of Hailes, near East Linton. *Knox* 1812 shows Hailes but also *Whitehill* at Wanton Walls; and this gave the names of WHITEHILL MAINS to the farm, WHITEHILL STREET to the row of cottages shown on *Ordnance Survey* 1852 as already developing beside the road earlier shown on *Roy* 1753, and WHITEHILL TERRACE to a row on the opposite side, suppressed in the redevelopment of the mining village in 1980. WHITEHILL ROAD, also figured on *Roy*, is named as the road leading to Whitehill Mains. The place name is Anglian *hwit hyll* or Scots *white hill*, evidently referring to a hill which, perhaps by reason of grassiness, showed up as paler amid the surrounding heathy landscape: possibly it was the knowe on which Whitehill House was later built; or else it may have been the low but prominent hill that rises to a summit in the west of Whitehill Mains.

WHITE HILL (Swanston) is recorded in 1709. Its name probably refers to the relative paleness of this grassy knowe (today obscured by the T-wood planting) against the background of Caerketton's crags and heather.

WHITEHORSE CLOSE (276 Canongate) *see* BOYD'S CLOSE.

WHITEHORSE CLOSE (31 Canongate) is listed on *Ainslie* 1780, but in *Maitland* 1753 as well as *PO Directory* 1827 it is given as DAVIDSON'S, for Robert Davidson, shoemaker, and his son John, brassfounder, who owned the tenements from 1752 until 1798. A Mrs Davidson was still resident in 1799. Earlier, the close was (LAURENCE) ORD'S, for former owners Laurence Ord, merchant burgess of Edinburgh in 1680, and his daughter Christian Ord or Graham, who sold the lands in 1695. Laurence Ord rebuilt the property, with a large gateway to the Canongate, and the present building north of the yard, despite much alteration, fits this late 17th-century date. The date 1623 carved on a windowhead has no significance whatsoever, for (as demonstrated in Harris: *Date Inscribed on Whitehorse Inn*, in Edinburgh City Library) it is only the latest of a series of widely differing dates which have appeared on the windowhead since Skene, in a print of 1819, first recorded a date 16?3, with the third digit doubtful. There is no record of the building being run as an inn, and Robert Chambers, making enquiries in about 1820, could find no one who could remember such a thing; but it seems to have been designed as one, with stabling entered from the North Back of the Canongate, and the name of the close strongly suggests that there was a 'White Horse' inn here at some time. Probably it was before the Davidsons' time, perhaps in that of John Mitchell of Alderston, who owned it between 1695 and 1745, or perhaps it was only in the time of the Ords, for it may have fallen victim to the decline of the Canongate in the last years of the Scottish Parliament.

WHITEHOUSE was enlarged along its south side in 1751 and 1816 by transfers totalling almost 6 Scots acres from the Grange and (mostly) from the Burgh Muir, but apparently originated as a *merkland* of some 33 Scots acres, marching with the Grange on its east side and the Muir on the other three; and like the GRANGE and BRUNTSFIELD (*which see*) it seems that it was not feued out of the Muir but independently created when (or before) the Muir was granted to the town in about 1120. Possibly, like Bruntsfield, it provided for some officer of the Crown; but the earliest indication of ownership is in *RMS* 1444, which confirms that HOGISTOUN in the Burgh Muir, owned by the prominent Edinburgh burgess Robert Hog of Hogistoun, and previously by the late Walter Hog, also a burgess, was now sold to Sir Alexander Home. The Hogs had long been a prosperous local family, one being listed in the *Ragman Roll* of 1296, while another figures in *RMS* 1350 as buyer of a quarter of Dalry. It is therefore possible that the estate had been called 'Hog's farm' for a considerable time; but by 1504 it was also being called 'the place and lands of Quhitehous' or WHITEHOUSE, no doubt referring to the lime-washed walls of its place or mansion house. The 17th-century successor of the house is shown on *Adair* 1682, and its remains were incorporated in the building of St Margaret's convent in 1835. WHITEHOUSE LOAN, shown on *Roy* 1753, was probably the access to Bruntsfield and Hogistoun from the 12th century onwards, and is named for Whitehouse. The estate was bought in 1819 by Ann Oliphant, widow of Francis Grant of Kilgraston in Strathearn; and after development began in about 1859 with STRATHEARN ROAD, Perthshire also supplied the names of BLACKFORD ROAD (1860) and KILGRASTON ROAD (1862). HOPE TERRACE (1860) was named for Mrs Grant's son, Sir James Hope Grant, joint heir to the estate; WHITEHOUSE TERRACE, on the south march, was named for the estate in about 1861; and STRATHFILLAN ROAD was named for that part of upper Strathearn in about 1908.

WHITEHOUSE (Cramond) was the principal manor place of the templelands in Cramond Regis. Recorded as *Quhit Hous* in 1615 and shown on *Laurie* 1763 it was presumably named for its lime-washed harling. WHITEHOUSE ROAD, shown on *Roy* 1753 as connecting Kirk Cramond with the old QUEENSFERRY ROAD now represented by Braehead Grove, was evidently named as 'by or to Whitehouse'. Its south end was extended to meet the new Queensferry road in about 1824.

WHITEHOUSE TERRACE (Corstorphine) was named in 1902. The name appears to have been fancy, the earlier *Whitehouse* in the neighbourhood having been at CORSTORPHINE BANK, *which see*. In

1966, in order to obviate any confusion with Whitehouse Terrace in Grange Loan, the street was renamed CORSTORPHINE HOUSE TERRACE, since it is in the vicinity of CORSTORPHINE HOUSE, *which see.*

WHITELAW (Currie) is recorded as *Wytelawe* in *Bain* 1335 and as *Whitlaw de Curry* in 1336. The variation *Whitehill* occurs in the 17th century, and it is shown thus on *Roy* 1753. The name is Anglian *hwit hlaw* or Scots *white law*, hill or little hill of a (comparatively) pale colour. It may refer to the knowe 150 yards west of the farm steading, once part of Currie Muir, which probably rose *white* (i.e. grassy) in contrast to the *black* or heathery muirland.

WHITELEA ROAD etc (Balerno) *see under* COCKBURN CRESCENT, Balerno.

WHITE MOSS (Ratho) is named on *Roy* 1753. The name is Anglian *hwit mos* or Scots *white moss*, boggy ground which is grassy, pale in contrast to the dark or black look of reeds or heather.

WHITE PARK (Gorgie) is built on part of Gorgie Muir, feued from the Merchant Company and developed in 1887 by David White, spirits dealer in the High Street.

ADAM WHITE'S CLOSE (Shore Place, South Leith) is named on *Kirkwood* 1817 and still shown on *Ordnance Survey* 1931 on ground, since cleared, east of Tolbooth Wynd. It was obviously named for an owner, as yet untraced.

WHITESIDE (Currie) is shown on *Laurie* 1763 as a settlement of some kind; on *Knox* 1812 it is *Whiteside Wa's* (i.e. wells or springs) and *Ordnance Survey* 1852 shows it as a *ree* or sheepfold beside the plantation which still carries on the name. This is Anglian or Scots *hwit side*, a slope which, being grassed, was 'white' or paler than the 'black' heathery muir round about it.

WHITINGFORD (Bonnyhaugh) *see under* BONNYHAUGH, Bonnington, *and also* WHITING ROAD.

WHITING ROAD (Granton) appears on *Cramond Roads* 1812 as the name of what is now Crewe Road North, or even the whole of Crewe Road; and the same road is given as *Whiteing road* about forty years earlier, on a map of the Granton district, *RHP 714*. The name also occurs at NEWHAVEN (*which see*) where a tale of use by fishwives bears every mark of having been invented to explain the name, on the assumption that it refers to fish; but it is possibly from Anglian *hwit eng* or *ing*, 'white' or grassy pasture, contrasting with the 'black' or heathery muirland which seems to have been general behind the shore in early times.

WHITSLADE'S CLOSE (493 High Street) *see under* JAMES COURT.

WHITSON CRESCENT etc (Saughton) *see under* STENHOUSE, Saughton.

WHYTE PLACE (Abbeymount) was named by 1902, presumably for its developer.

WILCOCKIESHAW (Queensferry) is recorded as a field name in Muirhall in 1662. It is Scots *will-cockis haw*, haugh frequented by wild birds; and is almost identical to the *Wilcockisholme* recorded near Kingscavil, West Lothian, in 1560, in which the final part is *-holm*, meadow beside water or marsh.

WILFRID TERRACE (Parson's Green) *see under* PARSON'S GREEN.

WILKIE'S CLOSE (125 Canongate) *see* BROWN'S CLOSE, Canongate.

WILKIESTON ROAD (Ratho) is shown on *Laurie* 1763 and named as leading to Wilkieston. This was the *Spittalton* or hospice, recorded in 1376 and still named thus on *Armstrongs* 1773. *Knox* 1812 shows it unnamed, beside *Linburn*, but shows the adjoining farm of Bonnyton as owned by *Wilkie Esq*. and the modern name appears on *Gellatly* 1834.

WALTER WILLES'S CLOSE (300 High Street) *see* BUCHANAN'S COURT.

WILLIAM BLACK PLACE (Queensferry) was built in Muirhall in 1956, and named for Senior Bailie William Black JP, who retired in that year.

WILLIAMFIELD (Portobello) is shown on *Wood's Portobello* 1824 as *Williamsfield*, owned by a Mr Macintosh and possibly named for him, even although, as shown on *Roads from Figget* 1783, it had once been part of the garden of *Rosefield*, home of William Jamieson, the 'Father of Portobello', who died in 1813. Listed as *Williamfield* in 1836, it was redeveloped as a row of cottages some time before 1887, and the name was continued when they were replaced by WILLIAMFIELD SQUARE in 1960.

WILLIAMSON'S CLOSE (599 High Street) *see* SEMPLE'S CLOSE.

WILLIAM STREET (Coates) *see under* COATES.

WILLOWBANK ROW (Newhaven) had taken its original shape by 1876 and got its name from a house, *Willow Bank* on the Whale Brae, so called because of a large old willow tree growing there. The street name was continued when new housing was built, on quite a different line, in the mid 1960s.

WILLOWBRAE (Duddingston) appears in *PO Directory* 1845 as the name of a house shown thus on *Lancefield* 1851 but previously shown on *Kirkwood* 1817 and *Pollock* 1834 as *Willow Bank*. The indications are that both names were coined for the house from the traditional name of WILLOW HEAD, *which see*. In 1881 a terrace of housing in Parson's Green began to be occupied as WILLOWBRAE TERRACE, a side name changed to WILLOWBRAE VILLAS in 1882 and extinguished in 1896. WILLOWBRAE ROAD is shown as 'the gait to Restalrig' on a map of Duddingston in 1564, printed in *Old Edinburgh Club XXIII*. It was known as 'the road by the Willowhead'; but in *PO Directory* 1889 the address 'Willowbrae' seems to be used for one or two houses beside the Villas, and in the following year *Willowbrae Road* appears as the address of farm people further south, probably extending to Duddingston Mill. WILLOWBRAE AVENUE began to be developed beside the Villas in 1889; and WILLOWBRAE GARDENS were begun in Northfield in 1910.

WILLOW HEAD (Duddingston) is shown on *Roads from Figget* 1783 as the name of the easterly spur of Arthur's Seat, while *Duddingston* c1800 gives it as the name of the field beside the summit of the road from Jock's Lodge to Duddingston Mill. The c1800 map also names the field next to the south, beside part of the road figured in 1783 as having a gradient of 1:15, as WILLOW CLEAVE; and since this derives from Old Norse *kleif*, a steep track up a hillside, it might have been an early name for WILLOWBRAE ROAD, *which see*. These are among many 'willow' names in the vicinity of Arthur's Seat, *see under* BINGHAM GARDENS etc, DRUMSELCH, PIERSHILL, *and* SALISBURY.

WILLOWTREE PLACE (Currie) *see under* CHERRYTREE GARDENS etc, Currie.

WILSON'S CLOSE (211 Cowgate) is listed on *Ainslie* 1780 and was named for Robert Wilson, wig maker, owner of *Wilson's land* here at some time before 1751.

WILSON'S CLOSE (probably in High Street) is mentioned in *Protocols of James Young* 1491 as *Wilsone cloise in Edinburgh*, in which a Michael Chalmer had property; but it is not known where it was, and the question is perhaps complicated by a reference in the *Acts of the Lord Auditors* 1478 to *Michell of Chaumer landis of Leith callit Wilson's clois*. Neither the coincidence nor the conflict can be ignored; but it may be that the local lawyer's 'Edinburgh' was more accurate than the national clerk's 'Leith'.

WILSON'S COURT (134 Canongate) is listed on *Ainslie* 1780, only two years after William Wilson of Soonhope, writer in Edinburgh, acquired this ground, formerly owned by Sir John Sinclair of Ulbster, as a site for a tenement.

WILSON'S PARK (Portobello) was laid out in the property of that name in about 1804, along with Maryfield and Tower Lane. Although the street is shown nameless on *Wood's Portobello* 1824 and *Sutter* 1856, it is listed in *Portobello Directory* 1836 and was probably the general address of houses within the original property until the street name was formalised, perhaps in about 1880. Wilson was one of William Jamieson's subfeuars.

WILTON ROAD (Craigmillar Park) *see under* CRAIGMILLAR PARK.

WINDY DOOR NICK (Swanston) is recorded in 1709 as the Scots descriptive name of this sharp and windswept dip in the crest of the ridge between Allermuir and Byerside Hill.

WINDING CLOSE (18 Cowgate) *see* MURRAY'S CLOSE, Cowgate.

THE WINDMILL (Bristo) was erected by the town in 1598 under its contract with the Society of Brewers (*see under* SOCIETY) to supply their breweries at Greyfriars with water from the South Loch. Although the Society was dissolved in 1619, the windmill with its cistern, 230 square yards in area, seems to have continued to operate; but it is described as 'now demolished' in 1768, when its site was conveyed to the adjoining Chapel (later Buccleuch Kirk) as a burial ground. WINDMILL CLOSE, obviously so named because it faced it across the street, is shown on *Scott* 1759. WINDMILL STREET, so named because it skirts the north of the windmill site, was part of James Brown's George Square scheme 1766 and is named on his feuing plan for *George Square* 1779. Shown on that plan as *Mews Street*, WINDMILL LANE is named thus on *Pollock* 1834. WINDMILL PLACE was coined in 1984 as a name for a redeveloped property adjoining Windmill Close, although never part of it.

WINDMILL BRAE (Murrayfield) is shown on *Ordnance Survey* 1852. The name derives from the windmill which, shown on *Adair/Cooper* 1735 and *Roy* 1753, is still visible as a ruin on the northwest boundary of the Gallery of Modern Art. In 1851 the *Ordnance Survey* reported that it had then been long disused, but noted a local tradition that for some time before that it had been used to mill whins for feeding stock.

WINDSOR PLACE (Portobello) appears on *Roads from Figget* 1783 as the way into the second of William Jamieson's brickfields in Portobello, *see under* MOUNT LODGE. Originally named NICHOLSON STREET for Jamieson's first wife, who died in 1800, it is shown on *Wood's Portobello* 1824 as JAMESON STREET, for Jamieson himself, who had died in 1813; but the *Portobello Directory* 1836 lists WINDSOR PLACE and WINDSOR TERRACE, and since the latter, built in 1834, extended the street into the grounds of a large house shown as existing in 1824 and named on *Portobello* 1856 as 'Windsor Cottage', it may be that the street name derived from the house name. Presumably it refers to Windsor Castle, and (at a guess) it may be a reflection of loyal enthusiasm aroused by the visit of George IV to Portobello in 1822, *see under* KING'S ROAD. Increasingly treated as a side name, Windsor Terrace was finally taken into Windsor Place when the street was further extended in about 1932.

WINDSOR STREET (Hillside) is named on *Calton* 1819 as part of William Playfair's CALTON NEW TOWN (*which see*) and building began in 1823. Presumably it was named for Windsor Castle, but what in particular prompted this in 1819 is not recorded.

WINDY EDGE (Queensferry) is recorded as *Vindhedge* and *Winiege* in 1607 and 1636 and appears in field names on *Dundas* 1757 and *Plewlandfield* 1769. The name is Scots, windy summit, referring to the broad knowe which centres around NT 211776 beside a part (now abandoned) of the old Builyeon road. An alternative and probably older name for the same feature was KETTLESLAW, *which see*.

THE WINDY GOUL or **GOWL** (Queen's Park) describes the place and the violent squalls which occur in it. Scots *goul* or *gowl*, a narrow defile, is from Gaelic *gobhal*, a crotch. The road connecting Duddingston to QUEEN'S DRIVE was formed out of an ancient footpath in 1856.

WINGS (Gilmerton) was in the Easter Quarry park of Drum, west of the Dalkeith road and just south of Ferniehill Road, at about NT 29756943. It is named on *Laurie* 1763, and still shown, although not named, on *Armstrongs* 1773; but there is no sign of it on *Knox* 1812, where the detail suggests that it may have been cleared in course of road works. The name is still preserved in the field name *Wings park* in Edmondston on the opposite side of the main road. In absence of early forms its origin can only be guessed at, but it might well be from Old Norse *vangr*, a field.

WINNELSTRAELEE (Wardie) was a large farm on the north side of Ferry Road and east of the Wardie burn. Recorded in 1657 and on all maps from *Adair* 1682 until the late 1930s (by which time it was displaced by the vapid invention of FERRYFIELD, *which see*) the name is Scots *winnelstrae* (English *windlestraw*) a wiry grass useful for making grass ropes or ties for *winnels* or bundles of hay or straw, together with -*lee*, grassland. It also occurs at Whitburn, West Lothian. The steading was near the west side of the housing development of Ferryfield, and its name is remembered in the naming of a nearby path WINNELSTRAELEE, and less directly in that of WEST WINNELSTRAE, built in 1981 in the westernmost field of the farm.

WINTON DRIVE and **TERRACE** (Fairmilehead) began a development in Mortonhall in 1936, when the estate was owned by Col. Algernon Richard Trotter, and the streets were named for his wife, Lady Edith Mary Montgomerie, daughter of the Earl of Eglinton and Winton. WINTON LOAN followed in 1963, and WINTON PLACE and GROVE in 1973, WINTON GARDENS in 1975 and WINTON PARK in 1976.

WISHAW TERRACE (Meadowbank) *see under* CAMBUSNETHAN STREET, Meadowbank.

THE WISP (Niddrie & Edmonston) was adopted in 1978 as a single name, long used locally, for the road previously named partly as NIDDRIE ROAD from Edmonston and EDMONSTON ROAD from the Dalkeith road. The name is from the 5-acre property of *The Wisp*, shown on *Laurie* 1763 and *Knox* 1812 and detailed on *Caldcoats etc* 1815. The most likely meaning of its name is Scots *wisp* or *wosp*, the bush or bunch of twigs that was the sign of a tavern, and by extension could mean one, an *ail wosp*, as mentioned by William Dunbar in about 1500; and although there is no record of a hostelry here, it would seem a likely place for such a staging post on the ancient road from Leith to Dalkeith by Restalrig, Niddrie and Newton. WISP GREEN was formed in 1979 in CLEIKIMIN (*which see*) but was named as a branch off *The Wisp* road.

WOLRIDGE ROAD (Liberton) *see under* CADOGAN ROAD, Liberton.

WOLSELEY CRESCENT, GARDENS, PLACE and **TERRACE** (Parson's Green) *see under* PARSON'S GREEN.

WOODBINE TERRACE (South Leith) was built by 1868 and was followed by WOODVILLE TERRACE (1869) THORNVILLE TERRACE (1870) ASHVILLE TERRACE (1873) BEECHWOOD TERRACE (1877) ELMWOOD TERRACE (1878) and OAKVILLE TERRACE (1880)—all fancy names, in accordance with the practice of their builders, the Edinburgh Co-operative Building Company.

WOODBURN PLACE and **TERRACE** (Morningside) were named by 1878 as being built in part of the grounds of Woodburn House, which is shown on *Pollock* 1834 and no doubt got its fancy name from the woodland planting beside the Jordan burn, shown on *Kirkwood* 1817.

WOODFIELD AVENUE (Colinton) was named for the adjoining property of *Woodfield*, so named on *Fowler* 1845 but given as *Woodville* on *Gellatly* 1832 and on *Ordnance Survey* 1852, the earlier form showing clearly that it was a play on the estate name of *Woodhall*. WOODFIELD PARK was named in 1981 as being in the grounds of WOODFIELD HOUSE.

WOODHALL (Colinton and Juniper Green) is recorded in 1374 as *Wodhalle* in the barony of Redhall, the other early forms of the name being *Wodhall* in 1438 and *the wodhall* in 1495. The name is Anglian, either *wuda heall*, hall of or at the wood, or (much more likely, inasmuch as there is no evidence for a hall here in early times) it may be *wuda halh*, haugh of or at the wood, which would fit the topography excellently. *Blaeu* 1654 (surveyed in about 1596) shows *Woodhall*, probably the tower house mentioned in *RMS* 1623, in the same position as WOODHALL HOUSE, dating from 1630. The estate included JUNIPER GREEN and other land north of the river between CURRIEMUIREND and ENTERKIN'S YETT, as well as land south of the river, stretching as far as the LADIE BURN south of TORPHIN, and at one time including BONALY. WOODHALL MAINS, shown on earlier maps, is named on *Ordnance Survey* 1893. Mills in Woodhall are mentioned in *RMS* 1582, and *Ordnance Survey* 1852 names WOODHALL MILL, WOODHALL BANK MILL, another WOODHALL MILL (a corn mill sometimes called CURRIEMUIREND MILL) as well as MOSSIE MILL (*which see*) sometimes called WOODHALL WAULK MILL. WOODHALL ROAD, named as the road *to Woodhall*, is shown on *Knox* 1812, and *Spylaw* 1799 shows how its Colinton end took its present form. WOODHALL MILL BRAE, formally so named after it had been altered to suit the new city bypass in 1986, is described in 1686 as 'a highway to the waterside and over the water' and was traditionally named as the access to the Woodhall (or Curriemuirend) corn mill. WOODHALL TERRACE (1912) DRIVE (1931) and AVENUE (1936) were named as being on Woodhall ground in JUNIPER GREEN (*which see*) whereas WOODHALL BANK (1936) in Fernielaw (part of Spylaw) took its name from Woodhall Road; and WOODHALL GROVE followed suit in 1965.

WOODHEAD PLACE (Sciennes) is shown on *Ordnance Survey* 1877 and was in use as a side name in Sciennes Road from 1867 until 1893. The name is probably fancy, and perhaps belonged to an earlier house on the site.

WOODLANDS GROVE (Duddingston) was developed in 1959, replacing a house named as *Woodlands* on *Ordnance Survey* 1852. This had itself replaced a property which is shown on *Duddingston* c1800 and *Kirkwood* 1817 as *The Hut* and *Duddingston Hut* (following the same fashion as the contemporary LOTHIAN HUT) and which had either replaced or been developed from the *Mains* shown on a plan of Duddingston in 1770 (copied in *Baird's Duddingston*) and figured 'Mr Mawr's' on *Figgate Roads* 1782. Known also as 'the earl's farm', this seems to have been built in the later 1760s to serve the policies of the earl of Abercorn's Duddingston House.

WOODSIDE TERRACE (Joppa) is shown named and partly developed at its western end on *Ordnance Survey* 1893. It was sited in the *Wardlands* field of Easter Duddingston, and none of the maps shows any woodland in the vicinity except in the grounds of Coillesdene at the street's east end.

WOODSTOCK ROAD (Inch) *see under* THE INCH, Nether Liberton.

WOODVILLE TERRACE (South Leith) *see under* WOODBINE TERRACE, South Leith.

WORLD'S END CLOSE (10 High Street) is recorded in 1725 and shown on *Edgar* 1742. The name may well be, as is generally assumed, a whimsical reference to the position of the close at the very foot of the High Street; but the even more curious name *Endmyleis well*, mentioned in the evidence at the trial of the murderers of Henry Darnley in 1567, possibly belongs in this general vicinity (*see* FOUNTAIN CLOSE, 28 High Street). The close is recorded in 1762 as *formerly* SWIFT'S, but although it is possible that there was a connection with the Swift family of OLD FISHMARKET CLOSE (*which see*) the references given in *Old Edinburgh Club XII* seem to be misreadings, and the point remains obscure. The alternative SWEIT'S, recorded in 1750, is either in mistake for *Swift's*, or else obscure. The close was also Sir JAMES STANFIELD'S, for Sir James Stanfield of Newmills, who had a house in it prior to his death in 1687 and whose son Philip, as related in *Wilson* and *Grant*, was convicted of his supposed murder, chiefly on the ground that the corpse bled when he touched it—according to superstition, a sure sign of guilt of secret murder. The close is listed in 1635 as ANDRO PURVES'S, for Andrew Purves, merchant, who had his house on the High Street frontage and owned other property in the close and in the little close off it, which may be the STEWART'S CLOSE listed in *Williamson's Directory* 1779 and 1799 and perhaps connected with Neil Stewart, merchant at the Netherbow, listed in the *Directory* 1780.

WRIGHT'S CLOSE (85 Cowgate) is listed on *Ainslie* 1780 but its name's origin is obscure.

WRIGHT'S CLOSE (239 Cowgate) is listed on *Ainslie* 1780, but the derivation of the name is obscure.

WRIGHTSHOUSES is recorded in *RMS* 1382 as the name of lands which were to be acquired in the next decade by a branch of the Napier family, about forty years before another branch acquired MERCHISTON (*which see*)—a family connection that has been obscured by the fact that Alexander, the first Napier of Merchiston, dropped his paternal arms in favour of those of the Lennox when his grandson was betrothed to a Lennox heiress. Shown on *Blaeu* 1654, the tower of Wrightshouses was extended or rebuilt in the 16th century, but by the late 18th century it had declined almost to the point of losing its name: on *Armstrongs* 1773 it is shown simply as *Mansionhouse*, and the Gillespie Trust knew it as *Balganie House* or *Burghmuir Castle* before they pulled it down in 1800 in order to build Gillespie's Hospital, itself replaced by sheltered housing in 1976. The estate lay entirely west of the Biggar highway: the area east of it, now known as *Wrightshouses*, was never part of the estate, but was open ground within the Burgh muir until 1716, when James Brownhill feued part of it (adding the rest in 1719) and built his *Golfhall* tavern to serve duty-free wines to the golfers on the Links. As shown on *Roy* 1753 and *Bypass Roads* 1763 a village rapidly developed, but the buildings on the west side of the highway were swept away when the highway was widened in 1792 (as confirmed by a plan of the estate in 1797, *RHP 20579*) and *Ainslie* 1804 shows the estate name ousted by that of Gillespie's Hospital and transferred to the eastern remnant of the village. The early spellings *Wrychyshousis* and *Wrichtishouis* leave the name obscure, insofar as it could be 'houses of the wrights or carpenters' or else 'houses belonging to Wright'. The first would scarcely fit this rural location in the 14th century or earlier, and it is more likely that (as seems to be the case with *Wrychtislands* in Restalrig) there was some early owner called Wright.

WRITERS' COURT (315 High Street) is shown on *Edgar* 1742. It was built, probably in the 1690s, by Robert Milne of Barfarg and Patrick Steel, and purchased in 1699 by the Writers to the Signet, as a home for their library. The principal building was a vast 8-storey tenement on the west side of Mary King's Close, which became part of the west frontage of the quadrangle of the Royal Exchange in 1754, with part of the close still in use in an open area in front of it; and thus it continued until 1898, when it was replaced by the burgh court development of the City Chambers. Cleriheugh's tavern was entered from the court. Although the buildings in the south of it were redeveloped as part of the Royal Exchange scheme of 1754, the Court itself survived until 1930-34, when in the course of the western extension of the City Chambers it was made into an access to the head of Warriston Close.

WYVERN PARK (Grange) *see under* THE GRANGE.

Y

YAIR'S CLOSE (232 Canongate) *see* PLAINSTANES CLOSE, Canongate.

THE YARDHEADS (South Leith) marked the north boundary of the lands of St Anthony's, sold to the town in 1724, as detailed in the report on the *Common Good* 1904; but the sett of the neighbourhood, as shown on *Naish* 1709, strongly suggests that the road had been built or adapted in 1548 as a military way serving the new ramparts of the town. It was evidently named for its position at the head of the yards or closes feued out from the LEES (*which see*) between Giles Street and Yardheads; and since these yards seem to be shown on *Siege of Leith* 1560 as at least partly developed, the street name probably dates back to that period.

YARIS or **YAIR'S CLOSE** (172 High Street) *see* OLD ASSEMBLY CLOSE.

YEAMAN PLACE (North Merchiston) was begun as YEAMAN TERRACE by 1879 and was renamed *Place* by 1881. YEAMAN LANE was formed about the same time and was named by 1887. The names derived from the owner of the ground, Alexander Yeaman, lawyer.

YEWLANDS CRESCENT and **GARDENS** (Liberton) took their name in 1958 from a house called *Liberton Cottage* from before 1852 but also *Yewlands* from before 1893, which had occupied the northern part of the site. Since *Ordnance Survey* 1852 shows its garden planted with trees, the name doubtless referred to yews included among them.

YOOLE'S PLACE (Portobello) was named for Thomas Yoole, who leased a pottery from William Jamieson in 1808 and, together with his son-in-law Thomas Rathbone, set up the business of Thomas Rathbone & Co, stoneware manufacturers, in 1810. The site was redeveloped as THE POTTERY in 1978.

YORK PLACE (New Town) was merely sketched on the plan for the first NEW TOWN 1766-67 as an indeterminate continuation of Queen Street, and it was not until 1791 that it was opened up to connect with the Broughton Loan at Picardy. Feuing began in about 1792, and by 1797 it was named (still following the theme of royal names begun in 1767) for George III's second son, the duke of York. YORK LANE, named about the same time, was developed from an existing track or right-of-way along the east boundary of the Broughton Parks, south of Broughton village.

YORK ROAD (Trinity) was developed in Trinity Mains in the 1820s, up to the boundary of Christian Bank, which ran some 50 yards north of Lennox Row. *Pollock* 1834 shows a link through Christian Bank to the Chain Pier at Trinity Crescent, but this had to be altered to a more easterly alignment to suit the track and station of the

Edinburgh, Leith & Newhaven Railway, constructed 1838-42. The street name, not shown on *Ordnance Survey* 1852 but appearing in *PO Directory* 1854, may have evolved from that of *York Buildings*, listed in Trinity in 1853. It seems likely that it derived ultimately from the city of York or from a personal surname, rather than from Frederick Duke of York, George III's third son and an eminent soldier, who died in 1827.

(JOHN) YOUNG'S CLOSE (276 Canongate) *see* BOYD'S CLOSE.

ALEXANDER YOUNG'S CLOSE (16 High Street) *see* TWEEDDALE COURT.

YOUNG STREET (New Town) *see under* NEW TOWN.

Z

ZAIR'S or **YAIR'S CLOSE** (172 High Street) *see* OLD ASSEMBLY CLOSE—the *z* is the Scots letter ȝ ('yogh') pronounced *y*.

ZETLAND PLACE (Trinity) was projected by 1887 and named and beginning to be occupied by 1890. Following a fashion started in the naming of LENNOX ROW, it was named for a ship, in this case the *Earl of Zetland*, registered in the port of Leith.

Other Reference Works on Place Names

Cameron K: *English Place-Names*, 3rd ed. London 1977.

Dixon N: *Place-names of Midlothian*, 1947. Typescript in University of Edinburgh Library; copy in ECL.

Ekwall E: *The Concise Oxford Dictionary of English Place-names*, 4th ed. Oxford 1960.

Ekwall E: *English River Names*. Oxford 1928.

Gelling M: *Place-names in the Landscape*. London 1984.

Johnston J B: *Place-names of Scotland*, 3rd ed. London 1934.

Macdonald A: *Place-names of West Lothian*. Edinburgh 1941.

Mackenzie W C: *Scottish Place-names*. London 1931.

Nicolaisen W F H: *Scottish Place-names*. London 1976, revised paperback edition 1986.

Padel O J: *Cornish Place-name Elements*. English Place-name Society, Cambridge 1985.

Smith A H: *English Place-name Elements*, 2 vols. English Place-name Society, Cambridge 1970.

Watson W J: *The History of the Celtic Place-names of Scotland*. Edinburgh 1926.

Index to Names by Localities

Since boundaries are not always precise—and indeed, may alter in the course of time—some names may be found listed under adjoining neighbourhoods. In certain cases, subdivisions of neighbourhoods have been given their own separate headings— e.g. *High Street* within *Old Town*.